HISTORICAL AND GEOGRAPHICAL
DICTIONARY OF JAPAN

Ama no Hashidate
Miyajima
Matsushima

HISTORICAL AND GEOGRAPHICAL DICTIONARY OF JAPAN

with 300 illustrations
18 appendices, and several maps

by E. PAPINOT, M.A.

and with an introduction to the new edition
by Terence Barrow, Ph.D.

CHARLES E. TUTTLE COMPANY
Rutland, Vermont & Tokyo, Japan

Representatives

Continental Europe: BOXERBOOKS, INC., *Zurich*

British Isles: PRENTICE-HALL INTERNATIONAL, INC., *London*

Australasia: BOOK WISE (AUSTRALIA) PTY. LTD.
104-108 Sussex Street, Sydney 2000

*Published by the Charles E. Tuttle Company, Inc.
of Rutland, Vermont & Tokyo, Japan
with editorial offices at
Suido 1-chome, 2-6, Bunkyo-ku, Tokyo, Japan*

Copyright in Japan, 1972, by Charles E. Tuttle Co., Inc.

Library of Congress Catalog Card No. 71-152116

International Standard Book No. 0-8048-0996-8

*First edition published 1910 by Kelly & Walsh, Ltd., Yokohama
First Tuttle edition, 1972
Fifth printing, 1979*

0220-000281-4615
PRINTED IN JAPAN

INTRODUCTION TO THE NEW EDITION

E. Papinot's *Historical and Geographical Dictionary of Japan*, which first appeared in English in 1910, has stood unchallenged by any competitor for over half a century. Students who search for it today often find a battered and dog-eared copy, guarded by their librarian. A reprint at this time will no doubt be greatly welcomed by scholars and librarians alike.

The object of this book is explained by Papinot in his preface, namely, to give "a summary account of the principal events and names that occur in the history and geography of Japan." In this matter the book succeeds admirably, subject of course to the reader's understanding the developments of scholarship since 1900. The entries and articles of the *Historical and Geographical Dictionary of Japan* are arranged alphabetically; so, if we wish, we can also call the book an encyclopedia of Japan. Of course, the word "geographical" in the title appertains to towns, districts, populations, and ethnical description and not earth sciences.

The appendices are an especially useful reference to the Western reader as he can quickly find facts such as Japanese terms for weights or measures, districts, historical dates, imperial successions, dynasties, genealogies of emperors and princes, and the relationship of Buddhist sects. Every Japanophile should have Papinot handy in his library.

The biographical supplement entitled "Principal Foreigners Connected with Japan Before the Restoration" provides us with a fascinating review of the hardships, frustrations, and all-too-frequent extermination of foreigners in early Japan. Papinot is influenced by his private religious zeal, concerned with Catholic missions in Japan. However, the sufferings of the Jesuits, Dominicans, and others he mentions as being "buried alive at Nagasaki," "burned alive at Edo," "crucified," and "condemned to the torment of the pit" are true records of the horrors of life of the time. Old Japan was not all butterflies, cherry blossoms, and dainty geisha.

Papinot was a careful researcher working in the best scholarly traditions of the Victorian times in which he lived. He ranks among that distinguished band of Westerners who went to Japan following the Meiji Restoration of 1868 and who left to posterity a contribution to Japanese culture.

Terence Barrow, Ph.D.

PREFACE.

This book does not intend to give more than a summary account of the principal events and names that occur in the History and Geography of Japan. Consequently, the alphabetical order has been adopted, an arrangement that will undoubtedly contribute to the usefulness of the book.

It contains but little discussion of dates and facts, as it is not meant to be a critical history. Therefore the official chronicle which assigns the year 660 B.C. as the date on which *Jimmu-tenno*, the first Emperor of Japan, ascended the throne, has been adopted. But, the critical study of Japanese history seems to place this event some 600 years later, and does not guarantee certainty, at least for its principal facts, beyond the VII century of our era. Nevertheless, as we want to give the traditions of Japan on the origin and development of the country, we deem it appropriate to place mythology, legend and history on the same footing, and usually leave the discernment of truth from error to the judgment of the reader.

History, in our days, has left the beaten track of merely narrating battles and giving a vocabulary of more or less famous names. It strives to explain the existence of the customs, morals and the common ideas of the people. We have followed this view, and our Dictionary gives an amount of information on the usages, customs, feasts, dignities, taxes, etc. of the country, and affords a deeper insight into the Genius of Japan which is still so enigmatical to the Western World. An alphabetical index of English names, which refers to the articles of the Dictionary, will be of help to those who use the book. (Appendix I).

It seemed logical to us to group in chronological order, under the family name, all biographical notices of those who rendered that name famous. However, as we often find eminent persons designated only by their forename, we have made an alphabetical list of forenames and refer to the family names where the desired information can be found (Append. II). Thus, the biographical sketch of *Nobunaga* will be found under the title of *Oda*, that of *Hideyoshi*, under that of *Toyotomi*; that of *Ieyasu*, under that of *Tokugawa*, etc.

The sketches of the Emperors are to be found under their posthumous title, the only one in fact, by which they are known in history: however, the name which they bore during their life-time, is given in the notice. It may be of interest to know that the name of the reigning sovereign is never pronounced; *Kinjō-heika*, *Konjō-heika*, *Tennō-heika*, (H.M. the Emperor), etc. are used instead.

The prefix *go* (coming after) written before the name of an Emperor, answers to the title "Second" thus *Go-Murakami* means *Murakami* II.

We add a number to each Sovereign to indicate his place in the chronological list, — thus, *Hanazono-tennō*, 95th Emperor of Japan. We could not of course, use the same word for the Empresses and therefore placed their number between brackets; thus, *Kōgyoku-tennō*, Empress (35) of Japan.

Officially a Sovereign begins to rule only in the year following the death or the resignation of his predecessor.

As to the *nengō* or periods of years, it is well to remember that the change of name (*kaigen*) was made at any time of the year and that the new name, by retroactive effect, was given to the part of the year already passed. Thus the year 1573 begins the 4th year of *Genki*. On the 28th day of the 7th month, the *nengō* was changed into that of *Tenshō*, which is then supposed to start with the beginning of the year and in history, *Genki* has no 4th year. Consequently, if any Japanese work assigns a given fact to the 4th year of *Genki*, it must be understood to refer to the year 1573, before the change of *Genki* into that of *Kenshō* had been made. In order not to give two different *nengō* to the same year for the end of the first and the beginning of the second, we have followed the official system and indicate: — *Genki*: *nengō*, 1570–1572; *Tenshō*: *nengō*, 1573–1591, etc.

Readers familiar with the history of the Empire of the Rising Sun may be astonished to see a modification in some historical names, the orthography of which had been generally accepted. Thus, instead of *Yamatodake* we say *Yamatotakeru*; *Takeshiuchi* instead of *Takenouchi*; *Ishida Kazushige* instead of *Ishida Mitsunari*; *Kiso Yoshinaka*, instead of *Yoshihide*, etc. A painstaking and deep study of ancient documents by some learned professors of the University has brought to light the real pronunciation of these names and we have adopted it.

There is no fixed rule in Japanese for the euphonic softening (*nigori*) of some syllables, — such as *da* for *ta*, *go* for *ko*, etc., and we may find in almost any book *Ukita* and *Ukida*, *Takikawa* and *Takigawa*, etc. We have followed the most common pronunciation.

The preposition *no* between the name and forename has been mostly omitted. Formerly in common use it has been gradually dropped; thus we say *Minamoto no Yoritomo* or *Minamoto Yoritomo*.

We have been obliged to limit ourselves in the Geographical part. With the exception of historical places, only such cities are mentioned in this Dictionary as possess at least 10,000 inhabitants, rivers of more than 100 kilometers or mountains over 1,000 meters in height.

Instead of giving the 639 districts (*kori*, *gun*) in their alphabetical order, we have put them together under the name of their respective provinces.

The illustrations are reproductions of famous Japanese paintings. The historical figures, anterior to the 14th century were mostly taken from the *Zenken-kojitsu* of *Kikuchi Yōsai* (1788–1878).

We have given the escutcheons (*mon*) of the principal noble families; explanations in this respect are furnished under the heading "*mon*."

As the Dictionary contains only Japanese names, we thought it would be agreeable to many readers to present, in a Supplement, a short sketch of the principal foreigners connected with Japan from the first arrival of the Portuguese (1542) down to the Imperial Restoration (1868).

Detailed information on some points may be found either in the several Appendices, or in synoptical tables.

In the choice of sources we have preferred Japanese treaties on History and Geography, the catalogue of which would be too extensive and of too little interest to be given here. But we have not entirely excluded European writers and owe much valuable information to *M. B.-H. Chamberlain's* books (*Things Japanese, Handbook for Japan, Moji no Shirube*, translation of the *Koji-ki*, etc.) which are all known for their high standard of erudition and trustworthy scholarship.

In transliterating Japanese sounds into Roman letters, we have followed the rules laid down by Dr. Hepburn, the pioneer-author of English-Japanese Dictionaries. This method has been generally adopted and is the standard of pronunciation. In this system:

a   has the sound of *a* in *father, arm*.

e   has the sound of *ey* in *they, prey*.

i   has the sound of *i* in *machine, pique* or like the sound of *e* in *mete*.

u   has the long sound of *u* in *rule, tune*, or *oo* in *moon*, excepting in the syllables *tsu, zu*, and *su*, when it has a close sound, resembling, as near as possible, the sound of *u* pronounced with the vocal organs fixed in the position they are in just after pronouncing the letter *s*.

o   has the sound of *o* in *no, so*. The horizontal mark over *ō* and *u* indicates merely that the sound of *o* and *u* is prolonged.

ai has the sound of *ai* in *aisle*, or like *eye*.

au has the sound of *ow* in *cow, how*.

ch is pronounced like *ch* in *cheek, cheap*.

sh is pronounced like *sh* in *shall, ship, shop*.

f   has a close resemblance to the sound of the English *f*, but differs from it, in that the lower lip does not touch the upper teeth ; the sound is made by blowing *fu* softly through the lips nearly closed, resembling the sound of *wh* in *who : fu* is an aspirate, and might for the sake of uniformity, be written *hu*.

g   in the *Tōkyō* dialect has the sound of *ng*, but in *Kyōto, Nagasaki*, and the southern provinces it has the hard sound of *g* in *go, gain*.

r   in *ra, re, ro, ru*, has the sound of the English *r ;* but in *ri* is pronounced more like *d*. But this is not invariable, as many natives give it the common *r* sound.

se in *Kyōto, Nagasaki* and the southern provinces is pronounced *she*, and *ze* like *je*.

The final *n*, when at the end of a word, has always the sound of *ng ;* as *mon* = *mong, san* = *sang, min* = *ming*, but in the body of a word, when followed by a syllable beginning with *b, m* or *p*, it is pronounced like *m*, as *ban-min* = *bamming, mon-ban* = *mombang ; shin-pai* = *shimpai*. Before the other consonants it has the sound of *n ;* as, *an-nai, bandai, hanjō*.

The sounds of the other consonants, viz., *b, d, h, j, k, m, n, p, s, t, w, y* and *z* do not differ from their common English sounds.

Finally, we also give the Chinese pronunciation (*kan-on* and *go-on*) of the most usual Geographical terms and of the words that most frequently enter into the composition of local and personal names.

Romaji Japanese		Pronunciation of Chinese Characters	
kuni	國	koku	country
agata	縣	ken, gen	department
	府	fu	1st class prefecture
kōri	郡	gun	district
	京都	kyō	capital
		to	„
ichi	市	shi, ji	city
machi	町	chō	town
furusato	郷	gō	district
mura	村	son	village
sato	里	ri	„
suji	條	jō	line
tokoro	所	sho, so	place
ba	場	chō, jō	„
mori	森	shin, sen	forest
hayashi	林	rin	wood
yama	山	san, sen	mountain
take	嶽	gaku	summit
nobori	登	tō	„
mine	峯	hō, fu	„
tōge	峠		mountain neck
utena	臺	dai	terrace
tsuka	塚	shō, jō	mound of earth
iwa	岩	gan, gen	rock
saka	坂	hen, han	ascent
hashi	橋	kyō, gyō	bridge
michi	道	tō, dō	road
tani, ya	谷	koku	valley
hatake	畠		field
ta	田	ten, den	rice field
hara	原	gen, gwan	moor, prairie
no	野	ya, e	„
shiro	城	sei, jō	castle
kura	倉	sō, shō	granary
kura	藏	sō, zō	„
seki	關	kwan, ken	barrier
kaki	垣	en, on	palisade
kata	方	hō	side
kata	片	hen	„
higashi	東	tō, tsu	East
nishi	西	sai, sei	West
minami	南	nan	South
kita	北	hoku	North
oku	奥	ō	back
fuchi	淵	en, on	deep pool (eddy)
tsuno	角	kaku	horn
umi	海	kai, kei	sea
nada	洋	yō	„
irie	灣	wan, en	gulf
e	江	kō	bay
ura	浦	ho, fu	„
tsu	津	shin	harbor, port
numa	沼	shō	marsh
mizu-umi	湖	ko, ku	lake
ike	池	chi, ji	pond
hori	堀	kutsu	canal
kawa, gawa	川	sen	river
shima	島	tō	island
minato	港	kō	port
moto	本	hon	source

ROMAJI JAPANESE		PRONUNCIATION OF CHINESE CHARACTERS	
on, o, mi	御	go	(term of respect)
kami, ue	上	shō, jō	above
shimo, shita	下	ka, ge	below
soto	外	gwai, ge	exterior
naka	中	chū	interior
uchi	内	dai, nai	„
moto	元	gen, gwan	source
ō	大	tai, dai	great
ko	小	shō	small
hito	人	jin, nin	man
otoko	男	dan, nan	boy
onna	女	jo, nyo	girl, woman
chi, tsuchi	土	do, to, tsu	earth
ame, ama	天	ten	heaven
hi	日	jitsu, nichi	sun, day
tsuki	月	getsu, gwatsu	moon, month
hoshi	星	sei	star
hi	火	kwa	fire
mizu	水	sui	water
yu	湯	tō	hot water
yuki	雪	setsu	snow
kōri	氷	hyō	ice
ki	木	boku, moku	tree, wood
matsu	松	shō, shu	pine
sugi	杉	san, sen	cedar
sakaki	榊		Cleyera Jap.
kiri	桐	tō, dō	paulownia
fuji	藤	tō, dō	wistaria
take	竹	chiku	bamboo
kusu	楠	nan, dan	camphor tree
suge, suga	菅	kwan, ken	sedge
ume	梅	bai, mai	plum
ine, ina	稲	tō, dō	rice before blossoming
shiba	柴	sai, se	brush-wood
shiba	芝	shi	lawn
hana	花	kwa, ke	flower
kane	金	kin, kon	metal
kama	鎌	ren, ron	sickle
ishi	石	seki, jaku	stone
ie	家	ka, ke	house
to	戸	ko, ge	door
kado	門	mon, bon	door, gate
tama	玉	gyoku	precious stone
iro	色	shoku, shiki	color
toyo	豊	hō, fu	abundance
tomi	富	fū, fu	wealth
nori	德	toku	virtue
yoshi	吉	kichi, kitsu	happiness
o	尾	bi, mi	tail
i, ido	井	sei, shō	well
taira, hira	平	hei, byō	flat (adj.)
kiyo	清	sei, jō	pure
hoso	細	sei, sai	slender
hiro	廣	kō	large, wide
maru	丸	kwan	round
taka	高	kō	high
aka	赤	seki, shaku	red
ao	青	sei, shō	blue, green
shiro	白	haku, byaku	white
kuro	黑	koku	black

ROMAJI JAPANESE	PRONUNCIATION OF CHINESE CHARACTERS	
haya	早	*sō*	rapid
omo	重	*chō, ju*	heavy
karu	輕	*kei, kyō*	light
fuka	深	*shin, son*	deep
asa	淺	*sen*	shallow
naga	長	*chō*	long
hisa	久	*kyū, ku*	long (time)
furu	古	*ko, ku*	ancient
nii, atarashi	新	*shin*	new
ima	今	*kin, kon*	at present
mae	前	*sen, zen*	in front, before
saki	先	*sen*	„
ato	後	*kō, go*	after
asa	朝	*chō*	morning
ban, yū	夕	*seki*	evening
haru	春	*shun*	spring
natsu	夏	*ka, ge*	summer
aki	秋	*shū*	fall or autumn
fuyu	冬	*tō*	winter
hotoke	佛	*butsu, futsu*	Buddh. divinity
kami	神	*shin, jin*	Shint. divinity
miya	宮	*kyū, gū*	Shint. temple
tera	寺	*shi, ji*	Buddh. „
	宗	*shū, sō*	religion
eda	派	*ha, he*	branch
nagare	流	*ryū, ru*	current, stream
	天皇	*tennō*	emperor
kisaki	皇后	*kōgō*	empress
miya	宮	*kyū, gū*	imperial prince
mi-ko	親王	*shinnō*	„ „
samurai	士	*shi*	knight
kerai, omi	臣	*shin, jin*	vassal
matsuri	祭	*sai*	religious feast
tsurugi	劒	*ken*	sword (long, double edged)
katana	刀	*tō*	sword
tate	舘	*kwan*	building
kasa	笠	*ryū*	hat
sake, saka	酒	*shu*	wine (from rice)
uma	馬	*ba*	horse
inu	犬	*ken*	dog
saru	猿	*en*	monkey
hachi	蜂	*hō*	bee
tsuru	鶴	*gaku*	crane
koma	駒	*ku, ko*	colt
tori	鳥	*chō*	bird
kuma	熊	*yū*	bear
hitotsu	一	*ichi, itsu*	1
futatsu	二	*ni*	2
mitsu	三	*san*	3
yotsu	四	*shi*	4
itsutsu	五	*go*	5
mutsu	六	*roku*	6
nanatsu	七	*shichi*	7
yatsu	八	*hachi*	8
kokonotsu	九	*ku*	9
tō	十	*jū*	10
momo	百	*hyaku*	100
chi	千	*sen*	1,000
yorozu	萬	*man, ban*	10,000

HISTORICAL INTRODUCTION.

The History of Japan may be divided into three periods, the first of which begins with the origin of the Japanese people and extends to the times of the *Kamakura Shōgun*. It comprises 18 centuries (660 B.C. — 1192 A.D.). During this period, the power was in the hands of the Emperors. The second extends from the *Minamoto Shōgun* (1192) to the end of the *Tokugawa* (1868) and is the age of military feudal sway. The third period begins with the Imperial Restoration. During this time the customs of the people undergo a complete transformation; the administration of the country follows modern ideas and Japan ranks among the great nations of the world.

We shall here give the whole of this history in a succinct form. It is narrated in detail in the pages of the book.

I. — Period of Autocracy (660 B.C. — 1192 A.D.)

According to Japanese traditions a tribe — probably of Malayan origin, — came to the shores of *Kyūshū* in the 7th century before the Christian era. Later on it is said to have gone northward, and to have subjected the Aborigines to its authority, and, after numerous struggles for many years, to have finally settled in the district of *Yamato*. The leader of these adventurers, *Hasanu no Mikoto* became the first Emperor of Japan (*Jimmu-tennō*). His enthronement, according to the aforesaid source of information, took place in the year 660 B.C. This event is considered as the foundation of the Empire, and the beginning of a dynasty of sovereigns who have ruled over Japan for more than 25 centuries.

From that date the Annals are silent for a space of 500 years, after which an attempt at civilization began under the reigns of *Sujin* (97-30 B C.) and *Suinin* (29 B.C. — 70 A.D.). Then comes the legend of the famous hero *Yamatotakeru* (81-113), who enters the western provinces on a tour of exploration and subjugates the aboriginal tribes at least temporarily to the sway of Imperial authority. *Yamatotakeru's* son reigns only a few years (*Chūai*, 192-200); his widow the Empress *Jingō* ascends the throne after him. Japanese chronicles attribute to her the conquest of the three small kingdoms (*San-Kan*) in the southern portion of the Korean peninsula, but Chinese and Korean annals do not mention this expedition. Moreover, the Empress, being with child at the beginning of the campaign, found means to retard her delivery until the following year when she returned to *Tsukushi*: a fact which seems to darken, according to some authorities, the pure sky of divine descent.

The child that was born became the Emperor *Ōjin*, lived 110 years and was honored as a god under the name of *Hachiman*.

Ōjin's son, *Nintoku*, ruled for 87 years (313-399). His reign is known as the golden time of a patriarchal age which however did not last very long. In the following century rivalry was the order of the day, bloody dramas were of frequent occurrence in the imperial family and ended by the disappearance of *Nintoku's* descendants, when its last scion, a young madman, a kind of Heliogabalus, *Buretsu-tennō* by name, was assassinated in his palace (506).

A lateral branch descendant from Ōjin was then raised to the throne, and under *Kimmei* (540-571), its fourth sovereign, Buddhism was introduced into Japan by bonzes who came from Korea (552).

From the very first, war broke out on the religious question between the principal ministers who were jealous of one another. The *Mononobe*, supporters of national Shintoism, were overthrown, and the *Soga*, the enthusiastic adherents of the new creed, found themselves at the height of undisputed power. They abused it and did not shrink even from murdering the Emperor *Sushun*, (592). This act roused the animosity of the princes and lords against them and fifty years after (644), they were murdered to make way for the *Fujiwara* whose influence was to extend over a longer period.

However, the introduction of Buddhism caused great changes in the ideas and customs of Japan. The bonzes from China and Korea imported a continental civilization: Chinese literature, arts, sciences, architecture, calendar, etc. Prince *Shōtoku* (573-621), who has been called the Constantine of Buddhism, favored these improvements and put the rudimentary administration of the country on a more advanced footing. But the honor of bringing this to a successful issue belongs to the Emperor *Kōtoku* (645-654), through his famous reform of the *Taikwa* era. Henceforth everything was copied from the Chinese mode of government: the ministers, the administration of the provinces, the dignities and ranks at court, the periods of years *(nengō)*, taxation, etc., and this system, if we except some trifling details, remained in vogue to the present time.

In the following century, the Empress *Gemmei* (708-714) removed the capital to *Nara*, where she remained for 75 years (710-784). The *Koji-ki* (712) and the *Nihon-shoki* (720), the two most ancient historical works were compiled during her reign. Buddhism continued to prosper, national poetry produced its first songs which have come down to us, in the anthology called *Man-yō-shū*.

The 50th Emperor, *Kwammu* (782-805), founded the city of *Kyōto* (794) which was built on the model of a Chinese capital and was to be the Court-residence to the time of the Imperial Restoration. The *Fujiwara* were all-powerful: the Empress was always chosen from that family. They thus became the uncles and grandfathers of the Emperors and were the natural regents of young sovereigns during their minority, and, even after the emperor had attained the legal age they continued to rule, under the title of *Kwampaku*.

Meanwhile the number of princes went on increasing in the imperial family and their maintenance was a heavy burden on a treasury that found it difficult to defray even the ordinary court expenses. To obviate this inconvenience, the princes received a family name : *Taira, Minamoto,* and the government of a province. Their descendants formed the military caste which soon took precedence over the effeminate nobility of the Court which had neglected the profession of arms, and found a congenial occupation only in poetical tilts and similar frivolous pastimes.

Owing to this decline of imperial authority, disorder arose on all sides, and revolts were of frequent occurrence : *Taira Masakado* (940), *Abe Yoritoki* (1056), the *Kiyowara* (1087) aimed at creating independent principalities and even the bonzes of important temples were not afraid of presenting petitions or complaints, arms in hand. To quell these rebels, the Court implored the help of the great military families, and rewarded them when peace was restored by increasing their domains, and thus unwittingly caused their power to become formidable.

The *Taira* and the *Minamoto,* descendants of the Emperors *Kwammu* and *Seiwa* (859-876), rose to great power. They vied with each other for preponderance, and during a space of 35 years their antagonism caused bloody conflicts all over Japan. The *Taira* conquered through the energy of the chiefs *Tadamori* (1096-1153), *Kiyomori* (1118-1181) ; their triumph was finally secured during the *Hōgen* (1156) and the *Heiji* (1159) civil wars. They felt confident of having overthrown the rival party. But *Kiyomori* had scarcely passed away, when the *Minamoto* rose in revolt and in a few years were able to annihilate their adversaries (1185).

Yoritomo, after his victory, placed a child of 4 years on the throne and assumed the title of *Sei-i-taishōgun.* That day saw a complete change in the system of government : a new era had begun in the history of Japan.

II. — Feudal Period (1192-1868).

Thus far, the rule of the *Kyōto* Court over the eastern and northern provinces had been little more than nominal. There was no tie of union between this region and the rest of the Empire : climate, race, customs, all were different. The West was the invading power, and with its Chinese civilization had exerted, it is true, a refining but at the same time, a weakening influence. The East represented the aboriginal race, backward no doubt, but animated by its native and somewhat fierce energy. Thus the tie binding these two races, was very loose and the aforementioned great revolts had all arisen in the East. This rivalry, the study of which has been more or less neglected by historians, continued to the time of the Imperial Restoration. Can we say that it has entirely disappeared even at the present time? It is a factor that has not yet been brought ully to light and which would help to solve many difficult questions of

Japanese history. *Yoritomo* knew how to make use of this rivalry to strengthen his own authority. When he was named *Shōgun*, he made *Kamakura* the seat of government and distributed the Northern and the Eastern provinces among his followers who had rendered his elevation possible. In the West and South he placed some members of his family and some of the *Fujiwara* whose fidelity he had secured ; thus, each province, instead of being as heretofore governed by an officer sent from *Kyōto* for the space of 3 to 5 years, formed one or several hereditary fiefs. Some of these families transmitted their rights in the same lineage for the space of fully 7 centuries : as for instance the *Shimazu* in *Satsuma*, the *Nambu* in *Mutsu*, the *Sō* in *Tsushima*, etc. Furthermore, *Yoritomo* resolved to reorganize the administration in such a way as to have full control in his own hands Unfortunately he died before he could carry out his plans (1199). His two sons and successors, *Yoriie* and *Sanetomo*, did not possess equal energy and allowed their power to pass to the *Hōjō*, to whom they were related through their mother. These latter could not or dared not take the title of *Shōgun* after the extinction of *Yoritomo's* direct lineage, and they selected for this office a child of the *Fujiwara* family (1219), and later on an imperial prince (1252) in whose name they governed at will. However, they took the name of *Shikken* (regent), and under that name were able to retain full power during an entire century, which was one of the most prosperous in Japanese history. Their authority was not always lenient and even became insupportable to more than one Emperor, but all efforts to check it proved futile and occasioned the overthrow or the exile of several emperors. Moreover, to forestall even the slightest desire of independence on the part of the *Kyōto* Court, which they watched very closely from their *Rokuhara*, the *Hōjō* took great care to elevate only children to the throne. Interior dissensions in the imperial family were also of great value to them, and an understanding was concluded which allowed an Emperor to rule only for the space of ten years, after which he was obliged to resign in favor of the rival branch. The *Fujiwara* however were still powerful at Court and to weaken their influence, it was decided that the offices of *Sesshō* and *Kwampaku* were alternately to be entrusted to members of the five branches (*go sekke*) of the family, who it will be seen were afterwards divided by jealousy. In the meantime, the only foreign invasion with which Japan was threatened in the course of her history, that of the Mongols, came to nought through the energy of *Hōjō Toki-mune* and a fortuitous tempest that destroyed the whole fleet of the enemy (1281).

The *Hōjō*, like the *Minamoto*, and as will be seen later on, the *Ashikaga* and the *Tokugawa* lost their influence. For a time the administration was carried on by men of genius, then followed a period of decline, interior dissensions increased, usurped authority was weakened and the way for the restoration of Imperial Power was thus prepared.

The instrument of this work of restoration was the Emperor *Go-Daigo* (1319-1338). Having been raised to the throne at the age of 30, he swore the destruction of the powerful *Shikken*. Herein he was aided by such faithful servants as *Nitta Yoshisada, Kusunoki Masashige, Nawa Nagatoshi,* and in less than two years, he overthrew the supreme power of the *Kamakura Shōgun* (1333).

But *Go-Daigo* had scarcely recovered his independence, and begun the work of reorganization as he had dreamed it, when disunion appeared among his generals. The revolt again started in the East, in the *Ashikaga* clan, a branch of the *Minamoto : Takauji,* its chief assumed the title of *Shōgun,* raised an emperor of his choice to the throne and thus established a new Shōgunal dynasty which remained in power for a space of over 200 years (1336-1573). The dethroned Emperor courageously entered into conflict with his rebel subject and his sons and grandsons kept up the fight after his death. The singular spectacle of two Emperors, ruling simultaneously could thus be seen, for a space of 56 years : the one, hidden in the *Yamato* mountains, but firmly adhering to his legitimate rights and the other, supported by the *Ashikaga,* occupying the palace of *Kyōto,* but deprived of the three sacred emblems of the Imperial dignity. This state of affairs could not however last very long, the contending forces being too unequal. The South yielded, a compromise being effected in 1392 between the two rival branches, from which the Emperor was alternately to be elected. This convention — which was not to be executed — closed the schism and completely established the influence of the *Ashikaga.*

But the belligerent spirit that had naturally invaded the military classes during these civil wars, could not be quenched in a short time. The first of the *Ashikaga Shōgun* were able by personal energy to confine it within just limits, but their successors soon found themselves overpowered. The East, once more, started hostilities. The junior branch of the *Ashikaga,* which, from the city of *Kamakura,* was ruling the *Kwantō* with the title of *Kwanryō,* would not be satisfied with less than the first place ; the *Shōgun* trusted their great vassals for the defence of their rights ; meanwhile other complications arose and rivalries took place. A terrible civil war inaugurated the *Ōnin* era (1467), and during one full century intestine wars were to be the order of the day in the whole Empire. Disorder was seen everywhere, misery was great among the people. Even the imperial Palace had to share in the general want ; old Court ceremonies were suppressed for want of money ; for the same reason the funeral of deceased Emperors could not be solemnized. The *Shōgun* became only tools in the hands of their great feudataries, the *Hosokawa,* the *Shiba,* the *Hatakeyama,* who deposed and replaced them at will, till both, suzerains and vassals were engulfed and disappeared in the same torrent.

At the time when the government of the *Ashikaga Shōgun* was meeting its fate, a small *daimyō* of the province of *Owari,* at first a vassal to the *Shiba,* profited by these intestine troubles to enlarge his own dominion. When he died (1549), his son whose name was *Oda Nobunaga* then 15 years of age, inherited his estates. A few years sufficed for him to become master of several provinces, and his fame for bravery and energy was so great that the Emperor *Ōgimachi,* sent a messenger, inviting him to re-establish order in the Empire. *Nobunaga* accepted this difficult task.

After having defeated the most turbulent among the *daimyō* and over-
awed the others, he deposed the last *Ashikaga Shōgun*, took the management of affairs in his own hands, and was repairing the ruins which a
century of civil wars had accumulated, when a treacherous vassal who
owed everything to him, killed him, and thus his work was left unfinished
(1582).

His power fell into the hands of a soldier who, by his intelligence and
his victories, had raised himself from the lowest to the highest rank among
the generals of *Nobunaga*. *Hideyoshi* put aside the sons of his former
master, and, feeling that he could not claim for himself the dignity of
Shōgun, forced the Emperor to confer on him the most elevated title
of the civil hierarchy, that of *Kwampaku*. He continued the work of
pacification undertaken by *Nobunaga*, and triumphed over all the rebel
daimyō. Having thus reached the zenith of honour and power he was
so blinded by pride that he thought of extending his sway over Korea
and even over China. It may be that he simply intended to turn the
warlike dispositions of his soldiers into another channel. The fact
remains that he undertook this unhappy campaign which could not
fail to end in disaster, in spite of an initial but transient success. At the
close of his life, he understood his mistake and his last words were to
recall his troops that had been decimated by continuous fighting and by
sufferings of all kinds (1598).

Hideyoshi had entrusted to five great *daimyō* the guardianship of his
son *Hideyori* then a young child. Among these five men, one was found
to whom the second rank would not suffice; this was *Tokugawa Ieyasu*
(1542-1616), a descendant of the *Minamoto*. When in 1590, he was
placed over the eight provinces of the *Kwantō*, he selected the small port
of *Edo*, in *Musashi* province, as the site of his new castle. After *Hideyoshi's* death, he soon separated himself from his colleagues, who
were faithful to their promise to the *Taikō* and fought against them.
The East was again about to struggle with the West; and again the East
conquered when, in the plains of *Sekigahara (Mino)*, it attained a
supremacy that was destined to last for the space of two and a half
centuries.

Ieyasu obtained the title of *Shōgun* three years after this victory,
(1603), and began the *Tokugawa* line which came to possess an authority
that was unknown both to the *Minamoto* and to the *Ashikaga*. Two
years later, he resigned the Shogunate to his son, retired to *Sumpu*, and
before his death, had the consolation to see *Hideyoshi's* lineage become
extinct at *Ōsaka*. (1615). From that moment, power was secure in
his family. His immediate successors, *Hidetada* (1605-1623) and
Iemitsu (1623-1651), continued his work and strengthened the iron rule
he had imposed upon his country :—Breaking off all relations with
foreign lands ; closing all ports of the country to foreign commerce if we
except the Dutch and the Chinese ; atrocious persecution of the Christians ;
close watching of all the proceedings of the *daimyō* and the *samurai ;*
adroit spying at the *Kyōto* Court ; Draconian laws on the press, on the
teaching of Confucianism, etc. ; such were the principles of the *Shōgun's*

government For two hundred years, every *daimyō*, *samurai* and the common people seemed to bear this yoke willingly which had secured them lasting peace after so many years of trouble and disorder. Then the well regulated machinery began to show signs of decay. The power, which was at first wielded by men of energy and talent, fell into the hands of children, subordinates ruled in their name, the *Edo* Court became as effeminate as had been that of *Kyōto*, and decay set in rapidly. The Western and Southern clans, who were kept aloof from the administration, notwithstanding their large estates, anxiously followed the downward movement and when they thought the moment propitious they threw off their allegiance and openly entered the fight. They did not however dare to supersede the government which they were bound to destroy, so they set up the imperial standard and took as the first article of their program, the restoration of the supreme power into the hands of the Emperor. Some Court noblemen, the *Sanjō*, the *Iwakura*, supported this plan with all the weight of their influence. Besides, the government of the *Shōgun*, had committed a great crime in the eyes of many. It had concluded treaties with the foreign barbarians, and polluted the country of the gods, by permitting foreigners to reside therein. The expulsion of these intruders formed the second article of the program of the discontented. Their rallying word henceforth was: *Sonnō-jōi* (to venerate the Emperor and to expel the foreigners). Vainly did the *Shōgun* try to divide his adversaries ; vainly did he slacken in his severity towards the *daimyō* ; it was too late. Nothing was to stop the forward movement. The last *Tokugawa Shōgun* for a whole year tried to face the thousand difficulties of his critical situation ; he was finally obliged to send his resignation to the Emperor. His adherents fought for some months to come, but the imperial army, composed especially of Southern and Western men, triumphed everywhere. The East met its defeat, the government of the *Shōgun* had passed and the Imperial Restoration was an accomplished fact. (1868).

III. — Imperial Restoration.

The Emperor rapidly grasped the situation. For over 200 years the people were used to see all the laws emanate from Edo ; he had therefore to take up his residence in that city, if he wished the people henceforth to understand that all authority was in his hands. *Edo* was then called *Tokyō* and became the capital of the Empire. The whole government system was modified and, as in olden times China had served as model in the reforms, so now Europe was looked upon as the standard for the new system of ruling. The fiefs of the *daimyō* were abolished and a new administrative division, that of departments, was adopted ; the Court-nobles and the feudal lords were amalgamated into one class, that of the *kwazoku* ; military service, which till then had been the privilege of only the *samurai* was extended by conscription to the whole nation; and the many centuries old proscription edicts against Christianity were recalled. In its foreign relations, the new government, not feeling itself sufficiently strong, carried its spirit of conciliation to extreme limits ; Korea even, weak Korea, always considered as an ancient vassal, might show itself insolent, without fearing to be rebuked.

Even among the promoters of the Restoration some were found who thought that the movement had swerved from its original path. The new order of things did not realize the dream of the fervent patriots who had helped to overthrow the *Shōgun*. Discontent was smothering for a long time, riots took place in different districts, at last, a formidable insurrection broke out in *Satsuma* (1877) and for several months, it was doubtful whether Japan would not return to the beautiful days of the ancient *samurai* with their two swords. The imperial army however carried the day, and this last attempt to bring back the ancient order of government only resulted in a firm consolidation of the new regime.

The reform plans were then put into execution : ministerial service, nobility, decorations, army, navy, justice, every thing was modified according to European ideas. At the same time all the resources of the country were worked and developed. The day then came, when the country conscious of its strength, wished to show to China that her old ideas of a quasi-suzerainty over Japan belonged to the domain of legends, and that Japan was in turn to become the guide of its old mistress in the way of contemporary civilization. Ten years had scarcely elapsed, when Europe awoke to an unexpected change. Japan no longer wished to bear with either her tutelage or her unreasonable requirements : it asked to take rank among the great powers. This story is only of yesterday and need not be related in detail.

Japan has completely changed in many points, and this in the small space of 30 years. One cannot help but ask the questions : what will be the next move, and what the consequence of so rapid and astonishing a stride ? It is God's secret and no human being can reasonably foretell it.

For some years passed, especially, Japan has been overwhelmed with praise: *beatum dixerunt populum cui haec sunt;* it has yet to acquire another glory : *beatus populus cujus Dominus Deus ejus !*

E. P.

Yokohama, January, 1909.

HISTORICAL AND GEOGRAPHICAL
DICTIONARY
OF JAPAN.

A

Abe, 安 倍. A family which, in the eleventh century governed a part of the province of *Mutsu.*

—— **Yoritoki,** 賴 時 (+ 1057). Son of *Tadayoshi*, possessed six districts, in the center of which he built the castle of *Koromogawa*, and established a sort of independent principality, keeping all the proceeds of the taxes, and refusing to contribute to the expenses of the province, etc. The governors of *Mutsu* and *Dewa* marched against him, but were defeated. Therefore the emperor appointed *Minamoto Yoriyoshi Chin-jufu-Shōgun* and commissioned him to quell the revolt. *Yoriyoshi* took his son *Yoshiie* with him —— *Yoritoki* was killed by an arrow, in one of the first engagements.

—— **Sadatō,** 貞 任 (1019-1062), the eldest son of *Yoritoki*, continued the war. Attacked by *Yoriyoshi* at *Kawasaki*, he defeated him and obliged him to retreat (1058). It was only four years later that, *Yoriyoshi*, who had been reinforced by *Kiyowara Takenori* of *Dewa*, succeeded in defeating him successively at *Komatsu*, *Koromogawa* and *Kuriyagawa*, where *Sadatō* lost his life.

—— **Munetō,** 宗 任, the 2nd son of *Yoritoki*, at first fought under his brother's banner, but eventually surrendered to *Yoshiie*. He was exiled to *Tsukushi* where he became a bonze. He is supposed to be the ancestor of the *Matsuura* family.

Abe, 阿 部. A family of *daimyō*, originating in *Mikawa*, and descended from *Ōhiko*, a son of the Emperor *Kōgen*.

Masakatsu { Masatsugu - Shigetsugu { Sadataka - Masakuni (a)
              { Masaharu - Masamune (b)
            { Masayoshi - Masaaki - Masayoshi- Masatake (c)

(*a*) —— The elder branch. —— **Masakatsu,** 正 勝 (1541-1600), served *Ieyasu* and, in 1590, received from him a revenue of 5000 k. at *Ichihara* (*Izu*).

—— **Masatsugu,** 正 次 (1569-1647), the eldest son of *Masakatsu*, was raised to the rank of *daimyō* after *Sekigahara* (1600). He established himself successively in *Hatoya* (*Musashi*) 1600, *Shikanuma* (*Shimotsuke*) 1610 ; *Ōtaki* (*Kazusa*) 1617 ; *Odawara* (*Sagami*-60,000 k.) 1620 ; and *Iwatsuki* (*Musashi*) 1623. — His descendants established themselves in 1681, at *Miyatsu* (*Tango*) ; in 1697, at *Utsunomiya* (*Shimotsuke*) ; and finally, from 1710 to 1868, at *Fukuyama* (*Bingo* — 110,000 k.) = To-day, Count.

(*b*) — The younger branch settled in *Ōtaki* (*Kazusa*) 1651 ; in *Kariya* (*Mikawa*) 1702 ; in *Sanuki* (*Kazusa* — 16,000 k.) from 1710-1868 = To-day, Viscount.

(*c*) — This branch settled in *Mibu* (*Shimotsuke*) 1635 ; in *Oshi* (*Musashi*) 1639, then in *Shirakawa* (*Mutsu* — 100,000 k.) from 1823-1868 = To-day, Viscount.

Abe, 安部. A family of *daimyō*, originating in *Suruga* and descended from the *Shigeno* branch of the *Seiwa-Genji*. Established at *Hambara* (*Mikawa*) 1636, they were transferred to *Okabe* (*Musashi* — 20,000 k.) 1751, where they remained until the Restoration = To-day, Viscount.

Abe Hirafu, 安倍比羅夫. A Governor of *Koshi*. He commanded an expedition against the *Ebisu* (658) another into *Korea* to aid *Kudara* (661) and was named *Shōgun*. He is said to be the ancestor of the *Abe*, *Andō*, and *Akita daimyō*.

Abe-kawa, 安倍川. A river which flows through *Suruga* and empties itself into the sea near *Shizuoka* (63 km.).

Abe Nakamaro, 安部仲麿 (701-770). A poet and man of letters. Sent to China in 716 with *Kibi no Makibi* to complete his studies, where he remained for more than thirty years. *Fujiwara Kiyokawa* persuaded him to return to Japan with him, but encountering a storm at sea, and having a narrow escape, they returned to China, where they remained.

Abeno, 安部野. A plain in *Settsu*, between the villages of *Tennōji* and *Sumiyoshi*. Here *Kitabatake Akiie* was defeated by *Kō Moronao* (1338) ; to whose honor a temple has been erected (*Abeno-jinja*). This place was the scene of several battles when *Nobunaga* besieged *Ishiyama-jō*, the castle of the *Hongwan-ji* temple (1576-1580), and also during the *Ōsaka* Campaign of 1615.

Abe Seimei, 安倍晴明 (+ 1005) a celebrated Astronomer.

Abukuma-gawa, 阿武隈川. A river which takes its rise at Mount *Asahi-yama* (*Iwaki*), enters *Iwashiro*, flows through *Shirakawa*, *Nihonmatsu*, *Fukushima*, and empties itself into the Pacific Ocean near *Iwanuma*. — Also called *Akuri-gawa*, (227 km.)

Aburakōji, 油小路. A family of *kuge* descended from *Fujiwara Uona*. = To-day Count.

ABE SEIMEI.

Abura-urushi-bugyō, 油漆奉行. A title created in 1645 and given to two officials, whose duty it was to keep an account of the oil, varnish, lacquer, etc., in all the administrations of the *Bakufu*.

Abutsu-ni, 阿佛尼 (+ 1283). At first maid of honor of the princess *Kuni-Naishinnō* (*Anka-mon-in*); she married *Fujiwara Tameie* (1197-1275). At the death of her husband, she shaved her head and took the names *Abutsu* and *Hokurin-zenni*. In 1277, she went from *Kyōto* to *Kamakura* and, under the title of *Izayoi-nikki*, published a very interesting account of her journey.

Achi no Omi, 阿知使主. A Korean prince descended from the Chinese dynasty of the latter *Han* (*Go-Kan : 25 B.C. — 221 A.D.*) In 289, he settled in Japan, with a large number of Korean emigrants. The emperor *Ōjin* gave them the village of *Hinosaki* (*Yamato*). In 307, he went to the country of *Go* (Eastern China) and brought back with him some women skilled in weaving, who taught their art to the Japanese. He was then named *Kurando*. He is the ancestor of the *Sakanoe*, the *Harada* and the *Akizuki*.

Adachi, 安達. An ancient family of *Dewa*, descended from *Fujiwara Yamakage* (824-888).

—— **Morinaga, 盛長,** (+ 1200). Sided with *Yoritomo* against the *Taira*, and after the triumph of his party, became a bonze under the name of *Rensai*.

—— **Kagemori, 景盛,** (+ 1248). The eldest son of *Morinaga*, served under *Yoriie*. In 1218, he recovered the fief of *Akita*, and was the first to take the title of *Akita-jō-no-Suke*. On the death of *Sanetomo* (1219) he shaved his head, took the name of *Gakuchi* and retired to *Kōya-san*, whence the title of *Kōya-nyūdō*, by which he is commonly known. At the time of the *Shōkyū* war (1221), he marched upon *Kyōto* with *Hōjō Tokifusa* and defeated the imperial army. His daughter who had married *Hōjō Tokiuji*, became the mother of *Tsunetoki* and of *Tokiyori*, and when the latter became *Shikken*, the influence of *Kagemori* was preponderant. He contributed with all his might to the ruin of the *Miura* family (1247).

—— **Yoshikage, 義景,** (+ 1255). Son of *Kagemori*, was *Akita-jō-no-Suke* and *Hyōjōshū*. After the death of the emperor *Shijō* (1242), *Fujiwara Michiie* desired to have his grandson *Tadanari-Shinnō* ascend the throne, to which *Hōjō Yasutoki* was opposed, wherefore the latter sent *Yoshikage* to *Kyōto* to enthrone Prince *Kunihito* (*Go-Saga-tennō*). Falling ill in 1254, *Yoshikage* shaved his head and took the name of *Gwanchi*. He died the following year.

—— **Yasumori, 泰盛,** (+ 1285). Third son of *Yoshikage*, succeeded to his father's titles and dignities. His daughter was married to *Hōjō Tokimune*, and became the mother of *Sadatoki*. When the latter became *Shikken*, (1284), *Yasumori* and his son *Munekage* enjoyed great authority for a time. But *Taira Yoritsuna*, the minister (*shitsuji*) of *Sadatoki*, accused them of plotting against the young *Shikken*, and even of aspiring to the shogunate. *Sadatoki* lent a willing ear to these insinuations and had the whole *Adachi* family put to death.

Agano-gawa, 阿賀野川. A river which takes its rise in the south-eastern part of *Iwashiro*, passes by *Wakamatsu*, enters into *Echigo*, flows through *Tsugawa* and empties itself into the Sea of Japan at *Matsugasaki*, a little above *Niigata*. In its upper course, it is also called *Aizugawa*, from the district it traverses, (175 Km.).

Agata, 縣. Primitively this name was applied to the plantations and rice-fields, belonging to the Court. Later on, it was extended to all the domains governed by an *Agata no miyatsuko*.

Agata no miyatsuko, 縣造. In ancient times a title for the governors of districts called *agata*. Below them were the *Agata-nushi*.

Aichi-ken, 愛知縣. A department formed from the provinces of *Owari* and *Mikawa*. — Pop. 1,692,750. Capital, *Nagoya* (285,000 inh.) chief cities : *Atsuta* (24,950), *Toyohashi* (20,000), *Okazaki* (16,900) *Ichinomiya* (14,150), *Tsushima* (12,800), etc.

Aikawa, 相川. Capital (13,000 inh.) of the province of *Sado*.

Aino, ア イ ヌ. The *Aino*, who call themselves *Ainu* (men) are the last remnants of the aboriginal race of Japan. Japanese history calls them *Ebisu* (barbarians). Gradually driven back by the invaders from the S.W., they were not brought under complete subjection before the 18th century. According to the latest census, their number does not exceed 18,000, nearly all residing in the island of *Ezo*.

Ai no take, 相嶽. One of the peaks of *Shirane-zan* (*Kai*) (3,100 m.).

Ainoura, 相浦. A family of *samurai* from *Saga* (*Hizen*) ennobled in 1895.=To-day, Baron.

Aizawa Seishi, 會澤正志 (1782-1863), Confucianist from *Mito*. Left several works.

Aizen-myō-ō, 愛染明王. The Buddhist god of love, represented with three eyes and six arms ; often found at the side of the goddess *Kwannon*.

Aizu, 會津. A district of the province of *Iwashiro*. The emperor *Sujin*, having appointed four *Shōgun* to go over and pacify the four grand regions (*shi-dō*) of the country (88 B.C.) ; two of them, *Ōhiko*, *Shōgun* of the *Hokurikudō* and *Takenukawa-wake*, *Shōgun* of the *Tōkaidō*, gave the name of *Aizu* (meeting) to the place where they met after accomplishing their mission. In the beginning of the 15th century, the *Ashina daimyō* built the castle of *Kurokawa* (*Wakamatsu*) there. — The people of *Aizu* have always been renowned for their high-spirited and warlike character ; they distinguished themselves by their fidelity to the *Shōgun* at the time of the Restoration.

Aizu no shi-ke, 會津四家. The four *daimyō* families, that resided in *Aizu* before the *Tokugawa* Shogunate : *Ashina, Date, Gamō* and *Uesugi*.

Ajiki, 阿直岐. A scholar from *Kudara* (Korea) said to have passed over to Japan in 284, A.D., (really in 404), bringing with him, as presents for the emperor *Ōjin*, horses, clothes, books, etc. He was the first to introduce Chinese literature into Japan. *Ajiki* became preceptor to Prince *Uji-no-Waki-iratsuko*, the son of *Ōjin*. According to some authors, his true name was *Aji Kishi*, *Aji* being his forename and *Kishi* his family name.

Akabashi Moritoki, 赤橋守時 (+ 1333). Descendant of *Hōjō Yoshitoki*, in the fifth generation. He, with *Koresada*, received the title of *Shikken*, when *Takatoki* became bonze (1326). When *Nitta Yoshisada* advanced to attack *Kamakura*, *Moritoki* attempted to check him at *Kobukuro-zaka*, but he was defeated and put an end to his life. His sister was married to *Ashikaga Takauji*.

Akagi-san, 赤城山. A volcano (1860 m.) in the eastern part of *Kōzuke*.

Akaishi-yama, 赤石山. A mountain (3,093 m.) on the limits of *Suruga* and *Shinano*.

Akamagaseki, 赤間ヶ關. See *Shimonoseki*.

Akamagaseki-kaikyō, 赤間ヶ關海峽. The eastern end of the *Shimonoseki* strait, between *Hondo* and *Kyūshū*, also called *Haya-tomo no seto*.

Akama-numa, 赤麻沼. A lake in the south of *Shimotsuke* (15 km. in circumference).

Akamatsu, 赤松. An ancient family of the *Harima daimyō*, descended from *Minamoto Morofusa* (*Murakami-Genji*).

—— **Suefusa,** 季房 descendant of *Morofusa* in the sixth generation, was the first to take the name of *Akamatsu*, from a village of *Harima*, where he settled and built the castle of *Shirahata*, towards 1110 A.D.

—— **Norimura,** 則村 (1277-1350). A fervent member of the *Zenshū* sect, shaved his head while still young and took the name of *Enshin* 圓心, by which he is mostly known. In 1333, by order of Prince *Morinaga-Shinnō*, he levied troops, marched on to *Kyōto*, defeated *Hōjō Nakatoki* and captured *Rokuhara*; shortly after, *Go-Daigo* re-entered the capital and rewarded *Norimura* by bestowing upon him the title of *Harima no Shugo* and giving him *Harima* province in fief. But shortly after, he was stripped of his province and limited to the possession (*Shō-en*) of *Sayō*. Incensed at this, *Norimura* passed over to the *Ashikaga* party and became the implacable adversary of the southern dynasty. While *Takauji* went to levy troops in *Kyūshū*, he stayed the progress of *Nitta Yoshisada*; then, returning towards the east with *Takauji*, he fought at *Minato-gawa* (1336).

AKAMATSU NORISUKE.

—— **Norisuke,** 則祐 (1312-1371). A son of *Norimura*, he was a bonze at *Hiei-zan*; but, in answer to the appeal of Prince *Morinaga Shinnō*, he threw off his religious garb, and with his father, levied troops against the *Hōjō*. Afterwards, he followed *Norimura* to the northern camp, and, on his death, became governor of *Harima*, next of *Bizen*.

Shigenori	Norimura (*Enshin*)	Norisuke	Yoshinori - Mitsusuke - Noriyasu.
			Yoshisuke (*Arima*).
		Sadanori - Akinori - Mochisada - Sadamura.
		Norisuke - Mitsunori - Mitsuhiro - Norihiro (*Hirose*).
	Enkō - Atsumitsu - Atsunori - Munesue - Noriharu (*Bessho*).

—— **Yoshinori,** 義 則 (1358-1427), was in great favor with the *Shōgun Yoshimitsu*, who numbered him among his ministers, and after the overthrow of the *Yamana* (1391), annexed the province of *Mimasaka* and several districts of *Inaba* and *Tajima* to his dominions. Later on *Yoshinori* shaved his head taking the name of *Shōshō*, and, as he was of very small stature, was surnamed *San-shaku-Nyūdō* (the bonze three feet tall).

—— **Mitsusuke,** 滿 祐 (1381-1441), succeeded his father, but his relative *Mochisada* intrigued at the Court of the *Shōgun Yoshimochi* to obtain the domains of *Mitsusuke*. The latter hearing that the *Shōgun* was about to consent, returned to *Harima* and began to fortify his castle of *Shirahata*. *Yoshimochi* sent *Hosokawa Mochimoto* and *Yamana Tokinori* against him, but the majority of the *daimyō* having declared in favor of *Mitsusuke*, the *Shōgun* thought it advisable to yield : *Mochisada* was invited to take his own life by committing harakiri, and his rival returned to *Kyōtō* (1427), where he shaved his head and took the name of *Shōgu*. Shortly after, *Yoshimochi* died and was succeeded by his brother *Yoshinori*; *Sadamura*, son of *Mochisada*, recommenced the intrigues of his father at the Court of the new *Shōgun*, to dispossess *Mitsusuke*. The latter, informed of this by his son, invited the *Shōgun* to a feast, during which he had him assassinated. Thereupon *Mitsusuke* fled to *Shirahata*, where he was soon besieged by *Hosokawa Mochiyuki, Akamatsu Sadamura, Takeda Nobukata, Yamana Mochitoyo*, etc. He killed himself, his son *Noriyasu* following his example.

Akamatsu, 赤 松. A family of *samurai* from *Shizuoka* (*Suruga*) ennobled in 1887 = To-day, Baron.

Akamatsu Sōshū, 赤 松 滄 洲 (1721-1801). Confucianist of the *Ako* clan (*Harima*). Left several works, among them a history of the 47 *gishi*.

Akanagi-yama, 赤 薙 山. A mountain north of *Nikkō* (*Shimotsuke*) 2.1 50 m.

Akasaka, 赤 坂. in *Kawachi*; an old castle, built in 1331 by *Kusunoki Masashige*, taken and destroyed in 1382 by the troops of the northern dynasty.

Akashi, 明 石. A city of *Harima* (21,000 inh.) In the 16th century it was the residence of the *daimyō Takayama, Hachisuka, Bessho*. Under the *Tokugawa* it was successively occupied by the *Kuroda* (1580), *Ogasawara* (1617), *Toda* (1633), *Ōkubo* (1641), *Matsudaira* (1649), *Honda* (1684), finally, from 1693 to 1868, by the *Matsudaira* (100.000 k.) — The meridian of this city determined the official time for all Japan.

Akashi-kaikyō, 明 石 海 峽. Strait of *Akashi*, between *Hondo* and the island of *Awaji*.

Akashi Morishige, 明 石 守 重 (+ 1618). vassal of *Ukita Hideie, daimyō* of *Okayama* (*Bizen*) ; he bore the title of *Kamon no Suke*. At *Sekigahara*, where he fought against *Ieyasu*, he defeated the troops of *Nakamura Tadakazu*; but his party having been vanquished, he surrendered to *Kuroda Nagamasa*, who sheltered him in his estates. When *Hideyori* appealed to all the *samurai* of good will to support him in his struggle against the *Tokugawa, Morishige* was one of the first to proceed to *Osaka*, where he fought valiantly. After the fall of the city (1615), he succeeded in escaping and lived the last three years of his life in extreme poverty.—*Morishige* has been baptised in 1596, and in the letters of the missionaries, he is known by the name of *John Akashi Kamon*.

Akayasu-yama, 赤安山. A mountain on the borders of *Kōzuke, Shimotsuke* and *Iwashiro;* also called *Mada-yama* (1950 m.)

Akazome Emon, 赤染衛門. A daughter of *Taira Kanemori* adopted by the *Kebiishi-Uemon, Akazome Tokimochi*. She attended *Fujiwara Rin-Ko,* wife of the *Kwampaku Michinaga*. She married *Ōe Tadahira;* and was remarkable for her poetical and literary talents. In 1027 she published the *Eiywa-monogatari,* which is a history of the supremacy of the *Fujiwara*.

AKAZOME EMON.

Akechi, 明智. An ancient family descended from *Toki Yorimoto (Seiwa-Genji)* also called *Koretō*.

—— **Mitsuhide,** 光秀 (1526-1582). A son of *Mitsukuni;* at first served the *Saitō* of *Mino*. When *Tatsuoki* revolted against his father and killed him (1556), *Mitsuyasu,* uncle of *Mitsuhide,* shut himself up in the castle of *Akechi,* but he was vanquished and killed. At the head of all his *kerai, Mitsuhide* entered the service of *Asakura Ujikage,* then that of *Nagaoka (Hosokawa) Fujitaka*. In 1566, he retired to *Gifu,* offered his services to *Nobunaga* and took rank among his officers. Five years later he received the castle of *Sakamoto* (*Ōmi*) in fief, with a revenue of 100,000 k. and the title of *Hyūga no Kami*. In 1575 he assumed the name of *Koretō* and received the mission to pacify *Tamba*. He besieged *Hatano Hideharu* in the castle of *Yakami,* but as the siege was protracted, he took the mother of *Hideharu* as a hostage, upon which the latter surrendered, only to be crucified by order of *Nobunaga*.

To avenge their lord, the retainers of *Hideharu* got possession of *Mitsuhide's* mother and massacred her (1577); thereupon *Mitsuhide* destroyed the castle and put all its inmates to death; moreover he conceived a mortal hatred against *Nobunaga* on whom he swore to wreak vengeance. He waited five years for a favorable occasion. In 1582, *Hashiba Hideyoshi,* who was fighting in the *San-yō-dō* against *Mōri Terumoto,* asked *Nobunaga* for reinforcements. Before he personally started, *Nobunaga* sent orders to *Mitsuhide* to muster thirty thousand men, and to lead them in all haste to *Hideyoshi*. *Mitsuhide* assembled his troops, but instead of directing them towards *Chūgohu,* he marched them upon *Kyōto,*

AKECHI MITSUHIDE·

entered the city and besieged *Nobunaga* in the temple of *Honnō-ji*. Wounded by an arrow, and judging that resistance was useless, *Nobunaga* set fire to the temple and killed himself. His eldest son *Nobutada* cut off

from all help in the *Nijō* palace met the same fate (22 June 1582) Thence
Mitsuhide hastened to the castle of *Azuchi* which he gave up to plunder ;
then returning to *Kyōto*, he obtained an audience with the emperor, who
received him warmly. He styled himself *Shōgun*, appointed a *Shoshidai*, a
Machibugyō, etc. ; to secure for himself the public sympathy, he exempted
the citizens of *Kyōto* from taxes, and made liberal grants to the principal
temples. Meanwhile *Hideyoshi*, on hearing of these events, hastened to
make peace with *Mōri* and set out to punish the traitor. The battle was
fought at *Yamazaki*, on the borders of *Settsu* and *Yamashiro* ; *Akechi*
completely beaten, fled to his castle of *Sakamoto*, but was massacred by
the mob in the village of *Ogurusu*. Only thirteen days had elapsed from
the time he began to muster troops against *Nobunaga*. Hence the saying : " *Akechi no tenka, mikka* " (the power of *Akechi* lasted only three
days) ; hence also the surname : " *Jū-san kubō* " (the *Shōgun* of thirteen
days) which has been given him. — *Mitsuhide* was a poet of note.

—— **Mitsuharu, 光春** (+ 1582), a son of *Mitsuyasu* and cousin to
Mitsuhide, followed the fortune of the latter. He endeavored to deter
him from plotting against *Nobunaga*, and although his advice was not
heeded, he entered *Kyōto* with his cousin, besieged the *Honnō-ji* temple
and himself buried the head of *Nobunaga*. During the engagement of
Yamazaki, he was at *Azuchi*, and arrived too late to prevent disaster. At
Uchide-hama, near *Ōtsu*, he met the troops of *Hori Hidemasa* and was
defeated ; then crossing a part of lake *Biwa* on horse he returned to
Sakatomo, slaughtered the wife and children of *Mitsuhide* as well as his
whole family, set fire to the castle and took his own life.

Aki, 安藝. One of the eight provinces of *San-yō-dō ;* it comprises
seven districts (*kōri*). Chinese name : *Geishū*. — Now-a-days, a part of
Hiroshima-ken.

Aki, 安岐 in *Bungo ;* an old castle, built in the thirteenth century by
Tawara Yasuhiro, whose descendants resided there for fifteen generations.
Towards 1550, the castle was captured by the *Ōtomo ;* *Hideyoshi* gave it
to *Kumagaya Naotsura*, who was killed at *Sekigahara*, (1600) after
which the castle was abandoned.

Akimoto, 秋元. A family of *daimyō*, descending
from the *Utsunomiya*, and through them from the *Fuji-*
wara. Towards 1450 they were named after the district
of *Akimoto* (*Kazusa*) which they possessed.

—— **Nagatomo, 長朝** (+ 1628), first served the *Hōjō*.
After the fall of *Odawara*, he was attached to *Ieyasu*
who gave him estates at *Sōsha* (*Kōzuke*) (1590), and later,
after *Sekigahara*, (1600) raised him to the rank of *daimyō*.

—— **Yasutomo, 泰朝** (1580-1642), *Tajima no Kami*, received the
fief of *Tanimura* (*Kai* — 18,000 k.) in 1641.

—— **Takatomo, 喬朝** (1647-1714), a son of *Toda Tadamasa*, was
adopted by *Akimoto Tomitomo*, who had no children. In 1704, he was
transferred to *Kawagoe* (*Musashi* — 50.000 k.). His descendants settled
in *Yamagata* (*Dewa*) in 1767, then from 1845 to 1868 resided at *Tate-*
bayashi (*Kōzuke* — 63.000 k.) = To-day, Viscount.

Aki no miya, 秋宮.—(Lit.: Palace of Autumn) Name formerly given to the Empress. Used yet in poetry.

Aki-no-yo naga-monogatari, 秋夜長物語.—(Lit.: Long recitals of autumn nights). A book of the 13th century, whose author is unknown. Relates the adventures of the bonze *Sensai* and *Umewaka-gimi*, son of *Minamoto Arihito, Hanazono no Sadaijin*.

Akita, 秋田. Capital of *Ugo* province and of *Akita-ken* (30,000 inh.). An ancient castle built in 733 A.D. to stop the incursions of the *Ebisu*. In the 13th century, the *Adachi,* governors of the province, bore the title of *Akita-jō no Suke*. In the 15th century, *Andō Sanesue,* the holder of the castle, took its name, and his descendants resided there until 1602. At that time, they were supplanted by the *Satake daimyō* (205,000 k.), who resided there until the Restoration. The name of *Akita* was formerly limited to the castle; the city which surrounds it, was called *Kubota.*

Akita, 秋田. A family of *daimyō* descending from *Abe no Sadatō.* From the middle of the 15th century, they possessed the castle of *Akita* and the title of *Akita no Suke.*

—— **Sanesue, 實季** (+ 1659), a son of *Yoshisue,* was transferred to *Shishido* (*Hidachi* — 50,000 k.) in 1602; later in 1632, he was banished to *Asama* (*Ise*) where he died.

—— **Toshisue, 愛季** in 1645 he was appointed to *Miharu* (*Mutsu* — 50,000 k.), where his descendants resided until the Restoration. = Today, Viscount.

Akita-ken, 秋田縣. A department consisting of eight districts of *Ugo* and one of *Rikuchū*. Pop.: 835,000 inh. Capital: *Akita* (30,000 inh.) Chief towns: *Noshiro-minato* (13,700 inh.), *Tsuchisaki-minato* (13,000 inh.), *Yokote* (12,300 inh.), *Aniai* (10,400 inh.), etc.

Akitsu-shima, 秋津洲, 蜻蛉洲.—(Lit.: land of the dragon-fly). According to a legend, *Jimmu-tennō* from the top of a mountain of *Yamato,* which dominates all the surrounding country, discovered land in the neighborhood, having the form of a dragon-fly, and gave it that name, which is yet used in poetry to designate Japan.

Akizuki, 秋月. In *Chikuzen,* was successively the residence of the *daimyō Akizuki* (1190-1587), *Kobayakawa* (1587-1600), and *Kuroda* (50,000 k.) from 1600 to 1868.

Akizuki, 秋月. A family of *daimyō* descending from *Achi-no-Omi.*

—— **Taneo, 種雄** towards 1190 received from *Yoritomo* the estate of *Akizuki* (*Chikuzen*); he built a castle on it and took its name.

—— **Tanemichi, 種道**, descended from *Taneo,* sided with the southern dynasty, but was defeated by *Ashikaga Takauji* at *Tatarahama* (1336) and fled to *Dazaifu,* where he was killed.

—— **Tanezane, 種實** (+ 1588) saw his father *Fumitane* and his brother *Harutane* fall in battle against *Ōtomo Sōrin* (1557) and crossed over to *Yamaguchi* to ask for the help of *Mōri Motonari*. Again defeated he appealed to the *Shimazu* and sided with them when *Hideyoshi* came to *Kyūshū* to subdue them (1587). After peace was restored, he was transferred to *Takanabe* (*Hyūga* — 20,000 k.)

—— **Tanenaga,** 種長 (+ 1614), a son of *Tanezane*, took part in the expedition against Korea, under the order of *Kuroda Nagamasa*. In 1600, he sided with *Ishida Kazushige*, but was able to retain his estates by the help of *Mizuno Katsushige*. —— Until the Restoration, his descendants resided at *Takanabe* (*Hyūga* — 27,000 k.) = Now, Viscount.

Akizuki no ran, 秋月亂. — Insurrection brought about in 1876 by *Miyazaki Kuranosuke, Imai Tomotarō, Masuda Masakata*, etc., who at the head of 400 *samurai* of the *Akizuki* clan joined the *Kumamoto* insurgents. *Kuranosuke* was defeated and killed himself; the others were arrested.

Akō, 赤穂, a town of *Harima* (6,700 inh.). An old castle built towards 1575 by *Ukita Naoie*. It passed into the hands of the *daimyō Ikeda* (1600) and *Asano* (1645). It was *Naganori* the last of these, who afforded a pretext for the famous vengeance of the forty-seven *rōnin* (See *Ōishi Yoshio*), In 1702, the castle of *Akō* was given to the *Nagai*, and from 1706 to 1868, it was the residence of the *Mori daimyō* (20,000 k.)

Akutagawa, 芥川, in *Settsu*. An ancient castle, which in the 14th century, belonged to a family of that name, faithful to the southern dynasty. Afterwards the castle fell into the hands of the *Miyoshi*, but *Nobunaga* captured it in 1568, gave it to *Wada Koremasa*, and later on, to *Araki Murashige* (1573); it was abandoned after the latter's death (1579).

Ama, 尼, a Buddhist nun. The *ama*, also called *bikuni* were bound to celibacy, and lived together in nunneries, called *ama-dera*.

Amagasaki, 尼ケ崎 A town (15,000 inh.) in *Settsu*. An ancient castle built by *Hosokawa Takakuni*, at the beginning of the 16th century. It passed successively into the power of the *daimyō Araki* (1573), *Ikeda* (1579), *Tatebe* (1590), *Toda* (1617), *Aoyama* (1634), then from 1711 to 1868, it was the residence of the *Matsudaira* (*Sakurai*) *daimyō* (40,000 k.).

Amako, 尼子. A family of *daimyō* descended from *Sasaki*, (*Rokkaku*), *Takauji* (*Uda Genji*).

—— **Takahisa,** 高久, a grandson of *Takauji*, was the first, in the 14th century, to take the name of *Amako* (son of a nun), because, having lost his parents at the age of three years, he was brought up by an *ama*.

—— **Tsunehisa,** 經久 (1458-1541), a great grandson of *Takahisa*, inherited from his father *Kiyosada* and his grandfather *Mochihisa*, the office of governor (*shugo*) of *Izumo*, and resided at the castle of *Toda* 富田. In 1518, he marched against *Ōuchi Yoshioki* of *Suwō*, but the *Shōgun Yoshiharu* brought about peace (1521). The next year, *Yoshioki*, having invaded the province of *Aki*, the war recommenced. *Tsunehisa* had *Kagamiyama* besieged by *Mōri Motonari*, who recaptured the place, but he himself was repulsed before the castle of *Kanayama*, (*Aki*) by *Ōuchi Yoshitaka* (1524) In 1532, his son *Okihisa* revolted; *Tsunehisa* defeated him and obliged him to flee to *Bingo*. Later on, *Mōri Motonari*, hitherto a retainer of the *Amako*, passed over to the service of the *Ōuchi* (1540): *Tsunehisa* attacked him but was defeated.

Takahisa-Mochihisa-Kiyohisa-Tsunehisa ⎰ Masahisa-Haruhisa ⎰ Yoshihisa ⎱ ⎱ Kunihisa-Katsuhisa ⎱ Hidehisa ⎰ Okihisa

—— **Kunihisa,** 國久 (+ 1554), joined his nephew *Haruhisa* to fight against *Takeda Tsunenobu* (1540). He perished by the hands of this very same *Haruhisa*, with whom he had quarrelled.

—— **Haruhisa,** 晴久 (1514-1562) invaded the states of *Ōuchi Yoshitaka*, when the latter having been appointed *Dazai-Daini*, crossed over to *Kyūshū* (1536); but he was repelled by *Sue Takafusa*. He attacked *Mōri Motonari* (1541) with no better success; after which, he was abandoned by most of his retainers, who passed over to the service of the *Ōuchi*. But after the assassination of *Yoshitaka* by *Sue Harukata* (1551) he retrieved his losses, captured *Mimasaka* and seventeen castles in *Harima* (1554).

—— **Katsuhisa,** 勝久 (+ 1578) son of *Kunihisa*, struggled incessantly against the *Mōri;* he conquered *Tajima*, and with the aid of *Ukita Naoie*, subdued all the *San-in-dō*. In 1571, he was defeated by *Mōri Terumoto* and fled to the *Oki* isles. On his return to *Izumo*, he expelled *Yamanaka, Yukimasu,* and *Yamana Toyokuni*, who had invaded that province, and reconquered *Tajima* and *Inaba*. Entrusted with the guard of the castle of *Kōzuki* (*Harima*) by *Hideyoshi*, he was besieged by *Kikkawa Motoharu* and *Kobayakawa Takakage* and put an end to his own life.

—— **Yoshihisa,** 義久 (+ 1610), son of *Haruhisa* listened with joy to the overtures of *Ōtomo Sōrin* who proposed to conquer and divide between themselves the domains of the *Mōri* (1563). He attacked *Motonari* at once but was defeated. Therefore, he shut himself up in his castle of *Toda*, where he was shortly afterwards, besieged by a powerful army, but held out valiantly. Having executed his bravest officer, *Moriyama Hisakane*, accused of conniving with the enemy, he estranged the affections of his retainers, many of whom abandoned him. Perceiving that further resistance was impossible, he secretly fled and retired to *Aki*, where he shaved his head and took the name of *Yūrin* (1566). With him, the *Amako* family disappeared from history.

Amakuni, 天國. A famous smith of the 7th century. A sword, which he had forged for the emperor *Mommu* (704) and which was offered by *Shujaku-Tennō* to *Fudō* the god of *Narita*, as a token of gratitude for the defeat of *Taira Masakado* (940) is still in existence. He fabricated the famous sword *Kojima-maru*, which was handed down as a sacred inheritance in the *Taira* family.

Amakusa-jima, 天草島. A group of islands, west of *Kyūshū* depending on the province of *Higo*. The principal are: *Kami-shima, Shimo-shima, Naga-shima, Shishi-jima, Gosho-no-ura-shima, Maki-shima, Hi-no-shima,* etc.

Amakusa-nada, 天草洋. The sea of *Amakusa*, west of the said group of islands.

Amakusa no ran, 天草亂.　The insurrection of *Shimabara* (See *Shimabara*).

Amakusa Tokisada, 天草時貞 (+ 1638) also called *Masuda Shirō*.　Born in *Hizen*, appointed by *Ashizuka Chūemon*, etc., chief of the insurgents of *Shimabara*, he was killed on the fall of the castle of *Hara* and his head was exposed at *Nagasaki*.

Amami-shima, 阿麻彌島.　See *Ō-shima* (*Ōsumi*).

Ama no hashidate, 天橋立.　One of the most beautiful landscapes (*san-kei*) of *Japan*, one league from *Miyazu* (*Tango*).　It is a strip of land three kilometers long and sixty meters wide, lined with pine-trees, and advancing into the bay of *Miyazu*, at the extremity of which stands a little *Shintō* shrine.

Ama no iwa, 天岩.　The cave where *Amaterasu* shut herself up to escape from the insults of her brother *Susano-ō*.

Amano Tōkage, 天野遠景.　Born at *Amano* (*Izu*); was a vassal of *Minamoto Yoritomo*.　He fought against the *Taira* and, later on, was ordered to pacify *Kyūshū*.　By order of *Hōjō Tokimasa*, he killed *Hiki Yoshikazu*, father-in-law of the *Shōgun Yoriie* (1203).

Amano Yasukage, 天野康景 (1537-1613), a vassal of *Ieyasu*; from 1601 to 1607, he was *daimyō* of *Kōkokuji* (*Suruga* — 10,000 k.)

Amanozan-Kongō-ji, 天野山金剛寺.　A Buddhist temple, built, in *Kawachi* (1165) by the bonze *Akwan* 阿觀.　It was a place of refuge for *Go-Shirakawa* (1207), *Morinaga Shinnō* (1331) and *Go-Murakami* (1346-1360).

Ama-Shōgun, 尼將軍.　A surname given to *Masa-ko*, widow of *Yoritomo*, after she had become an *ama*.　(See *Masa-ko*).

Amaterasu-ō-mikami, 天照大御神.　Goddess of the sun or of light (*Shintō*).　Born from the left eye of *Izanagi*, she received the country of *Takama-ga-hara* (*Japan ?*) as her portion. — She taught her subjects to plant rice and to weave cloth.　Her brother, *Susano-o*, having obtained permission from his father to visit his sister, came to see her in *Takama-ga-hara*, but his insolent behavior incensed her so much that she hid herself in a cave of the rock *ama-no-iwa*, closing the mouth thereof with an enormous stone.　At once the world was sunk in darkness.　This caused excitement among all the gods who assembled to consult about the means of enticing the goddess out of her hiding place.　According to the deliberations, *Ishikoritome no mikoto* made a mirror (*yata no kagami*), *Tama-no-oya no mikoto* made a jewel of precious stones (*yasakani no magatama*); *Ame no hiwashi no mikoto* prepared strips of hemp (*nigite*); meanwhile *Ame-no-koyane no mikoto* went to the heavenly Mount *Kagu* and brought back a *Masakaki* tree, to the branches of which were hung the above mentioned objects.　Now the divine *Ame-no-uzume no mikoto* began to dance to the sound of music.　The expected result was soon produced.　*Amaterasu*, impelled by curiosity, slightly moved the rock which closed the cave and peeped out to see what had made the gods so merry.　Just then *Tajikara-o no mikoto* thrust his hand in and pulled the rock door open.　*Amaterasu* then left her hiding place, and *Koyane-no-mikoto* and *Futotama-no-mikoto* stretched a rope across the mouth of the cave to hinder the goddess from returning there for evermore. Thus the world was restored to light.

AMATERASU COMING OUT OF THE AMA-NO-IWAYA CAVE.

Susano-ō was expelled and fled to *Izumo*, where he settled down. His descendants gradually took possession of the land that had given them hospitality; therefore *Amaterasu*, to regain possession of her domains, was obliged to send *Takemikazuchi* and *Futsunushi* with order to subdue the invaders. It was only then that her grandson *Ninigi no mikoto* came in person to rule over the land he had inherited from his ancestors. *Ninigi* was the great grandfather of *Jimmu-Tennō*, and thus the imperial dynasty of Japan claims *Amaterasu* as its first ancestor.

Amaterasu-ō-mikami, is also called *Ōhirume, Shimmei, Daijingū, Tenshōkō Daijin*. The shrine erected to her honor at *Ise* (*Naikū*) is the most ancient and venerated in Japan.

Amemori Hōshū, 雨森芳洲 (1668-1755). A historian and man of letters of *Tsushima*.

Ame-no-futotama no mikoto, 天太玉命. A son of *Takami-musubi no kami;* one of the faithful retainers of *Amaterasu*, ancestor of the *Imube*. He has a temple at *Ichinomiya* in *Awa* (*Tōkaidō*).

Ame-no-hiboko, 天日槍. A prince of *Shiragi* (Korea) said to have come to Japan, in the reign of *Suinin Tennō* (27 B.C.) according to the *Nihon-ki;* but according to others, at the time of *Ōkuni-nushi*, or in the 2nd century A.D.—He is said to have settled in *Tajima*.

Ame-no-koyane no mikoto, 天兒屋命. A son of *Takami-musubi no kami;* a retainer of *Amaterasu*. He accompanied *Ninigi no mikoto* in his expedition to *Hyūga*. He is the first ancestor of the *Nakatomi* or *Fujiwara*. His temple is at *Nara*, (*Kasuga no miya*) where he is honored as *Kasuga daimyōjin, Hiraoka daimyō-jin*.

Ame-no-minaka-nushi no kami, 天御中主神. A god who before the creation, stood motionless in the center of the world. He was the first to reside at *Takama ga hara*. *Izanagi* and *Izanami* are his descendants in the 16th generation. According to the *Nihon-ki*, the name of the first god is *Kuni-toko-tachi*.

Ame-no-murakumo no tsurugi, 天叢雲劍. The sword which *Susano-ō-no mikoto* found in the tail of the *Yamato no orochi*. At the moment he pulled the sword out, a cloud rose around the eight-headed monster, whence the name of *murakumo* (pile of clouds) *Susano-ō* offered the sword to *Amaterasu*, who, in turn, gave it to her grandson *Ninigi*, when he started for *Hyūga*. — Henceforth looked upon as one of the three divine treasures (*shinki sanshū*) of the imperial family, it was preserved with veneration in the palace itself. *Sujin-tennō* placed it together with the mirror in the temple of *Kasanui* (*Yamato*) in 92 B.C., afterwards in that of *Ise* (5 B.C.). There, before starting on the expedition against the *Ebisu, Yamato-takeru-no-mikoto*, went to receive it from the hands of *Yamato-hime*, the priestess of the shrine. In *Suruga*, while the prince was hunting the deer in a great plain, the *Ebisu* set fire to the high grass to burn him alive; but quickly drawing his sword, he cut the grass all round him and thus escaped from the imminent danger. The name of the sword was then changed to that of *Kusanagi no tsurugi* (grass-mowing sword). After the death of *Yamato-takeru*, it was deposited in the temple of *Atsuta* (*Owari*).

Ame-no-taneko no mikoto, 天種子命. A descendant of *Koyane no mikoto* and ancestor of the *Fujiwara*. Was one of the companions of *Jimmu-tennō* in the latter's conquests, and subsequently his minister. He defined the *amatsu-tsumi* (crimes against heaven) and the *kunitsu-tsumi* (crimes against the estate), which are the first traces we find of judicial legislature in Japan.

Ame-no-tomi no mikoto, 天富命. A descendant of *Futotama no Mikoto* and companion of *Jimmu-tennō*. Became the chief of the *Imube*, who were intrusted with the religious services, the sacrifices to the ancestors, etc.

Ame-no-uzume no mikoto, 天鈿女命. A goddess that sang and danced in front of the cavern in which *Amaterasu* had shut herself up. She attached herself afterwards to *Saruta-hiko*. Her descendants were called *Sarume-gimi*.

Amida, 阿彌陀 (sanskr. Amitâbha). The supreme *Buddha* of the Paradise of the Pure-Earth of the West (*sai-hō no gokuraku-jōdo*, 西方極樂淨土). He is the one especially honored by the *Jōdo-shū* sect. He is also called *Amirita, Amidabaya, Mida.* — The first mention of *Amida* in Buddhist literature cannot be placed much earlier than the middle of the first century A.D.

Ampin, 安平. Also *Amping*. A seaport (4.500 inh.) on the western coast of *Taiwan* (*Formosa*). Near that place are the ruins of the *Fort-Zelandia* built by the Dutch in 1626 and destroyed in 1661.

Anamizu, 穴水. A castle-town in *Noto*. Was for 400 years (12th-16th cent.) the residence of the *daimyō Hasebe*. It was taken from them in 1577 by *Uesugi Kenshin*.

Anan, 阿難. A relative of *Shaka* and one of his first disciples. He is also called *Ananda, Tamon*.

Anato, 穴門. The ancient name of the province of *Nagato*, or *Chōshū*.

Anayama Baisetsu, 穴山梅雪. A nephew of *Takeda Shingen*. He made an alliance with *Ieyasu* and served him as guide in his expedition against *Katsuyori*, son of *Shingen*. As a reward he obtained a district of the province of *Kai*, but was assassinated (1582) by his former companions in arms, whom he had betrayed.

Ando, 安藤. A family of *daimyō* that originated in *Mikawa* and descended from *Abe no Hirafu* and *Abe no Nakamaro*.

Motoyoshi { Shigenobu-Shigenaga-Shigeyuki-Shigehiro. (*a*)
{ Naotsugu. (*b*)

(*a*) — The elder branch. — **Shigenobu,** 重信 (1558-1622), took part in all the wars of *Ieyasu*, who, in 1612, raised him to the rank of *daimyō* and bestowed on him the fief of *Takasaki* (*Kōzuke*).

—— **Shigenaga,** 重長. (1600-1657), enjoyed the favor of the *Shōgun Hidetada* and *Iemitsu*.

His descendants were successively transferred in 1695, to *Matsuyama* (*Bitchū*); in 1711, to *Kanō* (*Mino*); in 1756, to *Iwakidaira* (*Mutsu*-30,000 k.).

—— **Nobumasa,** 信正. (1819-1871), *Tsushima no Kami*, was the assistant and afterwards the successor of *Ii Kamon no Kami* in concluding the first treaties with foreign powers. = Now Viscount.

(*b*) — The cadet branch. — **Naotsugu,** 直次. (1564-1635), received the fief of *Kakegawa* (*Tōtōmi*), and, in 1617, was transferred to *Tanabe*

(*Kii*-28,000 k.), where his descendants resided till the Restoration. =
Now Baron.

Ando-bugyō, 安堵奉行. A justice of the peace in the times of
the *Hōjō* and the *Ashikaga*.

Andō Seian, 安東省庵. (1622-1701). Confucianist of *Yanagawa* (*Chikugo*). At the time of the *Shimabara* insurrection, being
only 15 years old, he desired, in spite of sickness, to follow his lord
daimyō and to fight the insurgents. When *Shu Shunsui* came from
China (1660), he constituted him his teacher and divided with him the
pension he received from his lord. He left several works.

Andō Tameaki, 安藤爲章. (1659-1716). Man of letters and
historian. Born in *Tamba*, he was called to *Mito* by *Tokugawa Mitsukuni* and became one of the co-laborers of the *Dai-Nihon-shi*, etc. He
was the author of some literary works.

Ane-gawa, 姉川. A river which has its source in the north of
Ōmi province, and empties itself into lake *Biwa*. In 1570 it was the
scene of a victory gained by *Nobunaga* and *Ieyasu* against *Asakura
Yoshikage* and *Asai Nagamasa*.

An-ei, 安永. *Nengō*: 1772-1780.

Anenokōji, 姉小路. A family of *kuge* descending from *Fujiwara
(Sanjō) Sanefusa* (1146-1224) = Now Count.

Anenokōji, 姉小路. A cadet branch of the preceding family.
For 200 years this family governed *Hida* province.

—— **Tadatsuna,** 尹綱. The second son of *Takamoto*, was the
first to receive the title of *Hida no Kokushi*. He fought for the emperor
Go-Kameyama and was killed in 1411.

—— **Koretsuna,** 自綱. (1540-1587), *Hida no kami*, first defeated
Kiso Yoshimitsu, but was afterwards defeated and killed by *Kanamori
Nagachika*, sent by *Hideyoshi* to seize *Hida*.

Angen, 安元. *Nengō*: 1175-1176.

Ani-gawa, 阿仁川. A river (117 km.) which has its source at
mount *Moriyoshi* (*Uego*) and empties itself into the *Noshiro-gawa*.

Ani-shima, 兄島. One of the group of the *Ogasawara* islands;
it has 16 km. in circuit.

Anjō, 安祥. A castle in *Mikawa*; was the residence of the *daimyō
Matsudaira* (*Tokugawa*) from about 1480 till 1530, *Anjō* (1530-1545),
Oda (1545-1573).

Ankan-tennō, 安閑天皇. The 27th Emperor of Japan, (534-535)
was prince *Magari-no-ōine-hirokuni-oshi-take-kanahi*, the eldest son of
Keitai-tennō, whom he succeeded at the age of 68; he reigned only two
years. He sent *Ōtomo no Muraji* and *Ōtomo no Sadehiko* to Korea to
support *Kudara* against *Shiragi*.

Ankokuji Ekei, 安國寺惠瓊. A bonze, chief of the *Ankokuji*
temple in *Aki*. When 11 years old, he entered the *Tōfukuji* in *Kyōto*.
Thence he was taken to *Aki* by *Mōri Terumoto*, who made him his
counsellor, placed him at the head of the *Ankokuji* temple, and bestowed
on him considerable revenues. Having been commissioned to negotiate
peace between *Terumoto* and *Hideyoshi* (1582), he followed the fortune

of the latter. After the death of *Hideyoshi*, he supported the rights of *Hideyori*, and, having been vanquished at *Sekigahara* (1600), he was beheaded at *Kyōto* together with *Ishida Kazushige*, etc.

Ankō-tennō, 安康天皇. The 20th Emperor of Japan (454-456) was first known as prince *Anaho ;* he succeeded his father, *Inkyō-tennō*, at the age of 53. He had already caused the assassination of his elder brother *Karu no Ōji* in order to take possession of the throne ; he caused likewise the assassination of his uncle *Ōkusaka*, a brother of *Inkyō*, in order to marry his wife. But in the following year, *Mayuwa no Ō*, son of *Ōkusaka*, revenged his father's death by assassinating the emperor.

Annaka, 安中. A castle in *Kōzuke*. It was the residence of the *daimyō Hōjō*, *Annaka*, *Takeda*, *Takikawa*, and *Hōjō ;* afterwards, under the *Tokugawa*, of the *daimyō Ii* (1615-1644), *Mizuno* (1645-1667), *Hotta* (1667-1681), *Itakura* (1681-1702), *Naitō* (1702-1749), finally, from 1749 till 1868, of *Itakura* (30,000 k.).

Annei-tennō, 安寧天皇. The 3rd Emperor of Japan (548-511 B.C.), was prince *Shikitsuhiko-tamademi*, a son of *Suisei-tennō*. He was 19 years old when he succeeded his father, and died after a reign of 38 years, of which history is silent.

Anotsu, 安濃津. The ancient name of the town of *Tsu* (*Ise*).

Anrakuju-in. In the village of *Takeda*, near *Kyōto*. At first, the residence of *Toba-tennō*, after his abdication (1123), it was later on transformed into a temple. Therein may be seen the tombs of the emperors *Toba* (+ 1156) and *Konoe* (+ 1155).

Ansatsushi, 按察使. See *Azechi.*

Ansei, 安政. *Nengō :* 1854-1859.

Antei, 安貞. *Nengō :* 1227-1228.

Antoku-tennō, 安徳天皇. The 81st Emperor of Japan (1181-1183), was prince *Kotohito*, a son of *Takakura-tennō* and of *Kenrei-mon-in Toku-ko* the latter a daughter of *Taira Kiyomori*. He was placed on the throne when only 3 years old, by his maternal grandfather then all powerful. The following year, *Kiyomori* died, and the *Minamoto* recommenced their war against the *Taira*. Soon *Kiso Yoshinaka* entered Kyōto victoriously as a conqueror, and *Taira Munemori* fled, taking the young Emperor along with him. The *Minamoto* then replaced *Antoku-tennō* by his brother *Go-Toba* and pursued their enemies who had retired into the western provinces. The struggle lasted yet for two years and ended by the crushing defeat of the *Taira* at *Dan-no-ura* (*Nagato*). Seeing that the battle was lost, *Nii no ama*, the widow of *Kiyomori*, threw herself into the sea with her grandson *Antoku*, who was then only 7 years old.

Ao ga shima, 青ヶ嶋. An island (20 km. circ.) under the jurisdiction of the *Izu* province and situated 8 km. South of *Hachijō-jima*. Was formerly called *Oni ga shima* (Island of the goblins).

Anwa, 安和. *Nengō :* 968-969.

Aoki, 青木. A family of *daimyō* descending from *Tajihi Shima*, who from 1600, were established at *Asada* (*Settsu* — 10,000 k.) = Now Viscount.

Aoki, 青木. A family of *samurai* of *Yamaguchi* (*Suwō*), ennobled after the Restoration. The head of the family now bears the title of Viscount.

Aoki Kazunori, 青木一矩. (+1600), was a vassal of *Hideyoshi*, and, from 1590, *daimyō* of *Kita-no-shō* (now *Fukui*) in *Echizen*. He was deposed after the battle of *Sekigahara*, and died the same year.

Aoki Kon-yō, 青木昆陽, was a scholar of the eighteenth century. In 1739 he was commissioned to visit all the provinces of Japan in order to collect ancient manuscripts, and, after his return from this mission, was made *Shomotsu-bugyō*. He had learned the Dutch language, and translated several works on politics, political economy, natural history, etc. It was he who introduced throughout Japan the cultivation of sweet potatoes (*Satsuma-imo*).

Aomori-ken, 青森縣. A department formed of four districts of the province of *Rikuoku*, north of *Mutsu*. — Popul: 663,000 inh. — Capital, *Aomori* (28,000 inh.) — Principal towns: *Hirosaki* (35,000 inh.), *Hachinohe* (11,300 inh.), etc.

Aomori-wan, 青森灣. *Aomori* Bay.

Aono, 青野. A town in *Mino*. It was the residence of the *daimyō Inaba* from 1603 till 1684.

Aoto Fujitsuna, 青砥藤綱. A minister of the *shikken Tokiyori* and *Tokimune*, in the 13th century, was celebrated for his spirit of economy, his righteousness and disinterestedness. (As there is no mention made of him in the *Azuma-kagami*, some critics doubt of his existence).

Aoyama, 青山. A family of *daimyō* originating in *Mikawa* and descending from *Fujiwara* (*Kwazan-in*) *Ietada* (1062-1136).

Tadanari {Tadatoshi-Munetoshi-Tadao   (*a*).
          {Yukinari -Yukitoshi -Yukizane   (*b*).

(*a*) — The elder branch ennobled in 1601, resided in *Edo*, where *Tadanari* (1551-1613) was *Machi-bugyō* and *Kwantō-bugyō*; next in *Iwatsuki* (*Musashi*), in 1619. In 1623, *Tadatoshi* (1578-1643), *Hōki no kami*, was deprived of his dignity. In 1649, his son, *Munetoshi*, *Inaba no kami*, was re-established at *Komoro* (*Shinano*) and the family was removed successively to *Hamamatsu* (*Tōtōmi*) in 1678; to *Kameyama* (*Tamba*) in 1702; to *Sasayama* (*Tamba*) in 1748 (60,000 k.) = Now Viscount.

(*b*) — The cadet branch, ennobled in 1615, established in 1623, at *Kakegawa* (*Tōtōmi*); in 1634, at *Amagasaki* (*Settsu*); in 1711, at *Iiyama* (*Shinano*); in 1717, at *Miyazu* (*Tango*); in 1758, at *Hachiman* (*Mino* 50,000 k.) = Now Viscount.

Aoyama, 青山. A family of *samurai* of the *Fukui* (*Echizen*) clan, was ennobled after the Restoration = Now Baron.

Aoyama, 青山. Family of confucianists of the *Mito* clan.

—— **En-u,** 延于. (1776-1843), favored by *Mito Nariaki*, was the first director of the *Kōdō-kwan*.

—— **Enko,** 延光. (1805-1870), son of the foregoing, was professor, and afterwards director of the *Kōdō-kwan*. Together with *Aizawa*

Seishi, Fujita Tōko, etc., he spread instruction among the *samurai* of his clan.

Arai, 新井. An ancient castle in *Sagami;* was the residence of the *daimyō Miura* from the 12th century; it was taken by the *Hōjō* of *Oda-wara* in 1518 and was kept by them till 1590, when it was abandoned.

Arai Hakuseki, 新井白石. (1656-1725), also called *Kumbi*, was a celebrated man of letters and historian. He was born in *Kururi* (*Kazusa*), and was successively patronized by the *daimyō Tsuchiya Toshinao* and by the *rōjū Hotta Masatoshi*. Having been called to *Kōfu*, in 1693, by the subsequent *Shōgun Ienobu*, he followed his new master to *Edo* when the latter succeeded his uncle *Tsunayoshi;* he became the *Shōgun's* counsellor and received the title of *Chikugo no kami*. He enjoyed the same favor under the next *Shōgun Ietsugu*. He has written several much esteemed historical works. It was *Hakuseki* that was commissioned to examine

ARAI HAKUSEKI.

Father *Sidotti* brought as a prisoner to *Edo* (1709); he has left an interesting relation (*Seiyō-Kibun*) of the examinations.

Ara-kawa, 荒川. A river (78 km.), which has its source in *Shinano*, flows through *Takata*, and empties itself into the Japan Sea at *Naoetsu* (*Echigo*). It is also called *Seki-gawa*.

Ara-kawa, 荒川. The name of the *Sumida-gawa* in its superior course.

Araki Murashige, 荒川村重, was a descendant of the *Fujiwara*. He served first *Ikeda Katsumasa*, afterwards, having been made *Shinano no kami*, he built in 1568 the castle of *Ibaraki* (*Settsu*) where he resided. Later on he attached himself to *Nobunaga* and became *Settsu no kami*, with residence at *Itami* (1573). While he was taking a part in the campaign of *Hideyoshi* against *Mōri Terumoto*, he was accused before *Nobunaga* by *Akechi Mitsuhide*. Having been forewarned, he shut himself up in his castle of *Itami*, and prepared for resistance. The castle was taken after a siege of one year, but *Murashige* succeeded in escaping to *Aki*, where he lived unknown. He had a two year old child, who was adopted in another family, and became the celebrated artist *Iwasa Matabei*.

Arakida Hisaoi, 荒木田久老. (1746-1804), was a *kannushi* of the *Naikū* temple (*Ise*) and a disciple of the learned *Kamo Mabuchi*. He studied and commented the ancient writers. His school became a rival to that of the famous *Motoori Norinaga* from which it differed by broader and more liberal views. He has left about fifteen works, the most celebrated of which is his commentary on *Manyōshū*.

Arashi, 嵐. A family of actors from *Ōsaka*, famous during the 18th and the 19th centuries.

Aratawake no mikoto, 荒田別命. A great-grandson of the
emperor *Sujin*. Having been sent to Korea by the empress *Jingō* in
249, he subdued *Shiragi*, divided the country into districts, and established a Japanese administration. He came back in 285, bringing along
with him the scholar *Wani*.

Ariake no umi, 有明海. A gulf in *Kyūshū*, between the provinces of *Hizen*, *Chikugo*, and *Higo*.

Ariake-yama, 有明山. A mountain (2,450 m.) in the N.-W. of
Shinano. It is also called *Shinano no Fuji*.

Arichi, 有地. A family of *Chōshū samurai* ennobled in 1895. =
Now Baron.

Arima, 有馬. A village in *Settsu*, renowned for its hot-springs.

Arima, 有馬. A family of *daimyō* descending from the *Akamatsu*,
and by them, from the *Murakami-Genji*.

—— **Yoshisuke,** 義祐. The son of *Akamatsu*
Norisuke, was the first who took the name of *Arima*
from the district in *Settsu* where he settled towards the
end of the 14th century. He constructed the castle of
Sanda, which was occupied by his descendants for about
200 years.

—— **Noriyori,** 則頼. (+ 1602), served *Hideyoshi*,
who gave him the castle of *Miki* (*Harima*). He joined afterwards the
party of *Ieyasu*, who raised his revenues to 20,000 k.

—— **Toyouji,** 豊氏. (1570-1642), a son of *Noriyori*, had the title
of *Gemba no kami*. In 1600, he fought at *Akasaka* (*Mino*) against the
troops of *Oda Hidenobu*. After the campaign, he received the fief of
Fukuchiyama (*Tamba* — 80,000 k.). He participated in the siege of
Ōsaka (1615) and brought back 57 heads of enemies as trophies. In
1620, he was transferred to *Kurume* (*Chikugo* — 210,000 k.), where his
descendants resided till the Restoration. = Now Count.

—— A cadet branch ennobled in 1726, resided first at *Saijō* (*Isc*),
then, from 1841 till 1868, at *Fukiage* (*Shimotsuke* — 10,000 k.). = Now
Viscount.

Arima, 有馬. A family of *daimyō* descending
from *Fujiwara Sumitomo*, (+ 940).

—— **Tsunezumi,** 經澄. A descendant of *Sumitomo* in the 8th generation, served the *Shōgun Tanetomo*
and built a castle at *Arima*, from which he took his name.

—— **Haruzumi,** 晴澄. Was *Shōbanshū* of the
Shōgun Yoshiharu and governed 6 districts of *Hizen*.
He was defeated by *Ōtomo Yoshinori*.

—— **Yoshisada,** 義貞. (+ 1577) *Shuri-tayū*, a son of *Haruzumi*,
made peace with the *Ōtomo;* but having turned his arms against *Ryūzōji*
Takanobu, he was not more successful than his father: he was defeated,
and had to submit to the conditions of the conqueror; in order to cement
peace, he gave his grand-daughter in marriage to *Masaie*, a son of
Takanobu. By the advice of his brother *Bartholomew Ōmura Sumitada*,
Yoshisada was baptized under the name of *Andrew*. He had given the

government of his domains to his eldest son *Yoshizumi;* but the latter having died in 1571, was succeeded by his brother *Harunobu.*

—— **Harunobu, 晴 信** (+ 1612), united with the *Shimazu* of *Satsuma* against *Ryūzōji Takanobu,* who was defeated and killed at *Shimabara* (1584). After the campaign in *Kyūshū* (1587), *Hideyoshi* confirmed *Harunobu* in the possession of his domains, and he occupied the two castles of *Hara* (also called *Arima*) and *Hi-no-ura,* or *Hi-no-e* (*Hizen*) with a revenue of 40,000 k. He took part in the expedition to Korea under the command of *Konishi Yukinaga.* At the time of the campaign of *Sekigahara* (1600), he sent his son *Naozumi* with 2,000 men to fight for the cause of *Hideyori,* and, nevertheless was able to keep his fief. In 1608, a ship sent by *Harunobu* to *Macao,* spent the winter in that port. A dispute having arisen between the crew and the people of the port, the governor, *Andrew Pessoa,* repressed it with much severity; on their return, the sailors carried their complaints to the *Shōgun.* The following year, this same *Pessoa* commanded the vessel *Madre de Dios,* which came to *Nagasaki.* He sent to *Sumpu* explanations which were accepted; but *Harunobu* made *Ieyasu* revoke this decision and obtained from him an order to seize the Portuguese ship. He had it surrounded by numerous boats carrying 1,200 men, and it took him three days to reduce his adversary. *Pessoa,* seeing that all was lost, set fire to the powder-magazine, and blew up his ship, involving in her destruction many Japanese boats. That act of revenge did not profit *Harunobu:* having been denounced to the *Shōgun* for being a Christian (he had been baptized in 1579 under the name of *John-Protasius*) and accused of intending to seize the castle of *Isahaya* (*Hizen*), he was banished to *Yamura* (*Kai*) and afterwards condemned to death and executed.

—— **Naozumi, 直 純**, had been baptized under the name of *Michael;* but having married the great grand-daughter of *Ieyasu,* he openly apostatized and became a persecutor of the Christians. After having been deprived of his domains by the disgrace of his father (1612), he received, at the beginning of 1615, the fief of *Nobeoka* (*Hyūga* — 53,000 k).

—— **Kiyozumi, 清 純**, was a grandson of *Naozumi.* He was dispossessed in 1691 on account of his bad administration; but, four years later, he was transferred to *Maruoka* (*Echizen* — 50,000 k.), where his descendants resided till the Restoration. = Now Viscount.

Arisugawa no Miya, 有 栖 川 宮 . A family of princes of the blood founded, in 1672, by *Yukuhito-Shinnō* (1654-1699), third son of the emperor *Go-Sai-in.*

—— **Taruhito-Shinnō, 熾 仁 親 王** (1835-1895), took an active part in the imperial Restoration. Having been nominated *Sōsai* (a title equivalent to that of prime minister), he commanded the army sent to subdue the last partisans of the *Shōgunate* (1868-1869), as well as that which suppressed the *Satsuma* insurrection (1877). He received the title of field-marshal (1878), that of *Sadaijin* (1880). He died at the age of 60, during the war against China.

The actual chief of the family is prince *Takehito,* born in 1862, married in 1879 the daughter of *Maeda Yoshiyasu,* the former *daimyō* of *Kaga*. The prince is an admiral of the Imperial Navy.

Ariwara, 在原. A family name given towards 830 by *Junwa-tennō* to the children of prince *Aho-shinnō*, a son of the ex-emperor *Heijō*.

—— **Yukihira,** 行平 (818-893), was governor of the provinces of *Harima*, *Bizen*, *Shinano*, *Bitchū*; *Chūnagon*, *Mimbukyō*, inspector (*Azechi*) of *Mutsu* and *Dewa*, etc.

—— **Narihira,** 業平 (825-880), the brother of *Yukihira*, also held important posts and distinguished himself as a poet and painter. It is believed that his somewhat romantic adventures and, especially his love intrigues, furnished the theme of the *Ise-monogatari*.

ARIWARA NARIHIRA.

Asada, 麻田 (*Settsu*), was from 1600 till 1868 the residence of the *daimyō Aoki* (10,000 k.).

Asada Gōritsu, 麻田剛立 (1734-1799). Astronomer of *Ōsaka*; was the teacher of *Takahashi Sakuzaemon*.

Asahi-dake, 朝日嶽. A mountain (1,800 met.) between *Kōzuke* and *Echigo*.

Asahi-dake, 朝日嶽. A mountain (2,000 met.) between *Echigo* and *Uzen*.

Asahi-gawa, 朝日川. See *Nishi-ōkawa*.

Asahina-Yoshihide, 朝夷義秀, Also called *Saburō*, was a son of *Wada Yoshinori* and, according to the legend, of *Tomoe Gozen*. He was renowned for his Herculean strength, took part in the revolt of his father against the *Hōjō* (1213), and distinguished himself by his feats of prowess. His party having been defeated, he fled, as some say, to *Kikai-ga-shima* (*Ryūkyū*), and, according to others, to *Koma* (Korea).

Asahi no kata, 朝日方 (1543-1590). Also called *Suruga Gozen*, was a uterine sister of *Hideyoshi*, and was married with *Saji Hyūga no kami*. After the campaign of *Komaki-yama*, when *Hideyoshi* intended to make peace with *Ieyasu*, he thought of making her marry him. *Saji*, to whom the project was communicated, committed suicide in order not to be an obstacle to the wish of his brother-in-law, and the marriage was celebrated a short time afterwards. In 1589, when the mother of *Hideyoshi* and *Asahi-hime* became ill, *Ieyasu* visited her with his wife, who died the following year.

Asahi no Miya, 朝日宮. Name formerly given to the temple of *Tenshō-daijin* in *Ise*.

Asahi Shōgun, 朝日將軍. Title under which *Minamoto Yoshinaka* is sometimes designated.

Asai, 淺井. A family descending from the *Fujiwara*, was first vassal to the *Sasaki* in *Ōmi*, and after some time, made itself independent.

—— **Sukemasa,** 亮政 (1495-1546), revolted against his suzerain *Sasaki* (*Kyōgoku*) *Takaie*, took up his residence in the castle of *Odani*

(*Ōmi*) which he had built in 1516, and made himself master of all the northern part of the province, which *Sasaki* (*Rokkaku*) *Takayori* in vain tried to reconquer.

—— **Hisamasa,** 久 政 (1524-1573), a son of *Sukemasa*, succeeded his father, and continued the war against the *Sasaki;* but having been vanquished, he submitted. His principal vassals assembled then and invited him to have his head shaved and to transmit the administration of his domains to his son, *Nagamasa*. He underwent this humiliation and retired to his castle of *Odani*. Later on he committed suicide when the castle was besieged and taken. The downfall of the castle was the ruin of his family.

—— **Nagamasa,** 長 政 (1545-1573), was selected by the vassals of his clan to replace his father *Hisamasa*, who had submitted to the *Sasaki*. Having been attacked by *Rokkaku Yoshikata*, he defeated him and took several of his castles (1561). He vanquished also *Saitō Tatsuoki*, besieged him in *Ōgaki* and was going to make himself master of a part of his domains (1564), when he was opposed by *Nobunaga*, who made war against him. After a protracted struggle of 3 years, peace was signed and *Nagamasa* married the sister of *Nobunaga* (1568). However, in the following year, hostilities recommenced : *Nagamasa* made an alliance with *Asakura Yoshikage* and was aided by the bonzes of *Hiei-zan;* but he was vanquished at *Anegawa* (*Ōmi*). By the intervention of the emperor *Ōgimachi* and the *Shōgun Yoshiaki*, a truce was concluded, (1570). It was of short duration, and the final struggle was not slow to begin. *Hisamasa* was defeated by *Hideyoshi*, and *Nobunaga* besieged the castle of *Odani*. Seeing that all was lost, *Nagamasa* intrusted his wife and children to his brother-in-law, set fire to the castle, and, together with his father and his two sons, committed suicide. — Of his three daughters, the eldest, *Yodo-gimi*, was married to *Hideyoshi;* the second, to *Kyōgoku Takatsugu;* the third, to *Hidetada:* she was the mother of the *Shōgun Iemitsu* and of the *Dainagon Tadanaga*.

Asaji no ura, 淺 茅 浦. A bay at the W. coast of *Tsushima* where the Mongols (*Mōko*) landed in 1274. *Sō Sukekuni*, the governor of the island, tried to repel them, but was killed in the battle.

Asaka Gonsai, 安 精 艮 齋 (1790-1860), was born at *Kōriyama* (*Mutsu*). When 17 years old, he went to *Edo*, where he became a pupil of *Satō Issai* and, afterwards, of *Hayashi*. He has published several works on literature and history.

Asaka no Miya, 朝 香 ノ 宮. Princely title created in 1906, in favor of *Hatohiko*, born in 1887, son of prince *Kuni Asahiko* and betrothed to *Hisa-ko Kane no Miya*, 7th daughter of the Emperor *Mutsuhito*.

Asaka Tampaku, 安 精 澹 泊 (1656-1737), was a scholar of the *Mito* clan. He was one of the principal contributors of the *Dai Nihonshi*.

Asakawa Zen-an, 朝 川 善 庵 (1781-1849), was a learned confucianist of the *Hirado* clan. He received lessons from *Yamamoto Hokuzan*, and applied himself especially to Chinese literature.

Asakura, 朝 倉. A family of *daimyō* descending from prince *Kusa-kabe-ōji* (662-689), a son of *Temmu-tennō*.

—— **Hirokage, 廣景** . He was in the service of the *Shiba* and was charged, about 1340, with the guard of the castle of *Kuromaru* (*Echizen*).

—— **Toshikage, 敏景** (+ 1475), a descendant of *Asakura Hirokage*, was one of the three principal vassals (*rōshin*) of the *Shiba* family and occupied the castle of *Ichijō-ga-dani*. In 1467, he defeated *Kyōgoku Mochikiyo* of *Kaga*, and, during the war of *Ōnin*, took the side of *Yamana Sōzen*. A short time afterwards, the *Shōgun* made him governor (*shugo*) of *Echizen* (1470).

—— **Norikage, 敎景** (1474-1552), fought constantly against the troops of *Ikkō-shū* in *Echizen*, *Kaga* and *Noto*.

—— **Yoshikage, 義景** (1533-1573), defeated the troops of *Ikkō-shū*, forced them to accept peace and gave his daughter in marriage to the chief bonze of the *Hongwan-ji*, *Kyōto*, who was to be content with the single province of *Kaga* as his fief (1562). In 1566, *Ashikaga Yoshiaki* asked for his assistance in order to acquire the inheritance of his brother the *Shōgun Yoshiteru*, but *Yoshikage* declined that difficult task. *Yoshiaki* applied then to *Nobunaga*, who accepted the mission and installed the new *Shōgun* at *Kyōto*. *Yoshikage* was then called to the capital, but refused to go. Immediately *Nobunaga* took the field with *Ieyasu* (1570), invaded *Echizen* and was about to besiege *Ichijō-ga-dani ;* but *Yoshikage* applied for help to *Asai Nagamasa*, and *Nobunaga*, conscious that he was not strong enough, returned to *Kyōto*. Soon afterwards he issued from the capital with a more numerous army and defeated his adversaries on the banks of the *Ane-gawa*. By the intervention of the emperor *Ōgimachi*, peace was concluded. But in 1573, war recommenced and *Yoshikage*, besieged in *Ichijō-ga-dani*, killed himself with all his family.

—— **Nobumasa, 宣政** (1583-1637), a nephew of *Yoshikage*, served *Hideyoshi* and *Ieyasu*. In 1625, he received in fief the castle of *Kakegawa* (*Tōtōmi* — 25,000 k.), but being implicated in the plot of *Dainagon Tadanaga*, of whom he was a counsellor, he was dispossessed of his fief (1632) and banished to *Kōriyama*, where he died.

Asama-yama, 淺間山. A volcano (2,480 met.) in *Shinano*. There was a terrible eruption in 1783. It emitted fragments of rocks in 1894 and 1900.

Asami Keisai, 淺見絅齋 (1652-1711), was born at *Takashima* (*Ōmi*), cultivated first confucianism under *Yamazaki Ansai*, afterwards he applied himself to the study of national antiquities and contributed to the revival of Shintoism.

Asano, 淺野 . A family of *daimyō* descending from *Toki's* family of *Mino* and by them, from the *Seiwa-Genji*.

—— **Nagamasa, 長政** (1546-1610), was the brother-in-law of *Hideyoshi*, whom he accompanied in his campaign against the *Mōri* clan in *San-yō-dō*. In 1584, he intervened as pacifier between *Hideyoshi* and *Ieyasu ;* the following year, he was one of the 5 *bugyō* and received the title of *Danjō-shōsuke*. During the war against the *Hōjō* of *Odawara*, he fought in *Kōzuke* and *Musashi* and took the castles of *Iwatsuki*, *Edo*, etc. (1590). Afterwards he took part in the expedition conducted by *Hidetsugu* against *Tsugaru*. During the Korean war, he, together with *Kuroda Yoshitaka*, was intrusted with the office of inspector of the army (*kangun*). After the death of *Hideyoshi*, having relations with both parties, and not liking to join either of them, he withdrew from public life and lived in retirement in *Fuchū* (*Musashi*). In 1600 however, he followed *Hidetada* into *Tōsandō*, and, in return, received 10,000 k. as a reward.

Nagamasa { Yukinaga - Nagaakira { Mitsuakira - Tsunaakira (a)
Nagaharu - Nagateru (b)
Nagashige - Naganao - Naganori (c)

(*a*) — The elder branch. — **Yukinaga,** 幸長 (1576-1613), the eldest son of *Nagamasa*, served first *Hideyoshi* and accompanied his father during the war against the *Hōjō* of *Odawara*, when, then only 15 years old, he served his first compaign, with *Honda Tadamasa*. *Ishida Kazushige* tried to implicate him in the plot of the *Kwampaku Hidetsugu*, but he was exculpated by *Maeda Toshiie*. During the expedition to Korea, he marched with *Katō Kiyomasa*, whom he succored at *Urusan*. On his return to Japan, when his father retired from public life, he received the fief of *Fuchū* (now *Kōfu*) (*Kai* — 200,000 k.), and, after *Sekigahara* (1600), was transferred to *Wakayama* (*Kii* — 370,000 k.).

—— **Nagaakira,** 長晟 (1586-1632), succeeded his brother *Yukinaga*, who died without children. Being a nephew of *Hideyoshi*, he was brought up at *Ōsaka*. For that reason, when war broke out between *Ieyasu* and *Hideyori*, *Ōno Harunaga* bestirred himself to make him take side with *Hideyori*. But *Nagaakira* joined the party of *Ieyasu*, distinguished himself at the siege of *Ōsaka*, and, as a trophy, brought back forty-two heads of the enemies. In 1616, he married a daughter of *Ieyasu*, the widow of *Gamō Hideyuki*. In 1619, he was transferred to *Hiroshima* (*Aki* — 426,000 k.), where his descendants resided till the Restoration = Now Marquis.

—— In 1885, three cadet branches of the family received the title of Baron.

(*b*) —— a cadet branch which from 1637 till 1719 resided in *Miyoshi* (*Bingo* — 50,000 k.).

—— **Nagatsune,** 長經 died in 1719 without heir, and his domains reverted to the elder branch.

(*c*) —— a cadet branch which successively established itself: in 1606, at *Mōka* (*Shimotsuke*); in 1622, at *Kasama* (*Hitachi*); in 1645, at *Akō* (*Harima* — 55,000 k.) It was dispossessed of its domains in 1701,

—— **Naganori,** 長矩 (1667-1701), *Takumi no kami*, had been commissioned with *Kira Yoshinaka*, *Kōzuke no suke*, to receive and entertain the envoys of the emperor *Higashi-yama* and of the ex-emperor *Reigen* at the court of the *Shōgun* (1700). *Yoshinaka*, whose office corresponded to that of master of ceremonies at the palace of *Edo*, was well versed in the laws of etiquette to be observed in such a circumstance, and it was the custom that his colleague should give him some presents in order to get instruction from him and be thus enabled to avoid any error against those rules. *Naganori* not willing to submit to such a custom, abstained from giving any present. *Yoshinaka*, deeply offended, did not spare his colleague humiliations and disobliging remarks. One day, he went so far as to rebuke him severely in public : *Naganori* lost patience and, drawing the little sword (*wakizashi*) which he carried in his belt, he struck *Yoshinaka* and wounded him in the forehead. The bystanders hastened to separate the adversaries ; but the *Shōgun Tsunayoshi* had *Naganori* immediately arrested and banished to *Ichinoseki* (*Mutsu*), the castle of *Tamura Nobuaki*. It was at that place that the *rōchū Tsuchiya Masanao* officially invited him to commit suicide by *karakiri*. As to his family, it was dispossessed of the domains in *Harima*. The following year, 47 *samurai* of the *Akō* clan revenged their master by killing *Yoshinaka* in his own house. — See *Ōishi Yoshio*.

Asawara Tameyori, 朝原 爲 賴. A *samurai* of *Kai* and a relation to *Ogasawara*, was renowned for his physical strength and his skill in archery. At the head of a band of robbers he pillaged and ransacked the environs of *Kyōto*. Order was given to have him arrested. *Tameyori*, one night, penetrated into the palace with his two sons and tried to assassinate the emperor *Fushimi* who escaped by a private door. They were soon surrounded by the guards of the palace, and all three killed themselves by *harakiri* (1290). The ex-emperor *Kameyama*, being accused of complicity in this criminal attempt, was compelled to have his head shaved and become a bonze.

Asazuma, 淺 妻. In *Ōmi*, was, from 1583 till 1600, the residence of *Shinjō Naoyori* (1538-1612), *Suruga no kami*, who, after the battle of *Sekigahara*, was deprived of his possessions and banished to *Aizu*.

Ashi, 安 志. In *Harima*, **Anashi** 穴 師 village, was the residence of a branch of the *Ogasawara* family from 1716 till 1868.

Ashigara-zaka, 足 柄 坂, is a road constructed from the village of *Sekimoto*, N. of *Odawara* (*Sagami*), to *Takenoshita*, near *Gotemba* (*Suruga*). It is the road that was followed by *Yamato-takeru* in his expedition against the *Ebisu* (110), by *Minamoto Yoshimitsu* marching against *Kiyowara Takehira* (1087), etc. In the reign of *Daigo-tennō* (898-930), a gate was erected on that road to watch the travellers ; hence the names *Kwantō*, *Kwansai*, to designate the provinces east and west of that place.

Ashigaru, 足 輕. (Literally : light foot) Soldiers of inferior condition who occupied the last rank in the escort of a *daimyō*, etc.

Ashiha-gawa, 足 羽 川. A river (99 km.) in *Echizen*. It empties itself into the *Hino-gawa*. It is also called *Asuha-gawa*, *Fukui-gawa*, *Asamizu-gawa*.

Ashihara-no-nakatsu-kuni, 葦 原 中 國. (Literal : central land of the reed-plain.) An ancient name of Japan.

Ashikaga, 足 利. A town (21,500 inh.) in *Shimotsuke*. The *Nitta* resided in the castle of that town from 1150 till about 1350. The shōgunal dynasty of that name traces its origin to that place. For several centuries, *Ashikaga* possessed a celebrated school (See *Ashikaga-gakkō*).

Under the *Tokugawa*, it was the residence of the *daimyō Doi* (1644), then, from 1704 till 1868, of the *Toda* (12,000 k.).

Ashikaga, 足利. A branch of the *Minamoto* (*Seiwa-Genji*), which gave 15 *Shōgun* to Japan, from 1338 till 1573.

—— **Yoshiyasu,** 義康 (1126-1157), *Mutsu no kami*, a grandson of *Minamoto Yoshiie* and a son of *Yoshikuni*, was the first to bear the name of *Ashikaga*, from the village where his father had established his residence in 1150. In the civil war of *Hōgen* (1156), he was on the side of *Taira Kiyomori* and guarded the imperial palace with *Minamoto Yoshitomo*. He died the following year. — *Yoshiyasu* is the ancestor, not only of the *Ashikaga*, but also of several families that played an important part in the events of the 14th, 15th, and 16th centuries.

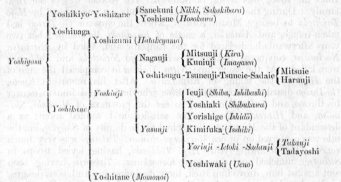

—— **Yoshikane,** 義兼 (1147-1196), *Kazusa no suke*, had married a daughter of *Hōjō Tokimasa* and was thus a brother-in-law of *Yoritomo*. For that reason he sided with the latter against the *Taira*. He took part in the campaign of *Noriyori* in *Kyūshū* (1185) and in that of *Yoritomo* in *Mutsu* (1189), and defeated a certain *Ōkawa Kaneto*, who pretended to be *Yoshitsune* having escaped from the disaster of *Koromogawa*. Soon afterwards he became a bonze.

—— **Yoshiuji,** 義氏 (1189-1254), *Sama no suke*, repressed the revolt of *Wada Yoshimori* against the *Hōjō* (1213). During the *Shōkyū* war (1221), he contributed greatly to the defeat of the troops of the emperor *Go-Toba*.

—— **Ietoki,** 家時, *Iyo no kami*, descendant in the 7th generation of *Yoshiie*. A writing of the latter said that the empire would be governed by his descendants in the 7th generation. Seeing that the prophecy of his ancestor was not realized, he went to the temple of *Hachiman*, the tutelary god of the *Minamoto*, and, offering up his life that the oracle might be fulfilled within three generations, he committed suicide.

I. — Shōgunal Branch (*Muromachi Shōgun*).

Takauji
{
Yoshiakira
{
Yoshimitsu
{
Tadafuyu

Yoshinori
{
Yoshimochi- Yoshikazu
Yoshitsugu

Yoshikatsu
Yoshimasa - Yoshihisa
Yoshimi - Yoshitane - Yoshifuyu- Yoshihide
Masatomo
{
Chacha
Yoshiharu
{
Yoshiteru
Shukei
Yoshiaki
Yoshizumi
{
Yoshitsuna
Yoshitada
Yoshinaga

Mitsunori

Motouji — (See II. Kamakura Branch).

—— **Takauji,** 尊 氏 (1305-1358), the first *Ashikaga Shōgun* from
1338 till 1358, was a son of *Sadauji*. His mother was of the *Hōjō*
family. During the war of *Genkō* (1331-1333), he was ordered by *Hōjō
Takatoki* to besiege Mount *Kasagi*, where the emperor *Go-Daigo* had
taken refuge, and *Akasaka*, a castle of *Kusunoki Masashige ;* but two
years afterwards he declared for the Emperor and, aided by *Akamatsu
Norimura*, conquered *Rokuhara*, where *Hōjō Nakatoki* and *Tokimasu*
were killed. At the same time *Nitta Yoshisada* completed the ruin of
the *Hōjō* by the taking of *Kamakura*. After his return to *Kyōto*,
Go-Daigo distributed rewards to those who had helped him to recover
his throne, and *Takauji* received in fief the provinces of *Musashi, Shimōsa*, and *Hitachi*. He was not satisfied and wanted more : as a
descendant of the *Minamoto*, he aspired to the dignity of *Shōgun*, but the
title was conferred on prince *Morinaga-shinnō : Takauji* was very much
vexed. The following year, *Hōjō Tokiyuki*, having levied troops in
Shinano, attacked and conquered *Kamakura. Takauji*, having been
sent against him, drove him back, then, disclosing his ambitious designs,
he distributed domains to his officers, established himself at *Kamakura*
and took the title of *Shōgun*. Having been declared a rebel, he prepared
to resist the imperial troops. Defeated by *Nitta Yoshisada* in *Mikawa*
and in *Suruga*, he intrenched himself in the *Hakone* mountains, where
he inflicted a bloody defeat on his adversary, who wanted to dislodge
him. A great number of *daimyō* then took his side, and, with their
assistance, he marched against *Kyōto*, defeated
the imperial army, and entered the capital, while
Go-Daigo fled to *Hiei-zan*. Meanwhile *Kitabatake Akiie* arrived from *Mutsu* with fresh
troops and, uniting with *Nitta Yoshisada, Kusunoki Masashige*, etc., expelled *Takauji* from
Kyōto. The latter, defeated again near *Hyōgo*,
went for help to *Kyūshū*. There, he defeated
Kikuchi Taketoshi at *Tatara-hama* (*Chikuzen*),
then hastened towards the capital. *Yoshisada*
and *Masashige* tried to ckeck his advance at the
Minato-gawa : they were defeated and *Masa-*

ASHIKAGA TAKAUJI.

shige committed suicide (1336). *Takauji* then entered *Kyōto* as a conqueror, declared that *Go-Daigo* had forfeited his throne, and installed *Kōmyō*, a son of *Go-Fushimi*, in his place. From that day dates the schism in the imperial descendance. For nearly 60 years, there were two emperors at the same time : one, the legitimate emperor, belonging to the so-called southern dynasty (*Nanchō*), because *Go-Daigo* had retired to the south of *Kyōto ;* the other belonging to the northern dynasty (*Hokuchō*), supported by *Takauji* and his successors, who finally obtained the abdication of his competitor. For 20 years, *Takauji*, aided by *Kō Moronao, Shiba Takatsune,* etc., continued the war, with alternate successes and reverses, it is true ; but he saw the supporters of the Southern Court fall one after another, such as, *Nitta,* the *Kusunoki,* the *Kitabatake,* etc. Then trouble came to his own family : his brother *Tadayoshi* and his son *Tadafuyu* took side with the adverse party, and he was obliged to wage war against them (1350). This cast a deep gloom over his last days. He died of a cancer in 1358, leaving his power to his son *Yoshiakira.*

—— **Tadayoshi,** 直義 (1307-1352). A brother of *Takauji,* first assisted him in his enterprises. In 1335, he was charged with the protection of the *Shōgun Narinaga-shinnō* at *Kamakura,* when *Hōjō Tokiyuki* came to attack that place. Not strong enough to resist him seriously, he had the ex-*Shōgun Morinaga-shinnō,* his prisoner, killed, and retreated to *Mikawa.* But soon he came back accompanied by *Takauji,* defeated *Tokiyuki* and re-entered *Kamakura.* When his brother revolted, he marched with him against *Kyōto* and took part in all the battles against the defenders of the legitimate dynasty. Unfortunately, *Takauji* chose, as first minister (*shitsuji*), *Kō Moronao,* who, proud of his success, soon misused his authority. *Tadayoshi* fell out with him, and tried to assassinate him. His design was discovered, and *Moronao,* to punish him, obliged him to have his head shaved and to become a bonze (1349). *Tadayoshi* apparently submitted and assumed the name of *Keishin ;* but soon afterwards, he offered his services to *Go-Murakami,* the emperor of the south, who appointed him general of all his troops. In 1351, he defeated his brother, killed his enemy *Moronao* at *Mikage* (*Settsu*), and entered *Kamakura ;* but at the beginning of the following year, he was in his turn defeated at *Sattayama,* taken prisoner and assassinated.

—— **Tadafuyu,** 直冬 (+ 1400). An illegitimate son of *Takauji,* and adopted by *Tadayoshi,* was appointed *tandai* of *Chūgoku* in 1349. When *Tadayoshi* joined the southern party, *Tadafuyu* also revolted against *Takauji.* Having been defeated by *Kō Moronao,* he fled to *Kyūshū,* where he married the daughter of *Shōni Yorihisa.* After the death of *Tadayoshi,* he fought under the command of *Yamana Tokiuji* and, in 1355, entered *Kyōto,* whence *Takauji* had fled ; but soon afterwards he was obliged to retreat to *Iwami.* At last he submitted to *Yoshimitsu* in 1376, and received the title of *Iwami no kami.*

—— **Yoshiakira,** 義詮 (1330-1368). The 2nd *Ashikaga Shōgun* from 1358 till 1367, was a son of *Takauji.* He was brought up at

Kamakura and then installed at *Muromachi* (*Kyōto*). When the southern army retook *Kyōto* in 1351, he went to *Kyūshū* for reinforcements, returned, re-entered the capital, deposed the emperor of the North and replaced him by *Sukō Go-Kōgon*, although the three imperial emblems were in possession of *Go-Murakami*, the emperor of the South. Having become *Shōgun* at the death of his father *Takauji* (1358), he continued the war against the southern dynasty, and by and by, obtained the submission of all the great *daimyō*, such as, *Ōuchi*, *Yamana*, *Nikki*, etc. Finally, overcome by illness, he abdicated in favor of his son *Yoshimitsu* then only 10 years old, and died some months afterwards in his 38th year.

—— **Yoshimitsu**, 義滿 (1358-1408). The 3rd *Ashikaga Shōgun*, from 1367 till 1395, being only 10 years old when succeeding his father *Yoshiakira*, had as minister (*shitsuji*) the celebrated *Hosokawa Yoriyuki*, to whom he greatly owed the success in his enterprises. Although the supporters of the southern dynasty had been defeated nearly everywhere, *Kyūshū* remained faithful to them owing to *Go-Daigo's* son, *Yasunaga-shinnō*, who being supported by *Kikuchi*, *Itō*, *Shimazu*, etc., kept up the war in that part of the country. *Yoshimitsu*, after having sent there *Imagawa Sadayo* with the title of *Tsukushi-tandai*, himself conducted an expedition in 1374. Resistance was short : *Kyūshū* submitted, and *Yasunaga* was obliged to flee and hide himself. Having returned to *Kyōto*, *Yoshimitsu* installed himself in the *Muromachi* palace and soon raised the prestige of the shōgunal power to its zenith. By frequent embassies he kept up his relations with the *Ming* dynasty recently established in China, cultivated letters and favored artists ; being a fervent adept of the Buddhist sect *Zen*, he was liberal to the bonzes and built the *Sōkoku-ji* temple, the most beautiful of the epoch (1382). Meanwhile the *Yamana*, a family of *daimyō*, availing themselves of the intestine wars, had become by and by the masters of 11 provinces. *Yoshimitsu* was uneasy at their increasing power. But, when, *Yamana Ujikiyo* attacked *Kyōto* in 1391, *Yoshimitsu* routed his army and distributed the immense domains of that family among his generals. This triumph definitively secured the power of the *Ashikaga*. The emperor of the South, *Go-Kameyama* himself submitted, and abdicated in favor of *Go-Komatsu*, the emperor of the North to whom he transmitted the imperial insignia under the condition that henceforth the emperors should be chosen from the two imperial branches alternately : it was the end of the schism which for 56 years had divided the country into two hostile camps (1392). Two years later, *Yoshimitsu* abdicated in favor of his son *Yoshimochi*, then 9 years old, and received the title of *Dajō-daijin* (prime minister).

ASHIKAGA YOSHIMITSU.

The following year he had his head shaved and became a bonze under the name of *Tenzan Dōgi*. Then, on a hill north of *Kyōto* (*Kitayama*), he built a splendid palace, which the people called "*Kinkaku-ji*" (golden temple), on account of the great richness in its ornamentation. From that place the powerful bonze continued to govern the land. He sent an embassy to China with rich presents : in return, the emperor of the *Ming* dynasty sent him a message in which he recognized him as king of Japan and authorized him to send a tribute only every tenth year. (However strange this letter of the Chinese emperor may seem, there is no doubt that he considered the presents sent to him from Japan as a tribute, and the embassies as a homage of vasselage) (1404). Having become dangerously ill, *Yoshimitsu* was visited by the emperor himself in the *Kinkaku-ji*. He soon afterwards died (1408) at the age of 50, requesting his son to stop the relations with China.

Yoshimitsu who carried the glory of his family to such a high degree, was, after *Takauji*, the most remarkable of the *Ashikaga Shōgun*.

—— **Yoshimochi, 義持** (1386-1428). Was, from 1395 till 1423, the 4th *Ashikaga Shōgun*. Having become *Shōgun* when 9 years old by the abdication of his father *Yoshimitsu*, he let the latter govern until his death. When, in 1412, *Go-Komatsu* abdicated, he nominated *Shōkō*, who also belonged to the northern dynasty, contrary to the agreement made in 1392 ; hence several revolts of the supporters of the southern dynasty in *Yamato, Kii, Mutsu*. In 1418 he killed, in the temple *Sōkoku-ji*, his brother *Yoshitsugu*, accused of aspiring to the shōgunate. In 1423, he abdicated in favor of his son *Yoshikazu* and became a bonze in the *Tōji-in ;* but *Yoshikazu* having died two years later, he resumed the power and kept it until his death in 1428.

SEAL OF ASHIKAGA YOSHIMOCHI.

—— **Yoshikazu, 義量** (1407-1425). The 5th *Ashikaga Shōgun*, from 1423 till 1425. He become *Shōgun* when 17 years old, by the abdication of his father *Yoshimochi* in 1423, and died two years afterwards.

—— **Yoshinori, 義教** (1394-1441). Was the 6th *Ashikaga Shōgun*, from 1428 till 1441. He was a bonze at the *Shōren-in* under the name of *Gi-en*, when, at the death of his brother *Yoshimochi*, he was chosen as his successor. The first act of his authority was to designate, as successor of *Shōkō-tennō, Go-Hanazono*, a great grandson of *Sukō-tennō* of the northern dynasty, which choice caused a revolt in *Ise*. *Yoshinori* had been elected *Shōgun* contrary to the advice of the *Kamakura Kwanryō, Ashikaga Mochiuji*, who aspired to the shōgunal dignity. On hat account their relations were so strained that *Yoshinori* ordered *Uesugi Norizane* to march with an army against *Mochiuji*. The latter was defeated at *Hakone* and invited to commit *harakiri* (1439). A little later, *Yoshinori* wanted to take a part of the domains of *Akamatsu Mitsusuke* in order to give them to *Akamatsu Sadamura*. *Noriyasu*, the son of *Mitsusuke*, having heard of that design, informed his father of it. The latter, concealing his irritation, invited *Yoshinori* to a feast, and had him assassinated in the middle of the entertainment (1441).

—— **Yoshikatsu,** 義勝 (1433-1443). The 7th *Ashikaga Shōgun*, from 1441 till 1443, succeeded his father when 8 years old and died two years later by falling from a horse.

—— **Yoshimasa,** 義政 (1435-1490). The 8th *Ashikaga Shōgun*, from 1443 till 1474, became *Shōgun* when 8 years old, at the death of his brother *Yoshikatsu.* In 1454, *Yamana Mochitoyo*, who had stirred up troubles in *Kyōto*, was banished to *Tajima*, where he raised an army. *Akamatsu Norinao* was sent against him, but was defeated, and *Mochitoyo* marched against *Kyōto*, which he entered as a conqueror, *Yoshimasa* being unable to check him. At the same time disturbances arose in *Kwantō :* the *Shōgun* sent his brother *Masatomo* to restore order in those provinces. Meanwhile the rivalries among the great families *Hosokawa, Hatakeyama, Yamana, Shiba,* etc., caused continual wars, and the misery of the people was aggravated day after day. Instead of trying to remedy this sad state of affairs, the *Shōgun* was thinking of nothing but pleasure in his palace of *Muromachi.* It was then that, having no children, *Yoshimasa* adopted his brother, the bonze *Gijin,* who reentered the world and took the name of *Yoshimi* (1464). But the following year, a son, *Yoshihisa,* was born to *Yoshimasa,* who immediately wanted to annul the promise made to his brother. The latter, to maintain his right, applied for help to *Hosokawa Katsumoto,* while the *Shōgun* addressed himself to *Yamana Sōzen* (*Mochitoyo*) for the support of his son. All the great *daimyō* took one or other side: *Hatakeyama Masanaga, Shiba Yoshitoshi, Akamatsu Masanori, Takeda Kuninobu,* etc., sided with *Katsumoto ;* while *Hatakeyama Yoshinari, Isshiki Yoshinao, Ōuchi Masahiro, Shiba Yoshikado, Toki Noriyori,* etc., were seen on the side of *Sōzen ;* and the civil war of *Ōnin* (*Ōnin no tairan*) commenced in 1467 to last for ten long years. *Kyōto* and the neighboring villages were reduced to ashes, and the artistic objects and documents which were then destroyed cannot be sufficiently regretted. Both *Sōzen* and *Katsumoto* died in 1473 : they had been fighting for seven years without any decided success. The following year, *Yoshimasa* abdicated in favor of his son *Yoshihisa,* then 9 years old. Meanwhile the hostile armies, tired of the war and unable to get provisions in the devastated districts, dispersed, each *daimyō* returning to his own province (1477). *Yoshimasa* then built on a hill east of *Kyōto* (*Higashi-yama*) a palace, which

ASHIKAGA YOSHIMASA.

in opposition to the *Kinkaku-ji* (golden temple) of his grandfather *Yoshimitsu,* was called *Ginkaku-ji* (silver temple). He lived there for ten years, surrounded by bonzes, poets, actors, etc., continuing to exhaust the treasury by his prodigality. His son *Yoshihisa* having died in 1489, *Yoshimasa* was reconciled with his brother *Yoshimi,* adopted the latter's son *Yoshitane,* whom he had nominated *Shōgun.* He died the following year, leaving the work built up by his predecessors in a very precarious state. On account of his palace at the *Higashi-yama*, *Yoshimasa* is often named *Higashi-yama-dono*, *Higashi-yama-Shōgun*.

—— **Yoshihisa**, 義 尚 (1465-1489). The 9th *Ashikaga Shōgun*, from 1474 till 1489, and a son of *Yoshimasa*, was raised to the shōgunate when 9 years old. His father continued to govern. In 1477, the *Ōnin* war came to an end, *Yoshimi* retired to *Mino*, and *Kyōto* was left in peace; but the authority of the *Shōgun* was shaken. *Yoshihisa* applied himself to strengthen it. In 1487, he himself led an expedition against *Sasaki Takayori*, besieged him in *Magari-no-sato* (*Ōmi*); but died of illness during the campaign. Although only 25 years old, he had given some hopes by his energy, but his untimely death did not permit him to realize them.

—— **Yoshimi**, 義 視 (1439-1491). The 4th son of *Yoshinori*, a brother of *Yoshikatsu* and *Yoshimasa*, was a bonze under the name of *Gijin* when *Yoshimasa*, then childless, adopted him as his heir (1464). He then took the name of *Yoshimi*. However *Yoshihisa* being born the following year, *Yoshimasa's* dispositions towards him underwent a complete change; hence the disastrous *Ōnin* civil war (1467). During the hostilities, *Yoshimi* established himself first at *Sakamoto*, afterwards he applied for an asylum to *Kitabatake Noritomo*, in *Ise*; finally he settled on *Hiei-zan*. Peace having been concluded, he retired to *Mino*; from thence *Yoshimasa* recalled him to *Kyōto* at the death of *Yoshihisa*, reconciled himself with him and adopted his son *Yoshitane* (1489). *Yoshimi* again became a bonze and died two years later at the age of 53.

—— **Masatomo**, 政 知 (1436-1491). Was the 3rd son of the *Shōgun Yoshinori*, a brother of *Yoshikatsu*, *Yoshimasa* and *Yoshimi*. He was a bonze when *Ashikaga Shigeuji*, the *Kwanryō* of the *Kwantō* provinces was expelled by *Uesugi Fusaaki*. *Yoshimasa* sent him to *Kamakura* to take *Shigeuji's* place; but, though supported by the troops of *Kai* and *Ise*, he could not install himself at *Kamakura*, and established his residence at ̣ *Horikoshi* (*Izu*), thence he governed *Kwantō*. Putting aside his eldest son *Chacha-maru*, he selected his second son *Yoshizumi* as his heir; but *Chacha* revolted against this decision, assassinated his father, and took his inheritance. Two years later he was himself deposed and killed by *Ise Nagauji* (*Hōjō Sōun*).

—— **Yoshitane**, 義 植 (1465-1522). The 10th *Ashikaga Shōgun*, from 1490 till 1493, and later from 1508 till 1521, was a son of *Yoshimi*. At the death of *Yoshihisa*, he was adopted by his uncle *Yoshimasa*, and succeeded him in 1490. The following year, he marched against *Sasaki Takayori*, whom he put to flight; then, supported by *Hatakeyama Masanaga*, he turned his arms against *Hatakeyama Yoshitoyo*, who hastened to ask *Hosokawa Masamoto* for help. The battle was fought at *Shogaku-ji* (*Kawachi*): the army of the *Shōgun* was completely defeated, *Masanaga* was killed, and *Yoshitane* had to flee into *Etchū*. *Masamoto* then recalled from *Izu Yoshizumi*, a son of *Masamoto*, and raised him to the shōgunate (1493). In 1498, *Yoshitane* left *Etchū* in order to seek an asylum with *Ōuchi*

Yoshioki in *Suwō*. He lived there for ten years, preparing his revenge. In 1508 *Yoshioki* having furnished him with an army, he marched against *Kyōto*, expelled *Yoshizumi* whose supporter *Masamoto* had been assassinated, and resumed the title of *Shōgun*. This unexpected success was soon afterwards crowned by a brilliant victory gained by *Yoshioki* over the *Hosokawa, Sasaki,* and *Miyoshi* families, leagued against him. In 1511, *Yoshizumi* having died, *Hosokawa Sumimoto* wished to raise *Yoshizumi's* son *Yoshiharu* to the shōgunate, and started with an army to install him in *Kyōto. Yoshioki* immediately went to *Tamba* to recruit an army. Having succeeded, he returned in great haste and completely defeated *Sumimoto*. After the latter's death in 1520, *Takakuni* replaced him as *Kwanryō;* but *Yoshitane* tried to thrust him aside : he did not succeed and was obliged to take refuge in *Awaji*. Then *Takakuni* nominated *Yoshiharu,* the son of *Yoshizumi* in his place. From *Awaji, Yoshitane* went to *Awa* (*Shikoku*), where he died in 1522, at the age of 58. As he died in exile in an island, he is often called *Shima-kubō*.

—— **Yoshizumi,** 義澄 (1478-1511). The 11th *Ashikaga Shōgun,* from 1493 till 1508, was a son of *Masatomo*. When his father died in 1491, he found an asylum in *Suruga* with *Imagawa Ujichika,* who took him to *Kyōto* and confided him to the *Kwanryō Hosokawa Masamoto*. When *Yoshitane,* defeated in *Kawachi,* left *Kyōto* and fled into *Etchū, Masamoto* replaced him by *Yoshizumi* then 16 years old (1493). *Masamoto* having been assassinated in 1507 and his successor *Sumimoto* being only 16 years old, *Yoshitane* raised an army in *Suwō* and reentered *Kyō-to,* hence *Yoshizumi* fled into *Ōmi* (1508). He died three years later, being 33 years old.

—— **Yoshiharu,** 義晴 (1510-1550). The 12th *Ashikaga Shōgun,* from 1521 till 1545, a son of *Yoshizumi,* was nominated *Shōgun* when 11 years old, after *Hosokawa Takaku* had expelled *Yoshitane* from *Kyōto* (1521). In 1528, *Miyoshi Nagamoto* having entered *Kyōto* with an army, *Yoshiharu* fled into *Ōmi,* to the residence of *Kuchiki Tanetsuna,* and returned to the capital only 4 years later. At that time the power of the *Shōgun* was at the mercy of the great *daimyō,* who, throughout the country, were at war with one another. It was the epoch of the great civil wars, which were brought to an end only when *Nobunaga* came into power. *Yoshiharu,* in order to escape from the *Miyoshi,* was again obliged to leave *Kyōto* in 1539, and retired to *Hatsuse* (*Yamato*), where he spent three years, and a second time, reentered the capital. At the end he abdicated the shōgunate in favor of his son *Yoshiteru* (1545); but, the following year, *Hosokawa Harumoto* obliged him again to flee to *Sakamoto* (*Ōmi*), where he died in 1550 at the age of 40.

—— **Yoshiteru,** 義輝 (1535-1565). The 13th *Ashikaga Shōgun,* from 1545 till 1565, was a son of *Yoshiharu*. Scarcely had he been made *Shōgun* (1545), when he was obliged to flee with his father to *Sakamoto* (*Ōmi*) ; afterwards, having been reconciled with *Miyoshi Chōkei,* the latter readmitted him to *Kyōto* (1553). But although invested with the title of *Shōgun*, he had no authority : *Chōkei* and his vassal *Matsunaga Hisahide* were the real masters. To get rid of their domination, *Yoshiteru* recalled *Hosokawa Harumoto ;* but *Chōkei* opposed his return, and the *Shōgun* was obliged to banish *Harumoto* to *Akutagawa* (*Settsu*). After that he invited *Uesugi Terutora* to pacify the *Kwantō* and *Mōri Motonari*, the *Kwansai*, but they refused to undertake such a difficult task. Finally, as he prepared to oppose the evil designs of *Matsunaga Hisahide*, the latter in haste repaired to Kyōto and invested the palace of the *Shōgun*. *Yoshiteru*, perceiving that any serious resistance was out of question, killed himself by *harakiri* (1565). He was only 30 years old.

—— **Yoshihide, 義 榮** (1564-1568). The 14th *Ashikaga Shōgun*, was a son of *Yoshifuyu* and a grandson of *Yoshitane*. He was chosen to succeed *Yoshiteru* by *Miyoshi Yoshitsugu* and *Matsunaga Hisahide*, when he was only three years old : the imperial investiture was however refused. Soon *Oda Nobunaga*, who patronized *Yoshiaki*, a brother of *Yoshiteru*, marched against *Kyōto*. Unable to resist, *Yoshitsugu* and *Hisahide* retired to *Awa* (*Shikoku*), taking along with them their *Shōgun*, who died soon afterwards, — some say of illness, others, that he was assassinated by *Hisahide*.

—— **Yoshiaki, 義 昭** (1537-1597). The 15th and last *Ashikaga Shōgun*, from 1568 till 1573, a son of *Yoshiharu* and brother of *Yoshiteru*, was a bonze under the name of *Gakkei*, at the *Ichijō-in* temple in *Nara*. After the death of *Yoshiteru*, his brother *Shukō*, then a bonze at the *Kokuon-ji* (*Kyōto*) was killed by the order of *Matsunaga*. *Yoshiaki* likewise was going to be put to death, when, aided by *Hosokawa Fujitaka*, he managed to flee to *Ōmi* where he found an asylum at the residence of *Sasaki Yoshitaka*. There he took the name of *Yoshiaki* (1565). Two years later he took refuge at the residence of *Asakura Yoshikage* in *Echizen*. As *Asakura* found it too difficult to lead him victoriously to *Kyōto*, *Yoshiaki* sent an emissary to *Oda Nobunaga*, who accepted the mission, entered the capital with his *protégé*, obtained the title of *Shōgun* (1568), for him rebuilt the *Nijō* palace, and intrusted the guard of *Kyōto* to *Kinoshita Hideyoshi ;* then in concert with *Tokugawa Ieyasu*, *Shibata Katsuie*, etc., he attacked *Sasaki*, *Asakura*, and all the other adversaries of *Yoshiaki*, and defeated them one after another. But soon the relations between the *Shōgun* and his protector began to be strained. *Nobunaga* dared to make representations to the *Shōgun* and presented a list of 17 articles containing the points in which the shōgunal administration ought to be reformed. His dignity wounded, *Yoshiaki* asked *Takeda Shingen* to rid him of the one to whom he owed his fortune. *Nobunaga* having been informed of the plot, seized the *Shōgun* and sent him a prisoner to the castle of *Wakae* (*Kawachi*). This put an end to the shōgunate of the *Ashikaga* (1573), who had governed Japan from 1336. In 1575, *Yoshiaki* became a bonze under the name of *Shōzan* and applied to *Mōri Terumoto* for an asylum. Later on he returned to Kyōto, where he lived almost ignored, and died in 1597, at the age of sixty one.

II. — KAMAKURA BRANCH (*Kwantō Kwanryō*).

```
                                      ┌ Yoshishisa
                                      │ Haruō-maru              ┌ Haruuji ┌ Fujiuji
                          ┌ Mochiuji ┤ Yasuō-maru    ┌ Takamoto ┤         └ Yoshiuji
               ┌ Mitsukane┤          │               │          └ Norihiro
               │          │          └ Shigeuji-Masauji┤ Yoshiaki ┌ Yoshizumi
               │          └ Mochinaka                 │          └ Yorizumi ┌ Kunitomo.
 Motouji-Ujimitsu ┤ Mitsunao                          └ Tomoyori            └ Yoriuji.
               │ Mitsutaka
               │ Mitsusada
               └ Mitsuhide
```

---- **Motouji, 基氏** (1340-1367). The 1st *Kamakura Kwanryō*, was a son of *Takauji*. After his revolt against *Go-Daigo*, having again set up the shōgunate in his own person, *Takauji* installed himself at *Kamakura*; but soon he perceived that the situation was not the same as in the time of *Yoritomo*, and that *Kyōto* was the right residence of the *Shōgun*. On the other hand, the difficulty of governing the turbulent eastern provinces from the capital, suggested to him the thought of not abandoning *Kamakura* entirely. Therefore reserving the succession to the shōgunate for his eldest son *Yoshiakira*, he intrusted the government of the eastern provinces to his 4th son *Motouji* with the title of *Kwantō Kwanryō* (1349). However, as *Motouji* was yet a child, the administration was put in the hands of *Uesugi Noriaki* and *Kō Morofuyu* with the title of *shitsuji*. But the very next year, when *Tadayoshi* joined the southern party, *Noriaki* followed his example and retired into *Kōzuke*. *Morofuyu*, remaining faithful to *Motouji*, marched against his colleague, but was killed in *Kai*. *Takauji* repaired then to *Kamakura* and defeated the troops of his brother, who was made a prisoner. A little later, *Nitta*, *Yoshioki*, and *Yoshimune* took *Kamakura* whence *Motouji* fled (1352): *Takauji* came back and defeated *Yoshimune*, who retired into *Echigo*. Having returned to *Kyōto*, *Takauji* sent *Hatakeyama Kunikiyo* to *Kamakura* as *shitsuji*. After the death of *Takauji*, as *Yoshioki* was going to attack *Kamakura* again, *Motouji* had him arrested and subsequently drowned in the *Rokugō-gawa* (1358). Peace was then restored in *Kwantō*, and *Motouji* sent troops to help his brother, the *Shōgun Yoshiakira*, to invest the *Yoshino* region, where the emperor of the South had entrenched himself. Betrayed by *Kunikiyo*, who, instead of accomplishing this mission, was going to attack *Nikki Yoshinaga*, he marched in person against his ministers, whom he defeated without difficulty, then, recalling his former *shitsuji Uesugi Noriaki*, he reinstalled him in his office (1364) and died three years later at the age of twenty-eight.

---- **Ujimitsu, 氏満** (1357-1398). The 2nd *Kamakura Kwanryō*, a son of *Motouji*, was only 10 years old when he succeeded his father in 1367. *Noriaki* continued his functions as minister; but dying the following year, he was replaced by his son *Yoshinori*, who, soon afterwards, had to lead an expedition against *Nitta Yoshimune* and *Wakiya*

Yoshiharu: Yoshimune was killed and *Yoshiharu* fled into *Shinano* (1370). Unfortunately, as *Ujimitsu* advanced in years, ambition entered the heart of the young *Kwanryō*. While *Yoshiakira* was subduing *Kyushū*, *Ujimitsu*, conceived the project of making himself master of *Kyōto* and having himself nominated *Shōgun: Uesugi Noriharu* to whom he spoke of his plan, first tried to dissuade him from that foolish enterprise; but seeing that his advice was of no avail, he committed suicide by *harakiri*. This tragic death made *Ujimitsu* reflect, and he abandoned his design (1379). Somewhat later, he sent *Uesugi Norikata* against *Oyama Yoshimasa*, a partisan of the South, who caused troubles in *Shimotsuke*. *Yoshimasa* was defeated and killed (1382). At last, in 1391, when *Yoshimitsu* fought against the *Yamana* clan, *Ujimitsu* was going to join him but the campaign was finished before he could take part in it. His jurisdiction was nevertheless extended to *Mutsu* and *Dewa*.

—— **Mitsukane, 滿兼** (1376-1409). The third *Kamakura Kwanryō*, a son of *Ujimitsu*, was 22 years old when his father died. *Uesugi Tomomune* was his minister. When *Ōuchi Yoshihiro* revolted in *Izumi* in favor of the southern dynasty, *Mitsukane* conceived the project of joining him and taking the place of the *Shōgun Yoshimochi;* but the revolt was promptly put down and he could not realize his plan (1399).

—— **Mochiuji, 持氏** (1398-1439). The 4th *Kamakura Kwanryō*, a son of *Mitsukane*, was eleven years old when he succeeded his father. *Uesugi Norisada, shitsuji*, ruled for him at the beginning and, at his death, was replaced by his son *Ujinori* (1411). Five years later, *Ujinori* formed the plot to replace *Mochiuji* by the latter's brother *Mochinaka*. *Mochiuji* immediately asked *Uesugi Morimoto* for help, and took refuge first in *Izu*, then in *Suruga*, whence *Imagawa Noritada* conducted him to *Kyōto*. The *Shōgun Yoshimochi* ordered all the *daimyō* of *Kwantō* to support *Mochiuji*. Meanwhile, *Norimoto*, who had been levying troops in *Echigo*, came back with great forces, and utterly defeated *Ujinori: Mochiuji* returned to *Kamakura*, where *Mochinaka* had committed suicide. At the death of *Yoshimochi* (1428), *Mochiuji* tried in vain to be nominated *Shōgun: Yoshinori* having been preferred, he swore to take revenge. Convinced that *Uesugi Norizane* was the cause of his failure, he tried to get rid of him. As however *Norizane* was so powerful as he was popular in *Kwantō*, the attempt was difficult. In the mean time *Mochiuji* concerted measures with *Isshiki Naokane* and *Uesugi Norinao;* but the plot was discovered, and the *Kwanryō* was obliged to apologize to *Norizane* and exile both his accomplices. New attempts having been directed against him, *Norizane* retired to his castle of *Hirai* (*Kōzuke*) and thence informed the *Shōgun* of the events. The answer was to put to death *Mochiuji*, who, besieged in the temple of *Eian-ji* (*Musashi*). committed suicide (1439): he was 42 years old. His uncle *Mitsusada* and his eldest son *Yoshihisa* did the same in the temple of *Hōkoku-ji*. — Thus finished, after 90 years, the administration of *Kwantō* by the *Kwanryō* of the *Ashikaga* family.

The three younger sons of *Mochiuji* had however succeeded in fleeing to *Nikkō*. In 1440, *Yūki Ujitomo, daimyō* of *Koga* (*Shimōsa*) led them to his castle and took up their party; but his castle was besieged and he lost his life. Two of his protégés were caught in their flight and put to death in *Mino*. *Haruō-maru* 春王丸, the eldest, was 13 and *Yasuō-maru* 安王丸, the second, was eleven years old.

—— **Shigeuji,** 成氏 (1434-1497). The 4th son of *Mochiuji*, was taken to *Shinano* after his father's death, into his mother's family. He was then five years old. His uncle, *Ōi Mochimitsu*, applied to *Nagao Kagenobu*, who obtained for *Shigeuchi* the title of *Kwanryō* (1449) : *Uesugi Noritada*, a son of *Norizane*, was *shitsuji*. At the same time *Yūki Shigetomo*, a son of *Ujitomo* came from *Mutsu* to join him at *Kamakura*, and both of them prepared to revenge the deaths of their fathers and brothers. The *Shōgun Yoshimasa*, mistrusting *Shigeuji*, had himself informed by *Noritada* of what was going on in *Kwantō* : this was a new motive of hatred, and, in 1454, *Noritada* was assassinated. At the news of this crime, all the vassals of the *Uesugi* rose in arms against *Shigeuji*, and civil war re-commenced. *Fusaaki*, *Noritada's* brother, established himself at *Kamakura*, whilst *Shigeuji* took refuge at *Koga*, hence the name of *Koga-kubō*, by which the people designated him and his successors. Meanwhile *Fusaaki* sent a report of the events to *Kyōto*, and asked the *Shōgun* to designate some one to replace *Shigeuji*: *Yoshimasa* then nominated his own brother *Masatomo* as *Kwanryō* of the *Kwantō*, and sent him to *Kamakura*. But as many *daimyō* and *samurai* had remained faithful to *Shigeuji*, *Masatomo* was obliged to establish himself in *Izu*, at *Horikoshi;* on that account he was called *Horikoshi-gosho*. Thus on the one side, *Masatomo* was supported by the whole clan of the *Uesugi;* on the other, *Shigeuji* was supported by the *Chiba*, the *Utsunomiya*, the *Oyama*, etc. *Norisada*, *Sadamasa* and the *Uesugi* having come to besiege *Koga*, *Shigeuji* retired to *Chiba* (1471). Finally, in 1478, by the intervention of the *Shōgun*, peace was concluded between the two parties, and *Shigeuji* was able to return to *Koga*, where he died in 1497, at the age of sixty-three.

—— **Masauji,** 政氏 (+ 1531). Was a son of *Shigeuji* and likewise lived in *Koga* (*Koga-kubō*). In 1506, his son *Takamoto* tried to revolt against him; but peace was restored owing to the intervention of *Nagao Kageharu*.

—— **Yoshiaki,** 義明 (+ 1538). Was the 3rd son of *Masauji*. Some disagreement having arisen between him and his father, he retired to the castle of *Oyumi* in *Mutsu*, hence the name of *Oyumi-gosho* that was given him. *Satomi Yoshihiro*, after having submitted to him, joined him against *Hōjō Ujitsuna*: they were defeated and *Yoshiaki* perished in the battle (1538).

—— **Haruuji,** 晴氏 (+ 1560). A grandson of *Masauji* and a son of *Takamoto*, married the daughter of *Hōjō Ujitsuna*, and afterwards took side with the *Uesugi*. When the latter waged war against *Ujitsuna* and besieged the castle of *Kawagoe* (*Musashi*), he was defeated with them.

—— **Yoshiuji,** 義氏. Was the last *Koga-kubō*. He had a daughter known by the name of *Koga-himegimi*, for whom he adopted *Kunitomo*, who established himself in 1590 at *Kitsuregawa* (*Shimotsuke*), where his descendants resided till the Restoration, with a revenue of 10,000 k. = Now Viscount.

Ashikaga-gakkō, 足利學校. Was a celebrated school founded by *Ono no Takamura* (801-852) according to some, and by *Ashikaga Yoshikane* (1147-1196) according to others. In 1350, *Ashikaga Motouji* enlarged it, and *Nagao Kagehisa* established it at *Ashikaga (Shimotsuke)* in 1394. Yet, its greatest patron was the *shitsuji Uesugi Norizane,* who in 1439 endowed it with considerable revenues, enriched it with numerous manuscripts, and put at its head the bonze *Kwaigen* renowned for his learning. Favored by the descendants of *Norizane,* this school soon became the most important center of the study of Chinese and Confucianism, but it declined by and by under the *Tokugawa* shōgunate.

Ashikaga-hon, 足利本. *Ieyasu* having founded a school in 1601 at *Fushimi (Yamashiro),* appointed the bonze *Sanyō* its director. Until then the latter had been a professor at the *Ashikaga* school. *Sanyō* ordered a great number of movable wooden characters to be engraved ; by means of these characters he printed books, which were called *Ashikaga* books, because the greater number came from that celebrated school.

Ashikaga-jidai, 足利時代. The period of the *Ashikaga* shōgunate : from 1336 till 1573.

Ashikaga-Shōgun, 足利將軍. The following were the *Ashikaga Shōgun* : — 1, *Takauji* ; 2, *Yoshiakira* ; 3, *Yoshimitsu* ; 4, *Yoshimochi* ; 5, *Yoshikazu* ; 6, *Yoshinori* ; 7, *Yoshikatsu* ; 8, *Yoshimasa* ; 9, *Yoshihisa* ; 10, *Yoshitane* ; 11, *Yoshizumi* ; 12, *Yoshiharu* ; 13, *Yoshiteru* ; 14, *Yoshihide* ; 15, *Yoshiaki.*

Ashimori, 足守. A town in *Bitchū,* which was the residence of the *daimyō Kinoshita* from 1600 till 1868.

Ashina, 蘆名. A family of *daimyō* descending from the *Miura* and by them from the *Taira.* This family was powerful in *Mutsu* during the 15th and 16th centuries. *Sawara Yoshitsuru,* the last son of *Miura Yoshiaki,* received the district of *Aizu* in fief. His grandson took the name of *Ashina. Morimasa* was his great-grandson.

Morimasa - Morihisa - Morinori $\left\{\begin{array}{l}\text{Moritaka}\\\text{Morikiyo - Moriuji}\left\{\begin{array}{l}\text{Moritaka - Morishige}\\\text{Morioki}\end{array}\right.\end{array}\right.$

—— **Morimasa,** 盛政 (1386-1432). Was a son of *Norimori.* In 1416 he joined the *Uesugi* clan in a war against *Ashikaga Mochiuji.* He resided at the castle of *Kurokawa* (now *Wakamatsu*), and was *Shuri-tayū.*

—— **Morihisa,** 盛久 (+ 1444), was *Shuri-tayū* and *Shimōsa no kami.*

—— **Morinori,** 盛詮 (1431-1466). Was *Shimōsa no kami.*

—— **Moritaka,** 盛高 (+ 1517), married the daughter of *Date Ujimune* in 1473. In 1478 a contention arose between him and his son : hence a war broke out between them, and lasted till 1506.

—— **Morikiyo,** 盛舜 (1490-1553), *Tōtōmi no kami,* succeeded his brother *Moritaka,* whose son had died. In 1547, he tried with *Date Harumune* to seize the domains of the *Sōma* family, but was defeated.

—— **Moriuji,** 盛 氏 (1521-1580), *Shuri-tayū*, was constantly at war with *Satake Yoshishige*, *Hōjō Ujiyasu*, etc.

—— **Moritaka,** 盛 隆 (1560-1583). Having sent presents to the Emperor and to *Nobunaga*, was created *Tōtōmi no kami* (1579). He waged war against *Date Masamune* and *Tamura Kiyozumi*, and was assassinated on account of his disorders by *Ōba Sanzaemon*, one of his *kerai*.

—— **Morishige,** 盛 重. Was a son of *Satake Yoshishige*, but was chosen to succeed *Moritaka*, who had died childless: he was then 12 years old. Many *kerai* of the *Satake* clan accompanied him to his new domains, which fact caused discontent among the former servants of the *Ashina* family, and many of them passed over to the clan of *Date Masamune*. The latter, who was only waiting for an opportunity, soon invaded the territories of his neighbor. In 1589, he besieged and took the castle of *Kurokawa*. *Morishige* escaped to *Edosaki* (*Hitachi*), where he lived in seclusion. Thus ended the *Ashina* family, after having been, for 2 centuries, one of the most powerful *daimyō* in the North.

Ashinazuchi, 脚 名 椎. A son of *Ōyamazumi no kami*, lived in *Izumo* with his wife *Tenazuchi*. Their daugher *Inada-hime* was on the point of being devoured by the monster *Yamata no orochi*, when *Susanono-o* came to her rescue, killed the serpent and married her.

Ashi no umi, 蘆 湖. A lake (20 Km. in circuit) south of *Sagami*, better known as *Hakone* lake.

Ashizuka Chuēmon, 蘆 塚 忠 右 衛 門 (1578-1638). Was a son of *Chūbei*, governor of the castle of *Udo* (*Higo*) in the time of *Konishi Yukinaga*. After his father's death, he took refuge in *Shimabara* (*Hizen*), and was one of the chiefs of the insurrection in 1637-1638. By prodigies of bravery he often triumphed over the besiegers: but want of provisions rendered the insurgents powerless, and he lost his life at the capture of the castle of *Hara* by the enemies.

Ashizuri-saki, 足 摺 崎. A cape south of *Tosa* (*Shikoku*).

Ashū, 阿 州, the Chinese name of *Awa* province (*Shikoku*).

Ashukū-nyorai, 阿 閦 如 來. One of the five Buddhist gods of wisdom (*Gochi-nyorai*).

Asō, 麻 生. A place in *Hitachi*. It was from 1624 till 1868, the residence of the *daimyō Shinjō* (10,000 k.).

Aso, 阿 蘇. The name of a *Kyūshū* family descending from *Kamu-ya-i-mimi no mikoto*, a son of *Jimmu-tennō*. *Asotsu-hiko no mikoto*, a son of *Kamu-ya-i-mimi*, was nominated *Aso-kuni no miyatsuko*. His descendants assumed the name of *Aso* and, in the reign of *Keikō* were in charge of the *Asojinja* temple in *Higo*.

—— **Korezumi,** 惟 澄. A son of *Korekuni*, sided with the southern dynasty, was defeated at *Tatara-hama* in 1336 by *Takauji*, but continued to support *Yasunaga-shinnō*. His residence was the castle of *Yabe* (*Chikugo*).

—— **Korenao,** 惟 直 (+ 1336). Was killed at the battle of *Tatara-hama* (*Chikuzen*).

—— **Koretoyo,** 惟 豊 (+ 1584). A descendant of the foregoing, was possessor of the *Yabe* castle, with a revenue of 300,000 k.

—— **Koremitsu,** 惟光 1581-1593). A son of *Koretoyo,* was but a child when his father died. In 1588, when the *Higo* province was divided between *Konishi Yukinaga* and *Katō Kiyomasa,* he took refuge with the latter. *Hideyoshi* ordered him to be killed when he was 13 years old.=A descendant of that family is now a Baron.

Aso-san, 阿蘇山. A volcano (1,700 met.) in the N.-E. of *Higo.* Its five principal peaks are: *Taka-take, On-take, Neko no take, Narao-take, Ikuyama no take.* There were eruptions in 1884, 1889, 1894.

Ason, 朝臣, or *Asomi,* the 2nd of the 8 classes (*hassei*) established by the emperor *Temmu* among the nobles of the Court (682). The title applied to ministers, and was added to the name; as, *Minamoto-ason.*

Asuha-gawa, 足羽川. See *Ashiha-gawa.*

Asuka, 飛鳥. A village in *Yamato,* which was the residence of the Court during the reigns of the emperors *Inkyō* (412-453), and *Suiko* (593-628). Referring to its distance from *Nara,* the palace was called *Tōtsu-Asuka* (farther *Asuka*).

Asuka, 飛鳥. In *Kawachi,* was the residence of the emperors *Richū* (400-405) and *Kensō* (485-487). It was called *Chikatsu-Asuka* (nearer *Asuka*) in contradistinction to *Tōtsu-Asuka.*

Asuka-shinnō, 飛鳥親王 (+ 835). A son of the emperor *Kwammu,* was *Kōzuke-taishu.* His descendants were known by the name of *Kuga.*

Asukabe Tsunenori, 飛鳥部常則. A celebrated painter of the 10th century.

Asukai, 飛鳥井. A family of *kuge,* descending from *Fujiwara Masatsune* (1169-1221).

—— **Masayo,** 雅世. Compiled the *Shin-zoku-kokin-waka-shū* (new anthology of Japanese poems, ancient and new) in 1438, by the order of the *Shōgun Yoshinori.*

—— **Masayasu,** 雅康. A son of *Masayo,* and celebrated poet. = Now Count.

Asuke, 足助. An ancient castle in *Mikawa:* it belonged successively to the *Asuke daimyō* (13th and 14th centuries), to *Suzuki* (1540-71), to *Takeda* (1571-82), to *Tokugawa* (1582-90).

Ata, 吾田. Ancient name of the S. part of the *Satsuma* province, where *Ninigi no mikoto,* his sons and grandsons resided.

Atago, 愛宕. An ancient family of *kuge.* = Now Viscount.

Atago, 愛宕. The god that protects towns from fires (*Shintō*): probably the same as *Homusubi* or *Kagutsuchi.*

Ataka, 安宅. In *Kaga,* was the scene of a battle in which *Taira Koremori* defeated *Hayashi Mitsuaki, Togashi Ietsune,* etc., (1183).

Atami, 熱海. A sea-port N.-E. of *Izu,* renowned for its hot-springs and mild climate.

Atsugashi-yama, 厚樫山. A mountain N.E. of *Iwashiro,* where *Yoritomo* defeated *Fujiwara Yasuhira* (1189). Also called *Kunimi-mine.*

Atsuta, 熱田. A town (25,000 inh.) in *Owari,* celebrated for the great Shintoist temple *Atsuta-daijingū,* where the great sword *Ame-no-*

murakumo no tsurugi (which see) is venerated. After the death of *Yamato-takeru*, one of his companions, *Takeinatane-kimi*, was in charge of the guard of the temple. Towards 1115, *Owari-no-sukune Kazumasa*, one of his successors, ceded his functions to *Fujiwara Suenori*. The latter's daughter having been married with *Minamoto Yoshitomo*, became mother of *Yoritomo*: thence the influence of the *Atsuta-daigūji*. Before making war on *Imagawa Yoshimoto*, *Nobunaga* went to pray at the *Atsuta* temple, and it was to the god *Atsuta-myōjin* that he attributed his victory at *Okehazama* (1560).

Atsuta-daigūji, 熱田大宮司. Title of the chiefs of the *Atsuta* temple, inheritable among the descendants of *Fujiwara Suenori.* = The chief of that family is now Baron *Chiaki*.

Atsuzane-shinnō, 敦實親王 (897-966). Also called *Ninnaji no miya*, was a son of the emperor *Uda*, and the ancestor of the *Uda-Genji*.

Awa, 安房. One of the 15 provinces of *Tōkaidō*, was detached from *Kazusa* in 710, and comprises one district belonging to the *Chiba-ken*. Its Chinese name is *Bōshū*.

Awa, 阿波. One of the 6 provinces of *Nankaidō*. It comprises 10 districts, which form *Tokushima-ken*. Its Chinese name is *Ashū*.

Awaji, 淡路. One of the provinces of *Nankaidō*, is a great island (152 Km. in circuit) which shuts up the Inland Sea in the East. It comprises 2 districts belonging to *Hyōgo-ken*, and has 195,000 inhabitants. Its Chinese name is *Tanshū*. According to the Japanese mythology, *Awaji* was the first island created by *Izanagi* and *Izanami*. The emperor *Junnin* was exiled to this island in 764, and prince *Sawara-shinnō* in 785. — The island belonged successively to the *daimyō Sasaki, Hosokawa, Asaka, Miyoshi, Wakizaka*. From 1615 it was a part of the domains of the *Hachisuka*, the *daimyō* of *Tokushima* (*Awa*). — In ancient times it was called *Hasawake-shima* 穗狹別島, *Mitsu-kuni* 御食津國.

Awaji no haitei, 淡路廢帝. (Lit.: the emperor exiled to *Awaji*). A name applied to the emperor *Junnin*, who was banished to *Awaji* by the empress *Shōtoku* in 764, and died in his exile the following year.

Awaji no kimi, 淡路君. A name applied to prince *Sawara-shinnō*, who was exiled to *Awaji* in 785 for having killed *Fujiwara Tanetsugu*, and died while proceeding to the place of his banishment.

Awaji no seto, 淡路瀬戸. Ancient name of the *Akashi* strait.

Awataguchi, 粟田口. The name of a family descending from *Fujiwara Yoshikado* and attached to the *Kōfuku-ji* temple (*Nara*). = Now Baron.

Awazu, 粟津. A place in *Ōmi*, near *Ōtsu*, where, in 1184, *Kiso Yoshinaka* and his four famous companions (*shi-tennō*), *Imai Kanehira, Higuchi Kanemitsu, Tate Chikatada*, and *Nenoi Yukichika*, were killed.

Aya, 阿野. A *kuge* family descending from *Fujiwara* (*Sanjō*) *Kinnori* (1103-1160). = Now Viscount.

Ayabe, 綾部. A place in *Tamba*, which was the residence of the *daimyō Bessho* (1583-1628) and the *Kuki* (1633-1868).

Aya-no-kōji, 綾小路. A *kuge* family descending from *Minamoto* (*Uda-Genji*). = Now Viscount.

Azana, 字. An assumed name; as, a nom de plume, a nom de guerre. In former times, when a student entered a school, he adopted an *azana,* under which he was matriculated. Confucianists went by that name all their life. *Arai Hakuseki's azana,* for instance, was *Zaichū.*

Azari, 阿遮利 or *Ajari* (Sanscr. *ajariya*). Buddhist dignity below that of *Risshi.* In Japan, it became an official title in 1034, and was given for the first time to the bonze *Kyōen-Hōshi.* — See *Sō-kwan.*

Azechi, 按察使. A sort of inspector created by the empress *Genshō* in 719, to superintend the administration of the governors of provinces. Later on, their office was intrusted to the *Chinjufu-shōgun.* = Syn. *Ansatsushi.*

Azuchi, 安土. A place in *Ōmi,* on the north-eastern shore of lake *Biwa,* where *Nobunaga* had a magnificent castle built by *Niwa Nagahide* (1576). The castle was pillaged by *Akechi Mitsuhide* in 1582. After the latter's death, *Oda Nobuo* governed from that place in the name of his nephew *Sambōshimaru.* On the site of the castle stands now the temple *Sōken-ji,* where some rare souvenirs of *Nobunaga* are kept.

Azukari-mōsu, 關白. The ancient name of *Kwampaku.*

Azuki-zaka, 小豆坂. A place in *Mikawa,* where *Oda Nobuhide* defeated *Imagawa Yoshimoto.* Later on *Ōkubo Tadatoshi* fought at the same place against the troops of the *Ikko-shū* bonzes.

Azuma, 吾妻. The name formerly given to the 15 eastern and northern provinces of *Honshū.* As the legend tells us, *Yamatotakeru no mikoto,* coming back from the expedition against the *Ebisu,* arrived at the top of *Usui-saka* (*Sagami*); at the sight of the plain extending way down to the sea, and recalling to mind the self-sacrifice of *Tachibana-hime,* he exclaimed : *Azuma wa ya !* (ah ! ma femme !) : hence the name *Azuma* given to these provinces.

Azuma-hyakkwan, 東百官, (Lit.: the hundred functions of the East), were titles conferred by the *Shōgun* on the *daimyō* and *samurai* by analogy to those granted by the imperial Court.

Azuma-kagami, 東鑑. A history (52 vol.) of Japan written towards the end of the 13th century by an unknown author : it extends from 1180 till 1266, and is a precious source of historical informations about that period.

Azuma-yama, 吾妻山. A mountain (2,350 met.) situated between *Kōzuke* and *Shinano.*

Azuma-yama, 吾妻山. A volcano (1,800 met.) in *Iwashiro :* it had been thought extinct for a long time, when in 1893 an eruption took place which has been followed since by several others.

Azumi no muraji, 安曇連. A title given to an official who formerly, with the *Kashiwade no omi,* had charge of all that concerned the food of the emperor.

B

Baba, 馬塲. The name of a *samurai* family in *Kai*. They were vassals of the *Takeda*.

—— **Torasada, 虎定.** A *samurai* of the *Baba* family : he was killed by *Takeda Nobutora*, to whom he had made some representations.

—— **Nobukatsu, 信勝** (1514-1575). Served under *Takeda Shingen*, and accompanied him in all his wars, but he lost favor when *Katsuyori* succeeded his father.

—— **Nobuharu, 信春** (+ 1582). Died fighting against *Nobunaga* when the latter wanted to seize the domains of the *Takeda*.

Baishin, 倍臣. An indirect vassal, in opposition to *jikisan*, direct vassal. A *daimyō's jikisan* were the *Shōgun's baishin*.

Bakin, 馬琴. See *Kyokutei Bakin*.

Bakufu, 幕府 (Lit.: government of the tent). Is the name first given to the shōgunal government organized in *Kamakura* by *Yoritomo* in 1190. It was thus denominated because the former *Shōgun*, in their expeditions, had no fixed residence and administered from their camp.

Bakufu-jidai, 幕府時代. Period of Japanese history during which authority was in the hands of *Shōgun*, from 1192 till 1867. This name is particularly applied to the *Tokugawa* shōgunate (1603-1867).

Bakuro-gashira, 馬口勞頭. The name given under the *Tokugawa* shōgunate to an official who was charged with providing for laborers and relay horses, etc. The title was hereditary in the *Yamamoto* family.

Bakwan, 馬關. See *Shimonoseki*.

Bamba, 番塲. See *Suribari-tōge*.

Bambetsu, 番別. When the emperor *Saga* fixed the family names by a law (815), the word *bambetsu* was used to designate foreigners ; as, Chinese, Koreans, etc., that had been naturalized Japanese.

Bandai-san, 磐梯山. Formerly called *Aizu-yama*, is a mountain group in *Iwashiro*, comprising the *Ō-Bandai*, *Ko-Bandai*, *Kushi-ga-mine*, and *Akahaniyama*. It was *Ko-Bandai* that collapsed suddenly on the 15th of July, 1888.

Bandō, 板東. The name formerly given to the *Tōkaidō* provinces east of the *Osaka* barrier.

Bandō Tarō, 板東太郎. Surname given to the *Tone-gawa* river, because it is the longest river of the *Bandō* or *Kwantō*.

Ban Kōkei, 伴蒿蹊. (1733-1806), Man of letters. Born in *Ōmi*, but lived at *Kyōto*. Left several works.

Ban Nobutomo, 伴信友. (1775-1848), Man of letters from *Obama* (*Wakasa*). The works he wrote, consist of more than 400 volumes.

Bansai, 板西. Name given to the provinces west of the *Osaka* barrier, in distinction from *Bandō*.

Bansai-shichi-yū, 板西七雄. The name by which are designated the seven most celebrated warriors of the western provinces in the
XVI. century; namely: *Miyoshi Chōkei, Ōuchi Yoshitaka, Amako
Haruhisa, Shimazu Yoshihisa, Mōri Motonari, Ōtomo Sōrin,* and *Chōsokabe Motochika.*

Bansho-shirabe-dokoro, 蕃書調所, (Lit.: place of study of the bar-
barbarians' books) was a school founded in 1856 at *Edo, Kudan-zaka-shita,*
for the study of European sciences, the correction of translations, etc. The
Wakadoshiyori Endō Tanenari, Tajima no kami, was its first director;
Minosaku Gempō, Sugita Narisato were among the first professors.—
In 1862, the school was transferred to *Hitotsu-bashi,* and its name
changed into *Yōsho-shirabe-dokoro* (place of study of European books).
Then the following year it was denominated *Kaiseijo* (which see).

Banshū, 播州. The Chinese name of *Harima* province.

Bashō, 芭蕉 (1644-1694), By birth *Matsuo Munefusa* 松尾宗房
was a literary man born at *Tsuge (Iga).* He brought into fashion the
kind of poetry called *haikai* or *hokku* (3 verses of 5, 7, and 5 syllables
respectively).

Bekki Shōzaemon, 別木莊左衛門. A *rōnin* who, in 1651,
with *Hayashi Tōemon* tried to stir up a rebellion at the death of the *Shōgun
Iemitsu.* The plot was discovered and the fomenters punished by death.

Ben-en, 辨圓 (+ 1279). Was a celebrated bonze of the *Tendai* sect
and the founder of the *Tōfuku-ji* temple (*Kyōto*).

Bengyoku, 辨玉.— (1818-1880). Also called *Kei-a Shōnin* 慶阿
上人, Bonze of the *Jōdo-shū* sect. Born at *Asakusa* (*Tōkyō*), he entered
the *Shōtoku-ji* temple (*Shitaya*) at the age of 10, then the *Zōjō-ji* (*Shiba*),
and became chief of the *Sambō-ji* at *Kanagawa.* He was a distinguished
poet.

Benkei (Musashi-bō), 辨慶 (武藏坊). The son of a bonze of the
Kumano temple (*Kii*). In his infancy he was called *Oniwaka-maru* 鬼
若丸; having become a bonze, he took the name of *Musashi-bō.* Contrary
to his calling, he always evinced a greater taste for fencing and other
military exercises than for the cenobite life. One day, on the *Gojō* bridge
(*Kyōto*), he attacked *Minamoto Yoshitsune,* then quite young. Having
been overpowered by the young lord, he became his faithful follower.
He accompanied him in his expedition against the *Taira,* and afterwards in his flight into *Ōshū* to the residence of *Fujiwara Hidehira,* and
finally died with him at the battle of *Koromo-gawa* after wonderful deeds
of valor (1189). Legendary accounts have embellished *Benkei's* adventures and popularized his strength, stratagems, and devotedness to *Yoshitsune.* It went so far as to suppose him to have escaped the disaster at
Koromogawa, and to have fled into *Ezo* with his master.

Benkei-saki, 辨慶崎. A cape on the W. shore of *Shiribeshi*
(*Hokkaidō*).

Benkwan, 辨官. The name formerly given to members of the
Council of State. They were the *sabenkwan* and the *ubenkwan.* Later
on, when the functions were divided among the 8 departments, there
were the *sadaiben* and the *udaiben,* the *sachūben* and the *uchūben,* the

sashōben and the *ushōben*, and finally the *gomben*; collectively, they were called the *shichi-ben*.

Ben no Naishi, 辨內待. A daughter of *Fujiwara Toshimoto* and a lady in attendance at the court of the emperor *Go-Daigo* and *Go-Mura-kami*. When the latter fled to mount *Yoshino* (1346), she was taken prisoner by *Kō no Moronao*: *Kusunoki Masatsura* having delivered her, the emperor wished to bestow her on him as his wife, but *Masatsura* refused her in a celebrated poem. *Ben no Naishi* became an *ama* and devoted her life to the memory of the young hero.

Benten, 辨天, or *Benzaiten* **辨才天**. An Indian goddess honored among the seven gods of luck. She is often represented as mounted on a dragon or a serpent. It is this goddess that is venerated at *Enoshima* (*Sagami*)

Beppu, 別府. A sea-port in *Bungo*. It is renowned for its hot springs, the temperature of which varies from 36° to 55°C.

Besshi, 別司. A little town in *Iyo* near which are some copper mines.

Bessho, 別所. The name of the *Harima daimyō* family, descended from *Akamatsu Enshin*.

——**Nagaharu, 長治** (1558-1580). Was fighting for 4 years against *Hashiba Hideyoshi*, commissioned by *Nobunaga* to subjugate *San-yō-dō*. Finally his castle of *Miki* was taken, and *Nagaharu* committed suicide at the same time as his brother *Tomoyuki*.

——**Toyoharu, 豐治**. Son of *Nagaharu*, he was only 2 years old at the death of his father. Later on he obtained from *Hideyoshi* the title of *Bungo no kami*, with the castle of *Ayabe* (*Tamba*) and a revenue of 20,000 k. He was dispossessed in 1628 on account of his bad conduct.

Bettō, 別當. Formerly the highest official in some administrations: *Kebiishi-bettō*, etc. — Likewise the superintendent of the household of a retired emperor, the superintendents of the five principal branches (*Sekke*) of the *Fujiwara* family; the dignitaries of certain imperial temples. — One of the titles of the *Tokugawa Shōgun* was that of *bettō* of the *Junwa-in* and the *Shōgaku-in* temples. At present, the title is applied to the superintendent of the household of the princes of the imperial family.

Bifuku mon-in, 美福門院 (1117-1160), *Fujiwara Toku-ko*, a daughter of *Dajō-daijin Nagazane*, was the wife of the emperor *Toba* and the mother of *Konoe-tennō*.

Biku, 比丘 (Sanskr.) Bonze, Buddhist monk or friar; esoteric mendicants (內乞) and exoteric mendicants (外乞).

Bikuni, 比丘尼 (Sanskr.), Bonzess, Buddhist nun; female religious mendicants. — Syn. *Ama* 尼.

Bikuni-gosho, 比丘尼御所. The temples where the daughters of emperors retired when becoming *bikuni*. The title is also applied to the princesses themselves.

Bingo, 備後. One of the 8 provinces of *San-yō-dō*. It comprises 9 districts belonging to the *Hiroshima-ken*. Anciently it was called *Kibi-no michi no shiri*, or *Kibi no ushiro*. — Its Chinese name *Bishū* includes *Bizen* and *Bitchū*.

Bingo-nada, 備後洋. One of the basins of the Inland Sea situated between *Harima-nada* in the East and *Mishima-nada* in the West.

Bingo no Saburō, 備後三郎. See *Kojima Takanori*.

Binzuru, 賓頭盧. Is said to be one of the 16 *Rakan*. He was excluded from among them for having taken notice of the beauty of a woman. The power of curing all sicknesses is attributed to him, which renders him very popular.

Birushana-butsu, 毘盧遮那佛. See *Roshana*.

Bishamon, 毘沙門. One of the 7 gods of luck and also one of the three gods of war (*San-senjin*), is represented as holding a spear in one hand, and a small pagoda in the other. He is also called *Tamon*, as one of the *Shi-dai-tennō*, and is charged with watching over the North.

Bishū, 尾州. The Chinese name of *Owari* province.

Bishū, 備州. The Chinese name of *Bizen*, *Bitchū*, and *Bingo*, all three joined together formerly constituted the land of *Kibi*.

Bitatsu-tennō, 敏達天皇. The 30th emperor of Japan, (572-585). Before he became emperor, his name was *Osada*, or *Nunakura-futotama-shiki*. He succeeded his father *Kimmei* when 34 years old. During his reign there was an ardent struggle between the fervent adherents of the newly imported Buddhism and those of the old national Shintoism. The former were supported by *Soga no Umako*, and *Monobe no Moriya* was at the head of the latter. In 577, bonzes and architects came from Korea for the construction of temples : they brought along with them Buddhist books and statues, which, by the order of *Moriya* were thrown into the *Naniwa* canal. *Bitatsu* sent several expeditions to Korea, in order to restore the kingdom of *Mimana* that had been invaded by *Shiragi*, but these expeditions were not successful.

Bitchū, 備中. One of the 8 *San-yō-dō* provinces : it comprises 7 districts belonging to *Okayama-ken*. The Chinese name is *Bishū* (given conjointly to *Bizen* and *Bingo*). Formerly the province was called *Kibi-no-michi no naka*.

Bitō Nishū, 尾藤二洲 (1745-1813). Famous professor of the *Shōhei-kō*, at *Edo*. He and two other savants of the time, *Koga Seiri* and *Shibano Ritsuzan*, are called the *Kwansei no san-suke*, or *San-hakase* (The 3 doctors of the *Kwansei* era).

Biwa-hōshi, 琵琶法師. In former times, singers that played the biwa (a four stringed lute), whilst declaiming the *jōruri*. The singers were usually bonzes that had become blind. — See *Jōruri*.

Biwa-ko, 琵琶湖. *Biwa* or *Ōmi* lake is 290 Km. in circuit, its length is 59 Km., and its breadth 20 Km. According to tradition it was formed in the 5th year of the emperor *korei* (286 B. C.) by the same earthquake that caused mount *Fuji* to rise. Formerly it was called *Awa-no-umi*. The governor of the land south of the lake was called *Awa-umi no miyatsuko ;* hence, by contraction, *Ōmi no miyatsuko*. Lake *Biwa* is renowned for its beautiful scenery, and has often been sung by poets. It is also called *Ōmi no umi*, *Nio* 鳰 *no umi*, *Shio-naranu-umi* (fresh-water sea).

Bizen, 備前. One of the 8 provinces of *San-yō-dō*, comprises 6 districts belonging to *Okayama-ken*. Formerly it was called *Kibi-no-saki,* or *Kibi-no-michi no kuchi*. *Bizen, Bitchū* and *Bingo* taken conjointly are designated by the Chinese name *Bishū.*

Bōdaiju, 菩提樹. The tree (*ficus indica* or *religiosa*) under which *Shaka* became *Buddha,* that is to say, obtained the perfect knowledge of things. On that account it became the sacred tree of the Buddhists.

Bōhan, 謀反. A word which formerly designated the crime of leze-majesty. The punishment was: the death of the culprit, of his father, mother, children, and servants; the banishment of his grand-parents, grand children, and brothers; and moreover the confiscation of all the property of the family.

Bōjō, 坊城. A *kuge* family, descended from *Fujiwara Morosuke* (908-960). = Now Count.

—— A branch of the same family possesses the title of Baron.

Bokkai, 渤海. A little kingdom of Korea, formed towards the end of the 7th century from that part of *Kōrai* which had not been annexed to China.

Bōmon Kiyotada, 坊門清忠 (+ 1338). Son of *Fujiwara Toshi-suke,* was a *kuge* of the court of *Go-Daigo-tennō,* who, first disclosed the ambitious designs of *Ashikaga Takauji* and insisted on having him declared a rebel by the emperor. He died on *Yoshino-san.*

Bon, 鬼節. The festival of the dead. It is celebrated from the 13th to the 15th of July. During these three days the deceased are supposed to return to the places where they once lived.

Bō no tsu, 坊ノ津. S. of *Satsuma, Nishi-minami-kata mura.* Formerly an important commercial sea port for foreign ships.

Bonten, 梵天. Is the Japanese name of *Brahmā.*

Bōryō, 坊令. A title formerly used to designate the chief of a ward, the mayor.

Bosatsu, 菩薩 (Sanscr. *Bōdhisattva*). Buddhist saints who have to pass only once more through a human existence before attaining the state of *hotoke* (*Buddha*).

Bōshin no eki, 戊辰役. The civil war of 1868, which ended in the ruin of the Shōgunate. (*Bōshin* is the Chinese reading of the cyclic characters of the year: 戊辰 *tsuchino-e no tatsu,* senior brother of the earth and the dragon).

Bōshū, 房州. Chinese name of *Awa* province (*Tōkaidō*).

Boshū, 防州. Chinese name of *Suwō* province.

Botansha, 牡丹社. A tribe of Aborigines in the south of Formosa.

Bōzu, 坊主. A bonze, a Buddhist monk or friar. Bonzes were formerly bound to celibacy and to abstain from fleshmeat. *Shinran-shōnin,* the founder of the *Shin* or *Ikkō* sect (1224), was the first that dispensed his disciples from this obligation.

Bugu-bugyō, 武具奉行. A title created in 1863 and given to the official having charge of all that concerned arms, armor, etc. His office comprised the functions of the *gusoku-bugyō,* the *yari-bugyō,* etc.

Bugyō, 奉行 . . The name formerly given to the chief of an administration. Thus, the *Machi-bugyō* had charge of the city affairs; the *Kanjō-bugyō*, of the finances; the *Jisha-bugyō*, of the temples, etc.

Bukaku, 舞鶴 . Another name for the town of *Maizuru*. Pronounced according to the Chinese characters *mai* (dance) and *tsuru* (crane).

Bukan, 武鑑 . The book of heraldry of the feudal nobility in the time of the shōgunate. It contained the names, residences, revenues, arms, etc. of all the *daimyō*, as well as the names of their principal *kerai*, a detailed account of the presents they had to offer every year to the *Shōgun* and of those they received from him in return, etc.

Buke, 武家 . The military class, the *samurai*.

Buke-jidai, 武家時代 . The period of Japanese history during which the government was in the hands of the military class. It extends from *Yoritomo's* shōgunate (1192) to the Imperial Restoration (1868).

Buke-keihō, 武家刑法 . A penal code in vigor from *Yoritomo* to *Ieyasu* (1190-1600).

Buke-seiji, 武家政治 . Government of military feudalism, as had been organized by *Yoritomo*.

Buke-shohatto, 武家諸法度 . A code promulgated by *Ieyasu*, containing in 13 chapters the laws to be observed by the *daimyō* and the *samurai*.

Bukkō-ji, 佛光寺 . This temple was founded in *Kyōto* by the bonze *Shimbutsu*, a brother of *Shinran*. It became the seat of a branch of the *Shin-shū* sect (1232). The chief bonze of this temple belongs to the nobility.

Bukkō-kokushi, 佛光國師 . See *Sogen*.

Bukkyō, 佛教 . The doctrine of *Buddha*, or Buddhism, which is also called *Butsudō* (way of *Buddha*), *Buppō* (law of *Buddha*). — *Shaka* (557-477 B. C.), first preached this religion and confined himself to diffuse it by word of mouth; later on his disciples put down in writing the teachings of their master, as far at least, as they remembered them: hence came a great number of books (*sûtras:* Jap., *keiten*). As the doctrines exposed in these different works, were far from being identical, there came into existence numerous sects claiming to be supported by the authority of the *sûtra*. Shortly after *Shaka's* death, his disciples were divided into two great schools: the *Mahâyâna* (*daijō*, great vehicle), and the *Hinayâna* (*shōjō*, small vehicle. The first known as the northern or Chinese Buddhism; the second, as the southern, or Siamese and Ceylon Buddhism. As Chinese and Korean bonzes brought their doctrine to Japan, Japanese Buddhism belongs principally to the northern school. — In 552, the king of *Kudara* (Korea) sent Buddhist statues and books as a present to the emperor *Kimmei*. Two years later, *Tonei* and *Dōshin* came to this country. They were the first bonzes that Japan had ever seen, and began at once to preach their religion. They found a powerful protector in the person of *Soga no Iname*, who built the first temple (*Mukuhara-dera*, or *Kōgen-ji*) at his residence. But they also met with resolute adversaries, such as *Mononobe no Okoshi, Nakatomi no*

Kamako, etc., who pretended that the admission of a new religion would be a gross insult to the *Shintō* gods, the creators and protectors of the land. Hence there arose a strife between the two parties which lasted for 35 years, i.e. until the triumph of Buddhism in 587. As the new doctrine was supported by prince *Shōtoku-taishi*, it made rapid progress, and shortly after his death, many sects made their appearance one after another. They were: *Jōjitsu* and *Sanron* (625), *Hossō* (653), *Kusha* (660), *Kegon* (739), and *Ritsu* (754). These are the 6 sects of the *Nara* era. After them came the three sects of the *Heiankyō* (*Kyōto*) era : *Tendai* (806), *Shingon* (806), and *Yūzū-nembutsu* (1123). Finally the *Kamakura* period saw five others coming into existence ; they were : *Jōdo* (1174), *Zen* (1191), *Shin* (1224), *Nichiren* (1253), and *Ji* (1275). Of these sects, three : *Sanron*, *Jōjitsu*, and *Kusha*, have disappeared from Japan long ago ; most of the others are divided into several branches. — Owing to the skill of the bonzes and the diffusion of the *Ryōbu-Shintō*, the two cults, Shintoism and Buddhism, lived in harmony with each other, and ministers of both religions could be seen alternately celebrating their ceremonies in the same temples, but after the Restoration, Buddhism, being no more recognized as the national religion, had to restore the Shintō temples of which it had possession. The decline of Buddhism in Japan dates from that epoch, notwithstanding its new philosophical and theological foundations, if we may so call the efforts of the bonzes to give a new form to the tenets of the creed and bring them to be more in harmony with the modern system of evolution as taught by a certain class of men both in Europe and America. Indeed, some have gone so far as to claim that the philosophy of Buddhism cannot attain its perfect development unless it be supported by the theory of evolution. Another current of thought among Buddhists, not yet well defined, but which would only require the stimulant of novelty produced by the adherence of some public men to Christianity, is to find a similitude with Christian thought. And yet philosophically speaking, two systems can hardly be said to be more opposite than the Buddhist assemblage of thought and Christian dogma, although in the ceremonial of the two religions we may find some superficial resemblance. — In the whole Empire, there are 71,992 temples (*tera*), 52,106 bonzes, and, in a population of 47,400,000 inhabitants, the statistics acknowledge 28,600,000 Buddhists.

Bumbai-ga-hara, 分倍河原. In *Musashi*, *Nishifu-mura*, was the scene of several battles : of *Nitta Yoshisada* against *Hōjō Yasuie* (1333), of *Ashikaga Shigeuji* against *Uesugi Fusaaki* (1455), of *Hōjō Ujiyasu* against *Uesugi Tomooki* (1530).

Bummei, 文 明. *Nengō*: 1469-1486.

Bummin-shikkushi, 問 民 疾 苦 使. An office created by the empress *Kōken* in 758. Its functions were to give information about the wants of the people, to succor the needy, etc.

Bumpō, 文 保. *Nengō*: 1317-1318.

Bun-an, 文 安. *Nengō*: 1444-1448.

Bun-ei, 文 永. *Nengō*: 1264-1274.

Bun-ei no eki, 文永役. This is the name given to the war resulting from the first expedition of the Mongols to Japan (1274). The

BATTLE AGAINST THE MONGOLS.

invaders, after having ravaged *Tsushima* and *Iki*, were repulsed from *Kyūshū*, their general was killed, and a tempest dispersed their fleet. — (See *Hōjō Tokimune*.)

Bungo, 豊後. One of the 12 provinces of *Saikaidō*; it comprises 10 districts belonging to *Ōita ken*. The Chinese give the name "*Hōshū*" to this province together with that of *Buzen*. In ancient times *Bungo* was called *Toyokuni-no-michi no shiri*.

Bungo-kaikyō, 豊後海峽. The *Bungo* strait or *Bungo* channel, is situated between *Kyūshū* and *Shikoku*.

Bungo no Fuji, 豊後富士. See *Yubu-zan*.

Bunji, 文治. *Nengō*: 1185-1189.

Bunki, 文龜. *Nengō*: 1501-1503.

Bunkwa, 文化. *Nengō*: 1804-1817.

Bunkwan, 文觀 (+ 1357). Was the chief bonze of the *Daigo-ji* temple near *Kyōto*. He entered the coalition formed by the emperor *Go-Daigo* against the *Hōjō* (1330), but was exiled to *Iwō-jima* (*Ryūkyū*) by *Takatoki*. After the conquest of *Kamakura*, he was recalled from his exile, re-entered his monastery, and joined the party that fought against *Ashikaga Takauji* but his troops having been defeated at *Yamazaki*, he was obliged to flee from the capital.

Bunkyū, 文久. *Nengō*: 1861-1863.

Bun-ō, 文應. *Nengō*: 1260.

Bunreki, 文曆. *Nengō*: 1234. — It is also called *Bunryaku*.

Bunroku, 文祿. *Nengō:* 1592-1595.

Bunroku no kenchi, 文祿檢地. *Hideyoshi* had a register made of all the provinces, from 1589-1595. New measures were used for that survey (1 *tan* = 300 *tsubo*, 1 *chō* = 10 *tan*). From that time, the revenues were no more appraised in money, but in *koku* of rice. This reform was called *Bunroku no kenchi,* or *Tenshō no koku-naoshi.*

Bunryaku, 文曆. *Nengō:* 1234.

Bunsei, 文政. *Nengō:* 1818-1829.

Bunshin, 文身, Tattooing. The ancient Aborigines such as the *Ezo, Kumaso* used to tattoo themselves. The fashion came back towards the end of the 18th century, and spread among the lower classes. The shogunal government prohibited it, but the law was not observed. The custom has now fallen into disuse.

Bunshō, 文正. *Nengō:* 1466.

Buntoku-tennō, 文德天皇. See *Montoku-tennō.*

Bunwa, 文和. *Nengō* of the northern dynasty: 1352-1355.

Bunya, 文屋. See *Fumiya.*

Buppō, 佛法. See *Bukkyō.*

Buretsu-tennō, 武烈天皇. The 25th Emperor of Japan (499-506) was Prince *O-hatsuse-waka-sasagi,* a son of *Ninken-tennō.* He succeeded his father in 499, when ten years old, and is remarkable only for his cruelties. According to the *Nihon-shoki,* he took pleasure in having pregnant women disemboweled, had the nails taken off from some people and forced the unhappy sufferers to dig the earth with their hands, obliged peasants to climb trees, which he then had cut down. One stormy day, some people entered the palace and assassinated the youthful tyrant. He was then 18 years old.

Bushi, 武士. *Samurai,* warrior, soldier; military class.

Bushidō, 武士道 (Lit.: the way of the *samurai*). This term is applied to the principles of loyalty and honor which were always to be followed by the *samurai. Bushidō* borrowed stoic endurance, scorn of danger and death from Buddhism; religious worship of country and sovereign from Shintoism; a certain literary and artistic culture, as well as the social moral of the five relations (*go-rin*), from Confucianism. This amalgam was to form the code of the perfect knight. It may be summed up in three words: The *samurai* is a man of few words — he does not serve two masters; — for duty he sheds his blood, "like the cherry-tree drops its flowers." Such was, or, at least, such was to be the ideal *samurai.*

Bushū, 武州. The Chinese name to designate *Musashi* province.

Bushū (Ni-jū-hachi), 部衆 (二十八). Designates the 28 attendants of the goddess *Kwannon;* they are the personification of the 28 constellations of Japanese astronomy.

Buson (Taniguchi), 蕪村 (谷口). A painter of the Chinese school, likewise renowned as a poet — He is also called *Yosa* 與 謝.

Busshin-shū, 佛心宗. A Buddhist sect, which goes also by the name of *Zen-shū.* The bonze *Dōshō,* after his return from China tried to spread this sect, and after him, *Dōei, Saishō, Gikaku, Giku,* etc., but without success. In 1174, *Kakua*, a bonze of *Hiei-zan*, brought the *Rinzai-shū* from China ; finally *Eisai*, in 1192, succeeded in implanting the sect, of which he is considered the founder in Japan. (See *Zen-shū*).

Busshi-ryū, 佛師流. An ancient school of sculpture that produced principally Buddhist statues. It was founded into 1020 by the bonze *Kōshō* and was brought to a high degree of perfection by his descendants *Jōchō, Kakujo, Raijo, Kōjo, Kōkei, Unkei, Tankei, Kōen,* etc.

Butsudō, 佛道. See *Bukkyō*.

Butsu Sorai, 物徂徠. See *Ogiu Sorai*.

Buzen, 豊前. One of the 11 provinces of *Saikaidō*. It comprises 6 districts belonging to the *Ōita-ken*. — Its Chinese name is *Hōshū* (together with *Bungo*). — Formerly it was called *Toyokuni-no-michi no kuchi*.

Byōdō-in, 平等院. A temple of the *Tendai* sect, at *Uji*, south of *Kyōto*. It was originally the villa of the minister *Fujiwara Yorimichi* : when he became bonze, he turned it into a temple (1052). It was in this temple that *Minamoto Yorimasa* took refuge after his defeat at the *Uji* bridge (1180), and committed *harakiri* sitting on his fan.

Byōji, 平治. *Nengō* : 1159. — Also called *Heiji*.

C

Chacha-maru, 茶々丸. See *Ashikaga Masatomo.*

Chacha-nobori, 茶々登. The name of a mountain (2,400 m.) in the island of *Kunashiri*, the most southern of the *Chishima* (Kurile) islands.

Chakudasei, 着駄政. A law which obliged the *Kebiishi* with his own hands to chain the feet of great criminals. This formality was performed twice a year, in the fifth and the twelfth month.

Cha-no-yu, 茶湯. Manner of preparing a powdered tea infusion (*matsu-cha* or *hiki-cha*); it gradually became a trifling and complicated ceremony. The bonze *Jukō* (1422-1502) established its first rules, which were perfected and definitely adopted by *Sen no Rikyu* (1520-1591). Although the *cha-no-yu* is not so much in vogue at the present time, it continues to form part of a young lady's education.

Cha-usu-yama, 茶臼山. A hill in *Settsu*, southwest of the *Tennōji* temple (*Ōsaka*); formerly it was called *Arahaka*. In 1546, *Hosokawa Harumoto* was defeated here by *Miyoshi Chōkei*. During the siege of *Ōsaka* (1615), *Sanada Yukimura* and *Honda Tadatomo* likewise fought against each other at the same place. Both perished in the battle.

Cha-usu-yama, 茶臼山. A mountain in *Shinano*, near *Nobusatomura*. *Takeda Shingen* established his camp there during his campaign against *Uesugi Kenshin* (1561).

Chi-an, 治安. *Nengō*: 1021-1023. — Also called *Ji-an*.

Chiba, 千葉. A town (26,500 inh.) in *Shimōsa* province, the capital of the *Chiba-ken*, was, from the 12th to the 16th century, the residence of the *Chiba daimyō*.

Chiba, 千葉. The name of a *daimyō* family descended from *Taira*. This family was very powerful in *Shimōsa* from the ·12th to the 16th century.

—— **Tsunetane,** 常胤 (1118-1201). Was *Chiba no suke*, and joined *Yoritomo's* party as soon as the latter rose against the *Taira* (1180). He took part in the campaign of *Noriyori* against *Yoshinaka*, fought at the battle of *Ichi no tani* (1184), and joined in the expedition of *Yoritomo* against *Fujiwara Yasuhira* (1189).

—— **Sadatane,** 貞胤 (1291-1351). First supported the *Hōjō*; after the capture of *Kamakura* (1333), he joined the party of the emperor *Go-Daigo*, and finally followed the party of the northern dynasty.

—— **Kanetane,** 兼胤. Supported *Uesugi Ujinori* against *Ashikaga Mochiuji* (1416).

—— **Tanenao,** 胤直. A son of the above he remained faithful to *Uesugi Norizane* but when *Shigeuji* became *Kwanryō*, he gave him his support. Having been defeated conjointly with him, he committed suicide by *harakiri* at the same time as his son *Tanenobu* (1455). The *Uesugi* chose his brother *Sanetane* at his successor.

—— **Sanetane, 實胤**. At the death of his brother (1455) he was governor of the *Ichikawa* castle (*Shimōsa*), and became *Chiba no suke*, as seen in the preceding article. Being besieged in his castle of *Ichikawa*, he was compelled to surrender, and was replaced as governor by his nephew *Takatane* (1456).

—— **Takatane, 孝胤**. Assisted by his father *Yasutane*, supported *Shigeuji's* party, fought against the *Uesugi* and their general *Ōta Dō-kwan*, who finally triumphed over him in 1479.

—— **Toshitane, 利胤** (1528-1559). A grand-son of *Takatane*, fought against *Uesugi Kenshin*, was defeated and killed in 1559.

—— **Shigetane, 重胤**. Belonged to the *Odawara Hōjō* clan; being besieged in his castle at *Sakura* by *Honda Tadakatsu* and *Sakai Ietsugu* (1590), he surrendered and was dispossessed. —— After this the family disappears from history.

Chiba-ken, 千葉縣. A department formed by the provinces of *Awa, Kazusa*, and 8 districts of *Shimōsa*. —— Its population amounts to 1,329,400 inh. —— Capital: *Chiba* (26,250 inh.). Chief towns : *Funabashi* (12,000 inh.), *Chōshi* (9,000 inh.), etc.

Chiburi-shima, 知夫里島. An island (25 Km. in circuit) belonging to the *Okishima* group. The emperor *Go-Daigo* was exiled to this island by *Hōjō Takatoki* in 1332, but succeeded in escaping from it the following year.

Chihaya, 千早. A place in *Kawachi*, where *Kusunoki Masashige* built a castle. In 1331 the *Hōjō* besieged it in vain. *Masanori*, a son of *Masashige*, defended it for a long time against the *Ashikaga*, but it was finally taken and destroyed in 1392 by *Hatakeyama Yoshitō*.

Chijingo-dai, 地神五代. A name designating the five generations of terrestrial spirits which after the seven generations of celestial spirits (*Tenjin-shichi-dai*), are the ancestors of the imperial dynasty. They are: (1) *Ama-terasu-ō-mikami*, (2) *Masaya-akatsukachi-hayabi-ame-no-oshihomimi no mikoto*, (3) *Amatsu-hiko-hikoho-no-ninigi no mikoto*, (4) *Hiko-hohodemi no mikoto*, (5) *Hikonagisa-take-ugaya-fuki-aezu no mikoto*, who was the father of *Jimmu-tennō*.

Chikamatsu Monzaemon, 近松門左衛門 (1653-1724). Was the most celebrated dramatic author of Japan. His true name was *Sugimori Nobumori ;* born in *Hagi* (*Nagato*), he entered the temple *Konshō-ji* at *Karatsu* (*Hizen*), in order to become a bonze, but left it to establish himself at *Ōsaka*. He composed 97 *jōruri* (dramas), of which 74 are historical. His works are still very popular.

Chika no yaso-shima, 値賀八十島. (Lit.: the 80 islands of *Chika*). The name given by the emperor *Keikō* to the islands belonging to *Hizen ;* that is, those of *Hirado* and of *Gotō*.

Chikara-ryō, 主税寮. See *Shuzei-ryō*.

Chikubu-shima, 竹生島. An island in the northern part of lake *Biwa*. This island is renowned for its temple dedicated to the goddess *Kwannon*, and is said to have suddenly sprung up in the year 82.

Chikugo, 筑後. One of the 11 provinces of *Saikaidō*. It comprises six districts belonging to *Fukuoka ken*.—Chinese name : *Chikushū* (collectively with *Chikuzen*). In ancient times, it was called *Tsukushi-no-michi no shiri*.

Chikugo-gawa, 筑後川. A river (137. Km.) which has its source in *Bungo*, passes through *Kurume*, and empties itself into the *Ariake-wan*, between *Saga* and *Yanagawa*. It is also called *Tsukushi Saburō*, *Chitose-gawa*, *Mii-gawa*, *Hitoyo-gawa*, *Sakai-gawa*.

Chikuma-gawa, 筑摩川. A river (373 Km.) which has its source at the *Jūmonji-tōge* (*Shinano*), passes through *Komoro*, *Ueda*, *Matsushiro ;* receives the *Sai-gawa* near *Nagano ;* passes near *Iiyama*, then enters *Echigo*, where it takes the name of *Shinano-gawa*.

Chikura-okido, 千座置戸. The tables on which a criminal was to bring the objects furnished by him in expiation of his crime. Anciently it designated the chastisement of great crimes. According to the Legend, *Susano-o*, had to undergo it for the outrages done to his sister *Amaterasu*, and, as he had nothing to offer in atonement, his nails and hair were torn off, after which *Koyane no mikoto* read the sentence to him which exiled him to *Ne-no-kuni* (Korea).

Chikusa, 千種. A castle in *Ise*, governed from the 14th to the 16th century by a *daimyō* of the same name.

Chikusa, 千種. A *kuge* family descended from *Murakami-Genji*. The chief of the family is now a Viscount.

Chikusa, 千種. An ancient family of *daimyō* in *Ise*.

―― **Takamichi,** 高道. Built the castle of *Chikusa* towards 1350.

―― **Tadaharu,** 忠治. (16th century), fought *Rokkoku Yoshikata* of *Omi*.

―― **Tadamoto,** 忠基. A son of the above submitted to *Nobunaga*, d was killed in a battle in *Mino*.

an**Chikushū,** 筑州. The Chinese name of the two provinces *Chikuzen* d *Chikugo* taken collectively.

an**Chikuzen,** 筑前. One of the 11 provinces of the *Saikaidō*. It mprises 9 districts belonging to *Fukuoka-ken*. The Chinese name is co*hikushū* (designating *Chikugo* and *Chikuzen* collectively). Anciently iC was called *Tsukushi-no-michi no kuchi*.

t **Chinda,** 鎮田. A village in *Bungo*, four *ri* east of *Takeda*. It is renowned for its high waterfall, from the height of which criminals condemned to death were precipitated. Those who survived the fall were pardoned.

Chinjufu, 鎮守府. Formerly the military prefecture. At the beginning, when the army was sent against the *Ebisu*, it was commanded by a *Chintō-shōgun*, 鎮東將軍, or a *Sei-Ezo-shōgun*, 征蝦夷 or a *Chin-teki-shōgun*, 鎮狄. These *shōgun* however bore their tittle only for the time of the expedition and had no fixed residence. In 725, *Ōno Azumabito*, was created *Azechi-ken-Chinju-shōgun*, 按察 使兼鎮守 and took up his residence at the castle of *Taga* (*Mutsu*). *Ōtomo no Otomaro* and *Sakanoe no Tamuramaro* were invested with the same title under *Kwammu-tennō*. But it was only in 812 that the castle of *Izawa* (*Mutsu*) was selected as the seat of the *Chinjufu*, which was composed of a *shōgun* (general), a *gunkan* 軍 監

(inspector), and several inferior officers. When *Yoritomo* had obtained the title of *Sei-i-taishōgun*, 征夷大將軍, that of *Chinjufu-shōgun* was suppressed. *Go-Daigo* re-established it in favor of *Kitabatake Akiie* (1326), but under the *Ashikaga*, it was definitively abolished. Now *Chinjufu* signifies a maritime prefecture. There are four in Japan, namely, *Yokosuka*, *Kure*, *Sasebo*, and *Maizuru*, to which may be added *Ryojun-kō* (Port-Arthur).

ANCIENT SEAL OF THE CHINJUFU

Chinu, 血沼 (Lit.: bloody lake). This name was anciently given to *Izumi* province. When *Jimmu-tennō*, was repulsed from *Yamato* by *Nagasune-hiko*, he returned by sea towards *Kii* province, and, off *Izumi*, his brother *Itsuse no mikoto*, who had been severely wounded, washed his wounds : hence the name given to the sea, and by extension, to *Izumi* province.

Chinzei, 鎮西, The name formerly given to the military government of *Kyūshū*. By extension, *Kyūshū* itself.

Chinzei, 鎭西. A branch of the *Jōdo* sect. It was founded in the 13th century in *Chikugo* by a bonze called *Shōkō-shōnin.* — See *Jōdoshū go-ha.*

Chinzei-bugyō, 鎭西奉行. The name formerly given to the military governor of *Kyūshū*. In 1186, *Yoritomo* created this function and intrusted *Amano Tōkage* with it. In 1223, *Ōtomo Yoshinao* obtained the same title, which became hereditary in his family. — Below the *bugyō* there was a *shugo*. The first one was *Mutō Sukeyori* (1191), who assumed the name of *Shōni*, and transmitted it to his descendants. In 1275, *Hōjō Sanemasa* was appointed *Kyūshū-tandai* and performed both the functions of *bugyō* and those of *shugo*. The title of *Kyūshū-tandai* was entirely reserved to the members of the *Hōjō* family.

Chinzei-hyōjōshū, 鎭西評定衆. A title created in 1299 and given to officials charged with dispensing justice in *Kyūshū*. It was suppressed under the *Ashikaga*.

Chinzei-keigoban, 鎭西警固番. Officials formerly charged to guard the *Kyūshū* coasts in order to prevent the landing of Mongols and the incursions of pirates.

Chion-in, 智恩院. A celebrated Buddhist temple in *Kyōto*, built in 1211 by *Genkū*. It was destroyed by fire in 1633, rebuilt by the *Shōgun Iemitsu*, and solemnly opened in 1639. It is the seat of the *Jōdo-shū*.

Chiryaku, 治暦. *Nengō:* 1065-1068.

Chishaku-in, 智積院. A Buddhist temple in *Kyōto*, built in 1601 from the ruins of the famous *Negoro-ji* temple (*Kii*) destroyed by *Hideyoshi* in 1585. It is now the seat of the *Tendai* sect.

Chishima, 千島, (Lit.: the thousand islands). The name given to the Kurile islands numbering 32, the principal ones of which are, from S. to N.: *Kunajiri*, *Etorū*, *Uruppu*, *Shinshiru*, *Shashikotan*, *Onekotan*, *Haramuchi*, and *Shimushu*. The total area is 16,940 Km².; the population amounts to 2115 inhabitants. They are divided into 9 districts (*kōri*) and are so governed.

Chishō-daishi, 智澄大師. See *Enchin.*

Chitsū, 智通. The name of a bonze who went to China in 658 and returned three years afterwards, bringing the *Kusha* sect to Japan. In 673, he was made *sōjō* (then the highest dignity of the Buddhist hierarchy).

Chō, 町. A surface measure equal to 10 *tan* 段 or 3000 *tsubo* 坪, about one hectare. — Formerly, a rectangle measuring 30 *bu* 步 in length and 12 *bu* in breadth (1 bu was then 5 *shaku*) formed one *tan*; one *chō* was equal to 10 *tan*. It was *Hideyoshi* that reformed the system of measures in use until then. (See *Bunroku no Kenchi*).

Chōchōshi, 調帳使. Formerly an official having charge, in every province, of the register of the revenues in kind, such as silk, cotton, etc., to be paid by every family. The articles were to be collected during the eighth month and deposited in the chief town of the province, then, before the end of the 12th month, they had to be conveyed to the capital, where the *kokushi* himself, accompanied by the *chōchōshi*, presented them to the Emperor.

Chō Densu, 兆殿司 (1352-1431). Whose true name was *Minchō*, was a bonze of the *Tōfukuji*, in *Kyōto*, and a celebrated painter. He founded the *Unkoku-ryū* school.

CHŌ DENSU.

Chōfu, 長府. A town (7900 inh.) in *Nagato*, was formerly the capital of the province. It is also called *Toyora, Toyoura.* It has an ancient castle of the *Nōri daimyō.*

Chōga, 朝賀. The solemn reception that took place at the imperial palace on the first day of the year. The Emperor dressed in 12 fine silk robes, repaired, on this occasion, with the Empress, to the *Daigoku-den* (the hall of the throne), where he received the congratulations of the court officials and the envoys of the provinces. This ceremony was also called *chōhai* 朝拜. In time of disturbances, that is, from the middle of the 10th century, a less solemn ceremony, called *ko-chōhai*, was substituted. The reception was then held in the *Seiryō-den* and the high officials alone were admitted.

Chōgen, 長元. *Nengō :* 1028-1036.

Chōhai, 朝拜. See *Chōga.*

Chōhō, 長保. *Nengō :* 999-1003.

Chōhōsōshi, 長奉送使. An official who was to accompany and protect the princess that repaired to the *Ise* temple of which she was to become the high-priestess (*saigū*). That office was also called *kansōshi* 監送使. The first that performed it was *Chūnagon Abe no Yasuhito*, in 852.

Chōji, 長治. *Nengō :* 1104-1105.

Chōjō, 長承. *Nengō :* 1132-1134.

Chōkai-zan, 鳥海山. A volcano (2200 met.) in the south of *Ugo.* Its last eruption took place in 1861. The mountain is also called *Tori-no-umi-yama* (according to the Japanese reading of the same characters).

Chōkei-tennō, 長 慶 天 皇. The 98th Emperor (1369-1373), was prince *Sanenari,* the eldest son of *Go-Murakami,* of the southern dynasty. He succeeded his father in the difficult conjunctures in which his party was at that time, and, after four years, abdicated in favor of his brother *Go-Kameyama.* Some historians do not reckon him among the emperors.

Chokkau, 勅 勘. A punishment which consisted in confining an official to his house with the prohibition to leave it or receive visits.

Chōkin, 朝 覲. Solemn visits which the reigning emperor paid to the ex-emperor or to the dowager empress at the beginning of the year that followed his accession to the throne (*sokui no chōkin*), after having performed the *gembuku* (*gembuku no chōkin*), etc. The emperor left his palace in a palanquin and was accompanied by a numerous suite. At the exterior gate of the ex-emperor's residence, the guard of the emperor stopped while he continued with his retinue. Having reached the interior gate, the emperor alighted as a sign of respect. The ceremonial was observed for the first time by *Saga-tennō* in 810. From the reign of *Ichijō* (987-1011) a curious custom was established: the emperor was to play on the flute before his predecessor.

Chōkōdō, 長 講 堂. A temple built by the emperor *Go-Shirakawa* after his abdication (1158) and where he lived for 30 years. He enriched it with considerable revenues. In the time of *Go-Fukakusa* (1259), 180 villages belonged to this temple; the rent (*Chōkōdō-ryō*) which they paid constituted the revenues of the retired emperors.

Chokunin, 勅 任. See *Kwantō.*

Chokusenka-shū, 勅 撰 歌 集. The generic name of 21 collections of poems compiled from the reign of *Daigo* (898-930) until that of *Go-Hanazono* (1429-1465).

Chōkwan, 長 寛. *Nengō:* 1163-1164.

Chōkyō, 長 享. *Nengō:* 1487-1488; also called *Chōkō.*

Chōkyū, 長 久. *Nengō:* 1040-1043.

Chōnan, 長 南. A castle built in 1445 by *Takeda Nobunaga* in *Kazusa.* It was taken by *Satomi Nariyoshi,* in 1480; by *Hōjō Ujimasa* in 1570. Finally *Ieyasu* gave it to *Honda Tadakatsu* in 1590.

Chōnen, 奝 然. See *Kōji-Daishi.*

Chōreki, 長 暦. *Nengō:* 1037-1039; also called *Chōryaku.*

Chōroku, 長 祿. *Nengō:* 1457-1459.

Chōsen, 朝 鮮. That is Korea. It is called by this name since 1392: before that epoch, it was called *Kōrai.* — See *San-kan, Kudara, Mimana, Shiragi, Koma,* etc.

Chōshū, 長 州. The Chinese name of *Nagato* province. This name is more in use than that of *Nagato.*

Chōsokabe, 長 會 我 部. A *Tosa* family of *samurai* that served successively the *Hosokawa,* the *Miyoshi,* and finally the *Ichijō.*

—— **Kunichika,** 國 親 (1503-1556). Built a castle at *Toyooka* and began to aggrandize his domains at the expense of his neighbours.

—— **Motochika,** 元 親 (1539-1599). Transferred his residence to the castle of *Nagahama,* and, by and by, made himself master of the whole *Tosa* province at the expense of *Ichijō Kanesada* (1573). In 1580, *Nobunaga* charged him with the conquest of the other provinces of *Shikoku*, which he destined for his own son *Nobutaka*. *Motochika* acquitted himself willingly of this mission. Meanwhile *Nobunaga* and his son having died, he was going to keep all his conquests for himself, when *Hideyoshi* interfered leaving him only *Tosa* (1585). He took part in the expedition against Korea, where he distinguished himself by his courage, and received the title of *Tosa no kami*. After his return, he transmitted his domains to his son, had his hair shaved and died at *Fushimi*.

CHOSOKABE MOTOCHIKA.

—— **Morichika,** 盛親. Embraced the party of *Hideyori* against *Ieyasu* (1600). Having been dispossessed of his domains, he became a bonze and retired to *Kyōto*. In 1615 he took part in the defense of the castle of *Ōsaka*. After the capture of the castle, he fled to *Hachiman-yama*, but he was discovered, conducted to *Kyōto*, condemned to death, and beheaded at the *Rokujō-gawara*.

Chotoku, 長德. *Nengō*: 995-998.

Chōwa, 長和. *Nengō*: 1012-1016.

Chōyō, 重陽. A popular feast celebrated on the 9th day of the 9th month. It is generally called the feast of chrysanthemums (*kiku no sekku*).

Chūai-tennō, 仲哀天皇. The 14th Emperor of Japan (192-200), was prince *Tarashi-nakatsu-hiko*, a son of *Yamatotakeru no mikoto*, and the husband of the celebrated *Jingō-kōgō*. In 193 he started on an expedition against the *Kumaso*, stopped at *Toyora* (*Nagato*), then passed over to *Chikuzen*. There a council was held to find out the best means to repress the rebels. The empress and the minister *Takeshiuchi no Sukune* were of opinion that, the *Kumaso* revolting only on account of being instigated and helped by *Shiragi* (Korea), war had first to be carried into that country. The emperor, afraid of the difficulty of the enterprise, was of the contrary opinion, although the empress supported her advice on a revelation of the gods. Did perhaps these gods punish him for his opposition? The fact is that, in the mean time, the emperor died suddenly, and the expedition was conducted by *Jingō Kōgō*. *Chūai* was then 52 years old. According to Korean documents, *Chūai's* death, the Korean expedition and *Ojin's* birth must be brought down to the year 346 as that date cannot be doubted.

Chūen, 忠圓. A celebrated bonze of the *Jōdo-ji* temple (*Kyōto*). At the request of *Go-Daigo-tennō*, he entered a complot the object of which was the overthrow of the *Hōjō* (1331). The latter exiled him to *Echigo*; but after the ruin of *Kamakura*, he returned to *Kyōto*.

Chūgoku, 中國. The name formerly given to the S.-W. part of *Hondo*, comprising the 16 provinces of *San-yō-dō* and *San-in-dō*.

Chūgoku-tandai, 中國探題. See *Nagato-tandai*.

Chūgū, 中宮. See *Sangū*.

Chūjō, 中乗. (Lit.: the middling conveyance, sc. to *Nirvâna*). An abstract category in which are classed all systems between *Daijō* and *Shōjō*.

Chūjō-hime, 中將姫 (753-781). Was a daughter of *Fujiwara Toyonari*. Being persecuted by her step-mother, she retired to the *Taimadera* temple (*Yamato*), assumed the name of *Zenshin-ni*, and employed the leisure left after her religious exercises in embroidering a tapestry representing the Buddhist paradise (*mandara*). The legend makes *Chūjō-hime* an incarnation of the goddess *Kwannon*.

Chūko, 中古. The middle ages of Japanese history; i.e., from the reign of *Kōtoku* till that of *Antoku* (645-1183).

Chūko san-jū-roku kasen, 中古三十六歌仙. See *San-jū-roku kasen*.

Chūkyō-tennō, 仲恭天皇. Prince *Kanenari*, the 85th Emperor of Japan (1221), was raised to the throne when only 4 years old, after the abdication of his father *Juntoku*. The latter in concert with the ex-emperor *Go-Toba*, his father, resolved to overthrow the *Hōjō*. Their army was defeated, both *Juntoku* and *Go-Toba* were exiled, and the young emperor was deposed after a reign of 70 days. He still lived 13 years in the *Kujō* ward at *Kyōto*, hence the name of *Kujō-haitei* by which he is known. It was only in 1870 that he received the posthumous name of *Chūkyō*, and was placed on the list of the emperors.

Chūnagon, 中納言. Counsellors at the Court, ranking after the *dainagon*. Their number was not always the same: at the end of the 12th century there were as many as ten.

Chūshi, 中祀. The feasts established by regulations of the *Jingi-kwan*, were divided into great (*daishi*), secondary (*chūshi*), and small feasts (*shōshi*). The *chūshi* were *Toshigoi no matsuri*, *Tsukinami no matsuri*, *Kanname no matsuri*, *Niiname no matsuri* and *Kamo no matsuri*. People prepared themselves for these feasts by a 3 days' fast and by purifications.

Chūson-ji, 中尊寺. A celebrated temple of the *Tendai* sect, near the village *Hiraizumi*, in the southern part of *Rikuchū*. This temple was founded by *Jikaku-daishi* (*Ennin*), and enriched by the *Fujiwara* of *Mutsu*, *Kiyohira*, *Hidehira*, etc., whose burial-place it was. The temple possesses also many souvenirs of *Yoshitsune* and *Benkei*, who died near that place.

Chūzenji-ko, 中禪寺湖. A lake (25 Km. in circuit) in *Shimotsuke*, W. of *Nikkō*. It is also called *Satsu-no-umi* (sea of happiness). It is 1300 met. above the level of the sea.

Chūzenji-san, 中禪寺山. See *Nantai-san*.

D

Dai, 大 (1527-1602). Was a daughter of *Mizuno Tadamasa,* a *dai-myō* of *Kariya* (*Mikawa*). She married *Tokugawa Hirotada,* and was the mother of *Ieyasu* (1542). In 1545 she was returned to her family, because her brother *Nobumoto* had submitted to the *Imagawa.* She married now *Hisamatsu Toshikatsu,* by whom she had three sons and four daughters. She died at the age of 75 at *Fushimi,* and received the posthumous name of *Denzū-in,* which was also given to the *Sōkei-ji* temple in *Edo* (*Koishikawa*), where she was buried.

Daibutsu, 大佛. Large statues of *Buddha Dainichi-nyorai* or *Birushana.* The most remarkable are those of :—

Kyōto (*Hōkō-ji*) ...... height	17m.40	erected in	1801 ;
Nara (*Tōdai-ji*) ...... ,,	15m.90	,,	746 ;
Kamakura .... ,,	15m.00	,,	1252 ;
Hyōgo (*Nōfuku-ji*) ... ,,	14m.40	,,	1891 ;
Tōkyō (*Ueno*) .... ,,	6m.60	,,	1660.

Daibutsu, 大佛. A branch of the *Hōjō* family, *shikken* of *Kama-kura.*

—— **Yorimori,** 賴盛. A son of *Hōjō Tokifusa* and grandson of *Tokimasa* was the first who took the name of *Daibutsu* or *Osaragi.*

—— **Sadafusa,** 貞房 († 1306). A grandson of *Yorimori,* was governor of *Kyōto* (*Rokuhara-tandai*) and distinguished himself as a poet. The family became extinct at the ruin of *Kamakura* (1333).

Dai-dairi, 大內裏, or *Ō-uchi.* The imperial palace erected in *Kyōto* by *Kwammu-tennō* in 794. The inclosure having the form of a rectangle, was surrounded by a moat, then by a wall measuring 10 *chō* (1.091 met.) from north to south, and 8 *chō* (873 met.) from east to west. The palace having been burnt in 960, 166 years after its erection, was rebuilt. Then from 960 till 1058, it was destroyed 15 times by fire, and rebuilt after each conflagration on a smaller scale. Finally, after the fire of 1227, the place was definitively abandoned : the Emperor then dwelt in a temporary palace (*rikyū*), or in the house of a prince or of a *Fujiwara,* which house then took the name of *Uchi-dairi.* It was only towards the end of the 16th century that the palace was rebuilt by *Hideyoshi; Ieyasu* enlarged it in 1611. The present imperial palace of *Kyōto* (*Gosho*) dates only from 1854. — See *Dairi, Daigoku-den, Seiryō-den, Shishin-den,* etc.

Daidō, 大同. *Nengō* : 806-809.

Daidō-ji, 大道寺. A *samurai* family descending from the *Taira.*

—— **Shigetoki,** 重時. Whose name was *Ise Tarō,* lived in the *Daidō-ji* temple (*Yamashiro,*) of which he took the name in 1471. His younger brother, *Ise Shinkurō,* became the famous *Hōjō Nagauji* (*Sōun*), and *Shigetoki* attached himself to his fortune.

—— **Shigeoki, 重興.** *Suruga no kami,* was charged by the *Hōjō* with the guard of the *Kawagoe* castle (*Musashi*).

—— **Masashige, 政繁.** *Suruga no kami,* had his revenues raised to 180,000 *koku.* In 1590 he was vanquished by *Maeda Toshiie* to whom he surrendered ; and, after the capture of *Odawara,* he killed himself by *harakiri* (1591).

—— **Naoshige, 直重** (1573-1628). Served successively *Maeda Toshinaga, Matsudaira Tadayoshi,* and *Tokugawa Yoshinao* (*Owari*).

—— **Shigehisa, 重久.** Followed the fortune of *Tokugawa Tadateru.*

—— **Shigesuke, 重祐** (1639-1730). Published some works on military art.

Daidō-kō, 大同江. Japanese name of the *Tatong* river (Korea), which passes through *Whang-ju, Pyeng-yang,* etc.

Daidōtei, 大稲埕. *Twatutia,* a part of the town of *Taihoku* (*Taipeh*) in Formosa, inhabited by Europeans.

Dai-ei, 大永. *Nengō :* 1521-1527.

Dai-en-reki, 大衍曆. See *Koyomi.*

Daigaku, 大學. (Lit.: great science) ; one of the 4 books of Confucius.

Daigaku-ryō, 大學寮. The ancient Imperial University in *Kyōto.* It depended on the Ministry of Ceremonies (*Shikibu-shō*). The rector had the title of *Daigaku no kami* 頭 ; he was assisted by the *suke* 助, *jō* 允, *sakwan* 屬, etc. The Faculty was composed of two professors of Chinese (*kyōgyō-hakase*), 2 professors of Law (*ritsu-gaku-hakase*), 2 professors of Mathematics (*san-hakase,*) etc. 400 pupils studied the Chinese Classsics, 10 studied Law, and 10, Grammar and Composition.

Daigakuryō no shi-dō, 大學寮四道. The four branches taught at the ancient University : History (*kiten* 紀傳), Chinese Classics (*myōkyō* 明經), Law (*myōho* 明法), and Mathematics (*san* 算).

Dai-geki, 大外記. An official dependent on the *Dajō-kwan,* having charge of correcting the imperial ordinances and the petitions addressed to the Emperor. The *Dai-geki* had as subordinate a *shō-geki* and 10 *shishō* 史生 (secretaries). To the *geki* corresponded the *naiki* 内記 that belonged to the *Nakatsukasa-sho ; geki* might be translated by secretary of the Council of State, and *naiki,* by secretary of the Minister of Archives. — The title of *geki* became hereditary in the two *kuge* families of *Kiyowara* and *Nakahara.*

Daigen no hō, 大元法. A Buddhist ceremony celebrated every year at the *Jibu-shō* from the 8th till the 15th of the first month. A sealed box containing some vestments of the Emperor was brought from the palace, some prayers were said over it and then it was carried back to the palace. It is said that this custom was brought from China by the bonze *Jōgyō* towards 840. This ceremony was also called *Daigensui-hō,* 大元帥法.

Dai-gensui, 大元帥. Generalissimo, a title exclusively given to the Emperor. — See *Gensui.*

Daigo, 醍醐. A *kuge* family descending from *Fujiwara Tadamichi,* = Now Marquis,

Daigo-ji, 醍醐寺. A Buddhist temple, S.E. of *Kyōto*, founded in 902 by the bonze *Shōbō* (*Rigen-daishi*). *Dōsei* and *Seiun,* two sons of the emperor *Kameyama* became its chief bonzes; their successors were generally princes, and the temple bore the title of *monzeki.* Having been partly destroyed during the *Ōnin* war (1467), it was rebuilt by *Hideyoshi.* At present it is the seat of *Shingon* sect.

Daigoku-den, 大極殿. Formerly the state-room in the palace of

DAIGOKU-DEN.

the Council of State. It was in that hall that the ceremony of the enthroning of the Emperor took place.

Daigo-tennō, 醍醐天皇. The 60th Emperor of Japan (898-930), was prince *Atsuhito,* the eldest son of *Uda-tennō.* He ascended the throne at the age of 13. Listening to the calumnies of the *Fujiwara, Tokihira, Sadakuni,* and of *Minamoto no Hikaru,* he exiled *Sugawara Michizane* to *Dazaifu* (901). During his reign, literature shone brightly: the works of *Ki no Tsurayuki, Miyoshi Kiyotsura, Fukane Sukebito,* etc., are still classical. For that reason the *Engi* era (901-922) is known in history as a period of prosperity, as it may be seen by the code called *Engi-shiki. Daigo* himself is often called *Engi no Mikado.* But during his reign already, notwithstanding the splendor of the ceremonies at the Court and the comfort enjoyed at the capital, disorder gradually crept into the interior of the land. Number of rich farmers obtained the charges of *toneri, efu,* etc. for money, and refused to submit to the orders of the *Kokushi.* The latter, too often, preferred to live at the Court rather than in their provinces, and the families of the military class then began to take the places of the *kuge. Daigo* died at the age of 46, and was buried in the *Daigo-ji* temple, which he himself had built : hence his posthumous name.

Daihō, 大賓. A castle in *Hitachi,* owned in the 14th century by the *Shimotsuma* family. *Masasue* having embraced the party of the South, was besieged in his castle in 1343. He was defeated and killed himself by *harakiri.* — See *Shimotsuma.*

Daiji, 大治. *Nengō :* 1126-1130.

Daijin, 大臣. The Minister secretary of State. This title was created at the *Taikwa* reform (645). A *Sadaijin* (minister of the left), an *Udaijin* (minister of the right), and a *Naijin* (minister of the interior), took the place of the *Ō-Muraji,* the *Ō-Omi,* etc. Later, in 702, a *Dajō-daijin* (prime minister) was placed at the head of the Council, and the title of *Naijin* was changed into *Naidaijin.* These denominations were in use until 1885. At that epoch, the *Dajō-daijin,* the *Sadaijin,* and the *Udaijin* were suppressed, and a cabinet (*Naikaku*) was constituted, comprising 10 *Daijin :* *Sōri-daijin* (Minister of the Council, president, without a department), *Naimu-daijin* (interior), *Gwaimu-daijin* (foreign affairs), *Ōkura-daijin* (finances), *Rikugun-daijin* (war), *Kaigun-daijin* (navy), *Mombu-daijin* (public instruction), *Shihō-daijin* (justice), *Nōshōmu-daijin* (agriculture and commerce), *Teishin-daijin* (post and telegraph), to which must be added, the *Kunai-daijin* (imperial Household), although not belonging to the Cabinet.

Daijingū, 大神宮. The great *Ise* temples dedicated to *Amaterasu-ō-mikami ;* also the goddess herself.

Daijin-zenji, 大臣禪師. A title bestowed in 764 by the Empress *Shotoku* upon the bonze *Dōkyō,* who enjoyed her entire confidence. The following year he was made *Dajō-daijin-zenji,* a unique occurrence in the history of Japan.

Daijō, 大乘 (Lit.: great vehicle, great conveyance). The northern or Chinese Buddhism (*mahâyâna*), in opposition to *shōjō* (small vehicle), the southern Buddhism of Siam, Ceylon (*hinayâna*). The characteristics of this system are an excess of transcendental speculation and the substitution of fanciful degrees of meditation in place of the practical asceticism of the *Shōjō.*

Daijō-e, 大甞會. A ceremony which was also called *daijō-sai, ōname, ōnie, ōmube.* Every emperor performed it once after his enthronement, to honor his ancestors, the *tenjin* and the *chijin.* *Go-Hanazono-tennō* celebrated it in 1430 ; after that date it was discontinued, on account of the civil wars, until performed again by *Higashi-yama-tennō* in 1680. The present Emperor performed it in 1871. It is the most solemn Shintoist festival.

Daikaku-ji, 大覺寺. A temple of the *Shingon* sect at *Saga,* W. of *Kyōto.* It was first a villa built for the emperor *Saga* after his abdication in 823, and became, in 876, a Buddhist temple, whose chief bonzes were always princes of the imperial family. *Kameyama* (1276) and his son *Go-Uda* (1288) having retired to this temple, their descendants were called *Daikakuji-tō* (*Daikakuji* line) ; while the descendants of *Go-Fukakusa,* who had retired to the *Jimyō-in* (1266), were called

Jimyōin-tō. The rivalry between these two branches of the imperial dynasty holds a great place in the history of the 13th and the 14th centuries.

Daikoku, 大黒. One of the 7 gods of luck, the special god of riches. He is represented sitting or standing on rice bags, which rats come to gnaw at under his indulgent eyes.

Daikwan, 代官. Officials who, under the *Hōjō* and *Ashikaga* governed the great fiefs. in the absence of the titulars (*kokushi*, *shugo*) then mostly at the capital. — Under the *Tokugawa*, the title was given to the administrators of the domains of the *Shōgun.*

Daikyō, 大饗. Great banquets formerly given at the Court. The *nikyū-daikyō* were offered by the dowager empress and by the reigning empress to the princes and ministers. When an official was raised to the rank of *daijin*, he invited his colleagues and the principal personages of the palace to a feast, which was called *daijin-daikyō.*

Daimuken-zan, 大無間山. A mountain (2.330 met.) between *Suruga* and *Tōtōmi.*

Daimyō, 大名 (Lit.: great name). A noble, a lord in feudal times. The possessors of great domains were first called *myōden;* then by and by the term *daimyō* prevailed. *Daimyō* were classified into

DAIMYŌ AND HIS RETINUE ON A VISIT TO THE SHŌGUN, ON THE FIRST OF THE YEAR.

kokushu, governors of one or several provinces ; *ryōshu,* governors of a smaller territory ; and *jōshu,* commanders of a castle. Before *Ieyasu,* there were 18 *kokushu,* 32 *ryōshu,* and 212 *jōshu.* From the time of *Ieyasu,* all those whose revenues were above 10,000 *koku* of rice were *daimyō*. He divided them into two classes: the *fudai-daimyō*, numbering 176, who had sided with him before the campaign of *Sekiga-hara* (1600), and the *tozama-daimyō*, numbering 86, who had submitted to his authority only after having been defeated. — See *Myōden*.

Dainagon, 大納言. Counsellors of the imperial Court. The *Taihō* code (702) created 4 *dainagon*. In 828, *Junwa-tennō* added some *gon-dainagon* (vice great-counsellors). Towards the end of the 12th century, the number of *dainagon* was raised to 8. At the beginning, they were called *Ōimono-mōsu-tsukasa*.

Dai-naiki, 大內記. Formerly the first secretary of the Department of the Archives (*Nakatsukasa-no-shō*). He was assisted by a *shō-naiki*.

Dainei-ji, 大寧寺. A temple of the *Zen* sect, near *Fukagawa* (*Nagato*), in which *Ōuchi Yoshitaka*, vanquished by his vassal *Sue Harukata*, committed suicide (1551).

Dai-ni, 大貳. A high official of the *Dazaifu*, below the *gon-no-sotsu* (governor). When there was a *gon-no-sotsu*, there was no *dai-ni*, and vice versa. The *dai-ni* replaced the governor.

Dainichi-dake, 大日嶽. A mountain (1950 met.) between *Echigo*, and *Iwashiro*.

Dainichi-gawa, 大日川. A river (70 Km.) in *Kaga*; it passes through *Kutani* and *Daishōji*. It is also called *Sakai-gawa*, 界川, *Daishōji-gawa*, 大聖寺川, *Sugao-gawa*, 菅生川.

Dainichi-Nyorai, 大日如來 (sanskr. *Vairotchana*). One of the persons of the Buddhist trinity. He personifies wisdom and purity, and is also called *Roshana-butsu*, or *Birushana*.

Dai-Nihon, 大日本. The great (empire of the) rising Sun, i.e., Japan. The empire of Japan, situated in the N.W. of the Pacific Ocean, lies between 119° 20′ and 156° 32′ long. E. and between 21° 18′ and 50° 56′ lat. N. It is composed of 5 great islands: *Hondo*, *Shikoku*, *Kyūshū*, *Hokkaidō*, and *Taiwan*, and of more than 500 small islands to which must be added the southern half of Saghalin (*Karafuto*) acquired by Japan in 1905. The surface of the empire is 417,500 square kilom., and its population amounts to 48,542,736 inhabitants (Dec. 31, 1903), viz.: 116 inhabitants per square kilometer. This population is divided into 5,200 *kwazoku* (nobles) 2,228,000 *shizoku* (former *samurai*), and 46,310,000 *heimin* (common people).

Japan is divided into 10 great regions comprising 88 provinces: those are:—*Kinai* (5 provinces), *Tōkai-dō* (15 provinces), *Tōsan-dō* (13 provinces), *Hokuroku-dō* (7 prov.), *San-in-dō* (8 prov.), *San-yō-dō* (8 prov.), *Nankai-dō* (6 prov.), *Saikai-dō* (12 prov.), *Hokkai-dō* (11 prov.), *Taiwan* (3 prov.). For the Administration, it is divided into 3 *fu* (prefectures), 43 *ken* (departments), and 2 *chō* (governments), namely those of *Hokkai-dō* and *Taiwan*. Those of *Taiwan* not counted, there are 622 *kōri* (districts), 57 *shi* (cities), 1,163 *machi* (towns), and 14,034 *mura* (villages).

The following figures, for reference, are taken from the official statistics of 1904 :—

Foreigners residing in Japan	13,848
Newspapers and magazines	1,328
Post-offices	4,177
Telegraph offices	633
Post and telegraph offices	1,466
Post and telegraph officials	25,274
Letter carriers	23,251
Length of rail-roads in operation ... ...Km ,	11,054
Telephone offices	180
Primary schools	27,168
Number of pupils in primary schools	5,137,600
Hospitals	858
Physicians	36,660
Police stations and offices	16,329
Police inspectors and agents	39,850
Jinrikisha (*rikisha*)	200,991

	Steamers	1,395
Merchant vessels :	Sailing vessels	4,020
	Japanese junks	1,355

Senators	327
Deputies	379
Electors (for the Chamber of Deputies)	757,788
Prefectural Assemblies	45
Members of Pref. Assemblies	1,594
Electors (for Pref. Assemblies)	2,009,725
District Assemblies	531
Members of District Assemblies	12,585
Municipal Assemblies	12,462
Members of Mun. Assemblies...	147,645

In olden times, Japan was called *Ō-yashima no Kuni* 大八州國, *Ō-Yamato-toyo-akitsu-shima* 大日本豊秋津嶋, *Ō-Yamato-hidakami no Kuni* 大倭日高見國, *Yamato no Kuni* 倭國, etc.

Dai-Nihon-shi, 大日本史. A great history of Japan in 243 volumes published through the care of *Mitsukuni*, prince of *Mito* (1622-1700). This work, which was finished only in 1715, contributed much to raise the prestige of the imperial dynasty, and to cause the *Tokugawa* to be regarded as usurpers.

Dairen, 大連. *Dalny*, in *Liao-tong* peninsula.

Dairi, 内裏. That part of the palace specially set apart for the service of the Emperor. The *shishin-den*, the *seiryō-den*, etc. belonged to it. When the Court was unable to rebuild the imperial palace, and the Emperor was obliged to reside elsewhere, his residence was called *sato-dairi*. By extension, the word *dairi* applied to the Emperor himself.

Dairyō, 大兩. An ancient coin equivalent to 72 *shu* 銖. The *shōryō* 小兩 was only 24 *shu*. Later, the *bu* 分 was created : then 6 *shu* made 1 *bu*, and 4 *bu* one *ryō*.

Daisanji, 大参事. The name given, at the time of the suppression of the *han* (feudal domains), to the officials until then called *karō* 家老. The *daisanji* came immediately after the *han-chiji* 藩知事 (prefect), just as the *karō* came after the *daimyō*.

Daiseishi, 大勢至. Or simply **Seishi.** A *bosatsu* belonging to the retinue of *Amida*.

Daisen, 大山. See *Ōyama (Hōki)*.

Daishi, 大師 (Lit: great master). An honorific title added to the posthumous name of certain bonzes, considered as the holiest, or most learned. This practice was imported from China. It was the emperor *Seiwa* who for the first time conferred this title in 866 : that of *Dengyō-Daishi* on the celebrated bonze *Saichō*, and that of *Jikaku-Daishi* on another celebrated bonze called *Ennin*.

Daishi, 大祀. The great Shintoist ceremonies as regulated by the *Jingi-kwan*. They were of three different rites or degrees of solemnity : *daishi, chūshi,* and *shōshi.* — See *Saishi.*

Daishōji, 大聖寺. A town (10,000 inh.) and ancient castle in *Kaga*. The castle was successively occupied by the *daimyō*: *Tsuba* (15th cent.), *Asakura, Mizoguchi* (1583–1592), *Yamaguchi* (1592–1600), *Maeda* (1600–1868).

Dai-Sōjō, 大僧正. The highest dignity in the Buddhist hierarchy. The *dai-sōjō* ranked with the *dainagon*. — See *Sō-kwan.*

Daiten-Zenji, 大典禪師 (1634–1716). A chief bonze of the *Shōkoku-ji* temple in *Kyōto*. He was renowned for his knowledge of Chinese literature. He left numerous writings.

Daitoku-ji, 大徳寺. A temple in *Kyōto*. It is the seat of a subdivision of the *Rinzai* branch of the *Zen* sect, and was built by *Myōchō (Daitō-kokushi)* in 1323. Among its chief bonzes were several celebrities : *Ikkyū* in the 15th century, *Takuan* in the 17th century. In the precincts of the temple are the tombs of *Oda Nobunaga* and of his sons *Nobutada* and *Nobuo.* — The branch of the Daitoku-ji comprises 4 divisions : *Kita no ha, Minami no ha, Kwantō no ha,* and *Ikkyū no ha.*

Daizen-shiki, 大膳職. Formerly the office of the Minister of the Imperial Household (*Kunai-shō*), having charge of the collection and employment of taxes in kind destined for the palace. The chief of the office had the title of *Daizen-tayū*, which, from the time of *Ieyasu*, was hereditary in the family of the *Chōshū Mōri.*

Dajō-daijin, 大政大臣. The Prime Minister and president of the Supreme Council (*dajō-kwan*). This title was created in 671 by the emperor *Tenchi* for his son *Ōtomo no Ōji*, and for a long time was reserved for the imperial princes. The empress *Shōtoku* was the first to depart from this custom by conferring the title of *Dajōdaijin-Zenji* on the bonze *Dōkyō*.

Dajō-kō, 太上皇. See *Dajō-tennō.*

Dajō-kwan, 太政官. Supreme Council of the Emperor, established in 702. It was composed of the *Dajō-daijin* (minister-president), the *Sadaijin* (minister of the left), the *Udaijin* (minister of the right), the *Naidaijin* (minister of the Interior), the four *Dainagon* (first class secretaries), the three *Shōnagon* assistant secretaries). Afterwards the *Chūnagon* were created and the number of *Dainagon* and *Shōnagon* increased.

Dajō-tennō, 太上天皇. Or simply *Dajō-kō*, *Jōkō*, the title of the emperors after their abdication. They were called *Dajō-hōō* or *Hōō*, when they became bonzes. The empress *Jitō* was the first to take this title (696). Later, it was customary for the new emperor to offer this title to his predecessor: *Junwa-tennō* did so to his brother *Saga* in 824. The ex-emperor refused by

ANCIENT SEAL OF DAJŌKWAN.

a writing (*songō no jisho*) ; the successor insisted (*songō go-hōsho*). *Uda-tennō* (897) refused as many as six times. This custom was interrupted at the time of the troubles of *Ōnin* (1467), and taken up again by *Sakura-machi-tennō* (1736).

Dan, 男. A title of nobility corresponding to that of baron= *Danshaku*.

Danii, 太泥. Ancient Japanese name of the island of *Borneo*.

Danjōdai, 彈正臺. Or *Tadasu-tsukasa*. Formerly a high Court of justice. There were four ranks of officials: *Kami* 尹 (president), *Suke* 弼 (vice-president), *Jō* 忠 (secretaries), *Sakwan* 疏 (assessors). In 836, the greater part of the attributions of the *Danjōdai* devolved upon the *Kebiishi*.

Dan-no-ura, 檀浦. A bay in *Nagato*, near *Shimonoseki*, where, in 1185, the celebrated naval battle was fought that consummated the ruin of the *Taira* and the triumph of the *Minamoto*. The latter's victory was principally due to the bravery of *Yoshitsune*, who, among other feats, in one bound, leaped over eight (?) boats (*hassō-tobi*) to reach an enemy. The ex-emperor *Antoku*, 7 years old, and his grandmother *Nii-no-ama*, the widow of *Kiyomori*, perished in the sea with a great number of their partisans. — See *Taira Munemori*.

Danrin-fū, 談林風. A kind of *haikai* (Poetry of 17 syllables) created by *Nishiyama Sōin* (1610-1682).

Danrin-kōgō, 檀林皇后. The name given to *Tachibana Kachi-ko*, wife of the emperor *Saga*.

Dansen-bugyō, 段錢奉行. A title created in 1371. By *dansen* were specified the extra taxes levied for the crowning of the emperor, or some other important circumstances ; later on, they were called *go-yōkin*. The functions of the *bugyō* were to assess the taxes according to the fortunes of the families and to collect them. This title existed only in the time of the *Ashikaga*.

Danzan-jinja, 談山神社. See *Tamu-no-mine*.

Daruma, 達摩 (sanskr. *Bodhidharma*). A son of a king of southern India, who, having become a bonze, went to China and introduced the Buddhist *Zen* sect into that country. He is represented clad in red and in deep meditation, sometimes even without legs. He is supposed to have lost them by a nine years' uninterrupted contemplation.

Daruma-ki, 達摩忌. A feast of *Daruma*, which is celebrated on the 5th day of the 10th lunar month.

Date, 伊達. A family of *daimyō* in *Mutsu*, descending from the *Fujiwara*.

—— **Tomomune, 朝宗**. A descendant in the 16th degree of *Fujiwara Uona*, residing at *Isa*, in *Hitachi*. In 1189 he transferred his residence into *Mutsu*, *Date* district, of which he took the name. He is the ancestor of *Masamune*.

Masamune { Tadamune { Tsunamune-Tsunamura-Yoshimura. (a).
Muneyoshi-Takeaki-Nobuaki (*Tamura*). (b).
Hidemune { Munetoshi-Muneyoshi-Munetoshi. (c).
Munezumi-Muneyasu-Muratoyo. (d).

(*a*) — **Masamune, 政宗** (1566-1636). Was a son of *Terumune* (+1584). His father having been killed by *Nihonmatsu Yoshitsugu*, *Masamune* succeeded him at the age of 18, and continued to wage war against his neighbors to aggrandize his domains. In 1589 he made himself master of *Aizu*, domain of the *daimyō Ashina*, and established his residence at the *Kurokawa* castle (*Wakamatsu*); but the following year, *Hideyoshi*, having triumphed over the *Odawara Hōjō*, forced him to be satisfied with the *Yonezawa* fief (300,000 k.). At the time of the expedition to Korea, he accompanied *Hideyoshi* to *Nagoya* (*Hizen*), thence he passed into Korea with *Asano Nagamasa*. During his absence, he was accused of being implicated together with the *Kwampaku Hidetsugu* in a plot against *Hideyoshi*, but he succeeded in disculpating himself. In 1600, *Ieyasu* ordered him to make war against *Uesugi Kagekatsu*, and, assisted by *Mogami Yoshiteru*, he defeated *Naoe Kanetsugu*. He then received in fief the 12 districts possessed until then by the *Uesugi*, and changed the name of his castle from *Iwatezawa* to that of *Sendai* (620,000 k.). He took part in the siege of *Ōsaka* (1615), and repelled the troops of *Gotō Ujifusa*. When the *Shōgun Hidetada* persecuted the Christians at *Edo*, he obtained the release of Father Sotelo, who had been arrested, called the latter to *Sendai* and commissioned him to accompany an embassy he was sending to the Sovereign Pontiff and to the king of Spain, the embassy being headed by *Hasekura Rokuemon Tsunenaga* (1613). *Masamune* was then said to

DATE MASAMUNE.

be favorably disposed towards the Christians, and even inclined to embrace Christianity, but fearing to displease the *Shōgun*, he soon changed his dispositions and became a persecutor. He died at the age of seventy, renowned not only as a warrior, but still more as a diplomat and a protector of artists and scholars.

—— **Tadamune,** 忠宗 (+ 1658). Was a son of *Masamune* and enjoyed much credit with the *Shōgun Iemitsu*.

—— **Tsunamune,** 綱宗. Having been denounced at *Edo* on account of the licentiousness of his life, he was condemned to dig, at his own expense, the moat of the castle of *Edo* from *Megane-bashi* to the gate of *Ushigome* (1660). His descendants resided at *Sendai* (620,000 k.) until the Restoration. = Now Count.

(*b*) —— **Muneyoshi,** 宗良. The 2nd son of *Tadamune*, revived the name of *Tamura*, an ancient family of *Mutsu*, which had been dispossessed by *Masamune*. He established his residence at *Ichinoseki* (*Mutsu*—30,000 k.), where his descendants resided till the Restoration. = Now Viscount.

(*c*) —— The junior Branch was established at *Uwajima* (*Iyo*) in 1614 (100,000 k.).

—— **Muneki,** 宗城 (1817–1882). Played a conspicuous part at the time of the Restoration, and was among the first to ask for the suppression of the shōgunate. = Now Marquis.

(*d*) —— A Branch of the above which in 1657 received the castle of *Yoshida* (*Iyo* — 30,000 k.). = Now Viscount.

Date Chihiro, 伊達千廣 (1803–1877). Man of letters of the *Wakayama* clan (*Kii*). In his works he shows great attachment to the Imperial Restoration.

Dazaifu, 太宰府. A town in *Chikuzen*, which from the 6th century was the seat of the *Tsukushi* government. — It was at that place that, in 1182, the emperor *Antoku* took refuge, but the revolt of *Ogata Koreyoshi* compelled him to pass into *Nagato*. It was at *Dazaifu* too, that the Mongols tried to land in 1281.

Dazaifu, 太宰府. Formerly the military government of *Kyūshū*. When, during the reign of *Kemmei* (663), the kingdom of *Mimana* (Korea) had been destroyed by *Shiragi*, the Japanese posts which had been established in that country, were transferred to *Tsukushi*. An administration was charged with the defence of the coasts, and, gradually with all the civil services, such as, agriculture, taxes, posts, Communications, etc. The administration was composed of 1 *sotsu*, 3 *ni* (*dai-ni* and *shō-ni*), 2 *gen* (*dai-gen* and *shō-gen*), 2 *ten* (*dai-ten* and *shō-ten*,) etc. In 740, the *Daizai-shōni Fujiwara Hirotsune* having revolted, the *Dazaifu* was suppressed and replaced by a *Tsukushi-chinzeifu*, but was re-established in

ANCIENT SEAL OF DAZAIFU.

745. After the downfall of the *Taira*, *Yoritomo* created a *Chinzei-bugyō* (1186) as governor of *Kyūshū*, which title was afterwards changed to that of *Kyūshū-tandai* (1275), which in its turn, was later on modified to the original *Daizaifu-sotsu*.

Dazai no gon-no-sotsu, 太宰權帥. The head of the government of *Kyūshū* had the title of *Dazai no sotsu*. As this title was generally reserved for princes of the imperial family who did not leave the capital, a sub-governor (*gon-no-sotsu*) with the rank of *nagon* took his place.

A *daijin* occupied this position when sent into exile, as it happened to *Sugawara Michizane.*

Dazai-shōni, 太宰少貳. The title of one of the principal officials of the *Dazaifu.* In 1196, *Mutō Sukeyori* received this title from *Yoritomo,* and his descendants made it their family name, *Shōni.*

Dazai Shuntai, 太宰春臺 (1680-1747). Was born at *Iida* (*Shinano*), and became a pupil of *Ogiu Sorai,* and a renowned Confucianist. His instructions were very well attended, and his works, numbering over 50, are still much appreciated.

Dembu, 傳符. A written authorization given by the *Dajōkwan,* which entitled the bearer to receive relay horses when charged with an official mission.

Den-chōrō, 傳長老 (+ 1633). Was born in the *Isshiki* family, became a bonze of the *Zen* sect and the head of the *Nanzen-ji* and the *Konchi-in* temples and is known under the name of *Sūden.* He accompanied *Ieyasu* in all his campaigns as a secretary. At the battle of *Mikata-ga-hara* (1572), he himself fought, and took the heads of 3 enemies as a trophy. *Ieyasu* allowed the *Konchi-in* as a reward, to have three black stars on its arms. In 1608, *Sūden* was charged with the high office of administrator of the Buddhist and the Shintoist temples, as well as with the redaction of the letters to be sent to foreign countries. He is also called *Konchi-in Sūden.*

Dengaku, 田樂. The name given to amusements in which peasants formerly indulged after certain periods of hard labor in the fields. Later on historical scenes of olden times were represented. Over 50 pieces of that kind were composed. They resembled the *nō* and were much in vogue during the *Kamakura* and the *Muromachi* éras (1200-1570). Gradually however, the *dengaku* gave way to the *sarugaku* or *nō*.

Dengyō Daishi, 傳教大師 (767-822). The posthumous name by which the bonze *Saichō* is known. *Saichō* was born in *Ōmi,* in the *Miura* family, became bonze when 12 years old, and was a disciple of *Gyōhyō.* By order of the emperor he went to China in 802, visited many Buddhist temples, among others the *Kokusei-ji,* on mount *Tendai* in *Tchekiang* 浙江 province. After his return in 805, he diffused the doctrines he had imbibed: it was the beginning of the *Tendai* sect, the seat of which was established at the *Enryaku-ji* temple, which he had built on *Hiei-zan* in 788. He also brought from China many religious books and the ceremony of Buddhist baptism (*kwanchō*), which he himself administered to the dying *Kwammu-tennō.* Shortly before his death, *Saichō* received the title of *Dengyō-hōshi,* which was changed by the emperor *Seiwa* into that of *Dengyō-daishi* in 866.

DENGYŌ DAISHI.

Denjō-bito, 殿上人. The name primitively given to the dignitaries of the Court who enjoyed the privilege of being admitted to the *Seiryōden* hall called *Denjō-no-ma:* they were the *kurando* of the 4th,

5th, and 6th ranks. Later, this title was given to all those who, although not *kurando*, were authorized to visit the Emperor.

Denzū-in, 傳通院. The temple of the *Jōdo-shū* sect, erected in 1413 at *Edo* (*Koishikawa*) by the bonze *Shōkyō*. It was first called *Sōkei-ji*, but had its name changed when *Denzū-in*, the mother of *Ieyasu* was buried in that temple in 1602.

Dewa, 出羽. One of the 13 provinces of *Tōsandō*, detached from *Echigo* in 712. — Its Chinese name is *Ushū*. — In 1868, it was divided into *Uzen* and *Ugo*.

Dō, 道. A region or division of land containing several provinces. There are 7 *dō*: *Tōkaidō* (15 prov.), *Tōsandō* (13 prov.), *Hokurokudō* (7 prov.), *Sanindō* (8 prov.), *Sanyōdō* (8 prov.), *Nankaidō* (6 prov.), *Saikaidō* (12 prov.), to which may be added *Hokkaidō* (11 prov.).

Dōbō-gashira, 同朋頭. Under the *Tokugawa* government it was the title given to the chief of the servants of the shōgunal palace. This office was generally entrusted to a bonze. To prepare the reception halls, to offer tea, run errands for officials, etc.: such were the occupations of the *dōbōshū*, also called *bō-ami*. They were supressed in 1866.

Dōbō-shū, 同朋衆. Under the *Ashikaga* administration, servants in the service of the *Bakufu*. Their function was to receive the guests. Bonzes were generally charged with this office.

Dochō, 度牒. A sort of diploma given by the government to bonzes and *ama* after their admission into the congregation. It was also called *doen*.

Dōgen, 道元. See *Shōyō-Daishi*.

Dōgo, 道後. A village in *Iyo* renowned for its hot springs, in which, according to legend, *Ōnamuji* and *Sukuna-bikona* were the first to bathe; after them followed many emperors and high personages. — In 1335, *Doi-Michiharu* built a castle there, which he called *Yuzuki-jō*, where his descendants resided and governed the province. *Fukushima Masanori* took it in 1588. The castle of *Dōgo* was demolished when *Katō Yoshiaki* established himself at *Matsuyama*, in 1600.

Dōgo, 嶋後. The largest of the *Oki* island, (120 Km. in circuit); the three smaller ones are called *Dōzen*. — *Dōgo* is also called *Haha-jima*.

Doi, 土井. A family of *daimyō*, native of *Mikawa*.

—— **Toshikatsu, 利勝** (1573-1644). Was a son of *Mizuno Nobumoto*, an uncle of *Ieyasu*. He was adopted by *Doi Toshimasa* and brought up with *Hidetada*. In 1601, he was made *daimyō* and received a revenue of 10,000 k. in *Shimōsa*; afterwards he successively passed to *Sakura* (30,000 k.) and to *Koga* (132,000 k.). Together with *Sakai Tadayo* and *Aoyama Tadatoshi*, he was chosen counsellor of *Iemitsu*. *Toshikatsu* had three sons, hence the three branches of the family.

Toshikatsu
{ Toshitaka-Toshishige-Toshimasu-Toshizane. (a)
{ Toshinaga-Toshitomo-Toshitsune-Toshinobu. (b)
{ Toshifusa-Toshitomo-Toshihiro-Toshisada. (c)

(*a*) — The elder branch resided at *Koga* (*Shimōsa* 132,000 k.) until 1675. The same year, *Toshihisa* the eldest son, having died without children, *Toshimasu* his uncle, became his successor, and was transferred to *Toba* (*Shima* — 60,000 k.). The family having been transferred to *Karatsu* (*Hizen*) in 1691, returned in 1762, to *Koga* (*Shimōsa* — 80,000 k). = Now Viscount.

(*b*) — The younger branch was founded by *Toshinaga*, the second son of *Toshikatsu*. The family was established at *Nishio* (*Mikawa*) ; afterwards, in 1747, at *Kariya* (*Mikawa* — 23,000 k.) = Now Viscount.

(*c*) — The youngest branch descended from *Toshifusa*, the 3nd son of *Toshikatsu*. It was established, in 1682, at *Ōno* (*Echizen* — 40,000 k.) = Now Viscount.

Doi Michiharu, 土居通治. Was a native of *Iyo* and father of *Kōno*. In 1333, when *Go-Daigo* fled from *Oki* and established himself at *Funanoe-sen* (*Hōki*), *Michiharu* and his kinsman *Tokunō Michitoki* took his side and defeated the *Nagato-tandai*, *Hōjō Tokinao*, at *Hoshioka*. Afterwards they made war against the *Ashikaga*. *Michiharu* was killed at the taking of the castle of *Kanasaki* (*Echizen*) in 1337.

Doi Sanehira, 土肥實平. A descendant of the *Taira*, who, having been established at *Doi* (*Sagami*), took its name. In 1180, answering the call of *Yoritomo*, he took part in the campaigns against *Yoshinaka* and the *Taira*. Peace having been restored, he received 5 provinces of *Sanyōdō* as a fief, and afterwards was appointed governor of *Kinai*. He died in 1220.

Dōjō-ji, 道成寺. A Buddhist temple in *Kii*, known by the legend of the bonze *Anchin* (928), too long to be reproduced here.

Dōki-jidai, 銅器時代. The brazen age of the anthropologists, coming after the stone age (*sekki-jidai*) and before the iron age (*tekki-jidai*).

Dōkō-Daishi, 道興大師. The posthumous name of *Jitsue* (785-847), a celebrated bonze of the *Shingon* sect, who enjoyed great credit with the emperors *Saga* and *Seiwa*.

Dōkyō, 道鏡. A bonze who, by his intrigues, obtained a great influence over the ex-empress *Kōken*. *Fujiwara Nakamaro*, a favorite of the emperor *Junnin*, took umbrage, raised an army against him, but was defeated and killed in *Ōmi* (764). *Dōkyō*, then more powerful than ever, had *Junnin* exiled to *Awaji* and induced *Kōken* to re-ascend the throne, whilst he himself was created *Dajōdaijin-Zenji*, and even *Hō-ō*, a title reserved to emperors. All authority was in his hands, and soon his party went so far as to publicly proclaim him worthy of the throne. The empress already shaken was about to yield ; but before doing so, she ordered a faithful servant, *Wake no Kiyomaro*, to repair to the temple of the god *Hachiman*, at *Usa*, for consultation. The answer was that a simple subject could never become emperor. This exasperated *Dōkyō*, who exiled *Kiyomaro* to *Ōsumi*, after having ordered the tendons of his legs to be cut (768). But the empress had changed her mind. The following year, *Kōnin-tennō* having ascended the throne at the death of the empress, his first act of authority was to banish *Dōkyō* to *Shimotsuke*, where he died in 772.

Donchō, 曇徵. A Korean bonze. It is said that he came to Japan in 610, bringing Buddhist books along with him, that he was a skilful draughtsman and taught the Japanese to make paper and Indian ink.

Dōryū, 道 隆 (1214–1278). A Chinese bonze who came to Japan when 33 years old, and introduced the *Zen* sect. The *shikken Hōjō Tokiyori* put him at the head of the *Kenchō-ji* temple, which he had just erected at *Kamakura* (1253). Later he became chief of the *Saimyō ji* temple. After his death, he received the posthumous title of *Daigaku-Zenji*. He is also called *Rankei*.

Dōsen, 道 璿. A Chinese bonze who came to Japan in 735, and introduced the *Kegon* sect.

Dōshō, 道 昭. A bonze of the *Genkō-ji* temple, who, in 653, accompanied the embassy sent to China, and who, after his return (654), commenced to preach the *Hossō* or *Yuishiki* sect. He also contibuted to the propagation of the *Ryōbu-shintō*. In the provinces where he passed, he built bridges, dug wells, made rivers navigable, etc. He died in the year 700, and was cremated. It was the first time that cremation was performed in Japan.

Dōso-jin, 道 祖 神. The god of roads and ways (*Shintō*). Also called *Dōroku-jin* 道 陸 神, *Sae no kami* 塞 神, *Kunado* 久 那 斗 神, etc.

Dōwa-chōhen, 童 話 長 篇. Work in which *Kurozawa Okinamaro* (1795–1859) has compiled in poetical form, the most popular fables for children: *Momotarō, Kachikachi-yama, Shita-kiri-suzume,* etc.

Dōzen, 島 前. A collective name given to the 3 islands, *Chiburi-shima, Nishi no shima* and *Naka-shima,* of the *Oki* group.

E

Ebisu, 夷 (Barbarians). A name given to the Aborigines in the East and North of Japan. Those that lived in the most remote provinces were called *Ara-Ebisu, Tsuga ru-Ebisu*. The *Aino* are their descendants.

Ebisu, 惠 比 須. Was the 3d son of *Izanagi* and *Izanami*, and is one of the 7 gods of luck. He is represented with a fishing-line and a fish *(tai)* in his hand. He is also called *Hiruko*.

Ebisu-kō, 惠 比 須 講. A festival celebrated, especially by merchants, on the 20th of the eleventh lunar month, in honor of *Ebisu*.

Eboshi-na, 烏 帽 子 名. At the time of the *gembuku*, a kinsman or a friend was chosen as *eboshi-oya* (sponsor) who, putting the *eboshi* (a kind of hat) on the head of the young man, gave him a name : it was the *eboshi-na*, or *kammei*.

Echi, 越. An ancient province on the western coast of *Hondo*. In 680 it was divided into *Echizen, Etchū*, and *Echigo*.

Echigo, 越 後. One of the seven provinces of *Hokurokudō*. It comprises 15 districts which belong to the *Niigata-ken*. Its Chinese name is *Esshū*, which is also given to *Echizen* and *Etchū*.

Echizen, 越 前. One of the 7 provinces of *Hokurokudō*. It comprises 8 districts which belong to the *Fukui-ken*. Its Chinese name is *Esshū*, which designates also *Etchū*, and *Echigo*.

Edo, 江 戶. Now *Tōkyō*, the capital of Japan, was originally but a little village of fishermen, near which *Ōta Sukenaga (Dōkwan)*, a vassal of the *Uesugi*, built a castle in 1456, and fighting against his neighbors of *Iwatsuki, Hachigata*, etc., became master of the whole *Musashi* province. Afterwards *Edo* came into the possession of the *Kubō* of *Koga*, but in 1524 fell into that of *Hōjō Ujitsuna*. At the downfall of the *Hōjō* (1590) when *Tokugawa Ieyasu* received *Kwantō* as a fief, he selected *Edo* for his residence, and erected a castle, which, for 260 years, was the seat of the shōgunate. The palace, repeatedly destroyed and rebuilt, was reduced to ashes in 1863. The town also was several times partially destroyed by fire ; the conflagrations of 1621, 1657, 1668, and 1845, left scarcely anything but ruins. The earthquakes of 1633, 1650, 1703, 1707, and 1855 caused considerable damage. Meanwhile the *Shōgun* and their ministers applied themselves to embellish the city. From that period date the *Nihonbashi* (1603) the temple of *Kwannon* in *Asakusa* (1618) the temple *Kwan-ei-ji* in *Ueno* (1626), the *suidō* (waterworks) which bring the water from the *Tamagawa* to *Edo* (1653), the *Ryōgokubashi* (1659), the *Higashi-Hongwanji* temple (1680), the *Eitai-bashi* (1698), etc.. At the Restoration the name of *Edo* was changed into that of *Tōkyō* (1868), and, in the following year, the town became the residence of the Emperor and the seat of government. — See *Tōkyō*

Edo-jidai, 江戶時代. The period of the *Tokugawa* shōgunate in *Edo*, from 1603 till 1867 ; it is also called *Tokuyawa-jidai.*

E-dokoro, 繪所. During the *Ashikaga* period, an officer superintending affairs relating to painting.

Efu, 衛府. Offices of the Imperial Guard. The *Taihō* code (702) had created five of them : *emon-fu, sa-eji-fu, u-eji-fu, sa-hyōe-fu* and *u-hyōe-fu.* Successively there were added the *chūe-fu* (728), the *jutō-e-fu* (759) which was afterwards changed into *konoe-fu* (775), the *gwai-e-fu,* which together numbered 8 in all. In 772, the *gwai-e-fu* was suppressed.

E-fumi, 繪踏 (Lit. : — picture trampling). The obligation to trample on the cross at the taking of the census. This law was enacted in 1716 in order to make certain of the extinction of Christianity. It is said to have been applied even to foreigners who landed in Japan.

Egawa-Tarōzaemon, 江川太郎左衛門 (1801-1855). A certain *samurai* in the service of the *Shōgun.* In his youth, he studied Dutch. At his father's death (1835), he succeeded him as *daikwan* of *Nirayama* (*Izu*). In 1839, *Torii Yōzō,* having been charged with the inspection of *Shimōsa, Kazusa, Awa, Sagami, Izu, Ōshima,* he accompanied him and on his return, he drew up a statement on the best means of defending the coasts. He was then made professor of target shooting and military drill. He soon had 4000 pupils, to whom he gave a hat of particular form, which was called the *Nirayama-bōshi.* When, in 1849, an English vessel came to anchor at *Shimoda,* he sent her off without parley. After the arrival of Commodore Perry, he took a very active part in the construction of the *Shinagawa* forts.

Eguchi, 江口. In *Settsu,* a place where *Miyoshi Masanaga* (*Sōzan*) built a castle, and where, besieged in 1549 by *Miyoshi Chōkei,* he was defeated and killed.

Ehime-ken, 愛媛縣. A department formed by the province of *Iyo.* — Pop. 1,056,000. — Capital, *Matsuyama* (36,600 inh.). — Principal towns : *Imabaru* (15,000 inh.), *Uwajima* (13,250 inh.), *Besshi-yama* (11,600 inh.), etc.

Eichō, 永長. *Nengō :* 1096.

Ei-en, 永延. *Nengō :* 987-988.

Eigen-ji, 永元寺. A temple founded in *Ōmi,* by the bonze *Genkō* (1322), which became the seat of a subdivision of the *Rinzai* branch of the *Zen* sect.

Eigwa-monogatari, 榮華物語. A work composed in 1027 by *Akazome no Emon.* It embraces the history of two centuries (850-1027) and especially describes the magnificence (*eigwa*) of *Fujiwara Michinaga.*

Eihō, 永保. *Nengō :* 1081-1083.

Eiji, 永治. *Nengō :* 1141.

Eijō, 永承. *Nengō :* 1046-1052. — It is also called *Eishō.*

Eikwan, 永觀. *Nengō :* 983-984.

Eikwan-ji, 永觀寺. A Buddhist temple erected in *Kyōto* (855) by the bonze *Shinsho.* It is the seat of the *Seizan* branch of the *Jōdo* sect. The temple was rebuilt on a new and greater plan in 983, (*Eikwan* 1 *nen*) by the bonze *Eikwan,* hence its name.

Eikyō, 永亨. *Nengō:* 1429-1440.

Eikyō no ran, 永亨亂. A civil war which arose in *Kwantō* when the *Kwanryō Mochiuji,* irritated at not having been made *shōgun,* refused obedience to the elected *Shōgun Yoshinori,* commenced war against *Uesugi Norizane* and was finally condemned to commit *hara-kiri* (1439).

Eikyū, 永久. *Nengō:* 1113-1117.

Eiman, 永萬. *Nengō:* 1165.

Einin, 永仁. *Nengō;* 1293-1298.

Einin-shinnō, 桀仁親王, (1356-1416). Was the son of the emperor *Sukō* of the northern dynasty. The latter disposed of his throne (1352) in favor of his brother *Go-Kōgon,* who, in his turn, abdicated in 1371. *Einin* then desired to succeed him, but the *Kwanryō Hosokawa Yoriyuki* caused *Go-Enyū,* the son of *Go-Kogon,* to be elected: hence the rivalry between the two ex-emperors. At the death of *Sukō* (1398) his domains returned to the crown to the great disappointment of *Einin,* who then retired to *Daikōmyō-ji* to become a bonze under the name of *Tsūchi.* However shortly after he inherited the palace and possessions of prince *Naohito* in *Harima.* In 1403, he took up his residence in *Saga* (*Yamashiro*). He is the ancestor of the princes *Arisugawa.*

Eiraku-sen, 永樂錢. Copper coins made in *China* during the *Eiraku* era (1403-1424) and imported in great quantities into Japan. They circulated for a long time, and were also called *eisen.*

Eiroku, 永祿. *Nengō:* 1558-1569.

Eiroku-ji, 永祿寺. See *Namban-ji.*

Eiryaku, 永曆. *Nengō:* 1160.

Eisai, 榮西 (1141-1215). A famous bonze born in *Bitchū* of the *Kayō* family. At the age of 14, he entered the monastery at *Hiei-zan.* In 1168, he went to China, visited the temples of *Tendai-zan,* and soon came back to Japan. Then, with the intention of going as far as India, he embarked again in 1187, and went first to *Tchekiang.* However contrary winds prevented the voyage he had projected. He therefore remained at the *Tendai-zan,* and came back to Japan in 1191. The following year, he erected the *Shōfuku-ji* in *Hakata* (*Chikuzen*). The *Shōgun Yoriie* having had the *Kennin-ji* built in *Kyōto* appointed *Eisai* chief (1202). It was then that he propagated the *Zen* sect doctrine which he had brought from China. In 1203, he was raised to the dignity of *Dai-sōjō.* After having been called to *Kamakura* in order to erect the *Jūfuku-ji,* he died at the age of 75 years. He was given the posthumous title of *Zenkō-kokushi. Eisai* introduced the cultivation of tea into Japan. After his return from China, he planted some in *Chikuzen,* then in the neighborhood of *Kyōto* but the people rejected the beverage as a poison. *Eisai* then composed a book (*Kissa-yōjō-ki*) in which he enumerated the hygienic qualities of tea; he more-over had, the good fortune of curing the *Shōgun Sanetomo* with tea. From that time, the cause was gained: the cultivation of tea spread, and soon was in daily use among the people.

Eishō, 永正. *Nengō:* 1504–1520.

Eisō, 永祚. *Nengō:* 989.

Eitoku, 永德. *Nengō* of the northern dynasty: 1381–1383.

Eiwa, 永和. *Nengō* of the northern dynasty: 1375–1378.

Ei-zan, 叡山. See *Hiei-zan.*

Eji, 衛士. Soldiers of the imperial guard belonging to the *Ejifu.* Towards 900, their number was limited to 600. They guarded the gates of the palace, the eight ministries. etc.

Ejifu, 衛士府. A corps of the imperial guard. Besides guarding the palace, they escorted the carriage of the emperor. In 808, the *emonfu* was suppressed and its duties joined to the *ejifu.* Gradually the functions of the *ejifu* were ascribed to the *Kebiishi.*

Ekei, 惠瓊. See *Ankokuji Ekei.*

Ekiba, 驛馬. Relay horses at the disposal of express messengers of the government. In case of urgency, they suspended a little bell (*ekirei*) at the collar of the horse in order to give notice of their arrival, and thus found fresh horses day and night. According to the importance of the roads, every relay had to keep 20, 10, or 5 horses.

Ekwan, 慧觀. A Korean bonze who came to Japan in 625. He established his residence at the *Genkō-ji,* and began to preach the two sects *Sanron* and *Jōjitsu,* which no more exist.

Embun, 延文. *Nengō* of the northern dynasty: 1356-1360.

Emi no Oshikatsu, 惠美押勝. See *Fujiwara-Nakamaro.*

Emma-ō, 閻魔王. The king of the Buddhist hell, who judges the souls of the dead and determines the punishment due to their sins.

Emonfu, 衛門府. A guard of the imperial palace. At the beginning, this function was performed by the two families *Ōtomo* and *Kumebe,* and, after the extinction of the latter, by the *Ōtomo* and the *Saiki.* In 643, the empress *Kōgyoku* created the *Emonfu* which comprised the *Kadobe,* the *Mononobe,* the *Eji,* the *Hayato,* etc.

Empō, 延實. *Nengō:* 1673–1680.

Emura Sensai, 江村專齋, (1533–1633). His true name was *Munemoto.* He was a physician in the service of *Katō Kiyomasa.* After the fall of the *Katō* family (1632), he went to *Kyōto.* He was then 100 years old. The ex-emperor *Go-Mi-no-o* wished to see him, and asked for the secret of his longevity:—"It is temperance (*sessei*)", he answered. The emperor loaded him with presents. Soon afterwards he died. One of his friends, *Itō Tan-an,* under the title of *Rōjin-monogatari* (statements of an old man), collected the propositions *Sensai* liked to propound.

Enami, 榎並. In *Settsu,* a castle in which *Kusunoki Masanori* established himself after his defection (1369), and from which he fought against his former partisans, the *Wada,* etc. At a later epoch, the castle was the scene of the wars between *Miyoshi Chōkei* and his relation *Masanaga* (1549).

Ena-zan, 惠那山. A mountain (2,240 met.) between *Mino* and *Shinano.*

Enchin, 圓珍 (814-891). A bonze who went to China in 853 and brought back the doctrine of the *Jimon* branch of the *Tendai* sect (858). In 927, the emperor *Daigo* bestowed on him the posthumous title of *Chishō-Daishi*.

Enchō, 延長. *Nengō:* 923-930.

Endō, 遠藤. A *daimyō* family originating in *Mino* and descended from the *Taira*. The family first resided at *Hachiman* (*Mino*), from 1600 to 1698, then at *Mikami* (*Ōmi*-12,000 k.). After the Restoration, they resumed the name of *Tō* which they bore before the shōgunate of the *Tokugawa* = Now Viscount.

Endō Moritō, 遠藤盛遠. See *Mongaku-Shōnin*.

Engaku-ji, 圓覺寺. A temple built at *Kamakura* in 1282 by *Hōjō Tokimune*. It became the seat of a subdivision of the *Rinzai* branch of the *Zen* sect. The bonze *Sogen* (*Bukkō-Zenji*) was its first chief.

Engen, 延元. *Nengō:* 1336-1339.

Engi, 延喜. *Nengō:* 901-922.

Engi-shiki, 延喜式. A collection in 50 volumes of the regulations concerning the ceremonies of the palace, the audiences of the officials, the customs of the provinces, etc. It was published during the *Engi* era (927), hence its name. It was the emperor *Daigo* that charged his minister *Fujiwara Tokihira* with superintending this publication; after *Tokihira's* death (909) his brother *Tadahira* continued the work. — In 1818, *Matsudaira Naritake*, *daimyō* of *Matsue* (*Izumo*), revised it and added ten supplementary volumes.

Enkei, 延慶. *Nengō:* 1308-1310.

Enkō-Daishi, 圓光大師. See *Genkū*.

Enkwan, 圓觀. A bonze, chief of the *Tōji* temple in *Kyōto*. In 1331, he joined a plot against the *Hōjō* and was exiled into *Mutsu*. After the taking of *Kamakura* in 1333, he returned to his temple, where he died in 1356.

Enkyō, 延亨. *Nengō:* 1744-1747.

Enkyū, 延久. *Nengō:* 1069-1073.

Ennin, 圓仁. See *Jikaku-Daishi*.

En no Matsubara, 役松原. The name of an old garden in the precincts of the imperial palace at *Kyōto*. The garden has often been sung in poetry.

En no Shōkaku, 役小角. Was born in 634 in the *Yamato* province. He studied Buddhism and, when 32 years old, retired to mount *Katsuragi*, where he lived in solitude for over 30 years. Having been accused of sorcery, he was exiled in 699 into one of the *Izu* islands, but was pardoned some years later. It is said that one of his practices was to ascend the highest mountains in order to consecrate their summits to *Shaka*.

EN NO SHŌKAKU.

En-ō, 延應. *Nengō:* 1239.

Enomoto, 榎本. A *samurai* family which was ennobled in 1885 ; the chief of the family to-day is Viscount.

—— **Takeaki, 武揚.** Was born in *Edo* in 1836. After having finished his studies at the *Shōhei-gakkō*, he became an officer in the *Shōgun's* navy, was sent to Holland in 1860 and came back in 1866. At the time of the Imperial Restoration, he left with several men-of-war for *Hakodate*, where, with *Ōtori Keisuke*, he continued the struggle for six months. He surrendered to general *Kuroda Kiyotaka*, on the condition that he alone would be responsible for this campaign. He was imprisoned in *Tōkyō* and set free three years later at the request of his conqueror, general *Kuroda* and of Marshal *Saigō*. Soon after, he was appointed general secretary of the *Kaitakushi* (department of the *Yezo* colonization) ; it was then that he caused the mines of *Ishikari* and *Sorachi* to be worked. In 1873, he was nominated vice-admiral, afterwards ambassador to Russia. It was in this capacity that he concluded the treaty by which the southern part of Saghalien (*Karafuto*) was exchanged for the Kurile Islands (*Chishima*). Ambassador to *Peking* in 1882, Viscount in 1885, Admiral *Enomoto* has since been Minister of Communications, Minister of Education, and of Foreign Affairs. He is now a member of the Privy Council.

Enomoto Kikaku, 榎本機角 (1661-1707.) A pupil of *Bashō;* he became famous in the composition of *haikai* (poetry of 17 syllables).

E-no-shima, 江島. A little island in *Sagami*, near *Kamakura*, dedicated to the goddess *Benten*, who is said to have caused it to rise from the bottom of the sea, in the sixth century.

Enryaku, 延曆. *Nengō:* 782–805.

Enryaku-ji, 延曆寺. A temple founded by *Dengyō-Daishi* during the *Enryaku* era, at the summit of *Hiei-zan*. For centuries it was the seat of the *Tendai* sect. It was built to protect the Imperial palace against "noxious" influences of the N-E. Gradually other temples were erected around it, and the power of the bonzes steadily increased. They even kept a considerable army, which became the terror of *Kyōto* and its neighbourhood. It is especially with regard to them that the emperor *Shirakawa* said : "There are three things which I cannot bring under obedience : the water of the *Kamo-gawa*, the dice of the *sugoroku* game, and the bonzes on the mountain." To reduce them to obedience, the iron-hand of *Nobunaga* was necessary : in 1571 he burnt the temples and massacred all the bonzes. Since then some temples have been rebuilt, but are greatly inferior in grandeur to the former ones.

Enshi, 園司. Formerly the governor, or administrator of a *shō-en*.

Enshū, 遠州. The Chinese name of the *Tōtōmi* province.

Enshū-nada, 遠州灘. The sea of *Enshū*, or *Tōtōmi*.

Enshū-ryū, 遠州流. See *Kobori Masakazu*.

Entoku, 延德. *Nengō:* 1489-1491.

Enya Takasada, 塩谷高貞. A descendant of *Sasaki Yoshikiyo* and son of *Sadakiyo* who was the first to assume the name of *Enya;* he was appointed *Kebiishi* and *Izumo no shugo*. When *Go-Daigo* escaped from *Oki* and established himself at *Funanoe-sen*, *Takasada* submitted to him and escorted him to *Kyōto* (1333). In 1335, when vanquished by *Ashikaga Takauji*, he surrendered and joined the party of the northern dynasty. Three years later, he was ordered to collect three hundred boats in *Izumo* and *Hōki* in order to attack *Wakiya Yoshisuke* in *Echizen*: he was about to start, when he was assassinated by *Kō-Moronao* (1338).

En-yu-tennō, 圓融天皇. The 64th Emperor of Japan from 970–984, was prince *Morihira*, the 5th son of *Murakami-tennō*. He succeeded his brother *Reizei* when 11 years old. The *Dajō-daijin Fujiwara Kanemichi*, and then his brother *Yoritada*, governed the empire. Under his reign, *Kyōto* and its neighborhood were infested by robbers. *Minamoto Yorimitsu* was ordered to reduce them and received the title of *Shōgun*. The imperial palace was burnt three times: in 976, 980 and 982. *En-yū* abdicated when 25 years old (984), and died 7 years later.

Erimo-saki, 襟裳岬. A cape south of the *Hitaka* province (*Hokkaidō*).

Eshin, 惠心, (942–1017). A bonze renowned as a scholar, painter and sculptor. He was first called *Urabe Genshin*, entered the *Hiei-zan* at a very early age and became a disciple of *Jie-Daishi*. He then built the *Eshin-in* temple at *Yokawa*, and prepared the foundation of the *Jōdo* sect.

Esshū, 越州. The Chinese name of the 3 provinces, *Echizen*, *Etchū* and *Echigo*.

Eta, 穢多. An inferior class of ancient society, a sort of pariah to whom those trades were reserved which were considered impure, such as those of flayers, tanners, curriers, etc.—It is said that the *eta* were descendants of ancient Korean prisoners or of shipwrecked people that settled in Japan.—The *eta* in *Edo* had the *Danzaemon* for their chief, who gradually became very rich.—In 1871, the name *eta* was abolished, all became *heimin*: hence the name of *shin-heimin* (new *heimin*) often applied to them.

Eta-ga-saki, 穢多崎. A place on the right bank of the *Yodo-gawa*, in *Ōsaka*. During the siege of 1615, John *Akashi Kamon* (*Akashi Morishige*) established himself at that place but was vanquished by the troops of *Hachisuka Iemasa*.

Eta-jima, 江田島. An island (31 Km. in circuit) in the Inland Sea, near *Hiroshima* (*Aki*) where a naval school (*Kaigun-hei-gakkō*) has been established.

Etchū, 越中. One of the seven provinces of *Hokurokudō*. It comprises eight districts belonging to *Toyama-ken*. — Its Chinese name is *Esshū* which it bears together with *Echizen* and *Echigo*.

Etō-Daishi, 惠燈大師. See *Rennyo*.

Etō Shimpei, 江藤新平 (1835-1874). A *samurai* of the *Saga* clan (*Hizen*) who took an active part in the Imperial Restoration. He was successively Vice-Minister of Education, Minister of Justice (1872) *Sangi* (1873). Afterwards, dissatisfied with the policy followed with regard to Korea which he thought too pacific, he entered *Saga*, and tried to incite the whole *Kyūshū* to rebellion. *Ōkubo Toshimichi* was sent to repress the revolt. *Shimpei* was defeated, and fled to *Kagoshima*, where he endeavored to persuade *Saigō Takamori* to join him. From there he went to *Obi* (*Hyūga*), then to *Kōchi* (*Tosa*), everywhere seeking adherents, but he was arrested at *Shimoda* (*Tosa*), conducted to *Saga*, and beheaded on April 13 (1874) with six of his accomplices.

Etorū-jima, 擇捉島. The largest of the *Chishima* (Kurile islands); it is 180 Km. long, its average width is 40 Km.; its principal port is *Shana*. — It was explored in 1798 by *Kondō Morishige*.

Ezan-misaki, 惠山岬. A cape on the east of *Oshima* province (*Hokkaidō*).

Ezo, 蝦夷. See *Hokkaidō*.

Ezo-bugyō, 蝦夷奉行. An office created in 1718 for guarding the coast of *Ezo* and suppressing commerce with China.

Ezo-kwanryō, 蝦夷管領, or *Ezo-daikwan*. An official established in *Tsugaru* during the *Kamakura* era. He had charge of watching the doings of the *Ebisu* in *Mutsu*, *Dewa*, and *Watari-shima* (*Hokkaidō*). Formerly this charge belonged to the *Chinjufu-shōgun* and the *Akita-jō no suke*.

F

Fu, 府 . The seat of an administration ; the chief town of a clan ; a capital ; a storehouse where treasures were kept. — To-day, departments having as chief-city one of the 3 following great towns, *Tōkyō*, *Kyōtō* and *Ōsaka*.

Fubito. 史 . (Lit. : literary men, writers). Officials created by the emperor *Richū* in 403. They collected historical documents in every province. — See *Fumi no obito.*

Fuchū, 府中 . A place in *Hitachi* now called *Ishioka* ; formerly the capital of the province. It was the residence of *Taira Sadamori* whose descendants took the name of *Daijō*. Their castle was called *Fuchū-Ishioka-jō*. In 1590, this castle was destroyed by *Satake Yoshishige*. In 1602, it became the residence of *Rokugō Masanori*, and from 1623 till 1645 that of *Minagawa Takatsune*. In 1700, *Matsudaira Yoritaka*, the 5th son of *Yorifusa* of *Mito* received it in fief (30,000 k.) and his descendants remained there till the Restoration.

Fuchū, 府中 . A place in *Nagato*, the name of which is now *Chōfu*, or *Toyoura*. It was the residence of the Court (*Toyoura no miya*) under the emperor *Chū-ai*, from 193 to 199 and, later on, the capital of the province. *Atsugashi Yoshitake*, after having been appointed *shugo* by *Takauji*, was deposed in 1370 by *Ōuchi Hiroyo*. In 1557 *Fuchū* came into possession of the *Mōri*.

Fuchū, 府中 . A place in *Tsushima*, now called *Izu-no-hara*. It was formerly the capital of the province. In 1666 the *daimyō Sō Yoshizane*, residing until then at *Kanaishi*, transferred his residence to *Fuchū*.

Fuchū, 府中 . A place in *Kai*. — See *Kōfu.*

Fuchū, 府中 . A place in *Suruga*. — See *Shizuoka.*

Fuchū, 府中 . A place in *Echizen*. — See *Fukui.*

Fudai, 譜代 . A hereditary vassal or retainer. *Ieyasu* gave the title of *fudai-daimyō* to those who had embraced his party before the campaign of *Sekigahara* (1600) ; they numbered 176. All important functions were reserved for them.

Fu-Daishi, 傳大師 . A Chinese bonze of the 6th century, generally called *Warai-botoke* (the laughing *Buddha*). He is generally represented between his two sons *Fuken* and *Fujō*.

Fudō, 不動 . A Buddhist divinity (probably the same as *Dainichi*) which has power to foil the snares of the devils. *Fudō* is represented with a dreadful expression and surrounded by flames ; in the right hand he holds a sword, (*gōma no ken*) to strike the demons, in the left hand, a cord (*baku no nawa*) to bind them.

Fudoki, 風土記 . In 713, the Empress *Gemmei* ordered all the provinces to give a report describing the towns, villages, rivers, mountains, productions, customs, etc. These reports were called *fudoki ;* only four are still extant: they are those of *Hitachi, Harima, Izumo* and *Bungo*.

Fuefuki-gawa, 笛 吹 川. A river, the source of which is in *Kokushi-ga-take* (*Kai*) and which by its union with the *Kamanashi-gawa*, forms the *Fuji-kawa*. It is also called *Netori-gawa*.

Fuefuki-toge, 笛 吹 峠. A pass in the north of *Musashi*. *Nitta Yoshimune* was defeated there in 1352 by *Ashikaga Takauji*.

Fugen, 普 賢. A Buddhist god, patron of those who practise *hokke-zammai* (ecstatic contemplation). His statue is often seen at the right hand of that of *Shaka*.

Fugo, 封 戶. Formerly the number of houses, or of families given as serfs to princes and Court officials according to their rank (*i*) and their office (*kwan*): the *Dajōdaijin* were accorded 2000; the *San-gū*, 1500; the princes, 800; the nobles of the first rank (*ichi-i*), 300, etc.

Fujieda, 藤 枝. A town in *Echizen*. From 1583 till 1600 it was the residence of *Niwa Nagamasa* who was dispossessed of it after the battle of *Sekigahara*.

Fujii, 藤 井. A place in *Mikawa* where *Matsudaira Nobukazu* defeated the troops of *Ikkō-shū* (1563).

Fujii, 藤 井. A *kuge* family, descended from the *Fujiwara*. Its head is now Viscount.

Fujii-dera, 葛 井 寺. A temple founded by *Gyōgi Bosatsu* in *Nagano* (*Kawachi*) in 725. It was the scene of *Kusunoki Masatsura's* victory over *Hosokawa Akiuji* (1348). In 1615, *Sanada Yukimura, Mōri Katsunaga,* and *Gotō Mototsugu* fought a battle near that temple against the army of the *Shōgun*.

Fujii Takanao, 藤 井 高 尙 (1764-1840). A man of letters, pupil of *Motoori Norinaga*. He was the head of the *Kibitsu-jinja* temple (*Bitchū*).

Fujii Teikan, 藤 井 貞 幹 (1722-1789). A man of letters and a historian of *Kyōto*.

Fujii Umon, 藤 井 右 門 (1720-1767). His true name was *Nao-akira, Yamato no kami*. He was beheaded for having composed and published a book favorable to the imperial authority and hostile to the shōgunate.

Fuji-kawa, 富 士 川. A river (118 Km.) formed by the junction of the *Fuefuki-gawa* and the *Kamanashi-gawa*. It flows from the west of Mount *Fuji* and empties itself into *Suruga* bay at *Iwabuchi*. It is renowned for its rapids.

Fujimi-hōzō-bangashira, 富 士 見 寶 藏 番 頭. A title created in 1639 and applied to the guardian of the storehouses which contained the treasures of the *Tokugawa Shōgun*. These storehouses were situated in the quarter of *Edo* called *Fujimi-chō*.

Fujin, 夫 人. Also *mime, kisaki, ōtoji,* names to designate secondary wives of the emperor. The *Taikō* code fixed their number at three; they were to be selected from among the daughters of the ministers. The term *fujin* ceased to be in use towards 850.

Fujinami, 藤 波. A *kuge* family descended from *Fujiwara Moro-zane* (1042-1101). The head of the family, is now Viscount.

Fuji no makigari, 富士牧狩. Hunting expeditions of the *Shōgun* or the regents of *Kamakura* in the neighborhood of mount *Fuji*. For that purpose they established a hunting-seat at *Gotemba;* hence the name of that place.

Fuji no yama, 富士山. Also *Fuji-san*, a mountain (3780 met.) between the provinces of *Kai* and *Suruga*. Before the annexation of Formosa, it was the highest mountain in the Japanese Empire. According to tradition, it was formed in 286 B. C. by an earthquake which sunk the bed of lake *Biwa*. It is a volcano, that had been several times in a state of eruption. Those of 800, 864 and 1707 were especially remarkable. The last eruption produced *Hōei-zan* and lasted from December 16, 1707 to January 22, 1708. The mountain is also called *Narusawa no takane, Tokiwa-yama, Hatachi-yama, Chiri-yama, Mie-yama, Nii-yama, Midashi-yama, Mikami-yama, Hagoromo-yama, Otome-yama, Higashi-yama, Taketori-yama, Sennin-yama, Fuku-kaze-ana-yama, Tōki-shiranu-yama*, etc. Mount *Fuji* has always been an inexhaustible theme for poets, painters, etc.

Fujiōji, 藤大路. A *kuge* family, descended from *Fujiwara Nagayoshi* (800-854). The head of the family is now Viscount.

Fujioka, 藤岡. A *samurai* family of the *Kōchi* clan *(Tosa)* ennobled after the Restoration. The head of the family is Viscount.

Fujishima, 藤島. A place in *Echizen*, where *Nitta Yoshisada* was killed by an arrow (1338) in a fight against *Ashikaga Takauji*. In 1876, a temple was erected there in his honor.

Fujita, 藤田. A *samurai* family of the *Mito* clan *(Hitachi)*.

—— **Tōko, 東湖** (1806-1855). A counsellor of the famous *Nariakira* whom he encouraged in his hatred against foreigners and with whom he was shut up at *Komagome (Edo)* (1844). At the great earthquake in 1855, he was crushed to death under the ruins of the house of *Nariakira*.

—— **Koshirō, 小四郎** (1842-1865). The 4th son of the above. Full of indignation that, despite the orders of *Kyōto*, the *Bakufu* was not in haste to expel the foreigners, he in 1864 united with *Tamaru Naosuke*, called about him the *samurai* of like disposition, and with them formed an army which encamped at *Tsukuba-san* and defeated the troops sent from *Edo* to reduce them. After that, *Koshirō* fought all those of the *Mito* clan who showed themselves favorable to Europeans. Later he repaired to *Kyōto*, but was arrested on the road and decapitated by order of the *Shōgun*.

Fujitani, 藤谷. A *kuge* family descended from *Fujiwara Nagaie* (1005-1064). = Now Viscount.

Fujitani, 藤谷. A renowned family of literati under the *Tokugawa*. The best known among them are: *Shigeaya* (1738-1779) and *Mitsue* (1768-1823).

Fujito, 藤戸. A village in the peninsula of *Kojima (Bizen)*. In 1184, the *Taira* anchored their numerous boats near that place. The *Minamoto*, who were pursuing them on land, had no boats at their disposal and did not know how to engage in battle, when *Sasaki Moritsuna*, measuring the depth of the water with a bamboo, advanced towards the

Taira and defeated them. As a reward, *Moritsuna* received the peninsula of *Kojima* as a fief.

Fujito-kyō, 藤戸峽. The isthmus of the peninsula of *Kojima* (*Bizen*).

Fujiwara, 藤原. A place in *Yamato*, which was the residence of *Nakatomi no Kamatari*; hence the privilege given him by the emperor *Tenchi* to take for himself and his descendants the name of *Fujiwara* (669).

Fujiwara, 藤原. A family which descended from *Ame no Koyane no Mikoto*, one of the faithful followers of *Amaterasu* and of *Ninigi no Mikoto*. Until *Kamatari*, the members of that family bore the name of *Nakatomi*.

I. — MINISTERS, STATESMEN, WARRIORS, ETC.

Kamatari-Fuhito
- Muchimaro
  - Toyonari -Tsuginawa
  - Nakamaro -Asakari
- Fusasaki
  - Nagate
  - Kiyokawa
  - Matate -Uchimaro-Fuyutsugu
    - Yoshifusa-Mototsune
    - Yoshisuke
    - Yoshikado(*Kwanjuji*)
  - Uona -Fujinari -Toyozawa -Murao -Hidesato.
  - Kaedemaro-Sonondo.
- Umakai
  - Hirotsugu
  - Kiyonari -Tanetsugu-Nakanari
  - Yoshitsugu
  - Momokawa-Otsugu
  - Kurajimaro
- Maro —Hamanari

—— **Kamatari**, 鎌足 (614–669). First called *Nakatomi no Kamako*, was a faithful servant of *Karu no Ōji*, and with him plotted the ruin of the *Soga* whose ambition was unlimited. One day, whilst the empress *Kōgyoku* gave public audience to the envoy of Korea, *Soga no Iruka* was assassinated in her presence, and *Soga no Emishi*, his father was killed in his own house (644). The empress then abdicated and *Karu no Ōji* succeeded her under the name of *Kōtoku-tennō*. The new emperor inaugurated his reign by introducing great changes in the form of government. This system was called the reform of *Taikwa* (*Taikwa no kaishin*). *Kamatari* was appointed *Naijin* and took an active part in public affairs during the reigns of *Kōtoku*, *Saimei*, and *Tenchi*. In 669, he fell dangerously ill. The emperor then nominated him *dai-shokukwan* and granted him and his descendants the family name of *Fujiwara*. His temple is in *Tamu-no-mine* (*Yamato*).

FUJIWARA KAMATARI.

—— **Fuhito**, 不比等 (659–720). A son of *Kamatari*, and minister during the reigns of *Jitō*, *Mommu*, *Gemmei*, and *Genshō*. In 708, he was nominated *Udaijin*, and in 718 refused the title of *Dajō-daijin*, which title the empress however conferred on him after his death. In 760, he received the posthumous name of *Tankai*. His eldest daughter, *Miyako no Iratsume*, had been married to *Mommu-tennō* and was the mother of *Shōmu;* his second daughter, *Kōmyō-shi,* married *Shōmu,* and became the mother of the empress *Kōken. Fuhito* also had 4 sons who are the ancestors of the four branches of the house of *Fujiwara: Muchimaro,* the *Nan-ke; Fusasaki,* the *Hoku-ke; Umakai,* the *Shiki-ke, Maro,* the *Kyō-ke.*

—— **Muchimaro,** 武智麿 (680–737). Became *Udaijin* in 734, and *Sadaijin* on the eve of his death. As his domains were situated south of those of his brother *Fusasaki,* his family was called *Nan-ke* (southern branch), and that of *Fusasaki, Hoku-ke* (Northern branch).

—— **Fusasaki,** 房前 (682–737). Had charge of the inspection of *Tōkaidō* and *Tōsandō* (702); he became minister of Police (*Mimbu-kyō*).

—— **Umakai,** 宇合 (694–737). The third son of *Fuhito,* was *Hitachi no kami.* He was charged with inspecting *Awa, Shimōsa,* and *Kazusa.* He suppressed a rebellion of the *Ebisu* in *Mutsu* (724) and was appointed *Sangi* when this title was created (731). As he was at the same time *Shikibu-kyō* (master of ceremonies), the name of *Shiki-ke* was given to his family.

—— **Maro,** 麿 (695-737). The 4th son of *Fuhito,* was *Hyōbu-kyō, Sangi, Sayu-kyō-tayū;* hence the name of *Kyo-ke* given to his family. The four brothers died of small-pox the same year.

—— **Toyonari,** 豊成 (704–765). A son of *Muchimaro,* was minister during the reigns of *Genshō* and *Shōmu.* In 757, he intended to have prince *Shioyaki-ō* nominated *taishi* but his brother *Nakamaro,* who enjoyed the full confidence of the empress *Kōken,* caused prince *Ōi-ō* to be elected and *Toyonari* was exiled to *Tsukushi,* to the *Dazaifu,* whence he was recalled only after the death of *Nakamaro* (764). He is also called *Naniwa no Daijin.*

—— **Nakamaro,** 仲麿 (710-764). Was a son of *Muchimaro.* In 757, he succeeded in having prince *Ōi-ō* nominated *taishi.* The latter having ascended the throne two years later, loaded him with favors and bestowed the title of *Emi no Oshikatsu* on him. Afterwards, jealous of the influence the bonze *Dōkyō* had over the ex-empress *Kōken, Nakamaro* raised troops in order to seize him but pursued as far as *Ōmi* by his cousins *Yoshitsugu* and *Kurajimaro,* he was defeated and killed with his two sons *Materu* and *Kuzumaro.*

—— **Nagate,** 永手 (714-771). A son of *Fusasaki,* was minister during the reigns of *Shōmu, Kōken, Junnin, Shōtoku.* At the latter's death, he aided in the nomination of the emperor *Kōnin,* who conferred on him the first rank of the first class (*shō-ichi-i*). As he resided at *Naga-oka,* he is often known by the name of *Nagaoka-Daijin.*

—— **Kiyokawa,** 清河. Son of *Fusasaki,* became *Sangi,* (749) and ambassador to China (*Kentō-shi*) the following year. He went as far as *Tchang-ngan* in the province of *Chensi,* where he was received by the emperor *Gensō* (*Hiuen-hoan*). He embarked for Japan with *Abe no Nakamaro,* but their vessel was driven by a storm to the coasts of Annam where the natives massacred many of their servants. They were however able to reach the coasts of China where they settled and obtained offices and dignities from the emperor. *Kiyokawa* died when 73 years old.

—— **Matate,** 眞楯 (716-767). Was another son of *Fusasaki*, and was successively *Sangi, Dainagon,* and *Shikibu-kyō.*

—— **Uona,** 魚名 (721-783). A fourth son of *Fusasaki,* was in the service of *Shōmu, Kōken, Junnin,* and *Kōnin.* He was *Sadaijin* when at the accession of *Kwammu* to the throne (782), he was implicated in a conspiracy against the new emperor, and exiled to *Tsukushi.* Having been pardoned soon afterwards, he returned to the capital where he died the following year. He is the ancestor of the *Mutsu, Fujiwara,* the *Date,* etc.

—— **Hirotsugu,** 廣嗣 (715-741). Was the eldest son of *Umakai.* In his youth, he simultaneously studied Buddhism, military art, astronomy, etc. Having been made governor of the *Dazaifu,* he took umbrage at the great influence of the bonze *Gembō* over the Court, and rebelled. *Ōno no Azumabito* and *Ki no Iimaro* were sent against him. *Hirotsugu* was defeated, arrested at *Nagano* (*Hizen*) and beheaded.

—— **Yoshitsugu,** 良繼 (716-777). Was the second son of *Umakai.* When his brother *Hirotsugu* revolted, he was exiled to *Izu* (740). Having been recalled at the death of *Gembō* in 746, he was appointed *Kōzuke no kami.* Afterwards, hostile to his cousin *Nakamaro,* then all-powerful, he was degraded and banished to *Ōmi.* In 764, he contributed to the defeat of *Nakamaro* and was nominated *Dazai-shi,* and afterwards *Nai-daijin.* His daughter *Otomuro* became the consort of *Kwammu* and mother of *Heijō* and *Saga.*

—— **Momokawa,** 百川 (722-779). Was a son of *Umakai.* He was minister during the reign of *Kōken* and *Shōtoku.* At the latter's death (770) notwithstanding the opposition of the *Udaijin Kibi no Mabi,* he succeeded with the help of *Nagate* and *Yoshitsugu* in having *Kōnin,* who was 62 years old, nominated. When there was question of choosing the *taishi* (crown prince), *Momokawa* proposed *Yamabe-shinnō,* the eldest son of *Kōnin* but the emperor was in favor of *Sakabito-naishinnō,* a daughter of one of his concubines. *Momokawa* did not desist and remained before the gate of the palace, without returning to his residence, for forty days, when finally the emperor yielded to his advice. So he gained his cause and *Yamabe-shinnō* (later on the emperor *Kwammu*) was nominated (773).

—— **Kurajimaro,** 藏下麿 (734-775). Another son of *Umakai,* was *Izumo no suke* and *Bizen no kami.* He took part in the campaign against his cousin *Nakamaro* (764). In 767 he had charge of inspecting the provinces of *Iyo* and *Tosa,* and afterwards became successively *Hyōbu-kyō, Dazai-shi* and *Sangi.*

—— **Hamanari,** 濱成 (716-782). A son of *Maro,* was *Sangi, Danjō no suke, Gyōbu-kyō,* finally *Dazai-shi* (781).

—— **Tsuginawa,** 繼繩 (727-796). Was a son of *Toyonari.* The *Ebisu* of *Mutsu* having revolted in 780, massacred the *Azechi Ki no Hirozumi. Tsuginawa,* having been nominated *Sei-i-taishi,* together with *Ki no Kosami,* was ordered to reduce them to submission. In 783, he was appointed *Dainagon* and afterwards, *Dazai-shi,* and, in

790, *Udaijin*. He is also known by the name of *Momozono no Udaijin*.

—— **Uchimaro,** 内麿 (756–812). A son of *Matate*, was successively *Chūnagon*, *Dainagon*, *Udaijin*. He is also known by the name of *Nagaoka-Daijin*.

—— **Sonondo,** 園人 (756–818). A son of *Kaedemaro*, was *Mino no kami*, *Yamato no kami*, *Ukyō-tayū*, *Kunai-kyō*. He was charged with the inspection of *San-yō-dō*, then of the compilation of the *Shōjiroku* (genealogy of the Court Nobles). He is also known by the name of *Yamashina-Daijin*.

—— **Tanetsugu,** 種繼 (737–785). Was a son of *Kiyonari*. The *taishi*, *Sawara-shinnō*, having asked that *Saeki no Imagebito* be nominated *Sangi*, *Tanetsugu* opposed the nomination. In order to escape the hatred of the prince, he retired to *Nagaoka* (*Yamashiro*) but while the emperor *Kwammu* was at *Nara*, in 785, the *taishi* had *Tanetsugu* assassinated. He received the posthumous title of *Sadaijin*, and later, that of *Dajō-daijin*.

—— **Otsugu,** 緒嗣 (773–843). A son of *Momokawa*, was minister during the reigns of *Saga*, *Junwa*, *Nimmyō*. He was also charged with the publication of the *Nihon-kōki*, a history of Japan from 792 till 830 (40 vols.).

—— **Asakari,** 朝獦. A son of *Nakamaro*, was *Mutsu no kami*, *Azechi*, *Chinjufu-Shōgun*. He constructed the forts of *Momonō* (*Mutsu*) and *Okatsu* (*Dewa*) against the *Ebisu*. He was deprived of his domains at the time of the revolt of his father (764).

—— **Oguromaro,** 小黒麿 (733–794). A grandson of *Fusasaki*, took a prominent part in the campaign against the *Ebisu* in 780. He was *Ise no kami*, *Mutsu no kami*, *Dainagon*, etc.

—— **Tsunetsugu,** 常繼 (796–840). A son of *Kadonomaro*, was *Dazai-shi* (837), afterwards ambassador to China (*Tō*).

—— **Nakanari,** 仲成. A son of *Tanetsugu*, was made *Sangi* by *Kwammu*. In 810, he was put to death for being implicated in a conspiracy with his sister *Kusuriko*, the object of which was to restore *Heijō* to the throne and to transfer the capital to *Nara*.

—— **Fuyutsugu,** 冬嗣 (775–826). A son of *Uchimaro*, cultivated literature and the military arts. He was minister during the reigns of *Kwammu*, *Heijō*, *Saga*, and *Seiwa*. He is known by the name of *Kan-in no Daijin*. His daughter *Nobu-ko*, married *Nimmyō-tennō*, and became the mother of *Montoku*.

—— **Yoshifusa,** 良房 (804–872). Was a son of *Fuyutsugu*, and minister during the reigns of *Seiwa* and *Nimmyō*. *Montoku* made him *Dajō-daijin* in 857 and allowed him to wear his sword even when coming to the palace but *Yoshifusa* refused that honor. At the accession of *Seiwa* (859), *Yoshifusa* being his grandfather, became *Sesshō* (regent). In order to give the young emperor an idea of what field-labour was like, he ordered *Ki no Imamori*, governor of *Yamashiro*, to send a certain number of labourers that they might till the soil in the emperor's presence (864). In 866, he asked to be relieved from his functions, but the emperor never would give his assent. He published the *Shoku-Nihon-kōki* (the history of Japan from 833 to 850) in 30 volumes. *Yoshifusa* is known by the name of *Somedono no Daijin* or *Shirakawa-dono*. His wife was the daughter of the emperor *Saga ;* his daughter *Aki-ko* was the mother of *Seiwa*. It is with him that the great power of the *Fujiwara* House and the line of the *Sesshō* and the *Kwampaku* began.

—— **Yoshisuke,** 良 相 (813–867). A son of *Fuyutsugu*, was *Sakon-e-shōshō*, *Udaijin* (857). He is known by the name of *Nishi-Sanjō-daijin*.

—— **Yoshikado,** 良 門 . A son of *Fuyutsugu*, was *Dajō-daijin*, and the first that bore the name of *Kwanjuji*. He was the ancestor of the *Ucsugi*, the *Ii*, of *Nichiren*, etc.

—— **Mototsune,** 基 經 (836–891). A son of *Nagayoshi*, was adopted by his uncle *Yoshifusa*, and, in 872, appointed *Udaijin*. At the accession of *Yōzei* (877) then only ten years old, he became *Sesshō*, and afterwards *Dajō-daijin*. The emperor giving signs of insanity, *Mototsune* deposed him and wished to replace him by prince *Tsune-sada-shinnō*. The latter having refused, he chose a son of *Nimmyō-tennō*, *Tokiyasu-shinnō*, 55 years old who became the emperor *Kōkō* (885). When this emperor died in 888, *Mototsune* raised the latter's son *Uda* to the throne, and continued to govern in his name. *Mototsune* was the first who received the title of *Kwampaku*, which was given him instead of *Sesshō* when *Yōzei* attained majority (882). He has written a historical work in ten volumes, the *Montoku-jitsuroku* (the history of the reign of *Montoku*). He is often designated by the name of *Horikawa-daijin*.

—— **Sugane,** 菅 根 (856–908). A son of *Yoshitoshi*, became *Shikibushōsuke*. He took part in the accusations of *Tokihira*, etc. against *Sugawara Michizane*, and was nominated *Sangi*.

—— **Yamakage,** 山 蔭 (824–888). A son of *Takafusa*, was *Chūnagon*, and *Mimbu-kyō*.

—— **Yasunori,** 保 則 (825–895). A son of *Sadao*. In 878, when the *Ebisu* of *Dewa* revolted and burnt the castle of *Akita*, *Yasunori* was sent against them. Having been appointed *Dazai-daini* in 887, he feigned ill-health in order not to be obliged to go to *Tsukushi*. He was *Sangi* and *Mimbu-kyō*.

—— **Tokihira,** 時 平 (871–909). A son of *Mototsune*, was successively *Kebiishi* (892) *Dainagon* (897), and finally *Sadaijin*. Then, jealous of the increasing influence acquired by *Sugawara Michizane*, in concert with *Minamoto Hikaru*, *Fujiwara Sugane*, etc., he accused *Sugawara Michizane* of plotting to dethrone the emperor *Daigo* in order to replace him by the emperor's brother *Tōkiyo no Shinnō*, who was the son-in-law of *Michizane*. The emperor then only 17 years old gave credit to the calumny, and *Michizane* was banished to *Tsukushi* with the title of *Dazai no gon-no-sotsu* (901). *Tokihira* now governed according to his pleasure. He presided at the redaction of the *Sandai-jitsuroku* (the history of the reigns of *Seiwa*, *Yōzei*, and *Kōkō*). He is known by the name of *Hon-in-daijin*.

—— **Nakahira,** 仲平 (875-945). A brother of *Tokihira*, was minister during the reigns of *Daigo* and *Shujaku*. He is known by the name of *Biwa no Daijin*.

—— **Tadahira,** 忠平 (880-949). A son of *Mototsune*, continued the compilation of the *Engi-shiki* code, which had been begun by his brother *Tokihira*, and published it in 50 volumes (927). Having become *Sadaijin* in 924, he was made *Sesshō* at the accession of *Shujaku-tennō* (931), *Kwampaku* in 941, and *Dajō-daijin* in 943. He is known by the name of *Ko-Ichijō-Dajō-daijin*. Towards the end of his life, he being *Dajō-daijin, Saneyori* his eldest son, became *Sadaijin* and *Morosuke*, his second son, *Udaijin*; thus the three great ministries (*san-kō*) were under his control.

SEAL OF
FUJIWARA TADAHIRA
(920).

```
            Tokihira { Akitada
                      { Atsutada
            Nakahira
                       Saneyori { Yoritada { Sanesuke - Sukehira
                                {          { Kintō - Sadayori
                                { Atsutoshi - Sukemasa
                                  Koretada { Korenari
                                           { Yoshikane
                                           { Yoshitaka - Yukinari
Mototsune {                       Kanemichi - Akimitsu
                                            Michitaka { Korechika
                                           {          { Takaie
            Tadahira            Kaneie { Michikane
                      Morosuke {                   Yorimichi-Morozane { Moromichi
                               {                                      { Ietada
                               { Michinaga                           { Masazane
                                            Nagaie (Reizei)
                                            Yorimune (Ishino, Ishiyama, Sono)
                                            Norimichi - Toshiie - Mototoshi
                                 Tamemitsu - Tadanobu
                                 Kinsue - Sanenari - Kinnari - Sanesue - Kinzane
                                 Moromasa- Naritoki - Sanekata
```

—— **Arihira,** 在衡 (892-970). A grandson of *Yamakage*, and adopted by *Ariyori*, was a celebrated man of letters. He was first *Udaijin* and afterwards *Sadaijin*. He is known by the name of *Awada no Sadaijin*.

—— **Tadabumi,** 忠文 (873-947). In 940 he was appointed general (*seitō-taishōgun*) of the army sent against *Taira Masakado* who had revolted: the revolt was promptly suppressed. He was also chosen to reduce *Fujiwara Sumitomo* in *Tsukushi*, but before he arrived the rebellion was at an end. He was then appointed *Mimbu-kyō* and *Kii no Kami*. He is known by the name of *Uji no Mimbu-kyō*.

—— **Hidesato,** 秀郷. A son of *Murao*, who was a descendant of *Uona*. He was governor of *Shimotsuke* when the revolt of *Taira Masakado* broke out (939). Uniting his forces with those of *Taira Sadamori*, governor of *Hitachi*, he marched against the rebel, who was defeated at *Kushima* (*Shimōsa*): *Masakado* having been wounded fell from his horse and *Hidesato* beheaded him with his own hand. Afterwards he was appointed *Chinjufu-Shōgun* and *Musashi no Kami*. He is the ancestor of the *Mutsu Fujiwara* (see *Hidehira, Yasuhira*) and of the *Yamanouchi*, the *Tosa daimyō*.

—— **Akitada,** 顯 忠 (898-965). A son of *Tokihira*, was *Sangi*, afterwards *Udaijin* (960). He is known by the name of *Tomikōji-udaijin*.

—— **Atsutada,** 敦 忠 (906-943). A son of *Tokihira*, was *Gonchūnagon*, but is especially celebrated as a poet. He is known by the name of *Hon-in-Chūnagon*.

—— **Saneyori,** 實 賴 (900-970). The eldest son of *Tadahira*. After having been *Udaijin, Sadaijin, Dajō-daijin*, he became *Kwampaku* in 968, then *Sesshō* at the accession of *En-yū-tennō* (970). He is known by the name of *Ono-miya-dono*.

—— **Morosuke,** 師 輔 (908-960). A son of *Tadahira*, became *Udaijin* in 947. He is known by the names of *Kujō-dono* and *Hōjō-udaijin*.

—— **Yoritada,** 賴 忠 (924-989). A son of *Saneyori*, became *Udaijin* in 971, and succeeded *Koredata* in the functions of *Sesshō* (973), and *Kanemichi* in those of *Kwampaku* (977) ; finally he became *Dajō-daijin* in 978. After his death, he received the title of *Suruga-kō*, but he is better known by the name of *Sanjō-daijin*.

—— **Koretada,** 伊 尹 (924-972). A son of *Morosuke*, became *Udaijin* in 970, *Sesshō* at the death of his uncle *Saneyori* (971), and afterwards *Dajō-daijin*. He received the title of *Mikawa-kō*, and is known by the name of *Ichijō-Sesshō*.

FUJIWARA MOROSUKE.

—— **Kanemichi,** 兼 道 (925-977). Was the second son of *Morosuke*. At the death of his brother *Koretada* (972), he succeeded him as *Kwampaku*, and was made *Dajō-daijin* in 974. A fire having destroyed the imperial palace (976) the emperor retired to the residence of his father-in-law *Kanemichi*, and remained there for more than a year. After his death, *Kanemichi* received the title of *Tōtōmi-kō*. He is known by the name of *Horikawa-dono*.

—— **Kaneie,** 兼 家 (929-999). The third son of *Morosuke*, was raised to the dignity of *Chūnagon*, then to that of *Dainagon* before his brother *Kanemichi*, which fact excited the latter's jealousy and was the cause why the two brothers never lived on good terms with each other. After *Kanemichi's* death (977), he was made *Udaijin ;* afterwards his daughter *Sen-shi* was married to the emperor *En-yū* and became the mother of *Ichijō-tennō*, at whose accession, *Kaneie* became *Sesshō* (987). *Yoritada* having died the following year, he succeeded him as *Dajō-daijin*, and was made *Kwampaku* when the emperor attained majority (989). After his death, his house was changed into a temple under the name of *Hōkō-in*, and *Kaneie* himself was called *Hōkōin-daijin ;* he is also called *Higashi-Sanjō-dono*.

—— **Kinsue,** 公 季 (958-1029). The fifth son of *Morosuke*, and like his brothers, successively *Udaijin* (1017), *Sadaijin, Dajō-daijin*

(1021). His sister married the emperor *Murakami*. After his death he received the title of *Kai-kō*.

—— **Sanesuke, 實資** (957-1046). A son of *Yoritada*, became *Udaijin* in 1021. He died when 90 years old and is known by the name of *Go-Ono no miya*.

—— **Kintō, 公任** (966-1041). A son of *Yoritada*, became a famous poet. As he was *nagon* at the same time as *Minamoto Toshikata*, *Fujiwara Yukinari*, and *Minamoto Tsunenobu*, all poets like himself, the name *Shi-nagon* (four *nagon*) was given to the group. He drew up the list of the 36 most celebrated poets of Japan, (*San-jū-roku-kasen*) and is known by the name of *Shijō-dainagon*.

—— **Sukemasa, 佐理**. A son of *Yoritada*, was renowned as a calligrapher, became *Dazai-daini* and afterwards *Usa-jinshin*. He died when 55 years old.

—— **Korenari, 惟成** (953-989). A son of *Koretada*, was in the service of the emperor *Kwazan*, and became a bonze with him at the *Kwazan-in* (986).

—— **Yoshikane, 義懷** (957-1008). The second son of *Koretada*, was a faithful servant of the emperor *Kwazan*, whom he prevented from committing suicide at the death of his much beloved wife *Tsune-ko*, and became bonze with him (986).

—— **Akimitsu, 顯光** (944-1021). A son of *Kanemichi*, rose to the rank of *Sadaijin*. His daughter *En-shi* was married to *Ko-Ichijō*, a son of the emperor *Sanjō*. A daughter of *Michinaga* being taken as a second wife, *En-shi*, out of spite, returned to her father who struck with consternation suddenly turned grey. His daughter having died of grief soon after, *Akimitsu* applied to the bonze *Dōman* to throw a spell over *Michinaga*. The people gave him the surname of *Akuryō-safu* (the *safu* with the evil spirits).

—— **Sumitomo, 純友**. Was a son of *Dazai-Shōni Nagazumi*. After a secret understanding with *Taira Masakado*, while the latter revolted in *Shimōsa*, he started from *Iyo* (939) and invaded *Harima*, *Bizen*, and the whole *Sanyō*. The emperor sent *Ono Yoshifuru* and *Minamoto Tsunemoto* against him. *Sumitomo* retired to *Dazaifu* and was defeated at *Hakata*. He then fled to *Iyo*, where he was arrested and put to death by *Tachibana Tōyasu* (941). His head was sent to *Kyōto*. He was the ancestor of the *Arima daimyō* of *Hizen*.

—— **Michitaka, 道隆** (953-995). A son of *Kaneie*, succeeded his father as *Sesshō* (990); afterwards the emperor *Ichijō* having performed the ceremony of the *gembuku*, he took the title of *Kwampaku* (993). He is known by the name of *Nijō-kwampaku*.

—— **Michikane, 道兼** (955-995). The second son of *Kaneie*, was a bonze at the *Kwazan-in* when his nephew *Ichijō* ascended the throne. He then resumed secular life, became *Udaijin* in 994, and the following year, succeeded his brother *Michitaka* as *Kwampaku*. He died one week later. The people called him *Nanuka no Kwampaku* (the seven days' *Kwampaku*). He was replaced by his brother *Michinaga:* thus the three brothers, *Michitaka*, *Michikane* and

Michinaga, succeeded one another in the dignity of *Kwampaku ;* for that reason they are called the *San-michi* (the three *michi*,—from the first character of their names).

—— **Michinaga, 道長** (966–1027). Was the fifth son of *Kaneie.* At the death of his brother *Michikane* (995), he was nominated *Kwampaku* in spite of the intrigues of his nephew *Korechika* who aspired to that dignity, and brought the power of the *Fujiwara* to its zenith. In 999, he gave his daughter *Aki-ko* to the emperor *Ichijō.* The latter having died in 1012, he raised *Sanjō* to the throne and obliged him to marry his second daughter *Ken-shi.* *Sanjō*, having become blind, abdicated (1016), and *Michinaga* replaced him by his own grandson, *Go-Ichijō* then only 9 years old, and as soon as the latter was of age to perform the *gembuku*, he gave him his 3d daughter *I-shi.* Moreover, he caused *Atsunaga-shinnō*, his other grandson, to be declared *taishi* (heir to the throne) who was afterwards the emperor *Go-Shujaku ;* gave the post of *Kwampaku* to his son *Yorimichi*, he receiving the title of *Dajō-daijin ;* then having secured the welfare of his family, he became bonze at the *Tōdaiji* temple (1018). In 1020, he commenced, in his domain of *Kyōgoku*, the erection of the temple *Hōjō-ji*, which was solemnly inaugurated two years later, the emperor in person assisting at the ceremony; the three

FUJIWARA MICHINAGA.

daughters of *Michinaga*, two ex-empresses and one reigning empress, repaired there too; his uncle, *Dajō-daijin Kinsue*, his sons, *Yorimichi Kwampaku*, *Norimichi Naidaijin*, finally the whole imperial court surrounded the renowned old man. After this triumphant day, trials began : he lost two of his daughters successively, *Ken-shi*, the widow of *Sanjō*, and *Yoshi-ko* the wife of prince *Atsunaga-shinnō*. He himself fell ill and notwithstanding the prayers ordered by the empresses in all the great temples, he died aged 62. For thirty years he had governed the country : three emperors were his sons-in-law, four his grandsons. After his death, he was called *Hōjōji no Kwampaku.* His greatness was celebrated by *Akazome Emon* in the *Eigwa-monogatari.*

—— **Tadanobu, 齊信** (967–1035). Was a son of *Tamemitsu* and renowned as a man of letters and a poet. He was *Dainagon.*

—— **Sadayori, 定頼** (995–1045). A son of *Kintō*, was *Dainagon, Hyōbu-kyō*, and renowned as a poet.

—— **Korechika, 伊周** (974–1010). A son of *Michitaka*, was *Naidaijin* when only 21 years old. At the death of his father (995) he expected to succeed him in the dignity of *Kwampaku*, but his uncle *Michikane* supplanted him. To avenge himself, *Korechika*, following the custom of his time had recourse to magic, and by that or by something else, *Michikane* died some days afterwards. He was however disappointed a second time, for the title of *Kwampaku* was not given to him, but to his uncle *Michinaga.* The following year, having become the rival of the ex-emperor *Kwazan* in a love-affair, he wounded the latter in the side with an arrow and for that was exiled to *Dazaifu*. He was recalled in 997, because his sister had given a son to the emperor. *Korechika* is known by the names of *Gidō-sanshi*, *Sotsu no Naidaijin*.

—— **Takaie,** 隆 家 (979-1044). Another son of *Michitaka*, was *Chūnagon* and *Izumo no kami* at the age of 18, and afterwards became *Hyōbu-kyō*. Having been appointed governor of *Dazaifu*, he led an expedition to deliver *Iki* and *Tsushima* from foreign pirates who often attacked those islands (1019).

—— **Yorimichi,** 賴 道 (992-1074). Was the eldest son of *Michinaga*. At the accession of *Go-Ichijō*, he was made *Naidaijin*, and at the death of his father (1027), he succeeded him as *Kwampaku* governing the country for nearly fifty years. Like his father, he had his daughters married to the emperors *Go-Shujaku* and *Go-Reizei*. At *Uji* he erected a splendid palace, the *Byōdō-in*, for himself, in which he entertained the Emperor. In 1068, he resigned the office of *Kwampaku* in favor of his brother *Norimichi*, and retired to *Uji*, where he died at the age of 83. He is known by the name of *Ujidono*. With *Yorimichi*, the *Fujiwara* clan reached its highest degree of prosperity, but already signs of decline began to appear. The great military families of the *Taira* and the *Minamoto* were rising in power in their provinces and it was evident that they would soon replace those in the government, who had learned no other accomplishments but poetry, music, dancing and the like.

—— **Norimichi,** 敎 道 (996-1075). A son of *Michinaga*, was associated with his brother *Yorimichi* in the government of the empire, and succeeded him in the functions of *Kwampaku* (1069) ; but the emperor *Go-Sanjō*, who had just ascended the throne, was resolved to reign and govern, hence *Norimichi* could not exercise the functions of his charge. The people gave him the name of *Ō-Nijō-dono*.

—— **Morozane,** 師 實 (1042-1101). A son of *Yorimichi*, was appointed *Sadaijin* by the emperor *Go-Reizei*, but was excluded from public affairs by *Go-Sanjō*. *Shirakawa* appointed him *Kwampaku* (1075) ; he was replaced in 1083, but became *Sesshō* at the accession of *Horikawa* (1087), and later *Dajō-Daijin*. In 1094 he transferred the dignity of *Kwampaku* to his son *Moromichi*; but the latter died in 1099 and had no successor. The ex-emperor *Shirakawa* himself governed with his ministers (*bettō*). *Morozane* is known by the names of *Go-Uji-nyūdō*, *Kyōgoku-kwampaku*. He has left memoirs bearing the title of *Kyōgoku-kwampaku-ki*.

—— **Moromichi,** 師 通 (1062-1099). Was a son of *Mōrozane*. In his youth, he studied literature under the direction of *Ōe-Tadafusa*. He became *Naidaijin* in 1082 and succeeded his father as *Kwampaku* in 1094. He is known by the name of *Go-Nijō-dono*. He left memoirs bearing the title of *Go-Nijō-kwampaku-ki*. Promoting letters and military art, *Moromichi* made himself respected by all, but a premature death did not allow him to realize all the good which might have been expected.

—— **Mototoshi, 基俊** (1055-1138). Was a son of *Toshiie* and renowned as a man of letters and a poet.

—— **Kinzane, 公實** (1053-1107). Was a son of *Sanesue* and the ancestor of the *Sanjō, Tokudaiji, Saionji, Saga, Kikutei* and other families.

—— **Tametaka, 爲隆** (1070-1130). Was a son of *Tamefusa*. He was in the service of the emperors *Shirakawa, Horikawa* and *Toba*. He was *Sangi* and *Sadaiben*. He left memoirs bearing the title of *Eishō-ki*. He is the ancestor of the *Bōjō*, the *Honomi* and the *Hozumi*.

—— **Tadazane, 忠實** (1078-1162). A son of *Moromichi*, was *Kwampaku* in 1105, became *Sesshō* at the accession of the emperor *Toba* (1108), then again *Kwampaku* on the latter attaining majority (1113) and *Dajō-daijin*. In consequence of the disputes with the ex-emperor *Shirakawa* he retired to *Uji*, but when the ex-emperor *Toba*, his son-in-law, took the reins of government (1129), he was recalled. Later he had his hair shaved and established himself again at *Uji* where he died. He is known by the name of *Fuke-dono*.

—— **Koremichi, 伊通** (1093-1165). A son of *Munemichi*, was a favorite of the emperor *Sutoku*, who successively appointed him *Udaijin* (1156), *Sadaijin* (1157). After the death of *Fujiwara Nobuyori* who had revolted, he became *Dajō-daijin*.

—— **Tadamichi, 忠通** (1097-1164). Was a son of *Tadazane* succeeded his father as *Kwampaku* in 1121, became regent (*Sesshō*) at the accession of *Sutoku-tennō* (1123), and *Dajō-daijin* in 1129. The following year, the emperor married his daughter *Masa-ko*. But the ex-emperor *Toba* recalled *Tadazane* from *Uji*, and *Tadamichi* was obliged to yield the title of *Kwampaku* to the former which he however assumed again when his father definitively retired from public life (1140). Being a fervent Buddhist, he founded the *Hōshō-ji* temple in 1148, hence the name of *Hōshō-ji-kwampaku* by which he is known, and the title *Hōshōji-kwampaku-ki* given to his memoirs.

—— **Yorinaga,** 賴長 (1120-1156). A son of *Tadazane*, was successively *Dainagon, Ukon-e-taishō, Naidaijin, Sakon-e-taishō, Sadaijin.* When the emperor *Konoe* had performed the *gembuku, Yorinaga* gave him his adopted daughter *Masu-ko* in marriage (1150) but soon afterwards the emperor having also married *Tei-shi*, an adopted daughter of *Tadamichi*, there was disunion between the two brothers. This disunion was aggravated by the fact that their father *Tadazane* showed preference for *Yorinaga*, and tried to raise him above his eldest son. After the death of *Konoe* (1155), *Tadamichi*, wished to have *Masahito*, a son of *Toba*, elected ; *Yorinaga* tried to place the ex-emperor *Sutoku* on the throne again, but the first was elected, and *Yorinaga* was deprived of his charge of *Nairan*. He levied troops in the neighboring provinces of *Kyōto* and tried to raise a revolt in the capital (*Hōgen no ran*) : his partisans were all of the *Minamoto* clan with the exception of *Yoshitomo*, and were opposed by the whole *Taira* clan. He was killed by an arrow and his three sons were exiled.

—— **Nobuyori,** 信賴 (1133-1159). A descendant of *Michitaka*, son of *Tadataka*. Being favored by *Go-Shirakawa* he was appointed *Kebiishi-bettō.* He applied for a higher position, but the ex-emperor guided by the counsels of *Fujiwara Michinori* refused to comply. He then united with *Minamoto Yoshitomo* against the ex-emperor and the *Taira.* Hence the civil war known by the name of *Heiji no ran.* The insurgents began by burning the palace of the *Jōkō Go-Shirakawa*, then massacred *Michinori*, and secured the two emperors, after which *Nobuyori* took the title of *Dajō-daijin*, and began to govern according to his desire. Meanwhile *Taira Kiyomori* having been apprised of the events which had taken place in *Kyōto*, returned in great haste and sent his son *Shigemori* to fight the rebels. *Yoshitomo* defended himself bravely, but being defeated he fled into *Owari. Nobuyori* was captured and beheaded.

—— **Michinori,** 通憲 (+ 1159). A son of *Sanekane*, was in the service of the emperors *Toba, Sutoku*, and *Konoe*, and was made *Hyūga no kami* and *Shōnagon.* In 1145 he had his hair shaved and took the name of *Shinsai.* His wife had been the nurse of the emperor *Go-Shirakawa*, who kept no secrets from her and did nothing without her advice. It was *Michinori* who, after the *Hōgen* civil war (1156), obtained the pardon of *Tadazane.* But that influence brought upon him the hatred of *Fujiwara Nobuyori* and *Minamoto Yoshitomo*, who, at the time of the *Heiji* insurrection (1159) tried to dispose of him. *Michinori* fled to *Nara* and hid himself in a cavern, but he was discovered and put to death. He was a poet and a man of letters, and left several works.

—— **Narichika,** 成親 (1138-1178). A son of *Ienari* was *Sakon-e-chūjō.* During the *Heiji* war (1159), he sided with *Nobuyori* and was made prisoner by *Taira Shigemori.* Having been set free soon afterwards, he became *Sangi, Chūnagon, Owari no kami* and *Dainagon.* He applied for the dignity of *Sakon-e-taishō* but it was given to

Taira Shigemori (1177). Irritated by this, *Narichika* plotted the ruin of the *Taira ;* but *Minamoto Yukitsuna*, one of the conspirators, revealed the plot to *Kiyomori*. *Narichika*, was exiled to *Kojima, (Bizen)* and soon afterwards put to death.

—— **Naritsune, 成 經** (+ 1202). A son of *Narichika*, took part in the plot organized by his father against the *Taira*, and was exiled to *Oni-ga-shima, (Satsuma)* in 1177. Recalled the following year, he became *Sangi*.

—— **Moromitsu, 師 光** (+ 1177). Was appointed *Saemon no jō* through the influence of *Michinori*, who, before dying, changed his name to *Shinkō*. He succeeded to the confidence which *Michinori* enjoyed with the emperor *Go-Shirakawa*. Having conspired with *Narichika* against the *Taira* (1177), he was taken prisoner and put to death with his two sons, *Morotada* and *Morotsune*.

—— **Korekata, 惟 方**. A son of *Akiyori*, was *Kebiishi-bettō*. During the *Heiji* war, he helped the ex-emperor *Go-Shirakawa* and the emperor *Nijō* to escape from the palace where *Nobuyori* kept them confined and brought them to *Rokuhara*. Later, on account of a contention between him and *Go-Shirakawa*, the latter charged *Kiyomori* to arrest him and put him to death, but owing to the demand of the *Kwampaku Tadamichi*, they were content to exile him to *Nagato*, from whence he was recalled in 1166. He is known by the name of *Awada no bettō*.

—— **Motozane, 基 實** (1143-1166). A son of *Tadamichi*, became *Kwampaku* at the age of 16 ; afterwards *Sesshō* when *Rokujō* only 2 years old ascended the throne. He died the following year at the age of 24. He is known by the name of *Umezu-dono*.

—— **Motofusa, 基 房** (1144–1230). Was a son of *Tadamichi*, succeeded his brother *Motozane* in the office of *Sesshō* (1166), and afterwards was appointed *Dajō-daijin* and *Kwampaku* in 1171. In concert with the ex-emperor *Go-Shirakawa*, he endeavored, after the death of *Taira Shigemori*, to have the latter's domains confiscated : *Kiyomori* irritated had him exiled to *Tsukushi*, with the title of *Dazai no gon-no-sotsu* (1179) ; thence he went to *Bizen*, but was recalled at the death of *Kiyomori* (1181). When *Minamoto Yoshinaka* had become master of *Kyōto*, *Motofusa* joined him against the *Taira*, gave him his daughter in marriage, and had his own son *Moroie* then 12 years old appointed *Kwampaku*. After the death of *Yoshinaka* (1184) *Moroie* was deprived of his office, and henceforth *Motofusa* lived in retirement. He is known by the names of *Matsudono* and *Bodai-in no Kwampaku*.

—— **Kanezane, 兼 實** (1147–1207). Was the third son of *Tada-michi*, and was minister during the reigns of *Go Shirakawa*, *Nijō*, *Rokujō*, and *Takakura*. After the young emperor *Antoku* had been carried off from *Kyōto* by the *Taira*, he prevailed upon *Go-Shirakawa* to replace him by *Go-Toba* (1184) and was himself appointed *Sesshō*, afterwards *Dajō-daijin* (1189) and *Kwampaku* (1190), owing to *Yoritomo* who supported him. He is known by the name of *Tsuki-no-wa no Kwampaku*. He was the first that assumed the name of *Kujō*.

—— **Moronaga,** 師長 (1137–1192). Was a son of *Yorinaga*. Having taken part with his father in the *Hōgen* war (1156), he was exiled to *Tosa*, but was recalled in 1164, and became *Naidaijin* (1175) and *Dajō-daijin* (1177). Having again been exiled to *Owari*, by *Kiyomori* (1179), he came back the following year. He is known by the name of *Myō-on-in daijin*.

—— **Kiyohira,** 清衡 (+ 1126). A descendant of *Hidesato* in the 7th degree, was a son of *Tsunekiyo* and of a daughter of *Abe Yoritoki*. He became inspector (*ōryōshi*) of *Mutsu* and *Dewa*, and afterwards *Chinjufu-Shōgun*. He was the first of the great *Mutsu Fujiwara*, whose power later on gave umbrage to *Yoritomo*.

—— **Motohira,** 基衡 (+ 1157). A son of *Kiyohira*, had the same titles as his father, and maintained the glory of his family.

—— **Hidehira,** 秀衡 (1096–1187). A son of *Motohira*. His mother was a daughter of *Abe Munetō*. He received the title of *Chinjufu-Shōgun* in 1170. When *Yoritomo* levied troops against the *Taira* (1180), the latter vainly appealed to *Hidehira*, who declared in favor of *Minamoto*. *Yoshitsune*, after having escaped from the temple of *Kurama*, (1174), had recourse to his hospitality and sought refuge at his residence when *Yoritomo* attempted his assassination (1185). *Hidehira* protected him and gave him lands at *Koromogawa*, and, when dying (1187) exhorted his sons always to support him, and to unite their efforts to have him appointed *Shōgun*.

—— **Yasuhira,** 泰衡 (+1189). A son of *Hidehira*, and after his father's death governor of the provinces of *Mutsu* and *Dewa*. Having been ordered by *Yoritomo* to put *Yoshitsune* to death, he forgot the exhortations of his father, attacked *Yoshitsune* at *Koromogawa*, defeated him and sent his head to *Kyōto*. This base servility did not save him from ruin. *Yoritomo*, wishing to become master of *Mutsu* and *Dewa*, marched against him with a numerous army. The latter having been defeated tried to escape into *Ezo*, but he was assassinated by one of his *kerai*, *Kawata Jirō*, and his immense dominions were divided among *Yoritomo's* officers.

—— **Tadahira,** 忠衡. See *Izumi Saburō*.

—— **Motomichi,** 基通 (1160–1233). Was a son of *Motozane*. Favored by the ex-emperor *Go-Shirakawa*, he became *Sadaijin* at the age of 19. Shortly after, *Kiyomori*, whose daughter he had married, had him appointed *Kwampaku* (1180). At the accession of *Antoku* (1181) he became *Sesshō*, but refused to follow the *Taira* in their flight and retired to *Hiei-zan* with *Go-Shirakawa* Later he re-entered *Kyōto* with the army of *Yoshinaka*, (1183) and was *Sesshō* for the new emperor *Go-Toba*. Deposed by *Yoshinaka*, he was re-established in his functions at the death of the former (1184), but was deposed anew two years later. Re-appointed *Kwampaku* in 1196, he became *Sesshō* for the young emperor *Tsuchi-mikado*, resigned his functions in 1202, and from that time lived in retirement.

—— **Yoshitsune,** 良経 (1169–1206). Was a son of *Kanezane*. He became *Sadaijin* in 1199, *Sesshō* for the emperor *Tsuchi-mikado* in 1202, then *Dajō-daijin* in 1204. The emperor announced that he would visit him in his residence, but *Yoshitsune* was assassinated the night preceding the promised visit. He was renowned as a poet. People gave him the name of *Go-Kyōgoku*.

—— **Kintsugu, 公繼** (1175–1227). Was a son of *Sanesada*, became *Udaijin* in 1211. He was opposed to the design of the ex-emperor *Go-Toba* who desired to make war against *Hōjō Yoshitoki*. After the *Shōkyū* war, he was appointed *Sadaijin* (1221). He is known by the name of *No-no-miya Sadaijin*.

—— **Iezane, 家實** (1180–1243). Was a son of the *Kwampaku Motomichi*, and during 16 years held the offices of *Sesshō Kwampaku*, and *Dajō-daijin*. He is the ancestor of the *Konoe* and the *Takatsukasa*.

—— **Michiie, 道家** (1192–1252). A son of *Yoshitsune*, was *Sadaijin* when the *Shōgun Sanetomo* died without an heir. The *Shikken* of *Kamakura*, *Hōjō Yoshitoki* applied to *Michiie*, in order to raise his son *Yoritsune* two-years old to the shogunate (1219). *Michiie* became *Sesshō* during the short reign of *Chūkyō* (1221) and *Kwampaku* in 1228. He is the ancestor of the *Ichijō*, the *Nijō*, and the *Kujō* families.

—— **Kanehira, 兼平** (1228-1294). A son of *Iezane*, was *Dajō-daijin* and *Kwampaku*. He was the first to assume the name of *Takatsukasa*.

—— **Saneuji, 實氏** (1194-1269). Son of *Dajō-daijin Kintsune*, was minister under six emperors and became *Dajō-daijin* in 1246. In 1260, he shaved his head and took the name of *Jikku*. He is often called *Tokiwai-nyūdō*.

—— **Yoritsune, 賴經** (1218-1256). Was the third son of *Michiie*. When, in 1219, the *Shōgun Sanetomo* was assassinated, the *Shikken Yoshitoki* sought a successor to the *Minamoto* family. For the direct line of *Yoritomo* was extinct, but his sister had been married to *Fujiwara Yoshiyasu* and her daughter married *Kintsune*. The daughter of the latter, married to *Michiie*, had a son *Yoshitsune*, then 2 years old, who was destined to succeed the *Minamoto Shōgun*, while *Masa-ko* the widow of *Yoritomo* was regent. She was aided in her functions by her brother *Yoshitoki* and after the latter's death (1224), by her nephew *Yasutoki*. In 1226, *Yoritsune* then 8 years old was made *Sei-i-taishōgun*, but the authority remained in the hands of the *Hōjō*. In 1244, he transferred the shōgunate to his son *Yoritsugu*. Later, in 1252, he tried to create a revolt against the powerful *Shikken*, but the only result was the deposition of his son.

—— **Yoritsugu, 賴繼** (1239-1256). A son of *Yoritsune*, became *Shōgun* when 5 years old, at the abdication of his father in 1244, but the *Shikken Tsunetoki* and *Tokiyori* continued to govern. His father having been implicated in a plot against the *Hōjō*, the latter deposed the young *Shōgun* (1252) and replaced him by *Munetaka-shinnō*, a son of the emperor *Go-Saga*.

—— **Kanesue, 兼季**. The 3rd son of *Saionji Sanekane*, became *Udaijin* in 1322, but resigned his office the following year. He is known by the name of *Kikutei-Udaijin*, and is the ancestor of the *Kikutei* or *Imadegawa* family.

—— **Fujifusa,** 藤 房. A faithful follower of the emperor *Go-Daigo*, and at one time was *Chū-nagon*, and *Kebiishi-bettō*. In 1331, when *Go-Daigo* was forced to flee from *Kyōto* before the troops of *Hōjō Takatoki*, *Fujifusa* accompanied him to *Kasagi-san*. When the emperor was taken prisoner, *Fujifusa* was exiled to *Hitachi*, whence he came back after the downfall of the *Hōjō*. He tried to prevent *Go-Daigo* from favoring *Ashikaga Takauji*, to whom with good reason, he attributed ambitious designs, but seeing that his advice was of no avail, he became a bonze in the temple of *Kitayama* (1335).

FUJIWARA FUJIFUSA

—— **Toshimoto,** 俊 基 (+ 1330). When the emperor *Go-Daigo* endeavored to throw off the yoke of the *Hōjō*, *Toshimoto* was commissioned to gather adherents to his cause in *Kinai*, *Sakai*, etc. *Hōjō Takatoki* had him arrested, conducted to *Kamakura* (1325), and assassinated. His daughter is the celebrated *Ben no Naishi*.

—— **Tameaki,** 爲 明. A son of *Tamefuji*, he served *Go-Daigo* and accompanied *Takanaga-shinnō* in his exile to *Tosa* (1332). Later having come back to *Kyōto*, he received offices from the northern emperors *Sukō* and *Go-Kōgon*. By the latter's order he compiled a collection of Japanese poems (1360) and died soon afterwards.

—— **Morokata,** 師 賢. See *Kwazan-in Morokata*.

II. — MEN OF LETTERS, POETS, ETC.

—— **Akisue,** 顯 季 (1054-1122). A son of *Takatsune*, was adopted by *Sanesue*. He founded a school of poetry, was *Shuri-tayū*, hence the name of *Rōkujō Shuri-tayū* by which he is known. He was a great admirer of *Kakinomoto no Hitomaro* in whose honor he instituted a festival which he celebrated every year with *Minamoto Toshiyori*.

—— **Akisuke,** 顯 輔. A son of the above, was like his father a celebrated poet. By order of the emperor *Sutoku*, he compiled the *Jikwa-waka-shū* (1144).

—— **Kiyosuke,** 清 輔 (1084-1177). A son of the above. He with *Fujiwara Toshinari* and the bonze *Saigyō*, were the most celebrated poets of their time.

—— **Akihira,** 明 衡. A celebrated poet of the eleventh century, who has written several works. His sons *Atsumoto* and *Atsumitsu* were also distinguished as literary men.

—— **Ietaka,** 家 隆 (1158-1237). A son of *Mitsutaka*, was a pupil of *Fujiwara Toshinari* and rival of *Sadaie*. The emperor *Go-Toba* wishing to study poetry, asked the *Sesshō Yoshitsune* to find a master for him. *Yoshitsune* immediately proposed *Ietaka*, who then was called the *Hitomaro* of his century. With *Sadaie* he compiled the *Shin-kokin-waka-shū* (1205). He is known by the name of *Mibu-ni-i*.

—— **Yasumasa, 保昌** (958-1036). Was a celebrated poet and flutist. Legend tells us that, attacked at night by a robber, he charmed him so effectually with the music of his flute, that the robber was disarmed and followed him to his house.

—— **Tamenari, 爲業**. A son of *Tametada*, was *Izu no kami* during the reign of *Sutoku* (1124-1141), and was renowned as a poet and historian. He has written the history of Japan from *Montoku* to *Go-Ichijo* (851-1036).

—— **Toshinari, 俊成** (1114-1204). A son of *Toshitada*, was a celebrated poet. His master was *Fujiwara Mototoshi*. He was a great favorite of the emperors *Go-Toba* and *Tsuchimikado*, the latter even deigned to assist at the feast at *Waka-dokoro* on the occasion of the 90th anniversary of his birth. *Toshinari* is often called *Gojo-san-i*. He published several works.

—— **Takanobu, 隆信** (1142-1205). A son of *Tametaka*. His mother, married a second time to *Toshinari*, gave birth to *Sadaie*. Both were distinguished poets; *Takanobu* devoted his time also to painting and was the pupil of *Kasuga Mitsunaga*. He is often called *Hoshoji*. His son *Nobuzane* (1177-1265) likewise was a renowned painter.

—— **Sadaie, 定家** (1162-1241). Was a son of *Toshinari* and, like him, a poet. He contributed to the publication of several collections of poetry among which the best known is the "*Hyaku-nin isshu*" (Poems of a hundred poets); and the most important, the "*Shin-kokin-waka-shu*" (a new anthology of ancient and modern poetry). He is often called *Teika*.

—— **Tameie, 爲家** (1197-1275). A son of *Sadaie*, compiled several collections of poems. He is known by the name of *Mimbukyo-Nyudo*.

—— **Seikwa, 惺窩** (1561-1619). Was a descendant of the above. His father *Tamezumi* having died in the service of *Bessho Nagaharu* (1580), *Seikwa*, patronized by *Hideyoshi*, continued his studies and became a bonze under the name of *Myoju-in* in order to be initiated in Buddhist theology and philosophy. Dissatisfied with the doctrines which were expounded to him, he resolutely separated from the Buddhists, who until then enjoyed the monopoly of teaching philosophy. He founded a school of Confucianism (*Teishu-gaku-ha*) and made the Chinese philosophy of the *So* dynasty (960-1279) popular. He was patronized by *Ieyasu* who helped him to establish his school. He left numerous disciples who continued his work. The most celebrated among them was *Hayashi Razan*.

III. — EMPRESSES, ETC.

—— **Miyako no Iratsume, 宮子娘** (+ 754)). Also called *Fuji-wara-kogu*, was a daughter of *Fuhito*, the wife of *Mommu-tenno* and the mother of *Shomu-tenno*.

—— **Kusuri-ko, 藥子**. A daughter of the *Chunagon Tanetsugu*, was married to *Fujiwara Tadanushi*, and afterwards to the emperor *Heijo*. After the latter's abdication in favor of his brother *Saga* (809) *Kusuri-ko* together with her brother *Nakanari* tried to induce *Heijo* to transfer his residence to *Nara* and re-ascend the throne. The plot was discovered, *Nakanari* was put to death, *Heijō* had his head shaved and *Kusuri-ko* took poison (810).

—— **Aki-ko,** 明 子 (829-900). Was a daughter of *Yoshifusa*, the wife of the emperor *Montoku*, and the mother of *Seiwa-tennō*.

—— **On-shi,** 温 子 (872-907). Was a daughter of *Mototsune* and the wife of the emperor *Uda*.

—— **On-shi,** 穩 子 (885-954). Another daughter of *Mototsune*, was the wife of the emperor *Daigo*, and the mother of *Shujaku* and *Murakami*.

—— **Sen-shi,** 詮 子 (967-1006). Was a daughter of *Kaneie*, the wife of *Enyū-tennō*, and the mother of the emperor *Ichijō*. After the death of her husband (991) she had her head shaved and became *ama* under the name of *Higashi-Sanjō-in*. It is the first instance of an empress embracing religious life.

—— **Sada-ko,** 定 子 (977-1000). Was a daughter of *Michitaka* and the wife of *Ichijō-tennō* ; she had three children.

—— **Aki-ko,** 彰 子 (988-1074). Was a daughter of *Michinaga*, the wife of *Ichijō-tennō*, and the mother of *Go-Ichijō* and *Go-Shujaku*. In 1026 she had her head shaved and assumed the name of *Jōtō-mon-in*. She was the first empress that received the title of *mon-in*.

—— **Ken-shi,** 妍 子 (994-1027). Was another daughter of *Michinaga* and the wife of *Sanjō-tennō*.

—— **I-shi,** 威 子 (999-1036). Was the third daughter of *Michinaga* and the wife of *Go-Ichijō-tennō*.

—— **Toku-ko,** 得 子 (1117-1160). A daughter of *Nagazane*, the wife of *Toba-tennō*, and the mother of *Konoe*. She had her head shaved and assumed the name of *Bifuku-mon-in* (1145).

—— **Tama-ko,** 璋 子 (1101-1145). A daughter of *Kinzane* was the wife of *Toba-tennō* and the mother of the emperors *Sutoku* and *Go-Shira-kawa*. In 1124 she had her head shaved and received the name of *Tai-ken-mon-in*.

—— **Masa-ko,** 聖 子 (1122-1182). Was a daughter of *Tadamichi* and the wife of *Sutoku-tennō*. In 1150 she assumed the name of *Kōka-mon-in*.

—— **Masu-ko,** 多 子 (1140-1201). Was a daughter of *Kinyoshi*, the wife of *Konoe-tennō* and afterwards of *Nijō-tennō*.

—— **Yoshi-ko,** 姞 子 (1225-1292). Was a daughter of *Saneuji*, the wife of *Go-Saga-tennō*, and the mother of the emperors *Go-Fukakusa* and *Kameyama*.

—— **Kimi-ko,** 公 子 (1232-1304). Was a daughter of *Saneuji*, and the wife of *Go-Fukakusa-tennō*. In 1259, she took the name of *Higashi-Nijō-in*.

—— **Yasu-ko,** 寧 子 (1292-1357). Was a daughter of *Kinhira* and the wife of *Go-Fushimi-tennō*. She is known by the name of *Kōgi-mon-in*, and was the mother of the emperors *Kōgon* and *Kōmyō* of the northern dynasty.

—— **Ren-shi,** 廉 子 (1301-1359). Was an adopted daughter of *Kintaka*, the wife of *Go-Daigo* and the mother of the emperor *Go-Mura-*

kami. She accompanied *Go-Daigo* in his exile to *Oki* (1332). In 1351 she took the name of *Shin-Taiken-mon-in.*

—— **Izu-ko,** 厳子 (1351-1406). Was a daughter of *Kintada,* the wife of the emperor *Go-Enyū* of the northern dynasty and the mother of *Go-Komatsu-tennō.* In 1386 she took the name of *Tsuyō-mon-in.*

Fujiwara-no-miya, 藤原宮. A place in *Yamato,* was the residence of the Court during the reigns of *Jitō, Mommu* and *Gemmyō* from 687 to 710. At the latter date the capital was transferred to *Nara.*

Fuju-fuze, 不受不施 (Lit.: neither receive nor give). A branch of the *Nichiren* sect, founded in 1595 by *Nichi-ō,* a bonze of the *Myō-gaku-ji* temple (*Bizen*). It was interdicted at the same time as Christianity in 1614, and reauthorized in 1876. Its seat is in *Bizen.*

Fuju-fuze-kōmon, 不受不施與門. A branch of the *Nichiren* sect founded towards 1680 by the bonze *Nikkō.* It has its seat in *Bizen.*

Fukanden-sō, 不堪田奏. A petition addressed to the emperor every year on the 7th day of the 9th month to obtain the dispensation from taxes for rice-fields having produced a bad crop.

Fukanden-fusui-shi, 不堪田風水使. An official sent from *Kyōto* to ascertain damage done to rice-fields by wind, inundation, drought, earth-quakes, etc.

Fukashi, 深志. A place in *Shinano,* now *Matsumoto* In 1504, *Shimadate Sadanaga,* one of the *kerai* of the *Ogasawara,* governors of the province built a castle there on the site of the old castle of the *Matsumoto,* and called it *Fukashi-jō.* In 1533 *Ogasawara Nagatoki* made it his residence, and thence for 10 years waged war against *Takeda Shingen.* After his victory of *Kikyō-ga-hara* (1549), *Shingen* made himself master of *Fukashi* and committed its guard to his relative *Masatoki, Hyūga no kami. Oda Nobunaga* and afterwards *Uesugi Kagekatsu,* in their turn, took possession of it. Finally, in 1582, at the downfall of the *Takeda, Hideyoshi* established *Ishikawa Kazumasa* in that castle.—See *Matsumoto.*

Fuke-shū, 普化宗. A branch of the *Zen* sect, founded by the Chinese bonze *Fuke-Zenji.* In 1248, the bonze *Kakushin* went to China, where the famous *Busshō-Zenji* of the *Gokoku-ji* temple taught him the doctrines of the sect. There was a certain *Chōyū* in the temple who was very skilful in playing the flute (*shakuhachi*) and from him *Kakushin* received lessons. After his return to Japan (1254), he went through the country preaching and playing the flute. His successors *Kichiku* and *Komu* did likewise, and the name of the latter, *Komu-sō* has become the generic name by which travelling bonzes of the sect were designated. Under the *Tokugawa,* many *samurai* without masters enrolled in the *Fuke-shū* sect, dressed in the traditional costume and wore large hats so as to hide their faces. They went through the country begging and playing the flute. To avoid justice or the supervision of the shogunate, it became customary to become a *Komusō;* but disorders having ensued, *Ieyasu* published a regulation to fix their privileges and their obligations. The sect had seventy-three temples, all depending on *Ichigetsu-ji* at *Koganei* (*Shimōsa*). It was interdicted at the Restoration.

Fukiage, 吹上. A place in *Shimotsuke*, was from 1841 to 1868 the residence of a branch of the *Arima* family (10,000 *koku*).

Fukki, 服忌. Formerly a leave of absence granted to officials during the period of mourning customary after the death of a parent. The time varied from one year to seven days, according to the degree of relationship.

Fukko-ha, 復古派. A school of Confucianist philosophy founded in the seventeenth century, by *Itō Jinsai*, *Ogiu Sorai*, *Itō Tōgai*, etc.

Fukoku, 普國. Abbreviation of 普魯亞 Prussia.

Fukuba, 福羽. A *samurai* family of the *Tsuwano* clan (*Iwami*) ennobled in 1884. — The head of the family is Viscount.

Fukuchi-yama, 福智山. In *Tamba*. After the ruin of *Akechi Mitsuhide* (1582), *Hideyoshi* built a castle there for his adopted son *Hidekatsu* the fourth son of *Nobunaga*. At the death of *Hidekatsu* (1593), *Onoki Shigekatsu* replaced him, but was dispossessed in 1600. Afterwards the castle was the residence of the *Arima daimyō* (1600-1620) the *Okabe* (1621-1624) *Inaba* (1624-1648) *Matsudaira* (1649-1669) and finally of the *Kuchiki* (1669-1868).

Fukue, 福江. The chief town of *Fukue* island (*Hizen*), was for centuries the residence of the *Gotō daimyō*. The castle having been destroyed by fire in 1614, was rebuilt in 1849 by *Gotō Moriakira*, *Yamato no kami*.

Fukue-jima, 福江嶋. The largest of the *Gotō* islands (*Hizen*). Its circuit is 235 Km.

Fukui, 福井. The capital (44,500 inh.) of the department of the same name, was formerly called *Kita-no-shō ; Shibata Katsuie*, resided at the castle in that place (1575-1583). After *Shibata's* death *Hideyoshi* installed *Hori Hidemasa* there (1583-1590), and after the latter, *Aoki Kazunori* (1590-1600). In 1601, *Ieyasu*, established there his 2nd son *Yūki Hideyasu*, whose son *Tadanao* changed the name of *Kita-no-shō* to that of *Fukui*. The descendants of *Hideyasu* held the castle till the Restoration, forming the principal branch of the *Echizen-ke* (the family of the *Echizen Matsudaira*).

Fukui-ken, 福井縣. Department formed with the provinces of *Echizen* and *Wakasa* — (Pop. : 656,000 inh.). — Capital *Fukui :* 44,500 inh.).— Principal towns : *Tsuruga* (18,000 inh.), *Takebu* (16,000 inh.), etc.

Fukujin, 福神. — See *Shichi-Fukujin*.

Fukuoka, 福岡. A *samurai* family of *Kōchi* (*Tosa*) ennobled in 1884. The head of the family is Viscount.

Fukuoka, 福岡. The capital (70,000 inh.) of the *Fukuoka-ken*, was formerly called *Najima*. In 1587, *Hideyoshi* having given *Chikuzen* as a fief to *Kobayakawa Takakage*, the latter established his residence at *Najima ; Kuroda Nagamasa* succeeded him in 1600, and changed the name of the town into that of *Fukuoka*. His descendants resided there till the Restoration.

Fukuoka-ken, 福岡縣. The department formed with the provinces of *Chikuzen* and *Chikugo*, and 6 districts (*kōri*) of *Buzen*. — Pop. : 1,476,000 inh. — Cap.: *Fukuoka* (70,000 inh.). — Principal towns : *Kurume* (29,000 inh.), *Kokura* (27,500 inh.), *Moji* (25,300 inh.), *Ōmuta* (18,000 inh.), *Yanagawa* (12,000 inh.), *Wakamatsu* (12,000 inh.).

Fukurokuju, 福祿壽. One of the 7 *Fukujin*, the god of popularity. He is represented with a bald, unusually high skull. A crane is found at his side, on account of which some probably think him to be the god of longevity.

Fukushima, 福嶋. The capital (21,000 inh.) of the *Fukushima-ken*. Towards 1180, *Sugitsuma Yukinobu* built a castle at that place called *Sugitsuma-jō* where his descendants resided for a long time. Later it was the residence of the *Gamō daimyō* (1590-1600), of *Uesugi* (1600-1601); then it became the property of the *Shōgun* ; later from 1679 to 1684, it was the residence of *Honda*, from 1685 to 1700, that of *Hotta*, and finally that of *Itakura* from 1700 till 1868.

Fukushima, 福嶋. A *samurai* family native of *Owari*.

—— **Masanori,** 正則 (1561-1624). An adopted son of *Masamitsu*, first served *Hashiba Hideyoshi*, who in 1583 had him appointed *Saemon-no-suke*, and afterwards gave him the castle of *Kiyosu* (*Owari*) as a fief with a revenue of 200,000 *koku*. After the death of *Hideyoshi* in order to attach *Masanori* to his party, *Ieyasu* gave his adopted daughter in marriage to *Masayuki*, *Masanori's* son. In 1600, *Masanori* besieged *Gifu*, and made himself master of the place ; then at the battle of *Sekigahara*, he routed the troops of *Ukida Hideie*. He received as a reward the daimyate of *Hiroshima* (*Aki*) with a revenue of 498,000 *koku*. In 1610, he was charged by *Ieyasu* with the reconstruction of the castle of *Nagoya ; Masanori* did all he could to evade that ruinous corvee, but it was in vain. From that time, the relations with the *Shōgun* became continually more strained. At the time of the *Ōsaka* campaign (1615) *Masanori* asked to accompany the shogunal army ; *Ieyasu* obliged him to remain in *Edo*. Finally in 1619, he was accused of bad administration ; his *Hiroshima* daimyate was taken from him and that of *Kawanaka-jima* (*Shinano*) with a revenue of 45,000 *koku* was given him in exchange.

—— **Masayori,** 正頼. A younger brother of the above, was *Kamon-no-suke*, and *daimyō* of *Nagashima* (*Ise* — 12,000 k.) ; in 1600, he was transferred to *Uda* (*Yamato* — 30,000 k.) and deprived of his possessions in 1615.

Fukushima-ken, 福嶋縣. A department formed of the province of *Iwashiro* and of 11 districts of *Iwaki* — Pop : 1,146,000 inh. — Cap. *Fukushima* (21,000 inh.). — Principal towns : *Wakamatsu* (29,200 inh.), *Shirakawa* (14,600 inh.), *Kōriyama* (12,000 inh.), *Taira* (10,700 inh.).

Fukutsuka, 福塚. A place in *Mino ;* in the time of *Hideyoshi*, was the residence of *Marumo Chikayoshi* (20,000 k.) who was dispossessed in 1600.

Fukuwara, 福原. The name of a palace built by *Taira Kiyomori* in 1157 where *Kōbe-Hiōgo* now stands. In 1180, he transferred the Court to that palace together with his grandson the emperor *Antoku* only 2 years old ; but 4 months later he reinstalled them in *Kyōto*. The *Fukuwara* castle abandoned by *Taira Munemori* when he fled to the West (1183), came into the possession of the chief (*chōja*) of the *Fujiwara* family and afterwards to that of the *Ichijō*.

Fukuyama, 福山. A town (18,000 inh.) in *Bingo*. In 1619 *Mizuno Katsushige* built a castle there, where his descendants resided until 1698; then it became the residence of the *daimyō Okudaira* (1700-1710); afterwards that of the *Abe* (1710-1868).

Fukuyama, 福山. A town of *Oshima* (*Hokkaidō*) which before the Restoration, was called *Matsumae.* — See *Matsumae.*

Fukuzawa Yukichi, 福澤諭吉 (1835-1901). Was born of a southern *samurai* family. He learned Dutch at *Ōsaka*, then came to *Edo* in 1853. Having been attached to the embassy of 1860, he gave up every official position on his return in order to work at the Europeanization—or rather at the Americanization—of his country. His first work, on the "Condition of Europe" *Seiyō jijō* (1866) created a sensation. Two years later, he founded a school, the *Keiō gijuku*, renowned in Japan to such a degree, that it competes with the Imperial University. *Fukuzawa's* publications amount to 50 works, the best known are: One hundred Essays, (*Fukuō-hyaku-wa*) 1897, Autobiography (*Fukuō-jiden*) 1899. *Fukuzawa* exercised a considerable influence on his epoch: more than half the men who now conduct public affairs have been formed by him. His philosophy was an agglomeration of thoughts borrowed from every school without any originality. Religion, in his eyes, was only useful for "preserving peace in society and keeping the ignorant under the yoke." The cause of *Fukuzawa's* success was principally in the novelty of his subjects and the remarkable lucidity of his style either in writing or in speaking. He was surnamed the Sage of *Mita* (*Mita seijin*) from the name of the quarter of *Tōkyō* where he resided.

Fumi-e, 蹈繪. Religious images, crucifixes, etc. which were to be trodden upon by the people at the taking of the census, in order to prove that they did not belong to the proscribed Catholic religion.

FUMI-E.

Fumi no obito, 史首. Officials whose function formerly was to write the history and the geography of the provinces: *Wani* a Korean scholar, who came to Japan in 285, is said to have been their founder. The emperor *Richū* ordered that the history of every province should be written (403). The greater number of the documents were destroyed at the downfall of the *Soga* (644); however the *Funa-fubito Esaka* succeeded in saving some of them from the fire. According to the object of their occupation, the *fubito* were divided into *kuni-fubito, funa-fubito, tsu-fubito, gwa-fubito* etc.

Fumiya no Watamaro, 文屋綿麿 (763-821). Contributed to the suppression of the revolt of the ex-empress *Kusuri-ko* (811). He afterwards succeeded *Sakanoe no Tamuramaro* in the office of *Sei-i-taishōgun* and led an expedition against the *Ebisu* (812). He was *Ukon-e-taishō, Hyōbu-kyō, Chūnagon*, etc.

Fumiya no Yasuhide, 文屋康秀. Was a celebrated poet of the 9th century. He ranks among the *Rokkasen* (six great poets).

Funabashi, 船橋. A *kuge* family descended from the *Kiyowara*. The head of the family is now Viscount.

——— **Hidekata,** 秀賢 (1555-1614). A son of *Kunitaka, Jibu-shō-suke,* was a distinguished scholar.

Funai, 府内. Formerly the capital of *Bungo* which successively was the residence of the *Ōtomo daimyō* (13th century — 1593); *Hayakawa* (1593-1597); *Fukuwara* (1597-1600); *Takenaka* (1600-1634); *Hineno* (1634-1656) the *Matsudaira* (1658-1868).— It is now called *Ōita.*

Funakoshi, 船越. A *shizoku* family of *Hiroshima* (*Aki*) ennobled in 1900. The head of the family is a Baron.

Funanoe-sen, 船上山. A castle in *Hōki,* in which *Nawa Naga-toshi* received the emperor *Go-Daigo* after the latter's return from *Chi-buri-shima* (1333). He soon afterwards, at the head of an army, escorted him to *Kyōto.*

Funaoka, 船岡. A place in *Yamashiro,* where *Minamoto Tame-yoshi* and his sons were defeated in 1156 (*Hōgen no ran*) by *Kiyomori.*

Funate-gumi, 船手組. Officials under the *Tokugawa,* who were superintendents of the vessels belonging to the *Shōgun.* In 1632, four chiefs were created; they were called *funate-gashira;* superior to them was a *waka-toshiyori.*

Funatobe no Naoshi, 船戸部直. A painter of the 7th century, one of the first mentioned in history.

Fūren-numa, 楓蓮沼. A lake (59 Km. in circuit) in *Nemuro* (*Hokkaidō*).

Furuhito-Ūji, 古人皇子. Also called *Furuhito-oine-shinnō,* a son of the emperor *Jomei.* At the abdication of *Kyōgoku* (644), the throne was offered him, but he refused it and became bonze at the *Yoshino-san,* hence the name *Yoshino-taishi* is given him. The following year, regretting his decision, he excited a revolt, but was forestalled and put to death. His daughter married the emperor *Tenchi.*

Furuta, 古田. A *daimyō* family of the 16th and 17th centuries.

——— **Shigenari,** 重然 (1545-1615). Was *Oribe no shō.* He received 10,000 k. in 1600, but was dispossessed in 1615 for having communicated with the besieged in *Ōsaka.* He is the founder of the tea ceremony school, called *Oribe-ryū.*

——— **Shigekatsu,** 重勝 (1561-1600). Was *Hyōbu-shōsuke.* He served *Hideyoshi,* who gave him the castle of *Matsuzaka* (*Ise* — 37,000 k.). After *Sekigahara* his revenue was raised to 60,000 k. He died the same year.

——— **Shigeharu,** 重治. Was *Daizen-tayū* and was transferred in 1619 to *Hamada* (*Iwami*).

——— **Shigetsune,** 重恒 (1598-1648). Was *Hyōbu-shōsuke,* but was dispossessed in 1648 on account of the tyranny he exercised over his *kerai.*

Furuwatari, 古渡. In *Owari,* a castle which *Oda Nobuhide* built and occupied when he gave his own castle to his son *Nobunaga* (1535):

some remnants may still be seen in the precincts of the *Higashi-Hon-gwanji* temple in *Nagoya*.

Fusa no kuni, 總國. The ancient name of the provinces of *Kazusa* and *Shimōsa*.

Fushimi, 伏見. A town in the province of *Yamashiro*, south of *Kyōto*. In 1593 *Hideyoshi* built a magnificent castle there. Before the *Sekigahara* campaign (1600) *Ieyasu* entrusted it to *Torii Mototada*; but the army of *Ishida Kazushige* reduced it to ashes. In 1620, a *bugyō* (governor) was established in the place. One of the favourite walks of the people of *Kyōto* was to the ruins on the *Momoyama* hill — On the 27th and the 28th of January 1878, *Fushimi* was the scene of a battle in which the imperialists routed the army of the *Shōgun*.

Fushimi, 伏見. A family of princes of the imperial blood descended from *Sadatsune-shinnō* (1425-1474), a brother of the emperor *Go-Hanazono*. The actual chief of the house is prince *Sadanaru*, a general of the army. He was born in 1858, and married *Toshi-ko*, a daughter of prince *Arisugawa Takahito*, in 1876.

Fushimi-bugyō, 伏見奉行. An official created in 1620 and entrusted with the defence of the *Fushimi* castle.

Fushimi-tennō, 伏見天皇. The 92nd Emperor of Japan (1278-1298), was prince *Hirohito*, a son of *Go-Fukakusa*. He succeeded *Go-Uda* at the age of 23, and permitted his father to govern. The latter was forced to submit to the authority of the *Kamakura Hōjō*. In 1289, the *Shōgun Koreyasu-shinnō*, having displeased *Hōjō Sadatoki*, was deposed and replaced by *Hisaakira-shinnō*, a younger brother of the emperor. After a reign of 11 years, *Fushimi* abdicated in favor of his son in whose name he continued to govern. He died in 1317 at the age of 53.

Fushin-bugyō, 普請奉行. An office created in 1652 and entrusted to two officials whose functions were to superintend the reparations of the walls, moats, etc. of the *Edo* castle as well as other undertakings of the *Bakufu* in the town.

Fusō, 扶桑. One of the 10 sects of Shintoism established towards the middle of the 16th century. It especially honors the 3 gods of the creation (*Zōkwa no san-jin*).

Fusō-koku, 扶桑國. An ancient name of Japan, still used in poetry.

Fusō-ryakuki, 扶桑畧記. Historical work of the bonze *Kōen* of the *Hiei-zan*. It extends from the reign of *Daigo* (898) to that of *Go-Toba* (1198).

Fusōshū-yōshū, 扶桑拾葉集. An historical work in thirty volumes, compiled in the 17th century by order of *Tokugawa Mitsukuni* of *Mito*.

Futama, 二間. An apartment in the imperial palace, east of the *Seiryō-den*, in which the most celebrated *Bosatsu* were represented and where the bonzes assembled for certain ceremonies.

Futamata, 二俣. A castle town in *Tōtōmi*. In 1502, *Futamata Masanaga* built a castle there, which successively passed to the *Imagawa* and the *Oda*. It was in that castle that *Nobuyasu*, the eldest son of *Ieyasu*, was invited by his father to kill himself by *harakiri* (1579).

Futara, 二荒. A noble house descended from prince *Kitashira-kawa Yoshihisa* (+ 1895). The chief of the family is a Count.

Futomani, 太占. An ancient mode of divination consisting in calcining the shoulder blade of a male deer, on which some notches had previously been made. According to the fracture produced by the fire, a good or bad omen was signified.

Futsunushi no kami, 經津主神. Was also called *Mikafutsu no Kami, Iwainushi no Kami*, and was the son of *Iwatsutsu-no-o no Kami*. He was sent to earth with *Takemikazuchi* in order to prepare the coming of *Ninigi no mikoto*. His temple is situated at *Katori* (*Shimōsa*).

Futtsu-saki, 富津崎. The cape west of *Kazusa*, commanding the entrance to *Tōkyō* bay.

Fuwa no seki, 不破關. A barrier raised in *Ōmi* by the emperor *Temmu* (673). It has given its name to the village of *Seki-ga-hara* (the plain of the barrier), the scene of the famous battle of 1600.

Fu-yuso-den, 不輸租田. Formerly rice-fields taxed not for the government, but for the temples, schools, etc.

G

Gagaku-ryō, 雅樂寮. Formerly a building belonging to the *Jibu - shō*, and reserved for the study of music and dancing.

Gakkwan-in, 學館院. A school founded during the reign of *Saga* (810-823) by the empress *Tachibana Kachi-ko* (*Danrin-kōgō*) and her brother *Ujigimi* for the children of the *Tachibana* family. The principal of the school was a *Bettō*, always chosen from the members of the founders' family. Towards 960, *Tachibana Yoshifuru* had the *Gakkwan-in* affiliated to the *Daigaku* (University).

Gakuden, 樂田. A place in *Owari*, where *Oda Hisanaga* built a castle. The castle was taken by *Tsuda Nobukiyo*, and retaken towards 1560 by *Oda Nobunaga*, who entrusted its defence to *Sakai Masahisa*. In 1584 it was the scene of a battle in which *Ieyasu* defeated the troops of *Hashiba Hidetsugu*. — See *Komaki-yama*.

Gaku-dokoro, 樂所. A school of music which in 951 replaced the *Gagaku-ryō* and where Chinese music (*Tō*) especially was studied.

Gakumon-jo, 學問所. *Ieyasu* was the first who established a school in *Edo* and entrusted its direction to *Hayashi Dōshun* and to his son *Shunsai*. *Iemitsu* gave it the name of *Kōbun-in* and endowed it with revenues (1632). In 1692 the school was transferred to *Yushima* (*Hongō*) under the name of *Shōhei-kō*. Finally in 1797, having been improved and increased, it became the *Gakumon-jo*. It always continued under the direction of the *Hayashi* family.

Gakumon-jo-bugyō, 學問所奉行. The title of the director of a school founded in 1842 in *Edo* (*Kojimachi, Zenkokuji-dani*), and of which the *Hayashi* were professors.

Gakumonjo-kimban, 學問所勤番. A title given to the director of the *Gakumon-jo* according to the new regulations of 1797.

Gakushū-in, 學習院. A school founded in 1842 at *Kyōto* by the emperor *Ninkō* for the education of the children of the *kuge*. To-day the Nobles' school in *Tōkyō*.

Gamō, 蒲生. A *daimyō* family in *Ōmi*, descended from *Fujiwara Hidesato*.

——— **Katahide, 賢秀** (1534-1584) *Sahyō-e-tayū*, first in charge of the castle of *Hino* (*Ōmi*) for the *Sasaki*, he later entered the service of *Nobunaga*.

——— **Ujisato, 氏鄉** (1557-1596). A son of *Katahide*. When 13 years old, he distinguished himself at the taking of *Ōkōchi* castle (*Ise*) in the presence of *Nobunaga*, who soon afterwards, gave him his daughter in marriage. At the death of *Nobunaga* (1582), *Ujisato* asked his widowed mother-in-law to reside in his castle of *Hino*. Later he was made *Hida no kami* and *daimyō* of *Matsusaka* (*Ise*) with a revenue of

120,000 k. In 1590, after the war of *Odawara*, he was transferred to *Aizu* (*Mutsu* — 420,000 k.), with the object of bringing all the *daimyō* of the North to submit to *Hideyoshi*. *Kunohe Masazane* resisted, and an expedition was sent against him. *Ujisato* assisted by *Asano Nagamasa*, besieged him in his castle of *Kunohe* and defeated and killed him. After this exploit, his revenues were raised to 1 million *koku*. He then went to *Kyōto* where he was appointed *Sangi* At the time of the expedition to Korea, he accompanied *Hideyoshi* to *Nagoya*. Meanwhile he rebuilt his castle of *Kurokawa* (*Aizu*) and changed its name to *Wakamatsu*. He died at the age of 40. Several accused *Hideyoshi* of having poisoned him. *Ujisato* was baptized "Leo," in 1584.

—— **Hideyuki, 秀行** (1583-1612). Was a son of *Ujisato*. As he was only 13 years old at the death of his father, he was deprived of the immense daimyate of *Aizu*, and in return received that of *Utsunomiya* (*Shimotsuke* — 180,000 k.). After *Sekigahara* (1600), he returned to *Wakamatsu* (600,000 k.) where he died. He was only 30 years old. *Hideyuki* was a Christian.

—— **Tadasato, 忠郷** (1603-1627). The eldest son of *Hideyuki*. He succeeded to the daimyate of *Aizu*, but died without an heir.

—— **Tadatomo, 忠知** (1605-1634). The second son of *Hideyuki*, was chosen as his brother's heir, the latter having died without issue. He was transferred from *Aizu* to *Matsuyama* (*Iyo*—240,000 k.) He died when 30 years old, without an heir, and was the last of the *Gamō* family.

Gamō Kumpei, 蒲生君平 (1768-1813). Was first called *Fukuda Hidezane*, but having heard that his family was descended from *Gamō Ujisato*, he took that name. He was born at *Utsunomiya* and went to *Edo*, where he studied history, after which he travelled through the country. In the works he published, he deplores that the authority of the emperors was disregarded, that their tombs were neglected and left in ruins, etc. He also wrote a book on the importance of coast defence and the means to secure it. *Kumpei* is one of the few writers who, under the *Tokugawa*, dared support the imperial cause.

Gamōda-misaki, 蒲生田崎. A cape east of *Awa* (*Shikoku*).

Ganjū-san, 岩手山. A mountain (2,050 met.) in *Rikuchū*, northeast of *Morioka*. It is also called *Iwate-yama, Nambu no Fuji*.

Ganku, 岸駒 (1749-1838). Was the founder of a school of Painting—Chinese style,—which bears his name, (*Ganku-ryū*). He was born at *Kanazawa* (*Kaga*) of the *Saeki* family and came to *Kyōto* where he first served prince *Arisugawa* and then the imperial court.

Garan, 伽藍 (sanskr.) or Buddhist temple. When the dependencies are included, the name *shichi-dō-garan* is given.

Geba-shōgun, 下馬將軍. Surname given by the people to the *Tairō Sakai Tadakiyo* (1626-1681) ; he was also called *Takasago-shōgun*.

Gebu-kwan, 外武官. In opposition to *naibu-kwan*. The six *efu* who formed the imperial guard were called *naibu-kwan ;* the officers and *samurai* who took part in an expedition, under the conduct of the *Shōgun*, were known by the name of *gebu-kwan*.

Geishū, 藝州. The Chinese name of *Aki* province.

Geki, 外記. Secretary.—See *Dai-geki*.

Gekkei-unkaku, 月卿雲客. (Lit.: moon-ministers, cloud-nobles). Court nobles of the 3rd rank (*san-i*); those above were called *gekkei* or *kandachime*; those of the 4th and 5th ranks *unkaku* or *denjō-bito*. (A figure borrowed from the Chinese: the emperor is the sun, — the moon and the clouds are his servants).

Gekū, 外宮. One of the great temples of *Ise,* formerly dedicated to *Kuni-tokotachi no Mikoto,* but at present to *Ukemochi no Kami (Toyo-uke-bime).*

Gekwan, 外官. Generic name of all the offices and functions exercised outside the capital.

Gemba-ryō, 玄蕃寮. An official subordinate to the *Jibu-shō* and having charge of the registration of the bonzes and *ama,* the reception of ambassadors, and the superintendence of foreigners living in *Kyōto,* etc.

Gembō, 玄昉. A bonze of the *Kōfuku-ji* in *Nara.* In 716 he went to China and returned in 735. He was nominated *Sōjō* and built the *Kwanzeon-ji* in *Tsukushi,* denounced the revolt of *Fujiwara Hirotsugu,* and died in 746.

Gembuku, 元服. A ceremony during which a minor is declared to be of age. For the emperor, since the reign of *Seiwa* (864), it consisted in the receiving of a collar. The sons of *Kuge,* had their head-dress arranged according to the court fashion and received the *kammuri.* Among the officials, the young man changed the name he bore in childhood and received the *eboshi* from a relation or a patron, called *eboshi-oya* or *kammuri-oya.* During the *Tokugawa* period, the *gembuku* for boys consisted in having the top of the head shaved; and for girls, in having the eyebrows shaved and the teeth blackened.

Gembun, 元文. *Nengō:* 1736-1740.

Gemmei-tennō, 元明天皇. An empress (43) who reigned from 708-714. She was *Abe* or *Yamato-neko-amatsu-mihiro-toyokuni-nari hime,* a daughter of the emperor *Tenchi,* and at the age of 46, succeeded her son *Mommu.* In 710, she transferred the capital to *Nara.* By her wish the *Kojiki* (712) and the *Fudoki* (713) were written to embody the ancient traditions. She caused the first copper money (*Wadō-kaichin*) to be coined. After a reign of 7 years, she abdicated in favor of her daughter, and died when 61 years of age.

Gempei, 源平. (*Gen* and *Hei,* or *Minamoto* and *Taira*). The *Gempei* war; i.e. the war between these two families. It was the longest war of the 12th century. — See *Genji, Heike,* etc.

Gempei-seisui-ki, 源平盛衰記. A "History of the rise and fall of *Minamoto* and *Taira.*" A historical work in 48 volumes, from 1160 to 1185. It is attributed to *Hamuro Tokinaga.*

Genchū, 元中. *Nengō:* 1380-1382.

Gen-e, 玄慧 (1269-1352). A bonze who in the time *Go-Daigo,* expounded the Confucianist doctrines of the Chinese philosophers that lived during the *Kan* (206 B. C.—221 A. D.) and the *Tō* dynasty (619-907). He worked successfully to rouse the people against the tyranny of the *Kamakura Hōjō*. The composition of the *Taihei-ki* is attributed to *Gen-e*. With the help of the bonzes *Ze-en*, *Shin-e*, etc. he wrote the *Kembu-shiki-moku*, the *Shinka-seishiki*, and the *Teikun-ōrai*.

Gen-ei, 元永. *Nengō :* 1118-1119. — Also called *Gwan-ei*.

Genji, 元治. *Nengō :* 1864. — Also called *Gwanji*.

Genji, 源氏. The *Minamoto* family. In the 9th and 10th centuries, several emperors transmitted the name of *Minamoto* to their descendants (*Gen* in Chinese); hence the *Seiwa-Genji*, *Uda-Genji*, *Murakami-Genji*, and *Saga-Genji* branches, descended respectively from the emperors *Seiwa*, *Uda*, *Murakami*, and *Saga*.

Genji-monogatari, 源氏物語. (Lit.: History of the *Genji*). The most celebrated Japanese classical work, composed in the 10th century by *Murasaki Shikibu*.

Genji no shi-sei, 源氏四姓. The four branches of the *Minamoto* family ; *Seiwa-Genji*, *Saga-Genji*, *Murakami-Genji* and *Uda-Genji*.

Genkai-nada, 玄海灘. The sea situated N. N. W. of *Kyūshū*, also called *Kyūshū-nada*.

Genka-reki, 元嘉暦. The first calendar brought to Japan by the Korean bonze *Kwanroku ;* it was in use from 604 till about 680.

Genkei, 元慶. *Nengō :* 877-884.

Genki, 元龜. *Nengō :* 1570-1572.

Genkō, 元弘. *Nengō :* 1331-1333.

Genkō no eki, 元寇役. The name given to the war against the Mongols towards the end of the 13th century. It is also called *Bun-ei no eki* and *Kō-an no eki*, from the names of the *nengō* during which it took place.

Genkō no ran, 元弘亂. The civil war during the *Genkō* era. In 1326, the *Kōtaishi Kuninaga-shinnō* having died, the emperor *Go-Daigo* wished to replace him by his son *Morinaga-shinnō*, but was prevented by *Hōjō Takatoki* who had *Kazuhito-shinnō* a son of *Go-Fushimi*, nominated. *Go-Daigo* appointed *Morinaga-shinnō* chief of the temple *Enryaku-ji* of the *Tendai* sect, and with the help of the bonzes, prepared to get rid of the *Hōjō*. It was then that *Takatoki* marched against *Kyōto* with a numerous army : the emperor fled to mount *Kasagi*, but being taken prisoner, he was confined to the *Rokuhara* and afterwards exiled to *Chiburi* island (*Oki*).

Genkū, 源空 (1133-1212). Was born in the province of *Mimasaka*. At the age of 15, he entered the monastery of the *Enryaku-ji* temple (*Hiei-zan*), where he astonished his teachers by the rapidity of his progress. Afterwards he went to the *Kurodani* temple where he received lessons from *Ajari Eikū*. Later having found a work (*ōjō-yōshū*) of the bonze *Genshin*, he learned from it the doctrines of the *Jōdo* sect, which he embraced and began to propagate with great success. Abandoning the observances of the *Tendai* sect, he professed that salvation, i.e , entrance into the " pure land " (*Jōdo*) can be obtained only by prayer, and giving the example, he repeated the name of *Amida* as many as 60,000 times per day. The bonzes of the *Enryaku-ji* succeeded in having him exiled to *Sanuki* (1206). He returned to *Kyōto* in 1210, and built the temple *Chion-in* where he died, at the age of 76. He was known by the name of *Hōnen-Shōnin*. Later he received the posthumous title *Enkō-Daishi*.

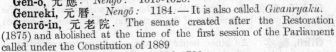

GENKŪ.

Genkyō, 元亨. *Nengō:* 1321-1323.

Genkyū, 元久. *Nengō:* 1204-1205.

Gennin, 元仁. *Nengō:* 1224.

Gen-ō, 元應. *Nengō:* 1319-1320.

Genreki, 元暦. *Nengō:* 1184.— It is also called *Gwanryaku.*

Genrō-in, 元老院. The senate created after the Restoration (1875) and abolished at the time of the first session of the Parliament called under the Constitution of 1889

Genroku, 元祿. *Nengō:* 1688-1703.

Gensan, 元山. Also called *Yuensan*, a sea-port in Korea.

Genshin, 源信 942-1017. Was born in *Yamato*, in the *Urabe* family. He entered the *Hiei-zan* and received lessons from *Jie-Daishi* (*Ryōgen*). He published several works, in which he propounds especially the efficacy of prayer. He had numerous disciples.

Genshi-sai, 元始祭. A feast celebrated at the palace on the third day of the new year. The emperor personally makes offerings to heaven and to his ancestors.

Genshō-tennō, 元正天皇. An empress (44) who reigned from 815-823. She was *Hitaka* or *Yamato-neko-takamizu-kiyotarashi hime*, and, at the age of 36, succeeded her mother *Gemmei*, whom she imitated by fostering the letters and sciences, arts and agriculture, etc. The *Nihon-ki* was published during her reign (720). She abdicated at the age of 45, in favor of her nephew, *Shōmu*, and died in 748 at the age of 69.

Gensui, 元帥. An ancient title corresponding to general. This dignity has been recently re-established and may be translated as Marshal of the Empire. The Emperor, as generalissimo of the army and the navy, has the title of *Dai-gensui.*

Gentoku, 元德. *Nengō:* 1329-1330.

Genwa, 元和. *Nengō:* 1615-1623.

Getsurin-Daishi, 月輪大師.— See *Shunjō*

Gidayū, 義太夫. A dramatical recital accompanied with music named after *Takemoto Gidayū* (1651-1714) who made it popular.

Gifu, 岐阜. The capital (32,000 inh.) of *Gifu-ken* and formerly the capital of *Mino*.— In 1097, *Minamoto Kunifusa*, *Mino no kami*, attempted a revolt which was suppressed by *Yoshiie*. Later *Nikaidō*, an officer of the *Kamakura Shōgun*, built a castle there on the hill called *Inaba-yama* (1203). In 1539, *Saitō Hidetatsu*, leaving *Kanō* (*Mino*) took up his residence at *Gifu*. His grandson *Tatsuoki* was turned out of the castle by *Nobunaga* (1564) who, leaving his castle of *Kiyosu* (*Owari*), in his turn established himself at that place. Later, *Nobunaga* built the castle of *Azuchi* (1576), and was replaced at *Gifu* by his son *Nobutada*. The latter died in 1582, and his brother *Nobutaka* resided at *Gifu* for a while ; the following year *Hideyoshi* intrusted the defence of the castle to *Ikeda Terumasa* (1583) then to *Hashiba Hidekatsu* (1591). After the latter's death (1593), his nephew *Oda Hidenobu* moved from *Kiyosu* to *Gifu*, where besieged in 1600 by *Fukushima Masanori*, he was taken prisoner, and exiled to *Kōya-san*. The castle was not rebuilt and no *daimyō* resided at *Gifu* under the *Tokugawa* shogunate.

Gifu-ken, 岐阜縣. A department formed by the provinces of *Mino* and *Hida*. — Pop : (1,046,000 inh.). — Cap. *Gifu* (32,000 inh.). Principal towns : *Ōgaki* (19,000 inh.), *Takayama* (15,500 inh.), etc.

Gi-jijū, 擬侍從. Dignitaries of the court who stood beside the Emperor during the ceremony of the coronation. They were also called *jijū-dai*.

Gikū, 義空. A Chinese bonze who came to Japan towards 815 and was the first to preach the doctrines of the *Zen-shū* sect in this country. The emperor *Saga* installed him at the *Tōji* temple in *Kyōto* and the empress had the *Danrin-ji* built for him at *Saga*. Later *Gikū* returned to China, where he died.

Gikyō-Daimyōjin, 義經大明神. The Japanese name of a divinity honored by the *Aino* and supposed to be *Minamoto Yoshitsune*. (The pronunciation of the characters of the name *Yoshitsune* is *Gikyō* or *Gikei*).

Ginkaku-ji, 銀閣寺. In 1473 *Yoshimasa* having abdicated the shogunate in favor of his son *Yoshihisa* built a palace on the eastside of *Kyōto* (*Higashi-yama*) in the precincts of which a silver pavilion (*Ginkaku*) was erected in imitation of the gold pavilion (*Kinkaku*) of *Yoshimitsu*. The most celebrated artists of the time worked at the ornamentation of the apartments, gardens, etc. After *Yoshimasa's* death (1490), the palace was converted into a temple under the name of *Jishō-ji*, or more commonly *Ginkaku-ji*.

Ginza, 銀座. Under the *Tokugawa*, an office dependent on the *Kanjō-bugyō* and having charge of the coining of silver money.

Gion, 祇園. A ward of *Kyōto*, formerly celebrated for its cherry-trees which, when in blossom, attracted thousands of visitors. It has given its name to the *Gion no yashiro*.

Gion Nankai, 祇園南海 (1677-1751). A painter who propagated in Japan the Chinese style called *Nan-gwa* or *Bunjin-gwa*. He was also a distinguished poet.

Gion no yashiro, 祇園社. The most popular temple in *Kyōto*. It was formerly a Shintoist temple, dedicated to *Susano-o no Mikoto* under the name of *Yasaka-jinja*. The *Ryōbu-shintō* gave it the name of *Gion-ji* ; it then became a dependency of the *Kōfuku-ji*, afterwards of the *Enryaku-ji*. Since the Restoration, it has again become purely Shintoist, with the exception of the name of *Gion* which has been preserved. It is also called *Kanshin-in*.

Gisō, 議奏. Officials chosen from among the *dainagon*, *chūnagon*, *sangi*, and charged with transmitting the answers of the emperor to the demands of the *daimyō* and the *samurai*. Their number was from 3 to 5. — See *Tensō*.

Gō, 郷. A family originating in *Mino* and ennobled in 1900. To-day the chief of the family is Baron.

Go-bugyō, 五奉行. The 5 magistrates appointed by *Hideyoshi* in 1585, for the administration of the city of *Kyōto*. *Maeda Gen-i*, *shoshi-dai*, had charge of the police and the temples; *Nagatsuka Masaie*, of finance; *Asano Nagamasa*, of the laws; *Ishida Kazushige*, of the public works; *Masuda Nagamori*, of justice.

Go-Chi-Nyorai, 五智如来. The five gods of wisdom or contemplation: *Yakushi*, *Tahō*, *Dainichi*, *Ashuku* and *Shaka*.

Go-Daigo-tennō, 後醍醐天皇. The 96th Emperor of Japan (1319-1338), was prince *Takaharu*, a son of *Go-Uda*. He succeeded his cousin *Hanazono* at the age of 31. Resolved to govern alone and to rid himself of the domination of the *Kamakura Shikken*, he had recourse to the

mediation of some *kuge*, and of the most influential bonzes in order to rouse the people. *Hōjō Takatoki* sent a large army against *Kyōto;* the emperor fled to mount *Kasagi*, but was arrested, brought back to *Rokuhara*, deposed, and exiled to *Chiburi* island (*Oki*), while prince *Kazuhito* was placed on the throne in his stead (1331). In the beginning of 1333, *Go-Daigo* succeeded in escaping from *Chiburi*, landed in *Hōki*, where *Nawa Nagatoshi* gave him hospi-

GO-DAIGO-TENNŌ.

tality at *Funanoe-sen;* then, having raised an army, *Nawa* conducted him to *Kyōto* which *Ashikaga Takauji* and *Akamatsu Norimura* had just taken from the *Hōjō*, whilst *Nitta Yoshisada* made himself master of *Kamakura*, and overthrew the power of the *Shikken*. Having re-entered his capital, the emperor rewarded his rescuers, by distributing fiefs and dignities among them. *Ashikaga Takauji* was not satisfied, although he had received the provinces of *Musashi*, *Shimōsa*, and *Hitachi;* soon afterwards, a son of *Takatoki*, *Tokiyuki*, the last of the *Hōjō*, having tried to retake *Kamakura, Takauji* marched against him, defeated his army, established himself at *Kamakura* and assumed the title of *Sei-i-taishōgun* (1335). The emperor pronounced him a rebel and sent *Nitta Yoshisada* against him, but the latter, at first victorious in *Mikawa* and *Suruga*, was defeated at *Hakone* (*Sagami*) and *Takauji* marched against *Kyōto*. *Kusunoki Masashige* and *Nawa Nagatoshi* in vain tried to stop him; they were defeated, and the emperor was again obliged to flee to Mount *Yoshino*. Meanwhile, *Kitabatake Akiie* arrived from the North with an army, defeated the troops of *Takauji* at *Miidera*: and the emperor again re-entered *Kyōto*. But *Takauji* had gone as far as *Kyūshū* to recruit his forces, and came back with a new army. *Nitta Yoshisada* and *Kusunoki Masashige* met him at *Hyōgo*, but were defeated. The first fled and tried to reassemble his soldiers, the second, after prodigies of valor and covered with wounds, committed *harakiri*. The emperor again fled from *Kyōto*, which he never re-entered and *Takauji* raised prince *Yutahito* (*Kōmyō*,), the brother of *Kazuhito* (*Kōgon*) to the throne (1336). Thus began the rivalry which was to last for nearly 60 years between the southern dynasty (*nanchō*) because *Go-Daigo* had retired to the South of *Kyōto*, the dynasty which historians of the Restoration consider as the legitimate one, and the northern dynasty (*hokuchō*) supported by the *Ashikaga*. *Go-Daigo* reigned two more years and saw the fall of all his supporters viz.: *Nawa Nagatoshi, Nitta Yoshisada, Yoshiaki, Kitabatake Akiie*, etc.; the northern provinces of *Mutsu* and *Dewa*, and those of *Kyūshū* were about the only ones that had remained faithful. It was in such circumstances that he transmitted his rights with the three imperial insignia to *Norinaga Go-Murakami*, a child of 12 years.

Gōdo, 合渡. A place in *Mino*. Before the battle of *Sekigahara* (1600) the van-guard of the army of *Ishida Kazushige* fought a battle there against the troops of *Tōdō Takatora*.

Go-efu, 五衛府. The five divisions of the imperial guard: *emon, saeji, ueji, sahyōe,* and *uhyōe.* — See *Efu.*

Go-En-yū-tennō, 後圓融天皇. An Emperor of the northern dynasty (1372-1382). *Ohito,* born in 1359, succeeded his father *Go-Kōgon,* when 13 years old. He abandoned the government to *Ashikaga Yoshimitsu,* who weakened the southern party more and more. After a reign of 10 years, *Go-En-yū* abdicated in favor of his son *Go-Komatsu* and died in 1393, 35 years old.

Go-Fukakusa-tennō, 後深草天皇. The 89th Emperor of Japan (1247-1259), was prince *Hisahito,* a son of *Go-Saga,* whom he succeeded when 4 years old. *Hōjō Tokiyori, Shikken* of *Kamakura* then governed according to his will and pleasure. Thus, having been displeased with the *Shōgun Fujiwara Yoritsugu,* he deposed him and chose, as his successor, prince *Munetaka,* a brother of the emperor (1252). When 17 years old, *Go-Fukakusa,* following the counsels of his father, abdicated in favor of his brother *Kameyama,* and retired to the *Jimyō-in,* but at the death of *Go-Saga* (1272), he regained his influence, and governed during the reign of *Fushimi* and *Go-Fushimi*, his son and his grandson. He died in 1304, at the age of 62.

Go-Fushimi-tennō, 後伏見天皇. The 93d Emperor of Japan (1299-1301), was prince *Tanehito*, a son of the emperor *Fushimi*. He succeeded his father when 11 years old, and his grandfather *Go-Fukakusa* governed for him. As he had been elected in opposition to *Go-Saga's* will which stated that the emperors should be taken alternately from among the descendants of his two sons *Kameyama* and *Go-Fukakusa*, *Go-Uda* obtained the consent of *Hōjō Sadatoki* that *Go-Fushimi* be deposed and replaced by his own son *Go-Nijō*. After his forced abdication, *Go-Fushimi* lived 35 years in retirement.

Go-gaku, 五嶽. Formerly five sacred mountains; *Takachiho*, *Kongōhō*, *Nyoi*, *Hiei*, and *Atago*.

Gō-gawa, 鄉川. A river (157 Km.) which, under the name of *Yoshidagawa*, has its source in *Aki*, flows through *Iwami*, and empties itself into the Japan Sea north of *Hamada*. It is also called *Iwamigawa*, and formerly *Eno-gawa*.

Go-gembuku-bugyō, 御元服奉行. An official who, during the *Kamakura* period, regulated the *gembuku* of the shōgunal family.

Go-haiga-bugyō, 御拜賀奉行. An official who, during the *Kamakura* period, regulated the ceremonies of congratulation on the accession of a *Shōgun* or a promotion in the court. *Nikaidō Yukimura* was the first who received this title when *Sanetomo* was made *Udaijin* (1218).

Go-Hanazono-tennō, 後花園天皇. The 102nd Emperor of Japan (1429-1465), was prince *Hikohito*, a son of prince *Sadanari*. At the age of 10, he succeeded the emperor *Shōkō* who had died without children. This reign, during which the *Ashikaga* attained the zenith of their power under the *Shōgun Yoshinori* and *Yoshimasa*, was one of civil wars which arose successively between the two *Ashikaga* families (1437-1441), the *Akamatsu* and the *Yamana*, the *Hosokawa* and the *Hatakeyama*, etc. These strifes were mere fore-runners of the war of *Ōnin*, which was to cause agitation throughout the country for over a hundred years. After a troubled reign of 36 years, *Go-Hanazono* abdicated in favor of his son *Fusahito Go-Tsuchimikado* and died 6 years later.

Gohommatsu, 五本松. A place in *Mikawa*, where, towards the middle of the 16th century, *Saigo Nobukazu* built a castle. His son *Masakatsu* was besieged in this castle and defeated by *Hōjō Ujinao* (1562).

Go-Horikawa-tennō, 後堀河天皇. The 86th Emperor of Japan (1222-1232), was *Toyohito*, grandson of *Takakura-tennō;* when ten years of age he was raised to the throne by *Hōjō Yoshitoki*, who had just deposed *Chūkyō* and exiled three ex-emperors. During his reign all authority was in the hands of the *Hōjō: Yoshitoki*, then *Yasutoki*, at *Kamakura ; Tokifusa, Tokiuji* and *Shigetoki*, at *Kyōto (Rokuhara)*. *Go-Horikawa*, after having abdicated in favor of his son *Shijō*, 2 years old died two years after, at the age of 23.

Goi, 五 井. A place in *Kazusa*, which from 1727 to 1841 was the residence of a younger branch of the *Arima* family (10,000 k.).

Go-Ichijō-tennō, 後一條天皇. The 68th Emperor of Japan (1017-1036), was prince *Atsuhira*, a son of *Ichijō-tennō*. He succeeded *Sanjō-tennō* when 9 years old. *Fujiwara Yorimichi*, an all powerful minister governed. In 1028, *Taira Tadatsune* revolted in *Shimōsa; Taira Naokata* sent against him was defeated. The *Minamoto, Yorinobu* and his son *Yoriyoshi* checked the revolt (1031). *Go-Ichijō* died when 29 years old.

Gojō, 五 條. A place in *Yamato*, was from 1600 to 1616 the residence of the *Matsukura daimyō* (25,000 k). Afterwards the castle became the property of the *Shōgun* who installed therein a *daikwan*. In 1863, at the time of the troubles which preceded the Restoration the *daikwan Suzuki Gennai* was assassinated in that castle.

Gojō, 五 條. A *kuge* family descended from *Sugawara Michizane*. The head of the family is now Viscount.

Go-kaidō, 五 街 道. Under the *Tokugawa*, the 5 great roads which, starting from *Nihon-bashi* (*Edo*), connected the provinces with the shōgunal city:

—— **1° The Tōkaidō,** 東 海 道: from *Edo* to *Kyōto*, through *Odawara, Fuchū* (*Shizuoka*), *Hamamatsu, Okazaki, Atsuta, Kuwana, Ōtsu*: 53 relays (*eki*) ; — 514 Km.

—— **2° The Nakasendō,** 中 仙 道, or **Kiso-kaidō,** 木 曾 街 道: from *Edo* to *Kyōto*, through *Ōmiya, Takasaki, Karuizawa, Shimo-Suwa, Fukushima, Ōta, Sekigahara, Kashiwabara, Kusatsu,* where it joined the *Tōkaidō:* 69 relays ;—542 Km.

—— **3° The Nikkō-kaidō,** 日 光 街 道: from *Edo* to *Nikkō*, through *Iwatsuki, Koga, Oyama, Utsunomiya, Tokujirō*. As it was the road on which the *Shōgun* travelled to go to *Nikkō*, it was called *O-nari-michi.*— 146 Km.

—— **4° The Kōshū-kaidō,** 甲 州 街 道: from *Edo* to *Fuchū* (*Kōfu*), through *Hachiōji, Katsunuma.*— 139 Km. After *Kōfu*, the road continued through *Nirazaki, Kanazawa,* and joined the *Nakasendō* at *Shimo-Suwa.*

—— **5° The Ōshū-kaidō,** 奧 州 街 道: from *Edo* to *Aomori*, through *Utsunomiya, Shirakawa, Fukushima, Sendai, Ichinoseki, Morioka, Ichinohe, Nobechi.*— 786 Km. It was also called *Riku-U-kaidō* and *Ō-U-kaidō.*

Besides these five main roads, there were the *waki-kaidō* : the *Hokkokukaidō,* (北 國 街 道), the *Chūgoku-kaidō,* (中 國 街 道), the *Nagasaki-kaidō,* (長 崎 街 道), and the *Mito-kaidō* (水 戶 街 道). The road on which the Emperor travelled when going to *Nikkō*, was called *Reihei-shi-kaidō,* (例 幣 使 街 道). This road connected *Takasaki* (*Kōzuke*) and *Nikkō*, passing through *Ashikaga* and *Mibu*.

Go-Kameyama-tennō, 後 龜 山 天 皇. The 99th Emperor of Japan (1373-1392), was prince *Norinari*, a son of *Go-Murakami*, who, at the age of 13, succeeded his brother *Chōkei* as emperor of the southern dynasty, whilst the *Ashikaga* supported *Go-Enyū* of the northern dynasty. He continued the struggle for 20 years, but all his supporters were defeated by the powerful *Shōgun Yoshimitsu*. In the end, he consented to come to an agreement. *Ouchi Yoshihiro* served as intermediary between the two rival courts. *Go-Kameyama* abdicated in favor of *Go-Komatsu*, since 10 years recognized as emperor of the North, but on the condition that the successors should alternately· be chosen from the two branches of the imperial family. This act put an end to the struggle which had lasted 60 years. After this event *Go-Kameyama* lived 32 years in the *Daigaku-ji* (*Saga*), long enough: to see the first two successors of *Go-Komatsu* chosen from the same branch, contrary to the treaty of 1392. His descendants were never to ascend the throne.

Go-kase-gawa, 五ケ瀬川. A river (118 Km.) which flows through *Hyūga* and empties itself into the sea near *Nobeoka*. — In its superior course it is called *Yakai-gawa*.

Go-Kashiwabara-tennō, 後柏原天皇. The 104th Emperor of Japan (1501-1527), was prince *Katsuhito*. He succeeded his father *Go-Tsuchimikado* at the age of 37. His reign was a succession of intestine wars: the family of the *Ashikaga Shōgun* was divided into two parties since the *Ōnin* dissensions; the great *daimyō* also were divided, and all Japan was in a state of revolution. But already *Mōri Motonari* and *Hōjō Sōun* appeared on the scene. They soon became masters of immense domains, thus preparing the road for *Nobunaga* and *Hideyoshi*, who were to pacify the country.

Go-kenin, 御家人. A name given to the *samurai* in the service of the *Shōgun* In the beginning, this term even applied to high officials, such as the *shugo* and the *jitō*. Under the *Tokugawa* it was only given to *samurai* inferior in rank to the *hatamoto*.

Go-kinai, 五畿内. The five provinces nearest to the ancient capital: *Yamashiro, Yamato, Kawachi, Settsu* and *Izumi*. Formerly only the first four provinces (*shi-ki*), existed but in 716 *Izumi* having been constituted a separate province, they were called *Go-ki*, or *Go-Kinai*.

Go-kō, 御幸. Or *gyōkō*, or *mi-yuki*. The journey of the emperor. At one time *gyōkō* or *go-kō* were indifferently used, but since the middle-ages *gyōkō* was reserved for the reigning emperor and *gokō* for the ex-emperors. The first journey of the emperor, after having been enthroned, was called *go-kō hajime*.

Go-Kōgon-tennō, 後光巖天皇. *Iyahito*, a son of *Kōgon*. An Emperor of the northern dynasty from 1352 to 1371, he succeeded his brother *Sukō* at the age of 15 and was enthroned without receiving the three imperial emblems (*shinki*), then in possession of the southern Emperor, *Go-Murakami*, who had surprised and captured *Kōgon, Kōmyō* and *Sukō*, two ex-emperors, and the reigning emperor of the North, giving them their freedom only five years after. *Go-Kōgon* witnessed the wars which the *Shōgun Takauji* and *Yoshiakira* waged against the South; he was even obliged to take refuge for some time in *Ōmi* (1361). After 20 years of an agitated reign, although less precarious than that of his Southern rival, he abdicated in favor of his son *Go-Enyū* and died 3 years later at the age of 37.

Gokoku-ji, 護 國 寺. A Buddhist temple at *Koishikawa* (*Tōkyō*), now the seat of the *Shingi* branch of the *Shingon* sect. Adjoining this temple, are the new burial grounds of the imperial family.

Go-Komatsu-tennō, 後 小 松 天 皇. Prince *Motohito*, a son of *Go-Enyū*. The 100th Emperor of Japan (1393-1412). When 7 years old, he succeeded his father as emperor of the Northern dynasty (1382). Ten years later, the emperor of the South, *Go-Kameyama*, having abdicated in his favor, and transmitted the imperial emblems to him, he became the sole legitimate sovereign ; but he exercised his power only as far as the *Shōgun Yoshimochi* allowed. After his abdication (1412) in favor of his son *Mihito* (*Shōkō-tennō*) he lived 20 years in retirement.

Go-Kōmyō-tennō, 後 光 明 天 皇. The 110th Emperor of Japan (1644-1654), was prince *Tsuguhito*, a son of *Go-Mi-no-o-tennō*. He succeeded his sister *Myōshō* at the age of 11 and died when 22 years old. The *Shōgun Iemitsu* and *Ietsuna* governed the empire during his reign.

Gokurakuji-zaka, 極 樂 寺 坂. A hill in *Sagami*. When *Nitta Yoshisada* intended to take *Kamakura* (1333), he sent *Ōtate Muneuji* and *Eda Yukiyoshi* to occupy that position, but they were repulsed by *Daibutsu Sadanao*, a general of the *Hōjō*, and *Muneuji* was killed in the battle. *Yoshisada* then took possession of the hill, and, from that place was able to attack *Kamakura*.

Go-Mi-no-o-tennō, 後 水 尾 天 皇. Prince *Kotohito*, a son of *Go-Yōzei*, whom he succeeded at the age of 17. The 108th Emperor of Japan (1612-1629). His reign witnessed the ruin of the *Toyotomi* and the last civil war before the Restoration. The power of the *Tokugawa* was then without a rival. *Hidetada* obliged the emperor to marry his daughter and, when the child born of this marriage was 7 years old, *Go-Mi-no-o* abdicated in his favor. He lived 50 years in retirement and died in 1680.

Go-Momozono-tennō, 後 桃 園 天 皇. Prince *Hidehito*, a son of *Momozono-tennō*. The 118th Emperor of Japan (1771-1779). He succeeded his aunt *Go-Sakuramachi*, when 14 years old, and died after a reign of 8 years during which the *Shōgun Ieharu* governed the empire.

Go-Murakami-tennō, 後 村 上 天 皇. Prince *Norinaga*, a son of *Go-Daigo*, whom he succeeded when 12 years old. The 97th Emperor of Japan (1339-1368). He continued the war against the Northern dynasty, but without more success than his father. However the dissensions in the *Ashikaga* family proved advantageous to him. In 1351, while *Takauji* was in *Kwantō*, *Kusunoki Masanori* and *Kitabatake Akiyoshi* made an attack on *Kyōto*, where they took the two ex-emperors *Kōgon* and *Kōmyō* and the emperor *Sukō*, of the Northern dynasty prisoners. *Go-Murakami* re-entered the capital but was soon besieged by *Ashikaga Yoshiakira* and again fled to *Yoshino* mountain, taking along with him the three prisoners whom he liberated only five years later.

In 1358 he was besieged in his retreat on *Yoshino*, and retired to *Kongō-san* (*Kawachi*), then to *Sumiyoshi* (*Settsu*) where he died at 41 years of age, having seen the greater number of his partisans abandon the struggle and side with the *Ashikaga*.

Go-Nara-tennō, 後奈良天皇. Prince *Tomohito* and son of *Go-Kashiwabara* whom he succeeded at the age of 31. The 105th Emperor of Japan (1527-1557). During his reign, Japan was a prey to civil war. The *Ashikaga Shōgun* had no authority whatever; the *daimyō* were at war with one another; the *Hōjō* and the *Mōri* were asserting themselves, whilst the *Ōuchi*, the *Hosokawa*, etc. disappeared. At the death of *Go-Nara*, *Nobunaga* was 24 years old, *Hideyoshi* 21, and *Ieyasu* 15: they were soon to exert themselves in restoring order and in pacifying the country exhausted by a century of uninterrupted civil war. It was during the reign of *Go-Nara* that Europeans made their first appearance in Japan (1542), and that St. Francis Xavier came to preach the Gospel (August 1549—November 1551).

Gongen, 權現. A name given in the *Ryōbu-Shintō* to a certain number of gods of the pure *Shintō*, that, according to the bonzes, were but the temporary manifestations of *Buddha*. This name is especially applied to *Tokugawa Ieyasu*, honored after his death by the name of *Tōshō-daigongen*, and commonly called *Gongen Sama*.

Go-Nijō-tennō, 後二條天皇. Prince *Kuniharu*, a son of *Go-Uda*. The 94th Emperor of Japan (1302-1308). At the age of 17, he succeeded *Fushimi-tennō*. The ex-emperors *Kameyama* and *Go-Uda* at *Kyōto*, but especially the *Shikken Hōjō Sadatoki* at *Kamakura*, governed in the name of the young emperor, who died at the age of 24 years.

Gonkengyō, 權檢校. The amalgamation of two offices by imperial order. Later it was called *gonkwan*.

Gonkwan, 權官 or *Kenkwan*. A temporary amalgamation of two offices.

Gon no ben, 權辨. Formerly a deputy *chūben* or *shōben:* he was styled *gon no chūben* or *gon no shōben*, or simply *gon no ben*.

Gon no kami, 權守. Formerly a vice-governor of a province. Generally the *kokushi* (governor) resided at *Kyōto*, and the *gon no kami* administered the province in his name. Only the large provinces (*taikoku, jōkoku*) had a *gon no kami* (*chūkoku, shōkoku*). When a *dainagon* or a *chūnagon* was sent to a province in disgrace, he received the title of *gon no kami*.

Go-Reizei-tennō, 後冷泉天皇. Prince *Chikahito*, a son of *Go-Shujaku*, whom he succeeded when 21 years old. The 70th Emperor of Japan (1046-1068). During his reign occurred the revolt of *Abe-Yoritoki*, the 9 years' war in *Mutsu* (1053-1062). The fame of the *Minamoto*, *Yoriyoshi* and *Yoshiie* dates from that campaign. *Go-Reizei* died at the age of 44 years after having thrice witnessed the conflagration of his palace.

Goryō-bayashi, 五靈林. A place, existing formerly north of *Kyōto*. In 1467, *Hatakeyama Masanaga* was defeated there by *Hatakeyama Yoshinari*.

Goryū-zan, 五龍山. A mountain in *Hizen, Kita-Matsuura-gōri*. It was there that the Mongols arrived in 1281.

Go-Saga-tennō, 御嵯峨天皇. *Kunihito*, a son of *Tsuchimi-kado*. The 88th Emperor of Japan (1243-1246). He succeeded *Shijō-tennō* when 23 years old. At the latter's death, the *Kwampaku Fuji-wara Michiie* wished to have *Tadanari*, his grandson, and son of *Jun-toku-tennō*, elected, but the *Shikken Hōjō Yasutoki* opposed the election on account of the part taken by *Juntoku* in the war of *Shōkyū* (1221) and had the son of *Tsuchimikado* elected. *Go-Saga* abdicated after a reign of 4 years, but as his two immediate successors were his two sons *Go-Fukakusa* and *Kameyama*, he practically governed for a period of 25 years. He lived in peace with the *Hōjō*, so much so, that when *Tokiyori* deposed the *Shōgun Yoritsugu* (1252) he chose as his successor *Munetaka-shinnō*, a son of *Go-Saga*. Before dying 1272, *Go-Saga* established the rule that henceforth the emperors should be chosen alternately from among the descendants of his two sons, *Go-Fukakusa* and *Kameyama:* this clause of his will subsequently occasioned rivalries and frequent troubles.

Go-sai-e, 御齊會. The most solemn of the Buddhist ceremonies, celebrated at the imperial palace; they were performed at the *Daigoku-den*, and consisted principally in the explanation of a sacred book. They

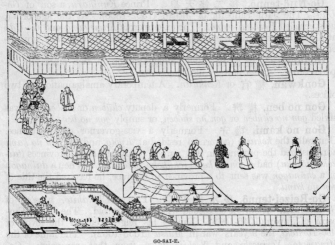

GO-SAI-E.

were inaugurated in 767, under the empress *Shōtoku* and henceforth performed annually, from the 8th to the 14th day of the 1st month.

Go-Sai-in-tennō, 御西院天皇. Prince *Nagahito*, a son of *Go-Mi-no-o*. The 111th Emperor of Japan (1655-1662). He succeeded his brother *Go-Kōmyō*, when 18 years old, and abdicated in favor of his brother (*Satohito-Reigen-tennō*) after a reign of 8 years, during which the *Shōgun Ietsuna* governed according to his will. *Go-Sai-in-tennō* died in 1685.

Go-Sakuramachi-tennō, 御櫻町天皇. An Empress (117) who reigned from 1763 to 1770. She was princess *Toshi-ko*, daughter of *Sakuramachi-tennō*, and succeeded her brother *Momozono* when 22 years old. After permitting the *Shōgun Ieharu* to govern the country, she abdicated at the age of 30, in favor of her nephew *Hidehito* (*Go-Momozono-tennō*), and lived 44 years in retirement.

Go-Sanjō-tennō, 御三條天皇. Prince *Takahito* and a son of *Go-Shujaku*. The 71st Emperor of Japan (1069-1072). He succeeded his brother *Go-Reizei* at the age of 35. *Go-Sanjō* is entitled to special mention for his active share in the government of the country at an epoch when, in conformity with a popular tradition, the emperor was to reign, but not to govern. Scarcely had he ascended the throne, than he expressed the wish to judge all matters of state personally. For this purpose he created the *Kiroku-sho*, a sort of council over which he presided and which decided all important questions. He reformed the abuses of the administration, suppressed a number of *shō-en*, weakened the power of the *Fujiwara*, and, in short, proved himself a remarkable sovereign. Unfortunately, after a reign of 4 years, he became ill, abdicated in favor of his son *Sadahito* (*Shirakawa-tennō*), and died the following year.

Go-sanke, 御三家 — See *Sanke*.

Go-sankyō, 御三卿. — See *Sankyō*.

Go-san-nen no eki, 後三年役. The 3 years' war (1086-1089). During the 9 years' war (1053-1062), *Kiyowara Takenori* had helped *Minamoto Yoriyoshi* to defeat *Abe Yoritoki* and his sons, and in return for his services, had been nominated *Chinjufu-shōgun*. His son *Sadahira* governed 6 *kōri* of the province of *Mutsu*, when *Iehira*, the latter's brother, aided by his uncle *Takehira*, revolted against him ; soon the war extended over the whole province. *Minamoto Yoshiie* was sent to support *Sadahira*. He besieged *Iehira* and *Takehira* in the castle of *Kanazawa* (*Dewa*). The rebels set fire to the castle and escaped, but were killed in their flight (1089).

Gose, 御所. A place in *Yamato*, the residence of the *Kuwayama daimyō* (26,000 k.) from 1590 till 1629.

Go-sechi-e, 五節會. Five festivals formerly celebrated at the palace : *gwanjitsu, hakuba, tōka, tango* and *toyoakira*.

Go-sechi no mai, 五節舞. Dances formerly performed by five dancing-girls in the 11th month, on the day of the ox. In 742, the emperor *Shōmu* had them performed at the palace on the first day of the year. Since that time, it was customary to have them performed on the five principal festivals.

Go-sekke, 五攝家. The five branches of the *Fujiwara* family ; *Konoe, Kujō, Nijō, Ichijō,* and *Takatsukasa* among which the Empress, the *Kwampaku* and the *Sesshō* were to be chosen.

Go-sekku, 五節句. Five traditional, popular festivals in Japan : *jinjitsu* (the 1st day of the 1st month), *jōmi.* (the 3rd day of the 3rd month), *tango,* (the 5th day of the 5th month), *tanabata* (the 7th day of the 7th month) and *chōyō* (the 9th day of the 9th month). It is said that this institution dates as far back as the reign of the emperor *Uda* (889-897).

Go-shichi-nichi no mishiho, 五七日御修法. In 833, *Kōbō-Daishi* asked the Emperor to have an oratory built in the palace, where, conformably to a Chinese custom, solemn prayers should be said for the peace and prosperity of the empire. The *Shingon-in* was then erected and the following year, from the 8th to the 15th of the first month, *Kōbō-Daishi* himself performed the ceremony, which, from that time, has been renewed every year by the chief bonze of the *Tōji* temple.

Go-Shirakawa-tennō, 後白河天皇. Prince *Masahito,* a son of *Toba-tennō.* The 77th Emperor of Japan (1156-1158). At the age of 29, he succeeded his brother *Konoe.* At the latter's death (1155), the ex-emperor *Sutoku* tried to have his son *Shigehito* nominated, but *Toba* succeeded in having another of his sons (*Masahito*) elected. *Sutoku* displeased, brought a great number of the nobles over to his party: at their head was *Fujiwara Yorinaga* and all the *Minamoto,* with the exception of *Yoshitomo.* The latter, with all the *Taira,* sided with *Toba:* this was the *Hōgen* war (1156). The *Taira* conquered: *Sutoku* was exiled to *Sanuki,* and *Shigehito* became a bonze. Two years later, *Go-Shirakawa* abdicated in favor of his son *Morihito* (*Nijō-tennō*), but he continued to govern during the reigns of his three immediate successors, and died at the age of 67 years (1192).

Gosho, 御所. The imperial palace in *Kyōto.* It was built by *Kwammu* in 794, and frequently destroyed by fire. *Nobunaga* and *Hideyoshi* repaired and embellished it. After the fire of 1788, *Matsudaira Sadanobu* rebuilt it on the model of the ancient palace. It was burnt last in 1854, and was rebuilt the following year: it is the present palace.

Go-shō, 五將. A name to designate the five most celebrated generals of the middle-ages: *Taira Kiyomori, Minamoto Yoritomo, Ashikaga Takauji, Oda Nobunaga,* and *Toyotomi Hideyoshi.*

Gosho-bugyō, 御所奉行. The superintendent of the shōgunal palace during the *Kamakura* shōgunate. The first who received the title was *Hōjō Tokifusa,* in 1204. Those who had performed the functions of *hyōjōshū* or those of *hikitsukeshū* were generally raised to that dignity.

Gosho-dokoro, 御書所. Formerly the imperial library. It was superintended by a *Bettō.*

Go-sho-Hachiman, 五所八幡. The five great temples in *Kyūshū,* dedicated to *Hachiman,* the god of war: *Ōwake no miya* (*Chikuzen*), *Chiguri no miya* (*Hizen*), *Fujisaki no miya* (*Higo*), *Nitta no miya* (*Satsuma*), and *Shō-Hachiman* (*Ōsumi*).

Gōshū, 江州. The Chinese name of *Ōmi.*

Go-shuin-bune 御朱印船. Under the *Tokugawa,* those authorized to carry on trade with foreign countries received a patent sealed with the red seal (*go-shu-in*) of the *Shōgun;* hence the name given to their vessels. The principal houses that enjoyed this privilege were, — in *Kyōto: Sumikura, Chaya, Fushimiya,* — in *Sakai, Iyoya;* — in *Nagasaki, Suetsugu,*

Araki, Funamoto, Itoya, etc. Besides, certain *daimyō,* the *Matsuura, Arima,* the *Sō,* the *Shimazu,* etc., enjoyed the same privilege.

GO-SHUIN-BUNE.

Go-shuin-chi, 御朱印地. Under the *Tokugawa,* the temples received a deed sealed with the red seal *(shu-in)* of the *Shōgun* confirming their grant of land, hence the name given to their possessions. The object of this custom was to prevent the sale of the said grounds. Sometimes the *kuge* received domains under the same conditions.

Go-Shujaku-tennō, 後朱雀天皇. Prince *Atsunaga,* a son of *Ichijō-tennō.* The 69th Emperor of Japan (1037-1045). He succeeded his brother *Go-Ichijō* at the age of 28 and died after a reign of 9 years, during which time the *Kwampaku, Yorimichi,* his uncle, exercised full authority.

Gosō-goe, 五僧越. A mountain road between *Waki-ga-hara (Ōmi)* and *Tokiyama (Mino).* It was on that road that *Shimazu Yoshihiro,* being defeated at the battle of *Sekigahara* (1600), fled towards *Osaka.* On this account it is also called *Shimazu-goe.*

Go-Sukō-in, 御崇光院 (1372-1456). *Sadafusa,* grandson of the emperor *Sukō,* and son of prince *Yoshihito-shinnō.* When *Shōkō-tennō* died without an heir (1428), *Hikohito,* the son of *Sadafusa,* was raised to the throne *(Go-Hanazono,)* and at the death of his father, bestowed on him the name of *Go-Sukō. Sadafusa* died when 85 years of age. He was a poet and a remarkable historian.

Go-tairō, 五大老. The five members of the council of state created by *Hideyoshi* and who were to assist his son in the government: *Tokugawa Ieyasu, Maeda Toshiie, Mōri Terumoto, Uesugi Kagekatsu* and *Ukita Hideie.* They were above the five *bugyō* and were to form the council of the regency during the minority of *Hideyori.*

Go-Takakura-in, 後 高 倉 院 . — See *Morisada-shinnō*.

Gotō, 五 島 . A group of islands north-west of *Kyūshū*, belonging to the province of *Hizen*. The most important are : *Fukue-jima, Nakadōri-shima, Wakamatsu-jima, Naru-shima* and *Hisaka-jima*.

Gotō, 五 島 . A family of *daimyō* in *Hizen*, descended from *Seiwa-Genji*. *Uku-Iemori* a descendant of *Takeda Nobuhiro*, established in the *Gotō* islands, took the name of *Gotō Iemori*. His successors resided there until the Restoration (12,000 k.). In the 16th century two of them, *Moriharu* (+ 1579) and *Sumiharu* (+ towards 1620) were Christians, and, following their example, a great number of their vassals embraced Christianity.—The head of the family is now Viscount.

Gotō, 後 藤 . A family of *samurai* in *Tosa* ennobled after the Restoration. — The head of the family is now Count.

—— **Shōjirō,** 象 二 郎 (1837-1897). Born at *Kōchi*, became counsellor of his *daimyō*, and was the initiator of the memorial addressed to the *Shōgun* in order to induce him to restore the authority to the emperor, usurped by his ancestors (1867). He has, several times been minister since the Restoration.

Gotō Shizan, 後 藤 芝 山 (1722-1782). Confucianist of the *Takamatsu* (*Sanuki*), clan.

Gotō, 後 藤 . *Samurai* family of the 16th century, vassal to the *Kuroda daimyō*.

—— **Mototsugu,** 基 次 . Also called *Matabei*, son of *Motokuni ;* served *Kuroda Yoshitaka*, then *Hideyoshi* and distinguished himself in Korea, at *Sekigahara*, etc. He afterwards sided with *Hideyori* and was killed at the siege of *Ōsaka* (1615). Some say that he fled with *Hideyori* into *Satsuma*. *Mototsugu* was a catholic.

—— **Ujifusa,** 氏 房 (1570-1615). Son of *Mototsugu*, after having served *Kuroda Nagamasa*, sided with *Hideyori* and, like his father, died at the siege of *Ōsaka*.

Gotō, 後 藤 . Family of artists renowned in metallurgy : ornaments for swords, armor, etc.

—— **Yūjō,** (1435-1512), 祐 乘 . Founder of the family, was born in *Mino*, came to *Kyōto*, where he was employed by the *Shōgun Yoshimasa* and *Yoshihisa*. He based his work especially on the designs of *Kanō Motonobu*, his neighbor. His descendants continued his work. The best known among these are : *Sōjō* (1487-1564), *Jōshin* (1505-1562), *Kōjō* (1529-1620), *Eijō* (1576-1617), *Kenjō* (1615-1662), *Sokujō* (+ 1668), *Teijō* (1604-1673), *Renjō* (1628-1709), *Tsujō* (1671-1722), *Jujō* (1685-1742), *Enjō* (1721-1784), *Keijō* (1740-1804), etc.

Go-Toba-tennō, 後 鳥 羽 天 皇 . Prince *Takahira*, a son of *Takakura-tennō*. The 82nd Emperor of Japan (1184-1198). Was raised to the throne when only 4 years old, after his brother *Antoku* had been carried off to the West by the vanquished *Taira*. His grandfather, *Go-Shirakawa*, governed in his name. He witnessed the elevation of the *Minamoto* and the downfall of the *Taira*. It was *Go-Toba* that bestowed the title of *Sei-i-taishōgun* on *Yoritomo* (1192), giving him

an influence that increased daily, while the
imperial authority, by degrees became
merely honorary. After a reign of 15
years *Go-Toba* abdicated in favor of his
son *Tsuchimikado*, who in turn, was
succeeded by his brother *Juntoku* (1211).
During these two reigns, *Go-Toba* governed
in the name of his sons. After the death
of *Sanetomo*, the 3rd and last *Minamoto
Shōgun* (1219), the power entirely passed
into the hands of the *Hōjō. Go-Toba*,
wishing to take it from them, entered into
open war against the powerful *Shikken ;*
unfortunately his troops were defeated at
Uji, Seta and even in *Kyōto* (*Shokyū no
ran* — 1221). The conquerors showed

GO-TOBA-TENNŌ.

themselves merciless : *Chūkyō* only 4 years old was deposed after a reign
of 70 days ; his father *Juntoku* was exiled to *Sado, Tsuchimikado* to
Tosa ; and *Go-Toba* was relegated to *Amagōri* (*Oki*), where he lived for
18 years more.

Go-Tsuchimikado-tennō, 後土御門天皇. Prince *Fusahito*,
a son of *Go-Hanazono* whom he succeeded when 20 years of age was
103rd Emperor of Japan (1466–1500). His reign began with the
Ōnin civil war (*Ōnin no tairan*), caused by rivalries existing among the
families of the *Ashikaga*, the *Hosokawa*, the *Yamana*, the *Hatakeyama*,
the *Shiba*, etc. The troubles lasted for 10 years and came to an end
only by the exhaustion of the two parties ; they began again after the
death of the *Shōgun Yoshimasa* (1490) and continued for a hundred
years. The misery caused by these wars affected even the imperial
palace, and when *Go-Tsuchimikado* died at the age of 59, his body
remained for 40 days without burial, the necessary money for solemn
funerals being wanting. Finally a great *daimyō* of *Ōmi, Sasaki Takayori*, had them performed at his own expense.

Go-Uda-tennō, 後宇多天皇. Prince *Yohito*, a son of *Kameyama-tennō*. The 91st Emperor of Japan (1275–1287). He was eight
years old, when he succeeded his father, who governed in his name.
The most noteworthy event that took place during his reign was the
destruction of the fleet sent in 1281 by *Koppitsuretsu* (*Kublai-khan*) to
conquer Japan (See *Hōjō Tokimune*). After a reign of 13 years, *Go-Uda*
abdicated in favor of his cousin *Fushimi*. When his son *Go-Nijō* ascended the throne (1302), he regained influence, but in 1307 at the death of
his wife *Yūgi-mon-in*, he had his head shaved and retired to the temple of
Daikaku-ji at *Saga* (*Yamashiro*), where he died in 1324 at the age of
57 years.

Go-yō-beya, 御用部屋. The council of the *Tokugawa Shōgun ;*
it was composed of the *Tairō*, five *Rōjū* and five *Waka-doshiyori*.

Go-Yōzei-tennō, 後陽成天皇. Prince *Katahito*, a grandson
of *Ogimachi-tennō*, and son of *Masahito-shinnō*. The 107th emperor

of Japan (1587–1611). He succeeded his grandfather at the age of sixteen. His reign commenced when *Hideyoshi* was at the zenith of his power and there was peace and prosperity throughout the country. *Hideyoshi* rebuilt the imperial palace and paid all the expenses of the Court: he was rewarded by a visit of *Go-Yōzei* to his palace of *Momoyama*, and by a poem written by the emperor himself. The expedition to Korea (1592–1598), the death of *Hideyoshi* (1598), the battle of *Sekigahara*, the triumph of *Ieyasu* (1600), the latter's nomination to the shōgunate (1603) and his abdication in favor of his son *Hidetada* (1605) such were the events which made his reign one of the most important in the history of Japan. The Court was the mere witness of these events and took but little part in them. After a reign of 25 years, *Go-Yōzei* abdicated in favor of his son (*Kotohito-Go-Mi-no-o-tennō*) and died in 1617, aged 47.

Go-yū, 五 雄 (Lit.: the five brave). A name to designate the five most celebrated generals of the 16th century: *Mōri Motonari*, *Hōjō Ujiyasu*, *Uesugi Terutora*, *Takeda Harunobu*, and *Oda Nobunaga*.

Go-zan, 五 山. In imitation of India and China, the order of precedence of the five principal temples of the *Zen* sect was fixed under the *Hōjō*: they were the *Enkaku-ji*, the *Kenchō-ji*, and the *Jufuku-ji*, in *Kamakura*, together with the *Kennin-ji* and the *Tōfuku-ji* in *Kyōto*. Later, the chief temples were distinguished as the *Kamakura go-zan* and the *Kyōto go-zan* (1336). The former were the *Kenchō-ji* the *Enkaku-ji*, the *Jufuku-ji*, the *Jōchi-ji*, and the *Iken-ji*; the latter the *Tenryū-ji* the *Shōkoku-ji*, the *Kennin-ji*, the *Tōfuku-ji* and the *Manju-ji*, superior to them was the *Nanzen-ji*.

Gozen, 御 前. Formerly honorary title added to the name of ladies of a certain rank: *Tamae-gozen*, *Shizuka-gozen*.

Gozu-tennō, 牛 頭 天 皇 (Lit.: the emperor with an ox head). One of the names by which *Susano-o* is honored.

Gujō, 郡 上. A town in *Mino*, also called *Yawata* or *Hachiman*. It has an ancient castle, built by the *Asakura* towards the end of the 15th century. The castle was successively the residence of the *Endō daimyō* of the *Inaba* (1590–1600), *Endō* (1600–1692), *Inoue* (1692–1697) *Kanamori* (1697–1758); finally from 1758 till 1868 that of the *Aoyama* (50,000 k.).

Gūke, 郡 家. Formerly the seat of the administration of the *gun* or *kōri*.

Gumma-ken, 郡 馬 縣. The department formed with the province of *Kōzuke*. — Pop.: 850,000 inh. — Capital: *Maebashi* (35,000 inh.) — Principal towns: *Takasaki* (31,000 inh.) *Kiriu* (20,000 inh.) etc.

Gun, 郡 (Jap.: *kōri*.) District. At the *Taikwa* reform, the country was divided into 66 provinces, comprising 592 *gun*. This division changed at times. At present there are 645 *gun*. (See App. V).

Gundan, 軍 團. A corps of troops formerly recruited and maintained in the provinces; the soldiers of 5 or 6 districts formed a *gundan*. Their number varied. It was commanded by a *taigi* and 1 or 2 *shōgi*. A *kō-i* commanded 200 men; a *ryoshi* a hundred; a *taisei* 50; 10 men formed a *kwa* and 5 a *go*. — In case of war, several *gundan* united to form an army corps (*gun*); every army corps was commanded by a *shōgun*, whose inferior officers were one *fuku-shōgun*, 1 or 2 *gunkan*, from one to four *gunsō*, and from 2 to 4 *rokuji*. A *Taishōgun* was at the head of 3 army corps. — These regulations were not applied to the provinces of *Saikaidō*, administered by the *Dazaifu*; nor to those of *Mutsu*, which had its *Chinjufu*; nor to those of *Dewa*, the military division of which was stationed at the castle of *Akita*. — The emperor *Kwammu* abolished the *gundan* and troops were only maintained in the provinces of *Mutsu*, *Dewa*, *Sado*, and in the *Dazaifu*.

Gunji, 郡司. Officials charged with the administration of districts (*gun*) since the *Taikwa* reform (645). According to their importance, the districts were divided into 5 classes, and were administered as follows:

1° *Taigun* 大郡, (from 16 to 20 leagues in circuit): 1 *tairyō*, 1 *shōryō*, 3 *shusei*, 2 *shuchō*.

2° *Jōgun* 上郡 (from 12 to 16 leagues in circuit): 1 *tairyō*, 1 *shōryō*, 2 *shusei*, 2 *shuchō*.

3° *Chūgun* 中郡 (from 8 to 12 leagues in circuit): 1 *tairyō*, 1 *shōryō*, 1 *shusei*, 1 *shuchō*.

4° *Gegun* 下郡 (from 4 to 8 leagues) 1 *tairyō*, 1 *shōryō*, 1 *shuchō*.

5° *Shōgun* 小郡 (from 2 to 4 leagues) 1 *tairyō*, 1 *shuchō*.

The *gunji* under the authority of the *kokushi* regulated all questions of taxes, instruction, agriculture, registration, etc. With the increase of the *shō-en* in the 11th century, the members of the *gunji* diminished and they were gradually replaced by the *nanushi*, the *satonushi*, etc.

Gunkan-bugyō, 軍艦奉行. A title created in 1829 and given to the official charged with the naval forces of the shōgunate.

Gunken, 郡縣. System of centralization in contradistinction to the feudal system (*hōken*).

Gunsho-ruijū, 郡書類集. A collection of 1821 volumes of ancient and rare works, published by *Hanawa Hokiichi* in 1782

Gūshū, 隅州. The Chinese name of the province of *Ōsumi*.

Gusoku-bugyō, 具足奉行. A title created in 1641 and conferred on the officials charged with the manufacture and repair of armor, helmets, etc. In 1863, this office was joined to that of the *Yumi-ya-bugyō* under the name of *Bugu-bugyō*.

Gwaikoku - bugyō, 外國奉行. A title created in 1858 for the official whose function it was to treat with foreigners; the following year it was joined to that of *Kanagawa-bugyō*. Gradually the number of these officials was raised to 10; their superintendent was a *Gwaikoku-sōbugyō*.

Gwaimu-shō, 外務省. The Department of Foreign Affairs created in 1885.

Gwakkō-Bosatsu, 月光菩薩. A Buddhist divinity who resides in the moon.

Gwakō-shi, 畫工司. An official created in 808, who had charge of all that concerned painting, etc. The title was suppressed at the foundation of the *e-dokoro*.

Gwan-ei, 元永. *Nengō:* 1118-1119.

Gwanjitsu no sechi-e, 元日節會. A festival celebrated at the palace on the first day of the year. The Emperor, after having received the felicitations of the Court in the *Daigoku-den*, invites all the officials to a feast, in the *Hōraku-den*.

Gwanryaku, 元曆. *Nengō:* 1184.

Gwassan, 月山. (Lit.: mountain of the moon). A mountain (1750 met) in *Uzen*. It is also called *Tsuki no yama*.

Gyōbu-shō, 刑部省. The ministry of Justice since the time of the *Taikwa* reform (645). It had charge of the prisons, the punishment of criminals, etc. Later, its authority passed to the *Kebiishi*, and only the name of *Gyōbu-shō* and the titles, all purely honorific of *Gyōbu-kyō* (minister), *Gyōbu-tayū*, etc. remained.

Gyōgesha, 凝花舍 or *Umetsubo*. A building reserved for the women employed in the imperial palace.

Gyōgi-Bosatsu, 行基菩薩 (670-749). A celebrated bonze of Korean birth, who when young, came to Japan and after having studied under the most renowned masters travelled through the provinces preaching Buddhism and constructing bridges, dikes, etc. In order to triumph over the opposition of the ardent Shintoists, he began to diffuse the doctrine of the *Ryōbu-shintō*, according to which the ancient gods, venerated in Japan, had been but the temporary manifestations (*gongen*) of Buddha, or other *Bosatsu*. Owing to this compromise, Buddhism made rapid progress. *Gyōgi* exercised a great influence over the emperor *Shōmu*, who nominated him *Dai-sōjō*, and bestowed on him the title of *Bosatsu*.

GYŌGI-BOSATSU.

Tradition attributes to him the invention of the potter's wheel, used in making a kind of rough porcelain (*gyōgi-yaki*) and he is supposed to have made innumerable sculptures and works of art.

Gyōkei, 行啓. The name given to the journeys and visits paid by the empresses or the imperial prince They set out in a special carriage (*itoge-guruma*) and were accompanied by an escort prescribed by the ceremonial of the Court.

Gyōkyō, 行敎. A celebrated bonze of the 9th century descended from *Takeshiuchi no Sukune*. He spent 90 days in prayer in the temple of *Hachiman* in *Usa* (*Buzen*), after which the god appeared to him and expressed the desire to have a temple erected near the capital: upon this revelation the emperor *Seiwa* built the temple of *Otoko-yama* (859).

Gyoshi-taibu, 御史太夫. In 648 the emperor *Kōtoku* having appointed prince *Ōtomo*, while still a child, *Dajō-daijin*, created three officials, with the title of *Gyoshi-taibu*, to assist him. When *Ōtomo* ascended the throne (*Kōbun-tennō*) in 672, he nominated his assistants *Dainagon*, and the title of *Gyoshi-taibu* was suppressed.

H

Hachi-daishū, 八 大 集. The eight principal collections of Japanese poetry from the *Kokin-shū* (905) to the *Shin-kokin-shū* (1205).

Hachi-dō, 八 道. The 8 great territorial divisions of Japan —See *Dō*.

Hachigata, 鉢 形. A castle (*Musashi*), which belonged successively to the *daimyō Fujita*, and the *Hōjō* (1537-1590). *Uesugi Kagekatsu* took it at the downfall of the *Hōjō* (1590).

Hachihon, 八 品. A branch of the *Hokke* sect, founded in the 14th century by the bonze *Nichiryū*. In 1898, its name was changed to that of *Hommon-Hokke-shū*.

Hachijō, 八 條. A *kuge* family descended from *Fujiwara Uona*. The head of the family is now Viscount.

Hachijō-jima, 八 丈 嶋. The most southern of the 7 *Izu* islands (40 Km. in circuit).

Hachiman, 八 幡. A name under which the emperor *Ōjin* (201-312) is honored as a god. He is also called *Yawata* (the corresponding Japanese word). *Hachiman* was the tutelary god of the *Minamoto*.

Hachiman, 八 幡. A place in *Ōmi*, near lake *Biwa*. In 1586, *Niwa Hidetsugu* built a castle there using the remains of the *Azuchi* castle. At the dealth of *Hidetsugu*, it was abandoned, and the temple of *Hachiman*, which had given its name to the village, was rebuilt.

Hachiman, 八 幡. In *Mino*. — See *Gujō*.

Hachiman-gū 八 幡 宮. The name of the temples dedicated to the god of war. The most celebrated are: *Usa-Hachiman* (*Higo*), *Otoko-yama no Hachiman* (*Yamashiro*), *Tsurugaoka no Hachiman*, at *Kamakura*.

Hachiman Tarō, 八 幡 太 郎. — See *Minamoto Yoshiie*.

Hachinohe, 八 戸. A town (11,300 inb.) in *Mutsu ;* from 1664 till 1868 it was the residence of the younger branch of the *Nambu* family (20,000 k).

Hachiōji, 八 王 子. A town (23,200 inh.) in *Musashi*. *Hōjō Ujiaki* built a castle there which was besieged and taken by *Maeda Toshiie* (1590). *Ieyasu* gave it in fief to *Ōkubo Nagayasu*, who was dispossessed in 1613.

Hachirō-gata, 八 郎 瀉. A lake (59 Km. in circuit) in *Ugo*.

Hachisuka 蜂 須 賀. A family of *daimyō* descended from the *Seiwa-Genji* by *Shiba Takatsune* (+ 1367)

——**Masakatsu,** 正 勝 (1525-1585). A son of *Masa-toshi*. He successively served *Saitō Toshimasa*, *Oda Nobunaga*, finally *Hideyoshi*, who had him nominated *Shuri-daibu*, and bestowed on him a revenue of 10,000 k.

——**Iemasa,** 家 政 (1558-1638). A son of the above. He took part in the expedition sent by *Hideyoshi* to

Shikoku and established himself at *Tokushima* in *Awa* (1585). He also took part in the Korean war, and after his return resigned the administration of his domains to his son. *Iemasa* was a Christian.

—— **Yoshishige** 義鎮 (1581-1615). Sided with *Ieyasu* in 1600 ; after the battle of *Sekigahara*, his revenues were raised to 186,000 k. and he received the title of *Awa no kami*. After the siege of *Ōsaka* (1615), *Awaji* island was added to his domains, which raised his revenue to 258,000 k.—His descendants resided at *Tokushima* till the Restoration. The head of the family is now Marquis.

Hachi-suke, 八助. In the middle-ages there were 8 provinces the governors of which had the title of *suke: Akita-jō no suke* (*Dewa*), *Miura no suke* (*Sagami*), *Chiba no suke* (*Shimōsa*), *Kazusa no suke* (*Kazusa*), *Kano no suke* (*Izu*), *Togashi no suke* (*Kaga*), *Ōuchi no suke* (*Suwō*), and *Ii no suke* (*Tōtōmi*).

Haga, 芳賀. A place in *Shimotsuke*. Towards 1185, *Haga-Takachika* built a castle there. In 1577, the residence was transferred to *Mōka*.

Hagi, 萩. A town (16,000 inh.) in *Nagato*. In the 13 century, *Hōjō Naomoto* built a castle there which became the possession of the *Yoshimi*. From 1600 to 1862, it was the residence of the *Mōri daimyō* (369,000 k.).

Hagiwara, 萩原. A *kuge* family descended from the *Urabe*. The head of the family is now Viscount.

Hahoro-gawa, 羽幌川. A river (79 Km) in *Teshio* (*Hokkaidō*).

Haichō, 廢朝. Formerly a 3 days' mourning observed by the Court at the death of a high dignitary. The curtain of the *Seiryō-den* was lowered, music and dancing were forbidden etc.

Haimu, 廢務. A holiday formerly granted to officials at an eclipse of the sun, at the anniversary of the death of the preceding emperor, etc.

Haishitsu, 廢疾. (Lit. : lame, infirm). According to the *Taihō* code, all invalids, such as : insane, deaf, dumb, dwarfs, hump-backed, etc. were exempt from taxes.

Hai-taishi, 廢太子. The imperial prince who after having received the title of heir apparent (*taishi*) was deprived of it for some grave reason. Such was the case with *Sawara-shinnō*, a son of *Kōnin* : *Kōgaku-shinnō*, a son of *Heijō* : *Tsunesada-shinnō*, a son of *Seiwa*, etc.

Hai-tei, 廢帝. A deposed emperor. Thus *Junnin-tennō* deposed by the empress *Shōtoku* and exiled to *Awaji*, is know by the name of *Awaji-haitei* ; *Chūkyū-tennō* deposed by *Hōjō Yoshitoki* is called *Kujō-haitei*.

Hakata, 伯太. A place in *Izumi* ; it was the residence of the *daimyō Watanabe* from 1661-1868.

Hakata, 博多. A port in *Chikuzen*, formerly very flourishing. It is now the commercial port of *Fukuoka* which it touches. It was near *Hakata* that a tempest destroyed the fleet sent by *Kublai-khan* (1281). A monument erected in the public garden recalls the event. In 1333 *Kikuchi Taketoki* faithful supporter of *Go-Daigo*, was defeated and killed at that place by the troops of *Shōni*, *Ōtomo*, etc.

Hakkai-zan, 八 海 山 . A group of 8 mountains forming one range north of *Echigo.* It has 8 lakes

Hakkōda-yama, 八 甲 田 山 . A mountain (1960 m.) in *Mutsu.*

Hakodate, 函 舘 . A seaport (85,000 inh.) in the province of *Oshima* (*Hokkaidō*). It was the last stronghold of the *Shōgun's* partisans at the Restoration : *Enomoto Takeaki* conducted the *Shōgun's* fleet thither and resisted the imperial troops for 6 months. He surrendered finally on the 27th of June (1869) and his capitulation put an end to the civil war.

Hakodate-bugyō, 函 舘 奉 行 A title created in 1864 and equivalent to governor of that part of *Ezo* island which was not under the authority of the *Matsumae daimyō.*

Hakodate-wan, 函 舘 灣 . The gulf or bay of *Hakodate.*

Hakone, 函 根 . A village in *Sagami,* renowned for its hot springs and the freshness of its climate. Formerly a barrier (*Hakone no seki*) was established there for the surveillance of the travelers.

Hakone-ji, 函 根 路 . A mountain road connecting *Odawara* (*Sagami*) with *Mishima* (*Izu*), passing through *Hakone.* Since the *Kamakura* shōgunate, it replaced the ancient *Ashigara* road. In 1335, *Ashikaga Takauji* intrenched himself at *Hakone* and severely defeated *Nitta Yoshisada.* It was also the road followed by *Hideyoshi,* marching against the *Odawara Hōjō* (1590). The present road dates from 1618.

Hako-saki, 箱 﨑 . A cape west of *Sanuki.*

Haku, 伯 . A title of nobility corresponding to that of earl or count. *Hakushaku* is also used.

Hakuba no sechie, 白 馬 節 會 . Or *Ao-uma-no sechie.* A festival celebrated on the 7th of the first month at the imperial palace ; the principal feature of the festival was the procession of 21 white horses.

Hakuchi, 白 雉 . *Nengō:* 650-654.

Hakuchō, 白 鳳 . *Nengō:* 673-685.

Hakusai, 百 濟 . — See *Kudara.*

Haku-san, 白 山 . (Lit.: White mountain). A mountain group on the borders of the provinces of *Mino, Hida, Echizen,* and *Kaga.* Its three principal summits are *Bessan* (2,320 met.) *Gozen-mine* (2,680 met.) and *Ōnanji.* — It is also called *Shira-yama, Ten-zan, Koshi no shirane.* — History mentions eruptions in 1239 and 1554.

Hakushū, 伯 州 . The Chinese name of the province of *Hōki.*

Hamada, 濱 田 . A town (10,600 inh.) in *Iwami.* It was the residence of the *daimyō Furuta.* (1619-1648), the *Matsui* (1649-1759), the *Honda* (1759-1769), the *Matsui* (1769-1836), finally from 1836 till 1868, of the *Matsudaira* (61,000 k.).

Hamamatsu, 濱 松 . A town (19,600 inh.) in *Tōtōmi.* Before 1570 it was called *Hikuma. Tokugawa Ieyasu* ordered *Honda Shigetsugu* to build a castle there, which he occupied in 1571. When he transferred his residence to *Edo* (1590), *Hideyoshi* replaced him at *Hamamatsu* by *Horio Yoshiharu.* Under the *Tokugawa* the castle belonged successively to the *daimyō Sakurai* (1601-1609), the *Mizuno* (1609-

1619), the *Kōriki* (1619–1638) the *Ōgyū* (1638–1645), the *Ōta* (1645-1681) the *Aoyama* (1681–1702), the *Honjō* (1702–1729), the *Ōkōchi* (1729–1749) the *Honjō* (1749-1758), the *Inoue* (1758-1817), the *Mizuno* (1817–1845), finally from 1845–1868, to the *Inoue* (60,000 k.).

Hamana-ko, 濱名湖. A lagoon, (157 Km. in circuit) in *Tōtōmi*. In olden times it was called *Tō-tsu-awa-umi*, (the remote foamy sea in contradistinction to lake *Biwa*, then called *Chika-tsu-awa-umi*, the near foamy sea) ; *Tō-tsu-awa-umi* by contraction became *Tōtōmi*, the name of the province.

Hamuro, 葉室. A *kuge* family, descended from *Fujiwara Yoshikado*. — The head of the family is now Marquis.

—— **Tokinaga,** 葉室時長 (13th century). Was *Dainagon* and related to the *Taira*. People attribute to him the composition of the *Heike-monogatari*, the *Hōgen-monogatari*, the *Heiji-monogatari*, the *Gempei-seisui-ki*, etc., but proof is wanting.

Han, 藩 (Lit. : hedge, palisade). Formerly a fief or territory governed by a *daimyō*. The *han* were established by degrees during the 12th century and regularly organized by *Yoritomo*. Under the *Ashikaga* it was not by the will of the emperor or of the *Shōgun* that the titulars were designated, but by force of arms. *Ieyasu Tokugawa* renewed the regulation of the ancient *Bakufu* and raised the number of the *han* to over 300. They were divided into 3 classes, according to the importance of their revenue : the *dai-han*, above 400,000 *koku* of rice ; the *chū-han* from 100,000 to 400,000 *koku* ; the *shō-han* below 100,000 *koku*. In 1868, the *han* passed under the authority of the emperor and every *daimyō* continued to govern under the title of *han-chiji*. In 1871, they were suppressed, and changed into *ken* (departments), and the *daimyō* received a pension from the Government in proportion to the revenues of which they were deprived.

Hanabusa, 花房. A *shizoku* family of *Okayama* (*Bizen*) ennobled in 1896. — The head of the family is Baron.

Hanabusa Itchō, 英一蝶 (1652–1724). A celebrated painter born in *Ōsaka*. He came to *Edo* at the age of 15, received lessons from *Kanō Yasunobu* and took the name of *Kanō Shinkō*. Having published a collection of satirical designs which offended the shōgunal government, he was banished to *Miyake-jima*, one of the 7 *Izu* islands (1698), where he lived for 12 years. It was after his return from exile that he changed his name to *Hanabusa Itchō* by which he is known.

Hanaguma-jō, 華隈城. Formerly a castle in *Settsu* near the present town of *Kōbe*. It belonged to *Araki Murashige* and resisted *Nobunaga* for a long time (1579) ; *Ikeda Nobuteru* succeeded in taking the castle.

Hana-shizume no matsuri, 鎮華祭. In ancient times a festival which was celebrated at the end of spring in honor of the *Shintoist* gods *Ōmiwa* and *Sai*, in order to be preserved from epidemic disease during summer.

Hanawa Hokiichi, 塙保己一 (1746–1821). A celebrated literary man and professor. He was born in *Edo*, became blind when 7 years

old, lost his mother soon afterwards and was brought up by a bonze.
He was taught music and acupuncture ; but he did not show any
aptitude. He then launched into the study of Japanese antiquities :
here he was in his element. Gifted with a prodigious memory, he
acquired extensive knowledge in a short time. In 1782 he published the
Gunsho-ruijū, a collection in 1821 volumes of ancient and rare works.
Ten years later he founded a school of literature and history (*Wagaku-
kōdan-jo*) which soon became so prosperous that the shōgunal government
appropriated it to itself. He published several other works.

Hanawa Naotsugu, 塙 直 次. A *samurai* of *Owari*, who successively served *Oda Nobunaga*, *Katō Yoshiaki*, *Kobayakawa Hideaki*,
Tokugawa Tadayoshi, *Fukushima Masanori*, finally having joined the
party of *Hideyori*, he was killed at the siege of *Ōsaka* (1615).

Hana-yama, 花 山. A hill near *Uji* (*Yamashiro*), on which the
Genkyō-ji temple stood, better known by the name of *Hanayama-dera*
or *Kwazan-in*. It was in that temple that the emperor *Kwazan* retired
after his abdication (986), hence his posthumous name. It was also at
that temple that *Yoshimine Munesada* served as bonze after the death
of the emperor *Nimmyō* (850). He became the celebrated *Sōjō Henjō*
and was buried in the temple.

Hanazono, 花 園. A *kuge* family descended from *Fujiwara* (*Sanjō*)
Sanefusa (1146-1224). — The head of the family is now Viscount.

Hanazono-tennō, 花 園 天 皇. The 95th Emperor of Japan (1308-
1318), was prince *Tomihito*, a son of *Fushimi-tennō*. He succeeded
Go-Nijō at the age of 19, but his father governed in his name. After
a reign of 11 years, he abdicated in favor of his cousin *Go-Daigo*, retired
to the *Myōshin-ji* temple, where he lived for 30 years.

Han-chiji, 藩 知 事. A title which from 1868-1871 (i.e. from the
Restoration to the Suppression of the *han*) was given to the *daimyō*
who continued to govern their domains.

Handen-shi, 班 田 使. In former times an official having charge
of the apportionment of the rice-fields. This office created by the
empress *Jitō* (691), was first called *handen-taifu* ; then in 732, the
emperor *Shōmu* created the *Sakyō-handen-shi*, the *Ukyō-handen-shi*
and the *Kinai-handen-shi*.

Handen-shuju-hō, 班 田 授 受 法. At the reform of the *Taikwa*
(645), it was regulated that every 6 years at the time of the census,
the rice-fields should be apportioned among the families of every village.
Each man received two *tan* (about 2 Hectares 40 ares) and each woman
two thirds of that amount. One twentieth of the harvest was to be
taken as taxes.'' At the death of the owners, the rice-fields reverted to
the State.

Hanibe, 土 部. In ancient times a potter's guild under the authority of the *Hanishi no Muraji*.

Hanishi, 土 師. In ancient times, artisans whose special occupation was to make earthen statuettes (*haniwa*) used at funerals.

Haniwa, 埴 輪. In ancient times, it was the custom at the death
of a person of high rank, that his servants be buried alive with

him. In the second year before Christ, *Yamato-hiko*, a brother of the emperor *Suinin*, having died, the custom was observed and 4 or 5 days after the funeral, the earth could still be seen to heave from the convulsions o the unfortunate victims. The emperor was moved to pity and, upon the advice of *Nomi no Sukune*, ordered earthen statuettes to be substituted for human victims. Those statuettes were called *haniwa*. *Nomi no Sukune*, received the title of *Hanishi no Muraji* and became the chief of the guild which from that time had charge of making the statuettes and other objects employed at funerals. From time to time such *haniwa* are found: they afford valuable information regarding the dress, etc, of ancient times.

HANIWA.

Haniyasu hiko, 埴安彦. The god of the earth (*Shintō*).

Haniyasu-hime, 埴安媛. The goddess of the earth (*Shintō*).

Hannin. — See *Kwantō*.

Hannya-zaka, 般若阪. A hill north of *Nara* (*Yamato*). In 1180, *Taira Shigehira* defeated there the troops of the bonzes of *Nanto*, after which he burnt the temple *Tōdai-ji*. In 1338, *Momonoi Naotsune*, of the northern party, here defeated *Kitabatake Akiie*.

Hansatsu, 藩札. Paper-money issued in the time of the *Tokugawa* by the *daimyō* and current only in their own *han*.

Hanshō-tennō, 反正天皇. The 18th Emperor of Japan. (406-411), was prince *Mizuha-wake*, a son of *Nintoku-tennō*. He succeeded his brother *Richū* at the age of 54 and died after a reign of 6 years. Tradition says that he was 9 feet in height. Under the reign of *Richū* (400) he caused the assassination of his brother *Naka-no-Ōji*, who had revolted against the emperor.

Hara, 原. A place in *Hizen* in the southern part of the *Shimabara* peninsula. It formerly had a castle called the castle of *Hara* or *Arima*: it was at that place, that in 1637 the peasants of *Amakusa*, *Shimabara*, etc. excited beyond endurance, by the exaction of their *daimyō*, entrenched themselves. — See *Shimabara*.

Hara, 原. A *samurai* family in the service of the *Tokugawa*.

——**Katsutane,** 勝胤. *Oki no kami* was governor of the castle of *Okasaki* (*Mikawa*) till 1590. In 1600, having fought against *Ieyasu*, he was taken prisoner and beheaded at *Kyōto*.

——**Mondo,** 主水. Thus named from his title *Mondo no suke*. Was a son of *Tanenari*, *Shikibu-shōsuke* (+ 1590). He was commander of a company of *Ieyasu's* guards. He was degraded in 1612, for professing Christianity (he was baptized, John). After having lived 11 years in retirement at *Edo*, he was betrayed by a servant and burned alive (1623).

Harada, 原田. A *samurai* family of *Kyūshū* related to the *daimyō Akizuki*. No more mention is made of it after the conquest of *Kyūshū* by *Hideyoshi* (1587).

Haraka no sō, 腹赤奏. A ceremony formerly performed at the palace, on the first day of the year. At that ceremony, some *haraka* (now *masu*, salmon-trout) from *Tsukushi* was offered to the Emperor.

Harakiri, 腹切 (Chinese ; *seppuku*). A manner of suicide peculiar to Japan. It was of two kinds, one obligatory and the other voluntary. The first took place after condemnation to death : *daimyō* and *samurai* then had the privilege of opening the abdomen, instead of being beheaded by the executioner. Such is the meaning of the words *harakiri* or *seppuku*. This was the case with the 47 *rōnin* of *Akō* (1702), with the murderers of the French sailors at *Sakai* (1867), etc. The principal motives in committing voluntary *harakiri* were : the desire of not falling alive into the hands of the enemy after a defeat ; to give proof of fidelity by committing suicide on the tomb of a deceased master ; to protest against the conduct of a superior, etc. Formerly *harakiri* was performed in a most brutal manner, and at times death came only after hours of suffering. Subsequently the patient made only a slight incision, and at the same time a faithful friend cut off his head with a sword. Obligatory *harakiri* has been completely expunged from the present legislation, but the voluntary *harakiri* occurs yet from time to time.

HARAKIRI.

Haramuchi-jima, 波羅茂知島. One of the Kurile (*Chishima*) islands (227 Km. long and 70 Km. broad) It is also called *Paramushiri*.

Harima, 播磨. One of the eight provinces of *San-yō-dō*. It comprises 13 districts belonging to the *Hyōgo-ken*. — Chinese name : *Banshū*

Harima-nada, 播磨灘. The eastern section of the Inland Sea.

Harinoki-tōge, 針木峠. A mountain pass (2,400 met.) between Shinano and Etchū.

Hario-jima, 針尾島. An island (65 Km. in circuit) at the entrance of the bay of Tai-no-ura (Hizen).

Haruna-ko, 榛名湖. A lake near Ikao (Kōzuke). It is also called Kami no se, Ikao-ko.

Haru no miya, 春宮. — See Tōgū.

Hase, 長谷. A village in Yamato, known for its temple Hase-dera, or Kwannon-dō, also Chōkoku-ji, one of the 33 temples dedicated to the goddess Kwannon in the neighborhood of Kyōto.

Hasebe, 長谷部. A family descended from Ki no Haseo.

—— **Nobutsura,** 信連 (+ 1217). A son of Tametsura, was attached to prince Mochihito-shinnō. The latter together with Minamoto Yorimasa and Nobutsura plotted to ruin the Taira (1180). The plot having been divulged, Kiyomori had the prince besieged in his palace of Takakura, but Nobutsura helped him to escape disguised as a woman. Nobutsura having been arrested was exiled to Hino (Hōki). Yoritomo recalled him and gave him the province of Noto in fief, which his descendants governed for 20 generations.

—— **Tsunatsura,** 綱連. Was the last of his family. He was besieged in his castle of Anamizu by Uesugi Kenshin, escaped to Nanao (Noto), where he was defeated and killed (1576).

Hasedō, 長谷堂. A village in Uzen, where Uesugi Kagekatsu was defeated by the troops of Date Masamune and Mogami Yoshiaki (1600).

Hasegawa, 長谷川. A samurai family of Chōshū ennobled in 1895. — The chief of the family is now a Baron.

Hasegawa-ryū, 長谷川流. A branch of the school of painting called Unkoku-ryū. It was founded by Hasegawa Tōhaku towards the end of the 16th century, and is represented by Tōteki, Sōchi, Kyūsai, Tōrin, Tōsaku, etc.

Hasekura Tsunenaga, 支倉常長 (1561–1622). Also called Rokuemon, a samurai of the Sendai clan, was attached to Date Masamune from his youth, and chosen by him to be at the head of the embassy for Europe. This embassy left Japan in October 1613, passed through Mexico, and arrived in Spain after a voyage of one year. King Philip III gave them a solemn audience and Tsunenaga was baptized at Madrid in presence of the king and the whole Court (February 17, 1615). In Rome, the ambassadors were received with great pomp: Hasekura was honored with the title of Roman citizen by Pope Paul V. He returned to Japan only in 1620, but found Masamune in quite different dispositions from those he had manifested some years previously. Orders to apostatize were given to all those who had received baptism, but Tsunenaga remained firm and, having retired into solitude, he persevered in the faith, his master not daring to persecute him. His son Tsuneyori, a Christian like his father, was put to death in 1640 because of his religion, by order of Tadamune, a son of Masamune.

Hashiba, 羽柴. Patronymic name adopted by *Hideyoshi* in 1575 ; he formed it by borrowing two characters from the names of two generals, his friends. *Niwa* (*ha*) and *Shibata* (*shiba*). Ten years later he changed it for that of *Toyotomi*, but some members of his family, who had adopted the name *Hashiba*, retained it.

—— **Hidenaga,** 秀長 (1540–1591). A half-brother of *Hideyoshi*, who accompanied him in all his campaigns. In 1582, he was appointed *Mino no kami* and became *daimyō* of *Kōriyama* (*Yamato*). In 1585, with *Hidetsugu*, he led an expedition into *Shikoku* against *Chōsokabe Motochika*, took part in a campaign to *Kyūshū* against the *Shimazu* (1587) and was appointed *Gon-dainagon*.

—— **Hidetoshi,** 秀俊 (1577–1594). A nephew and adopted son of the above. His mother was the eldest sister of *Hideyoshi*. He died when 17 years old.

—— **Hidekatsu,** 秀勝 (1567–1593). The 4th son of *Oda Nobunaga*, was adopted by *Hideyoshi*, (1582), became *daimyō* of *Kameyama* (*Tamba*) and *Tamba no kami*. He took part in an expedition to *Kyūshū*, against the *Shimazu* (1587), then in the campaign against the *Hōjō* of *Odawara* (1590), and died in Korea at the age of 27.

Hashimoto, 橋本. A *kuge* family descended from *Fujiwara* (*Saionji*) *Kintsune* (1171–1244). — The chief of the family is now Count.

Hashi no Nakatomo, 土師仲友. A noble of the Court, who, having been exiled to *Musashi* under the reign of *Suiko* (593-628) became a simple fisherman. He is said to have drawn the statue of *Kwannon* from the *Sumida-gawa* since that time venerated in the famous *Sensō-ji* temple (*Asakusa-Kwannon*) in *Edo*.

Hashiri-mizu, 走水. (Lit.: running water) *Yamatotakeru no mikoto*, in his expedition against the *Ebisu*, crossed the passage now called *Uraga* Channel (between *Sagami* and *Kazusa*), and called it *Hashiri-mizu* on account of its rapid current.

Hashiri-shū, 走衆. In the time of the *Kamakura* shōgunate, a guard on foot that accompanied the *Shōgun*. Thus, when *Yoritomo* went from *Kamakura* to *Kyōto* (1190), 30 *hashiri-shū* or *kachi-hashiri-shū* escorted him during the whole journey.

Hassaku, 八朔. An exchange of presents that formerly took place between masters and servants on the first day of the 8th month. This ceremony was first called *ta-no-mi* (fruit of rice-fields), on account of the objects offered ; hence the word *tanomi* (recourse, demand), and the ceremony took the nature of a festival celebrating good relations between *kimi* and *kerai*.

Hassei, 八姓. The eight titles (*kabane*) created by the emperor *Temmu* (685) for the nobles and officials of the Court : *Mabito* or *Mando, Asomi* or *Ason, Sukune, Imiki, Michi no shi, Omi, Muraji,* and *Inagi*. These titles were first added to the family name (*uji*), and finally became a part of it.

Hasshū, 八宗. The first eight Buddhist sects : *Sanron, Hossō, Kegon, Ritsu, Jōjitsu, Kusha, Tendai,* and *Shingon,* all founded during the *Nara* and the *Heian-jō* (*Kyōto*) period.

Hasuike, 蓮池. A place in *Hizen* which from 1635-1868, was the residence of a branch of the *Nabeshima* family (52,000 k.).

Hata, 秦. A family descended from *Yuzuki no kimi,* a Korean prince who came to Japan in 283. During the reign of *Nintoku,* the members of the clan were sent to divers parts of the country to teach sericulture.

—— **Sake no kimi,** 酒公. A grandson of *Yuzuki no kimi,* who caused mulberry-trees to be planted everywhere and greatly developed the production of silk. The emperor *Yūryaku,* in reward, bestowed on him the name of *Uzumasa* (471).

Hata-bugyō, 旗奉行. Under the *Tokugawa,* an official charged with the making and preserving of flags, banners, etc. for the shōgunal family (*masshiro no hata, kin-ōgi no ō-uma-jirushi, hangetsu no ko-uma-jirushi,* etc.). Important as it was during war, this office became a sinecure in time of peace, the banners being used only on the occasion of some annual festivals.

Hata Tokiyoshi, 畑時能. A warrior of the 14th century who, with *Nitta Yoshisada,* and *Wakiya Yoshisuke,* courageously supported the cause of the emperor *Go-Daigo.* He died pierced by an arrow whilst fighting against *Shiba Takatsune.*

Hatakeyama, 畠山. A *daimyō* family of *Musashi* descended from *Taira Takamochi.* The family being extinct in 1205, *Yoshizumi,* a son of *Minamoto Yoshikane* was chosen to represent it. Thus, the new family was descended from the *Seiwa-Genji.* This branch was one of the three *san-kwan* from among which the *Kwanryō* of *Kyōto* were selected.

—— **Shigetada,** 重忠 (1164-1205). Was a son of *Shigetoshi.* His ancestors who for several generations were in possession of *Hatakeyama* (*Musashi*) took its name. When *Minamoto Yoritomo* started his campaign (1180) *Shigetada,* although descended from the *Taira,* joined his party and, under the command of *Noriyori* and *Yoshitsune,* fought against *Yoshinaka,* and distinguished himself in the battle of *Ichi-no-tani* (1184). He also accompanied *Yoritomo* in the expedition against *Fujiwara Yasuhira* (1189). After the death of *Yoritomo* (1199) he became counsellor of *Yoriie.* In 1205 he and his son having been calumniated with *Hōjō Tokimasa,* they were summoned to *Kamakura,* but refused to go. In consequence, *Tokimasa* sent troops to arrest them. *Shigetada* gave battle, was defeated and killed together with his son *Shigeyasu.* This was the end of the first branch of the *Hatakeyama* family.

—— **Yoshizumi,** 義純. A son of *Minamoto* (*Ashikaga*) *Yoshikane,* was chosen by *Hōjō Tokimasa* to revive the name of *Hatakeyama,* after the death of *Shigetada* and *Shigeyasu.* He married the widow of *Shigeyasu,* a daughter of *Tokimasa* and inherited the domains of the *Hatakeyama* (1205).

—— **Kunikiyo,** 國清 (+ 1364). Was a son of *Iekuni,* and a descendant in the 6th degree of *Yoshizumi.* In 1335, he accompanied *Ashikaga Tadayoshi* in his campaign against *Nitta Yoshisada,* followed

Takauji into *Kyūshū* and was made *Kii no shugo*. When *Motouji* was sent to *Kamakura* as *Kwanryō* of *Kwantō*, *Kunikiyo* became his *shitsuji* (minister), shaved his head and took the name of *Dōsei* (1349). In 1358, he was ordered to put *Nitta Yoshioki* to death, and accordingly had him drowned in the *Rokugō-gawa*. He took part in the expedition of *Yoshiakira* against *Kusunoki* and *Wada*, the chiefs of the southern party. Later, on account of differences with the *Shōgun*, he lost favor, fled to *Shuzen-ji* (*Izu*), then to *Kyōto* where he died.

—— **Yoshitō,** 義深 (1331-1379). Shared the fortune of his brother *Kunikiyo*, and after the latter had lost favor, he replaced him and vanquished *Shiba Takatsune*.

—— **Motokuni,** 基國 (1352-1406). A son of *Yoshitō*, received the province of *Yamashiro* in fief (1392), then that of *Kawachi* (1394) ; in 1398, he was made *Kwanryō* of *Kyōto* and was the first of his family to bear that title. Soon afterwards he had his head shaved and took the name of *Tokugen.*

—— **Mitsuie,** 滿家 (+ 1433). Was a son of *Motokuni.* In 1399, he repressed the revolt of *Ōuchi Yoshihiro* (*Ōei no ran*) and received the province of *Kii*. In 1410, he became *Kwanryō*, shaved his head and took the name of *Dōsui.* After having been replaced as *Kwanryō* by *Hosokawa Mitsumoto* (1412), he was again invested with this office in 1421.

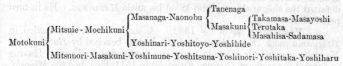

```
                              ┌ Masanaga-Naonobu ┌ Tanenaga
          ┌ Mitsuie - Mochikuni ┤                  └ Masakuni ┌ Takamasa-Masayoshi
          │                   │                              ┤ Terutaka
Motokuni ┤                   └ Yoshinari-Yoshitoyo-Yoshihide └ Masahisa-Sadamasa
          └ Mitsunori-Masakuni-Yoshimune-Yoshitsuna-Yoshinori-Yoshitaka-Yoshiharu
```

—— **Mochikuni,** 持國 (1397-1455). Was a son of *Mitsuie.* In 1441, he had his head shaved and took the name of *Tokuhon ;* the following year, he was made *Kwanryō*, but in 1445, was replaced by *Hosokawa Katsumoto.*

—— **Masanaga,** 政長 (+ 1493). A son of *Mochitomi, Owari no kami,* was adopted by *Mochikuni,* who had no children ; but a son, *Yoshinari,* having been born to him, he wished to disinherit *Masanaga* (1454). The latter applied to *Hosokawa Katsumoto* who set fire to the house of *Mochikuni,* and obliged him to flee to *Kawachi,* and *Masanaga* took possession of his domains. The following year *Yoshinari* raised troops to fight against *Masanaga,* but the *Shōgun Yoshimasa* succeeded in reconciling them. The *Hatakeyama* family was thus divided into two branches. In 1460 the struggle began anew. *Yoshinari* having been defeated fled to *Yoshino.* Soon afterwards, *Masanaga* was made *Kwanryō* (1464). Then began the *Ōnin* war. *Yoshinari* fought on the side of *Yamana Sōzen,* and *Masanaga* on that of *Hosokawa Katsumoto.* The two parties were alternately victorious and defeated. The hostilities ceased in 1485 and recommenced in 1493. At that time *Masanaga* attacked *Yoshitoyo,* a son of *Yoshinari* in *Kawachi,* but he was defeated and committed suicide.

—— **Yoshinari,** 義就 (+ 1493). Was the son of *Michikuni*. The latter had adopted his nephew *Masanaga* before *Yoshinari's* birth. *Masanaga* revolted, when he was deprived of his right to succession. The whole life of *Yoshinari* was one long struggle against his rival. *Hosokawa Katsumoto* and *Yamana Sōzen* having joined the party of *Masanaga*, *Yoshinari* was obliged to flee to *Iga* (1454). After a short period of peace, the war recommenced and *Yoshinari* retired to *Kawachi* (1460), then to *Kōya-san*. During the *Ōnin* war (1467), he was supported by *Yamana Sōzen*, and fought till his death.

—— **Yoshimune,** 義宗 (+ 1480). Was a son of *Masakuni* and belonged to the *Noto Hatakeyama* branch. He first served *Yamana Sōzen*, then, by the order of the *Shōgun Yoshimasa*, he joined the party of *Hosokawa Katsumoto* and was made *Kwanryō* (1473).

—— **Naonobu,** 尚順 (+ 1534). A son of *Masanaga* followed the *Shōgun Yoshitane* in his campaign against *Sasaki Takayori*, and afterwards retired to *Kii* (1492). In 1504, he transferred his castle of *Takaya* (*Kawachi*) to his son *Tanenaga* and shaved his head. 30 years later, he tried to create trouble, but was arrested and exiled to *Awaji*; where he soon afterwards died.

—— **Yoshitoyo,** 義豊 (+ 1499). Was a son of *Yoshinari*. In 1493, the *Shōgun Yoshitane* together with *Masanaga* carried on war against him in *Kawachi*: *Yoshitoyo*, aided by *Hosokawa Masamoto*, defeated the shōgunal army and killed his uncle *Masanaga*. He in turn perished in a battle.

—— **Yoshihide,** 義英 (+ 1532). A son of *Yoshitoyo*, resided in *Takeyama* castle (*Kawachi*). In 1507, he was besieged by *Hatakeyama Naonobu*, resisted for a whole year, and finally fled to *Izumi*. Having re-entered the castle of *Takaya* (*Kawachi*) in 1511, he joined the *Miyoshi*, but being attacked together with *Kaiun* by *Hosokawa Harumoto*, he committed suicide.

—— **Takamasa,** 高政 (+ 1576) A son of *Masakuni* inherited the province of *Kawachi*. He fought against *Miyoshi Chōkei* and was defeated in 1559 He was more fortunate in his campaign against *Miyoshi Jikkyū* (*Yoshikata*) the following year. In 1568, the *Shōgun Yoshiaki* again put him in the possession of the *Takaya* castle which had been taken from him by *Chōkei*. In a war with *Yuza Nobunori*, one of his *kerai*, who had seized the castle of *Takaya* and slain *Terutaka*, the son of *Takamasa* (1573), *Takamasa* raised troops and tried to take revenge, but without success. Then *Nobunaga* came, defeated *Nibunori* and kept the *Takaya* castle for himself. As to *Takamasa*, he lived 3 years more almost in a state of destitution; he received baptism in 1575.

—— **Yoshitaka,** 義隆 (1557–1574). Was a son of *Yoshinori* of the *Noto* branch, He was assassinated by one of his *kerai*, *Yuza Yoshifusa*. — From this epoch the family disappears from history.

Hatamoto, 旗下 (Lit.: at the foot of the standard). Formerly the camp of a *Shōgun*, next the *samurai* that guarded it. — Under the *Tokugawa*, the direct vassals of the *Shōgun*, ranking below the *daimyō* and above the *go-kenin*. The class of the *hatamoto* comprised three degrees : the *kōdai-yoriai*, the *yoriai* and the *kofushin*.

Hatano, 波多野. A family of *Tamba daimyō* descended from *Fujiwara Hidesato*. *Tsunenori* was the first that took the name of *Hatano*. After the *Ōnin* war (1467) a branch settled at *Yakami*, and was called *Higashi-Hatano ;* another at *Higami*, the *Nishi-Hatano*.

—— **Hideharu,** 秀治. Resided at *Yakami*, while his brother *Hidetoshi* occupied the castle of *Kameyama* (*Tamba*). He refused to submit to *Nobunaga*, who had him besieged in his castle by *Akechi Mitsuhide*. *Akechi*, to overcome his resistance, took his mother as a hostage : then *Hideharu* surrendered and was conducted to *Nobunaga*, who ordered him to be put to death (1575). His vassals in their turn, took the mother of *Mitsuhide* and put her to death. Hence probably the hatred of *Akechi* against *Nobunaga*.

Hatori, 服部. In ancient times a guild of silkgrowers and weavers, whose chief bore the title of *Hatori no Muraji*. He had charge of everything relating to the breeding of silkworms, weaving, etc. The *Kure-hatori* and the *Aya-hatori* were under his authority. This title was hereditary in a family that pretended to descend from *Ame-no-mihoko no mikoto*, the 11th descendant of *Ame-no-minakanushi no mikoto*.

Hatsu-kuni-shirasu-sumera-mikoto, 御肇國天皇 (Lit. : the 1st emperor pacificator of the country). Is the name given by the people to *Sujin-tennō* after his death (97–30 B. C.).

Hatsuta Tomoie, 八田知家. A warrior of *Shimōsa*, who followed *Yoritomo* in his expeditions against the *Taira* (1184), and *Fujiwara Yasuhira* (1189), etc. After the death of *Yoritomo*, he had a great share in the government together with *Hōjō Tokimasa*, *Ōe Hiromoto*, etc.

Hatto-gaki, 法度書. A collection of ancient laws compiled in a code of 15 volumes by the *Shōgun Yoshimune* (1725).

Hayachine-zan, 早池峯山. A mountain (2,000 m.) in *Rikuchū*. It is also called *Sōchihō-zan*.

Haya-saki, 早崎. A cape south of the *Shimabara* peninsula (*Hizen*).

Hayasaki-kaikyō, 早崎海峽. The strait which separates the *Shimabara* peninsula (*Hizen*) from the *Amakusa* islands (*Higo*).

Hayashi, 林. An ancient castle in *Shinano*. It was the residence of the *Ogasawara daimyō* from the 12th to the 16th century.

Hayashi, 林. A *samurai* family of *Chōshū* ennobled in 1887. —— The chief of the family is now Viscount.

Hayashi, 林. A *samurai* family of the *Shizuoka* clan (*Suruga*) ennobled in 1895. — The chief of the family is now Viscount.

—— **Tadasu,** 董. Was born in 1850, and fought under the command of admiral *Enomoto* in 1868. He was ambassador at *Peking* (1896), at St. Petersburg (1898), at *London* (1899). He became Viscount in 1902.

Hayashi, 林. A family of scholars, celebrated during the time of the *Tokugawa* as men of letters and professors.

—— **Dōshun,** 道 春 (1583–1657). Also called *Razan*, was born in *Kaga*. His father *Nobutoki* brought him to *Kyōto* at the age of 14 ; he studied literature at the temple of *Kennin-ji*, and then followed the lessons of the famous *Fujiwara Seikwa*. In 1606 *Ieyasu* bestowed on him the title of doctor (*hakase*) and 1st secretary of the *Bakufu*. In this capacity he recorded all the official acts of that epoch. He was a fervent Confucianist and endeavored to persuade *Ieyasu* to deprive the bonzes of all influence in the government. *Ieyasu* arranged a conference for him with the famous bonze *Tenkai*, but the discussion did not turn to the advantage of *Dōshun*, who, furious at his defeat, published two books in favor of Shintoism. His historical, philosophical and religious works amount to several hundred volumes.

—— **Shunsai,** 春 齊 (1618-1680). A son of *Dōshun*, was 17 years old when his father settled in *Edo* (1634). In 1643, by the order of the *Shōgun Iemitsu*, he published the *Kwan-ei keizu*, in 300 volumes, containing the genealogies of all the great families of Japan. Next he collected all the ancient and curious books he could find. In 1671, he published his principal work, the *Honchō-tsūgan*, a history of Japan in 300 volumes. Besides the above works, he wrote a great number of others, among which is the *Nihon-ō-dai ichiran*, translated into French by Klaproth in 1834 under the title of "Annals of the *Dairi*."

—— **Jussai,** 述 齊 (1768-1841). An adopted son of the above. His master was *Shibui Taishitsu*. He published several hundred volumes.

Hayashi Shihei, 林 子 平 (1754-1793). After having visited the whole country in order to discover the ancient traditions, he published the *Kaikoku-heidan* and the *Sangoku-tsūran*, two works in which he exalts the authority of the Emperor to the prejudice of the *Shōgun*, and for this reason, the *Bakufu* sent him back to *Sendai*, where, confined in his brother's house, he died at the age of 40. After the Restoration he received a posthumous rank at court (*shō-go-i*).

Hayashi Toemon, 林 戸 右 衛 門 . A *samurai* who, together with *Bekki Shōzaemon*, *Miyake Heiroku*, *Fujie Matajūrō*, etc., organized a revolt in 1652 against the *Shōgun Ietsuna*. Before the plot was carried out, the conspirators were arrested and put to death.

Hayashi-bugyō, 林 奉 行 . A title created in 1685 and given to 4 officials having charge of the superintendence of the shōgunal forests. The *Hayashi-bugyō* were under the authority of the *Kanjō-bugyō*.

Hayashida, 林 田 . A place in *Harima*. It was the residence of the *Tatebe daimyō* from 1617-1868 (10,000 k.).

Hayato, 隼 人 . In ancient times, warriors from *Hyūga* and *Ōsumi*, renowned for their bravery. A certain number among them guarded the palace and when on duty covered their heads with a kind of white or red wig which gave them the appearance of dogs whose barking they imitated in order to inspire greater fear.

Hayato-mai, 隼 人 舞. An ancient dance recalling the submission of *Hosuseri no mikoto*, to his younger brother *Hiko-hohodemi no mikoto*, the grandfather of *Jimmu-tennō*. As a pledge of his submission, he promised for himself and his successors to have the palace guarded by *haya-bito* (*hayato*). This dance is performed by the descendants of the ancient *hayato*.

Hayatomo no seto, 早 鞆 瀬 戸. The eastern part of the strait of *Shimonoseki*.

Hayato-zukasa, 隼 人 司. During the time of the *Taikwa* (645) reform, an office depending on the *Emon-fu* and having charge of recruiting the *hayato*, of teaching them singing and dancing, etc. The chief bore the title of *hayato no kami*. After the suppression of the *Emon-fu* (808), the *hayato* were placed under the jurisdiction of the *Hyōbu-shō*.

Heguri, 平 群. A family descended from *Takeshiuchi no Sukune*.

—— **Tsuku,** 木 兎. A son of *Takeshiuchi no Sukune*, was born on the same day as the emperor *Nintoku* (290). A wren (*sazaki*) entered the room where he was born and at the same time an owl (*tsuku*) made its appearance in the palace : now the owl being a bird of ill omen, the emperor *Ōjin* gave his son the name of *Ō-sazaki* and to his minister's child that of *Tsuku*. *Heguri Tsuku* led an expedition against *Shiragi* (Korea) in 329 and was minister under the emperor *Richū*. He died 128 years old.

—— **Matori,** 眞 鳥. A son of *Tsuku*, was minister (*Ō-omi*) under the emperors *Yūryaku*, *Seinei*, *Kensō* and *Ninken*. At the accession of *Buretsu*, he was accused of revolt: *Ōtomo no Kanamura* was sent to subdue him and *Matori* and his son *Shibi no Shin* were killed (498).

Heian-chō-jidai, 平 安 朝 時 代. The period extending from the foundation of *Kyōto* by *Kwammu* to the reign of *Montoku* (794-858), before the *Fujiwara* seized the power.

Heian-jō, 平 安 城. The imperial palace built by *Kwammu* in 794.

Heian-kyō, 平 安 京. (Lit.: the capital of peace and tranquillity). The name given by the emperor *Kwammu* to the new capital (*Kyōto*) which he had built in *Yamashiro* (794). It was laid out on the model of the Chinese town *Tchang-ngan* (*Chō-an*) in the province of *Chensi*, then the capital of the *Tang* (*Tō*). It was a rectangle of five kilometers in length and four and a half in breadth, surrounded by moats and palisades, the imperial palace occupying the centre of the northern part. The streets were straight and at right angles. A great thoroughfare, called *Shujaku-ōji*, starting from the southern gate of the castle (*Shujaku-mon*) and ending at the southern gate of the city (*Rajō-mon*) divided the town into two parts ; *Sakyō* on the left and *Ukyō* ou the right. The capital numbered nearly 40,000 houses (*ko* ; unit taken as a basis, 30 m. by 15); 8 *ko* made 1 *gyō* ; 4 *gyō*, 1 *chō* ; 4 *chō*, 1 *ho* ; 4 *ho*, 1 *bō* ; 4 *bō*, 1 *jō*. All these divisions were numbered, and it was from the *jō* in which certain great families lived, that they took their names : *Ichijō*, *Nijō*, etc.

Heigun-jima, 平 郡 嶋. An island (28 Km. in circuit) in the Inland Sea, S.E. of the *Suwō* province.

Heii-saki, 閉伊崎. A cape on the eastern coast of *Rikuchū*.

Heiji, 平治. *Nengō* : 1159.

Heiji-monogatari, 平治物語 (Lit.: narratives of the *Heiji* period). A classical work relating the *Heiji* war (1159). It is attributed to *Hamuro Tokinaga*, but the authorship is doubtful.

Heiji no ran, 平治亂. The civil war of the *Heiji* period (1159), *Fujiwara Nobuyori* and *Minamoto Yoshitomo* revolted against the *Taira*, but they were vanquished and killed.

Heijō, 平城 (Lit.: Castle of Peace). The name given to the imperial palace in *Nara*.

Heijō-kyō, 平城京. A name given to the town of *Nara* (*Yamato*) when it was the residence of the Imperial Court (709–784). It was also called *Taira no miyako*.

Heijō-tennō, 平城天皇. The 51st Emperor of Japan, (806–809) was prince *Ate*, a son of *Kwammu-tennō ;* he succeeded his father at the age of 32. After a reign of 4 years, he abdicated in favor of his brother *Saga*. Afterwards, he regretted his decision, and formed a plot, the chief instigator of which was his wife *Kusuri-ko*. He hoped thus to re-ascend the throne and transfer the capital to *Nara*. *Sakanoe no Tamuramaro* was ordered to repress the revolt. *Heijō* had his head shaved and lived yet 14 years. He is often called *Nara-tennō*.

Hei-ke, 平家. The *Taira* family. — See *Heishi*.

Heike-monogatari, 平家物語 (Lit.: narrations about the *Taira* family). A celebrated work written towards the end of the 12th century, and attributed to *Hamuro-Tokinaga*.

Heimin, 平民. A class of people comprising farmers, artisans and merchants. Above them were the *samu-*

HEIMIN.

rai, and below, the *eta* and the *hinin*. At present there are only three classes : the *kwazoku* (nobles), the *shizoku* (the ancient *samurai*), and the *heimin*, the latter comprising not only the ancient *heimin*, but also the *eta* and the *hinin*, who are called the *shin-heimin* (new *heimin*).

Heimon, 閉門. Under, the *Tokugawa* a punishement inflicted upon a *samurai* guilty of some offence. It consisted in being confined to one's home for 50 or 100 days, according to the gravity of the offence.

Heishi, 平氏. The *Taira* family. In 889, prince *Takamochi*, great grandson of *Kwammu-tennō*, was the first to receive the name of *Taira* (Chin.: *Hei*), from the emperor *Uda*. He is the ancestor of a great number of families, the principal branches being : in *Ise* and *Iga*, the *Ise-Heishi ;* in *Izu*, the *Hōjō* and the *Doi ;* in *Hitachi*, the *Daijō ;* in *Echigo*, the *Jō ;* in *Sagami*, the *Miura* and the *Kamakura ;* in *Shimōsa*, the *Chiba ;* in *Musashi*, the *Hatakeyama* and the *Kumagaya* etc. The clan of the *Taira* was at the zenith of its power in the time of *Kiyomori*, but only a few years after the latter's death, its glory was eclipsed by its rival, the *Minamoto* clan (1185). — See *Taira*.

Heki Masatsugu, 日置正次 (16th century). A *samurai* who founded a school of archery called by his name *Heki-ryū*. He was born in *Yamato*, distinguished himself at the battle of *Uchino* (*Iga*), visited the provinces to teach his art, and, at the age of 59, became bonze at mount *Kōya*.

Henjō (**Sōjō**), 遍照 (僧正). — See *Yoshimine Munesada*.

Hibiki-nada, 響灘. The sea which washes the W. coast of *Nagato*.

Hiburi-shima, 日振島. An island (24 Km. in circuit) S.W. of *Iyo* province. *Fujiwara Sumitomo*, when in revolt, started from that place to seize the *Dazaifu* (939).

Hida, 飛彈. One of the 13 provinces of *Tōsandō*. It comprises 3 districts belonging to the *Gifu-ken*. — Chin. name : *Hishū*.

Hida, 日田. A district (*kōri*) in the province of *Bungo*. In ancient times, it formed a *kuni* at the head of which was a *Hida no kuni no miyatsuko*. In the middle-ages, *Miyagi Nagatsugu* built a castle there. *Hideyoshi* bestowed it on *Mōri Takamasa* who, in 1600, went to *Saeki* and was replaced by *Ogawa Morimitsu*. It was afterwards occupied by the *Ishikawa* (1616–1633) the *Ogasawara* (1633–1645), the *Hosokawa* (1645–1682), and the *Matsudaira* (1682–1686) families ; finally it became a shōgunal domain.

Hida-gawa, 飛彈川. A river (118 Km.) which has its source in *Hida*, flows through *Mino* and empties itself into the *Kisogawa* near *Ōta*.

Hidaka, 日高. One of the eleven provinces of *Hokkaidō*. It comprises 7 districts.

Hidaka-gawa, 日高川. A river (220 Km.) in *Kii*.

Hidakami-ji, 日高見路 The ancient name of the region which now forms the provinces of *Hitachi*, *Iwaki* and *Rikuzen*, then inhabited by the *Ebisu*.

Hida no takumi, 飛彈匠. The province of *Hida*, very rich in forests, has always been renowned for its carpenters supposed to be the most skilful in the whole country. For that reason the custom was established to dispense the inhabitants of *Hida* from all taxes and corvées, in exchange for which they had to furnish the capital and especially the imperial palace with the necessary carpenters, who were called *Hida no takumi*. As they replaced one another every year, some coming from the province and others returning, they were also called *banshō*.

Hidari Jingorō, 左甚五郎 (1594-1634). A son of *Itami Masatoshi*, and a *samurai* in the service of the *Ashikaga*. He was educated by his mother, became a carpenter, afterwards a carver in wood, and is considered the most celebrated sculptor of Japan. He was left-handed, hence his name *Hidari*. His principal works of art are in the *Nishi-Hongwan-ji* temple of *Kyōto* and in the funerary temple of *Ieyasu* at *Nikkō*.

Hiden-in, 悲田院. An asylum founded by the empress *Kōmyō*, the consort of *Shōmu-tennō*, was destined for sick people, abandoned children, etc. of the capital (730). In the Buddhist language, *hiden* means pity, compassion.

Hie, 日吉. — See *Hiyoshi*.

Hieda no Are, 稗田阿禮. A descendant of *Ame-no-uzume no mikoto*. Endowed with a wonderful memory, she never forgot what she once heard. For this reason the empress *Gemmei* ordered her to dictate to *Ō no Yasumaro* all that she knew of the ancient traditions, the result of the work was the *Kojiki*. This was in the year 711, when *Hieda* was 65 years old.

Hiei-zan, 比叡山. A mountain (830 m.) N.E. of *Kyōto* on the boundary of the provinces of *Yamashiro* and *Ōmi*. In 788, the bonze *Saichō* (*Dengyō-Daishi*) founded a temple on it, which from the era was called *Enryaku-ji* and became the seat of the *Tendai* sect. Gradually other temples were erected about the first one, and in subsequent centuries, their number amounted, it is said, to as many as 3,000. In that immense enclosure, flourishing schools were soon established, where all the illustrious men of Japanese Buddhism *Shinran, Hōnen, Nichiren*, etc., were formed. Prosperity caused their ruin. The bonzes maintained troops (*sōhei*). These troops, not content with burning down the rival temple in *Nara* from time to time, spread terror even in *Kyōto*. *Nobunaga*, to punish them for having sided with *Asakura Yoshikage* against him, burned the temples and put all the bonzes to the sword (1571). Under the *Tokugawa Shōgun*, only a few temples were rebuilt.

Hie no yama, 比叡山. Another name of *Hiei-zan*.

Higashi-Fushimi, 東伏見. A family of princes of the blood descended from *Fushimi Kuniie*.

—— **Yoshiaki,** 嘉彰 (1846-1903). The fifth son of *Kuniie*, in 1870 received the title of *Higashi-Fushimi no miya*. In 1882, he took the name of *Akihito, Komatsu no miya;* but after his death, the family resumed the title of *Higashi-Fushimi*.

—— **Yorihito,** 依仁. A brother and heir of *Akihito* and officer of the navy, was born in 1867. In 1892, he married the daughter of *Yamanouchi Yōdō*, the former *daimyō* of *Kōchi* (*Tosa*).

Higashi-Hongwan-ji, 東本願寺. In the time of *Nobunaga, Kōsa,* head of the *Hongwan-ji* temple in *Kyōto,* and his son *Kōjū,* fortified themselves on *Ishiyama (Ōsaka),* and withstood a siege against *Sakuma Nobumori* (1580); for that reason, *Hideyoshi* selected *Kōchō,* another son of *Kōsa,* as head of the sect. But when *Ieyasu* was *Shōgun,* he had another temple built for *Kōjū,* and that temple being east of the former one, was named *Higashi-Hongwan-ji* (1602). From that time dates the division of the sect: the western (*Nishi-Hongwan-ji*), was the ancient, and the eastern, the new one. The *Higashi-Hongwan-ji* temple in *Kyōto,* built in 1602, was destroyed by fire four times since its foundation, the last time in 1874. It has been rebuilt from 1879 to 1895, and is now the largest temple in Japan: it measures 63 met. in length, 57 in breadth, and 38 in height.

Higashi-Kirishima-yama, 東霧島山. A volcano (1,600 m.) on the limits of *Hyūga* and *Ōsumi.* — According to the legend, it was on this mountain, also called *Takachiho no mine, Hoko no mine,* that *Ninigi no mikoto,* a grandson of *Amaterasu* and great-grandfather of *Jimmu-tennō,* set foot when he descended from heaven to earth.

Higashikuze, 東久世. A *kuge* family descended from the *Murakami-Genji.* — The head of the family is now Count.

—— **Michitomo,** 通禧. Was born in 1833, and acted an important part at the time of the Restoration; he was *Sangi,* president of the *Kaitakushi,* Vice-president of the House of Peers (1890-1891), and Vice-president of the Privy-Council since 1891.

Higashi-ōkawa, 東大川. A river (122 Km.) which has its source at *Mikuni-yama* (*Mimasaka*), passes through *Tsuyama,* traverses *Bizen,* and empties itself into the Inland Sea, S.E. of *Okayama.* It is also called *Yoshii-gawa, Nishi-Ōtera-gawa* and in its superior course, *Tsuyama-gawa.*

Higashi-Sanjō, 東三條. A branch of the *Sanjō* family. — After the Restoration its head received the title of Baron.

Higashi-Sanjō-dairi, 東三條内裏. A palace built in *Kyōto* for the emperor *Shirakawa* after his abdication in 1086. During the *Heiji* war (1159) the ex-emperor *Go-Shirakawa,* leaving his palace of *Takamatsu,* retired to the *Higashi-Sanjō,* which was subsequently burnt by *Fujiwara Nobuyori* and *Minamoto Yoshitomo.*

Higashi-yama, 東山. A hill E. of *Kyōto,* on which a number of celebrated monuments have been erected: the *Ginkaku-ji,* the *Nanzen-ji,* the *Kiyomizu-dera,* etc.

Higashi-yama-tennō, 東山天皇. The 113th Emperor of Japan (1687–1709), was prince *Asahito,* a son of *Reigen-tennō,* whom he succeeded at the age of 12. The *Shōgun Tsunayoshi* was then governing. The epoch is known by the name of *Genroku* era, and was the most prosperous of the whole *Tokugawa* Shōgunate. *Higashi-yama* died after a reign of 23 years, being 35 years old.

Higashizono, 東園. — A *kuge* family descended from *Fujiwara Yorimune* (993–1065). — The head of the family is now Viscount.

Higo, 肥後. One of the 12 provinces of *Saikaidō*; it comprises 12 districts, belonging to the *Kumamoto-ken.*—The Chinese name

Hishū designates both *Higo* and *Hizen*. — Formerly *Higo* was called *Hi-no-michi no shiri*.

Higuchi, 樋 口 . A *kuge* family descended from *Fujiwara Naga-yoshi* (800–854). — The head of the family is now Count.

Higuchi Kanemitsu, 樋 口 兼 光 . A warrior of the 12th century, and a son of *Nakahara Kanemichi*, governor of *Shinano*. He attached himself to *Kiso Yoshinaka* and became one of his 4 body-guards (*shi-tennō*). He distinguished himself especially at the battle of *Tonami-yama* (1183), and was killed together with *Yoshinaka* (1184).

Higyōsha, 飛 香 舍 . Or *Fujitsubo*. An apartment in the *Seiryō-den* reserved for women.

Hii-gawa, 斐 伊 川 . — See *Hi no kawa*.

Hii-zaki, 比 井 崎 . A cape S.W. of the province of *Kii*.

Hiji, 日 出 . An ancient castle in *Bungo*, also called *Ao-yanagi-jō* and *Ukitsu-jō*. In 1586, it was besieged and taken by *Shimazu Yoshihisa*. The following year, *Hideyoshi* gave it to *Hayakawa Yukishige*. Finally, from 1601 to 1868, it was the residence of the *Kinoshita daimyō* (25,000 k.).

Hijikata, 土 方 . A family of *daimyō* native of *Owari* and descended from the *Seiwa-Genji* by *Yorichika*, a son of *Mitsunaga*. They resided in *Komono* (*Ise* — 11,000 k.) from 1600 to 1868. = To-day, Viscount.

Hijikata, 土 方 . A family of *samurai* of the *Kōchi* clan (*Tosa*); they were ennobled after the Restoration in the person of *Hisamoto*. The head of the family is now Viscount

Hiki Yoshikazu, 比 企 能 員 . A warrior of the 12th century, who took the side of *Yoritomo* and accompanied him in all his expeditions against the *Taira* (1184) and against *Fujiwara Yasuhira* (1189). He was made *Kebiishi* and gave his daughter in marriage to the *Shōgun Yoriie*. When the latter became ill (1203) and his mother *Masa-ko* proposed to divide the right of succession between his brother *Sanetomo* and *Yoriie's* son, *Ichiman*, *Yoshikazu* found the part allotted to his grandson insufficient and protested (See *Yoriie*): *Hōjō Tokimasa* had him assassinated. His son *Munetomo* and his grandson *Ichiman* tried to escape, but were killed by *Hōjō Yoshitoki*.

Hiki-mawashi, 引 廻 . A punishment in the time of the *Toku-gawa Shōgun*. The criminal was led on horseback through the town of *Edo*, whilst a man following behind carried the cause of his condemnation written in large characters. After this ordeal he was executed.

Hikitsukeshū, 引 付 衆 . During the *Kamakura* shōgunate, secre-taries of the Council of administration (*hyōjōshū*) of the *Bakufu*. They were created in 1252, and their number was gradually raised from 3 to 8. A similar office, also called *Naidenshū*, existed under the *Ashikaga* at *Muromachi* (*Kyōto*).

Hiko, 彦 (Lit. : son of the sun). Formerly a title equivalent to that of prince.

Hiko-hohodemi no mikoto, 彦火
々出見尊. The 3d son of *Ninigi no
mikoto* and of *Konohana-sakuya hime*.
In consequence of contentions with his
brother *Hosuseri*, he went to *Watatsumi*,
the god of the sea (probably in the *Ryūkyū*
islands), where he remained for three years,
and married his daughter *Toyotama-hime*.
Having returned to his country, he forced
his brother to swear obedience to him.   He
is the grandfather of *Jimmu-tennō*.   The
legend says that he died on mount *Takachiho (Hyūga)* 580 years old.

HIKO HOHODEMI NO MIKOTO.

Hiko-isaseri-hiko no mikoto, 彦五
十狹芹彦命. — See *Kibitsu-hiko*.

Hiko-itsuse no mikoto, 彦五瀬命.
The elder brother of *Jimmu-tennō*.   He accompanied him in his expedition toward the East; in *Kawachi* he was wounded by an arrow in
in a combat against *Nagasune-hiko*, and died from his wound in *Kii*.

Hiko-nagisatake-ugayafukiaezu no mikoto, 彦瀲建 鸕鷀草
葺不合尊.   A son of *Hiko-hohodemi no mikoto* and *Toyotama hime*.
He married *Tamayori hime*, a younger sister of his mother, and had
4 sons of whom the last is *Jimmu-tennō*.

Hikone, 彦根.   A town (16,700 inh.) in *Ōmi*.   It was the residence
of the *daimyō Ii Kamon no kami* (340,000 k) from 1623-1868.

Hiko-san, 彦山.   A mountain (1,240 m.) in *Buzen*, celebrated for its
temples dedicated to *Masaya-kachi-kachi-hayabi-ame-no-oshiho-mimi no
mikoto*, the eldest son of the goddess of the sun.   The bonzes that served
at these temples belonged to the *Yamabushi* sect (*Shugen-dō*); their
revenues amounted to 128,000 k.   Since the Restoration, they are gradually declining.

Hiko-shima, 彦島.   An island (25 Km. in circuit) S.W. of the
strait of *Shimonoseki* and belonging to the province of *Nagato*.

Hikuma, 引間.   An ancient castle in *Tōtōmi*, where the town of
Hamamatsu now stands.   The castle was built towards 1505 by *Okōchi
Sadatsuna* who was killed during the siege of the castle by *Imagawa
Ujichika* in 1514.

Hime, 姫.   (Lit.: daughter of the sun).   In ancient times, a title
equivalent to that of princess. — See *Hime-miko*.

Himeji, 姫路.   A town (35,300 inh.) in *Harima*.   Towards 1350,
Akamatsu Sadanori built a castle there and intrusted it to the care of
his vassal *Kodera Yorihide*.   At the overthrow of the *Akamatsu* (1441),
Harima province came into the possession of the *Yamana*.   In 1467,
Akamatsu Masanori retook the province and returned it to *Kodera Masamoto*.   When *Hideyoshi* was sent by *Nobunaga* into *Sanyōdō*, he took
Himeji (1577), rebuilt and enlarged the castle.   In 1585, he gave
it to *Kinoshita Iesada*, his relation.   After *Sekigahara* (1600), *Ieyasu*
established *Ikeda Terumasa* therein; the latter changed the name

Himeyama, until then given to the castle, to *Himeji*. It was successively occupied by the *Honda* (1617-1639), the *Okudaira* (1639-1648), the *Matsudaira* (1648-1649), *Sakakibara* (1649-1667), the *Matsudaira* (1667-1684), the *Sakakibara* (1684-1704), the *Honda* (1704-1741), the *Matsudaira* (1741-1749), and, finally, from 1749 till 1868, by the *Sakai* (155,000 k.) — The castle of *Harima* is at present one of the best preserved of old Japan.

Hime-miko, 皇女. A title given in ancient times to imperial princesses. They were also called *Nyo-ō*. Since the *Taikwa* reform (645), the sisters and daughters of emperors were called *Nai-shinnō;* the relatives of the second and third degree, *Nyo-ō*. Later, in the time of feudalism, many princesses became Buddhist nuns and were called *Bikuni-gosho*.

Hime-shima, 姫島. An island (16 Km. in circuit) N.E. of *Bungo*.

Hineno, 日根野. A *daimyō* family native of *Mino*.

—— **Hironari,** 弘就 (+ 1602). Was a vassal of *Saitō*, served *Yoshitatsu* and *Tatsuoki* When the latter had been completely vanquished by *Nobunaga*, *Hironari* had his head shaved and took the name of *Jibukyō-hōin*.

—— **Takayoshi,** 高吉 (+ 1600). A son of the above, took part in the campaign against *Odawara Hōjō* and as a reward, received the castle of *Takashima* in *Shinano* (28,000 k.).

—— **Yoshitomo,** 吉朋 (1588-1658). A son of the above, was transferred in 1601 to *Mibu* (*Shimotsuke*), afterwards, in 1634, to *Funai* (*Bungo* — 20,000 k.). He died without an heir and his domains were confiscated.

Hinin, 非人 (Lit.: not man). Formerly the lowest class of society, below the *eta :* it was especially composed of mendicants, etc. The name was suppressed in 1871.

Hino, 日野. A place in *Ōmi* where *Koretoshi*, a descendant in the 7th generation of *Fujiwara Hidesato*, built a castle and then took the name of *Gamō*, from the district (*kōri*) in which it was situated. His descendants resided at *Gamō* till 1590.

Hino, 日野. A *kuge* family descended from the *Fujiwara*. The head of the family is now Count.

—— **Kanemitsu,** 兼光 (1145-1196). A son of *Sukenaga*, was made *Kebiishi-bettō* in 1191.

—— **Suketomo,** 資朝 (+ 1332). A son of *Toshimitsu*, became *Sangi* in 1321, *Kebiishi-bettō* in 1323, and supported *Go-Daigo* in his struggle against the *Hōjō*. Having been commissioned by the emperor to recruit supporters, he brought *Toki Yorinaga* and *Tajimi Kuninaga* with their troops from *Mino*, but *Hōjō Takatoki* from *Kamakura* ordered him to be arrested and banished to *Sado*. Afterwards, when *Takatoki* exiled *Go-Daigo* to the *Oki* islands, he had *Suketomo* assassinated by *Homma Yamashiro-nyūdō*, governor of *Sado*.

—— **Sukena,** 資名. A brother of the above, first served the emperor *Go-Daigo*, but, when *Takauji* himself had assumed the title of *Shōgun*,

(1335), he accepted an office from him, remaining however attached to the person of the ex-emperor *Hanazono*.

—— **Sukeaki**, 資明 (1309-1365). A brother of the two mentioned above, followed *Sukena* in the service of *Go-Daigo*, and afterwards of *Kōmyō*. *Takauji* even bestowed on him a part of the domains belonging to the *Daijingū* of *Ise*.

—— **Kunimitsu**, 邦光. A son of *Suketomo*, who, having heard of the death of his father in *Sado*, left for the island, entered the house of *Homma* and killed him; then, having returned to *Kyōto*, he faithfully served the emperors *Go-Daigo* and *Go-Murakami*. In 1350, he went to *Kyūshū* to aid *Yasunaga-Shinnō* and defeated the *Shōgun Yoshiakira* (1361).

—— **Arimitsu**, 有光. A son of *Sukenori*, was *Go-dainagon*. In 1425, he resigned his office and shaved his head. In 1443, at the head of 300 men, he entered the palace during night, took the three imperial insignia and brought them to prince *Ogura-shinnō*, who was bonze on *Hiei-zan*. The *Shōgun Yoshinori* sent *Hatakeyama Mochi-kuni* to pursue them: the prince committed suicide and *Arimitsu* was put to death (1444).

Hino-gawa, 日野川. A river (93 Km.) which has its source in *Ōmi*, flows through *Echizen*, passes near *Fukui*, and empties itself into the sea near *Sakai*. It is also called *Shirakijo-gawa*.

Hi no kawa, 簸川. A river in *Izumo* in which *Susano-o* killed the monster *Yamata no orochi*. It empties itself into lake *Shinji-ko*. It is also called *Izumo no Ōkawa*, *Yokota-gawa*, *Kai-gawa*, *Hii-gawa*.

Hi no kuni, 火國. The ancient name of the provinces of *Hizen* and *Higo*.

Hi-no-moto, 日本. Japanese synonym of *Nihon*. Still used sometimes in poetry.

Hino-nishi, 日野西. A *kuge* family descended from *Hino Kane-mitsu* (1145-1196). The head of the family is now Viscount.

Hi-no-ura, 肥浦. A place in *Hizen*, which, until 1612, was the residence of the *Arima daimyō*.

Hi-oki, 日置. In ancient times an approximate way of calculating the days, months and years according to the changes of the moon and the succession of the seasons. The system was abandoned at the introduction of the Chinese calendar in 602.

Hirado-jima, 平戸島. An island (169 Km. in circuit) N.W. of *Kyūshū* and belonging to *Hizen*, was the center of a flourishing commercial district. It was a trading place for the Portuguese from about 1550 till their expulsion from the country, and of the Dutch from 1610 till their confinement to *Deshima* in 1641; the English too had a factory there from 1613-1624. The Chinese and the Koreans continued to exchange the products of their countries there for those of Japan.— *Hirado* was since the 12th century the fief of the *Matsuura daimyō* (61,000 k.).

Hirado-kaikyō, 平戸海峡. Strait between the *Hirado* island and *Kyūshū*.

Hiraga-Gennai, 平賀源內 (1723-1779).   A celebrated botanist.
He was born in *Sanuki* and studied in *Edo ;* thence his reputation spread
throughout the land.   He died in prison having assassinated the
publisher of his books.

Hiraga Tomomasa, 平賀朝雅 (+ 1205).   A son of *Yoshinobu*
and great-grandson of *Minamoto Yoshimitsu,* married a daughter of
Hōjō Tokimasa.   In *Ise* and *Iga* he suppressed a revolt of *Motomori*
and *Moritoki,* the last of the *Taira.*   He was then nominated *Ise no
shugo* (1204).   His father-in-law, after having assassinated *Hatakeyama
Shigetada,* conceived the project of doing away with the *Shōgun Sanetomo* and of replacing him by *Tomomasa.*   The plot was discovered ;
Tokimasa was forced to shave his head ; the residence of *Tomomasa*
in *Kyōto,* was invested by *Gotō Motokiyo* and *Sasaki Hirotsuna,* and he
was killed by an arrow.

Hirai, 平井.   An ancient castle in *Kōzuke,* built in 1471 by *Uesugi
Akisada.*   The castle was taken by *Takeda Shingen* in 1551 ; then it
came into the possession of the *Odawara Hōjō* and was destroyed in
1590.

Hiraiwa Chikayoshi, 平岩親吉 (1542-1611).   A *samurai* of
Mikawa, was brought up with *Ieyasu,* who intrusted him with the
education of his eldest son *Nobuyasu.*   After the downfall of the *Takeda* (1582) he was made governor of *Kai.*   In 1590, he received the
castle of *Umayabashi* (*Kōzuke*) with a revenue of 30,000 k.   Having
been appointed guardian of *Yoshinao,* the 7th son of *Ieyasu,* he returned
to *Fuchū* (*Kai*), followed his ward to *Kiyosu* (1607) and to *Nagoya*
(1610) whence he governed the whole province of *Owari.*   He possessed
the castle of *Inuyama* with a revenue of 100,000 k.   He died the following year without an heir.

Hiraizumi no tate, 平泉館.   A place in *Rikuchū.*   In 1094,
Fujiwara Kiyohira, left *Toyoda,* took up his residence at *Hiraizumi no
tate* and built a castle which was occupied by his descendants *Motohira,
Hidehira,* and *Yasuhira.*   The latter was deprived of his domains and
the castle was destroyed in 1189.

Hirakata, 枚方.   In *Kawachi* on the *Yodo-gawa.*   Boats sailing
between *Ōsaka* and *Fushimi* stopped here.

Hiramatsu, 平松.   A *kuge* family descended from the *Taira.*
— The head is now Viscount.

Hirano, 平野.   A *daimyō* family descended from the *Kiyowara.*
They resided at *Tawaramoto,* (*Yamato* — 10,000 k.). — The head is now
Baron.

Hirano-jinja, 平野神社.   A Shintoist temple in *Kyōto,* where
the gods *Imaki, Kudo, Furuaki,* and *Hime* are worshipped.   Their
identification is very difficult.   The annual feast (*Hirano no matsuri*)
of the temple on the 2nd day of the 5th month, has been very popular
since the time of the emperor *Kwammu.*

Hirata, 平田.   A noble family.   The first to receive the title of
Baron was *Tōsuke.*   (1902).   He was born in 1849 and was minister of
Agriculture and Commerce.

Hirata-Atsutane, 平田篤胤 (1776-1843). One of the most learned writers of Japan. He was born in *Akita* (*Dewa*) and was first called *Ōwada Masayoshi*. In 1800 he was adopted by *Hirata Atsuyasu*, a *samurai* of *Matsuyama* (*Bitchū*). He made a special study of history and ancient literature. His principal works are: the *Kishin-shinron* (1805), a new treatise on the gods, and especially the *Koshi-seibun*, the *Koshi-chō*, the *Koshi-den*, which are extensive commentaries on the *Kojiki* and the *Nihonki*, in which he showed himself the defender of the Shintoist myths. He contributed much to the renovation of Shintoism and the raising of the imperial prestige. Probably for that reason, he was requested by the shōgunal government to cease writing (1841). He then retired to *Akita*, where he died (1843).

Hiratsuka Tamehiro, 平塚爲廣. A *daimyō* of *Mino* (50,000 k.) who having joined the party against *Ieyasu* in 1600, was despoiled of his domains.

Hirayama, 平山. An ancient castle near *Miki* (*Harima*), in which *Bessho Harusada*, a brother of *Nagaharu* for a long time resisted *Hideyoshi* (1579).

Hirohashi, 廣橋. A *kuge* family descended from the *Fujiwara*. — The head is now Count.

Hirohata, 廣幡. A *kuge* family descended from prince *Tomohito* (1579-1629) a grandson of the emperor *Ōgimachi*. — The head is now Marquis.

Hirosaki, 弘前. A town (35,000 inh.) in the province of *Rikuoku*. In 1600, *Tsugaru Nobuhiro* built a castle at that place where his descendants resided till the Restoration (217,000 k.).

Hirosawa, 廣澤. A *samurai* family of the *Yamaguchi* (*Suwō*), clan, ennobled after the Restoration. — The head is now Count.

Hirose, 廣瀬. A place in *Izumo*, was first a part of the fief of *Matsue*. In 1666, *Matsudaira Chikayoshi* built a castle there where his descendants resided till the Restoration (30,000 k.).

Hiroshima, 廣島. A town (113,500 inh.) in *Aki*, capital of the department of the same name. In 1593, *Mōri Terumoto* built a castle at *Hiroshima*, which, in 1600, passed over to *Fukushima Masanori*, and then, in 1619, to *Asano Nagaakira*, whose descendants resided in that castle till the Restoration (420,000 k).

Hiroshima-ken, 廣島縣. A department formed with the provinces of *Aki* and *Bingo*.—Pop.: 1,517,000 inh.— Capital: *Hiroshima* (113,500 inh.).—Principal towns: *Onomichi* (22,300 inh.) *Fukuyama* (17,800 inh.), *Kurahashijima* (14,000), *Nioshima* (14,000), *Hiromura* 13,600 inh.), etc.

Hiroshima-wan, 廣島灣. The *Hiroshima* bay.

Hiru-ga-kojima, 蛭小島. In *Izu*, now called *Nirayama*. It was to this place that *Minamoto Yoritomo* was exiled in 1160; he here communicated with the *Hōjō*, who afterwards helped him to triumph over the *Taira*. The ruins of his residence are still seen near *Nirayama*.

Hiruko, 蛭子.—See *Ebisu*,

Hiru-no-omashi no mitsurugi, 晝 御 座 御 劍. A sacred sword the origin of which is rather obscure According to some, it was made during the reign of *Ichijō* (987-1011) by the famous artists *Sukenari* and *Tomonari,* father and son, living in *Bizen ;* according to others, it was fabricated under *Go-Toba* (1184-1194) ; a third opinion, reconciling the two above, says that the sabre made under *Ichijō,* was swallowed up by the sea with *Antoku-tennō* at *Dan-no-ura* (1185) and that *Go-Toba* had a similar one made. It is the sword handed to the emperor at the ceremony of his enthronement and which he carries with him in his changes of abode Go-Toba made it one of the three treasures or emblems of the imperial dynasty (*san-shū no jinki*) but later on, another sword offered by the *Ise* temple was substituted.

Hiru-numa, 涸 沼. A lagoon (27 Km. in circuit) in *Hitachi.*

Hisaakira-shinnō, 久 明 親 王 (1276-1328). The 7th son of the emperor Go-*Fukakusa.* During the reign of his elder brother *Fushimi-tennō,* he was chosen by *Hōjō Sadatoki* to succeed the *Shōgun Koreyasu-shinnō* who was deprived of his dignity (1289). Having in his turn displeased the powerful *Shikken,* he was deposed and replaced by his son *Morikuni-shinnō* (1308) 7 years old. He then retired to *Kyōto,* where he lived 20 years.

Hisai, 久 居. In *Ise,* which, since 1632, was the residence of a branch of the *Tōdō* family (53,000 k.).

Hisaka-jima, 久 賀 島. An island (51 Km. in circuit) of the *Gotō* group (*Hizen*). It is also called *Kuga-shima.*

Hisamatsu, 久 松. The name of several families descended from the three brothers of *Tokugawa Ieyasu.* After some time, they were authorized to adopt the patronymic name of *Matsudaira.*

Toshikatsu				
Yasutoshi - Katsumasa - Katsuyoshi - Katsuyasu				(a)
Yasumoto - Tadanaga - Tadanori - Yoshihisa				(b)
Sadayuki - Sadayori - Sadanaga				(c)
Sadakatsu { Sadatsuna - Sadayoshi - Sadashige (*Matsudaira*)				(d)
Sadafusa - Sadatoki - Sadanobu				(e)

(*a*)—**Toshikatsu,** 俊 勝. In a second marriage he took to wife *Dai* the mother of *Ieyasu* and widow of *Tokugawa Hirotada* (+ 1549), by whom he had three sons.

—— **Yasutoshi,** 康 俊 (1556-1586). The eldest son of *Toshikatsu.* It was only in 1713 that his descendants were ennobled and received the *Tako* domain (*Shimōsa* — 12.000 k.), which they held till the Restoration. — The head of the family is now Viscount.

(*b*)—**Yasumoto,** 康 元 (1559-1610). Was *daimyō* of *Sekiyado* (*Shimōsa*). His descendants resided successively at *Ōgaki* (*Mino*), *Komoro* (*Shinano*), *Nagashima* (*Ise*). The family became extinct in 1702.

(*c*)—**Sadakatsu,** 定 勝 (1560-1624). Was *daimyō* of *Kakegawa* (*Tōtōmi*), *Kuwana* (*Ise*), *Nagashima* (*Ise*). His son *Sadayuki* was transferred in 1634 to *Matsuyama* (*Iyo* — 150,000 k.), where his descendants resided till the Restoration. — The head of the family is now Count.

(*d*) —— This branch continues under the name of *Matsudaira* — See
Matsudaira (Hisamatsu).

(*e*) **Sadafusa,** 定房. At first he resided at *Nagashima (Ise),*
then at *Imabaru (Iyo* — 35,000 k.), where his descendants continued to
live till the Restoration. — Now Viscount.

Hishigawa Moronobu, 菱川師宣 (1645-1715). A painter and
engraver. He studied in the *Tosa* school, then in that of *Iwasa Matabei.* He is also called *Kichibei.* His sons, *Morofusa* and *Moronaga,*
followed in the footsteps of their father.

Hishū, 飛州. The Chinese name of *Hida.*

Hishū, 肥州. The Chinese name of *Hizen* and *Higo* taken collectively.

Hissoku, 逼塞. Under the *Tokugawa,* a punishment inflicted on
samurai. It consisted in confining them to their house, in which
visitors were allowed to enter only at night. This punishment, lighter
than the *heimon,* was of three degrees: the *enryo,* the *tsutsushimi,* and
the *hissoku.*

Hitachi, 常陸. One of the 15 provinces of *Tōkaidō,* comprises
11 districts belonging to *Ibaraki-ken.* — The Chinese name is *Jōshū.* —
This region occupied by the *Ebisu* till the 2nd century, was incorporated
into the empire after the campaigns of *Takeshiuchi no Sukune* and
Yamatotakeru no mikoto (113). *Seimu-tennō* constituted it a province
over which he placed a *kuni no miyatsuko.* *Montoku-tennō* changed
its name *Hidakami* to *Hitachi.* In 826, it was decided that in
commemoration of *Yamatotakeru,* the governor of *Hitachi,* as well as
those of *Kazusa* and *Kōzuke,* should always be a prince of the imperial
family, with the title of *taishu.* For this reason, these three provinces
never had a *kami* but a *suke* or assistant *taishu.*

Hitori-bito, 朝夕人. Under the *Ashikaga,* a *samurai* of inferior
rank (*ashigaru*) who marched behind the *Shōgun* and carried the
things necessary for his use.

Hitotsubashi, 一橋. A branch of the *Tokugawa* family, founded
by *Munetada* (1721-1764) a son of the *Shōgun Yoshimune.* — See
Tokugawa (Hitotsubashi).

Hitotsu-yanagi, 一柳. A *daimyō* family native of *Mino* which descended from *Kōno Michinao.* It was divided into two branches for the
two sons of *Naomori* (1565-1636).

(*a*). — The elder branch resided successively at *Kambe (Ise), Saijō
(Iyo),* and, since 1670, at *Ono, (Harima* — 10.000 k.). — At present
Viscount.

(*b*). — The younger branch, since 1644 was established at *Komatsu
(Iyo* — 10,000 k.). — At present Viscount.

Hitoyoshi, 人吉. In *Higo,* the residence of the *Sagara daimyō*
(22,000 k.) since the end of the 12th century until the Restoration.

Hiuchi, 燧. An ancient castle in *Echizen,* in which *Kiso Yoshinaka*
was besieged and vanquished by *Taira Koremori* in 1183.

Hiuchi-nada, 燧灘. A small basin of the Inland Sea, north of
Iyo.

Hiuchi-take, 燧嶽. A mountain (1980 m.) on the boundary of *Iwashiro*, *Echigo* and *Shinano*.

Hiyoshi, 日吉 or *Hie*. There was an ancient temple on mount *Hiei* called *Hiyoshi-jinja* or *Sannō*. After the construction of the *Enryaku-ji* temple, the bonzes continued to honor the god venerated in the former temple, and even when they had a petition to present to the emperor, they never failed to transport the car (*mi-koshi*) with the image of the god to the capital. It is believed that *Hiyoshi*, *Hie*, *Sannō* are different appellations of the Shintoist god *Ōnamuji* or *Ōkuni-nushi no mikoto*.

Hizen, 肥前. One of the provinces of *Saikaidō* It comprises 14 districts, of which 6 belong to *Nagasaki-ken* and 3 to *Saga-ken*. The Chinese name *Hishū* comprises *Hizen* and *Higo*; anciently, *Hi-no-michi no kuchi*.

Hō-an, 保安. *Nengō*: 1120-1123.

Hodaka-take, 穂高嶽. A mountain (3,000 met.) on the limits of *Hida* and *Shinano*.

Hōe-bugyō, 法會奉行. During the *Kamakura* period, an official whose duty it was to preside over the meetings held in the temples for the regulation of ceremonies, etc

Hōei, 寶永. *Nengō*: 1704-1710.

Hōei-zan, 寶永山. An upheaval produced on the southern slope of Mount *Fuji* during the eruption in 1707-1708. It was so called from the name of the era during which it happened.

Hōen, 保延. *Nengō*: 1135-1140.

Hōgen, 保元. *Nengō*: 1156-1158.

Hōgen-monogatari, 保元物語. An historical work written towards the end of the 12th century and relating the *Hōgen* war. It is attributed to *Hamuro Tokinaga*.

Hōgen no ran, 保元亂. The civil war of the *Hōgen* era (1156) At the death of the emperor *Konoe*, the ex-emperor *Sutoku* expected to see his son *Shigehito-shinnō* raised to the throne, but, despite his efforts, *Toba-tennō* had another of his sons, *Shirakawa* nominated. *Sutoku* was supported by the *Minamoto* and *Shirakawa* by the *Taira* who ultimately conquered. *Sutoku* was exiled to *Sanuki*, *Shigehito* was obliged to become bonze and the others were put to death or banished, but the most striking result was the strengthening of the ever increasing authority of *Taira Kiyomori*.

Hōji, 保治. *Nengō*: 1247-1248.

Hōjō, 寶勝. One of the *Nyorai* that guard the four cardinal points. He is said to watch over the South.

Hōjō, 北條. In *Izu*, till the 12th century a fief of the *daimyō* of the same name. They left it in 1181, to follow *Yoritomo* to *Kamakura*. In 1205 *Yoshitoki* confined his father *Tokimasa* there.

Hōjō, 北條. In *Awa* (*Tōkaidō*) was, from 1600 till 1712 the residence of the *Yashiro daimyō* (10,000 k.).

Hōjō, 北條. A family descended from *Taira Sadamori* the head of which family, under the title of *Shikken* (regent) of *Kamakura*, was from 1200-1333 the actual ruler of Japan.

—— **Tokimasa,** 時 政 (1138-1215). A son of *Tokiie,* descendant in the 6th degree of *Taira Sadamori.* He was residing at *Hōjō* (*Izu*) when *Minamoto Yoritomo* exiled by *Kiyomori* (1160) arrived there and received hospitality first from *Itō Sukechika,* then from *Tokimasa.* In 1180, prince *Mochihito-shinnō* incited the *samurai* of *Kwantō* to revolt against the *Taira* *Tokimasa* set out with *Yoritomo,* killed *Taira Kanetaka,* but was defeated at *Ishibashi-yama* by *Ōba Kagechika* (1181). He then entered *Kai,* applied to *Takeda Nobuyoshi* for help and came back with an army of 20,000 men. *Yoritomo* established himself at *Kamakura* and married *Masa-ko* a daughter of *Tokimasa.* The latter was appointed governor of *Kyōto* (1185) and by degrees became more influential. After the death of *Yoritomo* (1199), he became guardian of *Yoriie,* and took the title of *Shikken.* From that time, *Tokimasa* together with his daughter governed without opposition. *Yoriie* having become ill (1203) *Tokugawa* regulated the order of his succession, gave the 28 provinces of the East to *Ichiman,* his son, and the 38 provinces of the West to *Sanetomo* his brother. *Hiki Yoshikazu, Ichiman's* grandfather, complained of the share given to his grandson: *Tokimasa* had him assassinated together with *Ichiman; Yoriie* still *Shōgun* having manifested his dissatisfaction, was exiled to *Shuzenji* (*Izu*) then put to death and replaced by his brother, *Sanetomo.* After that, the second wife of *Tokimasa* intrigued to have her son-in-law, *Hiraga Tomomasa,* appointed *Shōgun:* *Tokimasa* listened to her suggestions and intended to have *Sanetomo* assassinated but the plot was discovered, and *Tokimasa* in his turn was exiled (1205) to *Hōjō* (*Izu*) where he died when 78 years old.

—— **Masa-ko,** 政 子.—— See *Masa-ko.*

—— **Yoshitoki,** 義 時 (1163-1224). 2nd *Kamakura-Shikken,* was a son of *Tokimasa* and brother of *Masa-ko.* He took part in the expedition of *Minamoto Noriyori* against the *Taira* in *Kyūshū* and defeated

Harada Tanenao (1184) in *Bungo*. In 1205, he succeeded his father in the office of *Shikken* and governed in concert with his sister. After the death of *Sanetomo* (1219), he chose *Fujiwara Yoritsune* as *Shōgun* who was then only 2 years old, a son of *Sesshō Michiie*, and great-grand-son of the eldest sister of *Yoritomo*. Soon afterwards, the ex-emperor *Go-Toba* endeavored to overthrow the power of *Yoshitoki*, but his army was defeated at *Uji*, *Seta*, and at *Kyōto* (1221 — *Shokyo no ran*). *Go-Toba* was exiled to *Sanuki* as were also his sons *Tsuchimikado* and *Juntoku*, the first to *Tosa*, the second to *Sado*, and his grandson *Chūkyō* was deposed after a reign of 70 days. To watch more closely the intrigues of the Court, he installed his son *Yasutoki* and his brother *Toki-fusa* in the *Rokuhara* (*Kyōto*). Thus, all authority was in the hands of the *Hōjō*: the *Shōgun*, the very Emperors, were chosen, and deposed according to the *Hōjō's* will and pleasure. *Yoshitoki* died at the age of 62, assassinated by a servant of the imperial Court.

—— **Tokifusa,** 時 房 (1175-1240). A brother of *Yoshitoki*, who re-pressed the revolt of *Wada Yoshimori* (1213). After the *Shōkyū* war (1221), he was governor of *Kyōto* together with *Yasutoki* and established himself at the *Minami-Rokuhara*. At the death of his brother *Yoshi-toki* he returned to *Kamakura* to assist the new *Shikken Yasutoki* with his counsels. He is called *Daibutsu* from the name of the temple to which he had retired.

—— **Yasutoki,** 泰 時 (1183-1242). Was the third *Kamakura Shik-ken*. At the time of the *Shōkyū* war, his father *Yoshitoki* sent him to fight against the army of the ex-emperor *Go-Toba*. It was he that deposed the young emperor *Chūkyō*, replaced him by *Go-Horikawa*, and exiled the three ex-emperors to distant provinces, after which he installed himself in the *Rokuhara* palace and governed the capital. In 1224, he returned to *Kamakura*, to succeed his father and sent his son *Tokiuji* and his cousin *Tokimori* as governors to *Kyōto*. At the death of the emperor *Shijō* (1224), he sent *Adachi Yoshikage* to *Kyōto* in order to prevent the election of the candidate of the *Sesshō Michiie* and to raise *Go-Saga* to the throne. He died the same year at the age of 60. During his 18 years' administration, *Yasutoki* introduced numerous reforms and worked efficaciously at improving the state of the country which had been im-poverished by long civil wars. By his order, *Miyoshi Yasutsura* drew up a Code of 50 articles for the use of *samurai*; it was called *Jōei-shiki-moku* from the era during which it was published (1232). The bonze *Kōben* (or *Myō-e*) was his counsellor.

—— **Tomotoki,** 朝 時 (1193-1245). Was a brother of *Yasutoki*. At the time of the *Wada Yoshimori* revolt he fought against the famous *Asahina Yoshihide* (1213). During the *Shōkyū* war (1221), he brought troops from *Hokurokudō* and led them to *Kyōto*. He was then appointed *Hyōjōshū*.

—— **Shigetoki,** 重 時 (1198-1261). A brother of the two mentioned above, replaced *Tokiuji* in the northern *Rokuhara* with the title of *Sagami no kami* (1230) returned to *Kamakura* in 1247, where he was *rensho* (assistant) of the *Shikken Tokiyori*.

—— **Masamura, 政村** (1205-1273). A brother of the above was *Hyōjōshū*, then *Shikken-rensho* (1256), *Mutsu no kami*, *Sagami no kami*. In 1264 he replaced *Nagatoki* at the *Rokuhara*, and returned to *Kamakura* to assist the *Shikken Tokimune* (1271).

—— **Tokiuji, 時氏** (1203-1230). A son of *Yasutoki* who with his father took part in the *Shōkyū* war (1221). In 1224, he was sent as governor to *Kyōto* with *Tokimori* and took up his residence in a palace separate from that of *Tokimori*, hence the name of *Ryō-Rokuhara* (the two *Rokuhara*), which was given to their residences. Having become ill he returned to *Kamakura*, where he died at the age of 28.

—— **Nagatoki, 長時** (1230-1264). Was a son of *Shigetoki* He was sent to the northern *Rokuhara*, and returned to *Kamakura*, to assist the young *Shikken Tokimune* in 1256. He was made *Musashi no kami* and *Saburai-dokoro-bettō*. He died at the age of 35.

—— **Tsunetoki, 經時** (1224-1246). The fourth *Kamakura Shikken*, was a son of *Tokiuji*. He succeeded his grand father *Yasutoki* as *Shikken* (1242) and was *Musashi no kami*. Having become ill, he abdicated in favor of his brother *Tokiyori* and died soon afterwards.

—— **Tokiyori, 時賴** (1226-1263). The fifth *Kamakura Shikken*, was a son of *Tokiuji* and succeeded his brother *Tsunetoki* as *Shikken* in 1246. He had scarcely taken possession of his office, when *Mitsutoki*, *Echigo no kami*, supported by the ex-*Shōgun Yoritsune*, tried to have him assassinated in order to take his place; but the plot was discovered: *Mitsutoki* was exiled to *Izu* and *Yoritsune* sent back to *Kyōto*. The following year, *Miura Yasumura*, accused of endeavoring to re-establish *Yoritsune* in his former office of *Shōgun*, was put to death with all his family. *Yoritsune* having continued to conspire against *Tokiyori*, the latter deposed the *Shōgun Yoritsugu*, a son of *Yoritsune*, whom he sent back to *Kyōto*, and replaced him by prince *Munetaka*, a brother of the then reigning emperor *Go-Fukakusa* (1252). In 1256, his health failed. He shaved his head, assumed the name of *Dōsō*, and retired to the *Saimyō-ji* temple (hence the name of *Saimyō-ji-nyūdō*, by which he is known), letting *Nagatoki* govern in the name of his son *Tokimune*. It is said that he travelled incognito through the country, in order to judge personally of the needs of the people, of the abuses of the administration, etc. *Tokiyori* signalized his government by a wise economy and a close and constant interest in agriculture. He had, as minister, *Aoto Fujitsuna* of legendary fame.

—— **Tokimune, 時宗** (1251-1284). The 6th *Kamakura Shikken*, only 6 years old when his father *Tokiyori* resigned the office of *Shikken* in his favor, but he was assisted by the *Rensho Nagatoki*. From an early age he evinced a resolute, energetic character. In 1266, having had some disputes with the *Shōgun Munetaka-shinnō*, he deposed him and replaced him by *Koreyasu-shinnō*, only 3 years old, a son of prince *Munetaka*.—— In 1260, the celebrated *Kublai-Khan* (Jap. *Koppitsu-retsu*) had dethroned the *Song* dynasty (Jap. *Sō*) and having established his capital at *Khan-Baleck* (now *Peking*), he called upon all the former tributary states of China to acknowledge their fealty to the

Yuen (Jap. *Gen*) dynasty. In 1268, he sent an ambassador to Japan with a letter which *Tokimune* considered offensive to the country; it was left unanswered. In 1271, another ambassador was sent with the same result. In 1274, a fleet of 150 war-vessels arrived at *Tsushima*: *Sō Sukekuni*, the governor of the island, tried to resist, but he died in a battle at *Asaji no ura*, and the island was laid waste. The invaders after having devastated *Iki-shima*, tried to land at *Imatsu* (*Chikuzen*); the *Kyūshū daimyō-Shōni*, *Ōtomo*, *Matsuura*, *Kikuchi*, etc., — had intrenched themselves at *Hakozaki* and offered a vigorous resistance. The Mongols provided with fire-arms inflicted serious losses on the Japanese army and would undoubtedly have gained the victory in the end, had not *Liu*,

HŌJŌ TOKIMUNE.

their general, been killed in battle and many of their vessels wrecked in a tempest. The remainder of the fleet escaped and returned to China. *Kublai-Khan* did not consider himself vanquished: in 1276, he sent another ambassador with the same proposal. *Tokimune* had him beheaded at *Tatsu no kuchi* (*Kamakura*); two others met with the same fate at *Hakata* (*Chikuzen*) in 1279, and by the orders of *Tokimune*, *Kyūshū* and the western provinces of *Hondo* made themselves ready to repel any invasion. In June 1281, 100,000 Mongols and 10,000 Koreans, after having devastated *Iki-shima* and massacred all the inhabitants, came to the coast of *Dazaifu*, where they encountered an energetic resistance. Having landed at *Goryū-san* (*Hizen*), they met with a large army upon which they inflicted great losses by their artillery without however being able to vanquish them: after a week of desperate fighting the situation had not changed, when, for the second time, a tempest came to the succor of the Japanese. The Mongolian fleet was scattered, and thousands of soldiers perished in the sea. The survivors took refuge in the island of *Takashima*, where *Shōni Kagesuke* pursued them, slew a great many, and brought back a thousand prisoners who were put to death. Only three escaped to carry the news of the disaster to China. Meanwhile expecting a new invasion, *Tokimune* continued to fortify the coasts. In fact, *Kublai-Khan* began to prepare a new expedition, but his plan could not be realized, and thus Japan was preserved from the only foreign invasion that threatened her in the course of her history. *Tokimune* did not survive this triumph, which was greatly due to his energy; he died soon after at the age of 34.

—— **Sadatoki,** 貞 時 (1270-1311). The 7th *Kamakura Shikken*, and a son of *Tokimune*, was only 14 years old at the death of his father. He had his kinsman *Naritoki* as assistant. His first act of authority was to put *Adachi Yasumori* his maternal grandfather with his entire family to death. His only crime had been to seek the honours of the Shōgunate for his son *Munekage* (1285). Soon afterwards, displeased with the *Shōgun*

Koreyasu-shinnō, he sent him to *Kyōto*, and replaced him by *Hisa-akira-shinnō*, a brother of the reigning emperor *Fushimi* (1289). In 1292, a Korean envoy came to advise him to re-open relations with China in order to avoid another war : *Sadatoki* had him imprisoned and scorned his advice. In 1301, he had his head shaved, assumed the name of *Sōen*, and retired to the temple of *Saishōkoku-ji*, which he had built. *Sadatoki* was obliged to settle continual disputes between the two branches of the imperial family, concerning the succession to the throne. *Go-Saga* saw his two sons *Go-Fukakusa* (1247-1259) and *Kameyama* (1260-1274) crowned after him ; the latter abdicated in favor of his son *Go-Uda* (1275-1287), whose successor was *Fushimi* (1288-1298), a son of *Go-Fukakusa*. When *Fushimi* abdicated in favor of *Go-Fushimi*, the ex-emperor *Go-Uda* requested *Sadatoki* to respect the will of *Go-Saga* according to which the emperor should be chosen alternately from the two branches of his descendants. *Sadatoki* deposed *Go-Fushimi*, replaced him by *Go-Nijō*, a son of *Go-Uda* and decided that henceforth the emperors should abdicate after a reign of 10 years to surrender the throne to the rival branch. He also decided, in order to weaken the power of the *Fujiwara*, that the *Sesshō* (regent) and the *Kwampaku* should alternately be chosen from among the five branches called for this reason *Go-Sekke*. These arrangements were evidently made with a view to fortifying the authority of the *Hōjō* by dividing their adversaries. They were efficacious as long as energetic men like *Tokimune*, *Sadatoki*, were in power ; but in weak hands they became a cause of trouble and finally brought about the ruin of the powerful *Shikken*. *Sadatoki* continued to govern during ten years after his abdication, and died when 41 years old.

—— **Takatoki,** 高 時 (1303-1333). The 9th and last *Kamakura Shikken*, was a son of *Sadatoki*. After *Sadatoki* had his head shaved, his son-in-law *Morotoki* became regent ; at his death (1311) *Takatoki* then only 8 years old received the title of *Shikken* and was assisted by his kinsmen *Terutoki* and *Mototoki*. In 1316 he officially took the power ; but being of weak intelligence and dissolute morals, he spent his time in assisting at dances and dogfights, leaving the government in the hands of his minister *Nagasaki Takasuke*. The latter by his bad administration excited general discontent, and troubles arose in different provinces (1322). The emperor *Go-Daigo* thought the time favorable for the overthrow of the powerful *Shikken ;* emissaries sent by him found adherents even in *Kamakura*. But *Takatoki* having heard of it, obliged the emperor, under pain of deposition, to disown his emissaries and profess his good dispositions towards the *Hōjō* (1325). The following year prince *Kuninaga*, heir to the throne, having died, *Go-Daigo* wished to have his own son *Morinaga* nominated but *Takatoki* opposed his nomination, and chose *Kazuhito-shinnō*, a son of *Go-Fushimi*. The emperor, wishing to get the support of the powerful *Tendai* sect, nominated *Morinaga-shinnō* chief of the *Hiei-zan* temples, and a conspiracy was prepared · in secret. *Takatoki* now sent *Sadafuji* with 3,000 men to arrest *Go-Daigo*, who had time to flee to Mount *Kasagi*, south of *Kyōto* (1331). *Takatoki* then pronounced his deposition, raised *Kazuhito* (*Kōgon*) to the throne, and sending troops to surround *Kasagi-yama*, he made *Go-Daigo* prisoner, confined him for some time in the *Rokuhara* (*Kyōto*), and, at the beginning of the following year, exiled him to *Chiburi* (*Oki*). Defenders of the deposed emperor now arose everywhere: the *Kusunoki* in *Kawachi*, the *Nitta* in *Kōzuke*, the *Akamatsu* in *Harima*, etc. After one year's exile, *Go-Daigo* escaped from *Chiburi* island, landed in *Hōki* and asked *Nawa Nagatoshi* for protection. *Takatoki* sent an army to *Kyōto* under the command of *Ashikaga Takauji*; but the latter had no sooner arrived at the capital, than he declared himself in favor of *Go-Daigo* and besieged the *Rokuhara*, where the *Hōjō Nakatoki* and *Tokimasu* lost their lives. Meanwhile *Nitta Yoshisada*, having brought an army from *Kōzuke*, besieged and burned *Kamakura*, and *Takatoki*, after an attempt at resistance, committed suicide by *harakiri* with all his kinsmen and servants (May 22, 1333). Thus ended the power of the *Hōjō* who, for over a century, had been the real rulers of Japan.

—— **Tokiyuki**, 行時 (+ 1353). Was a son of *Takatoki*. At the taking of *Kamakura*, a servant led him to the residence of *Suwa Yorishige* in *Shinano*, who brought him back with an army, put *Ashikaga Tadayoshi* to flight and re-entered *Kamakura* (1335), only to be soon afterwards expelled by *Takauji*. *Tokiyuki* then presented himself to the emperor *Go-Daigo*, was pardoned and joined the partisans of the emperor. He fought under the command of *Kitabatake Akiie*, and then under *Munenaga-shinnō*. In 1352, he assisted at the capture of *Kamakura* by *Nitta Yoshioki*; afterwards, when the latter, defeated by *Takauji*, took refuge in *Echigo*, *Tokiyuki* hid himself in *Sagami*, but was discovered and beheaded at *Tatsu no kuchi*.

Hōjō, 北條. A *daimyō* family descended from *Taira Sadamori*. It was very powerful in *Kwantō* during the 16th century. As the family resided in *Odawara* (*Sagami*), it was generally called the *Odawara Hōjō* family, in order to distinguish it from the *Kamakura Hōjō Shikken*.

—— **Nagauji**, 長氏 (1432-1519). Was first called *Ise Shinkurō*. Being a native of *Suruga*, he served *Imagawa Yoshitada* and his son *Ujichika*. He had charge of the castle of *Hachiman-yama* and then of *Kōkokuji*. When *Ashikaga Masatomo* was assassinated by his own son *Chacha-maru* (1491), *Nagauji* marched against the latter, put him to death, took the province of *Izu* and installed himself at *Nirayama*. Having married his son *Ujitsuna* to a descendant of the ancient *Hōjō Shikken* he changed his family name to that of *Hōjō*, had his head shaved, and assumed the name of *Sōun*, 早雲, by which he is better known. At that epoch the two branches *Yamanouchi* and *Ōgigayatsu* of the *Uesugi* family

HŌJŌ SŌUN.

were at war with each other; *Sōun* offered his assistance to *Sadamasa*

(*Ōgigayatsu*) against *Akisada* (*Yamanouchi*). Having entered *Sagami* he took the castle of *Odawara* where he established himself (1495). In 1510, *Akisada* having been defeated and killed by *Nagao Tamekage*, the power of the *Uesugi* declined gradually and *Sōun* profited by it to increase his dominions. He besieged *Miura Yoshiatsu* in his castle at *Arai*, took it, and thus became master of the whole *Sagami* province (1518). He died the following year at *Nirayama*, at the age of 88. *Hōjō Sōun* was not only a remarkable warrior, but also a skilful administrator ; he left his son a code of laws in 21 chapters, which bears witness to his political talents.

Nagauji-Ujitsuna	Ujiyasu	Ujimasa		Ujinao
				Ujifusa (*Ota*)
				Naoshige
				Ujisada
		Ujiteru		
		Ujikuni		
		Ujinori - Ujimori		Ujinobu - Ujimune - Ujiharu
				Ujitoshi - Ujizumi
				Ujishige
		Ujitada		
		Ujimitsu		
		Kagetora		
	Tsunanari - Ujishige			Ujikatsu - Shigehiro
				Tokinari
				Tanemura

—— **Ujitsuna, 氏 綱** (1487-1541). A son of *Nagauji*, attempted to realize the plan conceived by his father, i e. to annihilate the *Uesugi* and to take their place. In 1524 he took the castle of *Edo* from *Tomo-oki*, who fled to *Kawagoe*. He gave his daughter in marriage to *Ashikaga Haruuji*, an enemy of the *Uesugi*, and made an appeal to all the *samurai* of *Kwantō*. *Tomooki* having died in 1537, his son *Tomosada* succeeded him. *Ujitsuna* then made himself master of the castle of *Kawagoe*, while *Tomosada* retired to *Matsuyama*. The following year, attacked by *Ashikaga Yoshiaki* and *Satomi Yoshihiro*, he defeated them ; *Yoshiaki* was killed and *Yoshihiro* submitted. The whole *Kwantō* now obeyed him, and, from his castle at *Odawara*, he applied himself to repair the injuries caused by long wars. With peace, prosperity reigned everywhere ; numbers of *samurai* came from *Kinai* and even from *Shikoku* to settle in the domains of the *Hōjō* in order to find tranquillity. *Ujitsuna* died when 55 years old.

—— **Ujiyasu, 氏 泰** (1515-1570). Was a son of *Ujitsuna*. In 1544, the two *Uesugi* leagued with *Imagawa Ujichika* against the *Hōjō* : *Ujiyasu* intrusted the defence of the *Kawagoe* castle to his brother *Tsunanari* and successively defeated *Uesugi Tomosada*, *Uesugi Norimasa* and *Ashikaga Haruuji*. *Norimasa* having taken refuge at *Hirai* (*Kōzuke*), *Ujiyasu* besieged him and took the castle, whilst *Norimasa* fled into *Echigo* to the residence of *Nagao Terutora*. This was the end of the two *Uesugi* branches in *Kwantō*, and the *Hōjō* took their place (1551). In 1554, *Ujiyasu* besieged *Haruuji* at *Koga*, made him prisoner, and kept him at *Kamakura*. Meanwhile, *Nagao Terutora* yielding to the entreaties of *Uesugi Norimasa*, came to besiege *Odawara* with a numerous army (1560), but was unable to take the place and so retired. Soon afterwards, *Ujiyasu* had to withstand the coalition of the *Imagawa* and the *Takeda*, but peace was brought about and cemented by marriage: *Ujinao*, a grandson of *Ujiyasu*, married the daughter of *Takeda Shingen*, and the latter's son married the daughter of *Ujiyasu*. In 1563, *Mogami Yoshihiro* together with *Ōta Sukemasa* besieged the castle at *Edo*: *Ujiyasu* routed them and *Yoshihiro* was forced to cede to him his possessions in *Kazusa*. Soon afterwards he made peace with *Uesugi Kenshin* (formerly *Nagao Terutora*), who adopted a son of *Ujiyasu*. Finally he sided with *Imagawa Ujizane* against *Takeda Shingen* (1568), and died two years afterwards at the age of 56. It was *Ujiyasu* who raised the glory and power of the *Odawara Hōjō* to their greatest height. He left 7 sons to continue his work.

—— **Ujimasa**, 氏 政 (1538-1590). Was the eldest son of *Ujiyasu* and took part in all his father's campaigns. In 1568, *Takeda Shingen* attacked *Imagawa Ujizane* and took *Fuchū* (*Shizuoka*), after which he proposed to the *Hōjō* to divide *Imagawa's* domains with them; but *Ujiyasu* and *Ujimasa* disgusted with such dishonesty raised an army against him. *Shingen* was obliged to retreat and *Ujizane* was re-established at *Fuchū*. Soon afterwards, *Shingen*, attacked *Nobunaga* (1570), and made peace with *Ujimasa*. The latter endeavored to maintain peace in *Kwantō* and even succeeded in preventing a war between *Satomi* and *Satake*. Having given his domains to his son *Ujinao*, he had his head shaved and took the name of *Ryūsai*. He served as mediator between *Takeda Katsuyori* and *Nobunaga* and restored peace (1574). In 1578 *Uesugi Kenshin* having died, *Kagetora*, a brother of *Ujimasa* whom he had adopted, was to take possession of his domains, but *Kagekatsu*, a nephew of *Kenshin* reclaimed his rights. *Kagetora* applied to his brother, and *Kagekatsu* asked help from *Takeda Katsuyori*: hence a war was about to ensue, but before *Ujimasa* could take part in it, *Kagetora* was killed and *Kagekatsu* had conquered the whole province of *Echigo*. *Nobunaga* admitted the rights of the *Hōjō* to the possession of *Kwantō*: when *Hideyoshi* asked them to acknowledge their vassalage, they refused. In 1590 *Odawara* was besieged and *Ujimasa* committed suicide.

—— **Ujinao,** 氏 直 (1562-1591). Was a son of *Ujimasa*. When *Uesugi Kagekatsu* aided by *Takeda Katsuyori* had taken the succession of *Kenshin*, *Ujinao* applied to *Nobunaga* and *Ieyasu* for aid; then marching against *Katsuyori* he defeated him (1579). At the death of *Nobunaga*, one of his generals *Takigawa Kazumasu* leaving the castle of *Umayabashi*, marched towards *Kyōto*; *Ujinao* thinking it a favorable occasion to make himself master of *Kōzuke*, went thither with an army, but *Kazumasu* returned in haste and defeated him. *Ujinao* applied to *Daidōji Masashige* for help, and now *Kazumasu* was vanquished and *Kōzuke* province was added to the

SEAL OF THE
ODAWARA HŌJŌ.

domains of the *Hōjō* (1582). A campaign in *Kai* and *Shinano* against *Tokugawa Ieyasu* and *Uesugi Kagekatsu* was without result, peace was signed and *Ujinao* married a daughter of *Ieyasu*. In 1589, the *Kwampaku Hideyoshi* ordered *Ujimasa* and *Ujinao* to repair to *Kyōto*, but *Ujinao* did not comply. *Hideyoshi*, irritated, gathered a numerous army and the following year, invested *Odawara*. Having been defeated in several en-counters, the besieged began to lose courage. *Matsuda Norihide* was put to death for having secretly communicated with the enemy. *Hide-yoshi* sent *Kuroda Yoshitaka* to *Ujinao* to invite him to surrender, promising to leave him *Sagami* and *Izu* in fief; but *Ujinao* refused. *Ieyasu* sent a similar invitation, but was likewise refused, and the siege continued. After some time, *Ujinao* was finally forced to yield and to submit to the conditions of the conqueror. *Ujimasa* was ordered to commit *harakiri*, and *Ujinao* was exiled to *Kōya-san*. He died the following year after having seen *Kwantō* transferred to *Tokugawa Ieyasu*.

—— **Ujinori, 氏規** (+ 1600). The 4th son of *Ujiyasu*, held the castle of *Nirayama* (*Izu*) when *Hideyoshi* began his campaign against the *Hōjō*. He was besieged by *Oda Nobuo* and *Fukushima Masanori*. After a stout defence, he surrendered the castle to *Ieyasu* and joined the besieged in *Odawara*. This town also having been surrendered, he accompanied *Ujinao* to *Kōya-san*. Soon afterwards, he obtained from *Hideyoshi* the small fief of *Sayama* (*Kawachi* — 10,000 k.) where his descendants resided till the Restoration. — The chief of the family is now Viscount.

Hōjō go-dai, 北條五代. The five generations of the *Odawara Hōjō*: *Nagauji, Ujitsuna, Ujiyasu, Ujimasa* and *Ujinao*.

Hōjō-ki, 方丈記. (Lit.: history of a room 10 feet square). A classical work composed in 1212 by *Kamo Chōmei* in which he relates the wars of the latter part of the 12th century.

Hōjō ku-dai, 北條九代. The 9 generations of the *Kamakura Shikken*: *Tokimasa, Yoshitoki, Yasutoki, Tsunetoki, Tokiyori, Tokimune, Sadatoki, Morotoki,* and *Takatoki*.

Hōjū-ji, 法住寺. An ancient temple in *Kyōto*. Towards the year 1000, *Fujiwara Tamemitsu* built a residence to which he retired ; later on it became the residence of the emperors *Toba* and *Go-Shirakawa* after their abdication, and finally was converted into a temple known by the name of *Hōjū-ji*. *Go-Shirakawa* besieged (1183) there by *Kiso Yoshi-naka*, fled but returned in 1191.

Hōken, 封建. Feudal government.

Hōki, 寶龜. Nengō: 770-780.

Hōki, 伯耆. One of the 8 provinces of *San-in-dō*. It comprises 3 districts belonging to *Shimane ken*. — Chinese name : *Hakushū*.

Hokkaidō, 北海道. (Lit.: region of the northern sea), *Yezo* or *Ezo* island. — Surface : 78,000 Km.²; length from north to south 470 Km. ; breadth from east to west 630 Km. — Population : 844,000 in-habitants (of whom 18,000 *Ainos*). — It was formerly called *Watari-shima* and was inhabited by the *Ebisu*, the aboriginal race of Japan.

Abe no Hirafu was the first to penetrate into that island in 662, and established a garrison in *Shiribeshi* to stop the incursions of the *Ainos*. In the 16th century, the island was colonized by *Takeda Nobuhiro*, one of whose descendants *Matsumae Yoshihiro*, had his authority recognized by *Ieyasu* in 1604. The *Matsumae* family continued to govern the south-western part of the island till the Restoration. — In 1868 *Enomoto Takeaki*, taking the shōgunal fleet along with him, formed the project of making *Yezo* an independent fief for the *Tokugawa ;* he took *Hakodate, Matsumae*, etc. and repulsed the imperial army for several months, but was finally obliged to surrender (June 1869). *Yezo* was then placed under a special administration named the *Kaitakushi*, received the name of *Hokkaidō* and was divided into 9 provinces. In 1881, the *Kaitakushi* was suppressed, and the island was divided into three departments, *Hakodate-ken, Sapporo-ken*, and *Nemuro-ken*. In 1886 the departments were suppressed and an independent administration, called *Hokkaidō-chō* was established with its seat at *Sapporo*. The actual 10 provinces of *Hokkaidō* are : *Oshima, Shiribeshi, Ishikari, Teshio, Kitami, Iburi, Hidaka, Tokachi, Kushiro*, and *Nemuro ;* to which the *Chishima* (Kurile islands) must be added. Those provinces contain 88 districts (*kōri*) and number 756 towns or villages.

Hokke-shū, 法華宗. — See *Nichiren-shū*.

Hōkō-Daishi, 法光大師. — See *Shinga*.

Hōkō-guntō, 澎湖群島. The Pescadores archipelago. It comprises 47 islands, having a total surface of 221 Km.^{2} and a population of 50,000 inhabitants.

Hōkō-ji, 方廣寺. A temple built in *Kyōto* by *Hideyoshi*, in which he placed a *Daibutsu* 19 met. high. The temple was destroyed by an earthquake in 1596, and rebuilt in 1612 by *Hideyori* who placed a monumental bell in it (4m. 20 in height, 2m. 75 in diameter, and 33 cm. in thickness). In the inscription were the two characters composing the name of *Ieyasu*, who, seeking a pretext to make war with the *Toyotomi*, declared himself offended, insisted upon an apology and the eradication of the inscription. Hostilities began soon afterwards. The *Daibutsu* was destroyed by fire in 1798 but three years afterwards, it was replaced by the present wooden *Daibutsu*.

Hōkō-ji, 豐光寺. — See *Sōkoku-ji*.

Hōkō-tō, 膨湖嶋. The largest island (79 Km in circuit) of the Pescadores. It has given its name to the archipelago.

Hoku-chō, 北朝. The northern dynasty, from 1336 to 1392. It was a branch of the imperial family, descended from *Go-Fukakusa*. It was so called to distinguish it from the descendants of *Go-Daigo*, who had retired south of *Kyōto*.

Hoku-ke, 北朝. One of the four primitive branches of the *Fujiwara* family, founded by *Fusasaki* (682-737).

Hokumen no bushi, 北面武士. Formerly nobles attached to the person of an emperor after his abdication. The title was created by *Shirakawa-jōkō*.

Hokurei, 北嶺. Another name given to the "ensemble" of the temples on *Hiei-zan*.

Hokurokudō, 北陸道. (Lit.: region of the northern land). One of the great territorial divisions of Japan. It comprises 7 provinces: *Wakasa, Echizen, Etchū, Echigo, Kaga, Noto,* and *Sado.*

Hokuroku no Miya, 北陸宮 (1165-1230). An imperial prince, grandson of *Go-Shirakawa* and son of *Mochihito-Ō.* At the death of his father (1180), he was led into *Hokuroku,* hence his name. He is also called *Kiso no Miya* and *Gensoku no Miya.* When the *Taira* had taken the young emperor *Antoku* to the South (1183) and the capital was without a ruler, *Kiso Yoshinaka* conceived the design of putting *Hokuroku no Miya* on the throne, but the attempt was unsuccessful. In 1185, the prince came back to *Kyōto* and took up his residence at *Saga,* where he lived in retirement until his death.

Hokusai, 北齊 (1760-1849). A celebrated painter born in *Edo.* He was called *Nakajima Tetsujirō.* Having received lessons from *Katsukawa Shunshō,* he changed his name to *Katsukawa Shunchō,* and later to that of *Katsushika Hokusai.* He applied himself especially to engraving and the illustrations of a great number of works are due to him. His best known works are: Divers Sketches (*mangwan*), Hundred Views of Mt. *Fuji,* the 53 Stages of the *Tōkaidō,* etc. Notwithstanding his numerous productions, *Hokusai* lived in poverty approaching to misery; his old age however was sweetened by the admirable devotedness of his daughter. He enjoys

HOKUSAI.

a greater celebrity among foreigners than among his compatriots.

Hōkwan-shō, 寳冠章. Decoration of the Crown. — See *Kunshō.*

Homma Tadahide, 本間忠秀. A warrior of the 14th century, celebrated for his skill with the bow and arrow. At first he served *Ashikaga Takauji,* but when the latter revolted against *Go-Daigo,* he left him and followed *Nitta Yoshisada.* He was beheaded by order of *Takauji.*

Hommoku-misaki, 本牧岬. A cape in *Sagami,* south of *Yokohama.*

Homusubi, 火結. The last child of *Izanagi* and *Izanami.* His birth was the cause of his mother's death, and he was therefore beheaded by his infuriated father. He is also called *Hi no Kagutsuchi* and is honored as the god of fire. The god *Atago,* who is supposed to protect towns against fire, is probably the same as *Homusubi.*

Hon-ami, 本阿彌. A family whose members were renowned as experts in the matter of sabres, swords etc. — The most renowned are *Myōhon* (1252-1355), *Kōtoku* (1554-1620), *Kōetsu* (1557-1637) *Kōho* (1603-1684), etc.

Hon-bugyō, 本奉行. Under the *Kamakura* shōgunate, a jury formed of the chiefs of families, who had to examine the charges brought against the accused.

Honchi-suijaku, 本地垂跡. According to theories of the *Ryōbu-Shintō* developed by *Gyōgi, Kūkai,* etc. the gods (*kami*) of Shintoism and those (*hotoke*) of Buddhism are but manifestations of the same divinities ; India is, so to say, the land of their origin (*honchi*) ; in Japan, they made their appearance for some time, leaving traces of their passage (*suijaku*). Thus *Tenshō-Daijin* is but the *avatar* of *Amida-Butsu, Hachiman,* that of *Kwanzeon,* etc.

Honchō-tsūgan, 本朝通鑑. An historical work of 300 volumes compiled under the direction of the *Hayashi* family (18th century) by order of the Shōgunal government.

Honda, 譽田 or *Konda.* A place in *Kawachi,* where *Kusunoki Masatsura* defeated *Hosokawa Akiuji* in 1347. During the siege of *Ōsaka,* the generals of *Hideyori, Sanada Yukimura, Mōri Katsunaga, Gotō Mototsugu,* fought a battle there against the army of *Ieyasu* (1615).

Honda, 本多. A *daimyō* family originating in *Mikawa,* and descended from *Fujiwara Kanemichi* (925-977).

Tadakatsu
   Tadamasa
      Tadatoki -Masatomo   (a)
      Tadayoshi
         Tadahira -Tadatsune -Tadanao (b)
         Tadatoshi -Tadatsugu -Tadahide (c)
         Tadaharu -Tadamichi -Tadayuki (d)
   Tadatomo -Masakatsu -Masanaga
         Tadakuni -Tadataka (e)
         Masanobu -Tadahide (f)

(*a*) — The elder branch. —— **Tadakatsu,** 忠勝 (1548-1610). Was a companion of *Ieyasu* in all his campaigns. When the latter received *Kwantō* as a fief (1590) he nominated *Tadakatsu daimyō* of *Ōtaki* (*Kazusa* — 100,000 k.), and, after *Sekigahara* (1600) transferred him to *Kuwana* (*Ise* — 150,000 k.).

—— **Tadamasa,** 忠政 (1575-1631). A son of *Tadakatsu.* In 1617 he was transferred to *Himeji* (*Harima* — 250,000 k.).

—— **Masatomo,** 政朝 (1597-1638). Having died without an heir, his cousin *Masakatsu* was chosen to continue the branch. — See (*e*).

(*b*) —— A younger branch that resided successively at *Kakegawa* (*Tōtōmi*), *Murakami* (*Echigo*), *Shirakawa* (*Mutsu*), *Utsunomiya* (*Shimotsuke*) ; in 1685, it was transferred to *Kōriyama* (*Yamato* — 120,000 k.), and became extinct in 1723.

HONDA TADAKATSU.

(*c*) — A branch which installed at *Koromo,* (*Mikawa*) in 1681, was transferred to *Sagara* (*Tōtōmi* — 10,000 k.) in 1749. In 1758, *Tadayoshi* was dispossessed for having been implicated in the plot of *Kanamori Yorikane.*

(*d*) — A branch which, from 1746 resided at *Izumi* (*Mutsu* — 20,000 k.). — At present Viscount.

(*e*) — **Tadatomo,** 忠朝 (1582-1615). *Daimyō* of *Ōtaki* (*Kazusa* — 50,000 k.), next of *Tatsuno* (*Harima*).

—— **Masakatsu,** 政 勝 (1614-1671). Was selected in 1639 to continue the elder branch and was made *daimyō* of *Kōriyama* (*Yamato* — 90,000 k.).

—— **Masanaga,** 政 長. In 1679 was transferred to *Fukushima* (*Mutsu*), and in 1684, to *Himeji* (*Harima* — 150,000 k.).

—— **Tadataka,** 忠 孝. In 1704 was transferred to *Murakami* (*Echigo*), and died without an heir in 1709; a relative was chosen as the adopted son, but was made *daimyō* of *Kariya* (*Mikawa* — 50,000 k.), afterwards of *Koga* (*Shimōsa*). His descendants resided successively: in 1759 at *Hamada* (*Iwami*), in 1769 at *Okazaki* (*Mikawa* — 50,000 k.), where they remained till the Restoration. — To-day Viscount.

(*f*) —— Younger branch of the above resided at *Yamasaki* (*Harima* — 10,000 k.) from 1639. — At present Viscount.

Honda, 本 多. A *daimyō* family originating in *Mikawa* and descended, like the above from the *Fujiwara*.

Toshimasa { Masanobu - Masazumi   (a)
              { Masashige - Masatsura - Masanao - Masanaga   (b)

(*a*) — The elder branch —— **Masanobu,** 正 信 (1539-1617). Was in the service of *Ieyasu*. In 1589, he was made *Sado no kami*, was the minister of *Ieyasu* in *Kwantō*, and became *daimyō* of *Takatori* (*Yamato* — 30,000 k.).

—— **Masazumi,** 正 純 (1566-1637). A son of *Masanobu*, was minister (*shitsuji*) of *Ieyasu* in *Sumpu* (*Shizuoka*), next of *Hidetada* in *Edo*. He had the title of *Kōzuke no suke*. In 1619, he became *daimyō* of *Utsunomiya* (*Shimotsuke* — 145,000 k.), but was dispossessed in 1622 and exiled to *Dewa*, where he died.

(*b*) — The younger branch which resided successively: in 1616, at *Sōma* (*Shimōsa*); in 1703, at *Numata* (*Kōzuke*); in 1730, at *Tanaka* (*Suruga* — 40,000 k.) where it remained till the Restoration — At present Viscount.

Honda, 本 多. A *daimyō* family native of *Mikawa* and descended from the *Fujiwara*.

—— **Yasushige,** 康 重 (1554-1611). *Bungo no kami* and, in 1590, *daimyō* of *Shirai* (*Kōzuke*), was transferred in 1601 to *Okazaki* (*Mikawa* — 50,000 k.). — His descendants resided in 1645, at *Yokosuka* (*Tōtōmi*); in 1682, at *Murayama* (*Dewa*); in 1701, at *Itoigawa* (*Echigo*); finally since 1717, at *Iiyama* (*Shinano* — 20,000 k.). — Now Viscount.

Honda, 本 多. A *daimyō* family native of *Mikawa* and descended from the *Fujiwara*.

Tadatsugu - Yasutoshi { Toshitsugu { Yasunaga - Yasuyoshi   (a)
                     {   { Yasumasa - Tadatsune   (b)
                     { Tadasuke   -Tadamasa - Tadayoshi   (c)

(*a*) — **Tadatsugu,** 忠 次 (1549-1613). Inherited the castle of *Ina* (*Mikawa*), which his descendants occupied for several generations.

—— **Yasutoshi,** 康 俊 (1570-1622). Was nominated *daimyō* by *Ieyasu*, in 1601, at *Nishio* (*Mikawa*), then, in 1607, at *Zeze* (*Ōmi* — 30,000 k). — His descendants resided at *Nishio* (*Mikawa*) in 1620, at

Kameyama (*Ise*) in 1636, at *Zeze* (*Ōmi*) in 1651 where they continued to reside till the Restoration (60,000 k.). —Now Viscount.

(*b*) — Younger branch which was first installed at *Nishishiro* (*Kawachi*), and since 1732 resided at *Kambe* (*Ise* — 15,000 k.). — To-day Viscount.

(*c*) — A branch which until the Restoration resided at *Nishibata* (*Mikawa* — 10,500 k.). — To-day Viscount.

Honda, 本田. A *samurai* family of *Satsuma* ennobled after the Restoration. — To-day Baron.

Hondo, 本土 or *Honshū*. The great isle of *Nippon*. — Surface: 226.580 Km.². — Population : 33,328.000 inh. — It comprises, 57 provinces, 34 departments, 439 districts, 10,658 towns or villages.

Hondō, 本堂. A *daimyō* family, descended from the *Seiwa-Genji*. The *han* of *Shitsuku* (*Hitachi* — 10,000 k.) is in its possession. — To-day Baron.

Hōnen-Shōnin, 法然上人.— See *Genkū*.

Hongaku-Daishi, 本覺大師.— See *Yakushin*.

Hongwanji, 木願寺. The principal branch of the Buddhist *Shin* or *Monto* or *Ikkō* sect, founded by *Shinran* (*Kenshin-Daishi*) in 1224. It took its name from the great temple in *Kyōto*, the seat of the sect, built in 1272 by the daughter (*Gakushin*) and the grandson of *Shinran*. At the time of the 8th chief bonze *Rennyo*, expelled from *Kyōto* by the bonzes of *Hieizan*, the seat was transferred to *Chikamatsu* (*Ōmi*) then to *Yoshizaki*, in *Echizen* (1470), and finally to *Yamashina*, near *Kyōto* (1480). In 1532, the chief bonze *Shōnyo* transferred it to *Ishiyama* (*Ōsaka*), thence to *Temman-zan* (*Ōsaka*) in 1585. Finally in 1591 the principal temple was erected on the site of the present one in *Kyōto* But, the chief bonze *Kōju* being opposed to *Nobunaga*, *Hideyoshi* replaced him, as chief of the sect, by his brother *Kōchō*. *Ieyasu* having come into power, erected another temple for *Kōju* (*Junnyo-Shōnin*) east of the former one, and, it was called *Higashi-Hongwanji* (1602) : hence the division of the sect into two branches. Since 1521, the *Hongwan-ji* temple has the title of *Monzeki*.

Honji-fure-gashira, 本寺觸頭. All the Buddhist sects, made a distinction between the *hon-ji* (central temple) and the *matsu-ji* (secondary temples). One among the latter is designated in every province to receive and transmit the orders and communications (*fure*) of the *hon-ji*. This temple is called *Honji-fure-gashira*.

Honjō, 本荘. An ancient castle in *Musashi*. From 1590 to 1608, it was the residence of a branch of the *Ogasawara* family.

Honjō, 本庄. An ancient castle in *Dewa* (*Ugo*), built in the 16th century by *Tateoka Mitsushige*, a vassal of the *Mogami*. When the latter were dispossessed of their domains (1623), the castle was transferred to *Rokugō Masanori* whose descendants resided there till the Restoration (20,000 k.).

Honjō, 本莊. A *daimyō* family native of *Yamashiro*.

Munemasa	Munesuke	- Suketoshi	- Sukenori	(a)
	Munenaga	- Munehisa		(b)
	Michiyoshi	- Michitaka	- Michiakira	(c)

(*a*) — the elder branch —— **Munesuke, 宗資** (1629-1699). Was the uncle on his mother's side of the *Shōgun Tsunayoshi* who ennobled him in 1688, and bestowed *Kasama* (*Hitachi* — 50,000 k.) on him as a fief. — His descendants resided in 1720, at *Hamamatsu* (*Tōtōmi*) ; in 1729, at *Yoshida* (*Mikawa*) ; in 1749, at *Hamamatsu ;* at last, from 1758, at *Miyazu* (*Tango* — 70,000 k.). — Now Viscount.

(*b*) — The younger branch installed at *Nibu* (*Echizen* — 20,000 k) became extinct in 1711.

(*c*) — The youngest branch resided at *Takatomi* (*Mino* — 10,000 k.) since 1706. — Now Viscount.

In 1705, the three branches were authorized to assume the name of *Matsudaira*.

Honjō-ji, 本成寺. A temple founded in *Echigo* by the bonze *Nichi-in* (1320), which temple became the seat of a branch of the *Hokke-shū* sect. In 1898, the name of the branch was changed to *Hokke-shū*.

Honkoku-ji, 本國寺. A temple built by *Nichiren* in 1253 at *Kamakura*. In 1341, *Komyō*, the emperor of the North, transferred it to *Kyōto*. It is the principal temple of the *Hokke-shū* sect. — In 1569, the *Shōgun Yoshiaki* was besieged in it by *Miyoshi Iwanari* and rescued by *Nobunaga*.

Honnō-ji, 本能寺. A temple in *Kyōto* in which *Akechi Mitsu-hide* attacked *Nobunaga*, who, having been wounded, committed suicide (1582).

Honomi, 穗樸. A *kuge* family descended from *Fujiwara Taka-fuji* (838-900). — The head of the family is now Viscount.

Honryū-ji, 本隆寺. A temple founded in *Musashi* by the bonze *Nisshin* towards 1520, and which became the centre of a branch of the *Hokke-shū* sect. In 1898, the name of the branch was changed to *Hommyō-Hokke-shū*.

Honshū, 本洲. — See *Hondo*.

Hō-ō, 法皇. The abbreviation of *Dajō-hō-ō*, a title borne by the emperors who after their abdication had their head shaved and became bonzes.

Hōō-zan, 鳳凰山, A mountain (2,900 m.) in the west of *Kai*.

Hōrai-zan, 蓬萊山. According to a Chinese legend, one of the 3 mountainous islands of the Eastern Sea inhabited by genii (*tennin*). This tradition probably has its origin in the vague notions of the Chinese concerning the existence of Japan It was to that island that the emperor *Shikō* of the *Shin* dynasty sent the physician *Jofuku*, to search for the elixir of life : he arrived in Japan in 221 B.C , and this may have been the first communication between the two countries.

Hōreki, 寶曆. *Nengō :* 1751-1763.

Hori, 堀. A *daimyō* family descended from *Fujiwara Uona* and native of *Mino*.

	Hideharu - Tadatoshi	(a)
Hidemasa	Chikayoshi - Chikamasa - Chikasada	(b)
	Toshishige	(c)

(*a*) — The eldest branch — **Hidemasa** 秀 政 (1553-1590). Served *Oda Nobunaga* and then *Hideyoshi*. In 1581 he received the castle of *Obama* (*Wakasa*). The following year he took part in the battle of *Yamasaki* against *Mitsuhide* and afterwards made himself master of *Sakamoto* castle. He received the fief of *Sawayama* (*Ōmi* — 90,000 k.) as a reward (1583). He died during the siege of *Odawara*.

—— **Hideharu,** 秀 治 (1575-1606). A son of *Hidemasa* received at the death of his father, the daimyate of *Kasuga-yama* (*Echigo*), and, in 1598, that of *Takata* (*Echigo* — 350,000 k.).

—— **Tadatoshi,** 忠 俊. A son of *Hideharu*, was dispossessed in 1610 and exiled to *Mutsu* on account of maladministration.

(*b*) — The younger branch. —— **Chikayoshi,** 親 良 (1580-1637). *Daimyō* of *Zōō* (now *Nagaoka*) (*Echigo* — 40,000 k). He was dispossessed at the same time as his nephew *Tadatoshi*, but two years later, he received the little fief of *Mōka* (*Shimotsuke*), and in 1627, that of *Karasu-yama* (*Shimotsuke*). — His descendants were transferred to *Iida* (*Shinano* — 17,000 k.) in 1672, and remained there till the Restoration. — Now Viscount.

(*c*). — The cadet branch installed at *Katori* (*Hitachi* — 10,000 k.), and dispossessed in 1679.

Hori, 堀. — See *Okuda*.

Horikawa, 堀 河. A *kuge* family descended from *Fujiwara Nagayoshi* (800-854). — Now Viscount.

Horikawa go-zō, 堀 河 五 藏. The scholar *Itō Jinsai*, who lived at *Horikawa* (*Kyōto*), had five sons, whose names ended in *zō* : *Genzō, Jūzō, Shōzō, Heizō,* and *Saizō,* all distinguished scholars like their father. They were called *Horikawa go-zō*.

Horikawa-tennō, 堀 川 天 皇. The 73d Emperor of Japan (1087-1107), prince *Taruhito*, was a son of *Shirakawa-tennō*, whom he succeeded at the age of 9, but the ex-emperor continued to govern. It was during his reign that the 3 years' war (*go-san-nen no eki*) (1087-1089) against the *Kiyowara* who had revolted in *Mutsu* took place. *Horikawa* died when 29 years old.

Horikoshi, 堀 越. The *Nirayama* village in *Izu*. In 1457, the *Shōgun Yoshimasa* sent his brother *Masatomo* to govern *Kwantō*. *Kamakura* being in the power of the *Uesugi*, *Masatomo* established himself in *Izu*, hence the name of *Horikoshi-gosho* that was given him. In 1491, *Chacha-maru* assassinated his father, in order to succeed him, but two years later, he was vanquished and killed by *Ise Nagauji*.

Horio, 堀 尾. A *daimyō* family of *Owari*.

—— **Yoshiharu,** 吉 晴 (1543-1611). A son of *Yoshihisa*, was in the service of *Hideyoshi* and successively occupied the castles of *Takahama* (*Wakasa*) and *Hamamatsu* (*Tōtōmi* — 60,000 k.) in 1590. He was one of the 3 *Chūrō* nominated by *Hideyoshi* before his death. After *Sekigahara* (1600), *Ieyasu*, whose cause he had espoused, made him *daimyō* of *Matsue* (*Izumo* — 235,000 k.).

—— **Tadauji,** 忠 氏 (1575-1604). A son of *Yoshiharu*, took part in the campaign of *Sekigahara*. He died before his father.

—— **Tadaharu,** 忠晴 (1599-1633). A son of *Tadauji*, succeeded his grandfather in the daimyate of *Matsue* ; but he died childless, and his domains reverted to the Shōgunate.

Horojiri-yama, 幌尻山. A mountain (1850 met.) on the boundary of *Ishikari* and *Teshio* (*Hokkaidō*).

Horomoshiri-jima, 波羅茂知島.—— See *Haramuchi-jima*.

Hōryū-ji, 法隆寺. A Buddhist temple founded in 607, near *Nara*, by prince *Shōtoku-taishi*. It is the most ancient temple in Japan. It is also called *Ikaruga-dera*.

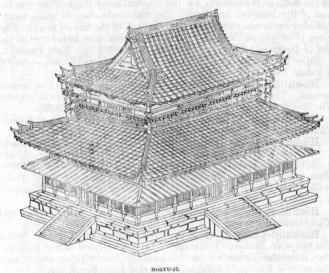

HŌRYU-JI.

Hoshina, 保科. A *daimyō* family of *Mikawa* and descended from *Minamoto Yorisue* (*Seiwa-Genji*).

Masanao {
  Masamitsu - Masayuki - Masatsune   (a)
  Masasada - Masakage - Masakata   (b)
}

(*a*) —— The elder branch.—— **Masanao,** 正直 (1542-1601), guarded the castle of *Takatō* (*Shinano*) for the *Takeda*. In 1590, *Hideyoshi* gave him the little fief of *Tako* (*Shimōsa*).

—— **Masamitsu,** 正光 (1561-1631). Was a son of *Masanao*. After *Sekigahara* (1600), he received the daimyate of *Takatō* (*Shinano* — 30,000 k.) from *Ieyasu*.

—— **Masayuki,** 正之 (1609-1672). An adopted son of *Masa-mitsu*, was in reality the 4th son of the *Shōgun Hidetada* and a brother of *Iemitsu*. It was on that account that in 1636, after the death of

Masamitsu, he exchanged the domain of *Takatō* for that of *Yamagata* (*Dewa* — 200,000 k.). Eight years later he was transferred to *Waka-matsu* (*Mutsu* — 230,000 k.). Before dying, *Iemitsu* entrusted him with the guardianship of his son *Ietsuna*. *Masayuki* is celebrated both as an administrator and a scholar. He and his successors bore the name of *Matsudaira*.

—— **Katamori, 容保**. Was the last descendant of the foregoing. At the time of the Restoration, he showed himself an energetic defender of the Shōgunal power. He resisted to the very last and the conquest of the castle of *Wakamatsu* by the imperial army (Sept. 1868) was the end of the hostilities in *Hondo*. He was condemned to confinement; but afterwards was offered the post of guard of the funeral temple of *Ie-yasu* (*Tōshōgū*) in *Nikkō*. His son *Kataharu* was transferred to the fief of *Tonami* (to-day *Tanabu*) (*Mutsu* — 30,000 k.). — Now Viscount.

(*b*) — The younger branch was established at *Iino* (*Kazusa* — 20,000 k.) since 1648. — Now Viscount.

Hō-shinnō, 法親王. A title given to princes (*shinnō*) that became bonzes. The first that bore this title was the brother of the emperor *Horikawa*. He had become chief of the *Ninnaji* temple (1099).

Hoshi no oka, 星岡. A place in *Iyo*, where the *tandai* of *Nagato*, *Hōjō Tokinao* was defeated in 1333 by the troops of the *Kōno*.

Hōshō, 寶生. A family of *nō* composers, founded by *Ren-ami* (+1468), a brother of *Kwanze Seami*. The best known are: *Hōzan* (+1585), *Katsuyoshi* (+1630), *Shigefusa* (+1665), *Shigetomo* (+1685), *Tomoharu* (+1728), *Nobuhide* (+1730), *Tomokiyo* (+1772), *Tomo-michi* (+1775), *Tomokatsu* (+1791), *Hidekatsu* (+1811) *Tomoyuki* (+1863).

Hōshū, 豐州. The Chinese name of the two provinces *Buzen* and *Bungo* taken together.

Hōshunji-yama, 芳春寺山. A mountain in *Wakasa*. When the troops of *Asakura Yoshikage* began the conquest of that province, they intrenched themselves on this mountain, and starting thence took the castle of *Kuniyoshi* defended by *Kuriya Katsuhisa* (1564).

Hosoi Heishū, 細井平洲 (1728-1801). A celebrated teacher of Confucianism. After having attended the lessons of *Akimoto Tanjun* at *Nagoya*, he studied Chinese at *Nagasaki* during 3 years, after which, he taught at *Edo*, *Nagoya*, *Yonezawa* and acquired a great reputation.

Hosokawa, 細川. A place in *Harima*, often mentioned in poetry. It was the residence of *Fujiwara Sadaie* and the birth-place of *Fuji-wara Seikwa*.

Hosokawa, 細川. A *daimyō* family descended from *Minamoto Yoshisue* (*Seiwa-Genji*) very powerful from the 14th to the 16th century. It was one of the three families (*san-kwan*) from which the *Kyōto Kwanryō* had to be chosen.

—— **Yoriharu, 賴春** (1299-1352). *Sanuki no kami*, from the beginning, joined the party of *Ashikaga Takauji*, who was likewise a descendant of the *Minamoto*. In 1337, he besieged and took the castle of *Kanasaki* (*Echizen*) and prince *Takanaga-shinnō, Nitta Yoshiaki, Doi Michiharu*, with the rest of the garrison were killed. In 1340, he took the castle of *Seta* (*Iyo*) and brought the whole of *Shikoku* under the rule of the *Ashikaga*. Later on, he with *Kō Moronao*, fought against, *Kusunoki Masanori* (1348-1351).

```
                              Kimiyori
    ┌───────────────┬──────────┴──────────────┬──────────┬─────────┐
  Kazuuji         Yoriharu                  Morouji   Yorisada
    │         ┌──────┼──────────────┐
 Kiyouji  Yoriyuki Yorimoto     Yorimochi  Ujiharu  Akiuji  Jōzen
    │               │               │
 Yorikazu       Mitsumoto       Yorinaga
                Mochiyuki        Mochiari
                Katsumoto        Noriharu
                Masamoto         Tsuneari
                    │                │
      Takakuni Sumitomo Sumiyuki   Masaari
         │                          │
      Ujitsuna  Harumoto          Motoari
                                  Mototsune
                                    │
                                  Fujitaka
```

—— **Kiyouji, 清氏**. A son of *Kazuuji, Sagami no kami*. He took part in the battle of *Shijō-nawate* (1349) against *Kusunoki Masatsura*, and in all the campaigns against the partisans of the Southern dynasty. Later on, on account of disputes with the *Shōgun Yoshiakira*, he offered his services to the emperor *Go-Murakami* (1361). Soon afterwards, aided by *Kusunoki Masanori*, he drove the emperor of the North and the *Shōgun* out of *Kyōto ;* but in a short time a numerous army compelled him to leave the capital. He retired into *Kawachi*, thence into *Sanuki*, where he built the castle of *Shiramine* and prepared again to take *Kyōto ;* but, having been attacked by his cousin *Yoriyuki*, he was defeated and killed in battle (1362). His sons took refuge in *Awaji*.

—— **Yoriyuki, 頼之** (1329-1392). Was a son of *Yoriharu*. By order of *Takauji*, he went into *Bitchū* and pacified *San-yō-dō*. Thence he passed into *Shikoku*, besieged his cousin *Kiyouji* in the castle of *Shiramine* (*Sanuki*) and, having defeated him (1362), subjected the whole island to the *Ashikaga*. Before dying, the *Shōgun Yoshiakira* named him *Shitsuji* (minister) and instrusted him with the guardianship of his son *Yoshimitsu*, then only 11 years old. The latter soon grew tired of the counsels of his mentor, and *Yoriyuki* seeing this, retired into the temple of *Saihō-ji* near *Kyōto* (1372). He nevertheless took part in the *Kyūshū* campaign (1374) ; but having been calumniated by jealous adversaries, he was banished to *Sanuki* (1379). It was only 12 years later that *Yoshimitsu*, seeing himself threatened by the ever

HOSOKAWA YORIYUKI.

increasing power of the *Yamana*, recalled his minister. *Yoriyuki* then took the field, and soon afterwards the *Yamana* were defeated (1391). *Yoriyuki* died the following year. Being childless, he had adopted his two brothers *Yorimoto* and *Mitsuyuki*.

—— **Yorimoto,** 賴元 (1343-1397). A brother of *Yoriyuki*, was *Shitsuji* i.e. minister of the *Shōgun Yoshimitsu*, afterwards *Kwanryō* in the place of *Shiba Yoshimochi* (1391). His descendants alternately bore the title of *Shitsuji* and that of *Kwanryō*.

—— **Ujiharu,** 氏春. A son of *Morouji*, *shugo* of *Awaji*. In 1361 he followed his cousin *Kiyouji*, who joined the party of the South, entered *Kyōto* with him and accompanied him to *Sanuki;* but when *Kiyouji* was defeated and slain by *Yoriyuki* (1362), *Ujiharu* returned to the *Ashikaga*. He died in 1387.

—— **Akiuji,** 顯氏 (+ 1352). Was a son of *Yorisada* and *Mutsu no kami*. Siding with *Takauji*, he fought against the party of the South, but when *Tadayoshi* quarrelled with his brother *Takauji* and abandoned the cause of the North, *Akiuji* followed him. In 1352 he was killed when with *Kiyouji* he fought against the troops of *Ashikaga Yoshiakira*.

—— **Jōzen,** 定禪. Was a brother of *Akiuji*. When *Hōjō Tokiyuki* attacked *Kamakura* (1335), *Jōzen* with *Ashikaga Tadayoshi* fled into *Musashi* and afterwards retired into *Sanuki* where he raised troops for *Takauji*, after which he fought against *Nitta Yoshisada*, *Wakiya Yoshisuke*, etc. The date of his death is unknown.

—— **Mitsumoto,** 滿元 (1378-1426). A son of *Yorimoto*, became *Kwanryō* in 1412.

—— **Mochiyuki,** 持之 (1400-1442). Was a son of *Mitsumoto*. In 1432, he succeeded *Shiba Yoshiatsu* in the office of *Kwanryō*. After the assassination of the *Shōgun Yoshinori* (1441), he secured the right of succession to the *Shōgun's* son *Yoshikatsu* and sent troops to punish the murderer *Akamatsu Mitsusuke*.

—— **Katsumoto,** 勝元 (1430-1473). A son of *Michiyuki* inherited the domains of his ancestors, i.e., nearly all *Shikoku*. Having been made *Kwanryō* at the age of 15 (1445), he was replaced in this office by *Hatakeyama Norimoto* in 1449, but recovered it in 1452. He married the daughter of *Yamana Mochitoyo*. The two sons of *Hatakeyama* having caused disturbances in *Kyōto* at that time, the *Shōgun Yoshimasa* called on all the great *daimyō* to aid in restoring peace; but *Katsumoto* and *Mochitoyo* did not comply with the invitation. *Yoshimasa* having adopted his brother *Yoshimi* as his successor (1464), *Katsumoto* was appointed his *Shitsuji*. The following year, a son was born to *Yoshimasa*, and *Mochitoyo* (then called *Sōzen*) was called upon to support his rights.

HOSOKAWA KATSUMOTO.

At this same time commenced the strife between *Shiba Yoshitoshi* and *Shiba Yoshikado* for the succession of their family and they soon faced each other: on one side, we find *Katsumoto* supporting *Ashikaga Yoshimi*, *Hatakeyama Masanaga*, and *Shiba Yoshitoshi*; on the other, *Yamana Sōzen* defending the interests of *Ashikaga Yoshihisa*, *Hatakeyama Yoshinari*, and *Shiba Yoshikado*. The other *daimyō* were divided between the two camps. It was the beginning of the disastrous *Ōnin* civil war (1467). *Katsumoto*, at the head of 100,000 men was posted on the east of *Muromachi* in order to guard the residence of *Yoshimi*, but *Sōzen*, having assembled 90,000 men, established himself on the West of *Muromachi;* and then ensued a series of almost daily combats, generally without any decisive result. The war had thus lasted for seven years, when *Katsumoto* died at the age of 44.

—— **Masamoto,** 政 元 (1466-1507). Was a son of *Katsumoto*. In 1493, he assisted *Hatakeyama Yoshitoyo* attacked by the *Shōgun Yoshitane* and *Hatakeyama Masanaga*. The latter were defeated at *Shōkokuji* (*Kawachi*), *Masanaga* was killed and the *Shōgun* fled to *Echū*. *Masamoto* then replaced him by *Yoshizumi*, a son of *Masatomo*, who was but an instrument in his hands. *Masamoto* having been made *Kwanryō* in 1494, established himself at *Kyōto*, and named *Miyoshi Nagateru* and *Kōsai Motochika* to replace him in the government of his provinces of *Awa* and *Sanuki*, but disputes arose between them and troubles ensued. *Masamoto* being childless, adopted three sons: *Sumiyuki*, *Sumimoto*, and *Takakuni*. *Nagateru* sided with *Sumimoto*, whilst *Motochika* was a partisan of *Sumiyuki*, and as *Masamoto* intended to make *Sumimoto* his heir, *Motochika* caused him to be assassinated (1507.)

—— **Sumimoto,** 澄 元 (1496-1520). A son of *Yoshiharu*, was adopted by *Masamoto*. He was only 11 years old when the latter died, and *Kōsai Motochika* declared against him. *Sumimoto* took refuge in the castle of *Sasaki Takayori* in *Ōmi*. *Miyoshi Nagateru* supported his cause and killed *Sumiyuki*, his rival. *Sumimoto* now could take possession of his *Shikoku* domains and was nominated *Kwanryō* (1507). But the following year, the *Shōgun Yoshitane* having re-entered *Kyōto* with *Takakuni*, *Sumimoto* fled to *Awa* (*Shikoku*). Supported by *Akamatsu*, he defeated *Takakuni* and re-entered the capital in 1511, but was driven from it soon afterwards. He allied himself with *Miyoshi Motonaga*, and again defeated *Takakuni* in 1519. The latter aided by *Sasaki Sadayori*, vanquished him in turn, and *Sumimoto* again fled to *Awa*, where he died some months after.

HOSOKAWA SUMIMOTO.

—— **Sumiyuki,** 澄 之 (+ 1507). A son of the *Kwampaku Kujō Masamoto*, was adopted by *Hosokawa Masamoto*, who, having chosen him as his heir, afterwards preferred *Sumimoto* and gave *Sumiyuki* some domains in *Tamba*. At the death of *Masamoto* (1507), *Kōsai Motochika* supported *Sumiyuki* against *Sumimoto;* but having been attacked near

Kyōto by *Miyoshi Nagateru, Sumiyuki* and *Kōsai Motochika* were defeated and killed in the battle (1507).

—— **Takakuni,** 高國 (+ 1531). A son of *Masaharu*, was adopted by *Masamoto* like *Sumimoto* and *Sumiyuki*. The antipathy of *Takakuni* for his adopted father was such that, when *Ōuchi Yoshioki* desired to re-establish *Yoshitane* in the office of *Shōgun*, he joined the party, which *Masamoto* had always opposed. *Sumimoto*, who supported the *Shōgun Yoshizumi* was defeated and fled into *Awa*, while *Yoshizumi*, retired into *Ōmi* (1508). In 1511, *Sumimoto* sent his kinsman *Masakata* to take *Kyōto*, but he was defeated and lost his life in the battle. When *Ōuchi Yoshioki* returned into his province of *Suwō* (1518), *Takakuni* succeeded him as *Kwanryō*. In 1519 having been defeated by *Sumimoto*, he retired into *Ōmi* to ask *Sasaki Sadayori* for assistance. He returned with an army and obliged *Sumimoto* to flee into *Awa*. Then he built a castle at *Amagasaki* (*Settsu*) and assumed so much authority that the *Shōgun Yoshitane* determined to give the office of *Kwanryō* to *Hatakeyama Tanenaga*. *Takakuni* revolted against the *Shōgun* whom he had always supported, obliged him to flee into *Awaji* and put *Yoshiharu*, a son of *Yoshizumi*, in his place (1521). In 1527, *Miyoshi Kaiun*, with *Harumoto*, a son of *Sumimoto*, attacked *Kyōto*. *Takakuni* again went into *Ōmi*, to apply to the *Sasaki* and the *Asakura* for aid and re-entered the capital. Four years later however *Kaiun* and *Harumoto* having attacked him anew, he was defeated at *Amagasaki*, and at *Tennōji*. He retired toward *Awa*, but was killed in his flight.

—— **Harumoto,** 晴元 (1519-1563). A son of *Sumimoto*, was only two years old at the death of his father. In 1527 *Miyoshi Nakamoto* (*Kaiun*) marched against *Takakuni* and made himself master of *Kyōto*, whence the *Shōgun Yoshiharu* and the *Kwanryō Takakuni* fled into *Ōmi*. *Harumoto* soon afterwards was driven from the capital but returned in 1531, defeated his rival, who was killed. The following year, *Harumoto* was reconciled with *Yoshiharu* and appointed *Kwanryō*. Having a dispute with *Nagamoto*, he slew him at *Sakai* (*Izumi*). He also repressed the troubles created by the bonzes of *Ikkō-shū*. In 1546, *Yuza Junsei* having sided with *Ujitsuna*, a son of *Takakuni*, raised an army. *Harumoto* sent *Miyoshi Chōkei* against him but he was defeated. The *Shōgun Yoshiharu* opened negotiations with *Ujitsuna*, and proposed terms of peace promising him the title of *Kwanryō* in return. *Harumoto* irritated re-entered *Kyōto*. The *Shōgun* and his son *Yoshiteru* fled to *Sakamoto* (*Ōmi*). The following year, peace was made and *Harumoto* was made *Kwanryō*, while *Ujitsuna* returned to *Awa*. Soon afterwards *Chōkei* having had some quarrels with *Harumoto*, became a partisan of *Ujitsuna* (1548), made himself master of the castles of *Nakajima, Miyake* and *Eguchi*, and defeated *Harumoto* at *Ōtsu* (1550). The latter became reconciled to the *Shōgun Yoshiteru*; but being attacked by *Chōkei*, they were compelled to flee to *Kuchiki* (*Ōmi*); the *Shōgun* negotiated for peace and returned to *Kyōto* (1553). Finally in 1558, *Chōkei* and *Matsunaga Hisahide* again made themselves masters of the capital. *Yoshiteru* and *Harumoto* fled to

Sakamoto (Ōmi), and thence opened negotiations. Peace was signed: the *Shōgun* came back to *Kyōto*, but *Harumoto* was kept prisoner at *Akutagawa (Settsu)*, where he died five years later. He was the last of the *Hosokawa Kwanryō*. The family had occupied that office for 180 years.

—— **Nobuyoshi, 信良** (+ 1615). Was a son of *Harumoto* and remained prisoner at *Akutagawa*. *Nobunaga*, after having seized *Settsu*, (1568) gave him 2 *kōri* in *Tamba*, but he was deprived of them by *Hideyoshi*, and died in obscurity.

Hosokawa, 細川. A *daimyō* family descended from the above —— **Fujitaka, 藤高** (1534-1610). A son of *Mibuchi, Harusada, Iga no kami*, was adopted by *Hosokawa Mototsune*, who descended, in the 7th generation, from *Yorimochi*, a brother of *Yoriyuki*. When the *Shōgun Yoshiteru* was assassinated (1565), he sided with *Yoshiaki* and prevailed on *Nobunaga* to take up the latter's cause. In 1573, he received the districts of *Otokuni (Yamashiro)* in fief, and assumed the name of *Nagaoka*. He took part with *N .bunaga* in the campaign against the troops of the *Hongwanji* at *Ōsaka* (1576), then in that of *Hideyoshi* in the *San-yō-dō* (1580). At the death of *Nobunaga* he had his head shaved and took the names of *Genshihōin* and *Yūsai* (1582). Afterwards he accompanied *Hideyoshi* in his expeditions into *Kii* (1585), *Kyūshū* (1587), and *Sagami* (1590), and wrote a history of these campaigns. In 1600, he was invited by *Ikeda Kazushige* to join him against *Ieyasu*, but he refused without however taking any part in the campaign of *Sekigahara*. He lived 10 years in retirement at *Kyōto*, cultivating poetry and history in which he excelled.

Fujitaka	Tadaoki	Tadatoshi-Mitsunao	Tsunatoshi	(a)
			Toshishige	(b)
		Tatsutaka -Yukitaka -Aritaka		(c)
	Okimoto -Okimasa	-Okitaka -Okichika		(d)

(a) — The elder branch. —— **Tadaoki, 忠興** (1564-1645). The eldest son of *Fujitaka*, first served *Nobunaga*, who gave him the province of *Tango* in fief (1580). He married the daughter of *Akechi Mitsuhide* who asked his assistance when he was going to revolt against *Nobunaga*, but *Tadaoki* indignantly refused and confined his wife in a retired place. During the *Kyūshū* war (1587), the latter was baptized at *Ōsaka* under the name of *Gracia*. In 1590, *Tadaoki* took part in the *Odawara* campaign and was commissioned to besiege the *Nirayama* castle *(Izu)*. After the death of *Hideyoshi*, *Tadaoki* whose eldest son had married the daughter of *Maeda Toshiie*, made use of all his influence to prevent the latter from separating from *Ieyasu*, whom he accompanied in his expedition against *Uesugi Kagekatsu*. During that time *Ishida Kazushige*, in order to detach the *daimyō* who had followed him from *Ieyasu*, ordered their wives and children to be seized and to be kept in the castle of *Ōsaka* as hostages. When the emissaries presented themselves at the house of *Hosokawa* the *Karō Ogasawara* informed his mistress that he had

received orders from *Tadaoki* to put her to death rather than to give her up to her enemies. *Gracia* submitted to the will of her husband and died courageously; she was 38 years old (1600). After the battle of *Sekigahara*, *Tadaoki* was transferred from *Tango* to *Buzen*, with his residence at *Kokura* and a revenue of 370,000 k. It was then that he assumed the name of *Hosokawa*. During the first campaign of *Ōsaka* (1614) he was charged to watch the *Shimazu*, but he took a brilliant part in the siege, which terminated in the ruin of the *Toyotomi* (1615). In 1619 he had his head shaved, assumed the names of *Sōritsu* and *Sansai*, and gave up the administration of his domains to his son *Tadatoshi*. He died aged 81, renowned as a warrior, a poet and a literary man.

—— **Tadatoshi,** 忠 利 (1586-1641). Was a son of *Tadaoki*, and had been baptized when 9 years old; but he dared not resist the orders of *Ieyasu*, and banished all Christians from his domains. In 1632 he was transferred to *Kumamoto* (*Higo* — 540,000 k). He took part in the suppression of the *Shimabara* insurrection (1638).

—— **Shigekata,** 重 賢 (1718-1785). Distinguished himself by his good administration and his zeal for the instruction of the *samurai*. It was for that purpose that in 1752 he founded the *Jishu-kwan* at *Kumamoto*, a school which has become celebrated. — The family resided at *Kumamoto* till the Restoration. — Now Marquis.

(*b*) — The junior branch, which, in 1666, settled at *Takase* (*Higo* — 35,000 k.). — Now Viscount.

(*c*) — A branch founded by *Tatsutaka*, 2nd son of *Tadaoki*.

—— **Tatsutaka,** 立 孝 . Who had been baptized in 1587 under the name of John, received the fief of *Udo* (*Higo* — 30,000 k.) at the death of his father (1646), where his descendants resided till the Restoration. — Now Viscount.

(*d*) — Branch founded by *Okimoto*, a brother of *Tadaoki*.

—— **Okimoto,** 興 元 (+ 1618). The second son of *Fujitaka*, first served *Nobunaga* and then *Hideyoshi*. He was baptized in 1594, and was always a fervent Christian. In 1610, he was made *daimyō* of *Mogi* (*Shimotsuke* — 10,000 k.) and in 1616, was transferred to *Yatabe* (*Hitachi* — 16,300 k.), where his descendants resided till the Restoration. — Now Viscount.

Hosokawa, 細 川 . A family of *Tosa*, ennobled in 1900. — Now Baron.

Hosokawa roku-kū, 細 川 六 候 . The six most celebrated members of the family of the *Hosokawa Kwanryō : Yoriyuki, Yorimoto, Mitsumoto, Mochimoto, Mochiyuki* and *Katsumoto*.

Hossō-shū, 法 相 宗 . A Buddhist sect also called *Yuishiki*. It was introduced into Japan from China by the bonze *Dōshō* in 654, and was especially propagated by *Chitsū* and *Chiyū* (657), later by *Chihō* and *Chiran* (703). Hence its two branches : that of *Nanji-den* or *Genkōji-den*, and that of *Hokuji-den* or *Kōfukuji-den*. The celebrated bonzes *Gi-en*, *Gyōgi*, *Gembō* belonged to this sect, which, at present, has about 45 large temples and 14 chief bonzes.

Hosuseri no Mikoto, 火闌降命. The eldest son of *Ninigi no Mikoto* and of *Konohana-saku-ya hime*. He had some contests with his younger brother *Hiko-hohodemi* and was compelled to submit to him. He is the ancestor of the *hayato*.

Hō-taikō, 豊太閤. The *Taikō Toyotomi Hideyoshi* (*Hō* is the Chinese pronunciation of the first character of the name *Toyotomi*).

Hotei, 布袋. A Chinese bonze of the 10th century, who is ranked among the seven gods of luck (*fukujin*). He personifies kindness and joviality and is represented with a monstrous abdomen.

Hōten, 奉天. *Mukden*, the capital of *Manchuria*.—During the Russo-Japanese war, a great battle was fought at that place, lasting from the 1st to the 10th of March, 1905.

Hotoke, 佛. Name given by the Buddhists to all those who have attained the state of illumination and the *nirvâna* (*nehan*). Is the Japanese equivalent of Buddha.

Hōtoku, 寶德. *Nengō*: 1449-1451.

Hotta, 堀田. A *daimyō* family of *Owari*, descended from *Takeshiuchi no Sukune*.

Masamori $\begin{cases} \text{Masanobu -Masayasu - Masatomo - Masanobu} & \text{(a)} \\ \text{Masatoshi} \begin{cases} \text{Masanaka - Masatora - Masaharu} & \text{(b)} \\ \text{Masataka - Masamine - Masanaga} & \text{(c)} \end{cases} \end{cases}$

(*a*) — The elder branch —— **Masamori, 正盛** (1606-1651). *Kaga no kami*, had great influence over the *Shōyun Iemitsu*. In 1635, he was made *daimyō* of *Kawagoe* (*Musashi* — 26,000 k.), in 1638, of *Matsumoto*, (*Shinano* — 95,000 k.), and in 1642, of *Sakura* (*Shimōsa*, 145,000 k.). At the death of *Iemitsu*, he committed suicide (*junshi*) in order not to survive the *Shōgun*.

—— **Masanobu, 正信** (1629-1677). A son of *Masamori* and *Kō-zuke no suke*, was dispossessed (1660) and exiled to *Iida* (*Shinano*) and later to *Tokushima* (*Awa*) for having addressed a letter of remonstrance to the Shōgunal government which was considered disrespectful.

—— **Masayasu, 正休**. A son of *Masanobu* received a revenue of 10,000 k. In 1682, he established himself at *Yoshii* (*Kōzuke*), and in 1698, at *Miyagawa* (*Ōmi* — 13,000 k.), where his descendants resided till the Restoration. — Now Viscount.

(*b*) — Junior branch —— **Masatoshi, 正俊** (1631-1684). Was a son of *Masamori*. At the death of his father (1651) he received a revenue of 13,000 k. at *Moriya* (*Shimōsa*); thence he passed in 1667, to *Annaka* (*Kōzuke* — 20,000 k.). He was successively *Waka-doshiyori* and *Rōjū*; was nominated *Tairō* and *Chikuzen no kami* (1681), and transferred to *Koga* (*Shimōsa* — 115,000 k.).

—— **Masanaka, 正仲** (1660-1694). *Shimōsa no kami*, passed to *Yamagata* (*Dewa*) (1685) and in 1686, to *Fukushima* (*Mutsu*).

—— **Masatora, 正虎** (1662-1729). *Izu no kami* returned to *Yamagata* in 1700.

—— **Masaharu, 正春**. In 1745, was transferred to *Sakura* (*Shimōsa* — 115,000 k.) where his descendants resided till the Restoration.

—— **Masamutsu,** 正睦 (1810-1864). Was *Jisha-bugyō, Ōsaka-jōdai, Rōjū* (1841). In 1856, the *Bakufu* charged him with regulating the intercourse with foreigners and it was in this capacity that, the following year, he received Mr. Harris, the envoy of the United States, and procured for him an audience with the *Shōgun Iesada* to discuss the opening of certain ports. This question roused the hostility of the *daimyō* of *Mito, Tosa,* and others; *Masamutsu* was sent to *Kyōto* but failed to obtain at Court the acceptance of the proposals. Though he was of the same opinion as the minister of the *Shōgun Ii Naosuke,* who made use of him, the party hostile to foreigners prevailed, and *Masamutsu* confined to his residence was removed from public affairs. He soon afterwards died, leaving the reputation of a skilful administrator and a distinguished literary man. — His descendant is a Count.

(*c*) — The second junior branch, which, in 1698, settled at *Katata* (*Ōmi*), and in 1812 was transferred to *Sano* (*Shimotsuke* — 18,000 k.). — Now Viscount.

Hōzō-in In-ei, 寶藏院胤榮 (1521-1607). A bonze of *Nara,* the founder of a fencing school called *Hōzōin-ryū.* He belonged to the *kuge* family *Nakamikado.* His descendants, *Inshun* (1589-1648), *Insei* (1624-1689), *Infū* (1682-1731), *Inken* (1746-1808), all bonzes of the same temple, continued the traditions of their ancestor.

Hozumi, 穗積. A *kuge* family descended from *Fujiwara Yoshi-kado.* — Now Baron.

Hozumi-shinnō, 穗積親王 (+ 715). The eighth son of the emperor *Temmu,* was minister under the reign of *Mommu* and was distinguished for his administrative talents.

Hyaku-nin isshu, 百人一首. A collection of one hundred poems (*tanka*) of one hundred different authors that lived between the seventh and the thirteenth centuries. The collection was compiled in 1235 by *Fujiwara Sadaie* and is very popular in Japan.

Hyōbu-shō, 兵部省. Formerly the War department. In ancient times, military affairs were superintended by the *Ōtomo* and *Mononobe* families. In 683, the emperor *Temmu* created the *Hyōseikwan* which in 702 was changed into the *Hyōbu-shō* or *Tsuwamono no tsukasa.* The minister was called *Hyōbu no kami,* later *Hyōbu-kyō.*

Hyōe-fu, 兵衛府. Formerly the imperial guard divided into *Sahyōe-fu* and *Uhyōe-fu,* having charge of the gate of the palace, of escorting the emperor, etc.

Hyōgo, 兵庫. A town, which with *Kōbe* forms the capital of the department of *Hyōgo* — See *Kōbe.* — Formerly it was called *Muko no minato, Wada no tomari.* It was there that *Kiyomori* built his splendid *Fukuwara* palace (1160), and that *Kusunoki Masashige* was killed at the battle of *Minato-gawa* (1336).

Hyōgo-ken, 兵庫縣. A department formed by the provinces of *Harima, Tajima, Awaji,* 3 districts of *Settsu* and 2 of *Tamba.* — Pop.: 1,776,000 inh.). — Capital: *Kōbe-Hyōgo,* (283,800 inh.). — Principal towns: *Himeji* (35,300 inh.), *Akashi* (21,200 inh.), *Amagasaki,* (15,000 inh.), *Nishinomiya* (14,000 inh.), etc.

Hyōgo-ryō, 兵庫寮. A magazine containing arms, flags, musical instruments, etc., employed in the ceremonies of the imperial palace.

Hyōjō-bugyō, 評定奉行. A title created in 1249 and corresponding to President of the Council of Administration under the *Kamakura* Shōgunate. *Adachi Yoshikage* was the first to bear this title. — The same office was created at *Kyōto* under the *Ashikaga*.

Hyōjō-sho, 評定所. Under the *Tokugawa*, an office where the *Jisha-bugyō*, *Machi-bugyō*, and *Kanjō-bugyō* assembled; sometimes the *Rōjū*, the *Ō-metsuke*, etc., joined them. This office was created in 1636, and established in *Edo*, *Tatsu no kuchi*, near the gate (*Wadagura-mon*) of the castle.

Hyōjōsho-jusha, 評定所儒者. Officials of the *Hyōjō-sho*. In 1693, this title was changed into that of *Hyōjōsho-meyasu-yomi*. They were subject to a *Waka-doshiyori*.

Hyōjōshū, 評定衆. Under the *Kamakura* shōgunate, high officials who, with the *Shikken*, assembled at the *Mandokoro* in order to deliberate on government affairs. This title was created in 1225. The number of officials was 15 or 16. They were formerly chosen among the families of literati: *Ōe*, *Kiyowara*, *Nakahara*, *Miyoshi*, *Nikaidō*, *Saitō*, etc., among whom this office became hereditary; later they were chosen among the principal *daimyō*: *Miura*, *Chiba*, *Adachi*, *Yūki*, *Sasaki*, *Utsunomiya*, etc., but without hereditary privileges. — Under the *Ashikaga* the *hyōjōshū* who had been re-established in 1354, were chosen from the families of *Settsu*, *Ōta*, *Machino*, *Ii-o*, *Fuse*, etc., all descended from the *Nakahara* or the *Miyoshi*.

Hyūga, 日向. One of the 11 provinces of *Saikaidō*. It comprises 8 districts belonging to the *Miyazaki-ken*. — Chinese name: *Nisshū*.

Hyūga-nada, 日向灘, The sea of *Hiūga*, East of *Kyūshū*.

I

I, 位. (Jap. *kurai*), Rank in the Court hierarchy. — See *Ikai*.

Ibara Saikwaku, 井原西鶴 (1642-1693). The author of several writings and the founder of a school of popular literature, of novels, tales, etc.

Ibaraki, 茨木. An ancient castle in *Settsu*, successively belonging to the *Hosokawa*, the *Miyoshi*, the *Nakagawa* (1568), and the *Katagiri daimyō*. The latter possessed it from 1583 to 1613.

Ibaraki-ken, 茨木縣. The department formed by the province of *Hitachi* and 5 districts of *Shimōsa*.— Pop.: 1,205,000 inh.— Capital : *Mito* (34,000 inh.). — Principal towns : *Minato* (12,300 inh.), *Ishioka* (11,800 inh.), *Yūki* (11,600 inh.), *Tsuchiura* (11,300 inh.), etc.

Ibi, 揖斐. A place in *Mino*. From 1600 to 1623, it was the residence of the *Nishio daimyō* (30,000 k.).

Ibi-gawa, 揖斐川. A river (118 Km.), which has its source in *Mino* and empties itself into the *Kiso-gawa* at its entrance into *Ise*. It is also called *Kuise-gawa, Roku-gawa, Sawato-gawa*.

Ibuki-yama, 伊吹山. A mountain (1,360 met.) in *Ōmi*. According to legend, a bad genius dwelt on it formerly. *Yamatotakeru no Mikoto*, returning from his expedition against the *Ebisu*, undertook to combat it. The genius took the form of a serpent and remained sleeping on the road. The prince having put his foot on the serpent, a thick fog surrounded the mountain and, at the same time, a subtle poison penetrated the body of the hero, who, with great difficulty, descended from the mountain to die in *Ise* (113). A *Shintō* temple (*Ibuki-jinja*) was erected to his memory.

Iburi, 膽振. One of the eleven provinces of *Hokkaidō*. It comprises 8 districts. — Capital : *Mororan*.

Iburi-wan, 膽振灣. The gulf of *Iburi*. It is also called *Uchi-ura* and, by Europeans, Volcano Bay.

Ichibashi, 市橋. A *daimyō* family descended from the *Seiwa-Genji*.

—— **Nagakatsu,** 長勝 (1558-1621). *Shimōsa no kami*, first resided at *Imao* (*Mino*) ; in 1608, he was transferred to *Yabashi* (*Hōki*) and in 1616, to *Sanjō* (*Echigo* — 40,000 k.). As he died without issue, his nephew *Nagamasa, Izu no kami*, was chosen to succeed him, and established himself at *Nishi-Ōji* (*Ōmi* — 18.000 k.), where his descendants lived until the Restoration. — Now Viscount.

Ichibu, 一分. Another name sometimes given to the *Shijō*, officials attached to the governors of a province.

Ichibu-ichigen, 一蔀一元. The *gen* is a period of 60 years beginning in the year of the *Mizu-no-e no inu* and finishing in the year *Ka-no-to no tori*. The *bu* is composed of 21 or 22 *gen*, beginning in the year *Ka-no-to no tori* and finishing in the year *Ka-no-e no saru*. Thus, from the advent of *Jimmu* (660 B.C. — *Ka-no-to no tori*) to the 6th year of the reign of *Saimei* (660 A.D. — *Ka-no-e no saru*), one *bu* (1320 years) elapsed. The *bu* that extends from the second year of *Jimmu* to the 9th year of *Suiko* (601) has only 1260 years. — See *Kaigen*.

Ichiburi, 市 振. A place in *Echigo*, where the battles between *Miyazaki Sadanori* and *Hōjō Tomotoki* (1221), and between *Nagao Tamekage* and *Uesugi Sadanori* (1509) were fought.

Ichibusa-yama, 市 房 山. A mountain (1820 m.) between *Higo* and *Hyūga*.

Ichijō, 一 條. A *kuge* family descended from *Fujiwara Michiie* (1192-1252). It was one of the five *go-sekke* in which the Empress, the *Kwampaku* and the *Sesshō* had to be elected.

—— **Tsunetsugu,** 經 嗣 (1358-1418), a son of the *Kwampaku Nijō Yoshimoto*, was adopted by *Ichijō Fusatsune* and himself became *Kwampaku*. He was renowned for his knowledge of Japanese and Chinese literature and is known by the name of *Shō-on-ji Kwampaku*.

—— **Kaneyoshi,** 兼 良 (1402-1481). A son of *Tsunetsugu*, was successively *Sadaijin*, *Dajō-daijin* (1446), and *Kwampaku* (1447). During the *Ōnin* war, he retired to *Nara* (1470). He has left numerous writings and received the name of *Go-Shō-on-ji Kwampaku*.

—— **Norifusa,** 敎 房 (1423-1480). A son of *Kaneyoshi*, became *Kwampaku* in 1458. In 1469, he retired into *Tosa*, where he died. Two sons, *Masafusa* and *Fusaie* survived him. The elder succeeded him and the younger became lord suzerain of *Tosa*. — See below.

—— **Fuyuyoshi,** 冬 良 (1464-1514). The second son of *Kaneyoshi*, was *Dajō-daijin* and *Kwampaku*. He has left several valuable writings. Having no children, he adopted *Fusamichi*, a son of *Fusaie*. — The descendant of the family is now Duke.

Ichijō, 一 條. A branch of the preceding family, from 1470 to 1573, governed the province of *Tosa*.

—— **Fusaie,** 房 家 (1445-1511). The second son of *Norifusa*, accompanied his father when the latter, to escape from incessant troubles in *Kyōto*, took refuge in *Tosa* (1469). At that time, the *Hosokawa* had lost all their authority in *Shikoku*, and the principal *samurai* chose *Fusaie* as lord (*kokushi*) of *Tosa*. — His successors were *Fusafuyu* (1496-1541), *Fusamoto* (1520-1549).

—— **Kanesada,** 兼 貞 (1543-1581). He had married the daughter of *Ōtomo Yoshishige*. He alienated all by his bad conduct and had to flee into *Bungo*, to the residence of his father-in-law (1573), where he was baptized under the name of *Paul* (1576). He tried in vain, to recover his domains. His former *kerai*, *Chōsokabe Motochika* had become too powerful, and *Kanesada* was obliged to live in retirement. He was assassinated by *Irie Sakon-tayū*, one of his former servants.

—— **Uchimasa,** 內 正 (1560-1580). A son of *Kanesada* and a Christian like his father, married a daughter of *Chōsokabe Motochika*, who gave him the title of *Tosa no kokushi*, but retained his authority. In 1580, he revolted against his father-in-law, but having been defeated, he had to flee to *He-no-ura* in *Iyo*, where, it is said, he was poisoned by *Motochika*. His son *Chikamasa* was entrusted to *Kureda Sadasuke*, hence the name of *Kureda-Gosho* that was given him. At the downfall of the *Chōsokabe*, he went to *Kyōto* where he lived in retirement.

Ichijō-ga-tani, 一 乘 谷. A place in *Echizen*, where, in 1470, *Asakura Toshikage* built a castle which his descendants occupied for four generations. *Yoshikane*, one of his descendants, was vanquished by *Nobunaga*, who entrusted the guard of the castle to *Katsurada Nagatoshi* (1573); but the latter was attacked and killed by the bonzes of *Ikkō-shū*. *Nobunaga* returned, defeated the rebels and gave *Echizen* in fief to *Shibata Katsuie*.

Ichijō-tennō, -- 條 天 皇. The 66th Emperor of Japan (987-1011), was prince *Kanehito*, a son of *En-yū-tennō;* he succeeded his cousin *Kwazan* when 7 years old. The *Fujiwara, Kaneie, Michitaka,* and *Michinaga* governed in his name. He died at the age of 32.

Ichimokuren, 一 目 連. A divinity honored at *Tado* (*Ise*) under the form of a dragon having but one eye. It is especially invoked to obtain rain.

Ichinobe-oshiha no Ōji, 市 邊 押 磐 皇 子 (+ 456). Was a son of the emperor *Richū*. At the death of *Ankō-tennō*, he was assassinated by his rival *Ō-hatsuse* (*Yūryaku-tennō*). He is the father of the emperors *Kensō* and *Ninken*.

Ichi no hito, 一 人. A title given to the *Kwampaku* or the *Sesshō*.

Ichi no kami, 一 上. A name given to the *Sadaijin*. When the latter at the same time was *Kwampaku*, it was the *Udaijin* that was called *Ichi no kami*.

Ichi-no-Miya, 一 宮. Formerly a title given to the eldest son of the Emperor.

Ichi-no-Miya, -- 宮. In former times, the principal Shintoist temple of the province. The name *Ichinomiya* has remained attached to many villages where such temples had been erected.

Ichinomiya, 一 宮. A place in *Kazusa*, which, from 1796 to 1868, was the residence of the *Kanō* branch of the *Matsudaira* (14,000 k.).

Ichinomiya, 一 宮. A place in *Bingo*. It received its name from an ancient temple (*Kibitsu-jinja*) dedicated to *Kibitsu-hiko no mikoto*. In 1331, *Sakurayama Koretoshi* built a castle there but being besieged, he retired to the temple and killed himself.

Ichinomiya, 一 宮. A place in *Mikawa*, where in 1564 *Ieyasu* built a castle, the guard of which he entrusted to *Honda Nobutoshi;* the latter being besieged by *Imagawa Ujizane*, applied to *Ieyasu* for help, and *Ujizane* retired to *Ushikubo*.

Ichinomiya, 一 宮. A place in *Awa* (*Shikoku*), where, in the 14th century, *Ichinomiya Narisuke* built a castle, which was taken by *Chōsokabe Motochika* in 1580. *Hideyoshi* took it in 1585 gave it and the whole province, to *Hachisuka Iemasa*, who established his residence at *Iyama* (*Tokushima*), and the castle gradually fell into ruins.

Ichinose-gawa, 一 瀬 川. A river (120 Km.) which has its source in mount *Ichibusa* and traverses *Hyūga* from West to East. It is also called *Ninose-gawa*.

Ichinoseki, 一 關. A place in *Rikuchū*, which, until 1671, was the residence of *Date Munekatsu*, a son of *Masamune*. Afterwards, from 1695 till 1868, it was the residence of the *Tamura* (30,000 k.) a branch of the *Date* family. This place it also called *Iwaimachi*.

Ichi-no-tani, 一 谷. A place in *Settsu* near *Hyōgo*, where *Minamoto Yoshitsune* defeated the *Taira* (1184). It was at that battle that the episode between *Kumagaya Naozane* and *Taira Atsumori* took place.

Ichi no tokoro, 一 所. Like *Ichi no hito*, a title given to the *Kwampaku* and the *Sesshō*.

Ichi no tsukasa, 市 司. An ancient title of the governors of *Kyōto*.

Ichi-ri-zuka, 一 里 塚. Equivalent to mile-stones, and placed from *ri* to *ri* on the main roads. It was *Nobunaga* who, fixing the *ri* to be of 36 *chō* (3,927 met.), placed such mark-stones in the neighboring provinces of *Kyōto*. In 1604, *Ieyasu*, taking *Nihon-bashi*, a bridge in *Edo*, as the starting point, erected them throughout the empire.

Ida, 井 田. A branch of the family of the counts *Toda*, former *daimyō* of *Ōgaki* (*Mino*). — The chief of the branch is now Baron.

Ida-ten, 韋 駄 天. A tutelary god of Buddhism represented in the form of a fair youth.

Iden, 位 田. Formerly rice-fields distributed among members of the nobility, from the 5th class (*go-i*) up to the imperial princes. Their extent varied, according to the rank, from 40 *chō* (39 hectares 66) to 80 *chō* (79 hectares 32) : they were not exempted from taxes.

Ie, 伊 江. A family related to the former princes of the *Ryūkyū* islands. It was ennobled after the annexation of the archipelago to Japan (1879). — Now Baron.

Iga, 伊 賀. One of the 15 provinces of *Tōkaidō:* it has been separated from *Ise* since 680, and comprises two districts which belong to the *Mie-ken*. — Its Chinese name is *Ishū*.

Iga Mitsusue, 伊 賀 光 季. Was the eldest son of *Satō Tomomitsu*. His sister had been married to *Hōjō Yoshitoki*, who appointed him *Sae-mon no suke*, *Kebiishi* (1215) and *Iga-hangwan*. After the assassination of the *Shōgun Sanetomo* (1219), he was sent to *Kyōto* to watch the intrigues of the Court. At the time of the *Shōkyū* war, the ex-emperor *Go-Toba* asked for his assistance against the *Hōjō;* *Mitsusue* refused. Having been attacked by *Miura Taneyoshi*, he killed him with an arrow, then set his house on fire, killed his eldest son *Mitsutsuna*, and committed *harakiri*. His second son *Suemura* inherited his domains.

Igaku-kwan, 醫 學 館. In 1765, *Taki Rankei*, a physician of the *Bakufu*, founded a medical school in *Edo*. It was called *Saijū-kwan*. Later, the shōgunal government claimed it and called it *Igaku-kwan*. Until the end it remained under the direction of the *Taki*, who it would seem, were a family of physicians.

Ihō, 位 袍. Formerly the color of the clothes that the officials had to wear according to their rank (*i*). The *Taihō* code fixed it as follows: first and second *i*, dark violet; third *i*, light violet; fourth *i*, red; fifth *i*, pink; sixth *i*, dark green; seventh *i*, light green; eigth *i*, dark blue; below 8th *i*, azure blue. These regulations have been modified several times.

Ii, 井 伊. A *daimyō* family native of *Tōtōmi* and descended from *Fujiwara Yoshikado*.

Naomasa { Naotaka - Naozumi - Naomori . . . . . Naosuke (a) }
         { Naokatsu- Naoyoshi - Naotake (b) }

(*a*) — The elder branch. —— **Naomasa** (1561-1602), served under *Ieyasu*, who, in 1590 gave him the castle of *Minowa* (*Kōzuke* — 12,000 k.). Thence he went to *Takasaki* (1589). At the battle of *Sekigahara* (1600), he defeated *Shimazu Yoshihiro*. *Ieyasu* then appointed him to *Sawayama* (*Ōmi* — 180,000 k.).

—— **Naotaka, 直 孝** (1590-1659). The second son of *Naomasa* in 1605 attached himself to the new *Shōgun Hidetada*, who gave him a revenue of 10,000 k. in *Kōzuke* (1610) and the title of *Kamon no kami*. At the time of the siege of *Ōsaka* in 1615, his elder brother *Naokatsu*, having refused to take part in the expedition, *Hidetada* ordered *Naotaka* to replace him and, at the conclusion of the war, gave him the domains of his brother. *Naotaka* finished the castle of *Hikone*, which had been begun by *Naokatsu* in 1603, and made it his residence in 1623. His revenues were raised to 290,000 k. then to 340,000 k. (1633). His descendants inherited the title of *Kamon no kami*, as well as the domains of *Hikone*, which they possessed till the Restoration.

—— **Naosuke, 直 弼** (1815-1860). Was the 14th son of *Naonaka*. With the exception of his eldest brother, who was to succeed his father, all the others had been adopted by *daimyō* families. He alone lived on a small pension taken from the revenues of *Hikone*. In 1845, his eldest brother died childless and *Naosuke* unexpectedly became *Kamon no kami* and lord of *Hikone*. In 1858, he became prime minister (*tairō*) of the *Shōgun Iesada*. The latter having died the same year without heir, the prince of *Mito*, *Nariaki*, desired to have his son *Hitotsubashi Keiki* nominated, but *Naosuke* opposed the nomination, and succeeded in having the 12 year old *Iemochi*, prince of *Kii*, elected. He had just signed a treaty with the United States (July 29th, 1858). Soon after he signed another with England (August 26th) and with France (October 9th). These treaties raised a strong opposition party throughout the country, and the Court in *Kyōto* in particular, demanded the expulsion of the barbarians (*jō-i*). *Naosuke* put 40 or 50 of the malcontents into prison at *Edo*, then he sent the *Rōjū Manabe Norikatsu* to *Kyōto* who imprisoned 57 *kuge, samurai*, etc., confined *Nariaki* to his house in *Edo*, and obliged the princes of *Owari*

II NAOSUKE.

and *Echizen* to resign the administration of their affairs to their sons. This series of energetic measures is known by the name of "great execution of the *Ansei* era " (*Ansei no taigoku*). The opening of the *Kanagawa* port (January 1859), the sending of an embassy to the United States, the treaty with Portugal, all served to exasperate the party hostile to foreigners, and, on the 24th of March, 1860, as *Naosuke* was going to the palace of the *Shōgun*, he was assassinated by 17 *rōnin* of the *Mito* clan (*Arimura Jizaemon Kanekiyo*, *Ōseki Washichirō*, *Sano Takenosuke Mitsuakira*, *Kurozawa Chūzō*, etc.). His death was officially announced only on the 20th of May and, on the 30th of the same month, he was buried in the temple of *Gotoku-ji*, near *Edo*. The following year, his son *Naonori*, who had succeeded him, had his revenues reduced to 240,000 k. — Now Count.

(*b*) — The junior branch —— **Naokatsu, 直 勝**. The eldest son of *Naomasa*, succeeded him in 1602 and, although inhabiting the castle of *Sawayama*, was obliged to build that of *Hikone* (*Ōmi*). At the time of the *Ōsaka* war, he remained in his castle. *Hidetada* irritated replaced him by his brother *Naotaka*, and instead of the immense domains of *Ōmi*, he gave him the little fief of *Annaka* (*Kōzuke* — 30,000 k.) (1615). — Thence his descendants removed successively to *Nishio* (*Mikawa*), in 1645 ; to *Kakegawa* (*Tōtōmi*), in 1658 ; and in 1705 to *Yoita* (*Echigo* — 20,000 k.). — Now Viscount.

Iida, 飯 田. A place in *Shinano*. A castle was built there towards 1195 by *Kondō Kaneie ;* the castle was afterwards occupied by the *Sakanishi* family and passed to the *Ogasawara* in 1360, to the *Takeda* in 1548. *Oda Nobunaga* gave it to *Mōri Hideyori* (1582) ; *Hideyoshi*, bestowed it upon *Kyogōku Takatomo* (1592). Under the *Tokugawa* it belonged successively to the *daimyō Ogasawara* (1601), the *Wakizaka* (1617), finally from 1672-1868, to the *Hori* (15,000 k.).

Iide-san, 飯 豊 山. A mountain (2,150 m.) between *Echigo* and *Uzen*. It is also called *Iitoyo-yama*.

Iimori-yama, 飯 盛 山. A mountain in *Kawaji*, one of the summits of mount *Ikoma :* the ruins of a castle are to be seen there. *Kusunoki Masashige* defeated the troops of the *Hōjō* (1333) on this mountain. The *Hatakeyama* and the *Miyoshi* for a long time were disputing about it. At the foot of the mountain is the *Shijō-nawate-jinja* temple.

Iino, 飯 野. A place in *Kazusa*, and from 1648 to 1868 was the residence of a branch of the *Hoshina daimyō* (20,000 k.).

Ii-no-ya, 伊 井 谷. A place in *Tōtōmi* where *Ii Tomosuke* built a castle (1093), which was the residence of his descendants for five centuries. In 1336, prince *Munenaga-shinnō* took refuge in it when fighting the *Ashikaga*. *Takeda Shingen* encamped there before the battle of *Mikata-ga-hara* (1572).

Iitoyo-ao no kōjo, 飯 豊 青 皇 女 (440-485). Was a daughter of *Ichinobe-oshiha no Ōji* and a grand-daughter of the emperor *Richū*. After the death of *Seinei-tennō* (484), she governed for one year, because her two brothers *Ōke* and *Oke* refused to assume the power. After her death, *Oke*, the younger, was elected. He is the emperor *Kensō*. *Iitoyo* later received the posthumous title of *Seitei-tennō*.

Iiyama, 飯山. A place in *Shinano*, where, in 1577 *Uesugi Kagetora* built a castle which, in 1584, was transferred to *Mori Tadamochi*. Under the *Tokugawa*, it belonged successively : to the *daimyō Minagawa* (1603), the *Sakuma* (1616), the *Sakurai* (1639), the *Nagai* (1706), the *Aoyama* (1711), finally from 1717 till 1868, to the *Honda* (20,000 k.).

Iizasa Chōisai, 飯篠長意齊. Born at the village of *Iizasa* (*Shimōsa*), he was called *Ienao* and was *Yamashiro no kami*. He founded a fencing school called *Shintō-ryū*, because it was established in fulfilment of a vow made by *Chōisai* to the Shintoist god *Katori* (*Shimōsa*).

Ijichi, 伊地知. A *samurai* family of *Satsuma*, ennobled after the Restoration. — Now Count.

Ijūin, 伊集院. A *samurai* family of *Satsuma*, ennobled after the Restoration. — Now Viscount.

—— **Goro, 伊集院五郎**. Was born in 1852 in *Satsuma*. While still a minor, he took part in the War of the Restoration. In 1871, he entered the Naval Academy ; in 1878 he was sent to England to study, and served on board the *Triumph* as cadet from 1879-1882 He returned home as a Lieutenant on the *Naniwa* 1886, was attached to the Naval Staff Board (1892-1895). He was made Captain and was on board the *Saikyō-Maru* in the battle of the Yellow Sea (1895) for which he was rewarded with the 4th class of the Golden Kite. In 1899 he became Rear-Admiral, invented the *Ijūin* fuse, and obtained the 3rd class of the Rising Sun. He was again rewarded for his splendid conduct during the Boxer trouble, and received the 2nd class of the Rising Sun. In 1903 he was appointed Vice-Admiral, then Vice-Chief of the Naval Staff. Finally he was honored with the 1st class of the Golden Kite and Grand Cordon of the Rising Sun for services rendered during the Russian-Japanese war.

Ikago, 五十子. A place in *Musashi*. In the 15th century, it was the residence of the *Uesugi* (*Yamanouchi*), who, at that place, fought *Ashikaga Shigeuji* and *Nagao Kageharu*.

Ikai, 位階. The gradation of the ranks at Court. This hierarchy borrowed from China, was introduced into Japan in 702, under the emperor *Mommu*.

During the reign of the empress *Suiko* (603), prince *Shōtoku-Taishi* created 12 ranks at Court (See *Kwan-i jū-ni kai*) ; these ranks were distinguished by the head-gear (*kammuri*) and the color of the clothes. The emperor *Kōtoku* (649) raised the number to 19 (See *Kwan-i jū-ku kai*) ; *Tenchi-tennō* (662), to 26 ; *Temmu* (682), to 48.

The *Taihō* Code (702) modified those regulations. It created a special hierarchy for princes having the title of *Shinnō* and another for the nobles, in which the princes that had not the title of *Ō* were comprised (*Shinnō* was applied only to the sons and the brothers of the emperor ; *Ō*, to his grandsons and great-grandsons).

The imperial princes were divided into four ranks : 1 *hon* 品, 2 *hon*, 3 *hon*, 4 *hon*. They said, for instance, 2 *hon Shinnō* X*** Y***.

The nobles and the Court officials were divided into 10 ranks (*i*), the first three and the last two having only 2 degrees, the others had 4, as is seen in the following table :

1st rank	{ 1st degree:	*Shō-ichi-i*	正一位	
	{ 2nd „	*Jū-ichi-i*	従一位	
2nd rank	{ 1st „	*Shō-ni-i*	正二位	
	{ 2nd „	*Jū-ni-i*	従二位	
3rd rank	{ 1st „	*Shō-san-i*	正三位	
	{ 2nd „	*Jū-san-i*	従三位	*Chokujū* 勅授
4th rank	{ super. 1st degree:	*Shō-shi-i-jō*	正四位上	nominated by the Emperor.
	{ infer. 1st „	„ „ -*ge*	正四位下	
	{ super. 2nd „	*Jū* „ -*jō*	従四位上	
	{ infer. 2nd „	„ „ -*ge*	従四位下	
5th rank	{ super. 1st „	*Shō-go-i-jō*	正五位上	
	{ infer. 1st „	„ „ -*ge*	正五位下	
	{ super. 2nd „	*Jū* „ -*jō*	従五位上	
	{ infer. 2nd „	„ „ -*ge*	従五位下	
6th rank	{ super. 1st „	*Shō-roku-i-jō*	正六位上	
	{ infer. 1st „	„ „ -*ge*	正六位下	*Sōjū* 奏授
	{ super. 2nd „	*Jū* „ -*jō*	従六位上	submitted to the approbation
	{ infer. 2nd „	„ „ -*ge*	従六位下	of the Emperor.
7th rank	{ super. 1st „	*Shō-shichi-i-jō*	正七位上	
	{ infer. 1st „	„ „ -*ge*	正七位下	
	{ super. 2nd „	*Jū* „ -*jō*	従七位上	
	{ infer. 2nd „	„ „ -*ge*	従七位下	
8th rank	{ super. 1st „	*Shō-hachi-i-jō*	正八位上	
	{ infer. 1st „	„ „ -*ge*	正八位下	
	{ super. 2nd „	*Jū* „ -*jō*	従八位上	
	{ infer. 2nd „	„ „ -*ge*	従八位下	*Hanjū* 判授
9th rank	{ 1st degree:	*Dai-so-i-jō*	大初位上	nominated by the ministers.
	{ 2nd „	„ „ -*ge*	大初位下	
10th rank	{ 1st „	*Shō-so-i-jō*	少初位上	
	{ 2nd „	„ „ -*ge*	少初位下	

The rank at Court (*i*) did not always agree with the office (*kwan*) of the individual. If the rank was superior to the office, the character *gyō* 行 was introduced in the titles ; for instance, *Shō-ni-i-gyō Dainagon X*** Y****. If the office was superior to the rank, *shu* 守 was introduced ; for instance, *Jū-san-i-shu Dainagon X*** Y****.

This hierarchy was preserved, but simplified at the time of the Restoration (1869) : the ranks henceforth numbered only 2 degrees, so that their total sum amounted to 20.

The consistency of the rank at Court with the dignities, functions and titles of nobility is established as follows :

Rank at Court.		Dignity.	Function.	Nobility.
1st rank	1st degree: Shō-ichi-i	Shinnin-kwan.		(posthumous)
	2nd „ Jū „			Duke
2nd rank	1st „ Shō-ni-i			Marquis
	2nd „ Jū „			Count
3rd rank	1st „ Shō-san-i	Chokunin-kwan.		Viscount
	2nd „ Jū „			
4th rank	1st „ Shō-shi-i		1 tō	Baron
	2nd „ Jū „			
5th rank	1st „ Shō-go-i		2 tō	
	2nd „ Jū „		3 tō	
6th rank	1st „ Shō-roku-i	Sōnin-kwan.	4 tō	
	2nd „ Jū „		5 tō	
7th rank	1st „ Shō-shichi-i		6 tō	
	2nd „ Jū „		7 tō	
8th rank	1st „ Shō-hachi-i		8 tō	
	2nd „ Jū „		9 tō	
9th rank	1st „ Shō-ku-i	Hannin-kwan.		
	2nd „ Jū „			
10th rank	1st „ Dai-so-i			
	2nd „ Shō „			

— See *Kwan-i*, *Kwan-tō*, etc.

Ikao, 伊香保. A village in *Kōzuke*, known for its hot-water springs.

Ikao-numa, 伊香保沼. — See *Haruna-ko*.

Ikari-yama, 碇山. A place in *Satsuma*, containing an ancient castle where the *daimyō Shimazu* resided in the 14th century.

Ikaruga-dera, 班鳩寺. Another name given to the *Hōryū-ji* temple, near *Nara*.

Ikaruga no miya, 班鳩宮. In *Yamato*, an ancient palace built by *Shōtoku-Taishi*, in 601, in which he died (621). His son *Yamashiro no Ō*, attacked by *Soga no Iruka* committed suicide in the same palace (643).

Ikazuchi, 雷. The generic name of the 8 gods of thunder (*Shintō*) : *Ō-Ikazuchi*, *Ho no Ikazuchi*, *Kuro-Ikazuchi*, *Saku-Ikazuchi*, *Waki-Ikazuchi*, *Tsuchi-Ikazuchi*, *Naru-Ikazuchi*, and *Fushi-Ikazuchi*.

Ikeda, 池田. An ancient castle of the *Ikeda daimyō* in *Settsu*. *Nobunaga* took it from them in 1572 and gave it to *Araki Murashige*.

Ikeda, 池田. A *daimyō* family native of *Ōmi* and descended from the *Seiwa-Genji*.

```
                                                   ┌ Tsugumasa-Munemasa      (a)
                          ┌ Toshitaka -Mitsumasa-Tsunamasa ┤ Masatoki  -Masayori      (b)
                          │                        └ Terutoshi -Masaharu      (c)
                          │                                   ┌ Tsunakiyo-Yoshiyasu    (d)
          ┌ Terumasa ┤ Tadatsugu -Tadao    -Mitsunaka ┤ Nakazumi -Nakateru      (e)
          │               │                                   └ Kiyosada -Sadakata      (f)
Nobuteru ┤               │ Terzumi                                               (g)
          │               └ Masatsuna-Teruoki   -Masanao                         (h)
          └ Nagayoshi -Nagayuki -Nagatsune                                       (i)
```

(*a*) —— **Nobuteru,** 信輝 (1536-1584). *Kii no kami*, first served *Oda Nobuhide*, then *Nobunaga*, who, in 1579, gave him a part of the province of *Settsu* and the castle of *Amagasaki* in fief. He was killed in the battle of *Nagakute* where *Hideyoshi* fought *Oda Nobuo*.

—— **Terumasa,** 輝政 (1564-1613). A son of *Nobuteru*, took part in the last campaigns of *Nobunaga* and participated in the battle of *Nagakute* (1584). By the order of *Hideyoshi*, he married the second daughter of *Ieyasu* and, after the battle of *Sekigahara*, he received the province of *Harima* in fief (520,000 k.) and the name of *Matsudaira*. He left 8 sons, who divided his domains among themselves.

—— **Toshitaka,** 利隆 (1584-1616). The eldest son of *Terumasa*, took part in the siege of *Gifu* (1600), and married the daughter of *Saka-kibara Yasumasa*, who had been adopted by *Hidetada* (1606). At the death of his father (1613), he inherited the castle of *Himeji* and the greater part of *Harima*. He was present at the siege of *Ōsaka* and died soon afterwards.

—— **Mitsumasa,** 光政 (1609-1682). A son of *Toshitaka*, inherited *Harima* and later, in 1617, was transferred to *Tottori* (325,000 k.), receiving the two provinces of *Inaba* and *Hōki* in fief. In 1632, he exchanged his domains for the daimyate of *Okayama* (*Bizen* — 315,000 k.). He loved science, and fostered education to the utmost of his power. In 1672, he gave up the administration of his domains in favor of his son. —— His descendants resided at *Okayama* till the Restoration. — Now Marquis.

— A junior branch which has been ennobled since the Restoration. — Now Baron.

(*b*) — A junior branch that resided at *Kamokata* (*Bitchū* — 25,000 k.). Now Viscount.

(*c*) — A branch that resided at *Ikusaka* (*Bitchū* — 15,000 k.). —— Now Viscount.

(*d*) —— **Tadatsugu,** 忠継 (1599-1615). Was son of *Terumasa*. At the death of his father, he received the daimyate of *Okayama* (*Bizen* — 315,000 k.). He took part in the siege of *Ōsaka* and died the same year, at the age of 17.

—— **Tadao, 忠雄** (1602-1632). A son of *Terumasa*, inherited the domains of his brother *Tadatsugu*, who had died childless. Later, in 1632, he was transferred to *Tottori* (*Inaba* — 325,000 k.), where his descendants resided till the Restoration. — Now Marquis.

(*e*) — A branch that resided at *Shikano* (*Inaba* — 30,000 k.). — Now Viscount.

(*f*) — A branch that resided at *Wakaza* (*Inaba* — 20,000 k.). — Now Viscount.

(*g*) —— **Teruzumi, 輝澄** (1603-1662)). The fourth son of *Terumasa*, received the fief of *Yamasaki* (*Harima* — 60,000 k.) in 1615, but was deprived of his fief on account of bad administration, and banished to *Shikano* (*Inaba*) (1640). His descendants resided at *Fukumoto* (*Harima*). (10,000 k.). — Now Baron.

(*h*) —— **Masatsuna, 政網** (1604-1632). The 5th son of *Terumasa*, received the fief of *Akō* (*Harima* — 54,700 k.) together with the name of *Matsudaira* in 1615. He died childless at the age of 29.

—— **Téruoki, 輝興** (1611-1647). The 6th son of *Terumasa*, succeeded his brother *Masatsuna* in the fief of *Akō*. Having become insane, he was relegated into *Bizen* (1643).

—— **Masanao, 政直**. A son of *Teruoki*, died in 1665 without heir. The family became extinct with him.

(*i*) —— **Nagayoshi, 長吉** (1570-1614). The 3rd son of *Nobuteru*, was adopted by *Hideyoshi* in 1581 and appointed *Bitchū no kami* (1585). He took part in the siege of *Gifu* (1600), and received the fief of *Tottori* (*Inaba* — 90,000 k.).

—— **Nagayuki, 長幸** (1587-1632). Was a son of *Nagayoshi*. He took part in the siege of *Ōsaka* (1615) and, in 1617, was transferred to *Matsuyama* (*Bitchū* — 65,000 k.).

—— **Nagatsune, 長恒** (1607-1638). Was a son of *Nagayuki*. He died without children and his domains returned to the shogunate.

Ikeda, 池田. A family native of *Echigo*, ennobled in 1899. — Now Baron.

Ikeda-ko, 池田湖. A lake (20 Km. in circuit) in *Satsuma*.

Ikegami, 池上. A village in *Musashi*, between *Tōkyō* and *Yokohama*. It contains the great Buddhist temple *Hommon-ji*, where *Nichiren* died in 1282.

Ikejiri, 池尻. A *kuge* family descended from *Fujiwara Motoie*. — Now Viscount.

Ikeno Taiga, 池野大雅 (1723-1776). Was a painter and a talented poet. He was a pupil of *Gion Nankai*. He is also called *Mumei*.

Iki, 壹岐. One of the eleven provinces of *Saikaidō*, formed by the island (137 Km. in circuit) of the same name. It comprises one district. Its Chinese name is *Ishū*. — (Pop. : — 37,000 inhab.). — It belongs now to the *Nagasaki* prefecture. — It was devastated by the Mongols in 1274 and in 1281.

Iki Hakatoko, 伊吉博德. Was a member of the embassy sent to China in 659. He accompanied prince *Hōshō* to Korea in 662. At the death of the emperor *Temmu* (686), he joined a conspiracy formed with the object of raising prince *Ōtsu no Ōji* to the throne, but he was pardoned. He took part in the compilation of the *Taihō* code (702).

Iki-shiki, 位記式. The ceremony of promotion to a higher rank at Court. This very solemn ceremony was performed for civil officials (*bun-kwan*) at the department of Rites (*Shikibu-shō*), and for military officers, (*bukwan*) at the War department (*Hyōbu-shō*). The details are minutely described in the *Engi-shiki*, the *Chōya-gunsai*, etc. — Since the Restoration, it is performed at the department of the Imperial Household (*Kunai-shō*).

Ikitsuki-shima, 生月島. An island (26 Km. in circuit) N.W. of *Kyūshū*. It belongs to the province of *Hizen*.

Ikkō-shū, 一向宗. A branch of the *Jōdo* Buddhist sect founded in 1224 by *Shinran-Shōnin* (*Kenshin-Daishi*). It is also called *Jōdo-shinshū, Monto-shū*. It has its seat at the *Hongwan-ji* temple in *Kyōto*. — See *Jōdo-shinshū*.

Ikkōto no ran, 一向徒亂. (Lit.: the civil war of the adherents of the *Ikkō* sect). The eighth successor of *Shinran, Rennyo-Shōnin* (1415-1499) forced to flee from *Kyōto*, spread the doctrines of the sect in the provinces of *Echizen, Kaga*, and *Noto*, where it became prosperous. The bonzes, not content with the domains they received from their adherents, made themselves masters of a great number of others and declared war against the *daimyō*. The 16th century to the times of *Nobunaga* was full of these wars, which were felt especially in *Echizen, Ise, Settsu*, and *Mikawa*.

Ikkyū-oshō, 一休和尚 (1394-1481). A celebrated bonze of the *Rinzai* sect, was the son of a concubine of the emperor *Go-Komatsu*. When quite young, he entered the *Daitoku-ji* temple in *Kyōto*, of which he became the 47th superior. He is renowned as a literary man, a poet, and a painter.

IKKYŪ.

Ikoma, 生駒. A *daimyō* family native of *Owari*, and descended from *Fujiwara Tokihira*.

—— **Chikamasa, 親正** (+ 1598). Was in the service of *Hideyoshi*. In 1578, he besieged the castle of *Shichijō* (*Mimasaka*), took part in the battles of *Shizu-ga-take* (1583) and *Komaki* (1584), he then received the fief of *Takashima* (*Ōmi* — 20,000 k.), later he was transferred to *Kambe* (*Ise* — 60,000 k.), and thence to *Takamatsu* (*Sanuki* — 60,000) (1587). He took part in the campaigns of *Odawara* (1590), and of Korea (1592). Before dying, *Hideyoshi* appointed him one of the three *chūrō*.

—— **Kazumasa, 一正** (+ 1610). A son of *Chikamasa*, sided with *Ieyasu* against *Ishida Kazushige* and, after *Sekigahara* (1600), had his revenues raised to 170,000 k.

—— **Masatoshi, 正俊** (+ 1621). A son of *Kazumasa*, joined the party against *Ieyasu* in 1600, and took part in the expedition sent to *Tango* against the *Hosokawa*. The party was defeated, but *Ieyasu* pardoned him in consideration of his father's services. In 1615, he assisted *Tōdō Takatora* in besieging the southern part of the castle of *Ōsaka*

—-– **Takatoshi,** 高 俊 (1611-1659). A son of *Masatoshi,* whom he succeeded. On account of bad administration, he was dispossessed and banished to *Dewa* (1640). His son *Takashige* obtained the little fief of *Yashima* (*Dewa* — 10,000 k.), where his descendants lived till the Restoration. — Now Baron.

Ikoma-yama, 生 駒 山. A small mountain range (520 met.) on the limits of *Yamato* and *Kawachi* It has been a favorite theme for poets. — See *Iimori-yama.*

Ikuchi-jima, 生 口 島. An island (27 Km. in circuit) in the Inland Sea, S.W. of the province of *Aki* to which it belongs.

Ikuha no Toda no Sukune, 的 戸 田 宿 禰. Was a warrior of the 4th century. In 324, the king of *Koma* (Korea) sent targets and iron bucklers as a tribute. The emperor *Nintoku* assembled his Court and ordered arrows to be shot against the bucklers in order to try their solidity : *Toda no Sukune* pierced one at the first shot, to the great astonishment of the Koreans. As a reward he received the name of *Ikuha* (target).

Ikusa no kimi, 行 軍 元 帥. Formerly the principal general during a war. Later he was called *Shōgun.*

Ikusa no san-bugyō, 軍 三 奉 行. Under the *Tokugawa,* in time of war, the *Ōmetsuke* became chief of staff and, with the *Hata-bugyō* and the *Yari-bugyō,* formed what the people called the three *bugyō* of the war.

Ikuta-jinja, 生 田 神 社. A Shintoist temple in *Settsu,* which, according to legend, was founded by *Jingō-kōjō* at *Ikuta no ura* (now *Kōbe*) and which is dedicated to her as well as to *Waka-hirume no mikoto.*

Imabaru, 今 治. A town (15,000 inh.) in *Iyo* (*Shikoku*). It has an ancient castle which was built in 1602 by *Tōdō Takatora,* and belonged successively to the *Tōdō daimyō* (1602), the *Tomita* 1608, and from 1635 to 1868, to the *Hisamatsu* (35,000 k.).

Imadegawa, 今 出 川. — See *Kikutei.*

Imadegawa-Kubō, 今 出 川 公 方. A name given by the people to *Ashikaga Yoshimi.*

Imadegawa no tei, 今 出 川 第. A palace in which *Ashikaga Yoshimi* resided when in *Kyōto :* it was situated in the district called *Imadegawa, Kita-Muromachi.*

Imado-yaki, 今 戸 燒. Kind of porcelain made at *Imari* (*Hizen*).

Imae-gata, 今 江 潟. A lake (8 Km. in circuit) in the western part of *Kaga.* It is drained by the *Kakehashi-gawa.*

Imagawa, 今 川. A *daimyō* family descended from the *Seiwa-Genji.*

Kuniuji-Motouji {
　Yorimoto-Yorisada
　　Noriuji -Yasunori -Norimasa -Noritada -Yoshitada
　Norikuni Sadayo {Sadakane
　(*Ryōshun*) Sadaomi -Sadatomo -Noriyoshi-Sadanobu
　Ujikane Sadatsugu
　　　　　-Naotada
}

—— **Kuniuji,** 國 氏. Grandson of *Ashikaga Yoshiuji,* established himself in the 13th century at *Imagawa* (*Mikawa*) and took its name.

—— **Norikuni,** 範 國 (1295-1384). Was a relation to *Ashikaga Takauji,* who gave him the province of *Tōtōmi* and, later, that of *Suruga.* He took part in the battle of *Shijō-nawate* (1348).

—— **Noriuji,** 範 氏. A son of *Norikuni,* served *Takauji* and *Yoshiakira,* and was *Kazusa no suke.*

—— **Sadayo,** 貞 世 (+ 1429). The second son of *Norikuni.* He inherited the province of *Tōtōmi,* his brother keeping that of *Suruga.* He accompanied the *Shōgun Yoshiakira* in his campaign against *Go-Murakami* in *Yoshino* (1359). When *Hosokawa Kiyouji* joined the southern party, *Sadayo* marched against and defeated him in 1361, after which he had his head shaved and took the name of *Ryōshun,* by which he is known. In 1371, the *Shōgun Yoshimitsu* nominated him *Chinzei-tandai.* First defeated by *Kikuchi Takemitsu,* he vanquished him in turn with the aid of *Ōuchi Yoshihiro* (1372). He also defeated *Shōni Fuyusuke* (1375). During 10 years he continued to fight against the partisans of the South in *Kyūshū,* then, having been calumniated with the *Shōgun* by *Ōuchi Yoshihiro,* he was recalled and returned to *Tōtōmi,* his province (1399), where he cultivated literature and history, and published several works, among which was a Commentary of the *Taihei-ki,* the *Imagawa-sōshi,* the *Kyūshū-kassen-ki,* etc.

—— **Yasunori,** 泰 範. Was a son of *Noriuji* and fought against *Yamana Ujikiyo.*

—— **Norimasa,** 範 政 (+ 1417). Was a son of *Yasunori.* The *Shōgun* sent him to combat *Uesugi Ujinori,* whom he defeated in 1396, after which he was surnamed *Fuku-Shōgun* (Vice-shōgun).

—— **Noritada,** 範 忠. A son of *Norimasa.* He was sent by the *Shōgun Yoshinori* to combat *Yūki Ujitomo* in *Kwantō* (1439) and defeated him. He then received the name of *Fuku-Shōgun.* In 1455 he drove *Ashikaga Shigeuji* out of *Kamakura,* where he reinstalled *Uesugi Fusaaki.*

—— **Yoshitada,** 義 忠 (+ 1480). Was a son of *Noritada.* He was killed at the battle on *Shiozuki-saka.*

Yoshitada-Ujichika
{
Ujiteru
Yoshimoto-Ujizane { Norimochi-Norihide
Takahisa
Yasunobu
Yoshitoyo
}

—— **Uiichika,** 氏 親. A son of *Yoshitada,* still a child at the death of his father, was brought up in his mother's family and obtained possession of his domains owing to *Ise Nagauji.* He was *Shuri-tayū.*

—— **Yoshimoto,** 義 元 (1519-1560). The third son of *Ujichika* 氏 親. Was at first bonze, but his elder brother *Ujiteru* having died without children, he succeeded him. He was *Jibu-Ōsuke* and *Suruga no kami.* He was defeated in *Owari* by *Oda Nobuhide* (1542), but nevertheless succeeded in bringing the three provinces of *Mikawa, Tōtōmi* and *Suruga* under his authority. In 1559 he raised an army and again attempted to conquer *Owari,* but he met *Nobunaga* and the following year he was defeated and killed at the battle of *Okehazama.*

—— **Ujizane, 氏眞** (1538-1614). Was a son of *Yoshimoto*. After the death of his father, he lost a great number of his *samurai*, who joined *Ieyasu* then established at *Okazaki* (*Mikawa*). In 1568, *Takeda Shingen* attacked and defeated him almost without striking a blow. *Ujizane* fled. Two years later, *Shingen* again took the field and *Ujizane*, defeated a second time, took refuge with *Ieyasu*, who bestowed on him a small pension. Later he went to *Kyōto*, had his head shaved and took the name of *Sōkwan*. He died in *Edo* at the age of 77. His descendants served the *Tokugawa Shōgun* and were numbered among the families called *kōke*.

Imai Kanehira, 今井兼平 (+ 1184). Was a son of *Kanetō*, governor of *Shinano*. He and his brother *Higuchi Kanemitsu*, belonged to the 4 body-guards (*shi-tennō*) of *Kiso Yoshinaka*, whom they followed in all his campaigns. He committed suicide when *Yoshinaka* was defeated and killed at *Awazu* (*Ōmi*).

Imai Sōkun, 今井宗薫 (+ 1627). Whose true name was *Hiratsuna*, assumed the name of *Sōkun* when he had his head shaved. He was a son of *Sōkyū* and, like his father, a renowned master in the manner of preparing tea for which purpose he founded a school. He served under *Hideyoshi*, afterwards under *Ieyasu*.

Imaki, 今城. A *kuge* family descended from *Fujiwara Morozane* — Now Viscount.

Imao, 今尾. A castle in *Mino*, which was the residence of the *Mōri*, and the *Ichibashi daimyō* from 1584-1608. It was then annexed to the domains of *Yoshinao* (*Owari*), who intrusted the guard of the castle to *Takenokoshi Masanobu*.

Imazono, 今園. A family descended from *Fujiwara Yoshikado*. It was attached to the *Kōfuku-ji* temple in *Nara*. — Now Baron.

Imba-numa, 印幡沼. A lake (47 Km. in circuit) in *Shimōsa*.

Imi-kura, 齊藏. Formerly store-houses where all objects used in Shintoist ceremonies were kept.

Imizu-gawa, 射水川. A river (219 Km.) rising in *Hida*, where it is called *Shira-kawa*; it traverses *Etchū* and empties itself into the Japan Sea at *Fushiki*. — It is also called *Shō-gawa*.

Imube, 齊部. Anciently persons having charge of the confection and keeping of the objects necessary to the Shintoist ceremonies. The chief had the title of *Imube no Obito*. There were the corporations of *Sanuki, Awa, Kii, Tsukushi, Ise*. The *omi*, the *shizuri*, the *tamatsukuri* belonged to the *Imube*.

Imube, 齊部. A family descended from *Ame-no-tomi no mikoto* who, having been appointed chief of the *Imube* by *Jimmu-tennō*, took that name. His descendants and the *Nakatomi* shared the direction of all matters concerning Shintoist worship.

—— **Hironari, 廣成**. Author of a work of researches concerning the language, customs, etc. of ancient times. It was published in 808 and is known as the *Kogo-shūi*.

Ina, 伊奈. A *daimyō* family, descended from *Seiwa-Genji*.

—— **Tadatsugu,** 忠 次 (1551-1607). Was in the service of *Ieyasu*, who, when he established himself in *Kwantō*, gave him a revenue of 13,000 k. at *Kōnosu* (*Musashi*). After the battle of *Sekigahara*, his revenue was raised to 20,000 k. *Tadatsugu* was remarkable for his zeal in developing agriculture, digging canals, draining rice-fields, etc.

—— **Tadamasa,** 忠 政. A son of *Tadatsugu*, was dispossessed for participating in the conspiracy of *Ōkubo Nagayasu*.

Inaba, 因幡. One of the 8 provinces of *San-in-dō*. It comprises 3 districts belonging to the *ken* of *Tottori*.—Chinese name : *Inshū*.

Inaba, 稲庭. An ancient castle of *Ugo*, built in 1190 by *Ono Shigemichi*, where his descendants resided for 16 generations. *Uemichi* having transferred his residence to *Numatate*, left the castle to his brother *Harumichi*, whose grandson was dispossessed by *Shimizu Yoshiyasu* (1595).

Inaba, 稲葉. A *daimyō* family native of *Mino* and descended from *Kōno Michitaka*.

Michihiro {	Michitoshi-Yoshimichi-Sadamichi-Norimichi-Kazumichi -Nobumichi					(a)
	Michikane - . . . . . -Masanari - . . . . -Masamichi {	Masatomo	(b)
		Masakazu	(c)

(*a*) — The elder branch. —— **Sadamichi,** 貞 通 (1451-1606). Received the fief of *Hachiman* (*Mino* — 40,000 k.) in 1585 and was afterwards (1600) transferred to *Usuki* (*Bungo* — 56,000 k.) where his descendants resided till the Restoration. — Now Viscount.

(*b*) — Junior branch. —— **Masanari,** 正 成 (+ 1628). Was first in the service of *Nobunaga*, then in that of *Hideyoshi*, and took part in the expedition to *Korea* under the command of *Kobayakawa Hideaki*. In 1619, he received the fief of *Itoigawa* (*Echigo* — 25,000 k.) His descendants resided successively at *Odawara* (*Sagami* — 105,000 k.) in 1632, at *Takata* (*Echigo*) in 1685, at *Sakura* (*Shimōsa*) in 1701, finally, from 1723 till the Restoration, at *Yodo* (*Yamashiro* — 115,000 k.). — Now Viscount.

(*c*) — A branch ennobled in 1781, which, from 1785, resided at *Tateyama* (*Awa* — 10,000 k.). — Now Viscount.

Inaba-yama, 稲葉山. An ancient castle in *Mino*, built in 1203, and which successively belonged to the *daimyō Toki*, *Saitō*. *Nobunaga* took it in 1564 and changed its name to *Gifu*. — See *Gifu*.

Inada-hime, 稲田媛. A daughter of *Ashinazuchi* and *Tenazuchi*. She was to be devoured by the monster *Yamata no orochi*, but *Susano-o* saved her. He took her to wife and with her settled in *Izumo*. She is the mother of *Ōnamuji* or *Ō-kuni-nushi no mikoto*.

Inagaki, 稲垣. A *daimyō* family native of *Mikawa* and descended from the *Seiwa-Genji*.

Shigekata-Shigemune-Nagashige {	Shigetsuna-Shigemasa	(a)
	Shigemoto -Shigesada	(b)

(*a*) — The elder branch successively resided: in 1601 at *Isezaki* (*Kōzuke* — 10,000 k.), at *Fujii* (*Echigo* — 20,000 k.) in 1615, at *Sanjō* (*Echigo* — 25,000 k.) in 1619 ; at *Kariya* (*Mikawa*) in 1651 ; at *Karasu-yama* (*Shimotsuke*) in 1702 ; finally, from 1725 to 1868, at *Toba* (*Shima* — 30,000 k.). — Now Viscount.

(*b*) — Junior branch, which from 1685-1868 resided at *Yamakami* (*Ōmi* — 13.000 k.). — Now Viscount.

Inagi, 稻置 . One of the 8 classes (*hassei*) of officials in ancient times. They collected the taxes of rice and other cereals. History gives the names of only 7 or 8 persons that had this title.

Inahi no Mikoto, 稻冰命 . A brother of *Jimmu-Tennō*, who, having emigrated into Korea, is said to have become king of *Shiragi*. Some authors identify him with *Hyukkusa* 赫居世 founder of the *Pak* 朴 dynasty, which reigned from 57 to 4 B. C.

Inamura, 稻村 . An ancient castle in *Awa* (*Tōkaidō*) It was built by *Satomi Yoshizane* towards 1450. His descendants resided in that castle for nearly a century.

Inari, 稻荷 . The goddess of rice, also called *Uga no mitama*, is perhaps the same as *Toyo-uke-hime*. Her very numerous temples are guarded by two stone foxes ; hence the common belief that the fox is the god of rice.

Inawashiro-ko, 猪苗代湖 . A lake (65 Km. in circuit) in *Iwashiro*, which, according to tradition, was formed in 806 at the time of an eruption of mount *Bandai*. It is also called *Aizu* lake, *Bandai-ko*, *Yama no i*.

Indo-yō, 印度洋 . The Indian Ocean.

Ingen-Zenji, 隱元禪師 (1592-1673) A Chinese bonze who, at the age of 29, entered the temple of *Ōbaku-san* (*Fukien*) and became its superior. Having been invited to Japan, he arrived in 1654, and spread the *Ōbaku* branch of the *Zen* sect. The ex-emperor *Go-Mi-no-o*, the *Shōgun Ietsuna*, and many high personages embraced his doctrine. He established himself at *Uji*, in the *Mampuku-ji* temple erected in 1661 on a hill, which he called *Ōbaku-san ;* hence the name of his sect. He died 83 years of age and received the posthumous title of *Daikō-ōshō-kokushi*.

Ingyō-tennō, 允恭天皇 . The 19th Emperor of Japan (412-453). was prince *O-asa-tsumawakuko no Sukune*, the 4th son of *Nintoku*. He succeeded his brother *Hanshō*, when 36 years old. During his reign, there was confusion among the family names (*uji* and *kabane*), some officials having changed their names, and others having assumed names to which they were not entitled. A reform was carried out in this respect. It was by the trial of hot water, that the parties concerned were obliged to prove their pretentions (415). *Ingyō* died at the age of 78.

In no chō, 院廳 . The Court of an emperor who governed after his abdication. This name originated in the time of the ex-emperor *Shirakawa*, who governed 40 years after his abdication (1087-1129).

In no shima, 因嶋 . An island (39 Km. in circuit) in the Inland Sea, and belonging to the province of *Bingo*.

In no tsukasa, 院司 . A grand master at the Court of an emperor who had abdicated.

Inō Tadayoshi, 伊能忠敬 (1745-1821). A historian and geographer, who, during 18 years, was engaged in drawing the map of Japan. He finished his work in the very year of his death. He is generally called *Inō Chūkei.*

Inoe no Naishinnō, 井上內親王 (717-775). A daughter of the emperor *Shōmu,* was at first a high-priestess of the *Ise* temple, and, somewhat later, married prince *Shirakabe no Ōji.* When the prince ascended the throne, she received the title of empress (770); but two years later, having plotted to have her son nominated heir to the throne, she was degraded and confined to *Yamato,* where she died. Her memory was rehabilitated in 800.

Inoue, 井上. A *daimyō* family native of *Mikawa* and descended from *Minamoto Yorisue* (*Seiwa-Genji*).

Kiyohide {
Masanori -Masatoshi-Masatō {
Masamine-Masayuki (a)
Masanaga -Masaatsu (b)
Masashige-Masakiyo -Masaakira -Masachika (c)

(*a*) — The elder branch which resided successively: at *Yokosuka* (*Tōtōmi* — 55,000 k.) in 1623, at *Kasama* (*Hitachi*) in 1645, at *Gujō* (*Mino*) in 1692, at *Kameyama* (*Tamba*) in 1697, at *Shimodate* (*Hitachi*) in 1702, at *Kasama* (*Hitachi*) in 1703, at *Iwakidaira* (*Mutsu* — 60,000 k.) in 1747, at *Hamamatsu* (*Tōtōmi*) in 1758, at *Tanakura* (*Mutsu*) in 1817, at *Tatebayashi* (*Kōzuke*) in 1836, at *Hamamatsu* (*Tōtōmi*) in 1845; finally, shortly before the Restoration, the family was transferred to *Tsurumai* (*Kazusa*). — Now Viscount.

(*b*) — Junior branch established since 1712 at *Shimotsuma* (*Hitachi* — 10,000 k.). — Now Viscount.

(*c*) — 3rd branch which, since 1640, resided at *Takaoka* (*Shimōsa* — 14,000 k.). — Now Viscount.

Inoue, 井上. A *samurai* family of the *Yamaguchi* (*Suwō*) clan, ennobled in 1884. — Now Count.

—— **Kaoru,** 馨. Born in 1835, furtively left Japan and went to England with *Itō Hirobumi.* After his return (1864), he was the object of ill-usage on the part of the *samurai* of his clan. After the Restoration, he became Vice-Minister of the Treasury, Minister of Foreign Affairs, Minister of the Home Department, Minister of the Treasury, finally Minister of Agriculture and Commerce. He retired from public life in 1898, and belongs to the *genrō.*

Inoue, 井上. A *samurai* family of the *Yamaguchi* (*Suwō*) clan, ennobled in 1887. — Now Viscount.

Inoue, 井上. A *samurai* family of the *Kumamoto* (*Higo*) clan, ennobled after the Restoration. — Now Viscount.

Inoue, 井上. A *samurai* family of the *Kagoshima* (*Satsuma*) clan, ennobled in 1887. — Now Baron.

Inoue Harima-no-jō, 井上播磨椽 (1632-1685). A celebrated composer of *jōruri* and founder of a dramatical school that bears his name.

I-no-yama, 猪山. A hill in *Awa* (*Shikoku*) near *Tokushima*, where a castle formerly stood. Towards the middle of the 16th century, it belonged to the *Mōri daimyō*. In 1582 *Chōsokabe Motochika* took the castle and intrusted its keeping to *Yoshida Yasutoshi*. *Hideyoshi* having sent his brother *Hidenaga* into *Shikoku* (1585), the province of *Awa* passed over to *Hachisuka Iemasa* who built a castle on a larger scale. It is the present *Tokushima* castle.

Insei, 院政. The administration of an emperor after his abdication. The first was that of *Shirakawa* (1087-1129).

Inshū, 因州. The Chinese name of the province of *Inaba*.

Inubō-ga-saki, 犬吠崎. A cape at the eastern extremity of *Shimōsa*.

Inui, 犬居. An ancient castle in *Tōtōmi*, which belonged successively to the *Amano daimyō*, and the *Imagawa*. *Takeda Shingen* took it in 1568, and intrusted it to *Miyauchi Kagezane*, who was besieged and defeated by *Ieyasu* in 1576.

Inu-kubō, 犬公方. (Lit.: the *Shōgun* of the dogs) a surname given by the people to *Tsunayoshi*, the fifth *Tokugawa Shōgun*. As he was disconsolate at being childless, the bonze *Ryūkō* of the *Chisoku-in* temple informed him that the privation of children in this world is a chastisement that those undergo who, in a former existence had deprived other beings of their life. He was therefore to prohibit the destruction of any living creature and, as it was the year of the dog, the prohibition should especially affect the preservation of dogs. Following this advice, *Tsunayoshi* published a decree to this effect in 1687, moreover he constructed an asylum at *Nakano* (*Musashi*), where dogs were lodged, fed, etc. Hence his surname.

Inu-ou-mono, 犬追物. A sport of the *samurai* in the time of the *Kamakura* shogunate. It consisted in confining dogs in an enclosure surrounded by a bamboo fence. They were then pursued on horseback and killed with arrows.

Inu-yama, 犬山. An ancient castle in *Owari*, built towards 1435 by *Shiba Yoshitake*, who intrusted its safety to the *Oda* family. In 1584, *Ikeda Nobuteru* besieged *Nakagawa Sadanari* in that castle and conquered it. In 1607, *Owari* became the fief of *Tokugawa Yoshinao* and, since that epoch, the *Inuyama* castle was guarded by *Naruse Masanari* and his descendants.

I-ō-jima, 伊王嶋. An island (6 Km. in circuit) at the entrance of the *Nagasaki* roadstead (*Hizen*).

I-ō-ji-yama, 醫王子山. In *Mikawa*, near *Nagashino*. It was the scene of a battle between *Takeda Katsuyori* and *Nobunaga* (1575).

Ippen-Shōnin, 一遍上人 (1239-1289). A celebrated bonze, called *Ochi Michihide*. At the age of 7, he entered the *Keikyō-ji* temple of the *Tendai* sect, on *Tokuchi-yama* (*Iyo*), where he successively studied the *Tendai*, the *Jōdo*, and the *Nembutsu* sects. He afterwards traveled through the provinces, preaching a new doctrine, namely that of the *Ji* sect. On

IPPEN-
SHŌNIN.

account of his peregrinations, the people surnamed him *Yūgyō-Shōnin* (traveling bonze). He died at the *Shinkō-ji* temple (*Settsu*). In 1886, he received the posthumous title of *Enshō-Daishi*.

Irako-saki, 伊良湖崎. A cape south of *Mikawa*.

Iratsuko, 郎子. Anciently signified young man.

Iratsume or **Iratsuhime,** 郎女. Anciently signified young girl.

Irie, 入江. A *kuge* family descended from *Fujiwara Nagaie* (1005-1064). — Now Viscount.

Iroha-uta, 伊呂波歌. A poem composed of the 48 sounds or syllables of the Japanese language, none of them being repeated. Some attribute it to *Kōbō-Daishi* (774-835); but it is probably posterior to him, and the author is unknown.

I-roku, 位祿. Formerly a pension in kind which the government paid officials of the 4th and 5th ranks (*shō-4-i, jū-4-i, shō-5-i,* and *jū-5-i*). It consisted of a fixed quantity of hemp, linen, cotton, etc. The quantity allotted to women was only half of that given to men.

Irō-saki, 石廊崎. A cape south of *Izu*.

Isa, 伊佐. An ancient domain of the *Date* family, in *Hitachi*. In 1189, *Tomomune* moved to *Mutsu*, in the *Date* district, but left one of his sons *Tamemune* in *Isa*, who took the name of *Isa*. His descendants were dispossessed in 1343.

Isahaya-kyō, 諫早峡. The isthmus which connects the peninsula of *Shimabara* with the province of *Hizen*.

Isawa, 石和. A place in *Kai* which was the residence of the *Takeda daimyō*, the lords of the province, during the shogunates of *Kamakura* and *Kyōto*. Towards 1530, *Nobutora* established himself at *Tsutsuji-ga-saki*.

Ise, 伊勢. One of the 15 provinces of *Tōkaidō*. It comprises 10 districts belonging to the *Mie-ken*. — Chinese name: *Seishū*. — The Shintoist temples of *Ise* are the most ancient and the most venerated in Japan. — See *Naikū, Gekū,* etc.

Ise, 伊勢. A *daimyō* family descended from *Taira Masanori*. The eighth descendant of *Masanori, Toshitsugu, Buzen no kami,* was the first that took the name of *Ise*.

| Sadayuki-Sadakuni | Sadachika-Sadamune | (a) |
| | Sadafuji - Nagauji | (b) |

(*a*) The senior branch. — **Sadayuki,** 定行. *Ise no kami* served the *Shōgun Ashikaga Yoshimitsu*.

—— **Sadachika,** 貞親 (1417-1473). A son of *Sadakuni*, sided with *Hosokawa Katsumoto* during the *Ōnin* war.

(*b*) The junior branch. — **Nagauji,** 長氏 (1432-1519). — See *Hōjō Nagauji*.

Ise Gorōdayū Shōzui, 伊勢五郎太夫祥瑞. Born in the village of *Kurobe* (*Ise*) applied himself to ceramics, first at *Matsuzaka* (*Ise*), then went to the *Kiang-nan* province in China, whence he brought back the Chinese processes of the art. In 1513, he established a factory at *Imari* (*Hizen*), where, for the first time, porcelain was manufactured with blue designs on a white ground under the glaze.

Ise Yoshimori, 伊勢義盛. One of the four body-guards (*shitennō*) of *Minamoto Yoshitsune*. He was born in *Ise*, hence his name, and was compelled to flee into *Kōzuke* for having committed a murder. It was there that *Yoshitsune* going to *Mutsu* became acquainted with him and took him into his service. He engaged in all the campaigns of his master and, when the latter was no longer on good terms with his brother and had to leave *Kyōto*, he went to *Ise* to levy recruits for him. At their head he attacked *Fujiwara Tsunetoshi*, governor of the province, was defeated and killed himself on *Suzuka-yama* (1186).

Ise-monogatari, 伊勢物語. (Lit : narrations from *Ise*), a classical work written at the beginning of the 10th century ; the author is unknown. It is believed that the hero of the novel is no other than the famous *Ariwara Narihira*, whose adventures are related under another name

Ise no Ōsuke, 伊勢大輔. A poetess of the 11th century ; she was the daughter of *Ōnakatomi Sukechika*, and a lady in waiting to the empress *Jōtō-mon-in*, the consort of *Ickijō-tennō*. She afterwards married *Takashina Narishige*, *Echizen no kami*. She has been numbered among the 36 celebrated poets of her epoch (*chū-ko san-jū-roku kasen*).

Ise no umi, 伊勢海. The gulf of *Ise* or *Owari*

Ise san-gū, 伊勢三宮. The 3 great Shintoist temples of *Ise :* the *Naikū*, the *Gekū* and the *Izatsu-gū*.

Isezaki, 伊勢崎. In *Kōzuke*, an ancient castle which belonged to the *Akashi daimyō*, who took the name of *Isezaki* (1500). *Uesugi Kagetora* made himself master of it in 1560. The troops of the *Odawara Hōjō* were defeated at that place in 1590. Under the *Tokugawa*, it was transferred to the *Inagaki daimyō* (1601-1615), finally from 1681 to 1868, it became the possession of the *Sakai* (20,000 k.).

Ishibashi, 石橋. A *daimyō* family descended from the *Seiwa-Genji*.

—— **Kazuyoshi,** 和義. Sided with *Ashikaga Takauji* and fought against the southern dynasty. Being besieged in the castle of *Mitsuishi* (*Bizen*) by *Wakiya Yoshisuke*, he was delivered by *Takauji*. In 1361 he received the province of *Wakasa* in fief.

Ishibashi-yama, 石橋山. A place in *Sagami* where *Minamoto Yoritomo* was defeated by *Ōka Kagechika* shortly after he had risen against the *Taira* (1184).

Ishida, 石田. A *samurai* family of the *Kōchi* (*Tosa*) clan, ennobled after the Restoration. — Now Baron.

Ishida Kazushige, 石田三成. Or **Mitsunari.** Descended from the *Fujiwara* and a son of *Tameshige*, was born in *Ōmi* and, at the age of thirteen, entered the service of *Hideyoshi*. In 1585, he was made *Jibu-shōsuke* (hence the name of *Gibounochio* by which he was known to the ancient missionaries) ; was one of the 5 *bugyō* chosen by *Hideyoshi*, and received the *Sawa-yama* castle in fief (*Ōmi* — 186,000 k.). He took part in the expedition to Korea as a member of the staff of *Ukita Hideie*, the generalissimo. After the *Taikō's* death, suspecting the ambitious designs of *Ieyasu*, he resolutely supported the rights of *Hideyori* against him. He persuaded *Uesugi Kagekatsu* to be the first to take the field, and, whilst *Ieyasu* was combating *Uesugi*, he formed his party: *Mōri Terumoto*, *Ukita Hideie*, *Kobayakawa Hideaki*, *Shimazu Yoshihiro*, *Nabeshima Katsushige*, *Tachibana Muneshige*, *Konishi Yukinaga*, *Kikkawa Hiroie*, *Chōsokabe Morichika*, etc., declared for *Hideyori*, raised an army of 130,000 men, and marched against *Ieyasu* who, in haste, came southward. The two armies met on the 21st of October 1600 at *Seki-ga-hara* (*Mino*). The defection of some of the allies caused the defeat of *Kazushige*, who fled to mount *Ibuki*. His father, his brother *Shigenari*, his son *Shigeie*, took refuge at *Sawayama*, but being pursued by the victorious army, they put their wives and children to death and committed suicide. *Kazushige* was arrested six days later at the village of *Iguchi*, conducted to *Kyōto* and decapitated at *Rokujō-ga-hara*, with *Konishi Yukinaga*, *Ankokuji Ekei*, etc.

Ishidō, 石堂. A *daimyō* family descended from the *Seiwa-Genji*.

—— **Yorishige,** 賴重. He was the first that took the name of *Ishidō*.

—— **Yoshifusa,** 義房. A son of *Yorishige*, sided with *Ashikaga Takauji*, his relative, and was made *Chinjufu-Shōgun* of *Mutsu*. When *Takauji* fell out with his brother *Tadayoshi*, *Yoshifusa* followed the latter to the South and, after the death of *Tadayoshi* (1351), he with *Nitta Yoshioki* fought against the northern party, and contributed to the taking of *Kamakura* (1352). The southern army having been repulsed soon afterwards, he retired into *Suruga*, and when *Yoshiakira* had vanquished *Wada Masatada*, he seeing the precarious situation of the legitimate dynasty, again submitted to the *Ashikaga*.

—— **Yorifusa,** 賴房. A son of *Yoshifusa*, continued to serve *Tadayoshi* after the latter's quarrel with his brother *Takauji*, and inflicted several defeats on the northern troops in *Settsu* and *Harima*. Having been defeated by *Takauji* in *Ōmi*, he retired to the castle of *Kwannon-ji*. When the *Shōgun* had retaken *Kamakura*, he submitted to him (1352) and hence sided with the North.

Ishigaki-jima, 石垣嶋. An island (43 Km. in circuit) of the *Yaeyama* group of the *Ryūkyū* archipelago.

Ishigaki-yama, 石垣山. A hill south-west of *Odawara* (*Sagami*), from the top of which *Hideyoshi* conducted the siege of that town (1590).

Ishiguro, 石黒. A *shizoku* family of *Echigo* ennobled in 1895. — Now Baron.

Ishii, 石井. A *kuge* family descended from the *Taira*. — Now Viscount.

Ishikari, 石狩. One of the eleven provinces of *Hokkaidō*, comprising 9 districts. — Cap.: *Sapporo*, 55,600 inh. — Principal town: *Asahigawa*.

Ishikari-dake, 石狩嶽. A mountain (2,100 m.) in *Ishikari*.

Ishikari-gawa, 石狩川. A river (655 Km.) which flows through *Ishikari* and empties itself into the gulf of *Otaru*. It is the longest river in Japan.

Ishikawa, 石川. A place in *Kawachi*, which was formerly the residence of the *Minamoto* branch of *Kawachi*. This branch is also called *Kawachi-Genji*, or *Ishikawa-Genji*.

Ishikawa, 石川. A *daimyō* family native of *Kawachi* and descended from *Minamoto Yoshitoki*, a son of *Yoshiie* (*Seiwa-Genji*).

			Noriyuki-Yoshitaka	(a)
Kiyokane	Ienari	-Yasumichi-Tadafusa	Fusanaga-Fusayoshi	(b)
	Yasumasa	-Kazunori	Yasunaga	(c)
			Yasukatsu -Kazunori	(d)

(*a*) — The senior branch — **Ienari, 家成** (1534-1609) *Hyūga no kami*, served *Ieyasu* and accompanied him in all his campaigns against the *Imagawa* (1569), the *Takeda* (1572), etc.

—— **Yasumichi, 康通** (1554-1607). *Nagato no kami*, received the *Naruto* fief (*Kōzuke* — 20,000 k.) from *Ieyasu* in 1590. After the battle of *Sekigahara* (1600), he was transferred to *Ōgaki* (*Mino* — 50,000 k.).

—— **Tadafusa, 忠房** (1572-1650). A son of *Ōkubo-Tadachika*, *daimyō* of *Odawara*, was adopted by *Yasumichi* and succeeded him, but, implicated in a plot of which *Tadachika* was accused in 1614, he was dispossessed. After the siege of *Ōsaka*, he received the daimyate of *Hida* (*Bungo* — 60,000 k.). In 1633 he was transferred to *Sakura*, (*Shimōsa*) and, the following year, to *Zeze* (*Ōmi*). — His descendants resided successively at *Kameyama* (*Ise*) from 1651 to 1669; at *Yodo* (*Yamashiro*) from 1669 to 1711; at *Matsuyama* (*Bitchū*) from 1711 to 1744, and at *Kameyama* (*Ise* — 60,000 k.) from 1744 to 1868. — Now Viscount.

(*b*) — The junior branch detached at the death of *Tadafusa* (1650), resided at *Kambe* (*Ise*), then from 1732 to 1868 at *Shimodate* (*Hitachi* — 20.000 k.). — Now Viscount.

(*c*) **Yasumasa, 康政**. A son of *Kiyokane*, was *Hōki no kami* and in 1590 received the fief of *Fukashi* (now *Matsumoto*) (*Shinano* — 100,000 k.). — His grandson, *Yasunaga*, implicated in the plot of *Ōkubo Nagayasu*, was dispossessed in 1613.

(*d*). — **Kazunori, 数矩**. *Higo no kami*, who possessed a revenue of 15,000 k. in *Shinano*, was dispossessed thereof at the same time and for the same reason as his uncle *Yasunaga*.

Ishikawa, 石川. A *samurai* family of *Mino* ennobled after the Restoration. — Now Baron.

Ishikawa Goemon, 石川五右衛門. Belonged to a *kerai* family of the *Miyoshi*. When 16 years old, he committed a theft in the house of his master; and, when they tried to arrest him, he killed three men, fled and became a robber. In 1595, *Hideyoshi* sent soldiers to capture him. He was condemned together with his son *Ichirō*, to be thrown into a cauldron of boiling oil, which sentence was executed in the dry bed of the *Kamo-gawa* in *Kyōto*. He was then 37 years old. Before dying he composed a poem which has remained celebrated. (Another version places his death in 1632).

Ishikawa Jōzan, 石 川 丈 山 (1583-1672). Of a *samurai* family of *Mikawa*, applied himself to fencing and horsemanship, then to literature. At the age of 33, he began to attend the lessons of *Fujiwara Seikwa*, and afterwards was employed as professor by *Asano Nagaakira, daimyō* of *Hiroshima*. Having been in service for 13 years, he came back to *Kyōto*, established himself at the *Shisen-dō*, where he lived for 40 years writing books and composing poems.

Ishikawa Sadakiyo, 石 川 貞 清. A *daimyō* who in the service of *Hideyoshi* received the castle of *Inuyama* (*Owari* — 12,000 k.) in fief. Having joined the party against *Ieyasu* in 1600, he was deprived of it and died in obscurity at *Kyōto*.

Ishikawa-ken, 石 川 縣. A department formed with the provinces of *Kaga* and *Noto*. — Pop.: 807,000 inhabitants. — Capital: *Kanazawa* (84,000 inh.), Principal towns: *Komatsu* (13,200 inh.), *Nanao* (11,700 inh.), *Wajima* (10,600), etc.

Ishikoritome no Mikoto, 石 凝 姥 命. Grandson of *Ame-no-koyane no Mikoto*. It was he that, while *Amaterasu* was hiding in the cave, fabricated the mirror (*Yata no kagami*) which became one of the three imperial treasures. Later he accompanied *Ninigi no Mikoto* in his expedition into *Hyūga*. He is honored in the *Hi-no-kuma-jinja* temple (*Kii*).

Ishino, 石 野. A *kuge* family descended from the *Fujiwara Yori-mune* (993-1065). — Now Viscount.

Ishiyama, 石 山. Another *kuge* family descended from *Fujiwara Yoshimune* (993-1065).

Ishiyama, 石 山. A place in *Wakasa*, where, towards 1560, *Mutō Kōzuke no suke* built a castle, the guard of which he intrusted first to *Hemi Suruga no kami*, next to *Hongō Jibu-shōsuke*. The castle was abandoned towards the end of that century.

Ishiyama-dera, 石 山 寺. A celebrated Buddhist temple in *Ōmi*. It was built by the bonze *Ryōben* by order of the emperor *Shōmu*, was consumed by fire in 1078, and was rebuilt by *Yoritomo*. Having been destroyed a second time, it was rebuilt by *Yodo-gimi, Hideyoshi's* widow. It belongs to the *Shingon* sect, and is one of the 33 temples dedicated to *Kwannon*.

Ishiyama-Hongwanji, 石 山 本 願 寺. Also called *Ishiyamamidō*, *Ōsaka-gobō* is a Buddhist temple erected in *Ōsaka* in 1532. After the burning of the great *Hongwanji* temple in *Kyōto*, it became the principal temple of the sect. Being surrounded by ramparts and moats, it was a real fortress, and it took *Nobunaga* about 10 years to conquer it (1580). The *Hongwan-ji* was then transferred to *Nakajima* (*Settsu*), afterwards to *Kyōto* in 1601.

Ishizu, 石 津. A place in *Izumi*, where *Kitabatake Akiie*, a general of the Southern dynasty was defeated and killed in 1338 by *Kō Moronao*.

Ishizuchi-yama, 石 槌 山 . A mountain (1,500 m.) in *Iyo*. It is also called *Iyo no takane, Omoga-yama.*

Ishū, 伊 州 . The Chinese name of *Iga*.

Ishū, 壹 州 . The Chinese name of *Iki*.

Iso-no-kami, Futsu no ō-kami, 石 上 布 都 大 神 . The *Shintō* god whose temple is in *Tamba-ichi* (*Yamato*).

Iso-no-kami-jingū, 石 上 神 宮 . A celebrated Shintoist temple in *Yamato*, built by the emperor *Sujin* (72 B. C.) in honor of *Futsu no kami*. The guard of the temple was intrusted to the *Mononobe* family.

Isshiki, 一 色 . A *daimyō* family descended from the *Seiwa-Genji*. Under the *Ashikaga* shōgunate it was one of the four families (*shishoku*) in which the minister (*shitsuji*) of the *Kyōto Kwanryō* was chosen.

—— **Kimifuka,** 公 深 . The 7th son of *Minamoto Yasuuji*. He established himself at *Isshiki* (*Mikawa*) towards the end of the 13th century. Hence his name.

—— **Akinori,** 詮 範 (+ 1406). Defeated *Yamana Ujikiyo* in 1391 and received the fief of *Imatomi* (*Wakasa*).

—— **Yoshitsura,** 義 貫 . A grandson of *Akinori* and son of *Mitsunori* (+ 1414), divided his domains with his brother *Mochinori* in 1411, the latter received the province of *Tango*, and *Yoshitsura* kept *Wakasa*. Thus the family was divided into two branches. In 1440, he revolted against the *Shōgun Yoshinori*, but was defeated and killed by *Takeda Nobukata*.

—— **Yoshinao,** 義 直 (+ 1483). A son of *Yoshitsura*, sided with the *Yamana Sōzen* party during the *Ōnin* war and was defeated by *Hosokawa Katsumoto* (1467).

—— **Yoshiharu,** 義 春 . A son of *Yoshinao*, accompanied *Ashikaga Yoshimi* in his flight into *Ōmi* (1488) and remained there till the nomination of *Yoshitane* to the shōgunate (1490).

The family lost its domains during the civil wars of the 16th century.

Isshin (go), 一 新 (御) . The Imperial Restoration of 1867-1868. — See *Kōmei-tennō, Tokugawa Iemochi, Keiki,* etc.

Isuzu-gawa, 五 十 鈴 川 . A small river (15 Km.) in *Ise*, where the faithful, before entering the temples of *Yamada*, purify themselves by washing their mouth and hands. It is also called *Uji-gawa, Mimosuso-gawa.*

Itagaki, 板 垣 . A *samurai* family of the *Kōchi* (*Tosa*) clan, ennobled in 1887. — Now Count.

Itagaki Nobukata, 板 垣 信 形 (+ 1547). General of the *Takeda*, *daimyō* of *Kai*, was governor of the *Suwa* district and resided in the *Ina* castle (*Shinano*). In 1546, he defeated *Murakami Yoshikiyo* and *Uesugi Norimasa*. The following year he gained another victory over *Ueda*, but lost his life in the battle.

Itakeru no kami, 五 十 猛 神 . A son of *Susano-o*. He was led into *Shiragi* (Korea) by his father, and is said to have become king of that country. He is also called *Ōyabiko no kami*.

Itakura, 板 倉 . A *daimyō* family native of *Mikawa* and descended from the *Seiwa-Genji* by the *Shibukawa* branch.

Kats-shige
{
Shigemune
{
Shigesato -Shigetsune-Shigefuyu (a)
Shigekata -Shigeatsu -Katsukiyo (b)
}
Shigemasa -Shigenori
{
Shigetane -Shigehiro (c)
Shigeyoshi-Shigetaka (d)
}
}

(*a*) — The senior branch. — **Katsushige**, 勝重 (1542-1624). Was a bonze till the age of 40, when he abandoned his profession to follow the call of *Ieyasu*, who, in 1586, made him *Suruga-bugyō*, then *Kwantō-daikwan* (1591). After *Sekigahara*, he became *Shoshidai* of *Kyōto* (1601) and occupied this office for 20 years. He received the title of *Iga no kami*, had his revenues raised to 40,000 k., but no castle was confided to him.

—— **Shigemune**, 重宗 (1587-1656). The eldest son of *Katsushige ;* he succeeded his father in 1620 in the office of *Shoshidai*, which office he held till 1654. In 1656, he became *daimyō* of *Sekiyado* (*Shimōsa* — 50,000 k.), and died the same year.

—— **Shigesato**, 重郷 (1620-1660), the eldest son of *Shigemune*, was *Awa no kami* and *Jisha-bugyō*. — His descendants resided successively at *Kameyama* (*Ise*) from 1669 to 1710; at *Toba* (*Shima*) from 1710 to 1717; at *Kameyama* from 1717 to 1744; finally at *Matsuyama* (*Bitchū* — 50,000 k.) from 1744 to 1868. — Now Viscount.

(*b*) — The junior branch resided at *Annaka* (*Kōzuke* — 15,000 k.) in 1681; at *Izumi* (*Mutsu* — 20,000 k.) in 1702; at *Sagara* (*Tōtōmi* — 25,000 k.) in 1746; finally, from 1749 to 1868, at *Annaka* (*Kōzuke* — 30,000 k.). — Now Viscount.

(*c*) —— **Shigemasa**, 重昌 (1588-1638). The second son of *Katsushige*, received a revenue of 15,000 k. in *Mikawa* for his conduct during the siege of *Ōsaka* (1615). In 1637, he was commissioned by the *Shōgun Iemitsu* to suppress the *Shimabara* insurrection (*Hizen*), and was killed by an arrow at the siege of the castle of *Hara*.

—— **Shigenori**, 重矩 (1617-1673). A son of *Shigemasa ;* he was governor of the castle of *Ōsaka* and *Rōjū*, afterwards *Shoshidai* of *Kyōto* (1668). In 1672, he received the daimyate of *Karasu-yama* (*Shimotsuke* — 60,000 k.).

—— **Shigetane**, 重胤 (1640-1705). A son of *Shigenori*, was transferred to *Iwatsuki* (*Musashi*) in 1680, and, the following year, to *Sakamoto* (*Shinano*). Two years later, he became bonze and divided his revenues between his son *Shigehiro* and his brother *Shigeyoshi*.

—— **Shigehiro**, 重廣. Was transferred to *Fukushima* (*Mutsu* — 80,000 k.), where his descendants resided till the Restoration. — Now Viscount.

(*d*) — A junior branch which, from 1699 to 1868, resided at *Niwase* (*Bitchū* — 20,000 k.). — Now Viscount.

Itakura-numa, 板倉沼. A lake (15 Km. in circuit) in *Kōzuke*.

Itami, 伊丹. An ancient castle in *Settsu*, built by the *daimyō Itami*. *Nobunaga* took it in 1573 and confided it to *Araki Murashige*, who was dispossessed of it in 1579. Under the *Tokugawa*, the *Itami* domain belonged to the *kuge Konoe*. — *Itami* is renowned for its *sake* (liquor brewed from rice).

Itami, 伊 丹．A *daimyō* family of *Settsu*, which, in the 16th century, resided at *Itami*.

—— **Chikaoki,** 親 興．Was deprived of his domain in 1573 by *Nobunaga* for having taken part in a plot formed against him by the *Shōgun Yoshiaki*.

Itami, 伊 丹．A *daimyō* family native of *Suruga*.

—— **Yasukatsu,** 康 勝 (1571-1649). *Harima no kami*, was in the service of *Ieyasu*. In 1632, he was intrusted with the guard of the *Kōfu* castle with a revenue of 12,000 k. at *Tokumi* (*Kai*).

—— **Katsunaga,** 勝 長 (1601-1662). A son of *Yasukatsu*, was assassinated by *Isshiki Kura-no-suke*.

—— **Katsumori,** 勝 守．A grandson of *Katsunaga*, killed himself in a fit of insanity (1698), and his domains returned to the *Shōgun*.

Itashima, 板 嶋．The ancient name of the town of *Uwajima* (*Iyo*).

Ito, 怡 土．An ancient district (*agata*) of *Chikuzen*.

Ito, 怡 土．An ancient castle in the district of the same name (*Chikuzen*). The castle was anciently the residence of the *agata-nushi*, afterwards the abode of the governor of the *Dazaifu*. *Yoritomo* gave the district of *Ito* to *Harada Tanenao*. Later it was bestowed on *Takaso*, the chief of the Shintoist temple, whose descendants held it for 20 generations, the last scion being *Uehara Nobutane*, who was dispossessed of it by *Hideyoshi* in 1587. When *Kuroda Nagamasa* received the province of *Chikuzen*, he intrusted the guard of the castle of *Ito* to his 4th son *Masafuyu*. Later the castle was abandoned. It was also called the castle of *Takaso*.

Itō, 伊 東．A place in *Izu*. *Minamoto Yoritomo*, when exiled by *Taira Kiyomori*, resided at this place from 1160 to 1180.

Itō, 伊 東．A *daimyō* family descended from *Fujiwara Korekimi* (727-789) by *Kudō Ietsugu*.

Ietsugu ⎰ Sukeie -Sukechika ⎰ Sukeyasu ⎰ Sukenari / Tokimune (*Soga*)
⎱ Sukekiyo
⎱ Sukutsugu-Sukutsune -Suketoki -Mitsusuke-Sukemune

—— **Sukechika,** 祐 親 (+ 1181). Received the domain of *Kawazu* (*Izu*) at the death of his father *Sukeie*, and on account of his domain, is often called *Kawazu Jirō*. His uncle *Suketsugu*, having become ill, intrusted his son to him, to be brought up and to receive the *Itō* (*Izu*) domain; but, as soon as *Suketsugu* was dead, *Sukechika* sent *Suketsune* away to *Kyōto* and took possession of his inheritance. *Suketsune* swore to avenge himself and, one day, when all the family had accompanied *Yoritomo* to a hunting party, he killed *Sukeyasu*, the son of *Sukechika*, and severely wounded the latter. This murder was the cause of the subsequent vengeance of the *Soga* brothers, the sons of *Sukeyasu*. *Sukechika* recovered from his wounds, but having refused to follow *Yoritomo* in his campaign against the *Taira*, he was arrested and invited to kill himself, notwithstanding the intercession of his daughter married to *Miura Yoshizumi*.

—— **Sukekiyo,** 祐清. The second son of *Sukechika,* went to *Kyōto* after the death of his father, and joined the party of the *Taira.* He was killed at *Shinowara* (*Ōmi*) while fighting against *Kiso Yoshinaka* (1183).

—— **Suketsune,** 祐經. — See *Kudō Suketsune.*

—— **Yoshisuke,** 義祐 (+ 1584). A descendant of *Suketsune,* he inherited the fief of *Agata* (*Hyūga*) in 1533. In 1541, he defeated *Satsuma :* the war continued for 10 years, and he increased his domains by a part of *Ōsumi* (1551) and *Satsuma* (1557), but he was finally defeated by *Shimazu Yoshihisa* (1576) and fled into *Bungo,* to the residence of *Ōtomo Sōrin,* thence he went to *Kyōto,* where he died.

—— **Yoshimasu,** 義益 (+ 1569). The eldest son of *Yoshisuke,* died before his father. His two sons, *Yoshikata* and *Yoshikatsu,* were baptized in 1582 under the name of *Bartholomew* and *Jerome.*

—— **Suketaka,** 祐丘 (1541-1600). Another son of *Yoshisuke,* was defeated together with his father, and with him, fled into *Bungo* (1577) and then to *Kyōto* (1579). After the death of *Nobunaga,* he adhered to *Hideyoshi,* who appointed him *Mimbu-ōsuke* and gave him estates in *Kawachi.* After the campaign in *Kyūshū* (1587), he was reinstated in *Hyūga* at the castle of *Obi* (50,000 k.). He took part in the expedition to Korea and was nominated *Bungo no kami* in 1599.

—— **Sukeyoshi,** 祐慶 (1588-1636). A son of *Suketaka,* served his first campaign when only 12 years old, at the battle of *Sekigahara ;* then, having returned into *Hyūga,* he joined the campaign of *Kuroda Yoshitaka* and *Katō Kiyomasa* against the *Shimazu.* He had the title of *Shuri-tayū* — His descendants resided at *Obi* (*Hyūga* — 50,000 k.) till the Restoration. — Now Viscount.

—— A junior branch resided at *Okada Bitchū* — (10,000 k.) from 1615 to 1868. — Now Viscount.

Itō, 伊藤. A *samurai* family of the *Yamaguchi* (*Suwō*) clan, ennobled in 1884. — Now Prince.

—— **Hirobumi,** 博文. Born in 1841, studied at the family school of *Yoshida Torajiro* and attracted notice of the seniors of the *Chōshū* clan. In 1863, he visited England and returned from Europe with *Inouye Kaoru,* when the squadrons of the allied powers were about to bombard *Shimonoseki* (1864). He obtained a delay to confer with the *daimyō,* but failed in his attempt to reconcile the parties. Afterwards patronized by the late *Kido,* he was intrusted with works of the greatest responsibility ; thus he helped towards the overthrow of the *Shōgunate* and the organisation of the *Meiji* Government. He acted as interpreter to the boy Emperor when he first saw the foreign representatives in February 1868. He was governor of *Hyōgo,* vice-Minister, and a member of the *Iwakura* embassy when this prince was sent as special envoy to approach the Powers and lead them to revise the old treaties (1872). After the assassination of *Ōkubo Toshimichi* and the death of *Kido*, he became the most conspicuous politician of Japan. He signed the treaty of *Tientsin* with China (1885), was sent to Europe and America to study the system of Parliamentary work and returned home to draw up the Constitution that was promulgated in 1889. He was repeatedly President of the Ministry, negotiated the treaty of *Shimonoseki* (1895). Later, he leaned in favor of party Cabinet; he then undertook to form a "model party." In 1891, he became President of the Privy Council, and in this capacity showed his skill in governing men, when, opposed by the conservative party, he admitted in the Privy Council the head of the opposition. During the Russo-Japanese war, he was twice sent to Korea and in the fall of 1906 filled the post of Resident General in that country.

Itō, 伊東. A *samurai* family of the *Kagoshima* (*Satsuma*) clan, ennobled after the Restoration. — Now Viscount.

Itō, 伊東. *Samurai* family of *Kagoshima* (*Satsuma*) made noble in 1895. — To day, Viscount.

—— **Sukeyasu, 祐亨.** Born in 1843, entered the marine service. He commanded the fleet during the Chinese war (1894-95) and was victorious in the battles of the Yalu and Port-Arthur. During the Russian war, he was chief of the General Staff of the Marine. Viscount in 1895 and Admiral.

Itō, 伊東. A family of *Hizen*, ennobled in 1895. — Now Baron.

Itō, 伊東. A family of *Tango*, ennobled in 1895. — Now Baron.

Itō, 伊藤. A family of celebrated scholars of the 17th and 18th centuries.

—— **Jinsai, 仁齋** (1627-1705). Was for 50 years the great commentator of Confucius, in *Kyōto*. Until then, the commentaries were limited to the Chinese philosophical writings of the *Sō* epoch; but *Jinsai* rejected these Chinese interpretations and commented on the very text of the master: he thus established the Confucianist school called *Fukko-ha*. He also studied ancient Japanese literature and published numerous writings. He is often called *Ko-gaku-sensei*.

—— **Tōgai, 東涯** (1670-1736). A son of *Jinsai*, continued the traditions of his father. He left several works which were formerly much appreciated.

Itoigawa, 糸魚川. A place in *Echigo*, which was the residence of the *Inaba daimyō*, from 1619 to 1632, of the *Matsudaira*, from 1632 to 1681, of the *Inaba* again, from 1685 to 1701, of the *Honda*, from 1701 to 1717, finally of the *Matsudaira* from 1717 to 1868. (10,000 k.).

Itoku-tennō, 懿德天皇. The 4th Emperor of Japan, was *Ō-Yamato-hiko-sukitomo no Mikoto*. He succeeded his father *Annei* at the age of 43 and died at 77. History is silent about this reign.

Itosaki, 糸崎. A place in *Bingo*, where, in 1570, *Kobayakawa Takakage* built a castle which was abandoned at the end of the same century.

Itōzu, 到津. A family descended from *Usatsu-hiko*, and which governed the land of *Usa* (*Buzen*) in the time of *Jimmu-tennō.* Later, the same had charge of the guard of the *Itōzu-Hachiman* temple in the same province. — Now Baron.

Itsuki-no-Miya, 齋宮. — See *Saigū-ryō.*

Itsuku-shima, 嚴嶋. An island (31 Km. in circuit), in the Inland Sea, south-west of *Hiroshima,* belonging to the province of *Aki.* It forms one of the three most beautiful landscapes (*san-kei*) of Japan. It is celebrated for its Shintoist temples dedicated to the three daughters of *Susano-o* : viz., *Tagori-hime, Takitsu-hime,* and *Itsukushima-hime,* the last of whom has given her name to the island which is also called *Onga-shima, Miya-jima.* — In 1555, *Mōri Motonari* built a castle in *Itsuku-shima.* It was also in this island that he defeated *Sue Harukata.*

Itsuse no Mikoto, 五瀬命. — See *Hiko-Itsuse no Mikoto.*

Itsutsuji, 五辻. A *kuge* family descended from the *Uda-Genji.* — Now Viscount.

Iwadono, 射場殿. An ancient castle in *Kai,* belonging to the *Oyamada daimyō,* the lords of *Gunnai. Nobushige,* the last lord, was deprived of his domains by *Nobunaga* (1582).

Iwafune no ki, 岩船柵. A sort of fortified wall built in the *Iwa-fune* district (*Echigo*), to stop the incursions of the *Ebisu* (648). — See *Nutari no ki.*

Iwai, 岩井. Governor of *Tsukushi.* He made a treaty of alliance with *Shiragi* (Korea) and revolted. He was defeated and killed by *Mononobe no Arakabi* (528). His domains were confiscated, and thus ended the nearly independent sovereignty which the descendants of *Watatsumi* had exercised for centuries over the north of *Kyūshū* : the *Dazaifu* took its place.

Iwaki, 磐城. One of the 13 provinces of *Tōsandō* formed of the 10 southern districts of *Mutsu,* in 1868. At present, seven belong to the *Fukushima-ken* and three to the *Miyagi-ken.*

Iwaki, 岩城. A *daimyō* family descended from the *Taira.*

—— **Tsunetaka, 常隆** (1566-1590). Inherited the *Iwakidaira* fief (*Mutsu*), which had been in the possession of his ancestors for several centuries. Having been defeated by *Date Masamune* in 1585, and by *Satake Yoshishige* in 1587, he submitted to *Hideyoshi.*

—— **Sadataka, 貞隆** (1584-1621). A son of *Satake Yoshishige,* was adopted by *Tsunetaka* and succeeded him. Having joined the party hostile to *Ieyasu,* together with his brother *Satake Yoshinobu* and *Uesugi Kagekatsu,* he lost his fief of *Iwakidaira* (180,000 k.) and in 1602 was transferred to *Kameda.* (*Dewa*—20,000 k.), where his descendants resided till the Restoration. — Now Viscount.

Iwakidaira, 磐城平. Or *Taira,* a town (10,300 inh.), of *Iwaki.* Its ancient castle successively belonged to the *Kitabatake daimyō* (14th century), to the *Iwaki* (15th and 16th centuries), to the *Torii* from 1602 to 1622, to the *Naitō* from 1622 to 1747, to the *Inoue* from 1747 to 1756, finally to the *Andō* from 1756 to 1868 (50,000 k.).

Iwaki-gawa, 岩木川. A river (87 Km.) which has its source at *Tomari-dake*, in the south of *Mutsu*, passes near *Hirosaki*, receives the *Aseshi-gawa* and the *Hirata-gawa*, then, flowing northward, empties itself into lake *Jūsan-gata*. It is also called *Hirosaki-gawa*.

Iwaki-yama, 岩木山. A mountain (1580 met.) in *Mutsu*. It is also called *Oku-fuji, Tsugaru-fuji*.

Iwakuni, 岩國. A town (7,600 inh) in *Suwō*, which from 1600 to 1868, was the residence of the *Kikkawa daimyō* (60,000 k.), a branch of the *Mōri* family. Near that town is the famous *Kintai-kyō* bridge over the *Nishiki-gawa*. It is composed of five arches, 135 met. long and of a very bold curvature.

Iwakuni-gawa, 岩國川. A river (94 Km.) which has its source in the north of *Suwō*, receives several tributaries, passes through *Iwakuni*, then divides into two branches, the *Imatsu-gawa* and the *Monzen-gawa*, which empty into the sea of *Aki*. It is also called *Nishiki-gawa, Kuga-gawa* and, in its superior course, *Ōse-gawa, Tawara-gawa*.

Iwakura, 岩倉. A place in *Hōki*, formerly the residence of the *Ogamo samurai*, who were deprived of their estates by *Amako Tsunehisa* towards 1520, and were reinstated by *Mōri Motonari* (1566). *Hideyoshi* installed *Nanjō Motokiyo* in that place (1583). Under the *Tokugawa*, it became a Shōgunal domain.

Iwakura, 岩倉. An ancient castle in *Owari*. It belonged to a branch of the *Oda* family. *Nobunaga* seized it in 1560.

Iwakura, 岩倉. A *kuge* family descended from *Murakami-Genji*. — Now Duke.

—— **Tomomi,** 具視 (1825-1883), figured very conspicuously in the Imperial Restoration. In 1862, he was imprisoned by order of the *Shōgun Iemochi*, but having been set free in 1867, he was appointed *gitei*, a title corresponding to that of Minister (1868). In 1869 he was sent on a mission to the *Nagato* and *Satsuma daimyō* to invite them to share in the administration of public affairs. Towards the end of 1871, he was ambassador to the United States and Europe. On his return in 1873, he found the Council of State divided into two parties, concerning the relations with Korea, which had refused to receive an imperial letter. *Tomomi* together with *Ōkubo Toshimichi*, sided with the peace party ; the other *sangi*, partisans of war, sent in their resignation, and the influence of *Iwakura* became still greater. Until his death, he was the most conspicuous politician in Japan.

Iwakura, 岩倉. A junior branch of the above, ennobled in the person of *Tomotsune* (1853-1890), the third son of *Tomomi*. — Now Baron.

Iwakura, 岩倉. Another junior branch. — Now Viscount.

Iwakura, 岩倉. A third junior branch. — Now Baron.

Iwamatsu Mitsuzumi, 岩松滿純 (+ 1417). A son of *Nitta Yoshimune*, married the daughter of *Uesugi Ujinori* and sided with the latter against *Ashikaga Moshiuji*, but was taken prisoner and put to death.

Iwami, 石見. One of the 8 provinces of the *San-in-dō*. It comprises six districts belonging to the *Shimane-ken*. — Chinese name : *Sekishū*.

Iwami-nada, 石見灘. The sea of *Iwami* on the western coast of Japan.

Iwamura, 岩村. An ancient castle in *Mino*. It originally belonged to the *Tōyama daimyō* (12th–16th centuries). *Takeda Shingen* took it and intrusted its guard to *Akiyama Haruchika*, who was expelled from it by *Nobunaga* (1575). *Hideyoshi* gave it to *Tamaru Tomotada*. Under the *Tokugawa*, it was occupied by the *Ōgyū daimyō* (1601-1638), by the *Niwa* (1638-1702), finally by the *Ishikawa* from 1702 to 1868 (30,000 k.).

Iwamura, 岩村. A *samurai* family of the *Kōchi* (*Tosa*) clan, ennobled after the Restoration. — Now Baron.

Iwamurata, 岩村田. A place in *Shinano*, which from 1693 to 1868, was the residence of the *Naitō daimyō* (15,000 k.).

Iwanaga hime, 磐長姫. A daughter of *Ōyamatsumi*, the mountain god, and of *Kayanu hime* the meadow goddess (Shintoism). She is the sister of *Ko-no-hana-saku-ya hime*, the goddess of mount *Fuji*, and has her temple on mount *Ōyama* in *Sagami*.

Iwa no hime, 磐之媛. The consort of the emperor *Nintoku* (314). The latter having also married *Yata-no-waki iratsume* (342), *Iwa no hime* retired to *Tsuzuki* (*Yamashiro*), where she died in 347, without having consented to return to the Court.

Iwarehiko no Sumera-Mikoto, 磐余彦天皇. The Emperor *Jimmu Tennō's* name during his life time.

Iwasa Matabei, 岩佐又兵衛. Was a son of *Araki Murashige*, *daimyō* of *Itami* (*Settsu*). When his father was dispossessed of his domains by *Nobunaga* (1579), *Matabei*, then only 2 years old, was taken by his mother into *Echizen* and brought up in the *Iwasa* family of which he took the name. Towards 1600, he went to *Kyōto*, to attend the drawing lessons of *Tosa Mitsunori* and afterwards he founded a new school. Rejecting the conventional methods and subjects of the traditional school, he applied himself faithfully to reproduce nature. His drawings in that style are known by the name of *ukiyo-e*, and *Matabei* himself is called *Ukiyo Matabei*.

Iwasaki, 岩崎. A place in *Ugo*, the residence of the *Satake daimyō* since 1762 (20,000 k.).

Iwasaki, 岩崎. A place in *Owari*, where *Niwa Ujikiyo* built a castle in 1538. The castle was taken by *Ikeda Nobuteru* in 1583. The following year, *Hideyoshi* gave it to *Inaba Michitomo*. After the battle of *Sekigahara*, it was abandoned and its debris used in the construction of the *Nagoya* castle (1610).

Iwasaki, 岩崎. A *samurai* family of *Kōchi* (*Tosa*), ennobled in 1900. — Now Baron.

Iwasaki, 岩崎. A junior branch of the above ennobled at the same time. — Now Baron.

Iwasaki Yataro, 岩崎彌太郎 (1834-1885). Was famous for his spirit of enterprise in commercial and industrial pursuits. He is the founder of the *Mitsubishi-Kwaisha* Shipping Co., etc.

Iwashimizu, 石清水. — See *Otoko-yama*.

Iwashiro, 岩代國. One of the 13 provinces of *Tōsandō*, formed by 10 districts of the southern part of the ancient province of *Mutsu*, in 1868. The 10 districts now belong to the *Fukushima-ken*.

Iwashita, 岩下. A *samurai* family of *Kagoshima* (*Satsuma*), ennobled after the Restoration. — Now Viscount.

Iwasuge-yama, 岩菅山. A mountain (2,515 met.) on the limits of *Kōzuke* and *Shinano*.

Iwate-ken, 岩手縣. A department formed of 10 districts of *Riku-chū*, 1 of *Rikuzen*, and 1 of *Mutsu*. — Pop.: 761,200 inh. — Capital: *Morioka* (33,000 inh.).

Iwate-yama, 岩手山. — See *Ganjū-san.*

Iwatezawa, 岩手澤. The ancient name of the castle and town which *Date Masamune* called *Sendai* (*Rikuzen*) when he established his residence there in 1602.

Iwatsuki, 岩槻. An ancient castle in *Musashi*, built in 1458 by *Ōta Mochisuke*. In 1544, the castle became the property of the *Hōjō*. In 1590, *Ieyasu* bestowed it on *Kōriki Kiyonaga*. Afterwards it belonged to the *Aoyama daimyō* (1619-1623), to the *Abe* (1623-1681) to the *Itakura* (1681-1682), to the *Toda* (1682-1688), to the *Matsudaira* (1688-1697), to the *Ogasawara* (1697-1711), to the *Nagai* (1711-1756), and from 1756 to 1868, to the *Ōoka* (23,000 k.).

Iwaya-kaikyō, 岩屋海峽. The strait which separates *Awaji* from *Hondo*. It is also called *Akashi-kaikyō.*

Iwō-dake, 硫黄嶽. A volcano in *Kushiro* (*Hokkaidō*). It is also called *Atosa-nobori.*

Iwō-jima, 硫黄嶋. A small island, (12 Km. in circuit), 40 Km. from the southern point of *Ōsumi*. It is the *Kikai-ga-shima* (island of the demons) of the legend. In 1177, *Fujiwara Naritsune, Taira Yasu-yori,* and the bonze *Shunkwan* were exiled to this island by *Kiyomori,* and the bonze *Bunkwan* by *Hōjō Takatoki* in 1330. There was a Shintoist temple in the island, called *Kumano jinja* and administered by the *Nagahama* family. Since the end of the 16th century, the island belonged to the *Shimazu daimyō* of *Kagoshima* (*Satsuma*).

Iyo, 伊豫. One of the 6 provinces of *Nankaidō* in *Shikoku*. It comprises 12 districts which form the *Ehime-ken*. — Chinese name: *Yoshū.*

Iyo-nada, 伊豫灘. The *Iyo* sea, west of *Shikoku*.

Iyo-Shinnō, 伊豫親王 (+ 807). A son of the emperor *Kwammu* was nominated *Jibukyō* and *Nakatsukasa-kyō* in 796. After the death of his father, he was accused of plotting against his brother *Heijō-tennō*. Imprisoned with his mother in the temple of *Kawara-dera,* they took poison, thus putting an end to their lives.

Izanagi, 伊弉諾. ⎱ The creative couple of Japan, forming the 7th
Izanami, 伊弉冊. ⎰ generation of the heavenly spirits (*tenjin shichi-dai*). Having been ordered by the gods, their ancestors, to give shape to the matter created by them, they descended from heaven by the bridge *Ukibashi*. As they came near our future earth, *Izanagi* dipped the extremity of his spear (*hoko*) into the muddy liquid; and, when he withdrew it, some drops fell from its point, which having become solid, formed an island, *Onogoro-shima*. The couple descended on that island and built a dwelling (*Yahiro-dono*). Here *Izanagi* and *Izanami* con-

tracted marriage, and from their union were born the 8 great islands
(*Ō-ya-shima*): *Awachi no shima* (*Awaji*), *Iyo-no-futa-na no shima*
(*Shikoku*), *Tsukushi-shima* (*Kyūshū*), the twin islands *Oki* and *Sado*,
Iki-shima, Tsushima, and *Akitsu-shima* (*Hon-
do*); then 6 smaller islands: *Kibiko-shima,
Azuki-shima, Ō-shima, Hime-shima, Chika-
shima,* and *Futago-shima.* Afterwards, birth
was given to the gods of water, wind, trees,
mountains, rivers, roads, thunder, rain, etc.
Finally the god of fire, *Kagutsuchi*, was born;
but his birth having caused the death of his
mother, *Izanagi*, in his sorrow, cut off the
head of the child and soon afterwards repaired
to the region of the shadows (*yomotsu-kuni*)
in order to intreat his spouse to come back to
him. To dispel darkness, he lit the comb
(*yutsutsuma-gushi*) which held his hair; then,
having seen the already decomposed corpse
of *Izanami*, he fled in horror. Having returned
to the surface of the earth at *Awaki-ga-hara*
(*Hyūga*), he hastened to purify himself from
the stains contracted in the land of the dead.
From every vestment he took off and from
every part of his body which he washed in
the river, new gods were born, numbering 26.
From his left eye, *Ama-terasu-ō-mikami* was
born; from his right eye, *Tsukiyomi no kami;*
from his nose, *Takehaya-Susano-o no Mikoto:*
these are the last three gods. *Amaterasu*
became the goddess of the sun; *Tsukiyomi,*
the goddess of the moon; and *Susano-o,* the

IZANAGI AND IZANAMI.

god of the earth. Certain commentators are of opinion that *Takama-
ga-hara*, the domain of *Amaterasu*, is represented by the *Go-Kinai*
region; *Unabara*, the domain of *Tsukiyomi*, by the *Ryukyū* islands
and perhaps *Korea;* finally *Ame-ga-shita*, the portion of *Susano-o*, by
the occidental provinces of *San-yō* and *San-in.* — After this division of
his domains, *Izanagi* retired to *Hi-no-waka-miya.*

Izawa, 膽澤. An ancient fortress in *Rikuchū*, built in 802 by
Sakanoe no Tamuramaro to check the inroads of the *Ebisu.* It was
for a long time the residence of the *Chinjufu-shōgun.*

Izayoi-nikki, 十六夜日記. (Lit.: journal of 16 nights). In
1277, *Abutsu-ni*, widow of *Fujiwara Tameie*, went from *Kyōto* to *Kamakura* in order to obtain from the *Shikken Hōjō Tokimune* that the domain
of *Hosokawa* (*Harima*) be granted to her son *Tamesuke.* The *Izayoi-
nikki* is the picturesque description of this journey.

Izayoi no ki, 十六夜記. A celebrated literary work containing
the relation of a journey from *Kyōto* to *Kamakura* in 1277 by *Abutsu*,
the widow of *Fujiwara Sadaie.*

Izu, 伊豆. One of the 15 provinces of *Tōkaidō :* it was separated from *Suruga* in 681, and comprises 2 districts which belong to the *Shizuoka-ken.* — Chinese name: *Zushū.*

Izu-ga-hara, 嚴原. The principal town of *Tsushima.* Its former name was *Fuchū.*

Izu no shichi-tō, 伊豆七嶋. The seven islands of *Izu: Ō-shima, Toshima, Nii-jima, Shikine-jima, Kōzu-shima, Miyake-jima,* and *Mikura-jima.* — Administratively they belong to the *Tōkyō-fu.*

Izumi, 和泉. One of the 5 provinces of *Kinai,* separated from *Kawachi* in 716. It comprises 2 districts belonging to the *Ōsaka-fu.* — Chinese name: *Senshū.*

Izumi, 泉. A place in *Iwaki,* which was the residence of the *daimyō Niwa* (1619-1628), *Naitō* (1628-1702), *Itakura* (1702-1746), and *Honda* (1746-1868). — (20,000 k.).

Izumi Chikahira, 泉親平. A *daimyō* of *Shinano* and a relative of the *Minamoto,* was in the service of the *Shōgun Yoriie* (1199-1204). Wishing to raise *Senju-maru,* the third son of *Yoriie,* to the shōgunate, he revolted against the *Hōjō,* deputed the bonze *Annen* to all the provinces to recruit adherents to his cause; but *Chiba Shigetane* revealed the plot to *Hōjō Yoshitoki.* An army was despatched against *Chikahira,* who was defeated and killed (1213). — *Chikahira* was renowned for his physical strength, and is compared to *Asahina Yoshihide,* his contemporary.

Izumi-gawa, 泉川. A river (79 Km.) in *Kazusa.* It is also called *Ōtaki-gawa.*

Izumi-nada, 和泉灘. Another name of the *Ōsaka* gulf.

Izumi Saburō, 泉三郎 (+ 1189). Name by which *Fujiwara Tadahira,* 3rd son of *Hidehira,* is usually designated. He is the only one of *Hidehira's* children, who, mindful of the last words of his father, remained faithful to *Minamoto Yoshitsune* and died with him.

Izumi-Shikibu, 和泉式部. A celebrated poetess of the 11th century, was a daughter of *Ōe Koretoki.* She married *Tachibana Michisada, Izumi no kami,* and had a daughter, poetess like herself, known by the name of *Ko-Shikibu. Izumi Shikibu* was called to the Court by *Michinaga,* became lady in waiting of the empress *Jōtō-mon-in* and was remarried to *Fujiwara Yasumasa.*

IZUMI SHIKIBU.

Izumo, 出雲. One of the 8 provinces of *San-in-dō* It comprises 6 districts which belong to the *Shimane-ken.* — Chinese name: *Unshū.*

Izumo Hirosada, 出雲廣貞. A celebrated physician in the reign of the emperors *Kwammu* and *Heijō.* In 808, he published a medical work of 100 volumes.

Izumo no kuni no miyatsuko, 出雲國御臣. Title borne during many centuries by the descendants of *Ama no Hohi no Mikoto,* who were, by right of inheritance, superiors of the large Shintoist temple of *Izumo.*

Izumo no ō-yashiro, 出雲大社. A great Shintoist temple in *Izumo*, dedicated to *Ōkuninushi no kami*. Its chiefs were the two families *Senge* and *Kitajima*, descended from the ancient *Kuni no miyatsuko*, now Barons. — The temple is also called *Kizuki no ō-yashiro*.

Izushi, 出石. A castle in *Tajima*, built in 1574 by *Yamana Suketoyo Hideyoshi* took it in 1580 and gave it to his brother *Hidenaga*, afterwards to *Maeno Nagayasu* (1582). Later it belonged to be *daimyō Koide* (1595-1696), *Matsudaira* (1697-1706); and from 1706 to 1868, to the *Sengoku daimyō* (30,000 k.).

J

Jakushū, 若州. The Chinese name of the province of *Wakasa*.

Ji-an, 治安. *Nengō :* 1021-1023. — Also *Chi-an.*

Jibu-shō, 治部省. One of the eight executive departments created by the *Taikwa* Reform (649). The administrator of this department had charge of the genealogies, successions, marriage and funeral rites, and public mourning, of theaters and music, of the imperial tombs, the reception of foreigners, etc. — The principal officials below the Minister (*Jibu-kyō*) were : 2 *suke* 輔, 2 *jō* 丞, 4 *sakwan* 錄, 10 *shisei*. — The *Gagaku-ryō* and the *Gemba-ryō* were dependencies of this department, which was at first called *Osamuru-tsukasa.*

Jie-Daishi, 慈慧大師. — See *Ryōgen.*

Jigen-Daishi, 慈眼大師. — See *Tenkai.*

Jijō, 治承. *Nengō :* 1177-1180.

Jikaku-Daishi, 慈覺大師 (794-864). A celebrated bonze of the *Tendai* sect. He was born in *Shimotsuke* of the *Mibu* family, and entered the *Hiei-zan* monastery, where he was the pupil of the famous *Saichō* (*Dengyō-Daishi*). In 838, he accompanied the embassy of *Fujiwara Tsunetsugu* to China. He remained for 9 years in that country, visiting the most renowned Buddhist temples and copying many religious works. After his return to Japan, he published the results of his researches in 21 works numbering 559 volumes. In 854, he was made chief of the *Tendai* sect (*Tendai-zasu*). Ten years later, he died in *Kyōto.* *Jikaku-Daishi* is a posthumous title ; during his life-time, he was called *Ennin.*

Jikifu, 食封. Formerly lands granted to princes and nobles of high rank, who personally collected the revenues for their subsistence. The revenues of the imperial princes were called *hompu* 品封 ; those of the nobles, *ifu* 位封, those granted for some great deed, *kōfu* 功封.

Jikisan, 直參. Formerly direct vassals, in opposition to *baishin*, indirect vassals.

Jikken-shi, 實撿使. — See *Kamakura-bakufu-shoshi.*

Jikoban, 平埔蕃. Half-civilized aborigines of the island of Formosa, half Chinese, half savage. In their dialect, they call themselves *Pepohoan.*

Jikōji, 慈光寺. A *kuge* family descended from the *Uda-Genji.* — Now Viscount.

Jikoku, 持國. One of the *Shi-tennō* (4 heavenly kings), that watches over the East (Buddh.).

Jikuan, ヂクアン. A Christian of *Anam*, who accompanied the last Jesuit missionaries that came to Japan (1644). He was imprisoned with them in the *Kirishitan-yashiki* (*Edo*), where he died in 1700 at the age of 78. He was buried in the *Muryō-in* temple.

Jimmu-tennō, 神武天皇. The first Emperor of Japan (660-585 B.C.) and the founder of the present reigning dynasty. His name was *Kamu-yamato-Iwarehiko no Mikoto*, and he was the 4th son of *Hiko-nagisatake-ugayafuki-aezu no Mikoto* and of *Tamayori-hime*. He was born in 711 B. C. and, from childhood, was distinguished for his intelligence and courage. When 45 years old, he started from mount *Takachiho (Hyūga)*, where his ancestors had been living for several generations, in order to undertake the conquest of the eastern province (667 B. C.). At *Usa (Buzen)*, *Usatsu-hiko*, the chief of the district, made his submission. Thence *Jimmu* went to the seaport of *Yamaga (Chikuzen)* where he stayed for one year. Then crossing the strait, he landed in *Aki*, penetrated into the land of *Kibi*, where he finished his preparations. Afterwards guided by *Shiin-etsu-hiko* through the Inland Sea, he arrived at *Naniwa no misaki (Ama-ga-saki)* and ascended the *Yodo-gawa* as far as the present village *Kusaka (Kawachi)*, where he landed. Taking a southern direction, he marched towards *Yamato*, where he met *Nagasune-hiko*, the chief of the country. *Jimmu* was defeated. During the battle *Itsuse no Mikoto*, the elder brother of

JIMMU-TENNŌ.

Jimmu, was dangerously wounded and died soon afterwards. Going back, *Jimmu* embarked at *O-no-minato (Izumi)* and went towards *Kii*: having landed at the seaport of *Arasaka*, he marched towards *Yoshino*, being guided by *Michi no Omi* and *Ōkume*. On his way, he easily defeated several chiefs of small tribes: *Nishiki-tobe, E-ukashi, Yaso-takeru, Eshiki;* next he again encountered *Nagasune-hiko*, whom he called upon to surrender. *Nagasune-hiko* refused and prepared for battle, when he was assassinated by his nephew *Umashimate*, who agreed to become the vassal of the emperor. The neighbouring tribes submitted likewise, and *Jimmu* was master of the whole of *Yamato*. He then selected the plateau of *Kashiwabara* at the foot of mount *Unebi*, as a site for the erection of his palace and made that place the capital of the empire. There he was solemnly enthroned on the 11th of February (The first day of the first lunar month) of the year 660 before the Christian era, and that date has been adopted as the beginning of the Japanese era (*kigen*). The following year, the Emperor distributed rewards to all those that had helped him in his conquest, and applied himself to organize his dominions. The three imperial emblems were kept in the palace: *Ame no Taneko* (the ancestor of the *Fujiwara*) and *Ame no Tomi* (the ancestor of the *Imube*) received charge of the cult and ceremonies; *Umashimate*, a son of *Nigihayabi* (the ancestor of the *Monobe*) and *Ōkume* (the ancestor for the *Kume*) were intrusted with the guard of the palace. Next he created the offices of *kunitzuko* (governors of provinces) and *agata-nushi* (chiefs of districts), as well as the corporations of *yukibe* (soldiers), *kumebe* (farmers), *hataoribe* (weavers), etc. According to the *Nihon-ki*, he died at the age of 127; and according to the *Koji-ki*, at the age of 137. He was buried on mount *Unebi*. The present critical history, on the strength of Chinese and Korean documents, places the existence of the first Japanese Emperor, at a date 6 centuries later: he would then have been born towards the year 62 or 63 B. C. and died in the year 1 before the Christian era.

ENTHRONEMENT OF JIMMU-TENNŌ.

Jimoku, 除目. The promotion of officials. In 676, the custom was established to have two promotions a year: in spring, for officials of the provinces; in autumn, for those of the capital. These promotions were called *haru no jimoku* and *aki no jimoku,* or *ge-kwan* and *kyōkwan no jimoku*. The promotion made during the annual feast of the *Kamo* temple, was called *matsuri no ji-moku*. When the promotions took place at another time, they were generally known by the name *rinji no jimoku*. There were also other promotions, such as, the *kokushi-jimoku*, the *gūji-jimoku* the *ko-jimoku* the *tsukasa-meshi no jimoku*, the *agata-meshi no jimoku*, etc.

Jimon, 寺門. A branch of the *Tendai* sect, founded in 858 by the bonze *Enchin* (*Chishō-Daishi*). Its seat is at the *Mii-dera* (*Ōmi*)

Jimvō-in, 持明院. A *kuge* family descended from *Fujiwara Yorimune* (993-1065). — Now Viscount.

Jimyō-in, 持明院. Formerly a residence situated in *Kyōto* and belonging to a branch of the *Fujiwara* family. It was so called on account of a small temple which it contained. At the end of the twelfth century, it was the residence of *Motoie*, who married his daughter to *Morisada-shinnō*, a son of the emperor *Takakura*. The prince came to reside there, and was known by the name of *Jimyō-in no miya*. After the *Shōkyū* war (1221), the *Hōjō* raised to the throne *Go-Horikawa*, a son of *Morisada* who received the title of *Dajō-tennō*, although he had never reigned. When *Go-Fukakusa* abdicated in favor of his brother *Kameyama* (1259), he retired to the *Jimyō-in* and his descendants, *Fushimi*, *Go-Fushimi*, etc. were known by the name of *Jimyō-in-tō*, while the descendants of *Kameyama* were called *Daikoku-ji-tō*. — The *Jimyō-in* was destroyed by fire in 1350.

Jimyō-in hō-ō, 持明院法皇. The name given to the emperor *Fushimi* after his abdication (1298).

Jimyō-in-tō, 持明院統. The name given to the descendants of the emperors *Go-Fukakusa* and *Fushimi*, who had retired to the *Jimyō-in*.

Jindai, 神代. (Lit.: the age of the gods). The period anterior to the advent of *Jimmu-tennō*. It is also called *taiko*, remote antiquity.

Jingi-kwan, 神祇官. The department of the Shintoist cult since the *Taikwa* reform (645). It had charge of the ceremonies, the superintendence of the Shintoist priests, etc. The principal officials were: 1 *kami* 伯, 2 *suke* 副, 2 *sakwan* 史, 30 *kamube* 神部, 20 *urabe* 卜部, 30 *tsukaebe* 使部. — The *Jingikwan* was primitively called *Kamitsukasa*.

Jingi-kwan no hasshin, 神祇官八神. 8 *Shintō* gods whose feasts were solemnly celebrated at the *Jingi-kwan*; they were: *Kami-musubi*, *Takami-musubi*, *Tamatsume-musubi*, *Iku-musubi*, *Taru-musubi*, *Ō-mi-yama*, *Miketsu*, and *Kotoshiro-nushi*.

Jingo-keiun, 神護景雲. *Nengō*: 767-769.

Jingō-kōgō, 神功皇后 (170-269). Was first known as *Okinaga-tarashi hime*, and was a daughter of *Okinaga no Sukune*, a grandson of the emperor *Kaikwa*. She married *Chūai-tennō*. The *Kumaso* having revolted in *Tsukushi*, the emperor went in person to subdue them. It was then revealed to the empress by the gods that, before punishing the *Kumaso*, the emperor should make the conquest of *Shinra* (Korea), that had incited the revolt. *Chūai* however did not consent to such a perilous expedition, and died soon afterwards (200). *Jingō*, then pregnant, put a stone in her sash to delay the birth of the child, and hastening the preparations, she carried war into Korea. On her passage to Korea, the god *Sumiyoshi* served her as pilot. A storm having arisen, big fishes came to the surface of the sea in order to support the boats

JINGŌ KŌGŌ.

and prevent them from foundering. The king of *Shinra* promptly submitted and promised to send 80 boats laden with gold, silver, cloth, etc. every year as a tribute. The kings of *Kōrai* and *Hakusai*, likewise acknowledged the suzerainty of Japan, and thus was effected the conquest of the *San-kan*. *Jingō* left her minister *Yada no Sukune* in Korea and returned to Japan, where she gave birth to a son that became the emperor *Ōjin*. She refused to ascend the throne and was content with the regency, which she exercised for 69 years, until her death. Soon after her return, the two princes *Kagosaka-Ō* and *Oshikuma-Ō*, sons of a concubine of *Chūai*, revolted in *Yamato*, claiming the succession of the throne by right of primogeniture. *Jingō* sent her famous general *Takeshiuchi no Sukune* against them, who put them to death. After that, the tranquillity of the regent was no more disturbed. She died 100 years old and was honored after her death by the name of *Kashi-dai-myōjin*. According to modern critics the Korean expedition, under *Jingō-Kōgō*, took place in the year 346 and not in the year 200, and the empress died towards the year 380.

Jingūji, 神宮寺. At the beginning of the 8th century, when the bonzes *Gyōgi, Ryōben,* etc. spread the *Ryōbu-shintō* throughout the land, *Fujiwara Muchimaro* built the first temple in which the ceremonies and prayers of both cults (Buddhist and Shintoist), were performed. The temple was called *Jingūji (miya-tera),* and its practices spread rapidly over the land. It was also at that epoch that, in imitation of the Buddhist custom, the Shintoist temples were classified into great (*taisha*) intermediate (*chūsha*), and small (*shōsha*) temples.

Jingū-kyō, 神宮敎. Formerly a branch of Shintoism. In 1900, it was officially suppressed as religious sect.

Jinjitsu, 人日. A popular festival (*sekku*) celebrated on the 1st day of the 1st month of the year.

Jinki, 神龜. *Nengō*: 724-728.

Jinkōshōtō-ki, 神皇正統記. (Lit.: History of the true succession of the divine emperors). A work published in 1339 by *Kitabatake Chikafusa*: it contains 6 volumes, and includes a period of history from the era of the gods to the year 1335. It supports the legitimacy of the southern dynasty.

Jin no za, 陣座. The place, in the imperial palace, reserved for the body-guard of the emperor. The guard on the left (*Sakon-e*) was placed near the gate, called *Nikkwa-mon;* the guard on the right (*Ukon-e*), near the gate called *Gekkwa-mon*.

Jinsen, 仁川. The Japanese name of the sea-port of *Chemulpo* (Korea), where Japan obtained a concession in 1883.

Jinshin no ran, 壬申亂. The civil war that occupied the short reign of the emperor *Kōbun* and was brought to a close by the triumph of his uncle *Temmu*. It took its name from the year of the sexagesimal cycle during which it happened (672).

Jinzū-gawa, 神通川. A river (204 Km.) which has its source in *Hida*, receives the *Kumano-gawa* and the *Ida-gawa*, flows through *Takayama, Furukawa, Toyama*, and empties itself into the Sea of Japan. It is also called *Ari-iso-gawa*.

Jippensha Ikku, 十返舍一九 (1775-1831). Whose true name was *Shigeta Teiichi*. He was an official of the *Bakufu* at *Sumpu* (*Shizuoka*).

Having been replaced by his brother, he came to *Edo* in 1794 and applied himself to write *jōruri* and comical novels. His best known work is the *Hizakurige* a humorous story of two queer fellows travelling in divers provinces.

Jireki, 治 暦.   *Nengō :* 1065-1068.

Jisetsu-Daishi, 慈 覺 大 師. — See *Shinjō.*

Jisha-bugyō, 寺 社 奉 行. The official who, under the *Kamakura* shōgunate, had charge of things concerning the Buddhist and Shintoist priests, the temples and their properties, the ceremonies, etc. This title was created in 1293, and *Hōjō Tokitsura* was the first who received it. — The function was reestablished by the *Tokugawa* in 1613. In 1635, three *jisha-bugyō* were nominated : they performed their office alternately, each during one month.

Jishi, 寺 司. The superintendent of a Buddhist temple. Prince *Shōtoku-taishi*, having finished the construction of the *Hōkō-ji* temple in 596, placed the bonze *Zentokushin*, a son of *Soga no Umako* at its head, with the title of *Hōkō-jishi*. This custom was gradually applied to all the great temples.

Jishō, 治 承.   *Nengō :* 1177-1180.

Ji-shū, 時 宗. A Buddhist sect founded in 1275 by the bonze *Ippen.* It now has 509 temples throughout Japan. The sect gradually separated into 13 branches. Its seat is at *Fujisawa* (*Sagami*).

Ji-shū jū-san ha, 時 宗 十 三 派. The 13 branches of the *Ji-shū* sect :

1.	**Honzan**	(princ. seat):	the *Seijōkō-ji* temple, at *Fujisawa* (*Sagami*).
2.	**Yūkō-ha**	,,	the *Kinkō-ji* temple, at *Kyōto, Shichijo.*
3.	**Ikkō-ji**	,,	the *Renge-ji* temple, at *Baba* (*Ōmi*).
4.	**Okutani-ha**	,,	the *Hongwan-ji* temple, at *Okutani* (*Iyo*) (Extinct)
5.	**Taima-ha**	,,	the *Muryōkō-ji* temple, at *Taima* (*Sagami*).
6.	**Shijō-ha**	,,	the *Kinren-ji* temple, at *Kyōto, Shijō.*
7.	**Rokujō-ha**	,,	the *Kwankikō-ji* temple, at *Kyōto, Rokujō.* ,,
8.	**Kai-i-ha**	,,	the *Shinzenkō-ji* temple, at *Ebishima* (*Hitachi*). ,,
9.	**Reizan-ha**	,,	the *Shōhō-ji* temple, at *Kyōto, Reizan.*
10.	**Kōkua-ha**	,,	the *Sōrin-ji* temple, at *Kyōto, Higashi-yama.*
11.	**Ichiya-ha**	,,	the *Kinkō-ji* temple, at *Kyōto, Gojō.* ,,
12.	**Tendō-ha**	,,	the *Bukkō-ji* temple, at *Tendō* (*Dewa*).
13.	**Mikagedō-ha**	,,	the *Shinzenkō-ji* temple, at *Kyōto, Gojō.* ,,

Jitō, 地 頭. Formerly the administrators of the domains of high court officials. This title existed before the *Kamakura* Shōgunate, and those invested with it had charge of collecting the taxes. In 1186, *Yoritomo* placed the *shugo* at the head of provinces and the *jitō* at the head of the *shō-en* (domains taken from the jurisdiction of the *shugo*). After the *Shōkyū* war (1221), bonzes and even women received this title, which became hereditary. — Under the *Ashikaga* shōgunate, the domains bestowed on nobles were called *ryōchi*, and their possessors, *ryōshu*. During the long civil wars of the 15th and 16th centuries, many *ryōshu* lost their possessions, which passed over to *samurai* vassals of the *shugo*, and the *jitō* were replaced by simple *hatamoto* ; this was continued under the *Tokugawa.*

Jitō-dai, 地頭代. An official replacing the *jitō*. The latter usually resided at the capital, and the *jitō-dai* replaced him in the administration of his domains, just as the *kokushi* was replaced by the *mokudai*, and the *shugo* by the *shugo-dai*. The *jitō-dai* were also called *gandai*, *daikwan*.

Jitō-tennō, 持統天皇. The empress (41) that reigned from 687 to 696. She was *Hironu hime*, or *Uno no Sasara*, a daughter of the emperor *Tenchi*, the consort of *Temmu*, and succeeded the latter at the age of 42. She signalized her reign by important administrative reforms, favored the development of agriculture, struck the first silver coin, etc. After a reign of 11 years, she abdicated in favor of her nephew *Mommu* and was the first to receive the title of *Dajō-tennō*, and the first too to be cremated after her death in 701.

JITŌ-TENNŌ.

Jitsue, 實慧. — See *Dōkō-Daishi*.

Jizō, 地藏, The god of mercy (Buddhist), patron of travellers, of children, and of pregnant wives. He is represented by the image of a bonze with shaved head, holding a gem in one hand, and a staff (*shakujō*) in the other, at the top of which metal rings are attached.

Jizō-ga-take, 地藏嶽. A mountain (2650 m.) in the western region of *Kai*.

Jizō-saki, 地藏崎. A cape north-east of *Izumo*.

Jizō-saki, 地藏崎. A cape east of *Bungo*.

Jō, 城. An ancient *daimyō* family of *Echigo*, descended from *Taira Yoshikane*.

—— **Sukenaga**, 資永. Was defeated and killed by *Kiso Yoshinaka* in 1182.

—— **Nagamochi**, 長茂. A brother of *Sukenaga*. Having been defeated with him, he fled into *Aizu*; afterwards, he was nominated *Echigo no kami*, and took part in the expedition of *Yoritomo* against *Fujiwara Yasuhira* (1189). After the death of *Yoritomo*, he revolted against the *Hōjō*, but was defeated and killed in 1201.

—— **Sukemori**, 資盛. Tried to continue the struggle after the death of his father, but was likewise defeated by *Sasaki Moritsuna*, and with him the family became extinct (1202).

Jō-an, 承安. *Nengō*: 1171-1174. — It is also called *Shō-an*.

Jōchō, 定朝. A celebrated sculptor of the 11th century and bonze like his father *Kōshō*. He was charged by *Fujiwara Michinaga*, to carve the statue of *Buddha* for the *Hōshō-ji* temple, which the latter was erecting (1022). As a reward, *Jōchō* received the title of *Hōkyō*. He is the ancestor of a long line of sculptors, the most celebrated of whom is *Unkei*. They are generally known by the name of *Nara-horimonoya* (sculptors of *Nara*).

Jōdai, 城代. Anciently the military governor of a castle in the absence of the lord. Under the *Tokugawa*, the castles of *Ōsaka*, *Fushimi*, etc. belonging to the *Bakufu*, were guarded by a *jōdai*..

Jōdo-shinshū, 浄土眞宗 (Lit.: the true *Jōdo* sect). Also called *Ikkō-shū*, or *Monto-shū*, is a Buddhist sect founded by *Shinran-shōnin* in 1224. It teaches that man cannot be saved by his works or prayers, but only by the mercy of *Amida*. It is the Buddhist Protestantism of Japan. Its temples are commonly called *Hongwan-ji* or *Monzeki*, and are the largest and most beautiful temples in Japan. The *Jōdo-shinshū*, or, by abbreviation, the *Shin-shū*, has presently 19,608 temples and 12,656,800 followers: it is the most prosperous sect. It is divided into about 10 branches.

Jōdo-shinshū jū-ha, 浄土眞宗十派. The 10 branches of the *Shinshū* sect:

1.	**Hongwanji-ha**	—Seat: *Kyōto, Horikawa-Hongwan-ji*;	founder,	*Shinran* (1224).
2.	**Ōtani-ha**	— „ *Kyōto, Shichijō-Hongwan-ji*;	„	*Kōju* (1602).
3.	**Takada-ha**	— „ *Isshinden (Ise), Senshū-ji*;	„	*Shimbutsu* (1226).
4.	**Bukkōji-ha**	— „ *Kyōto, Bukkō-ji*;	„	*Ryōgen* (14th cent.).
5.	**Kōshōji-ha**	— „ *Kyōto, Kōshō-ji*;	„	*Renkyō* (14th cent.).
6.	**Kibe-ha**	— „ *Kibe (Ōmi) Kinshoku-ji*;	„	*Shōshin* (13th cent.).
7.	**Senshōji-ha**	— „ *Echizen, Senshō-ji*;	„	*Jōdō* (1280).
8.	**Chōseiji-ha**	— „ *Echizen, Chōsei-ji*;	„	*Dōshō* (14th cent.).
9.	**Jōshōji-ha**	— „ *Echizen, Jōshō-ji*;	„	*Jogaku* (14th cent.).
10.	**Gōshōji-ha**	— „ *Echizen, Gōshō-ji*;	„	*Shōsen* (14th cent.).

Jōdo-shū, 浄土宗 (Lit.: sect of the pure earth). A Buddhist sect founded in 1174 by the bonze *Genkū (Enkō-Daishi)*: at present it has 8,322 temples, 2,586,000 followers in Japan, and is divided into about 5 branches.

Jōdo-shū-go-ha, 浄土宗五派. The 5 branches of the *Jōdo-shū* sect; the two first ones are subdivided in the following:

1.	**Chinzei** (*Shōkō-Shōnin*)	Shirahata-ha	—Seat: *Kyōto, Kōmyō-ji*;	founder,	*Jaku-ei*.
		Fujita-ha	— „ *Kyōto, Muryō-ji*;	„	*Ji-a*.
		Nakoshi-ha	— „ *Kōzuke, Zendō-ji*;	„	*Sonkwan*.
		Obata-ha	— „ *Yamashiro, Sensho-ji*;	„	*Ryōkū*.
		Sanjō-ha	— „ *Mikawa, Goshin-ji*;	„	*Dōkō*.
		Ichijō-ha	— „ *Yamashiro, Kōmyo-in*;	„	*Rei-a*.
2.	**Seizan** (*Shōkū-Shōnin*)	Nishidani-ha	—Seat: *Kyōto Kōmyō-ji*;	founder,	*Jō-on*.
		Fukakusa-ha	— „ *Kyōto Shinsō-in*;	„	*Enkū*.
		Higashi-yama-ha	— „ *Kyōto, Amida-in*;	„	*Kwanshō*.
		Saga-ha	— „ *Kyōto, Jō-Kongō-in*;	„	*Dōkwan*.
3.	**Chōraku-ji**	—Seat: *Chōraku-ji*; founder, *Ryūkwan Risshi*.			
4.	**Kuhon-ji**	— „ *Kuhon-ji*; „ *Kakumyō-Shōnin (Chōsei)*.			
5.	**Ichinengi**	— „ *Ichinengi*; „ *Jōkaku-Shōnin (Gyōsei)*.			

Jōe, 定慧 (+ 714). The eldest son of *Fujiwara Kamatari*, became bonze and went to China (669) to study the Buddhist doctrine. He remained there for 10 years, and, after his return, established himself on mount *Tamu no mine* (*Yamato*).

Jōei, 貞永. *Nengō*: 1232. — It is also called *Tei-ei*.

Jōei shikimoku, 貞定式目. A sort of code of the *samurai*, published in 1232 by *Miyoshi Yoshitsura*, by order of *Hōjō Yasutoki*.

It is divided into 51 chapters, and contains all the laws enacted since the time of *Yoritomo*.

Jofuku, 除福. A Chinese physician who came to Japan in 221 B. C. and established relations between the two countries. — According to a Chinese legend, *Jofuku* was sent by the emperor *Shikō* (*Shi-Houang*) to search for the elixir of life, and discovered *Hōrai-zan* (Japan), which he colonized with 300 young men and 300 young women. Such was the origin of the Japanese nation. — The Japanese tradition simply mentions that he arrived with his fellow countryman *Zokuden*, became a Japanese, and transmitted the name of *Shin* to his descendants. It is said that *Jofuku* introduced the books of Confucious into Japan. He died on mount *Fuji* and has a tomb in his honor at *Kumano* (*Kii*). For a long time, Chinese coins (*hanryō*) brought to Japan by *Jofuku*, have been discovered in *Kumano*.

Jōgen, 貞元. *Nengō*: 976-977. — Also called *Teigen*.

Jōgen, 承元. *Nengō*: 1207-1210. — Also called *Shōgen*.

Jōgū-taishi, 上宮太子. Another name of *Shōtoku-taishi*.

Jōgwan, 貞観. *Nengō*: 859-876. — Also called *Jōkwan*.

Jōhei, 承平. *Nengō*: 931-937. — Also called *Shōhyō*.

Jo-hikeshi-yaku, 定火消役. A title created in 1658 and given to 4 officials having charge of taking proper measures in case of fires, earthquakes, etc.

Jōhō, 承保. *Nengō*: 1074-1076. — Also *Shōhō*.

Jōi, 讓位. The abdication of the imperial dignity. The first emperor that abdicated was *Keitai* (531); *Kōgyoku* abdicated in 644, *Jitō* in 696. Gradually this practice became customary. The ceremonies concerning the abdication and the transmission (*jūzen*) of the imperial power were regulated by the emperor *Seiwa* in 871. At the appointed day, the Court assembled at the *Shishinden*, where the ceremony of the *Setsu-e* was first performed; next the sacred sword and the precious stone were solemnly remitted to the new emperor. If the elected emperor was not a son of his predecessor, custom required that he should first present a written document declining an honor of which he judged himself unworthy. At the time of the abdication of an emperor, the barriers of *Ise*, *Ōmi* and *Mino* were carefully guarded. — (See *Senso*).

Jōji, 貞治. *Nengō* of the Northern dynasty: 1362-1367.

Jōjitsu-shū, 成實宗. A Buddhist sect introduced into Japan in 625 by the Korean bonze *Ekwan*. In India and China, *Jōjitsu* was but a branch of *Sanron*, but in Japan, where it has been extinct a long time since, it formed an independent sect.

Jōkaku, 定覺. A sculptor of the 13th century and brother of the celebrated *Unkei*.

Jōko, 上古. A period of Japanese history from the reign of *Jimmu* to that of *Kōgyoku* (660 B. C. — 644 A. D.).

Jōkō, 上皇. The title given to an emperor after his abdication. When *Junwa* ascended the throne (824), there were for the first time two *Jōkō*, *Heijō* and *Saga*. In the reign of the *Go-Nijō* (1302), there were even five. They were distinguished from one another by the titles of *Ichi-in, Hon-in, Chū-in, Shin-in,* etc. — See *Dajō-tennō.*

Jōkō-jūnin, 成功重任. At the time of the power of the *Fuji-wara,* who multiplied the *shō-en* throughout the land, the Court, to obtain money, resorted to the sale of offices. The candidates were obliged to present their title (*jōkō*) to the office in addition to the sum to be paid, and, at the expiration of their term, they were reinstated by means of further payment. The emperor *Go-Sanjō* (1070) tried to reform such abuses, but it was in vain: they were continued and increased after the accession of *Yoritomo* to the shōgunate (1192).

Jōkyō, 貞享. *Nengō:* 1684-1687. — Also *Teikyō.*

Jomei-tennō, 舒明天皇. The 34th Emperor of Japan (629-641), was *Okinaga-tarashi-hi-hironuka no mikoto, Tamura no Ōji,* a grandson of the emperor *Bitatsu* and son of *Osaka-hikobito, Ōe no Ōji.* He succeeded his grandaunt *Suiko* at the age of 36, owing to the influence of *Soga no Emishi.* Under his reign, a revolt of the *Ebisu* was suppressed by *Kamitsukenu Katana* (637).

Jō-men-dori, 定免取. In order to fix the amount of taxes to be paid under the *Tokugawa* by the land-proprietors, a statement was made of the produce of the pieces of ground for 5, 6 or 10 years; the average thereof served as a basis to determine the taxes, and there was no hope for dispensation or diminution on account of tempests, inundations, etc.

Jōmi, 上巳. A popular festival (*sekku*) celebrated on the 3rd day of the 3d month, and commonly called *hiina-matsuri* (festival of the dolls). A Shintoist ceremony of purification (*harai*) was formerly performed on that day: a paper doll was obtained from a soothsayer, which, after certain prayers, was charged with all the faults and stains of the person that had received it, it was then thrown into the river, and the person was purified and sheltered from evil. Nowadays the paper dolls have been replaced by others of wax, wood, etc.; they are dressed as richly as possible, because they are supposed to represent the emperor and the empress (*dairi-bina*), and are exposed in the house.

Jō-ō, 貞應. *Nengō:* 1222-1223. — Also *Tei-ō.*

Jō-ō, 承應. *Nengō:* 1652-1654. — Also *Shō-ō.*

Jōreki, 承曆. *Nengō:* 1077-1080. — Also *Shōryaku.*

Jōruri, 淨瑠璃. Dramatic recital with music, in which the great achievements of ancient heroes were celebrated. Its origin runs as far back as the 13th century. It is said that *Hamuto Tokinaga,* after having composed the *Heike-monogatari,* taught a blind bonze to recite it whilst accompanying himself on the *biwa*: hence the name *biwa-hoshi.* The most celebrated composer of *jōruri* is a certain *Chikamatsu-Mon-zaemon* (1653-1724.)

Josetsu, 如雪. A celebrated painter, born in China. He came to Japan in 1370, became a bonze at the *Shōkoku-ji* temple, where he founded a school of painting according to Chinese principles. *Sesshū, Shūbun,* and *Kanō Masanobu* were his pupils.

Jōshō-ji, 證誠寺. A temple built in *Echizen* by the bonze *Jogaku* (13th century); it became later on the seat of a branch of the *Shinshū* sect.

Jōshū, 城州 . The Chinese name of the province of *Yamashiro*.

Jōshū, 常州 . The Chinese name of the province of *Hitachi*.

Jōshū, 上州 . The Chinese name of the province of *Kōzuke*.

Jōtoku, 承德 . *Nengō:* 1097-1098. — Also *Shōtoku*.

Jōtō-mon-in, 上東門院 . — See *Fujiwara Aki-ko*.

Jōwa, 承和 . *Nengō:* 834-847. — Also *Shōwa*.

Judō, 儒道 . } Doctrine or teaching of Confucius, Confucianism. —

Jukyō, 儒教 . } Confucius (Jap : *Kōshi*, 551-479 B.C.), as it is well known, did not pretend to found a religion; he laid down a code of morals based on filial piety and submission to authority. This system, developed and explained, has become a collection of maxims relating to all the acts of life, complicating them by a minute, affected ceremonial. Confucianism was introduced into Japan by *Wani* and *Ajiki* in 285, and, on account of its many points of resemblance with Shintoism, then alone practised, was received without difficulty. But after the introduction of Buddhism, it lost favor, and did not rise again until the 17th century, when *Ieyasu*, for the first time, caused the Chinese classics bo be printed in Japan. From that time, it was taught by such masters as *Fujiwara Seikwa, Hayashi Dōshun, Itō Jinsai*, etc., became the code of the *samurai*, and had a deep influence on Japanese society during the *Tokugawa* shōgunate. After the Restoration, when the European system of public education was adopted, Confucianism was again abandoned, as well as the Chinese classics which had been the base of education for 250 years. But it cannot be denied that many ideas at present still in favor among the higher classes, have a Confucianist origin, and it is perhaps desirable that they may not disappear too soon from a society of which they form one of the few remaining elements of stability.

Ju-ei, 壽永 . *Nengō:* 1182-1183.

Jukō, 珠光 (1422-1502). Was at first bonze in the *Shōmyō-ji* temple (*Kawachi*) ; but on account of his negligence in the discharge of his duties, he was dismissed, and then became a disciple of the famous *Ikkyū*. Being continually inclined to sleep, he used to drink tea to keep himself awake: he offered tea to visitors, and complicated its preparation with certain ceremonies which became greatly in vogue. The *Shōgun Yoshimasa* had him secularized, gave him a house in the *Sanjō* district (*Kyōto*) : it was the first school of the tea ceremony (*cha no yu*). *Jukō* is also called *Kyūshin-hōshi*.

Jūmonji-dake, 十文字嶽 . A mountain (2430 m) on the limits of *Musashi* and *Shinano*.

Jun-daijin, 准大臣 . Anciently an intermediate title between that of *Daijin* and that of *Dainagon*. It was created in 1005 by *Fujiwara Korechika*. *Gidō-sanshi* is another name for the same.

Jū-ni dōji, 十二童子 . The 12 retainers of the goddess *Kwannon*.

Junken-shi, 巡撿使 . — See *Kamakura-bakufu-shōshi*.

Jun-kunimochi-shū, 准國持衆 . The official immediately below the governor of a province (*kunimochi-shū*) during the *Ashikaga* shōgunate.

Junna-in, 淳和院. An ancient palace in *Kyōto*, the residence of the ex-emperor *Seiwa*, after whose death, in 881, it was converted into a school for young princes and the sons of *kuge* of high rank. At its head was a *bettō*. The title of *Junna-in-bettō* became honorific and, under the *Tokugawa*, was reserved to the *Shōgun*.

Junna-tennō, 淳和天皇. The 53rd Emperor of Japan (824-833), was prince *Ōtomo*, the 3rd son of *Kwammu*. He succeeded his brother *Saga* at the age of 38. After a reign of 10 years, he abdicated in favor of his brother *Nimmyō*.

Junnin-tennō, 淳仁天皇. The 47th Emperor of Japan (759-764), was prince *Ōi*, grandson of *Temmu* and son of *Toneri-shinnō*; he succeeded the empress *Kōken* at the age of 27. His minister, *Emi no Oshikatsu (Fujiwara Nakamaro)*, succeeded in having much influence over him and governed according to his own fancy. At the same time, the ex-empress *Kōken* allowed herself to be ruled by the bonze *Dōkyō*, who obtained from her every title and privilege he wished for. Soon the rivalry of the two men, equally ambitious and jealous of each other, became more and more acute. In 764, *Oshikatsu* raised an army and marched against *Dōkyō*: the latter resisted and his troops defeated the army of *Oshikatsu* in *Ōmi*. *Oshikatsu* was killed in the fight. Master of the situation, *Dōkyō* easily persuaded *Kōken* to reascend the throne: as to *Junnin*, he was banished to the island of *Awaji*, where he died the following year. Hence the name of *Awaji-haitei* by which he is known in history. His memory was rehabilitated in 1871 and he received the posthumous name of *Junnin*.

Jun no o-mari-bugyō, 旬御鞠奉行. During the *Kamakura* shōgunate, the opening of the tennis (*mari-hajime*) took place every year in the first month; after which the *kuge* and the *buke* played that game three times a month. A provost was chosen among them; he had charge of determining in advance the program of the exercises of the day: it was the *o-mari-bugyō*. *Hōjō Tokifusa* was the first to receive the title, in 1212.

Jun-san-gū, 准三宮. A title which guaranteed its possessor, the same revenue as that bestowed on any of the three empresses: the reigning empress, the dowager empress, and the archdowager empress. It could be given to princes and ministers. *Fujiwara Yoshifusa* was the first on whom it was bestowed, in 855. Later on, the title became merely honorific.

Junsatsu-shi, 巡察使. A title created in 694 and given to high officials in charge of inspecting the provinces, examining the administration of the governors, the condition of the people, the state of agriculture, the assistance given to old or sick, the abuses to be reformed, etc. This title, which was only temporary, disappeared from history towards 830.

Junshi, 殉死. Formerly at the death of a great personage, his servants were buried with him: it was the *junshi*. The emperor *Suinin*, on the advice of *Nomi no Sukune*, interdicted that practice (2 years B. C.). But the custom to commit suicide at the loss of one's master, was introduced as a sign of fidelity. In the 16th century, when a general or a *daimyō* died, many vassals put an end to their lives by *harakiri*. At the death of the *Shōgun Iemitsu* (1651), 5 great *daimyō* committed suicide in order not to survive him. It was only in 1668, that, by very severe ordinances, the *Shōgun Ietsuna* succeeded in suppressing that abuse.

Juntoku-tennō, 順徳天皇. The 84th Emperor of Japan (1211-1221), was Prince *Morinari*, the 6th son of *Go-Toba*. He succeeded his brother *Tsuchimikado*, when 14 years old. During his reign the shōgunal branch of the *Minamoto* became extinct by the assassination of *Sanetomo* (1219), and the authority of the *Hōjō* was consolidated. After a reign of 10 years, during which time the power was in the hands of the *Hōjō*, he abdicated in favor of his son *Kanenari* (*Chūkyō*), then only 3 years old. Having become *Dajō-tennō*, he supported his father when the latter tried to overthrow the powerful *Shikken* of *Kamakura*; but they failed in their plan: the imperial army was defeated, the young emperor deposed, and *Juntoku* exiled to the island of *Sado* (1221), where he lived yet 21 years. During his exile, he wrote a book (*Kimpi-misho*), in 3 volumes, in which he related with great detail the ceremonies and customs of the Imperial Palace. It was only in 1871 that his memory was rehabilitated and that he received the posthumous name of *Juntoku*.

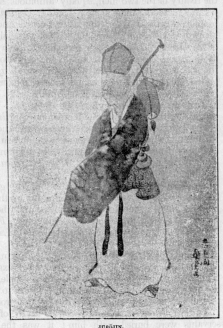

JURŌJIN.
BY OGATA KŌRIN.

Jūrakutei, 聚樂第 A palace built by *Hideyoshi* in *Kyōto* in 1586, in which he took up his residence the following year, and received the visit of the emperor *Go-Yōzei* and that of the ex-emperor *Ōgimachi*. When he transmitted the title of *Kwampaku* to his nephew *Hidetsugu*, he gave him the *Jūrakutei* also. After the death of *Hidetsugu* (1595), the palace was demolished and the remains were given to the *Nishi-Hongwan-ji* temple.

Jurōjin, 壽老人. One of the seven gods of luck: he is generally represented as an old man with a stag and a crane beside him as a sign of longevity.

Jū-san daishū, 十三代集. Thirteen collections of Japanese poems from the *Shin-chokusen* (1223), till the *Shinzoku-kokin-shū* (1438).

Jūsan-gata, 十三潟. A lake (26 Km. in circuit) in the N. W. of *Mutsu*; it receives the water of the *Iwaki-gawa*.

Jū-san meika, 十三名家. Anciently 13 families, the members of which cultivated literature, Confucianism, and, at the Court, performed the offices of *Benkwan, Dainagon*, and even that of *Daijin*. They enjoyed the privilege of wearing violet garments. They were: the *Karasumaru*, the *Yanagiwara*, the *Takeya*, the *Uramatsu*, the *Kanroji*, the *Hamuro*, the *Kwanjuji*, the *Madenokōji*, the *Seikanji*, the *Naka-mikado*, the *Bōjō*, the *Hino* and the *Hirohashi*.

Jusenshi, 鑄錢司. Anciently, officials having charge of minting money. *Ōyake Asomimaro* was the first that received the title in 694. The function was suppressed in the middle ages, the title alone remained.

Jutō-ei, 授刀衛. A body of the imperial guard created in 759; not long afterwards, it was called *Konoe-fu*. Its offices were in the *Jutō-toneri-ryō*, or *Tachihaki no toneri-tsukasa*.

K

Kaban, 加番. Under the *Tokugawa*, officials having charge of the castles of *Ōsaka* (1626) and *Sumpu* (1633) (*Shizuoka*). At *Ōsaka* there were 4 and replaced each other every 8 months. The 3 *Sumpu Kaban*, replaced each other every year.

Kabane, 姓. A title of dignity or rank. It became a family name. *Kabane* is different from *uji*, the real family name. The *uji* was bestowed by the Emperor according to the merit, the *kabane* was attached to the function; *Nakatomi*, *Fujiwara*, etc., are *uji*; *Omi*, *Muraji*, *Ason*, *Sukune*, etc., are *kabane*. Formerly there were only the *uji*; but the families increased and the *kabane* was instituted to distinguish their different branches. The principal *kabane* met with in history are: *Omi*, *Muraji*, *Tomo no miyatsuko*, *Kuni no miyatsuko*, *Waki*, *Kimi*, *Atae*, *Agata-nushi*, *Inagi*, *Suguri*, etc. When the functions became hereditary, the *uji* and the *kabane* together formed the family name. At the *Taikwa* reform (645), the heredity was suppressed but the families kept the title. In 682, the emperor *Temmu* created 8 *kabane* to reward his supporters in the *Jinshin* civil war: *Mabito*, *Asomi*, *Sukune*, *Imiki*, *Michi no shi*, *Omi*, *Muraji*, and *Inagi*. Later, those of *Kimi*, *Obito*, *Miyatsuko*, *Fubito*, *Ōkimi*, *Hafuri*, *Abiko*, *Kishi*, etc. were added. The emperor *Kwammu* gave some of his descendants the *uji* of *Taira* (*Hei*). As the *Fujiwara* family increased, branches kept the *uji* of *Fujiwara* and, besides, received the names of *Kondō*, *Naitō*, *Katō*, *Saitō*, etc., most of them borrowing the character *tō* (*fuji*) from the patronimic name. It was the origin of the actual family name (*myōji*). — See *Uji*, *Uji no kami*, etc.

Kabayama, 樺山. A *samurai* family of *Satsuma* ennobled in 1884. — Now Count.

—— **Sukenori, 資紀.** Born in 1837, entered the army while young, was lieutenant-colonel during the *Satsuma* war on the Staff of General *Tani*, then Governor of *Kumamoto*. He entered the navy in 1884, was promoted Vice-Admiral in 1885, became Minister of the Navy (1890-1892). During the Japan-China war, he was chief of the Naval Staff and on board of the " *Saikyo Maru*," assisted at the battle of the Yellow sea (Sept. 16th, 1894). He was named Count for services rendered on this occasion. He was the first Governor-General of Formosa, Minister of Home Affairs (1896-1897), then Minister of Education (1898-1900), a member of the Privy Council in 1904. He had been promoted to the rank of Admiral in 1895.

Kabuki, 歌舞伎. A kind of dance with singing introduced in *Kyōto*, towards the end of the 16th century by *O Kuni*, ex-*ama* of the temple of *Kizuki* (*Izumo*); by and by other actors were added, and it was the origin of the modern theater (*shibai*). The most frequented theater in *Tōkyō*, built in 1660, bears the name of *Kabuki-za*.

THEATRICAL SCENE.

Kachi-gumi, 徒士組. Bodyguards who accompanied the *Shōgun*, when he left his palace. In 1603, the *hashiri-shū* were created; they were divided into 4 squads of 30 men each: it was the origin of the *kachishū*.

Kachi-metsuke, 步目付. Police agents inferior to the *metsuke*, in the time of the *Tokugawa*. Before, they were called *yokome*.

Kachiyama, 勝山. Or *Katsuyama*, a place in *Awa* (*Tōkaidō*), was the residence of the *daimyō Naitō* (1601-1623), the *Matsudaira* (1624-1634), and from 1668 till 1868 that of the *Sakai* (12,000 k.).

Kada, 荷田. A family descended from the *Hagura*.

—— **Azumamaro,** 春滿 (1668-1736). Studied ancient history and classic literature of Japan. The *Shōgun Yoshimune* was his patron. He opened a national school at *Kyōto*, to oppose Chinese ideas.

—— **Arimaro,** 在滿 (1706-1769). An adopted son of the above, went to *Edo* towards 1730, established a school in that city and continued the traditions of his father.

Kadenokōji, 勘解由小路. A *kuge* family descended from *Fujiwara Mitsushiro*. — Now Viscount.

Kadobe, 門部. Company of 200 men belonging to the *Emon-fu*. They guarded the gates of the imperial palace. In 808, they were joined to the *Eji-fu*.

Ka-ei, 嘉永. *Nengō*: 1848-1853.

Kafu, 家扶. A steward of the houses of the nobility. — See *Karei*.

Kaga, 加賀. One of the 7 provinces of *Hokurokudō*. It comprises four districts, which belong to the *Ishikawa-ken*. It was separated from *Echizen* towards 820. — Chinese name: *Kashū*.

Kagae, 加々江. An ancient castle in *Mino*. It was occupied by the *Kagae daimyō* during the 16th century (12,000 k.).

Kagae, 加々江. A *daimyō* family native of *Owari*.

—— **Shigemune, 重宗** (+ 1584). *Suruga no kami*, served *Nobunaga* and was killed in the fight against *Hideyoshi*.

—— **Shigemochi, 重望** (+ 1600). A son of the above submitted to *Hideyoshi*, joined the party against *Ieyasu*, fought against *Mizuno Tadashige*, whom he defeated and killed. He himself lost his life soon afterwards.

Kagami, 加々見. A *daimyō* family descended from the *Sasaki*.

—— **Hisatsuna, 久綱.** A son of *Sasaki Sadashige*, was killed in the *Shōkyū* war (1221), when fighting against the *Hōjō*. His descendants resided at *Kagami-yama* (*Ōmi*), and served the *Sasaki daimyō*.

Kagami-gawa, 鏡川. A river (32 Km.) in *Tosa*: it flows through *Kōchi* and empties itself into the bay of *Urado*. It is also called *Ushioegawa*.

Kagami-yama, 鏡山. Formerly a castle of the *Kagami daimyō* in *Ōmi*.

Kagariya-shugonin, 篝屋守護人. In 1238, *Hōjō Yasutoki*, *Shikken* of *Kamakura* installed in *Kyōto* 48 posts of night guards. During the night the guards lit fires (*kagari*), hence their name. This custom was suppressed in 1370, when the *Shōgun* lived in *Kyōto*.

Kagawa, 香川. A *samurai* family of the *Mito* clan; it was ennobled in 1887. — Now Viscount.

Kagawa Kageki, 香川景樹 (1768-1843). A celebrated poet, author of several esteemed works.

Kagawa-ken, 香川縣. The department formed of the province of *Sanuki*. — Pop.: 731,000. — Cap.: *Takamatsu* (35,000 inh.) — Princ. towns: *Marugame* (25,000 inh.), *Kwannonji* (13,000 inh.), *Sakade* (12,500 inh.).

Kagen, 嘉元. *Nengō:* 1303-1305.

Kageyushi, 勘解由使. Officials created by the emperor *Kwammu* and sent to the provinces at the expiration of the powers of the governors, in order to see that the change was made without trouble.

Kagō, 勘合. The seal formerly put on patents authorizing the carrying on of commerce with China. It was the family of the *Ōuchi daimyō* of *Yamaguchi* (*Suwō*) which had the superintendence of it.

Kagoshima, 鹿兒島. Capital (53,000 inh.) of *Kagoshima-ken* and of *Satsuma* province. The town was known as far back as 764. The *Engi-shiki*, mentions the *Kagoshima jinja* temple. The castle was first called *Ueyama-jō* and belonged to the *Ueyama*. Later on, we find a *Tōfukuji-jō*, the lord of which, *Kimotsuki Kuneshige*, supported the southern dynasty. He was dispossessed in 1341 by *Shimazu Sadahisa*, who installed his son *Ujihisa* in the castle of *Tōfukuji*, which he left to settle at *Aira* (*Ōsumi*), next at *Shibushi* (*Hyūga*). *Motohisa*, a son of *Ujihisa*, returned to *Kagoshima*, built a new castle and called it *Shimizu-jō*. *Takahisa*, his descendant in the 9th generation, built the *Uchi-shiro* in the very town. Finally *Iehisa* erected the *Tsurumaru-jō* on the site of the ancient *Ueyama-jō*. His descendants resided in that castle till the Restoration (770,000 k.). — It was at *Kagoshima* that Saint Francis-Xavier landed on the 15th of August 1549. — In 1863, the English admiral Kuper, to revenge the murder of Richardson, bombarded the city. In 1877, the town was the center of a civil war called the *Satsuma* Rebellion. After 8 months of incessant fighting, the town was almost completely burnt down, the castle was destroyed, and *Saigō Takamori*, the head of the insurrection, killed himself by *harakiri*.

Kagoshima-ken, 鹿兒嶋縣. The department formed with the provinces of *Satsuma* and *Ōsumi*. — Pop.: 1,194,000 — Capital: *Kagoshima* (53,000 inh.). — Principal towns: *Taniyama* (26,000 inh.), *Ei* (22,000 inh.), *Higashi-minami-kata* (21,000 inh.) *Kushigino* (19,600 inh.), *Ibusuki* (16,400 inh.), *Akune* (16,000 inh.), *Kawanobe* (15,600 inh.), *Tarumizu* (15,000 inh.), *Nishikaseda* (14,900 inh.), *Kaseda* (14,700 inh.) *Higashi-ichiki* (12,300 inh.), etc.

Kagura, 神樂. A mime, the origin of which goes as far back as the

AME-NO-UZUME NO MIKOTO
DANCING IN FRONT OF THE CAVE OF AMATERASU.

dance performed in front of the cave of *Amaterasu*. It takes place at certain festivals, on a platform near Shintoist temples. The actors are masked and clad in damask silks ; fifes and drums form the accompaniment of the performance.

Kagura-ga-oka, 神樂岡. A hill N. E. of *Kyōto*, which was the scene of several battles : those of the bonzes of *Enryaku-ji* against *Utsunomiya Kintsuna* (1336), of *Kusunoki Masanori* against *Ashikaga Yoshiakira* (1352), of *Matsunaga Hisahide* against *Rokkaku Yoshikata* (1561), etc.

Kagutsuchi, 迦具土.— See *Homusubi.*

Kaharu, 香春. An ancient castle in *Buzen*, built towards 740 by *Fujiwara Hirotsugu*. In the 14th century, it belonged to prince *Yasunaga-shinnō*, of the Southern dynasty. Later it became the property of the *Harada*, afterwards of the *Takahashi*. In 1587, *Hideyoshi* bestowed it on *Kuroda Yoshitaka*. Under the *Tokugawa*, it formed a part of the domains of the *Hosokawa daimyō* (1600-1632), later of the *Ogasawara* (1632-1868).

Kahō, 嘉保. *Nengō*: 1094-1095.

Kai, 甲斐. One of the 15 provinces of *Tōkaidō*. It comprises 9 districts which form the *Yamanashi-ken.* — Chinese name : *Kōshū.*

Kaibara Ekiken, 具原益軒 (1630-1714). Was born at *Fukuoka (Chikuzen)*. He went to *Kyōto*, in 1657 and attended the lessons of *Yamasaki Ansai* and of *Kinoshita Junan*. After 3 years, he began to teach and published more than 100 works on Confucianist morals in an easy, flowing style. His books were much in vogue till the Restoration. In the "*Taigiroku*" (great doubt), the best known of his works he exposes the objections which, by and by, rose in his mind against the philosophic doctrines of *Shushi*.

Kaieda, 海江田. A *samurai* family of the *Satsuma* clan, ennobled in 1884. — Now Viscount.

Kaieki, 改易. A punishment inflicted on the *samurai* under the *Tokugawa :* they lost their revenues and became *heimin.*

Kaigane-zan, 甲斐根山. One of the peaks (3150 m.) of Mount *Shirane (Kai).*

Kaigen, 改元. Change of *Nengō.* — See *Nengō.*

Kaigun-bugyō, 海軍奉行. Minister of the Navy of the *Edo* shōgunate. This title was created in the 18th century, when, by the advice of *Matsudaira Sadanobu*, the *Shōgun Ienari* established foundries, docks, arsenals, etc. for the navy.

Kaigun-shō, 海軍省. The Department of the Navy, created in 1885.

Kaihoku, 海北. A family of painters of the *Kanō* school. The best known are : *Yūshō* (1533-1615), *Yūsetsu* (1598-1677), *Yūchiku* (1654-1728), *Yūsen* (18th century), *Yūtoku* (1763-1847), *Yūshō* (1818-1869).

Kaiki-shōhō, 開基勝寳. The first gold coins made in Japan, in 760. They are so called from the four characters engraven on them.

Kaikō, 開闔. Secretaries of the principal administrations under the *Kamakura* Shōgunate. They were : the *Mandokoro-kaikō*, the *Saburai-dokoro-kaikō*, the *Chihō-kaikō*, the *Jingū-kaikō*, etc. They were chosen from among the *hikitsukeshū.*

Kaikwa-tennō, 開化天皇. The 9th Emperor of Japan, (157-98 B. C.), was *Waka-yamato-nekohiko-ō-hibi no mikoto*, the 3rd son of the emperor *Kōgen*. He succeeded his father at the age of 50 and died 111 years old. History is silent about this reign of 61 years.

Kaimon-dake, 開聞嶽. A volcano (940 m.) in the southern part of *Satsuma*. According to tradition, this volcano was produced by an earthquake in the year 477 before the Christian era; it is also called *Hirakiki-dake*, *Satsuma-fuji*, *Utsubo-fuji*.

Kaimon-saki, 開聞崎. A cape in the southern part of *Satsuma*; it is also called *Hirakiki-saki*.

Kaimyō, 改名. Or *Hōmyō*, the posthumous name given by bonzes to the deceased faithful of their sect and inscribed on the funeral tablets. This name ends in one of the honorific titles *in*, *koji*, *shinji*, *shinnyo*, *dōji*, etc., according to the age, the sex, the rank of the deceased person.

Kainai san-kijin, 海内三奇人 (Lit.: the 3 originals). The 3 writers who under the *Tokugawa* shōgunate dared to defend the cause of the imperial authority against the encroachments of the *shōgun*: *Takàyama Masayuki* (1747-1793), *Hayashi Shihei* (1754-1793), and *Gamō Kumpei* (1768-1813).

Kairitsu-shū, 戒律宗. Or *Risshū*, a Buddhist sect introduced for the first time by *Zenshin-ni*, a daughter of the Chinese *Shiba Tattō*, who had established herself in Japan in the reign of *Keitai* (522). Later on, the bonzes *Dōkō* (704) and *Dōei* (735) after having studied the doctrines of the sect in China, tried, but without success, to propagate it. *Kanshin* who came from China in 754, succeeded in establishing it; for that reason, he is regarded as its founder. The ceremony of initiation into the sect consists in the solemn imposition of the ten moral precepts (*kai*), performed on a platform of earth (*kaidan*) raised near the temple. — This sect is so to say extinct since the 13th century.

Kaisei-jo, 開成所. Name given in 1863 to the School till then called *Bansho-shirabe-dokoro* (See that name). The teaching of English, French, German, mathematics, etc., was begun at that time. In 1877, it became part of the Imperial University.

Kaitakushi, 開拓使 (Lit.: colonization agency). A special administration that governed *Hokkaidō* from 1869 to 1881. It was helped by general Capron and several other Americans, founded model farms, built roads, developed the working of mines, etc. without, however, being able to realize the expectations that had been entertained.

Kaizu, 海津. A place in *Ōmi*, N. of lake *Biwa*. It was the residence of the *Kaizu daimyō* during the middle ages.

Kaizu, 海津. A place in *Shinano*. — See *Matsushiro*.

Kajiki, 加治木. A place in *Ōsumi*, where *Kajiki Chikahira* built a castle in 1190. *Hisahira*, his descendant in the 9th generation, was besieged by *Shimazu Tadamasa* (1495), transferred to *Ata* (*Satsuma*), and replaced by *Ijichi Shigesada*. The latter having also revolted against his suzerain, was defeated and committed suicide by *harakiri* (1527).

Kajino, 梶野. A family descended from the *Taira* and, for centuries, attached to the temple of *Kōfuku-ji* (*Nara*). — Now Baron.

Kajitori, 楫取. A *samurai* family of the *Yamaguchi* (*Suwō*) clan, ennobled after the Restoration. — Now Baron.

Kajitori-saki, 楫取崎 . A cape in the N. of *Iyo*. It is also called *Myōjinsaki, Miyazaki no hana.*

Kajiwara Kagetoki, 梶原景時 . A *samurai* of *Sagami*. When *Yoritomo* levied troops to fight the *Taira*, *Kagetoki*, under the command of *Ōba Kagechika*, fought against him : *Yoritomo*, having been defeated at *Ishibashi* (1181), together with *Doi Sanehira*, hid himself in the mountains. *Kagetoki* was sent to pursue him ; he discovered his retreat, but leading his troops in another direction, he allowed *Yoritomo* to escape, and, soon, afterwards espoused his cause. In 1184, he took part in the campaign of *Yoshitsune* against *Yoshinaka* and the *Taira ;* later on having had some contention with *Yoshitsune*, he calumniated him to *Yoritomo* and contributed much to embroil the two brothers. After the death of *Yoritomo*, he became a member of the Council of State. He then accused *Yūki Tomomitsu* of plotting against the *Shōgun Yoriie*: *Tomomitsu* together with *Miura Yoshimura, Wada Yoshimori* and several other officers, tried to get rid of *Kagetoki*, who fled to *Suruga* where, the following year, he was defeated and killed with his son *Kagesue* (1200).

Kajō, 嘉祥 . *Nengō:* 848-850. — Also called *Kashō.*

Kajō, 嘉祥 . Or *Kajō-shoku*, a ceremony that took place every year on the 16th day of the 6th month : in order to be preserved from any epidemic, 16 *mochi* (cakes made of rice flour) were offered to the *kami*, after which they were eaten. The ceremony is so called, because it was instituted in the first year of the *nengō Kajō.*

Kaiū, 家従 . Formerly steward of the household of a prince or a nobleman. — See *Karei.*

Kakegawa, 掛川 . A place in *Tōtōmi*, where *Imagawa Ujichika* built a castle in 1113, which castle he intrusted to the guard of *Asahina Yasutoshi*. The castle, later on, was transferred to *Ishikawa Ienari* (1569), next to *Yamanouchi Kazutoyo* (1590). Under the *Tokugawa*, it was successively occupied by the *daimyō Hisamatsu* (1601-1623), *Aoyama* (1623-1634), *Sakurai* (1635-1639), *Honda* (1639-1644), *Matsudaira* (1644-1648), *Fukushima* (1648-1658), *Ii* (1658-1705), *Sakurai* (1706-1711), *Ogasawara* (1711-1746), finally, from 1746-1868, *Ōta* (50,000 k.).

Kakei, 嘉慶 . *Nengō* of the northern dynasty: 1387-1388.

Kakimi Iezumi, 垣見家純 . Entered the service of *Hideyoshi*, who bestowed on him the castle of *Tomiku* (*Bungo* — 20,000 k.), he also took part in the expedition to Korea. Afterwards he sided with *Ishida Kazushige*, and was killed in the castle of *Ōgaki* (1600).

Kakimono - bugyō, 書物奉行 . A title created in 1633 and given to the 4 officials who had charge of the books, manuscripts, printings, etc. of the shōgunate.

Kakinomoto Hitomaro, 柿本人麿 . A celebrated poet of the 7th and the 8th centuries. He was in the service of the emperors *Jitō* and *Mommu* and died in *Iwami*, probably in 729. He is honored as the god of poetry and has his temple at *Akashi* (*Harima*)

KAKINOMOTO I ITOMARO.

Kakitsu, 嘉吉. *Nengō:* 1441-1443.

Kakitsu no hen, 嘉吉變. (Lit.: the advent of the *Kakitsu* era). An expression to designate the assassination of the *Shōgun Ashikaga Yoshinori* by *Akamatsu Mitsusuke* (1441). *Yoshinori* hated *Mitsusuke* and proved it to him in many ways; finally, he wished to despoil him of his domains in order to bestow them on *Akamatsu Sadamasa. Mitsusuke,* concealing his anger, invited the *Shōgun* to a feast during which he assassinated him; next he put fire to his own house and fled to *Harima.* There he proclaimed *Giun,* a bonze and grandson of *Ashikaga Tadafuyu,* heir of *Yoshinori.* Meanwhile, the *Hosokawa,* the *Takeda,* the *Yamana,* etc. recognized *Yoshikatsu,* the son of *Yoshinori,* and marched against *Mitsusuke,* who, being besieged in his castle at *Shirahata* and defeated after a short resistance, killed himself by *harakiri.*

Kakizaki, 蠣崎. A *daimyō* family descended from the *Takeda.* In the 15th century, the family installed itself in *Edo* and took the name of *Matsumae.* — See *Matsumae.*

Kako-gawa, 加古川. A river (76 Km.) that has its source in *Tamba,* passes through *Harima,* and empties itself into the Inland Sea at *Takasago.* It is also called *Innami-gawa, Hi-no-kō, Takino-gawa.*

Kakokujō, 下剋上 (Lit.: the inferior triumphs over the superior). The name given to the last period of the *Ashikaga* Shōgunate, during which time, the whole country being a prey to civil war, many powerful families were overthrown by their vassals.

Kakuhan, 覺鑁. — See *Kōkyō-Daishi.*

Kakui-jima, 鹿久居嶋. An island (28 Km. in circuit) in the Inland Sea, near the coast of the province of *Bizen,* to which it belongs.

Kakujo, 覺助. A son of *Jōchō,* and, like his father, sculptor and bonze at *Nara* (11th century).

Kakunotate, 角舘. A place in *Ugo* with a castle, the residence of the *Tozawa daimyō* in the 16th century (40,000 k.).

Kakushin-ni, 覺信尼. A daughter of *Zenhin-Daishi:* she married *Hino Hirotsuna* and was mother of the bonze *Shūe.* After the death of her husband, she had her head shaved, built the *Hongwan-ji* temple of *Yamashina* (1480) and was actively occupied in diffusing the *Shinshū* sect.

Kamae, 構. A punishment reserved to the bonzes in the time of the *Tokugawa,* and corresponding to a kind of excommunication. There were two degrees: the *ha-kamae,* exclusion of the branch, and the *shū-kamae,* exclusion of the whole sect.

Kamakura, 鎌倉. A small town (7250 inh.) in *Sagami,* which, for several centuries, was the second capital of Japan. When *Minamoto Yoritomo* left the province of *Izu,* where he had been exiled by *Kiyomori,* and began war against the *Taira,* he selected for his residence the village of *Kamakura,* which had been that of his ancestor *Yoriyoshi* (995-1082). After he had become *Shōgun* (1192), the town became more and more important. After the *Minamoto,* the *Fujiwara Shōgun* and those of the imperial family continued to reside at *Kamakura:* palaces, temples, residences of the nobles were built in great number, and it is said that, a century after *Yoritomo*, the population exceeded one million. During the *Genkō* war (1333), *Nitta Yoshisada* took *Kamakura* and a part of the town was reduced to ashes. The *Ashikaga* rebuilt it and in 1349, *Takauji* having appointed his son *Motouji* regent of the eastern provinces, (*Kwantō-kwanryō*), installed him at *Kamakura*. But the civil wars of the following century, the substitution of the *Uesugi* for the *Ashikaga* as *Kwanryō* (1439), the siege of 1454, and the conflagration of 1526 left almost nothing but ruins. At present there remain of the splendor of the past only the famous *Daibutsu* and the *Tsurugaoka-Hachiman* temple.

Kamakura-bakufu, 鎌倉幕府. The *Kamakura* shōgunate, of 1192-1333.

Kamakura-bafuku-kwansei, 鎌倉幕府官制. The system of administration established by the *Kamakura* shōgunate. Below the *Shōgun*, whose title after *Yoritomo*, became simply honorific, there was a regent (*Shikken*) of the *Hōjō* family, who wielded the full power. The *mandokoro* (central administration) attended to the territorial possessions of the nobles, the taxes, finances, etc.: it was composed of 15 or 16 *hyōjōshū* (councillors), the *hikitsukeshū* (secretaries), assisted by the *yoriaishū*. Military questions were regulated by the *saburai-dokoro;* justice was administered by the *keisatsu*. After these offices reserved to high personages, the *ko-saburai-dokoro* fixed the guards of the shōgunal palace, the escorts of honor, etc. — See the two following articles.

Kamakura-bakufu-shoshi, 鎌倉幕府諸使. Officials sent into the provinces on certain occasions by the *Kamakura Shōgun.* They were ranked under 5 titles :

—— **Jikken-shi,** 實撿使. Extraordinary envoys for grave reasons.

—— **Junken-shi,** 巡撿使. Officials that every year, at a fixed epoch, visited the country to examine the state of prosperity or misery of the people, to listen to their complaints, to judge differences, etc.

—— **Naiken-shi,** 內撿使. Officials that verified the rice crops in order to determine the taxes. Later they were called *kenken-shi*

—— **Kenchū-shi,** 撿注使. Officials delegated by the *shugo* or the *jitō* of every province to establish the exact cadaster and to prevent any arbitrary change thereof. Later, they were called *nawa-uchi* (line stretchers) and *sao-ire* (marking out with stakes).

—— **Kenken-shi,** 撿見使. Officials that, like the *jikken-shi*, were extraordinary delegates, but in less important circumstances.

Kamakura-banshū, 鎌倉番衆. Officials of inferior rank, having charge of certain services at the shōgunal palace of *Kamakura*. The principal among them were :

—— **Gakumonjo-ban,** 學問所番. Officials attending to horsemanship, archery, the study of ancient Japanese and Chinese customs, etc. (Created in 1213).

—— **Kinju-ban,** 近習番. Officials that selected and supervised the employées at the shōgunal Court (1225).

—— **O-ban,** 大番. *Samurai* recruited in the eastern provinces and, by turns, employed as guards of the shōgunal palace. They were on duty for one year at a time (1225).

—— **Kôshi-ban,** 格子番. Officials having charge in the morning of opening the grated doors and windows (*kôshi*) of the palace and in the evening of closing them (1252).

—— **Monkenzanketsu-ban,** 問見参結番. Officials who counted and watched the persons received in audience by the *Shôgun* (1252).

—— **Hisashi-ban,** 廂番. Guards of pavilions and villas outside of the palace.

—— **Hayahiru-ban,** 早晝番. Officials having charge of such arts as poetry, music, ball, games, etc. (1260).

Kamakura-dono, 鎌倉殿. The name given by the people to *Minamoto Yoritomo* after his installation at *Kamakura*.

Kamakura Gongorô Kagemasa, 鎌倉權五郎景政. A warrior of the *Minamoto* clan, who gained fame during the campaign of *Yoshiie* against the *Mutsu Kiyowara* (1091). Having had an eye pierced by an arrow he nevertheless continued to pursue his adversary and had the arrow extracted only after having killed his enemy: he was then 16 years old. He is the ancestor of the *Nagao*.

Kamakura-jidai, 鎌倉時代. The period of the *Kamakura* shôgunate, 1192-1333.

Kamanashi-gawa, 釜無川. A river which has its source at *Koma-ga-take* (*Kai*), passes through *Nirazaki*, receives the *Shio-gawa*, then the *Midai-gawa*, and, by its junction with the *Fuefuki-gawa*, forms the *Fuji-kawa*.

Kambe, 神戸. A person having charge of the finances in a Shintoist temple: collecting income, paying the salaries of employées, etc.

Kambe, 神戸. A place in *Ise*, where *Oda Nobutaka* built a castle in 1567. Later on, the castle belonged to the *Takigawa daimyô* (1585-1600), the *Hitotsuyanagi* (1600-1634), the *Ishikawa* (1634-1732), finally from 1732-1868, to the *Honda* (15,000 k.).

Kameda, 龜田. A place in *Ugo*, was, from 1602 to 1868, the residence of the *Iwaki daimyô* (50,000 k.).

Kamei, 龜井. A *daimyô* family descended from the *Uda-Genji* (a branch of the *Sasaki*); it settled in *Izumo* and was in the service of the *Amako*.

—— **Korenori,** 茲矩 (1567-1612). Left *Izumo* after the overthrow of the *Amako*, went to *Kyôto*, and attached himself to *Nobunaga*, afterwards to *Hidegoshi*, who bestowed on him the castle of *Shikano* (*Inaba* —— 13,000 k.). He took part in the expedition into *Kyûshû* (1587), espoused the cause of *Ieyasu*, and had his revenues raised to 43,000 k.

—— **Masanori,** 政矩. A son of *Korenori*, was transferred in 1617, to *Tsuwano* (*Iwami* —— 43,000 k.) where his descendants resided till the Restoration. —— Now Viscount.

Kameoka, 龜岡. A town (7,200 inh.) in *Tamba* (*Kyôto-fu*). Before the Restoration, it was called *Kameyama*. —— See *Kameyama*.

Kameyama, 龜山. A town in *Tamba* with an ancient castle which, towards the middle of the 16th century, belonged to the Christian *daimyô* John *Naitô Yukiyasu*. *Naitô* having been dispossessed by *Nobunaga* in 1573, the castle became the property of the *Hatano* (1573-79), next of *Akechi Mitsuhide* (1579-82). *Hideyoshi* bestowed it on *Maeda Munehisa* (*Gen-i Hō-in*). Under the *Tokugawa*, it belonged successively to the *daimyō: Okabe* (1609-21), *Matsudaira* (1621-34), *Suganuma* (1634-44), *Matsudaira* (1648-86), *Kuze* (1686-97), *Inoue* (1697-1702), *Aoyama* (1702-48), finally, from 1748 to 1868, to the *Matsudaira* (50,000 k.). — Since the Restoration, the name of the town has been changed to that of *Kameoka*.

Kameyama, 龜 山 . A town (7,400 inh.) in *Ise,* with an ancient castle built by *Seki Munekazu* towards the middle of the 16th century. After having been bestowed on *Gamō Ujisato* by *Nobunaga*, it was returned to the *Seki* (1584-86), who were again dispossessed of it by *Takigawa Kazumasu;* but *Hideyoshi* replaced the latter by *Okamoto Shigemasa* (1587-1600). Under the *Tokugawa* it belonged, in succession, to the *daimgō: Seki* (1600-10), *Okudaira* (1610-15), *Miyake* (1615-35), *Honda* (1636-51), *Ishikawa* (1651-69), *Itakura* (1669-1710), *Ogyū* (1710-17), *Itakura* (1717-44), and from 1744 till 1868, to the *Ishikawa* (70,000 k.).

Kameyama-tennō, 龜 山 天 皇 . The 90th Emperor of Japan (1260-74), was *Tsunehito,* the 7th son of *Go-Saga;* he succeeded his brother *Go-Fukakusa* when 11 years old. During his reign, the *Shikken Hōjō Tokimune* governed according to his own will. At the age of 26, *Kameyama* abdicated in favor of his son *Go-Uda.* In 1289, he had his head shaved and received the name of *Kongōgen.* He died in 1304, at the age of 56.

Kami, 神 . (Chinese, *shin,* spirit). The gods and goddesses of Shintoism.

Kami, 守 . A title corresponding to that of governor of a province: *Settsu no kami, Iga no kami.* From the time of the *Ashikaga,* the title, in most cases, became merely honorific: there were, for instance, several *Shinano no kami* at the same time, and having no jurisdiction over that province. The *Shimazu, daimyō* of *Kagoshima,* however bore the hereditary title of *Satsuma no kami;* the *Sō,* that of *Tsushima no kami,* etc.

Kami-ari-tsuki, 神 有 月 . (Lit.: month of the gods). The name given in *Izumo* to the 10th month (anc. cal.), because, according to legend, all the gods of Japan, leaving their own temples, assemble with *Okuninushi* at the great temple of *Izumo.*

Kami-kyō, 上 京 . The northern half of *Kyōto.*

Kaminari no jin, 雷 鳴 陣 . Formerly, in time of storm, after the third peal of thunder, the officers on duty, taking their bows and arrows guarded all the openings of the palace. The guards of inferior rank, wearing their *mino* (rain-coat made of straw), and their *kasa* (a kind of flat somewhat coneshaped hat), assembled in the garden of the southern pavilion (*nanden*). Meanwhile, the Emperor took refuge in the *shūhō-sha,* or *kaminari no tsubo.*

Kami-na-zuki, 神 無 月 . (Lit.: month without gods). A name given to the 10th month (anc. cal.), because, according to legend, all gods leave their temples to assemble with *Okuninushi* in *Izumo.*

Kami-no-mikawa, 上三川. A place in *Shimotsuke* with an ancient castle built by the *daimyō Utsunomiya*, who left it in 1249, for that of *Yokota*. From 1430 it was occupied by the *Imaizumi* family.

Kaminoseki-jima, 上關嶋. An island (37 Km. in circuit) in the Inland Sea, S. of the province of *Suwō* to which it belongs. It is also called *Naga-shima*.

Kami-no-yama, 上山. An ancient castle in *Uzen*, formerly called *Tsukioka-jō*. It was built by *Shiba Yoshitada* towards the middle of the 16th century; later on, it came into the possession of the *Satomi*. Under the *Tokugawa* it was the residence of the *Matsudaira daimyō* (1616-27), the *Toki* (1627-92), and from 1697-1868, the *Matsudaira* (30,000 k.).

Kami-shima, 上嶋. The northern part (198 Km. in circuit) of the island of *Tsushima*.

Kami-shima, 上嶋. An island (146 Km. in circuit) of the *Amakusa* group. It is also called *Seto-kami no shima*.

Kami-shima, 神嶋. An island (28 Km. in circuit) in the Inland Sea, belonging to the province of *Bitchū*. It is also called *Kōno-shima*.

Kamishimo, 社祢. Garments composed of the *kataginu* and the *hakama*; they were, from the end of the 15th century, the ordinary dress of the *samurai*. Under the *Tokugawa*, they formed the costume of ceremony.

Kamitsukenu, 上毛野. The ancient name of the province of *Kōzuke*.

Kamitsukenu Katana, 上毛野形名. A warrior of the 7th century. He was nominated *Shōgun* in 637, and marched against the *Ebisu;* but he was defeated and his army put to flight. Having been invested in his camp, he resolved to escape under cover of darkness, when his wife objecting that such conduct would be cowardice and an offence to the gods, assembled all the women shut up with her and taught them how to use the bow. It was at the head of this strange regiment that *Katana* marched against the enemy. The *Ebisu* believing themselves to be in the presence of a numerous body of warriors, raised the siege. The *Shōgun* then recalled his scattered troops and defeated the enemy.

Kamiya Sōdan, 神谷宗堪 (1551-1635). A *samurai* of *Hakata* (*Chikuzen*) who, after having traveled in China and the Philipine Islands, returned in 1588. *Hideyoshi* commissioned him to establish the camp of *Nagoya;* later, having entered the service of *Kuroda Nagamasa*, he built the castle of *Fukuoka*, and was engaged in the exploitation of mines, agriculture, weaving, etc.

Kamiyama, 神山. A *samurai* family of the *Kōchi* (*Tosa*) clan, ennobled after the Restoration. — Now Baron.

Kami-yo. 神代. The era of the gods. It is also called *Jindai, Taiko*.

Kammuri, 冠. Formerly the head-gear of princes, noblemen, and officials. It was a sort of flat cap, surmounted by a rounded plate and a fanion in the rear. Those of the emperor were of two kinds: the *usu-bitai* and the *hanbitai;* those of the nobles were the *atsubitai* and the

OIKAKE.

USU-BITAI.

KEN-EI.

sukibitai. Officials of inferior rank wore the *oikake,* the *ken-ei,* the *hoso-ei,* etc.

Kamo, 賀茂. A village north of *Kyōto,* renowned for its two great Shintoist temples, *Shimo-Kamo* and *Kami-Kamo,* the former is dedicated to *Tamayori-hime,* the latter, to her son *Wake-ikazuchi. Kwammu-tennō* selected these gods as protectors of *Heian-kyō* (*Kyōto*), his new Capital.

Kamo-Chōmei, 鴨長明. A bonze and writer of the 12th and 13th centuries. He first studied music and poetry, and was nominated director (*yoriudo*) of the *uta-dokoro* by the ex-emperor *Go-Toba.* Afterwards he asked to succeed his father as chief of the temple of *Kamo,* but his petition having been refused, he had his head shaved, took the name of *Ren-in,* and retired to mount *Ōhara-yama,* where he built a hut 10 feet square and 7 in height, and began to write books. The best known of his works are: the *Hōjō-ki* (history of 10 feet square), a kind of "A Journey Around My Room," relating incidentally the civil wars and conflagrations of which *Kyōto* was then the scene; — the *Mumyō-sō* (anonymous extracts); — the *Shiki-monogatari* (tales of the 4 seasons), etc.

Kamo Mabuchi, 加茂眞淵 (1697-1769). A son of a *kannushi* of the *Kamo* temple (*Tōtōmi*), was chosen as a son-in-law by the landlord of a hotel in *Hamamatsu.* The latter soon regretted his choice, for *Mabuchi* spent his time in reading instead of tending to the service of the house. After numerous discussions, he finally obtained the authorization to go to *Kyōto,* where he attended the lessons of *Kada Azumamaro,* and later went to *Edo* where he became a teacher. His talent was soon appreciated, and the most noted men of the epoch became his disciples. He was especially patronized by the *Chūnagon Tayasu Munetake,* a son of the *Shōgun Yoshimune* who took him into his service. In 1760 he resigned his position in favor of *Sadao,* his adopted son, and devoted himself to the study of antiquity and poetry. He was greatly instrumental in causing ancient history and ancient poems called *naga-uta,* to be appreciated.

Kamo-gawa, 加茂川. A river which rises in the northern part of *Yamashiro,* traverses the eastern part of *Kyōto,* receives the

Takase-gawa, and empties itself into the *Katsura-gawa*. Near its source it is also called *Nakatsu-gawa, Iwaya-gawa;* and towards its mouth, it is known as the *Semi-no-ogawa, Ishi-gawa, Hisage-gawa.*

Kamo no matsuri, 加茂祭. A festival which was celebrated at *Kyōto* during the 4th month in honor of the gods of *Kamo (Kamo-daijin).* It was instituted by the emperor *Kimmei* and observed on the day of the Cock. *Uda-tennō* (889) established a similar festival to be celebrated towards the end of the 11th month: it was called *Kamo rinji no matsuri.*

Kamo no mizu-umi, 鴨湖. A lake (20 Km. in circuit) in *Sado* Island, near the sea-port of *Ebisu-minato.* — It is also called *Koshi no mizu-umi.*

Kamōda-numa, 鴨生田沼. A lake (12 Km. in circ.) in *Chikuzen.*

Kamon, 家門. A title given to *daimyō* families related to the *Tokugawa.* They were: the different branches of the *San-ke (Owari, Kii, Mito),* of the *San-kyō (Shimizu, Tayasu, Hitotsubashi)* and of the *Matsudaira* of *Echizen,* all descended from the *Shōgun.*

Kamon no kami, 掃部頭. — See *Kanimori-zukasa.*

Kamui-zaki, 神威崎. A cape north-west of *Shiribeshi (Hokkaidō).*

Kan, 漢. The Chinese dynasty of the *Han* (206 B.C. — 221 A.D.). — *Kan no kuni,* China. — *Kan-go,* Chinese language. — *Kan-on,* pronunciation of the Chinese characters in the time of the *Han.*

Kan Shōjō, 菅相亟. — See *Sugawara Michizane.*

Kanagawa-bugyō, 神奈川奉行. A title created in 1858, and applied to the official who, after the opening of the *Kanagawa* sea-port, superintended the vessels, the importation, the exportation, etc.

Kanagawa-ken, 神奈川縣. The department formed of the province of *Sagami* and 3 districts of *Musashi.* — Popul.: 867.000 inh. — Capital: *Yokohama* (341,660 inh.) — Principal towns: *Yokosuka* (25,000 inh.), *Toda* (20,000 inh.), *Kanagawa* (19,000 inh.), *Odawara* (16,700 inh.), *Uraga* (13,500 inh.), etc.

Kanamori, 金森. An ancient *daimyō* family descended from the *Fujiwara.*

—— **Nagachika, 長近** (1524-1607). Was in the service of *Nobunaga* and afterwards in that of *Hideyoshi.* In 1585, being commissioned to conquer the province of *Hida,* he defeated and killed *Anenokōji Koretsuna,* wherefore he received the province in fief and the castle of *Takayama* as his residence.

—— **Yoshishige, 可重** (1559-1616). A son of *Nagao Kagenaga,* was adopted by *Nagachika.* He served *Nobunaga* and afterwards *Hideyoshi.* In 1600 he joined the party of *Ieyasu.* During the *Ōsaka* campaign (1615) he defended the castle of *Kishiwada (Izumi)* and fought so well that he secured the heads of 208 enemies slain by himself, as trophies. *Yoshishige* was renowned also for his skill in performing the tea ceremony which he had learned from *Sen no Rikyū.* — His descendants were transferred to *Yawata (Mino* — 20,000 k.) in 1697. The last one, *Yorikane,* was dispossessed on account of bad administration, and exiled to *Nambu* (1759).

Kanasaki, 金崎. An ancient castle in *Echizen* on the site of the present town of *Tsuruga*. In 1336, *Nitta Yoshisada* after having been defeated at the *Minato-gawa*, entrenched himself in this castle together with *Tsunenaga-shinnō*. The following year he was besieged by *Shiba Takatsune* but succeeded in escaping to *Soma-yama*. In the 16th century the castle belonged to the *Asakura*, but *Nobunaga* took it in 1570. — In *Tsuruga* there may yet be seen a Shintoist temple, *Kanasaki-jinja* dedicated to the princes *Tsunenaga-shinnō* and *Takanaga-shinnō*, both sons of *Go-Daigo*.

Kanayama, 金山. A hill in *Kōzuke* N. of the little town of *Ōta*, on which the ancient castle of the *Nitta* was situated. It was from that place that *Yoshisada* set out to support *Go-Daigo*. After the direct line of the descendants of *Yoshisada* became extinct, the castle was occupied by the *Yura*, a lateral branch. In 1553, *Nagao Kagetora* made himself master of the castle, but *Takeda Shingen* took it from him in 1566, and *Hōjō Ujimasa* took it in 1588. *Ieyasu*, in memory of *Yoshisada*, did not wish to install a *daimyō* in the castle, and *Kanayama* became a shōgunal property. Finally, after the Restoration, a Shintoist temple (*Nitta-jinja*) was erected on *Kanayama* to the faithful supporter of the legitimate dynasty.

Kanayama, 金山. An ancient castle in *Aki*, belonging to the *Takeda daimyō*, governors of the province under the *Ashikaga*. *Mōri-Motonari* took it in 1450, and the *Takeda* retired into *Wakasa*.

Kanayama, 金山. An ancient castle in *Ugo*, belonging to the *Mogami daimyō*.

Kanayama-hiko, 金山毘古. ⎫ *Shintō* gods, children of *Izanagi*
Kanayama-hime, 金山毘賣. ⎭ and *Izanami*. According to legend, they were born from the vomits of *Izanami* during her illness.

Kanazawa, 金澤. The capital (97,500 inh.) of *Ishikawa-ken* and *Kaga* province. — Towards 1475, the *Ikkō-shū* bonzes, having expelled the *Togashi daimyō* of the place, built the *Hongen-ji* temple, which they surrounded by a fortress. In 1575, *Nobunaga* took the fortress, in which he installed *Sakuma Morimasa*. *Hideyoshi* gave the province of *Saga* to *Maeda Toshiie* (1583), who built a new castle and made it his abode. His descendants resided in that castle till the Restoration (1,027,000 k.).

Kanazawa, 金澤. A village in *Musashi*, 10 Km. S. of *Yokohama*. It was celebrated in the Middle Ages for its famous library (*Kanazawa-bunko* — See below). It was the residence of the *daimyō Yonekura* from 1696 to 1868 (13,000 k.). — *Kanazawa* is renowned for its picturesque landscapes.

Kanazawa-bunko, 金澤文庫. A library founded at *Kanazawa* (*Musashi*) by *Hōjō Sanetoki* towards 1270: he collected a great quantity of manuscripts both Japanese and Chinese. The collection was increased by his successors *Akitoki* and *Sadaaki*. At the downfall of the *Hōjō* (1333), the library and the school connected with it, lost much of their importance, but *Uesugi Norizane* gave them preeminence again (1450).

Ieyasu, having established a library in *Edo*, ordered the transfer of all the ancient books to his new library.

Kandachime, 上 達 部. The name formerly given to the *kuge* of the 3rd rank (*san-i*) and above.

Kande-yama, 神 出 山. An ancient castle in *Harima*, built by *Akamatsu Noritsugu* and occupied by his descendants till 1570.

Kane-akira-shinnō, 兼 明 親 王 (914-987). The 11th son of the Emperor *Daigo*. In 920, he received the name of *Minamoto*. He was renowned for his literary attainments. He is also called *Miko-Sadaijin*, *Ogura-shinnō*.

Kaneko, 金 子. A family descended from the *Mononobe* and, for generations, attached to the *Mononobe-jinja* temple (*Iwami*). — Now Baron.

Kaneko, 金 子. A family of *Fukuoka* (*Chikuzen*) and ennobled in 1895. — Now Baron.

Kanenaga-shinnō, 懷 良 親 王. — See *Yasunaga-Shinnō*.

Kanezawa, 金 澤. A place in *Ugo*, formerly the residence of the *Kiyowara*, governors of *Dewa*. In 1087 *Takehira* and *Iehira* having revolted, *Minamoto Yoshiie* besieged and destroyed their castle.

Kani-e, 蟹 江. An ancient castle in *Owari*, built by *Watanabe Genjūrō* and, later on, occupied by *Oda Nobumasa*, next by *Sakuma Nobukatsu*, and then by *Maeda Kōjūrō*. In 1584, the latter surrendered the castle to *Takigawa Kazumasu*, who, being besieged by *Ieyasu* put *Kōjūrō* to death and fled into *Ise*.

Kanimori-zukasa, 掃 部 司. According to legend, at the moment of the birth of *Ugaya-fuki-aezu*, the father of *Jimmu*, *Ame no Oshibito*, with the aid of a broom, chased a crab (*kani*) from the house which was situated on the sea-shore. Hence the name of *Kani-mori* given to officials having charge of a portion of the imperial palace. Their chief was first called *Kanimori no Muraji*. Later the *Kanemori-zukasa* was created. At its head there were a *Kami*, a *Suke*, two *Jō*, two *Sawkan*, and below them, some *Kanibe*, *Tsukaibe*, etc. There was a *Kanimori-zukasa* of the *Ōkura-shō*, and one of the *Kunai-shō*, also called *Uchi-kanimori*. In 820, the two offices were united and called the *Kunai-shō* and gradually the name of *Kanimori* was contracted into *Kamon*. The chief officer was the *Kamon no kami*, a title which became merely honorific. Under the *Toku-gawa*, it was hereditary in the family of the *daimyō* of *Ii*, of *Hikone* (*Ōmi*).

Kan-in, 閑 院. The family of the princes of the blood descended from *Naohito-shinnō* (1703-1752), a son of the emperor *Higashi-yama*. The present representative of the family is prince *Kotohito*, born in 1865. He married the daughter of duke *Sanjō Sanetomi* in 1892.

Kan-in-dairi, 閑 院 内 裏. An ancient palace in *Kyōto*, first the residence of *Fujiwara Fuyutsugu*, and afterwards, that of the emperors *Shirakawa*, *Go-Toba*, *Tsuchimikado*, *Go-Saga*, *Go-Fukakusa*, etc., after their abdication.

Kanjō-bugyō, 勘 定 奉 行. Superintendents of the treasury under the shōgunate of the *Tokugawa*. *Ōkubo Nagayasu* was the first to discharge this function (1603). In 1682, their number was increased to

4, two of whom had the title of *Kujigata* and two others that of *Kattegata*. They had a great number of employees under their direction.

Kannabe, 河邊. An ancient castle in *Bingo* which in the 14th century was the residence of the governors of the province. In 1441, it became the property of the *Yamana*, then, towards 1530, that of the *Ōuchi* of *Suwō*.

Kanna-gawa, 神名川. A river which rises in *Kōzuke*, separates this province from *Musashi* and empties itself into the *Karasu-gawa*. It is also called *Kanra-gawa*. — In the 16th century its banks were the scene of numerous battles fought by the *Uesugi*, the *Takeda*, the *Hōjō*, the *Takigawa*, etc.

Kanname-matsuri, 神甞祭. A festival when new rice is offered to the ancestors of the imperial family. It was celebrated at the *Ise* temples: at the *Naikū*, on the 16th of the 9th month; at the *Gekū* on the following day. Since the adoption of the Gregorian calendar, the 17th of October has been fixed as the day of its celebration. It is also called *Shinjō-sai* (Chinese pronunciation of the same characters).

Kannarai-kyō, 神習教. One of the 7 sects of Shintoism.

Kannushi, 神主. The superior of a Shintoist temple. His functions consist in presenting the offerings destined to the *kami*, morning and evening. He has the *negi, hafuri, kannagi*, etc. under his command.

Kanō, 加納. A place in *Mino*, which successively was the residence of the following *daimyō*: the *Okudaira* (1601-10), the *Suganuma* (1610-32), the *Ōkubo* (1632-39) the *Toda* (1639-1711), the *Andō* (1711-56), and the *Nagai* (1757-1868)—(33,000 k.).

Kanō, 加納. A *daimyō* family, native of *Suruga* and descended from the *Fujiwara*. It was ennobled in 1726 and resided at *Ichinomiya* (*Kazusa*) from 1796 to 1868 (13,000 k). — Now Viscount.

Kanō-ryū, 狩野流. A school of painting founded by *Kanō Masanobu* in the 15th century. It sprang from the Chinese school of *Josetsu* and was divided into several branches.

—— **Masanobu, 正信** (1453-1490). The founder of the *Kanō* school of painting and a descendant of the *Fujiwara*, was born at *Kanō* (*Izu*), hence his name. After having attended the lessons of *Josetsu* and of *Shūbun* at *Kyōto*, he himself founded a school patronized by the *Shōgun Yoshimasa*, and after having his head shaved, received the title of *Hōgen*.

—— **Motonobu, 元信** (1476-1554). Also called *Ko-Hōgen, Eisen, Gyokusen*, attended the lessons of his father *Masanobu* and those of *Oguri Sōtan*. He adopted a special style, borrowing from the Chinese and the *Tosa* school. He was in great favor with the *Shōgun Yoshihisa, Yoshizumi, Yoshitane* and *Yoshiharu*. He received the title of *Echigo no kami* and that of *Hōgen* after having his head shaved. He was a friend of the sculptor *Gotō Yujō* whom he supplied with most of his subjects. *Motonobu* is the most celebrated painter of the *Kanō* school.

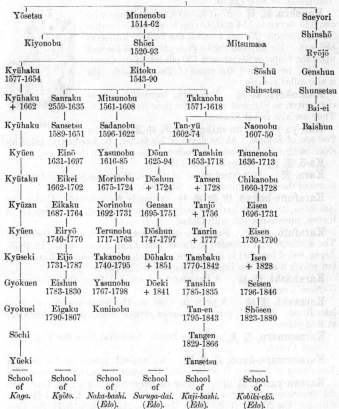

```
                              Masanobu
                              1453-90
                                 |
                              Motonobu
                              1476-1559

Yōsetsu           Munenobu                        Sueyori
                  1514-62                             |
                     |                             Shinshō
Kiyonobu          Shōei            Mitsumasa          |
                  1520-93                           Ryōjō
   |                 |                                |
Kyūhaku           Eitoku         Sōshū    Genshun
1577-1654         1543-90           |        |
                                 Shinsetsu  Shunsetsu
Kyūhaku  Sanraku    Mitsunobu   Takanobu      |
+ 1662   2559-1635  1561-1608   1571-1618   Bai-ei
                                              
Kyūhaku  Sansetsu   Sadanobu    Tan-yū   Naonobu   Baishun
         1589-1651  1596-1622   1602-74  1607-50

Kyūen    Einō       Yasunobu  Dōun     Tanshin   Tsunenobu
         1631-1697  1616-85   1625-94  1653-1718 1636-1713

Kyūtaku  Eikei      Morinobu  Dōshun   Tansen    Chikanobu
         1662-1702  1675-1724 + 1724   + 1728    1660-1728

Kyūzan   Eikaku     Norinobu  Gensan    Tanjō    Eisen
         1687-1764  1692-1731 1695-1751 + 1756   1696-1731

Kyūen    Eiryō      Terunobu  Dōshun    Tanrin   Eisen
         1740-1770  1717-1763 1747-1797 + 1777   1730-1790

Kyūseki  Eijō       Takanobu  Dōhaku    Tambaku  Isen
         1731-1787  1740-1795 + 1851    1770-1842 + 1828

Gyokuen  Eishun     Yasunobu  Dōeki     Tanshin  Seisen
         1783-1830  1767-1798 + 1841    1785-1835 1796-1846

Gyokuei  Eigaku     Kuninobu            Tan-en   Shōsen
         1790-1867                      1795-1843 1823-1880

Sōchi                                   Tangen
                                        1829-1866

Yūeki                                   Tansetsu

School   School   School        School       School      School
of       of       of            of           of          of
Kaga.    Kyōto.   Naka-bashi.   Suruga-dai.  Kaji-bashi. Kobiki-chō.
                  (Edo).        (Edo).       (Edo).      (Edo).
```

——**Tan-yū, 探幽** (1602-1674). The eldest son of *Takanobu*, restored the *Kanō* school, which had declined after *Motonobu*. His true name was *Morinobu*, but, after having had his head shaved, he took that of *Tan-yū*. The *Shōgun Hidetada* and *Iemitsu* patronized him and gave him ground near the *Kaji-bashi* bridge (*Edo*) to establish his school. In 1662, he was called to *Kyōto*, to paint the portrait of the ex-emperor *Go-Mi-no-o*.

—— **Naonobu,** 尚信 (1607-1650). A brother of *Tan-yū*, founded a school in the district *Kobiki-chō* (*Edo*).

—— **Dō-un,** 洞雲 (1625-1694). An adopted son of *Tan-yū*, founded a school in the *Suruga-dai* district (*Edo*).

Kanroji, 甘露寺. A *kuge* family descended from *Fujiwara Yoshikado*. — Now Count.

Kanshin, 鑑眞 (687-763). A Chinese bonze who came to Japan in 754 and, having been installed in the *Tō-daiji* temple (*Kyōto*), founded the *Ritsu* or *Kairitsu-shū* sect. He imposed the 10 precepts (*kai*) of the sect upon the emperor *Shōmu* and 430 officials of the Court. In 758, he received the name of *Taishin-oshō*. He is also called *Ganjin*.

KANSHIN.

Kantokoro, 神地. Formerly, territorial possessions given to Shintoist temples for their maintenance. They are also called *Shinryō*.

Kan-ya-i-mimi no mikoto, 神八井耳尊. The 2nd son of *Jimmu*. At the death of his father, he fought and killed his elder brother *Tagishi-mimi no mikoto*, who aspired to the throne.

Ka-ō, 嘉應. *Nengō*: 1169-1170.

Kara, 唐. An ancient name of China, the corresponding Japanese name of the *Tang* dynasty (*Tō*: 618-936).

Karafune-bugyō, 唐船奉行, or simply *Kara-bugyō*. Under the *Ashikaga*, an official having charge of superintending the relations of bonzes, merchants, etc. with China.

Karafuto, 樺太. Saghalien island (from N. to S. about 1,050 Km.) The southern part belonged to Japan from time immemorial. In 1875, Japan ceded her part to Russia in exchange for the *Chishima* (Kurile isl.), but retook it after the Russo-Japanese war (1905).

Karahashi, 唐橋. A *kuge* family descended from the *Sugawara*. — Now Viscount.

Karasaki, 唐崎. A place in *Ōmi* on the south-western shore of lake *Biwa*. In 1331, prince *Morinaga-shinnō* defeated *Hōjō Nakatoki* at that place.

Karasumaru, 烏丸. A *kuge* family descended from the *Fujiwara*. — Now Count.

Karasumaru-dono, 烏丸殿. An ancient palace of the *Shōgun Yoshimasa* in *Kyōto*. It is also called *Muromachi-dono* and *Hana-gosho*.

Karasu-yama, 烏山. A place in *Shimotsuke*, for a long time was the residence of the *Nasu daimyō*. Later it belonged to the following *daimyō*: the *Narita* (1590-1623), the *Matsushita* (1623-1627), the *Hori* (1627-1671), the *Itakura* (1672-1681), the *Nasu* (1681-1685), the *Nagai* (1685-1702), the *Inagaki* (1703-1725), and finally the *Ōkubo* (1725-1868) — (30,000 k).

Karatsu, 唐津. A place in *Hizen*, where during the Korean war (1592-98), *Hideyoshi* built a castle which he subsequently bestowed on *Terazawa Hirotaka*, whose family occupied it until 1647. Afterwards it came into the possession of the *Ōkubo daimyō* (1649-1678), the *Matsu-*

daira (1678-1691), the *Doi* (1691-1762), the *Mizuno* (1762-1817), and finally the *Ogasawara* (1817-1868) — (60,000 k.).

Karei, 家令. Formerly the superintendent of the household of a prince or nobleman.

Kareki, 嘉暦. *Nengō:* 1326-1328).

Kariya, 苅屋. An ancient castle in *Mikawa*, belonging to the *Mizuno* family from the middle of the 16th century till 1632. After that it passed over to the following *daimyō* families: the *Matsudaira* (1632-1651), the *Inagaki* (1651-1702), the *Abe* (1702-1709), the *Honda* (1709-1712), the *Miura* (1712-1747), and finally, to the *Doi* (1747 to 1868) — (23,000 k.).

Karizaka-tōge, 苅坂峠. A mountain pass (2,080 m) between *Kai* and *Musashi*).

Karō, 家老. Formerly the intendant of a *daimyō*.

Karoku, 嘉禄. *Nengō:* 1225-1226.

Karumi, 軽海. A hamlet of the *Mukawa* village (*Mino*), where the ruins of two ancient castles are seen. The eastern castle was the residence of the *Inaba daimyō* till 1468, then of the *Andō daimyō*, from 1540 to 1572. The western castle was built by *Katagiri Hanzaemon* towards 1550, and was transferred to *Hitotsu-yanagi Naomori* in 1589, who was dispossessed of it in the following year.

Kasa-ga-take, 笠嶽. A mountain (2120 m.) in the north-east of *Hida*.

Kasagi-yama, 笠置山. A mountain on the border of *Yamashiro* and *Yamato*, where the emperor *Go-Daigo* took refuge to escape from *Hōjō Takatoki* (1331). Soon afterwards he was besieged on the mountain, made prisoner, and banished to the *Oki* islands.

Kasai Kiyoshige, 葛西清重. A descendant of the *Taira*, who settled in *Musashi* and joined the party of *Yoritomo*. He accompanied *Noriyori* in his campaign against the *Taira* (1184), and *Yoritomo* in his expedition against *Fujiwara Yasuhira* (1189). He was then appointed governor of *Mutsu*. He contributed to the suppression of the revolt of *Wada Yoshimori* against the *Hōjō* (1213) and received the title of *Iki no kami*. Soon afterwards he had his head shaved and the people gave him the name of *Iki-nyūdo*. — His descendants, for several generations, continued to govern the province of *Mutsu*.

Kasakake, 笠掛. Formerly a sort of sport of the *samurai*. A hat was hoisted on a bamboo as a target. The *samurai* on horseback galoping past at full speed, were to pierce it with an arrow. During the *Kamakura* Shōgunate there were two varieties, the *tō-kasakake* and *kō-kasakake*.

Kasama, 笠間. An ancient castle in *Hitachi* built by *Taira Sada-michi*, whose descendants took the name of *Kasama* and, towards 1575, were dispossessed by *Utsunomiya Kunitsuna*. Under the *Tokugawa*, the castle was the residence of the following *daimyō* families: the *Matsui* (1601-07), the *Ogasawara* (1607-09), the *Toda* (1612-16), the *Nagai* (1616-1622), the *Asano* (1622-45), the *Inoue* (1645-92), the *Honjō* (1692-1702), the *Inoue* (1702-47) and the *Makino* (1747-1868). — (80.000 k.)

Kasanui no sato, 笠縫里. A village in *Yamato* where the emperor *Sujin* built a temple in honor of *Amaterasu* (92 B. C.,) and where he deposited two of the sacred treasures, the mirror and the sword. His daughter *Toyosuki-iri-hime* was its high-priestess. It was the first time that the imperial palace and the Shintoist temple were separated. — In the fourth year B. C., the temple, together with the sacred mirror, was transferred to *Ise* (*Gekū*.).

Kasato-iima, 笠戸嶋. An island (36 Km. in circuit) in the Inland Sea, south of the province of *Suwō*, to which it belongs.

Kashii, 香推. A place in *Chikuzen*, where the emperor *Chūai* established his camp at the time of his expedition against the *Kumaso*, and where he died (200).

Kashii, 樫井. A place in *Izumi*, where, during the *Ōsaka* war (1615) the troops of *Ōno Harufusa* were defeated by *Asano Nagaakira*.

Kashima, 鹿嶋. A place in *Hizen*, which was, from 1610 to 1868, the residence of a branch of the *Nabeshima* family (20,000 k.)

Kashima, 鹿嶋. A Shintoist temple in *Hitachi*, founded according to legend by *Jimmu-tennō* in honor of *Takemikazuchi*. Already in ancient times, it had the *Ōnokatomi* family at its head and possessed the whole district of *Kashima*. It had to be rebuilt every 21st year and always on the same plan. In the time of *Yoritomo*, *Kashima Munemoto* built a castle there of which his descendants were dispossessed by *Satake Yoshishige* in 1590.

Kashima-nada, 鹿嶋灘. The sea on the eastern coast of *Hitachi*.

Kashiwabara, 樫原. A place in *Tamba* which was the residence of a branch of the *Oda* family from 1695 to 1868 (20,000 k.).

Kashiwabara no miya, 樫原宮. A palace which *Jimmu-tennō* built at the foot of Mount *Unebi* (*Yamato*). It was at that place that *Jimmu-tennō* was enthroned (660 B. C.) and died.

Kashiwabara-tennō, 樫原天皇. *Kwammu-tennō* (782-805).

Kashiwade no Omi, 膳臣. Anciently an official in charge of all that concerned the table of the emperor. This title was hereditary in the *Ōtomo* family. Later on, the official was called *Kashiwade-zukasa*.

Kashō, 嘉祥. (Sanscr. *Kâsyapa*). Name of several Buddhist divinities: *Kashō-butsu* (*Kâsyapa Buddha*), one of the 7 ancient Buddhas; *Kashō* (*Mahâ-Kâsyapa*), one of the first disciples of *Shaka*: a legend tells us that having swallowed the sun and the moon, his body became more brilliant than gold; *Kashō-mato* (*Kâsyapa-Matanga*), etc.

Kashō, 嘉祥. *Nengō* 848-850.

Kashō, 嘉承. *Nengō* 1106-1107.

Kashō, 迦葉. One of the principal disciples of *Shaka*. Legend tells us that, having swallowed the sun and the moon, his body became brighter than gold.

Kashū, 河川. The Chinese name of the province of *Kawachi*.

Kashū, 加州. The Chinese name of the province of *Kaga*.

Kasuga-busshi, 春日佛師. The general name of all the members of the school of sculpture formerly annexed to the *Kasuga* temple of *Nara*.

Kasuga-daimyōjin, 春日大明神. The god honored in the *Kasuga* temple at *Nara*. — See *Ame no Koyane*.

Kasuga-jinja, 春日神社 . — See *Kasuga-yama.*

Kasuga no matsuri, 春日祭 . A festival celebrated at the *Kasuga* temple (*Nara*) in honor of the gods *Takemikazuchi, Futsunushi, Ame no Koyane,* etc. In 710, *Fujiwara Fuhito* selected the god *Takemikazuchi,* honored at *Kashima* (*Hitachi*), as the protector of his family, but on account of the distance, he built a new temple on the *Kasuga* hill at *Nara.* Hence the name *Kasuga-jinja* given to the temple and that of *Kasuga daimyōjin* to the god honored therein.

Kasuga no Miya, 春日宮 . — See *Shiki no Ōji.*

Kasuga no Tsubone, 春日局 (1579-1643). A daughter of *Saitō Toshizō* a *kerai* of *Akechi Mitsuhide;* she married *Inaba Masanori* a *samurai* of the *Ukita.* At the birth of *Iemitsu,* she offered herself as a nurse, and her services were accepted. Later, having heard that the wife of *Hidetada,* who preferred her second son *Kunichiyo* (*Tadanaga*), endeavored to have him appointed heir, and that the *Shōgun* seemed inclined to give his assent, *Kasuga no Tsubone,* pretending to go on a pilgrimage to *Ise,* went to *Sumpu,* (*Shizuoka*) and informed *Ieyasu,* who immediately repaired to *Edo* and spoke in favor of the elder of his grandsons. *Iemitsu,* having become *Shōgun,* did not forget the service rendered by his nurse and proved himself generous towards her. In 1629, she was called to *Kyōto* by the emperor *Go-Mi-no-o* who bestowed presents on her and gave her the second rank at Court with the name of *Kasuga no Tsubone.* She died at the age of 65.

Kasuga-ryū, 春日流 . A school of painting founded towards the end of the 10th century by *Fujiwara Motomitsu.* It sprang from the school of *Kose Kanaoka* The best known of its members are the *Fujiwara, Takayoshi, Takachika* (12th century) *Mitsunaga* (+ 1187) *Takanobu* (1142-1205), *Nobuzane* (1178-1266), next the *Shiba, Kwanshin, Sonkai, Keishun,* (15th century), *Ringen* (16th century), *Jiyū* (17th century).

Kasuga-yama, 春日山 . A hill east of *Nara,* upon which *Fujiwara Fuhito* erected a temple to his ancestors in 710 : it is the *Kasuga-jinja,* one of the most ancient and most venerated in Japan.

Kasuga-yama, 春日山 . An ancient castle in *Echigo,* built towards 1340 by *Uesugi Noriaki,* whose descendants were dispossessed of it by their *kerai Nagao Terutora* (*Kenshin*) in 1542. The latter's son *Kagekatsu* was transferred to *Aizu* in 1596, and replaced by *Hori Hideharu.* In 1610, *Ieyasu* bestowed the province of *Echigo* on his son *Tadateru,* who fortified himself at *Takata,* and the castle of *Kasuga-yama* was abandoned.

Kasumi ga ura, 霞浦 . A lake, (135 Km. in circuit) in *Hitachi.*

Kasuya Takenori, 糟屋武則 . A *samurai* of *Harima,* who entered the service of *Hideyoshi* in 1578. He received a revenue of 12,000 k. at *Kakogawa* (*Harima*). After the death of *Hideyoshi* he joined the party against *Ieyasu,* and after the battle of *Sekigahara,* was beheaded at *Kyōto* (1600).

Katagiri, 片桐 . A *daimyō* family of *Ōmi,* and descended from *Seiwa-Genji.*

—— A branch that resided at *Tatsuta* (*Yamato*) —— 10,000 k and became extinct in 1657.

—— Another branch, established at *Koizumi* (*Yamato* — 12,000 k.) in 1615, resided at that place till the Restoration. —— Now Viscount

Katakura, 片倉. A *samurai* family of the *Sendai* clan, ennobled after the Restoration. It had a revenue of 30,000 k. at *Shiraishi* (*Rikuzen*). —— Now Baron.

Katano, 交野. A *kuge* family descended from the *Taira*. —— Now Viscount.

Kataoka, 片岡. A family ennobled after the Restoration. —— Now Baron.

Kataribe, 語部. Formerly an association of public story-tellers. In certain solemn circumstances, they related ancient legends in presence of the emperor.

Katase, 片瀬. A village in *Sagami*, west of *Kamakura*. Anciently the place called *Tatsu no kuchi* was reserved for the execution of criminals. *Nichiren* (1271), the ambassadors of *Kublai Khan* (1275), etc., were taken there to be put to death.

Katata, 堅田. A place in *Ōmi*. Before 1600, it was the residence of the *daimyō* of the same name.

Katata, 堅田. A *daimyō* family that resided at the village of the same name towards the end of the 16th century (*Ōmi* — 20,000 k.).

—— **Hirozumi,** 廣澄. *Hyōbu-Shōsuke*, having joined the party against *Ieyasu*, was dispossessed and condemned to commit *harakiri* (1600).

Katei, 嘉禎. *Nengō:* 1235-1237.

Katō, 加藤. A *daimyō* family that resided at *Kumamoto* (*Hizen*) from 1588 to 1632.

—— **Kiyomasa,** 清正 (1562-1611). Born at *Nakamura* (*Owari*), he was called *Toranosuke* in his childhood. He lost his father when he was 3 years old. His mother being related to the mother of *Hideyoshi*, this latter who lived then at *Nagahama* (*Ōmi*), took upon himself to educate the boy. In 1585, he was nominated *Kazue no kami*; three years later, when the governor of *Higo*, *Sasa Narimasa*, had been dispossessed, *Kiyomasa* received in fief, half of this province with residence at *Kumamoto* (250,000 k.). He together with *Konishi Yukinaga*, commanded the van-guard of the Korean expedition (1592); his bravery and victories led the enemies to surname him *Kishō-kwan* (devil-general). *Ishida Kazushige, Konishi Yukinaga* and others having proposed peace,

[KATŌ KIYOMASA.]

Kiyomasa opposed the measure and was recalled to Japan by *Hideyoshi*. He returned to Korea when war broke out again (1597). Besieged in *Urusan*, by a numerous Chinese army, he offered a long and noble resistance and was at last delivered by *Kobayakawa Hideaki* and *Mōri Hidemoto*. He returned to Japan after the death of *Hideyoshi* (1598), and sided with *Ieyasu* who gave him in marriage the daughter of *Mizuno Tadashige* whom he had brought up, and after the battle of *Sekigahara*, he added to his domains the other half of *Higo* province that had been till then the property of *Konishi Yukinaga*. His revenues thus rose to

KATŌ KIYOMASA FIGHTING IN KOREA.

520,000 k. He died in 1611, and *Ieyasu* was suspected of having had a hand in his death, fearing as he did that *Kiyomasa* might side with *Hideyori*. *Kiyomasa* was a relentless enemy of the Christian name; he is honored in the temples of the *Nichiren* sect, to which he belonged, under the name of *Seishō-ko* (*Seishō* is the Chinese pronunciation of the Japanese *Kiyomasa*).

—— **Tadahiro,** 忠 廣 (1597-1653). *Kiyomasa's* son, being *Higo no kami*, was accused of having entered into a conspiracy to replace the *Shōgun Iemitsu* by his brother; for this purpose, he was dispossessed and banished to *Tsurugaoka* (*Dewa*), where he died. His son *Mitsuhiro* was at the same time exiled to *Takayama* (*Hida*): he died there the following year.

Katō, 加 藤. A family of *daimyō*, originating in *Mikawa* and descended from *Fujiwara Uona* (721-783).

—— **Yoshiaki,** 嘉 明 (1563-1631). At first served *Hideyoshi*. At the time of the Korean expedition, he commanded the fleet together with *Tōdō Takatora*. On his return, he sided with *Ieyasu*, was present at the battle of *Sekigahara* and was transferred from *Matsuzaki* (*Iyo* — 100,000 k.) to *Matsuyama* (*Iyo* — 200,000 k.) (1600). After the death of *Gamō Tadasato* (1627), he received the fief of *Aizu* (*Mutsu* — 400,000 k.).

—— **Akinari,** 明 成. Son of *Yoshiaki*, was dispossessed in 1643, owing to the tyranny with which he oppressed his subjects.

—— **Akitomo, 明 友**. Son of *Akinari;* after the deposition of his father, he received from the *Shōgun Iemitsu,* in consideration of his grandfather *Yoshiaki,* a revenue of 10,000 k. at *Yoshimizu (Iwami).* —— His descendants were transferred successively: in 1682 to *Minakuchi (Ōmi* — 20,000 k.); in 1695 to *Mibu (Shimotsuke);* and in 1712 to *Minakuchi (Ōmi* — 25,000 k.) where they resided till 1868. — Now Viscount.

Katō, 加 藤. A family of *daimyō,* originating in *Mino* and descended from the *Fujiwara.*

$$\text{Mitsuyasu - Sadayasu - Yasuoki} \begin{cases} \text{Yasuyoshi - Yasutsune} & \text{(a)} \\ \text{Yasukado - Yasuzane} & \text{(b)} \end{cases}$$

(a) — Elder Branch. —— **Mitsuyasu, 光 泰** (1537-1595). At first served *Nobunaga,* then *Hideyoshi,* who gave him a revenue of 20,000 k. at *Takashima (Ōmi).* In 1590, he was raised to 240,000 k. in *Kai.* He died in Korea.

—— **Sadayasu, 定 泰** (1581-1624). Son of *Mitsuyasu,* received, on his father's death, the castle of *Kurono (Mino* — 40,000 k.). He was transferred in 1610 to *Yonago (Hōki);* then, in 1617, to *Ōsu (Iyo* — 60,000 k.) where his descendants lived until the Restoration. — Now Viscount.

(b) — Junior Branch, installed since 1624 at *Niiya (Iyo* — 10,000 k.). — Now Viscount.

Katō, 加 藤. A family ennobled in 1900. — Now Baron.

—— **Hiroyuki, 弘 之**. Born in 1836 at *Izushi (Tajima),* senator (1875), director of the *Kaisei-gakkō* (1877), rector of the University of *Tōkyō* (1886-1893).

Katō, 加 藤. A family descended from *Fujiwara Toshihito.*

—— **Kagekazu, 景 員**. Son of *Kagemichi, Kaga no Suke,* lived in *Ise.* Having assassinated a *kerai* of the *Taira,* he left the province and fled with his two sons to *Kudō Shigemitsu (Ise)* who gave him his daughter in marriage. When *Yoritomo* rose in arms against the *Taira* (1181), *Kagekazu* sided with him, fought under him at *Ishibashi-yama* and afterwards served the *Bakufu.*

—— **Kagekado, 景 廉** (+ 1221). Son of *Kagekazu,* served in the campaign of *Noriyori* against the *Taira* (1184), then in that of *Yoritomo* against *Fujiwara Yasuhira* (1189). At the death of *Sanetomo* (1219), he became bonze.

Katō, 加 藤. Family which for 7 centuries has been directing the great porcelain manufactures of *Seto (Owari).*

—— **Shunkei, 春 慶** or *Shirōzaemon,* **四 郎 左 衛 門**. Seeing the imperfection of the processes employed so far, he repaired to China in 1223 with the bonze *Dōgen,* and remained there five years, spending his time in studying the Chinese methods. On his return to Japan, he settled down in the district of *Kasugai (Owari),* where he found a clay that seemed to possess all the qualities suitable for his purpose and set up a work-shop which grew steadily in importance.

—— **Tamikichi, 民吉**. A descendant of the former, is the hero of a famous legend. While he was still a pupil of *Tsugane Bunzaemon*, at the beginning of the 16th century, the latter desirous to know the secret of the fabrication of the *Hizen* potters, succeeded in negotiating a marriage between *Tamikichi* and the daughter of the principal potter of *Arita*. *Tamikichi* settled in his new family and remained there several years. He was initiated into all the secrets of fabrication, then, under pretext of wishing to see his native province again, he returned to *Owari*, where he made known all that he had learned and thus improved the *Seto* porcelains a good deal. The people of *Arita* wreaked their vengeance on him by crucifying his wife and children, who had remained among them.

Katori, 香取. In *Shimōsa*. A famous *Shinto* temple, founded, according to a legend, by *Jimmu-tennō* in honor of *Iwanushi no kami*.

Katsu, 勝. A family of *samurai* from the *Shizuoka* clan, ennobled after the Restoration. — Now Count.

—— **Yoshikuni,** (1823-1900) or **Yasuyoshi**. Better known by the name of *Awa* (on account of his title of *Awa no kami*) at the time of the Restoration, played the part of peacemaker between the two parties.

Katsukawa, 勝川. A family of painters of the realistic school (*ukiyo-e*), famous in the *Tokugawa* times. They dwelt at *Edo*. The most famous are : *Shunsui* (towards 1740), *Shunshō* (1726-1792), *Shun-ei* (1762-1819) : *Shunkō* (+ 1827) *Shunsei* (towards 1820), etc.

Katsumoto, 勝本. Principal town of the island *Iki*. From 1689 to 1868, was the residence of a branch of the *Matsuura daimyō* (10,000 k.).

Katsura, 桂. A family of *samurai* from *Chōshū*, ennobled in 1895. — Now Count.

—— **Tarō, 太郎**. Born in 1849, Vice-Minister of war from 1886 to 1891, commanded the *Nagoya* division during the war with China. Viscount in 1895, Governor of Formosa, Minister of war (1898-1900), Prime Minister (1901-1906), Count from the time of the formation of the Anglo-Japanese alliance (1902).

Katsurabara-Shinnō, 葛原親王 (786-853). Son of the emperor *Kwammu*, was *Hitachi no taishu*, *Shikibu-kyō*, *Dazai no sotsu*. He is the ancestor of the *Taira*.

Katsuragawa, 桂川. A family that during several generations filled in the *Bakufu* the office of translator for the Dutch. The best known members are : *Hoshū* (1751-1809), *Hosan* (1754-1808), *Hochiku* (1767-1827), *Hoken* (1797-1844), etc.

Katsuragi, 葛城. Name given by *Jimmu-tennō* to the village of *Taka-owari* (*Yamato*), where he defeated the *Tsuchigumo*, with the help of *katsura* nets. The emperor *Suisei*, resided there after the death of *Jimmu*. It is the birth-place of the *Soga*, the mighty ministers of the 7th century : they possessed the *agata* of *Katsuragi*.

Katsuragi Tsubura, 葛城圓. Son of *Tamata no Sukune*. Was minister in the reigns of *Richū*, *Hanshō*, *Ingyō*. When the young prince *Mayuwa no Ō* had assassinated the emperor *Ankō*, he fled to the house of *Tsubura*. The latter summoned by the new emperor *Yūryaku* to hand over the culprit, answered that he could not betray the confidence of the prince, who had asked him for protection He perished under the ruins of his house with all his family (456 A. D.).

Katsuragi-yama, 葛城山. A mountain on the limits of *Yamato* and *Kawachi*. A *Shintō* shrine has been erected on it in honor of the god *Hitokotonushi*. It is there that *En no Shōkaku* retired in 665 and for thirty years practised the art of sorcery.

Katsura-kawa, 桂川. A river (83 Km.) which takes its rise in *Tamba*, flows through *Yamashiro* and empties itself into the *Yodo-gawa*, south of *Kyōto*.

Katsusai ga yatsu, 葛西谷. A valley east of *Kamakura*, in which *Hōjō Yasutoki* built the temple of *Tōshō-ji*, to serve as the burial place for the members of his family. There *Hōjō Takatoki*, defeated by *Nitta Yoshisada*, put an end to his life with 283 of his *samurai* (1333).

Katsushika Hokusai, 葛飾北齋. — See *Hokusai*.

Katsuura, 勝浦. In *Awa* (*Shikoku*). In 1185, *Yoshitsune*, on his way to fight the *Taira*, was driven there by the wind. He landed and defeated *Sakurama Yoshitō* near the temple of *Denrin-ji*.

Katsuura, 勝浦. In *Kazusa*. Was from 1600 to 1751 the residence of the *Uemura daimyō* (12,000 k.).

Katsuyama, 勝山. In *Echizen*. Was from 1624 to 1691, the residence of a branch of the *Matsudaira* family; and from 1691 to 1868 that of the *Ogasawara* (22,000 k.).

Katsuyama, 勝山. In *Mimasaka*. Ancient castle built by *Miura Sadamune*, at the beginning of the 14th century. The descendants of the latter resided there for thirteen generations, but were dispossessed by *Ukita Naoie*, towards 1550. After *Sekigahara*, the castle passed over to the *Mōri daimyō*; but in 1764, it returned to the *Miura*, who held it until the Restoration (23,000 k.).

Katsuyama, 勝山. Ancient name of the castle of *Matsuyama* (*Iyo*).

Katsuyama, 勝山. In *Awa* (*Tōkaidō*). — See *Kachiyama*.

Kawabe, 河邊. A family descended from the *Fujiwara*, whose members were hereditarily attached to the *Kōfuku-ji* temple (*Nara*). — Now Baron.

Kawabe, 河邊. A family descended from the *Fujiwara*, and attached for centuries to the great temple of *Ise*. — Now Baron.

Kawachi, 河内. One of the 5 provinces of the *Go-Kinai*. Comprises 3 districts, which depend on the *Ōsaka-fu*. — Chinese name: *Kashū*.

Kawada, 河田. A family of *samurai*, from the clan of *Tottori* (*Inaba*), ennobled after the Restoration. — Now Vicount.

Kawada, 河田. A *samurai* family, from the clan of *Kōchi* (*Tosa*), ennobled after the Restoration. — Now Baron.

Kawa-fune-bugyō, 川船奉行. In the *Tokugawa* period, an official intrusted with the inspection of the boats on the rivers and canals of *Edo*, with the collection of the taxes, the delivery of patents, etc. At first the title was *Kawafune-shihai*, but in 1746 it was changed to that of *Kawa-fune-bugyō*, or *Kawa-fune-aratame-yaku*.

Kawagoe, 川越 . A city of *Musashi* province (20,000 inh.). Was first the residence of a family of the same name. *Kawagoe Shigeyori* served *Yoritomo*. In 1457, *Ōta Mochisuke*, *kerai* of the *Ōgigayatsu* (*Uesugi*), built a castle there which passed afterwards to the *daimyō* *Hōjō* (1537-90) *Sakai* (1591-1634), *Hotta* (1635-38), *Ōkōchi* (1639-94), *Yanagisawa* (1694-1704), *Akimoto* (1704-67), and finally to the *Matsudaira* (170,000 k.).

Kawaguchi, 河 口 . A family of *samurai* of the clan of *Wakayama* (*Kii*), ennobled after the Restoration. — Now Baron.

Kawaguchi-ko, 河 口 湖 . A lake in *Kai*, at the foot of Mt. *Fuji*. Also called *Benten-ko* (18 Km. in circumference).

Kawahire, 河 鰭 . A family of *kuge*, descended from *Fujiwara* (*Sanjō*) *Saneyuki* (1083-1162). — Now Viscount.

Kawajiri-misaki, 川 尻 岬 . A cape to the N. E. of *Nagato*.

Kawakami, 河 上 . A family of *samurai* from the clan of *Kagoshima* (*Satsuma*), ennobled after the Restoration. — Now Viscount.

Kawamura, 川 村 . A family of *samurai* from the clan of *Kagoshima* (*Satsuma*), ennobled after the Restoration. — Now Count.

Kawamura, 川 村 . A family originating in *Satsuma*, ennobled in 1896. — Now Baron.

Kawamura Zuiken, 川 村 瑞 軒 (1618-1700). Born at *Edo*, was at first a simple footman then a mail-carrier. A great fire having destroyed a part of the town, he repaired in haste to the mountains of *Kiso*, and brought a large quantity of building timber to *Edo*, which he sold at a great profit, or employed in erecting houses and stores. He afterwards engaged in cutting canals near some rivers to prevent inundations, such as the *Aji-kawa*, the *Yodo-gawa*, the *Nagara-gawa*, the *Nakatsu-gawa*, etc.

Kawanabe Kyōsai, 河 鍋 曉 齋 (1832-89). Born at *Koga*, (*Shimōsa*), he came to *Edo* and studied painting at the *Kanō* school. Was the last representative of the *Hokusai* "genre." Also called *Shōjō Kyōsai*.

Kawanakajima, 川 中 嶋 . A district comprised between the two rivers *Sai-gawa* and *Chikuma-gawa*, to the N. E. of *Shinano*. Was from 1553 to 1563 the scene of many engagements between *Uesugi Kenshin* and *Takeda Shingen*. In the *Tokugawa* period, it was the domain of the *Matsudaira daimyō* (1603-19), and the *Fukushima* (1619-24).

Kawasaki, 川 崎 . In *Rikuzen*, where *Minamoto Yoriyoshi* was defeated in 1056 by *Abe no Sadatō*.

Kawasaki, 河 崎 . A family of financiers, ennobled after the Restoration. — Now Baron.

Kawase, 河 瀨 . A family of *samurai* from the clan of *Yamaguchi* (*Suwō*), ennobled after the Restoration. — Now Viscount.

Kawatake Shinshichi, 河 竹 新 七 . A name of several artists, both actors and dramatists: *Shinshichi I.* (1747-95), *Shinshichi II.* (1816-93), also called *Furukawa Mokuami*; *Shinshichi III.* (1842-1901).

Kayano, 萱野. A place in *Tamba;* was until 1615 the domain of *Oda Nobukane,* brother of *Nobunaga.*

Kayanu-hime, 鹿屋野比賣. The prairie goddess (*Shintō*); daughter of *Izanagi* and *Izanami;* also called *Nozuchi no Kami.*

Kayo no Miya, 嘉陽宮. Princely title, created in favor of the 2nd son of prince *Kuni Asahiko, Kuninori,* who, born in 1867, married the daughter of Marquis *Daigo* in 1892; he is the superintendent of the great temple of *Ise.*

Kazahaya, 風早. A family of *kuge* descended from *Fujiwara* (*Sanjō*) *Saneyuki* (1083-1162) — Now Viscount.

Kazue-ryō, 主計寮. — See *Shukei-ryō.*

Kazusa, 上總. One of the 15 provinces of the *Tōkaidō.* Comprises 5 districts which depend on *Chiba-ken.* — Chinese name: *Sōshū* (with *Shimōsa*). — Formerly, *Kazusa* formed with *Shimōsa* only one province called *Fusa no kuni.* When it was divided in two, the southern part was called *Kami-tsu-fusa,* which was contracted into *Kazusa.*

Kebiishi-chō, 撿非違使廳. Formerly an office charged with the police and the punishment of crimes. Created in 839, it combined the functions of the *Efu* (arrest of criminals), the *Danjōdai* (judgment) and the *Gyōbu-shō* (punishment). It was directed by 1 *bettō,* 4 *suke* and 4 *tai-i.* Its importance increased with years. Notifications issued by it had the same value as imperial ordinances. The title of *Kebiishi-bettō* was much coveted and more than one civil war was caused by the rejection of a demand to obtain it. The emperor *Montoku* established a *Kebiishi-chō* in each province (857). When *Yoritomo* became *Shōgun* in 1192, he assigned to the *daimyō* the right of justice in their estates, and the influence of the *Kebiishi-chō* began to decline.

Kegon no taki, 華嚴瀧. A waterfall at *Nikkō,* the height of which is about 80 m. It has been called the "tomb" of Shopenhauer and Nietsche's philosophical theories, so many were the youths who practicing "the denial of the will to live" jumped into the great waterfall. The police has of late years tried to put a stop to this craze for suicide at the *Kegon no taki.*

Kegon-shū, 華嚴宗. A Buddhist sect, introduced into Japan by the Chinese bonze *Dōsen* in 735. At present, it possesses only about 20 temples in all the land.

Kei-an, 慶安. *Nengō:* 1648-1651.

Keibunkwai, 稽文會. A famous sculptor of Buddhist statues in the reign of *Shōmu* (8th century).

Keichō, 慶長. *Nengō:* 1596-1614.

Keichō no kwatsuji-hon, 慶長活字本. The first books printed in Japan with movable types, by order of *Ieyasu,* during the *Keichō* period.

Keichō-zan, 鷄頂山. Another name for Mt. *Takahara* to the N. of *Shimotsuke* (1800 m.).

Keichū, 契冲 (1640-1701). From his birth, he was called *Shimokawa Kūshin.* His father, *Genzen,* was *kerai* of the *Aoyama daimyō* of

Amagasaki (Settsu). At the age of 11, *Kūshin* left his father's house and placed himself under the direction of the bonze *Heijō* from the *Myōhō-ji* temple. Two years later, he went to *Kōya-san* to study and was appointed *ajari*. He then assumed the name of *Keichū*. He applied himself especially to the study of the ancient literature and history of Japan. *Mito Mitsukuni* tried to induce him to come to *Edo ;* but *Keichū* preferred to live in his solitude. He commented on the *Manyōshū*, the *Ise-monogatari*, the *Genji-monogatari*, etc. It was he that put in vogue the study of national antiquities.

Keijō, 京城. Japanese pronunciation of the two characters which the Koreans use for "capital." It stands for *Seoul* as formerly *Miyako* stood for *Kyōto.* — The Japanese pronunciation of the two characters of *Seoul* would be *Suigen.*

Keiju-in, 慶壽院 (+ 1565). Daughter of the *Kwampaku Konoe Hisamichi*, wife of the *Shōgun Ashikaga Yoshiharu* and mother of *Yoshiteru.* When the latter was attacked by *Miyoshi Yoshitsugu* and *Matsunaga Hisahide*, he set fire to his palace and committed suicide. Some servants offered to help *Keiju-in* to escape ; but she refused and jumped into the flames to die with her son.

Keikō-tennō, 景行天皇. 12th Emperor of Japan (71-130). *Ōtarashi-hiko-oshirowake no mikoto*, succeeded, at the age of 83, to his father *Suinin*. In the year 82, he went in person to *Tsukushi*, to quell a revolt of the *Kumaso*, and returned to *Yamato* only after an absence of 7 years. His son *Yamato-takeru no mikoto* headed other expeditions later on against the *Kumaso* (97) and the *Ebisu* (110). On his return, the emperor visited the *Tōkaidō* and the *Tōsandō* (123). In 128, he transferred his palace from *Makimuku (Yamato)* to *Shiga (Ōmi).* He died, according to the official chronology, at the age of 143 years ; according to the *Koji-ki* at the age of 137 ; according to the *Nihon-ki* at 106. — (See *Nihon-ki*). He had 80 children, most of whom became the founders of ancient noble families.

Keiō, 慶應. *Nengō :* 1865-1867.

Keiō-gijuku, 慶應義塾. A School founded in 1868, towards the end of the *Keiō* era, at *Mita (Tōkyō)* by *Fukuzawa Yukichi*. The founder remained at the head of the school for over thirty years and impressed his powerful stamp on a very large number of pupils who came flocking thither from all parts of Japan, seeking a direction in the muddle that necessarily followed the establishment of a new order of things. Thus the school became a center of intellectual and social influence and most of the leading minds of to day in Japan have adopted the amiable optimism of *Fukuzawa's* utilitarian philosophy. — At present the school is composed of University, Preparatory, Middle school and Primary departments. The University department is subdivided into four courses : law, politics, economy and literature.

Keishi-chō, 警親廳. The *Tōkyō* prefecture of Police.

Keitai-tennō, 繼體天皇. 26th Emperor of Japan (507-531). *Ohodo no mikoto* or *Hikofuto no mikoto*, descendant in the 5th generation of *Ōjin-tennō*, was raised to the throne at the age of 58, after the assassination of *Buretsu*. In his reign, a man from the country of *Ryō* (China), named *Shiba Tattō*, came to Japan, and made the first attempt to introduce Buddhism; but he did not succeed (522). In Korea, war continued against *Shiragi*, which would not submit to Japanese supremacy. At the age of 82, *Keitai* abdicated in favor of his son *Ankan* and died shortly afterwards. This is the first abdication mentioned in Japanese history.

Keiten, 經典. *Sûtras*, canonical books of Buddhism; they were written, after the death of *Shaka*, by his disciples. The first doctrines of the Buddha are contained in the *Kegon-kyō*, the last in the *Nehan-kyō* and the *Amida-kyō*. The whole forms 600 volumes or fascicles.

Keiun, 慶雲. *Nengo*: 704-707.

Kemmitori, 檢見取. Or *Mitori*. In the *Tokugawa* era, an official who went every autumn to ascertain the condition of the crop in the *Shōgun's* domains, in order to determine the amount of the taxes.

Kemmotsu, 監物. — See *Nakatsukasa-shō*.

Kemmu, 建武. *Nengō*: 1334-1335. — In 1336, *Go-Daigo* changed the name of the era to that of *Engen*; but the northern dynasty kept it still for two years; it was only in 1338 that it adopted the *Reki-ō* era.

Kemmu-chū-kō, 建武中興. (Lit.: Restoration of the *Kemmu*-era). When *Go-Daigo* escaped from *Oki*, where he had been exiled and returned to *Kyōto* (1333), he changed the *Shōkei nengo* established by *Kōgon* to that of *Kemmu* he then seized the government of the empire, created a court of justice (*kirokusho*), built barracks (*musha-dokoro*) for his troops, etc. and order seemed to be restored. But two years later, *Ashikaga Takauji* revolted and plunged the country once more into civil war.

Kemmu-shiki-moku, 建武式目. A code of laws in 17 chapters, published in 1336, which was in vigor during the whole *Ashikaga* period. It was compiled by the former *Hyōjōshū* of the *Bakufu* of *Kamakura*, *Shōni*, *Akashi*, *Ōta*, *Fuse*, and by the bonzes *Zeen*, *Gen-e*, etc.

Kempō, 建保. *Nengō*: 1213-1218.

Kempō jū-shichi jō, 憲法十七條. A code of laws in 17 chapters, which according to the *Nihon-ki*, is said to have been published by prince *Shōtoku-taishi*. More than a simple code of laws, it is a compilation of moral precepts, borrowed from Buddhism, Confucianism and Shintoism.

Ken, 縣. Department. — It is only since the Imperial Restoration that Japan is divided into *ken*. In 1868, a decree divided Japan into 13 *fu*, 273 *han* and 25 *ken*: In this division, the *han* comprised the land administered by the *daimyō*, and the domains of the *Shōgun* formed the *fu* and the *ken*. In 1871, the *han* were suppressed and Japan (except *Hokkaidō*), was divided into 3 *fu* (*Tōkyō*, *Kyōto*, *Ōsaka*) and 302 *ken*. At the end of the same year, the number of *ken* was reduced to 72. In 1876, a new handling maintained only 3 *fu* and 35 *ken*. In 1882, there were 3 *fu* and 40 *ken*; in 1906, 3 *fu* and 43 *ken*, plus the 11 provinces of *Hokkaidō* and the districts of *Taiwan* (Formosa).

Kenchō, 建長. *Nengō*: 1249-1255.

Kenchō-ji, 建長寺. A temple of *Kamakura*, founded in 1253, by the bonze *Dōryū*. It became the seat of a subdivision of the *Rinzai* branch of the *Zenshū* sect

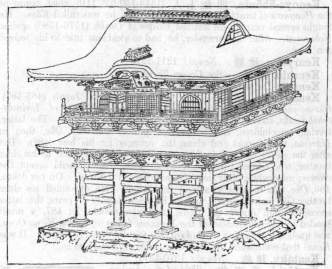

KENCHŌ-JI.

Kendan-bugyō, 撿斷奉行. In the *Kamakura* period, officials commissioned to visit the provinces, to reform abuses and render justice. Other officials, called *chi-bugyō*, were engaged in maintaining the roads, building houses, fostering commerce, etc. These two classes of officials constituted the *hoho-bugyō*.

Ken-ei, 建永. *Nengō*: 1206.

Ken ga mine, 劍峯. Eastern peak of the crater of Mt. *Fuji*. It is the true summit of the famous mountain.

Kengen, 乾元. *Nengō*: 1302.

Kenji, 建治. *Nengō*: 1275-1277.

Ken-jishin-shi, 撿地震使. A messenger sent by the Emperor, after a great earthquake, to the site of the disaster.

Kenjō, 儉仗. A *samurai* that followed a great lord and carried his sword. The *Azechi* of *Mutsu* and *Dewa* had 4 *kenjō*; the governor of *Mutsu* and the *Chinjufu-Shōgun*, two. The *Dazai no sotsu* and *Dazai-ni* had some also.

Kenju, 兼壽. — See *Rennyo-Shōnin*.

Kenkō-Hōshi, 兼好法師. — See *Yoshida Kenkō*.

Kenkyū, 建久. *Nengō*: 1190-1198.

Kennin, 建仁. *Nengō*: 1201-1203.

Kennin-ji, 建仁寺. Temple founded in *Kyōto*, in 1202, by the bonze *Eisai*. It was the first temple of the *Rinzai* branch of the *Zenshū* sect.

Kennyo-Shōnin, 顯如上人 (1543-1592). 11th chief bonze of the *Hongwan-ji* temple. During his life time, he was called *Kōsa*. He fought several years in his fortified temple of *Ōsaka* (1576-1580) against *Nobunaga*. After his surrender, he had to yield his title to his second son *Kōchō*.

Kenryaku, 建暦. *Nengō:* 1211-1212.

Kenshin, 謙信. — See *Uesugi Terutora*.

Kenshin-Daishi, 見眞大師. — See *Shinran*.

Kensō-tennō, 顯宗天皇. 23rd Emperor of Japan (485-487). *Oke-no-ihasu-wake*, grandson of *Richū-tennō* and son of *Ichinobe-oshihawake*, succeeded the emperor *Seinei* at the age of 35. The latter, having no children, called the two princes *Ōke* and *Oke*, then in *Harima*, to the court and chose the younger for his heir (482). But after the death of *Seinei*, *Oke* wanted to yield his place to his elder brother, who refused. During a whole year, neither would accept the crown; meanwhile, their sister *Iitoyo* governed the land. On her death, 485, *Oke* was induced to ascend the throne. He appointed his elder brother *Ōke*, heir apparent, and as he reigned only 3 years, the latter succeeded him under the name of *Ninken-tennō*. In 487, a revolt headed by the commander of the Japanese forces in Korea, *Ki no Ōiwa*, was quelled by the king of *Kudara*, the faithful vassal of Japan. It was *Kensō* that established the ceremony called *Kyokusui no en*.

Kentoku, 建德. *Nengō:* 1370-1371.

Kentōshi, 遣唐使. Title of the Ambassador sent regularly from Japan to China, in the times of the *Tō* dynasty (*Tang* — 619-907). The first Japanese embassy to China was headed by *Ono no Imoko* in 607. The messengers were called at first *Saikai-shi* (messengers towards the western sea). In 653, *Kishi no Nagami* was the first to receive the title of *Kentō-taishi*. The emperor *Uda*, following the advice of *Sugawara Michizane*, discontinued the embassies in 895.

ANCIENT SEAL OF THE
KENTŌSHI (733).

Kerai, 家來. Vassal of a *daimyō*, or servant attached to a house.

Kesa Gozen, 袈裟御前. — See *Mongaku-Shōnin*.

Kessho, 闕所. In the *Tokugawa* times, a punishment which consisted in depriving the culprit of a part or the whole of his goods or revenues.

Kessho-bugyō, 闕所奉行. In the *Tokugawa* days, an official intrusted with the execution of a sentence by which a criminal was deprived of his goods. When the home of the culprit was to be destroyed, the ground reverted to the *Fushin-bugyō*, the remains of the house to the *Sakuji-bugyō*, the furniture to the *Metsuke* who afterwards sold it.

Ki, 紀. An ancient family of warriors, literati, poets, etc.

—— **Oyumi, 小弓**. Was commissioned by the emperor *Yūryaku*, with *Soga Kanshi* and *Ōtomo Tan*, to fight in *Shiragi* (Korea) (465). The king of the country took to flight, but *Tan* was killed; as to *Oyumi*, he fell ill and died shortly afterwards.

—— **Ōiwa, 大磐**. Son of *Oyumi*, on hearing of the death of his father, repaired to *Shiragi*. He was not long there before he fell out with *Soga Kanshi* and killed him. In 487, he resolved to establish a kingdom for himself with the 3 western *Kan: Mimana, Koma* and *Kudara*. He built a capital which he called *Taizanjō* and took the name of *Shinsei*. Having intercepted convoys of provisions intended for *Kudara*, he was attacked by the troops of that country but put them to flight. However, he was unable to realize his ambitious views. It is not known how he died.

—— **Omaro, 男麿**. Was appointed *taishōgun* (562), sent to fight *Shiragi*, which had attacked *Mimana*, the ally of Japan, and obliged it to sue for peace. After the death of the emperor *Yōmei* (587), he assisted *Soga no Umako* to triumph over *Mononobe no Moriya*. In 591, he led another expedition into Korea.

—— **Hirozumi, 廣純**. *Chinjufu-Shōgun*, was commissioned to quell a revolt of the *Ebisu* in 774. Appointed *Mutsu no kami*, he went to fight some pillagers in *Dewa* and made them prisoners, but was assassinated by them while he was leading them into *Mutsu* (780).

—— **Kosami, 古佐美** (733-797). Was commissioned with *Fujiwara Tsuginawa* to avenge the death of *Hirozumi*. In 788, the *Ebisu*, having revolted again, *Kosami*, appointed *taishōgun*, mustered 50,000 men at the castle of *Taga* and marched against the rebels; after a first victory, he was defeated and returned to *Kyōto*.

—— **Natsui, 夏井**. Great grandson of *Kosami*, studied under *Ono no Takamura* and became a renowned caligrapher. He enjoyed the confidence of the emperor *Montoku* (851-858). After the latter's death, he was appointed governor of *Sanuki*, and proved a very clever administrator. When the *dainagon Tomo no Yoshio* set fire to a gate of the imperial palace (866), *Natsui* was banished to *Tosa*, because his brother-in-law belonged to the house of *Yoshio:* he died in exile. Besides his proficiency in handwriting, *Natsui* was renowned for his knowledge of medicine and for his skill in the game of *go*.

—— **Haseo, 長谷雄** (845-912). Was a pupil of *Sugawara Michizane* and one of the most famous literati of his time. In 894, he was to accompany *Michizane* to China, with the title of Vice-Ambassador (*fuku-shi*), but the embassy did not start, owing to the unsettled condition of China.

—— **Tsurayuki, 貫之** (883-946). Son of *Mochiyuki*, distinguished himself from his youth by his talents in caligraphy and poetry. Towards 925, he was appointed governor of *Tosa*, and published, under the title of *Tosa-niki*, a diary of his travels which has remained a classical work. In 905, he was commissioned, with his nephew *Tomonori, Ōshikōchi no Mitsune, Mibu no Tadamine,* etc. to publish the *Kokin-wakashū* (a collection of Japanese and Chinese poems both ancient and new). *Tsurayuki* is regarded as one of the great masters of Japanese poetry. His son *Tokibumi,* also held an honorable rank among the poets of his time.

KI TSURAYUKI.

— A branch of the family, intrusted with the *Shintō* temples of *Kii* and *Hizen,* was ennobled after the Restoration. — Now Baron.

Kibe, 木部. A branch of the *Jōdo-shin-shū* sect, which has its seat in the *Kinshō-ji* temple at *Kibe (Ōmi),* founded by the bonze *Kōgen.*

Kibe, 木部. A family descended from *Fujiwara Arinobu* and for centuries at the head of the temple and sect of *Kibe.* — Now Baron.

Kibi, 吉備. Ancient name of the region which comprises the provinces of *Bizen, Bitchū, Bingo* and *Mimasaka.* It was divided into *Kibi no kuchi, Kibi no naka* and *Kibi no shiri.*

Kibi-daijin, 吉備大臣. — See *Kibi Makibi.*

Kibi Makibi, 吉備眞吉備. Or *Mabi* (693-775). His true name was *Shimotsumichi Asomi;* he was descended from *Kibitsu-hiko no mikoto* and dwelt in *Kibi,* whence the name by which he is known. In 716, he went to China to study and there became famous with *Abe no Nakamaro.* He returned in 735, bringing over, it is said, to Japan the art of embroidery, the game of *go* (a kind of chess), the *biwa* (lyre with 4 strings), etc., and was appointed *Daigaku no suke.* He was chosen preceptor of the princess *Abe-naishinnō* (later on *Kōken-tennō* and *Shōtoku-tennō*). In 752, he returned to China as 2nd ambassador (*Kentō-fuku-shi*) and on his return, was appointed *Dazai-daini* (754), then *Udaijin* (766). On the death of the empress *Shōtoku* (769), the *Fujiwara, Nagate* and *Momokawa,* succeeded in raising prince *Shirakabe no Ōji* to the throne, against the will of *Makibi*: thereupon, *Makibi* tendered his resignation as minister and retired from public life. He died at the age of 82. He has been credited with the invention of the *kata-kana* (alphabet of 47 syllables).

Kibi-takehiko no mikoto, 吉備武彦命. Son of *Waka-takehiko.* Accompanied *Yamato-takeru no mikoto* in his expedition against the *Ebisu* (110 A. D.). After the submission of the latter, *Yamato-takeru,* proceeded to *Kōzuke* and commissioned *Kibi-takehiko* to explore the country of *Echi*: they met again in *Mino.* On the death of the prince (113), *Takehiko* carried the news to the emperor *Keikō.* He left several sons : *Okabe-hiko, Otomo-wake, Kamowake,* etc.

Kibitsu-hiko, 吉備津彦命. His true name was *Hiko-isaseri-hiko no mikoto.* Son of the emperor *Kōrei,* he received in the year 88 B. C., the title of *Shōgun* and was commissioned to inspect the western provinces, then to quell the revolt of *Take-haniyasu-hiko* brother-in-law of the emperor *Sujin* (81 B. C.). Later on, he headed an expedition into the country of *Kibi*, whence the name of *Kibitsu-hiko*, which was given him. Finally, in the year 38 B. C. he pacified *Izumo* province. — (As *Kōrei-tennō* was supposed to have died in the year 215 B. C., at the age of 128, his son, in the year 38 B. C., must have been over 200 years old!).

Kiden-dō, 紀傳道. One of the 4 classes of the old University (*Daigaku*). The study of Chinese history and literature took up most of the time. Later on, it was called *Bunshō-dō*.

Kido, 木戸. A family of *samurai* from the clan of *Yamaguchi* (*Suwō*) descended from the *Ōe*, ennobled after the Restoration. — Now Marquis.

—— **Takamasa** or **Kōin,** 孝允 (1834-1877). Played an active part in the Imperial Restoration. It was he that persuaded his lord *Mōri Yoshichika* of *Chōshū*, to surrender his domains to the emperor (1868).

After that, he proposed to change the former fiefs (*han*) to departments (*ken*), and was despatched to *Yamaguchi* to induce his former lord, to repair to *Tōkyō* and take a seat in the government. He was a member of the *Iwakura* embassy to Europe and America (1872), became Minister of Education, etc.

Kifune, 木船. In *Etchū*. An ancient castle built by the *Ishiguro* family; passed afterwards to the *Nagao* of *Echigo*. *Nobunaga* gave it to *Sasa Narimasa*, after the latter had pacified *Etchū* (1581). It was destroyed by an earthquake in 1585.

Kigen, 紀元. Beginning of the era of *Jimmu-Tennō*, fixed upon the 1st day of the 1st lunar month (11th of February) of the year 660 B.C. The date, adopted according to the *Koji-ki* and the *Nihon-ki*, had been calculated with the years of the sexagesimal cycle, and until the time comes when historical criticism will be able to establish a tolerably certain date, we are entitled to suppose an error of about ten cycles (600 years) in the above mentioned date, which brings the reign of the first emperor of Japan, down to the beginning of the Christian era. — See *Nihon-ki*.

Kigen-setsu, 紀元節. A feast celebrated every year on the 11th of February, in memory of the coronation of *Jimmu-tennō* at *Kashiwabara* (*Yamato*), which is regarded as the foundation of the Japanese empire. (660 B. C.). It was on February the 11th 1889, that the Constitution now in vigor, was promulgated.

Kii, 紀伊. One of the 6 provinces of *Nankaidō*. Comprises 9 districts of which 2 belong to *Mie-ken* and 7 to *Wakayama-ken*. — Chinese name: *Kishū*. Formerly called *Ki no kuni*. — In 1619, *Kii* province was assigned as fief (550,000 k.) to *Yorinobu*, 8th son of *Ieyasu*, who founded thus one of the 3 families (*san-ke*) from which the *Shōgun* could be chosen.

Kii-kaikyō, 紀伊海峽. Strait between *Kii* province and the island of *Awaji*.

Kiirun, 基隆. The port of *Keelung* (8,400 inh.) to the N. of Formosa.

Kikai-ga-shima, 鬼界嶋. — See *Iwō-jima*.

Kikkawa, 吉川. A family of *daimyō*, descended from the *Fujiwara*.

—— **Motoharu,** 元春 (1530-1586). 2nd son of *Mōri Motonari*, was adopted by *Kikkawa Okitsune*; distinguished himself in the wars waged by his father to extend his domains. Victorious over *Amako Katsuhisa*, he seized the provinces of *Izumo, Hōki, Tajima* and *Inaba* (1578). Later on, *Motoharu* fought two years against *Hideyoshi*, whom *Nobunaga* had sent to reduce the *Mōri*. Peace was restored on the death of *Nobunaga* (1582). After that, *Motoharu* fell sick, ceded his domains to his son *Motonaga*, and retired to *Kokura*, where he died.

Motoharu { Motonaga
Motouji
Hiroie
Hiromasa - Hiroyoshi - Hironao.

—— **Motonaga,** 元長 (1547-87). Eldest son of *Motoharu*, served in the campaigns of his father, and died shortly after him.

—— **Hiroie,** 弘家 (1561-1625). 3rd son of *Motoharu*, repaired to *Kyōto* in 1583 and received the title of *Kurando*. He succeeded his brother *Motonaga*, who had died without offspring, and enjoyed a revenue of 200,000 k. at *Toda* 富田 (*Izumo*). *Hideyoshi* made him marry the sister of *Ukita Hideie*, whom he had adopted and gave him the name of *Toyotomi* (1588). He served in the expedition to Korea (1592), with his cousin *Mōri Terumoto*. In 1600, having sided against *Ieyasu*, he was dispossessed. His younger brother *Hiromasa*, received from the *Mōri* family a revenue of 60,000 k. at *Iwakuni* (*Suwō*), where his descendants resided till the Restoration. — Now Viscount.

Kikkwa no en, 菊花宴. A festival celebrated in the palace on the 9th day of the 9th month, the time of the blossoming of the Chrysanthemums.

Kikkwa-shō, 菊花章. The order of the Chrysanthemum. — See *Kunshō*.

Kikōten, 乞巧奠. — See *Tanabata*.

Kikuchi, 菊地. A family of *daimyō* of *Kyūshū*, descended from *Fujiwara Takaie* (979-1044), *Dazai gon no sotsu*.

—— **Taketoki,** 武時 (1293-1334). Governor of *Higo*, declared himself for *Go-Daigo* in 1333, and with *Shōni Sadatsune* and *Ōtomo Sadamune*, defeated *Hōjō Hidetoki, tandai* of the *Chinzei*.

—— **Takeshige,** 武重. Son of *Taketoki*, was *Higo no kami*. After the death of his father, he followed *Nitta Yoshisada* and fought the *Ashikaga Takauji* and *Tadayoshi*. In 1337, *Isshiki Noriuji* having invaded *Higo*, *Takeshige* returned to *Kyūshū*, and with the aid of *Uji Korezumi*, chief of the temples of Mt. *Aso*, defeated *Noriuji* at *Ōtsuka-hara*.

—— **Takemitsu,** 武光 (+ 1364). Son of *Taketoki*, succeeded his brother *Takeshige*, who had died without offspring. He supported prince *Yasunaga-shinnō* in his efforts to maintain *Kyūshū* under the authority of the southern dynasty. He defeated *Isshiki Naouji* in *Chikuzen* (1358), *Hatakeyama Kunihisa* in *Hyūga* (1359) and *Shōni Yorihisa* in *Chikugo* (1360). The following year, he again defeated *Shōni Yorihisa* and with him, *Ōtomo Ujitoki* and *Matsuura Yasumasa*. He fought afterwards against *Shiba Ujitsune*, sent by the *Shōgun Yoshiakira*.

—— **Takemasa,** 武 政 (+ 1380). Son of *Takemitsu*, continued the struggle against the northern dynasty. In 1366, he mustered 20,000 men and defeated *Ōuchi Hiroyo*, of *Suwō ;* then he fought against *Imagawa Sadayo*, who was appointed *tandai* of *Kyūshū* (1371). Finally, when the *Shōgun Yoshimitsu*, came with an army of 170,000 men to subdue *Kyūshū*, *Takemasa*, notwithstanding a stubborn resistance, had to declare himself vainquished (1374) ; but the very next year, he took the field again and defeated *Ōtomo Chikayo*.

—— **Taketomo,** 武 朝 (1363-1407). Son of *Takemasa*, was present, when only 13, at the battle of *Mizushima*, where *Imagawa Sadayo* was defeated. He was vainquished by *Ōuchi Yoshihiro* (1377), but was victorious again over *Sadayo* (1378). That was his last success; exhausted, he had to retreat to *Higo*. In 1397, he tried to provoke a fresh rising which was at once quelled.

—— **Mochitomo,** 持 朝. Grandson of *Taketomo*, joined forces with *Ōuchi Masayo* and defeated *Shōni Sukeyori* in 1441. —— The family disappeared from history in the middle of the 16th century ; but in consideration of the fidelity they had displayed towards the southern dynasty, one of their descendants was ennobled after the Restoration. —— Now Baron.

Kikuchi, 菊 地. A family originating in *Mimasaka*, ennobled in 1902, in the person of **Dairoku,** 大 麓 (born in 1855), then minister of Education. — Now Baron.

Kikuchi Kōsai, 菊 地 耕 齋 (1618-82). A famous Confucianist of *Kyōto*. Has written several books.

Kikuchi Yōsai, 菊 池 容 齋 (1788-1878). A celebrated painter. At the age of 18, he became a pupil of *Takada Enjō* and applied himself to the study of the *Kanō* school. He afterwards repaired to the temple of *Nyoirin-dō*, of Mt. *Yoshino*, where he drew the portraits of over 100 persons famous for their loyalty or valor. The collection is called *Zenken-kojitsu*. At the advanced age of 88, he sent to an exhibition in the United States a painting which was awarded a prize.

Kikuta no seki, 菊 田 關. Formerly a mountain road connected the village of *Kubota* (*Iwaki*) with *Sekimoto* (*Hitachi*). A barrier was set up there for the inspection of travellers ; it was called *Kikuta no seki* or *Nakoso no seki*. *Minamoto Yoshiie* crossed it in 1087, to go and fight the *Kiyowara*, revolted in *Mutsu*. It has often been sung in poetry.

Kikutei, 菊 亭. A family of *kuge*, descended from *Fujiwara* (*Saionji*) *Michisue* (1090-1128). They bore at first the name of *Imadegawa ;* then, on account of the magnificent garden of Chrysanthemums (*kiku*) which they kept, they were called *Kikutei*. — Now Marquis.

—— **Kanesue, 兼季**. Was the first to receive the name of *Kikutei*. In 1322, he was appointed *Udaijin*. Was surnamed *Kikutei-Udaijin*.

—— **Harusue, 晴季** (1543-1617). Served as medium to have the title of *Kwampaku* granted to *Hideyoshi* (1585). Implicated in a conspiracy with his son-in-law *Hidetsugu*, he was banished to *Echigo*. He returned to *Kyōto* after the death of *Hideyoshi*, and became *Udaijin*.

Kikyō ga hara, 桔梗原. In *Shinano*, a place where *Ogasawara Nagatoki* was defeated by *Takeda Shingen* (1549).

Kimi, 君. In ancient times, a title given to officials who ruled the land subject to the authority of the *Kuni no miyatsuko*, or the *Agatanushi*. The title became a family name. Thus we find the *Honokimi*, in *Hizen*, the *Michigimi* in *Kaga*, the *Isshigimi* in *Ise*, etc.

Kimi ga yo, 君ヶ代. Japanese national hymn. Forms only one stanza of 31 syllables (*tanka*):

Kimi ga yo wa	The master's reign
Chi yo ni ya-chi yo ni	shall last 1,000 and 8,000 generations,
Sazare ishi no	till the pebbles
Iwao to narite	becoming rocks,
Koke no musu made,	shall be covered with moss!

This piece of poetry is extracted from the *Kokinshū* (book 7); its author is unknown. (In the *Kokinshū*, the first verse is: "*Waga Kimi wa*" (my master), and was changed into "*Kimi ga yo wa*"). *Hayashi Hiromori*, 林弘盛 (1821-1886) has adapted to these words a slow and solemn melody of the doric mode (whose rhythm does not however correspond to that of the poem, since it separates *sazare* from *ishi*). The melody differs from the lively mode of European national hymns.

Kimmei-tennō, 欽明天皇. 29th emperor of Japan (540-571). *Ame-kuni-oshi-haruki-hironiha no mikoto* succeeded his brother *Senkwa*, at the age of 32. His reign witnessed the last efforts made by the Japanese to hold their own in Korea and to support their allies *Kudara* and *Mimana* against the incessant attacks of *Shiragi*; but the victory remained with the latter, which, in 562, completed the conquest of *Mimana*. At that time, more, than 5,000 Korean families came to settle in Japan. The most important event of the reign of *Kimmei*, is the introduction of Buddhism. In 552, *Seimei*, king of *Kudara* (Korea), sent over as presents, some *sûtras* and a statue of Buddha: the emperor accepted them; but a dispute arose among his ministers on the question of worship. *Soga no Iname* approved the worship of the image, *Nakatomi no Kamako* and *Mononobe no Okoshi* maintained that this would be insulting to the tutelary gods of the land. The emperor allowed *Iname* to carry the statue to his house, where he erected a shrine (*Kōgen-ji*), which was the first *tera* in Japan. The next year, an epidemic afflicted the country; it was attributed to the vengeance of the *kami* and the statue was thrown into the *Naniwa* canal. Shortly after, two bonzes, *Ton-ei* and *Dōshin*, arrived from *Kudara;* but it was only 40 years later that Buddhism received legal sanction. *Kimmei* died at the age of 63, recommending the conquest of *Shiragi* and the restoration of *Mimana*, but his wishes were to remain ineffectual.

Kimon-numa, 喜門沼. A lake in *Tokachi* (*Hokkaidō*), 31 Km. in circumference.

Kimpoku-zan, 金北山. The highest mountain in the island of *Sado;* also called *Koshi no takane.*

Kimpu-zan, 金峯山. A mountain to the N. of *Kai,* on the borders of *Shinano* (2,550 m.).

Kimura, 木村. A family of *daimyō*, of the 16th century.

—— **Shigekore,** 重茲. Served *Hideyoshi*, went with an expedition to Korea, and received a fief in *Yamashiro;* but implicated in the conspiracy of *Hidetsugu*, he was dispossessed, and committed *harakiri* (1595).

—— **Shigenari,** 重成 (1594-1615). Son of *Shigekore*, was educated by his mother, who, after the death of her husband, sought refuge with a Christian family, whose religion she embraced, which fact allows us to suppose that *Shigenari*, then quite an infant, was baptized with her. Having grown up, he enlisted in the army of *Hideyori*, and perished in the siege of *Ōsaka.*

Kimura Hidetoshi, 木村秀俊. A *samurai* who served first *Akechi Mitsuhide*, then *Hideyoshi*. After the campaign of *Odawara*, he received a revenue of 300,000 k. in *Mutsu* (1590): thereupon, he established himself in the castle of *Toyoma* and his son *Shigemasa* in that of *Furukawa.* But their bad administration and other excesses provoked a revolt among the *samurai* and they were dispossessed the following year.

Kinai, 畿内. —— See *Shi-kinai* and *Go-kinai.*

Kinashikaru-Ōji, 木梨輕皇子. Son of the emperor *Ingyo*. In 434, he was appointed heir to the throne (*kōtaishi*). On the death of his father, he was attacked by his younger brother *Anaho* (*Ankō-tennō*), fled to the house of the *Mononobe*, and being pursued, committed suicide (453).

Kin-bugyō, 金奉行. In the *Tokugawa* days, officials of the finance department of the *Bakufu.* Established in 1646, they were at first 4 in number, under the authority of the *kanjō-bugyō;* later on, their number increased to 6 (1689). They had under their orders, 5 *moto-shimari-yaku*, 23 *dōshin*, 7 *minarai*, etc.

Kinchū-jōmoku, 禁中條目. A code of laws in 17 chapters, promulgated by *Ieyasu* in 1615, and laying down the rules to be observed by the *kuge* at the Court of *Kyōto.*

Kingo, 金吾. Abbreviation of *Shitsu-kingo.* Corresponding Chinese word for the Japanese *Eimon-fu* (corps of the Imperial guard). The officers of the *Eimon-fu* were also called *Kingo.* Thus *Kobayakawa Hideaki* is often styled *Kingo-chūnagon.*

Kinkaku-ji, 金閣寺．(Lit.: golden pavilion).　A pavilion built in 1397, by the *Shōgun Yoshimitsu*, on one of his estates N. W. of *Kyōto*.　It is 13 metres long and 10 wide, has two stories and has

KINKAKU-JI.

always been regarded as one of the most beautiful specimens of Japanese art of that period. — See *Rokuon-ji*.

Kinkaku-kō, キンカク港．The port of Vladivostock.

Kinko, 近古．The middle ages of Japanese history, from the *Kamakura* to the *Edo* Shōgunate (1192-1602).

Kinkwa-zan, 金華山．An island on the eastern coast of *Rikuzen* (11 Km. in circumference).　The temple of *Kogane-yama-jinja* is a very popular place of pilgrimage.　Also called *Hōrai-zan*.

Ki no kawa, 紀伊川．A river (120 Km.) which takes its rise in the *Yoshino* Mountains (*Yamoto*) whose name it takes, then enters *Kii*, flows through *Wakayama* and empties itself into the sea.　Also called *Kii-gawa*.

Kinoshita, 木下．A family of *daimyō*, originating at *Nakamura* (*Owari*).　*Hideyoshi*, still young and unknown, married the sister of *Kinoshita Iesada*, and took the name of *Kinoshita*, which he changed later on to that of *Hashiba* (1575).　That relationship was the cause of the fortune of the *Kinoshita*.

Iesada { Katsutoshi　　　　　　　　　　　　　　　　　　　　 (a)
　　　　 Toshifusa-Toshimasa-Toshisada-Kinsada　　　　 (b)
　　　　 Nobutoshi-Toshiharu-Toshinaga-Toshikazu.　　 (c)

(*a*) — Elder branch. — **Iesada,** 家定 (1543-1603).　Served his brother-in-law *Hideyoshi* and, in 1585, received as fief the castle of

Himeji (*Harima* — 40,000 k.). In 1600, he was transferred to *Ashi-mori* (*Bitchū*) and reduced to 25,000 k.

—— **Katsutoshi, 勝俊** (1568-1649). Eldest son of *Iesada*, received at first the castle of *Tatsuo* (*Harima*). He accompanied *Hideyoshi* to *Nagoya* (*Hizen*) at the time of the expedition to Korea and in 1594, was invested with the province of *Wakasa*, with residence at *Obama* (80,000 k.). Having sided against *Ieyasu*, he was dispossessed in 1600, retired to *Kyōto* and took the name of *Chōshōshi*. In his retreat, he cultivated his taste for poetry and published several books. *Katsutoshi* had been baptized in 1588 by the name of Peter.

(*b*) — Junior branch. — **Toshifusa, 利房** (1573-1637). 2nd son of *Iesada*, received in 1594, the castle of *Takahama* (*Wakasa* — 30,000 k.). He was dispossessed in 1600, for having fought against *Ieyasu*. But in 1614, when war broke out again, he abandoned the party of his family, and enlisted in the *Shōgun's* army. In return, he received the next year, the fief of *Ashimori* (*Bitchū* — 25,000 k.).

—— **Toshimasa, 利富** (1602-61). Succeeded his father at *Ashimori*. Fond of fencing with the lance (*sōjutsu*), he founded a school which has kept his name (*Kinoshita-ryū*). — His descendants dwelt at *Ashimori* until the Restoration. — Now Viscount.

(*c*) — Youngest branch. — **Nobutoshi, 延俊** (1577-1642). 3rd son of *Iesada*, sided with *Ieyasu* in 1600 and was commissioned to besiege *Onoki Shigetoshi* in the castle of *Fukuchiyama* (*Tamba*), which he captured. He received in return, the fief of *Hiji* (*Bungo* — 25,000 k.) where his descendants resided until the Restoration. — Now Viscount.

Kinoshita Jun-an, 木下順庵 (1621-98). A famous Confucianist. Born at *Kyōto*, he was remarkable for his precocity. At the age of 13, he already composed Chinese poems. He was a pupil of *Matsunaga Shōzō*; after that, he taught during 2 years, at *Higashi-yama* (*Kyōto*). Having entered the service of the *daimyō* of *Kaga*, he became the rival of *Yamazaki Keigi*, *Kumazawa Ryōkai*, etc. In 1682, the *Shōgun Tsunayoshi* made him come to *Edo* and entrusted him with several historical works. He left 2 sons, *Kyokan* and *Nyohitsu*, who continued his school.

Kinri, 禁裏. The Imperial Palace, and by extension, the Emperor himself. The *Kinri* was situated in the middle of the *Daidairi*, somewhat on the eastern side. It formed a square the sides of which were 300 metres long, surrounded by a double palisade, and comprised the *Shishinden* (hall of the throne), the *Naishi-dokoro* (where the imperial emblems were preserved), the *Seiryōden* (Emperor's apartments), the *Kōkyūkōshoden* (Hall of the Privy Council) etc. etc.

Kinri-gosho, 禁裏御所. — See *Go-sho*.

Kinri-zuki, 禁裏附. In the *Tokugawa* times, officials of the *Bakufu*, commissioned to inspect the Imperial Palace. Established in 1643, they were 2 in number, and were called at first *Kinchū on-mamorishū*. They depended on the *Shoshidai* and had under their orders, some *yoriki* and *dōshin*. Their duty was to keep watch over the interior and the exterior of the Palace, and to ascertain whether all the officials observed the rules, etc.

Kinsei, 近世. Modern period of Japanese history, covering the time of the *Edo* Shōgunate (1603-1867).

Kinshi-kunshō, 金鵄勳章. Order of the golden Kite. — See *Kunshō*.

Kintaiji, 金胎寺. In *Kawachi*. Ancient castle built in the 14th century by the *Kusunoki;* it passed over to the *Hatakeyama* and depended on their castle of *Takaya*.

Kinugasa, 衣笠. In *Sagami*. Ancient castle built towards 1060 by *Miura Tamemichi*, and was the residence of his descendants *Tametsugu, Yoshitsugu, Yoshiaki*. The latter, having sided with *Yoritomo*, was besieged there by *Hatakeyama Shigetada*, a *Taira* general, and committed suicide.

Kinu-gawa, 鬼怒川. A river (119 Km.) which takes its rise in Mt. *Akanagi*, flows through *Shimotsuke*, enters into *Hitachi* then into *Shimōsa*, and empties itself into the *Tone-gawa*. — Formerly called *Keno-gawa*.

Kinunuibe, 衣縫部. Ancient corporation or guild of tailors, founded in the reign of *Yūryaku* (457-479).

Kinza, 金座. In the *Tokugawa* times, an office depending on the *Kanjō-bugyō* and entrusted with the casting of gold coins and their withdrawal from circulation. The family of *Gotō Mitsutsugu* was in hereditary possession of the office.

Kira, 吉良. A family of *daimyō* descended from *Minamoto Yoshiuji* (1189-1254) (*Seiwa-Genji*).

—— **Mitsusada,** 滿貞. Sided first with his relative *Ashikaga Takauji*, then passed over to the southern dynasty. In 1352, he defeated *Hosokawa Kiyouji*, but was defeated in his turn by *Hatakeyama Kunikiyo* (1360) and submitted again to the *Ashikaga*.

—— In the *Tokugawa* era, the descendants of that family did not possess the title of *daimyō*, but were numbered among the *kōke* (see "*Koke*").

—— **Yoshinaka,** 義央. *Kōzuke no suke*, master of ceremonies in the *Shōgun's* palace, was, in that quality, commissioned in 1700, to receive and treat the envoys of the emperor *Higashi-yama* and the ex-emperor *Reigen*. Having, on that occasion, fallen out with *Asano Naganori, daimyō* of *Akō* (*Harima*), he reprimanded him publicly, and was struck by *Naganori* in the forehead with a dagger. The culprit was at once deprived of his possessions and exiled to *Mutsu;* but 47 of his *samurai*, having waited a year for a good occasion, avenged their lord and assassinated *Yoshinaka* in his house. — See *Shi-jū-shichi gishi*.

Kirimai, 切米. In the *Tokugawa* times, a pension paid in rice to the *samurai* of the *Bakufu*, who had no personal domains.

Kirimai-tegata-aratame, 切米手形改. In the *Tokugawa* days, an official commissioned, under the *Kanjō-bugyō*, to verify the demands for pension, presented by the *samurai* of the *Bakufu*. He resided at *Asakusa* (*Edo*), and had under him 9 *tedai* (employees). He was also called *Kakikae-bugyō*.

Kirino Toshiaki, 桐野利秋. A *samurai* of the *Kagoshima* clan (*Satsuma*). In 1867, he succeeded in having the guard of the Imperial Palace confided to his troops. Distinguished himself at the battle of *Fushimi*, at *Edo* (1868), and at the siege of *Wakamatsu*. After the Restoration, he received a high position in the imperial army. He insisted on an expedition to Korea, and retired to *Kagoshima*, when he saw that the government did not adopt his views. When *Saigō Takamori* rose in rebelion against the new regime, *Toshiaki* was his principal auxiliary. After having fought in *Higo, Satsuma, Hyūga, Ōsumi*, he returned for the last time to *Kagoshima*, and having been vainquished at the battle of *Shiroyama*, (Sept. 24th, 1877), committed *harakiri*.

Kirishima-yama, 霧嶋山. A mountain range between the provinces of *Hyūga* and *Ōsumi*. — See *Higashi-Kirishima* and *Nishi-Kirishima*.

Kirishitan-shū, 切支丹宗. (Altered form of the Portuguese *Cristan*). The Christian religion. — St. Francis-Xavier, who landed at *Kagoshima* on August the 15th, 1549, was the first Apostle of Japan. During 50 years, Catholicism made marvelous progress, especially in *Kyūshū* and the south-western provinces of *Hondo*. *Taikō-Hideyoshi* and, after him, the *Tokugawa Shōgun* prohibited the propagation of the Gospel and persecuted the converts. After the repression of the insurrection of *Shimabara*, (1638) Christianity was seemingly blotted out from the land.

SIGN BOARD.

BEARING PROHIBITION OF CHRISTIANITY.

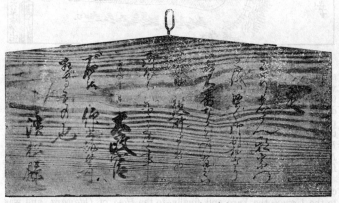

TRANSLATION OF TEXT. — Decreed : — The practice of the perverse Christian religion is severely prohibited. Suspected persons are to be denounced. Awards shall be given. Third month of the 4th year of *Keiō* (April 1868).

Council of State.

The above mentioned decree must be rigorously observed.

Department of Hamamatsu.

Nevertheless, a *Kirishitan-bugyō* was established to see to all matters relating to the prohibited religion. At *Edo*, in the ward of *Koishikawa*, an enclosure called *Kirishitan-yashiki*, was set aside, after the great persecutions, for the burial of the foreign missionaries, who still should dare to penetrate into Japan. History has preserved the names of *P. Pedro Marquez*, who was shut up there from 1646-1657 ; of *P. Francisco Cassala* (the date of his death is uncertain); of *P. Joseph Chiara* from 1646-1685 ; of Brother *Andrew Vieyra*, from 1646-1678 ; of *Jikuan*, an Annamite Christian, who died there in 1700 ; of Rev. *John Baptist Sidotti*, (1709-1715). The hill on which the prison was

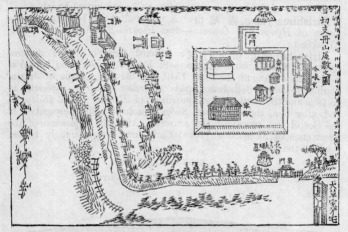

ANCIENT PLAN OF THE KIRISHITAN-YASHIKI

situated is still called *Kirishitan-zaka*. — Notwithstanding the edicts which severely prohibited Christianity, the annals of Japan bear witness to the fact that it was not entirely rooted out : Some Christians were discovered at *Ōmura* (*Hizen*) in 1658 ; in *Bungo*, in 1660 ; others were put to death in 1676, in 1683 ; in 1714 a certain number surrendered of their own accord to the judges ; in 1830, 6 were arrested and executed at *Kyōto*. Finally, in 1865, thousands of believers were found near *Nagasaki*, who had, for 7 or 8 generations preserved the faith of their fathers in secret.

Kiriu, 桐生 . A city in *Kōzuke* province (20,000 inh.). Ancient castle built in the 14th century, by *Kiriu Tameaki*. It passed afterwards to the *Uesugi*, the *Yura* and finally to the *Hōjō* of *Odawara*, and was abandoned in 1590. — Now-a-days, *Kiriu* is renowned for its manufactures of satin, crape, gauze, etc.

Kiroku, 季祿 . Formerly a distribution of pensions in kind (rice), which was made twice a year, in the 2nd and the 8th lunar months. An official, who had spent 4 months out of 6 without fulfilling his charge, lost all rights to a *kiroku*.

Kiroku-sho, 記録所. A council created in 1069 by the emperor *Go-Sanjō*, to deal with administrative and judicial matters. It was presided over by the emperor in person, and took cognizance of all the matters reserved until then to the *Kurōdo-dokoro*, with the aim of opposing the all-powerful influence of the *Fujiwara*. It cut down the number of *shō-en*, and endeavored to put the imperial finances on a surer footing. It ceased to exist at the close of the 14th century, in the reign of *Go-Komatsu*.

Kisaki, 后. In ancient times, the first wife of the emperor, had the title of *Ōgisaki*; the second, that of *Kisaki*; the mother of the emperor, that of *Sume-mi-oya no mikoto*. But after the *Taihō* code (702), the grandmother of the emperor was called *Taikōtaigō*; the mother of the emperor, *Kōtaigō*; the empress, *Kōgō*; the wives of lower rank, *Kisaki*, who comprised 2 *Hi*, 3 *Fujin*, 4 *Hin*. The empress had always to be of imperial blood; from the reign of *Shōmu* (724-748), the powerful *Fujiwara* succeeded in having her elected in their own family. — See *Sangū, Nyōgo*, etc.

Kiseki, 其磧 (1677-1736). A famous novelist. He called himself *Ejimaya Kiseki*. His works are stained with gross immorality.

Kishi, 吉士. Anciently, the title of an official sent from Japan to *Shiragi* (Korea), at the time when the *San-kan* were supposed to be under Japanese jurisdiction. The title became, later on, a family name.

Kishi-Bojin, 鬼子母神. A Buddhist goddess. According to the legend, she was an Indian woman, who had sworn to devour all the children of the city of *Bājagriha*. As a punishment, she was born again in the shape of a demon, and gave birth to 500 children, of whom she had to devour one every day. *Buddha* cured her of her cruel mania by making her eat pomegranates, and made her enter a convent. — In Japan, she is worshipped as the patroness of children. She is represented in the shape of a woman carrying a child and holding a pomegranate in her hand.

Kishiwada, 岸和田. A town of *Izumi* province. Pop.: 5,100 inh. In the Middle Ages, it was the fief of a family of the same name. It belonged afterwards to the *Miyoshi*. In 1582, *Nakamura Kazuuji* built a castle there, which was occupied by the *daimyō Koide* (1585-1619), *Matsudaira* (1619-40) and *Okabe* (1640-1868) — (60,000 k.).

Kishū, 紀州. Chinese name of the *Kii* province.

Kishū-nada, 紀州灘. Sea on the S. W. coast of *Kii*.

Kiso, 木曾. A mountainous region, comprising the S.W. of *Shinano* (*Nishi-Chikuma-gōri*) and the E. of *Mino* (*Ena-gōri*). In 702, a road was built there, called the *Kiso-kaidō* or *Nakasendō*. The ancient fief of *Kiso*, extended as far as the modern city of *Matsumoto* (*Shinano*). It was given to a branch of the *Minamoto*, among whom *Yoshinaka* became famous. In the *Ashikaga* times, the region belonged to the *Kiso* family, who resided first at *Suhara*, then at *Fukushima*. *Hideyoshi* gave it to *Ishikawa Sadakiyo*. In the *Tokugawa* period, it depended on *Nagoya* (*Owari*).

Kiso-gawa, 木曾川. A river which takes its rise in *Torii-tōge* (*Shinano*), traverses *Mino*, which it also separates from *Owari* and empties itself into the gulf of *Ise* at *Kuwana*. Also called *Ōta-gawa*, *Okoshi-gawa* (175 Km.).

Kiso-kaidō, 木曾街道.— See *Nakasendō*.

Kiso Yoshinaka, 木曾義仲.— See *Minamoto Yoshinaka*.

Kita, 喜多. A family, who from the beginning of the 17th century, have been famous for their skill in composing and executing "*nō*" or *sarugaku*.

Kitabatake, 北畠. A family of *daimyō* descended from *Naka-no-in Michikata* (*Murakami-Genji*).

—— **Chikafusa,** 親房 (1293-1354). Son of *Moroshige*, was successively *Chūnagon* (1319), *Dainagon* (1323), then *Daijin* (1333). He fought vigorously, with his sons *Akiie* and *Akinobu*, for the southern dynasty. He has left several works: the *Jinkō-shōtō-ki* (history), the *Shokugenshō* (administration), etc.

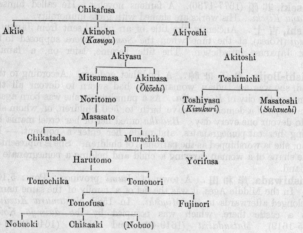

—— **Akiie,** 顯家 (1317-38). Eldest son of *Chikafusa*, was appointed in 1333, *Mutsu no kami* and preserved that province as well as *Dewa* under the authority of the southern dynasty. Appointed *Chinjufu-shōgun* (1335), he joined hands with *Nitta Yoshisada* against *Takauji* who was defeated at *Miidera*; which victory allowed *Go-Daigo* to re-enter *Kyōto*. *Akiie* returned to *Mutsu* with *Yoshinaga-shinnō*, (later on *Go-Murakami*) to raise troops, then returned to besiege *Kamakura*, which he captured in 1337. Then marching on *Kyōto*, he gained

victories at *Awa no hara*, *Yawata*, *Nara*, but was defeated and killed by *Kô Moronao* at *Sakai no ura* (*Izumi*).
He was only 21 years old.

—— **Akinobu, 顕信**. Son of *Chikafusa*, is known by the name of *Kasuga-shôshô*. He fought at first under his brother *Akiie* and succeeded him as *Mutsu no kami* and *Chinjufu-shôgun* (1338). After several campaigns in *Hitachi*, *Shimôsa*, etc. he repaired to *Kyûshû* with prince *Yasunaga-shinnô*, and was killed in a battle fought against *Shôni Yorihisa* at *Ôhara* (*Chikuzen*).

KITABATAKE AKIIE

—— **Akiyoshi, 顕能** (+ 1383). Son of *Chikafusa*, fought first in *Mutsu*, then in *Ise*, of which he was appointed governor (*kokushi*). Joining forces with *Wada Masatada* and *Kusunoki Masayoshi*, he defeated *Ashikaga Yoshiakira* and entered *Kyôto* (1352). Obliged to retreat before overwhelming odds, he remained until his death in the camp of the southern emperor, on Mount *Yoshino*, and received the title of *Udaijin*, *Sangû*, etc.

—— **Akiyasu, 顕泰** (1360-1402). Son of *Akiyoshi*, and like him governor of *Ise*, rallied round the *Shôgun* after the fusion of the two dynasties (1392), helped to quell the revolt of *Ôuchi Yoshihiro* (1399) and received from the *Shôgun Yoshimitsu* the district of *Kôga* (*Ômi*).

—— **Mitsumasa, 満雅** (1377-1440). Brother of *Akiyasu* and adopted by him as his heir. Seeing that contrary to the convention of 1392, the successor of *Go-Komatsu* was taken from the northern dynasty, he conceived the project of marching on *Kyôto* and raising to the throne prince *Ogura-shinnô*, son of *Go-Kameyama*, but he could not execute his design (1414). A second attempt, at the time of the accession of *Go-Hanazono* (1429), did not succeed better: *Mitsumasa* was defeated by *Toki Tokiyori*.

—— **Noritomo, 教具** (1423-1471). Son of *Mitsumasa*, *kokushi* of *Ise*, repressed in 1462 an attempt of *Hatakeyama Yoshinari* to revolt against the *Shôgun Yoshimasa*. At the time of the *Ônin* war (1467), he gave hospitality to *Yoshimi* who was obliged to flee from *Kyôto*.

—— **Masasato, 政郷** (1449-1508). Son of *Noritomo*, *kokushi* of *Ise*, had to proceed with rigor against one of his officers, *Enokura Ujinori*, who behaved badly towards those going on pilgrimage to *Ise* (1488).

—— **Harutomo, 晴具** (1496-1563). Grandson of *Masasato*, repressed the revolt of the *samurai* of *Tamaru* (*Ise*) who had massacred their lord, *Tamaru Tomotada*.

—— **Tomonori, 具教** (1528-1576). Son of *Harutomo*, saw several of his *kerai* revolt against him. *Nobunaga* came with an army to pacify the province, captured the castles of *Kambe* and *Kuwana*, and as a condition of the peace, obliged *Tomonori* to adopt his 2nd son *Nobuo* (1569). In 1576, *Tomonori* fell ill and was assassinated by his *samurai*.

—— **Nobuoki, 信興**. Eldest son of *Tomonori*, was invited to cede his rights to *Nobuo*, son of *Nobunaga*, who had received the province of *Ise.* Dissensions broke out between the two pretenders. *Nobuoki* was shut up at *Nagashima.* Later on, he dwelt in *Kawachi, Owari* and died at last at *Kyōto.* Two of his descendants, one of whom is the chief of the *Ryōzen-jinja* (dedicated to *Chikafusa, Akiie, Akinobu*) in *Iwashiro,* were ennobled after the Restoration. — Now Baron.

Kitagaki, 北垣. A family of *samurai* from the clan of *Izushi* (*Tajima*), ennobled after the Restoration. — Now Baron.

Kitagawa Utamaro, 北川歌麿 (1753-1805). A painter of the realistic school.

Kitagawara, 北河原. A family whose chief attached to the *Kōfuku-ji* temple, at *Nara,* was ennobled after the Restoration. — Now Baron.

Kitajima, 北嶋. A family which, for centuries, had been attached to the great temples of *Izumo ;* was ennobled after the Restoration. — Now Baron

Kitakami-gawa, 北上川. A river (240 Km.) which takes its rise on the *Nanashigure-dake* (*Rikuchū*), flows by *Morioka, Hanamaki, Mizusawa,* traverses *Rikuzen* and empties itself into the sea at *Ishinomaki.*

Kitaki-shima, 北木嶋. An island of the Inland Sea, depending on the province of *Bitchū* (20 Km. in circ.).

Kita-mandokoro, 北政所. — See *Mandokoro.*

Kitami, 北見. One of the 11 provinces of *Hokkaidō,* comprises 8 districts.

Kitamura Kigin, 北村季吟 (1618-1705). A man of letters; commented the *Genji-monogatari,* the *Makura no sōshi,* the *Hyaku-nin isshū,* etc.

Kitano, 北野. To the N. W. of *Kyōto.* In 836, a *Shintō* shrine (*Kitano-jinja*) was built there, in which, from 959, *Sugawara Michizane* was worshipped by the name of *Temman-tengū* or *Kitano-tenjin.* It was in the buildings of this temple, that *Hideyoshi* gave, in 1588, his famous tea festival (*Kitano dai-cha-no-yu*).

Kita-no-kōji, 北小路. A family of *kuge,* descended from *Fujiwara Arinobu.* — Now Viscount.

Kita-no-kōji, 北小路. A family of *kuge,* descended from the *Ōe.* — Now Viscount.

Kita-no-ōji, 北大路. A family descended from *Fujiwara Saneyuki,* whose chief is attached to the *Kōfuku-ji* temple of *Nara.* — To-day, Baron.

Kita-no-shō, 北荘. Ancient name of the city of *Fukui* (*Echizen*). — See *Fukui.*

Kitano-tenjin, 北野天神. Name by which *Sugawara Michizane* is worshipped in the temple of *Kitano* (*Kyōto*).

Kitashirakawa, 北白川. A family of imperial princes, issued from the *Fushimi no miya* branch.

—— **Yoshihisa,** 能久 (1847-95). Son of prince *Fushimi Kuniie,* was in 1868, chief of the temples of *Nikkō* and *Ueno* (*Tōkyō*), and bore the name of *Rinnōji no miya.* The last upholders of the shōgunate secured his person and carried him off with them to the north, to set him up against the lawful sovereign. After their defeat, he was secularized and sent to Europe, where he remained 7 years. He was appointed commander of the army sent to Formosa during the war with China and died in that island.

—— **Narihisa,** 成久. Born in 1887, is the present head of the family.

Kita-ura, 北浦. Lake in *Hitachi* (59 Km. in circ.)

Kitayama-gawa, 北山川. A river (83 Km.) which takes its rise in Mt. *Yoshino* (*Yamato*), enters *Kii* and empties itself into the *Kumano-gawa*. — Also called *Ikehara-gawa*.

Kitsuki, 杵築. In *Bungo*. Ancient castle built in 1250, by *Kitsuki, Chikashige,* relative of the *Ōtomo*. His descendants dwelt there for 17 generations. In 1593, when *Ōtomo Yoshimune* was dispossessed by *Hideyoshi*, the last *Kitsuki* committed suicide. The castle passed after that to the *daimyō Sugihara* (1596), *Hayakawa* (1597), *Hosokawa* (1600), *Ogasawara* (1632), and *Matsudaira* (1645-1868) (32,000 k.).

Kitsunegawa, 狐川. In *Yamashiro,* S. W. of *Kyōto,* where *Nagoshi Takaie* was defeated and killed by *Akamatsu Norimura* (1333).

Kitsuregawa, 喜連川. In *Shimotsuke,* was from 1590 to 1868, the residence of the *Ashikaga daimyō* (10,000 k.), descendants of the *Shōgun* of the same name.

Kiyomizu-dera, 清水寺. A famous temple on a hill of that name, E. of *Kyōto,* built in 780, by the bonze *Enchin* at the expenses of *Sakanoe Tamuramaro*. It depended formerly on *Tō-daiji* (*Nara*). The tenets of both the *Hossō* and the *Shingon* sects are taught there.

Kiyooka, 清岡. A family of *kuge,* descended from *Sugawara Michizane*. — Now Viscount.

Kiyooka, 清岡. A family of *samurai,* from the *Kōchi* (*Tosa*) clan; ennobled after the Restoration. — Now Viscount.

Kiyosu, 清洲. In *Owari*. An ancient castle, built at the beginning of the 15th century by *Shiba Yoshishige,* and entrusted to the *Oda* family. In 1553, *Oda Nobutomo* revolted against his suzerain and asserted his independence at *Kiyosu,* but he was himself put to death by his relative *Nobunaga*. In 1582, *Hideyoshi* gave the castle to his adopted son *Hidetsugu,* who was replaced there by *Fukushima Masanori* (1595). In 1600, *Ieyasu* stationed his son *Tadayoshi* there, who was succeeded by his brother *Yoshinao* (1607): the latter, having built the castle of *Nagoya* (1610), *Kiyosu* was abandoned.

Kiyosue, 清末. In *Nagato;* was from 1653 to 1868 the residence of a branch of the *Mōri daimyō* (10,000 k.).

Kiyosumi, 清棲, A family descended from *Ienori,* 12th son of prince *Fushimi Kuniie* and ennobled in 1888. — Now Count.

Kiyoura, 清浦. A family of *samurai* from the clan of *Kumamoto* (*Higo*), ennobled in 1902. — Now Baron.

Kiyowara, 清原. A family descended from the emperor *Temmu* (673-686) by his son *Toneri-shinnō*.

—— **Natsuno,** 夏野 (782-837). Grandson of *Toneri-shinnō* and son of prince *Ogura,* was *Udaijin;* is the author of the *Ryō no gige* (10 vol.), a commentary of the Chinese Code (*Myōhō*). Often called *Narabi-no-oka no Otodo* (*daijin*).

—— **Fusanori, 房則**. Grandson of *Natsuno*, had two sons: the elder is the ancestor of the *Dewa* branch; the younger, of the *kuge*.

—— **Takenori, 武則**. Descended in the 6th generation from *Fusanori*, served in the campaign of *Minamoto Yoriyoshi* against *Abe Yoritoki* and his sons. From his residence, *Yamagata* (*Dewa*), he brought a reinforcement of 10,000 men to *Yoshiie*, which enabled the latter to defeat *Sadatō* (1062). In return, *Takenori* was appointed *Chinjufu-shōgun*.

Takenori {Takesada {Sanehira {Narihira
         {Takehira {Iehira   {Kiyohira

KIYOWARA TAKENORI.

—— **Iehira, 家衡**. Grandson of *Takenori*, refused to submit to *Yoshiie*, when the latter was appointed *Chinjufu-shōgun*. Assisted by his uncle *Takehira*, he fought for 3 years, but shut up in his castle of *Kanezawa* (*Dewa*), he was defeated and killed with his whole family. Thus the *Dewa* branch of the *Kiyowara* became extinct (1087).

—— **Yorinari, 頼業** (1122-89). Son of the *dai-geki Suketaka*, belonged to the *kuge* branch and excelled in Chinese Law, Literature and History. He was *Etchū no kami*. — His descendants, all literati like himself, possessed hereditarily the office of *dai-geki*. — The family of *kuge Gojō* is descended from him.

Kizu, 木津. A small town (5,500 inh.) in *Yamashiro*, 35 Km. S. of *Kyōto*. Was formerly, before the foundation of *Kyōto*, the capital of the province. A castle was built there by the *Hatakeyama* in 1470. — Was also called *Okada-eki, Izumi no sato, Takase no sato*.

Kizu, 木津. A village, S. of *Ōsaka* (*Settsu*), near the mouth of the *Kizu-gawa*. The coast is called *Kizu-ura*. There it was that the wife of *Taira Shigehira*, after the execution of her husband, threw herself into the sea (1185). There, too, the boats of the *Mōri* brought provisions during the siege of the *Ōsaka Ishiyama-Hongwan-ji* (1576-1580).

Kizu-gawa, 木津川. A river (51 Km.) which takes its rise in *Iga*, enters *Yamashiro*, flows by *Kizu* and empties itself into the *Yodo-gawa*, near *Yawata*. — Also called *Yamashiro-gawa, Momo-gawa, Izumi-gawa*.

Kizu-gawa, 木津川. A branch of the *Yodo-gawa*, which strikes off in *Ōsaka*, and turning towards the South, flows into the sea.

Kizuki, 杵築. In *Izumo*. When *Ōkuninushi* yielded his rights to *Ninigi no mikoto*, the latter had a residence built for him, which has become the great *Shintō* temple of *Izumo* (*Izumo no ō-yashiro*).

Kō, 公. A title of nobility, corrresponding to "duke." In English books, it is translated by "prince," but the latter title should be reserved to the members of the imperial family. — Applied formerly to persons of very high rank; *Tankai-kō, Ieyasu-kō*, etc.

Kō, 侯. A title of nobility, corresponding to "marquis." — Formerly applied to the nobles of the military caste: *shokō*, under the *daimyō*.

Kō, 高. A family of warriors of the 14th century, in the service of the *Ashikaga.*

—— **Moronao,** 師直 (+ 1351). Served *Takauji.* He helped to destroy *Rokuhara* (1333), fought against *Kitabatake Akiie,* defeated and killed him at *Sakai-ura,* in *Izumi* (1338). In 1348, at the head of 60,000 men, he defeated *Kusunoki Masatsura* at *Shijō-nawate* (*Kawachi*); he triumphed also at *Kyōto,* over *Momonoi Naotsune* (1351), but one month later, he was defeated by *Ashikaga Tadayoshi* at *Mikage no hama* (*Settsu*) and killed in his flight.

$$\text{Moroshige} \begin{cases} \text{Moronao} \begin{cases} \text{Moronatsu} \\ \text{Moroaki} \end{cases} \\ \text{Morofuyu} \\ \text{Moroyasu-Moroyo} \\ \text{Moromochi} \end{cases}$$

—— **Morofuyu,** 師冬. Brother of *Moronao,* was *Mikawa no kami.* He fought for several years in *Hitachi* against *Kitabatake Chikafusa,* and succeeded in expelling him (1343). When *Ashikaga Motouji* was appointed *Kwanryō* of *Kwantō* (1349), *Morofuyu* became his minister (*shitsuji*) with *Uesugi Noriaki.* The latter having crossed over with *Tadayoshi* to the southern party, *Morofuyu* endeavored to fight him, but was defeated and obliged to flee to *Kai,* where *Suwa Takashige* pursued and killed him.

—— **Moroyasu,** 師泰. Brother of *Moronao,* was *Echigo no kami.* In 1335, he defeated *Hōjō Tokiyuki,* besieged *Nitta Yoshisada* at *Kanasaki* (*Echizen*) (1337) and captured the castle of *Ii* (*Tōtōmi*) (1340). In 1351, he besieged *Ishidō Yorifusa* in the temple of *Kōmyō-ji,* when he was assassinated with his son *Moroyo.*

Kōan, 弘安. *Nengō :* 1278-1287.

Kōan no eki, 弘安役. The *Kōan* war: name given to the campaign made to repel the Mongol invasion of 1281.

Kōan-tennō, 孝安天皇. 6th Emperor of Japan (392-291 B. C.). *Ō-Yamato-tarashi-hiko-kuni-oshihito no mikoto* succeeded his father *Kōshō-tennō,* at the age of 35. He died at the age of 137 (123, according to the *Koji-ki*) after a reign of 102 years, about which both legend and history remain silent.

Kōba-bugyō, 貢馬奉行. In the time of the *Kamakura* and *Kyōto* shōgunates, an official commissioned to select and bring to the capital the horses which the *Shōgun* presented to the emperor every year in autumn.

Kobayakawa, 小早川. A family of *daimyō* descended from *Mōri Motonari.*

—— **Takakage,** 隆景 (1532-96). 3rd son of *Mōri Motonari,* was adopted in the *Kobayakawa* family, vassals of *Ōuchi Yoshitaka.* He served in all the campaigns of his brother *Kikkawa Motoharu,* and their reputation became such, that they were commonly called *Ryō-kawa.* He defeated at *Itsukushima,* (1555), *Miura Etchū no kami,* general of *Sue Harukata ;* then in *Kyūshū, Ōtomo Sōrin* (1562). After a long struggle against the armies of *Nobunaga* and *Hideyoshi,* he had a large share in the conclusion of the peace (1582). *Hideyoshi* gave him the province of *Chikuzen* (1587). He distinguished himself by his valor in the campaign of Korea. At that time, as *Takakage* had no children, *Hideyoshi* gave him as adopted son, his own nephew *Hideaki*. Thereupon, he retired to his castle of *Mihara* (*Bingo*), where he died after two years.

—— **Hideaki,** 秀 秋 (1577-1602). 5th son of *Kinoshita Iesada* was adopted first by *Hideyoshi* and brought up by *Kita Mandokoro*, but in 1592, he became adopted son and heir to *Takakage*. On the resumption of hostilities in Korea (1597), although only 20 years old, he was appointed commander in chief of the expedition (*gensui*), on account of his relationship to *Hideyoshi* and *Kuroda Yoshitaka* was assigned to assist him with his counsel. The campaign was not successful. But the cause of the failure should be traced to the rivalry and jealousy of the generals, rather than to the incapacity of the commander in chief. The latter was nevertheless denounced as incompetent by *Ishida Kazushige*; the *Taikō* was displeased and ordered him to yield the command to another: *Hideaki* refused to obey. Relations became strained between uncle and nephew; but *Ieyasu* succeeded in reconciling them. *Hideaki* could forget neither the proceedings of *Kazushige*, nor the good offices of *Ieyasu*. After the death of *Hideyoshi*, *Ishida*, in order to win him over to his side, offered him the tutorship of *Hideyori* until the age of 15. Nor was *Ieyasu* slow in making him brilliant offers. *Hideaki*, although rather late, embraced the cause of *Hideyori*. At the battle of *Sekigahara*, he remained till towards evening simple spectator of the doubtful struggle. Then, suddenly, abandoning his party, he sent his *samurai* against the troops of *Ōtani Yoshitaka*, put them to flight, and secured the victory to *Ieyasu*. On the very morrow, he besieged the castle of *Sawayama* (*Ōmi*), where the whole family of *Kazushige* met their fate (1600). *Ieyasu* proved grateful to *Hideaki* and gave him in fief the provinces of *Bizen* and *Mimasaka* with a revenue of 520,000 k. But *Hideaki* did not enjoy his fortune long; he died in less than 2 years, aged only 26, and, as he had no heir, his domains reverted to the *Shōgun*.

—— A son of the last *daimyō* of *Chōshū*, *Mōri Motonori*, has saved his name and bears the title of Baron.

Kōbe, 神 戸 . Capital of *Hyōgo-ken*. Composed of two parts separated by the *Minato-gawa*: East, the port of *Kōbe*, opened to foreign trade in 1868, West, the Japanese city of *Hyōgo* (283,800 inh.).

Kōben, 高 辨 (1173-1232). A famous bonze. Born in *Kii*, he lost his parents at the age of 8, entered the temple of *Takao-zan* (*Yamashiro*) and studied there. He afterwards went over to the *Tō-daiji*, but returned to die at *Takao-zan*. He was one of the propagators of the *Ryōbu-shintō*, and is also called *Myōe*.

Kōbō-Daishi, 弘 法 大 師 . — See *Kukai*.

Kobori, 小 堀 . A family of *daimyō* in *Ōmi*, in the 17th and the 18th centuries.

—— **Masakazu,** 政 一 (1579-1647). Served *Ieyasu* and received in 1600, a revenue of 10,000 k. at *Komuro* (*Ōmi*), with the title of *Tōtōmi* *no kami.* In 1623, he was appointed *Fushimi-bugyō.* *Masakazu* won fame in all the branches of Japanese art, poetry, design, flowers, etc. To teach the solemn preparation of tea, he founded a school, which, from his title of *Tōtōmi no kami,* was called *Enshū-ryū* (*Enshū* being the Chinese name of *Tōtōmi*). He was chosen to teach that branch of art to the *Shōgun Iemitsu.* He is commonly called *Kobori-Enshū.*

—— **Masakata, 政方.** A descendant of *Masakazu, Izumi no kami* and *Fushimi-bugyō,* was dispossessed in 1788, on account of his bad administration.

Kobukuro-zaka, 小袋坂. A hill near *Kamakura* (*Sagami*), where *Akabashi Moritoki,* a relative of the *Hōjō,* was defeated and killed by *Nitta Yoshisada* (1333).

Kōbun-in, 弘文院. A school founded towards the year 800, by *Wake Hiroyo,* son of *Kiyomaro,* for the education of the children of his family. It was the first free school established in Japan. *Hiroyo* endowed it with a library of 5 to 6,000 volumes and a revenue of 40 *chō* (about 40 hectares) of rice fields.

Kōbun-tennō, 弘文天皇. 39th Emperor of Japan (671-672). *Ōtomo* or *Iga no Ōji,* son of *Tenchi-tennō,* succeeded his father at the age of 24 years. Hardly had he ascended the throne, when his uncle *Ō-ama no Ōji* (later on *Temmu-tennō*) revolted in *Yoshino* and claimed the succession of his brother. The emperor sent troops against the rebel, but they were defeated in several engagements, upon which the emperor committed suicide at *Yamazaki* (*Ōmi*), after a reign of 8 months. It was only in 1870, that he was inscribed on the official list of sovereigns, and received the posthumous name of *Kōbun.*

Kobushin-bugyō, 小普請奉行. In the *Tokugawa* days, an official entrusted with the maintenance and repairs of the shōgunal palace, the temples of *Momiji-yama,* and of *Shiba,* the ministries, the detached palaces, etc. Later on, all the temples of the Empire were included. That function, created in 1685, had first only one titular, afterwards two. They had under them 8 *kobushin-gata,* 7 *gimmi-yaku,* 17 *kari-gimmi-yaku.*

Kobushin-gumi, 小普請組. In the *Tokugawa* days, a guild intrusted with repairs of minor importance in the outhouses of the Shōgunal palace. At first, children and old men were employed to help the workmen. In 1689, a guild was formed with the *samurai* who had a revenue of from 200 to 3,000 *koku,* and who were without work; they were paid at the rate of 50 *koku* of rice and 2 *ryō* (*yen*) per year.

Kōbusho-bugyō, 講武所奉行. In 1855, was begun in *Edo* (*Tsukiji, Odawara-machi*), the *Kōbusho,* which was a sort of military school for young *samurai.* In 1859, it was transferred to *Kanda, Ogawa-machi,* and the next year, it was placed under a *bugyō.* In 1862, its name was changed to *Rikugunsho.*

Kōchi, 高知. Capital of *Kōchi-ken* and *Tosa* province (36,600 inh.) *Yamanouchi Kazutoyo,* appointed *daimyō* of the province in 1600, built a castle there, where his descendants resided up to the Restoration (242,000 k.).

Kōchi-ken, 高知縣. Department formed with the province of *Tosa* (*Shikoku*). — Pop.: 651,000 inh. — Capital *Kōchi* (36,600 inh.).

Kōchō, 弘長. *Nengō :* 1261-1263.

Ko-chōhai, 小朝拜. When circumstances hindered the solemn meeting of the New Year in the Palace, the high officials alone presented their felicitations to the Emperor in the *Seiryōden*. This ceremony, less solemn, was called *Ko-chōhai,* and after the 10th century it often took place. — See *Chōga.*

Kōdai-in, 高臺院 (1549-1624). Wife of *Hideyoshi*. Born at *Tsushima* (*Owari*), she was daughter of *Sugihara Yoshifusa,* sister to *Kinoshita Iesada,* and sister-in-law to *Asano Nagamasa*. By her wit, she rendered great services to her husband. After his death, she shaved her head and took the name of *Kōdai-in*. She is better known by the name of *Kita-Mandokoro.*

Kōdai-ji, 高臺寺. Buddhist temple of the *Zen-shū* sect, built at *Kyōto* in 1601 by *Kita-Mandokoro,* widow of *Hideyoshi*. In the precincts are preserved the tombs of *Taikō, Hideyori, Mandokoro,* and her nephew *Kinoshita Katsutoshi.*

Kodama, 兒玉. A family of *samurai* from *Chōshū,* ennobled in 1895. — Now Baron.

—— **Gentarō,** 源太郎 (1852-1906). Was vice-Minister of war in 1892, Governor of Formosa, Minister of war (1900-1902), Chief d'Etat Major of the army in Manchuria during the Russo-Japanese war (1904-1905), etc.

Kōden, 功田. Formerly rice-fields leased as a reward for services rendered to the country. There were 4 kinds: *taikō,* permanent lease; *jōkō,* leased for 3 generations; *chūkō,* for 2 generations; *gekō,* which passed over to the son, and after his death, reverted to the public domain.

Kodera, 小寺. A family of *daimyō,* who were entrusted with the guard of the *Himeji* castle (*Harima*), first for the *Akamatsu daimyō,* and then for the *Yamana ;* they finally, became independent. The last, *Norimoto,* was dispossessed by *Hideyoshi* in 1577.

Kōei, 康永. *Nengō* of the Northern dynasty: 1342-1344.

Kōen, 康圜. Sculptor of the 13th century, grandson of the famous *Unkei.*

Kōfu, 甲府. Capital of *Yamanashi-ken* and of *Kai* province (*Kōshū*) (37,600 inh.). Formerly called *Fuchū,* was during the *Kamakura* shōgunate, the residence of the *Ichijō daimyō*. Afterwards it became part of the domains of the *Takeda. Nobunaga,* having dispossessed *Takeda Katsuyori* (1582), gave *Fuchū* to *Kawajiri Shigeyoshi,* who was assassinated shortly afterwards. *Hideyoshi* replaced him by *Hashiba Hidekatsu,* who resided at *Fukuchiyama* (*Tamba*), and had the province of *Kai* administered by *Katō Mitsuyasu*. On the death of *Hidekatsu* (1593), *Asano Nagamasa* was appointed to *Fuchū* and built a castle there. In 1600, the province became a domain of the *Shōgun* and *Ieyasu* disposed of it in favor of his son *Yoshinao* (1603), *Hiraiwa Chikayoshi* being *jōdai*. When *Yoshinao* was transferred to

Nagoya (1607), *Fuchū* was left without a *daimyō*. In 1618, it fell to the lot of *Tadanaga*, brother of *Iemitsu*. In 1632, new interruption. In 1661, *Tsunashige*, son of *Iemitsu*, became *daimyō* of *Kōfu;* his son *Tsunatoyo*, who succeeded him, having been adopted by the *Shōgun Tsunayoshi*, was replaced by *Yanagisawa Yoshiyasu* (1704). Finally, from 1724 to 1868, *Kōfu* belonged to the *Shōgun*, who had himself represented by a *jōdai*, some *jōban*, etc.

Kōfu-saishō, 甲府宰相. Title by which was designated *Tokugawa Tsunashige*, *daimyō* of *Kōfu* and brother of the *Shōgun Ietsuna* and *Tsunayoshi*, from 1661 to 1678.

Kōfuku-ji, 興福寺. Buddhist temple of the *Hossō* sect, at *Nara*. *Nakatomi Kamatari*, had built at *Yamashina* (*Yamashiro*), in honor of his ancestors a temple which was called *Yamashina-dera*. His son *Fujiwara Fuhito*, transported it to *Heijō-kyō* (*Nara*), where it became very prosperous. In the Middle Ages, it possessed an army of troops (*sōhei*) who, more than once, carried disorder and confusion even to *Kyōto*.

Koga, 古河. A town in *Shimōsa* (11,000 inh.). Ancient castle built in the 13th century by *Shimokōbe Yukiyoshi;* it passed over to the *Uesugi*, and the *Oyama* (1382). In 1455, *Ashikaga Shigeuji* put up there; whence his name of *Koga-kubō*. Having reverted to the *Uesugi* in 1486, the castle was taken by *Hōjō Ujiyasu* in 1554. In the *Tokugawa* times, it belonged successively to the *daimyō Ogasawara* (1590), *Toda* (1601), *Ogasawara* (1609), *Nagai* (1622), *Doi* (1633), *Hotta* (1681), *Matsudaira* (1685), *Ōkōchi* (1694), *Honda* (1712), *Matsui* (1759), and *Doi* (1762-1868) (80,000 k.).

Kōga, 甲賀. A place in *Ōmi*, where the troops of the emperor *Kōbun* were defeated by his uncle *Temmu* (672). Later on, *Shōmu-tennō* built a palace there (724-748). In 1487, *Rokkaku Takayori* gave battle there to the army of the *Shōgun Yoshihisa;* his great-grandson *Yoshisuke* was defeated there by *Nobunaga* (1568).

Koga-kubō, 古河公方. Name given to *Ashikaga Shigeuji*, installed at *Koga* (*Shimōsa*) from 1455 to 1486.

Koga Seiri, 古河精里 (1750-1817). Professor of Chinese literature. Born of a *samurai* family of the *Saga* clan (*Hizen*), he came to *Kyōto* and followed the lessons of *Fukui Shōsha, Nishiyori Seisai;* at *Ōsaka*, he made acquaintance with *Bitō Nishū, Rai Shunsui*, etc. Having returned to his province, he filled an important office, was then called to *Edo* and appointed professor at the *Shōheikō*. In 1811, he was sent to *Tsushima* to consult with a Korean ambassador.

Kogai-gawa, 小貝川. A river which takes its rise in *Shimotsuke*, enters *Hitachi* and empties itself into the *Tone-gawa* (87 Km.).

Kōgaku-shinnō, 高岳親王. Son of the emperor *Heijō*, he was chosen in 810, by his uncle *Saga-tennō* as heir apparent, but replaced, the following year, by *Ōtomo-shinnō*, because he had been implicated in the conspiracy of *Kusuri-ko*. In 822, he shaved his head, took the name of *Shinnyo* and retired to the temple of *Tōji*, where he placed himself under the direction of *Kūkai*. After the latter's death (834), he wandered about the land, recruiting disciples everywhere; then, in 861, he left for China. He remained there only 6 months and went to India, in order to study Buddhism at its source, but he died in the mountains of *Laos* (865). — *Kōgaku-shinnō* is often called *Takaoka-shinnō* or *Shinnyo-Shōnin*.

Kōgen, 康元. *Nengō:* 1256.

Kō-gen ryō-ke, 江源兩家. The two branches of the *Sasaki*, which, in the Middle Ages divided *Ōmi* between themselves: to the South, the *Rokkaku;* to the North, the *Kyōgoku.*

Kōgen-tennō, 孝元天皇. 8th Emperor of Japan (214-158 B. C.) *Ō-Yamato-neko-hiko-kuni-kuru no mikoto* succeeded his father *Kōrei* at the age of 60. History does not tell us any thing about his reign of 57 years.

Kogi-ha, 古義派. Branch of the *Shingon* sect, founded in 806 by *Kūkai.* — See *Shingon-shū ni-ha.*

Kōgon-tennō, 光嚴天皇. *Kazuhito,* son of the emperor *Go-Fushimi,* was appointed heir apparent in 1326. When *Go-Daigo* had to flee from *Kyōto* before the *Hōjō* army, *Takatoki* declared him forfeit to the throne, and raised in his place prince *Kazuhito,* then 18 years old (1331). Less than 2 years later, *Akamatsu Enshin,* general of *Go-Daigo,* captured *Kyōto,* whence *Kōgon* had now to flee (1333). He retired to the temple of *Jōjō-ji* (*Tamba*) where he died in 1364 at the age of 52.

Kogō no Tsubone, 小督局. Daughter of *Fujiwara Narinori, gonchūnagon,* she was a lady of the Court of the emperor *Takakura* and won distinction by her skill in playing the *biwa* (guitar). The affection which *Takakura* showed her, excited the jealousy of the empress *Kenreimonin,* daughter of *Kiyomori,* and to escape her vengeance, *Kogō* fled to *Sagano* (1177). Recalled by the emperor, she returned to the palace and gave birth to the princess *Noriko-naishinnō.* Then, in 1179, aged 23, she shaved her head, and retired to the temple of *Seikan-ji* on *Higashi-yama* (*Kyōto*). Later on she settled down at *Ōhara,* where she died.

Kōgyoku-tennō, 皇極天皇. 35th sovereign of Japan (642-644). *Ame-toyo-takara-ikashi-hitarashi hime,* daughter of the prince *Chinu no Ōji,* and grand daughter of *Shōtoku-taishi,* succeeded her uncle and husband *Jomei-tennō,* at the age of 48. She yielded to the influence of the powerful *Soga* ministers, *Emishi* and *Iruka.* When they were assassinated, the empress abdicated in favor of her brother *Kōtoku* and received the name of *Sume-mi-oya no mikoto.* Ten years later, she re-ascended the throne. — See *Saimei-tennō.*

Ko-ha, 古派. (Lit.: the ancient sects). Name given to the Buddhist sects introduced into Japan during the *Nara* and *Hei-an* periods; those that sprang up during the *Kamakura* period, are called the *shin-ha* (new sects).

Kōhei, 康平. *Nengō:* 1058-1064.

Kohitsu, 古筆. In the *Tokugawa* days, a family of experts in works of art. The most renowned members are: *Ryūsa* (1572-1662), *Ryūnin* (1614-1677), *Ryūei* (1617-1678), *Ryūyū* (1648-1687), *Ryūchū*

(1656-1736), *Ryūon* (1664-1725), *Ryūen* (1704-1774), *Ryūi* (1751-1834), *Ryūhan* (1790-1853), *Ryūhaku* (1836-1862).

Kōhō, 康保. *Nengō:* 964-967.

Ko-Ichijō no In, 小一條院 (994-1051). . *Atsu-akira*, son of the emperor *Sanjō*, was appointed heir apparent at the accession of *Go-Ichijō* (1017); but the following year, as he showed symptoms of insanity, he was replaced as *taishi* by prince *Atsunaga-shinnō*, and given the title of *Ko-Ichijō no In*, by which he is known.

Koide, 小出. A family of *daimyō*, originating in *Owari* and descended from *Fujiwara Muchimaro* (680-737).

Masahide-Yoshimasa $\begin{cases} \text{Yoshihide-Yoshishige-Hidemasu} & \text{(a)} \\ \text{Yoshichika-Yoshihisa-Fusatoshi} & \text{(b)} \end{cases}$

(*a*) — Elder branch. — **Masahide,** 政秀 (1539-1604). Born at *Nakamura* (*Owari*), the birthplace of *Hideyoshi*, he married the sister of the latter's wife, and thanks to *Hideyoshi's* influence, was appointed *Harima no kami*, and received the fief of *Kishiwada* (*Izumi* — 60,000 k.). He was chosen by *Taikō* to be with *Katagiri Katsumoto*, preceptor of *Hideyori*. During the campaign of *Sekigahara*, *Masahide*, being ill, sent his son *Yoshimasa* to fight on the side of *Ishida Kazushige*.

—— **Yoshimasa,** 吉政 (1565-1613). Succeeded his father in the domain of *Kishiwada*.

—— **Yoshihide,** 吉英 (1586-1668). Son of *Yoshimasa*, divided his fief with his brother *Yoshichika* (1612) and when the latter was transferred to *Sonobe* (*Tamba*), he installed himself at *Izushi* (*Tajima* — 45,000 k.) — That branch became extinct in 1696.

(*b*) — Younger branch — resided at *Izushi* (*Tajima*), then at *Sonobe* (*Tamba* — 26,700 k.) — Now Viscount.

Koizumi, 小泉. In *Yamato*. Was from 1615 to 1868, the residence of the *Katagiri daimyō* (12,000 k.).

Kōji, 康治. *Nengō:* 1142-1143.

Kōji, 弘治. *Nengō:* 1555-57.

Kōji-Daishi, 弘濟大師. A bonze of *Tō-daiji* (*Nara*). Went to China in 982, remained there 7 years, and brought back statues and *sûtras*. He died in 1016. During his life, he was called *Chōnen*.

Koji-ki, 古事記. Or *Furu-koto-bumi*. The first Japanese history compiled by *Ō no Yasumaro*, from the recollections of an old woman *Hieda no Are*, then 65 years old, who had preserved the memory of all the old legends. The work began in 711, and was finished the following year; it forms 3 volumes and extends from the creation to the end of the reign of the Empress *Suiko* (628). The mythological part is nothing but a tissue of vulgar fables. Nor can the chronology bear the light of serious criticism. It does not agree with that of the *Nihon-ki*, published some years later (720). Thus the *Koji-ki* makes *Jimmu-tennō* die at the age of 137 years; the *Nihon-ki*, at the age of 127 (the latter number has been adopted by the official chronology). *Suisei*, son of *Jimmu*, died, according to the *Koji-ki* at the age of 45, — according to the *Nihon-ki*, at the age of 80 (the official chronology gives 84 years).

The emperor *Sujin* lived 168 years, according to the *Koji-ki* — 120, according to the *Nihon-ki*, etc. After all, the *Koji-ki* has its antiquity only to recommend it. From both a literary and a historical standpoint, it is notably inferior to the *Nihon-ki* and we shall see further on how much credibility the latter deserves. — See *Nihon-ki*.

Kojima, 小嶋. In *Suruga;* was from 1704 to 1868, the residence of a branch of the *Matsudaira* family (10,000 k.).

Kojima, 小嶋 (+ 1374). A bonze of *Hiei-zan*, author of the *Taihei-ki*.

Kojima Takanori, 兒嶋高德. Son of *Norinaga*, was born in *Bizen*, and in his youth, cultivated literature. When *Go-Daigo* had to flee before the army of the *Hōjō* (1331), *Takanori* levied troops and fought for the cause of the southern dynasty. As soon as *Go-Daigo* returned to *Kyōto* from his exile, *Takanori* arrived to escort him to his capital (1333). He contributed to the destruction of *Rokuhara*. He served afterwards under the orders of *Nitta Yoshisada* and fought in *Harima* against *Akamatsu Norimura*, who had just gone over to the *Ashikaga*. After the death of *Yoshisada* (1338), he followed *Wakiya Yoshisuke* into *Shikoku*, then returned to *Bizen* (1340). Besieged by *Takauji*, he returned to *Kyōto*, whence he fled to *Shinano*. There, he shaved his head and took the name of *Shijun*. He reappeared in 1352, and having levied troops, fought at *Otoko-yama*, which battle re-opened for *Go-Murakami* the gates of *Kyōto*. It is not known what became of *Takanori* afterwards. He is often spoken of by the name of *Bingo Saburō*. The best known incident of his life, is that of his writing on a tree a Chinese poem to console and encourage *Go-Daigo* on his way to exile.

Kōjin, 荒神. Deity of the hearth or the kitchen. According to Chinese legend, he was born in *Kiangsi;* he fled from his father's house, after having committed a theft, and became a beggar. A schoolmaster employed him as a cook and called him *Shimei*. Among the pupils of the school, there was one too poor to provide for his own maintenance, and every day *Shimei* fed him with what remained from his master's table. The pupil became in due time a high official, and remembering the charitable cook, had him called to reward him. He was told that *Shimei* had died some years before. Not able to assist him in life, he wrote poems in his honor, and gave him the title of Kitchen deity.

Kōjo, 康助. A sculptor of the 12th century, of the *Kasuga* temple (*Nara*). He was grandfather to the famous *Unkei*.

Ko-jū-nin-gumi, 小十人組. In the *Tokugawa* times, the guards that escorted the *Shōgun* when they went out. — There were the *homban*, the *o-tomo-ban*, the *o-tomo-kaban*, etc.

Kōka, 黃河. The Yellow River (China).

Kōkaku-tennō, 光格天皇. 119th Emperor of Japan (1780-1816). *Kanehito*, son of prince *Kan-in Sukehito* and great-grandson of the emperor *Higashi-yama*, was 8 years old when he succeeded *Go-Momozono-tennō*, who had died without offspring. He was chosen by the influence of the *Kwampaku Kujō Hisazane*. In his reign, a great fire destroyed 190,000 houses in *Kyōto*, together with the imperial palace (1788). The *Shōgun Ienari* had it rebuilt at once, and on taking possession of the new palace (1790), the emperor rewarded the *Shōgun* by sending him an autograph poem. In 1793, in accordance with an ancient custom, he intended to confer on his father the title of *Dajō-tennō*, although he had never reigned, to which, *Ienari* objected. Indeed, the powerful *Shōgun* governed entirely according to his fancy during the 50 years of his dictatorship. Nevertheless, the edifice raised by *Ieyasu* began to show symptoms of decay. It was at this time that *Gamō Kumpei* and *Takayama Hikokurō* distinguished themselves by their loyalty to the imperial dynasty, while several others were cast into prison or put to death for having dared to question the supreme rights of the *Shōgun*. At this period also the Russians made repeated attempts to open Japan to foreign trade. *Kōkaku* abdicated at the age of 43, in favor of his son *Ninkō* and lived still 25 years in retirement.

Kōka-mon-in, 皇嘉門院. — See *Fujiwara Masa-ko*.

Kokawa, 粉川. In *Kii ;* an ancient temple (*Kokawa-dera* or *Seon-ji*) built in 770 by *Ōtomo Sukoburu*. It became very prosperous, thanks to the liberalities of the ex-emperors *Kwazan* and *Shirakawa*. Towards the end of the *Ashikaga* period, the bonzes having caused disturbances, *Hideyoshi* besieged the temple and reduced it to ashes. It was rebuilt at the beginning of the 17th century, but never recovered its former splendor. It belongs to the *Tendai* sect and the principal deity worshipped there is the goddess *Kwannon* with a thousand eyes and a thousand arms (*Sengan-senju Kwanzeon*). — *Kokawa* was, in 1463, the scene of a battle between the *Hatakeyama, Masanari* and *Masanaga*.

Kōke, 高家. (Lit.: the high families). A title given in the *Tokugawa* days, to some great dispossessed *daimyō* : *Takeda, Yokose, Hatakeyama, Yura, Imagawa, Oda, Ōtomo, Ōsawa, Kira*, etc. They had neither castle nor domains and received from the *Bakufu* a pension of less than 1,000 k. But certain privileged missions were reserved to them : they carried the *Shōgun's* messages to the Imperial Palace ; they treated the Imperial envoys at *Edo ;* they represented the *Shōgun* at certain ceremonies of *Nikkō*, etc. They also regulated the ceremonies to be observed in the *Shōgun's* palace. They were instituted in 1608, and in 1845, their number was 26. — Below the *Kōke*, about 10 families bore the title of *Omote-kōke*.

Kōkei, 康慶. Sculptor of the *Kasuga* temple (*Nara*), father of the famous *Unkei* (12th century).

Kōken, 後見. Formerly the tutor of the *Shōgun* before his majority. It was always a *Tokugawa*.

Kōken-tennō, 孝謙天皇. 46th Sovereign of Japan (749-759). *Abe-naishinnō*, daughter of *Shōmu-tennō*, succeeded her father at the age of 33. Disciple of *Kibi-Daijin*, she proved a fervent Buddhist, gathering as many as 5,000 bonzes in the *Tō-daiji* temple to read the sacred books and forbidding under severe penalties to kill any living beings, etc. Under her reign, the *Daibutsu* of *Nara* was cast (752). In all government matters, she let herself be swáyed by her ministers, *Fujiwara*

Toyonari and his brother *Nakamaro*. The latter even persuaded her to abdicate in favor of *Junnin*. She shaved her head and took the name of *Takano-tennō;* 6 years later, she re-ascended the throne. — See *Shōtoku-tennō*.

Kokiden, 弘徽殿. Formerly a part of the Imperial Palace, reserved for the Empress, the Court ladies and their attendants.

Kokiden no ue no mitsubone, 弘徽殿上御局. The apartments reserved for women, in the former Imperial Palace. They were also called *Fujitsubo-ue no mitsubone* or simply *Ue no mitsubone*.

Kokinshū, 古今集. (Lit.: ancient and modern poems). A collection of poems made in compliance with an order of the Emperor *Daigo*, by *Ki no Tsurayuki*, his nephew *Tomonori*, *Ōshikōchi no Mitsune*, *Mibu no Tadamine*, etc. The work begun in 905 was not completed before 922. It forms 20 volumes comprising more than 1,100 poems, mostly *tanka* (31 syllables).

Kokki, 國忌. A ceremony celebrated every year, on the anniversary of the preceding emperor's death. This custom dates from the reign of the empress *Jitō* (687-696). All the bonzes of the principal temples came together to read the sacred Books, the Emperor and all the officials suspended all business, music was prohibited, etc. Since the Restoration, the ceremony is performed in the *Kōrei-den* (Hall sacred to the manes of the Emperors) of the Palace (*Kōmei-tennō-sai* on the 30th January).

Kōkō-tennō, 光孝天皇. 58th Emperor of Japan (885-887). *Tokiyasu*, son of the emperor *Nimmyō*, was 55 years old when he succeeded *Yōzei-tennō*, who had been deposed by *Fujiwara Mototsune*. To reward *Mototsune* for having chosen him, the new emperor created for him the title of *Kwampaku* or *Azukari-mōsu*. He died after a reign of 3 years.

Kōkoku, 康國. *Nengō:* 1340-1345.

Koku, 石. Measure of capacity, equal to 180 litres 40. — It was in *koku* of rice that from the 16th century onwards the revenues of *daimyō* and the salaries of officials were estimated. In the *Tokugawa* days, a revenue of 10,000 k. at least, was necessary to entitle one to the rank of *daimyō*. The value of the *koku* has naturally undergone variations. In 1787, for instance, it was 5 *ryō* $\frac{1}{2}$ (about 27fr. 50), so that the revenue of a domain of 30,000 k. was 165,000 *ryō* (825,000 frs.).

Kokubun-ji, 國分寺. (Lit.: provincial temples). In 737, the emperor *Shōmu* ordered that in every province a temple or monastery should be built for the bonzes (*sō-ji*) and another for the *ama* or Buddhist nuns (*ni-ji*): they were the *kokubun-ji*. In the former, called *Shinkōmyō-shitennō-gokoku-ji*, there had to be 20 bonzes, under the jurisdiction of the *Tō-daiji;* the latter, called *Hokke-matsuzai-ji*, received ten *ama* and depended on the *Hokke-ji*. The name *Kokubun-ji* has been applied in several provinces to the village where the temple so called was erected.

Kokudaka, 石高. (Lit.: the amount of *koku*). Until the close of the 16th century, the revenues of the *daimyō*, and the salaries of officials were valued in *kwan* (*kwandaka*), a coin equal to $\frac{1}{10}$ of a *ryō*. *Hideyoshi* substituted the valuation in *koku* of rice. From 1589 to 1596, a new survey was made of the whole empire (see *Bunroku no kenchi*). Until then, 360 *bu* made 1 *tan*, 10 *tan* made 1 *chō*; thenceforth, 30 *bu* made 1 *se*, 300 *bu* or *tsubo* made 1 *tan*, 3,000 *bu* made 1 *chō*. Thus the old *tan* was equalled to 1 *tan* and 2 *se* of the new system, and 1 *chō*, made 1 *chō* 2 *tan*. It was with these new measures, that the area of the domains and their revenues were estimated. This modification was termed *Bunroku no kenchi* or *Tenshō no koku-naoshi*.

Kokugun-bokujō, 國郡卜定. (Lit.: provinces and districts determined by divination). Before the *daijō-e* solemnity the two provinces that were to provide the ears of rice to be offered to the Imperial Ancestors were determined by the art of divination (*uranai*). In the Middle Ages, instead of provinces, 2 districts (*gun*) were designated.

Kokura, 小倉. A city of *Buzen* province (28,000 inh.). Ancient castle first called *Katsuyama* or *Katsuno*. It was built in 1442 by *Reizei Takasuke*, vassal of the *Ōtomo*. In the year 1587, *Hideyoshi* gave it to *Mōri Katsunaga*. In the *Tokugawa* times, it belonged to the *Hosokawa daimyō* (1600-1632) and then to the *Ogasawara* (1632-1868) — (150,000 k.).

Kokuryō-shi, 告陵使. Title given to the messenger sent by the Emperor after his accession, to offer the *gohei* on the tombs of his ancestors and other persons of high rank.

Kokusen-ya, 國姓爺 (1624-1662). By birth *Tei Seikō*. His father, *Tei Shiryō*, born in Fokien, passed over to Macao, where he was baptized Nicholas; he came afterwards to Japan, settled down at *Hirota* (*Hizen*), and married a Japanese woman of the name of *Tagawa*. Engaged in great commercial enterprises with China, he acquired considerable fortune, equipped a flotilla to support the *Ming* dynasty in their struggle against the Tartars, and was commander in Chief of the Imperial army (1629). He then repaired to Nanking, where his wife and son soon joined him. *Seikō*, having completed his studies, received from the emperor the title of Count with the name *Kokusen-ya* (1647), which European writers have changed to *Koxinga*. From that time onwards, he fought incessantly against the Manchus, who were supported by the Dutch. Finding it impossible to feed his troops in a country laid waste by the enemy, he embarked for Formosa, where he landed with 25,000 men, and in a few months, expelled the Dutch, who had been in the island for upwards of 40 years (1660). Retiring to the stronghold of *Fort Zelandia*, near *Amping*, he began to assume royal power. The following year, he repelled an attack of the Dutch who attempted to recover their colony; after which, he sent an Italian Dominican, Father Riccio to the governor of the Philippines, summoning him to pay tribute to the king of Formosa and threatening invasion in case of refusal. All the Chinese residing at Manila, were suspected of having some share in the matter, and were massacred. *Kokusen-ya* was preparing an expedition against the Philippines, when he died of fever, at the age of 39. After him his son and grandson following in his footsteps, endeavored to open Formosa to civilization, but the Tartars prevailed and the island became a Chinese possession. The grandson of *Kokusen-ya*, *Tei Kokuzō*, was called to Peking and received the title of Duke.

Kokushi, 國 司. The total number of officials, intrusted with the government of a province and more especially the governor himself. At first, the period in office for the provincial governors was 6 years; *Mommu-tennō* reduced it to 4 years (702); *Koken-tennō* lengthened it again to 6 years (755); later on, it came to be of 4 or 5 years' duration, depending on the distance from the capital. In ancient times the governor was called *Kuni no miyatsuko* and *Inagi: Jimmu-tennō* appointed 144 of them. In the reign of *Kōtoku* (645), they were called *Kokushu*. Later on, the empire was definitively divided into 66 provinces, which were known as *taikoku*, *jōkoku*, *chūkoku* and *gekoku*, all governed by a *Kokushu*, having under him 1 *Suke*, 1 or more *Jō*, *Moku*, etc. Moreover to each province was assigned a professor of literature, with a number of pupils varying from 50 to 20, according to the importance of the province, and a doctor of medicine with from 4 to 10 pupils. With the increase of the *shō-en*, the government of the provinces became more difficult. The *kokushu* resided at *Kyōto* and had themselves represented by a *Mokudai*. *Yoritomo* intrusted the administration of the provinc s to his vassals, who were called *Shugo* or *Jitō*. In the 14th century the title of *Kokushi* was reserved to the *kuge*. The military governors were called *shugo :* the former disappeared by degrees.

Kokushi-ga-take, 國 司 嶽. A mountain on the borders of *Kii* and *Shinano* (2,570 m).

Kokushu, 國 守. Governor of a province. — See *Kokushi*.

Kokusō-in, 穀 倉 院. An office created in 807 for the safeguarding of the warehouses (*kura*) where rice and other cereals were kept. Later on, it was presided by a *bettō*.

Kokūzō-Bosatsu, 虛 空 藏 菩 薩. A Buddhist deity, that resides in space. One of the personifications of wisdom.

Kōkwa, 弘 化. *Nengō :* 1844-1847.

Kōkyō-Daishi, 興 敎 大 師. Posthumous title of the bonze *Kakuhan* (1095-1144). Born in *Hizen*, he studied successively at *Ninna-ji*, *Mii-dera*, *Kōya-san ;* after which he founded the *Shingi* branch of the *Shingon* sect.

Koma, 高 麗. One of the ancient kingdoms of Korea, also called *Kōrai*. It existed from the year 37 B. C. to 668 A. D. — It was one of the 3 *Kan* (*san-Kan*), that called *Shin-Kan*. It became subject to Japan at the time of the expedition of *Jingō-kōgō* (200 A. D.) and proved a constant and faithful ally ; it was conquered by *Shiragi* (*Ba-Kan*).

Koma-ga-take, 駒 ヶ 嶽. A mountain in the W. of *Kai* (3,000 m.).

Koma-ga-take, 駒 ヶ 嶽. A mountain in the S. of *Shinano* (2,560 m.).

Koma-ga-take, 駒 ヶ 嶽. A mountain in the S. W. of *Iwashiro* (2,000 m.).

Koma-ga-take, 駒ヶ嶽. Another name for *Kurikoma-yama* (*Rikuzen*).

Koma-ga-take, 駒ヶ嶽. A mountain on the N. of *Echigo* (1,180 m.). It is the highest of the *Hakkai-san* group.

Koma-ga-take, 駒ヶ嶽. A volcano in *Oshima* (*Hokkaidō*) (1,000 m.); also called *Uchi-ura-dake, Kayabe-nobori*.

Komaki-yama, 小牧山. A hill in *Owari* (350 m.) ; also called *Higuruma-yama*. *Nobunaga* built a castle there (1563), where his son *Nobuo* was besieged by *Hideyoshi* (1584) ; *Ieyasu* came to the rescue of *Nobuo* and defeated *Hideyoshi*, whereupon the latter made peace.

Koma-shaku, 高麗尺. A long measure formerly used in Korea, and imported to Japan, at the time when the *San-Kan* became tributary to Japan, whence its name of "*Koma* measure." — It was equal to 35 cm. 56. At that time, the *jō* (10 ft.) was called *tsue ;* the *shaku* (foot), *saka ;* the *sun* (inch) *ki*.

Komata, 小俣. In *Shimotsuke*. Ancient castle which in the 16th century, belonged to the *Shibukawa daimyō*. It passed into the possession of the *Uesugi* and the *Hōjō*, and was captured by *Hideyoshi* in 1590.

Komatsu, 小松. In *Rikuchū*, near the present city of *Ichinoseki*, where *Abe no Sadatō* had a fortified camp which was captured by the troops of *Minamoto Yoriyoshi* and *Kiyowara Takenori* in 1062.

Komatsu, 小松. A city in *Kaga* province (13,300 inh.). Ancient castle built by the *Togashi daimyō*, and captured by *Asakura Yoshikage* (1560). The latter was dispossessed by *Nobunaga* (1573) and replaced by *Murakami Yoshiakira*. *Hideyoshi* installed there *Niwa Nagashige* (1597). From 1600 on, it belonged to *Maeda Toshinaga*.

Komatsu, 小松. In *Iyo*. Was from 1644 to 1868 the residence of a branch of the *Hitotsu-yanagi* family (10,000 k.).

Komatsu, 小松. A family of imperial princes, issued from *Fujiwara Kuniie*. In 1870, they received the name of *Higashi-Fushimi*.

—— **Akihito,** 彰仁. (Formerly *Yoshiaki*) (1846-1903). 5th son of *Fushimi Kuniie*, was first head bonze of the *Ninna-ji* temple. The Restoration secularized him and appointed him general of the Imperial Army. From 1870 to 1872, he studied in England. In 1882, his name *Yoshiaki* was changed to that of *Akihito*, and the name of his house, *Higashi Fushimi*, to that of *Komatsu no miya*. He had married in 1869 the daughter of *Arima Yorishige*, the former *daimyō* of *Kurume* (*Chikugo*). — After his death, his house took its former name of *Higashi-Fushimi* again.

Komatsu, 小松. A family descended from the *Taira* and attached, for centuries, to the *Kōfuku-ji* (*Nara*). — Now Baron.

Komatsu, 小松. A family of *samurai* from the clan of *Kagoshima* (*Satsuma*), ennobled after the Restoration. — To-day Count.

Kōmei-tennō, 孝明天皇. 121st Emperor of Japan (1846-1867). *Osahito*, son of *Ninkō-tennō*, born in 1821, appointed *Shinnō* in 1835 and *Kōtaishi* in 1840, succeeded his father in March 1846. In his reign, the arrival of foreigners hastened the overthrow of the *Shōgun*.

The latter, not daring to reject their demands, signed treaties with the Western Powers (1854-1857). These however were cancelled by the emperor, who issued orders to expel the barbarians (*jō-i*). Then, profiting of the *Bakufu's* perplexity, the emperor gained the adhesion of the great *daimyō* of *Mito*, *Nagato* and others, and, feeling himself supported, began to assert his authority, even against the *Shōgun*. *Iemochi* had to repair to *Kyōto* and receive his instructions (1863). The question of the guards of the Imperial Palace contributed to aggravate the situation : war broke out between the *daimyō* of *Nagato* (*Chōshū*) and the *Shōgun*. Meanwhile, the emperor was compelled to ratify the treaties, which the *Shōgun* had concluded with the foreign powers (1865). He died of smallpox, February 3rd, 1867 at the age of 37, too soon to see the Restoration which he had desired and prepared.

KŌMEI-TENNŌ.

Kome-Shōgun, 米將軍. (Lit.: rice-*shōgun*). Surname given by the people to the *Shōgun Yoshimune* (1716-1745), on account of the encouragements which he gave to agriculture, and the distributions of rice which he repeatedly made in times of famine.

Komoda, 小茂田. In *Tsushima*. A place where the Mongols landed in 1274 when they ravaged the whole island.

Kōmoku, 廣目. One of the *Shi-daitennō :* the one that watches over the West.

Kōmon, 黃門. A title at the Court of China, in the time of the *Tō* dynasty. In Japan it corresponded to *Chūnagon*. Thus *Fujiwara Sadaie* is called *Kyōgoku Kōmon ; Tokugawa Mitsukuni, Mito Kōmon*.

Kōmon, 興門. A branch of the *Nichiren* sect, founded by the bonze *Nikkō* (1290). In 1898, its name was changed to that of *Hommonshū*.

Komono, 薦野. Ancient castle in *Ise*, built in 1569, by *Takigawa Kazumasu*. From 1600 to 1868, residence of the *Hijikata daimyō* (11,000 k.).

Ko-mononari, 小物成. In the *Tokugawa* times, taxes levied on the revenues drawn from mountains, prairies, ponds, rivers, seas, etc. These taxes were called *ko-mononari*, to distinguish them from the *mononari*, or annual taxes paid by the country people. They were also called *uki-yaku* 浮役.

Komoro, 小諸. A small town in *Shinano* (8,500 inh.), on the *Chikuma-gawa*. Ancient castle, built in the 15th century by *Ōi Iga no kami*, who appropriated the domains of the ancient *Tetsuka* family. It was captured in 1553, by *Takeda Shingen*, who confided its guardianship to *Oyamada Bitchū no kami*. After the fall of the *Takeda*, *Hideyoshi* installed *Sengoku Hidehisa* there. In the *Tokugawa* times, it became successively the residence of the *daimyō*: *Hisamatsu* (1624), *Aoyama* (1649), *Sakai* (1662), *Nishio* (1679), *Ishikawa* (1682), and *Makino* (1702-1868). (15,000 k.).

Komparu, 金春. A family of writers and actors of "*nō.*" The best known are: *Ujinobu* (1316-1401), *Toyouji* (+ 1458), *Yasuteru* (+ 1628), *Kunihisa* (1680-1828), *Hiroshige* (+ 1896).

Kompira, 金比羅. — See *Kotohira-jinja.*

Komura, 小村. A family originating in *Hyūga*, ennobled in 1902. — Now Baron.

—— **Jutarō,** 壽太郎. Born in 1855, Minister at Seoul, and at Washington (1898) at St. Petersburg (1900), Minister of Foreign Affairs (1900-1906) and first Plenipotentiary, appointed to conclude peace with Russia (1905).

Kōmyō-ji, 光明寺. A Buddhist temple to the S.W. of *Kyōto*, founded by *Kumagaya Naozane* at the close of the 12th century. His successor *Seizan-Shōnin*, erected the principal temple, which received its name from the Emperor *Shijō.* It possesses the tomb of *Genkū* (*Hōnen-Shōnin*). It is the seat of the *Seizan* branch of the *Jōdo* sect.

Kōmyō-kōgō, 光明皇后 (701-760). Daughter of *Fujiwara Fuhito,* wife of the emperor *Shōmu* and mother of the empress *Kōken.* At the time of *Shōmu's* abdication, she shaved her head and took the name of *Mampuku* (749).

Kōmyō-tennō, 光明天皇. *Toyohito,* 9th son of the emperor *Go-Fushimi,* was raised to the throne in 1336, by *Ashikaga Takauji,* when *Go-Daigo* fled from *Kyōto* to the South. That was the beginning of the schism. *Go-Daigo,* entrenched on Mt. *Yoshino,* represented the legitimate southern dynasty; at *Kyōto, Kōmyō,* supported by *Takauji,* stood for the northern dynasty, which state of things lasted for 60 years. — In 1348, *Kōmyō,* aged 37, abdicated in favor of his nephew *Sukō.* In 1351, he was made prisoner, with his successor, by the army of the southern emperor, *Go-Murakami,* and was only set free in 1357. He died in 1380 at *Hatsuse* (*Yamato*), aged 59.

Konando-shū, 小納戸衆. In the *Tokugawa* days, young *samurai* that served in the *Shōgun's* palace. Their duty was to dress his hair, to shave him, serve him at table, look after his horses, his hawks, etc. Most of them were chosen from among the sons of *yoriai, kobushin, ryōban,* etc. — See *Koshō-shū.*

Kondei, 健兒. A sort of local militia which by and by replaced the troops that were sent from the capital to the provinces. In 762, sons of warriors and peasants were chosen in the 4 provinces of *Ise, Ōmi, Mino* and *Echizen,* to constitute the *kondei;* in 792, the practice was extended to the whole empire; towards 910, their number was fixed for every province and varied between 20 and 300; they were under the authority of the *Hyōbu-shō* (minister of war).

Kondō Morishige, 近藤守重 (1757-1815). A *samurai* of the *Bakufu,* who in 1795, was appointed assistant of the *bugyō* of *Nagasaki.* 3 years later, the Russians landed at *Etorū,* the largest of the Kurile Islands. They planted a cross there and a number of posts with Russian inscriptions, to show that they had taken possession of the island. *Morishige* was sent to the spot to investigate the matter; he tore down the cross and the posts and put up others, with the following inscription in large characters: *Dai-Nippon-Etorū*. On his return to *Edo*, he drew a map of *Ezo* and insisted on the necessity of appointing a *bugyō* for that island, which was done shortly afterwards. Thereupon, *Morishige* retired to *Shibuya*, near *Edo*. His son *Tomizō*, having assassinated a peasant, they were both confined at *Ōmizo* (*Ōmi*), domain of *Wakebe Mitsuyasu*, where *Morishige* died at the age of 58. In 1860, 45 years after his death, his memory was rehabilitated, on account of the services he had rendered in *Hokkaidō*.

Kon-e-fu, 近 衞 府. Formerly, a corps of the Imperial guard. It was divided into *Sakon-e* and *Ukon-e*. The officers bore the title of *taishō*, *chūjō*, *shōshō*, *shōgen*, *shōsō*, *fusei*, *banchō*, *toneri*, etc.

Kongara-dōji, 矜 羯 羅 童 子. One of the two attendants of the god *Fudō*.

Kongō, 金 剛. An ancient family famous for their skill in writing and performing "*nō*" and "*sarugaku*." The best known is *Shinroku* (1507-1576).

Kongōbu-ji, 金 剛 武 寺. The first temple founded at *Kōya-san* (*Kii*) by *Kūkai* in 816. Also called *Nanzan*. — See *Kōya-san*.

Kongō-sen, 金 剛 山. Mountain on the borders of *Yamato* and *Kawachi* (1,235 m.). On its western slope *Kusunoki Masashige* built in 1331, his castle of *Chihaya*, also called *Takama-yama*, *Katsuragi-yama*.

Kōnin, 弘 仁. *Nengō*: 810-823.

Kōnin-tennō, 光 仁 天 皇. 49th Emperor of Japan (770-781). *Yamato-neko-ame-mune-takatsuki no mikoto*, also called *Shirakabe-Ōji*, was grandson of *Tenchi-tennō* and son of prince *Shiki*. At the death of the Empress *Shōtoku*, the *Fujiwara*, *Momokawa* and *Nagate*, raised him to the throne. He was 62 years old. The first use he made of his authority was to banish to *Shimotsuke* the intriguing bonze *Dōkyō* and to recall from exile the faithful *Wake no Kiyomaro*, whom he appointed *Udaijin*. He had to quell two revolts of *Ebisu* in *Mutsu* (774-780). After a 12 'years' reign, he abdicated in favor of his son *Kwammu* and died the same year.

Konishi Yukinaga, 小 西 行 長 (+ 1600). Son of an apothecary of *Sakai* (*Izumi*), he was adopted by a *samurai* of *Ukita Hideie*, *daimyō* of *Okayama* (*Bizen*). In 1577, when *Hideie* had to submit to *Hideyoshi*, he chose *Yukinaga* to negotiate the peace; the young man pleased *Hideyoshi*, who attached him to his service, granted him a revenue of 10,000 k., with the title of *Takumi no suke*, then that of *Settsu no kami*. After the *Kyūshū* expedition, *Yukinaga* received as fief, half of the province of *Higo* (240,000 k.) and settled down at *Udo*. He had been baptized Augustine in 1583, and is spoken of in the letters of the ancient missionaries as Don Augustin. At the time of the Korean expedition (1592), he received, with *Katō Kiyomasa*, the command of the vanguard, and was the first to land at *Fusan*. Having stormed the place, he marched upon the capital, whence the king fled with all his court. *Yukinaga* pursued him as far as *Heijō* (*Hpyeng-yang*), on the frontiers of China, but without being able to overtake him. Attacked shortly after by a numerous Chinese army, he had to fall back on *Seoul*. He accompanied to Japan the Chinese embassy that came to treat of peace (1595); then, after the rupture of the negotiations, he returned to Korea, where all he could do, was to hold his own against the frequent attacks of the Chinese and Koreans. He returned to Japan after *Hideyoshi's* death (1598), sided with *Ishida Kazushige* against *Ieyasu* and was one of the vanquished of *Sekigahara*. He surrendered to *Kuroda Nagamasa*, was condemned to death and b headed at *Rokujō-ga-hara* (*Kyōto*) with *Kazushige*, *Ankokuji Ekei*, etc. (1600).

Kōno, 河野. *Daimyō* family descended from *Iyo-shinnō*, son of the emperor *Kwammu*, powerful during the Middle Ages.

—— **Michinobu,** 通信 (1156-1223). Sided with *Yoritomo*, when the latter rose against the *Taira* (1180). At first victorious, he was afterwards obliged to flee to *Aki*. There the *Numata* family furnished him with troops with which he re-entered *Iyo*; but he was defeated by *Taira Michimori* and fled again (1184). Hardly had he regained his province, when *Taira Munemori*, bringing along with him the young emperor *Antoku*, arrived at *Yashima* (*Sanuki*), and summoned him to join them and fight against the *Minamoto*: he refused, was defeated and again forced to flee. He met, on the way, *Noriyori* and *Yoshitsune*, who were coming to fight against the *Taira*; he joined them, contributed to their victory and was re-instated in the province of *Iyo*. He accompanied *Yoritomo* in his campaign to *Mutsu* against *Fujiwara Yasuhira* (1189). Having sided against the *Hōjō* in the *Shōkyū* war (1221), he was exiled to *Hiraizumi* (*Mutsu*), where he died.

—— **Michiari,** 通有. Grandson of *Michinobu*, was *Tsushima no kami*. He won fame in fighting against the Mongolian fleet that came to attack the castle of *Chikuzen* (1281).

—— **Michimori,** 通盛 (+ 1362). Son of *Michiari*, supported *Hōjō Takatoki* and *Ashikaga Takauji*, who confirmed him in the possession of *Iyo*.

—— **Michitaka,** 通尭 (+ 1374). Son of *Michimori*, abandoned the cause of the *Ashikaga* and offered his services to prince *Yasunaga-shinnō*. Joining forces with *Kikuchi Takemitsu*, he fought against *Hosokawa Yoriyuki*, and had at first some success, but was afterwards defeated and committed suicide.

—— **Michinao,** 通直 (+ 1587). *Danjō-shōsuke*, was attacked in 1568, by *Utsunomiya Toyotsuna* and implored the help of *Mōri Moto-nari*. *Kobayakawa Takakage* and *Kikkawa Motoharu* came to his rescue and re-instated him in his domains; but he was again defeated in 1580 by *Chōsokabe Motochika* who conquered *Iyo*. *Michinao* fled to *Aki* where he died.

It is from that family that the *daimyō Inaba* and *Hitotsuyanagi* descend.

Kōno, 河 野. A family of *samurai* from the clan of *Kōchi* (*Tosa*), ennobled after the Restoration. — Now Viscount.

—— **Togama,** 敏 鎌 (1844-1895). At first secretary in the Department of Justice, became afterwards Senator and Minister of Education and Commerce. In 1882, he resigned his post to devote his time to the formation of the Progressive party (*kaishin-tō*) and became president of the *Tōkyō* Exchange. When the Privy Council was created (1888), he was appointed one of its first members ; he became successively Minister of Agriculture and Commerce, of the Home Department, and of Education (1892). In 1893, he was ennobled with the title of Viscount.

Kōnodai, 鴻 ノ 臺. In *Shimōsa*, formerly, the capital of the province. *Satomi Yoshihiro* was defeated there by *Hōjō Ujitsuna* (1538) and by *Hōjō Ujiyasu* (1564).

Konoe, 近 衞. A family of *kuge*, descended from *Fujiwara Iezane* (1179-1242). It was one of the 5 branches (*go-sekke*), from which the empresses and the *Kwampaku* were chosen. — Now Duke.

—— **Tsunetada,** 經 忠 (1302-1352). Son of *Iehira* was *Kwampaku*. Remained faithful to the southern dynasty and accompanied *Go-Daigo* to Mt. *Yoshino*.

—— **Sakihisa,** 前 久 (1536-1612). Son of *Taneie*, was first called *Harutsugu*. In 1554, he was appointed *Kwampaku* and changed his name to *Sakitsugu*. In 1560, chosen suzerain lord by *Uesugi Terutora*, he repaired to *Echigo*, where he remained 5 years. Having returned to *Kyōto*, he took the name of *Sakihisa*, and retired to *Saga* (*Yamashiro*), where he wrote the *Saga-ki* (1573). Shortly after, having offended *Nobunaga*, he fled to *Satsuma*, where he sojourned 2 years. After which he returned to the capital, was appointed *Sangū*, then *Dajō-daijin* (1582). The same year, he shaved his head and took the name of *Ryūzan*.

—— **Nobutada,** 信 尹 (1565-1614). Son of *Sakihisa*, performed *gembuku* in 1577, and received from *Nobunaga* one of the ideographs of his own name : he was called *Nobumoto*. He asked permission to enlist in the expedition to Korea (1542), but the emperor *Go-Yōzei*, refused to grant his request. In 1602, he changed his name to *Nobutada*, became *Sadaijin* and *Kwampaku* (1605). He was a distinguished man of letters, and founded a literary school, known as the *Konoe-ryū*.

—— **Nobuhiro,** 信 尋 (1593-1643). Was the 4th son of the emperor *Go-Yōzei*, and was selected by his father as heir of *Nobutada*, who had no children. In 1623, he was appointed *Kwampaku*.

—— **Atsumaro,** 篤 麿 (1863-1904). Was director of the Noble School (*Gakushū-in*) and President of the Senate.

Konoe-tennō, 近 衞 天 皇. 76th Emperor of Japan (1142-1155). *Narihito*, 9th son of *Toba-tennō*, was raised to the throne at the age of 3, in place of his brother *Sutoku*. The ex-emperor *Toba*, governed with *Fujiwara Tadamichi*. *Konoe* died at the age of 17.

Ko-no-hana-saku-ya hime, 木 華 開 耶 姫. A *Shintō* goddess. Daughter of the Mountain deity, *Ōyamatsumi*, she married *Ninigi no* *mikoto.* Also called *Sengen* and *Asama*, she is honored as the deity of Mt. *Fuji.*

Kō-ō, 康 應 . *Nengō* of the northern dynasty : 1389.

Koppitsuretsu, 忽 必 烈 . Japanese name of *Koublai-khan (Hupilai)* — (1215-1294). It was he that failed to obtain allegiance from Japan and sent against her in 1280 an expedition of 100,000 Mongolians with 10,000 Koreans, almost all of whom perished in a tempest. — See *Hōjō Tokimune.*

Kōrai, 高 麗 . One of the ancient kingdoms of Korea ; also called *Koma* and *Shin-Kan.* It existed from 37 B. C. to 668 A. D., when it was conquered by *Shiragi (Ba-Kan).* The name *Kōrai* was applied for a long time to the whole of Korea, which took the name of *Chōsen* only in 1392.

Kōrei-tennō, 孝 靈 天 皇 . 7th Emperor of Japan (29)-215 B.C.). *Ō-Yamato-neko-hiko-futo-ni no mikoto,* succeeded his father *Kōan,* at the age of 52. He died at the age of 128 years, after a reign of 76 years. According to a tradition, in the 5th year of his reign (286 B. C.) a frightful earthquake had the double effect of sinking lake *Biwa* and raising Mt. *Fuji.* Another event — hardly more certain — was the arrival in Japan in 221 B. C., of the Chinaman *Shin no Jofuku,* physician to the emperor *Shikō (Chi-houang)* sent by the latter in search of the elixir of immortality.

Koremune Kinkata, 惟 宗 公 方 . In the reign of *Ōjin-tennō,* prince *Kōman-Ō,* descendant of the Chinese emperor *Shikō,* of the *Shin* dynasty, came with a large number of companions to dwell in Japan. His successors received the family name of *Shin.* Towards the year 880, this name was changed to *Koremune.* — *Kinkata* was doctor of Chinese law *(Mimpō-hakase) Kebiishi* and *Ōkura-gon-daisuke* (958). He it was that drew up all the regulations, laws, etc., promulgated at that time.

Koretaka-shinnō, 惟 喬 親 王 (844-897). Eldest son of the emperor *Montoku.* Was *Dazai no Sotsu* (858), *Dajō no Suke* (863), *Hitachi-Taishu, Kōzuke-Taishu* (872). Shortly afterward, he became a bonze. He is often called *Ono no Miya.* He was a distinguished poet.

Koretō-shōgun, 惟 任 將 軍 . Surname given by the people to *Akechi Mitsuhide,* whose patronymic name was *Koretō.*

Koreyasu-shinnō, 惟 康 親 王 . 7th *Shōgun* of *Kamakura* (1266-1289). Son of *Munetaka-shinnō,* he succeeded his father in the office of *Shōgun* at the age of 3, all the authority remaining in the hands of the *Shikken Hōjō Tokimune.* He was deposed by *Hōjō Sadatoki* and retired to *Saga* near *Kyōto,* where he shaved his head and lived for 37 years more.

Kōri, 郡 . District, — See *Gun.*

Kōriki, 高 力 . A family of *daimyō* originating in *Mikawa.*

—— **Kiyonaga,** 清 長 (1530-1608). Companion in arms of *Ieyasu,* became one of the *bugyō* of *Sumpu* (1565), *Kawachi no kami* (1586). In 1590, he received the fief of *Iwatsuki (Musashi* — 20,000 k.).

—— **Tadafusa,** 忠 房 (1583-1655). Was transferred in 1619, to *Hamamatsu (Tōtōmi),* and in 1638, to *Shimabara (Hizen* — 40,000 k.).

—— **Takanaga,** 高 長 (1604-1676). Was dispossessed and exiled to *Sendai* in 1668, on account of his bad administration.

Kōrin-ha, 光 淋 派. A school of painting founded at the close of the 17th century by *Ogata Kōrin* (1661-1716). — See *Ogata Kōrin.*

Kōriyama, 郡 山. A town in *Yamato* (14,000 inh.). Ancient castle built towards 1565 by *Odagiri Harutsugu, kerai* of *Tsutsui Junkei.* In 1585, *Hideyoshi* gave it to his brother *Hidenaga* with the 3 provinces of *Kii, Yamato* and *Izumi.* It passed afterwards to *Masuda Nagamori* (1594). In the *Tokugawa* days, it belonged successively to the *daimyō: Mizuno* (1615), *Okudaira* (1619), *Honda* (1639), *Matsudaira* (1679), *Honda* (1685) and *Yanagisawa* (1724-1868) (150,000 k.).

Kōrokwan, 鴻 臚 館. A building erected at the time of the foundation of *Kyōto*, for the reception of foreign guests, ambassadors, etc.

Koromo, 舉 母. In *Mikawa*, was in olden times, the seat of the *Koromo no kuni-miyatsuko.* — In the *Tokugawa* days, residence of the *daimyō Honda* (1681) and *Naitō* (1749-1868) (20,000 k.).

Koromo-gawa, 衣 川. A river in *Rikuchū* (41 Km.) which flows into the *Kitakami-gawa.* On its banks, *Yoshitsune* was defeated in 1189, by *Fujiwara Yasuhira.*

Koromogawa, 衣 川. A village in *Rikuchū*, on the *Koromo-gawa* river, where in the 11th century *Abe Yoritoki* had a fortified camp and where his son *Sadatō* was besieged and killed by *Minamoto Yoriyoshi* (1062).

Koropok-guru, — An *Aino* word, meaning cave-dweller. A race said to have occupied *Ezo* before the *Aino* and to whom are attributed the ruins seen in several places of *Hokkaidō*, especially in the environs of *Kushiro.* The Japanese call them *Kobito* (dwarfs).

Kōryaku, 康 暦. *Nengō* of the northern dynasty: 1379-1380.

Ko-saburai-dokoro, 小 侍 所. An office established at *Kamakura* in 1219, presided by a *Bettō*, who was always taken from among the *Hōjō.* Its duty was to settle all matters concerning the army of the *Bakufu :* military exercises, archery, lodging of the troops, etc. In 1241, a school was annexed to it, where the children of officers learned, besides Chinese characters and music, horsemanship, archery and a game like tennis, etc.

Kōsai Motochika, 香 西 元 近. Also called *Matarokurō. Kerai* of the *Hosokawa.* In 1507, he assassinated his suzerain *Masamoto*, and discarding the latter's adopted son, *Sumimoto*, chose to succeed him, *Sumiyuki*, son of the *Kwampaku, Kujō Hisatsune. Sumimoto* appealed to arms, and aided by *Miyoshi Nagateru*, defeated and killed both *Motochika* and his protégé *Sumiyuki* near *Kyōto*

Kōsaka, 高 阪. A family of *samurai* from *Shinano*, annihilated in 1561 by *Takeda Shingen*, who chose, to preserve the name, one of his *kerai* from *Kai*, who had been intrusted from 1556 with the guard of the castle of *Kaizu* (*Matsushiro*). The latter took the name of *Kōsaka Masanobu.* He held out a long time against *Uesugi Kenshin* and died in 1578.

Kōsaku, 視 告 朔. A ceremony borrowed from China according to which, the Emperor, on the first day of every month, repaired to the

Daigoku-den, where he inquired into all the official acts published during the preceding month. Later on that ceremony was held only 4 times a year, and by and by, was entirely abolished.

Kose, 巨勢. An ancient family descended from *Takeshiuchi no Sukune.*

—— **Saru,** 猿. Excelled in literature. In 570, he was commissioned to receive the ambassadors from *Koma* (Korea), whom a tempest had wrecked on the coast of *Echizen,* and to lead them to *Kyōto.*

—— **Tokotako,** 徳太古 (593-658). By order of *Soga no Iruka,* besieged prince *Yamashiro-Ōe* in his palace, and put him to death (643). After the fall of the *Soga,* he dispersed their adherents. In 649, he was appointed *Sadaijin.*

—— **Hito,** 比等. At the time of the *Jinshin* civil war (672), sided with the emperor *Kōbun,* and after the latter's defeat, was exiled by *Temmu.*

—— **Tayakasu.** 多益須 (+ 710). Helped to repress the revolt of prince *Otsu-Ōji,* who attempted to succeed *Temmu* (686). He afterwards became *Shikibu-kyō.*

—— **Maro,** 麿 (+ 717). Received in 709, the title of *Mutsu-Chintō-Shōgun* and was commissioned to quell a revolt of the *Ebisu* in *Mutsu* and *Echigo;* after which he became *Chūnagon.*

—— **Notari,** 野足 (745-812). Repressed with *Ōtomo Otomaro,* a revolt of the *Ebisu* in *Mutsu* and received the titles of *Mutsu no suke, Shimotsuke no kami, Hyōbu-tayū, Bitchū no kami, Chūnagon,* and others.

Kose-ryū, 巨勢流. The oldest school of painting in Japan. Founded by *Kanaoka* towards the middle of the 9th century. It is also called the First School or Buddhist School.

—— **Kanaoka,** 金岡. Son of *Chūnagon Notari* (which see), took as models the works of the Chinese painters of the *Tō* dynasty (619-907), and executed for the most part Buddhist religious subjects. The emperor *Uda* commissioned him to paint the sages of China in the *Seiryō-den* and the *Shishin-den.* Legend relates that a horse which he had painted in the *Ninna-ji* temple, escaped every night and galloped about in the neighborhood. It only remained motionless after its eyes had been effaced. *Kanaoka* was a friend of *Sugawara Michizane.* Only 5 or 6 authentic works of his are still extant. After him, his school was successively directed by: *Aimi* (910), *Kintada* (950), *Kimmochi* (980), *Hirotaka, Koreshige* (1030), *Nobushige* (1060), *Muneyoshi, Masumune* (1115), *Tomomune* (1155) *Sōshin* (1180), *Nagamochi* (1245), *Mitsuyasu* (1290), *Ariie* (1320), *Ariyasu,* etc.

KOSE KANAOKA.

Koshi, 越. Ancient name of the region comprising the provinces of *Echigo, Etchū, Noto, Kaga* and *Echizen.* — A district (*kōri*) of *Echigo,* still bears that name.

Kōshi, 孔子. Japanese name of Confucius (551-479 B.C.). Also called *Bunsen-Ō.* — See *Judō.*

Koshi-bito, 越 人. Ancient inhabitants of the country of *Koshi;* a branch of the *Ebisu,* they are believed to have come directly from the coasts of Korea and Manchuria.

Koshi-gawa, 古 志 川. A river in *Izumo* (75 Km.). Also called *Kando-gawa, Ottachi-gawa.*

Koshigoe, 腰 越. In *Sagami. Yoshitsune,* having taken *Munemori* prisoner, after his victory over the *Taira* (1185), came as far as *Koshigoe,* but was forbidden by *Yoritomo* to enter *Kamakura.* He fled thence to *Mutsu,* and 4 years later, his head was exposed at *Koshigoe.* In 1335, *Hōjō Tokiyuki* was defeated there by *Ashikaga Takauji.*

Koshiki-jima, 甑 島. A group of islands S.W. of *Kyūshū,* depending on the province of *Satsuma.* The principal are: *Kami-Koshiki* (67 Km. in circ.), *Naka-Koshiki* (17 Km.) and *Shimo-Koshiki* (78 Km.).

Ko-Shikibu no Naishi, 小 式 部 内 侍. Daughter of *Tachibana Michisada, Izumi no kami,* and of *Izumi Shikibu.* Was a maid of honour attending *Jōtō-mon-in,* widow of the emperor *Ichijō.* From her childhood, she evinced extraordinary talent for poetry, but the courtiers spread the report that the true author of her productions was her mother, a poetess of renown. Now, *Izumi Shikibu,* had to accompany her husband to *Tango,* leaving her daughter at court. During her absence, a poetical tournament (*uta-awase*) was held at court, and on the very morning of the day, the *Chūnagon Fujiwara Sadayori* said to *Ko-Shikibu :* " Has the messenger you sent to *Tango* already returned ? The absence of your mother must cause you a good deal of anxiety." The child, understanding the malicious purport of this question, approached *Sadayori* and improvised as answer a poem which the latter could not help admiring. *Ko-Shikibu* was then only 11 years old : from that day, her talent was no longer questioned.

Koshimizu, 越 水. A place in *Settsu* where *Ashikaga Tadayoshi* defeated his brother *Takauji* (1351). In 1509, *Miyoshi Motonaga* captured the castle, which belonged then to *Hosokawa Takakuni. Nobunaga* also took it in 1568.

Kōshin, 庚 申. The day on which the 2 terms of the cycle *ka-no-e* (the metal elder brother), and *saru* (ape) meet. On that day, feasts are held, the object of which is rather obscure. According to tradition, if a person sleep the preceding night, he is threatened with divers misfortunes Therefore, the fervent believers spend the whole night in worshipping a star which is also called *Kōshin,* and the night's vigil is known as *Kōshin-machi.* — As that occurrence is also called the day of the Ape (*saru*), the *Shintō* god *Saruta-hiko,* thanks to his name, has a share in the devotion of the believers. — Finally, feastings take place before big stones, numerous in country districts, on which 3 monkeys are engraved, one of which (*mi-zaru*), hides his eyes so as not to see, the 2nd (*kika-zaru*) stops his ears so as not to hear, and the 3rd, (*iwa-zaru*), covers his mouth so as not to speak.

Koshi no Fuji, 越富士. Another name for *Washigasu-yama* (*Echigo*).

Koshi no mine, 越ノ峰. Name given to the mountain ranges of *Kurohime-yama* and *Hashitate-yama* (*Echigo*).

Koshi no mizu-umi, 越ノ湖. A lake in *Echigo* (15 Km. in circumference). Also called *Fukushima-gata*. — Another name of the *Kamo no mizu-umi* (*Sado*).

Koshi no mono-bugyō, 腰物奉行. In the *Tokugawa* days, an official entrusted with the guard of the *Shōgun's* arms, his sabres of honor received for some great exploit, etc. He was always an expert-connaisseur of the quality of blades. The title created in 1653, was hereditary in the *Honnami* family but was abolished in 1866.

Kōshō, 康正. *Nengō:* 1455-1456.

Kōshō, 康尚. Bonze and sculptor of the 11th century, ancestor of *Nara-horimonoya*. He descended from the emperor *Kōkō*. The famous *Unkei* was one of his descendants.

Koshō-gumi, 小姓組. In the *Tokugawa* days, the guard commissioned to watch over the *Shōgun's* apartments in the Palace of *Edo*. Created in 1606, it was called at first *Hanabatake-ban* (guard of the flower garden).

Kōshō-ji, 興聖寺. A temple founded in 1233 at *Uji*, S. of *Kyōto*, by the bonze *Dōgen* (*Shōyō-Daishi*), who established there the *Sōdō* branch of the *Zenshū* sect.

Kōshō-ji, 興正寺. A temple founded at *Kyōto* in 1456, by the bonze *Renkyō*, and which became the seat of a branch of the *Shinshū* sect.

Koshō-shū, 小姓衆. In the *Tokugawa* days, *samurai* on duty in the *Shōgun's* palace. The palace was divided into 4 parts, called: *on-omote, naka-oku, oku* and *ō-oku*. In the first two were held the official ceremonies, receptions, etc. In the 3rd, the *Shōgun* attended to public business; the 4th was reserved for the ladies of the palace, therefore, the *koshō-shū* had no access to it. But on anniversary and other solemn days, when the *Shōgun* slept in the *oku*, 2 *koshō* watched near him. The *koshō-shū* were 30 in all.

Kōshō-tennō, 孝昭天皇. 5th Emperor of Japan (475-393 B. C.) *Mimatsu-hiko-kaeshine no mikoto*, succeeded his father *Itoku* at the age of 31. History is silent about this reign of 83 years.

Kōshū, 甲州. Chinese name of the province of *Kai*.

Kōtaifujin, 皇太夫人. Formerly a title given to the true mother of the emperor. She was also called *Fujin, Nyōgo, Chūgū*. — See *Kisaki*.

Kōtaigō, 皇太后. Formerly a title of the Empress Dowager, whether she had been before that time, *Kōgō* or *Chūgū* or *Nyōgo* or *Junkō* or *Jo-in*.

Kōtaishi, 皇太子. The heir apparent to the throne. He was also called *Taishi, Haru no miya, Tōgū, Shōyō, Chokun, Choni, Hitsugi no miya, Hitsugi no miko*, etc. The emperor *Keitai* was the first to appoint his successor by an imperial decree (531 A.D.): this custom was generally followed afterwards; neglected during the civil wars, it was re-established by *Reigen-tennō* in 1683. At the ceremony (*rittaishi*), in which the title of *Kōtaishi* was conferred, a sword called *Tsubokiri no tsurugi* was presented to the prince. Orders issued by the Prince Imperial were called *reishi;* his travels, *gyōkei;* petitions addressed to him, *jōkei*. He had a right to the title of *denka* His palace *Tōgū no miya*, was administered by a *taifu*. His wives were called *Nyōgo* or *Miyasudokoro*.

Kōtaitei, 皇太弟. A title borne by the heir apparent if brother to the emperor whom he was to succeed.

Koteda, 籠手田. A family of *samurai* from the clan of *Hirado* (*Hizen*) ennobled after the Restoration — Now Baron. — Among their ancestors of the 16th and 17th centuries, were several Christians, remarkable for their constancy in the faith.

Kotesashi ga hara, 小手差原. In *Musashi*. A place where *Nitta Yoshisada* defeated *Sakurada Sadakuni* (1334) and where his son *Yoshimune* gained a victory over *Ashikaga Takauji* (1352).

Koto, 古渡. In *Owari*. An ancient castle, built in 1534, by *Oda Nobuhide*. He had until then resided in the castle of *Nagoya*, but intending to give the latter to his son *Nobunaga*, he built that of *Koto* for himself, and resided therein. There *Nobunaga* performed *gem-buku*.

Koto-amatsu-kami, 別天神. The 5 *Shintō* gods, *Ame no Mina-kanushi*, *Takamimusubi*, *Kamimusubi*, *Umashi-ashikabi-hi-koji* and *Ame no Tokotachi*.

Kotohira-jinja, 琴平神社. Commonly called *Kompira*. A famous *Shintō* temple, founded at *Sanuki* (*Shikoku*), it is believed, by *Kūkai* (*Kōbō-Daishi*) at the beginning of the 9th century, after the model of which a great number of other temples have been constructed all over Japan. This temple whose true name was *Zōzu-san*, was sacred to *Kompira*, a divinity imported from India through China, and very difficult to identify. In 1872, the temple of *Kompira*, until then Buddhist, was given over to Shintoism, but the difficulty is to determine which deity was worshipped there. According to some, it was a certain *Koto-hira*, who, by similarity of name, was no other than *Kompira;* others say, it was *Susano-o* or *Ōnamuji*, or *Ōmononushi*, or *Kanayama-hiko*, etc. Moveover the emperor *Sutoku*, who died in exile not far from it (1164), is also worshipped in that place. In spite of the obscurity that shrouds his personality, *Kompira* is very popular and invoked especially by seamen and travellers.

Kōtoku, 享徳. *Nengō:* 1452-1454.

Kōtoku-tennō, 孝徳天皇. 36th Emperor of Japan (645-654). *Ame-yorozu-toyoshi no mikoto*, also called *Karu no Ōji*, succeeded his sister *Kōgyoku* at the age of 49 years. As heir apparent, he had prepared with *Naka no Ōe* (later on *Tenchi-tennō*) and *Nakatomi no Kamako*, the assassination of the *Soga*, *Emishi* and *Iruka*. His accession was the beginning of a new mode of government, to a large extent copied from

China The use of the *nengō* was adopted, and the reform inaugurated at that time bears the name of *Taikwa*, the first *nengō*. (*Taikwa no kai-*

KŌTOKU-TENNŌ AND NAKATOMI KAMATARI.

shin — which word see). The so-called reform was completed only 56 years later, in the reign of *Mommu*. *Kōtoku* died after a reign of 10 years.

Kotomari-saki, 小泊崎. A Cape N. of *Mutsu*, forms the bay of *Kotomari* (*Kotomari-wan*). Also called *Gongen-saki*.

Kōtō no Naishi, 勾當內侍. Lady superintendent of all the female personnel of the Imperial Court. This personnel was presided over by 4 *shōshi :* the first had the title of *Kōtō no Naishi :* the next two were known by their family name, e.g. *Gen-Naishi, Tō-Naishi*, etc.: the last was called *Shin-Naishi.* The apartment where the *Kōtō no Naishi* fulfilled her office was the *Chōkyō no tsubone ;* the orders, which by imperial command she transmitted to her subordinates, were called *johōsho.*

Kotoshironushi no kami, 事代主神. A *Shintō* deity. Also called *Katsuragi-hitokotonushi, Yae-kotoshironushi.* Son of *Ōkuninushi*, he assisted his father in the government of *Izumo*, when *Takemika-zuchi* was sent to request him to recognize the rights of *Ninigi no mikoto*. *Kotoshironushi* yielded to the grandson of *Amaterasu* and gave over his estates. He it is that is worshipped at *Futara-yama* (*Nikkō*) and at Mt. *Katsuragi* (*Yamato*).

Kotsubo-saka, 小坪坂. A place in *Sagami*, near the present village of *Tagoe*, where a battle was fought between *Wada Yoshimori* and *Hatakeyama Shigetada* (1180).

Ko-uji, 小氏. Lateral branches of a family; the main branch was called *Ō-uji*. — See *Uji, Ō-uji*.

Kōwa, 廉和. *Nengō:* 1099-1103.

Kōwa, 弘和. *Nengō:* 1381-1383.

Koyama, 小山. In *Tōtōmi*. An ancient castle built in 1571, by *Takeda Shingen* opposite that of *Hamamatsu*, then occupied by *Ieyasu*. He called it first *Nōman-jō*, then *Koyama-jō*. In 1575, *Ieyasu* besieged it, but he had to retreat before the army of *Takeda Katsuyori*. The castle was abandoned after the ruin of the *Takeda* (1582).

Koyama no ike, 湖山池. A lake in *Inaba* (14 Km. in circ.).

Kōya-san, 高野山. A mountain in *Kii*, also called *Takano-yama*, *Nanzan*, famous for its numerous Buddhist temples. The first, *Kongō-bu-ji*, was founded by *Kūkai* in 816. Thanks to the liberalities of the emperors and the *daimyō* of the province, the monastery became very prosperous. It occupied 223 hectares of land on which rose 723 main buildings, besides 440 outhouses. During the Middle Ages, it had soldiers of its own (*sōhei*), who, more than once, caused disturbance in the neighborhood. *Kōya-san* was for a long time, a place of exile for persons of rank. There *Hidetsugu*, nephew to *Taikō*, was invited to commit *harakiri* (1595); to that place too *Oda Hidenobu, Chōsokabe Morichika, Masuda Nagamori*, etc. were banished after *Sekigahara* (1600). A certain number of temples were destroyed by fire; and the decline of Buddhism, after the Restoration, dealt a last blow to the prosperity of the famous monastery. The immense cemetery of *Kōya-san* preserves the tombs, if not the bodies, of a great number of celebrated men: *Taira Atsumori, Kumagaya Naozane, Takeda Shingen, Akechi Mitsuhide, Ii Kamon no kami*, the bonzes *Kōbō-Daishi* (*Kūkai*), *Enkō-Daishi* (*Genkū*), etc. It is believed that those who have their tomb near that of *Kōbō-Daishi*, obtain through him the grace to start a new life in Paradise (*Jōdo*): hence, the great number of funeral monuments erected in this place.

Koyomi, 暦 (Chinese: *reki*). Calendar, almanac. We have very little knowledge of the manner in which months and years were counted in ancient times. The regular occurrence of the seasons and the phases of the moon, formed the basis thereof, and every year, some scholar of the time was commissioned to publish in advance a calendar (*hi-oki*), which was no doubt very summary. In 552, the king of *Kudara* (Korea), sent some astronomers (*reki-hakase*) to Japan, who drew up a calendar, which was however not accepted. In 602, the bonze *Kwanroku*, came also from *Kudara*, and brought with him the books (*reki-hon*) used in China to make out the calendar: this time, a Japanese, *Yakoshiso Tamafuru*, was appointed to study the new science, and from the first day of the year 604, the Chinese calendar was adopted. It was called *Genka-reki*. In 690, to the *Genka-reki*, was added the *Gihō-reki;* by and by, the latter alone remained in use, but underwent certain modifications called *Taien-reki* (763), *Goki-reki* (856). A new change produced the *Semmei-reki* (861), which was used during 823 years. In 1684, *Shibukawa Shunkai* published a new calendar (*Tenkyō-reki*), which was no more a simple reproduction of the Chinese calendar, adopted to things Japanese. Reformed in 1754, by *Abe Yasukuni* and *Shibukawa Kōkyō* (*Hōreki-kōjutsu-genreki*), in 1798, (*Kwansei-reki*), and in 1842 (*Tempō-reki*), it was abolished in 1872. An imperial decree determined that the morrow of the first day of the 12th month of that year, would be the first day of the 6th year of *Meiji* 1873 and that henceforth, the Gregorian calendar would alone be used. However, in the country districts especially, the old calendar is followed concurrently with the new.

Kōjō Sanjin, 紅葉山人. Nom de plume, chosen by *Ozaki Tokutarō* (1866-1903), a novelist who adopted for his works, a new kind of style, more akin to similar productions of the West.

Kōzuke, 上野. One of the 13 provinces of *Tōsandō;* comprises 11 districts, which have formed *Gumma-ken.* — Chinese name : *Jōshū.* — First called *Kamitsukenu*, it was formed with the western portion of the ancient provinces of *Kenu* (645). In memory of *Yamato-takeru*, who had sojourned there, the dignity of governor of the province was reserved to a prince of the blood, who bore the title of *Taishu*, and was represented by a *Suke*. In the *Kamakura* times, the *Adachi* family was *Kōzuke-shugo*. *Nitta Yoshisada*, native of the province, was appointed *Shugo* in 1334, prince *Narinaga-shinnō*, being *Taishu*. In the *Ashikaga* period, the title of *Shugo* was given to the *Uesugi*, who built the castle of *Shirai*, which was confided to the *Nagao*. The *Hōjō* of *Odawara* and *Takeda Shingen* divided the province afterwards between themselves, and in 1590, it passed into the possession of *Tokugawa Ieyasu*.

Kōzuke-shinnō, 上野親王. — See *Munenaga-shinnō*.

Kōzuki, 上月. In *Harima*. An ancient castle, which in the 16th century, belonged to the *Kōzuki* family. *Hideyoshi* took it in 1577, and entrusted it to *Amako Katsuhisa*, who, in the very next year, was besieged by *Kikkawa Motoharu* and *Kobayakawa Takakage* and committed *harakiri*.

Kōzu-shima, 神津島. One of the 7 isles of *Izu;* also called *Kamitsu-shima* (23 Km. in circ.).

Kubō, 公方. An honorific title at first reserved for the emperor. At the time of *Ashikaga Yoshimitsu*, it began to be applied to the *Shōgun*, then to the *Kwanryō* of *Kwantō*, etc. Thus we read of the *Kamakura-kubō, Koga-kubō, Horikoshi-kubō*, etc.

Kubota, 久保田. Ancient name of the castle of the *Satake daimyō* at *Akita* (*Dewa*), and by extension, of the city itself.

Kuchiki, 朽木. In *Ōmi*. Formerly, residence of the *daimyō* of the same name.

Kuchiki, 朽木. A family of *daimyō* descended from *Sasaki Nobutsuna* (+ 1242) and through him from the *Uda-Genji*.

—— **Yoshitsuna,** 義綱. Settled at *Kuchiki-dani* and took its name.

—— **Tanetsuna,** 植綱 (+ 1550). Gave hospitality to the *Shōgun Yoshiharu,* who was obliged to flee from *Kyōto* (1528). In 1539, he saved the son of *Yoshiharu, Yoshiteru,* then only 5 years old, and kept him at *Yase.* Having become *Shōgun,* in 1545, *Yoshiteru* gave *Tanetsuna* the title of *Mimbu-shōyū.* The latter died while fighting against *Takashima Etchū no kami.*

—— **Mototsuna,** 元綱 (1549-1632). Grandson of *Tanetsuna,* supported the *Shōgun Yoshiaki* (1568), fought against *Asai* (1570), and was appointed *Kawachi no kami* (1590). He sided with *Ieyasu* in 1600, and was present at the siege of *Ōsaka* (1615); he had then a revenue of 12,000 k. Shortly afterwards, he shaved his head.

—— **Nobutsuna,** 宣綱. Was transferred in 1627 to *Shikanuma* (*Shimotsuke* — 20,000 k.).

—— **Tanetsuna,** 植綱. Was transferred in 1649 to *Tsuchiura* (*Hitachi* — 30,000 k.). At last, in 1669, the family settled down at *Fukuchiyama* (*Tamba* — 32,000 k.), where it remained until the Restoration. — Now Viscount.

Kudara, 百済. An ancient kingdom of Korea, also called *Hakusai, Benkan.* Founded 15 years before the Christian era, it was supposed to have been conquered by Japan at the time of the expedition of *Jingō-kōgō* (200), proved constantly a faithful ally, and had often to ask for help against its turbulent neighbor *Shiragi,* which finally conquered it (663 A.D.). At that time, a large number of people from *Kudara* accompanied the remnants of the army that returned to Japan. They were made to dwell especially in *Settsu.* Whence it happened that formerly there was in that province a *Kudara-gōri,* (district) a *Kudara-mura* (village), a *Kudara-gawa* (river), a *Kudara-dera* (Buddhist temple), etc.

Kudara Kawanari, 百済河成 (+ 853). A descendant of the Koreans established in Japan, he won fame for his skill in handling both the pen and the sword. He became successively *Mimasaka gon no shōmoku* (823), *Harima no suke, Aki no suke,* and received the name of *Kudara Ason.*

Kudara Keifuku, 百済敬福 (698-766). A descendant of *Giji,* king of *Kudara,* became *Mutsu no kami.* At the time of casting the *Tō-daiji* (*Nara*) *Daibutsu,* the gold imported from China for the gilding was found to be insufficient. Just then gold mines were discovered in *Mutsu;* *Oda-gōri* and *Keifuku* presented the required quantity of the precious metal (746).

Kudara Sake no kimi, 百済酒君. Grandson of the king of *Kudara,* displayed arrogance towards *Ki no Tsunu no Sukune,* who was sent from Japan to fix the limits of the provinces and districts of *San-Kan* (353 A.D.), to inquire after their productions, etc. *Ki no Tsunu* complained to the king, who in reparation of the insult, sent his grandson as prisoner to Japan. After some time, the emperor *Nintoku* set him free, and learned from him the art of hunting with a hawk, art which had been practised already for a long time in Korea, but was still unknown in Japan.

Kudō, 工藤. A family of *daimyō* in *Izu,* descended from *Fujiwara Muchimaro.*

—— **Shigemitsu,** 茂 光 (+ 1181). Was commissioned to quell a revolt of *Minamoto Tametomo* (1170), who had been exiled to the island of *Ōshima* (*Izu*), after the *Hōgen* war (1156), and was causing disturbances. In 1180, he sided with *Yoritomo*, was defeated with him at *Ishibashi*, and killed shortly afterwards.

—— **Suketsune,** 祐 經 (+ 1193). Son of *Suketsugu* and nephew of the above was despoiled of his domains by his uncle *Itō Sukechika* and shut up in *Kyōto*. He revenged himself by wounding his uncle severely, and killing his son *Sukeyasu*. The son of the latter, *Soga Sukenari* and *Tokimune*, after having long waited for a favorable opportunity, at last succeeded in assassinating *Suketsune* in the very camp of *Yoritomo* (1193). This is the famous vengeance of the *Soga* brothers. —— See *Soga Sukenari.*

Kuga, 久 我. A family of *kuge*, descended from *Asuka-shinnō* (+ 835), son of *Kwammu-tennō.* —— Now Marquis.

Kuga-nawate, 久 我 畷. A place in *Yamashiro*, where *Nagoshi Takaie*, general of the *Hōjō*, was defeated and killed by *Akamatsu Enshin* (1333). In 1527, *Miyoshi Katsutoki* fought a battle against the *Shōgun Yoshiharu*.

Kugatachi, 盟 神 探 湯. In olden times, a kind of ordeal. In case of dispute, the two adversaries had to plunge their hands into boiling water, from which trial the innocent party was supposed to come out unscathed.

Kuge, 公 家. Nobles of the imperial Court. Most of them be-

CONCERT AT A KUGE'S HOUSE.

longed to the *Fujiwara, Sugawara, Taira, Minamoto, Kiyowara, Abe,*

Urabe, etc. This nobility was distinct from the military nobility (*daimyō*), over which it had precedence at Court.

Kuge-ryō, 公廨料. Formerly a pension paid to officials according to their rank.

Kuge-shohatto, 公家諸法度. A code of 17 articles, drawn up in 1615 relating to the princes and nobles of the Imperial Court. It was enacted after an agreement between *Ieyasu*, *Hidetada* and the *Kwampaku Nijō Akizane*. It was also called *Kinchūgata go-jōmoku*, *Kugechū go-hatto*.

Kugyō, 公卿. A title given to the Court nobles not lower than the 3rd rank (*san-i*). The name is sometimes used as synonymous with *kuge*.

Kugyō, 公曉 (1201-1219). 2nd son of the *Shōgun Minamoto Yoriie*. He was only 3 years old at his father's death; his grandmother *Masa-ko* intended to make a bonze of him and placed him in the temple of *Hachiman-gū* of *Tsuruga-oka* (*Kamakura*) where he received the name of *Kugyō*. With years also grew the hatred and jealousy which he had conceived against his uncle *Sanetomo*, who had been raised to the Shōgunate in his stead, and he swore vengeance. He waited long for a good chance. In 1219, *Sanetomo* received the title of *Udaijin* and repaired to the temple of *Hachiman* to thank the gods: *Kugyō* was hidden in the crowd. After the ceremony was over, the *Shōgun* descended the steps of the temple when *Kugyō* rushed upon him and struck him with a dagger. He profited of the disorder which followed, to make his escape, but was detected and killed by *Nagao Sadakage*.

Kuji-ki, 舊事記. A work on the origin of Japan, which was attributed to prince *Shōtoku-taishi*, but was lost at the time of the fall of the *Soga* (644 A.D.).

Kujō, 九條. A family of *kuge*, descended from *Fujiwara Michiie* (1192-1252). It was one of the 5 branches (*go-sekke*), from which the empress and the *Kwampaku* were chosen.

—— **Michiie,** 道家. — See *Fujiwara Michiie*.

—— **Norizane,** 敎實 (1210-1235). Son of *Michiie*, became *Kwampaku* in his father's place (1231), and *Sesshō* at the accession of *Shijō-tennō* (1233). He is often called *Dōin Sesshō*.

—— **Sukezane,** 輔實 (1669-1729). Son of the *Kwampaku Kaneharu*, became himself *Kwampaku* and *Dajō-daijin*. Was a distinguished painter. — The descendants of the family bear at present the title of Marquis.

Kujō-haitei, 九條廢帝. Name given to the emperor *Chūkyō*, deposed by *Hōjō Yoshitoki*, after a reign of 70 days (1221).

Ku-jū-ku ri no hama, 九十九里濱. (Lit.: coast of 99 leagues). Name given to the eastern coast of the provinces of *Kazusa* and *Shimōsa* for an extent of about 60 Km. It is also called *Yasashi no hama*, *Yadate no hama*.

Ku-jū-ku-shima wan, 九十九島灣. (Lit.: Gulf of 99 isles). A gulf W. of the province of *Hizen* (*Kyūshū*).

Kūkai, 空海 (774-835). Born at *Byōbu-ga-ura* (*Sanuki*), of the *Saiki* family, entered a Buddhist temple while still quite young, and at 19, took the name of *Kūkai*. In 804, he went to China, where for 2 years, he studied under the most

SEAL OF KUKAI.

famous masters. On his re- turn, he engaged in a discus- sion organized by the emperor between the most learned bonzes and surpassed them all in eloquence and science. After that, he began to preach the *Shingon* doctrines. In 816, he retired to Mt. *Kōya* (*Kii*), where he founded the temple

KUKAI.

of *Kongōbu-ji*, which became one of the largest in Japan. Many statues and paintings, whose authenticity is at least doubtful are attributed to him. He invented the alphabet called *hiragana*, and wrote the poem (*iroha-uta*) composed of 47 syllables after the manner of Japanese poems. In 921, *Kūkai* received from the emperor *Daigo* the posthumous name of *Kōbō-Daishi*, by which he is generally known.

Kuki, 九鬼. A family of *daimyō*, originating in the province of *Shima* and descended from *Fujiwara Tadahira* (880-949).

—— **Yoshitaka,** 嘉隆 (1542-1600). Governed the province of *Shima*, where he had built the castle of *Toba*. He submitted to *Nobunaga* (1569), and served in his campaigns against the bonzes of *Nagashima*, etc. *Hideyoshi* appointed him commander of the fleet which was to serve in the expedition of Korea (1592). In 1600, he sided against *Ieyasu*, was defeated and killed himself.

—— **Moritaka,** 守隆. Son of *Yoshitaka*, took in hand the govern- ment of *Shima* province (1599), and served under *Ieyasu's* colors, whilst his father sided with *Ishida Kazushige*. He was confirmed in his pos- sessions and saw his revenues increased from 26,000 k. to 46,000 k. On his death, his two sons divided his domains and formed the two branches of the family.

Yoshitaka-Moritaka {Hisataka - Takamasa - Takanori (a)
Takasue - Takatsune - Takanao (b) (c)

(*a*) — The Eldest branch — Resided first at *Toba* (*Shima*), then at *Sanda* (*Settsu* — 36,000 k.) (1634-1868). — Now Viscount.

(*b*) — Younger branch — Resided from 1633-1868 at *Ayabe* (*Tamba* — 19,500 k.). — To-day Viscount.

(*c*) — After the Restoration, a member of the above branch, until then a *samurai* of the *Ayabe* clan, was ennobled. — To-day Baron.

Kukunochi, 久々能智. Son of *Izanagi* and *Izanami*, worshipped as the tree god (*Shintō*).

Kuma-gawa, 球磨川. A river of *Higo* province (63 Km.) famous for its rapids. Also called *Yatsushiro-gawa.* — The *Kuma-gawa*, the

Fuji-gawa (*Suruga*), and the *Mogami-gawa* (*Ugo*), are called *Nihon san kyūryū* (the 3 rapid rivers of Japan).

Kumagaya, 熊谷. In *Mikawa*. An ancient castle built by *Kumagaya Bitchū* (1530), *kerai* of *Imagawa :* besieged in vain by *Matsudaira Kiyoyasu*, grandfather of *Ieyasu*, but captured by the latter (1566).

Kumagaya, 熊谷. A family of *daimyō*, descended from *Taira Sadamori.*

—— **Naosada, 直貞**. Settled down at *Kumagaya* (*Musashi*) and took its name.

—— **Naozane, 直實** (+ 1208). Son of *Naosada*, first served under *Taira Tomomori* and contributed with *Ōba Kagechika* to the defeat of *Yoritomo* at *Ishibashi-yama* (1181). Shortly afterwards, he passed over to the *Minamoto* and at the battle of *Ichi no tani* (1184), aided by his son *Naoie* and *Hirayama Sueshige*, obliged the *Taira* to escape by sea. There it was that he pursued and killed *Taira Atsumori* — Legend has embellished this episode so far as to pretend that *Naozane* substituted his own son for the young heir of his former masters. — In 1192, having fallen out with *Kuge Naomitsu* about the limits of their respective domains, he retired to the temple of *Kurodani* (*Kyōto*), where he took the name of *Renshō*, and put himself under the direction of the famous *Genkū*. He died in 1208.

Kumamoto, 熊本. Capital of *Kumamoto-ken* (60,000 inh.). Ancient castle built in the 15th century by *Ideta Hidenobu*, vassal of *Kikuchi :* it is called nowadays *Chiba-jō*. It was enlarged towards 1525 by *Kanokogi Chikamasa*. It passed into the possession of the *Ōtomo* and the *Shimazu*. In 1587, *Hideyoshi* gave it to *Sasa Narimasa*, and, the next year, to *Katō Kiyomasa*, who in 1599, undertook to rebuild it entirely on an enlarged plan. The *Katō*, dispossessed in 1632, were replaced by the *Hosokawa* (540,000 k.) who occupied the castle until the Restoration. — In 1876, a mutiny broke out there among some *samurai* dissatisfied with the new regime, but it was promptly quelled. — During the *Satsuma* war, Colonel *Tani Tateki* stood a siege of nearly 2 months, after which he was rescued by general *Kuroda* (April, 1877).

Kumamoto-ken, 熊本縣. Department in the province of *Higo*. Pop.: 1,212,000 inh. — Capital : *Kumamoto* (60,000 inh.) — Principal town : *Yatsushiro* (12,000 inh.).

Kumano, 熊野. Name of the S.F. part of *Kii* province.

Kumano-gawa, 熊野川. A river (138 Km.) which rises in *Yamato*, where it is called *Totsu-gawa*, enters *Kii* and empties itself into the sea at *Shingū*. Also called *Otonashi-gawa, Shingū-gawa, Narugawa*. — The sea which washes the S.E. coast of *Kii* has received the names of *Kumano no ura, Kumano-nada, Kumano no oki*.

Kumano-jirja, 熊野神社. Generic name for the 3 great temples of *Kumano : Hongū, Shingū* and *Nachi*. — The *Hongū* temple, founded 81 years B.C., is sacred to *Fusumi no mikoto, Hayatama no mikoto, Ketsu-miko* and *Amaterasu-ō-mikami*. — In the *Shingū*, founded in the first century of the Christian era, *Fusumi no mikoto, Haytama no mikoto* and *Ketsu-miko* are worshipped. The temple of *Nachi*, dedicated to the same deities and to *Izanagi*, is in the neighborhood of the famous cascade (140 m.), of the same name. — The 3 temples are also called *Kumano no san-zan*.

Kumaso, 熊襲. Ancient inhabitants of southern *Kyūshū*. The efforts of several centuries were necessary to bring about their subjection, which was completed only after the expedition of *Chūai* and *Jingō-kōgō* (193-200). They are believed to be a branch of the *Sow* tribe from Borneo, who seeking a more temperate climate, or being carried out of their way by storm, landed on the coasts of *Satsuma*, and settled in that country.

Kumazawa Ryōkai, 熊澤了介 (1619-1691). Also called *Banzan*. By birth, *Nojiri Jirōhachi*. He was brought up by *Kumazawa Morihisa*, his grandfather on the mother's side. He followed the lessons of *Nakae Tōju*. In 1645, he was engaged as professor by *Ikeda Mitsumasa*, *daimyō* of *Okayama*. In 1656, he came to *Kyōto*, and opened a school of political economy and administrative sciences. It was attended by quite a number of *kuge*. Its very success drew upon it the suspicion of the *Bakufu*, and *Ryōkai* had to seek shelter on Mt. *Yoshino* (1666). Invited by *Matsudaira Nobuyuki*, *daimyō* of *Akashi*, he accepted his offers and followed him when he was transferred to *Kōriyama* (1679), and *Koga* (1685). From that city, he addressed to the *Shōgun* a memorial on the reforms he deemed urgent in the administration. For this interference, he was condemned to prison and from that time abstained from all criticism.

Kumebe, 久米部. The guard established by *Jimmu-tennō* and commissioned to watch at the gates of the Imperial Palace. It became later on the *Konoe-hyōe*.

Kume-mai, 久米舞. An ancient dance performed in the Imperial Palace, at the time of the *Daijō-e*. When *Jimmu-tennō* advanced upon *Kii*, *Ōkume no mikoto* executed a dance while singing a war song. That was the signal for the attack, resulting in a victory over *Yasotakeru*. Such was the origin of the *Kume-mai*, so called from *Ōkume*, the ancestor of the *Kume*.

Kume no atae, 久米直. Chief of the *kumebe*. The first who received that title was *Ōkume no mikoto*, companion in arms of *Jimmu-tennō*. He transmitted it to his descendants, who took the name of *Kume*.

Kumon, 公文. In the *Kamakura* period, a written order, issued by the *Kumon-jo* or *Mandokoro*.

Kumon-jo, 公文所. The Department of the Archives, established by *Yoritomo* at *Kamakura* in 1184. *Ōe Hiromoto* was its first titulary. In 1191, the name was changed to *Mandokoro*. — See *Mandokoro*.

Kumotori-yama, 雲取山. A mountain on the borders of *Kai* and *Musashi* (2,090 m.).

Kunai-shō, 宮內省. Or *Miya no uchi no tsukasa*. Department of the Imperial Household. The *Taikwa* reform (645) had established a *Kunai-kwan* (office) which, in 702, was changed to *Kunai-shō*. The minister had the title of *Kunai-kyō* and was empowered to collect the revenues of the provinces and domains of the crown, etc. The *Kunai-shō* had under its direction : — 1 *shiki* (*Daizen*) ; — 4 *ryō* (*Moku, Ōi, Tonomo, Tenyaku*) : — 13 *tsukasa* (*Ōgi, Naizen, Zōshu, Kaji, Kwannu, Enshi, Dokō, Uneme, Mondo, Shuyu, Uchi-kamon, Kyotō, Uchi-some*) — (which names see).

Kunajiri-jima, 國後嶋. The southern of the Kurile Islands (628 Km. in circ.).

Kuni, 久邇. A family of imperial princes, issued from the *Fushimi* branch.

—— **Asahiko,** 朝彦 (1824-1891). Son of prince *Fushimi Sada-yoshi*, was adopted by the emperor *Ninkō* (1836) and entered the temple of *Seiren-in*. Secularized in 1863, he took the name of *Nakagawa no Miya* and was raised to the dignity of *Danjō-in*, high Inspector of justice, of good morals, of the conduct of officials, etc. Exiled to *Aki* (1868), and pardoned, he received in 1875, the name of *Kuni*, and in 1883, his family was declared a branch of the Imperial Family for two generations. The present head of the family is prince *Kunihiko*, born in 1873.

Kuni, 國. Province, country. By the *Taikwa* reform (645), Japan was divided into 54 provinces. *Temmu-tennō* in 681, separated *Iga* from *Ise*, *Izu* from *Suruga* and divided *Echi* into *Echizen*, *Etchū* and *Echigo*. *Gemmei-tennō* separated *Dewa* from *Echigo*, *Tango* from *Tamba*, *Mimasaka* from *Bizen*, *Ōsumi* from *Hyūga* (712). A little later, *Izumi* was formed with a part of *Kawachi*, *Noto* was taken from *Echizen*, and *Awa* from *Kazusa*. In 823, two districts of *Echizen* became the province of *Kaga*. The number of provinces was then 66, (without counting *Kinai*) which number did not change until the Restoration. — In 1868, the province of *Mutsu* was subdivided into *Iwaki*, *Iwashiro*, *Rikuzen*, *Rikuchū*, *Rikuoku*, and *Dewa* was divided into *Uzen* and *Ugo*. The following year, the island of *Ezo* (*Hokkaidō*) was cut up into 11 provinces. The kingdom of *Ryūkyū* (1879) and the island of *Formosa* (1895), having been annexed to Japan, the number of provinces is to day 87.

Kuni, 國. At first a *miko* (dancing girl), in the great temple of *Izumo*, she went to *Kyōto*, formed a group of dancing actresses, and had great success. She even played before *Hideyoshi*, who presented her with a coral necklace. Later on, she returned to her native province, shaved her head and died towards 1640. She is credited with having created the popular theatre, called *shibai* or *kabuki*. She is commonly called *Izumo o Kuni*.

KUNI.

Kun-i, 勳位. (Lit.: rank of merit). The *Taihō* code (702), established 12 ranks (*tō*), assigned not only to scholars and warriors but to those who built temples, who distinguished themselves by their filial piety, who fostered agriculture, etc. — Compared with the Court ranks (*i*), the first rank of merit (*ittō*) corresponded to the first degree of the 3rd rank (*shō-san-i*), and the 12th (*jū-ni tō*), to the 2nd degree of the 8th rank (*jū-hachi-i-ge*). — In 1875, the 12 ranks of merit were reduced to 8. — See *Ikai, Kwan-tō*, etc.

Kuni-bugyō, 國奉行. A title created in 1184 by *Yoritomo* and equivalent to military governor of province. Before that, there was a *shugo* at the head of every province. *Yoritomo* added a *bugyō*, whose special duty was to regulate military matters, to look to the punishment of crime, etc. He was also called *zatsumu-bugyō*.

Kuni-mochi-shū, 國持衆. In the *Ashikaga* days, a title given to the greatest *daimyō*, governors of one or more provinces, such as the *Hosokawa*, the *Yamana* the *Shiba*, the *Hatakeyama*, etc. Towards 1440, there were 19 of them; at the end of the 15th century, 15.

Kuninaka Kimimaro, 國中公麿 (+ 774). A Korean who came to Japan and settled down in the village of *Kuninaka* (*Yamato*), of which he took the name. He was an expert in the casting of metals, and commissioned to cast the *Tō-daiji Daibutsu* (*Nara*) (746).

Kunin-asayū-bito, 公人朝夕人. In the *Tokugawa* days, a servant who followed the *Shōgun* when he went to the Imperial Palace. He carried the utensils necessary for his master's service. That charge was hereditary in the *Tsuchida* family, which received for that purpose an allowance of rice for 10 persons (*jū-nin-guchi*).

Kunin-bugyō, 公人奉行. A title created in 1338, and assigned to a high official, commissioned to transmit the orders of the *Shōgun* to the provinces, which had from 10 to 30 days time to execute them, according to their distance from the capital. The first who received that title was *Suwa Enchū*.

Kuni no mikotomochi, 國司. In olden days, an official, who by express order of the emperor, was sent in case of urgency, to govern a province. Thus, in *Nintoku-tennō's* reign, there was a *Tōtōmi no kuni no mikotomochi*; and in *Yuryaku-tennō's* reign, one for *Shiragi* and *Mimana*.

Kuni no miyatsuko, 國造. The governors of provinces established by *Jimmu-tennō*. That title was first given as a reward to those who had conquered or pacified a province, which they continued to govern. *Jimmu-tennō*, established only 9 governors. In *Keitai-tennō's* time (507-531), there were 144. Those that governed an island were called *Shima no miyatsuko*. That title was suppressed by the *Taikwa* reform (645).

Kuni-tokotachi no mikoto, 國常立尊. A *Shintō* deity, who forms the first of the 7 generations of heavenly deities (*Tenjin shichi-dai*). At the time when the earth was separated from heaven, a new being appeared, resembling the stem of the plant called *ashi* (a kind of reed: *erianthus japonicus*), which by and by was changed into a deity: this was *Kuni-tokotachi*. He is honored mostly in *Ōmi*.

Kuniyoshi, 國吉 . In *Wakasa*, at present, *Sagaki*. An ancient castle belonging to the *Kuriya daimyō*. *Katsuhisa* was dispossessed by *Asakura Norikage* (1563). *Nobunaga* gave back the castle to *Katsuhisa* in 1569, and *Hideyoshi* confided it to *Kimura Hayato no suke* (1583).

Kunō, 久能 . In *Tōtōmi*. An ancient castle possessed by the *Kunō* family, *kerai* of the *Imagawa*, then of the *Tokugawa*. *Muneyoshi* having been transferred by *Ieyasu* to *Sakura* (*Shimōsa*), was replaced by *Matsudaira Shigetsuna* (1590). The castle was abandoned about the year 1620.

Kunohe, 九戸 . In *Mutsu*, near the present town of *Fukuoka*. Ancient castle, built towards 1575, by *Kunohe Masazane*, who revolted against his suzerain *Nambu Nobunao* and refused later on to submit to *Hideyoshi*. The latter sent *Gamō Ujisato* and *Date Masamune* against him: *Masazane* was besieged in his castle, and killed (1591).

Kunō-zan, 久能山 . A hill, near *Shizuoka* (*Suruga*), on the sea coast. It is 300 metres high, and commands a magnificent view. A Buddhist temple had been erected on its summit. In 1568, *Takeda Shingen* ordered it to be pulled down and replaced by a castle to resist the *Hōjō* and the *Imagawa*. On the fall of the *Takeda* (1582), it passed into the hands of *Ieyasu*. Towards the end of his life, *Ieyasu* commanded the castle to be razed and chose the site for his burial place. He was buried there in 1616, and the guard of his grave was confided to the *Yanagiwara*. A magnificent temple was erected near by (*Kunō-jinja*). The following year, the body of *Ieyasu* was transported to *Nikkō*, and the temple alone remained, where he is worshipped as *Tōshōgū-daigongen.* — *Kunō-zan* is also called *Fudarakusan.*

Kunshō, 勲章 . Decoration; order of Knighthood. There are in Japan 6 orders :

1° **Kikukwa-shō, 菊花章** The order of the Chrysanthemum, instituted in 1876, reserved for sovereigns and members of princely families. — Has but one class.

2° **Tōkwa-shō, 桐花章** . Order of the Paulownia, instituted in 1876, granted to princes and persons of very high rank. — Only one class.

3° **Kyokujitsu-shō, 旭日章** . Order of the Rising Sun, instituted in 1875, awarded for military or civil services. — 8 classes.

4° **Zuihō-shō, 瑞寳章** . Order of the Sacred Treasure, instituted in 1888, to reward civil or military services. — 8 classes.

5° **Hōkwan-shō, 寳冠章** . Order of the Crown, created in 1888, reserved for ladies. — 8 classes.

6° **Kinshi-shō, 金鵄章** . Order of the Golden Kite, created in 1890, rewards great military exploits and gives right to a pension. — 8 classes.

There are moreover several civil and military medals.

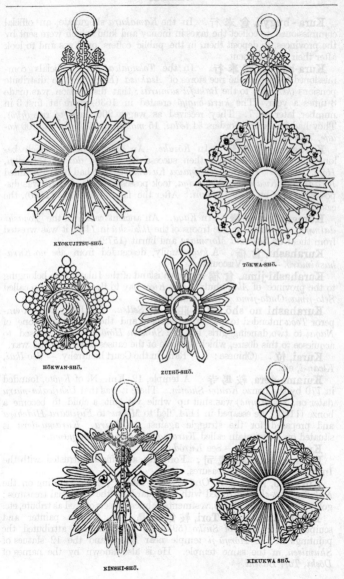

KYOKUJITSU-SHŌ.

TŌKWA-SHŌ.

HŌKWAN-SHŌ.

ZUIHŌ-SHŌ.

KINSHI-SHŌ.

KIKUKWA SHŌ.

Kura - bugyō, 倉奉行． In the *Kamakura* shōgunate, an official commissioned to collect the taxes in money and kind which were sent by the provinces, to deposit them in the public coffers or stores and to look after their management.

Kura-bugyō, 藏奉行． In the *Tokugawa* days, officials commissioned to inspect the rice stores of *Asakusa* (*Edo*), and to distribute pensions (*kirimai*) to the *Bakufu samurai :* that distribution was made 3 times a year. The *kura-bugyō* created in 1636, were at first 3 in number, later on, 7. They received as wages 200 bags of rice (*hyō*). They had under their orders 54 *tedai*, 15 *momban*, 35 *kuraban*, 200 *ko-age*, 70 *momibiki*, etc.

Kuragano, 倉賀野． In *Kōzuke*. An ancient castle, which belonged first to the *Kodama*, then successively to the *daimyō : Uesugi, Hōjō, Takeda*. In 1582, *Takigawa Kazumasa*, who had been appointed *Kwanryō* of *Kwantō* by *Nobunaga*, took possession of it, but he was dispossessed of it by *Hōjō Ujikuni*. After the fall of the *Hōjō* (1590), the castle was abandoned.

Kuragatake, 倉嶽． In *Kaga*. An ancient castle of the *Togashi daimyō*. Captured by the troops of the *Ikkō-shū* in 1488, it was wrested from them by *Sakuma Morimasa* and burnt (1572).

Kurahashi, 倉橋． A *kuge* family, descended from *Abe no Kura-hashimaro*. — Now Viscount.

Kurahashi-jima, 倉橋嶋． An island of the Inland Sea, belonging to the province of *Aki ;* shuts in the *Kure* bay to the south. Also called *Seto-jima, Ondo-jima*. (100 Km. in circ.).

Kurahashi no shō, 倉橋莊． In *Settsu*. In 1221, the ex-emperor *Toba* intended to grant this domain and the neighboring one of *Nagai* to two dancing girls, but the *Shikken Hōjō Yoshitoki* refused to acquiesce to this desire, which was one of the causes of the *Shōkyū* war.

Kurai, 位． (Chinese : *i*). Rank in the Court hierarchy. — See *Ikai, Kwan-i*, etc.

Kurama-dera, 鞍馬寺． A temple, 12 Km. N. of *Kyōto*, founded in 770 by the bonze *Kantei-Shōnin*. There it was that *Ushiwaka-maru* (later on, *Yoshitsune*) was shut up while yet quite a child to become a bonze (1160) ; he escaped in 1174, fled to *Mutsu* to *Fujiwara Hidehira* and prepared for the struggle against the *Taira*. *Kurama-dera* is situated on a mountain called *Kurama-yama* or *Matsuo-yama*.

Kurando, 藏人． — See *Kurōdo*.

Kura no tsukasa, 藏司． Formerly, an official intrusted with the Imperial Seal, Robes, Treasures, etc.

Kura-ryō, 内藏寮． One of the 6 offices (*ryō*) depending on the *Nakatsukasa-shō*, intrusted with the guard of the Imperial treasures : gold, silver, precious stones, vestments, fabrics; objects offered as tribute, etc.

Kuratsukuribe no Tori, 鞍作部鳥． A famous painter and sculptor, in the reign of *Suiko* (593-628). To him are attributed the paintings in the *Hōryū-ji* temple near *Nara*, and the 12 statues of *Shumisen*, in the same temple. He is also known by the names of *Dōshi, Tori Busshi*.

Kurayoshi, 倉吉. A small town in *Hōki* (8,600 inh.). Was, in the *Ashikaga* days, the residence of the *Yamana daimyō*, governors of the province, who in 1524, were despoiled by *Amako Tsunehisa*. There too, the *Satomi* family, formerly very powerful in *Awa* (*Tōkaidō*), became extinct in 1623.

Kure, 呉. A sea port in *Aki* province, 37 Km. S.E. of *Hiroshima* (62,800 inh.). Since 1887, the seat of a maritime prefecture (*Chinjufu*).

Kurikara-dani, 倶利加羅谷. In *Etchū*, near the borders of *Kaga*; the scene of a battle between *Kiso Yoshinaka* and *Taira Koremori* (1183).

Kurikoma-yama, 栗駒山. A mountain on the borders of *Rikuzen*, *Rikuchū* and *Ugo*. Also called *Koma-ga-take*. (1,650 m.).

Kuriko-yama, 栗子山. A hill near *Uji* (*Yamashiro*), also called *Kukome-yama*, *Kunimi-take*, *Shimmei-zan*. In 1113, the troops of the *Kōfuku-ji* temple of *Nara*, on their way to burn down the *Kiyomizu-dera* (*Kyōto*), were shattered there by *Minamoto Tameyoshi*. There too, the army of *Hōjō Yasutoki* camped before the battle of *Uji* (1221).

Kuriyagawa, 厨川. A village in *Rikuchū*, near which *Minamoto Yoriyoshi*, defeated and killed *Abe Sadatō* (1062).

Kurobane, 黒羽. In *Shimotsuke*. A place where *Hideyoshi*, after having defeated the *Nasu daimyō*, installed *Ōseki Takamasu*, whose descendants resided there until the Restoration (18,000 k.).

Kurobe-gawa, 黒部川. A river which waters the north of *Etchū* (78 Km.).

Kuroda, 黒田. A place in *Owari*, where in 1388, a battle was fought between *Toki Norinao* and *Shimada Mitsusada*. In the 16th century, *Wada Kawachi*, *kerai* of *Oda Nobunaga*, built a castle there, the guard of which was confided to *Sawai Saemon*. In 1590, *Hideyoshi* gave it to *Hitotsu-yanagi Naomori*, who, in 1600, was transferred to *Kambe* (*Ise*), and the castle of *Kuroda* was abandoned.

Kuroda, 黒田. A family of *daimyō*, descended from the *Sasaki* of *Ōmi* and through them from *Uda-Genji*.

—— **Mototaka,** 職隆 (1524-1585). *Mino no kami*, served first *Kodera Masamoto*, *daimyō* of *Himeji* (*Harima*), then *Nobunaga*. Shaved his head and took the name of *Sōen*.

—— **Yoshitaka,** 孝高 (1546-1604). Son of *Mototaka*, was first *kerai* of the *Kodera*; married the daughter of *Masamoto* and himself bore the name of *Kodera* until the fall of that family. Hence, the name of *Simeon Condera*, which the ancient missionaries give him in their writings. In 1569, he defeated the troops of *Akamatsu*, who had come to besiege *Himeji*. In 1573, he came to *Kyōto*, where for the first time, he saw *Nobunaga* and *Hideyoshi*: he headed the vanguard which the latter led into *Chūgoku*. He tried in vain to draw his former suzerain *Kodera Norimoto*, to *Nobunaga's* party: *Kodera* persisted in making alliance with the *Mōri* and was despoiled of his possessions (1577). *Yoshitaka* served as intermediary between *Hideyoshi* and *Kobayakawa Takakage* to bring about a peace. Afterwards, he served in the campaign of *Shi-koku* against the *Chōsokabe* (1585) and of *Kyūshū* against the *Shimazu* (1587) : whereupon he received as fief 6 districts of *Buzen* province (120,000 k.) and fixed his residence at *Nakatsu*. But his intelligence and ability having roused the jealous susceptibility of *Hideyoshi*, he yielded the administration of his domains to his son *Nagamasa* and took the name of *Josui* (1589). When *Kobayakawa Hideaki*, only 20 years old, was appointed commander in chief of the expedition to Korea (1597), *Yoshitaka* was ordered to accompany and counsel him. During the *Sekigahara* campaign (1600) he remained in *Kyūshū*, and in concert with *Nabeshima Naoshige*, *Katō Kiyomasa*, etc. captured the castles of *Usuki* (*Bungo*), *Yanagawa*, *Kurume* (*Chikugo*). *Ieyasu* tried to attach

SEAL OF
KURODA
YOSHITAKA.

him to his party and give him a high office in the government ; but after a courteous visit to *Edo*, *Josui* returned to *Kyūshū*, where he died after a few years. — *Yoshitaka* had been baptized in 1583, by the name of *Simeon*, and until death, proved faithful to the faith he had embraced.

—— **Nagamasa,** 長 政 (1568-1623). Son of *Yoshitaka*, came to *Kyōto* at the age of 10, and was intrusted by *Nobunaga* to the care of *Hideyoshi*, then *daimyō* of *Nagahama* (*Ōmi*). He served in the *Kyūshū* campaign (1587) and in Korea (1592). In 1600 he sided with *Ieyasu* and fought at *Sekigahara*. In reward for his services, he was transferred from *Nakatsu* (*Buzen* — 120,000 k.), to *Najima* (*Chikuzen* — 520,000 k.) ; he built a castle there and changed its name to *Fukuoka*. He fought at *Ōsaka* (1615), under the orders of *Hidetada*. — *Nagamasa* had been baptized, while still young, with the name of *Damian*, but he always remained lukewarm, and abandoned his religion when it was proscribed.

Yoshitaka - Nagamasa	Tadayuki - Mitsuyuki	Tsunamasa - Nobumasa		(a)
		Nagakiyo - Nagayoshi		(b)
	Nagaoki - Nagashige	-Naganori - Nagasada		(c)

(*a*) — Elder branch, which, from 1600 to 1868 resided at *Fukuoka* (*Chikuzen* —520,000 k.). — Now Marquis.

(*b*) — Branch, which, resided from 1688 to 1721 at *Naokata* (*Chikuzen* — 520,000 k.).

(*c*) — Younger branch, which from 1623 to 1868 resided at *Akizuki* (*Chikuzen* — 50,000 k.). — Now Viscount.

Kuroda, 黒 田 . A family of *daimyō*, originating in *Musashi* and descended from the emperor *Senkwa* (536-539), by *Tanji no Mabito*. Ennobled in 1700, resided at *Shimodate* (*Hitachi*) in 1703, was transferred to *Numata* (*Kōzuke*) in 1732 and to *Kururi* (*Kazusa* — 30,000 k.) (1742-1868). — Now Viscount.

Kuroda, 黒 田 . A family of *samurai* from the *Kagoshima* (*Satsuma*) clan, ennobled after the Restoration. — Now Count.

—— **Kiyotaka,** 清 隆 (1840-1900). Played a brilliant part in the Restoration and was commissioned to subdue the last remnants of the

Shōgun's army, who had fortified themselves in *Hakodate*. He besieged the city and received the capitulation of *Enomoto Takeaki*, the insurgent leader (1869). During the *Satsuma* war, he compelled the rebels to raise the siege of *Kumamoto*, after 2 months' fruitless efforts (1877). He was several times minister and president of the Privy Council.

Kuroda, 黒田. A family of *samurai* from the clan of *Kagoshima* (*Satsuma*), ennobled after the Restoration. — Now Viscount.

Kuroda, 黒田. A family of *samurai* from *Shizuoka*, (*Suruga*), ennobled after the Restoration. — One branch bears the title of Viscount, another that of Baron.

Kurōdo, 藏人. Or *Kurando* (for *Kura-bito*). Officials of the *Kurōdo-dokoro*.

Kurōdo-dokoro, 藏人所. An office created in 810, by the emperor *Soga*, to manage administrative matters and the wording of imperial decrees. *Fujiwara Fuyutsugu* and *Kose Notari* were its first titularies. In 897, its president received the title of *Bettō*, which was assigned to *Fujiwara Tokihira*. Its members were at first *kuge* of high rank. Later on 3 members of the 5th rank (*go-i*) and 4 of the 6th rank (*roku-i*) were added to their number. They were called *Higerō* and managed the daily routine work, the repasts of the Court, etc. Moreover, young men of high families were intrusted with the commissions, the messages, etc. They were the *Hikurōdo*. Besides, there were 8 *zōshiki*, 20 *tokoroshū*, 20 *takiguchi-bushi*, 3 *suitō*, 6 *kotoneri*, etc.

Kurohime-yama, 黒姫山. A mountain on the borders of *Shinano* and *Echigo* (2,095 m.).

Kuroishi, 黒石. A place in *Mutsu;* was from 1814 to 1868, the residence of a branch of the *Tsugaru* family (10,000 k.).

Kurokawa, 黒川. In *Mutsu*, a district of *Aizu*. Ancient castle built by the *Ashina daimyō*, who were despoiled in 1589 by *Date Masamune*. The latter left his residence of *Yonezawa*, and settled at *Kurokawa*, but the next year *Hideyoshi* obliged him to return to his former domains, and gave *Aizu* to *Gamō Ujisato*, who changed the name of *Kurokawa* to *Wakamatsu*. — See *Wakamatsu*.

Kurokawa, 黒川. In *Echigo*. — Was, from 1723-1868., the residence of a branch of the *Yanagisawa* family (10,000 k.).

Kurokawa, 黒川. A family of *samurai* from the clan of *Komatsu* (*Iyo*), ennobled after the Restoration. — Now Baron.

Kuroki, 黒木. A family of *samurai* from the clan of *Kagoshima* (*Satsuma*), ennobled in 1895. — Now Count.

—— **Tamesada,** 為楨. Born in 1844, chose a military career. At the time of the Chinese war (1894-1895), he was commanding the *Kumamoto* (*Higo*) division and assisted at the siege of Weihaiwei. In the Manchurian campaign (1904-1905) he was commander of the 1st army.

Kuroki-gosho, 黒木御所. A village in the *Oki* islands, where the emperor *Go-Daigo* dwelt during his exile (1332). A *Shintō* temple has been erected on the site of the emperor's dwelling.

Kurokuwa-gashira, 黒鍬頭. In the *Tokugawa* days, the chief of the *kurokuwa*. The latter, 470 in all, served as game-beaters in the

Shōgun's hunts. In ordinary times, they were employed in carrying messages, etc.

Kuromaru, 黒丸. In *Echizen*. An ancient castle of *Shiba Taka-tsune*. The latter was besieged there by *Nitta Yoshisada*. (1336).

Kuro-shio, 黒潮. The Black Current, whose waters, coming from the south, maintain a relatively mild temperature on the southern and south-eastern coasts of Japan. Its width is about 75 Km., its depth, about 900 m.; its rapidity varies with the direction of the winds.

Kurotani, 黒谷. A temple built in the 12th century, by the bonze *Genkū*, N.E. of *Kyōto*, where he began to preach the doctrines of the *Jōdo-shū* sect. There too *Kumagaya Naozane* retired in 1192.

Kurozumi-ha, 黒住派. One of the 10 Shintoist sects, established by *Kurozumi Munetada* (1779-1849). Claiming the sun to be the prin-ciple of all life in this world, it pays special honor to *Amaterasu-ō-mi-kami* and prescribes to its devotees the practice of long breathing, as a very healthful exercise.

Kurume, 久留米. A town of *Fukuoka-ken*, capital of *Chikugo* province (29,000 inh.). After his expedition to *Kyūshū*, (1587), *Hide-yoshi* installed *Mōri Hidekane* there, who was besieged in 1600 by *Nabe-shima Katsushige*. In the same year, *Tanaka Yoshimasa* became *daimyō* of *Kurume;* he was replaced in 1621, by *Arima Toyouji*, whose descendants resided there until the Restoration (210,000 k.).

Kururi, 久留里. In *Kazusa*. An ancient castle built in 1445 by *Takeda Nobunaga*, then *Shugo-dai* of the province. It passed to the *Satomi* (1480), then to the *Hōjō* (1575). In 1590, *Ieyasu* placed *Matsudaira Tadamasa* there. It became the residence of the *daimyō Tsuchiya* (1602), *Sakai* (1680), and *Kuroda* (1742-1868) (30,000 k.).

Kurushima, 來嶋. A village at the northern extremity of *Iyo*. Was, in the 16th century, the residence of a family of the same name, who entertained quite an army of pirates on the coasts of *Shikoku* and *Kyūshū*, and even sent flotillas to Korea and China.

Kurushima, 來嶋. A family of *daimyō*, originating in *Iyo* and descended from *Kōno Michiari*.

—— **Michifusa,** 通總 (1562-1597). Struggled against *Chōsokabe Motochika* who attempted to seize his domains, then submitted to *Hide-yoshi* (1585) who confirmed him in his possession of *Kurushima* (*Iyo* — 14,000 k.) At the time of the Korean expedition (1592), he commanded a flotilla of war junks, obtained some successes and was appointed *Izumo no kami*. He returned to Korea after the rupture of the negotiations, and was defeated and killed in an engagement.

—— **Michichika,** 通親 (1580-1611). Son of *Michifusa*, was in 1601 transferred to *Mori* (*Bungo* — 12,500 k.), where his descendants resided until the Restoration. — In 1616, the ideographs of the family's name were changed to 久留嶋 (*Kurushima*). — To-day Viscount.

Kurushima-kaikyō, 來嶋海峽. A strait between the northern extremity of *Iyo* and *Ōshima* island.

Kusaka, 日下. A district of *Kawachi*, where *Jimmu-tennō* was defeated by *Nagasunehiko*, when he attempted to penetrate into *Yamato*.

Kusanagi no tsurugi, 草薙劍.— See *Ame-no-murakumo no tsurugi*.

Kusatsu, 草津. A village in *Kōzuke*, renowned for its hot springs, the temperature of which varies from 35 to 70 degrees centigrade.

Kusatsu, 草津. In *Ōmi*; junction of the *Tōkaidō* and *Nakasendō*. In 1509, *Ōuchi Yoshioki* was defeated there by *Rokkaku Takayori*.

Kusha-shū, 俱舍宗. A Buddhist sect, brought from China to Japan by the bonzes *Chitsū* and *Chitatsu*, towards 660, at the same time as the *Hossō-shū* sect of which it is a branch.

Kushira, 櫛羅. A place in *Yamato*: it was from 1680-1868, the residence of a branch of the *Nagai* family (10,000 k.).

Kushiro, 釧路. One of the 11 provinces of *Hokkaidō*; comprises 6 districts. — Pr. town: *Kushiro* (5200 inh.), which contains many remnants ascribed to the *Koropok-guru*.

Kushizu, 櫛笥. A *kuge* family, descended from *Fujiwara Uona*. — Now Viscount.

Kusuishi, 鼓吹司. Formerly an office depending on the war department, intrusted with the teaching of the musical instruments: drum (*tsuzumi*), flute (*fue*), etc., used in time of war.

Kusunoki, 楠. A family of *daimyō*, descended from *Tachibana no Moroe* (683-757).

	Masayasu		
Toshichika	Masashige	(Wada) Masanji	Masasue
Masatsura Masatoki Masayuki Masanori		Yukitada Takaie Takasue	
Masakatsu Masamoto Masahide	Masahira		
Masamori	Tomoshige (Wada)		
Morinobu	Masataka		
Morimune	Masanao		
Morihide	Shigetoki		
Nagashige	Masamitsu		
Takashige	Masatoshi (Kusunoki)		
Masatora	Masanaga		
Masatora	Toshishige		
	Masahiro		

—— **Masashige**, 正成 (1294-1336). Resided E. of the temple of *Kongō-zan* (*Kawachi*). When the emperor *Go-Daigo* was expelled from *Kyōto* by *Hōjō Takatoki*, (1331), and fled to Mt. *Kasagi*, he appealed to *Masashige* and commissioned him to defend his cause. *Masashige* levied troops, fortified *Kongō-zan*, built the castles of *Akasaka* and *Chikaya*, and began the struggle with the *Hōjō*. After the capture of *Kamakura* by *Nitta Yoshisada* (1333), he defeated the bonze *Kembō* at Mt *Iiyama*, and pacified the region. In reward, he received the title of *Kawachi no* *kami* and the government of the provinces of *Settsu, Kawachi* and *Izumi*. When *Ashikaga Takauji* revolted in *Kwantō, Nitta Yoshisada* went to fight against him, whilst *Masashige* remained to protect *Kyōto* (1335). *Yoshisada* having been defeated at *Hakone, Takauji* marched upon the capital. *Masashige* advanced to check him, but was defeated at *Uji* and *Go-Daigo* had to seek shelter on *Hiei-zan* (1336). *Yoshisada*, joining forces with *Yūki Munehiro, Nawa Nagatoshi*, etc. once more attacked *Takauji*, put him to flight and re-installed the emperor at *Kyōto*. But *Takauji* soon returned from *Kyūshū* with a numerous army. *Masashige* and *Yoshisada* attacked him at *Hyōgo*, near the *Minato-gawa* river. After prodigies of valor, they yielded to overwhelming odds, and *Masashige* covered with wounds, 11 in all, committed *harakiri* with his brother *Masasue*. After his death, the

KUSUNOKI MASASHIGE.

emperor conferred on him the title of *Sakon-e-chūjō* and the rank of *shō-san-i*. After the Restoration, he was raised to the rank of *jū-ichi-i* and in 1871, a temple (*Nankō-san*) was erected in his honor on the spot where he died for the cause of the legitimate sovereign. — *Masashige* has remained as the type of loyalty and devotion to the imperial dynasty.

—— **Masaie, 正家** († 1348). A relative of *Masashige*, succeeded him as the head of his partisans, during the minority of *Masatsura*. After the battle of *Minato-gawa*, he repaired to *Urizura* (*Hitachi*). He was attacked there by the northern troops but put them to flight, killing their two generals, *Satake Yoshifuyu* and *Gotō Motoaki*. The following year (1337), he accompanied *Kitabatake Akiie* in his expedition to *Kyōto*. When *Masatsura* took the field, *Masaie* served under his orders, and with him was defeated and killed at *Shijōnawate*.

—— **Masatsura, 正行** (1326-1348). Eldest son of *Masashige*, was only 10 years old at his father's death. In 1347, he took the leadership of his partisans and rose against the *Ashikaga* ; he put to flight *Hosokawa Akiuji*, who had invaded *Kawachi*, and defeated *Yamana Tokiuji*, who had come to the rescue of *Akiuji*. Thereupon *Takauji* sent *Kō Moronao* and *Moroyasu* with 60,000 men to attack *Masatsura*. The latter, with his brother *Masatoki* and his cousin *Wada Takahide*, defended himself valiantly at *Shijōnawate* (*Kawachi*), but as his army was quite inferior to that of his enemies, he was overwhelmed and perished with all his

KUSUNOKI MASATSURA.

partisans. He was only 22 years old. A temple (*Shijōnawate-jinja*) has been erected on the spot where he died.

—— **Masanori, 正儀** († 1390). The youngest son of *Masashige* ; became head of the *Kusunoki* clan after the death of his brothers. He took the field in 1361, defeated the *Sasaki*, and then, joining sides with

Hosokawa Kiyouji, who had just embraced the southern cause, became master of *Kyōto*, whence he was expelled one month later by the *Shōgun Yoshiakira*. Then joining forces with *Wada Masatake*, he won a victory over the *Shōgun's* army and reappeared in *Kawachi*. On the death of *Go-Murakami* (1368), departing from his family traditions, he entered into a parley with *Hosokawa Yoriyuki* and submitted to the *Ashikaga*. He was then attacked by his former companion in arms, *Wada Masatake*, but with the aid of *Yoriyuki*, he succeeded in repelling him. After which, *Masanori* himself, besieged the southern emperor in his stronghold of *Kongō-zan* (1373). In 1378, he undertook a new campaign with his son *Masakatsu*. Then, after a defection of 12 years, he submitted again to *Go-Kameyama*, who was then confined to Mt. *Yoshino*. (1381). His castle of *Akasaka* was captured the following year by *Yamana Ujikiyo*.

—— **Masakatsu,** 正勝. Eldest son of *Masanori*, continued, even after the fusion of the two parties, to struggle against the *Ashikaga*. In 1399, he revolted in *Izumi* with *Ōuchi Yoshihiro*, but they were defeated.

—— **Masamoto,** 正元. Brother of *Masakatsu*, conceived the project of assassinating the *Shōgun Yoshimitsu*, but he was found out and put to death by *Urakami Yukikage* (1402).

—— **Mitsumasa,** 光正. A descendant of *Masanori*. Attempted to assassinate the *Shōgun Yoshinori* and to raise to the throne a prince of the southern dynasty, but he was arrested and beheaded at *Rokujōgahara* (*Kyōto*) (1429).

—— **Masatora,** 正虎. A descendant of *Masanori*, was *Kawachi no kami*. He served the *Shōgun Yoshiaki*, and was *Shitsuji* of *Nobunaga*. He shaved his head and received the title of *Shikibugyō-hōin*. By order of *Hideyoshi*, he wrote in 1588, a narrative of the visit of the two emperors to the *Jūrakutei*. — At the time of the Restoration, researches were made to discover an authentic descendant of *Màsashige*, to confer on him a title of nobility, in memory of his illustrious ancestor. Many candidates came forward, but none could prove his descent with certainty: thus it happens that the name of *Kusunoki* does not appear in the roll of Modern Japanese heraldry.

Kusuri-gari, 薬獵. A pastime, in former years, during which plants used in medicine were gathered in the fields. Later on, the 5th day of the 5th month was set aside for that purpose.

Kutani, 九谷. A district in the south of *Kaga* province; renowned for its porcelains: 3000 workmen are employed and the annual manufacture amounts to 200 or 300,000 yen.

Ku-tō-ko, 九等戸. Formerly the 9 ranks into which the families were divided according to the amount of taxes they had to pay: *jōjō-ko, jōchū-ko, jōge-ko ; chūjō-ko, chūchū-ko, chūge-ko ; gejō-ko, gechū-ko,* and *gege-ko*. — In 706, the number was reduced to 4 : *dai-ko, jō-ko, chū-ko* and *ge-ko*.

Kuwahara, 桑原. A family of *kuge*, descended from *Fujiwara Michizane* — Now Viscount.

Kuwana, 桑名. A town of *Ise* province (20,200 inh.). Was in the 16th century, the residence of the *Ise* family, vassals of the *Kitabatake*. In 1576, *Oda Nobuo* constructed a castle there which was confided to *Amano Masatoshi*. *Hideyoshi* gave it to *Ujie Yukihiro*. In the *Tokugawa* days, it was occupied successively by the *daimyō*: *Honda* (1601), *Hisamatsu* (1617), *Okudaira* (1710), and *Hisamatsu* (1823-68) (100,000 k).

Kuwayama, 桑山 A family of *daimyō*, originating in *Kuwayama* (*Owari*).

—— **Shigeharu, 重春**. (1524-1606). Served *Hideyoshi*. In 1585, he built a castle at *Wakayama* (*Kii*) and received a revenue of 30,000 k.

Shigeharu { Kazushige-Kazuharu............Kazutada   (a)
            { Motoharu -Sadaharu   (b)

(*a*) — Elder branch which resided from 1600 at *Shinjō* (*Yamato* — 16,000 k.) and was dispossessed in 1682.

(*b*) — Younger branch which settled down at *Gose* (*Yamato* — 26,000 k.) in 1600 and became extinct in 1629.

Kūya-Shōnin, 空也上人 (903-972). Was first called *Kōshō*. Having become a bonze, he took the name of *Kūya*. Wandered from province to province, building bridges, digging wells, opening up roads, and all the while preaching Buddhism. In 951, an epidemic ravaged *Kyōto*: *Kūya* carved a large statue of "*Kwannon* with 11 faces," set it on a chair, and carried it all about the city, after which the scourge ceased. Thereupon a temple was erected, called *Rokuhara no Kwannon-dō* or *Rokuhara-mitsu-ji*, to receive the wonderful statue, which is still worshipped there. *Kūya* then set to work preaching Buddhism in the provinces of *Dewa* and *Mutsu*, where it was still very little known. He died at the *Saikō-ji* temple, where he dwelt in the intervals of his peregrinations.

KŪYA SHŌNIN.

Kuze, 久世. A family of *daimyō*, originating in *Mikawa*, and descended from *Murakami-Genji*.

—— **Hironobu, 廣宣** (1561-1626). Was a *kerai* of *Ieyasu* and served in all his campaigns.

—— **Hiroyuki, 廣之** (1609-1679). On the death of his father, was raised to the rank of *daimyō* and received in 1665, the fief of *Sekiyado* (*Shimōsa* — 35,000 k.). His descendants established themselves successively: in 1683, at *Niwase* (*Bitchū*); in 1686, at *Kameyama* (*Tamba* — 45,000 k.): in 1697, at *Yoshida* (*Mikawa*) ; in 1705 at *Sekiyado* (*Shimōsa* — 53,000 k), where they remained until the Restoration, but their revenues were reduced in 1862, to 43,000 k — Now Viscount.

Kuzuryū-gawa, 九頭龍川. A river in *Echizen* (125 Km.). Also called *Funabashi-gawa*, *Kurotatsu-gawa*.

Kwachō, 華頂. A family of imperial princes, founded in 1868, by prince **Hirotsune, 博經** 6th son of *Fushimi Kuniie*. — The present head of the family is prince *Hirotada*, born in 1902, 2nd son of prince *Fushimi Hiroyasu* 博 恭.

Kwaifūsō, 懐風藻. The first collection of poems published in Japan; was compiled in the 8th century by *Ōmi no Mifune*.

Kwaikei, 會慶. A sculptor of the 11th century, pupil of *Jōkaku*.

Kwajiba-mi-mawari-yaku, 火事場見廻役. A title created in 1722 and borne by 10 officials of the firemen brigade, commissioned to command the firemen in case of fire and to ascertain the damages.

Kwambun, 寛文. *Nengō*: 1661-1672.

Kwambutsu-e, 灌佛會. A ceremony established in 843 and performed on the 8th day of the 4th month in memory of the birth of *Shaka*. In the Imperial Palace, a special apartment (*Kwambutsudō-jō*), was fitted up for the festival (891), which consisted in burning incense before the statues and images of Buddha. It was also called *Busshō-e*.

Kwammu, 官務. Another name given to the *Sadaishi*, official of the *Benkwan-kyoku*.

Kwammu-tennō, 桓武天皇. 50th Emperor of Japan (782-805). Prince *Yamabe* or *Yamato-hiko-sume-ragi-iyateru no mikoto*, eldest son of the emperor *Kōnin*, succeeded his father at the age of 44. He resided first at *Nagaoka* (*Yamashiro*); then, in 794, moved to *Uda*, in the district of *Kadono* and called the place *Heian - kyō* (*Kyōto*), which was to be the capital of Japan for more than 10 centuries. He commissioned the learned *Ōmi no Mifune*, president of the *Daigaku*, to fix the posthumous names of all the emperors. Until then, they were called by the name of their capital or their personal names: from that time, date the names

KWAMMU-TENNŌ.

of *Jimmu, Suisei, Nintoku*, etc., by which they are known in history.
Kwammu had to quell a revolt of the *Ebisu :* he sent against them, *Saka-noe no Tamuramaro* who expelled them from *Suruga*, which they had
invaded, to *Mutsu*, and built the fort of *Izawa. Tamuramaro* was the
first to receive the title of *Seii-taishōgun.* In 799, a ship coming from
India, brought cotton grains to Japan, unknown in the country till then.
They were planted in *Nankaidō* and *Saikaidō*, and from that time dates
the making of cotton fabrics *(momen).* — Before dying, *Kwammu* received
from the bonze *Saichō* a sort of Buddhist baptism, administered then for
the first time in Japan.

Kwampaku, 關白. From 882 to 1868, the highest dignity at the
Imperial Court. First called *Azukari-mōsu*, the *Kwampaku* was all
powerful at Court. He represented the emperor, and at times even
took his place in all important questions. He served as intermediary
between the emperor and the officials. — See *Sekkwan-seiji, Sesshō-kwam-paku*, etc.

Kwampō, 寛保. *Nengō :* 1741-1743.

Kwampyō, 寛平. *Nengō :* 889-897.

Kwampyō hō-ō, 寛平法皇. A name given to the emperor *Uda*,
because, in the 9th year of the *Kwampyō*-era (897), he abdicated and
had his head shaved.

Kwampyō go-ikai, 寛平御遺戒. A sort of political testa-ment, transmitted by the emperor *Uda* to his son *Daigo*, when he yielded
the throne to him in the 9th year of the *Kwampyō* era (897).

Kwan-ami, 観阿彌. — See *Kwanze*.

Kwan Sazan, 菅茶山 (1748-1827). Born in *Bingo*, came to
Kyōto, where he followed the lessons of *Nawa Rodō ;* then returning to
his native province, opened a school which became very flourishing.

Kwan-daka, 貫高. During the Shōgunate of *Kamakura* and
Kyōto, the revenue or produce of a domain was estimated in money
(kwammon): the amount of revenues of a *daimyō* or official was called
kwan-daka. Hideyoshi, towards the close of the 16th century, substi-tuted the valuation in *koku* of rice *(koku-daka)*.

Kwan-ei, 寛永. *Nengō :* 1624-1643.

Kwan-ei-ji, 寛永寺. A Buddhist temple built at *Ueno (Edo)* in
1625 by the bonze *Tenkai*, in the precincts of which were buried the
Shōgun Ietsuna (+ 1680), *Tsunayoshi* (+ 1709), *Yoshimune* (+ 1751),
Ieharu (+ 1786), *Ienari* (+ 1841) and *Iesada* (+ 1858). It always
had at its head a prince of the imperial family, whom the *Shōgun* thus
had at their disposal, with the possibility of opposing him to the reigning
sovereign, should the latter show any tendency towards independence.
The last *Rinnōji no miya*, was secularized at the time of the Restora-tion and became prince *Kitashirakawa*. The temple *Kwan-ei-ji* was
burnt down in 1868, during the battle of *Ueno* between the imperial
army and the *Shōgun's* followers.

Kwan-en, 寛延. *Nengō :* 1748-1750.

Kwangaku-den, 観學田. Formerly, rice-fields whose revenues
served to support the students of the *Daigaku. Shōmu-tennō*, was the

first to grant the University for that purpose, 30 *chō* (about 30 hectares) of rice-fields (733) ; the emperor *Kwammu* in 785, added 102 *chō* in *Echizen*. In the 11th century, the *Daigaku* declined by degrees and the *kwangaku-den* disappeared.

Kwangen, 寛元. *Nengō :* 1243-1246.

Kwangi-ten, 歡喜天. — See *Shōden*.

Kwan-i, 冠位. (Lit. : kinds of head-dress). In 603, the empress *Suiko*, following the counsel of *Shōtoku-taishi*, divided, after the Chinese fashion, the nobles and officials into 12 classes, distinguished by the color of their head-dresses (*kammuri* = *kwan*) ; *Kōtoku* increased the number to 19 (649), *Tenchi*, to 26 (662), *Temmu*, to 48 (682).

Kwan-i jū-ku kai, 冠位十九階. The 19 degrees in the hierarchy of nobles and officials, created by the emperor *Kōtoku* in 649 : *taishoku* (織), *shōshoku, taishū* (繡), *shōshū, taishi* (紫), *shōshi, taikwa* (華)-*jō, taikwa-ge, shōkwa-jō, shōkwa-ge, taizan* (山)-*jō, taizan-ge, shōzan-jō, shozan-ge, taiotsu* (乙)-*jō, taiotsu-ge, shōotsu-jō, shōotsu-ge* and *risshin* (立身). — In 662, *Tenchi-tennō*, leaving the first 6 degrees as they were, changed the character *kwa* to *kin* (錦), in the following four (7-10) ; thus we have : *taikin-jō, taikin-ge, shōkin-jō* and *shōkin-ge ;* the classes from 7 to 18, received between *jō* and *ge* the intermediary *chū, taikin-chū, shōkin-chū, taizan-chū, shōzan-chū, taiotsu-chū, shōtsu-chū,* finally, the *risshin* class was changed to *taiken* (建) and *shōken,* which brought the number of degrees to 26.

Kwan-i jū-ni kai, 冠位十二階. The 12 degrees in the hierarchy of nobles and officials created by the empress *Suiko* in 603 : *taitoku* (德), *shōtoku, taijin* (仁), *shōgin, tairei* (禮), *shōrei, taishin* (信), *shōshin, taigi* (義), *shōgi, taichi,* (智) and *shōchi*.

Kwan-i shichi shoku jū-san kai, 冠位七色十三階. The 7 colors, fixed for the *kammuri* of the 13 hierarchical degrees, established in 647. Two years later, the number was increased to 19.

Kwan-i sōtō, 官位相當. Concordance of court ranks (*i*) and offices (*kwan*). The *Taihō* code (702), had made it the rule that the title of *Dajō-daijin* should correspond to *jū-ichi-i ;* those of *Sadaijin* and *Udaijin*, to *shō-ni-i* and *jū-ni-i ; Dainagon,* to *shō-san-i ; Dazai no sotsu,* to *jū-san-i ;* the same with the whole hierarchy of officials. When the court rank was above the office, it was made known by the character *gyō* (行) : *Sangi jū-san-i gyō Gyōbukyō ;* whilst, when the office was above the rank, *shu* (守) was used : *Shō-san-i shu Udaijin.* — See *Ikai, Kwan-tō*.

Kwanji, 寛治. *Nengō :* 1087-1093.

Kwanjō, 灌頂. A Buddhist ceremony, in which the bonze pours a little water (*kanro,* sweet dew) on the head of the believer, to remit his sins, purify his heart, and aid him to attain perfection. The ceremony was performed when a person received the imposition of the Buddhist precepts or when he shaved his head. A Buddhist name was then taken. Thus the bonze *Gyōgi* gave the emperor *Shōmu* the name of *Shōman* (748), *Go-Takakura* received from *Getsurin-Daishi,* the name of *Gyōjō* (1212). This ceremony has been called the Buddhist baptism.

Kwanju-ji, 勧修寺. A great temple of the *Tendai* sect, founded south of *Kyōto* by the mother of the emperor *Daigo*, at the beginning of the 10th century. For a long time, it was governed by a prince of the imperial family.

Kwanjuji, 勧修寺. A *kuge* family descended from *Fujiwara Yoshikado*. — Now Count.

Kwanki, 寛喜. *Nengō*: 1229-1231.

Kwankō, 寛弘. *Nengō*: 1004-1011.

Kwannin, 寛仁. *Nengō*: 1017-1020.

Kwannon, 観音. Or better *Kwanzeon dai-bosatsu* (Sanscr. *Avalôkitésvara*). *Bosatsu*, assistant of *Amida-butsu*, who became, through the people's religious turn of mind, the goddess of pity (Buddh.). According to the Chinese legend, she was born in *Setchoan* province, and was daughter of the governor of the town of *Souilin*; her name was *Myō-In*. One day, at the age of 18, she repaired to *Hakujaku-ji*, a prosperous temple of 500 bonzes. The bonzes, struck by the beauty of the girl, kept her in the temple, and prevented her from going out. Her father, informed of the fact, put all the bonzes to death and burnt the temple; his daughter perished in the flames. The next night, she appeared to him and informed him that she had escaped from the fire and had become a goddess. Thereupon, she received the name of *Sengan-senju-kwanzeon-bosatsu* (goddess with a thousand eyes and a thousand arms, embracing the earth). — In Japan, she is represented in different ways: with several faces (*Jū-ichi-men Kwannon*), with thousand arms (*Senju Kwannon*), with a horse's head (*Batō Kwannon*). She is also called *Nyo-i-rin* (precious stone able to fulfil all the desires of those that possess it), which may be translated by "almighty."

Kwannonji, 観音寺. In *Ōmi*; an ancient castle, which, from the 12th century, belonged to the *Sasaki*, who were dispossessed by *Nobunaga* in 1568.

Kwannon-zaki, 観音崎. A cape in *Sagami*, which commands the entry of *Tōkyō* bay.

Kwan-ō, 観応. *Nengō* of the northern dynasty: 1350-1351.

Kwanroku, 観勒. A bonze from *Kudara* (Korea), who came to Japan in 602 and taught astronomy, the reckoning of the calendar, etc. He was named *Sōzu*.

Kwanryō, 管領. A title of two high officials in the *Ashikaga* days: one, *Kyōto-Kwanryō*, prime minister of the *Shōgun*, was always taken from the *Shiba*, *Hosokawa* or *Hatakeyama* families, which were for that reason called the *san-kwan*; the other, *Kwantō-Kwanryō*, governor of *Kwantō*, was first taken from the younger branch of the *Ashikaga*, then from the *Uesugi*, etc. — See *Shitsuji*, *Kwantō-Kwanryō*, etc.

Kwansei, 寛政. *Nengō*: 1789-1800.

Kwansei igaku no kin, 寛政異學禁. As the disputes between the different Confucianist schools of *Itō Jinsai*, *Ogiu Sorai*, etc., constantly increased, the *Bakufu*, following the advice of the *Kwanju Shibano Ritsuzan*, decreed in 1795, that all interpretations at variance with the teachings of *Shushi* (a celebrated commentator of Chinese classics, 1130-1200), would be regarded as heterodox (*i-gaku*) and consequently interdicted. But this measure only contributed to increase the rivalry among the schools. — See *Tokugawa-jidai no keigaku-ha*.

Kwansei no san-kijin, 寛政三奇人. *Takayama Hikokurō Masayuki, Gamō Kumpei Hidezane* and *Hayashi Shihei Tomonao*, who during the *Kwansei* era, won distinction by their loyalty to the Imperial cause.

Kwansei no san-suke, 寛政三助. Three famous Confucianists who, during the *Kwansei* era, commented on the works of the Chinese scholar *Shushi* (1130-1200): *Koga Seiri Yasuke, Bitō Jishū Ryōsuke* and *Shibano Ritsuzan Hikosuke*.

Kwanshin-ji, 観心寺. A Buddhist temple, founded in *Kawachi*, in the reign of *Montoku-tennō* (851-858) and enlarged by *Kukai*. It was also called *Hi-no-o*. It served as a shelter to the southern emperor *Go-Murakami*, who also was buried there (1368).

Kwanshō, 寛正. *Nengō :* 1460-1465.

Kwanshu, 貫首. A title given to the chief of the *Kurōdo ;* also to the chief-bonze (*zasu*) of the *Hiei-zan* temples.

Kwantō, 關東. (Lit.: east of the barrier). A name given first to the region which extended east from the *Ōsaka* (逢坂) barrier, (*Ōmi*), near lake *Biwa*, and later on to the provinces situated east from the old *Hakone* barrier.

Kwan-tō, 官等. Hierarchy of officials. — Officials are divided into 3 classes : *Shinnin, Kōtō-kwan* and *Hannin*.

—— **Shinnin, 親任**. Who constitute the highest class, are appointed by a decree bearing the seal of the Emperor, and the Imperial seal, and signed by the Prime Minister. The rank of *Shinnin* is held by the Prime Minister, the Ministers, the members of the Privy Council, by Marshals and Admirals, the Vice-Minister of Justice, the prefects of *Tōkyō, Ōsaka* and *Kyōto*.

—— **Kōtō-kwan, 高等官**. The *Kōtō-kwan*, or officials of high rank, are divided into 10 classes (*tō*) : the first 3 hold the title of *Chokunin* (勅任), the 7 others are called *Sōnin* (奏任). The *Chokunin* are appointed by a decree bearing the Imperial seal, and enforced by the Prime Minister. The *Sōnin* are appointed, on presentation of the Ministers, by a decree bearing the seal of the Privy Council.

—— **Hannin, 判任**. The *Hannin* or officials of inferior rank, are divided into 5 classes; they are appointed by the respective ministers. — See *Ikai, Kwan-i*, etc.

Kwanto-bugyō, 官途奉行. During the shogunate of *Kamakura*, an official serving as intermediary between the *daimyō*, officers of the *Bakufu*, etc., and the Court of *Kyōto*, for demanding and granting titles, offices, etc. That charge was maintained by the *Ashikaga* and, from 1370, it became hereditary in the family of *Settsu Mitsuchika*.

Kwantō-gundai, 關東郡代. Formerly an official intrusted with the management of the *Shōgun's* domains. His rank was below that of *Kanjō-bugyō* and above that of *Gimmi-yaku*.

Kwantō-hakke, 關東八家. During the Middle Ages, the 8 great families of *Kwantō: Chiba, Oyama, Yūki, Nagayama, Satake, Oda, Utsunomiya* and *Nasu.*

Kwantō-hasshō, 關東八將. The chiefs of the 8 great families of *Kwantō* who, towards 1450, sided with *Ashikaga Shigeuji* against the *Uesugi: Chiba, Yūki, Oyama, Utsunomiya, Nasu, Satomi, Satake* and *Oda.*

Kwantō-hasshū, 關東八州. The 8 provinces east of the *Hakone* barrier: *Musashi, Awa, Kazusa, Shimōsa, Shimotsuke, Hitachi, Kōzuke* and *Sagami.*

Kwantō-kwanryō, 關東管領. Governor of *Kwantō.* In 1335, a survivor of the *Hōjō, Tokiyuki,* attempted to seize *Kamakura. Ashikaga Takauji,* commissioned by *Go-Daigo* to repress the revolt, marched against *Tokiyuki* and defeated him, whereupon, he attributed to himself the titles of *Sei-i-taishōgun, Tōgoku no Kwanryō,* etc., and after the example of *Yoritomo,* began to deal out to his officers, titles and domains. When he returned to *Kyōto,* he appointed as *Kwanryō,* first his brother *Tadayoshi,* and then his son *Yoshiakira,* with *Uesugi Noriaki* as *Shitsuji* (minister). *Yoshiakira* was recalled to *Kyōto* in 1349 and replaced by his brother *Motouji,* in whose family, the title of *Kwanryō* was transmitted for 90 years. At that time, (1439) the *Uesugi,* until then *Shitsuji,* called themselves *Kwanryō,* and the descendants of the *Ashikaga* took the title of *Gosho* or *Kubō.*

Kwantō san-suke, 關東三介. The 3 great families of *Kwantō,* whose chiefs bore the titles of *Suke: Chiba no suke, Kazusa no suke,* and *Miura no suke.*

Kwantoku, 寛德. *Nengō:* 1044-1045.

Kwanwa, 寛和. *Nengō:* 985-986. It is also read: *Kwanna.*

Kwanze, 觀世. A family that excelled in composing and performing *sarugaku* or *nō.* They descended from the *Taira* and were first called *Yusaki.*

—— **Kiyotsugu,** 清次 (1354-1406). Also called *Kwan-ami,* founder of the school which bears his name (*Kwanze-ryū*), was a *Shintō* priest (*negi*) of *Kasuga* temple at *Nara,* where he had his dances performed. The *Shōgun Yoshimochi* engaged him in his service. He has composed 15 *nō.*

—— **Motokiyo,** 元清 (1375-1455). Or *Se-ami.* Son of *Kiyotsugu,* composed 93 *nō.* — *Motomasa* (+ 1459), *Motoshige* (+ 1473), *Masamori* (+ 1501), *Nobumitsu* (1435-1516), *Mototada* (1509-1583), *Kokusetsu* (+ 1626), *Motoaki* (1722-1774), *Kiyotaka* (1837-1888), etc., walked in the footsteps of their ancestor *Motokiyo.* They are all known by the title of *Kwanze-tayū.*

Kwasho, 過所. In the shogunate of *Kamakura,* a passport signed by the *Shikken* and *Rensho,* which travellers had to exhibit at the barriers (*sekisho*) in order to be allowed pass.

Kwasho-bune, 過所船. Formerly, boats allowed to circulate without permits (*kwasho*). Later on, the name was given to boats plying between *Kyōto* and *Ōsaka.* At present, the barks circulating on the *Yodo-gawa* are so called.

Kwazan-in, 華山院. An ancient palace of *Kyōto*, to which the emperor *Kwazan* retired after his abdication (986). *Go-Daigo-tennō* resided there for some time after the defeat of *Takauji* (1336). It was destroyed during the *Ōnin* war (1467).

Kwazan-in, 華山院. A *kuge* family, descended from *Fujiwara Morozane* (1042-1101). It was one of the 7 *Seika*.

—— **Ietada,** 家忠 (1062-1136). Son of *Morozane*, was the first to take the name of *Kwazan-in*.

—— **Morokata,** 師賢 (1300-1332). Son of *Moronobu*, supported *Go-Daigo* in his struggle against the *Hōjō*. When the emperor had to flee from *Kyōto*, *Morokata* put on the emperor's dress, and while the latter sought shelter on Mt. *Kasagi*, he repaired to *Hiei-zan*, to recruit troops. Arrested by the emissaries of *Hōjō Takatoki*, he was banished to *Shimōsa*, the domain of *Chiba Sadatane*, where he died in the following year. After his death, he received the posthumous title of *Dajō-daijin*. The temple of *Komikado-jinja* (*Shimōsa*), is erected in his honor.

—— **Iekata,** 家賢 (1331-1367). Son of *Morokata*, also distinguished himself by his loyalty to the southern dynasty. Their descendant bears at present the title of Marquis.

Kwazan-tennō, 華山天皇. 65th Emperor of Japan (985-986). *Morosada*, son of *Reizei-tennō*, succeeded his uncle *En-yū*, at the age of 17. After a reign of 2 years, the death of his favorite wife, *Tsune-ko*, caused him so much grief, that he abdicated and retired to *Kwazan-in* where he died at the age of 41.

Kwazoku, 華族. The nobility which comprises the ancient *kuge* and *daimyō*, and the persons that have been ennobled (*shin-kwazoku*) since the Restoration. — In 1869, the title of *kwazoku* was conferred upon 148 *kuge* families, 288 *daimyō* families, 12 *Shintō* priests and 30 Buddhist priests of noble birth; in all, 478 families. In 1884, all the noble families received one of the 5 titles created that year. In 1905, the nobility comprised 11 dukes (*kō*), 35 marquises (*kō*), 90 counts (*haku*), 360 viscounts (*shi*), and 285 barons (*dan*); in all, 781 families, numbering about 4,000 members, who constitute the Japanese aristocracy.

Kyōden, 京傳 (1761-1816). By birth, *Iwase Sei*. Born at *Edo*, became a skilful designer, but distinguished himself especially as a novelist. He introduced a new style of novel, which remained in vogue until the Restoration. He has also published some burlesque poems.

Kyō-ga-misaki, 經ケ岬. Cape N. of *Tango*.

Kyōgen, 狂言. A sort of comic play, which was performed during the intervals of the *nō*. The principal families that hereditarily composed and performed *kyōgen* were the *Ōkura*, the *Chōmyō*, the *Sagi*, the *Izumi*, etc.

Kyōgoku, 京極. A family of *daimyō*, descended from *Uda-Genji*, through *Sasaki Ujinobu*, *Ōmi no kami*.

Takayoshi {	Takatsugu {	-Tadataka	-Takakazu	-Takatoyo	{ Takamochi	-Takanori		(a)
					{ Takamichi	-Takayoshi		(b)
	Takatomo {	Takahiro	-Takakuni	-Takayori				(c)
		Takamitsu-Takanao	-Takamori-	Takazumi	-Takashige			(d)
		Takamichi-Takatomo	-Takaaki	- Takayuki	-Takanaga			(e)

(*a*) — Eldest branch. — **Takatsugu**, 高 次 (1560-1609). Served *Nobunaga*, who made him marry his niece, daughter of *Asai Nagamasa* and sister of *Yodogimi*. *Hideyoshi* his brother-in-law gave him the fief of *Ōtsu* (*Ōmi* — 60,000 k.). He sided with *Ieyasu*, and was besieged in his castle by *Tachibana Muneshige* and *Tsukushi Hirokado*, but he entered into a parley, concluded a peace and fled to *Kōya-san*. Notwithstanding his flight, he received the very same year (1600), the domain of *Obama* (*Wakasa* — 92,000 k.). Shortly after, yielding to the earnest entreaty of his mother, and his brother *Takatomo*, *Takatsugu* received baptism with his whole family (1602).

—— **Tadataka**, 忠 高 (1593-1637). Married, in 1607, the 4th daughter of the *Shōgun Hidetada*. He served in the siege of *Ōsaka* and carried off as trophies, more than 300 heads of the enemy (1615). His revenues were by and by increased and in 1634, he received the fief of *Matsue* (*Izumo* — 260,000 k.). But he died 3 years later, without leaving any heir and his domains were confiscated. — However the *Bakufu* appointed *Takakazu*, son of his brother *Takamasa*, as head of the family, and gave him the fief of *Tatsuno* (*Harima* — 50,000 k.). In 1658, the family was transferred to *Marugame* (*Sanuki*), where it resided until the Restoration. — Now Viscount.

(*b*) — Branch separated from the preceding in 1694 and installed at *Tadotsu* (*Sanuki* — 10,000 k.), where it remained until the Restoration. — Now Viscount.

(*c*) — Younger branch. — **Takatomo**, 高 知 (1571-1621). Served *Hideyoshi* and received in 1592 the fief of *Iida* (*Shinano* — 80,000 k.). He sided with *Ieyasu*, and besieged the castle of *Gifu* (*Mino*). After *Sekigahara*, he was transferred to *Tanabe* (*Tango* — 125,000 k.), and shortly after, built the castle of *Miyazu*, where he settled down. He served in the two campaigns of *Ōsaka* (1614-1615). — *Takatomo* had been baptized in 1596 by the name of *John*.

—— **Takahiro**, 高 廣 (1599-1677). Was only the adopted son of *Takatomo*. After the latter's death, he retained the fief of *Miyazu*, but had his revenues reduced to 75,000 k. His bad administration as well as that of his son *Takakuni* (1616-1675), caused them to be dispossessed by the *Shōgun Ietsuna* (1666). *Takakuni* was banished to *Nambu*; *Takahiro* shaved his head and was confined to *Okasaki*, near *Kyōto*.

—— **Takayori**, 高 賴. Grandson of *Takahiro*, and son of *Takakuni*, was banished to *Tsu* at the same time as his father (1666); in 1687, he was pardoned, received a pension of 2,000 k. and took rank among the *Kōke* (which word see).

(*d*) — Branch which in 1604, resided at *Tanabe* (*Tango*); then from 1688-1868, at *Toyooka* (*Tajima* — 15,000 k.). — To-day Viscount.

(*e*) — Youngest branch — **Takamichi**, 高 道 (1603-1665). Son of *Kuchiki Tanetsuna*, was adopted by *Takatomo*. In 1620, he received a revenue of 10,000 k. at *Mineyama* (*Tango*), where his descendants remained until the Restoration. — Now Viscount.

Kyōhō, 享保. *Nengō:* 1716-1735.

Kyō-ke, 京家. A branch of the *Fujiwara* family, founded by *Maro* (695-737), son of *Fuhito*. Thus called, because *Maro* had the title of *Sakyō-tayū*.

Kyō-kudari-bugyō, 京下奉行. In the *Kamakura* times, an official, commissioned to examine the complaints made against the officers in *Kyōto*, and to judge the crimes or offences which they might be guilty of. He was also called *Kyō-kudari-shippitsu*.

Kyokujitsu-shō, 旭日章. Order of the Rising Sun.— See *Kunshō*.

Kyokusui no en, 曲水宴. An amusement customary at the Imperial Court, from the time of the emperor *Kensō* (486). It was held on the 3rd day of the 3rd month: the amateurs of poetry met on the banks of a little stream, down which, cups of *sake* (rice-wine) were made to float. Every competitor had to compose a Chinese poem (*shi*), after which, he had the right to stop a cup and drink its contents.

Kyokutei Bakin, 曲亭馬琴 (1767-1848). A famous novelist. He was born in *Edo*, and received counsel and aid from *Kyōden*. He has written 142 novels, the best known of which are: *Hakken-den* (story of 8 dogs representing the 8 cardinal virtues), in 106 volumes, written from 1814 to 1841; *Shichiya no kura* (the pawn-broker's store-house), *Yumihari-zuki-den*, etc. In 1842, the censorship of the *Bakufu* prohibited the publication of the novels and *Bakin* was reduced to silence.

Kyōkwan, 京官. A generic name for all the charges or offices held in *Kyōto*. The others were called *Gekwan*.

Kyōroku, 享祿. *Nengō:* 1528-1531.

Kyōshoku, 京職. Formerly, a title of two officials attached to the administration of the two sections (*Sakyō* and *Ukyō*) of the capital. They kept the register of the social state, the census of the population, superintended the maintenance of the roads, bridges, etc. In the *Toku-gawa* days, the *Shoshidai* was so called.

Kyōto, 京都, A city of *Yamashiro* province (379,500 inh.). — In 792, the emperor *Kwammu*, then residing at *Nagaoka* (*Yamashiro*), commissioned *Fujiwara Kokuromaro* and *Ki Kosami* to look for a suitable site for the foundation of a new capital; they selected the village of *Uda*, in the district of *Kadono*. The works began at once and 2 years later, the emperor took possession of his new palace, which he called *Heian-jō* (castle of peace); the city itself received the name of *Heian-Kyō* (which see). It was also called *Kyōto* (capital), *Raku*, *Rakuyō*, and, in opposition to *Nara*, *Hokkyō*, *Hokuto* (northern capital). From 794 to 1868, *Kyōto* was the residence of the imperial court. From 1190 to 1333, the prosperity of *Kamakura*, injured somewhat that of *Kyōto*, but, when the *Ashikaga Shōgun* installed themselves there, it recovered its former importance; later, it suffered from the long civil wars, which often ruined it. In the *Tokugawa* days, in proportion as *Edo* prospered, *Kyōto* declined. Finally, at the time of the Imperial Restoration, the capital was transferred to *Edo*, which became *Tōkyō* (Eastern capital), and *Kyōto*, received the official name of *Saikyō* (western capital) (1868). — However *Kyōto*, remains to this day, the city of great memories, the Moscow of Japan, which preserves in its numberless Buddhist and *Shintō* temples, marvellous specimens of Japanese art — *Kyōto* is at present the capital of *Kyōto-fu.*

Kyōto daikwan, 京 都 代 官. In the *Tokugawa* days, an official commissioned to administer the 5 provinces of *Kinai*. The charge was first filled by the *Machi-bugyō ;* in 1680, it became a special office, under the authority of the *Shoshidai.* From the close of the 18th century, it became hereditary in the *Kobori* family. It was also called *Kyōto-gundai.*

Kyōto-fu, 京 都 府. A department formed with the provinces of *Yamashiro, Tango* and 5 districts of *Tamba.* — Pop.: 984,000 inh. — Capital : *Kyōto* (379,500 inh.). — Princ. town : *Fushimi* (21,000 inh.).

Kyōto machi-bugyō, 京 都 町 奉 行. In the *Tokugawa* days, an official, residing at *Kyōto* and intrusted with the collection of taxes in the 5 provinces of *Kinai* and of *Ōmi, Tamba* and *Harima.* This office was established in 1600, and was filled by an official first called *Kyōto-gundai.* In 1665, two officials were appointed who received the title of *Machi-bugyō,* and were moreover empowered to judge lawsuits and superintend the temples.

Kyōto nana-kuchi, 京 都 七 口. Formerly the 7 gates of the capital : *Higashi-Sanjō, Fushimi, Toba, Shichijō-Tamba, Nagasaka, Kurama* and *Ōhara.*

Kyōto shichi Kwannon, 京 都 七 觀 音. The 7 temples of *Kyōto* dedicated to the goddess *Kwannon : Kakudō, Kawasaki, Yoshida-dera, Kiyomizu-dera, Rokuhara-mitsuji, Rokkaku-dō,* and *Renge-ō-in.*

Kyōto shichi Yakushi, 京 都 七 藥 師. The 7 temples of *Kyōto* dedicated to *Yakushi-Nyorai : Kwankei-ji* of *Gion, Gokoku-ji* of *Yawata, Ōhata-dera, Hōun-ji* of *Tadekura, Enryaku-ji, Chinkō-ji* and *Byōdō-ji.*

Kyōto Shoshidai, 京 都 所 司 代. In the *Ashikaga* period, the chief of the *Samurai-dokoro* bore the title of *Shoshi.* He had himself sometimes replaced by a *Shoshidai.* The office of *Kyōto Shoshidai* was created by *Nobunaga.* In 1600, *Ieyasu* granted that title to *Okudaira Nobumasa,* then to *Itakura Katsushige.* The duty of the *Shoshidai,* official representative of the *Shōgun* at *Kyōto,* was to inspect the Imperial Court, the *kuge ;* to judge lawsuits, etc. He had authority over the *bugyō* of *Kyōto, Fushimi* and *Nara,* over the *Kyōto-daikwan,* over the officials of the *Nijō* (*Shōgun's* palace at *Kyōto*), etc. Every 5 years, he had to repair to *Edo* to render an account of his administration to the *Shōgun.* A former *Ōsaka-jōdai* or a *Waka-doshiyori* was generally selected for the office of *Shoshidai.* He received annually 10,000 k. and had under him 50 *yoriki* and 100 *dōshin.* The office was suppressed at the beginning of 1867.

Kyōtoku, 享 德. *Nengō :* 1452-1454.

Kyōtōshi, 筥 陶 司. Formerly an office belonging to the *Kunai-shō* and empowered with superintending the manufacture of porcelain, earthenware, etc.

Kyō-un, 慶雲. *Nengō:* 704-707. Also called *Kei-un.*

Kyōwa, 亭和. *Nengō:* 1801-1803.

Kyū-an, 久安. *Nengō:* 1145-1150.

Kyūhōji, 久寶寺. A village in *Kawachi,* where, during the *Ōsaka* campaign (1615), *Chōsokabe Morichika* was defeated by *Tōdō Takatora.*

Kyūju, 久壽. *Nengō:* 1154-1155.

Kyūshū, 九州. (Lit.: 9 provinces). One of the 5 large islands of Japan. Formerly called *Tsukushi, Chinzei,* it occupies a large space in the ancient national legends. It was in *Kyūshū,* on Mt. *Takachiho,* that *Ninigi no mikoto* descended from heaven to earth. It was from *Kyūshū,* that *Jimmu-tennō,* his great-grandson set out for the conquest of the other parts of Japan; it was also the scene of the expeditions of *Jingō-kōgō* (200), and *Hideyoshi* (1592) embarked there for Korea; there too the first Europeans landed (1542); it was *Kyūshū* that, in the *Satsuma* war (1877), made the last attempt to prevent the Europeanization of the land. — *Kyūshū,* besides the largest island known by that name, comprises 150 smaller ones, having an area of 43,615 Km². It is divided into 9 provinces, 8 departments and 82 districts (*kōri*), which contain 2,520 cities or villages. Its population numbers 6,811,250 inh.

Kyūshū no Miya, 九州宮. — See *Yasunaga-shinnō*

Kyūshū tandai, 九州探代. The military governor of *Kyūshū,* in the *Hōjō* and *Ashikaga* times. The title created in 1275, was first conferred on *Hōjō Sanemasa,* commissioned to organize the national defence against the Mongols, and until the end of the *Kamakura* shogunate, this office was always filled by a *Hōjō.* The last, *Hidetoki,* was defeated and slain in 1333 by the *Ōtomo.* — In the *Ashikaga* period, the title was maintained: *Imagawa Ryōshun* bore it from 1371 to 1396.

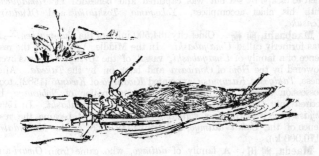

M

Mabechi-gawa, 馬淵川. River (98 Km.) which rises in the N.-E. part of *Rikuchū* flows through *Mutsu* and empties itself into the Pacific Ocean near *Hachinohe*.

Machi-bugyō, 町奉行. Under the *Tokugawa*, mayors or governors of the cities of *Edo, Kyōto, Ōsaka* and *Sumpu*. From the year 1719, there were, in the city of *Edo* two such governors who exercised their power by turns. They received 3,000 k., and had under their command 25 *yoriki* and 128 *dōshin*. — V. *Kyōto machi-bugyō*.

Machi-doshiyori, 町年寄. Under the *Tokugawa*, officers whose duty it was to maintain order among the people of *Edo*, to collect taxes, to watch over the chiefs of districts (*nanushi*), etc.

Machijiri, 町尻. Family of *kuge* descended from *Fujiwara Michitaka* (953-995). — Now Viscount.

Madenokōji, 萬里小路. Family of *kuge* descended from *Fujiwara Yoshikado*. — At present Baron.

Madenokōji, 萬里小路. Branch of the above family, from which it separated since 1882. — At present, Baron.

Maebara Issei, 前原一誠. A *samurai* of the *Chōshū* clan, who rendered great assistance to the imperial cause at the time of the Restoration and who, on this account, was appointed prefect of *Echigo*, then *Sangi* (1869) and Vice-Minister of the War (*Hyōbu-tayū*) (1870). But dissatisfied with the tendencies of the interior policy of 1871, he retired into his province and prepared for a revolt. Having learned that some tumult had occurred at *Kumamoto* (1876), he gathered some few hundreds of soldiers and started an agitation at *Hagi* (*Nagato*). Defeated, he tried to escape by sea but was captured and beheaded at *Yamaguchi*, with his chief accomplices, *Yokoyama Toshihiko* and *Okudaira Kensuke*.

Maebashi, 前橋. Chief city (34,500 inh.) of the *Gumma-ken*. — It was formerly called *Umayabashi*. In the Middle Ages it was the residence of a family of *Umayabashi*, vassal of the *Uesugi*. It was overpowered by the *Hōjō* of *Odawara* and later on by the *Takeda*. After these, *Takigawa Kazumasu*, appointed *Kwanryō* of *Kwantō* (1582), took possession thereof, but hearing of the assassination of *Nobunaga*, he retired into *Owari* and the *Hōjō* returned to *Umayabashi*. In 1590, *Ieyasu* gave it to *Hiraiwa Chikayoshi*. In 1601, it became the residence of the *Sakai daimyō*, and from 1749-1868, of the *Matsudaira* (170,000 k.).

Maeda, 前田. A family of *daimyō*, who came from *Owari* and descended from *Sugawara Michizane* (847-903).

—— **Toshiie,** 利家 (1538-1599). Served *Nobunaga* at first who intrusted to his keeping the castle of *Arako* (*Owari*). After the destruction of the *Asakura* (1573), he established himself at *Fuchū* (*Echizen* — 33,000 k.), obtained the province of *Noto* (1581) then that of *Kaga*

MAEDA TOSHIIE.

(1583). During the campaign against the *Hōjō* (1590), he, together with *Uesugi Kagekatsu*, received orders to take the castles in *Kōzuke* and *Musashi*. At the time of the Korean expedition (1592), he accompanied *Hideyoshi* to *Nagoya* (*Hizen*), and directed military affairs from that place, when the latter returned to *Fushimi*. He was one of the 5 *tairō* who had been appointed governors during the minority of *Hideyori* and it is to him more particularly that the *Taikō*, at the point of death, confided his son. It is not astonishing that he tried to combat the ambitious views of *Ieyasu* ; he died the following year. *Toshiie* is often called *Kaga-Dainagon*.

		Mitsutaka -Tsunatoshi	(a)
	Toshinaga - Toshitsune	Toshitsugu-Masatoshi	(b)
		Toshiharu -Toshiaki	(c)
Toshiie	Toshitaka - Toshitoyo	-Toshihiro -Toshiyoshi	(d)
	Toshimasa		(e)

(*a*) — Senior branch —— **Toshinaga, 利長** (1562-1614). Eldest son of *Toshiie* like his father, tried to prevent civil war, but did not succeed. Having no children, he adopted his youngest brother *Toshitsune*, who was betrothed to a daughter of *Hidetada*, whilst he himself married a daughter of *Ieyasu*. In 1600, he joined in the campaign against *Uesugi Kagekatsu*, and after the battle of *Sekigahara*, obtained the domains of his brother *Takamasa* (*Noto* — 215,000 k.), who had fought on the side of *Hideyori*. His income was then 1,250,000 k., a wealth never attained by any *daimyō* under the *Tokugawa*. He erected the castle of *Kanazawa* (*Kaga*), and resided therein. In the year 1615, *Hideyori* tried in vain to draw him to his party.

—— **Toshitsune, 利常** (1593-1658). *Toshinaga's* brother, succeeded him. Took part in the siege of *Ōsaka* (1615) and defeated *Ōno Harufusa's* army. In 1639, he made over to his son *Mitsutaka*, the administration of his domains and retired to *Komatsu*, whence the name *Komatsu-Chūnagon* which is often given to him. — Up to the Restoration, his descendants lived at *Kanazawa* (*Kaga* — 1,027,000 k.). — To-day, Marquis.

(*b*) — Junior branch, resided from 1639 to 1868 at *Daishōji* (*Kaga* — 100,000 k.). — To-day Viscount.

(*c*) — Junior branch, which resided from 1639 to 1868 at *Toyama* (*Etchū* — 100,000 k.). —-To-day Count. — After the Restoration, a branch of this family received the title of Baron.

(*d*) — Branch that from 1616 to 1868 resided at *Nanukaichi* (*Kōzuke* — 10,000 k.). —-To-day Viscount.

(*e*) —— **Toshimasa,** 利 政 . Third son of *Toshiie*, received from the hands of *Hideyoshi* the fief of *Nanao* (*Noto* — 215,000 k.) ; having taken side against *Ieyasu*, in 1600, he was deprived of his domains which returned to his eldest brother.

Maeda, 前 田 . Ancient *daimyō* family, issued from the *Fujiwara*, or, according to others, from the *Sugawara* and allied to the above family.

—— **Munehisa,** 宗 向 (1539-1602). Was first a bonze on the *Hiei-zan*, then adhered to *Oda Nobunaga* and was called *Gen-i* 玄 以 , *Gen-i Hō-in* 玄 以 法 印 (hence the name of *Ghenifoin* or *Guenifoin*, which was given him in the letters of the old missionaries), *Mimbukyō hō-in*, *Tokuzen-in Gen-i*. When *Nobutada* was attacked in the palace of *Nijō* by *Akechi Mitsuhide* (1582) he confided his son *Sambōshi-maru* (*Hide-nobu*) to *Munehisa*, who conducted him to *Gifu* and then to *Kiyosu*. *Hideyoshi*, having become *Kwampaku*, chose *Gen-i* as one of the 5 *bugyō* and gave him the fief of *Yakami* (*Tamba* — 50,000 k.). When the emperor *Go-Yōzei* and the ex-emperor *Ōgimachi* came to visit *Hideyoshi* in his new palace of *Jūrakutei* (1588), *Munehisa* had to regulate and prepare all the details of the reception : he studied with the utmost care the rules of the ceremonial adopted when the emperors *Go-Komatsu* and *Go-Hanazono* formerly visited the *Ashikaga Shōgun*, adapted it to the present circumstances and succeeded to the satisfaction of everybody. Named governor (*shoshidai*) of *Kyōto*, he embellished the city at the same time as he rendered it more healthy. Being obliged to search for the Christians of the capital, he endeavored to arrest only as few as possible, say the ancient Jesuits ; whilst the Japanese authors attribute to him the first idea of obliging those arrested to tread under foot the holy images in order to discover those who belonged to the forbidden religion — a process that was used with so much rigor under the *Tokugawa*. In 1600, feigning sickness, he was able to abstain from rejoining *Ieyasu*, without entering openly into the party of *Ishida Kazushige*, and could keep his domains. — *Munehisa* had two sons who were baptised in 1595, the elder one *Hidenori Sakon*, (1577-1602) under the name of Paul, and the other, *Munetoshi*, under the name of Constantine. This latter inherited the fief of *Yakami*, but, in 1608, he showed signs of insanity and was deposed.

Mae-ga-take, 前 嶽 . Mountain (2,800 m.) between *Kai* and *Shinano*.

Maejima, 前 嶋 . Family that came from *Echigo* and received a title of nobility in 1903. — To-day Baron.

Magari no sato, 釣 里 . In *Ōmi* An ancient castle belonging to the *Sasaki*. In 1487, the *Shōgun Yoshihisa* besieged *Takayori* therein ; during the siege, he took sick and died at the age of 25 (1489).

Maizuru, 舞 鶴 . Seaport (8,500 inh.) of the province of *Tango*. Since 1899, the seat of a maritime prefecture (*Chinjufu*). Formerly called *Tanabe* (See that name).

Maizuru, 舞 鶴 . Former name of the city of *Yonezawa* (*Uzen*).

Maki, 萬 喜 . Ancient family of *daimyō* that resided at *Maki* (*Kazusa* — 100.000 k.) in the 16th century. Was deprived of its possessions by *Hideyoshi* in 1590.

Maki, 眞木. A *samurai* family of the *Saga* (*Hizen*) clan, made noble after the Restoration. — At present Baron.

Makimuku, 纒向. In *Yamato*, was the residence of the Imperial Court under the rule of *Suinin* (29 B.C. — 70 A. D.) and of *Keikō* (71-130).

Makimura, 槇村. A *samurai* family of the *Yamaguchi* (*Suwō*) clan, made noble after the Restoration. — To-day Baron.

Makino, 牧野. A *daimyō* family that came from *Mikawa* and descended from *Takechi-uchi no Sukune*.

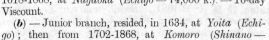

Narisada-Yasunari 1526-1567 1555-1609 { Tadanari { Mitsunari -Tadanari -Tadatoki (a) / Yasunari -Yasumichi-Yasushige (b) / Sadanari -Tadakiyo -Tadataka (c) / Narinori -Narisada -Nariharu -Narinaka (d)

(*a*) — Senior branch, resided successively : in 1590, at *Tako* (*Kōzuke*) ; in 1616, at *Nagamine* (*Echigo*) ; then from 1618-1868, at *Nagaoka* (*Echigo* — 74,000 k.). — To-day Viscount.

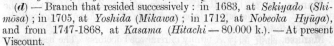

(*b*) — Junior branch, resided, in 1634, at *Yoita* (*Echigo*) ; then from 1702-1868, at *Komoro* (*Shinano* — 15,000 k.). — To-day Viscount.

(*c*) — Junior branch which, from 1634-1868, resided a *Mineyama* (*Echigo* — 11,000 k.). — At present Viscount.

(*d*) — Branch that resided successively : in 1683, at *Sekiyado* (*Shimōsa*) ; in 1705, at *Yoshida* (*Mikawa*) ; in 1712, at *Nobeoka Hyūga*, and from 1747-1868, at *Kasama* (*Hitachi* — 80.000 k.). — At present Viscount.

Makino, 牧野. *Daimyō* family from *Mikawa ;* installed in 1644 at *Sekiyado* (*Shimōsa*), it was transferred in 1668 to *Tanabe* (*Tango* — 35,000 k.) where it remained till the Restoration. — At present Viscount.

Makita, 蒔田. *Daimyō* family, which, before the Restoration, resided at *Asao* (*Bitchū* — 10,000 k.). — To-day Viscount.

Maku-bugyō, 幕奉行. Under the *Tokugawa*, an official whose duty it was to see to the making and the preservation of tents, curtains, etc. This office, created in 1637, had at first only one titulary ; later on, it had two.

Makura no sōshi, 枕草紙. A classical work in 12 volumes, written at the end of the 10th century by *Sei Shōnagon*, a Court lady.

Makyū, 媽宮 (Chin.: *Makung*). The chief port of the Pescadores.

Mameto no watashi, 摩兔戸渡. In former times, a ford of the *Kisogawa* from *Owari* province into that of *Mino*. During the war of *Shōkyū*, (1221), the imperial army was defeated at that place by *Hōjō Yoshitoki's* men.

Mamiya Rinzō, 間宮林藏 (1781-1845). From *Hitachi*, was commanded in 1805, to explore with *Matsuda Denjūrō*, the island of *Karafuto* (*Saghalien*). Thence, he passed into Eastern Siberia and returned, via China. He has published an illustrated account of his travels. He was the first Japanese who had ever penetrated into Siberia.

Mampuku-ji, 萬福寺. A temple built in 1661, near *Uji* (*Yamashiro*), by the Chinese bonze *Ingen*, who established therein the *Ōbaku* branch of the *Zen* sect. It is to the present day the principal seat of the sect and is also called *Ōbaku-san*. The architecture of the temple and its dependencies, in the purest Chinese style, differs considerably from any Japanese construction. *Ingen's* first successors were likewise Chinese bonzes. Among the great benefactors of the temple, we may mention the ex-emperor *Go-Mi-no-o* and the *Shōgun Tsunayoshi*.

Manabe, 間部. A *daimyō* family from *Mikawa*, descended from *Fujiwara Takafusa*.

— **Norifusa,** 詮房. The first raised to the rank of a *daimyō* (1707), receiving, in 1710, the fief of *Takasaki* (*Kōzuke* — 50,000 k.). — The family was transferred in 1717 to *Murakami* (*Echigo*), and, in 1720, to *Sabae* (*Echizen*), where it remained to the time of the Restoration. — To-day Viscount.

— **Norikatsu,** 詮勝 (1802-1884). *Rōchū*, was sent to *Kyōto* in Oct. 1858 by the *Tairō Ii Naosuke*, in order to defend the political views of the *Bakufu* and the conclusion of the treaties. He was successful in his endeavors to obtain the imperial sanction and to check the enemies of the shogunate; but after the assassination of the *Tairō*, he saw his revenues reduced to 40,000 k.

Man-an, 萬安 (1591-1654). Bonze of the *Zen-shū* sect; at the request of *Nagai Naomasa*, *daimyō* of *Yodo* (*Yamashiro*), he rebuilt the temple of *Kōshō-ji*.

Manase, 曲直瀬. A family of renowned doctors. The best known are: *Dōsan* 道三 (1506-1594), named also *Shōkei* 正慶, who was a Christian (baptised in December 1584, at *Kyōto*, his example was soon after followed by 800 of his pupils); *Shōrin* 正琳 (+ 1601), *Gensaku* 玄朔 (1551-1633), *Genkan* 玄鑑 (+ 1626), *Gen-en* 玄淵 (1636-1686), *Shōchin* 正珍 (1644-1728).

Mandokoro, 政所. Central Administration under the Shōgunate. In 1184, *Yoritomo* had created the *Kumonjo* at *Kamakura;* he afterwards changed its name to *Mandokoro* (1191). *Ōe Hiromoto* was its *Bettō* (president), *Fujiwara Yukimasa*, its *Rei* (vice-president), *Fujiwara Toshinaga* and *Nakahara Mitsuie* were its secretaries with the titles of *Anshu* 案主 and *Chikaji* 知家事 and all the orders emanating from the *Mandokoro* bore the seal of these four officials. Later on, the *Shikken* and the *Rensho* alone sealed these documents. The titles of *Anshu* and *Chikaji* were for a long time hereditary in the families of *Sugeno* and *Kiyowara*. — Under the Shōgunate of *Ashikaga*, the title of *Bettō* was suppressed, the president was called *Shitsuji*, and his substitute, *Shitsujidai*. — The name *Mandokoro* became also a title of honor: the *Kwampaku's* wife was called *Kita no Mandokoro*, and his mother *Ō-Mandokoro*.

Man-en, 萬延. *Nengō:* 1860.

Mangwan-ji, 滿願寺. A temple built at *Nikkō* in 810 by a pupil of *Shōdō-Shōnin*, *Kyōbin*, who became its first superior (818). It

Marune. 353

became the principal temple of *Nikkō*, and its chief bonzes were named by the Emperor. This rank was abolished in 1421, and then again re-established in 1614 and given to the famous *Tenkai*. In 1654, the second son of the emperor *Go-Mi-no-o*, *Shijō-shinnō*, became its superior; the temple was named *Rinnō-ji*, and the *Tendai* sect made thereof its principal house. From that time, its superior has always been a prince of royal blood, who was called *Rinnōji no Miya*. *Shijō-shinnō's* 12th successor, *Kōgen-hōshinnō*, was secularised and is known as prince *Kitashirakawa*. In 1871, the temple took its former name of *Mangwan-ji*, only to be renamed in 1884, *Rinnō-ji*. At the present day, it has lost much of its original splendor.

Manji, 萬治. *Nengō* : 1658-1660.

Manju, 萬壽. *Nengō* : 1024-1027.

Mannen-tsūhō, 萬年通寳. Copper money made in 760, under the reign of *Junnin-tennō*. It was valued at $\frac{1}{10}$th of the *Taihei-gempō*, a silver money piece struck at the same time.

Man-yō-shū, 萬葉集. (Lit.: collection of 10,000 leaves). A compilation of old poems, made towards 750 by *Tachibana no Moroe*. It contains over 4,000 pieces, mostly *tanka* (piece of poetry of 31

MANNEN TSŪHŌ.

syllables), much esteemed by connoisseurs, and constitutes at the present day a most precious source of philological, historical and archeological information.

Marishi-ten, 摩利支天 (sanskr. *Mâritchi*). In Brahmanic style, the personification of light; the same as *Krishna*. In the Chinese and Japanese Buddhistic style, Queen of Heaven, who resides in one of the stars of the Great Bear. She is represented as having eight arms, two of which carry the emblems of the sun and moon. — Some authors explain this name as a Chinese transcription of the name of the holy Virgin Mary.

Marubashi Chūya, 九橋忠彌. *Samurai* of *Yamagata* (*Dewa*) who called himself son of *Chōsokabe Motochika*. After more than 30 years, to avenge the death of his father, he came to *Edo* and plotted with *Yui Shōsetsu* against the *Shōgun Ietsuna* (1651). Both were to provoke an uprising, *Shōsetsu* at *Sumpu* (*Shizuoka*), and *Chūya* at *Edo*. But the plot was discovered : *Chūya* was arrested and crucified at *Shinagawa*

Marugame, 九龜. City (25,000 inh.) of *Sanuki*. Ancient castle, belonging successively to the *daimyō Ikoma* (1587), *Yamazaki* (1641), then from 1658-1863, *Kyōgoku* (50,000 k.).

Marumo Chikayoshi, 九毛親吉. *Daimyō* of *Fukuzuka* (*Mino* — 20,000 k.), who, having taken side against *Ieyasu* (1600), was besieged in his castle by *Ichibashi Nagakatsu*, deprived of his possessions and banished to *Kaga*.

Marune, 九根. In *Owari*. There, *Nobunaga* built a castle (1559) which he confided to *Sakuma Morishige* : the latter was besieged therein and defeated, the following year, by *Matsudaira Motoyasu*, vassal of *Imagawa Yoshimoto*.

Maruoka, 丸岡. In *Echizen*. An ancient castle, the residence of the *daimyō Aoyama* (1583), *Honda* (1600), then from 1695-1868, *Arima* (50,000 k.).

Maruyama Ōkyo, 圓山應舉 (1733-1795). Renowned painter. Born in *Tamba*, he came to *Kyōto* and took lessons from *Ishida Yūtei*, of the school of *Kanō*. Later on, putting aside the conventional principles admitted till then, he attempted a reform based on the faithful observation of nature. He established a school called *Maruyama-ryū* or *Enzan-ryū*, the principal representatives of which were *Gessen*, *Mori Sosen*, etc.

Masahito-shinnō. 誠仁親王 (1552-1586). Son of the emperor *Ōgimachi* and father of *Go-Yōzei*. He received the posthumous names of *Dajō-tennō* and *Yōkō-in* at the accession of his son (1587).

Masaki, 松前. In *Iyo*. Was in the 14th century the residence of the family of *Gōda*, which, having attached itself to the southern dynasty, was defeated and ejected by the *Kōno*. After the ruin of the *Kōno*, *Hideyoshi* gave this place to *Katō Yoshiaki* (1595), who in 1602, transferred his residence to *Matsuyama*.

Masa-ko, 政子 (1157-1225). Daughter of *Hōjō Tokimasa*, she married *Minamoto Yoritomo*, when this latter left *Izu* to go and fight the *Taira* (1180), and was the mother of *Yoriie* and of *Sanetomo*. At the death of her husband (1199), she had her head shaved and governed in the name of her son. After the assassination of *Sanetomo* (1219), she named *Shōgun Fujiwara Yoritsune* a child of two years, and continued to govern with her brother *Shikken Yoshitoki*. The nation has surnamed her *Ama-Shōgun* and *Ni-i no Zenni*.

Masuda Nagamori, 増田長盛 (1545-1615). Born at *Masuda* in *Owari*, he served *Hideyoshi* who chose him as one of the 5 *bugyō* and in 1594, gave him the fief of *Kōriyama* (*Yamato* — 200,000 k.). Having sided against *Ieyasu* in 1600, he was banished to the *Kōya-san*, then to *Iwatsuki* (*Musashi*). Before besieging *Ōsaka*, (1615), *Ieyasu* wished to entrust him with a threatening letter for *Hideyori*, but *Nagamori* refused to take it, and, as his son *Moritsugu* had enlisted in the army of *Ōsaka*, he was invited to perform *harakiri*. *Moritsugu* was enabled to escape and became *kerai* of the *Tōdō daimyō* of *Tsu* (*Ise*).

Masu-kagami, 増鏡. A great historical work, whose author is unknown, covers a period from *Go-Toba* (1184) to *Go-Daigo* (1333).

Masuyama, 増山. *Daimyō* family from *Shimotsuke*, descended from *Fujiwara Uona*. Made noble in 1647, they resided successively: in 1659, at *Nishio* (*Mikawa* — 20,000 k.); in 1663, at *Shimodate* (*Hitachi*); then from 1702-1868, at *Nagashima* (*Ise* — 20,000 k.). — At present Viscount.

Matsudaira, 松平. Village in *Mikawa* province. In 1368, *Minamoto Chikauji*, a descendant in the 11th generation of *Yoshiie*, married the daughter of *Matsudaira Nobushige* in that place, established himself there and transmitted to his progeny the name of *Matsudaira*.

Matsudaira, 松平. Patronymic name of a certain number of families, related to the *Tokugawa,* most of them descending from *Yasuchika,* son of *Chikauji* (+ 1407).

```
                        ┌Nobutada ┌Kiyoyasu              (Tokugawa)
                        │         │Nobutada              (Miki)
                        │         └Yasutaka -Yasusada    (Udono)
                        │Chikamori -Chikatsugu           (Fukama)
              ┌Nagachika│Nobusada -Kiyosada -Ietsugu     (Sakurai)
              │         │Yoshiharu -Ietada -Tadayoshi    (Tōjō)
              │         └Toshinaga -Nobukazu -Nobuyoshi  (Fujii)
     ┌Chikatada│                     ┌Norikatsu -Chikanori (Ogyū)
     │         │Norimoto -Norimasa   └Chikakiyo -Chikamasa (Ogyū)
     │         │Chikanaga                                 (Iwazu)
     │         └Norikiyo -Noritō -Masanori -Masatake     (Takiwaki)
     │         ┌Moriie -Morichika -Chikayoshi-Tōgorō -Kiyoyoshi (Takeya)
Yasuchika     │Okitsugu -Sadatsugu -Chikatada -Iehiro -Ietada   (Katahara)
     │Nobumitsu│Mitsushige -Nobusada -Chikamitsu-Kazumitsu -Masachika (Okusa)
     │         │Motoyoshi┌Genshin -Nobunaga -Tadatsugu -Kagetada (Goyu)
     │         │         └Tadakage -Tadasada -Yoshikage -Koretada (Fukamizo)
     │         │Mitsutada -Shigechika-Shigeyoshi -Shigekatsu -Shigetada (Nomi)
     │         └Nobushige -Nobutsugu-Nobumune -Nobunao  (Nagasawa)
     └Nobuhiro -Nagakatsu -Katsushige-Nobushige -Yasukuni -Yasuhiro (Yoda)
```

The other branches of the family were those of *Ōkōchi, Okudaira, Ochi, Matsui;* besides these, two issued from the *Tokugawa* of *Owari,* one from *Kii,* four from *Mito* and the *Takatsukasa* branch (for details, see further on).

Lastly, during the *Edo* shōgunate, the *Tokugawa* conceded to a certain number of noble families (*Maeda, Date, Kuroda, Asano, Nabeshima, Mōri, Ikeda, Hachisuka, Yamanouchi,* etc.) the priviledge of using the name of *Matsudaira,* and in the *daimyō* armory (*bukan*), we can see 52 families bearing that name. There are even 27 at present, of which 1 is a Marquis, 3 are Counts, 22 are Viscounts and 1 is a Baron.

Matsudaira (Echizen-ke), 松平越前家. A family issued from *Hideyasu,* 2nd son of *Ieyasu.*

—— **Hideyasu,** 秀康 (1574-1607). Was brought up by *Hideyoshi,* and took part in his campaign in *Kyūshū* against the *Shimazu* (1587). In 1590, *Yūki Harumoto, daimyō* of *Shimōsa,* having no children, asked *Hideyoshi* to get him an adoptive son; *Hideyoshi* selected *Hideyasu,* who, from that moment, bore the name of *Yūki* and entered into possession of the fief of *Yūki* (100,000 k.). In 1600, he accompanied his father in the war against *Uesugi Kagekatsu,* then assisted at the battle of *Sekigahara,* after which he received the daimyate of *Kita-no-shō* (*Echizen* — 670,000 k.). He died at the age of 33, leaving 5 sons, whose descendants formed the 8 branches of *Matsudaira* of *Echizen.*

Hideyasu					
Tadanao	-Mitsunaga	-Nobutomi	-Asagorō	-Nobuhiro	(a)
Tadamasa	Masachika	-Tsunamasa	-Yoshikuni	-Munemasa	(b)
	Mitsumichi-Naokata		-Naotomo	-Naoyuki	(c)
Naomasa	Tsunataka	-Tsunachika-Yoshitō		-Nobufusa	(d)
	Chikayoshi-Chikatoki		-Chikatomo-Chikaakira		(e)
	Takamasa	-Naotaka	-Naokazu	-Naomichi	(f)
Naomoto	-Naonori	-Motochika	-Akinori	-Tomonori	(g)
Naoyoshi	-Naoakira	-Naotsune	-Naozumi	-Naoyasu	(h)

(*a*) — Senior branch. —— **Tadanao, 忠 直** (1595-1650). Succeeded his father in the fief of *Echizen* and ceded to his brother *Naomoto* the name of *Yūki*, which he had borne till then. He was scarcely installed at *Fukui*, when he displeased his *kerai*, who appealed to the *Shōgun*, and *Honda Tomimasa* was named his counsellor. At the siege of *Ōsaka Tadanao* did not arrive at the appointed time; this disposed *Ieyasu* against him, but when he had joined the army, he distinguished himself and defeated *Sanada Yukimura's* troops: he then received the title of *Sangi*. Finding this reward not in proportion with the services rendered, he returned home dissatisfied, led a disorderly life, was deprived of his possessions in 1622, and banished to *Ogiwara* (*Bungo*). — It is believed that he was baptized in 1620, during his stay at *Kanazawa* (*Kaga*), and, if this fact is correct, it no doubt contributed to his disgrace. The fief of *Echizen* passed then into the hands of *Tadamasa*, *Tadanao's* brother.

—— **Mitsunaga, 光 長** (1615-1707). Oldest son of *Tadanao*, was, at the time of his father's disgrace (1622), sent to *Takata* (*Echigo* — 240,000 k.) to take possession of the fief of *Tadamasa*, the latter having been called to *Fukui*. He allowed evil counsellors to direct him, was dispossessed in 1681 on account of his arbitrary administration, and banished to *Matsuyama* (*Iyo*).

—— **Nobutomi, 宣 富**. Adopted son of *Mitsunaga*, received in 1699, the fief of *Tsuyama* (*Mimasaka* — 100,000 k.); his descendants remained in possession till the Restoration. — At present Viscount.

—— After the Restoration a branch of this family received the title of Baron.

(*b*) — Junior branch. —— **Tadamasa, 忠 昌** (1597-1645). Took part in the siege of *Ōsaka*, (1615), from thence he brought 57 heads of his enemies as a trophy. He obtained the fief of *Kawanakajima* (*Shinano* — 150,000 k.), and in 1619 was transferred to *Takata* (*Echigo* — 250,000 k.). When *Tadanao*, the head of the senior branch, was deprived of the daimyate of *Fukui* (1622), *Tadamasa* took his place, and his descendants kept it till the Restoration (320,000 k.).

—— **Yoshinaga** or **Keiei, 慶 永** (1829-1890). The last of his family, played an important role at the time of the Restoration. — At present Marquis.

(*c*) — Junior branch of the above, from 1717 to 1868, resided at *Itoigawa* (*Echigo* — 10,000 k) — At present Viscount.

(*d*) — Branch issued from **Naomasa, 直 政** (1601-1666), third son of *Hideyasu*, resided successively: in 1623, at *Ōno* (*Echizen* — 50,000 k.); in 1633, at *Matsumoto* (*Shinano* — 80,000 k.); then from 1638 to 1868 at *Matsue* (*Izumo* — 186,000 k. — At present Count.

(*e*) — Branch which from 1666 to 1868, resided at *Hirose* (*Izumo* — 30,000 k.). — At present Viscount.

(*f*) — Branch which from 1677 to 1868, resided at *Mori* (*Izumo* — 10,000 k.) — At present Viscount.

(*g*) — Branch issued from **Naomoto, 直基** (1604-1648), 4th son of *Hideyasu*. It resided successively : in 1624, at *Katsuyama*, (*Echizen* — 30,000 k.) ; in 1634, at *Ōno*, (*Echizen* — 50,000 k.) ; in 1644, at *Yamagata* (*Dewa* — 150,000 k.) ; in 1648, at *Himeji* (*Harima*) ; in 1649, at *Murakami* (*Echigo*) ; in 1667, at *Himeji ;* in 1682, at *Hida* (*Bungo*) ; in 1686, at *Yamagata ;* in 1692, *Shiragawa* (*Mutsu*) ; in 1741, at *Himeji ;* in 1749, at *Umayabashi* (*Kōzuke*) ; in 1767, at *Kawagoe* (*Musashi*) ; and from 1863 to 1868, at *Umayabashi* (170,000 k.). — At present Count.

(*h*) — Branch issued from **Naoyoshi, 直良**. 5th son of *Hideyasu*, who resided : in 1624, at *Kinomoto* (*Echizen* — 25,000 k.) ; in 1635, at *Katsuyama* (*Echizen* — 35,000 k.) ; in 1644, at *Ono* (*Eckizen* — 60,000 k.); then from 1682 to 1868, at *Akashi* (*Harima* — 100,000 k.). To-day Viscount.

Matsudaira (**Hisamatsu, 久松**). — See *Hisamatsu*.

Matsudaira (**Ōgyū, 大給**). — Family issued from *Norimoto* (1443-1534), which, residing at *Ōgyū* (*Mikawa*), took the name of that place.

Norimoto-Norimasa { Norikatsu-Chikanori -Sanenori { Ienori -Norinaga { Norihisa (a) / Norimasa (b) / Sanetsugu-Noritsugu-Norimori (c) / Chikakiyo-Chikamasa-Kazunori -Narishige-Tadateru -Terushige (d)

(*a*) — Senior branch —— **Norimasa, 乗正** (1480-1541). Sided with the *Imagawa*.

—— **Sanenori, 眞乗** 1553-1582). After the ruin of the *Imagawa*, offered his services to *Ieyasu*.

—— **Ienori, 家乗** (1561-1600). Received from *Ieyasu*, in 1590, the fief of *Nawa* (*Kōzuke* — 10,000 k.), then, in 1600, that of *Iwamura* (*Mino* — 20,000 k.). — His descendants were successively : in 1638, at *Hamamatsu* (*Tōtōmi*) ; in 1645, at *Tatebayashi* (*Kōzuke* — 50,000 k.) ; in 1661, at *Sakura* (*Shimōsa* — 60,000 k.) ; in 1678, at *Karatsu* (*Hizen*) ; in 1691, at *Toba* (*Shima* — 70,000 k.) ; in 1710, at *Kameyama* (*Ise*) ; in 1717, at *Yodo* (*Yamashiro*) ; in 1723, at *Sakura ;* in 1745, at *Yamagata* (*Dewa*) ; and finally from 1764 to 1868, at *Nishio* (*Mikawa* — 60,000 k.). — At present Viscount.

(*b*) — Branch which established itself, in 1682, at *Komoro* (*Shinano* — 22,000 k.) then from 1702 to 1868, lived at *Iwamura* (*Mino* — 30,000 k.). — This branch was also called *Ishikawa*. — At present Viscount.

(*c*) — Branch issued from **Sanetsugu, 眞次** (1577-1646), brother of *Ienori ;* from 1703, it had settled at *Okudono* (*Mikawa* — 16,000 k.). — To-day Viscount.

(*d*) — Branch which resided successively : in 1601, at *Sannokura* (*Kōzuke*) ; in 1617, at *Nishio* (*Mikawa* — 17,000 k.) ; in 1621, at *Kameyama* (*Tamba* — 20,000 k.) ; in 1634, at *Tsuruzaki* (*Bungo*) ; then, from 1658 to 1868, at *Funai* (*Bungo* — 22,000 k.) — To-day Viscount.

Matsudaira (Fujii, 藤井). Family issued from *Toshinaga* 利長 (+ 1560), which, residing at *Fujii* (*Mikawa*), took the name of that place.

—— **Nobukazu, 信一** (1548-1632). Accompanied *Ieyasu* into *Kwantō*, settled at *Nunokawa* (*Shimōsa*); then, in 1601, was transferred to *Tsuchiura* (*Hitachi* —30,000 k.); in 1617, to *Takasaki* (*Kōzuke* — 50,000 k.), and in 1619, to *Sasayama* (*Tamba*). The two sons of *Nobuyoshi* (1576-1621) became each the head of a branch of the family.

Toshinaga-Nobukazu-Nobuyoshi { Tadakuni -Nobuyuki-Tadayuki   (a)
                                { Tadaharu-Tadaaki -Tadachika   (b)

(*a*) — Senior branch, descended from **Tadakuni**, 忠國 (1597-1659). From *Sasayama*, it was transferred: in 1649, to *Akashi* (*Harima* — 70,000 k.); in 1679, to *Kōriyama* (*Yamato*); in 1685, to *Koga* (*Shimōsa*). In 1693, *Tadayuki* having become insane, was deposed; his son *Nobumichi* was sent to *Niwase* (*Bitchū*), and, in 1697, to *Kami no yama* (*Dewa* — 30,000 k.), where his descendants remained till the Restoration. —At present Viscount.

(*b*) — Junior branch issued from **Tadaharu**, 忠晴 (1598-1669). Resided successively: in 1642, at *Tanaka* (*Suruga* — 18,000 k.); in 1644, at *Kakegawa* (*Tōtōmi* — 28,000 k.); in 1648, at *Kameyama* (*Tamba*); in 1680, at *Iwatsuki* (*Musashi* — 38,000 k.); in 1697, at *Izushi* (*Tajima*); lastly from 1706 to 1868, at *Ueda* (*Shinano* —53,000 k.). — To-day Viscount.

Matsudaira (Sakurai, 櫻井). — See *Sakurai*.

Matsudaira (Takiwaki, 瀧脇). — Family descended from *Norikiyo*, son of *Chikatada*. From 1704 to 1868, resided at *Kojima* (*Suruga* — 10,000 k.). — Now Viscount.

Matsudaira, (Katahara, 形原). — Family descended from *Okitsugu*, son of *Nobumitsu*, who had settled at *Katahara* (*Mikawa*) and took the name thereof.

—— **Ietada, 家忠** (1547-1582). Took part in *Ieyasu's* campaigns.

—— **Ienobu, 家信** (1569-1638). Went, in 1619, from *Katahara* to *Takatsuki* (*Settsu* — 25,000 k.); then, in 1635, to *Sakura* (*Shimōsa* — 35,000 k.).

—— **Yasunobu, 康信** (1600-1682). Came back, in 1640, to *Takatsuki*; then, in 1649, was called to *Sasayama* (*Tamba* — 50,000 k.). — His descendants resided from 1748 to 1868, at *Kameyama* (*Tamba* — 50,000 k.). — To-day Viscount.

Matsudaira (Fukamizo, 深溝). — Family issued from *Motoyoshi*, whose son, *Tadakage*, stationed at *Fukamizo* (*Mikawa*), took the name of that place.

—— **Yoshikage, 好景** (1511-1556). Fought under *Kiyoyasu* and *Hirotada*, grandfather and father of *Ieyasu*, and was killed in a battle against *Kira Yoshiakira*.

—— **Koretada, 伊忠** (1537-1575). Assisted *Ieyasu* in his campaigns and was killed in a battle fought against *Oyamada Masayuki*, *kerai* of the *Takeda*.

—— **Ietada, 家忠** (1555-1600). Died whilst defending the castle of *Fushimi* against the army of *Ishida Kazushige.*

—— **Tadatoshi, 忠利** (1582-1632). Received in 1601, a revenue of 20,000 k. at *Fukamizo,* then was transferred, in 1612, to *Yoshida* (*Mikawa* — 30,000 k.). — His descendants lived: in 1632, at *Kariya* (*Mikawa*) ; in 1649, at *Fukuchiyama* (*Tamba* — 45,000 k.) ; in 1669, at *Shimabara* (*Hizen* — 70,000 k.) ; in 1749, at *Utsunomiya* (*Shimotsuke*); lastly from 1773 to 1868, at *Shimabara* (70,000 k.). — Now Viscount.

Matsudaira (**Nomi, 能見**). — Family descended from *Mitsuchika,* who took the name of his residence *Nomi* (*Mikawa*).

—— **Shigeyoshi, 重吉** (1498-1580). Served successively *Kiyoyasu, Hirotada,* and *Ieyasu.*

—— **Shigekatsu, 重勝** (1548-1620). Received in 1612, the fief of *Sanjō* (*Echigo* — 20,000 k.) ; he was transferred in 1617, to *Sekiyado* (*Shimōsa* — 20,000 k,), and in 1619 to *Yokosuka* (*Tōtōmi*). — His descendants resided : in 1626 at *Sanda* (*Settsu*) ; in 1630, at *Kami no yama* (*Dewa*); in 1632, at *Takata* (*Bungo*) ; then from 1645 to 1868, at *Kizuki* (*Bungo* — 30,000 k). — Now Viscount.

Matsudaira (**Nagasawa, 長澤**). — A family descended from *Nobushige,* son of *Nobumitsu. Masatsugu,* a descendant of *Nobushige,* adopted *Masatsuna,* son of *Ōkōchi Hidetsuna ;* thence the family took the name of *Ōkōchi.* (See that name).

Matsudaira (**Yoda, 依田**). — Branch issued from *Nobuhiro, Yasuchika's* son. Stationed in 1594, at *Fujioka* (*Kōzuke* — 50,000 k.), it died out in 1625.

Matsudaira (**Ōkōchi, 大河内**). — See *Ōkōchi.*

Matsudaira (**Okudaira, 奥平**). — Branch of the *Okudaira* family. (See that name).

—— **Tadaaki, 忠明** (1583-1644). Son of *Nobumasa,* was adopted by *Ieyasu,* whose grandson he was, and received for himself and his posterity the name of *Matsudaira.* He resided successively : in 1602, at *Sakute* (*Mikawa*) : in 1610, at *Kameyama* (*Ise* — 50,000 k.) ; in 1615, at *Ōsaka* (*Settsu* — 100,000 k.) ; in 1619, at *Kōriyama* (*Yamato* — 120,000 k.) ; in 1639, at *Himeji* (*Harima* — 180,000 k.).

—— **Tadahiro, 忠弘** (1628-1700). Was transferred in 1648 to *Yamagata* (*Dewa* — 150,000 k.) ; in 1668, at *Utsunomiya* (*Shimotsuke*) ; in 1681, at *Shirakawa* (*Mutsu*) ; in 1692, at *Yamagata.*

Tadaaki-Tadahiro { Tadamasa-Tadatoki -Tadahira -Tadakatsu   (a)
             { Tadanao -Tadaakira-Tadatsune-Tadatomi   (b)

(*a*) — Senior branch, which, after the death of *Tadahiro,* resided in 1700, at *Fukuyama* (*Bingo*) ; in 1710, at *Kuwana* (*Ise*) ; in 1823, at *Oshi* (*Musashi* — 100,000 k.). — At present Viscount.

(*b*) — Junior branch, issued from **Tadanao, 忠伺** (1651-1726), which, in 1700, took possession of *Handa* (*Mutsu*), was transferred in 1734 to *Usui* (*Kōzuke*), and, from 1767 to 1868, resided at *Obata* (*Kōzuke* — 20,000 k.). — At present Viscount

Matsudaira (**Matsui, 松井**). — See *Matsui.*

Matsudaira (Hisamatsu, 久松). — Family issued from *Sadatsuna*, third son of *Hisamatsu Sadakatsu* (1569-1623), uterine brother of *Ieyasu*.

—— **Sadatsuna, 定綱** (1592-1651). Third son of *Sadakatsu* and heir to his elder brother *Sadayoshi*, resided first at *Yamakawa* (*Shimōsa*); after the war of *Ōsaka* (1615), he was transferred to *Shimotsuma* (*Hitachi* — 30,000 k.) ; in 1619, to *Kakegawa* (*Tōtōmi* — 55,000 k.) ; in 1625, to *Yodo* (*Yamashiro* — 65,000 k.) ; in 1633, to *Ōgaki* (*Mino* — 85,000 k.) ; in 1634, to *Kuwana* (*Ise* — 100,000 k.). — His descendants resided : in 1710, at *Takata* (*Echigo*) ; in 1741, at *Shirakawa* (*Mutsu*).

—— **Sadanobu, 定信** (1758-1829). 7th son of *Tokugawa* (*Tayasu*) *Munetake*, was adopted by *Matsudaira Sadakuni* and succeeded him in 1783 at *Shirakawa*. He distinguished himself by a wise administration and, in 1787, was named *rōjū*, then *hosa* of the *Shōgun Ienari* (1790). He took henceforth a leading part in the government of the *Bakufu*, and to him the prosperity of the *Kwansei* era (1789-1801) is usually attributed. *Sadanobu* opposed the emperor *Kōkaku* who intended to give his father *Sukehito-shinnō*, the title of *Dajō-tennō*, although he had never reigned (1793). Several times the Russians tried to open communications with the Japanese : they were sent to *Nagasaki*, where they met always with an evasive answer ; moreover, *Sadanobu* had all the coasts inspected with care and forts

MATSUDAIRA SADANOBU.

constructed so as to prevent any attempt at landing. He withdrew from office in 1812, had his head shaved and took the name of *Gaku-ō*. *Sadanobu*, one of the great ministers of the Shōgunate of *Edo*, is also known as a writer ; he left several works. He is often called *Matsudaira Etchū no kami*. In 1823, his son *Sadanaga* was transferred from *Shirakawa* to *Kuwana* (*Ise* — 100,000 k.) where his family resided till the Restoration.

—— **Sadaaki, 定敬**. The last *daimyō* of *Kuwana*, took an important part in the defence of the Shōgunate at the time of the Restoration ; he was degraded in 1868. — His descendants at present bear the title of Viscount.

Matsudaira (Hoshina, 保科). — See *Hoshina*.

Matsudaira (Owari). — Branch issued from *Yoshiyuki*, son of *Yoshinao* (*Owari*) and grandson of *Ieyasu*. They reside, since 1700, at *Takasu* (*Mino* — 30,000 k.). — At present Viscount.

Matsudaira (Owari). — Branch issued from *Yoshimasa*, son of *Yoshinao* (*Owari*) and grandson of *Ieyasu*. Established in 1683, at *Yanagawa* (*Mutsu*), became extinct in 1729.

Matsudaira (Kii). — Branch issued from *Yorizumi*, son of *Yorinobu* (*Kii*) and grandson of *Ieyasu*. From 1670 to 1868, the family resided at *Saijō* (*Iyo* — 30,000 k.). — At present Viscount.

Matsudaira (Mito). — Branch issued from *Yorishige* (1622-1695), son of *Yorifusa* (*Mito*) and grandson of *Ieyasu*. Installed in 1639, at

Shimodate (Hitachi — 30,000 k.), it was transferred in 1642, to *Taka-matsu (Sanuki* — 120,000 k.), where it resided till the Restoration. — At present Viscount.

Matsudaira (Mito). — Branch issued from *Yorimoto*, son of *Yori-fusa (Mito)* and grandson of *Ieyasu.* Since 1700, it resided at *Moriyama (Mutsu* — 20,000 k.). — To-day Viscount.

Matsudaira (Mito). — Branch issued from *Yoritaka*, son of *Yorifusa (Mito)*, and grandson of *Ieyasu.* Since 1700, it resided at *Fuchū* (to-day *Ishioka*) *(Hitachi* — 20,000 k.). — At present Viscount.

Matsudaira (Mito). — Branch issued from *Yorio*, son of *Yorifusa (Mito)* and grandson of *Ieyasu.* Since 1682, it resided at *Shishido (Hitachi* — 10,000 k.). — To-day Viscount.

Matsudaira (Toda, 戸田). — See *Toda.*

Matsudaira (Ochi, 越智). — Branch issued from *Kiyotake* 清武, son of *Tokugawa Tsunashige* and brother of the *Shōgun Ienobu.* It resided successively : in 1706, at *Tatebayashi (Kōzuke* — 50,000 k.); in 1728, at *Tanakura (Mutsu)* , in 1746, at *Tatebayashi;* and from 1836 to 1868, at *Hamada (Iwami* — 60,000 k.). — To-day Viscount.

Matsudaira (Tōjō, 東條). — See *Tokugawa Tadayoshi.*

Matsudaira (Takeda, 竹田). — See *Tokugawa Nobuyoshi.*

Matsudaira (Echigo, 越後). — See *Tokugawa Tadateru.*

Matsudaira (Takatsukasa, 鷹司). — See *Yoshii*

Matsue, 松江. Chief town (34,700 inh.) of the *Shimane-ken* and of the *Izumo* province. Ancient castle built in 1601 by *Horio Yoshiharu* and occupied by his family till 1633. Was then the residence of the *daimyō Kyōgoku* (1634-1638), and, from 1638 to 1863, *Matsudaira* (186,000 k.).

Matsui (Matsudaira), 松井. *Daimyō* family, descended from *Minamoto Tameyoshi* (1096-1156). *Koreyoshi* son of *Tameyoshi*, resided at *Matsui (Yamashiro)* and took the name of the place.

—— **Yasuchika, 康親** (1521-1583). Served *Ieyasu* who authorized him to take the name of *Matsudaira.* Took part in the campaigns against the *Imagawa*, the *Asakura*, the *Asai*, the *Takeda*, and received a revenue of 20,000 k. in *Suruga.*

—— **Yasushige, 康重** (1568-1640). Resided successively : in 1590 at *Yorii (Musashi* — 20,000 k.); in 1601, at *Kasama (Hitachi* — 30,000 k.); in 1608, at *Yamaki (Tamba* — 50,000 k.) ; in 1615, at *Sasa-yama (Tamba)* ; in 1619, at *Kishiwada (Izumi* — 60,000 k.). — His descendants were transferred : in 1640, at *Yamazaki (Harima)* ; in 1649, at *Hamada (Iwami)* ; in 1759, at *Koga (Shimōsa)* ; in 1762, at *Okazaki (Mikawa)* ; in 1769, at *Hamada* (70,000 k.); in 1836, at *Tanakura (Mutsu* — 75,000 k.) and finally, in 1866, at *Kawagoe (Musashi* — 84,000 k.). —At present Viscount.

Matsui, 松井. *Samurai* family of the *Kumamoto (Higo)* clan, whose head was governor of the city of *Yatsushiro* and possessed a revenue of 30,000 k. — At present Baron.

Matsuida, 松井田 or **Matsueda, 松枝.** In *Kōzuke.* Old castle belonging to the *Annaka daimyō*, deserted in 1590.

Matsukata, 松方. *Samurai* family of *Kagoshima* (*Satsuma*), made noble in 1884. — To-day Count.

—— **Masayoshi,** 正義. Born in 1840, was one of the most remarkable politicians of the *Meiji* era. He was several times minister and president of the Council.

Matsuki, 松木. *Kuge* family descended from *Fujiwara Yorimune* (993-1065). — To-day Count.

Matsuki, 松木. Family whose head was chief of the temple of *Gekū* (*Ise*). Made noble in 1885. — At present Baron.

Matsukura, 松倉. In *Etchū*. Old castle built towards the middle of the 14th century by *Fumon Toshikiyo*, of the *Ashikaga* party. Became the property of *Momonoi Naotsune*, then of *Shiina Yasutane* ; *Uesugi Kagetora* captured it and confided it to the custody of *Kawada Buzen no kami*, who was besieged therein and defeated by *Shibata Katsuie* (1579).

Matsukura, 松倉. *Daimyō* family from *Yamato* and descended from the *Fujiwara*.

—— **Nobushige,** 信重 (1522-1586). Served the *Tsutsui* of *Iga*.

—— **Shigemasa,** 重政 (1574-1630). Sided with *Hideyoshi* who gave him the castle of *Futami* (*Harima*) (1587). He was transferred in 1600, to *Gojō* (*Yamato* — 25,000 k.) then in 1615, to *Shimabara* (*Hizen* — 60,000 k.). In 1624, some of his ships were carried by the wind towards the South and landed at Luzon : the sailors entered into communication with the inhabitants of the island and made some exchanges, then returned to *Hizen* and gave an account of it to their *daimyō*, *Shigemasa*, who told them to return to Luzon and to obtain all the information they could on these islands, and then asked at *Edo* the permission to lead an expedition against the Philippines, boasting that he would be as successful as the *Satsuma-daimyō*, *Shimazu Iehisa*, who, some 20 years before, conquered the *Ryūkyū*. The *Shōgun Iemitsu* seems to have given his consent to this foolish entreprise, but the death of *Shigemasa* hindered its realisation.

—— **Shigeharu,** 重治 (+ 1638). His tyranny towards his vassals, caused the insurrection of *Shimabara*. After the repression of the revolt he was dispossessed and banished to· *Tsuyama* (*Mimasaka*), where a message from the *Shōgun* came to invite him to commit *harakiri*. His son *Shigetoshi* was then banished to *Takamatsu* (*Sanuki*).

Matsumae, 松前. In *Oshima* (*Hokkaidō*). Old castle built in 1601, by *Matsumae Yoshihiro*, where the family resided till the Restoration. Was besieged in 1869, by *Enomoto Takeaki*, commander of the *Shōgun's* fleet. The same year, the name of the city was changed to *Fukuyama*.

Matsumae, 松前. *Daimyō* family from *Wakasa* and descended from the *Takeda*.

—— **Nobuhiro,** 信廣. Son of *Takeda Kuninobu*, in 1442, settled in *Ezo*, where he helped the governor *Kakizaki Shuri-tayū*, to repress the uprising of the *Ebisu*, married his daughter and took the name of *Kakizaki*.

—— **Suehiro, 季廣**. *Nobuhiro's* great-grandson, made laws for the *Ebisu*, encouraged them to commercial entreprises, etc.; he may be considered the first colonizer of *Ezo*.

—— **Yoshihiro, 慶廣** (1550-1618). *Suehiro's* son, submitted to *Hideyoshi* in 1587. He built in the district of *Matsumae*, a castle which he named *Fukuyama-jō*, and changed his name from *Kakizaki* to *Matsumae*. He continued the work of colonization which his father had begun and favored the immigration of the other provinces of Japan into *Ezo*.

—— **Akihiro, 章廣**. Not having been able to prevent an incursion of the Russians into the island, he was transferred to *Yanagawa* (*Mutsu*) (1807).

—— **Sadahiro, 定廣**. In 1821, returned to *Matsumae*, where his family resided till the Restoration (30,000 k.). — Now Viscount.

—— After the Restoration, a junior branch received the title of Baron.

Matsumine, 松嶺. Small city of *Ugo*, formerly called *Matsuyama* (See that word).

Matsumoto, 松本. Town (31,400 inh.) of *Shinano*. Was formerly the seat of a provincial governor and was called *Fukashi* (See that name). Under the *Tokugawa*, *Fukashi* became *Matsumoto* and was successively the residence of the *daimyō Ishikawa* (1583), *Ogasawara*, (1613), *Toda* (1617), *Matsudaira* (1633), *Hotta* (1638), *Mizuno* (1642), then from 1725-1868, *Toda* (60,000 k.). — Near *Matsumoto*, are the ruins of the castles of *Hayashi* and *Igawa*, where the *Ogasawara*, governors of the province, resided during the Middle Ages.

Matsumura, 松村. *Samurai* family from the *Kagoshima* (*Satsuma*) clan, made noble after the Restoration. — At present Baron.

Matsumura Gekkei, 松村月溪 (1742-1811). Founder of the *Shijō* School of Painting at *Kyōto*. Also called *Goshun*. — His brother *Keibun* 景文 (1780-1844) continued his traditions.

Matsunaga Hisahide, 松永久秀 (1510-1577). Also called *Danjō*. Vassal of the *Miyoshi*, he sided in 1529 with *Chōkei*, entered with him into *Kyōto* (1549) became governor of that city, fought against the *Sasaki*, who supported the *Shōgun Yoshiteru* (1558), pacified the province of *Izumi* and constructed the castle of *Shiki* (*Kawachi*) (1560), from which place he governed the provinces of *Yamato* and *Kawachi*. He then received the title of *Danjō-shōsuke* (whence his surname of *Danjō*). In 1563, he poisoned *Miyoshi Yoshioki*, son of *Chōkei*, and had *Yoshitsugu* declared his heir. Two years later, the *Shōgun Yoshiteru* having refused to name him *Kwanryō* in the place of *Chōkei*, who had died the year before, *Hisahide* with his son *Hisamichi*, came to attack the palace of *Nijō* and *Yoshiteru* killed himself. *Hisahide* then named a child of two years *Shōgun* and ruled as he pleased. Soon after, a war broke out between himself and *Miyoshi Yoshitsugu*, but being attacked at the same time by *Sasaki Yoshikata*, he made peace with *Yoshitsugu*. In 1568, he submitted to *Nobunaga* who named him governor (*shugo*) of the province of *Yamato*. A little later (1572), uniting his forces with those of *Yoshitsugu*, he revolted; defeated by *Nobunaga*, he abandoned his ally and thus contributed to the destruction of the *Miyoshi*. In 1577, he was contemplating a new revolt ; this time, *Nobunaga* sent his son *Nobutada* and *Tsutsui Junkei* to besiege him in his castle of *Shiki*. The castle was burned and *Hisahide* killed himself.

Matsu-no-o-yama 松尾山. Hill near the village of *Sekigahara* (*Mino*). In 1564, *Nobunaga* stationed *Fuwa Mitsuharu* on it, to oppose the *Asai* and the *Rokkaku*. At the battle of *Sekigahara*, the army of *Kobayakawa Hideaki* was stationed at that place (1600) : seeing *Ieyasu's* side would be victorious, he suddenly went over to him, entered the plain, defeated the troops of *Ōtani Yoshitaka*, and thus decided the fate of the battle.

Matsunoshima, 松嶋. In *Ise*. Was formerly called *Hosokubi*. Towards 1560, *Kitabatake Tomonori* built a castle there which was later on occupied by his son-in-law and heir *Oda Nobuo*. *Hideyoshi* gave it to *Gamō Ujisato*, who having taken up his residence in the castle of *Matsusaka* abandoned *Matsunoshima*.

Matsuoka 松岡. In *Settsu*. *Ashikaga Takauji*, defeated at *Uchidehama* by his brother *Tadayoshi* (1351), took refuge in the castle of *Matsuoka*, with the intention of killing himself ; but as peace was concluded, he returned to *Kyōto*.

Matsuoka, 松岡. In *Hitachi*. From 1622 to 1868, the residence of the *daimyō Nakayama* (25,000 k.).

Matsuo-matsuri, 松尾祭. The Shintoist temple of *Matsuo* (*Matsuo-jinja*), founded in 701, is situated in the western part of *Kyōto*. They venerate *Ōyamagui* and *Itsukushima-hime* in it. The annual feast of the temple begins in the 4th month on the day of the monkey, and lasts a full month. Later on, a second feast, celebrated in the 11th month, was added to the first one.

Matsuo-saki, 松尾崎. Cape N. of *Awaji* island.

Matsuo-saki. 松尾崎. Cape, S. of *Tosa*.

Matsurigoto-bito 判官. In certain administrations, an official below the *Suke*. When two, the first was called *Ōi-matsurigoto-bito* and the second, *Sunai-matsurigoto-bito*.

Matsusaka, 松坂. In *Ise*. Ancient castle built in 1570, by *Seta Chōsuke*, vassal of the *Kitabatake*. *Hideyoshi* gave it to *Gamō Ujisato* (1582) ; *Furuta Shigekatsu* succeeded him in that place (1590). In 1619, it belonged to the *Tokugawa* of *Kii*, and till the Restoration, it was left in the custody of a *jōdai*.

Matsushima, 松嶋. Archipelago, in the bay of the same name N.E. of *Sendai* (*Rikuzen*), composed of 800 small picturesque pine-clad islands. It is one of the three most renowned views (*san-kei*) of Japan.

Matsushiro, 松代. Town (8000 inh.) of *Shinano*. Ancient castle formerly called *Kaizu-jō*. Was the residence of the *daimyō Kiyono*. *Takeda Shingen* rebuilt it in 1537, and confided it to *Oyamada Bitchū no kami*. After the ruin of the *Takeda*, (1582), *Nobunaga* offered it to *Mori Nagakazu*. Under the *Tokugawa*, it belonged first to the domains of the *Shōgun*, then from 1622-1868, it became the residence of the *Sanada daimyō* (100,000 k.).

Matsushita, 松下. *Daimyō* family descended from *Sasaki Yasutsuna* and which took its name from a village of *Mikawa* where it was at first stationed.

—— **Yukitsuna,** 之綱. Lord of *Zudaji* (*Tōtōmi*), was *Hideyoshi's* first master. Once *Kwampaku*, the latter extended to the children and grandchildren the favors he was no more able to bestow on his former lord, *Yukitsuna* having died before that time.

—— **Yoshitsuna.** 吉綱 (1537-1598). *Yukitsuna's* son, served *Hideyoshi* who bestowed on him a revenue of 10,000 k. at *Kunō* (*Tōtōmi*,) with the title of *Iwami no kami*.

—— **Shigetsuna,** 重綱 (1580-1628). Resided at *Nihommatsu* (*Mutsu* — 30,000 k.)

—— **Nagatsuna,** 長綱. Son of *Shigetsuna*, was transferred to *Miharu* (*Mutsu*) at the death of his father and, in 1645, dispossessed on account of his excesses.

Matsushita Zenni 松下禪尼. Daughter of *Adachi Kagemori*, *Akitajō no suke*, wife of *Hōjō Tokiyuki* and mother of *Tokiyori*.

Matsuura 松浦. *Daimyō* family of *Hizen*, descended, according to some, from *Abe Yoritoki*, and according to others, from *Minamoto Tōru*, son of the emperor *Saga*. The latter say that *Minamoto Hisashi*, great-grandson of *Tōru*, settled in the district of *Matsuura* (*Hizen*) and took its name. *Yoshi* then would be his descendant to the 18th generation.

—— **Yoshi,** 義. At the time of the assassination of the *Shōgun Yoshinori*, (1441) shaved his head and built a temple at *Hirado* (*Hizen*), where he lived in retirement.

—— **Shigenobu,** 鎮信 (1549-1614). Son of *Takanobu*, followed *Hideyoshi* in his campaign against *Satsuma* (1587). Two years later, he shaved his head and took the name of *Sōsei-Hōin*. He fought in *Korea* under *Konishi Yukinaga*, and assisted *Kobayakawa Takakage* in defeating a Chinese army.

Takanobu-Shigenobu { Hisanobu-Atsunobu-Arinobu (a)
{ Masashi -Satoshi -Chikashi (b)

(*a*) —— Senior branch. —— **Atsunobu,** 篤信 (+ 1637). Through the care of his mother, a daughter of Barthélemy *Ōmura Sumitada*, he received baptism in his childhood, but, later on, far from keeping his faith, he became a persecutor of the Christians. His descendants resided, up to the time of the Restoration, at *Hirado* (*Hizen* — 60,000 k.) —— Now Count.

(*b*) —— Junior branch installed at *Katsumoto* (*Iki* — 10,000 k.). —— Now Viscount.

Matsuura Sayohime, 松浦佐用姫. Wife of *Ōtomo Sadehiko*. When her husband was sent to *Korea* to fight against *Shiragi*, (536) *Sayohime* ascended a mountain of the district of *Matsuura* (*Hizen*), gazed for a long time after the vessel that was carrying away her husband, and not being able to tear herself away from that place, died on the mountain and was changed into a stone, says the legend.

Matsuyama, 松 山   In *Yamato.* Ancient castle, belonging successively to the *daimyō Taga* (1588), *Fukushima* (1600), *Oda* (1615), and was finally abandoned in the year 1695.

Matsuyama, 松 山.   Town (36,600 inh.) in the province of *Iyo.* Ancient castle built in 1603 by *Katō Yoshiaki.* Was, later on, the residence of the *Gamō daimyō* (1627), then, from 1634 to 1868, of *Hisamatsu* (150,000 k.).

Matsuyama, 松 山.   In *Bitchū*   In 1333, *Takahashi Hidemitsu,* named governor of the province, settled in that place. It passed to the *Hosokawa,* then to the *Mōri* (1575), the *Ukita* (1582). Under the *Tokugawa,* it belonged successively to the *daimyō: Kobayakawa* (1600), *Kobori* (1602), *Asano* (1610), *Ikeda* (1617), *Mitsutani* (1639), *Andō* (1695), *Ishikawa* (1711), and from 1744 to 1868 to *Itakura* (55,000 k.). — Since the Restoration, it is called *Takahashi.*

Matsuyama, 松 山.   In *Musashi.* Ancient castle built in the beginning of the 15th century by the *Ueda daimyō.* The *Uesugi* took it in 1488, and the *Hōjō* in 1537; retaken in 1561 by *Uesugi Terutora,* it fell again, the following year, into the hands of the *Hōjō. Ieyasu* gave it in 1591 to *Matsudaira Ichiro;* it was at last abandoned in 1600.

Matsuyama, 松 山.   In *Dewa.* Was from 1647-1868 the residence of the *daimyō Sakai* (25,000 k.). — Is called to-day *Matsumine* 松 嶺.

Matsuzaki Hakkei, 松 崎 白 圭 (1682-1753).   *Samurai* of *Sasayama* (*Tamba*), studied Confucianism first at *Kyōto* under *Itō Tōgai,* then came to *Edo* and followed the teaching of *Ogiu Sorai* and of *Miwa Shissai.* Studied also military art. He wrote several very valuable books.

Matsuzono, 松 園.   Family descended from *Fujiwara Tadamichi* (1097-1164) and formerly attached to the temple of *Kōfuku-ji* (*Nara*). — Now Baron.

Mattō, 松 任.   In *Kaga.* Towards 1570, *Tokuyama Norihide* built a castle there which, in 1582, passed into the hands of *Maeda Toshinaga,* then of *Niwa Nagashige,* to return in 1600 to the *Maeda.* — Also called *Matsutō.*

Maya-Bunin, 摩 耶 夫 人.   Japanese name of the mother of *Shaka.*

Meiji, 明 治.   *Nengō* which began with the Imperial Restoration (1868). The year 1906, is its 39th year. The principal events of this period are:

1868. — Abolition of the *Shōgunate.* — Imperial Restoration.

1869. — *Edo,* chosen capital of the Empire, receives the name of *Tōkyō.* End of the resistance of the *Shōgun's* adherents (*Hakodate,* 25th of June).

1870. — Opening of *Tōkyō* and *Niigata* to foreigners.

1871. — Abolition of the *daimyō's* fiefs and division of Japan into departments.

1872. — Inauguration of the Railroad from *Tōkyō* to *Yokohama* (June 12th). — Law rendering the military service obligatory. — First National Exhibition at *Tōkyō.*

1873. — Adoption of the Gregorian Calendar, — Conflagration of the Imperial palace. — Repeal of the edicts against the Christians. — Erection of the primary schools.

1874. — *Saga's* insurrection. — Expedition to Formosa.

1875. — Japan cedes to Russia her rights to the island of *Saghaline* (*Karafuto*) in exchange for the Kuriles (*Chishima*).

1876. — Treaty with Korea. — Carrying two swords is forbidden. Riots at *Kumamoto* (*Higo*) and at *Hagi* (*Nagato*).

1877. — Insurrection of *Satsuma* (Feb.-Sept.).

1879. — Annexation of the *Ryūkyū* islands (*Okinawa-ken*).

1881. — Promise of a Constitution for the year 1890. — Organization of political parties.

1883. — First streetcars — Establishment of the Official Journal (*Kwampō*).

1884. — Creation of the 5 titles of nobility (*kō, kō, haku, shi, dan*).

1885. — Constitution of the Ministers' Council (*Naikaku*) : 10 Ministries. First Cabinet *Itō*. — Establishment of the *Yusen Kwaisha* S.S. Co.

1887. — The Emperor takes possession of the new Palace, begun in 1882.

1888. — Erection of the Privy Council (*Sūmitsu-in*). — Administration of *Kuroda* (April) — Eruption of the *Bandai-san* (*Iwashiro*) (July).

1889. — Promulgation of the Constitution (Feb. 11th) ; Assassination of Viscount *Mori Arinori*, Minister of Public Instruction. — Interdiction of the duel. — Adm. of *Yamagata* (Dec.).

1890. — First session of Parliament (Nov. 25th).

1891. — Burning of the house of the Senate and the Congress (Jan. 19th). — Attempt of *Tsuda Sanzō* against the life of the Czarowitz (Nicolas II) at *Ōtsu* (May 11th). — Adm. of *Matsukata* (May). — Great earthquake in *Mino, Owari*, etc. (Oct. 28th). — Dissolution of the Chamber (Dec.).

1892. — Second Adm. of *Itō* (Aug.).

1894. — War with China (Aug. 1st). (See for details, *Nisshin-sensō*).

1895. — Treaty of *Shimonoseki* (March 30th), ratified in *Cheefu* (May 8th). Intervention of Russia, France and Germany: retrocession of *Liao-tong* peninsula.

1896. — Erection of an administration (*takushokumu*) in Formosa.— Tidal wave in *Rikuchū* : 35,000 killed (July 2nd). Second Adm. of *Matsukata* (Sept.).

1897. — Death of Queen Dowager (Jan. 11th). — Adoption of the gold standard (Oct. 1st). — Germany occupies *Kiaochao* (Oct. 14th) and Russia, *Port-Arthur* (Dec. 20th).

1898. — 3rd Adm. of *Itō* (Jan.). — Revision of the Civil Code. — Adm. of *Ōkuma* (June). — 2nd Adm. of *Yamagata*.

1899. — The new treaties are put into execution : Japan opened to the world (Aug.).

1900. — Marriage of the Crown Prince (May 10th). — 4th Adm. of *Itō* (Oct.).

1901. — Adm. of *Katsura* (June).

1902. — Treaty of alliance with England.

1904. — War with Russia (Feb.) (For details, see *Nichiro-sensō*).

1905. — New treaty of alliance with England (Aug. 12th). — Peace of Portsmouth (Sept.) Riots in *Tōkyō*.

1906. — Adm. of *Saionji* (Jan.).

Mei-ō, 明應 . *Nengō:* 1492-1500.

Meireki, 明暦 . *Nengō:* 1655-1657.

Meirin-dō, 明倫堂 . Name of Schools existing at the time of the *Shōgun* at *Nagoya, Kanazawa* and *Nagasaki*. — For the two first, see *Shohan-gakkō;* for the 3rd, *Tokugawa-bakufu-gakkō.*

Meitoku, 明德 . *Nengō* during which the schism of the two dynasties ended. For the Northern dynasty it extended from 1390 to 1393 ; the dynasty of the South adopted it after the reconciliation and for the year 1393 only.

Meiwa, 明和 . *Nengō:* 1764-1771.

Men, 面 . Masks used by the performers of *sarugaku, kyōgen,* etc. Also called *omotegata.* The making of the masks became a special branch of art. The most renowned artists in that line were: — in the time of the *Hōjō, Akatsuru, Ryoëmon* and the bonze *Nitsuhyō ;* — under the *Ashikaga, Sankōbō, Iseki, Deinei, Joman ;* — under the *Tokugawa, Kawachi Ieshige.*

Meryō, 馬寮 . Formerly, official dependent on the *Hyōe-fu,* whose duty it was to watch over the food and the harnesses of the horses in the imperial stables. There were two of them : the *sa-meryō,* and the *u-meryō.* This title was hereditary in the family of the *Umakai-obito.*

Metsuke, 目付 . Under the *Tokugawa,* officials whose duty it was to watch over the keeping of the rules. The overseeing of the *daimyō* was made by the *ō-metsuke,* and that of the *hatamoto* by the *metsuke.* Every year, one of them was sent to *Nagasaki* to inspect. In the palace of the *Shōgun,* there were always two of them on watch, in the hall called *Kikyō-no ma.* The *metsuke* were created in 1617, and numbered 16 members. They were under the authority of a *Waka-doshiyori.*

Meyasu-bako, 目安箱 . In 1721, the *Shōgun Yoshimune* ordered a box to be placed in the hall of Council, on the days of audience, to receive the complaints, petitions, observations, etc., of any one who wished to address himself to the central government. The *Shōgun* alone possessed the key of this box, and opened it himself to examine the reclamations.

Mibu, 壬生 . In *Shimotsuke.* Ancient castle built in 1462, by *Mibu Tanenari.* The village, which until then had been called *Ueno-hara,* was named *Mibu.* The *Hōjō* of *Odawara* stormed it towards the middle of the 16th century. Under the *Tokugawa,* it was the residence of the *daimyō Hineno* (1600), *Abe* (1635), *Miura* (1639), *Ōkōchi* (1692), *Katō* (1695), then from 1712 to 1868, *Torii* (30,000 k.).

Mibu, 壬生 . *Kuge* family, descended from *Fujiwara Yorimune* (993-1065). — To-day Count.

Mibu, 壬生. Family descended from the emperor *Suinin* through *Otsuku no Sukune*. Had formerly the superintendence of the *Nijō* house. — At present Baron.

Mibu Tadamine, 壬生忠岑 (867-965). Famous poet. Was one of the compilers of the *Kokinshū*.

Michi-ae no matsuri, 道饗祭. An ancient festival, established to charm away the influence of the evil spirits: it took place in *Kyōto* on the 15th day of the 6th month.

Michi-bugyō, 道奉行. — See *Michigata-gakari*.

Michikata-gakari, 道方掛. In 1659, a *Michi-bugyō* was created whose duty it was to look after the repairing of the streets and roads of the *Shōgun's* capital ; in 1666, a *Jōsui-bugyō* was put in charge of the two aqueducts of the *Tama-gawa* and the *Kanda-gawa*. One hundred years later, these functions were added to those of the *Fushin-bugyō*.

Michinaga-shinnō, 陸良親王 (+ 1360). Son of prince *Morinaga* and grandson of the emperor *Daigo*. Was *Hitachi-taishu* and *Sei-i-tai-shōgun* of the southern dynasty. Fought in *Hitachi*, then in *Tamba* and in *Harima* against the *Ashikaga ;* then sided with the northern dynasty.

Michinoku, 陸奥. Ancient name of the province of *Mutsu*.

Michi-no-omi no mikoto, 道臣命. A descendant of *Takamimusubi no kami*. Was first called *Hi-no-omi no mikoto*. Companion in arms of *Jimmu-tennō*, he took part in his expedition to the East and when the conqueror was stopped in *Kumano* (*Kii*) by the difficulties he encountered in passing into *Yamato*, he made it easy of access by opening roads. It is on that account that *Jimmu* gave him the name of *Michi no omi*. He distinguished himself in the battles of *E-ukashi* and *Yasotakeru*. After the enthronement of *Jimmu* at *Kashiwabara* he was named chief of the *kumebe*, the guards of the imperial residence; the following year, he received grants of lands and the full administration of the war department.

Midō-dono, 御堂殿. Ancient residence of the *Fujiwara Michinaga* (+ 1027) at *Kyōto*. It was at first called *Kyōgoku-dono*, from the part of the city where it was located ; the name *Midō-dono* was given to it after *Michinaga* had built thereon the temple of *Hōshō-ji* (1022). *Michinaga* was called *Midō-kwampaku*. *Ichijō-tennō's* widow, daughter of *Michinaga*, had her palace in the same precincts. There were born the emperors *Go-Ichijō*, *Go-Shujaku* and *Go-Reizei*, and also the four daughters of *Michinaga* who consecutively became empresses. Next to the imperial palace, it was the richest house of *Kyōto*.

Mie-ken, 三重縣. Department formed by the provinces of *Ise*, *Iga*, *Shima* and two districts of *Kii*. — Pop.: 1,051,000 inh. — Chieftown : *Tsu* (32,520 inh.). — Principal cities : *Uji-Yamada* (27,700 inh.), *Yokkaichi* (25,200 inh.), *Kuwana* (20,150), *Ueno* (14,600 inh), *Matsuzaka* (13,000 inh.) etc.

Mihara, 三原. Town (9,500 inh.) of *Bingo*. Ancient castle built in 1549 by *Kobayakawa Takakage*. Passed into the hands of the *Fukushima* (1600), then of the *Asano* (1619).

Mihara-yama, 三原山, Volcano (800 m.) in the island of *Ōshima* (*Izu*).

Miharu, 三春. Small city (7,650 inh.) of *Iwaki*. Ancient castle that belonged successively to the *daimyō : Gamō* (1590), *Katō* (1627), *Matsushita* (1628), then from 1645 to 1868, *Akita* (50,000 k.). In 1868, it was captured by the troops of the *Shirakawa* clan that had joined the imperial cause.

Mii-dera, 三井寺. — See *Onjō-ji*.

Miike, 三池. In *Chikugo*. From 1621 to 1805, was the residence of one of the branches of the *Tachibana* family (10,000 k.).

Mikado, 御門. (Lit.: Noble gate). The Emperor. — This title is especially in use among foreigners: the Japanese say *Tenshi, Tennō,* etc.

Mikado-zukasa, 闈司. Official formerly in charge of the keys of the imperial palace and of the gates of the outside fortifications.

Mikage-hama, 御影濱. In *Settsu. Ashikaga Takauji* and *Kō Moronao* were defeated there by *Ishidō Yorifusa* (1351).

Mikami, 三上. In *Ōmi*. Was, from 1698 to 1868, the residence of the *Endō daimyō* (12,000 k). — *Mikami-yama*, the mountain situated in the neighborhood, is also called *Ōmi no Fuji, Shiojiri-yama, Mukade-yama :* its beauties have often been sung by the poets.

Mikata-ga-hara, 味方原. In *Tōtōmi. Takeda Shingen* was defeated there by *Tokugawa Ieyasu* (1572).

Mikawa, 參河. One of the 15 provinces of the *Tōkaidō.* Contains 10 districts, dependent on *Aichi-ken*. — Chinese name : *Sanshū.* — Is thus called on account of the three rivers that flow through it, the *Toyo-kawa,* the *Yahagi-gawa* and the *Ōhira-gawa.*

Mikawa san bugyō, 參河三奉行. The three vassals of the *Tokugawa,* entrusted with the government of the province of *Mikawa* at the time of *Nobunaga : Honda Shigetsugu, Kōriki Kiyonaga* and *Amano Yasukage.*

Mikazuki, 三日月. In *Harima.* Was from 1697 to 1868, the residence of the *Mōri daimyō* (15,000 k.).

Miki, 三木. In *Harima.* Ancient castle built in 1468 by *Bessho Naganori. Hideyoshi* captured it in 1580.

Miki-zukasa, 造酒司. Formerly an office entrusted with the *sake* (wine made from the rice) destined for the imperial table.

Mikkaichi, 三日市. In *Echigo.* Was from 1723 to 1868, the residence of a branch of the *Yanagisawa* family. (10,000 k.).

Mikkyō, 密教 or **Misshū,** 密宗. Another name of the *Shingon-shū* sect.

Miko, 御子. Title given formerly to the Emperor's children. — The *Taihō* code (702), regulated that the brothers and sons of the Emperor should bear the title of *Shinnō,* his grandsons and great-grandsons, that of *Ō. Junnin-tennō* decided that the title *Shinnō* should be conferred by an imperial decree (760). In the sequel, as the princes were increasing in number, and had thus become a heavy burden on the royal treasury, it became customary to give a family name (*Minamoto, Taira, Yoshi-mine, Tachibana,* etc.) to the Emperor's relatives and to force the others to become bonzes. — In the beginning of the 17th century, it was decreed that only three families should bear with right of inheritance, the title of *Shinnō : Fushimi, Katsura,* and *Arisugawa.* In the following century, they added the *Kan-in* family ; this constituted the *shi-Shinnō-ke,* i.e the four branches from which an heir could be chosen to any Emperor not having an heir. Moreover, 13 temples were designated (*Rinnō-ji, Ninna-ji, Daikoku-ji,* etc — See *Miya-monzeki*), over which princes were to rule that had become bonzes (*Hō-shinnō*). — At the time of the Restoration, this custom was abolished ; to the *Shi-shinnō,* were added other princes : the *Kitashirakawa,* the *Komatsu,* the *Kuni,* etc., whose descendants, after two generations lose their title of prince and enter into the ranks of the common nobility. The Emperor's sons bear by right, the title of *Shinnō :* they require no formal decree for that.

Mi-ko, 神子. Young girls, who perform the sacred dances, *kagura,* etc., in the large Shintoist temples. Some among the older ones pretend to have communication with the dead and with the gods, and to know the future — They are also called *kannagi.*

Miko-shiro, 神子代. The prince *Itoshiwake no Miko,* son of the emperor *Suinin,* having died without progeny, the *Itoshi-be* clan was formed, which was called *Koshiro no tami* (people replacing the children). Likewise, in order to perpetuate the memory of *Yamatotakeru no mikoto,* the *Takeru-be* were instituted. The Imperial Court took upon itself to administer the domains allotted to the *miko-shiro.* This strange custom was kept in vigour, during many centuries.

Mikoto, 尊, 命. In ancient times, a title of respect given to high personages. Was gradually reserved for the Shintoist gods. Even at the present day the imperial princes receive this title after their death.

Mikoto, 御言 or **Mikotonori.** Order, imperial decree. In ancient times, it was also called *ō-mikoto, tennō no ōse-goto, kami no ōse-goto.* At the time of the empress *Suiko* (604), the Chinese words *shō, choku, chokugo,* etc., were substituted for them. The name *shō,* was reserved for all important decrees solemnly promulgated before the whole Court ; for instance, a message to foreign ambassadors, the change of the *nengō,* the introduction of a new standard of money, a general amnisty, etc.

Mikuni-tōge, 三國峠. Pass (1,280 m.) on the boundaries of *Kōzuke, Echigo* and *Shinano.*

Mikuni-yama, 三國山. Name given to a great number of mountains situated on the boundaries of three provinces : *Etchū, Kaga* and *Noto ;—Shinano, Kōzuke* and *Musashi ;—Inaba, Hōki* and *Mimasaka ; —Izumo, Hōki* and *Bingo ;—Kii, Kawachi* and *Izumi ;—Chikugo, Higo* and *Bungo ;—Ise, Yamato* and *Iga ;—Tamba, Tango* and *Tajima,* etc.

Mikura-jima, 御倉嶋. One of the 7 islands of *Izu* (28 Km. in circuit).

Mikuriya, 御厨 or **Mikuri.** Ground formerly given to the temples, esp. to those of *Ise,* and the products of which served in the kitchen (*kuriya*). They were administered by the *Mikuriya-zukasa, Mikuriya-azukari.*

Mikusa, 三草. In *Harima.* Where *Yoshitsune* defeated the *Taira* in 1184.

Mi-kusa no kan-dakara, 三 種 神 器. The three sacred emblems, bestowed by *Amaterasu-ō-mikami* on *Ninigi no mikoto*, when he landed in *Hyūga*: *Yata no kagami, Ame no murakumo no tsurugi* and *Yasakani no magatama*. — They are also called *San-shū no shinki*.

Mimana, 任 那. One of the ancient kingdoms of Korea. Was conquered in 562, by *Shiragi*.

Mimasaka, 美 作. One of the 8 provinces of the *San-yō-dō*. Contains 5 districts, which belong to the *Okayama-ken*. — Chinese name: *Sakushū*. — Was separated from *Bizen* in 713.

Mimbu-shō, 民 部 省 or *Tami no tsukasa*. One of the 8 ministries created at the time of the *Taikwa* reform (646). Corresponded to the present Home ministry. Had to take up the census, to gather the taxes, to build new bridges and repair the old ones, etc., and to take charge of whatever pertained to agriculture. The Minister bore the title of *Mimbu-kyō*; he had under him a *taijō*, a *tayū*, a *gonkwan*, etc. The *Kazue-ryō* and the *Chikara-ryō* depended on the *Mimbu-shō*.

Mimi-nashi-yama, 耳 無 山. Mountain in *Yamato*. — It forms with the *Unebi-yama* and the *Ama no Kagu-yama*, the *Yamato san-zan* (the three mountains of *Yamato*). — Also called *Miminari-yama, Kuchi-nashi-yama, Tenjin-yama*.

Mimi-zuka, 耳 塚. (Lit.: Mount of the ears). A mount in the enclosure of the *Hōkō-ji* temple, near the *Daibutsu* (*Kyōto*). There were buried the noses and the ears of the Chinese and Koreans killed during the expedition of Korea (1592-1598). Not being able to follow the custom of those days, and send the heads of the enemies fallen in battle as trophy of their victory, the conquerors were satisfied with cutting off the noses and ears. — Is also called *Hana-zuka* (Mount of the noses).

Mimizu, 美 々 津. In *Hyūga*. Place where *Ōtomo Yoshishige* was defeated by *Shimazu Yoshihisa* (1578).

Mimizu-kawa, 美 々 津 川. River (110 Km.) in *Hyūga*.

Mimurodo, 三 室 戸. *Kuge* family, descended from *Fujiwara Kanemitsu*. — Now Viscount.

Min, 明. The Chinese dynasty of the *Ming* (1368-1644), which replaced the *Gen* (元 *Yuen*) and was deposed by the actually ruling dynasty of the *Shin* (清 *Tsin*).

Minabuchi Shōan, 南 淵 請 安. Descendant of the emperor *Ōjin*. In 607, went to China where he studied the system of administration and government of that country. Having returned to Japan, he enjoyed great influence and counted among his disciples the prince *Naka no Ōe* (*Tenchi-tennō*) and *Nakatomi Kamatari*.

Minagawa, 皆 川. In *Shimotsuke*. Was, in the 16th century, the residence of the *daimyō* of the same name, then of the *Toda* (1609-1612) and of the *Honda* (1615-1640).

Minagawa, 皆 川. *Daimyō* family from *Shimotsuke* and descended from the *Fujiwara*.

—— **Hiroteru,** 廣 照 (+ 1625). Fought first on the side of the *Hōjō* of *Odawara*, then submitted to *Hideyoshi* and obtained 30,000 k.

of revenue at *Minagawa* (*Shimotsuke*) (1590). In 1603, he was named preceptor of *Tadateru*, son of *Ieyasu* and transferred to *Iiyama* (*Shinano* — 40,000 k.) then, dispossessed, in 1616, at the time of *Tadateru's* conspiracy.

—— **Takatsune, 隆庸**. *Hiroteru's* son, received in 1623, the fief of *Fuchū* (*Hitachi* — 15,000 k). The family became extinct in him 1645.

Minagawa Kien, 皆 川 淇 園 (1734-1807). Renowned professor in *Kyōto*. Had as many as 3,000 scholars.

Minakuchi, 水 口. In *Ōmi*. Old castle, built towards the year 1583, by *Nakamura Kazuuji*; it passed then into the hands of *Nagatsuka Masaie*, who was besieged therein in 1600 and the castle destroyed. Having been rebuilt soon after, it became the property of the *Shōgun* and later on, the residence of the *Katō daimyō* (1682), the *Torii* (1695), and from 1712-1868, the *Katō* (25,000 k.)

Minami, 南. Family descended from *Fujiwara Kanemitsu*, and connected with the *Kōfuku-ji* temple (*Nara*). — Now Baron.

Minami Iwakura, 南 岩 倉 Family descended from the *Murakami-Genji* and connected with the *Kōfuku-ji* temple (*Nara*). — Now Baron.

Minamoto, 源. Family name given to a great number of sons and grandsons of emperors. — The princes of the imperial family steadily increasing in numbers and consequently the expenses of the Court becoming abnormal, *Saga-tennō*, gave the name of *Minamoto* (Chin. *Gen*) to his seventh son and younger brothers (814): it is the origin of the different *Minamoto-uji* or *Genji* families, distinguished from one another by the name of the emperor from whom they descended. Thus we have the *Saga-Genji*, the *Seiwa-Genji*, the *Uda-Genji*, the *Murakami-Genji*,

At first the families issued from these princes bore only the name of *Minamoto*; then, as their number increased, each branch, besides the patronymic (*uji*) name of *Minamoto*, adopted a special one (*myōji*), usually taken from the district or village in which they resided: *Ashikaga, Tokugawa, Matsudaira, Nitta, Takeda, Sasaki, Akamatsu, Kitabatake*, etc.—— (See *Seiwa-Genji, Uda-Genji, Murakami-Genji*). — The four principal

Minamoto families were those who descended from the emperors *Saga*, *Seiwa*, *Uda*, *Murakami*. Some of their branches had offices at Court and kept their rank as *kuge*, but most of them entered the military carrier and established the lineage of the *Shōgun* and the great *daimyō*. — Besides those four principal families, history mentions as having received the name of *Minamoto* : 5 sons of the emperor *Nimmyō*, 8 of *Montoku*, 3 of *Yōzei*, 14 of *Kōkō*, 4 of *Daigo*, 4 grandsons of *Sanjō*, and very many princesses ; but most of these branches became extinct after one or several generations.

Minamoto (**Saga-Gengi**). —— **Makoto,** 信 (810-869). 7th son of the emperor *Saga*, received the name of *Minamoto* in 814. He was *Sadaijin* (857), and as he lived in a quarter of *Kyōto* called *Kitabe*, he is often designated by the name of *Kitabe-Daijin*.

—— **Tsune,** 常 (812-854). 9th son of *Saga-tennō*, was *Udaijin* (840) and *Sadaijin* (849). He is often called *Higashi-Sanjō-Sadaijin*.

—— **Akira,** 明 (814-843). Brother of the two preceding, was *Daigaku no kami* (832), *Sangi* (849). When the emperor *Nimmyō*, his brother, died (850), he shaved his head and took the name of *Sosa*. He was called *Yogawa-Saishō-Nyūdō*.

—— **Sadamu,** 定 (815-863). Of the same family as the preceding, known by the name of *Shijō-Dainagon*, had great talent for music.

—— **Tōru,** 融 (822-895). Of the same family, was *Sadaijin* (872). He received the name of *Kawara-Sadaijin*.

—— **Hikaru,** 光 (845-913). Son of the emperor *Nimmyō*, joined *Fujiwara Tokihira* against *Sugawara Michizane* : the latter was accused of plotting against *Daigo* in order to replace him by his own son in law, the prince *Tokiyo-shinnō*. *Michizane* was exiled to *Tsukushi*, and *Hikaru* replaced him in the office of *Udaijin* (901). He is called *Nishi-Sanjō-Udaijin*.

—— **Shitagau,** 順 (911-983). Descendant of *Sadamu*, is known as a poet and a literary man. Was one of the compilers of the collection of poems called *Go-sen-waka-shū* (951). (See *Nashitsubo no go nin*). Received the titles of *Mimbu-ōsuke, Izumi no kami, Noto no kami*. Composed several works. Became bonze under the name of *Ambō-hōshi*.

Minamoto (**Daigo-Genji**). —— **Takaaki,** 高明 (914-982). 17th son of the emperor *Daigo*, received in 920, the name of *Minamoto*. Was *Udaijin* (966) and *Sadaijin* (968). He married *Fujiwara Yasu-ko*, daughter of *Morosuke*, who was later on married to the emperor *Murakami* and became the mother of the prince *Tamehira-shinnō*. In 969, *Takaaki* together with *Minamoto Mitsunaka* and *Tachibana Shigenobu*, planned to dethrone *Reizei-tennō*, and to replace him by his brother *Tamehira*. But the plot was discovered and *Takaaki* was sent in disgrace to *Tsukushi* with the title of *Dazai no gonno-sotsu*. He was re-called two years after by the emperor *En-yū*. He is usually known under the name of *Nishi-no-miya no Sadaijin*. A distinguished man of letters, he has written an Autobiography.

—— **Toshikata,** 俊賢 (959-1027). Son of *Takaaki*, was *Chūnagon* (1005), *Mimbukyō* (1010). He is one of the *Shi-Nagon* (See that name).

—— **Takakuni,** 隆 國 (1004-1077). Son of *Toshikata,* was *Gon-chū-nagon, Dainagon.* He is named *Uji no Dainagon.* Retired to *Uji,* he wrote several books.

—— **Toshiaki,** 俊 明 (1044-1114). Son of *Takakuni,* is the first who received the title of *Bettō* of the Court of the ex-emperor *Shirakawa* (1087) and that of *Shissei-Daijin.* Was also *Gon-dainagon* and Inspector (*azechi*) of the provinces of *Mutsu* and *Dewa.*

—— **Hiromasa,** 博 雅 (918-980). Grandson of the emperor *Daigo,* obtained fame as a musician. Wishing to receive lessons from the famous *Semimaru,* he went during three years, every evening, to the door of this musician's house, without gaining admittance. At last conquered by such perseverance, *Semimaru* accepted him as his scholar. *Hiromasa* is often designated by the name of *Hakuga no Sammi.*

Minamoto (Murakami-Genji).—— **Morofusa,** 師 房 (1003-1077). Son of the prince *Tomohira-shinnō,* is known as a writer and a poet. In 1020, he received the name of *Minamoto* and was successively *Naidaijin, Ukon-e-taishō, Udaijin, Sakon-e-taishō;* lastly, on the day of his death, he was named *Dajō-daijin.* He is known under the name *Tsuchimikado.*

Morofusa {Toshifusa-Moroyori
{Akifusa -Masazane-Masasada-Masamichi-Michichika

——— **Toshifusa,** 俊 房 (1035-1131) Son of *Morofusa,* after having occupied the highest positions including that of *Sadaijin* (1083) and of *Sakon-e-taishō* (1093), he had his head shaved and took the name of *Jakushun.* The people called him *Horikawa-Safu.* He has left an Autobiography. (*Suisa-ki*).

—— **Moroyori,** 師 賴 (1070-1139). Followed the steps of his ancestors and became a distinguished man of letters: he had studied under *Ōe Tadafusa.* He is called *Ono no miya.*

—— **Masazane,** 雅 實 (1059-1127). Rose to the dignity of *Dajō-daijin* (1122) and was above the *Kwampaku.* He is known under the name of *Kuga* and has left a diary called *Kuga-Shōkoku-ki.*

—— **Michichika,** 通 親 (1149-1202). Descendant of the above nobles, took part in the government during 7 consecutive reigns. His adopted daughter married the emperor *Go-Toba* and was the mother of *Tsuchimikado.*— *Michichika* is the ancestor of the *kuge Horikawa, Tsuchimikado,* and *Nakano-in.*

Minamoto (Uda-Genji).——— **Hideakira,** 英 明 (+ 940). Son of the prince *Tokiyo-shinnō* and grandson of the emperor *Uda,* his mother was the daughter of *Sugawara Michizane.* Was *Kurōdo no kami* and *Sa-chūjō.*

—— **Masanobu,** 雅 信 (920-993). Son of the prince *Atsuzane-shinnō* and grandson of the emperor *Uda,* was *Sadaijin.* He is known under the name of *Tsuchimikado.* His daughter married *Fujiwara Michinaga.*

Minamoto (Seiwa-Genji). — Branch issued from *Sadazumi-shinnō* (874-916), son of the emperor *Seiwa*, and from whom descend the three families of *Shōgun : Minamoto, Ashikaga* and *Tokugawa*.

—— **Tsunemoto**, 經基 (894-961). Son of *Sadazumi-shnnō*, took part in the campaign against *Taira Masakado* in 940, against *Fujiwara Sumitomo* in 941, and was named *Chinjufu-Shōgun*. In the year of his death, he received for himself and for his descendants the name of *Minamoto*.

—— **Mitsunaka**, 滿仲 (912-997). Son of *Tsunemoto*, was *Chinjufu-Shōgun*. He retired to *Tada* (*Settsu*): for this reason he is often called *Tada Manjū* and one of the branches of his family bears to the present day the name of *Tada*.

MINAMOTO MITSUNAKA.

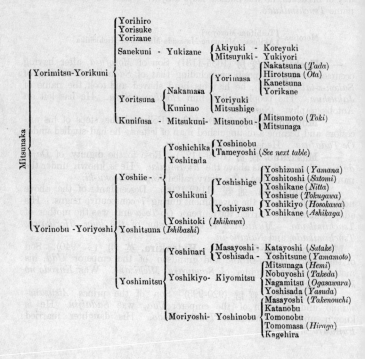

—— **Yorimitsu, 頼 光** (944-1021). Became famous on account of the feats he performed with his four companions (*shi-tennō*), *Watanabe no Tsuna, Sakata no Kintoki, Usui no Sadamichi,* and *Urabe no Suetake.* A fox having chosen the roof of the imperial palace for his abode, *Yorimitsu* shot a large arrow at it and killed it on the spot. Having received power to clear the city and its environs of banditti that terrorized the country, he exterminated them and closed the campaign with the death of the famous bandit *Ōe-yama* (*Tamba*).

MINAMOTO YORIMITSU.

—— **Yorinobu, 頼 信** (968-1048). Brother of the above, showed great valor and was named *Chinjufu-Shōgun.* In 1031, he repressed the revolt of *Taira Tadatsune* in *Shimōsa.*

—— **Yoriyoshi, 頼 義** (995-1082). Son of *Yorinobu,* accompanied his father to the war against *Taira Tadatsune* and was named *Sagami no kami,* then *Mutsu no kami.* He was ordered to fight against *Abe no Yoritoki,* who had rebelled in *Mutsu* : the war lasted 9 years (1055-1063) and finished with the defeat and death of *Yoritoki* and his sons. *Yoriyoshi* was then named *Iyo no kami,* and is known as *Iyo-nyūdō* because he had his head shaved soon after this occurrence.

—— **Yoshiie, 義 家** (1041-1108). Oldest son of *Yoriyoshi,* when a boy, was called *Genda.* At the age of 7, he performed the ceremony of the *gembuku* in the temple of *Hachiman,* at *Iwashimizu* (*Yamashiro*) and was from that moment called *Hachiman Tarō.* Having mastered in a

MINAMOTO YORIYOSHI.

very short time all the branches of military art, he made his first experiment at arms during the expedition conducted by his father against *Abe Yoritoki,* distinguished himself and on this account received the name of *Dewa no kami,* (1064). In 1081, the bonzes of the *Mii-dera* temple came to besiege *Hiei-zan* : *Yoshiie* was asked to repulse them. Named *Chinjufu-Shōgun,* he had to repress the *Kiyowara* revolt in 1087 ; at first defeated, he at last succeeded in his endeavors, owing to the timely help his brother *Yoshimitsu* brought him from *Kyōto. Yoshiie* has remained one of the most renowned heroes of the Middle Ages and legend has added some marvellous details to his eventful life.

YOSHIIE PURSUING ABE NO SADATŌ
(by Daihi, acc. t) Tosa Mitsuoki)

—— **Yoshitsuna,** 義綱 (+ 1134). *Yoshiie's* brother, made the *gembuku* in the temple of *Kamo* and was called *Kamo Jirō.* He took an active part in the campaign against *Abe no Sadatō* (1062), was called *Mutsu no kami* and repressed the revolt of the *Taira, Morosuke* and *Morosue,* in *Dewa* (1093). In 1109, his nephew *Yoshitada* having been murdered, *Yoshiaki,* son of *Yoshitsuna* was accused of the crime and condemned to death. *Yoshitsuna,* wishing to take revenge, levied an army, but was defeated by *Tameyoshi* and banished to the island of *Sado,* where he died.

—— **Yoshimitsu,** 義光 (1056-1127). *Yoshiie's* brother, made the *gembuku* in the temple of *Shinra-myōjin* and was called *Shinra Saburō.* Having been informed that his brother *Yoshiie* found it impossible to overpower the *Kiyowara,* who had revolted in the district of *Mutsu,* he came to his help with an army, and took a prominent part in the victory (1087). When he returned to *Kyōto,* he was named *Gyōbu-shōyū.*

—— **Yoshikuni,** 義國 (+1155). Son of *Yoshiie,* settled in the district of *Nitta* (*Kōzuke*). He was *Kebiishi* and repressed a sedition of *Satake Masayoshi* in *Hitachi.* After a quarrel with the *Udaijin Fujiwara Saneyoshi,* this latter's house was burned by the servants of *Yoshiukni,* who, on that account was obliged to retire to *Ashikaga* (*Shimotsu-*

ke) (1150), where he died. He is the forefather of the *Nitta* and the *Ashikaga* families.

—— **Yoshichika, 義親** (+1117) 2nd son of *Yoshiie*, was governor of *Tsukushi* and brought about troubles on account of his bad administration. Being recalled to *Kyōto*, he refused to obey and put the imperial envoy to death. Exiled to the *Oki* islands, he went into *Izumo*, killed the governor of the province and took his place ; but he was defeated by *Taira Masamori*, who had been sent against him (1107). Having become a bonze, he sought a retreat in *Mutsu*, tried again to raise the standard of revolt, but was defeated and put to death.

—— **Tameyoshi, 爲義** (1096-1156). Called first *Mutsu Shirō*. Son of *Yoshichika*, was heir of his grandfather *Yoshiie*. At the age of 13, he carried arms against his grand-uncle *Yoshitsuna*. Named *Kebiishi* in 1123, he checked the disturbances caused by the bonzes of *Hiei-zan*. During the *Hōgen* war (1156), he sided with the ex-emperor *Sutoku*, was defeated and put to death by order of *Kiyomori*, notwithstanding the prayers of his son *Yoshitomo*, who was unable to obtain his pardon.

—— **Yorimasa, 賴政** (1106-1180). Son of *Nakamasa* and a descendant of *Yorimitsu*, became famous, both as a poet and a warrior. In 1153, he killed with an arrow, the *nue* (a monster having the head of a monkey, the body of a tiger, and the tail of a serpent) which was seen flying over the imperial palace and shrieking horribly. A little later, he was named *Hyōgo no kami*. During the civil wars of *Hōgen* (1156) and *Heiji* (1159), he sided with the ex-emperor *Go-Shirakawa*, his protector. In 1178, he was raised to the 3rd rank in the Court (*san-i*), and as he shaved his head at that time, he was called *Gen san-i-nyūdō* : he is best known under this name. His connections however with the *Taira* were becoming more and more strained ; *Kiyomori's* tyranny brought about the climax. In 1180, *Kiyomori* wished to place his grandson *Antoku* on the throne, who was then only two years old, thus forcing his son-in-law *Takakura* to abdicate at the age on 20. *Yorimasa* then resolved to dethrone the *Taira* and to replace *Antoku* by the prince *Mochihito*, son of *Go-Shirakawa*. He secured the help of the bonzes of *Nara* and despatched *Minamoto Yukiie* into the provinces to recruit adherents to his cause. The plot was discovered to *Kiyomori*, who opposed the conspirators with an army commanded by his son *Tomomori*. *Yorimasa* sent the prince *Mochihito* to *Nara*, whilst he, with 300 resolute men, intrenched himself near the river *Uji-gawa*, and prepared to receive the enemy. He gave orders to destroy the bridge (*Uji-bashi*), but the assailants forded the river and began a bloody fight. *Kanetsuna* and *Nakatsuna*, sons of *Yorimasa* were killed; *Yorimasa* himself, wounded by an arrow and forseeing certain defeat, went to the temple *Byōdō-in* and there, sitting on his fan, committed *harakiri*

—— **Nakatsuna, 仲綱** (+ 1180). Son of *Yorimasa*, fought under his father against the *Taira*, and was killed at the battle of *Uji-bashi*. He was the ancestor of the *Ōta daimyō*.

—— **Yoshitomo, 義朝** (1123-1160). Son of *Tameyoshi*, was *Shimotsuke no kami*. During the *Hōgen* civil war (1156), he was the only member of the whole *Minamoto* family, who sided with *Taira Kiyomori* and besieged the palace of *Shirakawa* defended by his father and brother *Tametomo*. The latter were defeated; *Yoshitomo* begged in vain for his father's life: *Kiyomori* had him put to death. When peace was re-established, *Yoshitomo* was dissatisfied, because compared with that of *Kiyomori*, his reward was too small. Moreover, *Fujiwara Michinori* having refused to accept the hand of *Yoshitomo's* daughter for his son and accepted the daughter of *Kiyomori*, war soon broke out again. In 1159, *Kiyomori* being at *Kumano*, *Yoshitomo*, in concert with the *Kebiishi Fujiwara Nobuyori*, set fire to the palace of the ex-emperor *Go-Shirakawa*, secured the person of *Michinori* and put him to death. *Kiyomori* hastened to *Kyōto* and entrusted the repression of the insurrection to his son *Shigemori*. Being defeated, *Yoshitomo* fled to *Owari*, where he was murdered by one of his *kerai*, *Osada Tadamune*, who sent his head to *Kyōto*. His wife *Tokiwa Gozen* fled with her three children (See *Tokiwa Gozen*).

—— **Tametomo, 爲朝** (1139-1170). 8th son of *Tameyoshi*, is often called *Chinzei Hachirō Tametomo*. It is said that he was 7 feet high and of a Herculean strength. Being sent at the age of 13 to *Kyūshū*, he established himself in *Bungo*, where he caused disturbances in a very short time. He returned to *Kyōto* in 1154, joined his father during the *Hōgen* war (1156), and was banished to the island of *Ōshima* (*Izu*). Gradually, he took possession of the 7 islands of *Izu*, and again contemplated to overthrow the *Taira*. *Kudō Shigemitsu, Izu no suke* received orders to attack him (1170). Seeing the fleet of the latter coming towards him, *Tametomo* took an arrow and aim-

MINAMOTO TAMETOMO.

ing at the principal boat, shot it with such force that it pierced the hull and foundered the boat; he then returned home and committed *harakiri*. — *Tametomo's* exploits have passed into legend which even says that he was able to escape from *Ōshima* on a small skiff that landed at the *Ryūkyū*, on the island called *Oni-ga-shima*, and that he became the ancestor of the royal family of the archipelago.

—— **Yoshikata, 義賢** (+ 1155). Brother of the two preceding had a contest with his nephew *Yoshihira*, levied soldiers to fight him, but was defeated and killed.

—— **Yukiie, 行家** (+ 1186). 10th son of *Tameyoshi*, was first called *Yoshimori*. After his father and brothers had been defeated by the *Taira* (1156), he retired to *Shingū*, in the *Kumano* district (*Kii*), and was for this reason surnamed *Shingū Jūrō*. In 1180, he was selected to carry to the provinces prince *Mochihito's* invitation to rise against the *Taira ;* he then joined his nephew *Yoritomo* who was beginning the campaign. Not able to agree with *Yoritomo*, *Yukiie* left him, went to *Yoshinaka* in *Shinano* and followed him in his expedition against *Kyōto :* he was then named *Buzen no kami*. When *Yoshinaka* was defeated (1184), *Yukiie* fled into the province of *Kii* and, the following year, sided with *Yoshitsune* against *Yoritomo*. The latter having risen in arms, *Yukiie* fled to *Izumi*, where, by order of *Yoritomo*, he was put to death by *Fujiwara Yoshiyasu*.

—— **Yoshihira, 義平** (1140-1160). Eldest son of *Yoshitomo*, was only 15 years old when he bore arms against his uncle *Yoshikata*, whom he defeated and killed at *Ōkura* (*Musashi*) (1155). He had been surnamed *Kamakura Aku-Genda*. During the *Heiji* war (1159), he left *Kamakura* and joined his father at *Kyōto*, fought bravely against *Taira Shigemori*, but was defeated, and obliged to retreat to *Owari*. His father sent him to recruit troops in the North, where, having learned of the death of *Yoshitomo*, he secretly returned to *Kyōto*, but was soon discovered, arrested and beheaded at *Rokujōgahara*.

—— **Tomonaga, 朝長** (1144-1160). Son of *Yoshitomo*, accompanied his father when the latter fled from *Kyōto* after his defeat (1159) ; at *Ryūka-goe* (*Yamashiro*), in a battle against the troops of the *Yokokawa* bonzes, he was wounded by an arrow. Having arrived at *Aohaka* (*Mino*), his father ordered him to go with his brother *Yoshihira* and levy some troops in *Kai* and in *Shinano :* *Yoshihira* left at once, but inflamation having set in *Tomonaga's* wound, it was impossible for him to go further. Irritated with this mishap, *Yoshitomo* dreaded to desert him and to continue his route whereupon *Tomonaga* asked his father to kill him with his own hand. *Yoshitomo* following in this, the customs of the times accepted and despatched his own son. *Tomonaga* was buried on the spot; some time after, *Taira Munekiyo* violated his grave, beheaded him and sent the trophy to *Kyōto*.

—— **Yoritomo, 頼朝** (1147-1199). The first *Minamoto Shōgun*. 3rd son of *Yoshitomo*, made the *gembuku* at the age of 13, a little before the beginning of the *Heiji* civil war (1159). After the defeat of his father, he fled with him, left him at *Aohaka* (*Mino*) and took refuge at the house of the mayor (*ekichō*) of the village of *Ōi*. He was discovered by *Taira Munekiyo*, and taken to *Kyōto*. *Kiyomori* intended to put him to death, but at the petition of his mother, he was contented with exiling him to *Hiruga-oshima* (*Izu*) (1160): *Itō Sukechika* and *Hōjō Tokimasa* had charge of him. He had connexion with the *Sukechika's* daughter who bore him a son: in his fury, *Sukechika* wanted to kill him but *Yoritomo* managed to escape and took shelter in the house of *Hōjō Tokimasa*. There he acted in a similar manner with *Tokimaṣa's* daughter, the famous *Masa-ko*, and it was in vain that the father sent her to the governor of the province, *Taira Kanetaka;* she eluded his watchfulness and returned to *Yoritomo*. In 1180, when *Mochihito* sent orders to levy troops to fight against the *Taira*, *Yoritomo* was the first to respond to the call; he enrolled soldiers in *Izu* and in *Sagami* but was defeated at *Ishibashi-yama* (*Sagami*) by *Ōba Kagechika* (1181). He retreated then into the mountains of *Hakone*, where he gathered his adherents, stopped at *Kamakura* and summoned the whole *Minamoto* clan from the different provinces. *Kiyomori* sent an army against him, but the soldiers having heard of the superior numbers of *Yoritomo's* army, did not dare to attack him and retired without fighting. *Yoritomo* then sent his troops towards *Kyōto;* at the *Kiso-gawa*, between *Mino* and *Owari*, they joined the army brought

MINAMOTO YORITOMO.

up from *Shinano* by *Yoshinaka* and *Yukiie*, and defeated the soldiers of *Taira Shigehira*. Lastly, they came to *Kyōto*, from whence the *Taira* fled to the west, taking with them the young emperor *Antoku* (1183). *Yoshinaka*, once master of *Kyōto*, acted with such lawlessness, that he provoked the anger of the ex-emperor *Go-Shirakawa* and the jealousy of *Yoritomo*, who sent an army commanded by his own brothers *Noriyori* and *Yoshitsune* against him : *Yoshinaka* was defeated and killed (1184). The victors then turned their efforts against the *Taira*, whom they repulsed at *Ichi no tani* (*Settsu*), at *Yashima* (*Sanuki*) and at *Dan no ura* (*Nagato*). Dissensions having arisen between *Yoritomo* and *Yoshitsune* the latter, to escape from his brother who was watching for an opportunity to assassinate him, fled to *Mutsu*, where he was put to death by *Fujiwara Yasuhira*, acting by *Yoritomo's* command (1189). *Yoritomo* then had undisputed sway: in 1190, he was named *Sōtsuihoshi* (superintendent) of the 66 provinces; two years later, he received the title of *Sei-i-tai-shōgun*. A new era began for Japan, that lasted for nearly 7 centuries; the authority, no longer in the hands of the Emperor, was wielded by his powerful lieutenant-general, the *Shōgun*. *Yoritomo* showed himself cruel to opponents and all those whose influence he feared; his uncle *Yukiie* and his brother *Yoshitsune* had already been despatched by his order; he directed also that his other brother, *Noriyori*, be put to death (1193). We have however to concede that he was an eminent administrator, and his organization of the *Bakufu* of *Kamakura* proved that he had real genius for government. *Yoritomo*, often known under the title of *Kamakura-Udaishō* or *Kamakura-dono*, died at the age of 53, from the effects of a fall from horseback. — See *Kamakura, Kamakura-Bakufu*, etc.

—— **Noriyori, 範頼** (1156-1193). Brother of *Yoritomo*, was educated by *Fujiwara Norisue*. In 1180, he went at the head of an army and helped *Oyama Tomomasa* to defeat *Shida Yoshihiro* in *Shimotsuke*. By command of *Yoritomo*, he, with *Yoshitsune*, fought against *Yoshinaka*, defeated and killed him at *Awazu* (*Ōmi*) (1184). He then marched against the *Taira* and defeated them at *Ichi no tani*: he was in consequence named *Mikawa no kami*. Two months after, he carried on the campaign and went as far as *Bungo*; this prevented him from taking part in the battles of *Yashima* and *Dan no ura*. He then returned to *Kamakura*, and when *Yoritomo* proposed him to fight against *Yoshitsune*, he energetically refused. The union between the two brothers became more strained and matters were made worse by calumny. Finally *Noriyori* was banished to *Shuzenji* (*Izu*) and very soon after was put to death.

—— **Yoshitsune, 義經** (1159-1189). The youngest son of *Yoshitomo*, was named *Ushiwaka* in his childhood. After the *Heiji* war, he was pardoned by *Kiyomori* on condition that he would become a bonze; he was therefore placed in the temple *Kurama-dera*, under the care of the learned *Gakujitsu*. At the age of 11, reading the annals of his family, he resolved in his mind to walk in the footsteps of his ancestors. Vainly did *Gakujitsu* try to inspire him with love for religious exercises, *Yoshitsune* stealthily escaped from the temple and took refuge in the palace of *Fujiwara Hidehira*, in *Mutsu*: in this journey, he was accompanied by *Benkei*, whom he had beaten in a fencing pass on the bridge of *Gojō* (*Kyōto*) and who became his inseparable companion. In *Ōmi*, he made the *gembuku* and chose the name of *Yoshitsune*, a name which he was to bring to a great celebrity: he was then 16 years of age.

MINAMOTO YOSHITSUNE.

In *Mutsu*, *Hidehira* gave him shelter in the stronghold of *Hiraizumi*. As soon as he heard that *Yoritomo* had levied troops to march against the *Taira*, he hastened to join him with 2,000 horse (1180) : the two brothers met near the *Kise-gawa*, a river in *Suruga*. In the mean time, *Yoshinaka*, having arrived at *Kyōto* and excited disturbances, *Yoritomo* sent his two brothers *Noriyori* and *Yoshitsune* against him; he was defeated at *Uji*, then at *Seta* and at *Awazu* (*Ōmi*) (1184). *Yoshitsune* then entered *Kyōto*, where he was received by the ex-emperor *Go-Shirakawa* and lodged in the imperial palace After a few days' rest, he continued his campaign against the *Taira* who had erected a stronghold near the sea, at *Ichi no tani* (*Settsu*). With the help of *Noriyori*, he attacked the powerful *Heike* army from two different sides and completely defeated it : those who survived, fled by sea towards the West. *Yoshitsune* returned to *Kyōto*, was received with enthusiasm and obtained the title of *Kebiishi*. This increasing popularity of his younger brother bred jealousy in the mind of *Yoritomo*. Early in the following year, *Yoshitsune* re-opened the campaign. The *Taira*, after their defeat at *Ichi no tani*, had carried away the young emperor *Antoku*, and made a stronghold at *Yashima*, in *Sanuki* (*Shikoku*) : *Yoshitsune* attacked and obliged them to retreat to *Nagato*, where he closely pursued and completely crushed them at *Dan no ura* (1185). The emperor *Antoku* was drowned with his grandmother, *Kiyomori's* widow ; his mother, the empress *Kenrei mon-in* was saved. As to the *Taira*, most of them perished in the sea ; the prisoners were put to death. After this victory which secured the triumph of the *Minamoto*, *Yoshitsune* returned to *Kyōto* and then to *Kamakura*. *Yoshitomo's* jealousy was growing all the while ; a certain warrior, *Kajiwara Kagetoki*, who had had some dispute with *Yoshitsune*, calumniated him before his brother and when he arrived at *Koshigoe*, a small distance from *Kamakura*, he was forbidden to enter the city. *Yoshitsune* vainly tried to appease his brother, he had to return to *Kyōto*. There he was named *Iyo no kami*, but *Yoritomo* forbade him to take possession of his office and named a *Jitō* to replace him. Soon after, *Yoshitsune* was ordered to separate himself from his uncle *Yukiie* and to deliver the latter to *Yoritomo* : feigning some malady, he evaded the order ; his brother getting always more and more irritated, requested the ex-bonze *Tosabō Shōshun* to go to *Kyōto* and to assassinate *Yoshitsune* ; but the un-forseen happened : *Shōshun* was killed by his expected victim. Then, *Yorimoto* started for *Kyōto* : *Yoshitsune* resolved to fly to *Tsukushi*, but a storm drove him back to the shore ; he hid himself in *Yamato*, then at the *Yoshino-san*, at *Tabu no mine*, and even at *Kyōto* ; lastly, disguised as a pilgrim and accompanied by his wife, his faithful *Benkei* and some servants, he wended his way towards *Mutsu* to be again sheltered under the hospitable roof of *Fushiwara Hidehira*. The latter received him cheerfully and gave him the stronghold of *Koromogawa* as a place of refuge. But *Hidehira* died the following year and his son *Yasuhira* had not the courage to resist *Yoritomo's* order to march against *Yoshitsune* and to kill him. An army was sent to lay siege to *Koromogawa* : *Yoshitsune* defended himself with great valor, but finding it impossible to resist such great numbers, he killed his wife and children and then committed suicide. He was 31 years old. *Yasuhira* sent his head to *Kamakura*.—According to a legend, *Yoshitsune* did not die then. He was able to escape to the island of *Ezo* and is now honored by the *Aino* under the name of *Gikyō-daimyō-jin.*—According to others, who base their opinion on a similarity of name (the Japanese pronunciation of the Chinese characters of the name *Minamoto Yoshitsune* would be *Gen Gikyō*), he emigrated to *Mongolia*, where he became the famous *Gengis-Khan* (1157-1226).—At all events, *Yoshitsune* is, to the present day, one of the most popular heroes of Japan ; poetry and the theatre vie with each other in celebrating his exploits.

—— **Yoshinaka,** 義仲 (1154-1184). Son of *Yoshikata* and grandson of *Tameyoshi* was brought up by *Nakahara Kanetō*, in the mountainous district of *Kiso* (*Shinano*), hence his name *Kiso Yoshinaka* under which he is often known. At the age of 13, he made the *gembuku* in the temple of *Iwashimizu*. In 1180, obeying the orders of prince *Mochihito*, he levied troops in *Shinano* and marched against the *Taira ;* the governor of the province, *Ogasawara Yorinao* tried to oppose him, but he was defeated. The following year, *Jō Nagamochi* a *daimyō* of *Echigo*, came to attack him, but was likewise defeated. The *Taira, Michimori* and *Tsunemasa*, then made war against him : they were beaten in *Echigo*, and *Yoshinaka* remained thus sole master of several provinces. His uncle, *Yukiie*, after a quarrel with *Yoritomo*, joined him and both, with a large army, directed their steps towards *Kyōto* (1182). The *Taira*, vainly sought to oppose their progress ; they were defeated and, when they saw the enemy approaching their city, they fled, taking with them the young emperor *Antoku. Yoshinaka* entered *Kyōto* without difficulty, and was received as a liberator by the ex-emperor *Go-Shirakawa*, who named him *Iyo no kami. Yoshinaka* then resolved to put the prince *Hokuroku no Miya*, son of *Mochihito-Ō* on the throne, but the ex-emperor opposed his views. *Yoshinaka*, irritated at this opposition, gave full play to his anger and filled *Kyōto* with terror. He secured the person of the ex-emperor, burned the palace, deposed the *Kwampaku*, replaced him by a child 12 years old, and at last had himself named *Shōgun. Yoritomo*, hearing of this, placed his two brothers, *Noriyori* and *Yoshitsune* at the head of an army of 60,000 men and sent them against *Yoshinaka*, who was defeated at *Seta* and killed at the battle of *Awazu* (*Ōmi*) ; he was 31 years old.—— *Yoshi-*

SEAL OF
MINAMOTO YOSHINAKA
(1182).

naka had always been surrounded by 4 trusty companions at arms who died with him : *Imai Kanehira, Higuchi Kanemitsu, Tate Chikatada* and *Nenoi Yukichika :* they were called his *shi-ten.*

—— **Yoriie,** 頼家 (1182-1204). 2nd *Minamoto Shōgun.* Eldest son of *Yoritomo*, was at first called *Ichiman.* He was 17 years old when his father died, and, although he had then received the title of *Sō-shugo-jitō*, his mother *Masa-ko* formed a Council which was composed of her father *Hōjō Tokimasa*, of *Ōe Hiromoto* and of 11 other members ; these were entrusted with the Government affairs. *Yoriie* showed great ardor in learning the military art, fencing, horse-riding etc. ; but his morals were very low and this estranged all men from him. In 1202, he was named *Sei-i-tai-shōgun*, but fell ill the following year. *Masa-ko* then suggested that the 38 provinces of the *Kwansai* should be given to his brother *Semman* (*Sanetomo*), and the 28 provinces of the *Kwantō* to his son *Ichiman*. *Hiki Yoshikazu*, *Yoriie's* father-in-law, thinking the partition unfair to his grandson, presented a complaint to his son-in-law, and formed with him the design of destroying the *Hōjō*. *Masa-ko* heard of this and informed her father *Tokimasa* who sent *Amano Tōkage* to kill *Yoshikazu*. When the news of this murder had spread, the whole family of the *Hiki* rose in arms, but *Tokimasa* ordered the palace of *Ichiman*, where they had assembled, to be set on fire and all perished in the flames (1203). *Yoriie* was ordered to shave his head and was confined in *Shuzenji* (*Izu*), where *Tokimasa* had him assassinated the following year.

—— **Sanetomo, 實朝** (1192-1219). Third *Minamoto Shōgun*. *Yoriie's* brother, succeeded him as *Shōgun*, whilst the administration remained in the hands of his mother *Masa-ko*, his uncle *Yoshitoki* and his grandfather *Hōjō Tokimasa*. At the age of 12, he changed the name *Semman* which he had borne until then to *Sanetomo*. In the following year *Tokimasa* planned to destroy him, and to replace him by his son-in-law, *Hiraga Tomomasa*, but the plot was revealed to *Masa-ko* who hastened with her son to the palace of *Yoshitoki* : *Tokimasa* was obliged to shave his head and retire to *Hōjō* (*Izu*) whilst *Tomomasa* was put to death at *Kyōto* (1205). *Masa-ko* continued to govern with her brother *Yoshitoki*. At the beginning of the year 1219, *Sanetomo*, having received the title of *Udaijin*, ordered a ceremony of thanksgiving to be held at the temple of *Hachiman*, on the *Tsurugaoka* hill, near *Kamakura*. He was leaving the temple and standing on the steps, when he was assassinated by his nephew *Kugyō*, son of *Yoriie* ; he was then only 28 years old. He is the last of the *Minamoto Shōgun*.

—— **Ichiman, 一幡** (1200-1203). Eldest son of *Yoriie*, lost his life at the time when his relatives on the mother's side endeavored to secure for him his father's succession. — See *Yoriie*.

—— **Kugyō, 公曉** — See *Kugyō*.

—— **Senju-maru, 千壽丸** (1201-1214). Third son of *Yoriie*, was only 12 years old, when *Izumi Chikahira* levied an army against the *Hōjō* in order to raise him to the rank of *Shōgun*. *Chikahira* was defeated and *Senju-maru* was obliged to become a bonze under the name of *Eijitsu* (1213). The following year, *Wada Yoshimori* took up *Chikahira's* plan ; he was likewise defeated and *Senju-maru* fell with his party.

Minamoto Ari-ko, 在子 (1171-1257). Adopted daughter of the *Naidaijin Michichika*, married the emperor *Go-Toba* and was the mother of *Tsuchimikado*. In 1204, the emperor had his head shaved and took the name of *Shōmei mon-in*. She died at the age of 87.

Minamoto Chika-ko, 親子. *Morochika's* daughter, was the wife of the emperors *Kameyama* and *Go-Daigo*. By her second marriage she had several children among whom prince *Morinaga-shinnō*. She is known under the name of *Mimbukyō-san-i*.

Minase, 水無瀬. In *Settsu*. A famous Shintoist temple, where honor is paid to the emperors *Go-Toba, Tsuchimikado, Sutoku*.

Minase, 水無瀬. *Kuge* family, descended from *Fujiwara Michitaka* (953-995) and the chief, by right of inheritance, of the Shintoist temple of *Minase (Settsu)*. — Now Viscount.

Minato-gawa, 湊川. Small river of the province of *Settsu*, which enters the sea between *Kōbe* and *Hyōgo*. In 1336, it was the scene of a bloody battle, where *Kusunoki Masashige*, defeated by *Ashikaga Takauji*, killed himself.

Minchō-ryū, 明兆流. School of painting, Chinese style, established by the bonze *Minchō* or *Chō Densu* (1352-1431). The best known of its members are *Josetsu* and *Shūbun*.

Mine, 峯. In *Ise*, to-day, *Kawasaki*. Was under the *Ashikaga*, the residence of a family of *daimyō*, bearing the same name. *Nobunaga* dispossessed them in favor of *Takigawa Kazumasu* (1569), who was in turn dispossessed by *Hideyoski* (1591).

Mineyama, 峯山. In *Tango*. Since 1620, the residence of a branch of the *Kyōgoku* family. (13,000 k.).

Mino, 美濃. One of the 13 provinces of the *Tōsandō*. Comprises 15 districts depending on the *Gifu-ken*. — Chinese name: *Nōshū*. — In olden times, was called *Minu* (three plains) from the three plains *Kagami-no, Ao-no*, and *Kamo-no*.

Minobu, 身延. Village of *Kai*, famous on account of the great temple *Kuonji*, built in 1273 by *Nichiren*, whose remains are venerated in that place. It is to the present day the principal seat of the *Hokke-shū* sect. *Minobu-san* is also called *Fundari-mine*.

Mi-no-o no mikado, 水尾御門. The emperor *Seiwa* (859-876) received that name, because his grave is in the village of *Mi-no-o (Yamashiro)*.

Minowa, 箕輪. In *Kōzuke*. Old castle built towards 1525, by *Nagano Nobunari*, a vassal of the *Uesugi*. In 1565, *Takeda Shingen* besieged *Nagano* therein, who, being defeated, killed himself. After the destruction of the *Takeda* (1582), *Nobunaga* gave the province of *Kōzuke* to *Takigawa Kazumasu*, but the *Hōjō* secured it not long after that. *Ii Naomasa* to whom *Ieyasu* had given the castle of *Minowa* (1590), left it to take up his residence at *Takasaki*. (1598).

Mi-oya no kami, 御親神. Title under which, *Tamayori-hime*, the mother of *Jimmu-tennō*, is honored.

Miroku, 彌勒. (Sanscr. Máitreya). The *Bosatsu* who will be born again in the year 5,000 after *Shaka* entered Nirvâna and who in turn shall become *Buddha*.

Misaki, 三崎. In *Sagami*. Ancient castle belonging to the *Miura daimyō*. It passed, later on, to the *Satomi* (1556), then to the *Hōjō* of *Odawara*, and was abandoned in the year 1590. — In 1808, the *Bakufu* built a fort at *Misaki* to protect the coasts.

Misasagi, 山陵. Tombs of emperors or of some high officials. In ancient times, the emperors were placed in stone coffins and buried on the top of an eminence made for that purpose and surrounded with ditches. At the time of *Mommu*, the empress *Jitō*, his predecessor, was cremated

(701), and it became customary to deposit the remains of sovereigns in the large Buddhist temples, *Hokke-dō*, *Senyū-ji*, etc. The imperial tombs were placed under the care of the *Jibu-shō.* — See *Sanryō-bugyō.*

Misen-tō, 彌山嶋. Another name of the island of *Miya-jima*, whose highest mountain is called *Mi-sen.*

Mi-shima, 見嶋. Island (12 Km. circuit) on the N.W. coast of *Nayato.*

Mishima, 三嶋. Town (9,200 inh.) of the *Shizuoka-ken*, chief city of the *Izu* province.

Mishima, 三嶋. *Samurai* family of *Kagoshima* (*Satsuma*) made noble in 1887. — Now Baron.

——**Tsūyō,** 通庸 (+ 1888). Was prefect of the *Sakata* and the *Yamagata-ken*, Police inspector, etc.

Mishima-nada, 水嶋灘. One of the 5 principal basins of the Interior Sea, between the provinces of *Aki* (*Hondo*) and of *Iyo* (*Shikoku*).

Misshū, 密宗. (Lit.: secret religion). Another name of the *Shingon* Buddhist sect This sect demands 10 degrees of perfection or of self-knowledge, and it is only after having arrived at the last, that the faithful will be able to grasp the source and the depth of his own thought, and to discover the secret of becoming "*Buddha*" even in this world.

Misshū-ryōbu, 密宗兩部. The two parts, wisdom (*kongō-kai*) and reason (*taizō-kai*), of which the Buddhist perfection is composed in the *Misshū* or *Shingon* sect.

Mitake, 三岳. In *Tōtōmi.* Ancient castle belonging to the *Shiba daimyō* (15th century).

Mitake, 御嶽. The highest mountain of the *Tsushima* islands (487 m.). Also called *Nita-dake.*

Mi-take, 御嶽. Mountain situated 18 Km. W. of the city of *Kōfu* (*Kai*); famous for its temples.

Mito, 水戸. Chief town (33,800 inh.) of the department of *Ibaraki* and the province of *Hitachi.* — Ancient castle of the *Daijō* family; *Edo Michifusa* occupied it in the beginning of the 15th century, and his descendants held it till 1590. At that date it passed into the hands of the *Satake. Ieyasu* installed therein his sons *Nobuyoshi* (1600), *Yorinobu* (1603), then *Yorifusa* (1609); this latter formed the branch of the *Tokugawa* of *Mito* (350,000 k.), one of the three families (*san-ke*) from which the *Shōgun* could be chosen.

Mito, 水戸. Branch of the *Tokugawa* family.—See *Tokugawa* (*Mito*).

Mito Kōmon, 水戸黄門. — See *Tokugawa Mitsukuni.*

Mitori-ba, 見取場. Reclaimed land at the foot of mountains or on the banks of rivers, and which was taxed, not according to its surface, but according to the annual harvest it produced.

Mitoshiro, 御戸代. Rice-fields, the taxes of which went to the maintenance of the Shintoist temples.

Mitsui, 三井. Family of bankers, merchants and manufacturers, made noble in 1900. — Now Baron.

Mitsuke-ga-hara, 見附原. In *Tōtōmi.* Old castle built by the *Imagawa daimyō. Tokugawa Ieyasu* was defeated there in 1572 by *Takeda Shingen.*

Mitsukuri, 箕作 . Ancient castle in *Ōmi ;* it belonged to the *Rokka-ku daimyō* (*Sasaki*). *Nobunaya* secured it in 1573.

Miura, 三浦 . *Daimyō* family of *Sagami* descended from *Taira Takamochi*.

—— **Tamemichi, 爲通** . Settled, in the 11th century, in the district of *Miura* (*Sagami*) and took the name of the place. Towards 1060, he built the castle of *Kinugasa*.

—— **Yoshiaki, 義明** (1093-1181). Son of *Yoshitsugu* and great-grandson of *Tamemichi*, had the title of *Miura Ōsuke* and resided at the castle of *Kinugasa* (*Sagami*). When *Yoritomo* began his campaign against the *Taira*, he sent his son *Yoshizumi* and his grandson *Yoshi-mori* to the army. Having heard of the defeat of *Ishibashi-yama*, he levied other troops and routed *Hatakeyama Shigetada ;* but the latter soon came back and laid siege to *Kinugasa*, where *Yoshiaki* met his death.

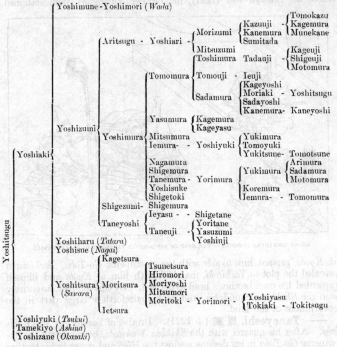

—— **Yoshizumi, 義澄** (1127-1200). Son of *Yoshiaki*, also called *Arajirō*, sided with *Yoritomo* against the *Taira* (1180) and, with the help of his brother *Yoshitsura*, defeated *Hatakeyama Shigetada* at *Kotsubo*

(*Sagami*). Defeated in his turn at *Kinugasa*, he retired into *Awa*, whence he returned to take part in *Noriyori's* expedition towards the West, and was intrusted with the defense of the *Suwō* province. He assisted at the battle of *Dan no ura* (1185) and took part in the campaign against *Fujiwara Yasuhira* (1189).

—— **Yoshitsura,** 義連. Brother of *Yoshizumi*, is also called *Sawara Jūrō*. He took part in the battles of *Kotsubo* and *Kinugasa*, then in the campaigns against *Yoshinaka* and against the *Taira*. His achievements at *Ichi no tani* made him famous. *Yoshitsura* is said to have been 7 and a half feet high and was gifted with Herculean strength.

—— **Yoshimura,** 義村 (+ 1239). Son of *Yoshizumi*, helped to repress the revolt of his cousin *Wada Yoshimori* against the *Hōjō* (1213). When *Kugyō* had murdered the *Shōgun Sanetomo*, he had him arrested by *Nagao Sadakage* and his head sent to *Hōjō Yoshitoki* (1219). A little before the *Shōkyū* war (1221), his brother *Taneyoshi*, then stationed

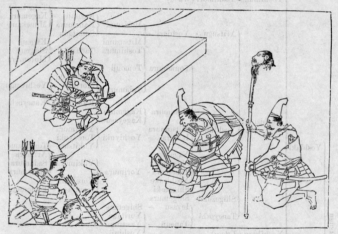

MIURA YOSHIMURA PRESENTING THE HEAD OF HIS BROTHER TANEYOSHI TO HŌJŌ YOSHITOKI.

at *Kyōto*, pressed him to side with the ex-emperor *Go-Toba*, *Yoshimura* revealed the plot to *Yoshitoki*, marched with him to *Kyōto* and himself presented his own brother's head to his lord. By this conduct, he entirely won the *Shikken's* confidence and took henceforth a large part in the government of the land.

—— **Taneyoshi,** 胤義 (+ 1221). Brother of *Yoshimura*, was *Kebiishi*. After his quarrel with the *Shikken Yoshitoki*, he supported the ex-emperor *Go-Toba* in his designs against the *Hōjō* and wrote to his brother to induce him to follow his steps, but *Yoshimura* delivered the letter to *Yoshitoki*. During the ensuing civil war, *Taneyoshi*, after having fought with great valor, was defeated and killed.

—— **Yasumura,** 泰村 (1104-1247). Son of *Yoshimura*, is also called *Suruga Jirō*. He followed his father to the *Shōkyū* war (1221), and was named *Wakasa no kami*, afterwards *Hyōjōshū* (1235). He enjoyed the full confidence of the *Shikken Tokiyori*, but could not agree with *Adachi Kagemori*. Their rivalry brought about the civil war : *Tokiyori* sided with his grandfather *Kagemori*, and *Yasumura* was defeated and killed with all his family in the premises of the temple *Hokke-dō* (*Kyōto*).

—— **Mitsumura,** 光村 (+ 1247). Brother of *Yasumura*, was *Kebiishi* and *Noto no kami*. He perished with his whole family in the war against the *Hōjō*. —— He was the last of the senior branch of the family.

—— **Yoshiatsu,** 義同 (+ 1516). Son of *Uesugi Takamasa*, was adopted by *Miura Tokitaka*, who had no heir. Some time after, a son, *Takanori*, having been born to him, he forced *Yoshiatsu*, to become bonze in the temple of *Sōsei-ji* (*Sagami*). *Yoshiatsu*, at first seemed to be resigned to his fate, but in 1496, he levied troops, laid siege to the castle of *Arai*, where *Tokitaka* was staying, defeated and killed him, and took possession of his domains. In 1499, he had his head shaved and took the name of *Dōsun*. Besieged in *Okazaki*, (*Sagami*) by *Hōjō Sōun*, he was defeated, took refuge in *Arai*, where, being again attacked, he committed *harakiri*, together with his son *Yoshimoto*. — Thus ended this family which for several centuries, had been at the head of the province of *Sagami*.

Miura, 三浦. *Daimyō* family, descended from *Miura Iemura*, son of *Yoshimura* (V. art. above). — Elevated to the rank of a *daimyō* in 1639, in the person of *Masatsugu* (1600-1641), the family resided successively : in 1639, at *Mibu* (*Shimotsuke*) ; in 1691, at *Nobeoka* (*Hyūga*) ; in 1712, at *Kariya* (*Mikawa*) ; in 1747, at *Nishio* (*Mikawa*) ; lastly, from 1764 to 1868, at *Katsuyama* (*Mimasaka* — 23,000 k.). — At present Viscount.

Miura, 三浦. *Samurai* family of the *Yamaguchi* clan *(Suwō*), made noble in 1884. — To-day Viscount.

Miwa, 三輪. In *Yamato*. *Isshiki Yoshitsura* was defeated in that place and killed in 1440, by the army of the *Shōgun Yoshinori*.

Miwa Shissai, 三輪執齋 (1669-1744). Confucianist from *Kyōto*. Taught *Ōyōmei's* Chinese philosophy, and published a translation of his book (*Denshūroku*).

Miya, 宮. In ancient times, the palace of the emperor was called *mi-araka* or *mi-ya*. The large temples of *Ise-Daijingū*, reproduce exactly their type of construction. Under *Ōjin-tennō's* reign (270), Korean carpenters came to Japan, and from that time, the imperial palace was built in Korean style. In 643, the Chinese style was adopted and used in the construction of the *Nara* (710) and *Kyōto* (794) temples

Miya, 宮. Shintoist temple. — Also called *jinja, yashiro*, etc.

Miya, 宮. Title of princes and princesses of the imperial family.— From ancient times the princes palaces were called *miya* and according to their situation, *Yotsu-tsuji no miya, Itsu-tsuji no miya, Tokiwai no miya*, etc. ; Gradually, the name of their residence was given to the princes themselves. Those among them, who became bonzes, took the name of the temple they entered : *Ninnaji no Miya, Rinnōji no Miya* etc. and were called *Miya-monzeki.*

Miyabe, 宮部 . *Daimyō* family of the 16th century.

—— **Tsugimasu,** 繼潤 (1528-1599). First a bonze at the *Hiei-zan*, followed *Asai Nagamasa*, who gave him the domain of *Miyabe* (*Ōmi*), which name he took. After the destruction of the *Asai* (1573), he served *Hideyoshi*, received the castle of *Toyokuni*, then that of *Tottori* (*Inaba*) (1582). After the *Kyūshū* campaign against the *Shimazu* (1587), he obtained an increase of revenues.

—— **Nagafusa,** 長房 . Son of *Tsugimasu*, succeeded him in the possession of the fief of *Tottori*, but having fought against *Ieyasu*, he was dispossessed (1600).

Miya-gawa, 宮川 . River (126 Km.) in *Ise*. Also called *Watarai-gawa, Kin-kawa*.

Miya-gawa, 宮川 . Name of the *Jinzū-gawa*, in its superior course, in *Hida*.

Miyagawa, 宮川 . In *Ōmi*. From 1698 to 1868, the residence of the *Hotta daimyō* (13,000 k.).

Miyagi-ken, 宮城縣 . Department formed by 14 districts of *Riku-zen* and 3 of *Iwaki*.—Pop., 899,000 inh.—Chief town : *Sendai* (93,500 inh.)—A principal city : *Ishinomaki* (18,600 inh.).

Miya-jima, 宮嶋 .— See *Itsuku-shima*.

Miyake, 屯倉 . In ancient times, name given to rice-fields belonging to the imperial domain, then by extension, to the granaries wherein they kept the rice produced in such fields, and finally to the officials having charge of same. It is to the emperor *Suinin*, that the construction of the first of these granaries is due, and under the rule of *Suiko*, they numbered 181. The officials who were at the head of these *miyake* had the title of *miyake-obito ;* the farmers who cultivated these rice-fields were called *tabe* and their chief, *tabe no muraji*.—Even to the present day, several villages bear the name *Miyake*, because they formerly possessed a rice granary.

Miyake, 三宅 . In *Settsu*. Ancient castle belonging to the *Hoso-kawa daimyō ;* was in 1549 the scene of a battle between *Hosokawa Harumoto* and *Miyoshi Chōkei*.

Miyake, 三宅 . *Daimyō* family, originally from *Mikawa* and descended from the *Uda-Genji*. It resided : in 1604, at *Ueno* (*Mikawa*) ; in 1615, at *Kameyama* (*Ise*) ; in 1635, at *Niiharu* (*Hitachi*) ; then from 1664 to 1868, at *Tawara* (*Mikawa* — 12,000 k.). — To-day Viscount.

Miyake-jima, 三宅嶋 . One of the 7 islands of *Izu* (30 Km. circuit).

Miyake Kwanran, 三宅觀瀾 (1674-1718). Confucianist. Born at *Kyōto*, was a disciple of *Asami Keisai* ; came to *Edo* and followed the teaching of *Kinoshita Jun-an*. Then served *Mito Mitsukuni*, and in 1712, succeeded *Arai Hakuseki* in the service of the *Bakufu*.

Miyake Shōsai, 三宅尚齋 (1662-1741). Confucianist. Born at *Akashi* (*Harima*), was disciple of *Yamazaki Ansai*. He left several works.

Miyako, 都. Town where the emperor resided ; capital. *Kyōto* was often designated under that name.

Miyako-Fuji, 都富士. Another name for *Hiei-zan*.

Miyako-gawa, 宮古川. River (49 Km.) in *Rikuchū* ; enters the Pacific Ocean at the *Miyako* port, Also called *Hei-gawa*.

Miyako-jima, 宮古嶋. Island (45 Km. circuit) of the *Ryūkyū* archipelago ; belongs to the *Okinawa-ken*.

Miyako Yoshika, 都良香 (848-879). Man of letters and savant. Of the *Kuwabara* family. His brother *Haraka* was also a distinguished man of learning.

Miya-Monzeki, 宮門跡. Title given to Buddhist temples that were governed by an imperial prince, and, by extension, to these princes themselves. 13 temples possessed this privilege :

Rinnō-ji, 輪王寺.— *Nikkō no Miya* —(*Nikkō* — *Tendai* Sect).
Ninna-ji, 仁和寺.— *Omuro-gosho* —(*Kyōto* — *Shingon* „).
Daikaku-ji, 大覚寺.— *Saga-gosho* —(„ — „).
Myōhō-in, 妙法院.— *Shin-Hiyoshi-Monzeki* — *Kyōto* — *Tendai* Sect).
Shōgo-in, 聖護院.— *Mori-goten* —(*Kyōto* — *Tendai* Sect).
Seiren-in, 青蓮院.— *Awata no Miya* —(*Kyōto* — *Tendai* Sect).
Chion-in, 知恩院.— *Kwachō-goten* —(*Kyōto* —*Jōdo* „).
Kwanjū-ji, 勧修寺.— *Minami-Yamashina-goten* —(*Kyōto* — *Shingon* Sect).
En-yū-in, 圓融院.— *Kajii no Miya, Nashimoto* —(*Kyōto* — *Tendai* „).
Manju-in, 曼珠院.— *Take no ura Go-Monzeki* —(„ — „ „).
Emma-in, 圓満院.— *Byōdō-in, Koma-Sakurai* —(*Uji*— „ „).
Shōkō-in, 昭高院.— (*Kyōto* — „ „).
Bishamon-dō, 毘沙門堂.— („ — „ „).

Miyanari, 宮成. A family attached for centuries to the Shintoist temple of *Usa* (*Bungo*). — Now Baron.

Miyanokoshi, 宮越. In *Shinano*. Was in the 12th century, the residence of *Kiso Yoshinaka*.

Miyanoshita, 宮下. Village of *Sagami*, known among the Europeans for its delightful climate, its scenery and hotsprings.

Miya-no-uchi no tsukasa, 宮内省. Old name for the *Kunai-shō*.

Mi-yasu-dokoro, 御息所. Apartment of the Palace where the Emperor takes his rest. Towards the 9th century, this word served to designate the secondary wives (*nyōgo, kōi,* etc.) of the Emperor. Later on, it was applied to the princes' wives.

Miyazaki-ken, 宮崎縣. Department of *Kyūshū*, formed by the province of *Hyūga*.— Pop.: 490,000 inh. — Chief town : *Miyazaki* (7,700 inh.) — Principal cities : *Miyakonojō* (13,200 inh.) *Kobayashi* (12,800 inh.).

Miyazu, 宮津. Town (8,900 inh.) of the *Tango* province. Old castle built in 1584, by *Hosokawa Tadaoki*. Under the *Tokugawa*, was successively the residence of the *daimyō Kyōgoku* (1600), *Nagai* (1669), *Abe* (1681), *Okudaira* (1697), *Aoyama* (1717), and from 1758 to 1868, *Honjō* (70,000 k.).

Miyoshi, 三好. *Daimyō* family, issued from the *Ogasawara* and, through them, from the *Seiwa-Genji*. At the beginning of the 14th century, *Ogasawara Nagafusa* settled in *Shikoku*. His descendant from the 8th generation came to the district of *Miyoshi* (*Awa*), took the name of the place and served the *Hosokawa*, then all powerful in *Shikoku*.

—— **Nagateru,** 長輝 (+ 1520). Also called *Yukinaga*, was *Chikuzen no kami*. At the time of the division which took place in the *Hosokawa* family at the death of *Masamoto* (1507), he took arms against *Sumiyuki*, defeated him near *Kyōto* and had *Sumimoto*, adopted son of *Masamoto*, nominated as *Kwanryō*. The following year, *Ōuchi Yoshioki* returned to *Kyōto* with the dispossessed *Shōgun Yoshitane*; *Nagateru* vainly tried to stop him, he was defeated and had to return to *Awa* with *Sumimoto*. In 1511, he had his head shaved and took the name of *Ki-un*. Having gathered an army, he marched against *Kyōto*, entered the city, but was defeated by *Asakura Takakage* (1519). He waited in vain for help from *Sumimoto*. Attacked a second time, he was again defeated and killed himself in the temple *Chion-in*.

—— **Masanaga,** 政長 (+ 1549). Brother to *Nagateru*, was *Echizen no kami*. Took the name of *Sōsan*. He became a bonze and having been defeated, together with *Hosokawa Harumoto*, by *Chōkei*, he was murdered by rovers.

—— **Nagamoto,** 長元 (+ 1532). Eldest son of *Nagateru*, was first called *Motonaga* and was *Chikuzen no kami*. In 1520, he entered *Kyōto* with the *Hosokawa* army: the *Shōgun* fled to *Awa* and was replaced by *Yoshiharu*. In 1532, *Nagamoto* had his head shaved and took the name of *Kai-un*. Some time after, having been calumniated to *Hosokawa Harumoto*, he was, by order of the latter, put to death in the temple *Hongwan-ji*. More than 70 of his servants committed suicide on the same occasion.

—— **Chōkei,** 長慶 (1523-1564). Eldest son of *Nagamoto*, first had the name of *Norinaga* and was *Chikuzen no kami*. At the age of 17, with the help of his relative *Masanaga* and of *Matsunaga Hisahide*, he invaded the *Kinai*. In 1548, he took the name of *Chōkei*. Having had some dispute with *Masanaga*, he asked his lord *Hosokawa Harumoto* for the authorization to levy troops in *Settsu*, *Izumi* and *Kawachi*, but instead of giving the required permission, *Harumoto* sided with *Masanaga*. *Chōkei* irritated, at once attacked and defeated *Masanaga*; then, establishing *Ujitsuna* as chief of the *Hosokawa* clan, he went and besieged *Harumoto* in his castle of *Miyake* (1549). He did not dare however to go so far as to oblige his former lord to kill himself, and, raising the siege, he again turned his arms against

Masanaga, whom he defeated. *Harumoto* fled into *Ōmi* and asked the *Shōgun Yoshiteru* for help. *Chōkei* meanwhile entered *Kyōto*, and intrusted the city into the hands of *Matsunaga Hisahide* (1550). Two years after, he returned, forced the *Shōgun* to submit, and had himself made *Shōbanshū* and *Shuri-tayū* (1560). After that he besieged *Hatakeyama Takamasa*, took his castle of *Iimori* (*Kawachi*), and installed himself there. *Takamasa* went into *Kii*, levied new troops and returned to attack *Chōkei*, but was again defeated and at last peace was restored in the *Kinai* (1562). The following year, *Yoshioki*, son of *Chōkei* died from the effects of poison given him by *Matsunaga Hisahide*. *Chōkei* then adopted *Yoshitsugu*, a son of his brother *Sogō Kazumasa*, but there never reigned great harmony between them. *Hisahide's* influence besides, was always on the increase: in 1564, he had *Chōkei's* brother, *Fuyuyasu*, put to death; shortly after, *Chōkei* himself fell sick and died at the age of 42.

—— **Jikkyū**, 實休 (+ 1559). Brother to *Chōkei*. His true name was *Yukitora*. Was *Buzen no kami*. He resided at the castle of *Miyoshi* (*Awa*). In 1552, he put *Hosokawa Mochitaka* to death and seized his possessions. *Hisamitsu Yoshioki*, *Mochitaka's* vassal, intending to revenge his master, levied troops against *Jikkyū*, but was defeated and killed. The *Shōgun* then sent an army into *Awa* and *Jikkyū* died on the battlefield.

—— **Fuyuyasu**, 冬康 (+ 1564). Brother of the former, defended the castle of *Araki* (*Settsu*) and was murdered by *Matsunaga Hisahide*. He was a distinguished poet.

—— **Yoshitsugu**, 義次 (+1573). Nephew and adopted son of *Chōkei*, allowed himself to be influenced by *Matsunaga Hisahide*. With him, he took part in the assassination of the *Shōgun Yoshiteru* and of his brother *Shukō* (1565). Once installed at the castle of *Takaya*, he soon fell out with *Hisahide*: *Nobunaga* restored peace and confirmed *Yoshitsugu* in the possession of half of the province of *Kawachi* (1568), with the castle of *Wakae*. In 1572, *Yoshitsugu*, hearing that a quarrel had arisen between the *Shōgun Yoshiaki* and *Nobunaga*, sided with the *Shōgun*; but *Nobunaga* besieged *Wakae* and *Yoshitsugu*, killed himself. About that time, the family disappeared from the records of history: its last representatives were defeated in *Shikoku* by the *Chōsokabe*.

Miyoshi, 三好. *Samurai* family of the *Chōshū* clan, made noble after the Restoration. — Now Viscount.

Miyoshi Kiyotsura, 三善清行 (847-918). In his youth, he was a scholar of *Kose Fumio*. Later he became minister under the emperors *Seiwa*, *Yōzei*, *Kōkō*, *Uda* and *Daigo*, and wrote the history of the 3 first mentioned. In 914, he presented the emperor *Daigo* with a memoir of 12 chapters on the ameliorations to be carried out in the administration of the government. He is one of the great men of the *Engi* era.

Miyoshi Yasunobu, 三善康信 (1140-1221). Son of *Yoritomo's* wet-nurse: whilst in *Izu*, *Yoritomo* kept him well informed of the events that happened at *Kyōto*. At the time of the organization of the *Bakufu*, he was named *Monchū-jo no shitsuji* and kept this office for over 30 years. At the age of 82 years, he transmitted the charge to his son *Yasutoshi*, and died in the same year.

Mi-yuki, 行幸. Name given to the places where the Emperor stopped in his excursions. They were also called *Gyōkō*. When he travelled to several places, his journey was called *Junkō*. The *Taihō* code (702), fixed the whole ceremonial of these journeys: the imperial guard (*hyō-e, eji*) watched the roads to prevent any one from leaving or from joining the procession on its way, etc. The *Engi* code (927) added to it a visit to the temples that were on the route, remunerations to officers and officials, etc.

Mizoguchi, 溝口. *Daimyō* family, originally from *Owari* and descended from *Minamoto Yoshimitsu* (*Seiwa-Genji*). From 1598 to 1868, it resided at *Shibata* (*Echigo*); its revenues, that were at first of 50,000 k. were raised to 100,000 k. in 1860. — Now Count.

Mizu-chō, 水帳. Under the *Tokugawa*, the surveying register.

Mizuha no me, 美都波. God of the waters (*Shintō*) Son of *Izanagi* and *Izanami*.

Mizu-kagami, 水鏡. Historical work treating of the period from the time of *Jimmu* to that of *Nimmyō* (660 B.C. — 850 A.D.). — The author is supposed to be *Nakayama Tadachika* (1131-1195).

Mizuki, 水城. In *Chikuzen*. In 664, a large dock was built, surrounded with strong embankments as a protection against the incursions of the Chinese and Korean pirates.

Mizuno, 水野. *Daimyō* family descended from *Minamoto Mitsumasa*, son of *Tsunemoto* (*Seiwa-Genji*). In the 15th century, *Mitsusada* settled at *Mizuno* (*Owari*) and took the name of the place.

—— **Tadamasa,** 忠政 (+ 1543). Occupied consecutively the castles of *Okawa* (*Owari*), *Ōtaka* (*Owari*) and *Kariya* (*Mikawa*). His daughter married *Tokugawa Hirotada* and was the mother of *Ieyasu*; whence the prosperity of the family.

			Katsushige-Katsutoshi-Katsusada	(a)
	Nobumoto-Tadashige	Tadakiyo	Tadamoto -Tadanao	(b)
			Tadamasu -Tadataka	(c)
Tadamasa	*Dai* (*Denzū-in*) wife of Tokugawa Hirotada and mother of Ieyasu.			
	Tadamori -Tadamoto -Tadayoshi-Tadaharu -Tadamitsu			(d)
	Norikata -Shigenaka			(e)

(*a*) — Eldest branch —— **Nobumoto,** 信元 (+ 1576). *Shimotsuke no kami*, in 1543, deserted the *Imagawa*, his liege lords, in order to follow *Oda Nobuhide*; this estranged the *Matsudaira* and the *Tokugawa* from him until the day when they also rallied round *Nobunaga*. Having had a quarrel with *Sakuma Nobumasa*, *Nobumoto* was accused before *Nobunaga* who gave orders to *Ieyasu* to put him to death: *Ieyasu* obeyed and sent the head of his uncle to *Nobunaga*.

—— **Tadashige,** 忠重 (1541-1600). Was the brother of *Nobumoto*, but at the death of the latter, he was chosen heir to his castle of *Kariya*

(*Mikawa*). He served *Hideyoshi* who named him *Izumi no kami* and raised his revenues to 40,000 k. He was murdered by *Kagai Hidemasu*.

—— **Katsushige, 勝成** (1564-1651). Took part in the *Kyūshū* expedition (1587) under the leadership of *Sasa Narimasa*. During the Korean war, his conduct was disgraceful. He passed from the army of *Konishi Yukinaga* to that of *Katō Kiyomasa*, then to that of *Kuroda Nagamasa*, of *Miura Shigekatsu*, etc. Having returned to Japan, he sided with *Ieyasu*, his cousin, and was named *Hyūga no kami*. In 1615, he was transferred from *Kariya* to *Kōriyama* (*Yamato* — 60,000 k.), and in 1619, to *Fukuyama* (*Bingo* — 100,000 k.). In 1638, he helped to repress the *Shimabara* insurrection. In 1646, he had his head shaved and took the name of *Sōkyū*. — His direct lineage stops in 1698. An heir was chosen for him in the person of one of his relatives, who, in 1703, received the castle of *Yūki* (*Shimōsa* — 17,000 k.), where his family remained till the Restoration. — To-day Viscount.

(*b*) — Branch which resided successively: in 1602, at *Obata* (*Kōzuke*); in 1616, at *Kariya* (*Mikawa*); in 1632, at *Yoshida* (*Mikawa*); in 1642, at *Matsumoto* (*Shinano*); in 1777, at *Numazu* (*Suruga* — 50,000 k.). At the Restoration, it was transferred to *Kikuma* (*Kazusa*). — Now Viscount.

(*c*) — Branch that resided at *Minakami* (*Tamba*), then at *Hōjō* (*Awa*), and, since 1827, at *Tsurumaki* (*Kazusa* — 15,000 k.). — Now Viscount.

(*d*) — Branch that resided successively: in 1615, at *Yamakawa* (*Shimotsuke*); in 1635, at *Tanaka* (*Suruga*); in 1642, at *Yoshida* (*Mikawa*); in 1645, at *Okazaki* (*Mikawa*); in 1762, at *Karatsu* (*Hizen*); in 1817, at *Hamamatsu* (*Tōtōmi*); in 1845, at *Yamagata* (*Dewa* — 50,000 k.). At the time of the Restoration, it was transferred to *Asahi-yama* (*Ōmi*). — Now Viscount.

(*e*) — Branch installed since 1619 at *Shingū* (*Kii* — 35,000 k.). — Now Baron.

Mizusawa, 水澤. Town (8,300 inh.) of *Rikuchū*. Was in the Middle Ages the seat of the *Chinjufu* or general government of the province of *Mutsu*.

Mizu-shima, 水嶋. Name given to two small neighboring islands, one (*Kami-Mizu-shima*) belonging to the *Bizen* province, the other (*Shimo-Mizu-shima*) to that of *Bitchū*. In 1183, *Kiso Yoshinaka's* army was defeated in that place by the *Taira*.

Mizutani, 水谷. *Daimyō* family which, remained at *Shimodate* (*Hitachi*), from the end of the 16th century, was transferred in 1639 to *Matsuyama* (*Bitchū*—50,000 k.), and died out in 1693.

Mochihito-Ō, 以仁王 (1150-1180). 4th son of the emperor *Go-Shirakawa*. His mother, daughter of the *Gon-dainagon Hidenari*, was not of sufficiently high rank to receive the title of *Shinnō*. When *Minamoto Yorimasa* rose against the *Taira* (1180), he called *Mochihito* to him promising to raise him to the throne in case he should be successful: the prince accepted and *Yukiie* was sent to the provinces to find supporters for their cause. Defeated with *Yorimasa* at *Uji-bashi*, *Mochihito* fled to *Nara* and was killed by an arrow whilst on his road there. He is also called *Sanjō no Miya*, *Takakura no Miya*. He left 6 sons : the eldest was the prince *Hokuroku no Miya ;* the 5 others became bonzes.

Mogami, 最上. Ancient *daimyō* family of *Dewa*.

—— **Yoshiakira,** 義光 (1546-1614). Son of *Yoshimori*, took advantage of the general confusion to increase his domains at the expense of his neighbors. He submitted to *Hideyoshi* and gave his daughter in marriage to *Hidetsugu ;* it was in vain that he interceded for her life ; she was beheaded at the same time as her husband (1595), and *Yoshiakira* kept a deep resentment against the *Taikō*. No wonder then that in 1600 he sided with *Ieyasu*, fought against *Uesugi Kagekatsu* and saw the revenues of his fief of *Yamagata* (*Dewa*) increased to 520,000 k.

SEAL OF
MOGAMI YOSHIAKIRA.

—— **Yoshitoshi,** 義俊. *Yoshiakira's* grandson, was dispossessed of his large estate on account of misgovernment and transferred to *Ōmori*. (*Ōmi*—10,000 k.) : he died in 1631 without leaving any heir.

Mogami-gawa, 最上川. River (242 Km.) that rises in the group of mountains of the *Azuma-yama*, S of *Uzen*, passes trough *Yonezawa*, flows towards the N., separates *Ugo* from *Uzen*, and enters the sea near *Sakata*. In its upper course, it is also called *Matsukawa*, and in its lower course, *Sakata-gawa*. The *Mogami-gawa*, the *Fujikawa* (*Suruga*), and the *Kuma-gawa* (*Higo*), are called the " *Nihon san kyūryū* " (three rapid rivers of Japan).

Mogishi, 喪儀司. Formerly an official depending on the *Jibu-shō* and having charge of whatever pertained to funerals, burials, imperial tombs, etc. In 808, this title was joined to that of *Kusuishi*.

Moitori no Muraji, 水取連. In olden times, officer of the corporation (*moitoribe*) whose duty it was to furnish the necessary water for the Imperial Palace. The first who received that title was *Otokashi*, *agatanushi* of *Taketa* and companion at arms of *Jimmu-tennō*.

Moitori-zukasa, 主水司. Formerly *Moitori no miyatsuko*. Since the *Taihō* code (702), an office depending on the *Kunai-shō*, and having charge of the water, ice, dishes, etc. required for the Shintoist and Buddhist ceremonies. The direction of this office became hereditary in the family of *Kiyowara Yorinari*. Gradually, *moitori* became *mondo*, and we find the titles of *Mondo no kami*, 正, *jō* 佑, *sakwan* 令史.

Mokudai, 目代. From the beginning of the 12th century it became customary for the governors of provinces (*kokushi*) to remain in *Kyōto*, whilst an official named *Mokudai* or *Rusu-shoku*, replaced them in their provinces.

Mombu-shō, 文部省. Office of Public Instruction, created in 1885.

Momiji-yama, 紅葉山. Hillock in the old castle of *Edo*, between *Hon-maru* and the *Nishi no maru*, where a temple was built on the tombs of the family of the *Tokugawa Shōgun*.

Mommu-tennō, 文武天皇. 42nd Emperor of Japan (697-707). *Ama no mamunetoyo-ihoji* or *Karu no Ōji*, grandson of the emperor

Tenchi, son of the prince *Kusakabe* (*Okanomiya no tennō*) and of the empress *Gemmei,* when only 14 years of age, he succeeded his aunt and grandmother *Jitō.* The *Taihō* code (*Taihō-ryō*) dates from his reign. This code copied the Chinese code of the time and completed the reforms inaugurated by the *Taikwa* era (645-649). *Mommu* died at the age of 25 and was succeeded by his mother *Gemmei.*

Momokubarino, 桃配野. In *Mino.* The emperor *Temmu* possessed a country house in that place and *Ieyasu* established his headquarters there before the battle of *Sekigahara* (1600).

Momonoi, 桃井. Old *daimyō* family descended from *Ashikaga Yoshikane* (+ 1199).

—— **Yoshitane, 義胤.** Son of *Yoshikane,* established himself at *Momonoi* (*Kōzuke*) and took the name of the place.

—— **Naotsune, 直常.** Great-grandson of *Yoshitane,* was named governor (*shugo*) of *Etchū* by *Takauji.* Defeated by *Kitabatake Akiie* at *Kamakura* and at *Aono ga hara* (*Mino*) (1337), he in his turn defeated him at *Nara* (1338). He likewise defeated *Akinobu, Akiie's* brother, on the *Otoko-yama.* When disunion set in between *Takauji* and his brother *Tadayoshi* (1350), *Naotsune* sided with the latter, passed with him to the side of *Go-Daigo* and went into *Etchū* to recruit his troops. He returned the following year and occupied *Hiei-zan:* he was dislodged from that place by *Takauji* and *Kō Moronao.* In 1354, he joined *Shiba Takatsune* and marched on to *Kyōto* whence *Takauji* had to flee into *Ōmi;* being in want of provisions, he returned into *Etchū,* where he had soon to defend himself against *Takatsune* and his son *Yoshimasa,* who, having passed to the Northern party, had received orders to combat him. He was defeated by *Yoshimasa* in 1369 and in 1370; after this date, history does not mention his name anymore; it is also certain that his whole family was destroyed in the struggle against the *Ashikaga.*

Momoshiki, 百敷. Ancient name given to the imperial Palace,— some say, because all the officials (*hyaku-kwan*) had their appointed place therein; — others say, this name was given to it, on account of the dimension of its outside enclosure.

Momo-yama, 桃山. Hill near *Fushimi* (*Yamashiro*), on which *Hideyoshi* built a magnificent castle in 1593; this castle was destroyed after his death and its remains distributed among the different temples of *Kyōto.*

Momoyasobe, 百八十部. In ancient times, name by which the ensemble of offices and functions were designated. Later, it was also called *hyakkwan-shoshi.*

Momozono-tennō, 桃園天皇. 116th Emperor of Japan (1747-1762). *Tōhito* eldest son of *Sakuramachi-tennō* succeeded him at the tender age of 7 and died after a reign of 16 years, during which reign the entire authority was in the hands of the *Shōgun Ieshige.*

Mon, 紋. Heraldry, escutcheon. The *Mon* was generally used in Japan, during the Middle ages. In time of war it could be seen on the banners, the helmets and the cuirasses of the warriors; in time of peace, they wore it on the overcoat (*haori*) at five different places, once on the back, twice on the sleeves and twice on the breast: hence the name *go-mon-baori*, by which it was known. The higher *daimyō* usually had three different *mon*, the others had two, and the simple *samurai* only one. The imperial family has the Chrysanthemum with 16 petals (*kiku no go-mon*) (1) and the paulownia (*kiri no go-mon*) on its escutcheon (2).—The best known *mon* of the high families are:

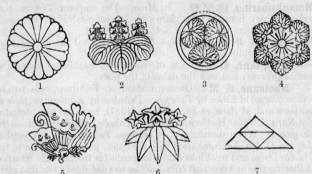

that of the *Tokugawa*, 3 leaves of asarum in a circle (*mitsu-aoi*) (3):—*Toyotomi, Ashikaga, Oda, Hosokawa, Uesugi*, the paulownia (2);—*Matsudaira*, 6 leaves of *asarum* in hexagonal form (4);—*Taira, Ikeda*, a kind of butterfly with unfolded wings (5);—*Minamoto*, 3 leaves of gentian (*rindō*) above 5 leaves of small bamboo (*sasa*) (6);—*Hōjō*, 3 triangles (*mitsu-uroko*) (7);—Besides flowers and plants, birds, butterflies, fans, Chinese characters, geometrical designs, crosses, the swastika (*manji*) and even Mount *Fuji* were used in heraldry. —Since the Restoration, the *mon* is not the exclusive right of the *kwazoku* and *shizoku*: the simple *heimin* have the power to use one.

Monchūjo, 問注所. High Court of Justice established at *Kamakura* in 1184 by *Yoritomo: Miyoshi Yasunobu* was its first president. Installed first in the palace of the future *Shōgun*, it was in 1199, transferred outside the city. It was the supreme court for all civil cases.—It continued in existence under the *Ashikaga Shōgun*, the charge of *Shitsuji* (president) being controlled in turn by the members of the *Ōta* and the *Machino* families.

Mondo, 主水.—See *Moitori-zukasa.*

Mongaku-Shōnin, 文覺上人. By birth, *Endō Moritō*. He lost his father *Shigetō*, when yet a child, and was brought up by *Haruki Michiyoshi*. At the age of 18, he became enamored of his cousin *Kesa Gozen*, who was married to *Minamoto Wataru*. After long hesitation and resistance, she feigned to yield to his solicitations on condition that he would first kill *Wataru. Moritō* consented and, the following night, he entered the house of his cousin; but *Kesa Gozen* took the place of her husband and received the fatal blow destined for him: *Moritō* then became a bonze and took the name of *Mongaku*. Some time later, he undertook to rebuild the temple *Shingo-ji* of Mount *Takao* (*Yamashiro*) and started on a begging tour for that purpose : he presented himself before the ex-emperor *Go-Shirakawa*, then residing at the temple *Hōshō-ji*, but having failed in some way in the respect due to his sovereign, he was banished to *Izu* (1179). There he met *Yoritomo* and pressed him to begin war with the *Taira* ; he secretly went to the palace of *Kiyomori*, at *Fukuhara*, whither the Court had been transferred, and, through the kind offices of *Fujiwara Mitsuyoshi*, obtained from *Go-Shirakawa* a rescript addressed to *Yoritomo*, commanding him to take up arms and deliver

MONGAKU-SHŌNIN.

the emperor from the tyranny of the *Taira*. *Yoritomo* hesitated no more and entered the lists. After his victory, he had the *Shingo-ji* repaired and always treated *Mongaku* with the greatest kindness. The ruling emperor *Go-Toba*, showed rather more ardor for pleasure and entertainments than for administration : *Mongaku* advised *Yoritomo* to replace him by his brother *Morisada-shinnō*, but the *Shōgun* recoiled from doing such an act. When *Yoritomo* died (1199), *Mongaku* believed the moment opportune to accomplish his design, but the plot was discovered and the turbulent bonze was exiled to the island of *Sado*, where he died miserably at the age of 80.

Mon-in, 門院. — See *Nyo-in*.

Mononobe, 物部. In olden times, a body of men whose chief had the title of *Mononobe no Muraji*. He had charge of the Palace guard, of the execution of criminals, etc. Later on, every *miyatsuko* (governor of province or district) had a guard of 20 *mononobe*. — In 808, the *mononobe* were joined to the *ejifu*. (See *Ejifu, Emonfu*.) The term *mononobe* was then given to the whole military class and became synonymous with *samurai*. The family which, for several generations had the title of *Muraji*, kept the name of *Mononobe*.

Mononobe, 物部. Ancient family descended from *Umashimade no mikoto*.

Irofu-Me-Arayama { Masara-Arakabi
{ Okoshi-Moriya

—— **Me,** 目. Son of *Irofu*, descendant in the 9th generation of *Umashi-made*. At the accession of *Yūryaku-tennō* (457) to the throne, he was named *Ō-muraji*. In 474, he defeated and killed *Asahirō*, who was plundering the province of *Ise*.

—— **Okoshi,** 尾興. Grandson of *Me*, received from *Kimmei-tennō* the title of *Ō-muraji*. In 552, the king of *Kudara* sent him a statue of *Buddha* and some Buddhist books as a present ; the emperor called on his ministers to ask their advice in reference to the reception to be given to this new divinity. *Soga no Iname* proposed to venerate it with the same honor that was given to the deities of the country. *Okoshi* and *Nakatomi no Kamako* opposed this as an insult to the *Kami*. *Kimmei* then gave the statue to *Iname*, who erected a temple in its honor in his own house. The following year, many fell victims to a contagious disease, and *Okoshi* attributed it to the vengeance of the outraged gods. By his advice, the new temple was burned and the statue thrown into the canal of *Naniwa*.

—— **Arakabi,** 麁鹿比 (+ 536). Was minister during the reigns of *Ninken, Buretsu, Keitai, Ankan* and *Senkwa*. In 512, *Kudara* asked the emperor for permission to annex the 4 districts (*agata*) of *Mimana*. The emperor consented and gave orders to *Akarabi* to carry his answer to the king of *Kudara*, but on the advice of his wife, *Akarabi* feigned sickness so as not to be burdened with a mission injurious to the gods, who had, at the time of the *Jingō-kōgō* expedition, shown clearly that they wanted *Mimana* to be subject to Japan. In 527, he repressed a revolt of the governor of *Tsukushi, Iwai*, whom he defeated and killed in the district of *Mii*.

—— **Moriya,** 守屋 (+587). Son of *Okoshi*, succeeded his father in the office of *Ō-muraji*. Like his father, he was an implacable enemy of anything that savoured of Buddhism, and, together with *Nakatomi no Katsumi*, opposed *Soga no Umako's* plans that were favorable to the new religion. Their party gained the advantage under the reign of *Bitatsu* (572-585), but his successor *Yōzei* himself became a Buddhist and the *Soga* triumphed. At the death of *Yōzei* (587), the two parties, pretending to have a right to present a candidate to the throne, came to open war: the battle was fought near Mount *Shigisen* (*Yamato*) ; *Moriya* and *Katsumi* were killed, as also the little prince they had intended to raise to the throne.

MONONOBE MORIYA.

Montoku-tennō, 文徳天皇. 55th Emperor of Japan (851-858). *Michiyasu*, eldest son of *Nimmyō-tennō*, succeeded him at the age of 24. He had to repress a revolt of the *Ebisu* in *Mutsu* (855) and an insurrection of the inhabitants of the island of *Tsushima* (857). Died at the age of 32.

Monto-shū, 門徒宗 . — See *Jōdo-shinshū*.

Monzeki, 門跡 . — See *Miya-monzeki*.

Monzen-barai, 門前拂 . Under the *Tokugawa*, punishment inflicted on the *samurai*. The guilty man was deprived of his pension, his swords were taken away and he was publicly driven before the gate of the *bugyō* or of his own *daimyō*. He then became " *rōnin*."

Mori, 母里 . In *Izumo*. From 1677 till 1868, residence of a branch of the *Matsudaira* of *Echizen* (10,000 k.).

Mori, 森 . In *Bungo*. Old castle that was built, according to tradition, by *Minamoto Tametomo* towards the middle of the 12th century. At the end of the following century, *Kiyowara Tomomichi* settled there and took the name of *Mori*. In 1470, it passed to the *Ōtomo*, then towards 1540, to the *Mori*. From 1601 to 1868, it was the residence of the *Kurushima daimyō* (12,500 k.).

Mori, 森. *Daimyō* family coming from *Mino* and descended from *Minamoto Yoshitaka* (+ 1159), 7th son of *Yoshiie* (*Seiwa-Genji*).

Yoshinari { Nagayoshi { Tadamasa-Nagatsugu { Nagatake-Naganari-Tadatsugu (a)
{ { Nagatoshi-Naganori-Toshiharu (b)

(*a*) — Elder branch. — **Yoshinari, 可成** (1523-1570). Son of *Yoshiyuki*, *Echigo no kami*, first served *Saitō Toshimasa*, then *Oda Nobunaga* and was killed whilst fighting against *Asai Nagamasa* and *Asakura Yoshikage*.

—— **Nagayoshi** or **Nagakazu, 長一** (1558-1584). Succeeded his father as lord of *Kanayama* (*Mino*) and took part in *Nobunaga's* campaigns against the bonzes of *Nagashima* (*Ise*) (1575) and against the *Takeda* (1582); after the destruction of the latter, he received 100,000 k. as revenue in *Shinano*. He was killed at the battle of *Nagakute*, whilst opposing *Ieyasu*.

—— **Tadamasa, 忠政** (1570-1634). Younger brother of *Nagayoshi*, succeeded him in his fief of *Matsushiro* (*Shinano*—120,000 k.). In 1603, he was transferred to *Tsuyama* (*Mimasaka* — 185,000 k.) with the title of *Mimasaka no kami*. — His great-grandson having died without issue in 1697, his domains return to the *Shōgun*; then a relative, *Tadatsugu*, was chosen to perpetuate his name and received 20,000 k. income; in 1706, he settled at *Akō* (*Harima*) where his descendants remained till the Restoration. — To-day Viscount.

(*b*) — Junior branch which from 1697 to 1868, resided at *Mikazuki* (*Harima* — 15,000 k.). — To-day Viscount.

Mori, 森. *Samurai* family of the *Kagoshima* (*Satsuma*) clan, made noble in 1887. — Now Viscount.

—— **Arinori, 有禮** (1847-1889). Was minister of Public Instruction since the year 1885, when, on the day of the proclamation of the Constitution (Feb. 11th, 1889), he was assassinated by a *Shintō* fanatic — *Nishino Buntarō*, by name. Rumor has it that one day, whilst visiting the temples of *Ise*, *Arinori* raised the sacred curtain with his cane in order to be able to look into the sanctuary, and it was this insult offered to the gods that *Buntarō* pretended to revenge. *Arinori* had studied in England and introduced many happy reforms in the management of different schools.

Mōri, 毛利. *Daimyō* family issued from the province of *Aki* and descended from *Ōe Hiromoto* (1148-1225).

—— **Suemitsu, 季光** (+1221). Son of *Hiromoto*, the first to take the name of *Mōri*.

—— **Tokichika, 時親**. Grandson of *Suemitsu*, settled at *Yoshida* (*Aki*).

—— **Motonari, 元就** (1497-1571). Descendant of *Tokichika* in the 9th generation. Resided at *Sarukake*, in the district of *Tajihi* (*Aki*). Having had a quarrel with his suzerain *Amako Tsunehisa*, he joined *Ōuchi Yoshitaka* and fought against him.

Ōuchi having been killed by his vassal *Sue Harukata* (1551), *Motonari* entered the lists against *Harukata*, defeated and killed him (1555) ; after this, he gradually occupied the domains of the *Ōuchi*, besieged *Yoshinaga* in *Yamaguchi* (*Suwō*) and conquered the city in 1557.   At that time, the financial state of the empire was in such a poor condition that the new emperor *Ōgimachi* had to wait two years before he could be crowned ; in 1560, *Motonari* took upon himself the expenses connected with the cere-mony and received in acknowledgment of his services the title of *Daizen-tayū* and the privilege to bear on his escutcheon the imperial chrysanthemum and the paulownia.
Meanwhile, his sons were fighting for him in all directions : nearly the whole *San-yō-dō* and the *San-in-dō* were under his power.   War broke out between him and *Ōtomo Sōrin*, the most powerful of the *Kyūshū daimyō*, but the *Shōgun Yoshiteru* acted as mediator between them : a daughter of *Sōrin* was betrothed to the grandson of *Motonari*, who was to keep only the castle of *Moji* (*Buzen*) in *Kyūshū*.   On the other side the *Amako* continued their resistance to their ancient

MŌRI MOTONARI.

vassal ; *Monotari* invaded *Izumo*, and after a long siege occupied the castle of *Toda* ; the last of the *Amako, Yoshihisa*, was confined in *Aki*, and *Motonari* became master of 10 provinces ; he has, on this account, been called *jū-koku no taishu* (1566).   He was the father of 9 sons ; the eldest, *Takamoto*, having died, *Motonari* was succeeded by his grandson, *Terumoto*.

	Takamoto-Terumoto {	Hidenari -Tsunahiro -Yoshinari	(a)
		Naritaka -Motokata -Mototsugu	(b)
Motonari {	Motoharu (*Kikkawa*)		(c)
	Takakage (*Kobayakawa*)		(d)
	Motoaki -Motoyasu		(e)
	Motokiyo -Hidemoto-Mitsuhiro-Tsunamoto-Mototomo		(f)
	Motomasa		
	Hidekane -Motonobu-Motofusa		(g)

—— **Takamoto.** 隆元 (1523-1563).   Eldest son of *Motonari*, helped his father in different campaigns, himself conquered *Bitchū* and governed the provinces of *Nagato, Aki, Bingo*.   He died before his father, at the age of 41.

(*a*) — Senior branch. —— **Terumoto,** 輝元 (1553-1625).   Son of *Takamoto*, succeeded his grandfather *Motonari*.   In 1570, with the help of his uncles *Kikkawa Motoharu*, and *Kobayakawa Takakage*, he raised an army against *Amako Katsuhisa* and *Yamanaka Yukimori*, and besieged them in the castle of *Suetsugu* (*Izumo*).   Having heard that his grandfather was dangerously ill, he left the command of the troops to *Motoharu* and hastened with *Takakage* to come to *Motonari*.   When *Suetsugu* surrendered, *Yukimori* was taken prisoner and sent to *Odaka* (*Hōki*), whence he was able to make his escape ; *Katsuhisa* fled to the *Oki* islands and from thence went to *Kyōto*.   In 1573, the *Shōgun Yoshiaki*, deposed by *Nobunaga*, sought shelter near *Terumoto*.

Nobunaga displeased, helped *Katsuhisa* and *Yukimoro* and enabled them to carry on the war : they invaded *Tajima*, and *Yamana Toyokuni* joined them ; in *Inaba*, they fortified themselves in the castle of *Tottori*. *Motoharu* marched against them and *Toyokuni* surrendered whilst *Katsuhisa* fortified himself in *Wakaza*. The following year (1575), *Terumoto* brought fresh supplies to *Motoharu* and *Katsuhisa* again entered *Tajima*. Two years later, *Katsuhisa* and *Yukimori*, re-entered the field, and forming the van-guard of *Hideyoshi's* army, they stopped at the castle of *Kōzuki* (*Harima*) ; *Terumoto* came and besieged them ; they were soon reduced to the last extremity and *Katsuhisa* committed *harakiri* (1578). Meanwhile, *Hideyoshi* was advancing, and having traversed *Inaba*, laid siege to the castle of *Takamatsu*, defended by *Shimizu Muneharu*, *Terumoto's* vassal. Having stormed the place, he sent the bonze *Ankokuji Ekei* to *Terumoto* to make peace. Whilst the deliberations were pending, *Hideyoshi* received the news of the assassination of *Nobunaga*. He at once invited *Muneharu* to commit *harakiri*, and announced his intention to *Terumoto* to continue the war : *Takakage* however brought his nephew to accept the propositions of peace. In 1587, *Terumoto* assisted in the *Kyūshū* expedition against the *Shimazu*. In 1591, he built the castle of *Hiroshima* and used it as his residence ; he now had a revenue of 1,200,000 k. Before dying, *Hideyoshi* chose him as one of the 5 *Tairō* who were to form the regency during the minority of his son *Hideyori*. In 1600, he fought against *Ieyasu* and during the campaign of *Sekigahara*, he was intrusted with the castle of *Ōsaka*. On the news of the defeat of his allies, he surrendered at once, and to gain favors with the victor, he went so far as to behead the son of *Konishi Yukinaga*, who had been intrusted to him. This shameful villany did not soften *Ieyasu* who took 8 provinces from him and left him only *Nagato* and *Suwō*, with a revenue of 369,000 k. Soon after, *Terumoto* shaved his head, took the name of *Sōzui* and left his domains to his son.

—— **Hidenari**, 秀就 (1595-1651). Son of *Terumoto*, succeeded his father in the government of *Nagato* and *Suwō* and, in 1601, built the castle of *Hagi* (*Nagato*), where he resided. In 1608, he obtained the privilege to bear the name of *Matsudaira* and the title of *Nagato no kami* ; at the same time he married an adopted daughter of the *Shōgun Hidetada*. In 1615, he assisted at the siege of *Ōsaka*.

—— **Narihiro**, 齊廣 (1814-1836). Descendant of *Hidenari* and, like his ancestor, lord of *Nagato* and *Suwō*, was a distinguished man of letters and wrote several books.

—— **Motonori**, 元德 (1839-1896). Son of *Hiroshige, daimyō* of *Tokuyama* (*Suwō*), was adopted in 1851 by *Yoshichika*, brother and successor of *Narihiro*. At the time when he assumed the administration of his domains, the shōgunate was endangered ; the expulsion of foreigners and the restoration of the imperial power was the order of the day. The emperor *Kōmei* secretly sent a letter to *Motonori*, asking his support, and the protection of *Kyōto* was intrusted to the two clans of *Satsuma*, and *Chōshū*. The *Shōgun Iemochi* received orders to expel foreigners and to bring about some reforms in the government. Following the instructions he had received, *Motonori* ordered his men to fire on the European vessels that passed the channel of *Shimonoseki* (1863). Being blamed for such a rash action, he attributed this disapproval to the influence of the *Shōgun* and in order to protect the emperor from evil counsellors, he resolved to become master of his person ; to that end, a a great number of *samurai* from *Nagato* assembled in *Kyōto* and soon entered into conflict with the toops of *Aizu* and *Satsuma*. The emperor published an edict, depriving *Motonori* and *Yoshichika* of the title of *daimyō* and ordering the *Shōgun* to march against *Chōshū*. In the meantime, the combined forces of the nations concerned in the affair were preparing to demand satisfaction for the aggression of the preceding year. At that time, two young *samurai* of the dreaded clan, were making their way to *Yokohama* : their names were *Itō Shunsuke* and *Inoue Bunda* ; they were destined to play a great part in the government of the Restoration, and become two of its great ministers. At the time of the aggression of their prince, they were in England ; they left at once, promising to obtain satisfaction from their *daimyō* ; they obtained a respite of 12 days, but their efforts remained fruitless : *Shimonoseki* was bombarded, and *Motonori* was obliged to promise an indemnity of 15 million francs and the free passage of the straits (Sept. 1864). Meanwhile the *Shōgun* had given orders to the neighboring *daimyō* to attack the rebel : assailed at the same time from three sides, *Chōshū* was everywhere victorious (1865-1866). Shortly after, the *Shōgun* died suddenly at *Ōsaka* (Sept. 1866) ; the emperor *Kōmei* soon followed him to the grave (Feb. 1867), and the expedition against *Nagato* was abandoned. In the beginning of 1868, the Shōgunate was abolished and *Motonori* reestablished in all his titles and dignities. His troops were conspicuous in the defeat of the *Shōgun's* army at *Fushimi*, at *Toba*, and at the capture of *Shizuoka*, *Edo*, *Wakamatsu* and *Hakodate*. On the advice of one of his *samurai*, *Kido Kōin*, when Councellor of State, *Motonori* was the first to propose that the *daimyō* should remit to the Emperor their fiefs and their revenues. — When the titles of nobility were created, *Motonori* received the title of Duke. His 5th son was entitled to found a branch with the title of Baron.

(*b*) — Junior Branch issued from **Naritaka,** 就 隆 (1603-1680). *Hyūga no kami*, 2nd son of *Terumoto*. From 1634 to 1868, it resided at *Tokuyama* (*Suwō* — 30,000 k.). — To-day Viscount.

(*c*) — See **Kikkawa.**

(*d*) — See **Kobayakawa.**

(*e*) — **Motoyasu,** 元 康 . Succeeded his brother *Motoaki*, who had died without issue. He fought under the command of his brother *Takakage* during the expedition to Korea. During the campaign of *Sekigahara* (1600), he besieged the castle of *Ōtsu*, was defeated and dispossessed.

(*f*) — **Motokivo,** 元 清 . Son of *Motonari*, was adopted when yet a child by the *Hoida* family, whose name he took. He fixed his residence in the castle of *Sarukake* (*Bitchū*). In 1577, he made a campaign in *Sanuki*, then, together with his brothers *Motoharu* and *Takakage*, he fought against *Amako Katsuhisa* and against *Ukita Naoie*. In 1583, he established himself in the castle of *Yamanaka*, again assumed the name of *Mōri* and received the title of *Iyo no kami*. He attended the expedition to Korea.

—— **Hidemoto,** 秀元 (1579-1650). Son of *Motokiyo*, first bore arms in the war against the *Hōjō* of *Odawara* (1590) and took part in the expedition to Korea. He returned a little before the death of *Hideyoshi* and received a revenue of 200,000 k. in the provinces of *Nagato*, *Suwō*, and *Aki* ; but after *Sekigahara* (1600), he was reduced to the small domain of *Fuchū* (*Nagato* — 50,000 k.). *Hidemoto* is often called *Toyoura no Sangi.* — His descendants resided at *Fuchū* (or *Toyoura*) till the Restoration. — Now Viscount.

In 1653, a branch of this family settled at *Kiyosue* (*Nagato* — 10,000 k.), and remained there till the Restoration. — Now Viscount.

(*g*) — **Hidekane,** 秀包 (1566-1601). 9th son of *Motonari*, was adopted, when a child, by *Ōta Hidetsuna*. When *Hideyoshi* had made peace with the *Mōri*, he took *Hidekane* with him to *Kyōto* and later on gave him the name of *Toyotomi*. After the *Kyūshū* expedition against the *Shimazu* (1587), he received the fief of *Kurume* (*Chikugo* — 210,000 k.) and the title of *Jibu-tayū*. It was during this campaign that he became a Christian, having being brought to make that step by the advice of *Kuroda Yoshitaka*. He was baptized and received the name of Simon. He took part in the expedition to Korea. At the time of the *Sekigahara* campaign, he followed *Tachibana Muneshige*, *daimyō* of *Yanagawa*, and fought against *Ieyasu*. He had no success in besieging the castle of *Ōtsu* (*Ōmi*) that was defended by *Kyōgoku Takatsugu*. During his absence, *Nabeshima Naoshige*, *daimyō* of *Saga*, came to invest *Kurume*, but *Kuroda Yoshitaka* and *Katō Kiyomasa* invited the garrison to surrender. After the campaign, *Hidekane* was dispossessed and retired to the estate of his nephew *Terumoto* with his son *Francis Motonobu*.

Mōri, 毛利. *Daimyō* family of *Owari*, descended from the *Uda-Genji* through *Namazue Takahisa*. Was first called *Mori*, then assumed the name of *Mōri*.

—— **Takamasa,** 高政 (1556-1628). Followed the fortunes of *Hideyoshi*, took part in the expedition of Korea, and in 1594, received the fief of *Saeki* (*Bungo* — 60,000 k.) In 1600, he sided against *Ieyasu*, who was content with reducing his revenues to 20,000 k. — His descendants resided at *Saeki* till the Restoration. — Now Viscount.

Mōri, 毛利. *Daimyō* family of the 16th century.

—— **Katsunobu,** 勝信 (+ 1601). Served *Hideyoshi*, who gave him the fief of *Kokura* (*Buzen* — 60,000 k.). He assisted in the expedition to Korea, then, in 1600, having taken sides against *Ieyasu*, he was banished to *Tosa*, where he died soon after.

—— **Katsunaga,** 勝永 (+ 1615). Son of *Katsunobu*, was exiled with his father, but at the time of the siege of *Ōsaka*, he secretly fled from *Tosa* with his son *Katsuie* and came to offer his services to

Hideyori. Both killed themselves when the castle fell into the hands of the enemy.

Mōri san-ke, 毛利三家. The three principal vassal families of the *Mōri* in the 16th century : *Kikkawa, Kobayakawa* and *Shishido.*

Mori Sōi, 森宗意 (+ 1638). *Samurai* of *Konishi Yukinaga,* who, after the death of his master (1600), retired to *Amakusa* and was one of the chiefs of the *Shimabara* insurrection. He was killed at the capture of *Hara.*

Mori Sosen, 森祖仙 (1747-1821). Famous painter, was born in *Nagasaki* but lived in *Ōsaka.* He showed special skill in painting monkeys.

Morikawa, 森川. *Daimyō* family from *Owari* and descended from the *Seiwa-Genji.*

—— **Shigetoshi,** 重俊 (1584-1632). Son of *Ujitoshi,* was ennobled in 1627 and received a revenue of 10,000 k. at *Ikumi* (*Shimōsa*) with the titles of *Naizen no kami,* and *Dewa no kami.* When the ex-*Shōgun Hidetada* died, *Shigetoshi* killed himself (*junshi*) in order not to survive his master. — His descendants were at *Ikumi* till the Restoration. — At present Viscount.

Morikawa Kyoroku, 森川許六 (1641-1715). Poet (esp. in the *hokku* style) and painter, pupil of *Basho.*

Morikuni-Shinnō, 守邦親王 (1301-1333). Grandson of the emperor *Go-Fukakusa* and son of the *Shōgun Hisaakira-shinnō,* at the age of 7, succeeded his father who had been deposed by the *Shikken Hōjō Sadatoki* (1308). After the destruction of the *Hōjō* he became bonze and died the same year.

Morinaga-Shinnō, 護良親王 (1308-1335). Son of the emperor *Go-Daigo* and of *Minamoto Chika-ko,* daughter of *Morochika.* At the death of the crown-prince *Kuninaga-shinnō, Go-Daigo* had resolved to replace him by *Morinaga,* but *Hōjō Takatoki* opposed it, and brought the choice on *Kazuhito-shinnō,* son of *Go-Fushimi* (1326): *Morinaga* became bonze and took the name of *Son-un,* and the following year, was made chief (*zasu*) of the temples of *Hiei-zan.* He established himself in the village of *Ōtō* (*Yamato*), hence the name of *Ōtō no miya* which

MORINAGA-SHINNŌ

was given to him. In 1331, when *Takatoki* was marching against *Kyōto* to dethrone *Go-Daigo, Son-un* with his brother *Sonchō* (*Munenaga-shinnō*), placed himself at the head of the troops levied by the bonzes, and tried to arrest the advance of the enemy, but he was defeated. He then concealed himself in the district of *Kumano* (*Kii*) put aside the garb of bonze, took his name of *Morinaga* again and gathered together partisans to his father's cause. After the ruin of the *Hōjō* (1333) he was named *Sei-i-tai-shōgun,* but the following year, having been calumniated before *Go-Daigo,* he was deposed, imprisoned in the *Nikai-dō* of *Kamakura* and placed under the guard of *Ashikaga*

Tadayoshi. In 1335, *Hōjō Tokiyuki* came to attack *Kamakura.* *Tadayoshi* was defeated and fled. Before his flight he had his prisoner put to death by the hands of *Fuchibe Yoshihiro.*

Morioka, 盛岡. Chief town (33,000 inh.) of the *Iwate-ken* and of the province of *Rikuchū.*—After having defeated *Fujiwara Yasuhira* (1189), *Yoritomo* divided the provinces of *Mutsu* and *Dewa* among several of his officers: *Nambu Mitsuyuki* received 5 districts (*kōri*) and settled at *Tega-saki.* Later on, one of his descendants fixed his residence at *Sannohe*; finally, in 1596, *Toshinao* built the castle of *Morioka,* where his successors remained till the Restoration. — The city and the former fief of

ASSASSINATION OF MORINAGA-SHINNŌ.

its *daimyō* are to the present day known by the name of *Nambu.*

Morioka, 森岡. *Samurai* family from *Kagoshima* (*Satsuma*) ennobled after the Restoration. — Now Baron.

Morisada-shinnō, 守貞親王 (1179-1223). 2d son of the emperor *Takakura.* He was taken to the West with his brother *Antoku* by the *Taira* (1183) then brought back to *Kyōto* after the battle of *Dan no ura.* After the *Shōkyū* war, his son, then 10 years old, was chosen by the *Shikken Hōjō Yoshitoki* to succeed *Chūkyō-tennō* (1221); *Morisada,* who had his head shaved in 1212, received the title of *Dajō-hō-ō* and the name of *Go-Takakura-in*; it was the first time that a *prince* had the title of *Dajō-tennō.* He married the daughter of *Fujiwara Motoie* and lived in his palace, the *Jimyō-in*; for this reason he is often called *Jimyō-in.*

Moriyama, 守山. In *Owari.* Old castle built towards 1525 by the *Oda* family.

Moriyama, 守山. In *Iwaki.* Was, from 1700 to 1868, the residence of a branch of the *Matsudaira* family (20,000 k.), that came from the *Tokugawa* of *Mito.*

Moriyama, 守山. In *Etchū*. The *shugo* of the province, *Shiba Yoshimasa*, was besieged there by *Momonoi Naotsune* (1335). Towards the end of the 16th century, the castle became the residence of *Maeda Toshinaga*, who later on settled at *Toyama*.

Moriyoshi-yama, 森吉山. Mountain (1600 m.) in *Ugo*.

Mororan, 室蘭. Port (4200 inh.) of *Hokkaidō*, chief town of the *Iburi* province.

Morokoshi, 唐土, 諸越. Name formerly given to China and often extended to Europe.

Moruyama, 守山. In *Ōmi*. Was at the end of the 16th century the residence of a *daimyō*, *Ujie Yukitsugu* (15,000 k.). — Also called *Moriyama*.

Mōshi, 孟子. Japanese name of the Chinese philosopher *Mencius* (371-289 B. C.).

Motoda, 元田. *Samurai* family of the *Kumamoto* (*Higo*) clan ennobled after the Restoration.—To-day Baron.

Motojime-yaku, 元〆役. Under the *Tokugawa*, an official immediately below the *Kin-bugyō*.

Motoori Norinaga, 本居宣長 (1730-1801). Famous man of letters. His family came from *Taira Yorimori*. Born at *Matsuzaka* (*Ise*), applied himself to the study of Japanese antiquity, calling on the learned *Kamo Mabuchi* to obtain the explanation of difficult passages. He intended to counteract the exaggerated attention which was then given to Chinese literature (*kangaku*), and for this purpose, raised the ancient Japanese literature (*wagaku*) to its former place of honour. He published 55 works, containing in all more than 180 volumes ; his principal work, to which he devoted more than 30 years (1764-1796) is the *Kojoki-den*. His works contributed not a little to the revival of Shintoism and to the Restoration of the imperial power whilst they opened a new era to

MOTOORI NORINAGA.

national literature. — *Kada Azumamaro*, *Kamo Mabuchi* and *Norinaga* are called the three great literati (*san-daijin*) of Japan ; to them was added, later on, *Hirata Atsutane*, thus forming the *Kokugaku shi-daika* — The son of *Norinaga*, *Haruniwa* (1763-1828), his adopted son *Ōhira* (1758-1833), his grandson *Uchitō* (1792-1855), continued his teaching.

Motosu-ko, 本巣湖. Lake (12 Km. circumference) in *Kai* ; one of the 8 lakes that lie at the foot of Mount *Fuji*.

Mugi-saki, 麥崎. Cape, S. of the province of *Shima*.

Mukai-jima, 向島. Island (26 Km. circumference) of the Inland Sea, S. W. of the *Bingo* province, opposite the port *Onomichi*.

Mukai-jima, 向島. Island (14 Km. circumference) of the Inland Sea, opposite the port *Mitajiri*, S. W. of the *Suwō* province. Called also *Mukō-jima*.

Mukōjima, 向島. Village in *Yamashiro*, between the *Uji-gawa* and the *Ogura* pond. *Hideyoshi* erected a castle there, which he left in 1595 for that of *Fushimi*. After his death (1598) *Ieyasu* took up his residence in the same place. Towards 1620, this castle was abandoned at the same time as that of *Fushimi*.

Muko no minato, 武 庫 港. Ancient name of the port of *Hyōgo* (*Settsu*), very much visited even in olden times. It was the landing place of the ships carrying the tribute of the *San-kan* (Korea). Later on, it was called *Wada no tomari, Hyōgo*.

Mukwan, 無 關 (+ 1293). Also called *Fumon*. Renowned bonze of the *Tōfuku-ji* temple in *Kyōto*. After his death, he received the titles of *Busshin-Zenshi* and *Daimyō-kokushi*. He is the founder of the *Nanzen-ji* temple.

Munakata, 宗 像. Family descended from the *Minamoto* and by inheritance, the head of the Shintoist temple of *Munakata-jinja*, situated in the district of *Munakata* (*Chikuzen*), between the villages of *Tashima* and *Ōshima*.

—— **Kiyouji, 清 氏**. Named in 914 chief (*daigūji*) of the *Munakata* temple, from which he took his name.

—— **Ujikuni, 氏 國**. Descendant of *Kiyouji*, built in 1182, a castle on *Shira-yama*, to protect the temple and its dependencies. In 1216, he adopted *Ujitoshi*, son of *Ōtomo Toshinao*, and transmitted him his charge.

—— **Ujihiro, 氏 弘**. Became *daigūji* in 1444. He defeated *Shōni Noriyori* who had intended to strip him of his domains (1469), and obliged him to escape to *Tsushima*.

—— **Okiuji, 與 氏**. Son of *Ujihiro*, joined *Ōuchi Yoshioki* in order to repulse a new attack of *Shōni Noriyori* (1506).

—— **Ujio, 氏 男** (+ 1551). Sided with *Ōuchi Yoshitaka*, when this latter was attacked by his vassal *Sue Harukata ;* he was defeated and killed himself in the temple *Dainei-ji* at *Fukagawa*, (*Suwō*).

—— **Ujisada, 氏 貞**. Was constantly at war with his neighbors. He died in 1586, and at his death his family disappears.

Munenaga-shinnō, 宗 良 親 王 (1312-1385). 4th son of the emperor *Go-Daigo*. In 1326, he became bonze, took the name of *Sonchō*, resided in the temple of *Myōhō-in* and became head (*zasu*) of the *Tendai* sect. In 1331, together with his brother *Son-un* (*Morinaga-shinnō*), he fought against *Sasaki Tokinobu*, was captured at *Kasagi-san* and exiled to *Sanuki*. After the ruin of the *Hōjō*, (1333) he returned to *Kyōto*, and when *Takauji* revolted against *Go-Daigo*, he put aside his priestly garb and resumed his former name of *Munenaga* : he is also called *Kōzuke-shinnō* or *Shinano no Miya*. He was then named *Nakatsukasa-kyō* and, later on, *Sei-i-tai-shōgun*. He fought in *Tōtōmi*, in *Shinano* and in *Echigo* against the partisans of the *Ashikaga*. In 1377, he re-entered the temple *Hase-dera*, passed from thence to *Shinano* and came to *Ii-no-ya* (*Tōtōmi*), to die. A temple was built there in his honor in 1871. *Munenaga-shinnō* was a distinguished poet. His son, *Okinaga-Ō*, had died before him.

Munetaka-shinnō, 宗 尊 親 王 (1242-1274). 2nd son of the emperor *Go-Saga*, was chosen, in 1252, by *Hōjō Tokiyori* to succeed the deposed *Shōgun Yoritsugu*. In 1266, pressed by the bonze *Ryōki*, he took the resolution to free himself from the tutelage of the *Hōjō*, but the plot having become known, he was deposed and confined in the *Rokuhara* (*Kyōto*). He shaved his head and took the name of *Gyōshō* (1272). *Munetaka* had two sons : *Koreyasu-shinnō*, who succeeded him in the charge of *Shōgun*, and the bonze *Shintaku*, chief of the *Emma-in* temple. His two daughters married the emperor *Go-Uda*.

Munin-tō, 無 人 嶋 . (Lit. : Islands without inhabitants). — See *Ogasawara-jima*.

Muraji, 連 . One of the 8 *kabane* created in 682 by the emperor *Temmu*. It was given to the head of some corporations : *Mononobe no Muraji*, etc.

Murakami, 村 上 . Town (7,800 inh.) of *Echigo*. — Was first named *Honjō*, and was the residence of a family bearing that name, and vassal of the *Uesugi*. Passed then to the *daimyō Murakami* (1596), *Hori* (1618), *Honda* (1644), *Matsudaira* (1649), *Sakakibara* (1667), *Honda* (1704), *Ōkōchi* (1710), *Manabe* (1717) and, from 1720 to 1868, *Naitō* (70,000 k.).

Murakami, 村 上 . *Daimyō* family descended from *Tamehira-shinnō*, son of the emperor *Murakami*.

—— **Yorikiyo,** 頼 清 . Son of *Chinjufu-shōgun Minamoto Yorinobu*, was adopted by *Norisada*, son of *Tamehira-shinnō*, and was the first who took the name of *Murakami*.

—— **Yoshiteru,** 義 光 (+ 1333). Also called *Hikoshirō*, descendant of *Yorikiyo*, showed himself an ardent defender of the southern dynasty ; he was killed, whilst defending prince *Morinaga* in the mountains of *Yoshino*. His son *Yoshitaka* died before him, at the age of 18.

—— **Yoshikiyo,** 義 清 (1501-1573). Lord of *Kuzuo* (*Shinano*), fought during 30 years against the *Takeda*, *Nobutora* and *Shingen* ; in 1553, he asked help from *Uesugi Kenshin*, of *Echigo*, and assisted him in his campaign of *Kawanakajima*. In 1565, he resided at the castle of *Nechi* (*Echigo*), then had his head shaved (1569) and ceded his domains to his son *Kunikiyo*.

—— **Yoshiakira,** 義 明 (+ 1624). First served *Niwa Nagahide*, then *Hideyoshi*, who gave him the castle of *Honjō* (*Echigo* — 95,000 k.). After *Sekigahara*, he was one of the counsellors of *Tadateru*, son of *Ieyasu*, and when this latter, charged with having aspired to the shōgunate, was dispossessed, *Yoshiakira* was also deprived of his domains and banished to *Sasayama* (*Tamba*) (1618), where he died.

Murakami-Genji, 村 上 源 氏 . Patronymic name of the families descended from the sons of the emperor *Murakami*, who received the name of *Minamoto*.

Murakami-tennō, 村 上 天 皇 . 62nd Emperor of Japan (947-967). *Nariakira*, 16th son of *Daigo-tennō*, at the age of 21, succeeded his brother *Shujaku*. In order to diminish the influence of the *Fujiwara*, he did not, at the death of the *Kwampaku Tadahira* (949), give him a successor but assumed the government himself. The first fire that destroyed the imperial palace took place under his reign (960) : it was the palace that had been built by *Kwammu-tennō* in 794. *Murakami-*

tennō died at the age of 42. The following list indicates the principal families issued from him and bearing the name of *Minamoto*.

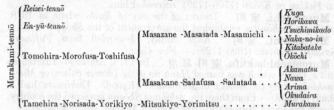

Murakami-tennō

Reizei-tennō

En-yū-tennō

Tomohira-Morofusa-Toshifusa

Masazane -Masasada -Masamichi . .

Kuga
Horikawa
Tsuchimikado
Naka-no-in
Kitabatake
Okōchi

Masakane -Sadafusa -Sadatada . . .

Akamatsu
Nawa
Arima
Okudaira

Tamehira -Norisada-Yorikiyo -Mitsukiyo-Yorimitsu . . . . *Murakami*

Murakuni Oyori, 村國男依 (+ 676). Faithful servant of prince *Ō-ama* (*Temmu*). At the time of the *Jinshin* civil war (672), he opposed the emperor *Kōbun* and defeated the imperial army in *Ōmi*. After *Kōbun* had killed himself, *Oyori* cut off his head and sent it to *Ō-ama*, who, once on the throne, rewarded him by conferring on him various domains. — His son *Shigamaro* succeeded him.

Muramatsu, 村松. City (7200 inh.) of *Echigo*. Was from 1644 to 1868, the residence of the *Hori daimyō* (30,000 k.).

Murasaki Shikibu, 紫式部 (+ 992). Daughter of *Fujiwara Tametoki*, *Shikibu no Jō*. She married *Fujiwara Nobutaka* and was maid of honor to the empress *Jōtō mon-in*, wife of *Ichijō-tennō*. At a very tender age, she showed an astonishingly good memory and great facility for poetry. She is the author of the *Genji-monogatari* and of the *Murasaki Shikibu Nikki*. When reading the *Genji-monogatari*, the emperor *Ichijō* said that the author must have known the *Nihon-ki* by heart; it is for this

MURASAKI SHIKIBU.

reason that she was surnamed *Nihonki no Tsubone*. — She had a daughter who married the *Dazai-daini Takashina Nariaki*, and was the nurse of *Go-Ichijō-tennō*; she is usually called *Dazai-sammi*; she cultivated poetry and wrote the *Sagoromo-monogatari*.

Murata, 村田. *Samurai* family of *Kagoshima* (*Satsuma*) ennobled after the Restoration. — Now Baron.

Murata Harumi, 村田春海 (1746-1811). Man of letters, a pupil of *Kamo Mabuchi*.

Muro Kyusō, 室鳩巣 (1658-1734). By his true name *Naokiyo*. Famous Confucianist. Received lessons from *Kinoshita Jun-an*. In 1711, with the recommendation of *Arai Hakuseki*, he became a functionary of the shōgunate and settled on *Surugadai* hill (*Edo*), whence his name *Shundai-sensei*. By his teaching, he made the philosophy of the Chinese *Tchou-hi* (1130-1200) popular. He left several works. — His son *Fukken* or *Kōkan* (1706-1739), succeeded him.

Muromachi, 室町. District of the city of *Kyōto* where in 1378, *Ashikaga Yoshimitsu* established the government of the *Shōgun*.

Muromachi, 室町. *Kuge* family, descended from *Fujiwara (Saionji) Michisue* (1090-1128). — Now Count.

Muromachi-bakufu, 室町幕府. In 1378, *Ashikaga Yoshimitsu* built a palace which was named *Hana no gosho* (flower palace) or *Muromachi-dono*, in the district of *Muromachi* (*Kyōto*). *Yoshimasa* had it rebuilt in 1459. — From there the *Ashikaga Shōgun* governed the country, whence the name *Muromachi-bakufu* given to their administration.

Muromachi-banshū, 室町番衆. Under the shōgunate of the *Ashikaga*, guards of the *Muromachi* palace. The *samurai* of *Kyōto* were divided in 5 sections (*go banshū* or *go kaban*) having a *ban-gashira* at their head. They kept guard in turn. Those who were with the *Shōgun* on the reception days of the 1st of the month and of the 5 *sekku*, were called *sessakushū*. The *tsumeshū* guarded the *Shōgun* whilst he was a minor. The *o-heya-shū* protected the *Shōgun* during his sleep. Lastly the guards that remained all the day in the apartment called *kosode no ma*, were known by the name *o-kosode go-banshū*.

Muromachi-dono, 室町殿. Name given to the shōgunal palace of the *Ashikaga* at *Kyōto*. The one built by *Yoshimitsu* in 1378, was properly named *Hana no gosho ;* the second built by *Yoshimasa* (1459), *Karasumaru-dono*.—The name *Muromachi-dono* was also employed to designate the *Shōgun* himself.

Muromachi-jidai, 室町時代. The period of the shōgunate of the *Ashikaga*, beginning in 1392, date of the fusion of the two dynasties of the N. and of the S, and lasting till 1490, accession of the *Shōgun Yoshitane*.

Muromachi jū-ichi i, 室町十一位. The 11 classes of officials under the *Ashikaga* : *ichizoku, daimyō, shugo, tozama, hyōjōshū, tomoshū, mōshitsugi, bangata, kunibito, bugyō,* and *sue-otoko*.

Muromachi san-kwanryō, 室町三管領. At the time of the shōgunate of the *Ashikaga*, the three families *Shiba, Hatakeyama,* and *Hosokawa* from which the *Kwanryō* (first minister of the *Shōgun*), was chosen.

Muromachi shi-shoku, 室町四職. During the shōgunate of the *Ashikaga*, the 4 families : *Yamana, Akamatsu, Isshiki* and *Sasaki* from which the ministers of the *Kwanryō* were chosen.

Muroto-misaki, 室戸岬. Cape S.W. of *Tosa*. Also called *Tōji-saki*.

Musashi, 武藏. One of the 15 provinces of the *Tōkaidō*. Has 20 districts (*kōri*), 8 of which depend at present on the *Tōkyō-fu*, 9 on the *Saitama-ken*, and 3 on the *Kanagawa-ken*. — Chinese name : *Bushū*.

Musashi-bō Benkei, 武藏坊辨慶. — See *Benkei*.

Musashi shi-ke, 武藏四家. The 4 most powerful families of the *Musashi* province during the Middle Ages : *Narita, Beppu, Nara* and *Goi*.

Musashi shichi-tō, 武藏七黨. The 7 vassal families of the *Uesugi*, who, at the time of the *Ashikaga*, divided among themselves the *Musashi* province. They were the *Tanji, Kisaichi, Kodama, Inomata, Nishino, Yokoyama,* and *Murayama*.

Musha-dokoro, 武者所. From the 10th century, the apartments of the *samurai* who attend an Emperor after his abdication.

Mushanokōji, 武者小路. *Kuge* family descended from *Fujiwara (Sanjō) Saneyuki* (1083-1162). — Now Viscount.

Musha roku-gu, 武者六具. The 6 principal parts of the armor of the ancient *samurai: sune-ate* (leg-armor), *hagi-te* (cuissart), *dō* (trunk), *kote* (armlet), *kubi-yoroi* (neck-piece) and *hō-ate* (helmet).

Musha - shugyō, 武者修行. At the time of the prosperity of the *bushidō*, a great number of fencing schools were established, whose graduates spread over the provinces to place their learning at the service of the *daimyō :* they were called *musha-shugyō*.

Musō - kokushi, 夢窓國師. — See *Soseki*.

Mutsu, 陸奥. Ancient province of the *Tōsandō,* which comprised the whole N.E. of *Hondo*. In 1869, it was divided into *Iwaki, Iwashiro, Rikuzen, Rikuchū* and *Rikuoku* or *Mutsu*. —Chinese name : *Ōshū*. — In ancient times, it was called *Michinoku,* then simply *Michi,* from whence the name *Mutsu*.

Mutsu, 陸奥. Northern part of the ancient

ARMOR OF THE 16TH CENTURY.

province of *Mutsu ;* named also *Rikuoku*. Comprises 9 districts (*kōri*), 8 of which depend on the *Aomori-ken,* and 1 on the *Iwate-ken*.

Mutsu, 陸奥. *Samurai* family of the *Wakayama* clan (*Kii*) ennobled after the Restoration. — Now Count.

—— **Munemitsu,** 宗光 (1844-1897). Studied at *Edo,* and supported the Imperial Restoration. He was, in 1875, a member of the Senate (*Genrō-in*) Implicated in the *Satsuma* rebellion, he was condemned to

5 years imprisonment : he left prison in 1883 and went to Europe. Later on, he became minister at Washington (1888), minister of Agriculture and Commerce (1890), then minister of Foreign Affairs (1892). As such, he aided in the revision of the treaties with the Powers and received the title of Viscount ; he was named a Count after the conclusion of the treaty of peace with China. His health obliged him to resign in May 1896, and he retired to *Ōiso* (*Sagami.*).

Mutsuhito, 睦 仁 . 122nd Emperor of Japan.—*Mutsuhito, Suke no miya*, son of *Kōmei-tennō*, was born at *Kyōto* Nov. 3, 1852. In 1860, he was named crown-prince and when his father died, Feb. 13, 1867, he succeeded him. He was then only 15 years old. The following year, the Shōgunate fell and the Imperial Restoration followed as a matter of course. A new era began, that of *Meiji* (See that name, to which is appended a summary of the principal events of the reign,) of which, 1909 is the 42nd year. The coronation ceremony took place at *Kyōto* on Nov. 12, 1868, and the following April, the capital was transferred to *Edo* which received the name of *Tōkyō*. On Feb. 9, 1869 the emperor married *Haru-ko*, 3rd daughter of the *kuge Ichijō Tadaka*, born May 28, 1850 ; they had not any children. — The crown-prince

SHINTOIST CEREMONY AT THE IMPERIAL PALACE.

Yoshihito, Haru no miya, was born on August 31, 1879, son of Mme *Yanagiwara Ai-ko* ; he was named heir presumptive on Nov. 3, 1889 On May 10, 1900, he married *Sada-ko*, the 4th daughter of the duke *Kujō Michitaka*, by whom he has 3 sons.

Myōchin, 明 珍 . Family of artisans which, during 22 generations (from 1200 to 1750), was famous in the art of forging and tempering swords. The best known of its members are : *Munesuke*, the founder of the family at *Kyōto*, and his son *Munekiyo*, who established himself at *Kamakura*.

Myōden, 名田. In the Middle Ages, when a person had cleared some waste land in order to change it into rice-fields, he became the proprietor thereof, and to distinguish these lands from the Government rice-fields (*kōden*), they received a special name and were designated by the general term of *myōden*. Their possessor was called *myōju* : if his domains were considerable, he was a *daimyō* ; if not, he was only *shōmyō*. At the time of the feudal system, these terms *daimyō* and *shōmyō* were reserved to the families of the military class according to the extent of their fiefs.

Myōe, 明惠. — See *Kōben*.

Myōgi-san, 妙義山. Mountain (600 m.) in *Kōzuke*. Has three principal summits, the *Shirakumo*, the *Kindō* and the *Kinkei*. Famous for its temple *Myōgi-jinja*, dedicated to *Yamatotakeru no mikoto*.

Myōhōdō, 明法道. Curriculum of the branches of study in the old University (*Daigaku*) : comprised esp. the Chinese law.

Myōji, 苗字. Family name. Before the Restoration, only the *samurai* and the nobles had a family name. It was generally taken from the name of the locality where one of their ancestors had resided. Since 1870, the lower classes were also obliged to adopt a family name. — See *Kabane, uji*, etc.

Myōkō-zan, 妙高山. Mountain (2,460 m.) on the boundaries of *Echigo* and *Shinano*.

Myōkyō-dō, 明經道. One of the branches of study of the old University (*Daigaku*), comprised especially Chinese classics.

Myōman-ji, 妙滿寺. Temple built in *Kyōto* in the 13th century by the bonze *Nichiju*, and which became the seat of a part of the *Nichi-ren* sect. In 1898, the name of this part of the sect was changed to *Kempon-hokke-shū*.

Myōshin-ji, 妙心寺. Buddhist temple, W. of *Kyōto*. At first, villa of *Kiyowara Natsuno* (782-837) and of his descendants, was afterwards the place of retreat of the ex-emperor *Hanazono* (1318). He presented it to the bonze *Egen* (*Kwanzan-kokushi*), who changed it into a temple of which he became the first superior (1350). Burned during the *Ōnin* war (1467) the temple was rebuilt and became the principal seat of the *Rinzai* branch of the *Zen-shū* sect. Besides 42 secondary temples in its precincts, the *Myōshin-ji* is overseer of 3,800 temples all over Japan.

Myōjō-tennō, 明正天皇. Empress (109) of Japan (1630-1643). *Oki-ko*, daughter of the emperor *Go-Mi-no-o* and of *Tokugawa Kazu-ko* (*Tōfuku-mon-in*) sister of the *Shōgun Iemitsu*, succeeded her father at the age of 6. After a reign of 15 years, during which the power was practically in the hands of her uncle *Iemitsu*, she abdicated in favor of her brother and withdrew to a place of retirement where she lived for 53 years.

N

Naba, 那 覇 . Or *Naha, Nawa.* Capital (35,500 inh.) of *Okinawa-ken (Ryūkyū).*—It is here that the troops of *Shimazu Iehisa* landed in 1609. When the Catholic missionaries, after two centuries of proscription, tried to re-enter Japan it was at *Naba* that they established themselves provisionally and there they resided from 1844 to 1848, and from 1855 to 1862.

Nabekake, 鍋 掛 . In *Shimotsuke. Satake Yoshinobu* was vanquished there in 1600 by *Sakakibara Yasumasa, Minagawa Hiroteru,* etc. generals of *Ieyasu.*

Nabeshima, 鍋 嶋 . Family of *daimyō* of *Hizen,* descendants of *Shōni Tsunefusa* and through him descendants also of the *Fujiwara.*

—— **Shigenao,** 茂 尙 . Son of *Tsunefusa,* established himself at *Nabeshima (Hizen)* towards the end of the 15th century, and took that name.

—— **Naoshige,** 直 茂 (1537-1619). Grandson of *Shigenao,* aided his suzerain *Ryūzōji Takanobu* in his war against *Ōtomo Sōrin* (1570). When, in 1584, *Takanobu* wished to attack *Satsuma, Naoshige* tried in vain to dissuade him : he took part in the campaign in which *Takanobu* was defeated and killed. *Masaie* son of *Takanobu,* succeeded him ; but little by little *Naoshige* became independent in his domains. He followed the campaign of *Hideyoshi* against the *Shimazu* (1587) and in 1590 established himself at *Saga (Hizen).* He also took part in the Korean war. In 1600, he sent his son *Katsushige* to assist *Ieyasu* in his expedition against *Uesugi Kagekatsu ;* but *Katsushige* did not arrive in time and let himself be induced by *Ishida Kazushige* to embrace his party, after which he laid siege to the castle of *Matsuzaka (Ise).* Being informed of these events, *Naoshige* hastened to call back his son and sent him against *Tachibana Muneshige, daimyō* of *Yanagawa (Chikugo),* who was then opposed to *Ieyasu.* Owing to this, *Naoshige* was confirmed in his fief of *Saga* and his revenues raised to 357,000 k.

Naoshige	Katsushige	Tadanao	-Mitsushige	-Tsunashige	(a)
		Motoshige	-Naoyoshi	-Mototake	(b)
	Tadashige	Naozumi	-Naoyuki	-Naotatsu	(c)
		-Masashige	-Naotomo	-Naomoto	(d)

(*a*)—Eldest branch-**Katsushige,** 勝 茂 (1580-1657). Son of *Naoshige.* Sent by his father to join the army of *Ieyasu* (1600), he was induced to join *Ishida Kazushige's* party, and besieged the castle of *Fushimi,* then that of *Matsuzaka (Ise).* Recalled to *Kyūshū* by *Naoshige,* he returned to *Ieyasu's* party and fought against *Tachibana Muneshige* of *Yanagawa (Chikugo).* During the *Ōsaka* campaign (1615), he stayed at *Saga,* to prevent, if necessary, any intervention of the *Satsuma* clan.

During the *Shimabara* insurrection (1637), he sent his two sons first, and afterwards took part himself in suppressing the rebellion. His descendants lived at *Saga* (*Hizen* — 357,000 k.) until 1868. — Marquis, at present. — After the Restoration, 3 branches of this family received the title of Baron.

(*b*) — Branch which from 1614 to 1868, resided at *Ogi* (*Hizen* — 73,000 k.).—Now Viscount.

(*c*) — Branch which from 1635 to 1868, resided at *Hasuike* (*Hizen* — 52,000 k.).—Now Viscount.

(*d*) — Branch which from 1610 to 1868, resided at *Kashima* (*Hizen* — 20,000 k.).—Now Viscount.

Naeki, 苗木. In *Mino*. Ancient castle which belonged successively to the *daimyō :* *Tōyama* (1573), *Kawajiri* (1583), then again, from 1600 to 1868, to the *Tōyama* (10,000 k.).

Nagahama, 長濱. Village (9,800 inh.) of the province of *Ōmi*, on the N. E. coast of lake *Biwa*. Formerly called *Imahama*. About the year 1510, *Uesaka Yasusada* built a castle there, which *Asai Hisamasa* afterwards captured. In 1573, *Nobunaga* gave it to *Hideyoshi* with a revenue of 180,000 k. *Hideyoshi* rebuilt the castle and changed its name to that of *Nagahama ;* after several years he repaired to *Himeji* (*Harima*) and confided the care of *Nagahama* to *Shibata Katsuie*, then to *Ishida Kazushige*. Under the *Tokugawa*, the *Naitō daimyō* resided there from 1606 to 1628, after which the castle was abandoned.

Nagai, 永井. Family of *daimyō*, native of *Mikawa* and descended from *Taira Yoshikane*.

Naokatsu	Naomasa	Naoyuki -Naonaga-Naomitsu	(a)
		Naotsune-Naohiro -Naohira	(b)
	Naokiyo -Naotoki -Naotane -Naomichi		(c)

(*a*) — Eldest branch—**Naokatsu, 直勝** (1563-1626). Served *Ieyasu* who gave him a revenue of 12,000 k. in 1600. After the *Ōsaka* campaign (1615), he received the fief of *Kasama* (*Hitachi* — 35,000 k.), then, in 1622, that of *Koga* (*Shimōsa* — 75,000 k.).

—— **Naomasa, 尙政** (1587-1668). Eldest son of *Naokatsu*, was transferred to *Yodo* (*Yamashiro* — 100,000 k.) in 1634.

—— **Naoyuki, 尙行**. In 1669, was transferred to *Miyazu* (*Tango* — 75,000 k.).

—— **Naonaga, 尙長**. Was killed during a ceremony at the temple of *Zōjō-ji* of *Shiba (Edo)* by *Naitō Tadakatsu* and his domains were confiscated (1680).

—— **Naomitsu, 直圓**. Brother of *Naonaga*, after whose death he received 10,000 k. of the revenues of *Kushira* (*Yamato*), where his descendants lived till the Restoration.—Now Viscount.

(*b*) — 2nd branch which resided successively : at *Karasuyama* (*Shimotsuke*) in 1687 ; at *Akō* (*Harima*) in 1702 ; at *Iiyama* (*Shinano*) in 1706 ; at *Iwatsuki* (*Musashi*) in 1711 ; finally, from 1756 to 1868 at *Kanō Mino* — 36,000 k.).—Now Viscount.

(*c*) — Branch which from 1649 to 1868, resided at *Takatsuki* (*Settsu* — 35,000 k.). — Now Viscount.

Nagakubo Sekisui, 長 久 保 赤 水 (19th century). *Samurai* of the *Mito* clan. Composed several works on Geography.

Nagakute, 長 久 手 . In *Owari*. During the campaign of *Komaki-yama* (1584), *Ieyasu* gained a victory there over the army of *Hideyoshi*, two of whose generals, *Ikeda Nobuteru* and *Mori Nagakazu*, were killed. This combat greatly raised the reputation of *Ieyasu*.

Nagamatsu, 長 松 . Family of *samurai* of the *Yamaguchi* clan (*Suwō*), ennobled after the Restoration.—Baron, at present.

Nagamori, 長 森 . In *Mino*. Ancient castle, which in the 14th entury was the residence of the *Toki daimyō*, governors of the province.

Nagano, 長 野 . In *Ise*. During the *Kamakura* shōgunate was the residence of the *Kudō daimyō*, descendants of *Suketsune*. It then passed to the *Kitabatake*, the *Nikki*, the *Toki*. In 1568, *Nobunaga* placed his brother *Nobukane* there.

Nagano, 長 野 . Capital (31,400 inh.) of *Nagano-ken*, also called *Zenkōji* on account of the large Buddhist temple of that name.

Nagano Kaku, 長 野 確 (1783-1837). Man of letters of the *Iyo* province.

Nagano-ken, 長 野 縣 . Department formed of the province of *Shinano*.—Pop. : 1,322,000 inh.—Capital : *Nagano* (31,400 inh.).— Prin. towns : *Matsumoto* (30,800 inh.) *Ueda* (23,700 inh.), *Iida* (14,000 inh.), *Kami-Suwa* (10,200 inh.), etc.

Naganuma, 長 沼 . In *Shinano*. From 1615 to 1688 was the residence of the *Sakuma daimyō* (13,000 k.).

Nagao, 長 尾 . Family of *Echigo daimyō*, descendants of *Taira* (*Muraoka*) *Yoshibumi*. They were for several centuries vassals of the *Uesugi* till *Terutora*, adopted by *Uesugi Norimasa*, became the head of that family.

—— **Kageharu,** 景 春 . Vassal of *Uesugi Akisada*, revolted against him and defeated him. They made peace in 1478 : *Kageharu* shaved his head and took the name of *Igen ;* the struggle was again renewed after the death of *Akisada* (1510).

—— **Tamekage,** 爲 景 . *Kerai* of *Uesugi Fusayoshi*, dared to reproach him for his negligence in directing his clan, and *Fusayoshi*, wishing to get rid of him, attacked him at *Nishihama* (*Etchū*) in 1509, but was overcome and killed. At that moment, a large number of *Uesu-gi's* vassals rallied to the cause of *Tamekage*. The following year, *Uesu-gi Akisada* came in his turn to fight him, but ended like *Fusayoshi*. *Usami Sadayuki*, to revenge his master, continued the war against *Tame-kage*, and it was not till 1538 that peace was concluded. *Tamekage* was killed a short time after, in fighting against the troops of the bonzes of *Ikkō-shū* of *Kaga*.—His son *Terutora* became the famous *Uesugi Ken-shin* (see that name).

Nagaoka, 長 岡 . Town (9,800 inh.) in *Echigo*. Ancient castle at first called *Zōō-san-jō*. Belonged successively to the *daimyō* : *Nagao*,

Hori (1598), *Tokugawa* (1610), *Hori* (1616), finally, from 1618 to 1868 to *Makino* (74,000 k.).

Nagaoka, 長岡. In *Yamashiro*. Was from 782 to 794 the residence of the emperor *Kwammu*, which place he left for *Kyōto*. The district of *Nagaoka* was given by *Nobunaga* to *Hosokawa Fujitaka*, who bore the name for several years. From 1626 to 1649, it became the domain of *Nagai daimyō* (10,000 k.).

Nagaoka, 長岡. Branch of the family of the *Hosokawa daimyō* of *Kumamoto* (*Higo*), ennobled in 1891. — To-day Viscount.

Nagara-gawa, 長良川. River (122 Km.) in *Mino*, which empties itself into the *Kiso-gawa*. — Also called *Gifu-gawa, Gunjō-gawa, Gotō-gawa*, etc.

Nagara-yama, 長柄山. Hill in *Ōmi*, near the town of *Ōtsu* and to the West of the temple of *Mii-dera*. It is there that the emperor *Kōbun* being defeated killed himself (672).

Nagasaki, 長崎. Capital (151,500 inh.) of *Nagasaki-ken*. — This was formerly but a poor fishing village called *Fukae no ura, Nigitatsu* or *Tama no ura*. In the 12th century, it was a part of the domains of *Taira Norimori*, then from the 13th to the 16th century, belonged to a family *Nagasaki*, which gave it its name. In the middle of the 16th century, it passed under the jurisdiction of *Ōmura Sumitada*, who, seeing foreigners trading chiefly at *Hirado*, opened for them the ports of *Yokose* and *Fukuda*, then in 1568, that of *Nagasaki*, which in a few years, became an important town. After the campaign of *Kyūshū* (1587), *Hideyoshi* seeing the increasing prosperity of that port, detached it from the domains of *Ōmura* and made it an imperial city under the direct control of the government. In 1603, *Ieyasu* placed a *bugyō* or governor there in the name of the *Shōgun*. From 1640 to 1859, *Nagasaki* was the only town in Japan where foreigners—Dutch and Chinese only — were permitted to traffic; it was also one of the 5 ports opened to Europeans by the treaty of 1857.

Nagasaki, 長崎. Family of which several members bore the title of *Naikwanryō* (minister) of the *Hōjō, Shikken* of *Kamakura*.

—— **Yoritsuna,** 頼綱 (+ 1293). Minister of *Shikken Sadatoki*, whom he induced to make away with his grandfather *Adachi Yasumori*, and for this purpose accused the latter of conspiring against his grandson (1285). Implicated in his turn in a conspiracy against *Sadatoki*, he was put to death with one of his sons.

—— **Takasuke,** 高資 (+ 1333). Minister of *Takatoki*, exercised a great influence on the feeble character of his master and governed according to his whims. His exactions and arbitrary doings caused several revolts and brought on the *Genkō* war (1331), which ended in the ruin of the *Hōjō*. *Takasuke* and his son *Takashige* perished with *Takatoki* in the burning of *Kamakura*.

Nagasaki-bugyō, 長崎奉行. Official charged with the administration of the town of *Nagasaki*, overseeing the commerce with Holland and China, the defence of the neighboring coast, etc. *Ogasawara Ichian* was the first that received the title (1603). — In 1808, the *bugyō Matsu-*

daira Yasuhide committed suicide, because he could not prevent the English ship "*Phaeton*" from entering the port of *Nagasaki*, nor burn it before it left.

Nagasaki-ken, 長崎縣. Department formed by the 6 districts of *Hizen*, the islands of *Iki, Tsushima* and a large number of smaller ones.—Pop.: 879,400 inh. — Capital : *Nagasaki* (151,500 inh.). — Prin. towns: *Sasebo* (52,500 inh.), *Nishi-Arie* (11,500 inh.), *Tomie* (10.000 inh.).

Nagasawa, 長澤. In *Etchū*. In the 14th century, was the residence of a *Nagasawa* family, which combated *Nagoshi Tokikane* and submitted to *Momonoi Naotsune* (1336). When the latter joined the southern party, his son *Naokazu*, besieged at *Nagasawa* by *Shiba Yoshimochi*, was vanquished and killed (1370).

Nagashima, 長嶋. In *Ise*. Ancient castle built, about 1555, by *Itō Shigeharu* and which passed into the hands of the bonzes of the *Kenshō-ji* temple of *Ikkō-shū*. *Nobunaga* seized it, and gave it to *Takigawa Kazumasu* (1574), with the northern districts of the province of *Ise*. In 1583, *Kazumasu* having sided with *Nobutaka* against *Nobuo*, the latter rendered himself master of *Nagashima*, which he confided to *Amano Kagetoshi*. The following year, *Hideyoshi* gave it to *Fukushima Masayori*. Under the *Tokugawa*, it was successively the residence of the *daimyō: Suganuma* (1600), *Hisamatsu* (1620), *Matsudaira* (1635), *Hisamatsu* (1649), then, from 1702 to 1868, *Masuyama* (33,000 k.).

Naga-shima, 長嶋. The most southern of the *Amakusa* group (86 Km. in circ). Belongs to *Satsuma* province.

Nagashino, 長篠. In *Mikawa*. Ancient castle of the *Suganuma daimyō*. In 1561, *Sadakage* left the *Imagawa* to serve *Ieyasu ;* 10 years after, he passed over to the *Takeda*. In 1573, *Ieyasu* took it and confided it to *Okudaira Nobumasa*, who was besieged there by *Takeda Katsuyori ;* but *Nobunaga* and *Ieyasu* came to his help and defeated the army of *Katsuyori* (1575).

Nagasune-hiko, 長髄彦. Governed the region of *Yamato* when *Jimmu-tennō* came to conquer it. He fought the invader, defeated him several times and obliged him to retreat. When *Jimmu* presented himself again, *Nagasune* prepared to fight him again, but was killed by *Umashimade no mikoto*, his nephew.

Nagatani, 長谷. Family of *kuge*, descended from *Taira Takamune*. Also called *Hase*. —To-day Viscount.

Nagato, 長門. One of the 8 provinces of *Sanyōdō*. Comprises 5 districts which belong to *Yamaguchi-ken*. — In ancient times, was called *Anato*. — Chinese name: *Chōshū*.

Nagato-keigo-ban, 長門警固番. Guard formed in 1275 to protect the coast of *Nagato* and the adjoining provinces and prevent the landing of the Mongols. Existed till 1330.

Nagatoro, 長瀞. In *Uzen*. Was from 1698 to 1868 the residence of the *Yonezu daimyō* (11,000 k.).

Nagato-tandai, 長門探題. Title created in 1275, and assigned to the official charged with the government of *Nagato* and of the coast-defence against the invasion of the Mongols. The first that received the charge was *Hōjō Muneyori* and, till the ruin of *Kamakura*, it was reserved to a member of the *Hōjō* family. The *Nagato-tandai* were also called *Chūgoku-tandai.*

Nagatsuka Masaie, 長塚正家 (+ 1600). At first *kerai* of *Niwa Nagahide,* he passed into the service of *Hideyoshi,* who gave him the fief of *Minakuchi* (*Ōmi* — 50,000 k.), and appointed him as one of the 5 *bugyō.* After the death of *Hideyoshi,* he opposed *Ieyasu,* and with *Chōsokabe Morichika,* besieged the castle of *Anotsu* (*Ise*); vanquished at *Sekigahara,* he fled to his castle of *Minakuchi,* which, soon after, was invested by *Ikeda Terumasa. Masaie* hid himself for some time at *Sakurai-dani* (*Settsu*), but was found out and committed suicide.

Nagayama, 永山. Family of *samurai* of *Kagoshima* (*Satsuma*), ennobled in 1895. — Baron at present.

Nagaya-Ō, 長屋王 (684-729). Son of prince *Takechi-shinnō* and grandson of the emperor *Temmu,* he was appointed *Sadaijin* in 724. Having conspired against *Shōmu-tennō,* he was besieged in his house by *Toneri-shinnō* and *Fujiwara Umakai:* he then killed his wife and children and committed suicide. *Nagaya-Ō* was remarkable as a literary man and a poet.

Nagi-nami futa-hashira, 諾册二柱. *Izanagi* and *Izanami.*

Nagi no yama, 奈岐山. Mountain (1590 m.) between *Mimasaka* and *Inaba.*

Nagoshi, 名越. Branch of the *Hōjō* family, descended from *Tomotoki,* 2nd son of *Yoshitoki, Shikken* of *Kamakura.*

—— **Takaie,** 高家 (+ 1333). Son of *Sadaie,* descended in the 5th generation from *Tomotoki.* He was charged by *Hōjō Takatoki* to march against *Kyōto* with *Ashikaga Takauji,* and depose *Go-Daigo* (1331). He was killed in a combat against *Akamatsu Enshin* at *Kuganawate.*

—— **Takakuni,** 高邦. Son of *Takaie,* served *Takauji* and aided him in the fight against the southern dynasty.

Nagoshi no harae, 名越祓. Shintoist ceremony of purification which takes place in the 6th month. Also called *Minazuki-barae.*

Nagoya, 名護屋. Capital (285,000 inh.) of *Aichi-ken* and of the *Owari* province. — In the 14th century, was the residence of a *Nagoya* family. About 1525, the governor of the province, *Shiba Yoshimune,* constructed a castle there which he confided to his son-in-law *Imagawa Ujitoyo. Oda Nobuhide* took it in 1532; then, when *Nobunaga* changed his residence to *Kiyosu, Nagoya* was abandoned. In 1610, *Ieyasu,* having given the province of *Owari* in fief to his 7th son *Yoshinao,* made all the *daimyō* contribute to the erection of a large castle which is to-day one of the best preserved in all Japan. The branch of the

Owari Tokugawa resided there from 1610 to 1868 with a revenue of 620,000 k.

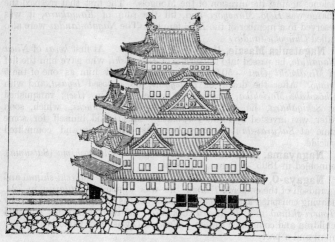

CASTLE OF NAGOYA.

Nagoya, 名護屋. Port of *Hizen*. In 1592, *Hideyoshi* built a residence there and dwelt in it at the beginning of the Korean expedition.

Naiben, 内辨. Officials charged to regulate the details of certain feasts (*sechi-e*) at Court. They were chosen from among the *Shōkei*.

Naidaijin, 内大臣. Formerly minister, who, under the *Udaijin* and the *Sadaijin*, took part in the administration of the Home Department. *Nakatomi Kamatari* was the first raised from the title of *Naijin* to that of *Naidaijin* (662); after him, *Yoshitsugu* (771) and *Uona* (779) bore the same title; but, as it was not embodied in the *Taikwa* and *Taihō* codes, it had no permanent possessor. It was first called *Uchi no Ō-omi* or *Uchi no Otodo*.

Naidantōnin, 内談頭人. Or *Hikitsuke-gashira*. Under the *Kamakura* shōgunate, president of the *Hikitsuke-shū*.

Naidōjō, 内道塲. Formerly a Buddhist temple in the interior of the Palace. As etiquette did not permit the Emperor, the Empress, etc., to go to the temples frequented by the people, the bonzes were called to the Court from time to time to perform their ceremonies at the *Naidōjō*.

Nai-en, 内宴. Feast (*sechi-e*), celebrated at the Palace the 21st, 22nd, and 23rd of the 1st month of the year: it took place in the *Ninju-den;* some poets read their works before the Emperor who then gave a banquet to the princes and the *kuge*.

Naifu, 内府. Chinese title corresponding to *Naidaijin* and sometimes used in that sense.

Nai-hyōgo-shi, 内兵庫司. Formerly a board charged with the keeping of the arms, armor, etc., of the Imperial Palace. In 808, it was joined to the *Hyōgo-ryō*.

Naijin, 内臣. — See *Naidaijin*.

Naijusho, 内豎所. Formerly, bureau of the employees and servants of the Imperial Palace. There were 300 *Naiju*, and the *Kwampaku* had the title of *Naijusho no bettō*.

Naikaku, 内閣. Since 1885, Cabinet, Council of Ministers.

Naiken-shi, 内撿使. — See *Kamakura-bakufu-shoshi*.

Naiki, 内記. — See *Uchi no shirusu-tsukasa*.

Naikū, 内宮. Shintoist temple, near the village of *Uji-Yamada* (*Ise*). It was built 4 years before Christ, and was dedicated to *Tenshōkō-daijin* (*Amaterasu*) and to *Tajikara-o no kami*. The sacred mirror, one of the 3 imperial emblems is preserved there. For centuries an imperial princess was at its head. It is customary to have it rebuilt every 20 years and always after the same model and the same dimensions. The present temple dates from 1900.

Naikubu, 内供奉. Or *Naigu*, 内供. Title of the superior of the bonzes, who, in the first month of the year was called to the palace to explain the Buddhist books, *Kongōmyō-kyō*, *Saishō-ō-kyō*, etc.

Nai-kwanryō, 内管領. Title borne by the prime minister of the *Hōjō*, regents (*shikken*) of *Kamakura* from 1200 to 1333.

Naikyōbō, 内教坊. Formerly pavilion of the Imperial Palace in which music, singing and dancing were taught to young maidens. At its head was a *Bettō* chosen from among the *Nagon*. Created in 765, it was afterwards suppressed.

Nairan, 内覧. Official created by *Yoritomo*, and charged with inspecting the Imperial Court, to inform the *Shōgun* of all that occurred there. This title corresponds to the *Shoshidai* of the *Tokugawa* shōgunate.

Nairei-shi, 内禮司. Former office, dependent on the *Nakatsu-kasa-shō*, and having charge of the protocol, the ceremonies, and etiquette to be observed in the Imperial Palace, also of the punishment of crimes that were committed there. — In 808, it was joined to the *Danjō-dai*.

Naishi-dokoro, 内侍所. Or *Kashiko-dokoro*, 賢所. Hall in the Imperial Palace in which the sacred mirror was venerated (*Yata no mi-kagami*). — The same name was given to the mirror itself.

Naishinnō, 内親王. Title given by decree to the princesses who were the nearest relatives of the Emperor. Those who did not marry became first high-priestesses of the *Shintō* temples of *Ise* or of *Kamo*, then, from the 13th century, *ama* (Buddhist nuns). The Restoration abolished this custom. When an emperor had no daughters, he adopted those of a prince and appointed them *Naishinnō*.

Naishi no tsukasa, 内侍司. Former bureau, charged with the service of the Empress' house. The personnel, composed of women only, had at its head 2 *Naishi no kami* 尚侍, 4 *Naishi no suke*, 典侍, 4 *Shōji* 掌侍 or *Naishi* 内侍 : it comprised 100 *Joju* 女繻.

Naitō, 內藤. Family of *daimyō*, native of *Mikawa* and descended from *Fujiwara Hidesato*.

Yoshikiyo ┤
Kiyonaga ┤ Ienaga -Masanaga┤ Tadaoki ┤ Yoshiyasu (a)
Masasuke (b)
Nobunari -Nobumasa-Nobuteru -Nobuyoshi ┤ Masaharu -Masachika (c)
(d)
Tadasato -Tadamasa┤ Kiyonari -Kiyotsugu-Masakatsu (e)
Masatsugu-Masakatsu-Masatomo (f)
Tadashige-Tadatane -Tadakatsu (g)

(*a*) — Eldest branch —— **Ienaga,** 家長 (1546-1600). Served *Ieyasu* who in 1590, gave him the fief of *Sanuki* (*Kazusa* — 20,000 k.). Charged with the guard of the castle of *Fushimi*, he killed himself rather than surrender.

—— **Masanaga,** 政長 (1568-1634). For his services at the siege of *Ōsaka* (1615), saw his revenues raised to 50,000 k., was then transferred to *Iwakidaira* (*Mutsu*— 70,000 k.) in 1622. — Transferred to *Nobeoka* (*Hyūga* — 70,000 k.) in 1747, his family lived there till the Restoration. — Now Viscount.

(*b*) — Younger branch, which, from 1670 to 1868, resided at *Unagaya* (*Mutsu* — 14,000 k.). — Viscount at present.

(*c*) — Branch which resided : in 1628, at *Izumi* (*Mutsu*) ; in 1702, at *Annaka* (*Kōzuke*) ; then, from 1748 to 1868, at *Koromo* (*Mikawa* — 20,000 k.). — Viscount to-day.

(*d*) — **Nobunari,** 信成 (1545-1612). Son of *Tokugawa Hirotada* and step-brother of *Ieyasu*, was adopted by *Naitō Kiyonaga*. He served *Ieyasu* and in 1590 made himself master of the castle of *Nirayama* (*Izu*), which belonged to the *Hōjō*, and received it in fief with a revenue of 10,000 k. In 1601, he was transferred to *Fuchū* (*Suruga* — 30,000 k.), then in 1606, to *Nagahama* (*Ōmi* — 50,000 k.). — After him, his family lived at *Tanakura* (*Mutsu*) in 1628 ; at *Tanaka* (*Suruga*) in 1705, finally at *Murakami* (*Echigo* — 50,000 k.) from 1720 to 1868. — Now Viscount.

(*e*) — Branch which from 1691 to 1868 resided at *Takatō* (*Shinano* — 33,000 k.). — Now Viscount.

(*f*) — Branch which from 1693 to 1868 resided at *Iwamurata* (*Shinano* — 15,000 k.). — Now Viscount.

(*g*) — Branch which resided at *Sano* (*Shimotsuke*) in 1626 ; at *Toba* (*Shima* — 32,000 k.) in 1634.

—— **Tadakatsu,** 忠勝. Was dispossessed and invited to commit *harakiri* for having killed *Nagai Naonaga* in the temple of *Zōjō-ji* at *Shiba* (*Edo*) (1680).

Naitō, 內藤. Family of *daimyō* of the 16th century, native of *Tamba*.

—— **Genzaemon,** 源左衛門. Served *Nobunaga* and received from him the fief of *Kameyama* (*Tamba* — 200,000 k.).

—— **Yukiyasu** or **Joan,** 如安 (+ 1626). Also called *Tokuan*, 德庵 succeeded his father in the fief of *Kameyama* ; but having sided with the *Shōgun Yoshiaki*, he was dispossesed by *Nobunaga* in 1573. In the Korean expedition, he fought under the command of *Konishi Yukinaga* and was chosen, on account of his knowledge of the Chinese characters to treat for peace at Peking. The emperor of China having proposed to confer on *Hideyoshi* the title of king of Japan, *Yukiyasu* was told that his mission had ended in a failure and he retired to the domains of *Yukinaga* in *Higo*, then to *Maeda Toshinaga* in *Kaga*, who gave him a revenue of 4,000 k. He had been baptized in 1564 by the name of *John*; on account of his faith, he was banished to Manila in 1614 with *Takayama Ukon, Ukita Hisayasu, Shinagawa Uhei, Shinagawa Gombei,* etc. He died after 12 years of exile.

Naiyaku-shi, 內 藥 司. Or *Uchi no kusuri no tsukasa*. Formerly an office depending on the *Nakatsukasa-shō*, having charge of medicines, consultations of physicians, etc., at the Palace. In 736, it was joined to the *Tenyaku-ryō*.

Nai-zenshi, 內 膳 司. Or *Uchi no kashiwade no tsukasa*. Office depending on the *Kunai-shō*, and having to provide for the Emperor's table. The office of *kami* 奉 膳 was hereditary in the two families of *Takahashi* and *Azumi*; upon the latter being banished under *Kwammu-tennō*, the *Takahashi* remained sole titulars.

Najima, 名 嶋. — See *Fukuoka*.

Nakadōri-shima, 中 通 嶋. An island (246 Km. in circ.) north of the *Gotō (Hizen)* archipelago. It is the largest of the group and is also called *Higashi-jima*.

Nakae Tōju, 中 江 藤 樹 (1608-1648). Born at *Ogawa (Ōmi)*, he lost his father while yet quite young, and was brought up by his grandfather, *kerai* of *Katō Yasuoki, daimyō* of *Ōsu (Iyo)*. He fled from *Shikoku* to find his mother in *Ōmi*, and continued there the studies he had commenced; he then began to teach moral, insisting on the notions of respect and mutual affection. He it was, who first taught the philosophy of the Chinese *Ōyōmei* 王 陽 明 in Japan, whose doctrines are generally opposed to those of *Shushi* 朱 熹. *Tōju* left more than 20 works and has been surnamed the sage of *Ōmi (Ōmi-seijin)*.

Nakae Tokusuke, 中 江 篤 介 (1847-1901). Materialist, a philosopher principally known by his last work *Ichi-nen-yū-han* (one year and a half), which is, so to say, the resumé of the doctrines which he professed during life. He had studied in France (1871-1874). After his return, he was named Secretary of the Senate (*Genrō-in*), then Director of the School of Foreign Languages. He translated the works of J. J. Rousseau into Japanese.

Naka-gawa, 那 賀 川. River (110 Km.) which takes its rise in *Tsurugi-yama*, waters the province of *Awa (Shikoku)*, and empties into the Pacific Ocean at *Tomioka*.

Naka-gawa, 那 珂 川. River (94 Km.) which rises in *Shimotsuke*, flows into *Hitachi*, waters *Mito* and empties itself into the Sea at *Minato*. In its upper course, it is called *Masu-gawa*.

Nakagawa, 中 川. Family of *daimyō*, native of *Settsu* and descended from *Minamoto Yorimitsu (Seiwa-Genji)*.

—— **Kiyohide,** 清 秀 (1542-1583). Was first in the service of *Araki Murashige* and, in 1573, overcame and killed *Wada Koremasa,* a partisan of the *Shōgun Yoshiaki*. At the time of the revolt of *Mura-shige*, he abandoned the latter and attached himself to *Nobunaga*, who gave him the fief of *Akutagawa* (*Settsu* — 120,000 k.). He was killed at the battle of *Shizu-ga-take*.

—— **Hidemasa**, 秀政. Eldest son of *Kiyohide*, died during the Korean war.

—— **Hidenari**, 秀成 (1570-1612). Succeeded his brother *Hidemasa* and received the fief of *Takeda* or *Oka* (*Bungo* — 70,000 k.), where his descendants lived till the Restoration.—Count at present.

Nakagawa, 中川. Family descended from *Fujiwara Yoshikado*. Was one of the 5 families attached to the temple of *Kōfuku-ji* (*Nara*). — Baron at present.

Nakahara Chikayoshi, 中原親能 (1142-1207). Descendant of *Fujiwara Michinaga* (966-1027), he served *Yoritomo*, was appointed chief of the *Kumonjo* (1184), then *Kuji-bugyō* (1191). He succeeded *Amano Tōkage* as governor of a part of *Kyūshū*; his adopted son *Yoshinao* took the name of *Ōtomo* and is the ancestor of the *daimyō* of that name.

Nakai Riken, 中井履軒 (1732-1816). Born in *Ōsaka*. Man of letters and a Dutch translator.

Nakai Shuan, 中井甃庵 (1693-1758). Confucianist of *Ōsaka*.

Nakajima, 中嶋. In *Mikawa*. Was, from 1623 to 1672, the residence of a branch of the *Itakura* family (50,000 k.).

Nakajima, 中嶋. Family of *samurai* of the *Kōchi* (*Tosa*) clan, ennobled after the Restoration. — Baron at present.

Naka Michitaka, 那河通高 (1828-1879). *Samurai* of *Morioka*. Pedagogue and historian.

Nakamikado, 中御門. Family of *kuge* descended from *Fujiwara Yoshikado*. — Marquis at present. —After the Restoration, a branch received the title of Baron.

Nakamikado-tennō, 中御門天皇. The 114th Emperor of Japan (1710-1735). *Yasuhito*, the 5th son of *Higashi-yama-tennō*, succeeded him at 9 years of age. His reign, during which the power was wholly in the hands of the *Shōgun Yoshimune*, was the most prosperous epoch of the *Tokugawa* (era of *Kyōhō*) shōgunate. At 35, *Nakamikado* abdicated in favor of his son and died two years later.

Nakamochi-bugyō, 中持奉行. An official under the *Kamakura* shōgunate, who, when the *Shōgun* travelled, carried the box (*karahitsu*) containing the necessary objects for the voyage. When *Yoritomo* went to *Kyōto* in 1190, that office was confided to *Horifuji Tsugichika* and his family: he was the first that bore that title.

Nakamuda, 中牟田. Family of *samurai* of the *Saga* (*Hizen*) clan, ennobled in 1884. — Viscount at present.

Nakamura, 中村. In *Owari*. Birthplace of *Hideyoshi* and *Katō Kiyomasa*: the former is honored in the temple of *Tōsen-ji*, where a holly (*hiragi*) planted by him, is seen; the second is venerated in the *Myōkō-ji* temple.

Nakamura, 中村. In *Iwaki*. Was from the middle of the 16th century till 1868, the residence of the *Sōma daimyō* (60,000 k.).

Nakamura, 中村. In *Tosa*. Ancient castle where the *daimyō Ichijō* resided from 1470 to 1572. A branch of the *Yamanouchi* family also lived there from 1656 to 1689.

Nakamura, 中村. Family of *daimyō* of the 16th and the 17th centuries.

—— **Kazuuji,** 一氏. (+ 1600). Served *Hideyoshi*, who gave him successively the fiefs of *Kishiwada* (*Izumi*) (1577), *Minakuchi* (*Ōmi*) (1585), *Fuchū* (*Suruga*—140,000 k.) (1590). He died just when he had made preparations to accompany *Ieyasu* in his campaign against *Uesugi Kagekatsu*.

—— **Tadakazu,** 忠一 (1590-1609). Son of *Kazuuji*, was transferred to *Yonago* (*Hōki* — 175,000 k.), but died at the age of 19 without an heir.

Nakamura Keiu, 中村敬宇 (1832-1891). Pedagogue and man of letters. Founded the school called *Dōjin-sha* at *Koishikawa* (*Tōkyō*) in 1868.

Nakamura Ranrin, 中村蘭林 (1697-1761). Confucianist of *Edo*.

Nakamura Ritsuen, 中村栗園 (1816-1881). Confucianist of *Minakuchi* (*Ōmi*).

Nakamura Tekisai, 中村惕齋 (1629-1702). Celebrated Confucianist of *Kyōto*, rival of *Itō Jinsai*.

Nakane, 中根. Family of *samurai* of the *Fukui* (*Echizen*) clan, ennobled after the Restoration. — Baron at present.

Naka-no-in, 中院. Family of *kuge*, descended from *Minamoto Morofusa*, (*Murakami-Genji*). — Count at present

Naka no Ōe, 中大兄. — See *Tenchi-tennō*.

Naka no shima, 中嶋. Island (65 Km. in circ.) in the *Oki* group. It was here that the emperor *Go-Toba* was banished by *Hōjō Yoshitoki* (1221) and died after 18 years of exile.

Naka no shima, 中嶋. Island (25 Km. in circ.) in the group called *Kawabe-shichi-tō* (*Kagoshima-ken*), S. of *Kyūshū*.

Naka-oku, 中奥. One of the apartments in the shōgunal palace of *Edo*, where the ceremonies took place. — See *Koshōshū*.

Nakasendō, 中仙道. (Lit.: Road in the Mts of the Centre). Route constructed in 702: it connects *Kyōto* and *Edo* passing through the provinces of *Yamashiro, Ōmi, Mino, Shinano, Kōzuke* and *Musashi*. As it follows the *Kiso-gawa* for a long distance, it is also called *Kiso-kaidō*. It counted 69 relays (*eki*).

Nakatomi, 中臣. Ancient family descended from *Ame no Koyane no mikoto*, a faithful servant of *Amaterasu ō-mikami*.

—— **Kamako,** 鎌子. Minister under the emperor *Kimmei* (540-571), he was a great opponent of Buddhism when it was first imported from Korea in 552, and commenced the contest against the *Soga*, partisans of the new religion.

—— **Katsumi,** 勝海 (+ 587). Son of *Kamako*, made common cause with *Mononobe no Moriya*, to hinder the introduction of Buddhism.

After the death of *Yōmei-tennō*, civil war broke out between the two parties in regard to the succession to the throne : the *Soga* triumphed and *Katsumi* was killed at *Shigi-sen* (*Yamato*).

—— **Kamatari,** 鎌足 (614-669). Grandson of *Katsumi*, succeeded in supplanting the *Soga* and had them put to death (644) Before dying, he received from the emperor *Tenchi* the family name of *Fujiwara* for himself and his descendants. — See *Fujiwara*.

—— **Omimaro,** 意美麿 (+ 711). Nephew of *Kamatari*, although he had adopted the name of *Fujiwara*, was authorized by the emperor *Mommu* to take that of *Nakatomi* again. He was put at the head of the temples of *Ise* and charged with every thing that regarded Shintoism.

Nakatsu, 中津. Town (15,000 inh.) in the *Buzen* province. Belonging successively to the *daimyō Kuroda* (1580-1600), *Hosokawa* (1600-1632), *Ogasawara* (1632-1716), and from 1717 to 1868, to *Okudaira* (100,000 k.).

Nakatsukasa-shō. 中務省. One of the 8 offices created at the *Taikwa* reform (649). Placed between the Emperor and the Council of State (*Dajōkwan*), he transmitted the imperial orders and the petitions of the functionaries, drew up the laws, decrees, and historical annals, kept the registers of the employments, dignities, taxes, etc. The minister had the title of *Nakatsukasa-kyō:* he had under him : 1 *tayū,* 1 *shōyū,* 1 *taijō,* 2 *shōjō,* 2 *sakwan,* etc. 8 *jijū* (chamberlains) attended the emperor ; 90 *toneri* formed the body-guard ; 2 *dai-naiki,* 2 *chū-naiki* and 2 *shō-naiki* were charged with drawing up the imperial messages ; 2 *dai-kemmotsu,* 4 *chū-kemmotsu* and 4 *shō-kemmotsu* kept the keys of the storerooms (*kura*) and supervised the entrance and exit of all the necessary objects. Finally, the *Nakatsukasa-shō* had as dependants : 1 *shoku* (*Chūgū-shoku*), 6 *ryō* (*ōtoneri-ryō, tosho-ryō, kura-ryō, naidono-ryō, on-yō-ryō* and *takumi-ryō*) and 3 *shi* (*nai-yaku-shi, nairei-shi* and *gwakō-shi*).

Naka-umi, 中海. Lake (64 Km. in circ.) N. E. of *Izumo*. Also called *Nawa no ura, Yonago-fuka-ura.*

Nakayama, 中山. Family of *kuge* descended from *Fujiwara* (*Kwazan-in*) *Ietada* (1062-1136).

—— **Tadachika,** 忠親 (1131-1195). Grandson of *Ietada* and son of *Tadamune,* wrote the history of Japan from *Jimmu-tennō* to *Nimmyō* (850), under the title of *Mizu-kagami.* He also left a Journal. The chief of the family bears at present the title of Marquis.

Nakayama, 中山 Family of *daimyō* descended from *Tanji no Mabito* and through him from the emperor *Senkwa.* Was vassal to the *Hōjō* of *Odawara.*

—— **Nobuyoshi,** 信吉 (1576-1642). *Bizen no kami,* was tutor of *Tokugawa Yorifusa* of *Mito* (1608). — From 1622 to 1868, his family resided at *Matsuoka* (*Hitachi* — 25,000 k.). — Baron at present.

Nakazono, 中園. Family of *kuge* descended from *Fujiwara Kosemaro,* son of *Muchimaro* (680-737). — Now Viscount.

Nakinin, 今歸仁. Family related to the ancient royal dynasty of *Ryūkyū,* and ennobled after the annexation of the archipalago. — Now Baron.

Nakoso no seki, 勿來關. — See *Kikuta no seki*.

Namazue, 鯰江. In *Ōmi*. Ancient castle belonging to the *daimyō Sasaki*: in 1568, *Yoshikata* and his son *Yoshisuke* took refuge there after the taking of their castle of *Kwannonji*, but *Shibata Katsuie*, sent by *Nobunaga*, besieged them also in that place, and made himself master of the castle (1573).

Namba, 難波. Family of *kuge* descended from *Fujiwara Tadanori* (1076-1141). — Now Viscount.

Namban-ji, 南蠻寺. (Lit.: temple of the southern barbarians). The Jesuit missionaries, who, as early as 1560, had formed a Christian community at *Kyōto*, were obliged to leave that town on account of the troubles which followed the tragic death of the *Shōgun Yoshiteru* (1565). Father Froez returned in 1568 and obtained from *Nobunaga* permission again to make his abode in the capital and there to preach. Japanese authors even assure us that *Nobunaga* gave to the chapel erected then and there and to its dependencies the name of *Eiroku-ji* (temple *Eiroku*: the year 1568 was the 11th of the *Eiroku* era); but the people called it by the name of *Namban-ji*. All was destroyed in 1588, after the first edict of proscription by *Hideyoshi*. — The *Namban-ji* was situated near the gate called *Shijō-bō-mon*. At the time of its fall, a bell was brought to the *Myōshin-ji* temple, where it remained for over 3 centuries. In 1906, it was put into the *Ueno* Museum (*Tōkyō*).

Namboku-chō, 南北朝. The two branches of the imperial family, that of the South (*nan*) and that of the North (*hoku*), who in the 14th century, contended for power.

Namboku-chō jidai, 南北朝時代. Period of the history of Japan from 1336 to 1392, during which there were two reigning dynasties at the same time: one, called the southern dynasty, which was the lawful one; the other, called the northern, upheld by the *Ashikaga Shōgun*.

Nambu, 南部. In *Kai*. *Mitsuyuki*, descended from *Takeda Yoshi-kiyo*, installed himself there in 1180 and took the name. In 1189, he went to *Mutsu*.

Nambu, 南部. Name formerly given to the domains of the *daimyō* of that name, that is, to the present province of *Rikuchū*.

Nambu, 南部. Family of *daimyō* descended from *Takeda Yoshi-kiyo* (*Seiwa-Genji*).

—— **Mitsuyuki, 光行.** Great-grandson of *Yoshi-kiyo*, established himself at *Nambu* (*Kai*) and took that name. After the campaign of *Yoritomo* against *Fujiwa-ra Yasuhira*, he received the domain of *Sannohe* (*Mutsu*) (1189).

—— **Nobunao, 信直** (1546-1599). Was adopted by his uncle *Yasunobu* who had no children, and to preserve his domains, he had to war against *Kunohe Masazane*, who wished to adopt his brother *Sanechika*. He demanded assistance from *Hideyoshi*, who sent troops under *Hidetsugu*, and *Masazane* was vanquished (1591). The following year, *Nobunao* accompanied *Hide-yoshi* to *Nagoya* (*Hizen*).

—— **Toshinao, 利直** (+ 1632). Son of *Nobunao*, constructed the castle of *Morioka*, where his descendants lived till the Restoration.

Nobunao-Toshinao-Shigenao
{
Shigenobu
{
Yukinobu-Nobuoki (a)
Masanobu-Nobumitsu (b)
}
Naofusa -Naomasa -Michinobu (c)
}

(*a*) — Eldest branch which, from 1601 to 1868, resided at *Morioka* (*Mutsu* — 130,000 k.). — Now Count.

(*b*) — Branch which from 1680 to 1868, resided at *Shichinohe* (*Mutsu* — 10,000 k.). — Viscount at present.

(*c*) — Branch which from 1664 to 1868, resided at *Hachinohe* (*Mutsu* — 20,000 k.). — Viscount at present.

Nambu, 南部. Family of *samurai* of the *Kōchi* (*Tosa*) clan, ennobled after the Restoration. — Now Baron.

Nami-ai, 波合. Village in the south of *Shinano*. It was there that *Wakiya Yoshiharu*, defeated by *Takauji*, retired with prince *Munenaga-shinnō* (1369). Prince *Korenaga-shinnō* died there in 1424, and has a temple erected in his honor at that place. There, finally, *Nobutada* brought to his father *Nobunaga*, the heads of *Takeda Katsuyori* and of his son *Nobukatsu* (1582).

Nanakoshi-mine, 七越嶺. Mountain on the borders of *Kii*, *Kawachi* and *Izumi*. Also called *Yoko-yama*.

Nanakusa no kayu, 七草粥. According to a custom brought from China, on the 7th day of the 1st month, the Emperor was presented with a dish composed of 7 plants (*nazuna*, *hakobera*, *seri*, *gogyō*, *aona*, *suzushiro* and *hotoke-no-za*), and all the Court ate of it in turn. This practice spread among the people little by little, and to its effects is attributed preservation from diseases.

Nanao, 七尾. Town (11,700 inh.) in the *Noto* province, south of a gulf which is divided in two by the island of *Noto-jima* : this is the finest harbor on the W. coast of Japan. — In 1398, *Hatakeyama Mitsunori*, named governor of the province, built himself a castle, which was taken by *Uesugi Kenshin* (1576).

Nanchin, 難陳. Gathering of savants called to choose a new *nengō* (name of era) ; after due discussion, the name was made known to the Emperor, who wrote it with his own hand and then had it published.

Nan-chō, 南朝. Southern dynasty during the civil wars of the 14th century (1336-1392). It descended from the emperor *Kameyama*, whilst that of the North came from *Go-Fukakusa*.

Nando-yaku, 納戸役. Under the *Tokugawa*, office charged with the jewels, clothing, furniture, etc , of the shōgunal palace, — stuffs offered by the *daimyō* and *hatamoto*, — objects given as rewards, etc. The head, appointed in 1635, was called *Nando-gashira* and had 60 *dōshin* under him. Later (1648) they distinguished the *moto-kata* from the *harai-kata*, the first having charge of all that entered the palace, the latter, of all that left it.

Naniwa, 難波. (Contraction from *nami-haya* : swift waves). Name given by *Jimmu-tennō* to that side of the *Settsu* province which borders on the delta of the *Yodo-gama*, then, later, to the whole province. The emperor *Nintoku* (313-399), had his palace (*Naniwa Takatsu no miya*) there, as also *Kōtoku* (645-654) (*Naniwa Nagara-toyosaki no miya*). The city of *Ōsaka* at present occupies about the centre of the ancient district of *Naniwa*.

Naniwa no horie, 難 波 堀 江. Canal dug by orders of the emperor *Nintoku* to preserve the capital from inundations (323). The work was done principally by Koreans that had emigrated to Japan. It is in this canal, that the emperor *Kimmei*, at the instigation of *Mononobe no·Okoshi* and *Nakatomi no Kamako*, threw the Buddhist statues sent by the king of *Kudara* (553).

Naniwa-ōgōri no murotsumi, 難 波 大 郡 舘. In the time when regular intercourse was held with Korea, a building erected in *Naniwa* to receive foreign envoys. It was also called *Naniwa no murotsumi*, *Tsu no murotsumi*.

Nanjō, 南 條. Family of *daimyō*, who, in the 16th century, occupied the castle of *Haneishi* (*Hōki* — 60,000 k.) and were deprived of it by *Ieyasu* in 1600.

Nankaidō, 南 海 道. (Lit.: Region of the South Sea). One of the grand division of Japan. It comprises 6 provinces : *Kii, Awaji, Awa, Sanuki, Iyo* and *Tosa*.

Nan-ke, 南 家. One of the 4 ancient branches of the *Fujiwara* family, founded by *Muchimaro* (680-737), son of *Fuhito*. It disappears from history towards the end of the 9th century.

Nanori, 名 乘. Or *jitsumyō*. Surnames *Takauji, Ieyasu, Yoritomo*, are *nanori*. Formerly distinct from the *tsūshō* or *zokumyō*, they are now confounded, every man being permitted to have only one surname.

Na-no-tsu, 名 津. Ancient port of *Tsukushi*, situated on the actual site of *Hakata* (*Chikuzen*). In former times, a very active emporium of commerce carried on between Korea and China. — The *San-shin* (three-ports) were formerly : *A-no-tsu* (*Ise*), *Bo-no-tsu* (*Satsuma*) and *Na-no-tsu*.

Nansō-gwa, 南 宗 畫. Style of drawing which the Japanese acquired from the school of *Shūbun* and of *Sesshū* ; it is also called *Bunjin-gwa*. *Ikeno Taiga, Watanabe Kwazan* became celebrated in this art.

Nantai-zan, 男 體 山. Mountain (2,490 m.) in *Shimotsuke*, N. of *Nikkō*. Also called *Kurogami-yama, Kita-Fuji, Chūzenji-san*.

Nanto, 南 都. (Lit.: Southern Capital). Name given to *Nara* after the removal of the capital to *Kyōto*. — Also used to designate the large temple *Kōfuku-ji* (*Nara*).

Nanto shichi-dai-ji, 南 都 七 大 寺. The 7 great Buddhist temples of *Nara* : *Tōdai-ji, Kōfuku-ji, Seidai-ji, Genkō-ji, Taian-ji, Yakushi-ji*, and *Hōryū-ji*.

Nanuka-ichi, 七 日 市. In *Kōzuke*. Was from 1616-1868, the residence of a branch of the *Maeda* of *Kaga* (10,000 k.).

Nanushi, 名 主. Under the *Tokugawa*, mayor of a town or village. The *nanushi* of *Edo* corresponded to the *kuchō* (mayors of counties) of to-day ; those of villages, also called *shōya*, to the *sonchō*. This office, filled by the most ancient families, was often hereditary.

Nanzen-ji, 南禪寺. Temple of *Kyōto*, central seat of the *Rinzai* branch of the *Zen-shū* sect. Being at first a palace to which the emperor *Kameyama* retired after his abdication (1274), it was converted into a temple by the bonze *Fumon* or *Mukwan* (*Busshin-Zenji*) in 1290.

Naoe Kanetsugu, 直江兼續 (1570-1619). Vassal of *Uesugi*, he supported *Kagekatsu* in his struggle with *Ieyasu*. When *Kagekatsu* was transferred to *Yonezawa* (*Dewa*) (1601), he gave *Kanetsugu* a revenue of 60,000 k. ; but the latter divided 55,000 k. among his *samurai*, and, contenting himself with 5,000 k., retired into solitude to occupy his leisure with art and literature.

Naohito-shinnō, 直仁親王 (1703-1752). Son of the emperor *Higashi-yama ;* he is the ancestor of the princes *Kan-in no miya*.

Nara, 奈良. Capital (30,600 inh.), of the department of the same name in *Yamato* province.—Was the capital of Japan from 710 to 784 (See *Nara no miyako*). The present town occupies only the western part of the old one. After the transfer of the capital to *Yamashiro*, *Nara* received the name of *Nanto* (southern capital). Its numerous temples, which harbored armies of mercenaries (*sōhei*), frequently caused troubles, owing to the continual strifes against the rival temples of *Hieizan*. The *Ashikaga* placed a governor (*Nanto-bugyō*) at *Nara* to forestall these troubles. *Nobunaga* and *Hideyoshi* deprived the temples of all their territorial possessions and made it impossible for them to levy troops. When *Hidenaga*, brother of *Hideyoshi*, received the government of *Yamato* province (1585) he placed a *machi-zukasa* at *Nara*. The *Tokugawa* changed that title to that of *Nara-bugyō*.—Of its former splendor there remain only the *Daibutsu*, some old temples and a fine park stocked with deer.

Narabara, 奈良原. Family of *samurai* of *Kagoshima* (*Satsuma*) clan, ennobled in 1896.—Baron at present.

Nara-bugyō, 奈良奉行. Title created in 1613 and given to an official who, under the authority of the *Shoshidai* of *Kyōto*, had charge of the administration of the town of *Nara*, the watch over the temples, etc.

Nara-chō, 奈良朝. ⎰ Period during which *Nara* was the re-
Nara-jidai, 奈良時代. ⎱ sidence of the imperial Court (710-784).

Nara-ken, 奈良縣. Department of *Yamato* province, — Pop. : 568,300 inh. — Capital : *Nara* (30,600 inh.). — Pr. towns : *Kōriyama* (14,000 inh.), *Totsukawa* (11,200 inh.), etc.

Nara no miyako, 平城京. In 710, the empress *Gemmei* transported the imperial Court to the district of *Sō-no-kami* (*Yamato*) and there had a town built which was called *Nara no miyako*, the palace itself being named *Heijō*. Contrary to the usage followed until then, the successors of *Gemmei* lived in the same place, and *Nara* was thus the capital during several consecutive reigns, till the day when *Kwammu* transferred it to *Yamashiro* (784).

Nara-tennō, 平城天皇. — See *Heijō-tennō*.

Narinaga-shinnō, 成良親王 (1325-1338). 10th son of the emperor *Go-Daigo*, was appointed *Kōzuke-taishu* and *Kwantō-kwanryō* in 1333, then sent to *Kamakura* and named *Sei-i-tai-shōgun* after the deposition of his brother *Morinaga*. In 1338, *Kōmyō*, the emperor of the North, chose him heir (*kōtaishi*) : he then returned to *Kyōto*, was dismissed shortly after, confined at *Kwazan-in*, and put to death with his brother *Tsunenaga-shinnō*. He was 13 years old.

Narita, 成田. Small town of *Shimōsa* (5,200 inh.) famous for its grand temple *Shinshō-ji* (see that word), dedicated to *Fudō* and where pilgrimages are made from all parts of Japan.

Narita, 成田. Family of vassal *daimyō* of the *Tokugawa*; from 1590 to 1623 it resided at *Karasu-yama* (*Shimotsuke* — 35,000 k). The last, *Ujimune*, dying without heirs (1623), his domains reverted to the shōgunate.

Naru-ita, 鳴板. (Lit.: sounding board). It was customary, in the corridors of the imperial Palace, to leave boards unfastened at certain intervals so that the noise they produced might give notice of some one approaching: it was the *naru-ita* or *kenzan no ita*.

Naruse, 成瀬. Family of *daimyō* descended from *Fujiwara Tadamichi* (1097-1164).

—— **Masakazu,** 正一 (1538-1620). Served *Ieyasu*, who, in 1607, gave him a revenue of 20,000 k. at *Kurihara* (*Hitachi*). Of the two sons of *Masakazu*, the elder, *Yukitora*, 行虎 died in 1639 without heirs, and his domains were confiscated. — The 2nd, *Masanari* 正成 entered the service of the *Tokugawa* of *Nagoya*, and was charged with keeping the castle of *Inuyama* (*Owari* — 35,000 k.), where his descendants lived to the Restoration. — Now Viscount.

Naruse - gawa, 鳴瀬川. River (98 Km.) in *Rikuzen*; empties itself into the gulf of *Ishinomaki*.

Naru-shima, 奈留島. Island (67 Km. in circ.) of the *Gotō* group (*Hizen*).

Narushima Shichoku, 成島司直 (1778-1862). Confucianist. Author of the *Tokugawa-jikki*.

Naruto-kaikyō, 鳴門海峡. Strait between *Awa* (*Shikoku*) and *Awaji*. Called also *Naruto no seto*.

Nashimoto, 梨本. Branch of the princely family of *Fushimi*, founded by *Moriosa* (+ 1881), son of *Fushimi Sadayoshi*, after the Restoration. — The present head of the house is prince *Morimasa*, born in 1874, son of prince *Kuni Asahiko*, adopted by *Moriosa*. In 1900, he married *Itsu-ko*, daughter of Marquis *Nabeshima*.

Nashitsubo, 梨壺. Or *Shōyō-sha*. Apartment reserved for the ladies of the Court in the ancient imperial Palace of *Kyōto*.

Nashitsubo no go-kasen, 梨壺五歌仙. Name given to 5 poetesses, all ladies of honor to the empress *Jōtō-mon-in*, widow of *Ichijō-tennō* : *Murasaki Shikibu*, *Izumi Shikibu*, *Akazome Emon*, *Uma no Naishi* and *Ise Ōsuke*. — Later were added *Sei Shōnagon* and *Ko-Shikibu*, which made up the *Nashitsubo no shichi-kasen*.

Nashitsubo no go-nin, 梨壺五人. Name given to *Ōnakatomi Yoshinobu, Kiyowara Motosuke, Minamoto Shitakō, Ki Tokibumi* and *Sakanoe Mochiki,* who, in 951, by order of the emperor *Murakami,* were united to the *Nashitsubo* to collect the *Go-sen-waka-shū* (collection of poems).

Nasu, 那須. Ancient family of *daimyō* of *Shimotsuke,* descended from *Fujiwara Michinaga* (966-1027).

—— **Sukeie,** 資家. Installed himself in the district of *Nasu* in 1125, and took that name. His descendants became more and more influential and under the *Ashikaga,* became one of the 8 great families of *Kwantō* (*Kwantō-hakke*). During the civil wars of the 15th and the 16th centuries, they vanquished their neighbors, the *daimyō Utsunomiya,* took their domains and built a castle at *Karasu-yama.*

—— **Sukeharu,** 資晴 (1546-1609). Was transferred by *Hideyoshi,* in 1590, to *Fukuwara,* in the district of that name (20,000 k.).

—— **Sukefusa,** 資房. Was dispossessed in 1685 for having disinherited his son *Suketoyo* in favor of *Sukenori,* son of *Tsugaru Nobumasa,* whom he had adopted.

Nasu shichi-ke, 那須七家. The 7 families, who, in the Middle Ages, divided the district of *Nasu* (*Shimotsuke*) among themselves: *Fukuwara, Ashino, Ōtawara, Ōseki, Okamoto, Sembon* and *Iōno.*

Nasu-zan, 那須山. Volcano (1910 m.), on the confines of *Shimotsuke, Iwashiro* and *Iwaki.* Also called *Cha-usu-dake.*

Nawa, 名和. In *Hōki.* Ancient castle of the *daimyō* of the same name. There *Go-Daigo* landed after escaping from the island of *Oki* (1333): he was received by *Nawa Nagatoshi,* who gave him an asylum at *Funanoe-sen.*

Nawa, 名和. Family of *daimyō* descended from *Akamatsu Suefusa* (*Murakami-Genji*).

—— **Tadafusa,** 忠房. Son of *Suefusa,* established himself at *Nawa* (*Hōki*) and took that name towards the end of 12th century.

—— **Nagatoshi,** 長年 (+ 1336). Received *Go-Daigo* who escaped from *Oki* where he was exiled, and installed him in the castle of *Funanoe-sen,* which belonged to him. Hearing of this, *Hōjō Takatoki* sent the *Sasaki, Kiyotake* and *Masatsuna,* to besiege *Funanoe-sen*; but they were repulsed: *Masatsuna* was killed and *Kiyotake* fled (1333). After this victory, *Nagatoshi* charged his son *Yoshitaka* to escort the emperor to *Kyōto.* The following year, he received as recompense the provinces of *Hōki* and *Inaba.* When *Ashikaga Takauji* revolted in *Kwantō, Go-Daigo* sent *Nitta Yoshisada* against him and charged *Nagatoshi* and *Kusunoki Masashige* to defend *Kyōto.* After the defeat of *Yoshisada* at *Hakone, Nagatoshi* tried to hinder the progress of *Takauji,* but was defeated at the bridge of *Seta* and killed in trying to re-take *Kyōto. Nagatoshi* is considered as one of the most generous defenders of the legitimate dynasty; a temple

NAWA NAGATOSHI.

(*Nawa-jinja*) is dedicated to him at *Nawa*. The family, which was hereditarily at the head of the temple, claimed descent from *Nagatoshi*, and was ennobled after the Restoration. — Now Baron.

Negi, 禰宜. Formerly, official charged with the offerings and petitions addressed to *Amaterasu* in the great temple of *Ise*. Later, this name was given to all the Shintoist priests (*kannushi*).

Negoro-dera, 根來寺. Temple founded by the bonze *Kakuhan* in 1130, at the village of *Negoro* (*Kii*); it belonged to the *Shingi* branch of the *Shingon* sect. Under the *Ashikaga*, it became very prosperous: it had as many as 2700 temples under its jurisdiction and supported an army of *sōhei* who caused frequent troubles in the province: it was besieged and destroyed by *Hideyoshi* in 1585, and the ruins served to rebuild the *Daigo-ji*, near *Kyōto*.

Nehan, 涅槃. The Buddhist *Nirvâna*. — *Nehan-e* is the feast held on the anniversary of the entrance of *Shaka* into *Nirvâna*.

Nemuro, 根室. One of the 11 provinces of *Hokkaidō*. Comprises 5 districts (*kōri*). — Capital: *Nemuro* (7,900 inh.).

Nengō, 年號. Era, period of years. — During the first 10 centuries of their history, the Japanese reckoned their years either from the enthronement of *Jimmu-tennō*, (660 B.C.), or after the sexagesimal cycle, or again from the commencement of each reign. *Kōtoku-tennō* borrowed from China the custom of giving a name to the years, and decided that the first year of his reign should be the 1st of the *Taikwa* era (645). Six years after, the emperor, having received the present of a white pheasant from the province of *Nagato*, concluded that this event merited to be handed down to history and changed the name of the era to that of *Hakuchi* (white pheasant): this was the first change of era (*kaigen*). *Kōtoku* died in the 5th year of *Hakuchi* (654), and his two immediate successors, *Saimei* and *Tenchi*, suppressed the nengō. *Temmu* re-established them in 672, and since then, the custom was followed without interruption: the accession of an emperor to the throne, an important event, happy or unhappy, brought about a change in the era. In the reign of *Murakami-tennō* (947-967) the astronomer *Abe Seimei* introduced the Chinese custom of changing the name of the era in the 1st (*ki-no-e no ne*) and the 57th (*ka-no-to no tori*) year of the cycle. The reigns which counted the greatest number of *nengō* are those of *Go-Daigo* (1319-1338) and of *Go-Hanazono* (1429-1465), which had, each 8. From the *Taikwa* era (645) to the *Meiji* (1868) there have been 229 *nengō*. At the imperial Restoration, it was decided that each reign should have only one *nengō*. — See *kaigen, nanchin,* etc.

Ne no hi no asobi, 子日遊. Custom introduced in the reign of *Uda-tennō* (889-897): on the first day of the Rat in the first month of the year, the people went to the country, rooted up some young pines, emblems of longevity, and took a repast in the open air.

Ne no kuni, 根國. Country to which *Izanagi* retired in his old age. Certain commentators presume it to be the province of *Izumo;* others, the land of the dead, in the next world, also called *Yomi, Yomi no kuni, Yomotsu-kuni.*

Nezu-ga-seki, 念珠關. Barrrier erected in former times on the frontiers of *Dewa* and *Echigo* to stop the incursions of the *Ebisu*.

Ni, 尼. (Abbreviation of *Bikuni*) *Ama*, a Buddhist nun.

Nichi-in, 日胤: (+1180). 7th son of *Chiba Tsunetane*, became a bonze in the temple of *Enjō-ji*, near *Nara*. When *Mochihito-Ō* rebelled against the *Taira*, he accompanied him, fought under him, and when the prince was killed at *Kōmyō-ji*, *Nichi-in* put 6 of his adversaries " hors de combat " before falling in his turn.

Nichi-in, 日印. Bonze of the *Nichiren* sect, who, in 1320, founded the temple of *Honsei-ji* in *Echigo* which became the seat of a branch of the sect.

Nichi-ō, 日奧. (1565-1630). Bonze of the *Nichiren* sect, founder of the *Fuju-fuze* branch. Chief of the temple of *Myōgaku-ji*, he displeased *Hideyoshi*, who exiled him to *Tamba* (1595), then to *Tsushima* (1600); pardoned in 1612 by *Ieyasu*, he returned to *Kyōto*, where he died.

Nichira, 日羅. Son or *Arisuto*, Japanese official in Korea, he lived in *Kudara*. The emperor *Bidatsu*, wishing to restore the power of *Mimana*, called him to ask his advice: the people of *Kudara* having resisted a long time, at last consented to his departure. He therefore went to Japan (583), conferred with the Emperor and was assassinated on his return to Korea.

Nichiren, 日蓮. (1222-1282). Celebrated bonze, founder of the *Hokke-shū* sect. A descendant of *Fujiwara Fuyutsugu*, *Tomosuke*, *Shōnagon* and *Bitchū no kami*, established himself at *Nukina* (*Tōtōmi*) in 1077, and *Masanao*, one of his descendants took the name of *Nukina*. *Shigetada*, great-grandson of *Masanao*, was dispossessed by *Hōjō Tokimasa* in 1203 and exiled to the district of *Nagasa*, in *Awa* (*Tōkaidō*): there he settled in the village of *Kominato*, where he espoused the daughter of a certain *Ōno Yoshikiyo*, a native of *Shimōsa*, and became a fisherman. This *Shigetada* was the father of *Nichiren*, who at his birth (1222) received the name of *Zennichi-maru*. From his youth, he applied himself to the study of Buddhism, became a bonze of the *Shingon* sect and took the name of *Nichiren* (lotus of the sun). In 1253, he commenced to propagate a new doctrine, preached by *Shaka* in his last days and contained chiefly in the *sūtra Myōhō-renge-kyō* (book of the Lotus of the good Law). The title of this

SEAL OF NICHIREN
(1274).

book was turned into a prayer used by his disciples, whose number increased from day to day. In 1260, he published a work (*Ankoku-ron*), in which he discussed the means to assure the peace of the State, violently attacked the other sects, and went so far as to predict the Mongol invasion. He dared to address his work to the *Shikken Hōjō Tokiyori*, who, being a fervent advocate of the *Zen-shū* sect, answered by exiling him to *Itō* (*Izu*). Pardoned after 3 years, he returned to *Kamakura* and renewed his attacks on the rival sects; this time, he was imprisoned with his disciple *Nichiro* and condemned to be beheaded at *Tatsu-no-kuchi*; but *Tokimune* commuted this sentence to that of exile and *Nichiren* was sent to the island of *Sado* (1271). He lived there only 2 years, and on his return, built the temple of *Kuon-ji* at *Minobu* (*Kai*), which became the seat of his sect. Several years after, he founded the temple of *Sōchū-ji* at *Ikegami* (*Musashi*), where he died at

NICdIREN.

the age of 61. His body was cremated and the ashes sent to *Minobu*. — To the Buddhists, *Nichiren* is an incarnation of *Bosatsu Jōgyō*, one of the first disciples of *Shaka*.

Nichiren-monka roku-rōsō, 日蓮門下六老僧. The 6 principal disciples of *Nichiren*: *Nisshō* 日昭 (+ 1323), *Nichirō* 日朗 (+ 1319), *Nikkō* 日興 (+ 1288), *Nitchō* 日頂 (+ 1317), *Nichiji* 日持 (+1293), and *Nikkō* 日向 (+ 1314).

Nichiren-shū, 日蓮宗. Or *Hokke-shū*. Buddhist sect founded by *Nichiren* in 1253. The doctrine of this sect is that of the *sûtra Myōhō-renge-kyō*, which contains the last instructions of *Buddha*; these instructions were preached for the first time by *Nichiren*. It is the doctrine of the 3 great secrets: adoration (*honzon*), law (*daimoku*) and moral (*kaidan*), which resume all the discourses of *Shaka*; it is however so profound that only the *Buddha* and the highest *Bosatsu* can comprehend it. It is no doubt on account of the excellent doctrines which they profess, that the followers of *Nichiren* have always been the most turbulent and fanatic Buddhists in Japan. Little by little the sect split into 9 branches, which at present, have 5,194 temples about 3,700 bonzes, chiefs of *tera*, and 1,283,600 adherents.

Nichiren-shū bumpa, 日蓮宗分派. The 9 branches of the *Nichiren* sect are:

1. **Itchi,**	一致	Founded by	*Nichirō*	(13th century)	at	*Ikegami* (*Musashi*)
2. **Shōretsu,**	勝劣	„	*Nichigetsu* („)	„	(„)
3. **Honseiji,**	本成寺	„	*Nichi-in*	(1320)	in	*Echigo.*
4. **Myōmanji,**	妙満寺	„	*Nisshū*	(1381)	at	*Kamakura.*
5. **Hachihon,**	八品	„	*Nichiryū*	(1420)	at	*Ikegami.*
6. **Honryū-ji,**	本隆寺	„	*Nisshin*	(1585)	at	*Hanazono* (*Higo*).
7. **Fuju-fuze,**	不受不施	„	*Nichiō*	(1595)	in	*Bizen.*
8. **Fuju-fuze-kōmon,**	不受不施講門	„	*Nikkō*	(16th century)	in	*Bizen.*
9. **Kōmon,**	與門	„	*Nikkō*	(about 1280)	at	*Ikegami.*

In 1898, the names of the still existing branches were modified and read as follows:

The *Myōmanji* branch became the	*Kempon-hokke-shū,*	顕本法華宗
„ *Hachihon*	„	„	*Hommon-hokke-shū,*	本門法華宗
„ *Honseiji*	„	„	*Hokke-shū,*	法華宗
„ *Honryūji*	„	„	*Hommyō-hokke-shū,*	本妙法華宗
„ *Kōmon*	„	„	*Hommon-shū,*	本門宗

Nichirō, 日朗 (+1319). Disciple of *Nichiren ;* was imprisoned with him at *Kamakura* (1271). He is the founder of the temples of *Hondo-ji* (*Shimōsa*), *Myōhon-ji* (*Kawakura*) *Hommon-ji* (*Ikegami*), *Honkoku-ji* (*Kyōto*), and of the branch *Itchi-ha.* He received the posthumous title of *Daikoku-Ajari.*

NICHIRŌ.

Nichiro-sensō, 日露戰爭. The Russo-Japanese war of 1904-1905, of which the following are the principal facts.

1904 — Feb. 6 — Rupture of diplomatic relations. — The Japanese fleet leaves the Port of *Sasebo* (*Hizen*).

1904 — Feb. 8 — Night attack on the Russian fleet at Port-Arthur. — Landing of the Japanese vanguard at *Chemulpo* (Korea).

„ 9 — Attack on Port-Arthur (Ad. *Tōgō*). — Two Russian ships (*Variag* and *Koreetz*) sunk at *Chemulpo.* (Rear-Ad. *Uryū*).

„ 11 — Declaration of war by the Emperor of Japan.

„ 24 — First attempt to block Port-Arthur.

March 6 — Demonstration of *Kamimura's* squadron before *Vladivostock.*

„ 27 — Second attempt to block Port-Arthur.

„ 28 — First engagement on land at *Chengju* (Korea).

April 7 — The first army (gen. *Kuroki*) occupies *Wiju* (Korea).

„ 13 — The Russian battleship *Petropaulovsk* strikes a mine and sinks: Admiral *Makarof* perishes with more than 600 men.

1904—April 30— The first army crosses the *Yalu*.
　　May　1 — Battle of the *Yalu*.
　　　,,　3 — Third attempt to block Port-Arthur.
　　　,,　5 — Landing of the second army (gen. *Oku*) at *Yentoa* (*Liaotong*).
　　　,,　6 — Occupation of *Kwantiencheng* (1st army).
　　　,,　15 — The *Hatsuse*, the *Yashima*, the *Miyako* strike mines and sink. — Collision of the *Kasuga* and the *Yoshino* : the latter sinks.
　　　,,　19 — Landing of the 3rd army (gen. *Kawamura*) at *Takushan*.
　　　,,　26 — Battle of *Nanshan* ; the Russians retreat towards Port-Arthur
　　　,,　28 — Occupation of *Dalny*. — General *Nogi* takes command of the investing army.
　　June　8 — The third army joins the first.
　　　,,　15 — Battle of *Telissu* ; general *Shackelberg* repelled.
　　　,,　16 — The *Vladivostock* squadron sinks the *Hitachi*, the *Izumi* and the *Sado-maru*.
　　　,,　23 — The Russian fleet at Port-Arthur makes a vain attempt to run the blockade.
　　July　3 — The Japanese occupy the passes of *Motienling*.
　　　,,　6 — Marshal *Ōyama* leaves *Tōkyō* with his Etat-Major to take the command in chief of the Armies in Manchuria.
　　　,,　20 — The *Vladivostock* squadron advances as far as the entry of *Tōkyō* Bay.
　　　,,　26 — Capture of *Tachikiao*.
　　　,,　30 — Capture of the second line of fortifications of Port-Arthur.
　　　,,　31 — Capture of *Tomucheng*.
　　Aug.　10 — The Russian squadron makes a sally, but is dispersed.
　　　,,　14 — Defeat of the *Vladivostock* squadron ; sinking of the *Rurik*.
　　　,,　27 — Battle of *Liao-yang* ; the Russians retreat beyond the
　–Sept.　3 — *Shaho*.
　　Oct.　9-18 — Battle of the *Shaho* ; the Russians retreat to *Mukden*.
　　Nov.　26 — Assault on Port-Arthur ; capture of the 203 Metre Hill.
1905 — Jan.　2 — Surrender of Port-Arthur (gen. *Stoessel*).
　　Jan.　25-29 — Battle of *Heikautai* : flank attack by general *Grippenberg* repelled.
　　March, 1-10 — Battle of *Mukden* ; the Russians retreat towards the north.
　　May, 27-28 — Naval Battle of *Tsushima* ; the Russian fleet (admiral *Rojestvensky*) is annihilated.
　　July, 7-30 — The Japanese take possession of *Saghalien*.
　　Aug.　9 — Opening of the peace negotiations at Portsmouth, U. S.

1905 — Aug. 29 — Conclusion of the treaty of peace.
Oct. 5 — Ratification of the treaty of peace.

CEREMONY OF THANKSGIVING PERFORMED AT THE TEMPLE OF ISE AFTER THE RUSSO-JAPANESE WAR.

Nichiryū, 日隆. A bonze of the *Nichiren* sect, founder of the *Hachihon* branch. It was he that built at *Kyōto*, the temple of *Honnō-ji*, where *Nobunaga* was assassinated.

Nie no ki, 贄柵. A fortified enclosure, erected in *Dewa* (near the present village of *Niida*), which had a little garrison to keep off the *Ebisu*. In 1189, *Fujiwara Yasuhira*, defeated by *Yoritomo*, sought refuge there but was put to death by *Kōda Yukibumi*, the commander of the castle.

Nigao, 仁賀保. An ancient family of *daimyō*, that, in the 16th century, occupied the castle of *Nigao* (*Dewa*). *Ieyasu* transferred them in 1602, to *Takeda* (*Hitachi* — 10,000 k.). On the death of *Takanobu* (1560-1623), his children became simple *samurai*.

Nigihayabi no mikoto, 饒速日命. Or *Kushitama-Nigihayabi*, a descendant of the elder brother of *Ninigi no mikoto*; he passed over from *Kawachi* to *Yamato*, where he married *Kashikiya-hime*, sister of *Nagasune-hiko*, who recognized him as his chief. He was the father of *Umashimade*.

Nigite, 幣. Banners or strips of hemp or paper, which are hung in *Shintō* shrines in memory of those that were made at the time of *Amaterasu's* retreat in the heavenly Rock-cave (*Ama no iwa.*) — (See *Amaterasu-ō mikami*).

Nihommatsu, 二 本 杉. A city of *Iwashiro* province (8,500 inh.) — An ancient castle built by *Hatakeyama Mitsuyasu*, which received the name of *Nihommatsu*. *Yoshitsugu*, his descendant in the 5th generation, was dispossessed in 1586 by *Date Masamune*. In 1590, the castle became a part of the domains of *Gamō Ujisato* later on, in the *Tokugawa* period, it was successively occupied by the *daimyō*: *Matsushita* (1602), *Katō* (1628), and *Niwa* (1642-1868) (100,000 k.).

Nihon, 日 本. (Lit.: origin of light). Japan. It was in 671 A. D. that the Chinese gave the name of *Jewpenn* to the archipelago situated east of their empire; the Japanese adopted this name, but modified its pronunciation. — See *Dai-Nihon*.

Nihon-gwaishi, 日 本 外 史. A history of Japan, from the shogunate of *Yoritomo*, (1192) down to the victory of *Ieyasu* (1600), published in 1827 by *Rai San-yō*. It contains 22 volumes.

Nihon jū-ni kei, 日 本 十 二 景. The 12 landscapes, considered to be the most beautiful in Japan: *Tago no ura* (*Suruga*), *Matsushima* (*Rikuzen*), *Hako-saki* (*Rikuchū*), *Ama no hashidate* (*Tango*), *Waka no ura* (*Kii*), Lake *Biwa* (*Ōmi*), *Itsukushima* (*Aki*), *Kisakata* (*Ugo*), Mount *Asama* (*Ise*), *Matsue* (*Izumo*), *Akashi* (*Harima*) and *Kanazawa* (*Musashi*).

Nihon-kai, 日 本 海. The Sea of Japan, between that country, Korea and China.

Nihon-ki, 日 本 紀. Or *Nihon-shoki*. 日 本 書 紀. A collection of ancient chronicles of Japan, from its origin to the end of the reign of *Jitō* (696), written with Chinese ideographs by prince *Toneri-shinnō*, *Ō no Yasumaro*, etc., in 720. It is also called *Yamato-bumi*. — The *Nihon-ki* is with the *Koji-ki*, the only authority for all that concerns the primitive period of Japanese history, and the two works often differ, especially in their chronological data. The official chronology follows sometimes one, sometimes the other, and at times, rejects them both, to follow a third opinion. To state an instance, the ages of the first emperors at the time of their death, are given as follows:

			Koji-ki, 137 years		— *Nihon-ki*, 127 years			— Official Chro., 127 years.		
1. Jimmu:	„	137 years		„	127 years			„	„	127 „
2. Suisei:	„	45	„	—	„	80		„	„	84 „
3. Annei:	„	49	„	—	„	57		„	„	57 „
4. Itoku:	„	45	„	—	„	77		„	„	77 „
5. Kōshō:	„	93	„	—	„	113		„	„	114 „
6. Kōan:	„	123	„	—	„	102	„ (of reign)—	„	„	137 „
7. Kōrei:	„	106	„	—	„	76	„ („)—	„	„	128 „
8. Kōgen:	„	57	„	--	„	57	„ („)—	„	„	116 „
9. Kaikwa:	„	63	„	—	„	60	„ („)—	„	„	111 „
10. Sujin:	„	168	„	—	„	120		„	„	119 „
11. Suinin:	„	153	„	—	„	140		„	„	141 „
12. Keikō:	„	137	„	—	„	196		„	„	143 „
13. Seimu:	„	95	„	—	„	107		„	„	108 „
14. Chūai:	„	...	„	—	„	...		„	„	52 „
15. Ōjin:	„	130	„	—	„	110		„	„	111 „
16. Nintoku:	„	83	„	—	„	87	„ (of reign) —	„	„	110 „
17. Richū:	„	64	„	—	„	70		„	„	70 „
18. Hanshō:	„	60	„	—	„	6	„ (of reign) —	„	„	60 „
19. Inkyō:	„	78	„	—	„	42	„ („)—	„	„	80 „
20. Ankō:	„	...	„	—	„	...		„	„	56 „
21. Yuryaku:	„	124	„	—	„	23	„ (of reign) —	„	„	62 „

The above table is enough to bring home to the reader how hard it must have been to make an authentic chronology of the first centuries of Japanese history, and at the same time, how little confidence the one merits that has been adopted. Moreover, the *Nihon-ki* is often at variance with itself, and, on analysing it closely, the student arrives at solutions which are quite unexpected. Thus, it is said, that the emperor *Keikō* was born in the 54th year of the reign of *Suinin*, or the 25th year A.D. Now, it is said elsewhere, that the same *Keikō* was appointed heir to the throne in the 37th year of his father's reign, at the age of 21; which is equal to saying that 17 years before his birth, he was already 21 years old.—Another instance. Prince *Ō-usu no mikoto*, twin brother to *Yamatotakeru*, was born in the 12th year of *Keikō* (82 A.D.); yet in the 4th year of the same reign, i.e. 8 years before he was born, he seduced the daughter of *Minotsukuri-kao*. — *Yamatotakeru* died in the 43rd year of *Keikō* (113 A.D.); now, his son *Chūai* was born in the 19th year of *Seimu* (149), i.e. 36 years after his father's death. Add to this, the improbable longevity of the first sovereigns, the age at which they have children (*Jimmu* at 80 years, *Itoku*, at 12 years, *Sujin*, at 90, *Suinin*, at nearly 100 years), and you can form an idea of the confidence which the *Nihon-ki* deserves. — *Motoori Norinaga* had already noticed between Japanese Chronicles and Korean Annals a discrepancy of two cycles (120 years). Such contemporary historians as dare to express an opinion on the matter, hold that the same proportion should be extended to the whole period between *Jimmu* and *Nintoku* (660 B.C.-399 A.D.), thus 10 cycles (600 years) seem to have been interpolated; the first emperor of Japan was probably contemporaneous with the Christian era. Be that as it may, Japanese history can hardly be considered as existing previous to the year 500 A.D. The annals of the 6th century ought to be accepted with the utmost reserve; and it is only from the 7th century, that we begin to tread on solid ground. On the whole, the *Nihon-ki*, is the first of a long series of official compilations (See *Riku-kokushi*), the authors of which were content to write down events in their chronological order, month after month, day after day, with neither criticism nor commentary. Interesting from a literary standpoint, it has but little historical value.

Nihon-ki no Tsubone, 日 本 紀 局 . — See *Murasaki Shikibu.*

Nihon san kei, 日 本 三 景 . The 3 landscapes, considered to be the most beautiful in Japan : *Itsukushima* (*Aki*), *Ama no Hashidate* (*Tango*), and *Matsushima* (*Rikuzen*)

Nihon-seiki, 日 本 政 記 . A history of Japan in 15 volumes by *Rai San-yō* (1780-1832).

Nihon shi-sei, 日 本 四 姓 . The 4 great family names in Japan : *Fujiwara, Taira, Minamoto, Tachibana.*

Niigata, 新 瀉 . Capital of *Niigata-ken* and of *Echigo* province (58,800 inh.). From 1869 to 1899, it was one of the 5 ports opened to foreigners. — Formerly called *Tsuchifuta no sato.*

Niigata-bugyō, 新 瀉 奉 行 . An office established in 1833, and assigned to a representative of the *Bafuku*, who had to inspect the boats coming and going on the river of *Niigata* (*Shinano-gawa*).

Niigata-ken, 新潟縣・ A department formed from the *Echigo* and *Sado* provinces. — Pop.: 1,882,600 inh. It is the most densely populated province of all Japan.—Capital: *Niigata* (58,800 inh.)—Chief towns: *Takata* (20,300), *Aikawa* (*Sado*) (12,500), *Shibata* (11,400), *Nuttari* (10,700), *Naoetsu* (10,600), etc.

Nii-jima, 新島・ One of the 7 isles of *Izu* (27 Km. in circ.).

Niimi, 新見・ In *Bitchū*, was from 1698 to 1868 the residence of the *Seki daimyō* (18,000 k.).

Niiname-matsuri, 新甞祭・ A ceremony held in the Imperial Palace, in which the emperor offers to the gods the first fruits of the new rice and afterwards partakes of it himself. This feast which can be traced up to remotest times was fixed for the "Rabbit" day of the 11th month. Since the introduction of the Gregorian calendar, it is held on the 23rd of November. It is also called *Shinjō-sai.*

Niiro, 新納・ The principal vassal family of the *Shimazu daimyō* (*Satsuma*).

Ni-i no ama, 二位尼 or *Ni-i dono,* 二位殿・ A name given to *Toki-ko,* wife of *Taira Kiyomori,* and to *Masa-ko,* wife of *Minamoto Yoritomo,* because they held the second Court rank (*ni-i*).

Niitabe-shinnō, 新田部親王 (+735), Son of the emperor *Temmu;* he was noted for his administrative talents, but would not consent to be appointed heir apparent (731).

Niitaka-yama, 新高山・ (Lit.: the new high mountain). The name given by Japanese to Mount *Morrison* after the annexation of Formosa. It is 3895 meters high and thus exceeds Mount *Fuji* (3,780 m.) by some 100 meters. The Emperor himself chose the name. — *Taka-yama* is another name for Mt. *Fuji.* — The Chinese called it *Yu-shan* (Jap.: *Gyoku-san*).

Niiya, 新谷・ In *Iyo,* was from 1623 to 1868 the residence of a branch of the *Katō daimyō* (10,000 k.)

Nijō, 二條・ A family of *kuge,* descended from *Fujiwara Michiie* (1192-1252). It was one of the 5 families (*go-sekke*) from which the empresses, the *Sesshō,* and the *Kwampaku* were chosen. — To-day Duke.

—— **Yoshizane,** 良實 (1216-70), Son of *Michiie,* was the first to take the name of *Nijō.* He became *Sadaijin* and *Kwampaku.* He has received the name of *Fukō-on-in.*

—— **Michihira,** 道平 (1287-1335). Great-grandson of *Yoshizane,* appointed *Kwampaku* in 1316, was replaced after the accession of *Go-Daigo* (1319) by *Ichijō Uchitsune,* and later on reinstated in his office (1327-29). He served the emperor *Go-Daigo* faithfully and received the name of *Nochi no Kōmyōshō-in.*

—— **Yoshimoto,** 良基 (1320-88). Son of *Michihira,* was successively: *Udaijin, Sadaijin, Kwampaku, Dajō-daijin, Sangū* (1376), *Sesshō* of the northern dynasty (1382). He has received the posthumous name of *Nochi no Fukō-on-in.* A distinguished poet and man of letters, he is the author of some 15 books.

—— **Mochimoto,** 持基 (1390-1445). Grandson of *Yoshimoto*, was *Kwampaku* (1424), *Sesshō* (1429), *Dajō-daijin* (1433), then again *Kwampaku* (1434) He has received the name of *Nochi no Fukushō-in*.

Nijō-dairi, 二條内裏. An ancient palace in *Kyōto*. At first occupied by *Fujiwara Michinaga* (966-1027) and *Norimichi* (996-1075), it became later on the residence of the emperors *Go-Reizei* (1051) and *Toba* (1124).

Nijō-jō, 二條城. At first the *Kyōto* residence of the *Shiba daimyō* of *Owari*, it passed over to the *Oda*, and, in 1569, *Nobunaga* built a castle there for the *Shōgun Yoshiaki*. After the deposition of the latter (1573), he offered it to prince *Masahito-shinnō*. In 1582, *Nobutada*, son of *Nobunaga*, after an attempt to save his father who was besieged in the *Honnō-ji* temple by *Akechi Mitsuhide*, retired to the *Nijō* castle where he was himself attacked and overpowered by the enemies of his family. He committed suicide, and the castle was burned. — It was located near the imperial Palace, in the ward called at present *Shimodachi-uri*.

Nijō-jō, 二條城. A palace built in 1600 by *Ieyasu*, west of *Kyōto*. It was the residence of the *Shōgun* when he visited *Kyōto*. *Ieyasu* resided there in 1611; *Hidetada* in 1617 and in 1626, received the visit of the emperor *Go-Mi-no-o*, his son-in-law at this place. *Iemitsu* sojourned there in 1634, after which, for more than 2 centuries, no *Shōgun* appeared in *Kyōto*. In 1863, *Iemochi* repaired thither, and received from the emperor *Kōmei*, orders to expel the foreign barbarians. Finally, it was from the *Nijō* palace, that *Keiki*, the last *Tokugawa*, handed over to the emperor his resignation as *Shōgun* (1867). It became imperial property by the name of *Nijō-rikyū* (detached palace of *Nijō*) and is still one of the richest and most interesting monuments of the former capital.

Nijō-jō jōban, 二條城定番. At the time of the *Tokugawa Shōgun*, an officer intrusted, under the authority of the *Shoshidai*, with the guard of the inner part of the *Nijō* palace.

Nijō-jō zaiban, 二條城在番. At the time of the *Tokugawa Shōgun*, a detachment of troops intrusted with the guard of the *Nijō* palace. Every year, a fresh guard was sent from *Edo ;* it numbered 150 men, divided into 3 sections who replaced one another every 4 months.

Nijō kura-bugyō, 二條藏奉行. A title created in 1625, and assigned to two officials intrusted, under a *Kanjō-bugyō*, with the guard of the stores (*kura*) belonging to the *Nijō* palace (*Kyōto*).

Nijō Takakura-dono, 二條高倉殿. An ancient palace of *Kyōto*, also called *Sanjō-bōmon-tei*. It was the residence of the *Ashikaga Shōgun Takauji, Yoshiakira, Yoshimochi, Yoshitane*. — It was located in the ward known to-day as *O-ike-dōri Takakura*.

Nijō-tennō, 二條天皇. The 76th Emperor of Japan (1159-1165). *Morihito*, son of *Go-Shirakawa*, succeeded his father at the age of 16. It was during his reign that *Taira Kiyomori*, for the second time victorious over the *Minamoto* (*Heiji no ran* — 1159), became the undisputed master of all Japan. *Nijō* died at the age of 23.

Nijō Tomi-no-kōji-dairi, 二條富小路内裏. An ancient palace in *Kyōto*, situated in the ward of *Tomi no kōji*. It was the residence of the emperors *Go-Horikawa, Go-Fushimi, Go-Daigo.* There also was held the coronation ceremony of *Go-Saga* (1243) and of *Go-Fukakusa* (1247).

Nijū-go Bosatsu, 二十五菩薩. The 25 most revered *Bosatsu* of Buddhism : *Kwannon, Seishi, Yakuō, Yakujō, Fugen, Bunshu, Shishikō, Darani, Kokūzō, Tokuzō, Hōzō, Sankai-e, Kongō, Konzō, Kōmyō-ō, Kwagen-ō, Shuhō-ō, Nisshō-ō, Gwakkō-ō, Sammai-ō, Seijison-ō, Taijizai-ō, Taiitoku-ō, Muhenshin* and *Hakugu-ō.*

Ni-jū-ichi dai-shū, 二十一代集. 21 collections of poems, from the *Kokin-shū* (905) until the *Shin-zoku-kokin-waka-shū* (1438).

Ni-jū-ni sha, 二十二社. The 22 most popular *Shintō* temples : *Ise, Iwashimizu, Kamo, Matsuo, Hirano, Inari, Kasuga, Ōharano, Iso-no-kami, Yamato, Hirose, Tatsuta, Sumiyoshi, Hiyoshi, Ume-no-miya, Yoshida, Hirota, Gion, Kitano, Nibu, Kibune,* and *Miwa.*

Ni-jū ryō, 二十寮. 20 dependencies of the imperial Palace, containing the head-offices of various administrations ; *Ōtoneri, Zusho, Kura, Nuidono, Takumi, Daigaku, Uta, Gemba, Misasagi, Kazue, Chikara, Moku, Sa-me,* and *U-me, Hyōgo, On-yō, Shuden, Ten-yaku, Ōi, Kamon* and *Saigū.*

Ni-jū-shi setsu, 二十四節. The 24 divisions of the year in the old calendar : *Risshun, Usui,* etc. — See Appendix XIV.

Nikai-dō, 二階堂. An ancient fortified temple of *Kamakura,* in the dungeon of which prince *Morinaga-shinnō* was confined and assassinated (1335).

Nikaidō, 二階堂. An ancient family of *daimyō* descended from *Fujiwara Yukimasa.*

—— **Yukimasa,** 行政. Son of *Yukitō,* was the first to take the name of *Nikaidō.* He served *Yoritomo* and became successively *Izumo-shugo, Yamashiro no kami* and *Shitsuji* of the *Mandokoro.*

—— **Yukimori,** 行盛 (1182-1254). Son of *Yukimitsu* and grandson of *Yukimasa,* served the *Shōgun* of *Kamakura* and was a minister of the *Shikken.* He was one of the authors of the *Jōei-shiki-moku.*

—— **Yukifuji,** 行藤 (1246-1302). Was *Kebiishi* (1282), *Dewa no kami* (1288), and *Rensho* (minister) of the *Shikken.*

—— **Sadafuji,** 貞藤. Was *Kebiishi* and *Dewa no kami,* and tried in vain to prevent *Hōjō Takatoki* from dethroning *Go-Daigo* (1331). He besieged *Morinaga-shinnō* at Mt. *Yoshino* and defeated *Murakami Yoshimitsu,* whose head he sent to *Kyōto.*

Nikkan, 日鑑. A bonze, disciple of *Nichiren,* became chief of the *Kuon-ji* temple of *Minobu (Kai).*

Nikki, 仁木. A family of *daimyō* descended from *Minamoto Yoshikiyo* (+1183) *(Seiwa-Genji).*

—— **Sanekuni,** 實國. Grandson of *Yoshikiyo,* was the first to take the name of *Nikki,* from the village of *Nikki,* in *Mikawa* where he fixed his residence.

—— **Yoriaki,** 賴章 (1299-1359). Descendant of *Sanekuni,* served *Ashikaga Takauji,* and fought for the northern dynasty. He became *Suwō no kami, Iga no kami* and *Shitsuji* (minister) of the *Shōgun.*

—— **Yoshinaga,** 義長 (+ 1367). Brother of *Yoriaki*, distinguished himself by his bravery in the campaigns against the southern dynasty. Having become an object of jealousy for his companions in arms, who attempted to take his life, he left the service of the *Ashikaga*, and fortified himself in the castle of *Nagano* (*Ise*), where he was besieged in vain. Later on, he became reconciled with the *Shōgun Yoshiakira* and was killed while fighting against *Kitabatake Akitoshi*. — The *Sakakibara daimyō* descended from a family of the same name.

Nikkō, 日 光. A small town in *Shimotsuke* province (7,500 inh.), renowned for the beauty of its temples and its picturesque scenery. — In 766, the bonze *Shōdō-Shōnin* built a temple there which he called *Shihonryū-ji*. In 808, *Tachibana Toshitō*, governor of the province, rebuilt the temple on a larger scale and called it *Honryū-ji*. Two years later, *Kyōbin*, disciple of *Shōdō*, built the *Mangwan-ji*, of which he became the first high priest. In 820, *Kūkai* (*Kōbō-Daishi*) visited these mountains and changed their name of *Futara-yama* (Chinese: *Nikō-zan*, 二 荒 山) to *Nikkō* (light of day). *Jikaku-Daishi* erected 3 other large temples, and 36 smaller ones (850). The emperors *Kwammu, Heijō, Nimmyō, Go-Toba*, later on *Yoritomo* and *Sanetomo*, granted landed property to the temples, which eventually came to possess, towards 1220, as many as 70 villages and a revenue of 180,000 k. — In 1590, *Hideyoshi* confiscated all their domains, leaving them nothing but the village of *Ashio* (600 k.): only 9 temples were preserved, all the others being demolished or transported elsewhere. — But in 1617, when the remains of *Ieyasu* were transferred to *Nikkō*, a magnificent temple was erected to receive them. From that time, under the able administration of the high-priest *Tenkai, Nikkō* gradually recovered its former prosperity. In 1645, the emperor *Go-Kōmyō* conferred on *Ieyasu* the posthumous title of *Tōshō-daigongen* and decreed that every year an imperial messenger (*reihei-shi*) should carry presents to his tomb. On the death of the *Shōgun Iemitsu* (1651), his remains were transported there and a temple was erected to his memory. In 1654, a son of the emperor *Go-Mi-no-o*, became high priest of the *Tendai* sect and established himself in *Nikkō*. The primitive temple then took the name of *Rinnō-ji*. — At the Restoration, all the revenues (240,000 k.) reverted to the crown. The temple of *Ieyasu* (*Tōshōgū*), was turned into a *Shintō* shrine, the temple of *Iemitsu* remaining Buddhist. — Although fallen from its pristine splendor, *Nikkō* is still one of the most interesting and most frequented resorts in Japan. The chief objects of interest at the present day are the temples built in and about the seventeenth century. The first object to claim attention is the Sacred Red Bridge closed to ordinary mortals except on certain festival days. The *Mongwan-ji* contains the *Sambutsu dō*, or Hall of the Three Buddha, so called because three gigantic images are found there. The Mausoleum of *Ieyasu* may be said to be the principal centre of interest. Prominent among the structures is a five storied pagoda of graceful form, 34 m. high and painted in pleasing colors. It is fronted by a granite *Torii* 9 m. high whose columns are 1 m. thick. The Holy of Holies is not accessible unless by special permission. Here Buddhist art is seen in its acme. Besides the mausolea of the *Shōgun* there are many other objects of great interest.

Nikkō, 日 與 (+ 1288) A bonze who accompanied *Nichiren* his exiled master to *Sado* (1271), and later on, built the temple of *Myōhon-ji* (*Awa*), where he died. He is the founder of the *Kōmon* branch of the *Hokkeshū* sect.

Nikkō, 日 講. A bonze of the *Nichiren* sect. ; disciple of *Nichiō*, he founded, in the 17th century, the *Fujufuze-kōmon* branch.

Nikkō-Bosatsu, 日 光 菩 薩. A Buddhist divinity that resides in the sun.

Nikkō-bugyō, 日 光 奉 行. Officials established in 1700, and intrusted with the maintenance and guard of the Shogunal temples of *Nikkō*, with the feasts and receptions, the administration of the town, the administration of justice in the provinces of *Shimotsuke* and *Kōzuke*, etc. They were two in number and served in turn six months at a time. They had under their command 6 *shihai-gimmi-yaku*, 36 *dōshin*, etc.

Nikkō-gongen, 日 光 權 現. Another name for the *Futara-jinja* or *Tōshō-gū* at *Nikkō*.

Ni-kwan, 二 官. The two great administrations of the *Taihō* Code. (702) : the *Jinji-kwan*, a kind of department of Worship and the *Dajō-kwan* or Council of State.

Nimbetsu-chō, 人 別 帳. In the *Tokugawa* days, the register of the social state, held by the mayors (*sato-osa, nanushi*). It came into use at the time when, to root out Christianity, every body was forced to present himself to the bonzes for the *Shūmon-aratame*. The formality had to be undergone at first every year, but from 1726, it recurred only in the years of the "Rat" and the "Horse."

Nimmyō-tennō, 仁 明 天 皇. The 54th Emperor of Japan (834-850). First called *Masara*, he was the 3rd son of *Saga-tennō*, and succeeded his uncle *Junwa* at the age of 24. He was a noted scholar and musician. He died after a reign of 18 years, and was buried at *Fukakusa*, whence the name of *Fukakusa-tennō*, by which he is also known.

Nimpyō, 仁 平. *Nengō* : 1151-1153.

Nin, 任. A promotion in dignity (*kwan*) ; e.g. *Ise no kami ni ninzu.* — The promotion to an office (*shoku*) was styled *ho* (*Samurai-dokoro-bettō ni hosu*) ; the promotion to a Court rank (*kurai*), was *jo* (*Shō-ni-i ni josu*).

Nin-an, 仁 安. *Nengō* : 1166-68.

Ninigi no mikoto, 瓊 々 杵 尊. Or better, *Amatsuhiko-hikoho no Ninigi*, grandson of *Amaterasu-ō-mikami*. The country of *Ō-yashima* (Japan), had by degrees fallen under the rule of the descendants of *Susano-o*, established in *Izumo*. *Amaterasu* wished her descendants to recover the regions they had been deprived of, and sent *Takemika-zuchi* and *Futsunushi*, who brought about the submission of *Ōkuninushi* and his son *Kotoshironushi*. Thereupon, *Amaterasu* presented her grandson with the 3 sacred treasures, the precious jewel (*Yasakani no magatama*), the sword (*Ame-no-murakumo no tsurugi*) and the mirror

Yata no kagami), which, to this very day, are still the symbols of the Imperial Power. After this, *Ninigi* descended from heaven, followed by a numerous suite, and alighted on the summit of Mount *Takachiho* (*Hyū-ga*) ; thence he proceeded to *Satsuma*, and established his residence at Cape *Ata no Kasasa*, where he married *Kono-hana-sakuya hime*, daughter of *Ōyamatsumi*. *Jimmu-tennō* was their great-grandson.

NINIGI NO MIKOTO.

Ninji, 仁治. *Nengō* : 1240-42.

Ninju, 仁壽. *Nengō* : 851-853.

Ninken-tennō, 仁賢天皇. The 24th Emperor of Japan (488-498).—*Oke*, son of *Ichinobe-oshiha no Ōji*, succeeded his brother *Kensō*, at the age of 39. Their father had been killed by *Yūryaku-tennō*, who looked upon him as a rival to the throne (457), whereupon, the two princes, still quite young, fled to the district of *Akashi* (*Hari-ma*), where they lived in seclusion. Discovered in the reign of *Seimei*, they were brought back to Court, resumed their rank, and the younger one, *Oke*, was appointed heir to the throne (482). He reigned by the name of *Kensō* (485-487), and was succeeded by his elder brother *Ninken*, whose reign of 11 years presents nothing remarkable. It was in 493, that the first tanners and curriers came over from Korea and the Japanese became acquainted with their art.

Ninkō-tennō, 仁孝天皇. The 120th Emperor of Japan (1817-46), *Ayahito*, son of *Kōkaku-tennō*, succeeded his father at the age of 18. During his reign of 30 years, the authority was in the hands of the *Shōgun Ienari* and *Ieyoshi* ; but already the prestige of the *Tokugawa* began to decline : every year some foreign ships appeared on the Japanese coasts, books were published, demanding the revival of Shintoism and the restoration of the imperial power ; dissenssions broke out in the very family of the *Shōgun*, and it was easy to foresee the impending ruin of the political structure raised 2 centuries before by *Ieyasu* and *Iemitsu*.

Ninna, 仁和. Or *Ninwa*. *Nengō* : 885-888.

Ninna-ji, 仁和寺. A temple of the *Shingon* sect, founded in 886, N. W. of *Kyōto*, by the emperor *Kōkō*. *Uda-tennō* retired thither after his abdication (899), had his head shaved and took the name of *Kongōhō*. Thereupon, the temple received the name of *O-muro*, by which it is commonly known. From that time, the head of the temple has always been an imperial prince.

Ninnaji no Miya, 仁和寺宮. — See *Atsuzane-shinnō*.

Ninshōji, 西大路. In *Ōmi* ; was from 1621 to 1868, the residence of the *Ichibashi daimyō* (18,000 k.). — To-day *Nishi-ōji*.

Nintoku-tennō, 仁徳天皇. The 16th Emperor of Japan (313-399). *Ō-sasagi*, 4th son of *Ōjin-tennō*, succeeded his father at the age of 23. On the day of his birth, an owl (*tsuku*) entered the room where he was born, whilst a wren (*sasagi*) flew into the house of *Take-shiuchi no Sukune*, to whom a son was born on the same day. Now the wren was a bird of good omen, whereas the owl was ill-omened. Therefore *Ōjin* gave his son the name of *Ō-sasagi* and his minister's child he named *Tsuku*. *Ō-sasagi* had an elder brother *Waki-ira-tsuko*, whom his father had destined for the throne, but who refused the honor. On the other hand, *Ō-sasagi*, not to go against the will of his father, declared he would never consent to take his brother's place. This state of things continued for 2 years, when *Wakiiratsuko* put an end to his own life, to oblige his brother to accept the throne. The latter proved worthy of the honor, and has, to the present day been looked upon as one of the most popular sovereigns, on account of the zeal he displayed for the welfare of his subjects: he fostered agriculture, exempted husbandmen from taxes for several years, dug canals, built dikes, erected houses for rice, etc. — After a reign of 87 years, he died at the age of 110, according to some (in which case, he must have been born when his father was 90 years old), — of 143, according to others.

NINTOKU TENNŌ.

Ninwa, 仁和. Or *Ninna*. *Nengō :* 885-888.

Ni-ō, 仁王. (Lit.: the two kings). The 2 statues, generally of frightful aspect, which may be seen on either side of the outer gate of the larger Buddhist temples. They represent *Indra* and *Brahma*, whose office it is to ward off the evil spirits. The gates they guard are called *Ni-ō-mon.*

NIŌ (BY UNKEI.)

Ni-ō-e, 仁王會. A ceremony which used to be held in the Palace, in the 3rd and the 7th months to secure good harvests and to ward off epidemics. The bonzes read the *Ni-ō-gokoku-hangya-kyō.*

Nippon, 日本. Japan. — See *Nihon* and *Dai-Nihon.*

Nirazaki, 韮崎. In *Kai* province. *Takeda Katsuyori* defeated by *Nobunaga* at *Nagashino* (*Mikawa*) built a castle at *Nirazaki* which he called *Shimpu-jō,* (1575) and which was captured at the time of the fall of the *Takeda* (1582).

Nirayama, 韮山. In *Izu* province. An ancient castle built towards the close of the 15th century by *Hōjō Sōun.* It was besieged in 1590 by *Oda Nobuo* and *Hachisuka Iemasa.* In the *Tokugawa* days, it belonged to the *Shōgun,* who confided it to a *daikwan* of the *Egawa* family,

Nire, 仁禮. A family of *samurai* from *Kagoshima* (*Satsuma*), ennobled after the Restoration. — To-day Viscount.

Nishi, 西. The name of two families of *samurai* from *Kagoshima* (*Satsuma*) ennobled in 1895. — To-day Barons.

Nishi, 西. A family of *samurai* from *Shizuoka* (*Suruga*), ennobled after the Restoration. — To-day Baron.

Nishigori, 錦織. A family of *kuge* descended from the *Fujiwara.* — Now Viscount.

Nishi-hachijō-dono, 西八條殿. Residence of *Taira Kiyomori,* W. of *Kyōto.* It was burnt after his death, in 1181.

Nishi-itsutsuji, 西五辻. A family descended from *Minamoto Nasa-nobu* (920-993) (*Uda-Genji*) and hereditarily attached to the *Kōfuku-ji* temple (*Nara*). — To-day Baron.

Nishijin, 西陳. (Lit.: western camp). A name given to the north-western ward of *Kyōto*, because, at the time of the civil war of *Ōnin* (1469), the western army, commanded by *Yamana Sōzen* had its camp there. Later on, this ward became renowned for its fabrics (*Nishijin-ori*).

Nishiki-e, 錦繪. Drawings of persons, birds, flowers, etc., reproduced by wood engravings. Devised for the first time by *Suzuki Harunobu*, an artist from *Edo* (1718-1770), they were also called *Edo-e*. *Utagawa Toyokuni, Katsushika Hokusai*, etc., became famous in this kind of art.

Nishi-Kirishima-yama, 西霧嶋山. A volcano on the boundary between *Hyūga* and *Ōsumi* (1650 m.). Also called *Karakuni-dake*.

Nishi-maru, 西丸. In the *Tokugawa* days, a palace, situated west of *Edo* castle, and serving as residence to the heir of the *Shōgun*. It had as officials, one *Rōjū*, 2 *Wakadoshiyori*, 2 *Sōsha-ban*, 6 *Sobashū*, etc.

Nishina, 仁科. A family, descended from *Taira Sadamori*, and, from the 12th century, established in *Shinano*.

—— **Moritō,** 盛遠 (+ 1221). Having gone to *Kumano* one day with his son, he met the ex-emperor *Go-Toba*, who took him into his service. *Hōjō Yoshitoki*, apprised of the fact, deprived him of his estates. *Go-Toba* tried in vain to have them restored to him : the *Shikken* remained inflexible. The emperor was highly incensed at this, and appealed to arms against the *Hōjō*. During the *Shōkyū* war, *Moritō* passed over into *Etchū*, to support the imperial cause, but was defeated and killed at *Tonami-yama*.

—— **Nobumori,** 信盛 (+1582). 4th son of *Takeda Shingen ;* was adopted by the *Nishina* family. After the defeat of his brother *Katsuyori*, he fortified himself in the castle of *Takatō* (*Shinano*) and prepared for resistance. *Oda Nobutada* sent a bonze to him and promised to let him go unhurt, if he surrendered. *Nobumori*, irritated at this proposal, had the unfortunate bonze's nose and ears cut off and sent him back to his master. Attacked shortly after, he resisted valiantly but was defeated and killed.

Nishino Buntarō, 西野文太郎 (1865-1889). A *samurai* of the *Yamaguchi* clan (*Suwō*). He came to *Tōkyō* (1887), where he held an office in the *Naimu-shō*, but was deeply engaged in politics. Having heard that the Minister of Education, *Mori Arinori*, had acted irreverently in a visit to the shrine of *Ise*, he repaired to the place to ascertain the fact, and returned with the resolution to avenge the insult offered to the Sun-goddess, by the Minister's blood. He carried his scheme into effect on the very day of the promulgation of the Constitution (Feb. 11, 1889), but was immediately attacked and killed by the attendants of his victim.

Nishi no shima, 西嶋. An island of the *Oki* group (81 Km. in circ.).

Nishio, 西尾. A small town in *Mikawa* (7400 inh.). An ancient castle occupied at first by the *Makino daimyō*, it passed into the hands of the *Tokugawa* in 1542 ; was afterwards the residence of the *daimyō*

Tanaka (1590), *Honda* (1601), *Matsudaira* (1617), *Honda* (1620), *Ōta* (1638), *Ii* (1645), *Masuyama* (1659), *Doi* (1663), *Miura* (1747), and *Matsudaira* (*Ōgyū*) (1764-1868) (60,000 k.).

Nishio, 西尾. A family of *daimyō*, descended from *Kira* (*Seiwa-Genji*).

——— **Yoshitsugu,** 吉次 (1530-1606). Son of *Kira Mochihiro*, successively served *Nobunaga, Hideyoshi* and *Ieyasu*. His descendants settled, in 1617, at *Tsuchiura* (*Hitachi*), in 1649, at *Tanaka* (*Suruga*), in 1679 at *Komoro* (*Shinano*), in 1682, at *Yokosuka* (*Tōtōmi*), where they remained until 1868. (350,000 k.). — To-day Viscount.

Nishi-ōhira, 西大平. In *Mikawa*. From 1748 to 1868 it was the residence of the *Ō-oka daimyō* (10,000 k.).

Nishi-ōji, 西大路. A family of *kuge*, descended from *Fujiwara Uona* (721-783). — To-day Viscount.

Nishi-ōkawa, 西大川. A river (125 Km.), which takes its rise in *Mimasaka*, where it is known as the *Takata-gawa*. It traverses *Bizen*, flows through *Okayama* and empties itself into the bay of *Kojima*.—Also called *Asahi-gawa, Sasase-gawa, Mino-gawa*.

Nishi-sanjō, 西三條. A family of *kuge*, descended from *Fujiwara* (*Sanjō*) *Sanefusa* (1146-1224). At first called *Sanjō-Nishi*. — Now Count.

Nishi-sanjō no dairi, 西三條內裏. An ancient palace of *Kyōto*, to which the emperors *Shirakawa* (1086) and *Toba* (1123) retired after their abdication.

Nishi-takatsuji, 西高辻. A family, descended from *Sugawara Michizane* and ennobled (1882) in the person of *Nobukane*, younger brother to *Takatsuji Fusanaga*. — To-day Baron.

Nishi-tō-in, 西洞院. A family of *kuge*, descended from the *Taira*. — Now Viscount.

Nishi-yotsutsuji, 西四辻. A family of *kuge*, descended from *Fujiwara* (*Saionji*) *Michisue* (1090-1128). — Now Viscount.

Nisshin, 日清. Japan and China.

Nisshin-sensō, 日清戰爭. The war between Japan and China (1894-1895). In the spring of 1894, troubles caused by bands of robbers, called *Tōgaku-tō*, broke out in Korea. The government of that country, unable to restore order, asked China to send some troops; Japan, in accordance with the treaty of 1885, also despatched troops to Korea. Hence the war, of which the principal events are as follows:

July   14, 1894 :   Rupture of diplomatic relations.

„   27, „   :   The *Naniwa* (Jap. cruiser, capt. *Tōgo*) sinks the *Kowshing* (Chin. Transport.)

„   29, „   :   The Japanese are victorious at *Gazan* (*Asan*) (Korea).

Aug.   1, „   :   Declaration of war by the two Emperors.

„   26, „   :   Treaty of alliance between Japan and Korea.

Sept. 16, „   :   Capture of *Heijō* (*Pyong-yang*) (gen. *Nozu*).

„   17, „   :   Naval victory of *Kaiyō-tō* (*Yalu*) (Adm. *Itō*).

Oct.   8, „   :   Victory of *Wiju* (marshal *Yamagata*).

Nov. 6-7, 1894 : Capture of *Kinchū* and of *Tailen-wan* (marshal *Ōyama*).

„ 22, „ : Capture of *Ryōjun-kō* (*Port-Arthur*) (marshal *Ōyama*).

Jan. 10, 1895: Capture of *Kaiping* (gen. *Nogi*).

Feb. 2, „ : Taking of *Ikai-ei* (*Wei-hai-wei*) (gen. *Ōdera*).

„ 17, „ : Surrender of the Chinese fleet to admiral *Itō*.

„ 19, „ : *Rikōshō* (*Li Hung-chang*) arrives at *Shimonoseki*.

March 4, „ : Taking of *Nyūchan* (gen. *Nozu*).

„ 24, „ : *Koyama Toyotarō* fires a revolver at *Li Hung-chang*.

„ 30, „ : Armistice for 21 days.

April 17, „ : Treaty of *Shimonoseki*.

May 8, „ : Ratification of the treaty of *Shimonoseki* at *Chefoo*. — Intervention of Russia, Germany and France.

May-June, „ : Taking possession of Formosa (*Taiwan*) and the Pescadores (*Hōko-tō*).

Nisshū, 日州. The Chinese name for *Hyūga* province.

Nisshū, 日什 (1314-1392). A bonze, founder of the *Gemmyō-ji* temple (*Kamakura*) and of the *Myōman-ji* branch of the *Nichiren* sect.

Nitchō, 日朝. A famous reformer of the *Nichiren* sect, in the 15th century; he was at the head of the *Kuon-ji* temple at *Minobu* (*Kai*) from 1472 to 1500.

Nitta, 新田. A district in *Kōzuke*, where *Minamoto Yoshishige*, grandson of *Yoshiie* established himself, towards the end of the 12th century, and of which place his descendants assumed the name.

Nitta, 新田. A family of *daimyō*, descended from *Minamoto Yoshishige*, son of *Yoshikuni* and grandson of *Yoshiie*.

Yoshishige {	Yoshikane- Yoshifusa- Masayoshi { Ieuji (*Ōtate*) Masanji-Motouji-Tomouji {	Yoshisada { Yoshiaki Yoshioki Yoshimune Yoshisuke (*Wakiya*)	
	Yoshinori (*Yamana*) Yoshitoshi (*Satomi*) Yoshisue (*Tokugawa*)		

—— **Yoshishige,** 義重 (+1202). Eldest son of *Yoshikuni*, received the name of *Nitta Tarō*. When *Yoshitomo* began war against the *Taira* (1180), *Yoshishige* sided with him and accompanied him to *Kamakura*. In 1611, the *Tokugawa*, whose ancestor he was, had the title of *Chinjufu-shōgun* conferred upon him.

—— **Yoshisada,** 義貞 (1301-1338). At first served in the army of *Hōjō Takatoki*, against *Kusunoki Masashige* in *Kawachi* (1333), but induced by prince *Morinaga-shinnō* to embrace the southern cause, he retired to *Kōzuke*, where he levied troops. Soon after, at the head of 20,000 men, he marched upon *Kamakura*, captured the place and put an end to the *Hōjō* domination. As a reward, he received the titles of *Sa-chūjō* and of *Harima no kami*, with the two provinces of *Kōzuke* and *Harima* as fiefs. When *Ashikaga Takauji* revolted against *Go-Daigo* (1335), *Yoshisada* was sent against him and defeated him on the banks of the *Yahagi-gawa* (*Mikawa*), and in *Suruga*, but he was defeated in his turn, at *Hakone* (*Sagami*). Recalled to *Kyōto*, he could not prevent

Takauji from getting possession of the city ; but shortly afterwards, aided by *Kitabatake Akiie*, he expelled him and defeated him at *Hyōgo* (*Settsu*). Having recruited a fresh army in *Kyūshū*, *Takauji* re-entered the field and at *Minato-gawa* (*Settsu*), won a signal victory over *Yoshisada* and *Masashige*, in which the latter lost his life (1336). Taking the princes *Tsunenaga-shinnō* and *Takanaga-shinnō* with him, *Yoshisada* sought refuge in the castle of *Kanasaki* (*Echizen*) ; besieged shortly after, he fled to *Soma-yama*, where he collected fresh troops and attacked *Shiba Takatsune* at *Fujishima* (*Echizen*). During the battle, he was struck by an arrow and died, scarcely 38 years old. *Yoshisada* is considered as one of the staunchest

NITTA YOSHISADA.

supporters of the legitimate dynasty ; he is honored in a temple (*Fujishima-jinja*) erected on the very spot where he died.

—— **Yoshisuke,** 義助 . — See *Wakiya Yoshisuke.*

—— **Yoshiaki,** 義顯 (+ 1337). The eldest son of *Yoshisada*, fought in all the campaigns of his father, and, when the latter, besieged in the castle of *Kanasaki* (*Echizen*), fled to *Soma-yama*, he remained to keep the enemy at bay, but when he saw that all further resistance was fruitless, he put an end to his life and prince *Takanaga-Shinnō* followed his example.

—— **Yoshioki,** 義與 (+ 1358). Second son of *Yoshisada*, aided *Kitabatake Akiie* to besiege *Kamakura*, and with him entered the place in 1337. *Akiie*, having been killed the following year, was replaced by his brother *Akinobu ;* *Yoshioki* with *Akinobu* fortified Mt. *Otoko*, but was defeated and obliged to seek refuge on Mt. *Yoshino*. In 1352, together with his brother *Yoshimune* and his cousin *Wakiya Yoshiharu*, he expelled *Ashikaga Motouji* from *Kamakura*, and took possession of the city ; but being himself dislodged by *Takauji*, he repaired to *Echigo* and retook the field in *Kōzuke* and *Musashi*. He was made a prisoner by *Takezawa Nagahira*. *Hatakeyama Kunikiyo*, minister of *Motouji*, condemned him to death. He was drowned in the *Rokugō-gawa*, at *Yaguchi no watari* (*Musashi*) where he is worshipped under the name of *Nitta-daimyōjin.*

—— **Yoshimune,** 義宗 (1332-1368). 3rd son of *Yoshisada*, who, on the death of his elder brother *Yoshiaki*, was chosen to inherit the domains of his father. He fought at first against *Ashikaga Yoshiakira*, on Mt. *Yoshino*, and then defeated *Takauji* at *Kanai-ga-hara* (*Musashi*). After that he fortified himself on Mt. *Fuefuki*, with prince *Munenaga-Shinnō ;* but he was besieged by *Takauji* and forced to seek shelter in *Echigo* (1352). He conquered half of that province and built a castle. He was killed in an engagement with *Uesugi Norimasa.*

—— **Sadakata,** 貞方 (+ 1410). Son of *Yoshimune*, continued to the end to fight for the southern dynasty, even after it had surrendered its rights to its northern rival (1392). In 1395, he was defeated and fled to *Mutsu*. The next year, he defeated the *Yūki* and the *Ashina* and established himself at *Shirakawa*. Made prisoner in a final attempt against *Kamakura*, he was put to death at *Shichi-ri-ga-hama*.—After the Restoration, a descendant of the above *daimyō* received the title of Baron.

Niwa, 丹羽. A family of *daimyō* originating in *Owari* and descended from the *Fujiwara*.

—— **Nagahide, 長秀** (1535-1585). Son of *Nagamasa*, served *Nobunaga*, who made him marry the daughter of his elder brother *Nobuhiro* and gave him the fief of *Sawayama* (*Ōmi* — 50,000 k.) (1571). He was afterwards intrusted with the construction ef the castle of *Azuchi* (1576), and in return received the domain of *Obama* (*Wakasa* — 100,000 k.).

—— **Nagashige, 長重** (1571-1637). Son of *Nagahide*, married, in compliance with *Hideyoshi's* order, a daughter of *Nobunaga*, and took up his abode at *Fuchū* (*Echizen*) (1583). He succeeded his father at *Obama ;* in 1598, he was transferred to *Komatsu* (*Kaga* — 100,000 k), and received the title of *Kaga no kami*. When the *Sekigahara* campaign broke out, he was engaged in a contest with his neighbor, *Maeda Toshinaga*, and was rather slow in answering the summons of *Ieyasu*, who after his victory, dispossessed him and had him closely watched in *Edo*. However, after several years, he gave him a revenue of 10,000 k. at *Futto* (*Hitachi*). In 1619, *Nagashige* received the fief of *Izumi* (*Mutsu* — 20,000 k.), then in 1622, that of *Tanakura* (*Mutsu* — 50,000 k.).

—— **Mitsushige, 光重.** Son of *Nagashige*, was transferred, in 1642, to *Nihommatsu* (*Mutsu* — 100,000 k.), where his descendants resided till the Restoration. — Now Viscount.

Niwa, 丹羽. A family of *daimyō*, originating in *Owari*, and descending from *Minamoto Yoshiuji* (*Seiwa-Genji*). — They resided successively at *Ibo* (*Mikawa*) (1603-1638), at *Iwamura* (*Mino*) (1638-1742), and at *Mikusa* (*Harima* — 10,000 k.) from 1742 to 1868. — To-day Viscount.

Niwase, 庭瀬. In *Bitchū*, an ancient castle built by *Ukita Naoie*. In the *Tokugawa* days, it belonged to the *daimyō Togawa* (1600), *Kuze* (1683), *Matsudaira* (1693), and lastly from 1699 to 1868 to *Itakura* (20,000 k.).

Niwata, 庭田. A family of *kuge*, descended from the *Uda-Genji*. —Now Count.

Ni-yodo-gawa, 仁淀川. A river (94 Km.) which takes its rise at Mt. *Ishizuchi* (*Iyo*), enters *Tosa*, receives the *Iwaya-gawa*, the *Morikawa*, the *Buntoku-gawa*, the *Kuroiwa-gawa*, the *Kusaka-gawa*, and empties itself into the Pacific Ocean, S. of *Kōchi*. Formerly called *Niedono-gawa*, *Kami-gawa*.

Nō, 能. In olden times, the only public plays were the sacred dances, *kagura*, etc., which were pantomimes of the old *Shintō* myths. In the 14th century, a spoken dialogue was added, recalling certain legends, or celebrating the exploits of popular heroes. Such was the origin of the "*Nō*," which were in great vogue at the time of the

Shōgun Yoshimitsu and *Yoshimasa*. Five families, which received a pension under the *Tokugawa* regime, hereditarily practised the profession of "*Nō*" actors; *Kwanze* (256 k.), *Komparu* (300 k.), *Hōshō* (100 k.), *Kongō* (100 k.) and *Kita* (200 k.). The chiefs of these families possessed the title of *tayū* and had under their orders, quite a number of musicians and "figurants" (*waki, tsure, kyōgenshi, fue, taiko, ōtsuzumishi, kotsuzumishi*, etc.). On the occasion of feasts in the shōgunal palace, they would give a performance of a "*Nō*." From the 16th century, the *Nō* still held a select place in the entertainments of the nobility, but they disappeared from the program of popular festivals, being superseded by the modern theatre (*shibai, kabuki*).

NÔ.

USHIWAKA AND BENKEI ON THE BRIDGE OF GOJÔ.

Nôami, 能阿彌. A celebrated artist of the 15th century, a painter (of the *Shūbun* school), and a professor of the tea ceremony.

Nobeoka, 延岡 or **Nobioka.** In *Hyūga*. It was formerly called *Agata* and received the name of *Nobeoka* only in 1693. It was the residence of the *daimyō Takahashi* (1587), *Arima* (1613), *Miura* (1692), *Makino* (1712), and *Naitō* from 1747 to 1868. (70,000 k.).

Nobono, 能褒野. In *Ise* (to-day, *Kawasaki-mura*). It was there that *Yamatotakeru no mikoto* died, on his return from his expedition to the East. (113). A temple was erected there in his honor in 1879.

Nochi no san-bō, 後三房. (Lit.: the 3 later *Bō*). Three learned *kuge* of the reign of *Go-Daigo* (1319-1338) whose names ended with the ideograph "*fusa*" (in Chinese, *bō*). They were *Kitabatake Chikafusa, Madenokōji Nobufusa*, and *Yoshida Sadafusa*. — They were called the later *bō*, in distinction to the three others, called the "*san-bō*," who flourished towards the end of the 11th century. They were *Fujiwara Korefusa*, *Fujiwara Tamefusa*, and *Ōe Tadafusa*.

Noda, 野田. A place in *Settsu*, where *Nobunaga* defeated the *Miyoshi* (1570).

Noda, 野田. A castle in *Mikawa*. In the 16th century it belonged to the *Suganuma daimyō*, vassals of the *Imagawa*, and of the *Tokugawa*. In 1575, *Ieyasu* fought a battle there against *Takeda Shingen*.

Noda, 野田. A family of *samurai* from *Kumamoto* (*Higo*), ennobled after the Restoration. — To-day Baron.

Nōden - bugyō, 納殿奉行. An official, at the time of the *Kamakura Shōgun*, intrusted with the care of the furniture, cloth and vestments, belonging to the *Shōgun's* palace and kept in an apartment called *nōden*. This office was later on called *Nando-yaku*.

Nogi, 乃木. A family of *samurai* from *Yamaguchi* (*Suwō*), ennobled in 1895.—Now Count.

—— **Kiten,** 希典. Born in 1849, was governor of Formosa in 1896. During the Russo-Japanese war, he commanded the army that invested Port-Arthur (1904).

Noguchi, 野口. A castle in *Harima*. In the 16th century, it belonged to the *Nagai daimyō*, vassals of the *Bessho*. *Hideyoshi* obtained possession of it in 1579.

Noheji-wan, 野邊地灣. The south-eastern part of *Aomori* bay.

Nojima, 野嶋. A castle in the island of *Ōshima* (*Iyo*). In the 16th century it belonged to the *Murakami*, vassals of the *Kōno*, who made themselves a name among the Japanese navigators of the time. Their ships traded not only with the neighboring provinces, but even with Korea and China. Their name disappeared from history at the beginning of the 17th century.

Nojima-ga-saki, 野嶋崎. A cape, S. of *Awa* province.

Nojiri-ko, 野尻湖. A lake in the north of *Shinano*. Also called *Fuyō-ko*. (13 Km. in circ.).

Noma-misaki, 野間崎. A cape S. W. of *Satsuma*.

Nomi no Sukune, 野見宿禰. Born in *Izumo*, was possessed of extraordinary strength. There lived at the same time a man in *Yamato*, *Taema no Kuehaya*, who boasted of having no rival for muscular power. The emperor *Suinin* pitted the two together, and *Taema* was beaten. (23 B.C.). This was, according to tradition, the origin of wrestling (*sumō-tori*). After his success, *Sukune* lived at the Court. It was he that advised to substitute clay statues (*haniwa*) for the human victims that were buried with persons of rank. These clay statues were first used at the burial of the empress *Hihasu-hime* (3. A.D.). Thereupon *Sukune* was put at the head of the potter's guild, with the title of *Hanibe no Omi*.

NOMI NO SUKUNE
AND
TAEMA NO KUEHAYA.

Nōmi-shima, 能美嶋. An island in the Inland Sea, dependent on *Aki* province (60 Km. in circ.).

Nomiya, 野宮. A family of *kuge*, descended from *Fujiwara Ietada* (1061-1135).—Now Viscount.

Nomo no misaki, 野母岬. A cape S. of *Hizen;* also called *Wakitsu-zaki.*

Nomura, 野村. A place in *Mino*, which was, from 1601 to 1631, the residence of a branch of the *Oda* family (20,000 k.).

Nomura, 野村. A family of *samurai* from *Yamaguchi* (*Suwō*), ennobled in 1887.—To-day Viscount.

Nonaka Kenzan, 野中兼山 (1616-1664). A *samurai* of the *Tosa* clan, to whom his lord, *Yamanouchi Tadatoyo*, gave an important share in the government of his fief. Having disputed with the other councillors of his lord, he was banished from the province and died the following year. His true name was *Yoshitsugu.*

Nonoguchi Takamasa, 野々口隆正 (1792-1871). *Samurai* of the *Tsuwano* clan (*Iwami*). Was one of the first to demand in his writings, the restoration of the imperial power.

Nonoichi, 野々市. A town in *Kaga*, formerly called *Nuno-ichi.* It was from the 11th to the 16th century, the residence of the *Togashi daimyō*, governors of the province.

Nonomura Ninsei, 野々村仁清. A celebrated potter and painter of the 17th century.

Norikura-dake, 乗鞍嶽. A mountain between *Hida* and *Shinano* (3160 m.).

Norikura-dake, 乗鞍嶽. A mountain between *Shinano* and *Etchū* (2730 m.).

Nori no tsukasa, 式部省. A former name for the *Shikibu-shō.*

Norito, 祝詞 or **Noritogoto.** *Shintō* prayers used especially in the purification ceremonies (*harai*).

Nori-yumi, 賭弓. A festival formerly held in the Imperial Palace, on the 18th day of the first month. The emperor assisted at an archery tournament between the different bodies of the Guard. (*Sakon, Ukon, Toneri,* etc.) The losers were condemned to drink *sake* (rice wine) and to perform dances.

Nosaki, 荷先. A part of the taxes of all the provinces, reserved for the principal temples and for the Imperial tombs.

Noshiro-gawa, 能代川. A river of *Ugo* (102 Km.). In its upper course it is also called *Yoneshiro-gawa*, and in its lower course, *Shi-jū-hachi-gawa.*

Nōshōmu-shō, 農商務省. The Department of Agriculture and Commerce, established in 1885.

Nōshū, 濃州. The Chinese name of *Mino* province.

Nōshū, 能州. The Chinese name of *Noto* province.

Nōso-numa, 納所沼. A lake in *Yamashiro*, source of the *Uji-gawa* (10 Km. in circ.).

Noto, 能登. One of the 7 provinces of the *Hokurokudō*, comprising 4 districts, which belong to *Ishikawa-ken*. It forms a peninsula, jutting into the Japan Sea. — Chinese name : *Nōshū*.

Noto-jima, 能登嶋. An island in the gulf of *Nanao* (*Noto*) (57 Km. in circ.).

Nozaki, 野崎. A family of *samurai* from *Kagoshima* (*Satsuma*), ennobled after the Restoration. — Now Baron.

Nozu, 野津. A family of *samurai* from *Kagoshima* clan (*Satsuma*), ennobled after the Restoration. — Now Count.

——**Michitsura,** 道貫. Born in 1842, was colonel during the *Satsuma* war. Brigadier-general in 1885, he commanded the division of *Hiroshima* (*Aki*) when the war with China broke out (1894). He began the campaign under the command of Marshal *Yamagata*, and, in the month of November, succeeded the latter who had fallen sick, in the command of the first army, with which he occupied a large part of Manchuria. After the war, he received the titles of Count and Marshal. He commanded the 4th army in the Manchuria campaign (1904-1905).

Nuidono-ryō, 縫殿寮. Formerly an office, belonging to the *Nakatsukasa-shō*, and intrusted with the needle-work and the artists that did it.

Nuimono-tsukasa, 縫司. Formerly an office in the Imperial Palace, intrusted with the vestments and needle-work.

Numadate, 沼舘. A castle in *Ugo* ; in the 16th century, it belonged to the *Onodera daimyō*, who were dispossessed by *Ieyasu* in 1600.

Numajiri, 沼尻. A place in *Shimotsuke*, where *Satake Yoshishige* defeated *Hōjō Ujiyasu* (1571) and was himself defeated by *Hōjō Ujinao* (1585).

Numata, 沼田. A small town in *Kōzuke* (6000 inh.), where *Numata Kagetoki* built a castle in 1153, which was captured by *Nagao Kageharu* in 1510, and afterwards came into the possession of the *Hōjō* of *Odawara*. *Ieyasu* gave it to the *Sanada daimyō* (1590), who were dispossessed in 1681, when the castle was abandoned. Rebuilt in 1703, it was until 1730 the residence of the *Honda daimyō*, then of the *Kuroda* (1730-1742), and finally of the *Toki* (1742-1868) (35,000 k.).

Numazu, 沼津. A town in *Suruga* (12,100 inh), with an ancient castle built by *Takeda Katsuyori* in 1579. The castle passed over to the *Nakamura* (1583) and to the *Okubo* (1600). That family having died out in 1613, the castle was demolished and was only rebuilt in 1777 by the *Mizuno* who resided there until the Restoration (50,000 k.).

Nureki-saki, 濡木崎. A cape on the E. coast of the island of *Sado*.

Nushiro, 淳代. To-day *Noshiro*, 能代, a town in *Ugo*, where *Abe no Hirafu* headed an expedition against the *Ebisu* and erected a fort with a garrison in 658 A.D. At the beginning of the 19th century, the *Tokugawa* placed a *bugyō* there to keep a lookout on the coast.

Nutari, 渟足. To-day *Nuttari* 沼垂, a town in *Echigo*, where in 648, a fortified "enceinte" was erected to keep off the *Ebisu* (*Nutari no ki*).

Nyaku-ōji, 若王子. A family descended from *Fujiwara Uona*, and hereditarily established at the head of the temple of *Nyakuō-ji*, near *Kyōto*. — To-day Baron.

Nyōgo, 女御. From the time of *Kwammu-tennō* (782-805), the title of the second wife of the Emperor. She was generally the daughter of a minister and came in rank immediately after the empress.

Nyo-in, 女院. The widowed mother of an Emperor, who shaved her head and took the title of *mon-in*. The mother of *Ichijō-tennō*, *Fujiwara Aki-ko*, was called *Higashi-Sanjō-in* (991). Later on, *Aki-ko*, widow of *Ichijō*, took the name of *Jōtō-mon-in* (1039), and from that time, the custom prevailed of adopting the title of *mon-in*. As to the name which preceded this title, it was taken first from the empress's place of retirement and afterwards, from the gates (*mon*) of the Imperial Palace. When the same name was held by two *nyo-in*, the prefixes *kō* (old), and *shin* (new) were used to distinguish them.

Nvokwan, 女官. Offices held formerly by the ladies of the Imperial Palace. The *Naishi-dokoro*, presided by the *Naishi no kami*, was the central office of this administration. The other officials were the *tenji*, *shōji*, *myōbu*, *nyo-kurōdo*, *tokusen*, *toji*, *uneme*, etc.

Nyo-ni no Miya, 女二宮. A title given to the second daughter of the Emperor. The terms, *Nyo-san no Miya* (3rd), *Nyo-shi no Miya* (4th), etc. were also used.

Nyo-ō, 女王. A title given to the female descendants of the emperors to the 4th generation, after which, they ceased to belong to the Imperial family.

Nyo-ō-roku, 女王禄. Formerly a pension granted to princesses (*nyo-ō*); the distribution was made in the Palace, on the 8th day of the first month.

Nyorai, 如來. A honorific title given to the Buddhas.

Nyotei, 女帝. Empresses that reigned and are numbered in the list of sovereigns with the title of *Tennō*. They were: *Suiko* (593-628), *Kōgyoku* (642-644), who reigned a second time by the name of *Saimei* (655-661), *Jitō* (687-695), *Gemmei* (708-714), *Genshō* (715-723); *Kōken* (749-758), who reascended the throne with the name *Shōtoku* (765-769). Then after a lapse of 9 centuries, *Myōshō* (1630-1645), and *Go-Sakura-machi* (1763-1770).

Nyūdō, 入道. Entering religion (Buddh.), becoming bonze or *ama*. —The person who did so.

Nyūdō-naishinnō, 入道内親王. A title given to Imperial princesses, that shaved their heads and entered a Buddhist monastery.

Nyūdō-shinnō, 入道親王. Title given to Imperial princes that became bonzes. When the title of prince was conferred upon them only after they had embraced the religious life, they were called *Hō-shinnō*.

Nyūgyū-in, 乳牛院. An office belonging to the *Kunai-shō* and placed under the authority of the *Ten-yaku-ryō* (Court physicians). It was intrusted with the supply of cow's milk for the Imperial table. The headman had the title of *Nyūgyū-in-bettō*; under him were the *nyūshi*, *azukari*, etc.

O

Ō-ama no Ōji, 大海人皇子. — See *Temmu-tennō*.

Ō-an, 應安. *Nengō* of the northern dynasty : 1368-1374.

Ōba, 大庭. A family of *samurai* from *Sagami*, descended from *Taira Takamochi*.

—— **Kageyoshi,** 景能 (+ 1210). Inherited the domain of *Ōba* (*Sagami*), and took its name. During the civil war of *Hōgen* (1156), he sided with *Minamoto Yoshitomo*, and besieged the palace of *Shirakawa*. When *Yoritomo* rose against the *Taira*, *Kageyoshi* joined his party, whilst his brother *Kagechika* fought on the opposite side. After the triumph of the *Minamoto*, he served the *Bakufu* of *Kamakura*.

—— **Kagechika,** 景親 (+ 1182). Brother of *Kageyoshi*, fought side by side with him in *Yoshitomo's* army during the *Hōgen* trouble (1156) ; he was condemned to death, but was spared through the intervention of the *Taira*, and from that time, he proved one of their most faithful partisans. It was he who defeated *Yoritomo* at *Ishibashi-yama* (1181) ; but the latter having received reinforcements from *Kai*, re-entered the field ; whereupon *Kagechika* finding resistance impossible, surrendered and was beheaded.

Ōba-gata, 大庭潟. A lake in *Kaga* (25 Km. in circ.). It is also called *Kahoku-gata*, *Yada-gata*.

Ōbaku-shū, 黄檗宗. A branch of the *Zen-shū* sect brought from China to Japan in 1655, by the bonze *Ingen*. In 1659, he obtained a piece of land at *Uji* (*Yamashiro*), on which he built a temple which he called *Mampuku-ji*, while the monastery bore the name of *Ōbaku-zan*, after the one in China of which *Ingen* had been superior. Protected by the emperors and the *Shōgun*, the *Ōbaku* sect which was an attempt to reform decaying Japanese-Buddhism, made rapid progress ; it possesses at present about 600 temples.

Obama, 小濱. A town in *Wakasa* province (8,800 inh.). It was successively the residence of the *Kinoshita daimyō* (1585-1600 inh), *Kyōgoku* (1600-1634) and *Sakai* (1634-1868) (103,500 k.). — It was formerly called *Kumo no hama*.

Ōban, 大番. In the *Tokugawa* days, the guard of the principal castles of the *Shōgun* : *Edo*, *Ōsaka*, *Fushimi*, *Kyōto* (*Nijō*), etc.

Ōban-bugyō, 椀飯奉行. Under the *Tokugawa Shōgun*, an official who regulated the ceremonies that were held on the 1st, 3rd, 7th, and 15th of the first month of the year, and on which the great families, *Hōjō*, *Chiba*, *Miura*, *Utsunomiya*, *Oyama*, etc., offered a banquet to the *Shōgun*.

Ōban-yaku, 大番役. Formerly *samurai* despatched from the provinces to guard the Imperial Palace. Their term of service was at first 3 years, but *Yoritomo* reduced it to 6 months.

Obata, 小幡. An ancient castle in *Kōzuke*, which, during the Middle Ages, belonged to a family of the same name, but afterwards passed to the *Odawara Hōjō*. Under the *Tokugawa*, it was occupied by the *daimyō Okudaira* (1590), *Mizuno* (1601), *Oda* (1615), *Okudaira* (1767-1868) (20,000 k.).

Obi, 飫肥. A castle in *Hyūga*, built towards 1475 by *Shimazu Tadakane*. It was captured in 1562, by *Itō Yoshisuke*, until then lord of *Tonokōri*; re-captured by *Shimazu Tadachika* the same year, it was taken again by *Itō* in 1568. It reverted to the *Shimazu* when the *Itō* emigrated to *Bungo* in 1577. Reinstalled in *Obi* by *Hideyoshi* (1587), the *Itō* remained there until the Restoration (50,000 k.)

Obito, 首. In olden times, a title (*kabane*) given to the heads of certain corporations: as, *Iwaibe no Obito*.

O Cha no Tsubone, 阿茶局 (+1637). Daughter of *Iida Kyūemon*, vassal of *Takeda Shingen*, she married *Kamio Magobei, samurai* of the *Imagawa*. When *Ieyasu* was sent as hostage to the *Imagawa*, *Kamio* and his wife treated him very kindly. *Magobei* having been killed with *Imagawa Yoshimoto* at *Okehazama* (1560), his wife returned to *Kai*. Later on, *Ieyasu* remembered the services she had rendered him, and called her to his castle of *Hamamatsu*, then to *Edo* and gave her the name of *O Cha no Tsubone*. Because of her superior intellect, she was often employed in delicate negotiations, which she conducted to the satisfaction of her protector. In 1614, she was sent to *Yodo-gimi* in *Ōsaka* and succeeded in bringing about a peace between the contesting parties. When the daughter of *Hidetada* married the emperor *Go-Mino-o*, (1624), *O Cha no Tsubone*, accompanied her to *Kyōto* and arranged all the details of the marriage ceremony. She was raised to the first rank (*ichi-i*) of the Court nobility, and died at a very advanced age.

Ochi, 越智. A town in *Yamato*. In the 14th century, it was the residence of a family of the same name, that fought for the southern dynasty.

Ochi, 越智. A family of *daimyō*, branch of the *Matsudaira* family. — See *Matsudaira* (*Ochi*).

Ochiai, 落合. A family of literati of the 19th century. The best known are: *Naoaki* (+ 1894), *Naozumi* (1840-1891), *Naofumi* (1861-1903).

Ōchō, 應長. *Nengō*: 1311.

Ōchō-jidai, 王朝時代. The period of Japanese history, in which the emperors governed in their own name, i.e. from the accession of *Jimmu-tennō* to the establishment of the *Kamakura* Shōgunate (660 B. C. — 1192 A. D.).

Oda, 小田. A castle in *Hitachi*, built towards the end of the 12th century by *Hatsuda Tomoie*. His descendants occupied it until 1574. At that time it was captured by *Ōta Sukemasa*, and abandoned at the time of the *Tokugawa*.

Oda, 織田. A family of *daimyō*, originating in *Owari*, and descended from *Taira Sukemori*, son of *Shigemori*.

—— **Chikazane, 親 實**. Son of *Sukemori*, established himself at *Oda* (*Echizen*) and took its name. His descendants, vassals of the *Shiba* family, followed the latter to *Owari*, and received the castle of *Inu-yama* in 1435.

```
Nobuhiro
                    Nobutada - Hidenobu
                              Hideo
                    Nobuo - -{Nobuyoshi -Nobumasa -Nobuhisa   (a)
                              Takanaga -Nagayori -Nobutake    (b)
                    Nobutaka
                    Hidekatsu
                    Katsunaga
          Nobunaga {Nobusada - Sadaoki - -Jisai
                    (6 other sons)
                    Daughter married to Gamō Ujisato
                         "          "   Tokugawa Nobuyasu
Nobuhide{                "          "   Maeda Toshinaga
                         "          "   Niwa Nagashige
                         "          "   Tsutsui Sadatsugu
                    (5 other daughters)
          Nobuyuki - Nobuzumi - Masakata
          Nobukane - Nobunori - Nobukatsu
          Nobuharu - Masatoshi
                    Yorinaga
          Nagamasu {Nagamasa - Nagasada - Nagaakira - Nagakiyo  (c)
                    Toshinaga - Nagashige- Hidekazu - Hidechika (d)
          Daughter married to {Daughter married to Hideyoshi (Yodo-gimi)
          Asai Nagamasa and   {     "          "    Kyōgoku Takatsugu
          to Shibata Katsuie  {     "          "    Tokugawa Hidetada
          Daughter married to Takeda Katsuyori
```

—— **Nobuhide, 信 秀** (+ 1549). Descendant of *Chikazane*, in the 17th generation, witnessed the ruin of his suzerains, the *Shiba* lords, and occupied half of *Owari* province. He fought against the *Saitō* and defeated *Imagawa Yoshimoto* in 1542, at *Azuki-zaka* (*Mikawa*).

—— **Nobuhiro, 信 廣** (+ 1574). Eldest son of *Nobuhide*, received the castle of *Anjō* (*Mikawa*), where he was besieged by *Imagawa Yoshi-moto* (1549), and was compelled to flee. He was killed at the battle of *Nagashima* (*Ise*).

—— **Nobunaga, 信 長** (1534-1582). 2nd son of *Nobuhide*, was 15 years old when his father died. Expert in all kinds of warlike exercises, he gave but little heed to the government of his domains. In vain, one of his best retainers, *Hirade Kiyohide*, endeavored to draw his attention to that point ; his remonstrances remained without effect. Thereupon the faithful servant committed his representations to writing, had them carried to his lord, and then put an end to his life. *Nobunaga* moved by such devotedness, changed his conduct for the better. In 1557, his younger brother, *Nobuyuki*, having treated with the *Hayashi*, who had invaded a part of *Owari*, *Nobunaga* sent against him *Ikeda Nobuteru*, who defeated him and put him to death. Three years afterwards, *Imagawa Yoshimoto*, daimyō of *Suruga* and of *Tōtōmi* entered *Owari* at the head of a numerous army. All the retainers of *Nobunaga* advised him to make overtures with the enemy rather than engage in an unequal contest ; but he rejected their timorous counsels, marched against his powerful adversary and defeated him completely at *Okehazama (Owari)* : *Yoshi-moto* fled, but he was pursued by *Hattori Koheida* and *Mōri Hidetaka* and put to death (1560). The provinces of *Suruga* and *Tōtōmi*, escheat-ed to *Nobunaga*, whose reputation began to spread far and wide. The emperor *Ōgimachi* sent *Tachiiri Munetsugu* secretly to him and com-missioned him to put an end to the troubles so long desolating the capital (1562). *Nobunaga* accepted the mission, and in 1564 he entered *Mino*, defeated *Saitō Tatsuoki* and established himself at *Gifu*. Before pene-trating into *Ōmi,,* he secured by family ties, the co-operation of *Asai Nagamasa, Takeda Shingen,* and *Tokugawa Ieyasu*. Another letter from the emperor urged him to hasten the pacification of the land ; shortly after, *Ashikaga Yoshiaki* asked his support to secure the suc-cession of his brother, the *Shōgun Yoshiteru*. *Nobunaga* set to work. He captured 18 castles in *Ōmi* and dispossessed the *daimyō Sasaki Yo-shikata ;* after this, he entered *Kyōto* with *Yoshiaki*, who received the title of *Shōgun*, (1568) ; again, breaking down the *Miyoshi*, he pacified *Settsu* and *Kawachi*. Whereupon, *Yoshiaki* wished to confer the title of *Kwanryō* on him, but *Nobunaga* refused. The next year, the *Miyoshi* and their vassal, *Matsunaga Hisahide*, re-entered *Kyōto* and besieged the *Shōgun* in the *Honkoku-ji :* *Nobunaga* returned in haste to the capital and defeated the assailants. Then he built the *Nijō* palace for *Yoshiaki*, repaired the Imperial Palace, determined the revenues of the Court, etc. After that, he went to *Ise* to fight against *Kitabatake Tomo-nori*, defeated him and gave him as son-in-law and heir his 2nd son *No-buo* (1569). The next year, he vanquished successively the *Asakura (Echizen)*, the *Asai (Ōmi)*, and the *Miyoshi (Settsu)*. The bonzes of *Hiei-zan* having sided against him, he led an army against them, seized their domains, set fire to their temples, and put them all to the sword. (1571) Mean-while, *Yoshiaki* plotted with *Takeda Shingen* to get rid of his formidable protector. But *Nobunaga* returned to *Kyōto*, deposed the *Shō-gun* and sent him as prisoner to the castle of *Wakae (Kawachi)* (1573) ; and thus after two centuries and a half, ended, the *Ashi-kaga* Shōgunate. After this, *Nobunaga* com-

ODA NOBUNAGA.

pleted the ruin of the *Asakura*, the *Asai*, the *Miyoshi*, and the *Sasaki*, and from this time forward, these 4 families disappear from history. In the following year, *Nobunaga* was received in the *Seiryōden* by the emperor, who offered him a cup and conferred on him the title of *Gon-Dainagon*. Thereupon, he built a superb castle for himself on the shores of lake *Biwa*, at *Azuchi (Ōmi)*, quelled the turbulent bonzes of *Ikkō-shū* (1576), besieged and defeated *Araki Murashige* in his castle of *Itami (Settsu)* (1579), and with the help of *Ieyasu*, crushed the *Takeda* at *Temmoku-zan (Kai)* (1582). Meanwhile *Hashiba Hideyoshi* was fighting with the *Mōri ;* he laid siege to the castle of *Takamatsu (Bitchū)* and asked for aid. *Nobunaga* commissioned *Akechi Mitsuhide* to bring him reinforcements, whilst he himself made preparations to direct the campaign in person. *Mitsuhide* mustered 30,000 men; but instead of leading them west, he entered *Kyōto* and suddenly invested the *Honnō-ji*, where *Nobunaga* had set up his residence. The latter hearing a tumult, went out to see what was happening but in a few moments, he fell mortally wounded. It was the 22th of June 1582. *Nobunaga* was only 48 years old; he left 12 sons and 11 daughters. The emperor conferred on him the posthumous name of *Sōgen-in*, the title of *Dajō-daijin* and the 2nd degree of the first rank (*jū-ichi-i*). — *Nobunaga* is one of the greatest figures in Japanese history. Bold and persevering, he rose from the rank of a petty *daimyō*, to the highest honors of the Empire. He put an end to the civil wars that had been ruining the country for upwards of a century, and resolutely began the work of re-organization, which the *Tokugawa* were to complete. He showed himself favorable to the Europeans, and in the interest of his country, encouraged foreign trade. From policy, if not from conviction, he supported the Catholic missionaries, who owed much of their astonishing success to his protection. His aim was to break down the barrier between Japan and other nations. His plan was delayed for 3 centuries owing to the distrustful policy of the *Tokugawa*.

ATTACK ON THE HONNŌ-JI TEMPLE BY AKECHI MITSUHIDE.

—— **Nobuyuki,** 信行 (+ 1557). Brother of *Nobunaga*. He received on the death of his father (1549), the castle of *Suemori* (*Owari*). In 1557, the *Hayashi*, *Oda's* retainers, attempted to make themselves independent, and to secure a part of *Owari*. *Nobuyuki* instead of crushing them, began to "parley" with them. *Nobunaga* incensed at this, sent *Ikeda Nobuteru* against him. He besieged him in *Suemori* and put him to death.

—— **Nobukane, 信包** (1548-1614). Brother of *Nobunaga*, was adopted by the *Nagao* family (1568), and received the title of *Kōzuke no suke*. He lived in *Kyōto*, and in 1594 shaved his head and took the name of *Rōtaisai*, yielding to his son the estates of *Kayano* (*Tamba* — 80,000 k.). He was a painter and a man of letters.

—— **Nobuharu, 信治** (1549-1570). Brother of *Nobunaga*, received the castle of *Usayama* (*Ōmi*) and was killed at *Sakamoto*, while fighting against *Asakura Kageharu*.

—— **Nagamasu, 長益** (1548-1622). Brother of *Nobunaga*, served *Hideyoshi* after the death of his brother. In 1586 he shaved his head and took the name of *Yūrakusai-Joan*. He had a revenue of 30,000 k. in *Yamato*. In 1615, he gave 10,000 k. to each of his two sons *Nagamasa* and *Toshinaga*, and keeping the rest for himself, retired to *Kyōto*, where he devoted his time to the study of the tea-ceremony. He had practised the art under the famous *Sen Rikyū*; he founded a school which his son *Yorinaga* continued. *Nagamasu* had been baptized in 1588.

—— **Nobutada, 信忠** (1557-1582). The eldest son of *Nobunaga*, served his first campaign at the age of 15 and accompanied his father in his expéditions. When *Nobunaga* fixed his residence at *Azuchi* (1576), *Nobutada* established himself at *Gifu*. The following year, he headed an expedition successfully into *Yamato* against *Matsunaga Hisahide*. He served in the campaign against *Takeda Katsuyori*, after which, intending to follow his father westward and subdue the *Mōri*, he entered *Kyōto* with him, and lodged in the *Myōdō-ji* temple. There he received intelligence of *Akechi Mitsuhide's* treachery. He hastened to his father's rescue, but arrived too late. Thereupon, he retired to the *Nijō* castle, made prince *Masahito-shinnō* leave the place for safety sake, ordered *Maeda Gen-i* to lead his son *Sambōshi* to *Kiyosu*, and defended himself valiantly against *Mitsuhide*, but soon yielding to overwhelming odds, he killed himself with 90 of his retainers.

—— **Nobuo, 信雄** (1558-1630). 2nd son of *Nobunaga*, was chosen to be the son-in-law of *Kitabatake Tomonori* after the latter's defeat (1569). *Kitabatake* ceded his domains and his title of *Ise-kokushu* in 1575. After the death of *Nobunaga*, all his grand vassals, assembled at *Kiyosu*, elected *Sambōshi*, son of *Nobutada*, as his heir and appointed as guardians his two uncles, *Nobuo* and *Nobutaka*. *Nobuo* was intrusted with the administration of the provinces of *Owari*, *Ise* and *Iga*, with a revenue of 1,000,000 k. ; he settled in *Kiyosu* and *Nobutada* in *Gifu*. Contentions arose between the guardians who appealed to the *daimyō* to defend their cause. *Shibata Katsuie, Takigawa Kazumasu, Sasa Narimasa, Maeda Toshiie*, etc. sided with *Nobutaka*; *Nobuo* was supported by *Hideyoshi, Niwa Nagahide, Ikeda Nobuteru*, etc. *Hideyoshi* then commissioned *Nobuo* to besiege his brother in the castle of *Gifu*, whilst he would fight against *Katsuie*. After resisting for a while, *Nobutaka* escaped from *Gifu*, but was slain in his flight (1583) ; *Katsuie*, defeated at *Shizu-ga-take*, took his own life in his castle of *Kita no shō* (*Echizen*). The following year, all the vassals repaired to *Azuchi* to offer their young suzerain *Sambōshi* and his guardian their New Year's wishes. *Hideyoshi* alone failed to appear, which greatly incensed *Nobuo.* He appealed to *Tokugawa Ieyasu*, and both mustered troops. *Hideyoshi* did the same, but in the very first engagement at *Nagakute (Owari)*, his van-guard was completely crushed. Meanwhile the bonzes of the *Negoro* temple (*Kii*), caused troubles in the provinces. *Hideyoshi* perceiving himself in a critical position, had recourse to diplomacy; he treated successively with his two adversaries and made them fair promises; he thus avoided certain disaster (1584). During the campaign against the *Hōjō* of *Odawara*, (1590) *Nobuo* came at the head of 15,000 men from the provinces of *Ise* and *Owari*. But again quarelling with *Hideyoshi*, he was consigned to a small fief of 20,000 k. in *Dewa*, after which, he shaved his head and took the name of *Jōshin*. Pardoned the following year, he returned to *Ise*, and on the death of *Hideyoshi* (1598), settled in *Fushimi*. Having sided against *Ieyasu* in 1600, he was dispossessed and retired to *Ōsaka*. When *Yodo-gimi* attempted to enlist him in her projects against *Ieyasu*, *Nobuo* always weak, declined and returned to *Kyōto*. After *Hideyori's* downfall (1615), he received from *Ieyasu* a revenue of 50,000 k. in *Yamato*, and died at the age of 73.— *Nobuo* had been baptized in 1588, but it is hard to say whether he persevered to the end in the practice of his religion.

—— **Nobutaka,** 信孝 (1558-1583). Third son of *Nobunaga* was chosen to be heir of the *Kambe* family (*Ise*). He established himself in the castle of the same name (1569). In 1582, he received in fief the 4 provinces of *Shikoku*, and headed an expedition to *Kii* against the chief of the *Hongwan-ji*, *Kōsa*, who was defeated and slain. On his father's death, hearing that his cousin *Nobuzumi* had been in league with *Akechi Mitsuhide*, he attacked him in *Ōsaka* and put him to death. Shortly after, he was appointed with his brother *Nobuo*, guardian of young *Sambōshi*. He resided at *Gifu*, and governed *Mino* province. His contentions with *Nobuo* led to war. *Nobutaka* was besieged in *Gifu* and took to flight, but being pursued by *Nakagawa Sadanari* and seeing himself on the point of being made prisoner he sought shelter in the *Shōhō-ji* temple at *Noma (Owari)* and killed himself.

—— **Hidekatsu,** 秀勝 (1567-1593). 4th son of. *Nobunaga*, was adopted by *Hideyoshi*. — See *Hashiba Hidekatsu.*

—— **Katsunaga,** 勝長 (1568-1582). 5th son of *Nobunaga*, received the castle of *Inuyama (Owari)* in 1581, and was killed with his father in the temple of *Honnō-ji.*

—— **Nobuzumi,** 信澄 (1555-1583). Son of *Nobuyuki*, married a daughter of *Akechi Mitsuhide*. In 1582, he served with his cousin *Nobutaka* in the campaign against the *Ikkō-shū* bonzes. On hearing of *Nobunaga's* assassination, he answered his father-in-law's appeal, joined his party and took up his position at *Ōsaka ;* but *Nobutaka* marched against him, defeated him and put him to death.

—— **Hidenobu,** 秀信 (1581-1602). Grandson of *Nobunaga*, and eldest son of *Nobutaka*, was only 1 year old when he lost his father and grandfather. He then bore the surname of *Sambōshi*. Recognized as heir of the family, he was transferred, by the care of *Maeda Gen-i*, from *Gifu* to *Kiyosu* and after the fall of *Mitsuhide*, to *Azuchi*. In 1585, *Hideyoshi* had him brought back to *Gifu*, and giving him an ideograph of his own name, called him *Hidenobu*. On the rupture between *Ieyasu* and *Ishida Kazushige*, the latter invited *Hidenobu* to join him. The *Gifu samurai* vainly endeavored to deter their young master from this alliance. He declared war against *Ieyasu*. Besieged in *Gifu* by *Fukushima Masanori* and *Kuroda Nagamasa*, he attempted to make a sally, but was repulsed. He surrendered to *Masanori*, who had him brought to *Imo-arai* (*Yamashiro*), there to await the decision of *Ieyasu*; the latter obliged him to shave his head and to repair to *Kōya-san*, where he died after two years, at the early age of 21. — *Hidenobu* was a Christian; he had been baptized at *Gifu* and received the name of *Paul*, with his younger brother *Hidenori*, who was called *Vincent*. History furnishes no information about the latter.

—— **Hideo** or **Hidekatsu**, 秀雄 (1573-1610). Eldest son of *Nobuo*, received in 1592, the castle of *Ōno* (*Echizen* — 50,000 k.). Dispossessed after *Sekigahara*, he repaired to *Asakusa* (*Edo*), where he lived in retirement. — At the time of the Restoration, there existed 4 *daimyō* families of the name of *Oda*.

(*a*) — The branch of *Nobuyoshi*, 信良 (+1626), 3rd son of *Nobuo*; they fixed their residence successively at *Obata* (*Kōzuke*) in 1615, at *Takabatake* (*Dewa*) in 1767; and at *Tendō* (*Dewa* — 20,000 k.). from 1828 to 1868. — To-day Viscount.

(*b*) — The branch of *Takanaga*, 高長 (+1659), 4th son of *Nobuo*; they settled at *Uda* (*Yamato*) (1615), and at *Kashiwabara* (*Tamba* — 20,000 k.). — To-day Viscount.

(*c*) — The branch of *Nagamasa*, 長政 4th son of *Nagamasu*; they resided at *Shibamura* (*Yamato* — 10,000 k.). — To-day Viscount.

(*d*) — The branch of *Hisanaga*, 尚長 5th son of *Nagamasu*; they resided from 1675 to 1868 at *Yanagimoto* (*Yamato* — 10,000 k.). — To-day Viscount.

Oda, 小田. An ancient family of *daimyō*, descended from *Hatsuda Tomoie*, son of *Minamoto Yoshitomo* (*Seiwa-Genji*).

—— **Tomoshige**, 知重. Son of *Tomoie*, fixed his residence, towards the end of the 12th century, at *Oda* (*Hitachi*) and took its name.

—— **Haruhisa**, 治久 (+1352). At first a vassal of the *Hōjō*, he rallied to the imperial cause after the fall of *Kamakura* (1333). He fought against *Takauji* and afforded shelter to *Kitabatake Chikafusa*; later on, he passed over to the *Ashikaga* party and in 1352 defeated *Nitta Yoshimune*. The family was dispossessed in 1573 by *Ōta Sukemasa*.

Odani, 小谷. An ancient castle in *Ōmi*, built in 1516 by *Asai Sukemasa*, who was besieged there the very same year, by *Kyōgoku Takamine*. *Nobunaga* captured it in 1573 and all the *Asai* perished in it.

Oda shi-ten, 織田四天. The 4 principal vassals of *Oda Nobunaga; Shibata Katsuie, Takigawa Kazumasa, Niwa Nagahide* and *Akechi Mitsuhide.*

Odawara, 小田原. A town of *Sagami* province and of *Kanagawa-ken* (16,700 inh). — An ancient castle which belonged to the *Doi daimyō* and passed in 1416 to *Ōmori Yoriaki. Hōjō Sōun* captured it in 1494 and fixed his residence there. *Uesugi Kenshin* besieged it in vain (1561) ; as did also *Takeda Shingen* (1573) ; but *Hideyoshi* attacked it with a powerful army in 1590 and captured it. This was the end of the *Hōjō.* Under the *Tokugawa*, it became the residence of the respective *daimyō, Ōkubo* (1590), *Abe* (1620), *Inaba* (1632) and *Ōkubo* (1686-1868) (116,000 k).

Ōe, 大江. An ancient family of scholars, literati and statesmen.

—— **Otondo,** 音人 (811-877). Was a disciple of *Sugawara Koreyoshi.* He rose to the post of *Kebiishi-bettō.* He is often called *Kōsō-kō* ; he contributed to the *Jōgwan-kyakushiki* (871), and has left several works.

—— **Chisato,** 千里. Son of *Otondo*, was a renowned poet.

—— **Asatsuna,** 朝綱 (886-957). Grandson of *Otondo*, distinguished himself as a man of letters and published a history of Japan (*Shinkokushi*). He is called *Nochi no Kōsō-kō.*

Otondo			
Kimiyoshi - Kiyotada		Yoshiteru- Tadayoshi-Morosue -Kiyoyoshi-Michikiyo	
		Narimichi	
Tamabuchi - Asatsuna			
Chisato			
Munebuchi		Kiyotoki	
Chiaki	Koreaki - Nakayoshi-	Masatoki	
		Koretoki	
		Yoshitoki	
Chifuru -	Koreshige		
	Koretoki	Shigemitsu- Tadahira -Takachika-Narihira -Tadafusa	
		Narimitsu - Tamemoto	

—— **Koretoki,** 維時 (888-963). Grandson of *Otondo*, filled important functions in the reigns of *Shujaku* and *Murakami.* He is also called *Kōsō-kō.*

—— **Tadahira,** 匡衡 (952-1012). A poet of renown and grandson of the above.

—— **Koretoki,** 以言 (955-1010). A relative of the above. Distinguished himself in literature.

—— **Tadafusa,** 匡房 (1041-1111). A descendant of *Tadahira*, was equally remarkable in prose and poetry. He became *Ōkura-kyō* and governor of *Dazaifu* (1098-1102). *Tadafusa, Fujiwara Nagafusa* and *Fujiwara Korefusa*, who all flourished at the same time, are styled the *Sam-bō* (3 *Bō* : *bō*) is the Chinese reading of the character "*fusa*").

ŌE TADAFUSA.

—— **Hiromoto,** 廣元 (1148-1225). Descendant of *Tadafusa*, served *Yoritomo* as soon as the latter rose against the *Taira* (1180). He was appointed *Bettō* of the *Kumonjo* (1183) and had a considerable share in the organization of the *Kamakura* Shōgunate. In return for his services, he received the domain of *Yamamoto* (*Higo*). He was afterwards *Bettō* of the *Mandokoro*. Councillor of the *Shōgun Yoriie* and *Sanetomo*, he proved a most able administrator. — From him the *Mōri*, *daimyō* of *Chōshū*, are descended.

Ō-ei, 應永. *Nengō* : 1394-1427 ; it is the longest Japanese era (34 years) after that of the *Meiji*.

Ōgaki, 大垣. A town in *Mino* (19,000 inh.), with an ancient castle built in 1535 by *Miyagawa Yasusada* by the orders of the *Shōgun Yoshiharu*. *Oda Nobuhide* captured it in 1546. After *Nobutaka's* defeat (1583), *Hideyoshi* gave it to *Ikeda Nobuteru*. It afterwards became the residence of the *daimyō Itō* (1590) *Ishikawa* (1600), *Hisamatsu* (1616), *Okabe* (1624), *Hisamatsu* (1633) and *Toda* (1634-1868) (100,000 k.).

Ogasawara, 小笠原. A family of *daimyō*, originating in *Shinano*, and descended from *Takeda Yoshikiyo* (*Seiwa-Genji*).

—— **Nagakiyo, 長清.** Great-grandson of *Yoshikiyo*. He was the first to take the name of *Ogasawara*. His descendants became by degrees masters of the whole province of *Shinano*.

—— **Sadamune, 貞宗** (1294-1350). Was governor of *Shinano* and at the same time had the administration of the provinces of *Hida* and *Tōtōmi*. At first he fought for *Hōjō Takatoki*, then, after the fall of *Kamakura*, joined the Imperial party. He levied troops in *Shinano* and *Hida*, and supported *Nitta Yoshisada*, but afterwards sided with the *Ashikaga*. He was sent by *Takauji* to besiege the castle of *Kanagasaki* (*Echizen*), where *Yoshisada* had intrenched himself but he was unable to take it (1336) ; thereupon, he attempted to check *Kitabatake Akiie* in his march to *Kyōto*, but was again defeated in *Mino*.

—— **Nagahide, 長秀.** Grandson of *Sadamune* and son of *Nagamoto*, was a famous master in the art of bow-shooting, horse-riding, etc. While a professor of the *Shōgun Yoshimitsu*, he was asked to compose with *Ise Mitsutada* and *Imagawa Ujiyori* a code of ceremonial for the *samurai*. These rules of etiquette were called *Ogasawara-ryū*.

—— **Nagatoki, 長時** (1519-1583). Descendant of *Sadamune*, was lord of *Fukashi* (later on, *Matsumoto*) and incessantly at war with the *Takeda* of *Kai*. When *Shingen* succeeded his father, *Nagatoki* formed a league against him with *Suwa Yorishige* ; but the latter let himself be duped by his powerful adversary and lost both his life and his domains (1553) ; *Nagatoki* too was soon defeated and compelled to seek refuge near *Murakami Yoshikiyo* in *Echigo*. The latter furnished him with an army. He then attempted to recover his castle of *Fukashi*, but being beaten, he sought shelter with *Uesugi Kenshin*. Thence he repaired to *Kyōto*, where he taught the *Shōgun Yoshiteru* the rules of archery and horsemanship, in which accomplishments his ancestors had excelled for centuries. He returned to *Shinano* after the death of *Yoshiteru*, but was assassinated by his servants.

—— **Hidemasa, 秀政** (1569-1615). Grandson of *Nagatoki*, served *Ieyasu* and received from him in 1590 the fief of *Koga* (*Shimōsa* — 20,000 k.). In 1601 he was transferred to *Iida* (*Shinano* — 50,000 k.), and in 1613, he recovered the castle of his ancestors at *Fukashi* (80,000 k.).

		Tadao - -Tadamoto -Tadafusa	(a)
	Tadazane	Naokata -Naomichi -Sadaakira	(b)
Hidemasa	Tadanaga - Nagatsugu-Nagakatsu-Nagatane		(c)
	Tadatomo - Nagayori -Nagasuke -Nagashige		(d)
Nobumine-	Nobuyuki - Masanobu -Sadanobu -Nobutoki		(e)

(*a*) — Branch which resided first at *Fukashi*, then at *Akashi* (*Harima* — 120,000 k.) (1617), and lastly from 1632 to 1868 at *Kokura* (*Buzen* — 150,000 k.). — Now Count.

(*b*) — Branch which resided until the Restoration at *Chizuka* (*Buzen* — 10,000 k.). — To-day Viscount.

(*c*) — Branch which fixed its residence in 1617 at *Tatsuno* (*Harima*) ; in 1632, at *Nakatsu* (*Buzen*) ; finally at *Ashi* (*Harima* — 10,000 k.) (1716-1868). — Now Viscount.

(*d*) — Branch which settled in 1632 at *Kizuki* (*Bungo*) ; in 1645, at *Yoshida* (*Mikawa*) ; in 1697, at *Iwatsuki* (*Musashi*) ; in 1711, at *Kakegawa* (*Tōtōmi*) ; in 1747, at *Tanakura* (*Mutsu*) ; and lastly from 1817 to 1868 at *Karatsu* (*Hizen* — 60,000 k.). — Now Viscount.

(*e*) — Family allied to the above and also descended from *Sadamune*. Established in 1590 at *Honjō* (*Musashi*), they moved in 1608 to *Koga* (*Shimōsa*) ; in 1619 to *Sekiyado* (*Shimōsa*) ; in 1637, to *Takasu* (*Mino*) ; and in 1691 to *Katsuyama* (*Echizen* — 22,000 k.). — To-day Viscount.

Ogasawara-jima, 小笠原島. A group of islands in the Pacific Ocean, more than 800 Km. south of *Tōkyō*. Discovered in 1593 by *Ogasawara Sadayori*, grandson of *Nagatoki* (See *Nagatoki*), they were given his name. The group contains 20 islands, the principal of which, starting from the N. are : *Muko-jima, Nakōdo-jima, Yome-jima, Ototo-jima, Ani-jima, Chichi-jima, Haha-jima, Ane-jima, Mei-jima, Imōto-jima*, etc. The population numbers about 2500 souls. Administratively, they belong to the *Tōkyō-fu*. They were formerly called *Munin-tō* (uninhabited islands). In European maps, they are named *Bonin* islands.

Ogasawara-ryū, 小笠原流. — See *Ogasawara Nagahide*.

Ogata, 尾形. A family of artists of the 17th and the 18th centuries.

—— **Kōrin, 光琳** (1661-1716). Born at *Kyōto*, he went to *Edo* and followed the lessons of *Kanō Tsunenobu ;* afterwards he studied the old masters of the *Tosa* school. He combined the teachings of both in his decorative painting so that both schools claim him ; but Japanese authorities generally, place him among the *Tosa* artists. He himself, founded the "*Kōrin-ha.*" This school was the first to use gold and silver dust in painting. *Sakai Hōitsu* (1761-1828), is the most famous artist of the *Kōrin* school.

—— **Kenzan,** 乾山 (1663-1743). Brother of *Kōrin*, excelled in painting, poetry and the ceramic arts.

Ogawa, 小川. A family of *daimyō*, who, at the end of the 16th century, occupied the castle of *Imabaru* (*Iyo* —— 70,000 k.). They were dispossessed by *Ieyasu* in 1600.

Ogawa, 小川. A family of *samurai* from the *Kokura* clan (*Buzen*) ennobled in 1895. —— To-day Baron.

Ogi, 小城. A town in *Hizen*, was from 1614 to 1868, the residence of a branch of the *Nabeshima* family (73,000 k.).

Ōgi-ga-yatsu, 扇谷. A place in *Sagami*, near *Kamakura*, where *Uesugi Sadamasa* fixed his residence. This name was given to his descendants.

Ōgigayatsu, 扇谷. A branch of the *Uesugi* family, established at *Ōgi-ga-yatsu* (*Sagami*), towards the middle of the 15th century. —— (See *Uesugi*.)

Ōgimachi, 正親町. A family of *kuge*, descended from *Fujiwara* (*Sanjō*) *Sanefusa* (1146-1224). —— To-day Count.

Ōgimachi-tennō, 正親町天皇 106th Emperor of Japan. (1558-1586). *Katahito*, son of *Go-Nara-tennō*, succeeded his father at the age of 41. Owing to lack of money, it was only 3 years later that the coronation ceremony could be performed with the help of *Mōri Motonari* who defrayed the expenses thereof. In 1562, *Ōgimachi* despatched *Tachiiri Munetsugu* to *Nobunaga*, inviting him to pacify the land disturbed for many years by civil wars. His reign witnessed the famous struggles between *Takeda Shingen* and *Uesugi Kenshin*, the end of the *Ashikaga* Shogunate, the rise and death of *Nobunaga*, the short dictatorship of *Akechi Mitsuhide* and the rise of *Hideyoshi*. *Ōgimachi* abdicated at the age of 70, in favor of his grandson *Go-Yōzei* and died 7 years later.

ŌGIMACHI-TENNŌ.

Ogino, 荻野. A dwelling in *Sagami*, was in the Middle Ages, the residence of a family of the same name, whose last scion, *Sueshige*, was killed in the battle of *Ishibashi-yama* (1181), where he fought against *Yoritomo*. After that, *Ogino* became the property of the *Engaku-ji* temple (*Kamakura*). Under the *Tokugawa*, it belonged to the *Ōkubo* family, a branch of which (13,000 k.) resided there from 1718 to 1868. —— It was then called *Ogino-yamanaka*.

Ogiu Sorai, 荻生徂徠 (1666-1728). A celebrated Confucian scholar of *Edo*, who founded a school where he taught the ancient Chinese philosophers. His disciple *Dazai Shuntai* continued his teachings. *Sorai* has left a great number of books. He is also called *Butsu Sorai*.

Ogiwara Shigehide, 荻原重秀 (1658-1713). Minister of finance (*Kanjō-bugyō*) of the *Bafuku*. It was he that advised the *Shōgun*

Tsunayoshi, to lower the value of the money then current in order to supply the deficiency of the Treasury (1695). The new coin was called *Genroku-kin* from the era during which it was struck. Until then, the *samurai* had received a pension in kind ; he substituted territorial possessions. The petty officials suffered greatly from this change, and bitter opposition broke out against *Shigehide*. Even *Arai Hakuseki* demanded his dismissal. He was discharged in 1712 and died the following year.

Oguma, 小熊 . In *Mino*, where *Minamoto Yukiie* was defeated by the *Taira* (1181).

Ogura, 小倉 . A family of *kuge* descended from *Fujiwara* (*Saionji*) *Saneo*. (1217-1273). — To-day Viscount.

Ogura-dono, 小倉殿. A dwelling erected in the village of *Saga*, near *Kyōto*, where the emperor *Go-Kameyama* lived for 30 years (1392-1424) after having yielded his rights to *Go-Komatsu* of the northern dynasty.

Ogura-ike, 小倉池 . A small lake in *Yamashiro*, with an outlet into the *Yodo-gawa ;* it is also called *Ō-ike* (circ. : 18 Km).

Ogura no Ōji, 小倉皇子 . Son of the emperor *Go-Kameyama*. When the latter abdicated in favor of *Go-Komatsu* (1392), who represented the northern dynasty, it was agreed that henceforward the emperors should be taken alternately from the two branches of the Imperial family. *Go-Komatsu* abdicated in 1412 in favor of his son *Shōkō*. On the latter's death (1428), prince *Ogura* claimed the right of succession, but the *Shōgun Yoshinori* proclaimed a descendant of *Sukō*, *Go-Hanazono*, of the northern dynasty the lawful emperor *Ogura* appealed to *Kitabatake Mitsumasa*, governor of *Ise*, who fought for his cause, but was defeated by *Hatakeyama Mochikuni* (1429). The prince had to return to *Ogura* and shave his head in the temple of *Manju-ji*. In 1440, a fresh attempt to rouse the *Kikuchi* of *Kyūshū* in his favor was quelled by the *Shōgun*.

Ogura-shinnō, 小倉親王 . — See *Kane-akira-shinnō*.

Ogura-yama, 小倉山 . A hill near the village of *Saga* (*Yamashiro*) where prince *Kane-akira-shinnō* had his estates. He was for this reason also called *Ogura-shinnō*. There too *Fujiwara Sadaie* compiled the *Hyaku-nin-isshū*.

Oguri Hangwan, 小票判官 (1398-1464), or as he is truly called *Sukeshige*, was the son of *Mitsushige*, lord of *Oguri* (*Hitachi*), who had been dispossessed by *Ashikaga Mochiuji*. *Oguri Hangwan* was the hero of many extraordinary adventures. One day (1426), some thieves had resolved to intoxicate him with *sake*, and murder him during the the night; but *Teruta-hime* revealed the plot which she had discovered and he jumped on a wild horse and fled to *Fujisawa* (*Sagami*). Another time, his enemies poisoned his bath and so he contracted leprosy ; thereupon *Teruta-hime* transported him in a little carriage, which she drove herself from *Kamakura* to the hot springs of *Yu no mine*, and a week sufficed to restore his health and strength. Later on, he became a bonze in the temple of *Sōkoku-ji* (*Kyōto*) and took the name of *Sōtan*. He studied painting under *Shūbun* and became one of the greatest artists of his time.

Ogurusu, 小栗栖. A town in *Yamashiro*, near the village of *Daigo*. *Akechi Mitsuhide* while attempting to reach his castle of *Sakamoto* (1582) after his defeat at *Yamazaki*, was assassinated here by the peasants.

Ōgyu, 大給. A family of *daimyō* — See *Matsudaira* (*Ōgyū*).

Ōhara, 大原. A family of *kuge*, descended from *Minamoto Masanobu* (920-973) (*Uda-Genji*). — To-day Count.

Ō-harai, 大祓. Formerly a solemn ceremony of purification (*Shintō*), which took place on the first day of the 6th and the 12th months.

Ōhashi Junzō, 大橋順藏 (1816-1862). A *samurai* of the *Utsunomiya* clan (*Shimotsuke*), renowned for his knowledge of Chinese literature. A staunch adversary of the opening of the country to foreigners, he opposed with all his might, the policy of the *Tairō Ii Naosuke*. Accused of complicity in an attempt to assassinate *Andō Nobumasa*, he was put to the torture and died shortly afterwards

O-heya-shū, 御部屋衆. — See *Muromachi-banshū*.

Ōhiko no mikoto, 大彦命. Son of the emperor *Kōgen*, was appointed *Shōgun* of the *Hokurokudō*, where he quelled a revolt of the *Ebisu* (88 B. C.). He defeated and killed *Take-haniyasu-hiko*, who had revolted against the emperor *Sujin* (81 B. C.)

Ohō, 應保. *Nengō :* 1161-1162.

Oide-bugyō, 御出奉行. Under the *Kamakura Shōgun*, an official commissioned to settle all the details of the *Shōgun's* journeys : escort, relays, etc. In 1263, the *Shōgun Munetaka*, repairing to *Kyōto*, appointed the *Gosho-bugyō Nikaidō Yukikata* to that charge and thenceforward it became customary to assign that title to the *Gosho-bugyō*. — This office continued under the *Ashikaga Shōgun*.

O-ie-ryū, 御家流. A way of writing the Chinese characters, taught by prince *Seiren-in no Miya* or *Son-en-Hōshinnō* (1298-1356), son of the emperor *Fushimi*. This school of calligraphy was also called *Son-en-ryū*.

Ōi-gawa, 大堰川. One of the names of the river *Katsura-gawa* (which see), also called *Hōzu-gawa*.

Ōi-gawa, 大井川. A river which takes its rise in the *Shirane-zan* (*Kai*) and is there called *Tashiro-gawa ;* it forms the limits between *Suruga* and *Tōtōmi*, flows by *Kanaya* and empties itself into the gulf of *Suruga* (180 Km.)

Oi-matsurigoto no tsukasa, 太政官. An ancient name of *Dajōkwan*.

Oimi, 生實. A town in *Shimōsa*, was from 1615 to 1868 the residence of the *Morikawa daimyō* (10,000 k.).

Oimi, 生實. An ancient family of *daimyō* in *Shimōsa*, destroyed in the 16th century by the *Hōjō* of *Odawara*.

Ōimikado, 大炊御門 A family of *kuge* descended from *Fujiwara Morozane* (1042-1101). — Now Marquis.

Ōi-mōchi-gimi, 大前君. (Corrupt form of *Ō-mae-tsukimi*). An ancient name given to the *Sadaijin* and *Udaijin*.

Ōi-mono-mōsu tsukasa, 大納言. An ancient name of the *Dainagon*.

O-inori-bugyō, 御祈奉行. Under the *Kamakura Shōgun*, an official chosen among the *Hyōjōshū* or the *Hikitsukeshū* and commissioned to ask prayers of the bonzes and *kannushi* in times of drought, epidemic and other calamities.

Oi no saka, 老坂. Formerly called *Ōe-yama*. A mountain on the boundaries of *Yamashiro* and *Tamba*, often mentioned in history and poetry. It was crossed by a road, guarded by a barrier (*Ōe no seki*). It was by this road that, in 1582, *Akechi Mitsuhide* went from *Kameyama* (*Tamba*) to *Kyōto* to attack *Nobunaga*.

Ōi-ryō, 大炊寮. Formerly an office of the *Kunai-shō*, intrusted with the reception and the distribution of the taxes in kind, sent in from the provinces. Thus the millet was handed over to the *Moitori-zukasa*, the peas to the *Daizen-shiki*, etc. It was ruled by one *Kami*, 1 *Suke*, 2 *Jō*, 2 *Sakwan*, etc.

Oishi Matora, 大石眞虎 (1792-1833). A celebrated painter of *Nagoya* (*Owari*).

Oishi Yoshio, 大石良雄 (1659-1703). Chief of the 47 *rōnin* of *Akō* (*Harima*). He was a *samurai* of *Asano Naganori*, when he received intelligence at *Akō* of his master's dispute with *Kira Yoshinaka*, of his death and the confiscation of his domains (1701). Thereupon he repaired to *Kyōto* and prepared a secret revenge. The son of *Yoshinaka*, adopted by *Uesugi Tsunakatsu* and raised to the rank of *daimyō* of *Yonezawa* (*Dewa*), began to suspect *Yoshio* and sent men to watch him : but they only saw in him a man addicted to drink and given up to pleasure without any apparent design in view.

OISHI YOSHIO.

Nearly two years had thus gone by, when one day, as *Yoshinaka* was banqueting, his house was suddenly surrounded by 47 *samurai* who broke into the festive hall ; their chief *Yoshio* cut off *Yoshinaka's* head, which was then placed on *Asano's* tomb. After which, they all surrendered to the officers of justice. *Yoshio* and 16 of his accomplices were confided to *Hosokawa Tsunatoshi*, *daimyō* of *Kumamoto* (*Higo*), 10 to *Matsudaira Sadanao* of *Matsuyama* (*Iyo*), 10 to *Mōri Tsunamoto* of *Fuchū* (*Nagato*), and 10 others to *Mizuno Tadamoto* of *Yamagata* (*Dewa*), and some months later, all were invited to take their own lives by *harakiri*. *Yoshio*, also called *Kuranosuke*, had his brother *Yoshikane*, only 15 years old, with him and a relative *Nobukiyo*, aged 27.

Oishi-zaki, 生石崎. A cape S. E. of *Awaji*.

Ōita, 大分. Capital of *Ōita-ken* and of *Bungo* province (13,100 inh.). It was formerly called *Funai*. — (See *Funai*).

Ōita-ken, 大分縣. A department formed of the province of *Bungo* and 2 districts of *Buzen.*—Pop. : 874,000. — Capital : *Ōita* (13,100 inh.). — Chief city : *Nakatsu* (15,100 inh.).

Ōiwa-yama, 大岩山. A place in *Ōmi*, near the village of *Kuroda*, where *Nakagawa Kiyohide* was defeated and killed by *Sakuma Nobumori*. (1583).

Ojika-shima, 小値賀嶋. One of the northern islands of the *Gotō* archipelago (*Hizen*) (30 Km. in circ.).

Ōjin-tennō, 應神天皇. 15th Emperor of Japan (201-310). This sovereign was first called *Honda-wake no mikoto ;* he was the 4th son of *Chūai-tennō* and of *Jingō-kōgō* and was born after his father's death.

His mother although pregnant, headed the expedition against the *San-kan* (Korea) and was delivered on her return to *Tsukushi*. She continued to govern as regent for 69 years and it is only after her death (269 A.D.) that *Ōjin* began to take the reins of government. He was also called *Ōtomowake*. It is in his reign (284-285) that the Korean scholars *Ajiki* and *Wani* are believed to have come to Japan, bringing with them Chinese literature and Confucianism. *Ōjin* died at the age of 110 years (130 according to the *Koji-ki*). In 712, the empress *Gemmei* had a temple erected in his honor in the district of *Usa* (*Buzen*), where he was honored by the name of *Hachiman-Dai-jingū*. The emperor *Seiwa*

ŌJIN-TENNŌ.

also dedicated to him the temple of *Otoko-yama* (*Iwashimizu-Hachiman-gū*), near *Kyōto*. He has become the god of war, and was the patron of the *Minamoto*.

Oka, 岡. A castle in *Sanuki*, taken by *Hosokawa Yoriyuki*, after he had dispossessed and killed his cousin *Kiyouji*, lord of *Sanuki* (1362). The castle was intrusted to the guard of his brother *Noriharu*, who received the title of *Sanuki no shugo*.

Oka, 岡. Another name for the city of *Takeda* (*Bungo*).

Okabe, 岡部. A town in *Musashi*, was from 1751 to 1868 the residence of the *Abe daimyō* (20,000 k.).

Okabe, 岡部. A family of *daimyō* originating in *Mikawa*, and descended from *Fujiwara Muchimaro* (680-737).

—— **Nagamori, 長盛** (1568-1632). Son of *Masatsuna*, served *Ieyasu*, who in 1590 gave him a revenue of 12,000 k. at *Matsufuji* (*Shimōsa*), and transferred him in 1600 to *Yamazaki* (*Harima* — 20,000 k.). He afterwards became governor of the *Fushimi* castle (1607), *daimyō* of *Kameyama*, (*Tamba*) (1609), of *Fukuchiyama* (*Tamba*) (1621) and of *Ōgaki* (*Mino*) (1624) —His descendants resided in 1632 at *Tatsuno* (*Harima*) ; in 1635, at *Takatsuki*

(*Settsu*); and finally at *Kishiwada* (*Izumi* — 53,000 k.) — Now Viscount.

O Kachi no kata, 料 勝 方. Or *O Kachi no Tsubone* (1578-1642). Daughter of *Ōta Yasusuke*, became a concubine of *Ieyasu*, to whom she bore 2 children. On the death of *Ieyasu*, she shaved her head. She died at the age of 65, and was buried in the temple of *Eishō-ji* (*Kamakura*), hence her name of *Eishō-in*.

Okada, 岡 田. A town in *Bitchū*, was from 1615 to 1868, the residence of the *Itō daimyō* (10,000 k.).

Ō-kagami, 大 鏡. A work in 8 volumes, written by *Fujiwara Tamenari* (12th century); it contains the history of 14 reigns from *Montoku* (851) to *Go-Ichijō* (1039).

Okami-yama, 大 神 山. — See *Ōyama* (*Hōki*).

Okamoto Shigemasa, 岡 本 重 政 (1542-1600). Native of *Owari*, he served *Nobunaga* then *Hideyoshi* who, in 1587, gave him the castle of *Kameyama* in *Ise* (20,000 k.). He served in the campaign against the *Hōjō* of *Odawara* (1590) and in the expedition to Korea (1592). After *Hideyoshi's* death, he sided against *Ieyasu*, and was condemned to perform *harakiri*.

Okanouchi, 岡 內. A family ennobled after the Restoration.—Now Baron.

Ō-kawa, 大 川. Another name for the *Hii-kawa* of *Izumo*, the *Yura-gawa* of *Tango*, the *Abu-gawa* of *Nagato*, etc.

Okayama, 岡 山. In *Settsu*, where the *Shōgun Hidetada* encamped during the siege of *Osaka* (1615) and where his generals *Kuroda Nagamasa* and *Katō Yoshiaki* defeated *Ōno Harunaga*.

Okayama, 岡 山. A place in *Ōmi*, where the *Shōgun Yoshizumi*, retired and died (1511), after he had been expelled from *Kyōto* by his rival *Yoshitane*. The *Sasaki* built a castle there.

Okayama, 岡 山. Capital of *Okayama-ken* and of *Bizen* province (80,000 inh.). — It possesses an ancient castle built in the middle of the 16th century by *Ukita Naoie*. Under the *Tokugawa*, it belonged to the *daimyō Kobayakawa* (1600) and *Ikeda* (1603-1868) (315,000 k.).

Okayama-ken, 岡 山 縣. A department formed of the provinces of *Bizen*, *Bitchū* and *Mimasaka*. — Pop.: 1,182,000 inh. — Capital: *Okayama* (80,000 inh). — Chief town: *Tsuyama* (12,000).

Okazaki, 岡 崎. Chief town (17,400 inh.) of *Mikawa*. — An ancient castle built towards 1440 by *Saigō Danjō Saemon*; in 1520, it came into the possession of *Tokugawa Kiyoyasu*, whose grandson *Ieyasu* was born there (1542). When the latter was transferred to *Kwantō* (1590), *Hideyoshi* gave the castle of *Okazaki* to *Tanaka Yoshimasa*. Under the *Tokugawa Shōgun*, it passed successively to the *daimyō*: *Honda* (1601); *Mizuno* (1645); *Matsudaira* (*Matsui*) (1762); and lastly to the *Honda* (1769-1868) (50,000 k.).

Okazaki, 岡 崎. A family of *kuge* descended from *Fujiwara Yoshikado*.—Now Viscount.

Okazaki Masamune, 岡 崎 正 宗 (1264-1344). A celebrated smith, renowned for his skill in forging sabre blades. He lived first at *Kama-*

kura, *Ima-kōji*, but left that city when it was captured by *Nitta Yoshi-sada* (1333) and repaired to *Kyōto*, where he forged a sabre for *Kusunoki Masashige*. Afterwards he returned to *Kamakura* where he died. His adopted son *Sadamune* succeeded him.

Okazaki Saburō, 岡崎三郎 — See *Tokugawa Nobuyasu.*

Okazawa, 岡澤. A family of *samurai* from the *Yamaguchi* clan (*Suwō*), ennobled after the Restoration.--To-day Baron.

Okehazama, 桶狭間. A place in *Owari*, where *Nobunaga* defeated *Imagawa Yoshimoto* (1560).

Oki, 隠岐. One of the 8 provinces of the *San-in-dō*, formed by the *Oki* islands. — Chinese name: *Inshū*.—It comprises 4 districts, which belong to *Shimane-ken*. — The 4 principal islands of the group are: *Dōgo-shima* or *Haha-jima* (120 Km. in circ.); *Naka no shima* (65 Km.) *Nishi no shima* (81 Km.), *Chiburi-shima* (25 Km.). The emperor *Go-Toba* was exiled to *Naka no shima* by *Hōjō Yoshitoki* (1221), and *Go-Daigo* to *Chiburi-shima* by *Hōjō Takatoki* (1332). — The population of the islands numbers 36,000 souls.

Oki, 沖. A family of *Owari*, ennobled after the Restoration.—Now Baron.

Ōki, 大木. A family of *samurai* of the *Saga* clan (*Hizen*) ennobled after the Restoration.—Now Count.

Ōkimi-tsukasa, 正親司. Formerly an office belonging to the *Kunai-shō*, and intrusted with the registers in which the names of princes, etc. were entered.

Okinawa-ken, 沖繩縣. The 55 islands of the *Ryūkyū* archipelago formed into a department at the time of their annexation to Japan (April 1879). — Pop.: 469,000. — Capital: *Naha* (35,500 inh.). — Chief towns: *Shuri* (25,000), *Motobu* (17,000), *Sunagawa* (16,000) *Gushi-chabu* (15,600), *Nishiharu* (14,500), etc.—The principal islands of the department, starting from the N. are: *Okinawa*, with a number of secondary islands; the *Miyako* and *Yaeyama* groups (See these names).

Okinawa-shima, 沖繩嶋. The largest island of the *Okinawa-ken*. Also called *Ryūkyū-shima*, *Nakagami-shima*; it is 118 Km. long, from 5 to 40 Km. wide, and is 405 Km. in circumference. Chief cities: *Naha*, (35,500 inh.) capital of the department; *Shuri* (25,000 inh.), etc.

Oki no shima, 沖嶋. An island in the middle of lake *Biwa*, also called *Okitsushima-yama*. (7 Km. in circ.).

Oki no shima, 沖嶋. An island south east of *Tosa* (17 Km. in circ.).

Ōkōchi, 大河内. An ancient castle in *Ise*, belonging to the *Kita-batake*, governors of the province. Captured by *Nobunaga* in 1569, it was afterwards abandoned.

Ōkōchi, 大河内. A family of *daimyō*, descended from *Minamoto Yorimasa* (1106-1180) (*Seiwa-Genji*).

—— **Akitsuna, 顕綱**. Grandson of *Yorimasa*, was the first to take the name of *Ōkōchi*.

—— **Masatsuna, 正綱** (1576-1648). Son of *Hidetsuna*, was adopted by *Matsudaira* (*Nagasawa*) *Masatsugu* and the family took the name of *Matsudaira*. He served *Ieyasu*, who in 1604, gave him a revenue of 20,000 k. in *Izu*. In 1627, he left the management of his domains to his son *Nobutsuna*.

Masatsuna { Nobutsuna { Terutsuna -Nobuteru -Nobunao (a) / Nobuoki -Terusada -Terumori (b) } / Masanobu -Masahisa -Masasada -Masatsune (c) }

(*a*) — Eldest Branch —— **Nobutsuna, 信綱** (1596-1662). Was educated with the future *Shōgun Iemitsu*. In 1633, he received the fief of *Oshi* (*Musashi* — 60,000 k.). In 1638, he succeeded *Itakura Shigemasa*, quelled the insurrection of *Shimabara* (*Hizen*) and on his return, was transferred to *Kawagoe* (*Musashi* —90,000 k.). — His descendants settled in 1694 at *Koga* (*Shimōsa*); in 1712 at *Yoshida* (*Mikawa*); in 1729 at *Hamamatsu* (*Tōtōmi*); at last from 1749 to 1868, at *Yoshida* (to-day, *Toyohashi*) (*Mikawa* — 79,000 k.). — Now Viscount.

(*b*) — Branch of *Nobuoki* 信與 (1630-1692), fifth son of *Nobutsuna*. Settled in 1681 at *Tsuchiura* (*Hatachi*); in 1692, at *Mibu* (*Shimotsuke*); in 1695, at *Takasaki* (*Kōzuke*); in 1710, at *Murakami* (*Echigo*); at last from 1717 to 1868 at *Takasaki* (*Kōzuke* — 80,000 k.). — Now Viscount.

(*c*) — Branch of *Masanobu, 正信*, brother of *Nobutsuna*, resided from 1703 to 1868 at *Ōtaki* (*Kazusa* — 25,000 k.). — Now Viscount.

Oku, 奧. An apartment in the palace of *Edo*, where the *Shōgun* treated with his ministers on the affairs of State — See *Koshōshū*.

Oku, 奧. A family of *samurai* from *Fukuoka* (*Chikuzen*), ennobled after the Restoration.—Now Baron.

—— **Yasukata, 保鞏**. Born in 1844, distinguished himself during the *Satsuma* war by cutting his way through the lines of the besiegers of *Kumamoto* to obtain assistance (1877). He commanded the 5th division (*Hiroshima*) during the war with China (1894-1895), and the 2nd army of Manchuria (1904-1905).

Ōkubo, 大久保. A family of *daimyō*, originating in *Mikawa* and descended from the *Utsunomiya* who were themselves descendants of *Fujiwara Michikane* (955-995).

—— **Tadakazu, 忠員** (1510-1582). Served the *Tokugawa* and helped in the defeat of *Imagawa Yoshimoto* (1555).

Tadakazu { Tadayo- -Tadachika-Tadatsune -Tadamoto -Tadatomo { Tadamasu (a) / Norihiro (b) } / Tadasuke (c) / Tadatame -Tadatomo -Tadataka -Tsuneharu-Tadatane - Tadasato (d) / Tadanori (e) }

(*a*) — **Tadayo, 忠世** (1531-1593). Served in all the campaigns of *Ieyasu*, who, in 1590, gave him the fief of *Odawara* (*Sagami* — 45,000 k.).

—— **Tadachika, 忠隣** (1553-1628). Succeeded his father at *Odawara* and had a revenue of 70,000 k. In 1614, accused of conspiring with *Tadateru* against his brother the *Shōgun Hidetada*, he was dispossessed and confined to *Hikone* (*Ōmi*). Later on, *Hidetada* invited him to *Edo*, but he refused to go and died in exile.

—— **Tadatsune, 忠常** (1580-1611). Followed *Hidetada* in his expedition to *Shinano* (1600). He died before his father.

—— **Tadamoto, 忠職** (1604-1670). Implicated at first in the disgrace of his grandfather, he received in 1632 the fief of *Kanō* (*Mino* — 50,000 k.); was transferred in 1639 to *Akashi* (*Harima*), and in 1649, to *Karatsu* (*Hizen* — 90,000 k.). — His descendants moved to *Sakura* (*Shimōsa*) in 1678, and to *Odawara* (*Sagami*) (1686-1868) (100,000 k.). — Now Viscount.

(*b*) — Branch coming from *Norihiro*, **敎寛** (1657-1737), which from 1718 to 1868, resided at *Ogino* (*Sagami* — 13,000 k.). — Now Viscount.

(*c*) — **Tadasuke, 忠佐** (1537-1613). 2nd son of *Tadakazu*, distinguished himself by his valor in all the wars of *Ieyasu*. In 1601, he received the castle of *Numazu* (*Suruga* — 20,000 k.), but, as he died without issue, his domains reverted to the *Shōgun*.

(*d*) — Branch coming from *Tadatame*, **忠為** (1554-1616), 6th son of *Tadakazu*, resided from 1725 to 1868 at *Karasu-yama* (*Shimotsuke* — 30,000 k.). — Now Count.

(*e*) — **Tadanori, 忠敎** (1560-1639). 8th son of *Tadakazu*, better known by the name of *Hikozaemon*, accompanied his elder brother *Tadayo* in his campaigns, and was involved in the disgrace of his nephew *Tadachika*. After the siege of *Ōsaka* (1615), *Ieyasu* offered to restore his domains, but *Tadanori* refused to accept them. However he remained at *Edo* and became the councillor and confidant of the *Shōgun Hidetada* and *Iemitsu*.

Ōkubo, 大久保. A family of *samurai* from *Kagoshima* (*Satsuma*), ennobled after the Restoration. — To-day Marquis.

—— **Toshimichi, 利通** (1832-1878). Played an important part in the Restoration. It was he that persuaded his suzerain, *Shimazu Narishige*, to surrender his fief of *Satsuma* into the hands of the Emperor (1867). Afterwards appointed minister of Finance, he was member of the *Iwakura* embassy to Europe and America (1868-1872). On his return, he opposed the war against Korea, and was appointed Minister of Home Affairs. He was commissioned to quell the revolt of *Etō Shimpei* at *Saga* (1874) and to obtain an indemnity from China after the expedition to Formosa. On the 14th of May 1878, he was assassinated in *Tōkyō* (*Kioi-zaka*) by *Shimada Ichirō* and 6 other *samurai* of the *Kaga* clan.

Ōkubo, 大久保. A family of *samurai* from *Shizuoka* (*Suruga*), ennobled after the Restoration. — Now Viscount.

—— **Ichi-ō, 一翁** (1817-1888). Served the last 5 *Tokugawa Shōgun*, was *Bugyō* of *Shizuoka* and of *Kyōto*. Before the entry of the Imperial army into *Edo* (1868), he was sent by the *Shōgun Keiki*, with *Katsu Yoshikuni*, to *Saigō Takamori*, to negotiate for peace. He was afterwards appointed governor of *Shizuoka* (1870), *Kyōto*, (1875), senator (1877), and received in 1887, the title of Viscount. — *Ichi-ō* won distinction not only in the art of warfare, but also in poetry and literature. He is also called *Tadahiro*.

Ōkubo Nagayasu, 大久保長安 (+1613) Son of *Komparu Shichirō*, an actor of *nō*, entered the service of the *Takeda* of *Kai*, and was raised to the rank of *samurai*. Afterwards he joined the party of *Ieyasu* to whom he rendered great pecuniary services by working the mines of *Izu*. In return, he received the title of *Iwami no kami* and the domain of *Hachiōji* (*Musashi* — 20,000 k.). After his death, from discoveries made in his dwelling he was suspected of fraudulent practices; letters were also found relating to a plot formed with the Christians and the Spaniards to overthrow the *Shōgun Hidetada*. His son *Tōjūrō* was arrested on the spot and put to death with 6 supposed accomplices.

Ōkubo Shibutsu, 大窪詩佛 (1767-1837). A scholar, poet and painter of *Edo*.

Oku-bōzu, 奥坊主. Servants of the *Shōgun's* palace in *Edo*. They numbered several hundreds and were intrusted with the sweeping and other household employments.

Okuda, 奥田. A family of *daimyō* descended from *Minamoto Yoshiuji* (1189-1254) (*Seiwa-Genji*). At the end of the 16th century, they took the name of *Hori*, but after the Restoration, they resumed the name of *Okuda*.

—— **Naomasa, 直政** (+1608). On entering the service of *Hori Hidemasa* he changed his family name of *Okuda* to *Hori*. Later on, he served *Hideyoshi* who confided the castle of *Sanjō* (*Echigo* — 50,000 k.). to him in 1598.

$$
\text{Naomasa}
\begin{cases}
\text{Naoyori -Naotsugu -Naosada -Naotaka} & \text{(a)} \\
\text{Naoyuki -Naokage -Naoyoshi-Naokatsu} & \text{(b)} \\
\text{Naoshige -Naotomo -Naonori -Naoyuki} & \text{(c)}
\end{cases}
$$

(*a*) — Eldest branch — **Naoyori, 直寄** (1577-1639). Occupied in 1616, the castle of *Nagaoka* (*Echigo*), and in 1618, that of *Murakami* (*Echigo*). His descendants were tranferred in 1644 to *Muramatsu* (*Echigo* — 30,000 k), where they remained till the Restoration. — Today Viscount.

(*b*) — Branch coming from *Naoyuki*, 直之 (1585-1642) that from 1698 to 1868 resided at *Shiiya* (*Echigo* — 10,000 k.). — Now Viscount.

(*c*) — Branch of *Naoshige* 直重 (+1615), who was killed in the siege of *Ōsaka*. The family resided from 1615 to 1868 at *Susaka* (*Shinano* — 15,000 k.). — To-day Viscount.

Okudaira, 奥平. A family of *daimyō* from *Mikawa* and descended, through the *Akamatsu*, from the *Murakami-Genji*.

—— **Nobumasa, 信昌** (1555-1615). Left in 1573 with his father *Sadayoshi*, the service of the *Takeda* of *Kai*, and placed

himself under *Ieyasu*. *Takeda Katsuyori*, incensed at this defection, put
the wife of *Nobumasa* to death but *Ieyasu* gave him his eldest daughter
Kame-hime in marriage and made him lord of *Nagashino* (*Mikawa*).
Here he was soon besieged by *Katsuyori*, who was however driven back
with heavy loss by *Ieyasu* and *Nobunaga*. In 1582, *Nobumasa*, in company with *Sakai Tadatsugu*, waged war against the *Takeda* in *Shinano*.
In 1590, he received the fief of *Miyasaki* (*Kōzuke* — 30,000 k); in
1600, he became governor of *Kyōto* and the next year, he was transferred to *Kanō* (*Mino* — 100,000 k.).

$$\text{Nobumasa} \begin{cases} \text{Iemasa -　-Tadamasa-Masayoshi-Masaakira} & (a) \\ \text{Tadamasa} & (b) \\ \text{Tadaakira} & (c) \end{cases}$$

(*a*) — Eldest branch descended from *Iemasa* 家昌 (1577-1614), who
resided successively : in 1601, at *Utsunomiya* (*Shimotsuke*) ; in 1619, at
Koga (*Shimōsa*) ; in 1622, at *Utsunomiya ;* in 1668, at *Yamagata* (*Dewa*) ;
in 1685, at *Utsunomiya ;* in 1697, at *Miyazu* (*Tango*) ; finally from 1717
to 1868 at *Nakatsu* (*Buzen* — 100,000 k.). — Now Count.

(*b*) — **Tadamasa,** 忠 政 (1580-1614). Was to inherit the fief of *Kanō*
(*Mino*) but dying before his father, his domain reverted to the *Shōgun*.

(*c*) — **Tadaakira,** 忠 明 (1583-1644). Was adopted by his grandfather *Ieyasu* and received the name of *Matsudaira* to be transmitted to
his descendants. — See *Matsudaira* (*Okudaira*).

Okudono, 奥 殿. In *Mikawa ;* from 1703 to 1868, the residence of
the *Matsudaira daimyō* (*Ōgyū*) (16,000 k.).

Oku-ishi, 奥 醫 師. Physicians of the *Shōgun's* palace, *Edo*. They
bore the title of *Hō-in*, or *Hōgan*, and were 20 in number. Their chief
was called *Osaji* and possessed great influence.

Okujiri-shima, 奥 尻 嶋. An island south west of *Hōkkaidō*,
belonging to *Shiribeshi* province (53 Km. in circ.).

Oku-jusha, 奥 儒 者. The 2 professors who attended the future
Shōgun, in the *Tokugawa* days. From 1655 the office belonged to the
Hayashi family ; towards 1725, one of them was a member of the *Naru-
shima* family.

Ōkuma, 大 隈. An ancient castle in *Chikuzen*, which in the 16th
century, belonged to the *Akizuki daimyō ;* there *Tanenaga* was besieged
by *Hideyoshi* in 1586.

Ōkuma, 大 隈. A family of *samurai* from the *Saga* clan (*Hizen*),
ennobled after the Restoration. — Now Count.

—— **Shigenobu,** 重 信. Born in 1838, eagerly joined the party of
the Restoration. Appointed *Sangi* (Councillor of State), he demanded the
establishment of the parliamentary system, and as soon as the Emperor
had promised (1881) to create two legislative assemblies in 1890, *Shigenobu*
tendered his resignation in order to set about organizing the Progressist
party (*kaishin-tō*). Appointed Minister of Foreign Affairs in 1887, he
began to negotiate the revision of the treaties with the Foreign Powers. A
afnatic threw a bomb at his carriage (1889) ; *Shigenobu* was badly injured
and had to submit to the amputation of his right leg. — Shortly after,

he left politics to devote his whole time to the great School which he had founded in the *Waseda* ward of *Tōkyō*. The school has since become a University.

Ōkume no mikoto, 大久米命. One of the companions in arms of *Jimmu-tennō*, chief of the outer-guard of the Imperial Palace (*kumebe*).

Okumura, 奥村. A family ennobled after the Restoration — Now Baron.

Okuni, 小國. An ancient castle in *Uzen*, which belonged to the *Mogami daimyō* and towards the end of the 16th century, passed over into the hands of the *Tozawa*.

O Kuni, 阿國. — See *Kuni*.

Ōkuninushi, 大國主. Son — or descendant in the 5th generation according to some — of *Susano-o*. He lived in *Izumo*, and governed the region of the *San-yō* and the *San-in*. *Takemikazuchi* was sent to invite him to recognize the suzerainty of *Ninigi no mikoto*. *Ōkuninushi* consulted his two sons; the elder, *Kotoshironushi*, consented to waive his rights in favor of a descendant of *Amaterasu ;* the younger, *Tateminakata*, refused to submit and was slain by *Takemikazuchi*. *Ōkuninushi* retired to *Kizuki* (*Izumo*), and is there worshipped in the great temple called *Izumo ō-yashiro*. He is also called *Ōnamuji*, *Ōmononushi*, *Ashihara-shiko-o*, *Yachihoko*, *Ōkunitama*, *Akitsukunitama*, etc.

Ōkura, 大藏. Formerly store-houses where the goods belonging to the Crown were kept. The first were built in the reign of *Yūryaku-tennō* (457-479), and confided to the *Hada* clan. — See *Uchikura*.

Ōkura-shō, 大藏省. Or **Ōkura no tsukasa.** From remote times store-houses were built to receive the objects sent to the Court as presents or taxes ; they were first called *iwaigura* and were intrusted to the *Imube* clan. In the reign of *Richū* (400-405), *uchi-kura* were built which were called *Ō-kura* in the reign of *Yūryaku*. At the time of the *Taikwa* reform (645), a ministry was established with an *Ōkura-kyō* at its head. It was intrusted with the collection of the taxes, the distribution of pensions, the verification of measures, the fixing of the prices of the most necessary staples. The Minister had under his control 5 secondary offices : *Tenju, Kamon, Urushibe, Nuibe, Oribe*. — In 1885, the name of *Ōkura-shō* was given to the Department of Finance.

Okurina, 謚. A posthumous name given to persons of rank. The *Taihō* Code (702), decided that an *okurina* should be given to the deceased according to their conduct and their deeds during life. Thus the emperor *Mommu* gave his predecessor, the empress *Jitō* (+701), the name of *Ō-yamato-neko-ame no hironu-hime no mikoto*. Later on, Chinese names were adopted : thus, the Chinese names of all the preceding sovereigns were fixed by *Ōmi Mifune* (784). These names were derived from their residences, as *Seiwa-tennō*, from the *Seiwa-in* palace ; sometimes from a temple, as *Kwazan, Enyū ;* sometimes from their place of burial as *Daigo, Murakami ;* from the name of a preceding emperor, with the prefix " *go* " (after) ; as *Go-Ichijō, Go-Shijaku ;* — the emperors that died in exile received the name of their place of banishment, as *Awaji-haitei* (*Junnin*), *Oki-in* (*Go-Toba*), *Sanuki-in* (*Sutoku*), *Sado-in* (*Juntoku*); others again, were named after the longest *nengō* of their reign : as, *Ninwa-tei* (*Kōkō*), *Engi-tei* (*Daigo*), etc.

Ōkuwa, 大桑. An ancient castle in *Mino*, belonging to the *Toki daimyō*, governors of the province ; it passed in 1540 to the *Saitō*.

Okuyama, 奥山. An ancient castle in *Tōtōmi*, built in 1384 by *Fujiwara Tomofuji* ; was destroyed during the civil wars of the 16th century.

Oku-yu-hitsu, 奥右筆. A title created in 1681 for two officials commissioned to draw up the text of certain important deeds for the government of the *Shōgun*. The first two that bore the title were *Kojima Jirōzaemon* and *Ninagawa Hikoemon*.

Omae-saki, 御前崎. A cape south of *Tōtōmi*.

Ō-mandokoro, 大政所. A title given to the mother of the *Kwampaku*. — It was especially applied to the mother of *Hideyoshi*. Nothing is known about the name of her family. A native of the village of *Nakamura* (*Owari*), she married *Kinoshita Yaemon*, by whom she had two children, a daughter (*Zuiryū-in*), and a son, who was *Hideyoshi*. After *Yaemon's* death, she married a certain *Chikuami*, by whom she had also two children : a son (*Hashiba Hidetoshi*) and a daughter (*Asahi no Kata*), who married *Ieyasu*. *Ō-mandokoro* died in 1593.

Ōma-saki, 大間崎. A cape north of *Mutsu*. It is the most northerly point of *Hondo*.

O-meshi-uma-azukari, 御召馬預. Under the *Tokugawa*, officials commissioned to procure the horses necessary for the service of the *Shōgun*. That office was hereditary in the *Suwa* and *Muramatsu* families.

Ō-metsuke, 大目附. Officials under the *Edo Shōgun*, commissioned to look to the exact observance of the laws, to revise law-suits, to control the proceedings of the *daimyō* and functionaries, to secure the execution of edicts against the Christians, to superintend the escort of the *Shōgun* when he travelled, to control the adoptions made by the *daimyō* families, etc. These officials, 4 in number, were first appointed in 1633, and bore the title of *Sōmetsuke* ; later on, their number was increased to 5 and their name was changed to *Ō-metsuke*.

Ōmi, 臣. One of the 8 titles (*hassei*) established by the emperor *Temmu* in 684. Like the other *kabane*, it was first added to the name (*uji*), and then confounded with it. — See *Kabane*.

Ōmi, 近江. One of the 13 provinces of the *Tōsandō*. It comprises 12 districts (*kōri*), which depend on *Shiga-ken*. — Chinese name : *Gōshū*. — In olden times, lake *Biwa*, which occupies the centre of the province, was called *Chika-tsu-awa-umi* (near foaming lake), in opposition with *Hamana-ko*, then named *Tō-tsu-awa-umi* (distant foaming lake), and these two names contracted into *Ōmi* and *Tōtōmi* have become the names of the two provinces.

Omigawa, 小見川. In *Shimōsa* ; in the 16th century, it was the residence of a family of the same name, and from 1724 to 1868 that of the *Uchida daimyō* (10,000 k).

Ōmi hakkei, 江近八景. The 8 famous sights of lake *Biwa* (*Ōmi*) : (1) the autumn moon at *Ishiyama ;* — (2). the evening snow at *Hira-yama ;* — (3). the setting sun at *Seta ;* — (4). the evening bell of *Miidera ;* — (5). the boats leaving the port of *Yabase ;* — (6). the sky and the breeze of *Awazu ;* — ,7). the night rain at *Karasaki ;* —(8). the wild geese alighting at *Katata.*—It was at the end of the 15th century that these *hakkei* were arranged similarly to the 8 views of *Shōshō* (瀟 湘, *Siaosiang*), near lake *Tōtei* (洞 庭, *Tongting*), in *Hunan* 湖 南, (China).

Ōmi Kenu, 近江毛野 (+ 530). Sent to *Mimana* by the emperor *Keitai* (527) to fight *Shiragi*, he was recalled on account of his bad administration and died in *Tsukushi:*

Ō-mikotomochi no tsukasa, 大宰府. An ancient name for the government of *Tsukushi*, called later on *Dazai-fu.*

Ōmi Mifune, 淡海三船 (722-785). Son of prince *Ikebe-Ō* and descendant of *Kadono-Ō*, received in 751 the name of *Ōmi no Mabito.* He repressed in *Ōmi* the revolt of *Fujiwara Nakamaro* (764), was commissioned to inspect several provinces and was appointed *Dazai-Shōni.* It was he that determined the posthumous names of the emperors from *Jimmu* to *Jitō.*

Ōmi-ryō, 近江令. The name of the code in use from the *Taikwa* Reform (645) to the *Taihō* era (701). — See *Taihō-ryō.*

Ōmi-ryōke, 近江兩家. The two branches of the *Sasaki* family which, in the Middle Ages, possessed *Ōmi* province. The *Echigawa* river separated the domains of the *Rokkaku* on the south, and the *Kyōgoku* on the north.

Ōmi-shima, 大三嶋. An island of the Inland Sea, north east of *Iyo* province, to which it belongs. (58 Km. in circ.)

Ōmiya, 大宮. A small town (5,000 inh.) of the district of *Kita-Adachi* (*Musashi*). There stands the temple of *Hikawa-jinja*, built by *Yamatotakeru no mikoto* in honor of *Susano-o.*

Ōmiya, 大宮. A small town (6,700 inh.) of the *Chichibu* (*Musashi*) district, near which is the temple of *Mitsumine-san*, which is said to have been dedicated by *Yamatotakeru* to his ancestors *Izanagi* and *Izanami.*

Ōmiya, 大宮. A family of *kuge* descended from *Fujiwara* (*Saionji*) *Kinhira* (1264-1315).—Now Marquis.

Ōmizo, 大溝. An ancient castle in *Ōmi*, built in 1115, by *Sasaki Nobutaka ;* it passed afterwards into the hands of the *Kaizu daimyō*, who were dispossessed by *Nobunaga* in 1572. The latter gave the castle to his nephew *Nobuzumi*, who was despoiled in his turn (1582), and succeeded by *Kyōgoku Takatsugu.* Under the *Tokugawa*, *Ōmizo* was from 1619 to 1868 the residence of the *Wakebe daimyō* (20,000 k.).

Ōmono-gawa, 大物川. A river in *Ugo*, flowing through *Akita* (118 Km. long). Also called *Toshima-gawa.*

Ōmononushi no kami, 大物主神. — See *Okuninushi.*

Omote, 御表. One of the 3 apartments (*oku*) reserved to the *Shōgun* in the former palace of *Edo.* — See *Koshōshū.*

Omoteban-ishi, 表番醫師. Physicians in attendance at the Shogunal palace of *Edo*. They were 30 in all.

Omoteyu-hitsu, 表右筆. Secretaries serving in the *Omote* of the Shogunal palace of *Edo*. The title was created in 1603 and first given to *Soga Toshisuke*.—See *Okuyu-hitsu*.

Ōmura, 大村. A town of *Hizen*, from the 12th century, residence of the *Ōmura daimyō*.

Ōmura, 大村. A family of *daimyō* from *Hizen*, and descended from *Fujiwara Sumitomo* (+ 941).

—— **Tadazumi,** 忠澄. A descendant of *Sumitomo* in the 8th generation, was the first to take the name of *Ōmura*, from the village in *Hizen*, where he lived.

—— **Sumitada,** 純忠 (1532-1587). Son of *Arima Haruzumi*, was chosen to succeed *Ōmura Sumiaki*. Baptized in 1562, by the name of Bartholomew, he was the first Christian *daimyō*, and remained faithful till his death. It was he that in 1568 opened the port of *Fukae* to foreign trade, which became the city of *Nagasaki*.

—— **Yoshiaki,** 喜明 (1568-1615). Son of the above, was also a Christian, he had received in baptism the name of *Sanche*. In 1600, he sided against *Ieyasu* and had to give up his domains to his son. He spent the rest of his life in profligacy.

—— **Sumiyori,** 純頼 (+ 1619). Son of the above. Was baptized and given the name of Bartholomew, like his grandfather. Towards the close of his life, he became persecutor of the Christian religion. — His family resided at *Ōmura* (*Hizen* — 28,000 k) till the Restoration. — Viscount in 1885, Count in 1891.

Ōmura, 大村. *Samurai* family of the *Yamaguchi* clan (*Suwō*), ennobled in 1887. — Now Viscount.

—— **Masujirō,** 益次郎 (+ 1869). Instructed the *samurai* of *Chōshū* in military arts. At the time of the Imperial Restoration, he fought against the army of the *Shōgun* at *Edo*, at *Wakamatsu* and pacified the N. E. part of *Hondo*. He had been named *Hyōbu-tayū* (Vice-Minister of War) and was working at the organization of the army, when he was murdered, with 5 of his officers (Nov. 8, 1869). He is the first Japanese in whose honor a bronze statue was erected. It stands in front of the *Shōkon-sha* temple, on the hill of *Kudan* (*Tōkyō*).

Ō-muraji, 大連. Title created by the emperor *Suinin*. Its bearer and the *Ō-omi* were the principal ministers.

Omura-wan, 大村灣. Bay, W. of *Kyūshū*; also called *Sonoki no irie, Tai no ura*.

Omuro, 御室. — See *Ninna-ji*.

Ōmuro-zan, 大室山. Volcano on the E. coast of *Izu*. Also called *Eboshi-yama, Sengen-yama, Fuji no imōto* (younger sister of Mt. *Fuji*).

Ōnakatomi, 大中臣. Ancient family, by right of inheritance, at the head of the *Jinji-kwan*. The best known members are: *Kiyomaro*

(702-788), *Morona* (743-797), *Fuchina* (774-850), *Yoshinobu* (922-991), *Sukechika* (954-1038), etc.

Ōnamuji, 大己貴. — See *Ōkuninushi*.

Onekotan-jima, 温禰古丹嶋. One of the *Chishima* (Kurile) islands.

Onga, 御賀. Ceremony at the Imperial Palace, during which the Empress, the princes, ministers, etc, offer their congratulations to the Emperor on the event of his 40th and 60th birthdays.

Oni, 鬼. Generic name for demons, goblins, gnomes, etc., who play a considerable part in the old folk lore.

Oni-ga-shima, 鬼嶋. An island (80 Km. circ.) south of *Hachijō-jima ;* also called *Ao-ga-shima*.

Ōnin, 應仁. *Nengō :* 1467-1468.

Ōnin no ran, 應仁亂. Civil war that broke out in the *Ōnin* era. — The *Shōgun Yoshimasa*, having no children, adopted his brother *Yoshimi*, and gave him as tutor (*hosa*) *Hosokawa Katsumoto* (1464). But the following year, a son, *Yoshihisa*, was born to him, upon which he intended to deprive his brother of his rights to the succession. Meanwhile, *Hatakeyama Mochikuni*, after having adopted his nephew *Masanaga*, also had a son, and dismissed his adopted son. Similar difficulties arose in the *Shiba* family, where two rivals, *Yoshitoshi* and *Yoshikado* disputed the inheritance of *Yoshitake* (+ 1452). The malcontents appealed to the great *daimyō* and two parties were formed, headed by *Hosokawa Katsumoto* and *Yamana Mochitoyo*. It was not long before war broke out, which continued without decisive advantage for either side, during 11 years (1467-1477). *Kyōto* and its environs were laid waste and the struggle was ended only by the exhaustion of both parties.

Onjō-ji, 園城寺. Or *Mii-dera ;* a temple north west of *Ōtsu* (*Ōmi*), seat of the *Jimon* branch of the *Tendai* sect. Built in 858 by the bonze *Enchin*, it became very prosperous and its rivalry with the *Enryaku-ji* (*Hiei-zan*), caused frequent disturbances. Both temples kept up armies of mercenaries (*sōhei*), and the 11th century especially rang with their broils. *Mii-dera* was burned 5 or 6 times by the enemy. The present edifice dates from 1690 and falls far short of its former splendor.

Ono, 小野. A place in *Harima*, where *Yoshitsune* defeated the *Taira* in 1184. It was from 1670 to 1868 the residence of the *Hitotsu-yanagi daimyō* (10,000 k.).

Ono, 小野. A family ennobled after the Restoration and hereditarily at the head of the *Shintō* temple of *Hi-no-misaki jinja* (*Izumo*).---Now Baron.

Ōno, 大野. A place in *Owari*, where *Oda Nobuo* built a castle in 1584, which he intrusted to *Yamaguchi Shigemasa ;* the latter was besieged there in vain by *Takigawa Kazumasu*.

Ōno, 大野. A small town of *Echizen* (9,600 inh.) ; was successively the residence of the *daimyō Oda* (1592), *Matsudaira* (1600), and *Doi* (1682-1868) (40,000 k.).

Ono Azumabito, 小野東人　　Was involved in the revolt of *Fuji-wara Hirotsugu* in *Tsukushi* (740), and exiled to *Mishima* (*Izu*). Pardoned 5 years later, he was appointed *Jibu-Shōsuke* and *Bizen no kami;* but was put to death for having shared in the conspiracy of *Tachibana Naramaro* (757).

Ōno Azumabito, 大野東人 (+ 742). Accompanied the expedition of *Fujiwara Umakai* against the *Ebisu* of *Mutsu* (724) and the next year built the castle of *Taga*. He was afterwards appointed *Chinjufu-shōgun* and *Azechi*. He quelled in 740 the revolt of the *Dazai-Daini Fujiwara Hirotsugu*. The latter was defeated and killed.

Ono Harukaze, 小野春風 (+ 899)　　Was appointed *Chinjufu-shōgun* in 878 and quelled a revolt of the *Ebisu* in *Dewa*.

Ōno Harunaga, 大野治長 (+ 1615). Served *Hideyoshi* and was *Shuri-tayū*. Having become an object of suspicion to *Ieyasu*, he was exiled to *Yūki* (*Shimōsa*) in 1599. The following year, he fought under the banner of *Fukushima Masanori*. He withdrew afterwards to *Ōsaka*, became the councillor of *Yodo-gimi*, encouraged her hos-

ONO HARUKAZE.

tility against *Ieyasu* and perished in the conflagration of the *Ōsaka* castle.

Ono Imoko, 小野妹子.　Was the first ambassador sent from Japan to China (*Zui*) in 607 and 608.

Ono Komachi, 小野小町 (834-900).　Daughter of *Yoshisada*, was believed to have been descended from *Ono Takamura*. She was renowned for her beauty, talents and misfortunes. She excelled in poetry and has been classed among the *Rokkasen*.

Ono Michikaze, 小野道風 (896-966).　Often called *Tōfū* (Chinese reading of *Michikaze*). Son of *Dazai-daini Kadotsuru*, excelled in pen-manship. The emperor *Daigo* made him write an inscription on the frontispiece of the *Daigo-ji* temple, which he was building. He also ordered from him two volumes of cursive (*sōsho*) and half cursive writing (*gyōsho*) and sent them to China (*Tō*) by the bonze *Kwanken*, to have them admired there (926). Towards the end of his life, he was subject to palsy, yet with his trembling hand, he continued to trace characters, some-what strange in form, which were nevertheless much admired. *Michikaze, Fujiwara Sari* and *Fujiwara Yukinari* are looked upon as the 3 masters in calligraphy (*san-seki*).

ONO MICHIKATA.

Ono Takamura, 小野篁 (802-852).　Son of *Sangi Kimmori*, followed his father when the latter was appointed governor of *Mutsu* and became expert in all the arts of war. He was reprimanded for his ignorance by the emperor *Saga*, and at once began his studies, in which he persevered to the end. He was appointed successively *Dai-naiki* (828), *Dazai-shōni* (832), then vice-ambassador to China (836). Delayed by a typhoon, he feigned illness to be relieved of his mission the following year. He wrote a poem against those traditional embassies, for which reason he was exiled to the *Oki* islands by the ex-emperor *Saga* (838), but pardoned two years later. In 847, he was raised to the rank of *Sangi*, and later on to that of *Danjō-Ōsuke* and *Sadaiben*. *Takamura* was considered one of the best writers of his time.

Ōno Yasumaro, 大安萬呂 (+ 723). Descendant of *Kamu-yai-mimi no mikoto*, 2nd son of *Jimmu-tennō*, cultivated literature and was commissioned, in 711, to write down from the reports of *Hieda no Are* the old traditions of the country; this work was published the following year in 3 volumes. It is the *Koji-ki*. In 716, *Yasumaro* was appointed *Mimbu-kyō*.

Ono Yoshifuru, 小野好古 (888-968). Was an elder brother to *Michikaze*. During the revolt of *Fujiwara Sumitomo* (939), he placed himself at the head of 200 war junks, and fought the rebel in *Iyo*; he pursued him to *Tsukushi*, defeated him at *Hakata* (*Chikuzen*) and made him prisoner. *Yoshifuru* was later on appointed *Sangi* (948).

Onodera, 小野寺. A family of *daimyō* who in the 15th and 16th centuries, possessed the district of *Semboku* (*Dewa*); they were dispossessed in 1600.

Ōno-gawa, 大野川. A river in *Bungo* (134 Km.); also called *Shirataki-gawa*, *Funaoka-gawa*.

Onoki Shigekatsu, 小野木重勝 (+1600). At first *samurai* from *Tamba*, received after the ruin of the *Hatano* (1579) the castle of *Fukuchiyama* (*Tamba* — 18,000 k.) After the death of *Nobunaga*, he served *Hideyoshi*, accompanied him in his expedition to *Kyūshū* (1587) and had his possessions doubled. In 1600, he sided against *Ieyasu*, asked pardon through the medium of *Ii Naomasa*, but was nevertheless invited to take his life by *harakiri* in the temple of *Jōdo-ji* at *Kameyama* (*Tamba*). — His wife, daughter of *Saionji Kintomo* was a Christian, and had been baptized in 1583 by the name of *Joanna*.

Onokoro-jima, 碬馭盧嶋. Island on which the creative deities, *Izanagi* and *Izanami*, alighted when they came down from heaven; there they built a dwelling for themselves which they called *Yahiro-dono*. — Quite a number of small islands around *Awaji* contend for the honor of having possessed this divine couple.

Onomichi, 尾道. A town of *Hiroshima-ken*, capital of *Bingo* province; seaport in the Inland Sea (22,300 inh.).

Ontake, 御嶽. A mountain on the borders of *Shinano* and *Hida*. Also called *Mitake*; — it is considered one of the holiest spots in Japan (3185 m.).

Ontake-kyō, 御嶽教. One of the 10 sects of modern Shintoism.

Ontaku-bugyō, 恩澤奉行. Under the *Tokugawa Shōgun*, an official commissioned to discuss merits, to fix rewards and to distribute domains. He was also called *Kunkō-bugyō*. This title was created in 1235 and given first to *Gotō Mototsuna*. — Under the *Ashikaga*, the office was preserved but the title changed to *Onshō-bugyō*.

Ōnuma, 大 沼 . A family of *samurai* from *Kurobane* (*Shimotsuke*), ennobled after the Restoration. — To-day Baron.

On-yō-ryō, 陰 陽 寮 . One of the 7 offices (*ryō*), depending on the *Nakatsukasa-shō*. It was intrusted with matters relating to astronomy, the calendar, omens, etc. In the reign of *Murakami* (947-967), *Kamo Yasunori* was appointed both *On-yō no kami* and *Temmon-hakase ;* but when he had initiated *Abe Seimei* in the study of astronomy, the two branches were separated and the *On-yō* was limited to divination.

Ō-oka, 大 岡 . A family of *daimyō*, originating in *Mikawa*, and descended from *Fujiwara* (*Kujō*) *Norizane* (1210-1235).

Tadamasa	Tadayo -Tadazane -Tadasuke-Tadayoshi	(a)
	Tadayoshi-Tadafusa -Tadanori -Tadatoshi	(b)

(*a*) — Elder branch — **Tadasuke,** 忠 相 (1677-1751). *Samurai* of the *Bafuku*, became successively *Yamada-bugyō* (1712), *Fushin-bugyō*, *Machi-bugyō* (1717), *Echizen no kami*, *Jisha-bugyō* (1736). At last, in 1748, he was raised to the rank of *daimyō* and received the little fief of *Nishi-Ōhira* (*Mikawa* — 10,000 k.). — *Tadasuke* has left the reputation of a remarkable administrator and a shrewd lawyer. A whole volume (*Ō-oka meiyo-seidan*), has been written about the judgments both striking and ingenious which he rendered during his administration. To him also is due the organization of the *Edo* corps of firemen. — His descendants resided until the Restoration at *Nishi-Ōhira*. — Now Viscount.

(*b*) — Younger branch, ennobled in 1751 in the person of *Tadamitsu* 忠 光 (1709-60) ; resided from 1756 to 1868 at *Iwatsuki* (*Musashi* — 23,000 k.). — To-day Viscount.

Ō-oku, 大 奥 . Apartments reserved for the ladies, in the Shogunal palace of *Edo*, which not even the *sobashū* nor the *koshōshū* were allowed to enter.

Ō-omi, 大 臣 . In olden times, a minister who shared the administration with the *Ō-muraji*. *Takeshiuchi no Sukune* was the first to receive that title (133).

Ōryōshi, 押 領 使 . A title created in 878, at the time of a revolt of the *Ebisu* in *Dewa*, and given to *Minabuchi Akisato*, commissioned to put down brigands, to render justice, etc. In 940, the title and functions of *Ōryōshi* were assigned to the governors of the provinces of *Shimōsa*, *Shimotsuke*, *Izumo*, *Awaji*, *Mutsu* and *Dewa*.

Osa, 日 佐 . In ancient times, interpreters of the Chinese and Korean languages. In the reign of *Kimmei* (540-571), a descendant of *Takeshiuchi no Sukune* brought from *Kudara* (Korea) 35 literati, to whom the emperor gave the family name of *Metsura-Omi*. They settled in the provinces of *Yamato* and *Ōmi* and performed the offices of *Osa*.

Ōsaka, 大 坂 . Capital of *Settsu* province and of *Ōsaka-fu* (1,100,000 inh.). The site occupied by the present city was in ancient times called *Naniwa no tsu* It was the Imperial residence during the reigns of *Nintoku* (313-342), *Kōtoku* (645-654), and *Shōmu* (744-748) ; it continued to be an important entrepot for goods shipped on junks to *Kyōto*. In 1532, the *Hongwan-ji* bonzes built a castle (*Ishiyama-jō*) there in which they erected their temple, and it was only after a pro- tracted siege of 10 years that *Nobunaga* succeeded in taking possession of it (1580). In 1583, *Hideyoshi* chose the city for his residence and built an immense castle, near which the greatest families also had an abode ; to this *Ōsaka* owes its prosperity. The siege of 1615 destroyed a great part of the buildings, but the fortifications remained. The *Toku- gawa* stationed there a *jōdai* and a *machi-bugyō*, and the city continued to prosper. It is now the greatest commercial centre in Japan.

Ōsaka-fu, 大坂府 . A department formed of the provinces *Kawachi*, *Izumi* and 4 districts of *Settsu*. — Pop. : 1.433,000. — Capital : *Ōsaka* (1,100,000 inh.). — Pr. town : *Sakai* (49,900 inh.).

Ōsaka-jō, 大坂城 . The *Ōsaka* castle built by *Hideyoshi* (1583- 1587) on the site of the *Hongwan-ji* temple, (*Ishiyama*) to be his official residence, (*Fushimi*, *Jūraku*, etc. being only temporary dwellings). The civil war of 1615 demolished a great part of it. *Ieyasu* gave it to his grandson *Matsudaira* (*Okudaira*) *Tadaakira ;* but in 1619, it became the property of the *Shōgun*, who intrusted it to a *jōdai*. Parts of the con- structions were then rebuilt but the battle of 1868 reduced all to ruins.

Ōsaka-jō-ban, 大坂城番 . A title created in 1619 and given to the two officers commissioned to guard the castle of *Ōsaka*. They resided there habitually and repaired to *Edo* every 5 or 6 years.

Ōsaka-jōdai, 大坂城代 . Representative of the *Shōgun* in the castle of *Ōsaka*. The first who filled this charge was *Naitō Masanobu* (1619). He was commissioned to maintain the fortifications in good condition, to settle lawsuits among the inhabitants of the city and the neighboring villages, to control the acts of the *machi-bugyō*, etc. It was one of the highest functions of the shogunate and was generally assigned to the *Sōsha-ban* or the *Jisha-bugyō* and at the end of his term, the *jōdai* be- came *Kyōto-shoshidai* or *Rōjū*. For some years (1652-1662) there existed at the same time 6 titulars who served in turns, but after 1662 the custom prevailed of appointing a single titular. The *Ōsaka-jōdai*, besides the revenues of his territory, received every year 10,000 k.

Ōsaka-machi-bugyō, 大坂町奉行 . A title created in 1617, and assigned to two officials commissioned to administer, in the name of the *Shōgun*, the city of *Ōsaka* and its environs. One was posted in the east of the city, the other in the west.

Ōsaka-metsuke, 大坂目附 . A title created in 1662, and assigned to two officials intrusted with the police of the city of *Ōsaka* and its environs. One was taken from among the *Tsukaiban*, the other, from the *Ryōban*. They were called at first *Kamiyata-metsuke*, then *Ōsaka- metsuke*. Their term of service was only one year, during which time they had to spend 10 days in the *Nijō* castle (*Kyōto*).

Ōsaka no seki, 逢坂關 . A barrier formerly established in *Ōmi*, near the present city of *Ōtsu*.

Ōsaka-wan, 大坂灣 . The gulf of *Ōsaka*, also called *Izumi-nada*.

Ōsaka-yama, 大坂山 . A mountain between *Yamato* and *Kawachi* ; also called *Nijō ga mine*, *Futago-yama*. A barrier (*seki*) was set up there in 796.

Ōsaka-zaiban, 大坂在番 . A title created in 1619, and assigned to two officials intrusted with the keys of the castle of *Ōsaka*, with the superintendence of the city temples and environs, etc. Chosen from among the *Ōbangumi* of *Edo*, they interchanged in the 8th month of every year.

Ōsaki-kami-shima, 大崎上嶋 . An island of the Inland Sea, south-east of the province of *Aki*, to which it belongs (48 Km. in circ.)

Ōsaki-shimo-shima, 大崎下嶋 . Island of the Inland Sea, S. E. of the province of *Aki*, to which it belongs (22 Km. in circ.).

Osamuru-tsukasa, 治部省 . An ancient name of the *Jibu-shō*.

Osaragi Sadanao, 大佛貞直 (+ 1333). Son of *Muneyasu* and descendant of *Hōjō Tokifusa*. When *Go Daigo* sought refuge on Mt. *Kasagi*, he was ordered to join *Ashikaga Takauji* and pursue the emperor ; he besieged the *Kusunoki* in their castle of *Akasaka* (*Kawachi*). Later on, he tried to check the advance of *Nitta Yoshisada* on *Kamakura*, but was defeated by *Ōtate Muneuji*, then by *Wakiya Yoshisuke* and slain in the engagement. He is also called *Daibutsu Sadanao*.

Ōseki, 大關 . A family of *daimyō* descended from *Tajihi Shima* (624-701) and through him, from the emperor *Senkwa*. From 1542 to 1868, they resided at *Kurobane* (*Shimotsuke* — 18,000 k.). — Now Viscount.

Ōseko, 大迫 . A family of *samurai* from the *Kagoshima* clan (*Satsuma*), ennobled after the Restoration. — Now Viscount

Oshi, 忍 . A small town (7,600 inh.) of *Musashi* ; ancient castle belonging to the *Narita* family, vassal of the *Hōjō* of *Odawara*, dispossessed in 1590. *Ieyasu* installed his son *Tadayoshi* there (1590-1600) ; it became afterwards the residence of the *daimyō Ōkōchi* (1633), *Abe* (1639-47) ; then, from 1823 to 1868, of the *Matsudaira* (*Okudaira*) (100,000 k.).

Oshima, 渡嶋 One of the 11 provinces of *Hōkkaidō* comprises 7 districts. — Capital : *Hakodate* (85,000 inh.).

Ōshima, 大嶋 . In *Shinano* ; ancient castle built in 1571 by *Takeda Shingen*, captured by *Oda Nobutada* in 1582, and abandoned shortly afterwards.

Ōshima, 大嶋 . A family of *samurai* from the *Yamaguchi* clan (*Suwō*), ennobled after the Restoration. — Now Baron.

Ōshima, 大嶋 . A family of *samurai* from the *Akita* clan (*Dewa*), ennobled after the Restoration. — Now Baron.

Ō-shima, 大嶋 . The largest of the 7 isles of *Izu* (42 Km. in circ.), called by the Europeans " *Vries* Island." It has an active volcano, the *Mihara* (800 m.) ; was for several centuries a place of banishment. *Minamoto Tametomo* was exiled there in 1156.

Ō-shima, 大嶋 . An island S. of the *Kii* peninsula (17 Km., in circ.)

Ō-shima, 大嶋. An island N. of *Chikuzen* (13 Km., in circ.)

Ō-shima, 大嶋. An island E. of *Chikugo* (8 Km., in circ.)

Ō-shima, 大嶋. An island N. of *Hirado* (*Hizen*) (27 Km., in circ.)

Ō-shima, 大嶋. An island W. of *Hizen* (33 Km., in circ.)

Ō-shima, 大嶋. An island S. E. of *Hyūga* (12 Km., in circ.)

Ō-shima, 大嶋. An island of the northern group of the *Ryūkyū* archipelago, (290 Km. in circ.). It belongs to *Osumi* province and *Kagoshima-ken*. Also called *Shō-Ryūkyū-shima, Amami-shima*.

Ō-shima, 大嶋. An island W. of *Ōshima* province (*Hōkkaidō*) (17 Km., in circ.).

Ō-shima-guntō, 大嶋群島. Northern group of the *Ryūkyū* archipelago, depending on *Osumi* province. The principal islands, going south, are: *Ō-shima, Kakeroma-jima, Toku no shima, Oki no shima, Erabu-jima*, etc.

Oshinokōji, 押小路. A family of *kuge*, descended from *Fujiwara* (*Sanjō*) *Sanefusa* (1146-1224). — Now Viscount.

Ōshio Heihachirō, 大鹽平八郎 (1792-1837). An officer (*yoriki*) of the *Ōsaka* police. In 1827, he arrested some Christians between *Ōsaka* and *Kyōto*. He was remarkable for his skill in discovering evil doers. In 1837, the rice crop being very bad, *Heihachirō* advised the *Machi-bugyō* to open the reserve stores to relieve the distressed people, but his counsel was not followed. Offended at this, he sold all his books and distributed the proceeds to the needy, whom he called and assembled from the neighboring provinces. Thereupon he endeavored to seize the castle, but was repulsed and forced to hide on Mt. *Yoshino ;* shortly after, he returned to *Ōsaka* and on being discovered, committed suicide. *Heihachirō* was a distinguished Confucianist, disciple of *Nakae Tōju* and propagator of the doctrines of *Ōyōmei*. He is also called *Chūsai*.

Ōshio-yama, 小鹽山. A hill north of *Kyōto*, where, in 1333, *Akamatsu Enshin* defeated the army of the *Hōjō*.—Also called *Ōhara-yama*.

Ōshū, 奥州. The Chinese name of the former province of *Mutsu*, which comprises at present *Iwaki, Iwashiro, Rikuzen, Rikuchū* and *Rikuoku*.

Ōshū-kaidō, 奥州街道. An old highway which connected the northern provinces with *Edo*. It was 750 Km. long, and had 87 stages (*eki*), between *Edo* and *Aomori*.

Ōshukubai, 鶯宿梅 (Lit.: The plum-tree with the nightingale's nest). In the reign of *Murakami* (947-967), a plum-tree near the *Seiryō-den* having withered, the emperor intended to replace it with a magnificent tree from the garden of *Ki no Tsurayuki's* daughter ; now it happened that a nightingale had made its nest in the tree, and the owner answered the request of the Emperor with this poem : " Respectfully do I receive the Imperial order ; but if the nightingale should come and ask me where his nest is, what shall I answer him ? " The emperor did not insist.

Ōshū-santō shichi-ke, 奥州山東七家 (Lit.: the 7 families E. of the *Ōshū* mountains). The 7 families, which in the Middle Ages, possessed the south-eastern part of *Mutsu : Yūki, Tamura, Nikaidō Nihom-matsu, Iwaki, Ōuchi* and *Ishikawa.*

Ōshū-sōbugyō, 奥 州 總 奉 行. After having defeated *Fujiwara Yasuhira,* governor of *Ōshū* (1189), *Yoritomo* invested *Kasai Kiyoshige* and *Izawa-Iekage,* with the title of *sōbugyō,* empowered them to render justice, etc. and the dignity was transmitted in these two families till the end of the *Kamakura* shōgunate (1333).

Ōsu, 大 洲. A town in *Iyo ;* ancient castle built in the 14th century, by the *Utsunomiya,* vassals of the *Kōno.* In 1569, *Toyotsuna* asked for the help of the *Chōsokabe* of *Tosa* and attempted to form an independent fief for himself, but he was defeated by *Kōno Michinao ;* his son *Naoyuki* succeeded in recapturing the castle of *Ōsu* and kept it until 1585. After that, the castle passed into the hands of the *daimyō Toda* (1585), *Tōdō* (1600), *Wakizaka* (1608), and finally of the *Katō* (1617-1868) (60,000 k.).

Ō-suke, 大 介. A title created in 935 by the emperor *Shujaku* and equivalent to sub-governor of a province. The governor (*kami*) resided at *Kyōto* and had himself replaced by an *Ō-suke,* who was generally chosen from among the *kuge.* This title was abolished by *Yoritomo.*

Ōsumi, 大 隅. One of the 11 provinces of the *Saikaidō.* Comprises 5 districts, which depend on *Kagoshima-ken.* — Chinese name : *Gūshū.* — It was separated from *Hyūga* in 713.

Ōsumi no hana, 大 隅 鼻. A cape north of *Iyo.*

Ōta, 太 田. In *Hitachi ;* ancient castle built in 802, by *Sakanoe Tamuramaro* to check the incursions of the *Ebisu. Fujiwara Michichika,* descendant of *Hidesato,* rebuilt it in 990 and received the title of *Ōta-tayū.* In the following century, it was captured by *Satake Takayoshi* and occupied by his descendants until 1602, when *Ieyasu* installed *Matsudaira Yasunaga* there. In 1707, the *daimyō* of *Mito* intrusted its guard to the *Nakayama* family, and it was definitively abandoned in 1803.

Ōta, 太 田. A family of *daimyō,* descended from *Minamoto Yorimasa (Seiwa-Genji).*

—— **Sukekuni,** 資 國. Descendant of *Yorimasa* in the 5th generation, settled down at *Ōta (Tamba)* and took that name.

—— **Sukekiyo,** 資 清 (1411-1493). Served *Uesugi (Ōgigayatsu) Mochitomo* and became his minister (*shitsuji*). Defeated by *Ashikaga Shigeuji* in 1451 and in 1454, he shaved his head and took the name of *Dōshin.*

—— **Sukenaga,** 資 長 (1432-1486). Eldest son of the above, succeeded his father in 1455. The next year, he built a castle at *Edo* and in 1458 shaved his head and took the name of *Dōkwan,* 道 灌 by which he is chiefly known. In 1464, he repaired to *Kyōto,* where he was received by the emperor *Go-Tsuchi-mikado* and by the *Shōgun Yoshimasa.* At that time, *Nagao Kageharu* was preparing to revolt against his suzerain *Uesugi Akisada :* after having tried in vain to deter him from his purpose, *Dōkwan* informed *Akisada* and *Kageharu* was defeated.

When war broke out between the two *Yamanouchi* and *Ōgigayatsu* branches of the *Uesugi*, *Dōkwan* sided with the former, and was assassinated by order of *Sadamasa*, the head of the latter branch.

—— **Suketaka, 資高**. Grandson of *Sukenaga*, served *Hōjō Ujitsuna*, and resided at the castle of *Iwabuchi* (*Musashi*).

—— **Yasusuke, 康資**. Son of *Suketaka*, served *Hōjō Ujiyasu*. He defeated the lord of *Oda* (*Hitachi*), who had revolted against the *Hōjō*. In 1563 he himself attempted to become independent, and with the help of *Satomi Yoshihiro*, tried to seize the *Edo* castle, but he was beaten by *Ujiyasu* at *Kōnodai* (*Shimōsa*). A daughter of *Yasusuke* was married to *Ieyasu* (See *O Kachi no kata*).

—— **Sukemune, 資宗**. Grandson of *Yasusuke*, received in 1638 the fief of *Nishio* (*Mikawa*), then, in 1645, that of *Hamamatsu* (*Tōtomi* — 35,000 k.). — His descendants resided successively at *Tanaka* (*Suruga*) 1687-1703 ; at *Tanakura* (*Mutsu*) (1703-1728) ; at *Tatebayashi* (*Kōzuke*) (1728-1746) ; and at *Kakegawa* (*Tōtomi*) 1746-1868 (53,000 k.). — Now Viscount.

Ota Kinjō, 大田錦城 (1765-1825). Born at *Daishōji* (*Kaga*), followed the lessons of *Minagawa Kien* at *Kyōto*, and at *Edo* those of *Yamamoto Hokuzan ;* but not satisfied with their teachings, he himself opened a school of Confucianism which he transported later on to *Kanazawa* (*Kaga*). He left many writings.

Ōta Nampo, 太田南畝 (1749-1823). A *samurai* of the *Bakufu*, who distinguished himself in literature and poetry.

Ōta-gawa, 太田川. A river in *Tōtomi* (63 Km.)

Ōta-gawa, 太田川. A river in *Kii ;* also called *Iro-gawa* in its upper course (86 Km.).

Ōta-gawa, 太田川. A river in *Aki* (81 Km.). Above *Hiroshima*, it branches out and forms the *Kyōbashi-gawa*, the *Motoyasu-gawa*, the *Nekoya-gawa*, the *Temmon-gawa*, which flow through the city. It is also called *Kabe-gawa*, *Yaki-gawa*, etc.

Ōta-gawa, 太田川. Another name of the *Kiso-gawa*.

Otagi, 愛宕. A family of *kuge*, descended from *Minamoto Morofusa* (*Murakami-Genji*). — Now Viscount.

Ōtaka, 太高. In *Owari ;* an ancient castle, belonging to the *Oda daimyō*. In 1558, it was intrusted to *Yamaguchi Sama no Suke*, who handed it over to *Imagawa Yoshimoto*. The latter confided it to *Tokugawa Ieyasu*, who, on the death of *Yoshimoto* (1560), returned to *Mikawa*.

Ōtaki, 大多喜. In *Kazusa ;* ancient castle built in 1240. At the end of the *Ashikaga* era, it belonged to a *Masaki* family, also called *Nekoya*. In 1590, *Ieyasu* installed *Honda Tadakatsu* there. It became the residence of the *daimyō Abe* (1652), *Inagaki* (1702), and *Matsudaira* (*Ōkōchi*) 1703-1868. (20,000 k.).

Ōtani, 大谷 . A family descended from the *Fujiwara*, which, from the time of *Shinran-Shōnin*, was at the head of the *Hongwan-ji* branch of the *Shin-shū* sect. At the end of the 16th century, they formed the two branches :—

$$\text{Kōkyō-Kōsa}\begin{cases}\text{Kōshō} & \text{(a)} \\ \text{Kōju} & \text{(b)}\end{cases}$$

(*a*) — Elder branch, who remained at the head of the *Nishi Hongwan-ji* temple (*Kyōto*) and of the sect of the same name — Now Count.

(*b*) — Younger branch, at the head of *Higashi Hongwan-ji* temple (*Kyōto*) and of the *Ōtani* branch of *Shin-shū* sect. — Now Count.

Ōtani-ha, 大谷派 . Branch of the *Jōdo-shinshū* sect, founded in 601 by the bonze *Kōju*. Also called *Higashi Hongwan-ji*.

Ōtani Yoshitaka, 大谷吉隆 (1559-1600). Born in *Bungo*. At the age of 15, he offered his services to *Hideyoshi*, who resided then at the castle of *Himeji* (*Harima*); received in 1582 the fief of *Tsuruga* (*Echizen* — 50,000 k.), and the title of *Gyōbu-Shōsuke*. In 1600, he sided at first with *Ieyasu* and leaving *Tsuruga* with his *samurai*, made ready to join him in his campaign against *Uesugi Kagekatsu*, but at *Sawayama* (*Ōmi*), he met *Ishida Kazushige*, who succeeded in winning him over to his party. He perished at *Sekigahara*.

Otaru, 小樽 . Port and capital of the province of *Shiribeshi* (*Hokkaidō*) (57,000 inh.).

Ōtate, 大館 In *Ugo* ; ancient castle which towards the middle of the 16th century, was occupied by the *Asari* family ; it passed into the hands of the *Akita* and the *Satake* (1602).

Ōtate, 大館 . A family of *daimyō*, descended from *Minamoto Yoshikane* (*Seiwa-Genji*) and connected with the *Nitta*.

$$\text{Yoshikane-Yoshifusa-Masayoshi}\begin{cases}\text{Masauji-Motouji-Tomouji-Yoshisada} & (\textit{Nitta}) \\ \text{Ieuji} \quad\text{-Muneuji-Ujiaki -Ujikiyo} & (\textit{Ōtate})\end{cases}$$

———**Ieuji, 家氏** . Was the first to take the name of *Ōtate*, his elder brother keeping that of *Nitta*.

———**Muneuji, 宗氏** . Fought under *Nitta Yoshisada* and entered *Kamakura* with him (1333).

———**Ujiaki, 氏明** (+ 1341). Fought under *Kitabatake Akiie* for the southern dynasty, defeated *Akamatsu Norimura*, at *Muroyama* and was appointed governor of *Iyo*. He joined forces with *Wakiya Yoshisuke* to conquer the province ; but on the death of *Yoshisuke* (1340), *Ujiaki* was besieged in the castle of *Seta* and committed suicide.

———**Ujikiyo, 氏清** (1337-1412). Fought under *Kitabatake Akiyoshi* and captured the castle of *Sekioka* (*Iga*) (1361). In 1373, he defeated *Nikki Yoshinaga* and received the title of *Iga no kami*. Later on he changed his name to that of *Sekioka*.

Ōtawara, 太田原 . In *Shimotsuke*. At first a part of the domains of the *Nasu daimyō* ; a vassal by the name of *Ōtawara* built a castle there in the 16th century, in which his descendants resided until 1868 (12,000 k.).

Ōtawara, 太田原. A family of *daimyō*, originating in *Shimotsuke* and descended from the emperor *Heijō-tennō*. At first vassals of the *Nasu daimyō*, they became independent in consequence of the civil wars of the 16th century, and built the castle of *Ōtawara* (*Shimotsuke*).

—— **Harukiyo, 晴清** (1567-1631). Was raised by *Ieyasu* to the rank of *daimyō* in 1602. — His descendants continued to reside at *Ōtawara*, until the Restoration. (12,000. k.). — Now Viscount.

Ōtera, 大寺. A family of *samurai* from the *Kagoshima* clan (*Satsuma*), ennobled in 1895. — To-day Baron.

—— **Yasuzumi, 安純** (+ 1895). Served in the expedition against Formosa (1874) and in the *Satsuma* war (1877). He was promoted to Brigadier general at the beginning of the war with China, and was killed at the siege of *Wei-hai-wei*.

Otodo, 大殿 (Contr. of *Ōtono*). A general term meaning a superior, a person of high rank, was applied especially to ministers.

Otokodate, 男達. Under the *Tokugawa*, associations of *samurai*, who made public profession of opposing the strong and helping the weak, even at the risk of their lives, but indulged in all sorts of excesses. They formed several gangs, *Jingi-gumi*, *Shiratsuka-gumi*, *Sekirei-gumi*, etc. At last they were suppressed by the *Shōgun Tsunayoshi*. Among their leaders, *Mizuno Jūrōzaemon*, *Banzui-in Chōbei*, *Karainu Gombei*, and others have remained famous.

Otoko-yama, 男山. A hill, 20 Km. south of *Kyōto*. On its summit stands the famous temple of *Iwashimizu-Hachiman-gū*, founded in 859. *Hachiman* being the tutelary divinity (*uji-gami*) of the *Minamoto*, his temple was always held by them in great veneration. There *Yoshiie* performed *gembuku* and received the name of *Hachiman Tarō* (1048); even emperors repaired thither in pilgrimage. During the civil wars of the 14th century, the southern army established its camp on *Otokoyama*. — It is also called *Yawata-yama*, *Obana-yama*, *Hato no mine*, *Kōro-zan*.

Ōtoku, 應德. *Nengō :* 1084-1086.

Ōtomo, 大伴. An ancient family, descended from *Michi-omi no mikoto*, companion in arms of *Jimmu-tennō*.

Kanamura-Sadehiko-Kuhi ⎰ Fukehi -Kojihi- -Otomaro -Katsuo ⎱ Makuta -Michitaru-Hahamaro

—— **Kanamura, 金村.** Son of *Katari*, descended in the 10th generation from *Michi-omi*. On the death of the emperor *Ninken* (498), *Heguri Matori* raised troubles regarding the imperial succession. *Kanamura* defeated and killed him, and was then appointed *Ō-muraji* by the emperor *Buretsu*. The latter having died without issue, *Kanamura* placed prince *Ōhodo* (*Keitai*), descendant of *Ōjin-tennō*, on the throne. He continued to be minister during the 4 next reigns.

—— **Sadehiko, 狹手彦.** Headed an expedition against *Shiragi* with his brother *Iwa*. The legend says that his wife *Matsu-ura no Sayo-hime*, unable to take her eyes off the ship that sailed with her husband, remained so long motionless on the beach, that she turned int a stone (*bōfu-seki*). The brothers pacified the *San-kan*, upon which, *Iwa* was appointed governor of *Tsukushi*, *Sadehiko* remaining in Korea. In 562, he was appointed *Tai-shōgun*, defeated the army of *Koma* and returned to Japan laden with rich spoils.

—— **Kuhi**, 咋. Fought under *Soga Umako* against *Mononobe Moriya* (587), then headed expeditions to Korea in 590 and 601.

—— **Fukehi**, 吹負. Supported *Temmu* in his struggle against the emperor *Kōbun* (672), and defeated the Imperial army in *Ōmi*.

—— **Kojihi**, 古慈斐 (695-777). Was ambassador to China in 752.

—— **Otomaro**, 弟麿 (731-809). Was sent to *Mutsu* against the *Ebisu* (791) and defeated them with the aid of *Sakanoe Tamuramaro*. He afterwards became preceptor of the Imperial Prince.

—— **Katsuo**, 勝雄 (776-831). Was governor of *Mutsu* and *Azechi*.

—— **Tabito**, 旅人 (665-731). Son of *Yasumaro*, governed the provinces of *Yamashiro* and *Settsu* and quelled a revolt of the *Hayato* in *Ōsumi* (720). He also became famous in poetry.

—— **Surugamaro**, 駿河麿 (+ 763). Shared in the revolt of *Tachibana Naramaro* and was exiled (757). Recalled shortly after, he was appointed *Azechi*, *Chinjufu-Shōgun* and defeated the *Ebisu*.

—— **Yakamochi**, 家持 (+ 785). Son of *Tabito*, was *Shōgun* in *Mutsu*. Shortly after his death, his relative *Tsugihito* killed *Fujiwara Tanetsugu* by order of prince *Sawara-shinnō*, and was arrested. He then declared that he had acted in obedience to *Yakamochi*; whereupon the latter, although dead, was declared to have forfeited all his titles and dignities, and his son *Nagate* was banished to the *Oki* islands. *Tsugihito* was exiled to *Sado*.

Ōtomo, 大友. A family of *daimyō*, descended from *Fujiwara Nagaie* (1005-1064).

—— **Yoshinao**, 能直. Descendant of *Fujiwara Hidesato*, was adopted by *Nakahara Chikayoshi*, and was the first to take the name *Ōtomo*. He served *Yoritomo* in his campaign against *Fujiwara Yasuhira* in *Mutsu* (1189). In 1193, he was appointed *Shugo-shoku* of *Buzen* and *Bungo*, and *Chinzei-bugyō*; thenceforth his family acquired great influence in *Kyūshū*.

—— **Sadamune**, 貞宗. Descendant of *Yoshinao* in the 5th generation, sided with the *Ashikaga* and fought against the *Kikuchi* in *Kyūshū*; then, under the orders of *Takauji*, besieged *Kyōto* (1336) and fought against *Nitta Yoshisada*.

—— **Sadanori**, 貞載 (+ 1336). Son of *Sadamune*, was killed while fighting against *Yūki Chikamitsu*. He was the first to take the name of *Tachibana* (which see).

—— **Chikayo**, 親世. Great-grandson of *Sadamune*, fought against the *Kikuchi*, supporters of the southern dynasty, and got possession of the 6 provinces of *Buzen*, *Bungo*, *Chikuzen*, *Chikugo*, *Hizen* and *Higo*. He received in 1396, the title of *Kyūshū-tandai*.

—— **Yoshinori**, 義鑑 (+ 1550) Descendant of *Chikayo* in the 9th generation, fought a long time against *Hoshino Chikatada*, who attempted to become independent in *Chikuzen*. In 1542, on learning that some Europeans had landed at *Tane-ga-shima*, he invited them to his court. Mendez Pinto repaired to *Funai* (*Ōita*) and caused profound stupefaction by showing the use of arquebuses, which were unknown in Japan. *Yoshinori* was assassinated by one of his retainers, *Tsukumi Mimasaka*, because he disregarded the rights of his eldest son *Yoshishige*, and intended to leave his succession to a bastard.

—— **Yoshishige, 義 鎮 (Sōrin)** (1530-1587). Gave hospitality to St. Francis Xavier for two months (1551), and was deeply impressed by the truths of Christianity, although he was to embrace the faith only many years afterwards. In the same year, he triumphed over *Kikuchi Yoshimune* who had revolted in *Higo ;* in 1556, he quelled the troubles caused by the priests of the great temple of *Usa* in *Buzen ;* the next year, he defeated *Akizuki Kiyotane* in *Chikuzen* and took possession of his domains. In 1562, leaving *Funai* to his son *Yoshimune*, yet quite a child, he built a castle for himself at *Niyūshima*, shaved his head and took the name of *Sambisai Sōrin :* it is by this name of *Sōrin* 宗 麟 that he is best known. Shortly afterwards, he invaded *Buzen* and prepared to cross over to *Suwō*, where *Mōri Takamoto* was preparing to resist him, but the *Shōgun Yoshiteru* intervened and made peace : a daughter of *Sōrin* was bethothed to *Terumoto*, son of *Takamoto*. Two years later, another expedition into *Chikugo :* *Akizuki Tanezane* was defeated. In 1569, *Kikkawa Motoharu* and *Kobayakawa Takakage* besieged the castle of *Tachibana* (*Chikuzen*) : *Sōrin* obliged them to raise the siege. In 1578, *Sōrin* was baptized and took the name of *Francis*. The rest of his life was spent in warring against the *Shimazu* of *Satsuma*, allies of the *Ryūzōji* and the *Akizuki*, and finding it impossible to hold out against them, he implored the support of *Hideyoshi* (1586), who led an expedition into *Kyūshū ;* peace was restored, but the *Ōtomo* retained only the province of *Bungo*. *Sōrin* died just when *Hideyoshi* returned to his castle of *Ōsaka*.

—— **Yoshimune, 義 統** (1558-1605). Took the administration of his father's extensive domains in hand in 1579. As early as the following year, he carried war into *Chikuzen*, where *Tawara Chikazane* had revolted. In 1584, he defeated *Ryūzōji Masaie*. After the campaign of *Hideyoshi* against the *Shimazu*, he saw his domains reduced to the single province of *Bungo* (1587). At the time of the Korean war, he set out at the head of 6,000 of his *samurai*, and fought under the orders of *Kuroda Nagamasa*. After some easy successes over the Koreans, the situation became more serious especially when the Japanese found themselves in presence of a strong Chinese army. *Konishi Yukinaga*, besieged in *Heijō* (*Pyong-yang*), asked for assistance from *Yoshimune ;* the latter, frightened by the number of the enemies, retreated in haste towards *Seoul*. *Hideyoshi*, on hearing of this conduct, recalled him to *Aki*, deprived him of his possessions and banished him to *Aki*, domain of *Mōri Terumoto* (1593). In 1600, he sided with *Ishida Kazushige*, returned to *Bungo* and fortified himself in the castle of *Ishitate*, where he was besieged and made prisoner by *Kuroda Yoshitaka*, and exiled to *Hitachi*.

Yoshimune had been baptized in 1587, by the name of *Constantine*, but he was never very strong in the faith.

—— **Yoshinobu, 義延** (+ 1639). Son of *Yoshimune*, baptized in his childhood by the name of *Fulgentius*, served the *Tokugawa* as a simple *samurai* and distinguished himself in the siege of *Ōsaka*.

—— **Yoshitaka, 義孝**. Grandson of *Yoshimune*. At the request of prince *Ninnaji no Miya*, he was raised to the rank of *Kōke* (1689). His descendants kept the title until the Restoration.

Ōtomo Kuronushi, 大友黒主. A famous poet of the 9th century. He is one of the *Rokkasen*.

Ōtomo hasshō, 大友八將. The 8 principal vassal families of the *Ōtomo daimyō* (*Bungo*) in the 16th century : *Tawara*, *Takita*, *Tsurusaki*, *Yoshioka*, *Ibi*, *Yoshihiro*, *Kawakubo* and *Shiroi*.

Ōtomo no Muraji, 大伴連. In ancient times, the chief of the *Ōtomo-be*, intrusted with the guard of the Imperial Palace. He was descended from *Ame-no-oshihi no Mikoto*.

Otomo-shū, 御供衆. In the *Ashikaga* era, the bodyguard of the *Shōgun*. Divided into 4 companies, they served him at table, escorted him when he went out, etc.

Ō-toneri, 大舍人. In ancient times, a soldier of the Imperial bodyguard ; the guard of the princes were called *toneri ;* those of the prince Imperial, *Higashi-no-Miya no toneri :* the number of these as fixed by the *Taihō* Code (1702) was 600. — See *Toneri*.

Ō-toneri-ryō, 大舍人寮. Formerly an office, depending on the *Nakatsukasa-shō*, and intrusted with all that concerned the Imperial guard.

Ōtō no Miya, 大塔宮. — See *Morinaga-shinnō*.

Ōtori, 大鳥. A family ennobled in 1900. — Now Baron.

—— **Keisuke, 圭介**. Born in 1833, high *samurai* of the *Bakufu*, fought to the end for the *Shōgun's* party. When the Imperial army entered *Edo* (April, 1868), he mustered troops in *Kazusa* and *Shimōsa*, but was defeated at *Utsunomiya* and at *Nikkō*, and rejoined *Enomoto* at *Hakodate*. After the surrender of that town (June, 1869), he was condemned to prison. Pardoned two years later, he entered the administration of *Hokkaidō*, became director of the Nobles' School, Minister to Korea (1894), and member of the Privy Council.

Oto-Tachibana hime, 弟橘媛. Wife of *Yamatotakeru no Mikoto*. When the latter, on his way to fight the *Ebisu* (110), was crossing the

OTO-TACHIBANA HIME.

bay between *Sagami* and *Kazusa*, he allowed himself to make some disparaging remarks about the sea-god, who, to revenge himself, raised a violent storm. Seeing the boats on the point of sinking, *Tachibana hime*, to appease the wrath of the god and save her husband, offered herself as a victim and leaped into the waves. On his way back, *Yamato-takeru*, beholding from the top of the *Usui-tōge* (*Kōzuke*), the plain which stretches out to the sea, and remembering the self-devotion of his wife exclaimed: "*Azuma wa ya!*" (Oh! my wife!). Hence the name of *Azuma* given to the eastern provinces of *Hondo*.

Ōtsu, 大津. Capital of *Shiga-ken* and of *Ōmi* province. (34,300 inh.). — Was the Imperial residence from 667 to 673 ; scene of a battle between the *Shōgun Yoshitane* and *Rokkaku Takayori* (1492). In 1582, *Akechi Mitsumasa*, a relative of *Mitsuhide*, was defeated there by *Hori Hidemasa*. Shortly afterwards, the castle of *Sakamoto* was rebuilt at *Ōtsu* and, in 1590, given to *Kyōgoku Takatsugu*, who sided with *Ieyasu* and was besieged by the army of *Mōri Terumoto* (1600). *Takatsugu* having been transferred to *Obama* (*Wakasa*), the castle of *Ōtsu* became the property of the *Shōgun* and was guarded by a *Bugyō*.

Ōtsuki, 大槻. A family of learned men from *Sendai ;* the most famous were : *Bansui* (1757-1827) ; *Banri* (1787-1838) ; *Bankei* (1801-1878), *Shuji*, *Fumihiko*.

Otsuki-yama, 御月山. A mountain between *Kōzuke* and *Echigo* (2,100 m.).

Ōtsu no Ōji, 大津皇子 (663-686). Son of the emperor *Temmu*. Following the counsel of the bonze *Gyōshin*, he endeavored to have himself crowned emperor on the death of his father, but was arrested and put to death.

Otsuso-bugyō, 越訴奉行. In the *Kamakura* and the *Kyōto* periods, officials commissioned to revise law-suits and judgments that had been appealed. The title was created in 1264.

Ō-u, 奥羽. The former provinces of *Mutsu* (*Ō-shū*) and *Dewa* (*U-shū*), comprising the whole northern part of *Hondo*.

Ōuchi, 大内. Formerly a name often given to the Imperial Palace. It was also called *Ō-uchi-yama* — See *Dairi*.

Ōuchi, 大内. A family of *daimyō* descended from *Rinsei-taishi*, a royal prince of Korea who emigrated to Japan in 611.

—— **Morifusa, 盛房.** Installed at *Ōuchi* (*Suwō*), was the first to take the title of *Ōuchi no Suke* (towards 1180), and was admitted to the military class.

—— **Hiroyo, 弘世.** Descendant of *Morifusa* in the 8th generation, governed the province of *Suwō*. He supported the southern dynasty at first, then passed over to the *Ashikaga* (1364) and received the provinces of *Nagato* and *Iwami*. He built the castle of *Yamaguchi* and resided there.

—— **Yoshihiro, 義弘** (1355-1400). Son of *Hiroyo*, served in the *Shōgun Yoshimitsu's* expedition to *Kyūshū* against the *Kikuchi* and received as reward the province of *Buzen* (1374). In 1391, he defeated *Yamana Ujikiyo* at *Kyōto*, and annexed *Izumi* and *Kii*, to his domains, which then comprised 6 provinces. The following year, after having defeated *Yamana Yoshisato* in *Kii*, he advanced to Mt. *Yoshino*, the last refuge of the southern dynasty, and opened negotiations with *Kitabatake Akinori*, delegate of *Go-Kameyama ;* he conducted the business skilfully and brought about the fusion of the two dynasties. Several years later, he responded to the advances of *Ashikaga Mitsukane*, the *Kwanryō* of *Kamakura*, who aspired to the shogunate and promised him his support ; for that purpose, he fortified himself at *Sakai* (*Izumi*), where he was besieged by *Hatakeyama Motokuni*, *Shiba Yoshishige*, etc , and perished in battle.

—— **Mochiyo**, 持世 (1395-1442). Son of *Yoshihiro*, was only 5 years old at his father's death ; his uncle *Morimi* governed his extensive domains, but was killed in *Chikuzen*, in an engagement with the *Shōni* (1431). *Mochiyo* then took the title of *Ōuchi no Suke* and entered *Yamaguchi*. After the assassination of the *Shōgun Yoshinori* (1441), he served in the campaign against the assassin, *Akamatsu Mitsusuke*, and contributed to the elevation of *Yoshikatsu* to the shogunate. After that, he marched against *Shōni Sukeyori*, who had sided with *Mitsusuke*, and wrested from him the province of *Chikuzen*. He died the following year without issue, and was succeeded by *Norihiro*, son of his brother *Mochimori*.

—— **Norihiro**, 教弘 (+ 1465). Nephew of *Mochiyo*, bore after him the title of *Ōuchi no Suke*. In an expedition headed by *Hosokawa Katsumoto* to quell some troubles in *Iyo*, he died of illness.

—— **Masahiro**, 政弘 (+ 1495). Son of *Norihiro*, sided with *Yamana Sōzen* in the *Ōnin* war (1467), defeated *Akamatsu Masanori* and entered *Kyōto*, but had to return in all haste to *Kyūshū*, where *Shōni Noriyori* had mustered troops in *Tsushima*, and, embracing the party of *Hosokawa Katsumoto*, tried to recover his domains in *Chikuzen*. —*Noriyori* was defeated.

—— **Yoshioki**, 義興 (1477-1528). Son of *Masahiro*, gave in 1499 hospitality to the *Shōgun Yoshitane*, who was expelled from *Kyōto* by *Hosokawa Masamoto*. *Yoshizumi*, appointed *Shōgun* by *Masamoto* in the place of *Yoshitane*, gave orders to the *Kyūshū daimyō* to unite their forces against *Yoshioki*, but fearing the power of a man who ruled over 6 provinces, they did not dare to obey. Having mustered a powerful army, *Yoshioki* set out from *Suwō* to reinstate the former *Shōgun*. The *Kwanryō Hosokawa Sumimoto* intended to check him in *Settsu*, but on ascertaining the strength of his adversary, did not dare to risk an engagement and fled to *Awa* with *Miyoshi Nagateru*, whilst *Yoshizumi* sought refuge in *Ōmi* with *Sasaki Takayori*. *Yoshioki* entered *Kyōto*, reinstalled *Yoshitane* after an absence of 15 years and received the title of *Kwanryō* (1508). Shortly afterwards, he was defeated by *Masakata*, a relative of *Sumimoto*, and went to *Tamba* to raise fresh troops ; then he returned and defeated *Masakata* at *Funaoka-yama* (1511). After that, *Yoshioki* applied himself to restore order in the State ; but *Amako Tsunehisa* having invaded *Bizen* and *Hōki*, he tendered his resignation as *Kwanryō*, returned to *Suwō* and defeated *Tsunehisa* (1518) The next year, he crossed over to *Kyūshū* and defeated successively *Shōni Masasuke* and *Ōtomo Yoshinori*. In 1522, he invaded *Aki* and built the castle of *Saijō* and *Kagami-yama ;* *Tsunehisa* resorted to arms once more, but was again defeated.

—— **Yoshitaka, 義隆** (1507-1551). Son of *Yoshioki*, quelled the disturbances raised in *Chikuzen* by *Shōni Sukemoto* and *Hoshino Chikatada* (1534) ; then, seeing his authority secure, he began to neglect military affairs and gave his time to literature, art and pleasure. Generous like his father, he paid the expenses of the coronation of the emperor *Go-Nara* (1536), and was appointed *Dazai-Shōni*. In 1543, he marched against *Amako Haruhisa*, but was defeated and returning to *Yamaguchi*, indulged more than ever in the amusements introduced into his castle by the *kuge* who had resorted thither, owing to the troubled condition of *Kyōto*. In vain did the principal *kerai*, *Mōri Motonari* and *Sue Harukata* endeavor to draw him away from this effeminate life ; their remonstrances remained without effect. Disunion then broke out among his subjects ; *Harukata* intrenched in his castle of *Wakayama* (*Suwō*), came to a secret understanding with *Ōtomo* of *Bungo* and prepared for revolt. It was the time when St. Francis Xavier came to *Yamaguchi*. He was on his way to *Kyōto* and intended staying only a few days at *Yamaguchi* but he prolonged his visit to 6 months (1551). He formed a Christian community which soon numbered 500 members. *Yoshitaka* received the foreign preacher kindly and listened to his instructions with interest, but went no further. He soon had other affairs to deal with. Hearing of the treacherous designs of *Harukata*, he called his retainers to arms against the rebel, but his appeal was disregarded by most of them. He then left his castle, where he felt too unsafe, and retired to the temple of *Hōsen-ji ;* this too he soon left and fled towards *Nagato ;* but a storm carried his boat to the village of *Fukawa*, where he landed and sought refuge in the temple of *Dainei-ji*. Here he was soon besieged by *Harukata*, and committed suicide ; his son followed his example.

—— **Yoshinaga, 義長** (+1557). Brother of *Ōtomo Yoshishige*, was chosen to continue the family of *Ōuchi*. In 1554, he quelled, with the help of *Sue Harukata*, a revolt of *Yoshimi Masayori* in *Iwami*. Meanwhile *Mōri Motonari* revolted too and *Yoshinaga* sent *Harukata* against him. *Harukata* was defeated and killed at *Itsuku-shima* (1555). The next year, *Motonari* invaded *Suwō* and was joined by a large number of *samurai*. *Yoshinaga* fled to *Chōfu* (*Nagato*), where he was soon overtaken by *Fukuhara Hiroyoshi*, the commander of *Motonari's* vanguard ; he sought refuge in the temple of *Chōfuku-ji* where he committed suicide. Thus the family became extinct. — A younger branch, descended from *Mochimori*, son of *Yoshihiro*, had taken the name of *Yamaguchi* (which see).

Ō-uji, 大氏. Patronymic name of a family of several branches, and often kept by the elder branch. Thus *Mononobe* is an *ō-uji ;* (*Mononobe*) *Asuka*, (*Mononobe*) *Ishikami*, etc. are *ko-uji*. — See *Uji*.

Ō-ura, 大浦. In *Mutsu*. Ancient castle, occupied by *Tsugaru Tamenobu*, towards the close of the 16th century.

Ō-uta-dokoro, 大歌所. Formerly, an office intrusted with the sacred poetry, music, dances etc. *Okiyo Kakinushi* was its first *Bettō* (816).

Ōwa, 應和. *Nengō* : 961-963.

Owari, 尾張. One of the 15 provinces of the *Tōkaidō ;* comprises 9 districts, depending on *Aichi-ken.* — Chinese name : *Bishū.* — Formerly called *Oharuda.*

Oyabe, 小矢部. (Now *Isurugi*). In *Etchū.* In 1183, the young emperor *Antoku* was taken by the *Taira* to *Etchū* and pursued by *Imai Kanehira,* general of *Niso Yoshinaka ;* the *Taira* army was beaten at *Oyabe* and forced to retreat to *Kaga.*

Oyama, 小山. In *Shimotsuke.* Ancient castle built by *Fujiwara Hidesato,* who, after his victory over *Taira Masakado,* was appointed governor of the province (940). *Tomomasa* his descendant in the 12th generation, won distinction under *Yoritomo.* At the time of the two dynasties, *Tomouji* remained faithful to the southern cause. In the *Ashikaga* era, the castle of *Oyama* passed into the hands of the *Yūki. Hideyoshi* sojourned there for a time in 1590, when he intended to subdue the northern *daimyō.* There *Ieyasu* learned that *Ishida Kazushige* had taken the field.

Oyama, 尾山. Ancient name of the city of *Kanazawa* (*Kaga*).

Oyama, 小山. A family of *daimyō,* descended from *Fujiwara Hidesato.*

—— **Masamitsu, 政光.** Descended from *Hidesato* in the 11th generation, was the first to take the name of *Oyama* towards the middle of the 12th century, from a castle in *Shimotsuke,* occupied by his ancestors for 300 years.

—— **Tomomasa, 朝政** (1155-1238). Son of *Masamitsu,* sided with *Yoritomo* as soon as the latter rose in arms against the *Taira* (1180) and received as reward some domains in *Hitachi.* He fought at *Ichi no tani* (1184), and in the campaign against *Fujiwara Hidehira* (1189). The following year, he accompanied *Yoritomo* to *Kyōto* and was appointed *Kebiishi* and *Shimotsuke no kami,* then *Harima-shugo* (1199). After that, he with *Hatakeyama Shigetada* quelled the uprising of *Hiki Yoshikazu* against the *Hōjō* (1203).

—— **Hidetomo, 秀朝** (+ 1335). Descendant of *Tomomasa* in the 6th generation, fought under the *Hōjō* against *Go-Daigo* and besieged the castle of *Akasaka.* After that, he rallied to the standard of *Nitta Yoshisada,* defeated *Kanazawa Sadamasa* at *Tsurumi* (*Musashi*) and took part in the siege of *Kamakura.* He was then appointed *Shimotsuke no kami.* In 1335, he was killed in *Musashi,* while fighting against *Hōjō Tokiyuki.*

—— **Yoshimasa, 義政** (+1382). Grandson of *Hidetomo,* raised an army in 1380 to defend the cause of the southern dynasty and defeated *Utsunomiya Mototsuna* at *Mobara,* but was obliged to fall back before *Uesugi Norikata,* sent against him by the *Kwanryō Ashikaga Ujimitsu.* Rallying his troops, he soon took the field again, but was defeated by *Uesugi*

Tomomune and committed suicide, after which his family became extinct.

Ōyama, 大山. A family of *samurai*, from *Kagoshima* clan (*Satsuma*), ennobled after the Restoration. — To-day Marquis.

—— **Iwao, 巌**. Born in 1842, was nephew of *Saigō Takamori*. He advanced rapidly in the army: Chief of the Etat-Major and Minister of war in 1884, he received the following year the title of Count, then the rank of Marshal (1891). During the war with China, he was appointed Commander in chief of the Second Army, whose greatest exploit was the storming of *Ryōjunkō* (*Port-Arthur*) (Nov. 22, 1894). After the treaty of peace, he was raised to the rank of Marquis, and when he title of *Gensui* was reestablished, he was one of the 4 that received it (1898). He was Commander in chief of the army in Manchuria during the war with Russia (1904-05).

Ō-yama, 大山. A mountain in *Hōki* (1815 m.); the highest in the *San-in-dō*; also called *Dai-sen, Ōkami-yama, Kakuban-san*.

Ō-Yamato-toyo-akitsu-shima, 大日本豊蜻蛉嶋. (Lit.: the great *Yamato*, the fertile island of the dragon fly). Name given in olden times to the largest island of Japan (*Hondo*). The legend says that *Jimmu-tennō*, ascending a high mountain and viewing in one glance all the outlines of the island, found in it some resemblance to a dragon fly and gave it the name.

Ōyamatsumi, 大山津見. Son of *Izanagi* and *Izanami*, honored as deity of the mountains (*Shintō*). His daughter *Ko-no-hana-saku-ya hime* married *Ninigi no mikoto*.

Ō-ya-shima no kuni, 大八嶋國. (Lit.: the country of the 8 islands). A name given to Japan in mythological times.

Oya-shio, 親潮. A polar current which issuing from the sea of *Okhotsk* meets the *Kuro-shio* (which see).

Ō-yashiro-ha, 大社派. One of the 10 sects of modern Shintoism, has its principal seat in the great temple (*ō-yashiro*) of *Izumo*.

Ōyodo-gawa, 大淀川. A river in *Hyūga*, formed by the junction of the *Iwase-gawa* and the *Hashino-gawa*. Also called *Akae-gawa*. (99 Km.)

Ōyori-yama, 大寄山. A hill in *Ōmi*, where *Asai Sukemasa* defeated the *Saitō* of *Mino* (1521) and *Nobunaga*, the *Asai* and the *Asakura* (1570).

Oyumi, 生實. In *Shimōsa*; ancient castle of the *Hara* family, vassal of the *Chiba*; was captured in 1525 by the *Takeda* of *Shimōsa*. Shortly afterwards, *Ashikaga Yoshiaki*, having had some contentions with his father *Masauji*, fled to *Mutsu*; all the *daimyō* of *Awa, Shimōsa* and *Kazusa*, the *Satomi*, the *Takeda*, etc., espoused his cause, recognized him as their lord and installed him in the castle of *Oyumi*; whence the name of *Oyumi-gosho*, which was given him. In 1538, *Yoshiaki* was defeated and killed at *Kōnodai* by *Hōjō Ujitsuna*. In 1627, the *Tokugawa* asssigned the castle to the *Morikawa daimyō*, who resided there up to the Restoration. (10,000 k.).

Ozaki, 尾崎. A family attached hereditarily to the temple of *Ninna-dō* (*Kyōto*), ennobled in 1896. — To-day Baron.

Ozaki Masayoshi, 尾崎雅嘉 (1755-1827). A learned scholar from *Ōsaka*.

Ozawa, 小澤. A family of *samurai*, from the *Kokura* clan (*Buzen*), ennobled after the Restoration. — To-day Baron.

Ōzutsu-yaku, 大筒役. In the *Tokugawa* days, an official charged to look after the reserve artillery in the military stores of the *Shōgun*. This title, created in 1138, was hereditary in the *Inoue* family.

BEN NO NAISHI.

P

Paramushiri, 波羅茂知里. — See *Haramuchi-jima.*
Pimisho, ピ ミ シ ョ. — See *Yamatsu-hime.*

R

Rahan. (Sanscr. *Arhat*) Abbreviation of *Arakan*. The fourth and last degree of Buddhist perfection. Title especially given to the 16 principal disciples of *Shaka* (*jŭ-roku Rakan*) and to the 500 members of the council of Rajagrila (*go-hyaku Rakan*).

Rai, 頼. A family of literati, famous in the 18th and 19th centuries.

—— **Shunsui, 春水** (1746-1816). Is the author of several esteemed historical works: *Fushin-shi, Shiyŭ-shi, Ittoku-roku, Zaishin-kiji, Zaikō-kiji, Takehara-bunchū, Shunsui-ikō*, etc.

—— **San-yō, 山陽** (1780-1832). Son of *Shunsui*, was a distinguished historian. His two principal works, *Nihon-gwaishi* and *Nihonseiki*, were all the more remarkable, because he pleaded already for the cause of the Imperial Restoration.

—— **Mikisaburō, 三樹三郎** (1825-1859). Son of *San-yō*, imbued with the ideas of his father, worked for the restoration of the Imperial power. He repaired to *Kyōto*, and obtained an order of the Emperor, commissioning *Mito Nariaki* to expel the foreigners; but his proceedings having leaked out, the *Tairō Ii Naosuke* had him arrested with about 30 followers by *Manabe Norikatsu*. He was taken to *Edo* and beheaded.

RAI SAN-YŌ

Rakan, 羅漢. Title given to the principal disciples of *Shaka*.

Raku, 洛. Formerly a name given to that part of *Kyōto* which was also called *Rakuyō, Sakyō*. Later on, the term was extended to the whole city.

Raku-chū, 洛中 . When *Hideyoshi* repaired the damages which
Raku-gwai, 洛外 . the capital had suffered from the time of the
Ōnin war (1467), the term, *Raku-chū*, stood for the city of *Kyōto* itself,
Raku-gwai, for the environs.

Rakuchū kei-ei, 洛中警衛 . In the *Kamakura* period, officials
intrusted with the police of *Kyōto*.

Rashō-mon, 羅城門 . Formerly the southern gate of *Kyōto*.
Often repaired from the time of *Kwammu*, it fell to pieces in the reign of
En-yū (970-984), and was not restored again.

Rebunjiri-shima, 禮文尻島 . An island N. E. of *Ezo* (47 Km.,
in circ.).

Reifuku-goran, 禮服御覽 . Ceremony at which were presented
to the emperor the robes he was to wear on the day of his coronation.

Reigen-tennō, 靈元天皇 . 112th Emperor of Japan (1663-1686).
Satohito, son of *Go-Mi-no-o-tennō*, succeeded his brother, *Sai-in*, at the
age of 9. During the 24 years of his reign, all the authority was in
the hands of the *Shōgun Ietsuna* and *Tsunayoshi*. He abdicated at the
age of 38, and died only in 1732, in his 79th year.

Reigi-ruiten, 禮儀類典 . An historical work in 510 volumes,
published at the end of the 17th century, under the auspices of *Mito
Mitsukuni*.

Reiheishi-kaidō, 例幣使街通 . A high way leading from
Takasaki (*Kōzuke*) to *Nikkō*, passing by *Ashikaga* and *Mibu*. It was
followed every year by the Imperial envoy (*reiheishi*), charged to carry
presents to the tomb of *Ieyasu*.

Reikei-den, 麗景殿 . In the ancient palace of *Kyōto*, a building
reserved, with the *Sen-yō-den*, for the ladies in attendance at the Court.

Reiki, 靈龜 . *Nengō* : 715-716.

Reishi, 令旨 . Name given to orders emanating from the dowager
empress, the reigning empress, or the Prince Imperial.

Reizei, 冷泉 . A family of *kuge*, descended from *Fujiwara Nagaie*
(1005-1064). The elder branch has at present the title of Count; a
younger branch, that of Viscount.

Reizei-tennō, 泉冷天皇 . 63rd Emperor of Japan (968-969).
Norihira, son of *Murakami-tennō* succeeded his father at the age of 18.
Hardly was he on the throne, when his brother *Tamehira*, supported by
Minamoto Takaakira and *Tachibana Shigenobu*, tried to usurp the
power, but the attempt failed and the culprits were banished to *Tsuku-
shi*. Shortly after, *Reizei* fell sick ; he abdicated in favor of his brother
Morihira (*En-yū*) and retired to the *Reizei-in*, where he lived 44 years.
He was the first to receive after his abdication, the title of *Dajō-tennō*.

Rekken, 列見 . Formerly a feast given at the *Dajō-kwan*, on the
11th day of the 2nd month, to which were invited the officials of the
War and Ceremony departments. Persons of high rank present wore
wreaths of flowers.

Remmon-kyō, 蓮門教 . A religious sect founded by *Shimamura-
Mitsu*, who was born in 1831 at *Yoshiga* (*Nagato*.) Although affiliated
with the *Taisei* sect (*Shintō*), it borrowed its doctrines from the *Fuju-fuze*

branch of the *Nichiren-shū*. Its ethics are those of Confucianism popularized by the *Kyūō-dōwa* and the *Shingaku-dōwa*.

Renge-zan, 蓮 華 山. A group of mountains (2,900 m.) on the
borders of *Etchū*, *Shinano* and *Echigo*.

Rennyo-Shōnin, 蓮 如 上 人 (1415-1499). Descendant in the 8th
generation of *Shinran-Shōnin*, and reformer of the *Shin-shū* sect. Son
of *Sonnyo* (*Enken-Hōshi*), he was adopted by *Chūnagon Kanesato*. At
the age of 16, he became a bonze of the *Hongwan-ji* temple, under the
name of *Kenju*, but was commonly called *Chūnagon-Hōshi*. His reputation for holiness and eloquence roused the jealousy of the bonzes of *Hiei-
zan*, who compelled him to leave *Kyōto*. After having wandered over the
eastern provinces as far as *Echigo*, preaching the doctrines of the sect, he
returned to the capital to claim his inheritance and become the 8th chief-
bonze of the *Hongwan-ji* (1457). Shortly afterwards, he obtained an audience from the emperor *Go-Hanazono*, who repaired the temple at his own
expense. This favor enraged the bonzes of *Hiei-zan*, who set fire to the
Hongwan-ji: *Rennyo* barely escaped with his life, carrying with him the
statue of *Shinran*. Then he resumed his wanderings, building temples at
Chikamatsu (*Ōmi*) and at *Yoshizaki* (*Echizen*). He had been already 5
years installed in the latter place, when the bonzes of the *Senshū-ji* temple,
of the *Takada* branch of the same *Shin* sect, jealous of his growing influence, attacked the temple and levelled it to the ground (1475). *Rennyo*
set out again, and founded the temples of *Kōzen-ji* (*Kawachi*) *Kyōgyō-ji*
(*Settsu*) and *Shinshū-ji* (*Kawachi*); after that, he chose a site in the village
of *Yamashina* (*Yamashiro*), to rebuild the *Hongwan-ji* temple, the seat of
the sect (1480); and there he died at age of 85. His immediate successor
received in 1521 the title of *Monzeki; Rennyo* himself was decorated in
1882, with the posthumous name of *Etō-Daishi*, and his present descendants, heads of the two *Hongwan-ji* branches, are the Counts *Ōtani*.

Rensha, 輦 車. A little hand carriage, which persons of high rank
could use, subject to permission from the emperor, even within the precincts of the Palace. It was also called *te-guruma*, *koshi-guruma*.

Rensho, 連 署. In the *Kamakura* period, the highest official after
the *Shikken*. Also called *Rempan*, *Gōhan*, *Kaban*. As he shared with
the *Shikken* the right to seal the official documents of the *Bakufu*, they
were called *ryō-shikken*, *ryō-shitsuji*, *ryō-kōken*. The *Rensho* was
always taken from the *Hōjō* family, and *Tochifusa* was the first to receive the title in 1224.

Ri, 里. League, long measure. Formerly the league had 50 *chō* (5
Km. 454) or 42 *chō* (4 Km. 582). At present, it has 36 *chō* (3 Km. 927);
It is called *kami-michi*, to distinguish it from a small league of 6 *chō* (655
m.) still in use in certain western provinces, and called *shi mo-michi*.

Ribu-Ō, 李 部 王. Name given to prince *Shige-akira-shinnō* (906-
954), son of the emperor *Daigo*. The prince had the title of *Shikibu-
kyō* (minister of Ceremonies), and as that Ministry is called *Ribu* in
China, he was surnamed *Ribu-Ō*.

Richū-tennō, 履 中 天 皇. 17th Emperor of Japan (400-405). *Ōe-
izao-wake* succeeded his father, *Nintoku*, at the age of 64. Hardly was

Nintoku dead, when his 2nd son *Suminoe no Nakatsu-Ōji* endeavored to secure the throne for himself. *Richū* sent against him his other brother *Mizuha-wake* (later on *Hanshō-tennō*), who had him put to death by one of his servants. *Richū* was the first to appoint 4 *Shōgun*, to watch over the defence of the empire: *Heguri-Tsuku, Soga Machi, Mononobe Irofu* and *Tsubura Ōkimi* (461). He died after a reign of 6 years.

Rigen-Daishi, 理 源 大 師 . — See *Shōbō*.

Rijiri-shima, 利 尻 島 . An island N. W. of *Hokkaidō* (60 Km., in circ) The highest point of the island has the shape of Mt. *Fuji* and is called *Kitami-Fuji*.

Rikuchū, 陸 中 . One of the 13 provinces of *Tōsandō*, formed in 1868 of 12 districts (*kōri*) of the former province of *Mutsu ;* at present 11 belong to *Iwate-ken* and 1 to *Akita-ken*.

Rikugun-bugyō, 陸 軍 奉 行 . Minister of War of the *Tokugawa*. That title was created only towards the close of the 18th century, when the regent *Matsudaira Sadanobu* adopted the European system for the army : infantry, cavalry, artillery, etc.

Rikugun-shō, 陸 軍 省 . The War Department, created in 1885.

Riku-kokushi, 六 國 史 . (Lit.: the 6 National Histories). The six historical collections which embrace the first 15 centuries of Japanese history :

— 1° **Nihon-shoki,** 日 本 書 記 (30 vol.), which dates from the creation to the reign of *Jitō* (696), a collection made in 720 by *Toneri-shinnō, Ō no Yasumaro, Ki no Kiyobito*, etc.; it is also called *Nihon-ki*.

— 2° **Shoku-Nihon-ki,** 續 日 本 記 (40 vol.), from 697 to 791, by *Ishikawa Natari, Fujiwara Tsuginawa, Sugeno Sanemichi*, etc.

— 3° **Nihon-kōki,** 日 本 後 記 (40 vol.) from 792 to 833, by *Fujiwara Otsugu* (840) ; only 10 vol. are still extant.

— 4° **Shoku-Nihon-kōki,** 續 日 本 後 記 (20 vol.), from 834 to 850, by *Fujiwara Yoshifusa* (869).

— 5° **Montoku-jitsuroku,** 文 德 實 錄 (10 vol.), from 851 to 858, by *Fujiwara Mototsune* (879).

— 6° **Sandai-jitsuroku,** 三 代 實 錄 (50 vol.), from 859 to 888, by *Fujiwara Tokihira* (901).

Rikuoku, 陸 奥 . — See *Mutsu*.

Rikuzen, 陸 前 . One of the 13 provinces of the *Tōsandō*, formed in 1868 with 14 districts (*kōri*) of the former province of *Mutsu*, of which 13 belong at present to *Iwate-ken*, and 1 to *Miyagi-ken*.

Rinji, 綸 旨 . An Imperial decree, written by a *Geki* (secretary) to appoint officials to public functions.

Rinnō-ji, 綸 王 寺 . — See *Mangwan-ji*.

Rinzai-shū, 臨 濟 宗 . A branch of the Buddhist sect *Zen-shū*, thus called after its founder, the Chinese bonze *Rinzai-Zenshi*. — In 1175, the bonze *Kakua* from *Hiei-zan* returned from China, where he had spent 4 years and learned from *Bukkai-Zenshi* the doctrines of the *Zen* sect, which made then its first appearance in Japan. A little later, *Eisai-Zenshi* repaired to China (1187) and, having been taught by *Kyoan-Zenshi*, he brought home the *Rinzai-shū* (1191), which he spread first in *Chikuzen*, then in *Kyōto* and *Kamakura*. — That branch has divided into 10 secondary branches, which possess at present in Japan altogether 6,120 temples, with about 4000 chief-bonzes and 1,818,000 believers.

Rinzai-shū jū-ha, 臨 濟 宗 十 派．The 10 branches of the *Rinzai-shū*, which have their seat in the following temples, of which they bear the names :

1. *Kennin-ji* (*Yamashiro*), founded by *Eisai* in 1202.
2. *Tōfuku-ji* (do.), „ „ *Ben-en* „ 1243.
3. *Kenchō-ji* (*Sagami*), „ „ *Dōryū* „ 1253.
4. *Enkaku-ji* (do.), „ „ *Sogen* „ 1282.
5. *Nanzen-ji* (*Yamashiro*), „ „ *Busshin* „ 1293.
6. *Eigen-ji* (*Ōmi*), „ „ *Genkō* „ 1320.
7. *Daitoku-ji* (*Yamashiro*), „ „ *Myōchō* „ 1323.
8. *Tenryū-ji* (do.), „ „ *Soseki* „ 1340.
9. *Myōshin-ji* (do.), „ „ *Egen* „ 1350.
10. *Shōkoku-ji* (do.), „ „ *Myōha* „ 1383.

Rinzō, 輪 藏．A large revolving library with 8 sides, containing the sacred Books of Buddhism.

Risshi, 律 師．A high Buddhist dignity, below that of *Sōzu ;* the titular held formerly the 5th Court-rank (*go-i*).

Risshū, 律 宗．The Buddhist sect *Ritsu* or *Kairitsu-shū* introduced into Japan in 754 by the Chinese bonze *Kanshin*. Has its principal seat at the *Tōshō-daiji* (*Yamato*). Little in vogue to-day.— See *Kairitsu-shū*.

Ritsu, 律．— See *Risshū* (*Ritsu-shū*).

Ritsu-ryō-kyaku-shiki, 律 令 格 式．Collections of the Codes published in the Middle Ages. *Ritsu* corresponds to the Criminal Law ; *Ryō*, to the Civil Law; *Kyaku* comprises ordinances of a later date ; *Shiki* treats especially of feasts and ceremonies. — The first Japanese Code, borrowed from the contemporay Chinese Code, was completed in 689, after more than 30 years of preparatory labors ; it was called *Ōmi-ryō ;* it contained 22 volumes and has not come down to us. — The emperor *Mommu* published a new Code of Laws in 701 : it is the famous *Taihō* Code (*Taihō-ritsuryō*). — In 811, (2nd year of *Kōnin* era), appeared 40 vol. of *Shiki* (*Kōnin-shiki*) and 10 vol. of *Kyaku* (*Kōnin-kyaku*), the whole collection being known as the *Kōnin-kyaku-shiki* and containing all the ordinances published since the promulgation of the *Taihō* Code.—In 868 (10th year of *Jōgwan*), appeared a new publication in 12 vol. of *Kyaku* (*Jōgwan-kyaku*) and 20 vol. of *Shiki* (*Jōgwan-shiki*), constituting the collection called *Jōgwan-kyaku-shiki*. Finally, in 907, (7th year of *Engi*) came the *Engi-kyaku-shiki*, comprising 12 vol. of *Kyaku* and 50 vol. of *Shiki*, thus completing the preceding compilations. — These 3 last collections are called the 3 great Codes (*San-dai-kyaku-shiki*).

Rōdō, 郎 黨．Formerly servants or vassals of a nobleman : this term is equivalent to *kerai, ie no ko,* etc.

Rōjū, 老 中 Or **Rōchū.** In the *Tokugawa* days, members of the *Shōgun's* Council. — This title, corresponding to the *Rensho* of *Kamakura*, the *Kwanryō* of *Kyōto*, was assigned to 5 officials chosen among *daimyō* having a revenue of a least 25,000 k. The *Ōsaka-jōdai*, the *Kyōto-shoshidai*, generally became *Rōjū* at the end of their term ; others were taken from among the *Soba-yōnin*, the *Wakadoshiyori*, the *Sōshaban*, etc. The *Rōjū* performed their duties in turn, each one serving a month. The Hall assigned to the *Rōjū* in the Shogunal palace was called *Go-yō-beya*, and was at first near that of the *Shōgun ;* but from the time when the *Tairō Hotta Masatoshi* was killed there by *Inaba Masayasu* (1684), it was transferred elsewhere and the *Rōjū* and *Wakadoshiyori* had rarely access to the *Shōgun.*

Rōjū-nami, 老中並. In the *Tokugawa* days, name given to a *Rōjū*, who had not a castle.

Rokkaku, 六角. A branch of the *Sasaki* family of *Ōmi.*

—— **Yasutsuna,** 泰綱. Son of *Sasaki Nobutsuna*, was the first to take the name of *Rokkaku* towards the middle of the 13th century. He possessed the full confidence of the *Shikken Hōjō*, was *Kebiishi, Ōmi no shugo, Iki no kami.*

—— **Ujiyori,** 氏頼 (1326-1370). Great-grandson of *Yasutsuna*, was also *Ōmi no shugo* and *Kebiishi.* He sided with the northern dynasty and fought under *Takauji* and *Yoshiakira.* He resided at the castle of *Kwannonji* (*Ōmi*), built by his ancestors.

—— **Mitsutaka,** 満孝 (+ 1413). Son of the *Shōgun Ashikaga Yoshiakira*, was adopted by *Ujiyori* and succeeded him in all his titles and possessions. He it was who, at the time of the reconciliation of the two Imperial Houses, came to *Kyōto* with the three sacred emblems, until then in the hands of *Go-Kameyama* (South), and handed them to *Go-Komatsu* (North).

—— **Takayori,** 高頼 (+ 1520). Son of *Masayori*, sided in the *Ōnin* war with *Yamana Sōzen* (1467), and conquered the whole province of *Ōmi* from the *Kyōgoku* (other *Sasaki* branch). In 1487, he was besieged in the castle of *Kwannonji* by the *Shōgun Yoshihisa*, and sought refuge on *Kōga-zan. Yoshihisa* died during the siege and was replaced by *Yoshitane* who took to arms again in 1492. *Takayori* was defeated and compelled to flee. On the death of the emperor *Go-Tsuchimikado*, he paid all the expenses of the funeral, and, in reward, was allowed to add to his arms the Chrysanthemum (*kiku*) and the Paulownia (*kiri*) of the Imperial family (1500). When the *Shōgun Yoshizumi* was expelled from *Kyōto* by his rival *Yoshitane*, he sought shelter with *Takayori.*

—— **Sadayori,** 定頼 (+ 1552). Son of *Takayori*, was first a bonze ; then, when his brother *Chikatsuna* died, he inherited the latter's right of succession. He contributed to the victory won by *Ōuchi Yoshi-oki* at *Funaoka-yama* over *Hosokawa Masakata* (1511), and was then appointed *Kwanryō* and *Danjō-shōsuke.* In 1518, he besieged *Asai Sukemasa* in his castle of *Odani* (*Ōmi*) in vain. Shortly afterwards, mustering fresh troops, he marched upon *Kyōto* and expelled *Miyoshi Nagateru* and *Hosokawa Sumimoto* (1520). He was killed in a fight against the *Miyoshi.*

—— **Yoshikata,** 義賢 (+ 1581). Son of *Sadayori*, aided *Hosoka-wa Harumoto* against *Miyoshi Chōkei* (1549). In 1555, coveting a part of the province of *Ise*, he laid siege to the castle of *Chikusa*, but the lord *Chikusa Tadaharu* negotiated a peace. After that, he fought against *Matsunaga Hisahide* at *Nyoi-ga-mine* (*Yamashiro*), and entered *Kyōto* with the *Shōgun Yoshiteru* (1558). In 1562, he made peace with *Miyoshi Chōkei*, ceded to his son the management of his estates, shaved his head, took the name of *Shōtei*, and was ranked among the *Shōban-shū*. He had learned archery from *Yoshida Shigekata*, horsemanship from *Saitō Jogen*, and he himself founded a school (*Sasaki-ryū*), to teach the arts of war. After his son was dispossessed, *Yoshikata* lived at the court of *Nobunaga*. He was baptized at *Azuchi* the very year of his death.

—— **Yoshisuke,** 義弼 (+ 1612). Son of *Yoshikata*, took in hand the administration of his father's domains (1562), with *Gamō Katahide* as councillor. In 1565, after the assassination of the *Shōgun Yoshiteru*, his brother, the bonze *Gakkei*, implored *Yoshisuke* to espouse his cause and help him to recover his rights to the shōgunate. *Yoshisuke* did not dare risk a war with the powerful *Miyoshi*. Then *Gakkei* turned to *Oda Nobunaga* who accepted the mission, raised an army and marched on to *Kyōto ;* in *Ōmi*, he captured several castles of the *Sasaki*, and compelled *Yoshisuke* to seek shelter on *Kōga-san*. The latter was besieged by *Shibata Katsuie* in his castle of *Namazue* (1572) ; forced to surrender, he lost all his domains and lived henceforth at the court of *Nobunaga*. — Later on, he entered the service of *Ieyasu*, and his descendants received the title of *kōke*.

Rokkaku, 六角. A family of *kuge*, descended from *Fujiwara Yorimune* (993-1065).—Now Viscount.

Rokkasen, 六歌仙. The 6 most famous poets of the 9th century : *Ariwara Narihira*, *Sōjō Henjō*, *Kisen-Hōshi*, *Ōtomo Kuronushi*, *Fumiya Yasuhide* and *Ono Komachi*.

Roku-buten, 六武天. The 6 gods of war : *Bonten*, *Taishaku*, and the *shi-tennō*, *Jikoku*, *Kōmoku*, *Zōchō* and *Bishamon*.

Roku-efu, 六衛府. Formerly the 6 sections of the Imperial guard. In the reign of *Shōmu* (724-748), they were called : *Emon*, *Chū-e*, *Sa-eji*, *U-eji*, *Sahyō-e*, *Uhyō-e ;* in 807, these names were changed to *Sa-konoe*, *U-konoe*, *Sa-eji*, *U-eji*, *Sahyō-e*, *Uhyō-e ;* in 811, they became *Sa-konoe*, *U-konoe*, *Sa-emon*, *U-emon*, *Sahyō-e*, *Uhyō-e*. Instead of *rokue-fu*, the term *shi-e ni-fu* was also used, and the *Emon* and *Hyō-e* were also called *Gwai-e*.

Roku-gi, 六議. According to the *Taihō* Code (702), 6 categories of persons, when guilty of a crime, could claim a diminution of the penalty by one degree. They were called the *roku-gi*, viz. : *gi-shin* 議親 (Imperial kinship), *gi-ko* 議故 (former services rendered), *gi-ken* 議賢 (great virtue), *gi-nō* 議能 (great talents), *gi-kō* 議功 (great merits), and *gi-ki* 議貴 (rank above *san-i*). The 8 more heinous crimes, called the *hachi-gyaku* were alone excluded from this measure of clemency.

Rokugō, 六郷. A family of *daimyō* descended from the *Fujiwara*.

—— **Masanori,** 政乘 (1567-1634). Son of *Michiyuki*, was first, like his ancestors, a vassal of the *Onodera* of *Dewa* and possessor of the domain of *Rokugō*. In 1588, he served in the campaign of his suzerain *Onodera Yoshimichi* against *Akita Sanesue*, and was defeated. After the fall of the *Onodera*, he served *Hideyoshi*, then *Ieyasu*, who in 1602, raised him to the rank of *daimyō* and gave him the fief of *Fuchū* (*Hitachi* — 10,000 k). In 1623, he was transferred to *Honjō* (*Dewa* — 20,000 k.), where his descendants resided till the Restoration. —— Now Viscount.

Rokugō-gawa, 六鄉川. —— See *Tama-gawa*.

Rokuhara, 六波羅. An old ward S. E. of *Kyōto*, where the representative of the *Kamakura Shikken* resided in the 13th and 14th centuries —— *Taira Tadamori* had owned a small estate there which steadily increased and covered, at the time of *Kiyomori*, 2,000 hectares; he built on it 5,000 houses for his officers. In 1183, *Munemori*, obliged to flee before the *Minamoto*, set it on fire, and reduced all to ashes. In 1220, the two governors (*tandai*) of *Kyōto* were established there by the *Hōjō* and resided in that place to the end of the *Kamakura Shōgun*. In 1333, *Rokuhara* was again attacked by *Kitabatake Akitada*, *Akamatsu Norimura*, etc., and totally destroyed.

Rokuhara-tandai, 六波羅探題. Title of the governors of *Kyōto*, at the time of the *Kamakura Shikken*. —— After the civil war of *Shōkyū* (1219), *Hōjō Yoshitoki* sent his son *Yasutoki* and his brother *Tokifusa*, to take over the administration of the capital and its environs; the former took a north position, the latter, south of *Rokuhara*; such was the beginning of what was called *Ryō-Rokuhara* (the two *Rokuhara*). In imitation of what had been done at *Kamakura*, they were assisted by some *Hyōjōshū* (1263), generally taken from among the *Gotō* and *Kamedani* families, by some *Hikitsukeshū*, etc. Gradually they came to rule over all the departments of administration. The two *tandai* were always taken from among the *Hōjō* family.

Roku Jizō, 六地藏. The 6 names by which the deity *Jizō* is honored : *Emmyō, Hōsho, Hōshu, Jichi, Hōin,* and *Kengoi*.

Rokujō, 六條. A family of *kuge* descended from *Minamoto Michichika* (1149-1202) (*Murakami-Genji*). —— Now Viscount.

Rokujō-gawara, 六條磧. A name given formerly to the part, usually dry, of the bed of the *Kamo-gawa* river, near the *Rokujō* ward in the S. E. p rt of *Kyōto*. It was there that after the battle of *Sekigahara* (1600) were beheaded *Ishida Kazushige, Konishi Yukinaga, Nagatsuka Masaie, Hara Katsutane, Katata Hirozumi, Ishikawa Yoriaki,* the bonze *Ankokuji Ekei*, etc.

Rokujō-tennō, 六條天皇. 79th Emperor of Japan (1166-1168). *Nobuhito*, 2nd son of *Nijō-tennō*, succeeded his father at the age of 3, while the ex-emperor, *Go-Shirakawa*, his grandfather governed with *Taira Kiyomori*. Three years later, the emperor, aged 6 years, was deposed and replaced by *Takakura*, son of *Go-Shirakawa* and son-in-law of *Kiyomori*. *Rokujō* died at the age of 13.

Roku-Kwannon, 六觀音. The 6 names by which the goddess *Kwannon* is worshipped : *Senju, Shō, Batō, Jū-ichi-men, Junchi* and *Nyoirin*.

Roku-nin-shū, 六 人 衆. — See *Wakadoshiyori*.

Rokuon-ji, 鹿 苑 寺. When *Ashikaga Yoshimitsu* ceded the shōgu-nate to his son *Yoshimochi* (1394), he retired to the hill of *Kita-yama*, near *Kyōto*, and, on a small estate belonging to the *Saionji*, built for himself a dwelling, which was completed in the space of 4 years, and called *Kitayama-den;* he annexed to it the famous *Kinkaku-ji*. After his death (1408), he received the posthumous name of *Rokuon-in-dono*, and his house was changed into a temple called *Rokuon-ji*. The *Kin-kaku-ji* alone remains.

Roku saibi, 六 齊 日. The 8th, 14th, 15th, 23rd, 29th and 30th of each month, which are days of abstinence for fervent Buddhists.

Roku-shaku, 六 尺. Formerly domestics of the *Goyō-beya* and other administrative offices in *Edo;* their duty was to carry messages, go on errands, etc. There were 500 *roku-shaku* and 306 *shingumi*.

Roku shō-ji, 六 勝 寺. Six ancient temples of *Kyōto*, in whose names the ideograph *shō* entered.

Hōshō-ji, 法 勝 寺,	founded by the emperor	*Shirakawa*	(1097) ;
Sonshō-ji, 尊 勝 寺,	„	„	„ *Horikawa*	(1102) :
Saishō-ji, 最 勝 寺,	„	„	„ *Toba*	(1152) :
Enshō-ji, 圓 勝 寺,	„	„ empress	*Taiken-mon-in*	(1128) ;
Seishō-ji, 成 勝 寺,	„	„ emperor	*Sutoku*	(1136) ;
Enshō-ji, 延 勝 寺,	„	„	„ *Konoe*	(1149) .

Rongo, 論 語. A Chinese classical book containing the discourses of Confucius to his disciples. It is said to have been brought to Japan in 284 A.D., by the learned Korean *Ajiki*.

Rōnin, 浪 人. A *samurai* who, freely or on compulsion, left the service of his lord and gained his living by pledging himself to any that needed bold men to make some daring attempt. The famous 47 *samurai* of *Akō* became *rōnin* after the death of their lord *Asano Naganori;* but the Japanese call them *gishi* (faithful *samurai*).

Rensō, 論 奏. Term applied to some important communication addressed to the Emperor by one of his subjects ; a less important matter was called *sōji;* a communication still less important, *bensō*.

Roshana, 盧 遮 那. Or *Birushana-butsu*, 毘 盧 遮 那 佛. (Sanscr. *Vairoçama*) *Buddha*, god of light ; he is typified by the *daibutsu* of *Kamakura, Nara, Kyōto*, etc. — Also called *Daibutsu-Nyorai, Dainichi-Nyorai*.

Rōya-bugyō, 牢 屋 奉 行. — See *Shugoku*.

Rusui-ban, 留 守 居 番. A title created in 1632, and assigned to the official commissioned to watch day and night over the apartments (*ō-oku*) reserved for the *Shōgun's* family. When a fire broke out in the neighborhood of the palace, he had to follow the wife and daughters of the *Shōgun* to the place where they retired. Later on, the number of the *Rusui-ban* was raised to 5, each having under his command 6 *yoriki* and 25 *dōshin*.

Rusui-toshiyori, 留 守 居 年 寄. In the *Tokugawa* era, official of the *Shōgun's* palace who regulated the passports of the daughters of *samurai* that served at Court, superintended the female attendants, inspected the store houses (*kura*) containing weapons, etc. In this latter charge, he was assisted by some *maku-gakari, bugū-gakari, teppō-dansu-gakari, yumi-ya-yari-gakari*, etc. He was also called *Oku-toshiyori*, and, in the absence of the *Shōgun*, he guarded the castle.

Rusu-kwan, 留守官. Formerly an official appointed to guard the Imperial Palace in the absence of the Emperor. Prince *Hirose-Ō* received that title in the reign of *Jitō*; likewise, when *Shōmu-tennō* visited the temples of *Ise* (741), prince *Suzuka-Ō* and *Fujiwara Toyonari* were appointed *Rusu-kwan*.

Ryakunin, 暦仁. *Nengō*: 1238.

Ryaku-ō, 暦應. *Nengō* of the northern dynasty: 1338-1341.

Ryōben, 良辨 (689-773). A bonze, disciple of *Dōsen*, propagated with him the *Kegon-shū* sect and the *Ryōbu-shintō*. He was at the head of the *Tō-daiji* temple (*Nara*), in which he erected, by order of the emperor *Shōmu* a large statue of *Budda* (746). He was a renowned writer and painter.

Ryōbu-shintō, 兩部神道. A doctrine holding that Shintoism and Buddhism are one and the same religion. Towards the beginning of the 9th century, Buddhism, owing to the efforts of the famous bonzes *Saichō, Kūkai, Gyōgi, Ryōben*, etc., had made great progress in Japan; nevertheless it was hard to induce the people to worship other divinities than the *Shintō* gods, founders and protectors of the land. Thereupon the bonzes, by a rather obscure application of the theory of the two parts (*ryōbu*: *kongō-kai* and *taizō-kai*) of the *Shingon-shū* sect, held that the tutelary deities of Japan, worshipped according to the *Shintō* rites, were nothing else than temporary manifestations (*gongen*) of the Buddhist divinities, whose true home (*honchi*) was India but who appeared in Japan, where they left traces (*suijaku*) of their passage. This theory, called *Ryōbu-shintō* or *Shimbutsu-kongō*, brought about the fusion of the two religions. With the exception of the two great temples of *Ise* and *Izumo*, which remained purely *Shintō*, most of the others were allotted to the bonzes, their architecture underwent changes inspired by Buddhism, etc. This state of things continued until the close of the 17th century. At that time rose a school of literati, *Kamo Mabuchi, Motoori Norinaga, Hirata Atsutane*, etc., who studied the national antiquities, and worked with all their might to bring about a revival of pure *Shintō*. Their ambition triumphed with the Imperial Restoration. In 1868, *Shintō* was declared to be the only State Religion and Buddhism was compelled to give back all the temples, into which it had penetrated through the influence of *Ryōbu-shintō*. Now-a-days, as formerly, the two religions have—at least officially, if not in the life of the people—become estranged, and this separation, without securing to the old Shintoism any remarkable revival, has dealt Japanese Buddhism a blow from which it strives in vain to recover.

Ryōchū, 良忠 (+ 1333). Grandson of the *Kwampaku Fujiwara Yoshizane*, and son of the *Gon-daisōzu Ryōhō*, became a bonze like his father and followed prince *Morinaga-Shinnō*. He accompanied *Go-Daigo* to Mt. *Kasagi* (1331), from whence he undertook to carry to the provinces an order of the Emperor, calling his faithful subjects to arms against the *Hōjō*. On his return, he endeavored to deliver *Go-Daigo*, then a prisoner at *Rokuhara*; but he failed and was arrested. He escaped at night by breaking the door of his prison, took to arms, and aided by *Akamatsu Norimura*, defeated his adversaries in many an encounter. Thereupon, he resolved with *Morinaga-Shinnō*, to do away with *Ashikaga Takauji*, whose ambitious designs he began to suspect; but when the prince, unjustly suspected by his father, was shut up in the *Nikaidō* (*Kamakura*) more than 30 of his followers were put to death, among whom was *Ryōchū*.

Ryō-gawa, 兩 川 . A name by which the two sons of *Mōri Motonari*, *Kobayakawa Takakage* and *Kikkawa Motoharu*, were known in the 16th century, because the ideograph *kawa* (川) entered into the composition of their names.

Ryōgen, 良 源 (912-985). A famous bonze of the *Tendai-shū* sect; was *Dai-sōjō* and chief of the *Hiei-zan* temples (966). He was a great favorite at Court and received the name of *Jie-Daishi*.

Ryōge no kwan, 令 外 官 . Name given to the functions established after the promulgation of the *Taihō* Code (702), such as *Naidaijin*, *Chūnagon*, *Kurando*, *Kebiishi*, etc.

Ryōjun-kō, 旅 順 口 . Port-Arthur. A Chinese naval station in the south of the *Liao-tong* peninsula. Captured by the Japanese, Nov. 22, 1894, and restored to China on the conclusion of the peace, it was leased to Russia in 1897 for 25 years. During the war of 1904-1905, it surrendered after a siege of more than 6 months. By the treaty of peace, the Russian rights were ceded to Japan. It is at present a naval prefecture (*Chinjufu*).

Ryōkami-yama, 兩 神 山 . A mountain to the west of *Musashi* (1700 m.); also called *Yōka-mi-yama*.

Ryōko, 陵 戸 . Formerly country families, intrusted with the guard and maintenance of the Imperial tombs (*sanryō, misasagi*). When there was no *ryōko*, some neighboring family was appointed to fill the office and was exempted from taxes and received the name of *shuko*.

Ryōnin, 良 仁 (1072-1132). A bonze, founder of the *Yūzū-nembutsu-shū* sect. Born at *Tomita* (*Owari*), he repaired to *Hiei-zan* and studied the doctrines of the *Tendai* sect. After 23 years, he retired to *Ōhara* (*Yamashiro*), where he founded the *Raikō-in* temple. There he adopted the habit of reciting 60,000 times a day the invocation (*nembutsu*) "*Namu-Amida-butsu*." His reputation soon spread. The emperor *Shirakawa* favored him and induced him to propagate the *Yūzū-nembutsu*. He afterwards founded at *Sumiyoshi* (*Settsu*), the temple of *Dainembutsu-ji*, which became the seat of the sect. His posthumous name is *Shō-ō-Daishi*.

Ryō no gige, 令 義 解 . A commentary on Chinese Law (*Myōhō*), in 10 volumes, published in 833 by *Kiyowara Natsuno*.

Ryō no shūge, 令 集 解 . A supplement to the *Ryō no gige*, published in 30 volumes by *Koremune Naomoto* (920). These two works completed the *Taihō* Code (702).

Ryō-Rokuhara, 兩六波羅. In the *Kamakura* era, the palaces of the two governors of *Kyōto*, one to the north, and the other to the south of *Rokuhara*..—See *Rokuhara*.

Ryōtō-hantō, 遼東牛嶋. The *Liao-tong* peninsula, a part of southern Manchuria.

Ryō-Uesugi, 兩上杉. The two branches of the *Uesugi* family, *Yamanouchi* and *Ōgigayatsu*, powerful at *Kamakura* under the *Ashikaga Shōgun*.

Ryōyō, 遼陽. *Liao-yang*, in southern Manchuria. Great battle, (Aug. 27, — Sept. 3, 1904).

Ryōzen, 靈山. In *Iwashiro*, where the *Chinjufu-taishōgun Kitabatake Akiie* built a castle in 1337. Abandoning that of *Taga*, he intrenched himself there to fight the better against the *Ashikaga*. The castle was besieged and destroyed while *Akiie* was fighting near *Kyōto*. On its site was erected in 1882 a temple (*Ryōzen-jinja*), dedicated to *Kitabatake Chikafusa* and his sons *Akiie, Akinobu*, etc.

Ryūkyū, 琉球. Name given by the Europeans to all the islands scattered between *Kyūshū* and *Formosa*. But the Japanese do not include the northern group (*Satsugū-shōto*), which have always belonged to the provinces of *Satsuma* and *Ōsumi*. The archipelago, formerly called *Uruma-jima*, forms 3 principal groups, which, going from north to south, are : *Okinawa, Miyako* and *Yaeyama*. It comprises 55 islands with a total surface of 2390 square kilometres and a population of about 455,000 souls. — The first mention of the *Ryūkyū* in Japanese history, is in the year 1187, date of the accession to the throne of a certain *Shunten*, said to be the son of *Minamoto Tametomo*. In 1451, the first embassy came to *Kyōto* and was received by the *Shōgun Yoshimasa ;* from that time, began the custom of sending periodical embassies. They ceased at the beginning of the 17th century ; for that reason, and also to demand satisfaction for the ill-treatment which some *Satsuma* fishermen wrecked on these coasts, had received at the hands of the natives, the *daimyō* of *Kagoshima, Shimazu Iehisa*, sent, in 1609, an expedition which captured the castle of *Shuri*, in the island of *Okinawa*, and annexed to his domains the group of *Ōshima*. Henceforward, the *Ryūkyū* paid tribute both to Japan and to China, which latter country, from the 15th century, claimed the suzerainty over these islands. In 1873, the king of the *Ryūkyū* came to *Tōkyō* and received the investiture of his domains ; in 1879, the archipelago was annexed to Japan and formed the department of *Okinawa*. China protested, but ex-president Grant, whose arbitration was requested, declared in favor of Japan. The former king is now Marquis, and two branches of his family possess the title of Baron.

Ryūkyū gō-take, 琉球五嶽. The 5 highest mountains of *Okinawa* island : *Kaso-dake, Nago-dake, Onna-dake, Ben-dake* and *Hattō-dake*.

Ryūsenji, 龍泉寺. In *Kawachi ;* ancient castle, which, in the 14th century, belonged to the *Kishiwada* family, vassals of the *Kusunoki*, and like them faithful to the southern dynasty. During the struggle between the two branches of the *Hatakeyama* family (1460-1466), the castle was in the hands of *Yoshinari*.

Ryūzōji, 龍造寺. A family of *daimyō*, originating in *Hizen*.

—— **Iekane,** 家兼 (1454-1546). Vassal of *Shōni Masasuke*, fought with him against *Otomo Yoshioki* of *Bungo*. When *Masasuke* was defeated and killed (1506), he raised fresh troops and defeated *Ōtomo*. Owing to that victory, his influence became considerable in his clan, and he succeeded at last in supplanting the sons of his former master.

—— **Takanobu,** 隆信 (1530-1585). Grandson of *Iekane*, was at first a bonze under the name of *Engetsu;* but at the age of 18, he returned to secular life. In 1553, he captured the castle of *Saga* (*Hizen*), where he established his residence; he was attacked the following year by *Shōni Tokinao*, but remained victorious. Always at war to increase his domains, he attacked successively his neighbors, *Arima Yoshisada, Ōmura Sumitada, Arima Haruzumi,* etc.; but was at last defeated by *Ōtomo Yoshishige* (1569), and perished in a bloody battle against *Shimazu Yoshihiro* of *Satsuma*.

—— **Masaie,** 政家 (1556-1607). Son of *Takanobu*, served in the expedition of *Hideyoshi* against the *Shimazu* (1587), and was confirmed in the possession of his fief of *Saga* (*Hizen* — 350,000 k.), which he ceded 3 years later to his vassal *Nabeshima Naoshige*.

Edo, DURING THE DAY.

Edo, AT NIGHT

S

Sabae, 鯖江. In *Echizen*. From 1720 to 1868, was the residence of the *Manabe daimyō* (50,000 k.).

Sachūben, 左中辨. Official below the *Sadaiben*, and his substitute. He was assisted by the *Sashōben*.

Sadaiben, 左大辨. Formerly an official having charge of the revision of the affairs of the *Nakatsukasa-shō*, the *Shikibu-shō*, the *Jibu-shō*, the *Mimbu-shō*, the *Dajō-kwan*, etc. When there was no *Uben-kwan*, he performed the latter's functions.

Sadaijin, 左大臣. (Lit.: Minister of the left). Formerly the second of the three principal ministers, inferior to the *Dajō-daijin*, and superior to the *Udaijin:* shared the administration with them, revised the judgments of the High Court (*Danjō*), but his special duty was to superintend the affairs pertaining to the Imperial palace. He was also called *Ichi no kami*, and *Safu*.

Sadaishō, 左大將. Abbreviation of *Sakon-e-taishō*.

Sadatsune-Shinnō, 貞常親王 (1425-1474). Son of prince *Sada-fusa-Shinnō* (*Go-Sūkō*) and great-grandson of the emperor of the North, *Sūkō*. Received the title of *Fushimi no Miya* from his brother, *Go-Hanazono-tennō*, and was the ancestor of the princely family of that name.

Sadayuki-Shinnō, 貞敬親王 (1765-1831). Descendant of the above and son of prince *Fushimi Kuniyori*. Was adopted by the emperor *Go-Momozono* (1797). He is the ancestor of the princes *Kwachō, Kita-Shirakawa, Yamashina, Nashimoto* and *Kuni*.

Sadazumi-Shinnō, 貞純親王 (874-916). 6th son of the emperor *Seiwa*. Was *Hyōbu-kyō, Nakatsukasa-kyō, Taishu* of *Hitachi* and of *Kazusa*. His son *Tsunemoto*, received the name of *Minamoto:* he is the ancestor of the *Seiwa-Genji*.

Sado, 佐渡. Large island (868 Km.²) on the W. coast of Japan. Forms one of the 7 provinces of the *Hokuroku-dō.* — Chinese name: *Sashū.* — Comprised three districts which were combined in 1896, (*Sado-gōri*). — Pop.: 115,000 inh. — Pr. cities: *Aikawa* (15,000 inh.), *Ebisu-minato* (4,300 inh.) — The island of *Sado*, for many years was a place of exile for important personages: the emperor *Juntoku* (1221), *Nichiren* (1271), etc. — It actually forms a part of the *Niigata* department.

Sado-bugyō, 佐渡奉行. Under the *Tokugawa*, an official who had charge of the island of *Sado*. Established at *Aikawa*, he administered justice, collected taxes, directed the working of the silver mines and guarded the island against any possible approach of foreign vessels. He was subject to the *Kanjō-bugyō*. *Ōkubo Nagayasu* was the first who received this title (1603).

Sadowara, 佐土原. In *Hyūga*. Formerly the seat of the provincial governor. During the 16th century, the *Shimazu* of *Satsuma* possessed a castle there wherein they defended themselves against the army of *Hideyoshi* (1587). From 1603 to 1868, it was the residence of a branch of the family (27,000 k.).

Saeki, 佐伯. In *Bungo*. Was, from 1594 to 1868, the residence of the *Mōri daimyō* (20,000 k.).

Saeki Imakebito, 佐伯今毛人 (719-790). Descendant of *Ōtomo Muroya*, and son of *Hitotaru*, became famous as architect and builder. He directed the works for the temple *Tō-daiji* (741). Together with *Fujiwara Tanetsugu* he was entrusted with the building of the new capital of the emperor *Kwammu* at *Nagaoka* (*Yamashiro*) (784).

Saga, 嵯峨. Village W. of *Kyōto*. The emperor *Saga* built a palace (to-day *Daikaku-ji*) in this village and retired in it after his abdication (823).

Saga, 佐賀. Chief town (33,000 inh.) of the *Saga* department. — Was the residence of the *Ryūzōji daimyō* (1553), then, from 1590 to 1868, that of *Nabeshima* (350,000 k.). In 1874, it was the scene of a small civil war brought about by *Etō Shimpei* and promptly checked by *Ōkubo Toshimichi*.

Saga, 嵯峨. *Kuge* family descended from *Fujiwara* (*Sanjō*) *Sane-fusa* (1146-1224). — Now Marquis.

Saga-Genji, 嵯峨源氏. Branch of the *Minamoto* family descended from the emperor *Saga*. — See *Minamoto*.

Saga-ken, 佐賀縣. Department formed of 8 districts (*kōri*) of the *Hizen* province. — Pop.: 666,000. — Chief town: *Saga* (33,000 inh.).

Saga-tennō, 嵯峨天皇. 52nd Emperor of Japan (810-823). *Kammu* second son of *Kwammu-tennō*, at the age of 24, succeeded his brother *Heijō* who retired to *Nara*. The following year, *Kusuri-ko*, *Heijō's* wife, and *Fujiwara Nakanari* plotted to restore *Heijō* to the throne and transfer the capital again to *Nara*, but *Sakanoe Tamuramaro* soon subdued the confederates: *Nakanari* was put to death, *Kusuri-ko* took poison, *Heijō* and his son *Takaoka-shinnō* were obliged to shave their heads. *Saga* was a remarkable administrator; the *Taihō* Code was completed by his orders; he created the offices of *Kurōdo*, of *Kebiishi* and others. After having reigned 14 years, he abdicated in favor of his brother *Junwa* and retired to *Saga* (whence his posthumous name), where he lived 19 years. *Saga* is known as a poet and a great calligraphist; he, with the bonze *Kūkai* and *Tachibana Hayanari*, form the *Sampitsu* (Lit.: the 3 brushes).

Sagami, 相模. One of the 15 provinces of the *Tōkaidō*. Comprises 8 districts, all depending on the *Kanagawa-ken*. — Chinese name: *Sōshū*.—In ancient times, called *Sashi no kuni*, then *Sashi-kami*, whence *Sagami*.

Sagami, 相模. Famous poetess of the 11th century. Daughter of *Minamoto Yorimitsu*; she married *Ōe Kinsuke*, *Sagami no kami*, whence the name under which she is known.

Sagami-gawa, 相模川. River (72 Km.), formed by the junction of the *Katsura-gawa* and the *Dōshi-gawa*, which rise in *Kai* and meet in *Sagami*. Also called *Banyū-gawa*.

Sagami-nada, 相摸洋. Sea, S. of *Sagami*.

Sagara, 相良. In *Tōtōmi*. Old castle built in 1576 by *Takeda Katsuyori* and rebuilt by *Tanuma Mototsugu* in 1772. His descendants lived there to the Restoration. (10,000 k.).

Sagara, 相良. *Daimyō* family, descended from *Fujiwara* and since the 13th century established at *Hitoyoshi* (*Higo*), where it remained to the Restoration (22,000 k.). — Now Viscount.

Sagiyama, 鷺山. In *Mino*. Old castle built towards the end of the 12th century by *Satake Hideyoshi*. During the 16th century, it passed into the hands of the *Saitō*: it was there that *Toshimasa* was besieged and killed by his son *Yoshitatsu* (1556).

Saibara, 催鳥樂. In former times, popular songs which the farmers sang especially whilst leading their horses. After the introduction of Chinese music, variations were added to them and they became a source of amusement among the nobility.

Saichō, 最澄. — See *Dengyō-Daishi*.

Saiga, 雜賀. In *Kii*. In the 16th century, was the seat of a clan, vassal of the temple *Ishiyama-Hongwan-ji* (*Ōsaka*). This clan, for a long time, fought against *Nobunaga*. There also, the chief bonze *Kōsa* took refuge after the capture of his castle at *Ōsaka* (1580).

Saigō, 西鄉. *Daimyō* family coming from *Mikawa*.

—— **Masakatsu,** 正勝 (+1561). At first a vassal of the *Imagawa*, he, in 1561, became a partisan of *Tokugawa Ieyasu*. Besieged in his castle by *Asahina Yasunaga*, general of *Imagawa Ujizane*, he set fire to it and perished therein with his son *Motomasa*.

—— **Iezane,** 家實 (+1597). Grandson of *Masakatsu*. After having fought on the side of *Ieyasu* in all his campaigns, he followed him to *Kwantō* (1590), and received a small fief in *Shimōsa*.

—— **Masakazu,** 正員 (1593-1638). In 1615 he received the castle of *Tōjō* (*Awa* — 10,000 k.) and the title of *Wakasa no kami*.

—— **Nobukazu,** 延員 (1614-1697) was dispossessed in 1693.

Saigō, 西鄉. *Samurai* family of the *Kagoshima* clan (*Satsuma*), ennobled after the Restoration.

—— **Takamori,** 隆盛 (1827-1877). In his childhood he showed a great liking for military exercises and rapidly acquired a high rank in the army of his *daimyō*. He performed a brilliant part in the Restoration war, and was named Marshal in 1874. Some time after, the question of intervention in Korean affairs was raised; *Takamori's* views being opposed by most of the ministers, he retired to *Kagoshima*. There he established a school, (*Shi-gakkō*) to which the youth of *Satsuma* and *Ōsumi* flocked in great number. The government, forseeing danger, did all in its power to bring *Takamori* back to *Tōkyō*, but in vain. The insurrectional movement was brewing during three full years and finally broke out at the beginning of 1877. On Feb. 15th, *Takamori*, at the head of 15,000 men, took possession of *Kagoshima*, then marching northward, he met the *Ku-*

mamoto army, defeated it and laid siege to that city, which was defended with great vigor by Colonel *Tani*. On hearing this news, the government declared *Takamori* to have forfeited all his titles and official rank and sent prince *Arisugawa Taruhito* with a considerable body of men against him. The rebels had to withdraw before superior numbers and entered *Hyūga*, where, notwithstanding their valor, they were defeated in several encounters. Making a supreme effort, *Takamori* after having defeated general *Miyoshi*, succeeded in entering *Kagoshima*. There, resistance soon became an impossibility : surrounded on all sides, by sea and by land, the insurgents prepared to sell their lives dearly. The last battle took place on *Shiro-yama*, Sept. 24th. *Saigō* fell, wounded in the leg by a ball, and one of his faithful retainers, *Beppu Shinsuke*, put an end to his life. — Such was the end of the once "great *Saigō*." A statue was erected in his honor in 1899 at the entrance of *Ueno* park in *Tōkyō* and his son received the title of Marquis in 1902.

—— **Tsugumichi**, 従道 (1843-1902). Brother to *Takamori* also took part in the Restoration war, but unlike his brother, remained always faithful to the government which loaded him with honors. He commanded the expedition to *Formosa* in 1874. Several times minister, he was at the same time Marshal and Admiral. — Now Marquis.

Saigū-ryō, 齊宮寮. Office charged with the administration of the *Ise* temples. — When *Suinin-tennō* had transferred the *Tenshō-Daijin* temple to *Ise*, (5 B.C.) he named his daughter *Yamato-hime*, high-priestess thereof. Later on, it became customary to change the titulary of this office at the accession of a new emperor : it was always a princess and she had the title of *Itsuki-Naishinnō* or *Sai-ō ;* her residence was called *Saigū*, and the bureau having charge of this administration was the *Saigū-ryō*. Under its jurisdiction, were ten secondary bureaus : *Tonari, Kurabe, Zembu, Suibu, Sakabe, Mizube, Tonobe, Saibe, Kadobe*, and *Umabe*.

Saigyō-Hōshi, 西行法師 (1118-1190). Descended from *Fujiwara Hidesato*, was called *Satō Norikiyo*. Very skilful in using the bow, he became a favorite with the ex-emperor *Toba*, who gave him rank among his *Hokumen no bushi* and enjoyed his poetry. But at the age of 23, he abandoned his wife and children, went to *Saga* (*Yamashiro*) and became a bonze under the names of *Saigyō* and *En-i*. He travelled through the provinces, preached and recited poetry. This manner of living displeased the famous *Mongaku-Shōnin*, who considering him the scandal of Buddhism, went so far as to say that if ever he crossed his path, he would break his head. Hearing this, *Saigyō* directed his

SAIGYŌ HŌSHI.

steps towards the temple *Takao-san* and presented himself before *Mongaku* who seemed quite satisfied with the interview, and, as one of his disciples expressed his surprise at this, *Mongaku* answered him ; " Have you then not seen *Saigyō ?* if we had fought together, I would certainly not have been victorious in the contest " ! — From there, *Saigyō* went to *Kamakura* and visited *Yoritomo,* who took delight in speaking with him about poetry and bow shooting ; at the moment of his departure, he presented him with a silver cat, which *Saigyō* offered to the first child he met in the street. He then bent his steps towards the North, where he usually resided with one of his relatives *Fujiwara Hidehira.* He died at *Kyōto,* at the age of 73. He left 2 volumes of poetry.

Sai-in-shi, 齊院司. In 810, the princess *Yūchi-ko-Naishinnō,* daughter of *Saga-tennō,* was named high-priestess of the *Kamo* temple and received the title of *Sai-in.* The *Sai-in-shi* was the bureau attending to the administration of her house. At its head was a *Bettō.* In 1204, at the death of princess *Rei-ko-Naishinnō,* 34th *sai-in,* this dignity was suppressed.

Saijō, 西條. In *Iyo.* Was in 1636, the residence of the *Hitotsu-yanagi daimyō ;* then from 1670 to 1868, of the *Matsudaira* (30,000 k.).

Saikai-dō, 西海道. (Lit.: Region of the Occidental Ocean). One of the 8 great divisions of Japan. Comprises the 9 provinces of *Kyūshū : Chikuzen, Chikugo, Buzen, Bungo, Hizen, Higo, Hyūga, Ōsumi* and *Satsuma,* also those of *Iki* and of *Tsushima.*

Sai-kawa, 犀川. River (118 Km.). After passing through *Shinano,* joins the *Chikuma-gawa,* near *Nagano,* thus forming the *Shinano-gawa.* The interior of the angle formed by the two rivers is called *Kawa-naka-jima.* During the 16th century, it was the scene of the great battles fought between *Takeda Shingen* and *Uesugi Kenshin.* — The *Sai-kawa* is also called *Narai-gawa.*

Saikoku, 西國. The western provinces of Japan, i.e. *Kyūshū* and the neighboring islands.

Saikoku-gundai, 西國郡代. Formerly an official established in the *Hida* district and charged with watching over the provinces of *Buzen, Bungo, Hyūga, Higo,* and *Chikuzen.*

Saiku-jo, 細工所. Under the *Tokugawa,* a bureau whose duty it was to keep the presents reserved for the emperor, the armour, harnesses, movable partitions and furniture of the Shōgunal palace, etc.

Saikusa no matsuri, 三枝祭. Formerly a feast during which, a barrel of *sake* (wine made out of rice) adorned with three branches of flowers was presented to the *Isagawa* temple.

Saikyō, 西京. (Lit.: capital of the West). Official name of *Kyōto* since the transfer of the capital to *Tōkyō* (capital of the East) in 1869.

Saimei-tennō, 齊明天皇. Empress (37th) of Japan (655-661). *Hitarashi-hime* who had already reigned under the name of *Kōgyoku-tennō* (642-644), reascended the throne at the age of 62, upon the death of her brother *Kōtoku,* and, for this reason, she has received the posthumous name of *Saimei-tennō.* She suppressed the use of the *nengō* which had been introduced by her predecessor ; built a palace at *Okamoto* (*Yamato*), the first that was covered with tiles, and sent *Abe no Hirafu* to subdue the *Ebisu* in *Ezo.* It was during her reign that, for the first time the feast of the dead (*bon-matsuri*) was celebrated (659). The kingdoms of *Koma* and *Kudara*, in Korea, having been attacked by the Chinese (660), asked help from Japan : the empress had intended to lead an army to Korea, and was already on her way thither, when she was surprised by death at *Asakura* (*Chikuzen*), at the age of 68.

Saimen no bushi, 西面武士. *Samurai* distinguished for their skill in things pertaining to war, and whom the emperor *Toba* attached to his person as a body guard after his abdication (1199). He had called them so, to distinguish them from the *Hokumen no bushi* created by *Shirakawa-tennō*.

Saimoku, 西牧. In *Kōzuke*. Old castle which, built by *Takeda Shingen*, passed into the hands of the *Hōjō* of *Odawara* and was destroyed in 1590.

Saionji, 西園寺. *Kuge* family, descended from *Fujiwara Kinzane* (1053-1107) It was one of the *Seiwa* (See that name). — Now Marquis.

—— **Kintsune,** 公經 (1171-1244). Son of *Sanemune*, married the niece of *Yoritomo*. In 1217, he tried to obtain the title of *Konoe-taishō*, to which the ex-emperor *Go-Toba* refused his consent. *Kintsune* resented it very much and laid a complaint before the *Shōgun Sanetomo*. *Go-Toba* now forbade him to reappear at Court. Later on, when he was prepared to attack the *Hōjō*, he attempted to imprison *Kintsune*, who succeeded in making good his escape (1221). At the accession of *Go-Hori-kawa*, he was named *Naidaijin*, and the *Dajō-daijin* (1222). — A daughter of *Kintsune*, married to the *Kwampaku Michiie*, was the mother of the *Shōgun Yoritsune ;* another became the wife of *Go-Saga*, and a third married *Go-Fukakusa*.

—— **Kinhira,** 公衡 (1264-1315). Son of *Sanekane*, often called *Chikurin-in* was *Sadaijin*. His daughter married the emperor *Go-Fushimi :* she was the mother by adoption of *Hanazono-tennō* and the true mother of *Kōgon* and *Kōmyō*, emperors of the North. The family was very influential at that time.

—— **Kimmune,** 公宗 (1309-1335). Grandson of *Kinhira*, having become acquainted with the designs of *Hōjō Takatoki*, he revealed them to *Go-Daigo*. *Takatoki* had him arrested and exiled to *Izumo*, where he was put to death by *Nawa Nagatoshi*.

—— **Kimmochi,** 公望. Descendant of the above. Born in 1849, he was one of the few *kuge*, who, after the Restoration, took any active part in the affairs of the government. Having studied in France (1870-1880), he became Minister at Vienna (1885), then at Berlin (1887). He was also charged to carry the answer of the Emperor *Mutsuhito* to his Holiness, Pope Leo XIII, in reply to a letter which had been addressed to him. President of the Bureau of Decorations, Vice-President of the House of Peers (1893), Member of the Privy Council, Minister of Public Instruction, and at intervals of Foreign Affairs (1895), he replaced Marquis *Itō* at the head of the political party called *Seiyū-kwai* (1903). President of the Council in Jan. 1906.

Saishi, 祭祀. Official ceremonies of the Shintoist religion, regulated by the *Jingi-kwan.* They are divided into 3 classes : *taishi, chūshi* and *shōshi.* The great feasts (*taishi*) were preceded by an abstinence of one month ; the middle feasts (*chūshi*), by one of 3 days ; the small feasts (*shōshi*), of one day only. In the first category was the *Daijō-e ;* in the 2nd, the first day of the year, the *Kanname* and the *Niiname-matsuri,* the feast of the *Kamo* temple ; in the 3rd, the feasts of *Hirano, Matsuo, Kasuga, Saikusa,* etc.

Saisho, 税所. *Samurai* family of the *Kagoshima* clan (*Satsuma*) made noble after the Restoration.—Now Viscount.

Saishō-e, 最勝會. Formerly a Buddhist ceremony, during which the prayers called *Saishō-ōkyō* were recited for the peace of the empire. Performed for the first time in 829 at the *Yakushi-ji* temple, it became soon a general custom.

Saitama-ken, 埼玉縣. Department formed by 9 districts (*kōri*) of the *Musashi* province.—Pop.: 1,249,000 inh.—Chief town : *Urawa* (6,900 inh.).—Pr. cities : *Kawagoe* (19,000 inh.) *Kumagaya* (12,000 inh.), etc.

Saitō, 齋藤. Ancient *daimyō* family coming from *Echizen* and descending from the *Chinjufu-Shōgun, Fujiwara Toshihito.*

—— **Sanemori,** 實盛 (1111-1183). Left the province of *Echizen* and established himself at *Nagai* (*Musashi*). He served *Minamoto Yoshitomo* but after the death of the latter, (1160) he attached himself to *Taira Mune-mori,* under whom he fought against *Kiso Yoshinaka.* He was killed at the battle of *Shinowara* (*Kaga*).

—— **Toshimasa,** 利政 (1494-1556). Born at *Kyōto,* was a bonze, but having returned to the world, he became an oil merchant. Protected by *Nagai Nagahiro,* he was adopted by the *Nishimura* family and took the name of *Hidemoto.* He murdered *Nagahiro* and changed his name into that of

SAITŌ SANEMORI.

Nagai Toshimasa. Not content with this, he expelled *Toki Yoshiyori,* then governor of *Mino,* and adopting the name of *Saitō,* he openly made war against *Oda Nobuhide,* but, fearing defeat, he sued for peace and gave his daughter in marriage to *Nobunaga.* His adopted son, *Yoshi-tatsu,* having asserted his independence, *Toshimasa* marched against him, but was defeated and killed.

—— **Yoshitatsu,** 義龍 (1527-1561). Son of *Toki Yoshiyori,* was adopted by *Toshimasa* who, having had other children, intended to deprive him of his succession. *Yoshitatsu* however with the help of *Nagai Mi-chitoshi,* put his two younger brothers to death and defeated his father in several battles. *Nobunaga* desired to revenge the death of his father-in-law, but he did not dare to enter into conflict with *Yoshitatsu.*

—— **Tatsuoki,** 龍興. Son of *Yoshitatsu,* was defeated by *Nobu-naga* in 1564, and fled. From that time, the name of his family is no more mentioned in history.

Saitō Chikudō, 齋藤竹堂 (1812-1849). Confucianist from *Sendai*. Pupil of *Asaka Gonsai*.

Saitō Hikomaro, 齋藤彥麿 (1768-1854). Confucianist from *Hamada* (*Iwami*). Disciple of *Motoori Norinaga*.

Saitō Setsudō, 齋藤拙堂 (1797-1865). Confucianist from *Ise*. Disciple of *Koga Seiri*.

Sai-un Hō-shinnō, 最雲法親王 (1104-1162), Son of the emperor *Horikawa*. Having become bonze, he was *Gon-sōzu* and head of the *Tendai* sect. He was the first prince who governed the *Kajii no miya*.

Sakabe, 酒部. In olden times, a corporation of men who prepared the *sake* (wine made out of rice) and whose chief bore the title of *Sakabe no kimi*.

Sakai, 境. Town (50,000 inh.) of *Osaka-fu*, chief city of *Izumi* province. — Was formerly called *Sakai no ura*. In 1336, *Kitabatake Akiie* was defeated there by *Kō Moronao*. Later on, *Yamana Ujikiyo*, named governor of the province, built a castle there (1373) which was called *Sempu*. After *Ujikiyo's* death (1391), it passed into the possession of *Ōuchi Yoshihiro*, then into that of the *Hosokawa* (1399), who confided it to the *Miyoshi*. During the whole Middle Ages, *Sakai* was the principal port of Japan. After the ruin of the *Miyoshi* (1577), *Nobunaga* established a governor there. Its prosperity declined when *Hideyoshi* tried to make *Ōsaka* the centre of all commerce. Under the *Tokugawa*, the *Shōgun* was represented in that city by a *bugyō*.

Sakai, 酒井. *Daimyō* family, coming from *Mikawa* and descended from *Minamoto Arichika*. *Arichika* had two sons: one, *Yasuchika*, took the name of *Matsudaira*; the other, *Chikauji*, that of *Sakai*, and is the ancestor of the family of that name. *Hirochika*, son of *Chikauji*, also had two sons who were the heads of the two principal branches of the family.

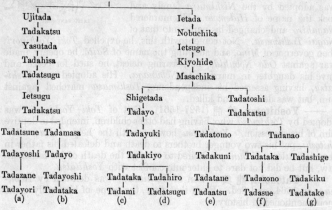

```
              Chikauji
                 |
              Hirochika
                 |
   ┌─────────────┼─────────────────────────────┐
 Ujitada                  Ietada
   |                        |
 Tadakatsu               Nobuchika
   |                        |
 Yasutada                Ietsugu
   |                        |
 Tadahisa                Kiyohide
   |                        |
 Tadatsugu               Masachika
   |                        |
   |            ┌──────────┼──────────┐
 Ietsugu      Shigetada           Tadatoshi
   |            |                     |
 Tadakatsu    Tadayo               Tadakatsu
```

Tadatsune	Tadamasa		Tadayuki		Tadatomo		Tadanao
Tadayoshi	Tadayo		Tadakiyo		Tadakuni	Tadataka	Tadashige
Tadazane	Tadayoshi		Tadataka	Tadahiro	Tadatane	Tadazono	Tadakiku
Tadayori	Tadataka		Tadami	Tadatsugu	Tadaatsu	Tadasue	Tadatake
(a)	(b)		(c)	(d)	(e)	(f)	(g)

(*a*) — Senior Branch. —— **Tadatsugu, 忠 次** (1527-1596). Served *Ieyasu,* had charge of the castle of *Yoshida* (*Mikawa*) and, in 1584, defeated and killed *Ikeda Nobuteru* at *Nagakute.*

—— **Ietsugu, 家 次** (1564-1619). In 1578, he succeeded his father in the possession of the castle of *Yoshida* (*Mikawa*). When *Ieyasu* had been transferred to *Kwantō* (1590), he gave him a revenue of 30,000 k. at *Usui* (*Kōzuke*); in 1604, *Ietsugu* took up his residence at *Takasaki* (*Kōzuke* — 50,000 k.), then in 1616, at *Takata* (*Echigo* — 100,000 k.). — Later on, the family resided : in 1619, at *Matsushiro* (*Shinano*) ; then from 1622 to 1868 at *Tsurugaoka* (*Dewa* — 120,000 k.). — Now Count.

(*b*) — Branch of the preceding family, which settled at *Matsumine* (*Dewa* — 20,000 k.) in 1647 ; built a castle there in 1779 and remained in it till the Restoration. — Now Viscount.

(*c*) — **Masachika, 正 親** (+ 1576). Served the *Tokugawa, Nobutada, Kiyoyasu* and *Hirotada.* In 1561, he took the castle of *Nishio* (*Mikawa*), which was afterwards entrusted to his care.

—— **Shigetada, 重 忠**. Son of *Masachika,* received the fief of *Kawagoe* (*Musashi* — 15,000 k.) in 1590, and in 1601, that of *Umayabashi* (*Kōzuke* — 35,000 k.). During the *Ōsaka* campaign (1615), he guarded the castle of *Edo.*

—— **Tadakiyo, 忠 清** (1626-1681). Governed during the illness of the *Shōgun Ietsuna* (1675-1680) and showed great talents for administration.—His descendants were transferred to *Himeji* (*Harima* — 150,000 k.) in 1749, where they remained till the Restoration.—Now Count.—Since then, two branches of the family have received the title of Baron.

(*d*) — Branch of the above which from 1681 to 1868, remained at *Isezaki* (*Kōzuke* — 20,000 k.).—Now Viscount.

(*e*) — Branch, which from 1668 to 1868 resided at *Katsuyama* (*Awa* — 12,000 k.).—Now Viscount.

(*f*) — **Tadatoshi, 忠 利** (1562-1627). Received the fief of *Tanaka* (*Suruga* — 10,000 k.) in 1601, then was transferred to *Kawagoe* (*Musashi* — 30,000 k.) in 1609.

—— **Tadakatsu, 忠 勝** (1587-1662). Was transferred to *Obama* (*Wakasa* — 103,500 k.) in 1634, where his descendants remained till the Restoration.—Now Count.

(*g*) — Branch of the above which, from 1682 to 1868, resided at *Tsuruga* (*Echizen* — 10,000 k.).—Now Viscount.

Sakai-bugyō, 境 奉 行. Under the *Tokugawa,* governor of the city of *Sakai* (*Izumi*). Established in 1600, he was first called *Sakai-mandokoro ;* then in 1618, this title was changed to that of *bugyō.* He was dependent on the *Jōdai* of *Ōsaka.*

Sakai Hōitsu, 酒 井 抱 一 (1761-1828). By birth *Tadayori,* was the brother of *Sakai Tadazane, daimyō* of *Himeji* (*Harima*). When very young, he entered the temple of *Nishi-Hongwan-ji* (*Kyōto*), studied the *Kanō* and *Tosa* school of painting, then adopted the style of *Ogata Kōrin.* Together with *Tani Bunchō,* he was the most celebrated artist of his time.

Sakaibe Iwazumi, 境部石積. Descendant of *Ōhiko no mikoto*. Went to China in 653, to complete his studies. When he returned, he published a collection of new words from Chinese characters, in 44 vol. now all lost (683).

Sakaibe Marise, 境部摩理勢 (+ 628). Son of *Soga Iname* and brother to *Umako*. At the death of *Suiko*, he intended to raise prince *Yamashiro*, son of *Shōtoku-taishi* to the throne. His nephew *Emishi*, then a minister, opposed this view, chose prince *Tamura* (*Jomei-tennō*) and had his uncle put to death.

Sakakibara, 榊原. *Daimyō* family descended from *Nikki Sadanaga* (*Seiwa-Genji*).

—— **Toshinaga,** 利長. Son of *Sadanaga*, settled at *Sakakibara* (*Ise*) and took the name of that place.

—— **Yasumasa,** 康政 (1548-1606). Served *Ieyasu* and in 1590 received the fief of *Tatebayashi* (*Kōzuke* — 100,000 k.).—His descendants resided: at *Shirakawa* (*Mutsu*) in 1643; at *Himeji* (*Harima*) in 1649; at *Murakami* (*Echigo*) in 1667; at *Himeji* in 1704; lastly from 1741 to 1868, at *Takata* (*Echigo* — 150,000 k.).—Now Viscount.

Sakamoto, 坂本. In *Ōmi*. Scene of a battle between the two rivals for the shōgunate, *Yoshizumi* and *Yoshitane* (1499). The latter being defeated, fled to *Suwō*. In 1547, *Yoshiharu* and *Yoshiteru* took refuge in that place to escape from *Hosokawa Harumoto*. *Nobunaga* built a castle there, which he entrusted to *Mori Yoshinari*, who, being attacked by the *Asakura*, the *Asai* and the troops of *Hiei-zan*, was defeated and killed (1571). *Nobunaga*, returning with an army, destroyed all the temples of *Hiei-zan*. He then gave the castle to *Akechi Mitsuhide* and after the defeat of the latter, his whole family committed *harakiri* (1582). *Hideyoshi* bestowed *Sakamoto* on *Niwa Nagahide* who, in 1584, went to *Otsu*.

Sakanoe, 坂上. Ancient family of warriors descended from *Achi no Omi*.

—— **Karitamaro,** 苅田麿 (728-786). Son of *Inukai*, helped in the repression of the revolt of *Nakamaro* (764). Was later on *Chinjufu-shōgun*.

—— **Tamuramaro,** 田村麿 (758-811). Son of the above, after having helped, under the orders of *Ōtomo Otomaro*, to check the advance of the *Ebisu*, he was given the command of an expedition against them (801); it was then that he received the title of *Sei-i-taishōgun*, created for the occasion. He defeated them completely and to stop their continuous incursions, built the castle of *Izawa* (*Mutsu*). He was buried at the village of *Kurisu*, near *Kyōto*, and it is believed that it is his tomb which is known

SAKANOE TAMURAMARO.

under the name of *Shōgun-zuka* (See that name). *Tamuramaro* is the founder of the famous temple *Kiyomizu-dera*. He is the ancestor of the *Tamura daimyō* of *Mutsu*.

Sakaori no miya, 酒折宮. In 112, *Yamatotakeru no mikoto*, after having defeated the *Ebisu*, passed into *Kai* and rested his troops. His temporary residence in that place was called *Sakaori no miya* (to-day, *Satogaki-mura*).

Sakimori-tsukasa, 防人司. Formerly title of the chief of the troops who guarded the *Dazaifu*.

Saki-shima, 先嶋. Southern part of the *Ryūkyū* archipelago, comprising the groups of *Miyako* and of *Yaeyama*.

Saki-shima, 佐木嶋. Island (14 Km. circ.) of the Inland Sea, S.E. of *Aki* province, of which it is a dependency.

Sakon, 左近. — See *Kon-e-fu*.

Sakuji-bugyō, 作事奉行. Under the *Kamakura Shōgun*, an official charged with the building of palaces and houses of the city. *Ōba Kageyoshi* was the first to receive this title in 1180. The official charged with the erecting of temples, had the title of *Zōei-bugyō;* the *Zaimoku-bugyō* attended to the transportation of the material to the place of construction.—Under the *Tokugawa Shōgun*, the *Sakuji-bugyō* attended to the repairs of the palaces, the castles, the tombs of *Ueno* etc. Created in 1632, a part of his functions were taken from him and given to the *Kobushin-bugyō* (1685): he had under him, 25 *hikwan* and 23 *kanjō-yaku*.

Sakuma, 佐久間. Ancient *daimyō* family, coming from *Owari*.

—— **Nobumori,** 信盛 (+ 1582). Served *Nobunaga*. In 1570, having the custody of the castle of *Nagahama* (*Ōmi*), he defeated the *Sasaki*. He besieged the temple of *Hongwan-ji* of *Ōsaka* for 5 years. Disgraced on that account (1580), he was confined on the *Kōya-san*, where he died.

—— **Morimasa,** 盛政 (1554-1583). Served *Shibata Katsuie* and was castellan of *Oyama* (*Kaga*). In 1583, he defeated and killed *Nakagawa Kiyohide* at *Shizu-ga-take*. After this success, *Katsuie* ordered him to draw back before the advancing army of *Hideyoshi;* *Morimasa* refused to obey, engaged the enemy and was defeated. He then fled, but was taken and beheaded at *Rokujō-gahara* (*Kyōto*).

—— **Yasutsugu,** 安次 (1556-1628). After the ruin of his party at *Shizu-ga-take* (1583), he submitted to *Hideyoshi*. After *Sekigahara* (1600), he received the castle of *Iiyama* (*Shinano*). His family became extinct in 1638.

Sakuma, 佐久間. *Samurai* family from *Chōshū*, ennobled in 1895.—Now Viscount.

Sakuma Shōzan, 佐久間象山 (1811-1864). *Samurai* of the *Matsushiro* clan (*Shinano*); came to *Edo* in 1839 in order to finish his studies and busied himself especially with the building of forts and ships. Twice, he sent reports to the *Bakufu* on the necessity of coast defence, but he was not listened to. When Commodore Perry arrived at *Shimoda*, some of *Shōzan's* adherents tried to board the American ship, but were taken prisoners together with *Shōzan* (1854). Liberated in 1862, he voted, contrary to the popular opinion for the opening of the ports to foreign trade, and was assassinated in *Kyōto* by some fanatical partisans of the conservative system.

Sakuma Tōgan, 佐久間洞巖 (1653-1736). Painter and writer from *Sendai*, has left several works.

Sakura, 佐倉. Small city (7,400 inh.) of *Shimōsa*. Ancient castle built by *Chiba Suketane*. In 1590, *Hideyoshi* gave it to *Kunō Muneyoshi*. Under the *Tokugawa*, was successively the residence of the *daimyō Matsudaira* (1602); *Doi* (1610), who rebuilt the castle; *Ishikawa* (1633), *Matsudaira* (1635), *Hotta* (1642), *Ōgyū* (1661), *Ōkubo* (1678), *Toda* (1688), *Inaba* (1701), *Ōgyū* (1723), and lastly from 1745 to 1868, *Hotta* (115,000 k.).

Sakura Sōgorō, 佐倉宗吾郎. Mayor (*nanushi*) of the village of *Kōzu* (*Shimōsa*). *Hotta Masamori* having died in 1651, his son and successor, *Masanobu*, then 22 years of age, increased the taxes to such an extent that great misery prevailed in his estates. As all representations were of no avail, 300 chiefs of villages joined and resolved to have their complaints brought to *Edo*. *Sōgorō* was chosen as their deputy and one day, as the *Shōgun Ietsuna* was going to the temple *Kwan-ei-ji* of *Ueno*, he handed in his petition. The *Shōgun* ordered *Masanobu* to

SAKURA SŌGORŌ presenting his petition to the SHŌGUN (by DAISHI).

appear before him; *Masanobu* obeyed, but irritated by this occurrence, threatened the signers of the petition with his vengeance. These poor men, being frightened, put the whole blame on *Sōgorō*, who was arrested with his whole family. *Sōgorō* and his wife were crucified, not however before they had witnessed the decapitation of their children (1655). Some years later however, *Masanobu's* tyranny received its punishment. He was deprived of his domains and banished to *Tokushima* (*Awa*) (1660). In the mean time, the memory of *Sōgorō* rose in the minds of his countrymen, who erected a temple (*Sōgo-jinja*) to him in the village of *Kōzu*.

Sakurai, 櫻井. In *Settsu*, famous as being the very place on which *Kusunoki Masashige*, when going to fight and die at *Minato-gawa*, parted from his son *Masatsura*, after having given him his last instructions (1336).

Sakurai, 櫻井. Branch of the *Matsudaira* family, descended from *Nobusada* (+ 1538), who, being governor of the castle *Sakurai* (*Mikawa*), took the name thereof. Under the *Tokugawa*, the family bore the name of *Matsudaira* and after the Restoration, that of *Sakurai*.

—— **Tadayori,** 忠頼. Served *Ieyasu*, who, in 1590, gave him the castle of *Yawata-yama* (*Musashi*), then in 1600, that of *Kanayama* (*Mino* — 25,000 k.), and the following year, that of *Hamamatsu* (*Tōtōmi* — 50,000 k.). — His descendants resided successively : in 1622, at *Sanuki* (*Kazusa*) ; in 1634, at *Tanaka* (*Suruga*) ; in 1635, at *Kakegawa* (*Tōtōmi*) ; in 1638, at *Iiyama* (*Shinano*) ; in 1706, again at *Kakegawa* ; and from 1711 to 1868, at *Amagasaki* (*Settsu* — 40,000 k.).—Now Viscount.

Sakurai, 櫻井. *Kuge* family descended from *Fujiwara Michitaka* (953-995).—Now Viscount.

Sakura-jima, 櫻島. Island (39 Km. circ.) in the bay of *Kagoshima*, opposite the city of that name. Called also *Mukō-jima*. According to tradition, it was produced by an upheavel of the earth's crust in 716. It is dependent on *Ōsumi* province.

Sakurajima-dake, 櫻島嶽. Volcano (1100 m.) in the island of *Sakura-jima* (*Ōsumi*) Also called *Ontake*.

Sakuramachi-tennō, 櫻町天皇 115th Emperor of Japan (1736-1746). *Akihito*, eldest son of *Nakamikado-tennō*, succeeded his father at the age of 15, and after a reign of 11 years, during which the power was in the hands of the *Shōgun Yoshimune*, he abdicated in favor of his son *Momozono*, then only 7 years old. He died 5 years later at the age of 31.

Sakushū, 作州. Chinese name of *Mimasaka* province.

Sakwanshō, 左官掌. Formerly a title of two officials inferior to the *Dajōkwan* ; kind of apparitors.

Sama, 娑麐. Port of *Suwō* province (now *Mitajiri*) ; the emperor *Keikō* sojourned in that place during the first part of his expedition against the *Kumaso* (82-83).

Sambō, 三房. Name given to three renowned literary men of the 11th century, of whose name the character *fusa* was a constituent (Chin. *bō*) : *Ōe Tadafusa*, *Fujiwara Korefusa* and *Fujiwara Nagafusa*.

Sammaibashi-jō, 三枚橋城. Old name of the castle built at *Numazu* (*Suruga*) by *Takeda Katsuyori* (1579). — See *Numazu*.

Sammon, 山門. Principal branch of the *Tendai-shū* sect, established in 805 by *Saichō* (*Dengyō-Daishi*). It formerly had its principal seat in the *Enryaku-ji* temple of the *Hiei-zan*.

Sammonto, 三門徒. Name given to three branches, *Senshōji*, *Chōseiji* and *Jōshōji* of the *Jōdo-shinshū* sect, founded in *Echizen* by the bonze *Jodō* (1253-1340) and his disciples.

Sampitsu, 三筆. The three famous calligraphists of the 9th century: the emperor *Saga*, *Tachibana Hayanari* and the bonze *Kūkai*.

Samurai, 士. Till the Restoration, military man, warrior, man of arms. This word comes from the verb *samurau*, or better *saburau*, which signifies: to be on one's guard, to guard; it applied especially to the soldiers who were on guard at the Imperial Palace. — The *samurai* received a pension from their *daimyō*, and had the privilege of wearing two swords. They intermarried in their own caste and the privilege of *samurai* was transmitted to all the children, although the heir alone received a pension. — In 1878, the corresponding Chinese term *shizoku* was substituted for the term *samurai*.

Samurai-dokoro, 侍所. Under the *Kamakura Shōgun*, a bureau that attended to all affairs concerning the military class: Guard of the *Shōgun's* Palace, nomination of officials, military tribunals, etc. In 1220, some of its functions were incumbent on the *Ko-samurai-dokoro*, but it retained the most important ones. — It was not abolished at the time of the shōgunate of *Muromachi*.

Samurai-dokoro bettō, 侍所別當. Title of the chief of the *Samurai-dokoro*. *Wada Yoshimori* was the first who bore that title (1180). His influence always increased, so much so, that even the *Shikken* had to submit to his will. In 1213, *Yoshimori* revolted against the *Hōjō*, but was defeated and put to death with all the members of his family. Since that time, the *Shikken* reserved the title and the functions of *Bettō* for himself.

Samurai-dokoro shoshi, 侍所所司. Under the *Kamakura Shōgun*, a title given to 4 officials who divided the functions of the *Samurai-dokoro* among themselves, when the *Shikken* had reserved the title of *Bettō* for himself (1213). The 4 first were *Nikaidō Yukimura*, *Miura Yoshimura*, *Oe Yoshinori* and *Iga Mitsuie*. — Under the shōgunate of *Muromachi*, *Yamana Tokiuji* and *Imagawa Sadayo* enjoyed the same privileges.

Samurai-dokoro yoriudo, 侍所寄人. Secretaries to the *Samurai-dokoro*. They were also called *Uhitsu*.

Samurai-odori, 士舞. (Lit.: warrior's dance). Formerly a diversion of the military class, consisting in a sort of a quadrille executed in war costumes.

Sanada, 眞田. *Daimyō* family, coming from *Shinano* and descended from the *Seiwa-Genji*.

—— **Yukitaka,** 幸隆. Son of *Unno Munetsuna*, castellan of *Iwao* (*Shinano*), settled at *Sanada* and took the name of the place at the beginning of the 16th century.

—— **Masayuki,** 昌幸 (1544-1608). Son of *Yukitaka,* served first *Takeda Shingen,* who entrusted the castle of *Ueda* to his care. After the ruin of the *Takeda* (1582), he offered his services to *Iegasu,* but the latter wanted to despoil him of his domains in order to give them to *Hōjō Ujinao* whose help he was then soliciting in his campaign against *Hideyoshi* (1584). *Masayuki* irritated, asked help of *Uesugi Kagekatsu* and defeated both the troops of *Ujinao* and of *Ieyasu.*
In 1586, the latter came to besiege *Ueda,* but *Masayuki,* through the good intervention of *Hideyoshi,* obtained peace. During the *Sekigahara* war (1600), he sided with *Ishida Kazushige* and sent his eldest son *Nobuyuki* to follow the party of *Ieyasu.* After the campaign, he was condemned to death, but his son obtained a commutation and he was banished to *Kudoyama (Kii),* where he died.

—— **Nobuyuki,** 信之 (1566-1658). Eldest son of *Masayuki,* was sent as a hostage to *Hamamatsu* upon his father's submission to *Ieyasu.* The latter gave him the daughter of *Honda Tadakatsu* in marriage, whom he had educated. In 1600, he sided with *Ieyasu* and received the castles of *Ueda (Shinano)* and *Numata (Kōzuke)* with a revenue of 65,000 k. In 1622, he was transferred to *Matsushiro (Shinano* — 100,000 k.) where his descendants remained till 1868. — To-day Count. — After the Restoration, a branch received the title of Baron.

—— **Yukimura,** 幸村 (1570-1615). 2nd son of *Masayuki,* married to the daughter of *Ōtani Yoshitaka,* served *Hideyoshi.* In 1600, he induced his father to side with him against *Ieyasu,* and after the campaign, was exiled to *Kudoyama (Kii).* When *Ieyasu* turned against *Hideyori,* he recalled him, but *Yukimura* declined to come and went to *Ōsaka.* There, he greatly helped in the defence of the place, defeated *Date Masamune* at *Hirano,* then, seeing that all resistance was useless, he attacked the troops of *Honda Tadatomo* and found his death on the battlefield.

San-chū, 三忠. The three great models of fidelity to the Emperor: *Taira Shigemori, Fujiwara Fujifusa* and *Kusunoki Masashige.*

San-chūrō, 三中老. The 3 *daimyō* chosen by *Hideyoshi* some time before his death (1598) to assist the 5 *Tairō* in the government during the minority of his son *Hideyori:* *Horio Yoshiharu, Nakamura Kazuuji* and *Ikoma Chikamasa.*

Sanda, 三田. In *Settsu.* Belonged to the *Akamatsu* of *Harima,* and later to the *Arima* (branch of the *Akamatsu*). When these were transferred to *Chikugo,* the castle of *Sanda* passed into the hands of the *Matsudaira* (1620). Lastly, from 1634 to 1868, it was the residence of the *Kuki daimyō* (36,000 k.).

San daibutsu, 三大佛. Formerly the 3 largest statues of *Buddha,* in the temples of *Tō-daiji (Yamato), Taihei-ji (Kawachi),* and *Kwan-ji (Ōmi).*

San daijin-ke, 三大臣家. The 3 branches of the *Fujiwara* family, whose members could become *Daijin* (civil title), but not *Taishō* (military title) thus differing from the *Go-sekke*, who could obtain both dignities. These were the following families :

(*a*) — **Ogimachi-Sanjō**, 正親町三條, descended from *Sanjō Sanefusa* (1146-1224).

(*b*) — **Sanjō-Nishi**, 三條西, descended from the above.

(*c*) — **Naka-no-in**, 中院, descended from *Kuga Masazane*.

San daika, 三大河. Formerly the 3 largest rivers : *Kiso-gawa*, *Tone-gawa* and *Shinano-gawa*.

San dai-kyakushiki, 三大格式. The 3 great collections of laws, customs, ceremonies etc.: *Kōnin-kyakushiki*, *Jōgwan-kyakushiki* and *Engi-kyakushiki*. — See *Ritsuryō-kyakushiki*.

San daikyō, 三大橋. The 3 large bridges of *Seta*, *Uji* and *Yamazaki*.

San daishū, 三大集. Formerly the 3 large collections of poems. *Kokin-shū* (published in 905) *Gosen-shū* (950) and *Shūi-shū* (986).

Sandō, 算道. In the old University (*Daigaku-ryō*), the section corresponding to the Scientific department. In it, Chinese, classics and mathematics were taught.

Sangi, 參議. Formerly high officials, counsellors of the *Dajō-kwan*. They took part in the deliberations but could not vote, this privilege being reserved to the ministers only. — This title was suppressed in 1885.

Sangū, 三宮. Under this title the 3 Empresses, archdowager, dowager and the reigning empress are known. They were also called *Chūgū ;* but from the 10th century, this name was applied only to the reigning empress ; later it was reserved to the favourite wife of the Emperor, even though she had not the title of Empress (*kōgō*).

San gyokushū, 三玉集. 3 collections of poetry : *Haku-gyokushū*, by the emperor *Go-Kashiwabara ; Heki-gyokushū*, by *Reizei Masatame ; Setsu-gyokushū*, by *Sanjō-nishi Sanetaka*.

San-in-dō, 山陰道. (Lit.: land in the shade of the mountains). One of the great divisions of Japan, S. W. of *Hondo*. Comprises 8 provinces : *Tamba, Tango, Tajima, Inaba, Hōki, Izumo, Iwami*, and *Oki ;* forming, with the *Sanyō-dō*, the country that was called *Chūgoku*.

San-ji-kyō, 三時教. (Lit.: 3 periods of teaching). According to the doctrine of the *Hossō-shū* sect, the preaching of *Shaka* was divided into 3 periods. In the first period the real existence of the ego is taught: it is the *U-kyō* contained in the *sûtras* called *Agon ;* in the 2nd period the nothingness of all things is taught, it is the *Kūkyō*, expressed in the *Hannya-kyō*, etc ; in the 3rd, he adopted the middle way, neither existence, nor nothingness, it is the *Chūdōkyō*, taught in the *Kegōn-kyō*, the *Shimmitsu-kyō*, etc. Now, of these three teachings, the last only contained the true doctrine, (*shinjitsu-ryōgi*) but as on account of its depth, it is accessible only to a few, the second divison was destined for those of medium intellects and the first division for the benefit of inferior minds.

Sanjō, 三條. *Kuge* family descended from *Fujiwara Kinzane* (1053-1107).

—— **Saneyuki,** 實行 (1083-1162). Son of *Kinzane*, is the first who took the name of *Sanjō*, from the district of *Kyōto* where he resided. He was *Udaijin* and *Dajō-daijin*.

—— **Kinnori,** 公教 (1103-1160). Son of *Saneyuki*, was *Naidaijin* (1157).

—— **Sanefusa,** 實房 (1146-1224). The son of *Kinnori*, had two sons; the elder, *Kinfusa*, was his heir; the other, *Kimiuji*, took the name of *Ōgimachi-sanjō* and was the ancestor of the family of that name.

—— **Kimiyori,** 公頼 (1495-1551). Descendant of *Sanefusa*, was *Sadaijin*. Not to be implicated in the broils that disturbed the city of *Kyōto*, he took refuge in the castle of *Ōuchi Yoshitaka* at *Yamaguchi*, and died when *Sue Hagukata* seized the castle of his lord.

—— **Sanetomi,** 實美 (1837-1891). Was one of the 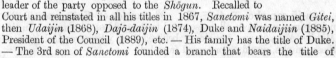 principal *kuge* leaders in the movement that brought about the Restoration. His influence at Court caused him to be suspected by the *Bakufu*, who in 1863 obtained his degradation and that of 6 other counsellors. All retired to *Chōshū*, under the protection of the *daimyō Mōri*, the leader of the party opposed to the *Shōgun*. Recalled to Court and reinstated in all his titles in 1867, *Sanetomi* was named *Gitei*, then *Udaijin* (1868), *Dajō-daijin* (1874), Duke and *Naidaijin* (1885), President of the Council (1889), etc.—His family has the title of Duke. —The 3rd son of *Sanetomi* founded a branch that bears the title of Baron.

Sanjō-nishi, 三條西. *Kuge* family, descended from *Fujiwara* (*Ōgimachi-Sanjō*) *Kimitoki*. It is at present called *Nishi-Sanjō*.—Now Count.

Sanjō-tennō, 三條天皇. 67th Emperor of Japan (1012-1016). *Okisada*, 2nd son of *Reizei-tennō*, at the age of 37 succeeded his cousin *Ichijō*. After a reign of 5 years he became blind, abdicated and died the following year.

San-jū-roku kasen, 三十六歌仙. The 36 most renowned poets who lived before the 11th century:

1. *Kakinomoto no Hitomaro* (+ 729).
2. *Ki no Tsurayuki* (883-946).
3. *Ochikōchi no Mitsune* (10th century).
4. *Ise* (favorite of *Uda-tenno*) (9th century).
5. *Otomo no Yakamochi* (+ 785).
6. *Yamabe no Akahito* (8th century).
7. *Ariwara no Narihira* (825-880).
8. *Henjō* (*Yoshimine Munesada* (816-890).
9. *Sosei* (*Yoshimine Harutoshi*)(9th cent.).
10. *Sarumaru-dayū* (8th century).
11. *Ki no Tomonori* (10th century).
12. *Ono no Komachi* (834-880).
13. *Fujiwara Kanesuke* (877-933).
14. *Fujiwara Atsutada* (906-943).
15. *Fujiwara Asatada* (+ 964).
16. *Fujiwara Takamitsu* (+ 994).
17. *Minamoto Kintada* (10th century).
18. *Mibu Tadamine* (10th century).
19. *Saigū* (*Yoshi-ko Jo-ō*) (929-985).
20. *Onakatomi Yorimoto* (10th century).
21. *Fujiwara Toshiyuki* (881-907).
22. *Minamoto Shigeyuki* (+ 1000).
23. *Minamoto Muneyuki* (+ 940).
24. *Minamoto Nobuaki* (10th century).
25. *Fujiwara Kiyotada* (10th century).
26. *Minamoto Shitagau* (911-983).
27. *Fujiwara Okikaze* (10th century).
28. *Kiyowara Motosuke* (908-990).
29. *Sakanoe Korenori* (　　"　　).
30. *Fujiwara Motoyoshi* (10th century).
31. *Ukon* (dau'r of *Fujiw. Suezumi*) (10 cent').
32. *Fujiwara Nakabumi* (10th century).
33. *Onakatomi Yoshinobu* (922-991).
34. *Mibu Tadami* (10th century).
35. *Taira Kanemori* (+ 990).
36. *Nakatsukasa* (dau'r of *Ise*, 4) (10th century)

This list was compiled by *Fujiwara Kintō* at the beginning of the 11th century. Later, 36 other poets were chosen who formed the *Chūko no 36 kasen*. These are:

1. *Izumi Shikibu* (11th century).
2. *Sagami*.
3. *Ekei Hōshi*.
4. *Akazome Emon*.
5. *Nō-in Hōshi* (*Tachibana Nagayasu*).
6. *Ise no Ōsuke*.
7. *Sone Yoshitada*.
8. *Dōmyō Ajari*.
9. *Fujiwara Sanekata*.
10. *Fujiwara Michinobu*.
11. *Taira Sadabumi* (+ 901).
12. *Kiyowara Fukayabu*.
13. *Oe Yoshitoki*.
14. *Minamoto Michinari*.
15. *Fujiwara Michimasa*.
16. *Sōki Hōshi*.
17. *Ariwara Motokata*.
18. *Oe Chisato*.
19. *Fujiwara Kintō* (966-1041).
20. *Onakatomi Sukechika* (954-1038).
21. *Fujiwara Takatō*.
22. *Uma no Naishi* (sister of *Akazome Emon*).
23. *Fujiwara Yoshitaka* (+ 974).
24. *Murasaki Shikibu* (+ 992).
25. The mother of *Fujiwara Michitsuna*.
26. *Fujiwara Nagayoshi*.
27. *Fujiwara Sadayori* (995-1045)
28. *Jōdō Mon-in no Chūjō*.
29. *Kane-Ō* (grandson of *Nimmyō-tennō*).
30. *Ariwara Munahari*.
31. *Fumiya Yasuhide*.
32. *Fujiwara Tadafusa*.
33. *Sugawara Sukemasa*.
34. *Oe Masahira* (962-1012).
35. *Ambō Hōshi* (*Minamoto Shitagau*).
36. *Sei Shōnagon*.

San-jū-san sho, 三 十 三 所. 33 temples of *Kyōto* and of the neighboring provinces, all consecrated to the goddess *Kwannon*. In the Middle Ages, it was commonly believed that whosoever had gone to these temples, would be preserved from hell.

1. *Nyoirin-ji*, at *Nachi* (*Kii*).
2. *Kongōhō-ji*, at *Kimiidera* (*Kii*).
3. *Kokawa-dera*, at *Kokawa* (*Kii*).
4. *Sefuku-ji*, at *Maki-no-o* (*Izumi*).
5. *Fujii-dera*, at *Nakano* (*Kawachi*).
6. *Minami-Hokke-ji*, at *Tsubosaka* (*Yamato*).
7. *Ryūkai-ji*, at *Okadera* (*Yamato*).
8. *Hase-dera*, at *Hase* (*Yamato*).
9. *Nan-en-dō*, at *Nara*.
10. *Mimurodo-dera*, at *Uji* (*Yamashiro*).
11. *Kami no Daigo-dera*, at *Uji* (*Yamashiro*).
12. *Shōhō-ji*, at *Iwima* (*Omi*).
13. *Ishiyama-dera*, at *Ishiyama* (*Omi*).
14. *Mii-dera* (*Onjō-ji*), at *Otsu* (*Omi*).
15. *Shin-Kumano-dera*, at *Kyōto*.
16. *Kiyomizu-dera*, at *Kyōto*.
17. *Rokuhara-Mitsu-ji*, at *Kyōto*.
18. *Rokkaku-dō*, at *Kyōto*.
19. *Gyōkwan-ji* or *Kōtō*, at *Kyōto*.
20. *Yoshimine-dera*, at *Kyōto*.
21. *Bodai-ji*, at *Anō* (*Tamba*).
22. *Sōzen-ji* (*Settsu*).
23. *Kacho-dera*, at *Toyokawa* (*Settsu*).
24. *Nakayama-dera*, at *Kōbe* (*Settsu*).
25. *Shin-Kiyomizu*, at *Kamogawa* (*Harima*).
26. *Hokke-ji* (*Harima*).
27. *Nyoirin-dō*, at *Shosha-zan* (*Harima*).
28. *Seisō-ji*, on *Nariai-yama* (*Tango*).
29. *Matsu-no-o-dera* (*Wakasa*).
30. *Chikubu-ji*, in the Island *Chikubu* (*Omi*).
31. *Chōmei-ji*, in the Island *Oku-shima* (*Omi*).
32. *Kwannon-ji*, at *Ashi-ura* (*Omi*).
33. *Kegon-ji*, at *Tanigumi* (*Mino*).

San kagami, 三 鏡. 3 famous historical works:—

1. *Mizu-kagami*, 水 鏡: 3 vol., from 660 B.C. to 850 A.D., by *Nakayama Tadachika*;

2. *Ō-kagami*, 大 鏡: 8 vol., from 851 to 1036, by *Fujiwara Tamenari*;

3. *Masu-kagami*, 増 鏡: 10 vol., from 1184 to 1338, by *Ichijō Fuyuyoshi*.

San kaidan, 三 戒 壇. Formerly the 3 temples in whose enclosure the platform (*kaidan*), required for the ceremony of the imposition of the 10 precepts (*kai*) of the *Risshū* sect, was erected: the *Tō-daiji*, (*Nara*);

the *Yakushi-ji* (*Shimotsuke*) and the *Kwannon-ji* (*Chikuzen*).—See *Kai-ritsu-shū*.

San kan, 三韓. Three kingdoms that were formerly in the southern part of Korea: *Bakan* or *Shiragi*, *Benkan* or *Kudara*, *Shinkan* or *Koma*.

San-kan seibatsu, 三韓征伐. The expedition led by the empress *Jingō* for the purpose of subjugating Korea (200).—See *Jingō-kōgō*. —The Korean annals do not mention the fact.

San-ke, 三家. The 3 branches of the *Tokugawa* family descended from the 3 last sons of *Ieyasu* : *Yoshinao*, who became *daimyō* of *Nagoya* (*Owari*) ; *Yorinobu*, *daimyō* of *Wakayama* (*Kii*), and *Yorifusa*, *daimyō* of *Mito* (*Hitachi*). They were usually called the families of *Owari*, *Kii* and *Mito*. When a *Shōgun* died without an heir, his successor could be chosen from these families only. Three times the *Kii* branch and once the *Mito* branch benefitted by this privilege.

San kei, 三景. — See *Nihon san-kei*.

Sankin-kōdai, 参勤交代. Law enacted by the *Tokugawa Shōgun* which obliged all the *daimyō* to reside alternately in their domains and in *Edo*, and to leave their wife and children as hostages in that city. The time of residence was not strictly determined but most of the *daimyō* remained one year at *Edo* and one year in their domains. Those of the *Kwantō* province changed their residence every 6 months. This law enacted in 1634 by the *Shōgun Iemitsu*, was abrogated in 1862.

San kisha, 三騎射. The 3 great sports of the *samurai* in the Middle Ages, being at the same time exercices of shooting and of horsemanship. — They were the *yabusame*, the *kasakake* and the *inu-ou-mono*.

San kō, 三公. Formerly, the 3 principal ministers : the *Dajō-daijin*, the *Sadaijin* and the *Udaijin*.

San kokushi, 三國司. In the 15th and the 16th centuries, the 3 great *daimyō*, governors of the provinces *Hatakeyama* in *Mutsu*, *Kitabatake* in *Ise* and *Amenokōji* in *Hida*.

San kwan, 三關. Formerly the 3 great barriers placed at some distance from *Kyōto* where travellers were inspected : *Fuwa* (*Mino*), *Arachi* (*Ōmi*) and *Suzuka* (*Ise*).

San kyō, 三教. The 3 great religions of Japan : Shintoism (*Dōkyō*), Buddhism (*Bukkyō*) and Confucianism (*Jukyō*).

San kyō, 三卿. The 3 branches of the *Tokugawa* family : *Tayasu*, *Hitotsubashi* and *Shimizu*. The first was established by *Munetake* (+1769), son of the *Shōgun Yoshimune* ; the 2nd, by *Munetada* (1721-1764), brother of the above ; the 3rd, by *Shigeyoshi* (1745-1795), son of the *Shōgun Ieshige*. — They did not possess castles, but resided at *Edo* and had their domains superintended by a *daikwan*.

Sannō, 山王. Another name of the Shintoist god *Ōkuninushi*. — See *Hiyoshi*.

Sannohe, 三戸. In *Mutsu*. Was from 1189 to 1597 the residence of the *daimyō Nambu*, who later settled in *Morioka*.

Sannomiya, 三宮. Family ennobled in 1895. — Now Baron.

San Nyorai, 三 如 來 . The 3 large statues of *Amida-Nyorai* in the temple *Zenkō-ji*, of *Shaka-Nyorai* at *Saga*, and of *Yakushi-Nyorai* in the *Inaba-dō* temple.

Sano, 佐 野 . In *Shimotsuke*. Old castle built, it is said, by *Fujiwara Hidesato* in the 10th century. Later it became the possession of the *Sano*, who kept it to 1614. It then became the residence of the *Naitō daimyō* (1626) and finally from 1684 to 1698 and from 1812 to 1868, that of the *Hotta daimyō* (18,000 k.).

Sano, 佐 野 . In *Izumi*. During the siege of *Ōsaka* (1615), the besieged army was defeated by the troops of *Asano Nagaakira*, then *daimyō* of *Wakayama* (*Kii*).

Sano, 佐 野 . Ancient family of *daimyō*, who, during the 12th century, resided at *Sano* (*Shimotsuke*). In 1614, *Masatsuna*, having been implicated in the *Ōkubo* plot, was dispossessed and banished to *Shinano*.

Sano, 佐 野 . *Samurai* family of the *Saga* clan (*Hizen*), ennobled after the Restoration. — Now Count.

Sanron-shū, 三 論 宗 . Buddhist sect so called because its doctrine is taken from the 3 *sūtras Chū-ron, Hyaku-ron* and *Jū-ni-mon-ron*. As it is supposed to propagate all the teachings of *Shaka*, it is also called *Ichi-dai-kyō-shū*. It was introduced into Japan in 625, by the bonze *Ekwan* from Korea. Later, it was divided into two branches *Gwankōji-ha* and *Taianji-ha ;* neither of which exist at present.

Sanryō-bugyō, 山 陵 奉 行 . Under the *Tokugawa*, an official charged with the care and repair of the Imperial tombstones (*sanryō* or *misasagi*). In 1703, the *Shōgun Tsunayoshi* had a hedge placed around the Imperial tombs which had been neglected during the civil wars of the 15th and the 16th centuries. *Yoshimune* protected the tombs by a ditch. At the beginning of the 19th century, researches were made to discover the neglected tombs. In 1862, *Toda Wasaburō* was named *Sanryō-bugyō* and ennobled in 1866. The Restoration completed the work then in progress.

Sansai, 散 齊 . Privations imposed upon officials, in preparation for certain Shintoist feasts : The duration was a whole month (*ara-imi*) before the great feasts (*taishi*) and 3 days (*ma-imi*) before the secondary feasts (*chūshi*). During that time, they were forbidden to enter a house containing a dead man, to visit the sick, to eat meat, to kill any living being, to punish criminals, to play on musical instruments, etc.

San sechie, 三 節 會 . 3 feasts celebrated by a banquet at the Imperial Palace : the 1st day of the year, the *Ao-uma no sechie* and the *Toyo-akari no sechie*.

San seki, 三 蹟 . The 3 famous calligraphists of the 10th century : *Ono Michikaze* (*Yaseki*), *Fujiwara Yukinari* (*Gonseki*) and *Fujiwara Sari* (*Saseki*). — Some substitute prince *Kane-akira-shinnō* for *Michikaze*.

San senjin, 三 戰 神 . The 3 gods of war : *Marishiten, Daikokuten* and *Bishamonten*. They are represented under the form of a man having 3 heads and 6 arms, and mounted on a wild boar.

San sha, 三社. The 3 most renowned Shintoist temples in the environs of *Kyōto: Ise, Iwashimizu* and *Kasuga.*

San shin, 三津. Formerly the 3 ports: *Bō-no-tsu (Satsuma), Hakata no tsu (Chikuzen)* and *Anotsu (Ise).*

Sanshū, 參州. Chinese name of *Mikawa* province.

Sanshū, 讃州. Chinese name of *Sanuki* province.

Sanshū jū-roku ke, 參州十六家. The 16 families, all related to the *Tokugawa,* who, during the 16th century, divided the *Mikawa* province among themselves: *Tokugawa, Matsudaira, Takeya, Katahara, Okazaki, Go-no-i, Ōkusa, Fukamizo, Nomi, Ōgyū, Takiwaki, Sakurai, Oshigamo, Fujii, Fukama* and *Nagasawa.*

Sanshū jū-roku shō, 參州十六將. The 16 generals of *Ieyasu,* who like himself natives of *Mikawa,* took part in his campaigns and most of whom became great *daimyō: Sakai Tadatsugu, Ishikawa Kazumasa, Ōsuka Yasutaka, Ii Naomasa, Honda Tadakatsu, Hiraiwa Chikayoshi, Sakakibara Yasumasa, Ishikawa Ienari, Matsudaira Nobukazu, Matsudaira Ietada, Matsudaira Yasuchika, Ōkubo Tadayo, Honda Yasutaka, Honda Tadatsugu, Torii Mototada* and *Uemura Iemasa.*

San shū no shinki, 三種神器. The 3 Imperial emblems. — See *Mi-kusa no kan-dakara.*

San son, 三尊. (Lit.: the three venerable men). A Buddha and his two assistants. The term is especially applied to *Amida* having *Kwannon* and *Seishi* at his side.

Santō Kyōden, 山東京傳. — See *Kyōden.*

Sanuki[i], 讃岐. One of the 6 provinces of the *Nankai-dō,* in the island of *Shikoku.* Comprises 7 districts that form the *Kagawa-ken.* — Chinese name: *Sanshū.*

Sanuki, 佐貫. Small city of *Kazusa.* Contains an old castle built in 1555 by *Satomi Yoshihiro.* His son *Yoshiyasu* was transferred to *Tateyama (Awa)* in 1590 and was replaced by *Naitō Ienaga.* Under the *Tokugawa,* it was the residence of the *daimyō Sakurai* (1622), *Matsudaira* (1639), *Yanagisawa* (1690), and from 1710 to 1868, *Abe* (16,000 k).

San-yō-dō, 山陽道. (Lit.: exposed region of the mountains). One of the great divisions of Japan, S. W. of *Hondo.* Comprises 8 provinces: *Harima, Mimasaka, Bizen, Bitchū, Bingo, Aki, Suwō* and *Nagato.* — Together with the *San-in-dō,* formed the *Chūgoku.*

San zenjō, 三禪定. Name given to the 3 high mountains: *Fuji-san, Haku-san,* and *Tate-yama,* because, like immovable beings raising their heads towards heaven, they seem to be in deep contemplation.

San-zō, 三藏. (Lit.: three collections) (Sanscr. *Tripitaka,* three baskets). The Buddhist law which comprises: doctrine (*Kei* 經, *sûtras*), discipline (*ritsu* 律, *vinayas*), and controversy (*ron* 論, *abhid-hamas*); all together they form 1662 works.

Sao-hiko, 狹穗彦. } Children of *Hiko-imasu no mikoto* and grand-
Sao-hime, 狹穗媛. } children of the emperor *Kaikwa. Sao-hime,*

also called *Sawaji-hime*, married *Suinin-tennō* and was mother of *Homutsu-wake*. In the year 26 B.C., *Sao-hiko* determined to rebel and provided his sister with a weapon with which she was to assassinate the Emperor. *Sao-hime* at first refused but being further urged, she finally consented. However when the moment came to commit the crime, she was seized with sudden fear and revealed the whole plot to her husband. *Suinin* sent *Kamitsukenu no Yatsunada* to the residence of *Sao-hiko* in order to surround it. *Sao-hime*, reproaching herself with having betrayed her brother, fled to his house and died with him.

Sapporo, 札幌. Chief town (55,600 inh.) of the *Ishikari* province (*Hokkaidō*). Started in 1870, this city, till 1881, was the seat of the *Kaitakushi* (Bureau of colonization); even to the present time, it possesses a school of agriculture.

Sarashi, 曝. Under the *Tokugawa*, a punishment reserved to certain criminals. — See *Tokugawa-keihō.*

Sarugaku, 猿樂, A popular representation, not unlike the *kyōgen.* Some believe it to have originated from the dance executed by *Uzume no mikoto* at the grotto where *Amaterasu* had hidden herself.

Sarugaku shi-za, 猿樂四座. The 4 families who practically had the monopoly of the composition and execution of the *Nō* and *Sarugaku*: *Kwanze, Komparu, Hōshō* and *Kongō.* — See *Nō.*

Saruma-numa, 猿間湖. Lake (about 79 Km. circuit.) in *Kitami* (*Hokkaidō*).

Sarumaru-dayū, 猿丸太夫. Famous poet of the 9th century, one of the 36 *kasen.* Some authors believe him to be the son of prince *Yamashiro no Ōe.*

Saruta-hiko, 猿田彦. A Shintoist god, also called *Sadabiko, Ōtsuchi no kami*, Led the van-guard of the escort of *Ninigi no mikoto*, when he descended to earth. Because his name begins with the character *saru* (monkey), his feast is celebrated on the day of the Monkey. — See *Kōshin.*

Sasa Narimasa, 佐々成政 (1539-1588). Born of a family vassal to the *Oda*, he served *Nobunaga* and defeated the *Asai* and the *Asakura* in *Echizen.* He received the fief of *Fuchū* (*Etchū* — 100,000 k.), and after having pacified the province, he settled at *Toyama* (1581). At the time of the troubles between *Oda Nobuo* and *Hideyoshi*, he sided with the former, but was defeated by *Maeda Toshiie* and reduced to submission. In 1587, *Hideyoshi* transferred him to *Kumamoto* (*Higo*), but he caused troubles in that place and in the following year, he was requested to kill himself.

Sasaki, 佐々木. *Daimyō* family, descended from *Minamoto Masanobu* (*Uda-Genji*), grandson of the emperor *Uda.*

—— **Nariyori,** 成賴. Great-grandson of *Masanobu* is the first who took the name of *Sasaki* from his domain in *Ōmi.*

—— **Hideyoshi,** 秀義 (1112-1184). Descendant of *Nariyori*, was adopted by *Minamoto Tameyoshi* when 13 years old. During the *Hōgen* war (1156), he fought under the command of *Yoshitomo*, and besieged the palace of *Shirakawa.* At the time of the *Heiji* war (1159), he helped *Yoshihira* and thus enabled him to withstand *Taira Shigemori*; but after the defeat of *Yoshitomo*, he fled. He intended to ask *Fujiwara Hidehira* to give him shelter in *Mutsu*, but he stopped on his way thither at *Shibuya* (*Sagami*) and *Taira Shigekuni* gave him his daughter in marriage. She was the mother of *Yoshikiyo*. *Hideyoshi* remained at that place for 20 years, and when *Yoritomo* rose in revolt against the *Taira*, he with his 4 sons sided with him (1180). He was killed at *Ōhara* (*Ōmi*) in a battle fought against *Hirata Ietsugu*, one of the *Taira's* partisans.

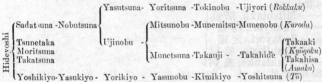

——— **Sadatsuna,** 定綱. Son of *Hideyoshi*, entered the field with *Yoritomo* and under the orders of *Hōjō Tokimasa*, attacked the governor of *Izu*, *Taira Kanetaka*, and defeated him. After the battle of *Ishibashiyama* (1181), he asked shelter from *Taira Shigekuni*, at *Shibuya* (*Sagami*), where he lived a long time with his father. When *Yoritomo* attacked *Satake Hideyoshi*, *Sadatsuna* joined him and came to besiege the castle of *Kanasa* (*Hitachi*). As reward, he was reinstated in the fief of *Sasaki* (*Ōmi*), of which his father had been deprived, and obtained in addition the government of the whole province, which his descendants kept for more than 3 centuries. In consequence of a quarrel in reference to the *Hie-jinja*, he was banished to *Satsuma*, and recalled after 4 years of exile. — *Sadatsuna* is the ancestor of the families *Rokkaku*, *Kuroda*, *Kyōgoku* and *Amako*.

——— **Moritsuna,** 盛綱. Son of *Hideyoshi*, sided with *Yoritomo* against the *Taira* (1180), then accompanied *Noriyori* in his expedition to the West. When the *Minamoto* army arrived at *Fujito*, it found *Taira Yukimori* entrenched in the peninsula of *Kojima* (*Bizen*). *Moritsuna* found a ford, spurred his horse into it, and, inducing his *samurai* to follow his example, decided the success of the battle (1184). In reward, he received the district of *Kojima* in fief, and the title of *Iyo no shugo*. After the death of *Yoritomo* (1199), he shaved his head and took the name of *Sainen*. In 1201, he defeated *Jō Sukemori* in *Kōzuke*.

——— **Takatsuna,** 高綱. Son of *Hideyoshi*, took a prominent part in *Noriyori's* campaign against *Yoshinaka* (1184). He was named governor of *Bizen* and of *Aki*. Some time after, he shaved his head, took the name of *Ryōchi* and retired to *Kōya-san*.

SASAKI TAKATSUNA.

——— **Nobutsuna,** 信綱 (+ 1242). Son of *Sadatsuna*, fought on the side of *Hōjō Yasutoki* during the *Shōkyū* war (1221), and was named *Kebiishi, Ōmi no shugo,* etc. He retired to *Kōya-san.*

—— **Yasutsuna,** 泰綱. — See *Rokkaku.*

—— **Ujiyori,** 氏賴. — See *Rokkaku.*

—— **Takauji,** 高氏 (1306-1373). Great-grandson of *Nobutsuna,* served *Hōjō Takatoki,* then *Ashikaga Takauji.* He assisted at the battle of *Shijō-nawate* against *Kusunoki Masatsura* (1348), at the investment of Mt. *Yoshino* by *Ashikaga Yoshiakira* (1356) and at all the campaigns against the Southern dynasty. — *Takauji* is the ancestor of the *Kyōgoku* and the *Amako.*

—— **Mitsutaka,** 滿高 ⎫
—— **Takayori,** 高賴 ⎪
—— **Sadayori,** 定賴 ⎬ — See *Rokkaku.*
—— **Yoshikata,** 義賢 ⎪
—— **Yoshisuke,** 義弼 ⎭

Sasaki, 佐々木. *Samurai* family of the *Kōchi* clan (*Tosa*), ennobled after the Restoration — Now Count.

Sasayama, 篠山. In *Tamba.* Was the residence of the *daimyō Matsudaira* (1608), then, from 1748 to 1868, of *Aoyama* (60,000 k.).

Sasebo, 佐世保. Port (52,500 inh.) of *Hizen* province and of *Nagasaki-ken ;* seat of a maritime prefecture (*Chinjufu*).

Sashiki, 佐敷. In *Higo.* Old castle that successively belonged to the *daimyō Nawa* (1335), *Kikuchi* (towards 1400), *Sashiki* (16th century). In 1562, it was taken by the *Shimazu* of *Satsuma.* *Hideyoshi* gave it to *Sasa Narimasa* (1587), then to *Katō Kiyomasa* (1588). It was abandoned by the *Hosokawa* (1632).

Sashima, 猿島. In *Shimōsa.* It was in this district, near the actual village of *Iwai,* that *Taira Masakado* rose in revolt, took the title of *Hei-shin-ō* and erected a palace for himself (939).

Sashōben, 左少辨. Formerly the secretary of the *Dajō-kwan,* inferior to the *Sadaiben* and the *Sachūben.*

Sashū, 佐州. Chinese name of *Sado* province.

Sasshū, 薩州. Chinese name of *Satsuma* province.

Satake, 佐竹. *Daimyō* family descended from *Minamoto Yoshimitsu,* brother of *Yoshiie (Seiwa-Genji).*

—— **Yoshinari,** 義業. Son of *Yoshimitsu,* was the first to take the name of *Satake.*

—— **Hideyoshi,** 秀義 (1151-1228). Great-grandson of *Yoshinari,* inherited the domain of *Satake (Hitachi).* When *Yoritomo* raised troops against the *Taira,* he refused to follow him and entrenched himself in his castle of *Kanasa,* where he was besieged by *Shimokōbe Yukihira* (1180) : he resisted for a long time and was successful in so far as to obtain peace whilst keeping his domains.

—— **Yoshinori,** 義仁 (1395-1462). Descendant of *Hideyoshi.* He supported the *Kwanryō* of *Kamakura, Ashikaga Mochiuji,* against the *Uesugi* (1416). After the death of *Mochiuji* (1439), the *Kwantō* appears to have been divided among 7 families, at whose head were the *Satake*. *Yoshinori* is known as a great painter and writer as well as a famous warrior.

—— **Yoshiaki, 義 昭** . Defeated a coalition of neighboring *daimyō* in 1569 ; he enlarged his domains at their expense.

—— **Yoshishige, 義 重** (1547-1612). Took the field against *Ashina Moriuji* (1576) ; but *Sōma Moritane* and *Ishikawa Akimitsu* reestablished peace. In 1581, he helped the *Sano* of *Shimotsuke* to defeat *Hōjō Ujimasa* by whom he was attacked. A large number of petty *daimyō* now placed themselves under the protection of *Yoshishige*. They were the *daimyō* of *Mibu, Kasama, Utsunomiya, Tagaya*, etc. Thus *Yoshishige* soon was master of the *Hitachi, Kazusa* and *Shimōsa* provinces. In 1585, he made war against *Hōjō Ujinao*, and then against *Date Masamune*. *Yoshishige* stormed the castles of *Ōhira, Mito, Ōta*, he established himself in that of *Ōta*, and his son *Yoshinobu* in that of *Mito* (1590).

—— **Yoshinobu, 義 宣** (1570-1633). Inherited the immense domains of his father in 1590. The same year, he took part in the expedition of *Hideyoshi* against the *Hōjō* of *Odawara* and was confirmed in the government of *Hitachi* province. Installed at *Mito*, he possessed an income of 800,000 k. In 1600, without an open rupture with *Ieyasu*, he lived on good terms with *Uesugi Kagekatsu* and *Ishida Kazushige*. It was due to his father's influence that he was not dispossessed ; he was however transferred to *Akita* (*Dewa* — 205,000 k.) where his descendants remained till the Restoration. — Now Marquis. — After the Restoration, 3 branches of this family received the title of Baron. — One branch, settled at the end of the 17th century at *Iwasaki* (*Dewa* — 20,000 k.), has at present the title of Viscount. — After the Restoration, a branch of the latter received the title of Baron.

Sata no misaki, 佐 田 岬 . Cape S. W. of *Iyo*.

Sata no misaki, 佐 多 岬 . Cape S. of *Ōsumi* : it is the most southern point of *Kyūshū*.

Sat-chō-to, 薩 長 土 . The 3 clans of *Satsuma, Chōshū* (*Nagato*) and *Tosa ;* they had taken the most prominent part in the Imperial Restoration and, on that account, occupy important positions, both civil and military.

Satō, 佐 藤 . *Daimyō* family, descended from *Fujiwara Hidesato*, possessing the fief of *Shinobu* (*Mutsu*) since the 11th century.—Besides *Saigyō-Hōshi*, the best known members of the family are the two brothers *Tsuginobu* (1158-1185) and *Tadanobu* (1160-1185), sons of *Motoharu*. They both belonged to the 4 body guards (*shi-tennō*) of *Minamoto Yoshitsune*, and died in his cause.

Satō Gōsai, 佐 藤 剛 齊 (1650-1719). Confucianist, disciple of *Yamazaki Ansai*.

Satō Issai, 佐 藤 一 齊 (1772-1859). Born at *Edo*, he followed the teaching of *Nakai Chikuzen, Minegawa Kien, Hayashi Kanjun*, and became a distinguished Confucianist. In 1805, he was director of the flourishing school kept by the *Hayashi* (*Shōhei-hō*) and had as many as 3,000 disciples upon whom he exercised a great influence.

Satō Norikiyo, 佐藤義清. — See *Saigyō-Hōshi*.

Sato-dairi, 里内裏. Name given to the houses temporarily occupied by the emperors in addition to the *Kyōto* Palace. Among them are the *Horikawa-in*, which was the residence of *Kwazan-tennō*, the *Ichijō-in*, of *Sanjō-tennō*, the *Nijō-Takakura*, of *Gō-Uda-tennō*, etc.

Satomi, 里見 *Daimyō* family descended from *Nitta Yoshishige* (+ 1202) (*Seiwa-Genji*).

—— **Yoshitoshi,** 義俊. Son of *Yoshishige*, was the first to take the name of *Satomi*, from his domain in *Kōzuke*.

—— **Yoshizane,** 義實 (1417-1488). Descendant of *Yoshitoshi*. He went from *Kōzuke* to *Awa* and built a castle at *Shirahama*.

—— **Yoshitaka,** 義堯 (1512-1574). Succeeded his father *Sanctaka* who had been assassinated by his nephew *Yoshitoyo* (1533). He marched against the murderer, besieged him in the castle of *Inamura*, put him to death and ruled over the province of *Awa*. Defeated together with *Ashikaga Yoshiaki* at *Kōnodai* by *Hōjō Ujitsuna*, he saw a great number of his vassals abandon him (1538). Some time after however, he was able to storm the castle of *Shiizu* belonging to *Takeda Nobumasa*. Rallying his troops, he resumed the campaign against the *Hōjō*, defeated them in several engagements and soon found himself again surrounded by a great number of *samurai* coming from *Musashi*, *Sagami*, *Kazusa*, and *Shimōsa*. He built a castle at *Kururi* and lived in it, leaving his son *Yoshihiro* at the castle of *Tateyama*.

—— **Yoshihiro,** 義弘 (+ 1578). Was defeated in 1564 at *Kōnodai* by *Hōjō Ujiyasu* and fled to *Kazusa*, but, in 1567, he in turn defeated the *Hōjō* army, that had come to besiege *Kururi*.

—— **Yoshiyori,** 義賴 (1555-1586). Continued the war against the *Hōjō*, who, in 1581, had entered *Kazusa* and *Awa*.

—— **Yoshiyasu,** 義康 (1573-1603). Took part in the campaign of *Hideyoshi* against *Odawara*, but lost *Kazusa* and *Shimōsa*; his possessions were reduced to the province of *Awa* (92,000 k.). In 1600, he sided with *Ieyasu* and his revenues rose to 120,000 k.

—— **Tadayoshi,** 忠義 (+ 1622). Being implicated in the *Ōkubo* plot, he was dispossessed in 1614, but at the petition of his *samurai*, he received a revenue of 40,000 k. at *Kurayoshi* (*Hōki*). He died without leaving an heir and his family became extinct.

Satsugū-shotō, 薩隅諸島. The islands dependent on the *Satsuma* and *Ōsumi* provinces, and consisting of the *Kumage*, *Gomu*, *Kawabe* and the *Ōshima* groups.

Satsuma, 薩摩. One of the 12 provinces of *Saikai-dō*. — Comprises 7 districts, which depend on *Kagoshima-ken*. — Chinese name: *Sasshū*. — *Satsuma* is derived from *Sachi-hama* or from *Satsu-shima*.

Satsuma-Fuji, 薩摩富士. — See *Kaimon-dake*.

Satta-yama, 薩埵山. In *Suruga*, near *Okitsu*. In 1352, *Ashikaga Takauji* at this place fought against his brother *Tadayoshi*. — Also called *Iwaki-yama*.

Sa-u-daijin, 左右大臣. The two ministers of the left and the right, below the *Dajō-daijin* (1st minister). They were formerly called *Ōi-machi-gimi, Ōi-ma-uchi-gimi.*

Sawa, 澤. *Kuge* family descended from *Kiyowara Natsuno.*—Now Count.—A junior branch has received the title of Baron.

Sawada, 澤田. Family, which, by hereditary right, was attached to the *Daijin-gū (Ise)* temple. — Now Baron.

Sawami, 澤海. In *Echigo.* From 1634 to 1687, was the residence of a branch of the *Mizoguchi* family (14,000 k.).

Sawara-shinnō, 早良親王 (757-785). 5th son of the emperor *Kōnin.* At the accession of his brother *Kwammu* to the throne, he was named heir presumptive (782). Having planned the murder of the *Chū-nagon Fujiwara Tanetsugu,* he was exiled to *Awaji* but starved himself to death whilst on the way.

Sawayama, 佐和山. In *Ōmi,* N. W. of *Hikone.* Old castle belonging, during the 16th century, to the *Isono* family, vassal to the *Kyōgoku.* *Oda Nobunaga* gave it to *Niwa Nagahide* (1573), who was replaced by *Hori Hidemasa* (1583), then by *Ishida Kazushige* (1590). After the battle of *Sekigahara* (1600), *Ii Naomasa* besieged the castle in which the whole family of *Kazushige* committed suicide. It became a domain of the *Ii* family but was abandoned for the castle of *Hikone.*

Sawa-zaki, 澤崎. Cape S. of *Sado* island.

Sayama, 狹山. In *Kawachi.* When *Hideyoshi* had overcome the *Hōjō* of *Odawara* (1590), *Ujinao* and his uncle *Ujinori* were confined to the *Kōya-san* and a revenue of 10,000 k. was allotted to them at *Sayama.* After the death of *Ujinori,* the property passed to his son *Ujimori,* whose descendants remained there till the Restoration.

Sayo, 佐用. In *Harima.* Old castle which, from the 12th to the 16th century, belonged to the *Akamatsu.* Passed into the possession of *Ukita Naoie.* In 1577, *Hideyoshi* took it.

Sechi-e, 節會. Formerly renowned feasts that took place at the Palace and terminated with a banquet for all the nobles and officials of high rank.

Segawa, 瀬川. In *Settsu,* where *Ashikaga Takauji* was defeated by *Nitta Yoshisada* (1336). There also, or near that place, *Kō Moronao* and *Moroyasu* were defeated and killed by *Ashikaga Tadayoshi* (1351).

Sei, 世. In the genealogical tables we find that the emperor *Go-Daigo* is of the 48th *sei* and of the 96th *dai.* *Sei* means the generations from father to son ; *dai,* the rank of succession. Thus, *Go-Daigo* is the 96th emperor of Japan, and he descends from *Jimmu-tennō* in the 48th generation. Likewise the 4 brothers *Myōshō, Go-Kōmyō, Go-Saiin* and *Reigen,* who followed each other on the throne, are the 109, 110, 111 and 112th *dai,* but all belong to the 61st *sei.* *Mutsu-hito* is the 122nd emperor (*dai*) of Japan and descends from *Jimmu* in the 68th generation (*sei*).

Seibi-kwan, 濟美舘. School established in 1863 at *Nagasaki ;* French, English, Russian, Dutch and Chinese languages were taught in t according to methods proper to each of these countries.

Seidō, 聖堂 . Temple built in 1690 at *Edo* (*Hongō*) in honor of Confucius. At the time of the Restoration it was transformed into an educational Museum.

Sei-i-shi, 征夷使 . (Lit.: sent against the Barbarians). The general staff of an army sent to fight the *Ebisu* ; it was composed of a *Taishō-gun*, a *Fuku-shōgun*, a *gunkan*, *gunsō*, etc. In 720, *Tajihi no Agatamori* received .the title of *Jisetsu-sei-i-shōgun ; Abe no Surugamaro*, that of *Jisetsu-chinteki-shōgun* and was ordered to repulse the *Ebisu* of the East and those of the North This is the first time we find the term *sei-i* mentioned in Japanese history. Later on , we read *Jisetsu-taishōgun*, *Seitō-taishōgun*, *Jisetsu-seitō-shōgun*, *Seitō-taishi*, etc. all temporary titles which were used only during the expedition. The emperor *Kwammu* gave the title of *Sei-i-taishōgun* to *Ōtomo Otomaro* (791) and to *Sakanoe no Tamuramaro* (797). This same title was bestowed by the emperor *Go-Toba* on *Minamoto Yoritomo*, but it was for life and hereditary. — *Sei-i-taishōgun* (commander-in-chief against the Barbarians) or, by abbreviation, *Shōgun* (general), such was the title under which the *Minamoto* (1192-1219), the *Fujiwara* (1220-1244), some Imperial princes (1245-1334), the *Ashikaga* (1336-1573), and lastly the *Tokugawa* (1603-1868), exercised unlimited power to which the emperors themselves were obliged to yield. This state of affairs caused Europeans for a long time to believe that Japan was governed by two emperors, one retired in his palace of *Kyōto*, the descendant of the gods, busied only with religious matters ; the other, the acting sovereign, governing and administering as he pleased. This notion though false was a correct estimate of the situation. The investiture of the *Shōgun* was at all times received from the emperor, who seems never to have had either the desire or the power to refuse it. From the time of *Yoritomo*, the title of *Shōgun* was reserved for the descendants of the *Minamoto* (*Seiwa-Genji*), and for this reason, *Nobunaga*, descendant of the *Taira*, and *Hideyoshi* who was of low extraction, never bore that title.

Sei-i-taishōgun, 征夷大將軍 . — See *Sei-i-shi*.

Seiji-sōsai-shoku, 政事總裁職 . In 1862, the power of the shōgunate was in the hands of *Iemochi*, then only 16 years old, and hence unable to cope with the ever increasing difficulties of the situation. The emperor *Kōmei* commanded him to give the title of *Seiji-sōsai* to *Matsudaira Yoshinaga* (1828-1890) of *Echizen*, and to entrust him with the direction of affairs, keeping however in the mean time *Hitotsubashi Keiki*, the future *Shōgun*, as counsellor (*hosa*). The following year, *Yoshinaga* was replaced by *Matsudaira Naokatsu, Yamato no kami*. The title was suppressed in 1864.

Seikanji, 清閑寺 . *Kuge* family descended from *Fujiwara Yoshikado*. — Now Count.

Seikō, 齊衡 . *Nengō* : 854-856.

Seikwa, 清華 . *Kuge* families, whose members could become *Udaijin*, *Sadaijin* and *Dajō-daijin*, but not *Sesshō* nor *Kwampaku*. They were also called *Kwazoku*. They are :

1. *Sanjō*, descended from *Fujiwara Sanesue* (1038-1162) ;

2. *Saionji,* descended from *Fujiwara Michisue* (1090-1123);
3. *Tokudaiji*   ,,   ,,   ,,   *Saneyoshi* (1066-1157);
4. *Kwazan-in,*   ,,   ,,   ,,   *Ietada* (1062-1136);
5. *Ōimikado,*   ,,   ,,   ,,   *Tsunezane* brother to *Ietada;*
6. *Kuga,*   ,,   ,, *Minamoto Morofusa* (*Murakami-Genji*)*;*
7. *Imadegawa,* ,,   ,, *Saionji Kanesue* (14th century).

These 7 families were for a long time called *Shichi-Seikwa;* later the following families were added to them:

8. *Hirohata,* descended from the emperor *Ōgimachi;*
9. *Daigo,* descended from *Ichijō Kaneka* (1692-1751), and thus we have the *Ku-Seikwa.*

Seikwan-in, 靜 寬 院 (+ 1877). Daughter of the emperor *Ninkō;* her true name was *Chika-ko, Kazu no miya.* In 1860, difficulties having arisen between the Emperor and the *Shōgun,* the *Tairō Ii Naosuke* proposed to betroth *Kazu no miya* to the young *Shōgun Iemochi,* then 14 years old. The emperor consented and they were married in the beginning of 1862. *Iemochi* died in 1866; in 1869, the princess, returned to *Kyōto* and took up her residence in the *Seigo-in.* She came back to *Tōkyō* in 1874 and died at *Tōnosawa* (*Sagami*).

Seimu-tennō, 成 務 天 皇. 13th Emperor of Japan (131-191). *Waka-tarashi-hiko,* son of *Keikō-tennō,* succeeded his father at the age of 47. He fixed limits to the provinces (*kuni*) and the districts (*agata*), and had them governed by some *Tsukasa no osa: kuni no miyatsuko, agata-nushi, wake, inagi,* etc. He died at the age of 107, after a reign of 60 years.

Seinei-tennō, 清 寧 天 皇. 22nd Emperor of Japan (430-484). *Shiragatake-hirokuni-oshiwaka-yamato-neko,* son of *Yūryaku-tennō,* succeeded his father at the age of 36 and died after a reign of 5 years. It was he who ordered the *Niiname-matsuri* to be celebrated for the first time (481).

Seiryō-den, 清 涼 殿. Building of the *Kyōto* Palace in which the emperor ordinarily lived; it is also called *Chū-den.* Its dimensions were 20m. (N.-S.) by 16m. (E.-W.) and was situated N. W. of the *Shishin-den.*

Seisen-tanizaku-shiki, 成 選 短 冊 式. Ceremony that took place every year at the Imperial Palace on the 5th day of the 5th month and at which the nobles of high rank presented a piece of poetry to the Emperor, written on a *tanizaku* (a long and narrow strip of paper on which poetry was usually written).

Seishi, 勢 至. — See *Daiseishi.*

Seishō-kō, 清 正 公. Name by which *Katō Kiyomasa* is known and honored in the *Nichiren* sect, of whose tenets he was a fervent adherent and a generous protector. (*Seishō* is the Chinese reading of the Japanese name *Kiyomasa*).

Sei Shōnagon, 清少納言. Daughter of *Kiyowara Motosuke* and lady of honor to the empress at the Court of *Ichijō-tennō* (10th century). In literature and poetry, she was the rival of *Murasaki Shikibu.* Her most renowned work is the *Makura no Sōshi.*

SEI SHŌNAGON.

Seishū, 勢州. Chinese name of *Ise* province.

Seitaka-Dōji, 制咤迦童子. One of the two followers of the god *Fudō;* the other was *Kongara-Dōji.*

Seitoku-kwan, 精得館. School of medicine established at *Nagasaki* in 1861 by *Matsumoto Ryōjun,* the professors of which were foreigners.

Seiwa-Genji, 清和源氏. Patronymic of the families descended from *Sadazumi-shinnō* (874-916), son of the emperor *Seiwa,* and which received the name of *Minamoto.* The table placed below indicates the principal ones.

Seiwa-Sadazumi-Tsunemoto {	Mitsunaka {	Yorimitsu-Yorikuni {	Yoritsuna (a) / Kunifusa (b)
		Yorinobu-Yoriyoshi {	Yoshiie (c) / Yoshimitsu (d)
	Mitsuyoshi- Mitsukuni-Tamemitsu Tamekimi (e)		

(*a*) — Yoritsuna-Nakamasa-Yorimasa-Nakatsuna .... *Ōta*

(*b*) — Kunifusa - Mitsukuni - Mitsunobu - Mitsumoto .... { *Toki / Akechi / Asano*

(*c*) — Yoshiie- {	Yoshichika- Tameyoshi {	Tametomo	(*Shōgun*) / *Hatsuda* / *Shishido*
		Yoshikata	*Kiso*
	Yoshikuni {	Yoshishige- { Yoshikane / Yoshinori / Yoshitoshi	*Nitta* / *Yamana* / *Satomi*
		Yoshisue	*Tokugawa* / *Matsudaira* / *Sakai*
		Yoshiyasu- { Yoshikiyo	*Nikki* / *Hosokawa* / *Sakakibara*
		Yoshikane	*Ashikaga* / *Hatakeyama* / *Momonoi* / *Kira*
			Imagawa / *Shiba* / *Shibukawa* / *Ishidō* / *Isshiki*

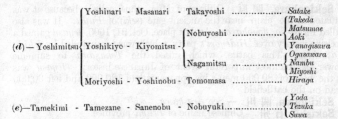

Seiwa-tennō, 清和天皇. 56th Emperor of Japan (859-876). *Korehito*, son of *Montoku-tennō*, ascended the throne at the death of his father. He was but 9 years old and he is the first child-emperor of whom Japanese history makes mention. His maternal grandfather *Fujiwara Yoshifusa* governed with the title of *Sesshō* and that of *Kwampaku* (864). When the emperor was 18 years old, he married him to one of his daughters, who was at the same time the aunt and wife of *Seiwa*, whilst he himself was his grandfather and father-in-law. It was during his reign (864) that an eruption of *Fuji-san* and *Asama-yama* caused a great number of victims, and that, in 871, the *Jōgwan-kyakushiki* (collection of laws) was promulgated. At the age of 27, *Seiwa* abdicated in favour of his son *Yōzei*, shaved his head and died 4 years later. His tomb is in the hamlet of *Mi-no-o* (*Yamashiro*) and for this reason, he is called *Mi-no-o no mikado*.

Seizan, 西山. In Hitachi, near the small city of *Ōta*. The *daimyō* of *Mito, Mitsukuni*, retired to that place after having transferred the administration of his domains to his son *Tsunaeda*. He died there in 1700.

Seizan, 西山. Branch of the *Jōdo-shū* sect founded during the 12th century by the bonze *Shōkū*. 4 of his disciples established 4 subdivisions of this branch:

1. *Nishidani-ryū*, 西谷流. Founded by *Jō-on* in the temple *Kōmyō-ji* (*Yamashiro*);

2. *Fukakusa-ryū*, 深草流. Founded by *Ryūshin* in the temple *Shinsō-in* (*Yamashiro*);

3. *Higashi-yama-ryū*, 東山流. Founded by *Kwanshō* in the temple *Amida-in* (*Yamashiro*);

4. *Saga-ryū*, 嵯峨流. Founded by *Dōkwan* in the temple *Kongō-in* (*Yamashiro*);

Seki, 關. Formerly a gate where the passports (*fuda, warifu*) were examined. The place where it was erected was called *sekisho*, and the post that guarded it, *sekimori*.

Seki, 關. In *Hitachi* (now, *Kawachi-mura*). Old castle of the *Seki daimyō*. *Munesuke* therein offered hospitality to *Kitabatake Chikafusa* and died there when the castle was besieged by *Kō Morofuyu* (1343).

Seki, 關. *Daimyō* family descended from *Fujiwara Uona*. Resided, from 1698 to 1868, at *Niimi* (*Bitchū* — 18,000 k.). — After the Restoration, Viscount; degraded in 1903.

Sekigahara, 關原. Village of *Mino*, thus called, because it was situated in the plain near the ancient gate (*seki*) of *Fuwa*. It was also called *Fuwa-no, Aonohara*. At that place, Oct. 21, 1600, *Ieyasu* gained a decisive victory over *Hideyori's* party, which was commanded by *Ishida Kazushige*. This battle, which raised the *Tokugawa* to supreme power, is the most important event of Japanese history. *Ieyasu* was at the head of 80,000 men; his opponents had 130,000 and left 30,000 dead on the battlefield.

Seki-gawa, 關川. — See *Ara-kawa*.

Sekishū, 石州. Chinese name of *Iwami* province.

Sekiyado, 關宿. In *Shimōsa*. Under the *Ashikaga*, a castle belonging to the *Yanada* family. In 1556, *Hōjō Ujiyasu* occupied it and gave it to his son-in-law *Ashikaga Haruuji*. *Uesugi Kenshin* stormed it in 1561. Under the *Tokugawa*, it was the residence of the *daimyō Hisamatsu* (1590), *Matsudaira* (1617) *Ogasawara* (1619), *Hōjō* (1637), *Makino* (1644), *Itakura* (1656), *Kuze* (1669), *Makino* (1682) and from 1705 to 1868 that of *Kuze* (48,000 k.).

Sekke, 攝家. — See *Go-sekke*.

Sekku, 節句. — See *Go-Sekku*.

Sekkwan-seiji, 攝關政事. (Lit.: government of the *Sesshō* and the *Kwampaku*). At the accession of the emperor *Seiwa*, (859) then only 9 years old, his grandfather *Fujiwara Yoshifusa* was named *Sesshō* (regent) and governed in his stead. Under the reign of *Yōzei* (877), *Mototsune* exercised the regency. *Kōkō*, who ascended the throne at the age of 55 (885), dispensed with a regent, but he created the title of *Kwampaku* for *Mototsune*, which remained henceforth in the *Fujiwara* family. When the Emperor was a minor, a *Sesshō* was named, who at the ceremony of the *gembuku*, changed his title to that of *Kwampaku* and continued to rule. These two titles could be bestowed only on the 5 branches of the *Fujiwara* family that were called *Go-Sekke*: *Konoe, Kujō, Nijō, Ichijō,* and *Takatsukasa*. During 3 centuries, the *Fujiwara* possessed an immense influence; but gradually, the authority passed into the hands of the military families. The first of these was the *Taira*, followed by the *Minamoto*, and the titles of *Sesshō* and *Kwampaku* became only honorary: their authority, if they possessed any, being limited to the interior of the Court at *Kyōto*. These titles however, remained in the same families till the Restoration. One single exception had been made in favor of *Hideyoshi* (1585).

Semimaru, 蟬丸. Servant (*zōshiki*) of prince *Atsuzane-shinnō* (897-966), son of the emperor *Uda*. He was blind, but excelled in poetry and music (*biwa*). He retired to *Ōsaka* (*Yamashiro*) and lived in retirement. — See *Minamoto Hiromasa*.

Semmyō, 宣命. In olden times, proclamations that were made to the people, of the most important events, such as: accession of a new emperor, choice of an empress, nomination of the successor, erection of a great temple or an Imperial sepulchre, etc.

Sen, 千. Under the *Tokugawa*, name of several families, whose members in different provinces were professors of the ceremony of the *cha no yu.* Those of *Wakayama* (*Kii*) all took the name of *Sen Sōsa :* those of *Kanazawa* (*Kaga*), the name of *Sen Sōshitsu ;* those of *Takamatsu* (*Sanuki*), *Sen Sōshu,* etc. — See *Sen Rikyū.*

Sendai, 仙臺. Chief town (93,500 inh.) of *Miyagi-ken* and *Rikuzen* province. In 1600, *Date Masamune,* who had been transferred from *Yonezawa* (*Dewa*), built a castle there and called it *Aoba-jō.* Its principal gate was taken from the palace which *Hideyoshi* had in *Nagoya* (*Hizen*) when he started for his Korean expedition (1592). The descendants of *Masamune,* the most powerful *daimyō* of the North, lived there till the Restoration (620,000 k.).

Sendai-gawa, 川內川. River (180 Km.) of *Satsuma,* rises at the *Shiraga - take,* passes through *Miyanojō* and enters the Ocean N. of *Hashima-saki.*

Sendanno, 栴檀野. Village of *Etchū,* formerly called *Hannyano.* In 1183, *Taira Koremori* was defeated there by *Imai Kanehira* and obliged to escape into *Kaga.* When *Nagao Tamekage* had resolved to conquer *Etchū,* he stopped at that place with his army, but he was defeated by the small *daimyō* of the provinces, *Kamio, Shiina, Enami,* etc. (1545). His son *Kagetora* (*Kenshin*) revenged the death of his father by offering to his spirit, 16 heads of the enemy, killed with his own hand (1563).

Sengaku, 仙覺. Bonze of the *Shaka-dō* temple at *Kamakura* (13th century). Is famous as a poet, and left a commentary of the *Man-yō-shū.*

Senge, 千家. Family descended from *Ame-no-oi no mikoto* and by right of inheritance, superior of the large Shintoist temple (*Ō-yashiro*) of *Izumo.*—Now Baron.

Sengen, 淺間山. — See *Ko-no-hana-sakuya-hime.*

Sengoku, 仙石. *Daimyō* family coming from *Mino* and descended from the *Toki* (*Seiwa-Genji*).

—— **Hidehisa, 秀久** (1551-1614). Son of *Hisamori,* served *Hideyoshi.* He subdued the island of *Awaji* and stormed the castle of *Sumoto* (1581), but was defeated in *Shikoku* by *Chōsokabe Motochika* (1583), and in *Bungo* by *Shimazu Yoshihisa* (1586). After the ruin of the *Hōjō* of *Odawara* (1590), he received the fief of *Komoro* (*Shinano* — 50,000 k.).

—— **Tadamasa, 忠政**. Son of *Hidehisa,* was transferred in 1622 to *Ueda* (*Shinano* — 60,000 k.). — In 1706, the family moved to *Izushi* (*Tajima* — 30,000 k.) and remained there till the Restoration.—Now Viscount.

Sengoku-jidai, 戰國時代. Period from 1490 to 1600, during which Japan was completely involved in civil war.

Sengoku shichi-yū, 戰國七雄. The 7 most renowned warriors of the civil wars of the 16th century : *Oda Nobunaga, Imagawa Yoshimoto, Takeda Shingen, Mōri Motonari, Uesugi Kenshin, Hōjō Ujiyasu* and *Toyotomi Hideyoshi.*

Senji, 宣旨. Mode of promulgating the Imperial decrees (*mikotonori*). The orders, when transmitted by a minister to the *benkwan*, who drew them up and published them, were called *dai-senji ;* those addressed only to the chiefs of the different sections of the Palace, were called *shō-senji ;* those transmitted by a special envoy (*taishi*) to the provinces, were called *kuni-senji*, etc.—The nobles and ladies of the Palace who had to transmit the orders of the Emperor were also called *senji*.

Senji-masu, 宣旨桝. Measures of capacity, fixed and imposed on the people by the emperor *Go-Sanjō* in the year 1072. That year being the 4th of the *Enkyū* era, they were called *Enkyū-senji-masu*. One *shō* of that time was worth only 0,81 of the present *shō* (1 litre 80.).

Senjimon, 千字文 (Lit.: book of the 1,000 characters). Classic Chinese book composed of 1,000 characters, none of them appearing twice, they are disposed in such a way that each series of 8 forms a complete sentence. It is said to have been brought to Japan, at the same time as the *Rongo*, by the Korean *Ajiki* in 284, but the Chinese annals tell us that it was composed in 525, by order of the emperor *Outi* (*Butei* — 502-549), founder of the *Leang* (*Ryō*) dynasty.

Senjō-dake, 千丈嶽. Mountain (2970 m.) on the borders of *Kai* and *Shinano*.

Senkwa-tennō, 宣化天皇. 28th Emperor of Japan (536-539). *Takeo-hiro-oshi-tachi*, 3rd son of *Keitai-tennō*, succeeded his brother *Ankan* at the age of 69. He sent *Ōtomo Sadehiko* to fight *Shiragi* (Korea) and died after a reign of 4 years.

Sennin, 仙人 (Lit.: mountain men). Superior beings having human form, but were subject neither to old age nor to death. A sort of *genii* of the mountains, they were venerated as demi-gods. The imagination of artists has had free scope in representing them. One (*Kokaku-sennin*) is carried through the air by a crane; an other (*Koi-sennin*) travels, mounted on a carp ; a third *Tsugen-sennin* draws a gigantic horse out of a diminutive calabash, etc.

Se-no-o Kaneyasu, 瀬尾兼康. Possessor of the domain of *Se-no-o* (*Bitchū*), was made prisoner at the battle of *Ataka* (*Kaga*) ; *Yoshi-naka* did not kill him but confided him to *Kuramitsu Nariuji* (1183). *Se-no-o* gained the latter's confidence and having intoxicated him, put him to death, massacred the officers and the guard of the governor of *Bizen*. He then intrenched himself in *Sasako*, where, being attacked by *Imai Kanehira*, he was defeated and killed, together with his son *Muneyasu*.

Sen Rikyū, 千利休 (1520-1591). Also called *Sōeki* 宗易. He was born a *Nakada Yoshirō*, at *Sakai* (*Izumi*) and became famous in the art of the arrangement of flowers, and in the solemn preparation of the tea ceremony (*cha-no-yu*), which he brought to such perfection that his regulations are kept to the present day. He first served *Nobunaga* and was called to the castle of *Azuchi*. He then entered the service of *Hideyoshi* whose favorite he became and, in 1588, was even allowed to appear in the presence of the emperor *Go-Yōzei*. *Rikyū* had a daughter of exquisite beauty and one day she was met by *Hideyoshi*, who asked her hand from her father ; the latter however resisted all the entreaties of the powerful *Taikō*. The following year, he was accused of bribery and invited to commit *harakiri*.

Senshū, 泉州. Chinese name of *Izumi* province.

Senshū-ji, 專修寺. Temple, built in the 13th century at *Takata* (*Shimotsuke*) by the bonze *Shimbutsu*. It was, till 1465, the principal seat of the *Takata* branch of the *Jōdo-shinshū* sect, which was transferred at that date to a temple of the same name *Isshinden* (*Ise*).

Senso, 踐祚. Accession to the Imperial throne. When the vacancy was created by the abdication of the actual emperor, it was called *Jō-i*. In olden times, there was only one ceremony. Since the 9th century, we have first the ceremony of the *Juzen*, made at the *Shishin-den*, during which the emperor-elect was acknowledged rightful heir and received the 3 emblems of the Imperial dignity ; then that of the *Soku-i*, celebrated at the *Daigoku-den*, which consisted in the proclaming the enthronement of the new emperor.

Sentō, 仙洞. Name given to the palace inhabited by an emperor after his abdication. Also called *Jōkō*. An order written by an ex-emperor is called *Inzen*. Immediately after his abdication, the emperor took the title of *Shin-in*, and should his predecessor be yet living, the latter changed his name into that of *Hon-in*. The empress who followed him in his retreat was called *Jo-in*.

Sen-yū-ji, 泉涌寺. Temple founded by *Kūkai* (*Kōbō-Daishi*) S.E. of *Kyōto*. Since *Shijō-tennō* (+ 1242), it became the burial place of the emperors. In its treasury is kept a tooth, said to be one of *Shaka's* which the famous *Tankai* (*Fujiwara Fuhito*) is supposed to have brought from China.

Seppuku, 切腹. — See *Harakiri*.

Serata, 世良田. Village of *Kōzuke*, in which *Minamoto* (*Nitta*) *Yoshishige* (+ 1202) settled towards the end of the 12th century and where his descendants continued to reside. In 1332, the *Hōjō*, in order to defray the expenses incurred by their war against the emperor *Go-Daigo*, sent men everywhere to collect the required amount. The collector sent to *Serata* showed himself so exacting, that *Nitta Yoshisada* had him put to death, levied an army against the *Hōjō*, and, the following year, occupied *Kamakura*. The *Nitta* or *Serata* family were the ancestors of the *Tokugawa*, who therefore endowed the temple *Chōraku-ji*, where *Yoshishige's* mausoleum can be seen.

Sesonji-ryū, 世尊寺流. School of calligraphy founded in the temple *Seson-ji*, during the rule of *Kamakura*, by *Yukiyoshi* and *Tsunetomo*, descendants of *Fujiwara Yukinari*.

Sesshō, 攝政. Regent of the empire. At the death of *Chū-ai* (200), *Jingō-kōgō* for 69 years acted as regent instead of his son *Ōjin* : it was the first time that this happened in Japan. Later on, *Umayado-Ōji* (*Shōtoku-Taishi*) was regent during the reign of the empress *Suiko* (593-621). At the death of *Montoku* (858), his successor *Seiwa* was only 9 years old, and his grandfather *Fujiwara Yoshifusa* was named *Sesshō* during the minority of the emperor, a custom that was followed afterwards. — *Shissei, Setsuroku*, are synonyms of *Sesshō*. — See the following article.

Sesshō-kwampaku, 攝政關白. From the earliest times, during the minority of the emperor, a minister acted as regent (*sesshō*); when the emperor came of age, the ex-regent continued the administration (*azukari mōsu—kwampaku*) but under the authority of the sovereign. Later on, these two terms, *sesshō* and *kwampaku*, became two distinct titles, and were the most honorable in the Court, more so even than that of *Dajō-daijin*. When there was a *sesshō*, there was no *kwampaku*, and vice versa. The *kwampaku*, on account of his high position, was also called *Ichi no za, Iehi no hito*. — See *Sekkwan-seiji*.

Sesshū, 攝州. Chinese name of *Settsu* province.

Sesshū, 雪舟 (1420-1506). Born at *Akahama* (*Bitchū*) he was by birth *Oda Tōyō*; at the age of 13, he became bonze in the temple *Hō-fuku-ji*. From his youth, he showed great aptitude for painting, and having become a disciple of the bonze *Kōtoku-Zenji* of the *Sō-koku-ji*, he went to *Kamakura*, where he applied himself to the study of the works of *Josetsu* and *Shūbun*. In 1463, he went to China, where he painted several Japanese scenes for the emperor, which were very much appreciated. After 6 years, he returned to his country, and settled at the *Unkoku-ji* temple in *Yamaguchi* (*Suwō*), then at the *Taiki-an* (*Iwami*). *Sesshū* is considered one of the greatest painters of the Chinese school, whose traditions he followed whilst adding to them a strong personal character; this latter trait has placed him even above his masters *Shūbun* and *Josetsu*.

SESSHŪ.

Sesson, 雪村 (1450-1506). *Satake Heizō*. Born at *Tokotaku* (*Hitachi*). His father having disinherited him in favor of an illegitimate son, he became a bonze in the *Jōdo-shū* sect and gave his time to painting, following *Shūbun's* and *Sesshū's* traditions; afterwards he painted according to the principles of the old Chinese masters of the *Sō* (960-1279) and *Gen* (1279-1368) dynasties. He ranks next to *Sesshū*.

Seta, 瀬田. Village of *Ōmi*, S. of lake *Biwa* on the *Seta-gawa*. A bridge across the river has given the place great importance; it was the scene of numerous encounters. Here in 672, *Murakuni Oyori*, *Temmu's* general, defeated *Chison*, *Kōbun's* partisan. Later on, *Kusakabe Komoro* burned the bridge in order to cut off the retreat of *Emi Oshikatsu*, who was defeated and killed (736). *Kiso Yoshinaga* was defeated here by *Noriyori* (1184). Here *Nobunaga* put up his tents, when he ordered the burning of the *Hieizan* temples (1571). After the assassination of *Nobunaga*, *Akechi Mitsuhide* summoned the castellan of *Seta*, *Kagetaka*; but the latter instead of obeying, burned the bridge, seized all the boats and thus prevented the escape of the murderer.

Seta, 世田. In *Iyo*. Old castle belonging to the *Kōno daimyō*. In 1335, *Ōtate Ujiaki* occupied it, but later on it was taken from him by *Hosokawa Yoriharu* (1340).

Seta-gawa, 瀬 田 川. River flowing out of lake *Biwa* (*Ōmi*). It runs 15 Km. south, and enters *Yamashiro*, where it takes the name of *Uji-gawa*.

Setchū-ha, 折 衷 派. School of Confucianism whose principal members were: *Nakanishi Tan-en* (1709-1752), *Inoue Randai* (1705-1761), *Uno Meika* (1698-1745), *Inoue Kinga* (1733-1784), *Katayama Kenzan* (1730-1782), etc.

Seto, 瀬 戸. Small city (8000 inh.), famous for its porcelain factories (*seto-mono*), established towards 1230 by *Katō Shirōzaemon*.

Seto-nai-kai, 瀬 戸 内 海.) The Inland Sea, or the Japanese
Seto-no-uchi, 瀬 戸 内. ∫ Mediterranean, lies between the 3 great islands of *Hondo*, *Shikoku* and *Kyūshū*, and is closed on the E. by the *Awaji* island; it is joined to the Ocean on the E. by the *Akashi* and the *Naruto* straits, on the W. by the straits of *Bungo* and *Shimonoseki*. It is divided into 5 large basins (*nada*), which are (from E. to W.) *Harima-nada*, *Bingo-nada*, *Mishima-nada*, *Iyo-nada* and *Suwō-nada*. The *Seto-nai-kai*, studded with nearly 300 islands, is famous all the world over for the beauty of its scenery.

Seto-zaki, 瀬 戸 崎. Cape S. of *Kii*; also called *Kanayama-saki*.

Setsu-zan, 雪 山 (Lit.: snowy mountain). Name given by the Japanese, after the annexation of Formosa, to mount *Sylvia* (3854 m.), in the N. of this land.

Settei-ryū, 雪 鼎 流. Branch of the school of painting called *Unko-ku-ryū*. Established by *Tsukioka Settei* (1760-1836), it has produced such men as: *Okada Gyokuzan*, *Ishida Gyokuzan*, *Nakai Rankō*, etc.

Settsu, 攝 津. One of the 5 provinces of *Kinai*. Comprises 7 districts, 4 of which belong to the *Ōsaka-fu* and 3 to the *Hyōgo-ken*.— Chinese name: *Sesshū*. — Formerly called *Naniwa*, *Tsu no kuni*.—In 683, was governed by a special administration (*Settsu-shiki*) having a *taifu* at its head; then in 793, the *shiki* was suppressed and *Settsu* was ruled like the other provinces.

Seyaku-in, 施 藥 院. Formerly a medical service at the Imperial Palace. The chief, at first called *In no bettō*, received the title of *Seyaku-in-shi* in 825: he had under his orders the *Hankwan*, *Shuten*, doctors, etc

Shaka, 釋 迦. *S'âkya-Muni*, the founder of Buddhism. Also called *Gautama* and by the Europeans, *Buddha*. According to Chinese authors, he was born in the year 1027 before the Christian era, but European critics bring the date down to the year 653, and even to 557 B. C.—*Shaka* is the name of a dynasty that reigned over the kingdom of *Kabilavastu* (*Kabirae*), in central India; *Muni* signifies anchorite.— *Shaka's* father was king *Suddhodana* (*Jōbon-dai-ō*) and his mother *Màyà* (*Maya-bunin*). At the age of 7, he thoroughly knew Astronomy, Geography, Mathematics and Military science. At 15 years of age, he was named heir apparent to the throne; hence the name *Shitta-Taishi*, given him by the Japanese. At 17 (according to some at 27) he married *Yasodhara* (*Yashudara*), and from that time, he resolved to quit a world, that appeared to him only a succession of pain and suffering, through birth, sickness, old age, and death. The night following the birth of his son *Rahoula*, he left his family and retired to the solitude of *Ourouwela* in order to meditate on the way to perfection : there at the age of 35, sitting under the tree *bodhi* (*bōdaiju* — ficus religiosa), he received the perfect knowledge of all things and became *Buddha*. He began to preach and his first teachings form the *Kegon-kyō*. He soon had a great number of disciples, among whom 1250 of the best disposed received the title of *Arakan*. After 5 years, *Shaka* came back to *Kabilavastu*, where he received a spendid reception and where he preached with great success. At the age of 9, *Rahoula* became a disciple of his father. Soon after one of his aunts embraced the perfect way and was the first *Bikuni* or *Ama*. At the age of 80, after 45 years of uninterrupted preaching, *Shaka* entered the *Nirvâna* (*nehan*).—See *Bukkyō, San-ji-kyō*.

Shake-bugyō, 社 家 奉 行. Under the *Ashikaga Shōgun*, an official whose duty it was to watch over all the Shintoist temples. To create this office, some functions were separated from the *Jisha-bugyō*.

Shaku-i, 爵 位. Formerly the rank which the governors of provinces gave to the Shintoist temples under their jurisdiction. Later, the sanction of the Emperor was required.

Shaku-i shi-jū-hachi kai, 爵 位 四 十 八 階. The 48 degrees of the hierarchy of the nobles and officials created in 685 by the emperor *Temmu*.—The two ranks of *myō-i* 明 位 and the 4 of *jō-i* 淨 位 , having each 2 degrees, thus making in all 12 degrees were reserved for the princes. — Below them were the :

Shō-i, 正 位 :	4 ranks with 2 degrees each (*tai, shō*), in all	8 degrees			
Jiki-i, 直 位 :	,,	,,	,,	8 ,,	
Gon-i, 勤 位 :	,,	,,	,,	8 ,,	48 degrees.
Mu-i, 務 位 :	,,	,,	,,	8 ,,	
Zu-i, 追 位 :	,,	,,	,,	8 ,,	
Shin-i, 進 位 ;	,,	,,	,,	8 ,,	

Shakuten, 釋 奠. Formerly a ceremony in honor of *Confucius* and his 10 principal disciples (*jū-tetsu*). It was performed twice a year at the *Daigaku* in the 2nd and the 8th months.

Shamu, 暹 羅. The kingdom of *Siam*.

Sharai, 射 禮. In former times, a ceremony that took place at the Palace on the 17th day of the 1st month and which consisted in a sort of trial of skill in bow-shooting ; the nobles and the princes took part in it.

Shashikotan-jima, 捨 子 古 丹 島. Island (about 53 Km long by 15 to 23 broad) of the *Chishima* Archipelago (Kurile).

Shi, 子. Title of nobility corresponding to that of Viscount

Shiba, 芝. One of the 15 districts of *Tōkyō*, S. W. of the city, remarkable for its large Buddhist temples which guard the tombs of 6 *Tokugawa Shōgun* : the 2nd, *Hidetada* (+ 1632); the 6th, *Ienobu* (+ 1713) ; the 7th, *Ietsugu* (+ 1716) ; the 9th, *Ieshige* (+1761) ; the 12th, *Ieyoshi* (+1853) ; and the 14th, *Iemochi* (+ 1866).

Shiba, 斯 波. *Daimyō* family descended from *Minamoto Yasuuji* (*Seiwa-Genji*). Also called *Bue* 武 衞 , from the district of *Kyōto* where the family resided. — During the *Ashikaga* shogunate, it was one of three families (*san-kwan*) from which the *Kwanryô* of *Kyôto* could be chosen.

—— **Ieuji, 家氏**. Son of *Yasuuji*, is the first who, at the end of the 13th century, adopted the name of *Shiba*.

—— **Takatsune, 高経** (+1367). Great-grandson of *Ieuji*, joined the party of *Ashikaga Takauji*, aided in the defeat of the Imperial army at *Takenoshita* (*Suruga*), and entered *Kyôto* (1335). The following year, he defeated *Wakiya Yoshisuke* and *Nitta Yoshiaki* at *Uryu* (*Settsu*), then he occupied the castles of *Kanagasaki* (*Echizen*) where *Nitta Yoshisada* had intrenched himself (1337), and of *Takanosu*, defended by *Hata Tokiyoshi* who was slain there (1338). After these victories, the Southern party had no longer any partisans in *Echizen* and the surrounding country. But *Takatsune*, after his quarrels with *Takauji*, supported *Tadafuyu*, who having been defeated, took refuge in *Echizen* (1354). However after the death of *Takauji*, *Takatsune* became reconciled with the *Shôgun Yoshiakira*, and his son *Yoshimasa* was named *Shitsuji* (minister) (1362). The peace did not last long: *Takatsune* quarrelled with *Sasaki Takauji* and *Akamatsu Norisuke*. *Yashiakira* sent against him *Sasaki Ujiyori* and *Hatakeyama Yoshitô*, who besieged him in his castle of *Somayama* (*Echizen*). He held out for more than one year, but finally died of sickness during the siege.

—— **Yoshimasa, 義将** (+1410). Son of *Takatsune*, received the title of *Shitsuji* in 1362; *Yoshimitsu* having become *Shôgun* (1367), changed it into that of *Kwanryô*. Favorite of the new *Shôgun*, *Yoshimasa* received the government of *Echizen*, *Etchû*, *Noto*, *Shinano*, *Sado*, and *Wakasa*. He is also known as a poet.

—— **Yoshitake, 義健** (+1452). Died without an heir, and his succession was disputed by *Yoshikado* and *Yoshitoshi*.

—— **Yoshikado, 義廉** (+ towards 1480). Was son of *Shibukawa Yoshino*. At the death of *Yoshitake*, his cousin was appointed to succeed him, but the great vassals of *Shiba*, the *Kai*, the *Asakura*, the *Oda* refused to sanction this choice and named *Yoshikado*. War ensued between the two rivals and their partisans. In 1459, the *Shôgun Yoshimasa* approved the nomination of *Yoshikado* and gave orders that all the domains of *Shiba* should be restored to him: *Yoshitoshi*, without relinquishing his claims, fled to *Suwô*. His cause came before the Court of *Kyôto*, and, in 1466, the *Shôgun*, repealing his first decision, recognised *Yoshitoshi* as the legitimate heir to *Yoshitake*. *Yoshikado* refused to submit and appealed to his father-in-law *Yamana Sôzen*; *Yoshimasa* alarmed, again abandoned *Yoshitoshi* and named *Yoshikado Kwanryô*. The following year, civil war (*Ônin no ran*) broke out: *Yoshikado* was naturally on the side of *Sôzen*. After peace was restored (1477), he retired to the castle of *Kiyosu* (*Owari*).

—— **Yoshitoshi, 義敏** (1430-1490). Son of *Ôno Yoshikane*. He had been adopted by *Shiba Mochitane*, uncle to *Yoshitake*. At the death of the latter (1452), the family named *Yoshitoshi* as his successor; but the great vassals refused to acknowledge him and began to divide the large domains of their lords among themselves; the *Oda* took *Owari*, the

Asakura, Echizen ; the *Kai, Tōtōmi*, etc. *Yoshitoshi* appealed to the *Shōgun Yoshimasa* to whom the rebel vassals deputed *Ise Sadachika* to explain their conduct, based, they said, on the incapacity of *Yoshitoshi*. The *Shōgun* admitted their reasons and accepted their candidate *Yoshikado*. *Yoshitoshi* now went to *Suwō* to ask help of *Ōuchi Norihiro*. At that time, the sister of *Yoshitoshi's* wife married *Ise Sadachika* and the latter returned to the *Shōgun* to plead the cause of his new ally : *Yoshitoshi's* rights were admitted (1466). *Yoshikado*, helped by his father-in-law *Yamana Sōzen* levied an army and marched against *Kyōto* : *Yoshitoshi* fled to the North and when the civil war broke out, he was naturally on the side of *Hosokawa Katsumoto, Sōzen's* adversary (1467). In 1475, he retired to *Owari*, but the *Oda* had already occupied the greater portion of the province of which they had been *shugo-dai* for several generations, and, *Yoshitoshi*, finding himself powerless to regain his lost domains, fled to *Echizen* where he died.

—— **Yoshisato,** 義達 (+1521). Grandson of *Yoshikado*. He tried in vain to regain authority over his vassals ; three had gradually become independent in the domains which had been confided to them.

—— **Yoshimune,** 義統 (+1554). Son of *Yoshisato*, was defeated by *Oda Nobutomo* and subsequently killed himself.

—— **Yoshikane,** 義銀 (+1572). Son of *Yoshimune*. He asked the help of *Nobunaga* against *Nobutomo*, whom he besieged at *Kiyosu*, and whom he defeated and killed. *Yoshikane* now resided at *Kiyosu*. He soon after tried to shake off the authority of *Nobunaga*, but had to leave *Owari*, passed into *Ise*, and afterwards into *Kawachi*, where he died, almost in misery. — With him, the family which, for over two centuries, had been so powerful, disappears from history.

Shiba Kōkan, 司馬江漢 (1747-1818). Painter, was a scholar of *Suzuki Harunobu*, then of *Tani Bunchō*. He went to *Nagasaki* and learned from the Dutch the principles of perspective, until then unkown to the Japanese. Here he also acquired a knowledge of copper-engraving, oil-painting, etc. He likewise learned Astronomy, History, Geography, and wrote several works.

Shibamura, 芝村. In *Yamato*. Was from 1615 to 1868, the residence of a branch of the *Oda* family, descended from *Nagamasu*, brother of *Nobunaga* (10,000 k).

Shiba-no-kōji, 芝小路. Family descended from *Fujiwara Tametaka* and attached to the temple *Kōfuku-ji* at *Nara*. — Now Baron.

Shibano Ritsuzan, 柴野栗山 (1748-1821). Born at *Takamatsu* (*Sanuki*), he studied at *Edo* and afterwards at *Kyōto*. Named in 1788 professor at the *Shōhei-kō*, his lectures on Japanese antiquities drew great crowds of hearers.

Shibata, 新發田. City (11,500 inh.) of *Echigo*. In the 16th century, domain of a family of the same name. *Uesugi Kagekatsu* occupied it in 1587 and when he was transferred to *Aizu* (1597), *Hideyoshi* gave it to the *Mizoguchi daimyō*, who occupied it until the Restoration (50,000 k.).

Shibata, 柴田. *Daimyō* family from *Owari* and descended from the *Minamoto* (*Seiwa-Genji*). Was vassal of the *Oda*.

—— **Katsuie,** 勝家 (1530-1583). Joined in the plot formed by *Hayashi Michikatsu* to replace *Nobunaga* by his brother *Nobuyuki* (1557); *Ikeda Nobuteru*, having been sent against them, defeated them and *Katsuie* submitted. In 1570, *Nobunaga* entrusted him with the keeping of the castle of *Chōkōji (Ōmi)*, taken from the *Sasaki : Yoshisuke* laid siege to the castle but was repulsed. After the campaign against the *Asai* and the *Asakura*, *Katsuie* received the *Echizen* and *Kaga* provinces in fief (1579) and established himself in the castle of *Kita-no-shō* (now, *Fukui*). In 1582, he invaded *Noto*, but the 3 *daimyō* of the province, *Yuza*, *Miyake* and *Nukui*, appealed to *Uesugi Kagekatsu*. *Katsuie* had made preparations to fight the powerful *daimyō* of *Echigo*, when he heard of the death of *Nobunaga*. He at once marched against *Akechi Mitsuhide*, but arrived only after the defeat of the latter. He took part in the conferences that ended in the election of *Sambōshi (Hidenobu)* as successor of *Nobunaga*. Very soon after, being jealous of the ever growing influence of *Hideyoshi*, he resolved to get rid of him, and

SHIBATA KATSUIE.

when some dispute occurred between *Nobutaka* and the future *Taikō*, he sided with the latter. War ensued : the army of *Katsuie* was defeated at *Shizu-ga-take (Ōmi)* owing to the imprudence of *Sakuma Morimasa*. and *Hideyoshi* laid siege to *Kita-no-shō*. Not being able to resist such a powerful foe, *Katsuie* set fire to the castle and killed himself together with his wife and some 30 servants. —— *Katsuie's* wife was the sister of *Nobunaga*. After having been married for some time, she left *Katsuie*, married *Asai Nagamasa* (1568), and had 3 daughters. At the death of *Nagamasa* (1573), she returned to her first husband. When *Kita-no-shō* was besieged, *Katsuie* begged her to escape with her children, but she refused and after having entrusted her 3 daughters to a faithful servant who led them to a place of safety, she met death with her husband. She was 37 years old. —— Of her 3 daughters, *Yodo-gimi*, the eldest married *Hideyoshi ;* the 2nd, *Kyōgoku Takatsugu ;* the 3rd, the future *Shōgun Hidetada*.

—— **Katsutoyo,** 勝豊 (+1583). Son of *Shibukawa Hachizaemon*, was adopted by *Katsuie* and entrusted with the keeping of the castle of *Nagahama (Ōmi)* (1582) : he was forced to surrender to *Hideyoshi* and died at *Kyōto*, the same year.

—— **Katsumasa,** 勝政 (1557-1582). Brother of *Sakuma Morimasa*, adopted by *Katsuie*, was killed at *Shizu-ga-take*.

—— **Katsuhisa,** 勝久 (1568-1583). *Katsuie's* nephew and adopted by him, fought at *Shizu-ga-take* and, after the defeat, fled into the mountains where he was pursued and killed.

Shiba Tattō, 司馬達等. Japanese name of the Chinese *Sumatah*, who, having come to Japan in 522, settled in *Yamato* and tried to spread Buddhism, but the people refused to accept foreign gods. Later on, his 3 daughters were the first *ama* (Buddhist nuns).

Shibata Zeshin, 柴田是眞 (1807-1891). Born at *Edo*, he studied painting under *Suzuki Nanrei,* later at *Kyōto* under *Okamoto Toyohiko,* and according to the testimony of the most competent critics, he became the most skilful artist in lacquer work that Japan has ever produced.

Shibatei, 芝亭. Family descended from *Fujiwara (Saionji) Saneo* (1217-1273) and attached to the *Kōfuku-ji* temple (*Nara*). — Now Baron.

Shibayama, 芝山. *Kuge* family descended from *Fujiwara Tamefusa.* — Now Viscount.

Shibukawa, 澁川. *Daimyō* family descended from *Ashikaga Yasuuji* (*Seiwa-Genji*).

—— **Yoshiaki,** 義顯. Son of *Yasuuji* in the 13th century took the name of *Shibukawa*.

—— **Yoshiyuki,** 義行. Descendant of *Yoshiaki,* was governor of *Musashi* and built the castle of *Warabi*.

—— **Mitsuyori,** 滿賴 (+ 1446). Son of *Yoshiyuki,* was named *Kyūshū-tandai* to replace *Imagawa Sadayo* (1395). Later on, he shaved his head and took the name of *Dōchin*.

—— **Yoshikane,** 義俊. Son of *Mitsuyori,* named *Kyūshū-tandai* in 1457, defeated *Ashikaga Shigeuji* and secured the office of *kwanryō* to the *Uesugi*. He continued to govern the *Musashi* province of which his descendants were deprived by the *Hōjō* of *Odawara*.

Shi bukwan, 四部官. The 4 titles, *kami, suke, jō* and *sakwan,* created by the emperor *Mommu* (701). These titles were the same for the 8 ministerial departments but were written with different characters.

Shibuya, 澁谷. Family descended from *Fujiwara Tadamichi* (1097-1164) and, by right of inheritance, at the head of the *Bukkō-ji* temple (*Kyōto*) and of the branch of the *Shinshū* sect bearing the same name. — Now Baron.

Shibuzawa, 澁澤. Family coming from *Musashi* and ennobled in 1900. — Now Baron.

Shichi Fukujin, 七福神. The seven gods of good luck: *Ebisu, Daikoku, Benten, Fukurokuju, Bishamon, Jurōjin* and *Hotei.* The origin of this group, partly Japanese, partly Chinese, partly Indian, is very obscure. On *Ieyasu's* request, the famous bonze *Tenkai* (*Jigen-Daishi*) defined their respective attributes and made each of them personify one of what he believed to be the 7 sources of happiness in this world: longevity wealth, probity, contentment, popularity, wisdom and strength. But

THE 7 GODS OF GOOD LUCK.

Daikoku
Fukurokuju   Bishamon
Benten
Jurōjin   Ebisu
Hotei.

this division of their attributes has remained very uncertain and the people often mistake their respective powers.

Shichi-hon yari, 七本鎗. (Lit.: the 7 spears). Under this name, those 7 warriors were known who most distinguished themselves in the battles of the time. — Thus the 7 *hon yari* of the *Azuki-saka* battle (*Mikawa*) (1542) are: *Tsuda Nobumitsu, Oda Nobufusa, Okada Naonori, Sasa Katsumichi, Sasa Katsushige, Nakano Sōchi* and *Shimogata Masanori.* — Those of *Shizu-ga-take* (*Ōmi*) (1583) are: *Fushima Masanori, Katō Kiyomasa, Hirano Nagayasu, Katō Yoshiaki, Wakizaka Yasuharu, Katagiri Katsumoto* and *Kasuya Takenori.* — Those of *Kanizaka* (*Owari*) (1584) are: *Ōkubo Tadatoshi, Ōkubo Junshirō, Ōkubo Tadayo, Ōkubo Tadasuke, Abe Tadamasa, Sugiura Shigezane* and *Sugiura Chin-ei,* — etc.

Shichijō, 七條. *Kuge* family descended from *Fujiwara Michitaka* (953-995). — Now Viscount.

Shichi seikwa, 七清華. — See *Seikwa.*

Shichi-tō, 七嶋. — See *Izu no shichi-tō.*

Shi Daishi, 四大師. The 4 most renowned bonzes honored with the title of *Daishi*: *Dengyō-Daishi* (*Saichō*), *Kōbō Daishi* (*Kūkai*), *Jikaku-Daishi* (*Ennin*) and *Chishō-Daishi* (*Enchin*).

Shi daitennō, 四大天王. (Lit.: the 4 great Kings of heaven). The 4 gods who protect the world from the attacks of demons, each guarding one of the 4 cardinal points: *Jikoku,* the East; *Zōchō,* the South; *Kōmoku,* the West; *Tamon,* the North.

Shido, 志度. In *Sanuki. Taira Munemori* there defeated the army of the *Minamoto* whilst on his way to *Yashima* with the emperor *Antoku* (1185).

Shi-dō, 四道. The 4 branches of learning in the old University (*Daigaku*). — See *Daigakuryō no shi-dō.*

Shi-dō Shōgun, 四道將軍. The 4 generals named by the emperor *Sujin* (88 B. C.) to repress the incursions of the *Ebisu*: *Ōhiko* in the North, *Takenunakawa-wake* in the East, *Kibitsu-hiko* in the West and *Michinushi* in *Tamba.*

Shiga, 滋賀. In *Ōmi,* (now, *Ōtsu*). Was the Imperial residence during the reigns of *Tenchi* and *Kōbun* from 668 to 672.

Shiga-ken, 滋賀縣. Department formed by the *Ōmi* province.— Pop.: 740,000 inh —Chief town: *Ōtsu* (34,500 inh.).—Pr. cities: *Hikone* (16,700 inh.), *Nagahama* (10,300 inh.), etc.

Shigeno, 滋野. *Samurai* family of the *Yamaguchi* clan (*Suwō*) ennobled after the Restoration. — Now Baron.

Shigeno Sadanushi, 滋野貞主 (785-852). Minister of the emperors *Junwa* and *Nimmyō*; distinguished legist and writer. Left many books.

Shigenoi, 滋野井. *Kuge* family descended from *Fujiwara* (*Sanjō*) *Kinnori* (1103-1160). — Now Viscount.

Shigi-san, 信貴山. Mountain (500 m.) between *Kawachi* and *Yamato.* Tradition tells us that here *Soga Umako* defeated *Mononobe Moriya* (587). A temple (*Kwanki-in Sonshi-ji*) is erected at the top, in honor of the god of war *Bishamon*. In 1333, the prince *Morinaga-shinnō* fortified himself here against the *Hōjō* army. Later on (1560), *Matsunaga Hisahide* constructed a castle at the same place, in which, being besieged by *Nobunaga*, he killed himself (1577).

Shihō-hai, 四方拝. Ceremony celebrated at the Palace on the 1st day of the year at the hour of the Tigre (3 to 5 a.m.) and during which the emperor turns towards the 4 cardinal points, venerates the tombs of the ancestors and prays for the prosperity of his reign and for preservation from all calamities during the year.

Shihō-shō, 司法省. Ministry of Justice created in 1885.

Shii, 志比. In *Echizen* (now *Shiidani*). In 1232, the bonze *Dōgen* built the temple *Eihei-ji* there, which became the seat of the *Sōdō-shū* sect. During the Middle Ages, it was the residence of the *Hatano daimyō*, governors of the province.

Shiinetsu-hiko, 椎根津彦. Called also *Chin-hiko, Kamishiritsu-hiko*. Submitted to *Jimmu-tennō* when he made his expedition to the East and served him as pilot. In return for that office he was named *Yamato no kuni no miyatsuko*.

Shiiya, 椎谷. In *Echigo*. Here it was that *Nagao Tamekage* defeated *Uesugi Akisada* (1510). Was from 1698 to 1868, the residence of a branch of the *Hori* family (10,000 k.).

Shijō, 四條. *Kuge* family issued from *Fujiwara Uona* (721-783).

—— **Takasuke,** 隆資 (+ 1352). Son of *Takazane*, served *Go-Daigo*. Named *Kebiishi-bettō*, he endeavored to induce all the bonzes of the *Hiei-zan* to join the party of the emperor, whom he accompanied in his flight to *Kasagi*. When *Go-Daigo* was taken prisoner, he shaved his head ; later, having again returned to active life at the downfall of the *Hōjō* (1333), he fought against *Ashikaga Takauji*, was defeated at *Otoko-yama* (1336) and at *Shijō-nawate* (1348). He was killed in a battle against the troops of the North.

—— **Takatoshi,** 隆俊 (+ 1373). Son of *Takasuke*, continued the war against the *Ashikaga*. In 1353, he defeated the governor of *Kii*, then, with *Yamana Tokiuji*, he laid siege to *Kyōto* and obliged the *Shōgun Yoshiakira* to seek refuge in *Mino ;* the latter soon returned and the party of the South was forced to retreat. In 1355, *Takatoshi* again attacked the army of the *Shōgun*, but was repulsed. He however continued the war, was successful in several encounters but was at last slain in battle.—His descendants at present bear the title of Marquis, and a parallel branch, that of Baron.

Shijō-ha, 四條派. School of painting founded in the 18th century at *Kyōto* by *Matsumura Gekkei*. It is also called *Shijō-ryū*. It produced such men as *Matsumura Keibun, Okamoto Toyohiko, Oda Kaisen, Sakuma Sōen*, etc.

Shijō-nawate, 四條畷. In *Kawachi*, where *Kusunoki Masatsura* was defeated and killed by *Kō Moronao* (1348). A temple (*Shijō-nawate jinja*) has been erected in his honor on the neighboring mountain of *Iimori*.

Shijō-tennō, 四條天皇. 87th Emperor of Japan (1233-1242). *Mitsuhito,* son of *Go-Horikawa-tennō,* was raised to the throne at the abdication of his father, when only two years old. *Fujiwara Norizane,* whose brother was *Shōgun* at *Kamakura,* was named *Sesshō;* he died two years later and was replaced by his father *Michiie,* who exercised authority in the Palace whilst the *Shikken Hōjō Yasutoki* administered the empire at his pleasure. *Shijō* died at the age of 12.

Shi-jū-shichi gishi, 四 十 七 義 士. (Lit.: the 47 faithful *samurai*). The 47 *rōnin* of the *Akō* (*Harima*) clan, who revenged the death of their master *Asano Naganori,* by killing *Kira Yoshinaka,* who had insulted him.—See *Ōishi Yoshio.*

Shika-dai-ji, 四 個 大 寺. Formerly the 4 largest Buddhist temples: *Tō-daiji, Kōfuku-ji, Enryaku-ji,* and *Onjō-ji.*

Shikazono, 鹿 園. Family descendant of *Fujiwara* (*Sanjō*) *Sanefusa* (1146-1224) and attached to the temple *Kōfuku-ji* (*Nara*). — Now Baron.

Shikibunden, 職 分 田. Or *Shikiden.* Formerly rice-fields allotted to the holders of certain offices. Thus the *Dajō-daijin* received 40 *chō* (about 100 acres); the *Sadaijin* and the *Udaijin,* 30 *chō;* the *Dainagon,* 20 *chō;* the *Dazai-sotsu,* 10 *chō;* the *Dazai-dai-ni,* 6 *chō; Dazai-shō-ni,* 4 *chō;* a governor of province, 2 *chō* 6, etc.

Shikibu-shō, 式 部 省. Or *Nori no tsukasa.* Ministry of Ceremonies, created in 649 and suppressed after the Restoration. Its functions were to examine into the merits of the officials in reference to their advancement, to fix the rewards, to superintend the University, etc. The minister had the title of *Shikibu-kyō;* subject to him were, 1 *tayū,* 1 *shōyū,* 2 *taijō* 2 *shōjō,* etc.

Shikifu, 職 封. Formerly domains allotted to officials according to the importance of their functions.

Shiki-hyōjōshū, 式 評 定 衆. Honorary members of the Council, under the *Kamakura Shōgun.* The title was given to military officers who could not hold with their own office that of *Hikitsukeshū, Mandokoro, Monchūjo,* etc., but who, in the ceremonies, were connected with the members of these administrations.

Shiki-ke, 式 家. One of the 4 branches of the *Fujiwara* family, founded by the 4 sons of *Fuhito.* The *Shiki-ke* comes down from *Umakai* (694-734), *Shikibu-kyō,* whence the name given to his lineage This branch was at its highest point of prosperity at the time of *Momokawa* (722-779). It became extinct during the revolt of *Kusuri-ko* and *Nakanari* (810).

Shi-Kinai, 四 畿 內. In 646, the emperor *Kōtoku* gave the name of *Kinai* to the country round about the capital. Later on, this region was divided into 4 provinces; *Yamato, Kawachi, Naniwa* and *Yamashiro,* which also received the name of *shi* (4) *Kinai.* In 716, *Izumi* was added to them, thus forming the *go* (5) *Kinai.*

Shikine-jima, 式 根 島. One of the 7 islands of *Izu.*

Shiki no Ōji, 施 基 皇 子 (+ 716). 4th son of the emperor *Tenchi* Had great influence during the reigns of *Jitō* and *Mommu.* More than

50 years after his death, when his son *Shirakabe no Ōji* was raised to the throne (769), *Shiki* received the posthumous title of *Tawara-tennō* or *Kasuga-no-miya no tennō*.

Shikitei Samba, 式亭三馬 (1757-1822). Renowned novelist of *Edo*. His best work is the *Ukiyo-furo*.

Shikken, 執權. First minister of the *Shōgun* of *Kamakura*. This title had its equivalent in the *Sesshō* and the *Kwampaku* of *Kyōto*. In 1203, *Yoriie* having handed over the shōgunate to his brother, then only 11 years old, their maternal grandfather *Hōjō Tokimasa* took upon himself the direction of affairs and received the title of *Shikken*, which he transmitted two years later to his son *Yoshitoki*. In 1213, after the defeat of *Wada Yoshimori*, *Yoshitoki* assumed the title of *Samurai-dokoro-bettō*, and, as he was already *Mandokoro-bettō*, he then held both the civil (*bun*) and the military (*bu*) authority, which his descendants inherited and exercised till 1333.

Shikoku, 四國. One of the 5 large islands of Japan, so called, because it comprised 4 provinces : *Awa, Sanuki, Iyo* and *Tosa*. Its area is 18,210 Km.[2] and its coast measures 2,659 Km. The population numbers 3,015,000 inh. The 4 provinces that composed it have formed 4 departments : *Tokushima, Kagawa, Ehime* and *Kōchi*, comprising 36 districts (*kōri*), 5 large cities (*shi*) and 817 boroughs or villages (*machi* and *mura*). 75 small islands are dependent upon *Shikoku*. It is the most densely populated of the 5 large islands of Japan, (165 inh. to Km.[2]).

Shima, 志摩. One of the 15 provinces of *Tōkaidō*. Comprises 1 district, which is dependent on the *Mie-ken*. It is the smallest in all Japan.—Chinese name : *Shishū*.

Shimabara, 島原. Peninsula, S. of *Hizen*. Was included until 1612, in the domains of the *Arima daimyō*, then passed to *Matsukura Shigemasa*. The latter died in 1630, and his son *Shigeharu* began a reign of unendurable tyranny. It happened that the inhabitants of the island of *Amakusa* had then also grievances against their *daimyō Terazawa Katataka*. In 1637, more than 30,000 men of the two clans united and under the leadership of several veteran *samurai* of *Konishi Yukinaga*, intrenched themselves behind the walls of the abandoned castle of *Hara* or *Arima* and prepared for the struggle. *Itakura Shigemasa* who was sent against them with 30,000 soldiers was killed whilst leading the attack upon the fortress. *Matsudaira (Ōkōchi) Nobutsuna* succeeded him and at the head of 100,000 men, besieged *Hara* for 2 months before he could take it. On April 14th 1638, he stormed the castle and all of the 37,000 men whom sword and famine had spared were put to death to a man. — The Japanese historians are nearly unanimous in saying that the *Shimabara* insurrection was a revolt of the persecuted Christians, but although a great number of the insurgents were indeed Christians, religion itself was in no way connected with the affair. The cause must be sought solely in the unrelenting cruelty of the local *daimyō*.

Shima-kubō, 島公方. Name given to the *Shōgun Ashikaga Yoshitane*, who died in exile in the island of *Awaji* (1523).

Shimane-ken, 島根縣 . Department formed by the *Izumo, Iwami* and *Oki* provinces.—Pop. : 743,000 inh.—Chief town : *Matsue* (34,700 inh.)—Pr. city : *Hamada* (10,400 inh.).

Shimazu, 島津 . *Daimyō* family governing *Satsuma* since the end of the 12th century.—*Minamoto Yoritomo* having had relations with the sister of *Hiki Yoshikazu*, she was found with child and the jealousy of *Masako* forced her to seek refuge in *Kyūshū*, where she brought forth a child, which received the name of *Tadahisa* and was the ancestor of the *Shimazu*.

—— **Tadahisa, 忠久** . Married the daughter of *Koremune Hironobu*, whose name he at first took. In 1186, he received the domain of *Shioda* (*Shinano*), and then was named governor of *Satsuma*. He sent *Honda Sadachika* to take possession of the province in his name and accompanied *Yoritomo* in his expedition to *Mutsu* (1189). He went to *Satsuma* in 1196, subdued *Hyūga* and *Ōsumi* and built a castle in the domain of *Shimazu* (*Hyūga*), which name he also adopted.

```
                          Tadahisa
                          Tadayoshi
   ┌────────┬──────────┬──────────┬──────────┬──────────┐
Tadayasu  Hisatoki  Hisatsune   Tadatsune  Hisanji
                     Tadamune
         ┌────────┬──────────┬──────────┬──────────┐
      Tadauji  Tadamitsu  Sadahisa   Sukehisa   Suketada
         │       (Sata)              (Kabayama)  (Hokugō)
      Tadanao              Ujihisa
      (Izumi)
                          Hisatoyo
                          Tadakuni
              ┌────────────────────┬──────────┐
           Tomohisa              Tatsuhisa
           Tadayuki              Tadamasa
           ┌──────────┐          ┌──────────┐
        Tadayoshi  Tadaharu            Katsuhisa
           Takahisa           Tadamasa
   ┌────────┬──────────┬──────────┬──────────┐
Yoshihisa Yoshihiro Iehisa   Mamahisa
           Iehisa  Toyohisa  Tadaoki
           Mitsuhisa          Hisao
           Tsunahisa          Tadataka
   (Branch of Kagoshima)   (Branch of Sadowara)
```

—— **Takahisa, 貴久** (1514-1571). Descendant of *Tadahisa*, governed the 3 provinces of *Satsuma, Ōsumi* and *Hyūga*. The Europeans upon their first arrival landed in his domains at *Tane-ga-shima*, and from them he learned the use of fire arms. In 1549, he received saint Francis-Xavier in his castle of *Kagoshima*.

—— **Yoshihisa, 義久** (1533-1611). Eldest son of *Takahisa*, in 1573, defeated *Itō Suketaka* who came to ask the help of *Ōtomo Sōrin*.

The latter came with a large army to attack the *Shimazu*, but was also defeated (1578). In 1583 *Yoshihisa* sent his brother *Iehisa* to assist *Arima Yoshizumi* who had been attacked by *Ryūzōji Takanobu*, and the latter was defeated. *Ōtomo Sōrin* appealed to *Hideyoshi* who ordered *Yoshihisa* to return all the land which he had occupied, with the exception of *Satsuma* and *Ōsumi*. *Yoshihisa* refused to obey (1586), and *Hideyoshi* then in person directed an expedition against the powerful *daimyō*, who, after some success, was defeated and obliged to submit. The conditions of the victor were lenient: the *Shimazu* retained *Satsuma*, *Ōsumi* and a part of *Hyūga*, but *Yoshihisa* had to cede his domains to his brother *Yoshihiro*, which he did in 1587. At his death, 30 *samurai* in order not to survive him, killed themselves.

—— **Yoshihiro,** 義弘 (1535-1619). Brother to *Yoshihisa*, in 1573 defeated *Itō Suketaka* in *Hyūga*. During *Hideyoshi's* expedition, he repulsed the vanguard of the latter, commanded by *Sengoku Hidehisa* and *Chōsokabe Motochika ;* but he was afterwards defeated and submitted (1587). He succeeded *Yoshihisa* and took part in the Korean expedition. In 1600, he fought against *Ieyasu* and, after the defeat of his party at *Sekigahara*, returned in all haste to *Satsuma*. At his arrival, *Yoshihisa* had him imprisoned at *Sakura-jima* and through the mediation of *Fukushima Masanori*, obtained his pardon from *Ieyasu*, who gave it on condition that he would shave his head and give over his domains to *Tadatsune*.

—— **Iehisa,** 家久 (+1587). Brother of the two preceding, in 1583 was sent against *Ryūzōji Takanobu*, who had invaded the domains of *Arima Yoshizumi ; Tadanobu* was defeated and killed, and *Iehisa* took the provinces of *Chikuzen*, *Chikugo*, *Hizen* and *Buzen*. In 1586, he assisted *Akizuki Tanezane* and defeated *Takahashi Shigetane*, whom he put to death. During *Hideyoshi's* campaign in *Kyūshū*, he defeated *Chōsokabe Motochika* and *Ōtomo Yoshimune*, and made *Funai (Ōita)* his stronghold. Being attacked by *Hashiba Hidenaga*, he was forced to retire into *Hyūga*, and finally to submit, but on the day he surrendered to *Hidenaga*, he died from the effects of poison.

—— **Tadatsune,** 忠恒 (1576-1638). Son of *Yoshihiro*, succeeded his father in 1602, and the following year came to *Fushimi* to pay homage to *Ieyasu*, who authorised him to take the name of *Matsudaira* and also gave him one character of his own name. *Tadatsune* then changed his name to that of *Iehisa* (not to be mistaken for his uncle cited above). In 1609, having to complain about the inhabitants of the *Ryūkyū* island, he sent *Niiro Kazuuji* to obtain satisfaction ; whereupon the son of the king and 10 of his servants were taken prisoners to *Kagoshima* and the Islanders had to pay an annual tribute to the *daimyō* of *Satsuma*. His revenues thus rose to 770,000 k. In 1617, he was named *Chūnagon*, then *Satsuma no kami* and *Ōsumi no kami*.

—— **Nariakira,** 齊彬 (1809-1858). Descended from the above, he in 1824 for the first time, saw the *Shōgun Ienari*, who gave him one of the characters of his name. In 1851, he personally administered the domains of the family. Two years later, fire having destroyed the Imperial Palace, he sent a large sum of money to aid in its reconstruction. He busied himself very actively in forming a good army in his clan and manifested a great attachment to the Imperial cause that was already beginning to agitate men's minds.

—— **Hisamitsu,** 久 光 (1820-1887). Was brother to *Nariakira,* and succeeded him. He is also called *Saburō.* In 1862, whilst at *Kyōto,* the Emperor asked him to escort *Ōhara Shigenori* his envoy (*chokushi*) to the *Shōgun Iemochi* to *Edo. Hisamitsu* accepted and the mission being fulfilled, the envoy's train returning to *Kyōto* met some English tourists at *Namamugi,* near the actual town of *Yokohama.* These men made way, but the *samurai* of the escort wanted to force them to alight from their horses. This they refused to do and were attacked, one of them *Richardson* being killed and two others wounded. The following year, the English government demanded satisfaction but the *Shōgun* giving an evasive answer, admiral Kuper with 7 vessels appeared before *Kagoshima* and bombarded the city. Some time later, *Hisamitsu* was charged with the defence of *Kyōto,* which had been taken away from the troops of *Chōshū ;* but owing to the tact of *Saigō Takamori,* the misunderstanding did not last long and the two clans united their efforts in favor of the Imperial Restoration. *Hisamitsu* was then named *Sangi, Sadaijin,* Duke, etc.

—— **Tadayoshi,** 忠 義 (1840-1897). Son of *Hisamitsu,* followed the line of conduct adopted by his father and showed himself a staunch supporter of the Imperial Restoration, which procured for him several titles, decorations, etc. — At present the *Shimazu* family numbers 2 dukes : the one, heir of the senior line, by *Tadayoshi,* adopted son of *Nariaki ;* the other, heir to *Hisamitsu ;* — 1 count, descended from a collateral branch which from 1603 resided at *Sadowara* (*Hyūga* — 27,000 k.) ; — and 8 barons, created after the Restoration.

Shimazu shichi-tō, 島 津 七 黨 . The 7 families, having the largest estates and being vassals to the *Shimazu* of *Satsuma : Niiro, Hokugō, Ijuin, Machida, Kawakami, Ata* and *Kajiki.*

Shimban, 新 番 . Under the *Tokugawa Shōgun,* the body guard of the *Shōgun.* Created in 1643, they were divided into 4 and later on into 8 sections.

Shimbetsu, 神 別 . At the time of the emperor *Saga,* there was a good deal of confusion about family names ; to obviate it somewhat. the people were divided into 3 classes : *Shimbetsu,* descendants of the gods ; *Kōbetsu,* descendants from the emperors ; *Hambetsu,* born in the different fiefs. The *Fujiwara,* for instance, were of the first class ; the *Tachibana,* of the second.

Shimbutsu, 眞 佛 . Descendant of *Taira Kunika* and son of *Kuniharu,* governor of *Shimotsuke,* whom he succeeded. Having great admiration for the noble virtues of *Shinran,* he transmitted his domains to his brother *Kunitsuna* and became a disciple of the renowned bonze (1225). In 1232, he was made chief of the *Kōshō-ji* temple (*Kyōto*). He is the founder of the two branches *Takada* and *Bukkōji* of the *Shin-shū* sect.

Shimizu, 清水. Branch of the *Tokugawa* family issued from *Shigeyoshi* (1745-1795), son of the *Shōgun Ieshige*. It possessed a revenue of 100,000 k. and formed one of the *San-kyō*. — See *Tokugawa* (*Shimizu*).

Shimizu, 清水. *Samurai* family of the *Yamaguchi* clan (*Suwō*), ennobled after the Restoration. — Now Baron.

Shimizu Hamaomi, 清水濱臣 (1776-1824). At first a doctor, he cultivated Japanese literature, received lessons from *Murata Harumi*, and later on, opened a school at *Edo*. He had great success in teaching.

Shimizutani, 清水谷. *Kuge* family descended from *Fujiwara* (*Saionji*) *Michisue* (1090-1128). — Now Count.

Shimmotsu-ban, 進物番. Under the *Tokugawa*, an official whose duty it was to accept the presents offered to the *Shōgun* by the *daimyō* and *hatamoto*, and to distribute the gifts sent by the *Shōgun*.

Shimmotsu-bugyō, 進物奉行. Under the *Kamakura Shōgun*, an official whose duty it was to attend to the presents received or sent by the *Shōgun*.

Shimoda, 下田. Port S.E. of *Izu* peninsula. In 1854, it was visited by Commodore Perry and opened to American commerce; the U.S. Minister, Townsend Harris, resided there till the port of *Kanagawa* was opened to international commerce (1859).

Shimoda-bugyō, 下田奉行. — See *Uraga-bugyō*.

Shimodate, 下舘. In *Hitachi*. Was the residence of the *daimyō Mizutani* (1590), *Matsudaira* (1638), *Masuyama* (1663), *Kuroda* (1703), then from 1732 to 1868, *Ishikawa* (20,000 k.).

Shimokōbe, 下河邊. Ancient family descended from *Fujiwara Hidesato*.

—— **Yukiyoshi, 行義**. Son of *Yukimitsu*, received the domain of *Shimokōbe* (*Shimōsa*) in the 12th century, and took the name of that place.

—— **Yukihira, 行平**. Son of *Yukiyoshi*. He at first served the *Taira*, then sided with *Yoritomo*. He took part in the Western campaign of *Noriyori* (1184) and with *Chiba Tsunetane* defeated and drove out the robbers that infested the environs of *Kyōto*; he then accompanied *Yoritomo* in his expedition to *Mutsu* (1189). He taught the art of using the bow to the *Shōgun Yoriie*.

Shimokōbe Chōryū, 下河邊長流 (1624-1686). Native of *Yamato*, was called *Ozaki Tomohira*. Studied Japanese antiquities and opened a school at *Ōsaka*. *Mino Mitsukuni* invited him to his castle, but *Chōryū* declined the offer. He was the friend of *Keichū*, who published his posthumous books. *Chōryū*, also called *Nagaru*, is known as the founder of the School which revived the study of ancient literature and poetry.

Shimo-kyō, 下京. Formerly the southern half of *Kyōto*.

Shimomura, 下村. In *Iwashiro*. From 1787 to 1823, residence of the *Tanuma daimyō* (10,000 k.).

Shimonoseki, 下關. Port (42,800 inh.) at the S.W. point of *Nagato*. Also called *Akamagaseki, Bakwan*. — It was there that the *daimyō* of *Chōshū*, *Mōri Motonori*, in June and July 1863, ordered his people to fire on the American, Dutch and French vessels that passed through the channel. As a consequence of this act of hostility, *Shimonoseki* was bombarded, at first by the French admiral *Jaurès* (July 1863), then by the English and the interested powers (Sept. 1864). — It was at *Shimonoseki* that the negotiations of peace took place after the Chinese war (1895). The Japanese plenipotentiaries were: Count *Itō Hirobumi* and Viscount *Mutsu Munemitsu ;* the Chinese envoy was *Li-hung-tchang* (*Rikōshō*) who arrived there on March the 19th. On the 24th of the same month, when *Li-hung-tchang* was leaving the house of the conference with the Japanese ministers, a certain *Koyama Toyotarō*, 26 years old, shot at him with a revolver and wounded him below the left eye. An armistice was agreed upon and on April 17 a treaty of peace followed, the ratification of which was signed at *Chefu*, May 8.

Shimōsa, 下總. One of the 15 provinces of the *Tōkaidō*. Comprises 9 districts, 6 of which depend upon the *Chiba-ken* and 3 upon the *Ibaraki-ken*. — Chinese name: *Sōshū* (with *Kazusa*). — In ancient times, *Shimōsa* with *Kazusa* formed only one province called *Fusa no kuni :* this province was later on divided into two, *Kami-tsu-fusa* and *Shimo-tsu-fusa*, names which were contracted into *Kazusa* and *Shimōsa*.

Shimo-shima, 下島. The largest island (532 Km. circuit) of the *Tsushima* group.

Shimo-shima, 下嶋. The largest island (276 Km. circuit) of the *Amakusa* (*Higo*) group.

Shimotedo, 下手渡. In *Iwashiro*. From 1805 to 1868, residence of the *Tachibana daimyō* (10,000 k.).

Shimotsuke, 下野. One of the 13 provinces of the *Tōsandō*. Comprises 8 districts, which depend upon the *Tochigi-ken*. — Chinese name: *Yashū*. — United to the *Kōzuke*, it formed in ancient times, the *Kenu no kuni* which was divided into the *Kami-tsu-kenu* and the *Shimo-tsu-kenu*, whence the names *Kōzuke* and *Shimotsuke*.

Shimotsukenu Komaro, 下毛野古麿 (+710). Descendant of prince *Toyo-shiro-iri-hiko*, son of the emperor *Sujin*. He greatly aided in compiling the Code (*ritsuryō*) of *Taihō* (701), and received orders to explain it to the princes and officials. Was *Shikibu-kyō* (708).

Shimotsuma, 下妻. In *Hitachi*. Old castle built towards 1455, by *Tagaya Ujiie*. In 1590, *Hideyoshi* made it a dependency of the domains of *Yūki* (*Shimōsa*). Under the *Tokugawa*, it belonged to the fief of *Mito*, and from 1712 to 1868, became the residence of the *Inoue daimyō* (10,000 k.).

Shimpō-bugyō, 神寶奉行. Under the *Kamakura Shōgun*, an official providing necessaries, required at certains Shintoist temples.

Shimpō-gata, 神寶方. Under the *Tokugawa*, an official whose duty it was to provide necessaries at the temples placed over the tombs at *Nikkō*, etc. In 1746, this office was united to that of the *Abura-urushi-bugyō*.

Shimpu-jō, 新府城. In *Kai*, to day, *Tanaka-mura*. Castle built by *Takeda Katsuyori* after his defeat at *Nagashino* (1581) ; the following year it was stormed by *Nobunaga*.

Shimushu-jima, 占守島. The most northern island of the Kurile (*Chishima*), 12 Km. from cape *Lopatka* (*Kamtchatka*). Measures 60 Km. from N. to S. and 40 from E. to W. — It is this island, that *Kôda Gunji* tried to colonize in 1892 and which he intended to make an out-post against the Russians.

Shina, 支那. China.

Shinagawa, 品川. A suburban town (92,000 inh.), lying S. W of *Tôkyô*, on the seashore. —In 1854, *Mito Nariaki*, officially commissioned to construct defenses against foreigners, ordered 7 forts to be built in the *Tôkyô* bay, to protect the capital of the *Shôgun*. At the end of 1868, *Enomoto Takeaki* with his men of war sailed from thence for *Hakodate*.

Shinagawa, 品川. *Samurai* family of the *Yamaguchi* clan (*Suwô*) ennobled after the Restoration — Now Viscount.

Shi-nagon, 四納言. 4 famous poets of the 11th century, all of whom had the title of *Nagon*: *Minamoto Tsunenobu, Fujiwara Kintô, Minamoto Toshikata* and *Fujiwara Yukinari*.

Shinai-numa, 品井沼. Lake (39 Km. circ.) in *Rikuzen*; its outlet is the *Naruse-gawa*.

Shina-kai, 支那海. Chinese sea.

Shinano, 信濃. One of the 13 provinces of the *Tôsandô* Comprises 16 districts that formed the *Nagano-ken.* — Chinese name : *Shinshû.*

Shinano-gawa, 信濃川. River (392 Km.) formed by the junction of the *Chikuma-gawa* and the *Sai-gawa*, near *Nagano*. It passes through *Iiyama* and enters *Echigo*, passing *Nagaoka, Sanjô* and flows into the Japan Sea at *Niigata.* — Also called *Hassen-hassui-gawa.*

Shinano no Fuji, 信濃富士. Name given to Mt. *Ariake-yama* (2,450 m.) in *Shinano*.

Shinatsu-hiko, 志那津比古) Son and daughter of *Izanagi* and
Shinatsu-hime, 志那津比女∫*Izanami*, honored as gods of the wind (*Shintô*).

Shindo, 神奴. Formerly, families of low extraction that lived on the domains of certain Shintoist temples The temple of *Kashima* (*Hitachi*) sheltered a great number of them.

Shinga, 眞雅 (801-879). Renowned bonze of the *Shingon* sect. Was much in favor during the *Seiwa-tennô* reign. Has received the posthumous title of *Hôkô-Daishi*.

Shingaku-dôwa, 心學道話. Treatise of Confucianist morals, composed, at the end of the 18th century, by *Ishida Kampei, Tejima Toan, Nakajima Dôni*, etc. It contained a great number of illustrations and was always in great demand.

Shingi, 新義. Branch of the *Shingon-shû* sect, founded in the 12th century by the bonze *Kakuhan* (*Kôkyô-Daishi*).

Shingo-keiun, 神護景雲. *Nengô*: 767-769.

Shingon-in, 眞言院. Temple in the precincts of the Imperial Palace, where the bonzes gathered at appointed times to pray for the peace of the country, a good harvest, etc.

Shingon-shū, 眞言宗. Buddhist sect founded in 806 by the famous bonze *Kūkai* (*Kôbô-Daishi*). — This sect, whose doctrine is contained in the *sûtras Dainichi-kyō* and *Kongōchō-kyō*, is based on the (*ryō-bu*): *Kongō-kai* (world of diamond), wisdom, and *Taizō-kai* (world of the bosom), reason, which are destined to help man to find out the origin of his soul and body, in order to purify all his actions and thus arrive at virtue and happiness without limit in the illumination of *Buddha.* — In Japan the *Shingon-shū* possesses no less than, 12,900 temples, more than 7,000 chief bonzes and 3,715,000 adherents.

Shingon-shū ni-ha, 真言宗二派. The two branches, *Kogi* and *Shingi* of the *Shingon* sect: the first was established by *Kūkai*, the second, by *Kakuhan*. In fact, it was 140 years after the death of the latter, towards 1280, that the bonze *Raiyu* erected *Negoro-dera* (*Kii*) as the head of a new branch; but as *Kakuhan* had founded *Negoro-dera*, and his tomb being in that place, he is considered as the founder of the *Shingi* sect.

Shingū, 新宮. City (14,000 inh.) S. E. of the *Kii* province, at the mouth of the *Kumano-gawa*. It is said *Jimmū-tennō* landed here when he made his incursion into *Yamato*. Ancient castle built towards 1180 by *Minamoto Yukiie*. In the middle of the 16th century, it belonged to the *Horiuchi daimyō*. Under the *Tokugawa*, it was annexed to the domains of the *Wakayama* and was entrusted to the care of a *jōdai* of the *Mizuno* family. — *Shingū* is known especially on account of its Shintoist temple bearing the same name. — See *Kumano-jinja*.

Shingun, 神郡. Formerly great tracts of land set apart for the support of the principal Shintoist temples: *Ise, Izumo, Kashima, Katori*, etc.

Shinji-ko, 宍道湖. Lake (51 Km. circum.) in *Izumo*. Also called *Shishiji-ko, Matsue no ko*.

Shinjō, 新庄. In *Yamato*. From 1680 to 1868, the residence of the *Nagai daimyō* (10,000 k.).

Shinjō, 新庄. In *Uzen*. Old castle at first belonging to the *Mogami* family, but from 1622 to 1868 residence of the *Tozawa daimyō* (68,000 k.).

Shinjō, 眞盛. Branch of the *Tendai-shū* sect founded in the 15th century by the bonze *Shinjō*.

Shinjō, 眞盛 (1442-1495). Bonze, founder of the *Shinjō* branch of the *Tendai-shū* sect. Received the posthumous name of *Jisetsu-Daishi*.

Shinjō, 新荘. *Daimyō* family descended from *Fujiwara Uona*.

—— **Naoyori,** 直頼 (1538-1612). Served *Hideyoshi*, who entrusted him with the keeping of the *Yamasaki* castle and styled him *Suruga no kami*. In 1600, he sided against *Ieyasu* and was banished to *Aizu*; when pardoned, he received the fief of *Aso* (*Hitachi* — 10,000 k.) (1604), where his descendants remained till the Restoration. — Now Viscount.

Shinjō-sai, 神嘗祭. — See *Kanname-matsuri*.

Shinjō-sai, 新嘗祭. — See *Niiname-matsuri*.

Shinken, 新撿. Name given to the new survey of land, which work was done under the *Tokugawa* from 1680 to 1700. It was called *Shingen* (new survey) to distinguish it from the one made by order of *Hideyoshi* 100 years before.

Shinkyū-shi, 賑給使. Formerly messenger sent by the emperor to the provinces that had suffered from storms, floods, etc. He brought help to the victims and dispensed them from taxes. — See *Fukan-den-fusui-shi.*

Shinnin, 親任. — See *Kwan-tō.*

Shin no Jofuku, 秦徐福. — See *Jofuku.*

Shinnō, 親王. Title of princes of the Imperial family. They were also called *Take no sono* (bamboo garden), *Teiyō* (imperial leaves), *Tenshi* (celestial branches), *Ryūshū* (dragon's den), etc. — The princesses bore the title of *Nai-shinnō.* — See *Mi-ko.*

Shinnyo-Shōnin, 眞如上人. — See *Kōgaku-shinnō.*

Shinnō no ningoku, 親王任國. The 3 provinces *Kazusa*, *Hitachi* and *Kōzuke*, which, in memory of *Yamatotakeru*, were governed only by a prince of the Imperial family having the title of *Tai-shu*. The emperor *Junwa* made this law in 826. When the prince could not reside in the province, he had a *Suke* to replace him.

Shinowara, 篠原. In *Ōmi*. It was there that *Yoshitsune*, acting by command of *Yoritomo* ordered *Tachibana Kiminaga Taira Munemori* to put his son *Kiyomune* to death, as well as all prisoners of war taken at the battle of *Dan no ura* (1185).

Shinozuka Iga no kami, 篠塚伊賀守. Descended from *Hatakeyama Shigetada*. Served *Nitta Yoshisada* and fought in his company against the *Hōjō* and the *Ashikaga*. After the death of *Yoshisada*, he followed *Ōtate Ujiaki* into *Iyo;* besieged in the castle of *Seta* by *Hosokawa Yoriharu* and on the point of being made prisoner, he fled to the *Oki* islands (1341). — His daughter, *Iga no Tsubone*, married *Kusunoki Masanori.*

Shinra, 新羅. Another name of the old kingdom of *Shiragi* (Korea)

Shinran-Shōnin, 親鸞上人 (1174-1268).

SHINRAN SHŌNIN.

Famous bonze, founder of the *Shinshū* sect. — Son of the *kuge Hino Arinori*, he was born at *Kyōto*. At the age of 9, he left his parents to become a disciple of *Jichin*, who initiated him into the doctrine of the *Tendai-shū* sect; later he followed *Genkū* (1203) who taught him the *Jōdo-shū* doctrine, but he was satisfied with neither of these systems. The question of celibacy and abstinence imposed upon the bonzes, made him reflect for a long time. One day, the goddess *Kwannon* appeared to him in the temple of *Rokkaku-dō*, and delivered him from all his doubts, for we see him very soon after, marrying the daughter of *Fujiwara Kanenori* and forming a new sect, the *Jōdo-shin-shū* (the true sect of *Jōdo*), also called *Monto-shū* and *Ikkō-shū* (1224). His preaching and his attacks on the other sects, brought upon him the animosity of the bonzes; being accused at *Kamakura*, he was banished to *Echigo* and was pardoned only after 5 years of exile. In 1272, the principal temple of his sect received the name of *Hongwan-ji* (*Kyōto*). — Since the Imperial Restoration, *Shinran* has received the title of *Kenshin-Daishi.* — See *Jōdo-Shinshū, Hongwan-ji, Ikkō-shū,* etc.

Shinri-kyō, 神理教. One of the 10 actual Shintoist sects; it was started only a few years ago by *Sano Tsunehiko.*

Shin-Rokkasen, 新六歌仙. 6 famous poets of the 12th and the 13th centuries : *Go-Kyōgoku* (*Fujiwara Yoshitsune,* + 1206), the bonze *Jien* (+ 1225, son of *Fujiwara Tadamichi*), *Shunzei* (*Fujiwara Toshinari,* 1114-1204), *Teika* (*Fujiwara Sadaie,* — 1171-1241, son of the above), *Karyū* (*Fujiwara Ietaka,* 1158-1237) and the bonze *Saigyō Hōshi* (1125-1198).

Shinsai, 眞濟 (798-858). Renowned bonze, disciple of *Kōbō-Daishi.* Born of the *Ki* family, he was initiated by *Kūkai* into the secrets of the *Shingon-shū* and became *Ajari.* In 836, whilst going to China, his boat was shipwrecked : *Shinsai* was able to hold on to a floating plank and after 23 days was rescued by some foreign fishermen. The emperor *Montoku* named him *Sōjō ;* but *Shinsai* declined to accept this title because his master *Kūkai* had never received it. The emperor gave then *Kōbō-Daishi* the posthumous title of *Sōjō* whereupon *Shinsai* was induced to accept the proffered title.

Shinshiru-jima, 新知嶋. Island (110 Km. long from N. E. to S. W.) of the *Chishima* (Kurile) archipelago.

Shinshō-ji, 新勝寺. Famous temple of *Narita* (*Shimōsa*), dedicat-

THE TEMPLE SHINSHŌJI AT NARITA.

ed to *Fudō*. It belongs to the *Shingon* sect. The statue of *Fudō* which is venerated there was, according to some, sculptured by *Kōbō-Daishi*, according to others, brought by him from China. At the time of the revolt of *Taira Masakado*, it was transferred to that place from the temple *Takao-zan* by the bonze *Kwanchō*, and it was due to the intercession of *Fudō* that the defeat of the rebel was attributed (940). When the civil wars were terminated, *Kwanchō* intended to return the statue to *Takao*, but all efforts to lift it proved ineffectual and, in a dream, the god declared his intention of staying at *Narita* in order to protect and to civilize the eastern provinces. The emperor *Shujaku* then ordered a large temple to be constructed, and endowed it with great revenues. The present building dates from 1704. In the treasury of the temple a sword is found presented by *Shujaku* to *Fudō* to thank him for his protection, and the touch alone of this sword is said to cure insanity and deliver from the possession of the fox.

Shinshū, 信 州. Chinese name of *Shinano* province.

Shin-shū, 眞 宗. Buddhist sect. — See *Jōdo-shin-shū.*

Shintō, 神 道. (Lit.: ways of the spirits.) Shintoism, national religion of Japan. — Properly speaking, Shintoism is not a religion: it has no dogma, no moral code nor sacred book, and really consists in a somewhat confused mixture of the veneration of ancestors and nature worship. The absence of a code of morals, is accounted for by the innate perfection of the Japanese people, who descending from the gods (*kami*), have no evil inclinations to overcome like the Chinese and the Western nations, and whose manners and customs never need reform. — The *Shintō* mythology mentions a first god *Ame-no-minakanushi* (lord of the middle of heaven) who remained motionless in the centre of the universe at the time of the creation, or who, according to others, was the first born at *Takama-ga-hara* (plain of heaven). After him, come *Takamimusubi, Kamimusubi, Umashi-ashikabi-hiko, Kunitokotachi, Kunisatsuchi, Toyokunnu ;* then *Uichini* and *Suichini, Tsunukui* and *Ikukui, Ōtonochi* and *Ōtomabe, Omotaru* and *Kashikone,* and finally *Izanagi* and *Izanami,* the two that created Japan and an infinite number of gods. Of them were born *Amaterasu-ō-mikami, Tsukiyomi no mikoto* and *Susano-o no mikoto. Amaterasu* sent her grandson *Ninigi no mikoto* to rule over Japan. He is the great-grandfather of *Jimmū-tennō,* first Emperor. — Shintoism has personified all the forces and all the phenomena of nature, and sought to render them propitious ; whence, the gods of the wind, of the sea, of the mountains, of epidemics, etc., it even added to them the gods of food, of the kitchen, of the hearth, etc. In the beginning, there was no other temple but the Imperial Palace, a very rudimentary construction, not differing from the common huts of the people except in size. The ceremonies consisted especially in purifications and ablutions. The temple of *Ise* was the first erected outside of the Palace, and an Imperial princess had to watch over the 3 treasures, the mirror, the sword and the jewel, transmitted by *Amaterasu* to her descendants. Shintoism, as a national and religious ceremonial, remained in this state of simplicity till the introduction of Buddhism (552). It was soon, supplanted by the new religion, which brought more profound metaphysics and a higher moral code as also a more solemn ritual. Some conservatives tried to uphold the ancient institutions, but they had to give way to the bonzes when they established the *Ryōbu-shintō*, and from that moment, if we except a few ceremonies peculiar to the Palace and the great temples of *Ise* and *Izumo*, the two cults were merged into one. This state of affairs continued to the 18th century, when the works of *Kamo Mabuchi*, *Motoori Norinaga*, *Hirata Atsutane*, etc. brought about a reaction in favor of the national religion and against Buddhism and Confucianism which were of foreign origin. The Restoration completed the work, and since 1868, Shintoism is the only State religion, which means that the State is without religion. — At present, Shintoism counts 163,861 temples served by 16,093 *kannushi*. It is divided into 10 sects or branches, which differ only in a few details of ceremony, their universal moral being comprised in this only precept : " Follow the impulse of your nature and obey your Emperor." These 10 branches are : 1 *Shintō-honkyoku* (to it are attached the *Tenri-kyōkwai*, *Kinkō-kyōkwai*, *Maruyama-kyōkwai*, etc.); 2 *Ō-yashiro-ha* (*Izumo*) ; *Taisei-kyōkwai* (to which belongs the *Remmon-kyōkwai* ; 4 *Ontake-kyō* ; 5 *Kannarai-kyō* ; 6 *Shusei-sha* ; 7 *Kurozumi-ha* ; 8 *Fusō-kyō* ; 9 *Shinri-kyō* ; 10 *Misogi-kyō* (formerly called *Tōkami-kyō*). — In 1900, the *Jingū-kyō* was officially declared not to be a religious sect. In a population of 47,400,000 inhabitants, statistics show 18,800,000 to be Shintoists.

Shintō-honkyoku, 神道本局. One of the 10 existing Shintoist sects. Its principal temple is that of *Ise*.

Shintō-kata, 神道方. Under the *Tokugawa*, an official subject to the *Jisha-bugyō* and especially charged with the care of the Shintoist temples and ceremonies. This title was hereditary in the *Yoshikawa* family.

Shiojiri-tōge, 鹽尻峠. Mountain pass (1060 m.) in *Shinano*, N. of lake *Suwa*. *Takeda Shingen* gained a victory there over the *Hōjō* of *Odawara* (1545).

Shionoritsu-hiko, 鹽乘律彦. Warrior who led the first expedition sent to Korea by the emperor *Suinin* (29 years B. C.) in order to help *Mimana* against *Shiragi*.

Shionoya-jō, 鹽谷城. Old castle built at the end of the 12th century by *Shionoya Tomoyoshi* in the district of *Shio-no-ya* in *Shimotsuke* (village of *Kawasaki*, *Horie-yama*) and which his descendants kept for several generations.

Shioyaki-Ō, 鹽燒王 (+764). Grandson of the emperor *Temmu* and son of *Niitabe-shinnō*. The rebel *Fujiwara Nakamaro* chose him as successor to *Junnin-tennō* ; but after the defeat of his party, he was put to death.

Shirabyōshi, 白拍子. Ancient dances established by *Shima no Chitose* and *Waka no Mae* (1115). Dressed in a white *suikan*, wearing an *eboshi* and carrying a large sword, girls performed dances that became fashionable and which, because of the costume, were also called *otoko-mai* (boys' dances). Later on, the *eboshi* and the sword were dispensed with.

— The name *shirabyōshi* applied equally to the dance and to those who performed it.

Shiragi, 新 羅. One of the ancient kingdoms of Korea. Also called *Shinra*, and habitually the enemy of Japan, which was frequently obliged to send expeditions thither to repel attacks upon *Mimana* and its other vassals or allied states. The *Shiragi* kingdom, established in the year 57 B. C., enlarged itself at the expense of its neighbors but was at last destroyed in the year 934.

Shirahata, 白 旗. In *Harima*. (*Akamatsu-mura*). Old castle built towards 1110 by *Minamoto Suefusa*, who from that time assumed the name of *Akamatsu*. His descendants resided in it for more than 3 centuries. When *Mitsusuke* had assassinated the *Shōgun Yoshinori*, he sought shelter in that place, but being attacked by *Yamana Mochitoyo*, he killed himself and the castle was destroyed. (1441).

Shirai, 白 井. In *Kōzuke* (*Nagao-mura*). Under the *Ashikaga*, domain of the *Uesugi*, who left its administration to the *Nagao* family. *Uesugi Norizane* went there at the time of his difficulties with *Ashikaga Mochiuji* (1438), and from there, governed the two provinces of *Kōzuke* and *Echigo*. Seized by *Takeda Katsuyori* in 1571, the castle was retaken by *Uesugi Kenshin*, from whom it was again captured by the *Hōjō* of *Odawara*. In 1590, *Ieyasu* gave it to *Honda Hirotaka*. It was abandoned in 1623.

Shirakami-misaki, 白 神 岬. Cape S. of *Oshima* (*Hokkaidō*).

Shirakawa, 白 河. Town (14,000 inh.) of the *Iwaki* province. — In 1189, *Yoritomo*, after having defeated *Fujiwara Yasuhira*, divided his domains among his officers : *Yūki Tomomitsu* received the district of *Shirakawa ;* his grandson *Sukehiro* built a castle there (1289) where his descendants resided and remained the faithful partisans of the Southern dynasty. They were dispossessed by *Hideyoshi* in 1590. Under the *Tokugawa*, the castle belonged successively to the *daimyō Gamō* (1590), *Niwa* (1627), *Sakakibara* (1643), *Honda* (1649), *Okudaira* (1681) *Matsudaira* (1692), *Hisamatsu* (1741) ; and lastly from 1823 to 1868, *Abe* (100,000 k.).

Shirakawa, 白 川. *Kuge* family descended from *Kiyohito-shinnō*, son of the emperor *Kwazan* (985-986). — Now Viscount.

Shira-kawa, 白 川. Small river that rises in the *Nyoi-dake*, E. of *Kyōto*, passes through the village of *Shirakawa*, around the *Higashiyama* and enters the *Kamo-gawa*. It has given its name to the whole region it traverses E. of the *Kamo-gawa :* thus we have the *Shirakawaden*, the *Shirakawa-kitadono*, etc.

Shirakawa-den, 白 河 殿. At first a villa of *Fujiwara Yoshifusa*, near *Kyōto*, became afterwards the retreat of the emperor *Shirakawa*. After his death (1129) it was transformed into a temple with the name *Hōshō-ji*, and in its precincts were gradually constructed the *Sonshō-ji*, the *Saishō-ji*, the *Enshō-ji* the *Seishō-ji*, and the *Enshō-ji* which were called the *Rokushō-ji*. They were nearly all destroyed during the *Shokyū* war (1221), and the *Hōshō-ji*, during the *Ōnin* war (1467).

Shirakawa-kita-dono, 白河北殿. Palace N.E. of *Kyōto*, where the emperor *Sutoku* resided, and which was burned by *Minamoto Yoshitomo* during the *Hōgen* war (1156).

Shirakawa-tennō, 白河天皇. 72nd Emperor of Japan (1073-1086). *Sadahito*, at the age of 10, succeeded his father *Go-Sanjō*. His reign was filled with the wars undertaken against the bonzes of *Hieizan* (*Enryaku-ji*) and of *Mii-dera*. At the age of 33, he abdicated in favor of his son *Horikawa*, then 9 years old; but, continuing to govern, he organized his own court, chose a minister to his liking, (*in-bettō*), guards (*hokumen no bushi*), etc. In 1096, he had his head shaved by the bonze *Ryōnin* and took the name *Yūkaku* with the title of *Hō-ō*. A fervent Buddhist, he spent considerable sums of money in building temples, and, in order to get the money, he sold the governorship of provinces, etc. The term of office was at first to last only 4 years, then 6, then for life, and finally became hereditary, thus establishing the feudal system in the country which gradually supplanted the nobility of the Court and substituted the rule of the *Shōgun* for the Imperial authority. — *Shirakawa* died in 1129, after a reign of more than 50 years.

Shirane, 白根. *Samurai* family of the *Yamaguchi* clan (*Suwō*), made noble after the Restoration. — Now Baron.

Shirane-zan, 白根山. A group of mountains on the boundaries of *Kai* and *Shinano*; the principal summits are the *Nōdori-zan* (3000 m.), the *Ai no take* (3100 m.), the *Kaigane-zan* (3150 m.).

Shirane-zan, 白根山. Volcano (2240 m.) on the boundaries of *Kōzuke* and *Shinano*. Also called *Ara-yama*.

Shirane-zan, 白根山. Volcano (2560 m.) between *Shimotsuke* and *Kōzuke*. Was in eruption in 1889.

Shiretoko-saki, 知床崎. Cape S.E. of *Kitami* (*Hokkaidō*).

Shiribeshi, 後志. One of the 11 provinces of *Hokkaidō*.- Comprises 17 districts (*kōri*). — Chief city : *Otaru* (57,000 inh.). — Formerly called *Shirebitsu*.

Shiribeshi-gawa, 後志川. River (135 Km.) rising in *Iburi*, passes through *Shiribeshi* and enters the Japan Sea at *Isoya*.

Shiribeshi-yama, 後志山. Mountain (2400 m.) on the boundaries of *Shiribeshi* and *Iburi*. Also called *Ezo-Fuji*.

Shiriya-saki, 尻矢崎. Cape, N. E. of *Mutsu*. Also called *Fujiishi-saki*.

Shiro, 城. Castle, redoubt, comprising a certain number of buildings protected by a wall and surrounded by large ditches. To erect a *shiro*, the *daimyō* needed special authorization from the *Shōgun* in default of which, they could only possess a *jin-ya* (kind of intrenchment).

Shiro, 代. In olden times, measure for surfaces. 1 foot (*Koma-shaku*) square formed 1 *bu* (4m.² 55), and 5 *bu* 1 *shiro* (22m.² 75).

Shiroishi, 白石. In *Iwaki*. Ancient castle belonging to the *Uesugi*. *Date Masamune* besieged it and occupied it in 1600, uniting it to the domains of his family. *Date, Uesugi*, and all the *daimyō* of the North, met together in council in that place, in 1868, and decided to help the *Aizu* clan against the Imperial army.

Shishibito-be, 宍 人 部. Formerly servants whose duty it was to prepare the meats of the royal table. Their chief bore the title of *Shishibito-ason*.

Shishin-den, 紫 震 殿. Or better, *Shishii-den*. Building of the Imperial Palace of *Kyōto*, which contained the throne hall. It measured 20 m. from E. to W. and 15 m. from N. to S. The sages of China were represented on the movable partitions. This hall was decorated by the most skilful painters of the time. It served for solemn receptions : coronations, New Year's receptions, etc.

Shi-shinnō-ke, 四 親 王 家. The 4 families of royal princes : *Fushimi no miya*, descended from *Einin-shinnō* (1356-1416), son of the emperor *Sukō* ; — *Arisugawa no miya*, descended from prince *Yukihito* (1654-1699), son of the emperor *Go-Sai-in* ; — *Katsura no miya*, descended from prince *Masahito* (1552-1586), son of *Ōgimachi-tennō* ; — *Kan-in no miya*, descended from *Naohito-shinnō* (1701-1752), son of the emperor *Higashi-yama*. — See *Miko*.

Shi-sho-kaidan, 四 所 戒 壇. The 4 temples where a *kaidan* was erected for the purpose of imposing the Buddhist precepts (*kai*) : *Tōdaiji*, *Yakushi-dera*, *Kwannon-ji* and *Enryaku-ji*. — See *Kairitsu-shū*.

Shi-shoku, 四 職. — See *Muromachi shi-shoku*.

Shishū, 志 州. Chinese name of the *Shima* province.

Shita san-bugyō, 下 三 奉 行. Under the *Tokugawa*, the people called the *Fushin-bugyō*, *Kobushin-bugyō* and *Sakuji-bugyō* by that name.

Shi-ten, 四 天. This name was formerly given to 4 faithful *samurai* who formed the body-guard of their suzerain, fought for him and frequently died with him. The best known are :

(*a*) — the *shi-ten* of *Minamoto Yorimitsu* (944-1021) : *Watanabe no Tsuna*, *Sakata no Kintoki*, *Usui no Sadamichi* and *Urabe no Suetake*.

(*b*) — the *shi-ten* of *Kiso Yoshinaka* (1154-1184) : *Imai Kanehira*, *Higuchi Kanemitsu*, *Tate Chikatada* and *Nenoi Yukichika*.

(*c*) — the *shi-ten* of *Minamoto Yoshitune* (1159-1189) : the 2 brothers *Kamada*, *Morimasa* and *Mitsumasa*, and the 2 brothers *Sato*, *Tsuginobu* and *Tadanobu*.

(*d*) — the *shi-ten* of *Oda Nobunaga* (1534-1582) : *Shibata Katsuie*, *Takigawa Kazumasu*, *Niwa Nagahide* and *Akechi Mitsuhide*. — Some families likewise had their *shi-ten*, i.e. their 4 principal vassals. Thus the *shi-ten* of the *Yūki* family were : *Tagaya*, *Mizutani*, *Yamakawa* and *Iwakami* ; — those of the *Ashina* were : *Hirata*, *Matsumoto*, *Sase* and *Tomita*.

Shi-tennō, 四 天 王. — See *Shi-daitennō*.

Shitoku, 至 德. *Nengō* of the Northern dynasty : 1384-1386.

Shitsubushi, 漆 部 司. Formerly, bureau of the Minister of Finance whose duty it was to watch over the manufacture of lacquerware.

Shitsuji, 執 事. Under the shogunate of *Kamakura*, vice-president of the *Mandokoro*. The president had the title of *Bettō*, reserved to the *Shikken Hōjō*. The *shitsuji* acted as first minister of the *Shikken*. —

Under the *Ashikaga, Takauji* named 2 *shitsuji* at *Kyōto, Kō Moronao* and *Uesugi Tomosada*. In 1362, the title of *shitsuji*, then borne by *Shiba Yoshimasa* was changed to *kwanryō*. — At *Kamakura*, the son of *Takauji, Yoshiakira*, having assumed the title of *Kwantō-kwanryō*, *Uesugi Noriaki* received that of *shitsuji*, which was however changed to *kwanryō*, when the *Ashikaga* of *Kamakura* were designated, as well as those of *Kyōto*, by the title of *Kubō*. — The vice-president of the *Monchūjo* also had the title of *shitsuji*, which, under the *Kamakura* and the *Kyōto Shōgun*, was hereditary in the *Ōta* and the *Machino* families.

Shizai, 死罪. Capital punishment inflicted upon great criminals. — In the *Taihō* code, there were only two ways of executing criminals: strangulation (*kōzai*) and decapitation (*zanzai*). Under the *Tokugawa*, 5 ways were introduced:

(*a*) — *Zanzai:* simple decapitation.

(*b*) — *Hi-aburi:* punishment by fire (reserved to incendiaries).

(*c*) — *Sarashi-kubi:* decapitation followed by the exposure of the criminal's head.

(*d*) — *Haritsuke:* the criminal was attached to a post (later on a cross) and pierced with a lance.

(*e*) — *Nokogiri-biki:* reserved for the foulest crimes. This punishment consisted in making wounds on the two shoulders of the guilty person, and besmearing a saw with blood from the wound, as if to indicate that the torture had been performed with that instrument. After two days exposure along the road side, the condemned was led through the streets and crucified. — These punishments were administered only to the lower classes. The *samurai* had the privilege of committing *harakiri*. — See *Tokugawa-keihō*.

Shizoku, 士族. Name given to the former class of *samurai* (military caste) since 1878. — Among a population of 46,601,688 inh., Japan, in 1899, numbered 2,104,698 *shizoku*, i.e. 4½%.

Shizu-ga-take, 賤岳. Hill in *Ōmi*, between the villages of *Kagu* and *Yogo*. *Shibata Katsuie's* army, commanded by *Sakuma Morimasa*, was defeated in that place by *Hideyoshi* (1583).

Shizuka Gozen, 静御前. Dancing girl of *Kyōto*, who became the mistress of *Minamoto Yoshitsune*. When *Yoritomo* intended to assassinate his brother through the agency of the bonze *Tosabō Shōshun* (1185), *Shizuka* gave notice of it to her lover, who thus had time to save himself and kill his assailants. Forced to take flight, *Yoshitsune* sent *Shizuka* back to *Kyōto*, from where *Yoritomo* brought her to *Kamakura* and vainly sought to make her reveal the hiding place of his brother.

SHIZUKA GOZEN.

Masako, knowing her great skill, asked her to dance before her, but

Shizuka obstinately refused. *Yoritomo* however forced her to dance, accompanied with the music of cymbals by *Hatakeyama Shigetada* whilst *Kudō Suketsune* played the tambourine. During the dance she improvised a doleful love song to the illustrious exile. *Yoritomo*, much displeased ordered her child which was born soon after, to be killed by *Adachi Kiyotsune*, and sent her back to *Kyōto*.

Shizuki-yama, 指月山. Hill near *Hagi* (*Nagato*), the possession of the *Mōri daimyō* who had a castle erected on its summit.

Shizuoka, 静岡. Chief town (42,200 inh.) of the *Shizuoka-ken* and *Suruga* province; formerly called *Sumpu, Funai, Fuchū.* Under the *Ashikaga*, this city was the residence of the *Imagawa daimyō*, the governors of *Suruga. Takeda Shingen* occupied it in 1569. After the ruin of the *Takeda* (1582), *Tokugawa Ieyasu*, receiving the 2 provinces of *Suruga* and *Tōtōmi* in fief, left *Hamamatsu* for *Sumpu*, where he erected a castle. Transferred to *Edo* in 1590, he was replaced by *Naka-mura Kazuuji.* After *Sekigahara* (1600), he placed *Naitō Nobunari* there, then in 1606, his own son *Yorinobu*, and after having transmitted the administration of the shōgunate to *Hidetada*, he retired thither himself and died at that place (1616). In 1625, *Tadanaga*, son of *Hidetada* was transferred thither from *Kōfu* (*Kai*) and when he was dispossessed, (1632), *Sumpu* remained the property of the *Shōgun.* — See *Sumpu-kaban, Sumpu-jōdai.* — At the time of the Restoration, the Imperial army on its march to *Edo*, entered *Sumpu*, March the 5th 1868. At the end of the civil war, *Sumpu* became, from 1869 to 1897, the place of re-tirement of the last *Shōgun, Keiki.* The name was changed to *Shizuoka.*

Shizuoka-ken, 静岡縣. Department formed by the provinces of *Tōtōmi, Suruga* and *Izu* (except the islands that belong to the last pro-vince). — Pop.: 1,295,000 inh. — Chief town : *Shizuoka* (42,200 inh.). Pr. cities : *Hamamatsu* (19,600 inh.), *Numazu* (12,000 inh.), *Nagata* (11,200 inh.), *Shimada* (11,000 inh.).

Shō, 尚. Family of the ancient kings of the *Ryūkyū* archipelago. — Now Marquis.

——— Tai, 泰 (1843-1901). Was dispossessed in 1879, and in com-pensation, was received into the Japanese nobility.

Shō-an, 承安. *Nengō* : 1171-1174.
Shō-an, 正安. *Nengō* : 1299-1301.

Shōbanshū, 相伴衆. Officials of high rank who, under the *Ashi-kaga Shōgun*, accompanied the *Shōgun* in his travels. In 1421, *Yoshi-mitsu*, being invited to visit *Ise Sadatsune*, for the first time gave this title to *Hatakeyama Mitsuie.* The members of the *Shiba, Hosokawa* and *Hatakeyama* families, before being named *kwanryō*, and also the *daimyō* skilful in military exercises, were chosen as *shōbanshū.*

Shōbikōchin, 燒尾荒鎮. Formerly a banquet given by a noble or an official upon the occasion of his promotion to a higher rank. This custom, having brought about many abuses, was suppressed by *Fujiwara Tokihira* at the beginning of the 10th century.

Shōbō, 聖寶 (832-909). Famous bonze of the *Shingen* sect. Son of a prince of the Imperial family, at the age of 16 he placed himself under the guidance of the famous *Shinga*, became *Ajari*, *Sōjō*, etc., and received the posthumous title of *Rigen-Daishi*.

Shōbutsu, 生 佛 . Bonze of the *Hiei-zan* ; having lost his sight, he became a player on the *biwa* (*biwa-hōshi*) and is the first who borrowed his long recitals from the *Heike-monogatari*, etc.

Shōchō, 正 長 . *Nengō :* 1427.

Shōchū, 正 中 . *Nengō :* 1324-1325.

Shōden, 聖 天 . God of wisdom .(Buddh.) especially invoked to remove obstacles from an undertaking. Also called *Kwangi-ten*.

Shōdo-shima, 小 豆 嶋 . Island (120 Km. circum.) of the Inland Sea, in the *Harima-nada*. Belongs to the *Sanuki* province.

Shōdō-Shōnin, 勝 道 上 人 . Bonze (735-817) who, in 767, built the first temple of *Nikkō* (then *Nikō-zan* or *Futara-yama*) ; and called it *Shihonryū-ji*. He rebuilt it on a larger scale in 808 and named it *Honryū-ji*. — See *Nikkō*.

Shō-en, 莊 園 . Formerly, domains with which the emperor rewarded princes or high officials. The possessors of *shō-en*, called *shōji*, at first had only the produce of these lands, the land itself remaining imperial property ; but they were exempt from taxes and not subject to the provincial government. Their number gradually increased ; some lords, on their own authority, gave the name of *shō-en* to their domains, dispensed justice, levied heavy taxes, etc. In the 11th century, half of the country was thus converted into *shō-en* domains. Vainly did some emperors enact laws against this state of affairs. *Yoritomo*, however succeeded in notably diminishing their number and imposed on all an annual taxation of 5 *shō* (9 litres) of rice per *tan* (10 acres). — The *shōji* were often absent from their domains and had them administered by a *jitō*.

Shōen-hōshinnō, 性 圓 法 親 王 (1292-1347). 4th son of the emperor *Go-Uda*. At the age of 15, he became bonze at the *Daikaku-ji* and obtained for this temple great donations from his father. Received the posthumous name of *Nanchi-in*.

Shōgaku-in, 奬 學 院 . School established at *Kyōto* in 881 by *Ariwara Yukihira* for the youth of noble families. The director, who bore the title of *Bettō*, was the highest *kuge* of the *Minamoto* clan. Under the reign of *Toba tennō* (1108-1123), this office became hereditary in the *Kuga* family. In 1383, *Go-Komatsu* gave this title to the *Shōgun Yoshimitsu*, he being the chief of the *Minamoto* (*Genji no chōja*), and from that time, it became but an honorary title added to those of the *Shōgun*. The *Tokugawa* bore it also.

Shōgen, 承 元 . *Nengō :* 1207-1210.

Shōgen, 正 元 . *Nengō :* 1259.

Shōgun, 將 軍 . — See *Sei-i-shi*.

Shōgun-zuka, 將 軍 塚 . When the emperor *Kwammu* had chosen *Kyōto* as his capital (794), he ordered a statue of clay, 8 feet high, to be made, covered it with armor, put into its hands a bow and arrows, and had it buried on a hill (*Kwachō-zan*), E. of the city. This was to be the god protecting the city and expected to keep away all evil minded men or spirits. The eminence covering this tomb is called *Shōgun-zuka* (tomb of the *Shōgun*) The popular belief is that the famous *Shōgun Sakanoe no Tamuramaro* (+ 811) is buried there and that when some danger threatens the city, a noise comes from the tomb.

Shohan-gakkō, 諸 藩 學 校 (Lit.: schools of the different clans). In the first 100 years that followed the accession of the *Tokugawa* to the shōgunate, the instruction of the young *samurai* had been very much neglected. If we except the *Shōhei-kō* of *Edo*, there was no public school, and it was in order to obviate this inconvenience that in the 18th century the *daimyō* of the large estates established schools in their residence to which the most distinguished professors were invited. The rules and curriculum were similar to those of the *Shōhei-kō* of *Edo*. At first, only Chinese literature and military art were taught, but later, the study of Japanese antiquities and the little of European sciences that had been able to gain admission into the country through *Nagasaki*, were introduced. There were boarders and day scholars, entering at the age of 7 or 8, and leaving at 20. Instruction was given free of charge, all expenses connected with the maintenance of the school being met by the *daimyō*. The principal schools of this kind were :

(*a*) — At *Nagoya*, the *Meirin-dō*, 明 倫 道 established in 1749, by *Tokugawa* (*Owari*) *Munechika :* its curriculum embraced Japanese, Chinese, mathematics, writing, ceremonies, and bow-shooting.

(*b*) — At *Mito*, the *Kōdō-kwan* 弘 道 舘 founded in 1838 by *Tokugawa Nariaki*, with the help of *Fujita Tōko*, etc. This school was divided into two sections one (*bunkwan*) for literary studies, and the other (*bukwan*), for military arts.

(*c*) — At *Kanazawa* (*Kaga*), the *Meirin-dō* 明 倫 堂 (1792). (Japanese, Chinese, medicine, mathematics, writing, politeness, astronomy) and the *Kyōbu-kwan*, 經 武 舘 and *Sōyū-kwan* 壯 猶 舘 (military arts).

(*d*) — At *Wakayama* (*Kii*), the *Gakushū-kwan*, 學 習 舘 (1713), which, to the ordinary studies, added the Dutch language.

(*e*) — At *Kagoshima* (*Satsuma*), the *Zōshi-kwan*, 造 士 舘 (1773) and the *Embu-kwan*, 演 武 舘 (school of medecine).

(*f*) — At *Kumamoto* (*Higo*), the *Jishū-kwan*, 時 習 舘 (1752), for literary studies, and the *Tōzai-ryōsha*, 東 西 兩 榭 for military arts.

(*g*) — At *Hagi* (*Chōshū*), the *Meirin-kwan* 明 倫 舘 (1718), and the *Denshū-dō* 傳 習 堂 for the European sciences.

(*h*) — At *Kōchi* (*Tosa*), the *Kyōju-kwan*, 敎 授 舘 founded in 1760 and replaced in 1860 by the *Chidō-kwan*, 致 道 舘 .

(*i*) — At *Sendai*, the *Yōken-dō* 養 賢 堂 (1736), where music and the Russian and Dutch languages were taught.

(*j*) — At *Wakamatsu* (*Aizu*), the *Nisshin-kwan*, 日 新 舘 (1788).

(*k*) — At *Yonezawa* (*Dewa*), the *Kōjō-kwan*, 興 讓 舘 (1797), was especially a school of Confucianism ; the *Embu-kō*, 演 武 校 and *Kōsei-dō*, 好 生 堂 for medecine and military arts.

(*l*) — At *Okayama* (*Bizen*), the *Kankoku-gakkō*, 閑 谷 學 校 (1669), founded by *Ikeda Mitsumasa* with *Kumazawa Ryōkai*. In the *Okayama* clan, learning was held in highest esteem.

(*m*) — At *Kyōto*, the *Horikawa-gakkō*, 堀 河 學 校 founded by *Itō Jinsai*.

(*n*) — At *Ōsaka*, the *Kwaitokusho-in*, 懷 德 書 院 (1720), established by *Nakai Shūan*.

Shōhata, 勝 幡. In *Owari*. Old castle of the *Shiba daimyō*, governors of the province, who entrusted its administration (as well as that of *Inuyama*, *Kiyosu*, etc.) to the *Oda* family. *Nobuhide*, profiting by the dissensions that were weakening his lords, occupied the castle of *Nagoya* in 1532, where he established himself after having abandoned the one of *Shōhata*.

Shōhei, 正 平. *Nengō*: 1346-1369. — Or *Shōhyō*.

Shōhei-kō, 昌 平 校. School founded by the *Shōgun Iemitsu* (1630), at *Shinobu-ga-oka* (*Edo*). It was but a library, at first called *Kōbun-in*, in which *Hayashi Razan* gave his lectures on literature. Later on, *Tokugawa Yoshinao* built a temple there where Confucius was venerated, and Japanese literature and history were taught. Transferred in 1690, to *Yushima-dai* under the name of *Seidō*, it received the name of *Gakumon-jo* in 1797, and was very prosperous till the middle of the 19th century.

Shōhō, 正 保. *Nengō*: 1644-1647.

Shōhyō, 正 平. *Nengō*: 1346-1369. — Or *Shōhei*.

Sho-in-ban, 書 院 番. Under the *Tokugawa Shōgun*, *samurai* guarding the interior of the Palace of *Edo*; they accompanied the *Shōgun* in his outings and attended him in the ceremonies.

Shōji, 正 治. *Nengō*: 1199-1200.

Shōji, 莊 司. Formerly a title given to the possessors of the *shō-en*.

Shōji-ko, 精 進 湖. Or *Shōjin no ko*. Lake (9 Km. in circum.) in *Kai*, N. W. of Mount *Fuji*. Called also *Ishise no mizu-umi*.

Shōjin, 聖 尋. Son of the *Kwampaku Fujiwara Mototada*, became bonze and rose to the highest dignities, *Dai-sōjō*, *Tōdaiji-bettō*, *Daigozasu*, etc. In 1331, he helped *Go-Daigo* to escape to Mt. *Kasagi*; made prisoner at the same time as the emperor, he was banished to *Shimōsa*, then returned to the *Tō-daiji* after the ruin of the *Hōjō* (1333).

Shōjō, 猩 々. Fantastic beings having the body of a monkey, with long red hair falling on the shoulders; they were believed to be especially fond of *sake* (rice-wine).

Shō-jō, 小 乘. (Lit.: small vehicle). *Shaka* classed men according to the knowledge they had of his doctrine, 1st the simple (*shōmon*), 2nd the enlightened (*engaku*) and 3rd the truly wise (*bosatsu*). To these 3 classes there are three corresponding periods or rather 3 degrees in the teaching of his doctrine. (See *san-ji-kyō*). The first, called small vehicle, (*shōjō* or *Hinayâna*) and especially spread at Siam and at Ceylon, is known under the name of Buddhism of the South; the 2nd, great vehicle (*daijō* or *Mahâyâna*) propagated at first in China then in Korea and Japan, is known as the Buddhism of the North.

Shōka, 正 嘉. *Nengō*: 1257-1258.

Shōkei, 上 卿. Formerly high officials of the *Kiroku-jo*. — Also *Daijin* or *Nagon* exercising a temporary office at the Palace, such as that of *Naiben*, etc.

Shōkoku, 相國 . Under the *Ashikaga Shōgun*, title borrowed from China and designating the *Dajō-daijin*.

Shōkon-sha, 招魂社 . Temples erected in several cities to the manes of the soldiers who died for the Imperial cause. — The best known is that of *Tōkyō* (*Yasukuni-jinja*) built on the heights of *Kudan* (*Kōjimachi*).

Shōkō-tennō, 稱光天皇 . 101st Emperor of Japan (1413-1428). *Mihito* succeeded his father *Go-Komatsu* at the age of 12. He was raised to the throne by the *Shōgun Yoshimochi* contrary to the treaty of 1392, by which the sovereign had to be chosen alternatively from the two branches of the Imperial family; no wonder then, that this election caused several revolts among the ancient partisans of the Southern dynasty. This reign, besides, is filled with the civil wars occasioned by the rivalry of the great families to obtain the title of *Kwanryō*, either of *Kyōto* or of the *Kwantō*. *Shōkō* died at the age of 27, leaving no heir.

Shōkyū, 承久 . *Nengō* : 1219-1221.

Shōkyū no ran, 承久亂 . The civil war of the *Shōkyū* era. — After the death of *Sanetomo*, last of the *Minamoto Shōgun* (1219), *Fujiwara Yoshitsune*, then 2 years old, was chosen by the *Hōjō* to succeed him, and *Yoshitoki* continued to govern. A little later (1221), the emperor *Juntoku* abdicated in favor of his son. There then were 3 ex-emperors : *Go-Toba* (*Ichi-in*), *Tsuchimikado* (*Chū-in*), and *Juntoku* (*Shin-in*). *Go-Toba* and *Juntoku* resolved to get rid of the *Hōjō*, and an order was sent to all the provinces to levy troops and march against them. On hearing this, *Hōjō Yoshitoki*, after taking the advice of his sister *Masa-ko* and *Ōe Hiromoto*, sent a large army against *Kyōto* under the command of his sons *Yasutoki* and *Tomotoki* and his brother *Tokifusa*. The several thousands of *samurai* who had answered the call of the Emperor, were defeated at *Uji* and at *Seta* : the *Kamakura* army victoriously entered *Kyōto*, and *Yoshitoki* took his revenge. The young emperor *Chūkyō* was deposed, his father *Juntoku* exiled to *Sado* and *Go-Toba* to *Oki*. Although *Tsuchimikado* had kept himself secluded, he was notwithstanding exiled to *Shikoku*. Thus ended the *Shōkyū* war. The *Hōjō* were thus to remain all powerful during one more century.

Shōmu-tennō, 聖武天皇 . 45th Emperor of Japan (724-748). *Ame-shirushi-kuni-oshiharuki-toyo-sakura-hiko*, son of *Mommu-tennō*, at the age of 25, succeeded his aunt *Genshō*. During his reign, lived the famous bonzes *Gyōgi*, *Dōsen*, *Ryōben*, etc. It was a period of prosperity for Buddhism : the *Hase-dera*, the *Tō-daiji*, the *Daibutsu* of *Nara*, etc. date from that period. A public drugstore (*Shiyaku-in*) was likewise established, bridges were built, a survey of all the provinces made, the houses began to be covered with tiles, examinations were prescribed for admission to public offices, etc. After a reign of 25 years, *Shōmu* abdicated in favor of his daughter *Kōken*. He had his head shaved by *Gyōgi*, and took the name of *Shōman*. He lived 8 more years.

Shōmyō, 小名 . Formerly,—especially under the *Ashikaga*, — lord of a small domain, as opposed to *daimyō*. — See *Daimyō*, *Myōden*.

Shōnagon, 少納言. Officials of the *Dajō-kwan*, whose duties were equivalent to that of a 2nd class secretary. Their number, fixed at first to 3, was afterwards increased. They were formerly called *Sunaimono-mōshi* or *Sunaimono-mōsu-tsukasa*, because they transacted business of small importance.

Shōnai, 庄内. — See *Tsurugaoka*.

Shō-naiki, 小内記. — See *Dai-naiki, Uchi no shirusu-tzukasa*.

Shō-ni, 小貳. Formerly an official of the *Dazaifu*, inferior to the *Gon no sotsu* and the *Dai-ni*. In case a *Dazaifu* existed, no *Dai-ni* was nominated; hence, the title of *Shō-ni* was equivalent to that of sub-governor of the *Dazaifu*. This title was given by *Yoritomo* to *Fujiwara* (*Mutō*) *Sukeyori*, and became a family name.

Shōni, 小貳. Ancient *daimyō* family descendant of *Fujiwara Hidesato*.

—— **Sukeyori, 資頼**. Descendant of *Hidesato* in the 9th generation, received the title of *Dazai Shō-ni* (1189) from *Yoritomo;* he settled at *Dazaifu* and took the name of *Shōni*.

—— **Kagesuke, 景資**. Was on duty, at the time of the Mongols' expedition against *Kyūshū*. He organized the defence, fought gallantly, and when the tempest had dispersed the invaders' fleet, pursued them as far as the *Takashima* island and massacred all those who had sought shelter there (1281).

—— **Sadatsune, 貞經**. Sided at first with *Go-Daigo;* but, hearing of the success of the *Ashikaga*, he went over to their side and fought for the Northern dynasty. In 1334, he defeated and killed *Kikuchi Taketoki;* but was in turn defeated and killed by *Taketoshi* son of *Taketoki*.

—— **Yorihisa, 賴尚**. Son of *Sadatsune*, who after having defeated *Taketoshi*, led 2,000 men to the help of *Takauji* and fought in the battles of *Minato-gawa* (1336) and *Amida-ga-mine*, where the Southern army was defeated. Having returned to *Kyūshū*, he fought against *Kikuchi Takemitsu*, but was defeated on the *Chikugo-gawa*.

—— **Fuyusuke, 冬資** (+ 1375). Son of *Yorihisa*, at first served *Imagawa Sadayo*, was nominated *tandai* of *Kyūshū;* then, after some contention with him, turned against him, but was defeated and killed.

—— **Yorizumi, 賴澄**. *Fuyusuke's* brother, whom he succeeded. He served prince *Yasunaga-shinnō* and was named *Kyūshū tandai* and *Echigo no kami* by him.

—— **Masasuke, 政資**. Descendant of the above, was killed whilst fighting against *Ōuchi Yoshioki*, who came to despoil him of his domains (1506).

—— **Sukemoto, 資元** (1497-1532). Son of *Masasuke*, tried to regain the inheritance of the family. He married the daughter of *Ōtomo Masachika;* the latter gave him help, and in 1529, he defeated the army of the *Ōuchi*.

—— **Tokinao, 時尚**. Son of *Sukemoto*, had to fight his vassal *Ryū-zōji Takanobu*, and was defeated by him in 1554. Having taken refuge in *Chikugo*, he levied a second army and again took the field, but being defeated a second time, he killed himself (1556). With him ended his family. — The *Nabeshima daimyō* descend from the *Shōni*.

Shōnin, 上人 . (Lit.: superior man). Title placed after the name of certain bonzes famous for their virtue. Corresponds to " His Eminence, or His Lordship."

Shō-ō, 正應 . *Nengō* : 1288-1292.

Shō-ō Daishi, 聖應大師 .— See *Ryōnin*.

Shōren-in, 青蓮院 . Temple of *Kyōto*. Was the residence of *Shinran-Shōnin* but after his death (1263), was changed into a temple, the superior of which was a prince of the Imperial family.

Shōryaku, 正曆 . *Nengō* : 990-994.

Shōryaku, 承曆 . *Nengō* : 1077-1080.

Shoryō-shi, 諸陵司 . Formerly an officer subject to the *Jibushō* and whose functions were to prepare the funerals, to take care of the Imperial tombs, to watch over the *Ryōko*, etc.

Shōryūji-jō, 勝龍寺城 . In *Yamashiro*, S. W. of *Kyōto*. Old castle built in 1339 by *Hosokawa Yoriharu*. In the next century, it passed into the hands of the *Hatakeyama*. *Hosokawa Fujitaka* rebuilt it in 1573. *Akechi Mitsuhide* confided it to the care of his vassal *Miyake*, who, after the defeat of *Yamazaki* (1582), killed himself. The castle was then abandoned.

Shosha-zan, 書寫山 . Hill (400 m.) in *Harima*, on which the bonze *Shōku*, at end of the 10th century, built the temple *Enkyō-ji* ; this temple became famous and even received a visit from the emperors *Kwazan* and *Go-Shirakawa*. *Go-Daigo* passed there, when returning from *Hōki* to *Kyōto* (1333). In 1351, it was the scene of a battle between *Ashikaga Takauji* and *Ishidō Yorifusa*.

Shō-shi, 小祀 . According to the *Jingi-kwan*, the small feasts or less solemn ceremonies of the Shintoist religion were so called. The principal among them were : *Ō-imi no matsuri, Kaze-no-kami no matsuri, Hana-shizume no matsuri, Saigusa no matsuri, Tama-shizume no matsuri, Ho-shizume no matsuri, Michi-ae no matsuri, Sonokarakami no matsuri, Matsuo no matsuri, Hirano no matsuri, Kasuga no matsuri, Ōharano no matsuri, Ume-no-miya no matsuri, Jingojiki no matsuri, Yaso-shima no matsuri*, etc.— See *Saishi*.

Shoshidai, 所司代 .— See *Kyōto-shoshidai*.

Shōsho, 詔書 . Formerly Imperial decrees on important subjects. (Those referring to less important things were called *Chokusho*). The *Shōsho* began with the following formula : *Akitsu-mikami to Ame-no-shita shiroshimesu Yamato no Sumera-mikoto no Ō-mikoto* (Decree of the Emperor who commands under heaven......), and terminated with the solemn sentence : *Kotogotoku kike* (listen all). The *Shōsho* carried, besides the Imperial seal, those of the *Nakatsukasa-kyō, tayū* and *shōyū*, of the *Dajō-daijin, Sadaijin, Udaijin* and *Dainagon*.

Shōsō-in, 正倉院 . Store house (*kura*) built in 756 in the precincts of the temple *Tō-daiji*, at *Nara*, in which many objects were kept pertaining to the times of *Shōmu* and *Kōken*, i.e. of the most prosperous times of the *Nara* era (724-748). It was happily preserved from fire for more than 1,000 years. It could not be opened without a special permission of the Emperor, and *Yoritomo, Michiie, Yoshimitsu,* and *Ieyasu* even, had to submit to that formality. Thanks to the care which was lavished upon it, it has reached the present day unimpaired, and is actually an archaeological museum of inestimable value.

Shōtai, 昌泰 . *Nengō*: 898-900.

Shōtetsu, 正徹 (1380-1458). By birth, *Ki Seigen*, bonze of the *Tō-fuku-ji* temple. Is the author of a great number of poems. He compiled 20,000 of them in a collection (*Sōkonshū*), the preface of which was written by *Ichijō Kaneyoshi*. Owing to certain criticisms which he inserted in his verses, he was banished for some time to *Yamashina*, then pardoned.

Shōtoku, 正德 . *Nengō*: 1711-1715.

Shōtoku-taishi, 聖德太子 (572-621). 2nd son of the emperor
Yōmei. He was sur-
named *Umayado*,
because his mother,
whilst walking in the
Palace, was sudden-
ly seized with the
pangs of child-birth
and brought forth
her child in the Impe-
rial stables (*umaya*).
At the accession of
his aunt *Suiko* (593),
he was named heir
to the throne (*taishi*)
and exercised a real
regency (*sesshō*).
The following year,
he gave great sup-
port to Buddhism of
which he was a fer-
vent disciple. He
fixed 12 court ranks,
distinguished by the
colour of their head-
gear (*kammuri*)
(603); promulgated
a Code of laws in 17
chapters, borrowed
from China (604);
with the help of
Soga no Umako, he

SHŌTOKU-TAISHI AND HIS TWO SONS..

published two historical works, the *Tennō-ki* and the *Koku-ki* (620). He died the following year, at the age of 49, leaving 8 sons and 6 daughters. — *Shōtoku-taishi* is one of the great figures of Japanese history, especially on account of his activity in the propagation of Buddhism. He follow-ed the teaching of *Eji*, bonze of *Koma* (Korea). As soon as he came to power, he selected the 3 *sūtras* of the *Mahâyâna* doctrine (*dai-jō*) and ordered them to be taught everywhere; he built the temples of *Shi-tennō-ji*, *Hōryū-ji*, *Chūkyū-ji*, *Hōkō-ji*, etc. and at the time of his death, Buddhism numbered already 46 *tera*, 820 bonzes and 560 *ama* (nuns) in Japan. It was *Shōtoku-taishi* who for the first time sent an embassy to China (607) and who adopted the Chinese calendar (604).

Shōtoku-tennō, 稱德天皇. Empress (48) of Japan (765-769). *Abe Nai-shinnō*, *Shōmu-tennō's* daughter, who had been empress (749-758) under the name of *Kōken*, but ascended the throne a second time at the age of 48, on the advice of the bonze *Dōkyō*. Because of this second term, she received the posthumous name of *Shōtoku-tennō*. — During the reign of *Junnin*, who occupied the throne after her first resignation, the ex-empress *Kōken*, who had taken the name of *Takano-tennō*, allowed herself to be completely guided by the ambitious bonze *Dōkyō*, on whom she bestowed many favors and dignities. This preference excited the jealousy of the nobles, and *Emi no Oshikatsu* (*Fujiwara Nakamaro*) rose in revolt but he was defeated and the ex-empress profited by the occasion to resume the reins of government. She exiled *Junnin* to *Awaji*, then nominated *Dōkyō Dajō-daijin-zenshi* and *Hō-ō* (this last title had till then been reserved for the emperors who had become bonzes after their abdication). Yet *Dōkyō* was not satisfied for he aspired to nothing less than the throne and would have probably succeeded in persuading *Shōtoku* to abdicate in his favor, but the empress, before placing a throne that had been held for 14 centuries by the same lineage, into the hands of a usurper resolved to consult the god *Hachiman* of the temple of *Usa*. She deputed the faithful *Wake no Kiyomaro*, who brought an answer from the god, stating that never should a subject become emperor. On the strength of this oracle, the empress kept the throne, but she died the following year. During her reign (767) *Shōdō-Shōnin* built the first temple (*Shihonryū-ji*) of *Nikkō*.

Shōwa, 正和. *Nengō*: 1312-1316.

Shōya, 庄屋. — See *Nanushi*.

Shōyō-Daishi, 承陽大師. Posthumous name of the bonze *Dōgen* (1200-1253). Son of the *Naidaijin Kuga Michichika*, he lost his mother when 8 years old, and entered the *Hiei-zan*, where he studied the doctrines of the *Tendai* sect under the direction of *Eisai*. In 1223, he went to China, remained there 5 years and on his return, settled at the *Kennin-ji* temple and began to preach the *Sōdō* sect. Later on, he founded the *Eihei-ji* (*Echizen*), which became the principal temple of his sect (1244). *Dōgen* was a famous poet. The posthumous title of *Shōyō-Daishi* was given him in 1880.

Shōyō-sha, 昭陽舍. — See *Nashitsubo*.

Shozai, 諸西. In *Kazusa*. From 1841 to 1868, residence of the *Hayashi daimyō* (10,000 k.).

Shōzuka no Baba, 三途河婆. Old sorceress who steals children's clothes when they pass the river of hell (*Sozu-kawa*).

Shū, 宗. Religion, sect. — *Hasshū*, the 8 oldest Buddhist sects. — *Tendai-shū*, the *Tendai* sect. — *Kirishitan-shū*, the Christian religion.

Shūbun, 秀文. Famous painter of the 14th and the 15th centuries. Towards 1375, he went to *Echizen* and married into the *Soga* family, whose name he took ; in order to distinguish him from the following, he is often named *Soga Shūbun*. He lived in the *Hida* province and painted according to the Chinese school : for this reason, he is also called *Tō* (China) *no Shūbun*.

Shūbun, 周文. Painter of the 15th century. Born in *Ōmi*, he came to *Kyōto* and was the chief of the *Sōkoku-ji* temple. In painting, he was the scholar of *Josetsu*. He is often called *Ekkei Shūbun*.

Shuchō, 朱鳥. *Nengō :* 686-689.

Shugen-dō, 修験道. Buddhist associations formed by the *Shingon* and *Tendai* sects. That of *Shingon*, the foundation of which is ascribed to *En no Shōkaku*, has its origin traced to the bonze *Shōbō* (834-909) of the *Daigo-ji* temple ; that of *Tendai*, to *Zōyo* (1090) of the *Shōgo-in*. Under the *Tokugawa*, the *Shugen-dō* of the *Shingon-shū* was named *Tōzan-ha*, and that of the *Tendai-shū*, *Honzan-ha*. Every year, members of the two branches met on Mount *Ōmine* in order to pray and to perform different works of devotion : this meeting was called *Nyōhō*. The adherents of the *Shugen-dō* are named *Shugenja*, and commonly *Yamabushi*.

Shugo, 守護. | In 1185, on the advice of *Ōe Hiromoto*,
Shugo-shoku, 守護職. | *Yoritomo* created an official in the provinces formerly belonging to the *Taira*, and not depending directly on him, to assist the *kokushi* (governor) : he named him *shugo* or *shugo-shoku*. In the *shō-en*, they were called *jitō*. At the head of the *Kwantō* provinces, which depended directly upon him he placed *kuni-bugyō*. — The *shoku*, who at first were called *sotsuibushi*, had to secure the payment of the taxes, render justice, levy troops in case of war, etc. Gradually they extended their power over the *shō-en*, and the *jitō* were reduced to a secondary position. Under the *Ashikaga*, the *shugo* became still more powerful, some governing several provinces, for in 1440, the *Yamana* lorded it over 11 provinces. After the *Ōnin* war (1469), they began to replace the *kokushi* and formed the class of *daimyō*, whilst the *jitō* and the *gokenin* were called *shōmyō*.

Shugo-bugyō, 守護奉行. Under the *Ashikaga*, official whose duty it was to watch over the conduct of the *shugo*, to attend to their changes etc. This title was suppressed the following century.

Shugo-dai, 守護代. | Official who replaced the *Shu-*
Shugo-daikwan, 守護代官. | *go*, when absent from his fief. As the case occurred very frequently, the *Shugo-dai* increased in importance and at times even over-threw the *Shugo*.

Shugo-funyū-chi, 守護不入地. (Lit. : lands where the *Shugo* entered not). Under the *Kamakura Shōgun*, the temples were more than once despoiled of their valuables by the *Shugo* or the *Jitō ;* on that account, the *Hōjō* and the *Ashikaga* revived the old laws that exempted the temples from all local jurisdiction : it was even forbidden any *samurai* to enter the temples armed, were it even to arrest a criminal. Whence it came that the domains of the temples were called *Shugo-funyū-chi*.

Shūgoku, 囚獄. Under the *Tokugawa*, keeper of the *Kodemma-chō* prison (*Edo*) : he was usually known by the name of *Rōya-bugyō*. The *Machi-bugyō*, the *Jisha-bugyō*, the *Kanjō-bugyō*, sent him their criminals. He had 50 *dōshin* and 30 *genan* subject to him. This office was hereditary in the *Izushi* family.

Shugo-shi, 守護使. Formerly an official sent by the *Shugo* to examine the state of the rice-fields before the harvest and to fix accordingly the amount of taxes on the farmers.

Shūhōsha, 襲芳舎. Room in the Palace where the Emperor retired during thunderstorms. In order to charm away the thunderbolt, besides the preventive measures taken to protect the Emperor (See *kaminari no jin*) the *meigen* was performed. It consisted in sounding a bowstring to expel the evil spirits. This room was also called *kaminari no tsubo.*

Shu-in-bune, 朱印船. — See *Go-shuin-bune.*

Shu-in-chi, 朱印地. — See *Go-shuin-chi.*

Shujaku-tennō, 朱雀天皇. 61st Emperor of Japan (931–946). *Yuta-akira*, son of *Daigo-tennō*, succeeded his father at the age of 7. *Fujiwara Tadahira* was *Sesshō*. During this reign occurred the revolts of *Taira Masakado* in *Kwantō* and of *Fujiwara Sumitomo* in *Iyo* (939). At the age of 24, he abdicated in favor of his brother *Murakami* and lived 6 more years.

Shukei-ryō, 主計寮. Formerly a bureau under the *Mimbushō* charged to receive and verify imposts and taxes, etc., sent from the provinces. It was composed of 1 *kami* (its head), 1 *suke*, etc. Also called *Kazue-ryō.*

Shūki-kōrei-sai, 秋季皇靈祭. Feast celebrated in the Palace, at the autumnal equinox (Sept. 23rd), in honor of the spirits of the Emperors.

Shukuji-kwasho-bugyō, 宿次過書奉行. In the time of the *Kamakura* and the *Kyōto Shōgun*, an official who obtained and distributed passports. The *Shikken* and the *Renshō* placed their seal thereon.

Shukushin, 蕭愼. Japanese name of an old Chinese tribe that, according to some, inhabited Manchuria, but most probably lived in the region of the actual *Kiangsou* province. During the 6th and the 7th centuries, pirates repeatedly made incursions on the coasts of *Sado, Dewa, Echigo*, etc., and the empress *Saimei* had to send an expedition against them under the leadership of *Abe no Hirafu* (658).

Shūmei, 州名. Chinese name of the Japanese provinces. This name was formed by taking one of the two characters—generally the first,—from the name of the province and adding the character *shū* to it. Thus *Sōshū* for *Sagami, Bishū* for *Owari*, etc. The provinces that later on were divided into several, distinguished by the word *zen, chū, go*, had only one *shūmei ;* thus *Esshū* comprises *Echizen, Etchū* and *Echigo*. Some of these *shūmei* are more in use than their corresponding Japanese expressions ; for inst.: *Kōshū (Kai), Shinshū (Shinano), Bōshū (Awa), Jōshū (Kōzuke)*, etc.

Shūmon-aratame, 宗門改. Legal formality which obliged every man to declare at the time of the census, to which religious sect he belonged. Established to secure the extinction of the Christian religion, this custom dates from 1641, or some time after the *Shimabara* insurrection. The better to attain their end, they added to it the practice of trampling on Christian images (*e-fumi*). The two officials who presided at this formality were called *Shumon-aratame-yaku* or *Kirishitan-yaku*; one of them was given by the *Ō-metsuke*, the other, by the *Zoku-bugyō*; they had 6 *yoriki* and 30 *dōshin* subject to them.

Shunjō, 俊芿 (1167-1228). Bonze of the *Shingon-shū* sect. Went to China in 1199, where he studied during 12 years and on his return, settled at the *Senyū-ji* temple (*Kyōto*) where he preached the *Ritsu* sect. He received the posthumous name of *Getsurin-Daishi*.

Shunkei, 春慶. — See *Katō Shunkei*.

Shunki-kōrei-sai, 春季皇靈祭. Feast celebrated in the Palace at the spring equinox (March 20th), in honor of the spirits of the Emperors.

Shunkwan, 俊寛 (1142-1178). Chief bonze of the *Hōshō-ji* temple. Born of the *Minamoto* family, he with *Fujiwara Narichika* plotted to destroy the *Taira*, but his plans were discovered and he was banished to *Kikai-ga-shima* (1177). The following year, his accomplices were pardoned, but he as instigator of the plot was put to death.

Shuri, 首里. Port (25,000 inh.) of the *Okinawa* island. Formerly the capital of the *Ryūkyū* and residence of the kings of the archipelago.

Shuri-shiki, 修理職. At one time called *Osame-tsukuru-tsukasa*. Formerly bureau whose office was to tend to the buildings and repairs in the Imperial Palace. At its head were 1 *kami*, 1 *suke*, 2 *jō*, 4 *sakwan*, etc.

Shusei-sha, 修成社. One of the 10 Shintoist sects, established in 1873, by *Nitta Kunimitsu*, which purposes to conciliate Buddhism with the national religion.

Shusen-shi, 主船司. Formerly bureau having charge of all that pertained to boats, their rigging, furniture, etc.

Shu-Shunsui, 朱舜水 (1600-1682). A Chinese literary man coming from the *Tchekiang* province. After the ruin of the *Ming* dynasty, came to *Nagasaki* (1659). He was living in extreme poverty when *Andō Shōan*, professor of *Yanagawa* (*Chikugo*) took him as his master and made him share half of the pension received from the *daimyō*. In 1665, *Mito Mitsukuni* called him near his person and treated him with great honor. He was one of principal authors of the *Dai-Nihon-shi*.

Shusse-hyōjōshū, 出世評定衆. Under the *Ashikaga Shōgun*, this name was given to some officials of the *Kira, Yamana, Ishibashi, Isshiki*, etc. families, who were ranked by special privilege (*shusse*) among the *Hyōjōshū* without having passed through the grade of *Hikitsukeshū*, (*shusse*). They were suppressed towards 1560.

Shuyō-shi, 主鷹司. Formerly bureau having the care of the falcons and dogs employed in the hunting expeditions at which the Emperor assisted. Also called *Taka-kai-be*.

Shuzei-ryō, 主税寮. Formerly bureau under the direction of the *Mimbu-shō*, charged to receive the taxes in kind that were levied in the provinces. Also called *Chikara-ryō*. It had at its head 1 *kami*, 1 *suke*. 2 *jō*, 4 *sakwan*, etc.

Shuzenji, 修善寺. Village of *Izu*, thus called on account of a temple built there by *Kūkai* in the 9th century. To this place *Minamoto Noriyori* (1193), *Yoriie* (1203), *Hōjō Tokimasa* (1205), etc. were banished. In 1360, *Hatakeyama Kunikiyo* intrenched himself there to resist the attacks of *Ashikaga Motouji*. Passed later on into the hands of the *Hōjō* of *Odawara*.

Sidotti, (John Baptist) (1668-1715). — Born at Palermo and ordained priest in Rome, he embarked from Genoa with Mgr. de Tournon, legate of the Holy See to China (1703). After some years spent at Pondichery and in the Philippine Islands, he left for Japan, which he intended to evangelize. He landed at *Yaku-shima* (island S. of *Ōsumi*) on Oct. 13, 1708. Arrested at once, he was taken to *Nagasaki*, then to *Edo*, where he arrived in Dec. 1709 and was confined in the *Kirishitan-yashiki*. He there converted two old persons, a man and a woman, who were his servants and who had already been instructed in the Christian religion by Rev. F. Chiara (+ 1685). He had the consolation of baptizing them (1714), but in punishment, he was enclosed in a pit 5 feet deep, at the top of which a small hole was left open to prevent him from being asphyxiated and through which food was passed to him. He lived thus one full year and died there on Dec. 15, 1715. In his *Seiyō-kibun*, *Arai Hakuseki*, relates the examination to which Abbé Sidotti was subjected.

Sō, 宗. *Daimyō* family descended from *Taira Tomomori*, and since the 13th century, chief of the *Tsushima* islands.

—— **Tomomune, 知宗.** 3rd son of *Taira Tomomori*, repressed the troubles in *Tsushima* in 1245, and was named governor of the place.

—— **Sukekuni, 助國** (+ 1274). Son of *Tomomune*, was killed at *Asaji no ura* whilst fighting the Mongols.

—— **Sadamori, 貞盛** (1385-1452). Had constant relations with Korea and agreed to send thither every year 50 junks laden with Japanese products. These junks were expected to return with Korean and Chinese merchandise.

—— **Yoshitomo, 義智** (1568-1615). Went to *Hakozaki* (*Chikuzen*) at the time of *Hideyoshi's* expedition in *Kyūshū* (1587), was presented to him and was confirmed in his possession of *Tsushima*. In 1590, he was sent on a mission to Korea, to oblige the king of that country to resume the periodical embassies, that seemed to have fallen into neglect. He was successful, but this did not prevent the war which the *Taikō* had already resolved upon. *Yoshitomo* took part in it under the command of his father *Konishi Yukinaga*. In 1600, he sided with *Ieyasu*, but remained in *Tsushima* and was not present at the battle of *Sekigahara*. The same year, he was again sent to Korea to conclude peace, and on his return, his revenues were increased to 100,000 k.—*Yoshitomo* had been baptised in 1591 but the fear of displeasing *Ieyasu* caused him to abandon his faith. — His descendants remained at *Fuchū* (*Tsushima* — 100,000 k.) till the Restoration. — Now Count.

Sōami, 宗 阿 彌 . Painter, poet and professor of the tea ceremony, was much esteemed by the *Shōgun Yoshimasa* (15th century).

Soba-shū, 側 衆 . Under the *Tokugawa, samurai* on duty at the Palace of *Edo*.—Among them, some had to read the reports of the *Rōjū* to the *Shōgun*, and to write down the observations he made ; they were called *Goyō-o-toritsugi.* They settled in advance the days of audience of the *daimyō* and the *hatamoto*. After a period judged sufficiently long, the *Sobashū* were usually raised to the rank of *Waka-doshiyori.* The custom for each *Shōgun* to raise one *Soba-shū* to the rank of a *daimyō*, began at the commencement of the 18th century.

Sobo-ga-take, 祖 母 嶽 . Mountain (1750 m.) on the boundaries of *Bungo, Higo* and *Hyūga ;* it is the highest mountain of *Kyūshū.* Also called *Uba-ga-take.*

Sōdō-shū, 曹 洞 宗 . Branch of the *Zen-shū* sect, brought from China in 1228 by the bonze *Dōgen (Shōyō-Daishi).* Its principal temple was the *Eihei-ji* temple *(Echizen)* and at present it numbers in Japan 13,700 temples, 11,000 bonzes and chiefs of temples, and 5,350,000 adherents.

Soejima, 副 嶋 . *Samurai* family descended from *Takeshiuchi no Sukune,* and through him from the emperor *Kōgen* (275-198 B.C.).

—— **Iname,** 稻 目 (+ 570). Was minister under the emperors *Senkwa* and *Kimmei.* In 552, the king of *Kudara* had sent some Buddhist statues as a present to the emperor , who asked the advice of his ministers on the subject. *Iname* answered : " These gods are honored in all the Western countries ; how could Japan afford to refuse to venerate them ? " But the other ministers, *Mononobe Ogoshi* and *Nakatomi Kamako,* were of different opinion. The emperor then gave the presents received from Korea to *Inabe,* and the latter erected the first Buddhist temple in his house which was called *Kōgen-ji.*

—— **Umako,** 馬 子 (+ 626). Son of *Iname,* was minister under the reigns of *Bidatsu, Yōmei, Sushun* and *Suiko.* In 584, more objects of the Buddhist cult having been sent from Korea, they were given to *Umako* who built a temple for them not in his house but in the village of *Ishikawa.* Before dying, *Yōmei* resolved to become a Buddhist : *Mononobe Moriya* did all in his power to make the emperor change his mind, but the counsels of *Umako* prevailed. *Yōmei* died a Buddhist, and immediately after his death, the two parties, each presenting its own candidate to the throne, came to blows. Under cover of religion, two rival families disputed the preeminence. A battle took place on mount *Shigisen* and the *Mononobe* were completely defeated, Buddhism triumphed with the *Soga.* The following year (588), *Umako* built the *Hōkō-ji,* and the new religion was on a fair way to prosperity. The emperor *Sushun,* however, strongly resented the independence with which his minister was acting and resolved to get rid of him, wherefore he gathered troops in his palace : *Umako,* having been apprised of the fact assassinated the emperor and replaced him by his sister *Suiko* (592), under whose reign he ruled together with prince *Shōtoku-taishi.*

—— **Emishi,** 蝦 夷 (+ 645). Son of *Umako,* was minister under the reigns of *Jomei* and *Kōgyoku.* At the death of *Suiko,* he rejected prince *Yamashiro* son of *Shōtoku-taishi*, and raised *Tamura no Ōji* (*Jomei*) to the throne. His influence was predominant during that reign. Having become ill, he transferred his office to his son. Both were after-wards assassinated.

—— **Iruka, 入鹿** (+ 645). Son of *Emishi*, after having in con-junction with his father secured the throne to the widow of *Jomei* (641), chose as her successor prince *Furuhito no Ōe*, relative of the *Soga*. But prince *Yamashiro* was an obstacle to this plan: *Iruka* therefore had him assassinated (643). This crime brought matters to a climax for the *Soga* were univer-sally hated. Prince *Naka no Ōe* (later on *Tenchi-tennō*) and *Nakatomi Kamatari* resolved to get rid of the *Soga*, and chosing a certain reception day when the Korean ambassadors were pre-sented to the Em-press, some of con-spirators entered the *Daigoku - den*, and under the eyes of the Empress, despatched *Iruka*, whilst others went to murder *Emi-shi* in his own house. —This was the end of the *Soga's* power; they had governed the land during a century: The *Fujiwara* soon after replaced them.

MURDER OF SOGA IRUKA.

Iname - Umako { Emishi · · Iruka
{ Kuramaro- { Akae
{ Kurayamada

—— **Akae, 赤兄**. Grandson of *Umako* and son of *Kuramaro*, was ordered in 658, to repress the revolt of prince *Arima*, who was aspir-ing to the throne. He besieged him in his house and put him to death.

Later, he was *Sadaijin* (671), but was banished by *Temmu-tennō* because he had sided with *Kōbun* (672).

— **Kurayamada Ishikawa-maro,** 倉山田石川麿. Brother to *Akae*, joined *Nakatomi Kamatari* against *Emishi* and *Iruka*, and was named *Udaijin* (645). He was the first to bear that title which had just been created. He took a leading part in the *Taikwa* reform ; but being calumniated to the emperor *Kōtoku*, he was put to death with all the members of his family. Afterwards his innocence was proved.

Soga, 曾我. *Samurai* family of the *Yanagawa* clan (*Chikugo*) made noble after the Restoration. — Now Viscount.

Soga Sukenari, 曾我祐成 . (1172-1193) ⎫ Grandsons of *Itō Su-*
Soga Tokimune, 曾我時致 . (1174-1193) ⎭ *kechika*. Their father *Sukeyasu* was murdered by his relative *Kudō Suketsune* (1177) and their mother then married *Soga Sukenobu,* who adopted the 2 children and gave them his name. While still young they had determined to avenge their father. But *Suketsune* was the favorite of *Yoritomo,* who, was much displeased with *Sukechika* for not having embraced his cause. He sent *Kagesue* to *Soga Kajiwara* with orders to bring the two children to *Kamakura.* He intended to put them to death but on the entreaties of *Kagesue, Hatakeyama Shigetada* and *Wada Yoshimori,* he agreed to spare their lives and sent them back to their mother. *Tokimune* became a disciple of the bonze *Gyōjitsu* of *Hakone ;* but at the age of 16, he secretly fled from the temple and joined his brother, and together, they sought protection from *Hōjō Tokimasa.* One day, *Yoritomo* being on a hunting expedition at the foot of Mount *Fuji,* they penetrated into his camp and and came to the tent of *Suketsune.* He was absent, but *Honda Chika-tsune,* a *kerai* of the *Hatakeyama,* told them where he was, and at once they fell upon him and put him to death. *Sukenari* was killed on the spot by *Nitta Tadatsune,* but *Tokimune* was arrested by a certain *Gorō-maru,* and led before *Yoritomo,* who, admiring his boldness, would have pardoned him, but *Inufusamaru,* son of *Suketsune,* interfered and he was put to death.—Such is, briefly, the story of the *Soga* brothers' vengeance (*Sukenari* or *Jūrō* and *Tokimune* or *Gorō*) to commemorate which, poetry, romance, and even the theatre vie with one another.

Sogen, 祖元 (1226-1286). Bonze, founder of the *Engaku-ji* temple (*Kamakura*), subdivision of the *Rinzai* branch of the *Zenshū* sect. Invited by *Hōjō Tokimune,* he came from China in 1279, and, 3 years after, was chief of this large temple, which *Tokimune* had just erected. He has received the posthumous title of *Bukkō-Zenji.*

Sogō, 十河 . In *Sanuki.* Old castle, in the 16th century occupied, by a family of the same name, descended from the *Miyoshi.* Was abandoned in 1586.

Sōgō, 僧綱 . The 3 highest dignities of the Buddhist hierarchy : *Sōjō, Sōzu* and *Risshi.*—See *Sō-kwan.*

Sō-go-shoku, 僧五職 . The 5 principal offices of a Buddhist monastery : *Jimu, Kengyō, Bettō, Zasu* and *Chōja.*

Sōhei, 僧兵 . Formerly, mercenaries maintained by large temples to protect their domains and to fight rival sects. The *Hieizan (Enryaku-*

ji) monastery, was the first to engage them, and the *sōhei* often caused trouble in the capital. The *Kōfuku-ji* of *Nara* and the *Mii-dera*, also had their standing army, commanded by bonzes, and the emperors had

SŌHEI-

to call on the power of the *Minamoto* to repress the disorders occasioned by their pretensions.

Sō-i, 僧位. — See *Sō-kwan*.

Sō-jitō, 總地頭. — See *Sōryō-jitō*.

Sōjō, 僧正. — See *Sō-kwan*.

Sōjō Henjō, 僧正遍照. — See *Yoshimune Munesada*.

Sōkoku-ji, 相國寺. Or *Shōkoku-ji*. Temple founded in 1383 by the *Shōgun Yoshimitsu* in order to receive the remains of the *Ashikaga*. It became the headquarters of the 10 branches of the *Rinzai* sect. The chief bonze for several centuries possessed great influence and his advice was often sought concerning governmental affairs.

Sokue, 觸穢. Formerly a state requiring purification. Death, funeral, pregnancy, child birth, etc. were its principal causes. Those who contracted it, had to be purified by abstinence and ablutions. During this state, it was forbidden to enter the Palace or even to have intercourse with anybody. This practice was abolished at the Restoration.

Soku-i, 即位. Announcement ceremony made to the people at the accession of a new emperor. At first the enthronement and the proclamation were made at the same time. From the 9th century, there were two distinct ceremonies, the *senso* (See this word) and the *soku-i*. This last was very solemn, and took place at the *Daigoku-den*. Formerly soothsayers (*on-yō-shi*) selected a propitious day, officials were named to partake in the ceremony, prayers were offered at the Shintoist and Buddhist shrines. Special envoys were sent to announce it at the *Ise* temple, as also at the tombs of the emperors and of some important personages. On the day of the *soku-i*, the Emperor gave his predecessor and the dowager empress an honorary name (*songō*). Later on the ceremony was preformed at the *Shishin-den*.

Sō-kwan, 僧官. Dignities in the Buddhist hierarchy. The most exalted is that of the *Sōjō*, which comprises 3 degrees: *Dai-sōjō* (created in 745 for *Gyōgi*), *Sōjō* (created in 624 for *Kwanroku*) and *Gon-sōjō*. The *Dai-sōjō* had the rank of *Dainagon*; the *Sōjō*, that of *Chūnagon*; the *Gonsōjō*, that of *Sangi*. — The second grade is that of *Sōzu*, which comprises 4 degrees: *Daisōzu* (created in 673 for *Dōshō*), *Gon-dai-sōzu*, *Shō-sōzu* (created in 673 for *Gisei*) and *Gōn-shō-sōzu*. — The third grade is that of *Risshi*, also created in 673 and later on divided into 3 degrees: *Dai-risshi*, *Chū-risshi*, and *Gon-risshi*. — The other titles (*Sō-i*) in use among the bonzes were those of *Hōkyō* (bridge of the law), *Hō-in* (seal of the law), *Hōgen* (eye of the the law), *Ajari* (spiritual master), *Zasu* (master of the seat), *Shuza* (principal seat), etc. The titles *Hōshi*, *Kokushi* and *Daishi* were only given after death.

Sōma, 相馬. In *Shimōsa*. Was the residence of the *Toki daimyō* (1600-1616), then of the *Honda* (1616-1723).

Sōma, 相馬. *Daimyō* family descended from *Taira Masakado*. From 1590 to 1868, it resided at *Nakamura* (*Mutsu* — 60,000 k.). — Now Viscount.

Somayama, 杣山. Ancient castle of *Echizen*, wherein *Nitta Yoshisada* sought shelter after the capture of *Kanasaki* (1337): from there, he set out to fight *Shiba Takatsune* at *Fujishima*, where he met his death.

Sonchō-hōshinnō, 尊澄法親王. — See *Munenaga-Shinnō*.

Sone, 曾根. *Samurai* family of the *Yamaguchi* clan (*Suwō*) made noble in 1902. — Now Baron.

Son-en-hōshinnō, 尊圓法親王 (1298-1356). 6th son of the emperor *Fushimi*. Was called *Morihiko*. Became bonze and chief (*zasu*) of the *Tendai* sect and was the 17th abbot of the *Seiren-in* temple. He had taken lessons in writing from *Fujiwara Yukifusa* in the *Seson-ji* temple, and some time later, established a school which was called *On-ke-ryū*.

Sōnin, 奏任. — See *Kwan-tō*.

Sonnō-jōi, 尊王攘夷. "Respect to the emperor and out with the Barbarians:" the rallying cry of the *Shōgun's* opponents at the time of the Restoration.

Sono, 園. *Kuge* family descended from *Fujiwara Yorimune* (993-1055). — Now Count.

Sonobe, 園部. In *Tamba*. Was from 1619 to 1868, the residence of the *Koide daimyō* (30,000 k.).

Sonoda, 園田. *Samurai* family of *Kagoshima* (*Satsuma*) made noble in 1897. — Now Baron.

Sonoike, 園地. *Kuge* family descended from *Fujiwara* (*Sanjō*) *Saneyuki* (1083-1162). — Now Viscount.

Sonokara-kami no matsuri, 園韓神祭. Formerly a feast celebrated at the *Kunai-shō* in honor of *Omononushi, Sukunabikona*. etc.

Son-un-hōshinnō, 尊雲法親王. — See *Morinaga-shinnō*.

Sorori Shinzaemon, 曾呂利新左衛門 (+1603). Born in *Izumi*, his trade was to make scabbards, but he also studied poetry, the tea ceremony etc., and was for 30 years, one of the favorites of *Hideyoshi*. He is also called *Sōyū*, that being the name he took when he shaved his head.

Sōryō-jitō, 總領地頭. Or **Sō-jitō.** The *Jitō* were the chiefs of the *shō-en* : those who possessed several *shō-en* appointed several *Jitō*, over whom a *Soryō-jitō* was placed. *Yoritomo* brought things back to their primitive state by reducing the number of of *shō-en*.

Sosei-Hōshi, 素性法師. — See *Yoshimine Hironobu*.

Soseki, 疎石 (1271-1346). Born in *Ise*, he was a descendant of the emperor *Uda* in the 9th generation. At the age of 4, he lost his mother and was placed in the temple of *Hirashio-yama* (*Kai*) under the guardianship of the bonze *Kū-a*. When 18 years old, he shaved his head and was named *Chikaku*. One night, he dreamed he was visiting the two famous temples *Sozan* and *Sekitō* in China : he then took the name of *Soseki*. In 1325, *Go-Daigo* received him at Court ; the following year, he founded the *Zen-ō-ji* temple (*Ise*), then in 1342, the *Tenryū-ji* (*Yamashiro*) which became the headquarters of a branch of the *Rinzai-shū* sect. *Soseki* was a distinguished poet. His posthumous name is *Musōkokushi*.

Sōsha-ban, 奏者番. Under the *Tokugawa Shōgun*, an official whose duty it was to introduce the *samurai* to audience with the *Shōgun* at New Year and certain festivals (*sekku*), to read the list of presents given by the *Shōgun*, to regulate the details of the ceremony etc. Created in 1632, this office was discharged by two *Sōsha-ban*, but their number was subsequently raised to 24, who performed their duties by turn. In 1658, the *Jisha-bugyō* exercised it in connection with his own office. It was suppressed in 1862.

Sōshi, 壯士. Unprincipled youths, who, not unlike the ancient *rōnin*, offer their services to whosoever has need of them. They especially attach themselves to politicians and play an important part during elections.

Sōshin-in, 崇親院. School established in 860 at *Kyōto* by the *Sadaijin Yoshisuke* for young ladies of the *Fujiwara* family.

Sōshū, 相州. Chinese name of *Sagami* province.

Sōshū, 總州. Chinese name of the united provinces of *Kazusa* and *Shimōsa*.

Sōsō go-kun, 草創五君. The 5 great statesmen, who, at different times, have created some new political organization : *Minamoto Yoritomo, Ashikaga Takauji, Oda Nobunaga, Toyotomi Hideyoshi* and *Tokugawa Ieyasu*.

Sotōri-hime, 衣通姫. Or *Oto-hime*. Younger sister of the empress *Osaka no Ōnakatsu-hime*, wife of *Inkyō-tennō* (412-453). She was remarkable for her beauty; for this reason, *Inkyō* gave her the *Fujiwara* Palace (*Yamato*), and created a special bodyguard for her, called *Fujiwara-be*, which was recruited from all the provinces.

SOTŌRI-HIME.

Sōtsuibushi, 總追捕使. In 1185, *Yoritomo* sent to all the provinces, high officials who replaced the governors. These officials were called *sōtsuibushi* (later on they were called *shugo*), and *Yoritomo* himself was known by the title of *Nihon-sōtsuibushi* or 66 *koku no sōtsui-bushi*.

Sōya, 宗谷. Small city of *Hokkaidō*, chief town of *Kitami* province.

Sōya-kaikyō, 宗谷海峡. Strait which separates *Hokkaidō* from *Karafuto* (Saghalien island). Also called Strait of La Perouse by Europeans.

Sōya-misaki, 宗谷岬. Cape N. of *Kitami*; it is the most northern point of *Hokkaidō*.

So-yō-chō, 租庸調. The 3 kinds of taxes formerly levied on the farmers. The 1st was the tax on rice, which at times rose as high as 4 per cent. of the harvest: it was called *so* or *denso*. The second was levied on silk, cotton, vegetables, fish, etc.: it was the *chō*. Lastly, each adult was obliged annually to perform 10 days of statute-labor, which were called *sai-eki*. In case of failure to do the work, a fine of about 9 m. of cotton cloth was imposed: this tax was called the *yō*. Two youths or 4 children had to pay the same impost as an adult.

Sōzu, 僧都. Buddhist dignity.—See *Sō-kwan*.

Sōzu-gawa, 三途川. Or *Sanzu-gawa*, or *Mitsuse-gawa*. River of the Buddhist hell. On its shores the old *Shōzuka* is stealing the clothes of little children.

Sue Harukata, 陶晴賢 (+ 1555). Vassal of *Ōuchi Yoshitaka*, *daimyō* of *Yamaguchi* (*Suwō*). This *daimyō*, having received into his castle many *kuge*, who had been expelled from the capital, devoted his time to literature and amusements in vogue at Court, but neglected military exercises and the administration of his provinces. His principal *kerai*, *Mōri*, *Sue*, *Sugi*, *Naitō*, complained to him about it, but in vain. In 1550, *Harukata* left *Yamaguchi* returning to his domains; he gathered some troops in his castles of *Tomita* and *Wakayama*, and prepared to rise against his lord. The following year, he even attacked *Yoshitaka* and stormed *Yamaguchi*: *Yoshitaka* fled to *Fukawa* (*Nagato*), where he was soon after besieged by the rebel and killed himself. *Harukata* then chose a successor in the person of the brother of *Ōtomo Sōrin*, who took the name of *Ōuchi Yoshinaga* and allowed his protector to rule as he pleased. Some vassals leagued against him but *Harukata* at once besieged *Sagara Taketō* in his castle of *Hanao* and having taken him prisoner, put him to death, but being in turn attacked by *Mōri Motonari*, he was defeated and killed at *Itsukushima* (1555).

Suematsu, 末松. Family of the *Fukuoka* clan (*Chikuzen*) made noble in 1895. — Now Baron.

Suemori, 末森. In *Owari*. Old castle of the *Oda daimyō*. After *Nobuhide's* death (1549), it passed into the hands of *Nobuyuki*, who was besieged there and killed by his brother *Nobunaga* in 1557.

Suemori, 末森. In *Noto*, near the present village of *Kashiwazaki*. Old castle of the *Toki daimyō*. *Yuza Tsugumitsu* who occupied it in 1550, was deprived of it by *Shibata Katsuie* (1580). Passed then to the *Maeda* of *Kaga* (1584) and was abandoned.

Suga, 須賀. In *Izumo*. *Susano-o no mikoto* retired there.

Suganuma, 菅沼. Ancient *daimyō* family coming from *Mikawa* and descended from *Fujiwara*.

—— **Sadamitsu,** 定盈 (1542-1604). Served the *Imagawa*, then the *Tokugawa* and in 1601, received the fief of *Nagashima* (*Ise* — 20,000 k.).

—— **Sadayoshi,** 定芳. Son of *Sadamitsu*, in 1619 was transferred to *Zeze* (*Ōmi*), then in 1634, to *Kameyama* (*Tamba* — 40,000 k.).—The family became extinct in 1647.

Sugawara, 菅原. Family of unknown extraction (some historians claim it to have descended from *Nomi no Sukune*) whose members, through their talents and merits, attained the highest dignities.

—— **Kiyogimi,** 清公 (770-842). At first attached to the Imperial Prince, passed several years in China and, on his return, was named *Owari no suke*. He applied to this province the mode of governing which he had found used by the *Tō* (China) and suppressed corporal punishments. Named *Daigaku no kami*, he reformed the University regulations and endeavored to introduce Chinese customs in the administration, ceremonies, etc.

—— **Koreyoshi,** 是善 (812-880). Son of *Kiyogimi*, who like his father, was preceptor of the Imperial Prince, professor of literature (*bunshō-hakase*) and rector of the University.

—— **Michizane,** 道眞 (845-903). Son of *Koreyoshi*, exercised great influence upon the emperor *Uda*. He endeavored with all his might to diminish the power of the *Fujiwara* and to reestablish the Imperial authority. Named *Dainagon*, (897) and *Ukon-e-taishō*, he advised *Uda* to abdicate in favor of his son *Daigo*. He then became *Udaijin* and governed together with the *Sadaijin Fujiwara Tokihira*. But the favor shown to him by the two emperors, soon gave umbrage to the other ministers, who leagued against him. The *Fujiwara, Tokihira, Sadakuni* and *Sugane*, united with *Minamoto Hikaru* accused *Michizane* of plotting to dethrone the emperor and of attempting to elevate his own son-in-law, prince *Tokiyo-shinnō*, brother to *Daigo*. The emperor gave credence to these calumnies, and *Michizane* was disgraced and sent to *Tsukushi* with the title of *Dazai no gon-no-sotsu* (901). On hearing the news, the ex-emperor *Uda*, hastened to the Palace to beg his son to reconsider his decision, but upon his arrival he found all doors closed and could not gain admission. *Michizane* survived his exile only two years. His greatest consolation was to ascend Mount *Tempai-zan*, and there, with his face turned towards *Kyōto*, to venerate the master who had disgraced him. People honor him under the names of *Kan Shōjō*, *Tenjin*, *Temmangū*, etc. 20 years after his death, he was reestablished in all his dignities and received the title of *Sadaijin*, then of the *Dajō-daijin*. At *Kyōto*, the temple of *Kitano* is consecrated to his honor. During his ministry, *Michizane* was able to suppress the embassies periodically sent to China (894). — *Michizane* is the ancestor of the *kuge* families *Gojō* and *Takatsuji*, and of the *daimyō* *Maeda* of *Kaga*.

SUGAWARA MICHIZANE.

Sugeno Mamichi, 菅野眞道. Descendant of the prince of *Kudara Shinson-Ō*, who settled in Japan. Was preceptor of the Imperial Prince and one of the principal editors of the *Shoku-Nihon-ki* (797). Received the titles of *Mimbu-kyō*, *Ōkura-kyō*, *Ōmi no kami*, etc. Died at the age of 74.

Sugi, 杉. *Samurai* family of the *Yamaguchi* clan (*Suwō*) made noble in 1887. — Now Viscount.

Sugihara, 杉原. Ancient *daimyō* family descended from *Taira Sadamori*. In 1601, it obtained the fief of *Toyo-oka* (*Tajima* — 35,000 k.), and became extinct in 1653.

Sugita Gempaku, 杉田玄伯 (1733-1817). Famous doctor. Together with *Maeno Ryōtaku*, he translated some Dutch books on medecine and surgery, and instructed a great number of scholars.

Sugitani, 杉溪. Family descended from *Fujiwara Uona* and by right of inheritance belonging to the *Kōfuku-ji* temple (*Nara*). — Now Baron.

Suguri, 村主. In olden times, chief of a village chosen among the most prominent inhabitants.

Suijin, 水神. God of the water, springs, wells, etc. (*Shintō*).

Suiko-tennō, 推古天皇. Empress (33) of Japan (593-628). *Toyo-mike-kashikiya-hime*, 3rd daughter of *Kimmei-tennō*, succeeded her brother *Sushun*, when she was 39 years old. In 576, she married the emperor *Bidatsu*, her brother from her father's side. *Bidatsu* was succeeded by his two brothers *Yōmei* and *Sushun*. At the death of the latter, *Suiko* ascended the throne. It was the first time that an empress as such ruled in Japan (*Jingō-kōgō* did not reign, but acted as regent for her son *Ōjin*). She placed the administration in the hands of her nephew, and encouraged him in all his efforts to implant Buddhism in the country. On her mother's side she descended from the *Soga*, who during her reign enjoyed unlimited influence. *Suiko* died at the age of 75.

Suikotō, 出擧稻. Formerly a custom very much in use and consisting in borrowing grains or other objects for a certain time and in returning them with interest. According to the *Taihō* code (702), a farmer who had borrowed seeds in spring, was obliged to return double the amount after the harvest.

Suinin-tennō, 垂仁天皇 11th Emperor of Japan (29 B. C. — 70 A. D.). *Ikume-iri-hiko-isachi*, 3rd son of *Sujin-tennō*, succeeded him at the age of 40. He repressed the revolt of his brother-in-law *Sao-hiko*, who tried to seize the throne (25 B. C), built the first temple of *Ise* (5 B. C.) and substituted earthen statues for the human victims which it was customary to immolate on the tombs of emperors and high personages. *Suinin*, according to tradition, died at the age of 139, after a reign of over 100 years.

Suisei-tennō, 綏靖天皇 2nd Emperor of Japan (581-549 B. C.). *Kamu-nuna-kawa-mimi* or *Takenu-kawa-mimi*, 3rd son of *Jimmu-tennō*, succeeded his father at the age of 51. During the interregnum of 3 years consecrated to mourning that followed *Jimmu's* death, a son, *Tagishi-mimi*, born of a first wife, tried to seize the throne but was defeated and killed by *Kamu-ya-i-mimi*, a brother of *Suisei*. History does not give any particulars about his reign of 33 years.

Suitengū, 水天宮. Temples erected in several places to the gods of the sea. These gods are difficult to identify : there are the Vedic god *Varuna*, the Shintoist gods of *Sumiyoshi* (*Settsu*), the young emperor *Antoku* and those who perished with him in the billows of *Dan-no-ura*, etc.

Sujin-tennō, 崇神天皇 10th Emperor of Japan (97-30 B. C.). *Mimaki-iri-hiko-inie*, 2nd son of *Kaikwa-tennō* whom he succeeded when 52 years old. In 92 B. C. he built a temple dedicated to *Amaterasu-ō-mikami*, at *Kasanui* (*Yamato*) into which were conveyed the 3 sacred emblems or Imperial treasures, till then kept at the Palace itself his daughter *Toyosuki-iri-hime* became the first priestess (*saigū*) of the place. He created 4 *Shōgun* to repel the *Ebisu* (88). His reign, the first about which history gives any details, was a period of organization. Taxes were fixed, lakes and canals dug, boats built, the census of the population taken, etc. During his reign the first embassy from *Mimana* (Korea) (87) came to Japan. *Sujin* is said to have died at the age of 119 years.

Suke, 介. Formerly a title signifying substitute, taking the place of ; and corresponding to the word " vice " before a noun : for inst. : *Hitachi no suke* — vice-governor of *Hitachi*, etc. There were two degrees, *dai* and *shō* or *ōi* and *sunai*.

Sukehito-shinnō, 典仁親王 (1733-1794). Son of prince *Kanin Naohito* and grandson of the emperor *Higashi-yama*. *Go-Momozono* having died without an heir, *Kanehito*, son of *Sukehito* was raised to the throne (*Kōkaku-tennō*). At the death of the latter, his son wished to give him the title of *Dajō-tennō*, but the *Shōgun* opposed it, and it is only since 1884, that he received it together with the name of *Kyōkō-tennō*.

Sukiya-gashira, 数寄屋頭. Under the *Tokugawa*, title given to 3 officials who attended to the arrangements of the tea ceremony at the Palace of the *Shōgun*. Subject to them were the *fukuro-shi, haritsuke-shi, furo-shi, kama-shi, himono-shi, hyōgu-shi*, etc.

Sukō-tennō, 崇光天皇. Emperor of the Northern dynasty (1349-1352). — *Okihito*, son of *Kōgon* succeeded his uncle *Kōmyō* at the age of 15. His short reign was troubled by the war between the two dynasties. In 1352 by a daring exploit, the generals of the South, *Kitabatake*

Akiyoshi and *Kusunoki Masanori* penetrated into *Kyōto* and took *Sukō* and his two predecessors prisoners. The *Shōgun Yoshiakira* then chose *Go-Kōgon*, brother of *Sukō*, to succeed him. *Sukō* was liberated 5 years after (1357) and died in the year 1398, at the age of 65.

Sukuna-bikona, 彦少名. *Shintō* god. Son of *Takamimusubi no kami*. He helped *Ōkuninushi* to establish his authority over the country of *Izumo*, before *Nimigi no mikoto* descended from heaven to rule Japan. He taught man sorcery and the use of medicines.

Sukune, 宿禰. One of the 8 classes (*hassei*) of nobles and officials created by the emperor *Temmu* (682). The title signifies noble, gentleman, and was added to the family name: *Nomi no Sukune, Takeshiuchi no Sukune*, etc.

Sukuri, 首里. Ancient name for the port of *Shuri* (*Okinawa*).

Suma, 須磨. Village in *Settsu*, on *Akashi* strait. Often praised in poetry on account of the beauty of its scenery.

Sumera, 皇. *Sumeragi, Suberagi, Subera, Sube*: all equivalent terms signifying " He who rules under the heavens " and was applied to Shintoist gods and to emperors. Arguing from a similarity of sound, some authors have thought the name *Sumera* was a corruption of *Semiramis*, in which case the goddess *Amaterasu* would be none other than the great queen of Babylon, and the invaders of Japan of the 7th century before our era were the Assyrians, who left their country willingly or by force. This is of course only a supposition, and as it includes so many unknown quantities, it admits of no early solution.

Sumida-gawa, 隅田川. River (290 Km.) which rises at the foot of *Kobushi-yama*, on the boundaries of *Musashi, Kai, Shinano* and *Kōzuke*. Is first called *Nakatsu-kawa*, then *Ara-kawa* and lastly *Sumida-gawa*. Passes *Kumagai, Urawa* and enters the bay of *Tōkyō* after passing through the E. part of the capital. Also called *Ō-kawa, Asakusa-gawa, Miyato-gawa*.

Suminoe, 住江. Or *Sumiyoshi*. In *Settsu*, between *Ōsaka* and *Sakai*. This famous Shintoist temple was first built by *Jingō-kōgō*, in *Chikuzen* in honor of the gods of the sea, who had aided him in his expedition against Korea. It was removed to its present site by the emperor *Nintoku* in the 4th century. It received many domains, and the *Tsumori* family in whose keeping it was, enjoyed great influence. During more than 10 years (1360-1372), it served as an asylum for *Go-Murakami* the emperor of the South. From there, *Shimazu Yoshihiro*, who had been defeated at *Sekigahara* (1600), took ship in order to return to *Hyūga*. There also *Ieyasu* remained during the 1st siege of *Ōsaka* (1614).

Suminoe no Nakatsu-Ōji, 住江仲皇子 (+400). Son of the emperor *Nintoku*, who, after the death of his father, tried to seize the throne. He was defeated and killed by his brother *Mizuha-wake* (later on *Hanshō-tennō*).

Suminokura Ryōi, 角倉了以 (1554-1614). Son of *Yoshida Sōkei*, physician of *Saga* (*Yamashiro*). He became an engineer. In 1603, by order of *Ieyasu* he built a large ship for trade with Annam. Later he converted the river *Ōi-gawa* into a canal, cleared the rapids of

Hōzu and opened the river to navigation ; when the *Daibutsu* temple was
built (1608), all the material was conveyed to *Kyōto* by this water way.
He likewise opened the *Kamo-gawa* to navigation (1611). In 1614, he
received the order to convert the *Fuji-kawa* into a canal, but he fell sick
and his son *Genshi* replaced him. Navigation on that river dates from
that time. *Ryōi* died in the same year at the age of 61.

Sūmitsu-in, 樞密院. Privy Council of the Emperor, created in
1888. In 1904, its members numbered 24.

Sumiyoshi, 住吉. — See *Suminoe.*

Sumiyoshi, 住吉. School of painting derived from that of *Tosa.*
It is represented by : *Hiromichi* (1599-1670) *Hirozumi* (1631-1705),
Hironatsu (1644-1735), *Hiroyasu* (1666-1750), *Hiromori* (1705-1777),
Hiroyuki (1754-1811), *Hironao* (1781-1828), *Hirotsura* (1793-1863).

Sumō-bugyō, 相撲奉行. During the *Kamakura* shogunate,
officials whose duty it was to organize and to preside over wrestling
matches (*sumō*) which took place at the Palace of the *Shōgun* or in the
enclosure of the *Hachiman* temple (*Tsuru-ga-oka*.).

Sumō-shiki, 相撲式. Wrestling matches which took place at the
Imperial Palace on the 7th and 8th days of the 7th month. The origin of
these contests is due to *Nomi no Sukune*, and his descendants, the *Sugawara*, had the supervision thereof.

Sumō-zukasa, 相撲司. Formerly officials charged to organize
wrestling contests in the Imperial Palace. As there were two sets of
wrestlers, so there was a *Sa-sumō-zukasa* and a *U-sumō-zukasa.*

Sumoto, 洲本. Principal city (8750 inh.) of *Awaji* island. Old
castle, was the residence of the *Wakizaka daimyō* during the 16th century.
Under the *Tokugawa*, it belonged to the *Ikeda* (1613) and the *Hachisuka* (1615-1868).

Sumpu, 駿府. Old name of the town of *Shizuoka* (*Suruga*).

Sumpu-jōdai, 駿府城代. Under the *Tokugawa Shōgun*, official
who guarded the castle of *Sumpu*, attended to its repairs, administered the domains that belonged to it, etc. As he was generally
chosen from among the *Ōban-gashira*, he lived in the castle with his
family and every 5 or 6 years came to *Edo*, to give an account of his
administration to the *Shōgun.*

Sumpu-kaban, 駿府加番. Title created in 1633 and given to 2
officials who assisted the *Sumpu-jōdai*. They were changed every year
in the 6th month.

Sunomata, 墨股. In *Mino*. During his expedition against *Saitō
Tatsuoki*, *Nobunaga* built a castle there (1562) which he entrusted to the
care of *Kinoshita Tōkichirō* (later *Hideyoshi*). *Tatsuoki* besieged the
castle without success. Later it belonged to *Ikeda Nobuteru*, and was
finally abandoned.

Sunshū, 駿州. Chinese name of *Suruga* province.

Suri-age-hara, 摺上原. Plain in *Iwashiro*, in which *Masamune*
defeated *Ashina Yoshihiro* (1589).

Suribari-tōge, 麿針峠. Mountain road N. E. of *Ōmi*, at the top
of which is the village of *Bamba*. In 1333, *Hōjō Nakatoki* and *Tokimasu*

the two governors of *Kyōto*, making their escape to *Kamakura*, were arrested there and killed themselves. *Rokkaku Sadayori* there defeated *Asai Sukemasa* (1526). In 1600, *Kobayakawa Hideaki* and *Ii Naomasa* from this place besieged the castle of *Sawayama*, which belonged to *Ishida Kazushige*.

Suruga, 駿河. One of the 15 provinces of *Tōkaidō*. Comprises 5 districts. — Chinese name : *Sunshū.* — Now belongs to *Shizuoka-ken*.

Suruga-Dainagon, 駿河大納言. — See *Tokugawa Tadanaga*.

Suruga - wan, 駿河湾. Gulf between the coasts of *Suruga* and the *Izu* peninsula.

Susaka, 須坂. In *Shinano*. Ancient castle in the 16th century belonging to the *Takanashi* family. Was from 1615 to 1868, the residence of the *Hori daimyō* (now, *Okuda*) (10,000 k.).

Susaka no ōji, 朱雀大路. Formerly a large street running from N. to S. and dividing *Kyōto* into two parts; it began at the southern gate (*Susaka -mon*) of the Imperial Palace and ended at the southern exterior gate (*Rakujō-mon*) of the city. — The same existed formerly at *Nara*.

Susano-o, 須佐之男. *Shintō* god. Born from the nose of *Izanagi*. From his youth he had a violent character (this being the signification of his name);

SUSANO-O'S ARRIVAL IN IZUMO

or was at least very eccentric, for he rooted up trees, put forests on fire, etc.

His father sent him to a country called *Ne no kuni* (*Izumo?*) : he asked and obtained permission to visit his sister *Amaterasu* before leaving. Having arrived at the *Takama-ga-hara*, he committed great extravagances, sowing cockle in the fields, destroying the harvests, going so far as to outrage his sister who retired into a cave, leaving the world in darkness. For all these misdeeds, *Susano-o* was exiled and went to *Izumo*, where having triumphed over the dreadful *Yamata no orochi* (serpent with 8 heads), he married *Kushi-Inada-hime*, daughter of *Ashinazuchi* and *Tenazuchi*, and settled in *Suga*. His descendants governed the region of *Izumo* and very likely enlarged their domains, since *Amaterasu* was obliged to send her grandchild *Ninigi* to recover her inheritance. --- *Susano-o* is honored by some as a god of the sea by others as the god of the moon. He is also venerated by the name of *Gozu-tennō* (the emperor with the ox head). His temples are called *Gion* in the *Ryōbu-shintō* and *Yasaka* in the pure Shintoism.

Sushun-tennō, 崇峻天皇. 32nd Emperor of Japan (588-592). *Hatsuse-be-wakasazaki*, 12th son of *Kimmei-tennō*, succeeded his brother *Yōmei* at the age of 68. At the death of the latter, *Mononobe Moriya* and *Nakatomi Katsumi* proposed prince *Anaho*, who like themselves was an enemy to Buddhism but the *Soga* supported *Hatsusebe*, their relative. Victory favored the *Soga*. *Soga Umako* soon after showed such arrogance that *Sushun* resolved to get rid of him, but the powerful minister was informed of the plot and had the emperor assassinated — It was during his reign that scales or balances were imported from China to Japan,

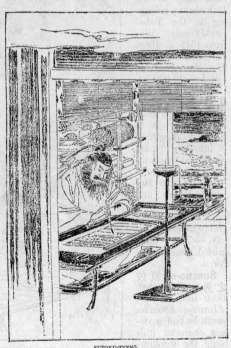

SUTOKU-TENNŌ.

and that for the first time, tiles were used for roofing the temple *Hōkō-ji*.

Sutoku-tennō, 崇徳天皇. 75th Emperor of Japan (1124-1141). *Akihito*, eldest son of *Toba-tennō* succeeded his father at the age of 5. His great-grandfather, *Shirakawa*, and later his father, in company, with *Taira Tadamori* their favorite acted as regents. In 1136, *Toba* had a son by his favorite wife, *Bifuku-mon-in* (*Fujiwara Toku-ko*), and 6 months later, had him named heir presumptive ; he then obliged *Sutoku* to resign in favor of his younger brother (*Konoe-tennō*) who, crowned when 2 years of age, died at 17. *Toba* now raised another of his sons *Go-Shira-kawa* to the throne but *Sutoku*, aided by *Fujiwara Yorinaga*, tried to seize the crown. The great *daimyō* divided into two factions, and soon the *Hōgen* civil war began (1156). The partisans of *Sutoku* were defeated and he was banished to *Sanuki*, where he died in 1164. He was 46 years old.

Suwa, 諏訪. In *Shinano*. — See *Takashima*.

Suwa, 諏訪. *Daimyō* family coming from *Shinano* and descended from *Minamoto Mitsumasa*, brother to *Mitsunaka* (*Seiwa-Genji*).

—— **Morishige,** 盛重. Descended from *Mitsumasa* in the 9th gene-ration, was the first to take the name of *Suwa*, from the district of *Shinano* where he settled and where his family remained for several centuries.

—— **Yorishige,** 頼茂 (+ 1542). For a long time fought *Takeda Shingen*, who coveted his domains. After making peace, he went to *Kōfu*, was treacherously arrested by *Itagaki Nobukata* and killed himself.

—— **Yoritada,** 頼忠 (1536-1606). Served *Ieyasu*, who in 1592, gave him the fief of *Sōsha* (*Kōzuke* — 15,000 k.). In 1601, he returned to *Suwa*, where his descendants remained till the Restoration (30,000 k.). — Now Viscount.

SUWA-KO.

Suwa-ko, 諏訪湖. Lake (18 Km. circum.) in *Shinano*. Its outlet is the *Tenryū-gawa*. Also called *Ga-ko*.

Suwō, 周防. Or *Suō*. One of the 8 provinces of *San-yō-dō*. Comprises 6 districts. — Chinese name : *Bōshū*. — At present belongs to *Yamaguchi-ken*.

Suwō-nada, 周防灘. Western basin of the Inland Sea, S. of the *Suwō* province.

Suzuka-Ō, 鈴鹿王 (+ 745). Son of prince *Takechi no Ōji* and grandson of emperor *Temmu*. Was minister under the reigns of *Gemmei, Genshō* and *Seimu ;* received the titles of *Ōkura-kyō, Sangi, Shikibu-kyō,* etc.

Suzuka-yama, 鈴鹿山. Group of mountains on the borders of *Ise, Iga* and *Ōmi*. In 702, a barrier was placed there : it became thus one of the 3 gates (See *San-kwan*) that protected the capital. After the ruin of the *Taira* (1185), the remnant of their clan apparently sought shelter in the recesses of that district, and for several centuries, committed robbery with impunity.

Suzuki, 鈴木, *Daimyō* family which in the 16th century, lived at *Asuke* (*Mikawa*). Dispossessed in 1571 by *Takeda Shingen*.

Suzuki, 鈴木. Name of several celebrated painters who lived during the 18th and the 19th centuries. The best known are : *Harunobu* (1718-1770), *Fuyō* (1749-1816), *Nanrei* (1776-1845), *Shōren* (1778-1803), *Gako* (1816-1870), etc.

T

Tabe, 田部. Formerly, families who cultivated ricefields belonging to the crown. They were under the jurisdiction of the *Ta-zukasa* or *Mita no tsukasa*.

Tabu no mine, 多武峯. — See *Tamu no mine*.

Tachibana, 立花. In *Chikuzen*. Old castle, built during the 16th century by the *Tachibana* family, vassal of the *Ōtomo*. Was captured in 1569 by *Mōri Motonari*, and recaptured the following year by *Ōtomo Sōrin*. In 1588, it passed into the hands of *Kobayakawa Takakage*; then became a part of the domain of the *Kuroda* (1600) and was abandoned.

Tachibana, 橘. Ancient noble family descended from prince *Naniwa-Ō*, son of *Shōtoku-Taishi*.

—— **Moroe, 諸兄** (684-757). At first called *Katsuragi*. He received the family name of *Tachibana* from the emperor *Shōmu*. He was *Udaijin* (738), *Sadaijin* (751), etc. and composed the anthology called *Man-yō-shū*.

—— **Naramaro, 奈良麿**. Son *Moroe*, was *Daigaku no kami, Mimbu-ōsuke, Sangi, Sadaiben*. At the death of his father, jealous of the ever increasing influence of *Fujiwara Nakamaro*, he, together with prince *Funado*, *Ono Azumabito* and others, plotted the ruin of the powerful minister, but their plans were discovered and the conspirators put to death (757).

TACHIBANA NO MOROE.

—— **Kiyotomo, 清友** (757-789). Son of *Naramaro*, was *Uchitoneri*.

—— **Kachi-ko, 嘉智子** (787-851). *Kiyotomo's* daughter, married the emperor *Saga* (815) and was the mother of *Nimmyō*. When the latter fell sick, she shaved her head and became an *ama* in order to obtain his cure, but it was in vain, and, the following year, she followed her son to the grave. A zealous Buddhist, she erected the temple *Danrin-ji*; whence the name of *Danrin-kōgō*, under which she is known. With the help of her brother *Ujikimi*, she founded the *Gakkwan-in*, a school established especially for the children of the *Tachibana* family.

—— **Hayanari, 逸勢**. Grandson of *Naramaro*, is famous as a calligraphist, especially in the kind of writing called *reisho* (square letters). He went to China, where he remained several years and returned with *Kūkai* (806). In 842, he was implicated in a conspiracy to raise prince *Tsunesada-shinnō* to the throne; for this reason, he was banished to *Izu* but died on the way.

—— **Yoshimoto,** 良 基 (823-885). Descended from *Moroe*. He was named *Shinano no kami* (859), favored agriculture, diminished the taxes and proved himself a remarkable statesman.

—— **Nagayasu,** 永 愷. Descendant of the above, was a distinguished poet. He is better known by the name *Nō-in Hōshi*.

Tachibana, 立 花, *Daimyō* family, descended from *Ōtomo Sadamune* and through him, from the *Seiwa-Genji*.

—— **Muneshige,** 宗 茂 (1567-1642). Son of *Takahashi Shigetane*, was adopted by *Tachibana Shigetsura* and inherited *Tachibana's* castle (*Chikugo*) In 1586, he defeated the *Shimazu*, and *Hideyoshi* gave him *Yanagawa* (*Chikugo* — 120,000 k.) in fief. He took part in the expedition to Korea and with *Kobayakawa Takakage* gained a victory over the Chinese army. Later, he rescued *Katō Kiyomasa*, who was besieged in *Uru-san* (*Ulsan*), and enabled him to rout his assailants. In 1600, he sided against *Ieyasu* and was dispossessed; sometime after he was again taken into favor, and in 1611, received the fief of *Tanakura* (*Mutsu* — 20,000 k.) and in 1620, was re-established in *Yanagawa*. He helped to repress the *Shimabara* revolt (1637-38). — His descendants remained at *Yanagawa* (*Chikugo* — 119,000 k.) till the time of the Restoration. — At present, Count. — A junior branch descended from *Naotsugu*, brother to *Muneshige*, in 1621 resided at *Miike* (*Chikugo*); then, from 1805 to 1868, at *Shimotedo* (*Mutsu* — 10,000 k.).— Now Viscount.

Tachibana Morikuni, 橘 守 國 (1679-1748). Born at *Ōsaka*, he received lessons from *Tsuruzawa Tanzan* and was one of the most skilful draughtsmen and engravers of his time.

Tachiiri Munetsugu, 立 入 宗 繼. Official of the Imperial Court, who seeing the desolation reigning in *Kyōto* because of the protracted civil wars, induced the *Chūnagon Fujiwara Korefusa* to advise the emperor to request *Oda Nobunaga* to restore order in the city. The Emperor *Ōgimachi* listened to the advice, and, in 1562, *Munetsugu* was intrusted with a letter to *Nobunaga* requesting the latter to repress the disorders. In 1567, he received a similar commission.—In reward for the service rendered the Imperial cause, *Munetsugu* in 1898, 300 years after his death, was raised to the 2nd degree of the 2nd rank in the Court (*ju-ni-i*).

Tachikawa, 立 河. In *Musashi*. During the 15th and the 16th centuries, residence of the *Tachikawa* family. In 1504, *Uesugi Akisada* was defeated at that place by *Imagawa Ujichika* and *Hōjō Sōun*.

Tada, 多 田. In *Settsu*. Old Shintoist temple (*Tada-jinja*) built by the emperor *Sujin* in memory of *Tatataneko*, son of *Ōmono-nushi no mikoto*. Was the domain of *Minamoto Mitsunaka*, who is for this reason often called *Tada Manjū*; his descendants resided there during several centuries. — *Tada* also possesses hot springs called *Hirano-onsen*.

Tada Manjū, 多 田 滿 仲. — See *Minamoto Mitsunaka*.

Tadami-gawa, 只 見 川. River (141 Km.) of *Iwashiro*, tributary of of the *Agano-gawa*.

Tada Yukitsuna, 多田行綱. Descended from *Minamoto Mitsu-naka*; also called *Tada Kurando*. In 1177, he with *Fujiwara Narichi-ka* plotted against the *Taira*, but changing his mind, he revealed all to *Kiyomori*, who put the conspirators to death. Later he served *Yoritomo*, fought against *Yoshitsune* at *Kawajiri* (*Settsu*), but was defeated and killed (1184).

Tadotsu, 多度津. Town (7800 inh.) of *Sanuki*. In the 16th century, the residence of the *Kagawa* family, who ruled 3 districts. *Amagiri-jō* was the name of the castle; it was captured by *Chōsokabe Motochika*. Under the *Tokugawa*, it belonged to the *Kyōgoku* of *Maru-game*, who there established a junior branch of their family (10,000 k.) in 1694.

Taga, 多賀. In *Rikuzen*. Ancient stronghold built in 724 to stop the raids of the *Ebisu* : *Ōno Azumabito* who built it, established in it the administration (*Chinjufu*) of the government of *Mutsu*. In 802, *Sakanoe no Tamuramaro* transferred it to *Izawa*. *Izawa Iekage* was placed in *Taga* by *Yoritomo*, with the title of *Rusu-shoku* (1190). During the civil wars of the 14th century, the governor (*Chinjufu-taishōgun*) *Kitabatake Akiie* entertained prince *Yoshinaga-shinnō* in it and with him fought bravely against the *Ashikaga*. Captured by *Ishidō Yoshi-fusa* in 1337, recaptured by the Imperial army in 1351, it definitely passed to the Northern dynasty in 1352, and was very soon after abandoned.

Tagaya, 多賀谷. *Daimyō* family that in the 16th century, possessed the *Shimotsuma* castle (*Hitachi* — 60,000 k.). Dispossessed in 1600.

Tagishi-mimi no mikoto, 手研耳命. Son of *Jimmu-tennō* and of *Ahiratsu-hime*. At the death of his father, he attempted to seize the throne, but was defeated and killed by his brother *Kamu-ya-i-mimi no mikoto* (583 B. C.).

Taga no ura, 田子浦. Bay and village of *Suruga*, famous for its picturesque scenery.

Taguchi Shigeyoshi, 田口成能. Nobleman of the *Awa* province (*Shikoku*). He at first sided with the *Taira* and built a palace for the emperor *Antoku* at *Yashima* (*Sanuki*) (1184). He fought the *Mina-moto* in *San-yō-dō*, then after the battle of *Dan-no-ura* (1185), he joined their party.

Taguchi Ukichi, 田口卯吉 (1855-1905). Historian and renowned professor. Wrote a great number of books.

Tahō, 田寶. Buddhist god, one of the *Go-chi-nyorai*.

Taichū-ken, 臺中縣. Department in the center of *Taiwan*, (Formosa). — Pop. : 820,500 inh. — Chief town : *Taichū* (4,000 inh).

Tai-ei, 大永. *Nengō* : 1521-1527.

Taihei-ji, 太平寺. Buddhist temple in the village of *Higashi-mizu-hiki* (*Satsuma*). *Hideyoshi* made this temple his headquarters during his campaign against *Satsuma*, and it was at the same place that he signed a treaty of peace with *Shimazu Yoshihisa* (1587).

Taihei-ki, 太平記. Historical work in 41 volumes, attributed to the bonze *Kojima* (+ 1374) of the *Hiei-zan*. It covers one of the most troubled epochs of Japanese history, from 1318 to 1368.

Taihō, 大寶. *Nengō:* 701-703.

Taihō no chihō-kwansei, 大寶地方官制. An administration created during the *Taihō* era. The capital was divided into two parts, *Sakyō and Ukyō,* each having a governor assisted by a *Ichi no tsukasa.* *Settsu* province enjoyed a special government (*Settsu-shoku*). *Kyūshū,* *Iki* and *Tsushima* were governed by the *Dazai-fu.* The other provinces according to their importance were ranked among the *dai-koku, jō-koku,* *chū-koku* and *ge-koku,* and received a uniform administration (See *Kokushi*).

Taihō-ryōritsu, 大寶令律. Code of laws promulgated in the 1st year of the *Taihō* era (701).—The emperor *Tenchi* had already in his time charged a commission with the work of collecting the laws then in force: the work was finished in 670, and as the capital was then at *Shiga,* in *Ōmi,* it was called *Ōmi-ryō:* it consisted of 22 vol.— Completed under the reign of *Temmu* (682), it was promulgated by the empress *Jitō* (689). The emperor *Mommu* gave orders to the princes *Osakabe-shinnō, Fujiwara Fuhito,* and others, to collect all anterior work into a complete code of laws. The work was finished in 701, and the same year, several doctors of Chinese law, (*myōhō-hakase*) were sent to all the provinces to promulgate and explain it. The empress *Genshō* had it revised during the *Yōrō* era (718), and this new edition was called *Shin-ryō* or *Yōrō-ryōritsu.* Excepting a few slight modifications, the *Taihō* code of laws remained in force to the time of the Restoration.—See *Ri-tsuryō-hyakushiki.*

Taihoku-ken, 臺北縣. Department in the North of *Taiwan* (Formosa). — Pop. 756,200 inh. — Chief town: *Taihoku (Taipeh)* (6,000 inh.).

Taiji, 大治. *Nengō:* 1126-1130.

Taiken-mon-in, 待賢門院. — See *Fujiwara Tama-ko.*

Taiko, 太古. Mythological period, from the creation to the accession of *Jimmu-tennō.*

Taikō, 太閤. Title taken by a *Kwampaku,* when he was succeeded in office by his son: if he transmitted it to another, he had no claim to that title. If, when being succeeded by his son, he shaved his head, and became bonze, he was called *Zenkō.* Although this title occurs several times in history, it is especially given to *Toyotomi Hideyoshi,* who took it when the office of *Kwampaku* passed to his adopted son *Hidetsugu* (1592).

Taikō-taigō, 太皇太后 Grandmother of the Emperor or archdowager Empress.

Taikun, 太君. Title taken by the *Shōgun* in his dealings with foreigners from 1854 to 1867.

Taikwa, 大化. *Nengō:* 645-649. It was the first *nengō* of Japan.

Taikwa no kaishin, 大化改新. Reform of the *Taikwa* era. This name was given to the modifications introduced into the administration from the *Taikwa* era till the promulgation of the *Taihō* code, a period of 56 years (645-701). At his accession to the throne, the emperor *Kōtoku* abolished the titles *Ō-omi* and *Ō-muraji* and created those of *Sadaijin*, *Udaijin* and *Naijin* (or *Uchi no Omi*); the first to posses these titles were : *Abe Kurahashi-maro*, *Soga Kurayamada Ishikawa-maro* and *Nakatomi Kamatari*, who with some advisers (*komon*) assisted in the government. The first year of his reign was the first year of the *Taikwa* era ; thus the *nengō* was introduced. Wishing to reform the abuses and to introduce the administrative system then in use in China (*Tō*) ; he ordered all the governors of provinces or of districts to become acquainted with the wants of the people. He had a box placed at the door of the Palace, wherein the people could place a statement of their grievances against officials. He fixed the limits of the provinces (*kuni*) and districts (*kōri*), ordered the census to be taken and established the *Handen-shuju-hō*. (See that word). In short the entire administration was revised and new offices created.

Tainan-ken, 臺南縣. Department, S. of *Taiwan* (Formosa isl.). Pop.: 1,050,000 inh. — Chief town : *Tainan* (47,300 inh.) : formerly called *Taiwan-fu*, was the capital of the island. Is situated 4 miles inland ; its port is *Ampin*.

Taira, 平. — See *Iwaki-daira*.

Taira, 平. Family descended from prince *Katsurabara-shinnō* (786-853), son of the emperor *Kwammu*. It exercised great power during the 11th and 12th centuries. Its protracted struggle with the rival family *Minamoto* covers some of the most interesting pages of Japanese history.

——— **Takamune, 高棟** (804-867). Eldest son of *Katsurabara-shinnō*, in 825 he received, for himself and his descendants the family name of *Taira*. He was *Dainagon*.

——— **Takamochi, 高望**. Son of *Takami-Ō* and grandson of *Katsurabara-shinnō*, in 889 received from the emperor *Uda*, the name of *Taira*.

——— **Kunika, 國香** (+ 935). Eldest son of *Takamochi*, was *Chinjufu-shōgun* and governor of *Hitachi* : he was put to death by his rebel nephew *Masakado*.

—— **Sadamori,** 貞盛. Also called *Joheida*, heard the news of his father's death, whilst he was at *Kyōto:* he left the city at once and together with his uncle, *Yoshikane, Shimōsa no suke,* fought *Masakado,* but they were defeated. He returned to *Kyōto,* levied new troops, and with the help of *Fujiwara Hidesato,* again offered battle to the rebel, who was now defeated and killed (940). *Sadamori* was then named *Chinjufu-shōgun,* and later *Mutsu no kami.*

—— **Masakado,** 將門 (+ 940). Son of *Yoshimasa,* received the name of *Sōma Shōjirō.* He served the *Sesshō Fujiwara Tadahira,* and demanded the office of *Kebiishi,* but was refused. In revenge he retired to *Kwantō,* settled in the district of *Toyoda* (*Shimōsa*) and began a guerrilla warfare in the surrounding country. He attacked his uncle *Kunika,* governor of *Hitachi,* and put him to death (935). The following year, *Yoshikane,* brother of *Kunika,* with *Sadamori* attacked him, but were defeated and forced to take refuge in *Kyōto.* After *Yoshikane's* death (939), *Masakado* occupied *Shimōsa, Shimotsuke* and *Kōzuke.* He then assumed the title of *Heishin-ō* (new emperor *Taira*), established his Court at *Ishii* (*Shimōsa*), named ministers and officials, etc. In the mean time, *Fujiwara Sumitomo,* to whom *Masakado* had promised the *Kwampaku* dignity, revolted in *Sakaidō.* In 940,

DEATH OF TAIRA MASAKADO.

Fujiwara Tadabumi who had received the title of *Seitō-taishōgun,* marched against *Masakado* with a large army. He came too late however, for *Sadamori,* with the help of *Fujiwara Hidesato,* and *Ōryōshi* from *Shimotsuke,* had already attacked the rebel, defeated and pursued him for 13 days, finally overtaking him at *Kōjima* (*Shimōsa*). In the last encounter, *Masakado*, having been wounded by an arrow, fell from his horse. *Hidesato* leaped to the ground, killed the wounded man and sent his head to *Kyōto*. This revolt is known in history by the name of *Tenkei no ran*.

—— **Korehira, 維衡**. Son of *Sadamori*, became famous in military art. Together with *Minamoto Yorinobu, Taira Muneyori* and *Fujiwara Yasumasa*, he forms the *Bushō shi-ten* (4 great warriors) of his epoch. He governed the provinces of *Ise, Mutsu, Dewa, Izu, Shimotsuke, Sado*, etc.; then after some dispute, he openly made war against *Muneyori* and was exiled to the island of *Awaji*. As he spent most of the time in *Ise*, his descendants were called *Ise-Heishi* (*Taira* of the *Ise* province).

—— **Koremochi, 維望**. Educated by his uncle *Sadamori*, settled in *Mutsu*, had some dispute with *Fujiwara Morotane*, whom he defeated and killed. This made him famous throughout all *Kwantō*. He was *Dewa no suke* and *Chinjufu-shōgun*. He died at the age of 80.

—— **Tadatsune, 忠常**. Was grandson of *Yoshibumi*, who lived at *Muraoka* (*Musashi*), and is known by the name of *Muraoka Gorō*. He settled in *Kazusa* and received the titles of *Kazusa no suke* and of *Ōryōshi* (inspector) of *Musashi*. In 1028, he became lord of *Awa* province by killing its governor. *Taira Naokata* was sent against him, but met with defeat. *Minamoto Yorinobu* had more success and forced him to retreat (1031). *Tadatsune* is the ancestor of the *Chiba daimyō*.

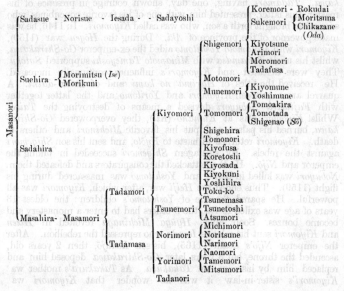

—— **Iesada, 家貞.** Served *Tadamori* and *Kiyomori*. During the *Heiji* war, (1159), he fought against *Hyūga Michinaga*, whom he defeated and killed in *Echizen*.

—— **Sadayoshi, 貞能.** Son of *Iesada*, was governor of *Higo* and *Chikugo*. In 1180, *Kikuchi Takanao* levied troops in *Kyūshū*, and sided with *Yoritomo ; Sadayoshi* marched against and defeated him Returning to *Kyōto*, he met *Munemori*, who was retreating in *Saikaidō* with the emperor *Antoku*. He vainly attempted to induce them to return to the the capital. After his arrival at *Kyōto*, he had the remains of *Shigemori* brought to the *Kōya-san*. He then again joined *Munemori* and served under him. After the ruin of the *Taira*, his life was spared owing to the intercession of *Utsunomiya Tomotsuna*. He shaved his head and in retirement was known by the name of *Higo-Nyūdō*.

—— **Tadamori, 忠盛** (1096-1153). Served the emperors *Shirakawa, Horikawa* and *Toba ;* governed the provinces of *Harima, Ise* and *Bizen*, and was named *Kebiishi*. In 1129, he was ordered to repress the high-sea pirates, who infested the coasts of *San-yō-dō* and *Nankai-dō*. The ex-emperor *Toba* ordered him to build the *San-jū-san-gen-dō*, and in reward he received the governorship of *Tajima* (1132). The credit he enjoyed created enemies who tried to kill him, but he escaped their snares.

—— **Kiyomori, 清盛** (1118-1181). The most renowned of the *Taira*, was, if tradition can be trusted, a son of the ex-emperor *Shirakawa*. *Tadamori*, having, one day, shown courage in presence of his master, this latter, presented him with one of his favorite concubines, who soon after, brought forth a son, who was called *Kiyomori*. In 1146, he was made governor of the province of *Aki*. During the *Hōgen* war (1150), *Kiyomori* with *Minamoto Yoshitomo* aided the ex-emperor *Go-Shirakawa*, whilst his uncle *Tadamōsa* with *Minamoto Tameyoshi* supported *Sutoku*. They were defeated and *Kiyomori's* influence continually increased. He received the titles of *Harima no kami* and of *Dazai-daini*. A quarrel arose between *Kiyomori* and *Yoritomo* and the latter together with *Fujiwara Nobuyori* devised a means of destroying the *Taira*. Whilst *Kiyomori* was at *Kumano* (*Kii*), they overpowered *Go-Shirakawa*, burned his palace, and put his favorite *Michinori* and others to death. *Kiyomori* returned in haste to *Kyōto*, and sent his son *Shigemori* against the rebels. By stratagem *Shigemori* succeeded in taking the emperor and *Nijō*. He then attacked the conspirators and defeated them. *Nobuyori* was killed in battle, and *Yoshitomo* was massacred during his flight (1159). Thus ended the *Heiji* war, after which, *Kiyomori* was all powerful. He spared the life of *Yoshitomo's* children : the oldest 13 years of age was exiled to *Izu*, the 3 others had to enter a monastery and become bonzes. Soon after, *Hyūga Michinaga* revolted in *Hizen* and *Kiyomori* sent his relative *Iesada* who repressed the rebellion. After the emperor *Nijō's* death (1165), his son *Rokujō*, then 2 years old, ascended the throne, but 3 years later, *Go-Shirakawa* deposed him and replaced him by his own son *Takakura*. As *Takakura's* mother wa *Kiyomori's* sister-in-law it was no wonder that *Kiyomori* wa named *Naidaijin*, then *Dajō-daijin* : it was the first time that a member of the military class was raised to that dignity. In 1168, he became ill, shaved his head and took the name of *Jōkai*, whilst the people called him *Dajō-nyūdō*. Whilst living in the spendid palace he had built at *Fukuhara*, near *Hyōgo* (*Settsu*), he governed the country as he pleased ; 60 members of his family possessed the highest offices of the land and were at the head of more than 30 provinces He had 300 young pages at his command who informed him of all they saw and heard. In 1171, his daughter *Toku-ko*, then 15 years old, married the emperor *Takakura* her junior by 4 years. His two sons (*Shigemori* and *Munemori*) were named *Sakon-e-taishō* and *Ukon-e-taishō* (1177) respectively. The *Fujiwara*, *Narichika* and *Moromitsu*, however a second time plotted the ruin of the *Taira*, but *Tada Yukitsuna*, their accomplice, revealed the whole design to *Kiyomori*, and his revenge was frightful. The principal leaders were executed, and many others were exiled ; he had even made up his mind to imprison *Go-Shirakawa*, who had given his approval to the plan, but on the advice of *Shigemori*, he pardoned him. The folllowing year (1179), a son was born to the emperor *Takakura*, and *Kiyomori* had him at once declared heir to the throne. Soon after, *Shigemori* died, at the age of 43 (1179). Deprived of the wise counsels and of the firm remonstrances of his son, *Kiyomori* gave full vent to his tyranny : he imprisoned *Go-Shirakawa* in the palace of *Toba*, exiled the *Kwampaku* and the *Dajō-daijin*, deposed 39 officials, and obliged his son-in-law *Takakura* to abdicate in favor of his grandson *Antoku*, then 2 years old. All these measures exasperated the nobles to such a pitch that a new plot was formed, headed by the prince *Mochihito-shinnō*, son of *Go-Shirakawa*. A call to arms was sent to the warriors throughout all the provinces and the first to answer was *Minamoto Yorimasa*, who, notwithstanding his 75 years, fought bravely, but was overwhelmed by superior numbers at *Uji-bashi* (1180). Prince *Mochihito* was killed at *Nara* and the bonzes who had given help to *Yorimasa* saw their temples burned. To prevent a coup-de-main, *Kiyomori* took the emperor with the whole Court to his palace of *Fukuhara*. Meanwhile, the *Minamoto* assembled their troops in *Kwantō* ; defeated by *Oba Kagechika*, at *I-shibashi-yama*, *Yoritomo*, far from being discouraged assembled a second army, and was able to rout the troops of *Koremori*. At this news *Kiyomori* fell sick and died after 8 days. He

TAIRA KIYOMORI.

made his sons and grandsons promise however, to bring *Yoritomo's* head to his tomb, which desire was not to be fulfilled.

—— **Norimori**, 敎盛 (1129-1185). Brother to *Kiyomori*, fought against *Fujiwara Nobuyori* during the *Heiji* war (1159) and was named *Etchū no kami*. In 1161, he in concert with *Taira Tokitada* tried to depose the emperor *Nijō* and to replace him by his brother *Norihito-shinnō*, on which account he was deprived of all his offices. *Norihito*, having become *Takakura-tennō* (1169), named *Norimori Kurando, Sangi*, etc. In 1183, he accompanied the emperor *Antoku* to *Saikai-dō*, defeated *Minamoto Yukiie* at *Muroyama* (*Harima*), and killed himself at *Dan-no-ura*.

—— **Yorimori,** 頼盛 (1132-1186). Brother to *Kiyomori*, assisted *Norimori*, when he besieged *Fujiwara Nobuyori* in the temple *Ninna-ji* (1159). He was named *Owari no kami*, then *Dainagon*, and as he usually lived at *Ike*, he was surnamed *Ike-Dainagon*. His wife, *Ike no Gozen*, pleaded for and obtained the pardon of *Yoritomo*, who always showed himself very grateful. *Yorimori* then having nothing to fear, remained in *Kyōto* when the *Taira* all fled to the West (1183). The following year, *Yoritomo* called him together with *Munekiyo* to *Kamakura*. The latter refused to go, but *Yorimori* was well treated and returned to *Kyōto* where he died.

—— **Tadanori,** 忠度 (1144-1184). Brother of *Kiyomori*, was brought up at *Kumano*, received lessons from *Fujiwara Toshinari*, and became a distinguished poet. Later on, he was *Satsuma no kami*. He was killed by *Okabe Tadazumi* at the battle of *Ichi-no-tani*, where he had shown wonderful courage.

—— **Yasuyori,** 康頼. In 1177, took part in the plot of *Fujiwara Narichika* and of the bonze *Shunkwan* against *Kiyomori*, for which he was exiled to *Kikai ga shima*, but was pardoned the following year.

—— **Moritoshi,** 盛俊 (+ 1184). Son of *Morikuni*, was *Etchū no kami*. He aided *Shigemori* and enabled him successfully to fight *Minamoto Yoshihira* at the *Rokuhara* (1159). In 1181, he defeated *Yukiie* and *Yoshinaka*, but died at *Ichi-no-tani*. His father, *Morikuni*, having been taken prisoner at *Dan-no-ura*, was brought to *Kamakura* where he starved himself to death in captivity.

—— **Tokitada,** 時忠 (1130-1189). Descendant of *Takamune* and son of *Tokinobu*, served the emperors *Konoe, Go-Shirakawa, Nijō*. Banished to *Izumo* in 1162, he was recalled 5 years after and named *Chūnagon*, but having been involved in a plot against *Kiyomori*, he was again exiled to *Izumo* (1177). Pardoned the following year, he defeated the troops of the *Hiei-zan* that had caused disorder in the capital. In 1183, he followed *Munemori* into *Saikai-dō*; he then surrendered to *Yoshitsune* and was banished to *Noto*, where he died.

—— **Tomoyasu,** 知康. Son of *Tomochika*, was *Kebiishi*. In 1183, the ex-emperor *Go-Shirakawa* ordered him to check the advance of *Yoshinaka's* army which was threatening the capital, but frightened at the great number of his enemies, he fled without offering battle. He then went to *Kamakura* and submitted to *Yoritomo*.

—— **Hirotsune,** 廣常. Son of *Tsunetaka, Kazusa no suke*, fought under *Minamoto Yoshitomo* during the *Hōgen* (1156) and *Heiji* (1159) wars and showed great valor. He then served *Yoritomo*, but in consequence of quarrels with some other generals, he was besieged and put to death by *Kajiwara Kagetoki*.

—— **Munekiyo,** 宗清. Son of *Suemune,* served *Yorimori,* who
created him *mokudai* of the *Owari* province, of which he was the governor. In 1160, *Minamoto Yoshitomo* having been killed, his son *Yoritomo* fled but was arrested by *Munekiyo,* who was on his way from
Owari to *Kyōto.* According to *Kiyomori's* orders, he was kept prisoner
at *Munekiyo's* house. The latter however had pity on a prisoner 14
years old and spoke in his behalf to *Yorimori's* wife, *Ike no Gozen,* who, being a daughter of *Fujiwara Munekane,* was *Kiyomori's* mother-in-law :
moved by her entreaties, *Kiyomori* spared *Yoritomo's* life, but exiled him
to *Izu.* When the *Taira* fled to *Saikai-dō* (1183), *Munekiyo* remained
at *Kyōto* with *Yorimori. Yoritomo* called them both to *Kamakura,* with
the intention of rewarding them for the favor he had received 20 years
before, but *Munekiyo* refused to accept the invitation and rejoined *Munemori* in the South. It is not known what became of him after the ruin
of his family.

—— **Kagekiyo,** 景清. Son of *Fujiwara Tadakiyo,* was adopted
by the *Taira* and showed great valor. He fought *Yoshinaka* at *Yukiie.*
Made prisoner at *Dan-no-ura* (1185), he was brought to *Kamakura* but
starved himself to death. Legends have embellished his life : they represent him taking the disguise of a bonze to assassinate *Yoritomo* during
some ceremony, or again, plucking out his own eyes, not to see the
triumph of the enemies of his family.

—— **Shigemori,** 重盛 (1138-1179). Eldest son of *Kiyomori,* took
a prominent part in the suppression of the *Hōgen* (1156) and *Heiji* (1159)
troubles, that had been caused by the tyranny of his father. He endeavored to moderate the impetuous character of *Kiyomori,* and at the time
of the revolt of *Fujiwara Narichika* (1177), he prevented the imprisonment of *Go-Shirakawa.* *Shigemori* remains, to the present day, one of
the most accomplished models of fidelity and respect due to one's sovereign. Unhappily he died before his father, and thus could not
prevent the excesses that occurred in the latter days of his father's life.

—— **Munemori,** 宗盛 (1147-1185). Son of *Kiyomori,* became his
heir at *Shigemori's* death. Instead of moderating the excesses of his
father, he became the executer of his evil designs, and, besieging *Go-Shirakawa* in his palace, imprisoned him at *Toba-in* (1179). When *Yoshinaka* marched upon *Kyōto, Munemori* sent his brother *Tadanori* and his
nephew *Koremori* against him, but they were defeated. He then
summoned the bonzes of *Hiei-zan* to help him, but they refused.
Meanwhile, *Yukiie* in *Yamato* and *Yukitsuna* in *Settsu* were getting
ready to march against *Kyōto. Munemori* now assembled the members
of his family and the principal officers, and told them his intention of
retiring into *Kyūshū.* All opposed his project but he, taking the young
emperor *Antoku,* his mother *Kenrei-mon-in,* his brother *Morisada* and
others with him, started on his way South, all his vassals being obliged
to follow. They had scarcely left *Kyōto,* when the ex-emperor *Go-Shirakawa* recovering power, deposed more than 200 officials of the *Taira*
clan and raised *Go-Toba,* the 4th son of *Takakura,* then 3 years old, to
the throne. *Munemori* had scarcely landed at *Dazaifu,* when he was

attacked by *Fujiwara Yoritsune, Ogata Koreyoshi*, etc. He retired then to *Hakozaki* (*Chikuzen*), then to *Sanuki* where he built a temporary palace for the emperor at a place called *Yashima*. As the *Minamoto* were divided into two factions, he profited of their disunion to return into *San-yō-dō*, went as far as *Settsu* and built a fort at *Ichi-no-tani*. Meanwhile, *Noriyori* and *Yoshitsune* after having defeated *Yoshinaka*, marched against the *Taira*. Simultaneously attacked on both sides *Munemori* was defeated but escaped by sea to *Yashima*, leaving the following among the dead; his uncle *Tadanori*, his brothers *Kiyosada* and *Kiyofusa*, his cousins *Tsunemasa, Tsunetoshi, Atsumori, Michimori, Narimori*, his nephews *Moromori, Tomoakira*, etc. (1184). Leaving *Yashima*, *Munemori* went to *Shido* (*Sanuki*), then to *Hikishima*, and returned to *Hakozaki* where he met *Noriyori* ready to attack him. He took to sea again and sailed for *Dan-no-ura* bay, near the present city of *Shimonoseki* (*Nagato*). *Yoshitsune* followed him and a desperate battle ensued, in which the advantage soon was on the side of the *Minamoto*. When doubt as to the issue of the battle could no longer be entertained, *Tomomori* approached the boat that bore the Imperial family and declared that all hope of success was over. *Kiyomori's* widow, *Nii-no ama*, then gathered all her children and grandchildren about her and told them that *Munemori* was neither her son nor *Kiyomori's*. Having only one son, *Shigemori, Kiyomori* was becoming very anxious when hopes were entertained for an heir. A girl was born, who was secretly exchanged for a son that had just been born to an umbrella merchant of *Kitazaka*, near *Kiyomizu-dera*. "This son of an umbrella merchant," she added vehemently, "is no other than *Munemori*: it is then not astonishing that we do not find the intelligence or the courage of the *Taira* in him!" Saying this, she seized her grandson *Antoku* and leaped with him into the sea. At this moment the battle was changed into a rout and *Tomomori, Norimori, Tsunemori, Sukemori, Yukimori, Arimori*, etc., were killed. The empress *Kenrei-mon-in*, daughter of *Kiyomori* and mother of *Antoku* was saved. *Munemori* and his son *Kiyomune*, were made prisoners and taken to *Kyōto* and then to *Kamakura*, but were put to death on the way, at a place called *Shinowara* (*Ōmi*).

—— **Tomomori,** 知盛 (1152-1185). Son of *Kiyomori*, defeated *Minamoto Yorimasa* at *Uji-Bashi*; *Yamamoto Yoshitsune* at *Mii-dera* (1180); and *Yukiie* at *Sakakura* (*Mino*) (1181). In 1183, he fought against *Yoshinaka* in *Ōmi*, but was defeated and retreated to *Kyōto*. *Munemori* then resolved to go South and *Tomomori*, who had vehemently opposed this plan had to follow him to *Yashima*. Defeated at *Ichi no tani* (1184), he escaped death by flight and built a fort at *Hikishima* (*Nagato*) against the *Minamoto*. He fought bravely at the battle of *Dan-no-ura*, went to *Nii no ama* to announce her that defeat was imminent; then, hearing that *Munemori* had not the courage to kill himself but had been made prisoner, he wept from very shame; finally, he, with his uncle *Norimori* committed suicide.

—— **Shigehira, 重衡** (1158-1185). Son of *Kiyomori*, took part in the battle of *Uji-bashi* against prince *Michihito* and *Yorimasa* (1180). From there, he went to *Nara* and burned the *Tō-daiji* and *Kōfuku-ji* temples that had given help to the *Minamoto*. He,then fought against *Yukiie*. When the *Taira* went South, (1183) *Yoshinaka* entrusted their pursuit to *Takanashi, Takanobu, Ashikaga Yoshikiyo, Nishina Moriie*, etc. A battle took place at *Mizushima* (*Bitchū*). The *Taira*, commanded by *Shigehira, Michimori* and *Norimori* were victorious and *Takanobu* and *Yoshikiyo* met death in battle. Made prisoner at *Ichi-no-tani*, *Shigehira* was taken to *Kamakura* and the following year, by request of the bonzes whose temples he had burned, was beheaded near *Nara*.

—— **Toku-ko, 徳子** (1155-1213). Daughter of *Kiyomori*, in 1171 married the emperor *Takakura* and in 1178, gave birth to the future *Antoku-tennō*. In 1181, at the death of *Takakura*, she took the name of *Kenrei-mon-in*. Having escaped death at *Dan-no-ura*, she was led to *Kyōto* and died in that city.

—— **Atsumori, 敦盛** (1169-1184). Son of *Tsunemori*, fought bravely at *Ichi-no-tani*. When the defeated *Taira* were obliged to take to flight, *Atsumori* was left behind and to gain the boats was obliged to spur his horse into the sea; *Kumagaya Naozane* having seen this, invited him to single combat, which challenge *Atsumori* accepted. He, however, was unhorsed and *Naozane* cut his head off. — This episode has often been sung in poetry, and acted on the stage.

—— **Noritsune, 教経** (1160-1185). Son of *Norimori*, was *Noto no kami*. He took part in the battles of *Mizushima, Ichi-no-tani* and *Dan-no-ura*. In this last battle, seeing defeat inevitable, he sought out *Yoshitsune's* boat to slay him but the soldiers came to the rescue of their chief. *Noritsune* kicked a soldier into the sea, then seizing one with each hand, he leaped into the sea.

—— **Koremori, 維盛**. Son of *Shigemori*, was sent to fight *Yoritomo ;* he went as far as *Fuji-kawa*, when his army, hearing of the great strength of the enemy, refused to advance, thus obliging him to return to *Kyōto* (1180). In 1183, he defeated *Yoshinaka* at *Hiuchi* (*Echizen*). He then followed *Munemori* to *Yashima ;* soon after however, he left the place, took to sea and landed in *Kii*. He caused the news to be spread that he was drowned, but in reality went to the *Kōya-san*, and became a bonze. He was then 25 years old. To escape all search, he remained hidden at *Fujinawa* (*Kii*). — *Koremori* had a son, called *Rokudai*, who, after the battle of *Dan-no-ura*, was spared through the intercession of *Mongaku-shōnin*, whose disciple he became, but when *Mongaku* was exiled to *Ōmi*, *Rokudai* was arrested and beheaded at *Tagoe* (*Sagami*) at the age of 26 years (1199).

Taira no miyako, 平安京. Name given by the emperor *Kwammu* to the capital (*Kyōto*) which he built in 794. It was only later on known by the name of *Heian-kyō* (the Chinese reading of the same characters).

Tairō, 大老. Under the *Tokugawa*, the first minister of the *Shōgun*. He was also called *Genrō* or *Ō-toshiyori*. The first to receive this title were *Doi Toshikatsu* and *Sakai Tadakatsu* (1638). Later on, the office was given to one official usually chosen from the *Sakai*, *Ii* and *Hotta* families. A *tozama-daimyō* was never raised to the dignity of *Tairō*. From the time of *Ienobu* (1709) till that of *Ieshige* (1760), this office was vacant. One of the best known *Tairō* is the famous *Ii Kamon no kami*, signer of the first treaty with the foreign powers. He was assassinated in 1860.

Tairō, 大老 . — See *Go-Tairō*.

Tairō, 大粮 . Formerly, food (rice, salt, *shōyu*, etc.) distributed monthly to the Imperial guard.

Taisei-kyōkwai, 大成教會 . One of the 10 present sects of Shintoism. The *Remmon-kyōkwai* is one of its branches.

Taisha, 大赦 . General pardon formerly granted on some important occasions, such as at the crowning of an Emperor, etc.

Taishaku, 帝釋 . The god *Indra* of Brahmanism ; one of the *Roku-buten*.

Taishi, 太子 . Imperial prince, proclaimed heir presumptive to the throne. If the prince was a brother of the ruling emperor, he was called *Taitei*. These titles subsequently were changed into those of *Kōtaishi* and *Kōtaitei*.

Taishō, 大將 . Title created in the 9th century and applied to the commanders of the two divisions of the Imperial bodyguards : *Sakon-e-taishō* and *Ukon-e-taishō*. Afterwards it denoted the general in chief of an army. — To-day it is the intermediary grade between the general of a division (*chūjō*) and a marshal (*gensui*) and corresponds to field-marshal.

Taishu, 大守 . Title created in 826, and applied to the provincial governors of *Hitachi*, *Kazusa* and *Kōzuke*. These 3 provinces, in memory of the sojourn of *Yamatotakeru* in them, were always governed by a prince of the royal family, and this latter, who generally resided at *Kyōto*, was represented in the provinces by a *Suke*.

Taishū, 對州 . Chinese name of the *Tsushima* province.

Taisō, 大喪 . In ancient times, solemn funerals of an emperor or a high dignitary. An official with the title of *Hinkyū-tayu* presided over the ceremony and the *Yūbu no tami* accompanied the procession. The *Taihō* code entrusted the organisation of the funerals to the *Jibu-shō*. In 701, the ex-empress *Jitō* was cremated (*kwasō*), and in 756, the emperor *Shōmu* was buried according to the Buddhist ritual ; hence the ancient ceremonies were abandoned. In the middle of the 17th century, a certain *Sakanaya Hachibei* protested to the emperor against cremation and, at the death of *Go-Kōmyō* (1654), the old customs were revived and have since then been in constant use.

Taitōtei, 大稻埕 . Japanese name of the city of *Twatutia* (31,600 inh.), on the Eastern coast of Formosa. Also called *Shingai*.

Taiwan, 臺灣 . Island of Formosa (1180 Km. circ., 34,745 Km². of surface). — Pop. : 2,830,000 inh., of which 42,000 are Japanese. — Originally called *Pokkan* or *Pekiande*, the island was named *Taiwan* by the Chinese, *Takasago* by the Japanese, *Formosa* (beautiful) by the Portuguese. In 1624, the Dutch occupied the Western coast and established 3 garrisoned forts near *Amping*. Two years later the Spaniards founded a colony near *Kelung*, but were driven away by the Dutch in 1624 who built a new fort at *Tansui*. In 1660, *Kokusen-ya* (*Koxinga*), driven from *Nanking* by the Mandchous, landed in Formosa with 25,000 men and, in a few months, occupied the whole island. His son, *Teikei* and his grandson *Teikokuzō* ruled the island, but the latter surrendered to a Tartar general and the island became a Chinese possession (1683). In 1722, a revolt of the aborigines was quelled with very great difficulty and a part of the island was devastated. In 1771, Count *Benyowsky*, a Hungarian who with a hundred other prisoners had escaped from *Kamtschatka*, tried to settle in that island, and with the help of some savage tribes, defeated the Chinese troops, but not trusting to the fidelity of the islanders he abandoned his former plan and took to sea to try a similar experiment in the island of *Madayascar*. A new revolt which lasted 30 years (1794-1833), left the whole island a heap of ruins. In 1874, Japan sent an expedition thither under the command of *Saigō Tsugumichi* to punish the islanders who had massacred some fishermen, shipwrecked on their coasts. Finally after the Chinese-Japanese war, Formosa became a Japanese possession (1895), and was divided into 3 departments : *Taihoku-ken*, *Taichū ken*, *Tainan-ken*, and into 3 prefectures of the second order : *Giran-chō Taitō-chō*, *Hōko-chō*. — The islands *Shō-Ryūkyū* (*Lambay* isl., 13 Km. circ.), *Kōtō* (*Botel-tobago* isl., 47 Km. circ.), *Kwashō* (*Samasama* isl.), etc., are dependent upon Formosa.

Taiwan-kaikyō, 臺灣海狹. Strait of Formosa.

Tajihi no Agatamori, 多治比縣守 (668-737). Son of *Sadaijin Shima*, was ambassador to China (717), then *Musashi no kami* and inspector (*azechi*) of *Sagami*, *Shimotsuke* and *Kōzuke* provinces (719). The following year he repressed a revolt of the *Ebisu*, and in reward, was named *Nakatsukasa-kyō*.

Tajikara-o no mikoto, 手力雄命. Shintoist god. Son of *Ame no Sokotachi no kami*. He took away the stone that closed the entrance of the grotto into which *Amaterasu-ō-mikami* had taken refuge.

Tajima, 伯馬. One of the 8 provinces of *San-in-dō*. Comprises 5 districts, all belonging to the *Hyōgo-ken*. — Chinese name : *Tanshū* (with *Tamba* and *Tango*).

Tajima-Fuji, 但馬富士. Name given to *Mi-hiraki-yama* (*Tajima*), because of its resemblance to the great mountain of *Suruga*.

Tajima Mori, 田道間守. He was of Korean origin, descended from *Ame no Hiboko*. In the year 61, he was sent to China to seek the fruit of perpetual scent (*tokijiku no kagu no konomi*). After 10 years, he returned to Japan to find *Suinin* dead and replaced by his son *Keikō*. He went to the tomb of the late emperor placed the fruits he had brought with him on it and killed himself. This fruit received the name of *tachibana* (orange).

Tajimi Kuninaga, 多治見國長. — See *Toki Yorikane*.

Tajiri, 田尻. *Samurai* family of the *Kagoshima* clan (*Satsuma*), made noble in 1896. — Now Baron.

Takachiho, 高 千 穂 . Family descended from *Go-Fushimi-tennō* and attached to the Shintoist temple of mount *Hiko-san* (*Bungo*). — Now Baron.

Takachiho no mine, 高 千 穂 峰 . — See *Higashi-Kirishima-yama*.

Takada-ha, 高 田 派 . Branch of the *Jōdo-shin-shū*, Buddhist sect, founded by the bonze *Shimbutsu* in 1226 at *Takada* (*Shimotsuke*). In 1465, *Shin-e*, superior of the sect, transferred its headquarters to *Isshinden* (*Ise*).

(**Takadate,** 高 舘 . In *Rikuchū* (*Hira-izumi mura*). *Yoshitsune* was received there as a guest by *Fujiwara Hidehira*, but being attacked by *Yasuhira*, under orders from *Yoritomo*, he put his wife and children to death and committed suicide (1189).

Takadaya Kahei, 高 田 屋 嘉 兵 衞 (1769-1827). Born in *Owari*, he went to *Hyōgo*, built a large ship which he filled with merchandise and sailed for *Matsumae* and *Etoru-jima*, where he transacted business with the islanders. In 1812, whilst returning from *Etoru*, he was made prisoner by the Russians and taken to *Kamtchatka*, where he learned the Russian language. At his request, the *Shōgun* consented to make an exchange of prisoners : *Kahei* and his companions being set free whilst the *Shōgun* liberated the crew of the *Diana*, commanded by *Golownin*. This ship had been taken by the Japanese at *Rebunjiri-shima*, in the preceding year. Having returned to his country, he was re-established in his offices and rewarded.

Takagi, 高 木 . *Daimyō* family descended from *Minamoto Yorichika* (*Seiwa-Genji*). From 1623 to 1868, it resided at *Tannan* (*Kawachi* — 10,000 k.). — Now Baron.

Takagi, 高 木 . Family of the *Satsuma* clan, made noble in 1905. — Now Baron.

Takahama, 高 濱 . In *Wakasa*. *Hideyoshi* in 1593, placed his relative *Kinoshita Toshifusa* (3000 k.) there. He was dispossessed by *Ieyasu* (1600).

Takahara-gawa, 高 原 川 . Name of the *Jinzū-gawa*, in its upper course, before entering *Etchū*.

Takahara-yama, 高 原 山 . Mountain (1800 m.) N. of *Shimotsuke*. Also called *Keichō-zan*.

Takahashi, 高 梁 . City (6100 inh.) of *Bitchū*. Before the Restoration, it was called *Matsuyama*. (See that name).

Takahashi, 高 橋 . Ancient *daimyō* family of *Kyūshū* ; during the 15th and the 16th centuries, vassal of the *Ōtomo* of *Bungo*.

—— **Shigetane,** 鎭 種 (1544-1585). Governed the district of *Mikasa* (*Bungo*) and resided at *Iwaya* castle. He shaved his head and took the name of *Shōgun* (1567). Besieged in his castle by *Shimazu Yoshihisa*, he bravely resisted but in the end killed himself.

—— **Mototane,** 元 種 . Adopted child of the above, in 1587, received the *Miyazaki* (*Hyūga* — 50,000 k.) fief from *Hideyoshi*. He took part in the Korean expedition under *Kuroda Nagamasa*. In 1600, he fought against *Ieyasu* and protected the *Ōgaki* castle. Owing to the influence of *Mizuno Katsushige*, he was allowed to retain his domain, but having been implicated in the plot of *Tomita Motonobu*, he was dispossessed and banished to *Tanakura* (*Mutsu*), where he died.

Takahashi, 高橋. A family which possessed many learned men during the 18th and 19th centuries.

—— **Sakuzaemon,** 作左衛門 (1764-1804). Better known by the name of *Tōkō*, was the son of *Motosuke*, one of the *samurai* guarding the castle of *Ōsaka*. He studied astronomy under *Asada Gōritsu* and reformed the calendar in use at that time. His reform, accepted by the government of the *Shōgun*, was published in 1795, and the new calendar was called *Kwansei-reki* (calendar of the *Kwansei* era).

—— **Sakuzaemon,** 作左衛門 (1783-1828). Son of the above was *Shomotsu-bugyō, Temmongata-kentai*. He learned the Dutch, the Manchou and the Russian languages, and translated several works. In 1826, the chief of the Dutch factory of *Deshima* came to *Edo*, accompanied by Siebold. *Sakuzaemon* entered into communication with the latter, and in exchange for some Dutch books, gave him the map of Japan made by *Inō Tadayoshi*. The fact became known, *Sakuzaemon* was imprisoned and died during the trial.

Takahoko-numa, 鷹架沼. Lake (26 Km. circum.) E. of *Mutsu*.

Takajō, 鷹匠. Under the *Tokugawa*, an official whose duty it was to supervise the raising and maintenance of the falcons and dogs employed in the *Shōgun's* hunting expeditions.

Takakura, 高倉. *Kuge* family descended from *Fujiwara Nagayoshi* (800-854) — Now Viscount.

Takakura no miya, 高倉宮. Palace in *Kyōto*, former residence of prince *Mochihito* (1150-1180), son of *Go-Shirakawa*. The prince himself was at times called by that name.

Takakura-tennō, 高倉天皇. 80th Emperor of Japan (1169-1180). *Norihito*, 7th son of *Go-Shirakawa*, at the age of 8 years, succeeded his nephew *Rokujō*. When 11 years old, he married *Taira Toku-ko, Kiyomori's* daughter, and a boy was born to him in 1178. Two years later, *Kiyomori* obliged his son-in-law to abdicate in favor of his grandson *Antoku*. *Takakura* died the following year, at the age of 21. His reign marks the period of the *Taira's* greatest power.

TAKAKURA-TENNŌ.

Takama-ga-hara, 高天原. (Lit.: the plain of the high sky). Country inhabited by *Izanagi* and *Izanami* whence they came to create Japan. They transmitted their former abode to *Amaterasu-ō-mikami*. Commentators have not as yet been able to identify *Takama-ga-hara*. It most probably designates the place of residence of the ancestors of *Ninigi no Mikoto*. They are said to have established themselves in *Izumo*, when they arrived from the South, and later on settled in *Ise*, from whence *Ninigi* repaired to Mount *Takachiho* (*Hyūga*).

Takamatsu, 高松. Chief town (34,500 inh.) of *Kagawa-ken* and of *Sanuki* province. — Ancient castle built in 1335 by *Yorishige*, governor of the province. *Hideyoshi* in 1585, placed *Sengoku Hidehisa* there, who, in 1587, was transferred and replaced by *Ikoma Chikamasa*. In 1640, *Ikoma Takatoshi* was dispossessed, and from 1642 to 1868, *Takamatsu* was the residence of the *Matsudaira daimyō* (120,000 k.).

Takamatsu, 高松 . In *Bitchū*. Ancient castle belonging to the *Mōri daimyō*. In 1582, *Hideyoshi* there besieged *Shimizu Muneharu* and compelled him to surrender by changing the course of the river and submerging the surroundings of the castle : this was called *Takamatsu-jō no mizu-zeme*.

Takamatsu, 高松 . *Kuge* family descended from *Fujiwara* (*Sanjō*) *Kinnori* (1103-1160). — Now Viscount.

Taka-mikura, 高御座 . Throne constructed for the Emperor at the time of the ceremony of the crowning. It was surrounded with mirrors and purple drapery and surmounted by the symbolical bird called *hō-ō*.

Takamimusubi no kami, 高皇産霊神 . Shintoist god. Together with *Ame-no-minaka-nushi* and *Kammimusubi*, he is, according to mythology, one of the creators of the world. He protected *Amaterasu* and helped her to rule *Takama-ga-hara*.

Takamuku Kuromaro. 高向玄理 (+ 654). Descendant of *Takeshiuchi no Sukune*, he accompanied the first embassy sent to China (607), and stayed there for 33 years. Having returned to Japan, he received the title of Doctor (*Kuni-hakase*) and shared in the work of bringing about the *Taikwa* reform (645). Sent to restore peace in *Shiragi* (Korea), he returned with the son of the king as hostage. Appointed chief of the embassy to China, (654) he died in that country after a sojourn of 5 or 6 months.

Takanabe, 高鍋 . City (5,800 inh.) of *Hyūga*. Ancient castle belonging to the *Itō daimyō*. The *Shimazu* occupied it in 1578, *Hideyoshi* gave it as fief to *Akizuki Tanenaga*, and his descendants kept it till the Restoration (27,000 k.).

Takanaga-shinnō, 尊良親王 (1311-1337). 2nd son of the emperor *Go-Daigo*. When *Ashikaga Takauji* revolted, he was named *Kwanryō* of the Eastern provinces and marched against the rebel. Besieged in the castle of *Kanagasaki* (*Echizen*) he killed himself.

Takanawa-san, 高縄山 . Mountain N. of *Iyo*, on which during the 13th and the 14th centuries, the castle of the *Kōno daimyō* was situated.

Takano, 高野 . *Kuge* family descended from *Fujiwara Yorimune* (993-1065). — Now Viscount.

Takano Chōei, 高野長英 (1804-1850). Born in *Mutsu*, of the *Gotō* family, he was adopted by his uncle *Takano Gensai*. He studied the Dutch language, came to *Edo* and took lessons in medicine from *Yoshida Chōshuku*. In 1824, he went to *Nagasaki* and became Siebold's scholar. Having returned to *Edo*, his fame as a doctor grew daily and disciples came from all parts. In 1838, the arrival of an English ship (Capt. Morrison) at *Uraga* produced a great commotion. The *Bakufu* prepared to repel any attack by force of arms. *Chōei* at this same time was publishing a book (*Yume-monogatari* : stories of dreams) in which whilst depicting the civilization of Europe, he criticized steps taken by the government. for which he was condemned to prison for life. Three years later, he escaped, owing to a fire that destroyed part of the buildings where he was confined, and went to *Uwajima* (*Iyo*), where he was employed by the *daimyō* as translator. Having returned to *Edo*, (1844), he lived in disguise under the name of *Takayanagi Ryūnosuke* and continued to translate books especially such as treated of military science. The *Bakufu* having discovered the place of his retreat and ascertained his identity, sent soldiers to arrest him. *Choei* defended himself, killed two of his assailants, then killed himself. In 1898, he was raised to the 4th rank (*shō-shi-i*).

Takao-jō, 高雄城. In *Kaga* (*Togashi-mura*). Ancient castle of the *Togashi daimyō*. Was captured in 1488 by the troops in the service of the *Hongwanji* (*Ikkō-shū*). Also called *Togashi-jō*.

Takaoka, 高岡. In *Shimōsa*. Was from 1640 to 1868, the residence of the *Inoue daimyō* (14,000 k.).

Takaoka, 高岡. *Kuge* family descended from *Fujiwara Kosemaro*. — Now Viscount.

Takaoka-jō, 高岡城. Ancient castle of the *Tsugaru daimyō*, near the present town of *Hirosaki* (*Mutsu*).

Takaoka-shinnō, 高岳親王. — See *Kōgaku-shinnō*.

Takasago, 高砂. Harbor (6,200 inh.) in *Harima*, at the mouth of the *Kako-gawa* river, famous for its picturesque scenery, which has often been celebrated in poetry.

Takasago, 高砂. Name given, towards the 16th century, to Formosa, on account of the similarily of its scenery to that of the shores of the *Takasago* (*Harima*).

Takasaki, 高崎. Town (31,000 inh.) of *Kōzuke*. — Ancient castle built in the 15th century by the *Wada daimyō* and for this reason called *Wada-jō*. Passed then into the possession of the *Uesugi*, and later into that of the *Takeda*. In 1582, *Takigawa Kazumasa*, having been named by *Nobunaga*, *Kwanryō* of the *Kwantō*, established himself at *Umayabashi*, and *Takasaki* became part of his domains. After *Nobunaga's* death, the *Hōjō* of *Odawara* occupied it. Under the *Tokugawa*, it belonged successively to the *daimyō Ii* (1590), *Sakai* (1604), *Toda* (1616), *Matsudaira* (1617), *Andō* (1619), *Ōkōchi* (1695), *Manabe* (1710), and finally to *Ōkōchi* (*Matsudaira*) from 1717 to 1868, (82,000 k.).

Takasaki, 高崎. *Samurai* family of the *Kagoshima* clan (*Satsuma*), made noble after ther Restoration. — Now Baron.

Takashima, 高島. In *Shinano* (*Shimo-Suwa-mura*). Ancient castle of the *Suwa daimyō*. *Takeda Shingen* occupied it in 1553 and entrusted it to *Itagaki Nobukata*. Burnt in 1582, by *Nobunaga's* troops it was rebuilt by *Hineno Takayoshi* (1590). In 1601, *Ieyasu* reinstated *Suwa Yoritada*, whose descendants remained in the castle till the Restoration (30,000 k).

Takashima, 高島. *Samurai* family of the *Kagoshima* clan (*Satsuma*) made noble in 1884. — Now Viscount.

Taka-shima, 高島. Island (40 Km. circum.) of *Hizen*, near the entrance of *Nagasaki* harbor. Center of an important mining district, its annual production amounts to over 800,000 tons of coal. — In 1282,

30,000 shipwrecked Mongols took refuge on this island, but, attacked by *Shōni Kagesuke*, they were defeated and all massacred.

Takasu, 高須. Small city (4800 inh.) of *Mino*. — Ancient castle built in 1574 by *Ōhashi Shigekazu*. Under the *Tokugawa*, it belonged to the *daimyō Tokunaga* (1600) *Ogasawara* (1640) ; and *Matsudaira* from 1700 to 1868, (30,000 k.),

Takasugi Shinsaku, 高杉晋作 (1839-1867). *Samurai* of the *Chōshū* clan, who during the troubled times that preceded the Restoration distinguished himself by his fidelity to his lord, his opposition to the shogunate, his hatred to foreigners and his military talents.

Takata, 高田. City (20,400 inh.) of *Echigo*. — In 1610, it became the fief of *Tadateru*, 6th son of *Ieyasu* (600,000 k.). Later belonged to the *daimyō Sakai* (1616), *Matsudaira* (1623), *Inaba* (1685), *Toda* (1701), *Hisamatsu* (1710), then from 1741 to 1868, to *Sakakibara* (150,000 k.).

Takata, 高田. In *Bungo* (*Shibazaki-mura*). Ancient castle built in the 13th century by *Takata Shigesaka*, vassal of the *Ōtomo*, *Hideyoshi* gave it to *Takenaka Shigetada* in 1593, and when the latter went to *Funai* (*Ōita*), *Takata* was abandoned (1600). *Matsudaira Shigenao*, who received it in 1632, repaired it, but his son *Hidechika* settled at *Kizuki*, and *Takata* was finally abandoned (1645).

Takata Motokiyo, 高田與清 (1783-1847). Disciple of *Murata Harumi*. He published more than 50 works on literature and history.

Takatenjin, 高天神. In *Tōtōmi*. Ancient castle built towards 1425 by *Imagawa Noritada*. In 1569, it passed into the hands of the *Takeda* and was occupied by *Ieyasu* in 1581.

Takatō, 高遠. Small city (4500 inh.) of *Shinano*. — Towads 1340, it was given in fief by *Ashikaga Takauji* to *Kiso Iemura*, whose descendants were dispossessed of it by *Takeda Shingen* (1549). The latter built a castle there and installed his son *Katsuyori* (1562). After the ruin of the *Takeda*, *Nobunaga* entrusted it to *Hoshina Masanao* (1582), whom *Hideyoshi* replaced by *Kyōgoku Takatomo* (1592). Under the *Tokugawa*, it belonged to the *daimyō Hoshina* (1600), *Torii* (1636), and from 1691 to 1868, to *Naitō* (33,000 k.).

Takatomi, 高富. In *Mino*. From 1706 to 1868, the residence of the *Honjō daimyō* (10,000 k.).

Takatori, 高取. In *Yamato*. Ancient castle which in the 14th century belonged to the *Ochi* family, faithful adherents of the Southern dynasty. In 1585, it was a part of the domains of *Hashiba Hidenaga*. Under the *Tokugawa*, it became the residence of the *daimyō Honda* (1600), and from 1640 to 1868, that of *Uemura* (25,000 k.).

Takatsuji, 高辻. *Kuge* family descended from *Sugawara Michizane* (847-903). — Now Viscount.

Takatsukasa, 鷹司. *Kuge* family descended from *Fujiwara Iezane* (1179-1242).

—— **Kanehira,** 兼平 (1228-1294). 6th son of *Iezane*, was the first to take the name of *Takatsukasa*. This family was one of the 5 principal branches of the *Fujiwara* family. —— Now Duke.

Takatsukasa, 鷹 司 . — See *Matsudaira* (*Taketsukasa*).

Takatsuki, 高 槻 . In *Settsu*. Ancient castle which during the 16th century belonged to the *Takayama daimyō*, who were dispossessed in 1579. Under the *Tokugawa*, was the residence of the families *Toki* (1617), *Matsudaira* (1619), *Okabe* (1635), *Matsudaira* (1640), and from 1649 to 1868, of the *Nagai* (36,000 k.).

Takatsuma-yama, 高 妻 山 . Mountain (2425 m.) on the borders of *Shinano* and *Echigo*.

Takaya, 高 屋 . In *Kawachi* (*Furuichi-mura*). Ancient castle built towards the end of the 14th century by *Hatakeyama Yoshitō*. His descendants were dispossessed of it by *Miyoshi Yoshitsugu* (1560), and the latter in turn by *Nobunaga* (1568).

Takayama, 高 山 . Principal city (14,700 inh.) of *Hida* province. Ancient castle and residence of the *daimyō Anenokōji* (1400 to about 1587), *Kanamori* (1587-1697). It became a part of the *Shōgun's* domain who had it governed by a *daikwan*.

Takayama, 高 山 . Ancient family of *daimyō* from *Settsu*.

—— **Hida no kami, 飛 驒 守** (+ 1596). Was governor of the castle of *Takatsuki* and became a vassal of *Araki Murashige* when the latter received the province of *Settsu* from *Nobunaga* (1573). When *Murashige* revolted (1579), he sided with him, was besieged in his castle and banished to *Kitanoshō* (*Echizen*), where he died in 1564. He was baptised *Darie*, and was always a fervent Christian.

—— **Nagafusa, 長 房** (1553-1615). Son of the above had the title of *Ukon-tayū*. He was baptised at the age of 11, at the same time as his father, and received the name of *Juste ;* for this reason he is mentioned in the writings of the old missionaries under the name of *Juste Ukon-dono*. The Japanese called him *Takayama Ukon*. He joined the campaign against the *Hongwan-ji* temple of *Ōsaka*. When his suzerain *Araki Murashige* revolted in 1579, he submitted to *Nobunaga*, who gave him the castle of *Akutagawa* (*Settsu*). When informed of the assassination of *Nobunaga*, he left in haste with *Ikeda Nobuteru* and helped to defeat *Akechi Mitsuhide* at *Yamasaki* (1582). During the campaign of of *Shizu-ga-take* (1583), having to defend the position of *Yanase*, he was attacked and defeated by *Sakuma Morimasa*. He took part in the expedition against the bonzes of the *Negoro-dera* (1585) and in the *Kyūshū* campaign against the *Shimazu* (1587). Having fallen into disgrace on account of being a Christian, he was banished to *Kaga*. It is believed that *Maeda Toshiie* took him to the siege of *Odawara* (1590), in the hope that his valor would obtain the favor of *Hideyoshi* for him, but in vain ; he was obliged to return to his place of exile. He remained there to 1614. At that time, an edict of *Ieyasu* banished all the missionaries from Japan, as well as the most prominent Christians. *Ukon* was among them. He left *Kanazawa* to go to *Nagasaki*, and from there he sailed for Manila with his whole family. The junk in which he embarked carried also some 30 missionaries, *John Naitō* and his family, and several Christian women among whom was a daughter of *Ōtomo Sōrin*. Sailing from *Nagasaki* on the 8th of November 1614, the exiles arrived at

Manila on the 28th of the same month and were received with great honor. But two months afterwards, *Ukon* died, having been ill for only a short time (Feb. 3, 1615). He was buried in the church of the Jesuits, where his tomb can be seen to the present day.

Takayama Masayuki, 高山正之 (1747-1793). Also called *Hikokurō*. Born at *Hosoya* (*Kōzuke*), he came to *Kyōto* at the age of 18, and had a powerful protector in the person of the *Dainagon Nakayama*. He devoted his time principally to the study of history and was astonished to see that, unlike the political condition during the Middle Ages, the *Shōgun* had usurped the power which the Emperor should have exercised. He traveled over different provinces to revive the prestige of the Imperial dynasty in the minds of the people. At *Kyōto*, he stationed himself at the *Sanjō* bridge, and there, turning towards the Palace, fell on his knees and venerated the Emperor from afar. Finally at the end of his peregrinations, he arrived at *Kurume* (*Chikugo*) where broken hearted at the sight of the poor state of the country, he offered himself as a victim to the Imperial cause and committed *harakiri*. — *Masayuki* to the present day, has remained a model of the fidelity due to a sovereign. With *Gamō Kumpei*, and *Hayashi Shihei*, he forms what is called the *Sankijin*.

Takayoshi-Ō, 尊義王 (+ 1444). Son of prince *Ogura no Ōji* and grandson of the emperor *Go-Kameyama* He was bonze at the *Manjū-ji* temple, when *Fujiwara* (*Hino*) *Arimitsu* plotted to elevate him in place of the reigning emperor, *Go-Hanazono*, descendant of the Northern dynasty. They levied troops in *Yamato*, *Kawachi* and *Kii*, and one night, entering the Palace, they sought to take the Emperor in person. The latter succeeded in making his escape to the residence of the *Sadaijin Fusatsugu*, but the 3 Imperial emblems fell into the hands of the conspirators. The *Shōgun* sent an army against them under the command of *Hatakeyama Mochikuni*. The rebels having intrenched themselves on mount *Hiei-zan*, were defeated and the prince killed himself.

Take, 多氣. In *Ise*. Ancient castle of the *Kitabatake daimyō*, governors of the province. Built in 1335 by *Akinobu*, it was captured by *Nobunaga* (1569).

Takechi no Ōji, 高市皇子 (+ 696). 2nd son of the emperor *Temmu ;* he helped his father to obtain the Imperial power and fought in *Ōmi* against the troops of *Kōbun-tennō* (672). In 690, he was named *Dajō-daijin*. He is the father of the princes *Nagaya-Ō, Suzuka-Ō*, etc.

Takeda, 竹田. City (6100 inh.) of *Bungo*. Formerly called *Oka*, from the name of the castle (*Oka-jō*) of its lords. Was from 1593 to 1868, the residence of the *Nakagawa* family (70,000 k.).

Takeda, 武田. *Daimyō* family descended from *Minamoto Yoshimitsu* (1056-1127), brother of *Yoshiie* (*Seiwa-Genji*).

—— **Yoshikiyo,** 義清 (+ 1163). Son of *Yoshimitsu*, was the first to take the name of *Takeda*.

—— **Nobuyoshi,** 信義 (1138-1186). Grandson of *Yoshikiyo*, sided with *Yoritomo* and levied troops for his support in *Kai* and *Shinano* (1180), then accompanied *Noriyori* in his campaign against the *Taira* (1184).

—— **Nobumitsu,** 信光 (1162-1248). Son of *Nobuyoshi*, assisted at the campaign against *Kiso Yoshinaka* and against the *Taira*. Being a favorite of *Yoritomo*, he obtained the *Suruga* province in fief. He repressed the revolt of *Wada Yoshimori* (1213). At the time of the *Shōkyū* war (1221), he did not even reply to the offers made him by *Go-Toba*, but helped the *Hōjō* and entered *Kyōto*. In reward, he was made governor of *Aki*. Soon after, he shaved his head and took the name of *Kōren*. *Nobumitsu* was famous for his skill in horsemanship and arrow shooting.

—— **Nobumitsu,** 信満 (+ 1417). Descendant of *Nobuyoshi* in the 9th generation, inherited the *Kai* and *Aki* provinces. Defeated at *Tokusa* (*Kai*) whilst fighting against *Uesugi Norimune*, he killed himself.

—— **Nobushige,** 信重 (+ 1450). Son of *Nobumitsu*, became a bonze at the *Kōya-san* at the death of his father, but when his uncle *Nobumoto*, governor of *Kai* died, he returned to succeed him.

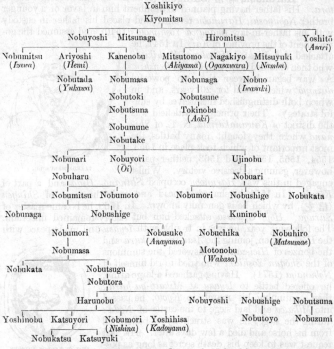

—— **Nobumasa,** 信昌. Grandson of *Nobushige*. He repressed the revolt of one of his most powerful vassals, *Atobe Kageie*, whose aim was nothing less than to become master of the whole province of *Kai*. He attacked *Atobe Kageie* at *Ishizawa* where he defeated and killed him and his son *Kagetsugu* (1465). *Nobumasa* was then but 19 years old.

—— **Nobutora,** 信虎 (1493-1573). Grandson of *Nobumasa*, built the castle of *Kōfu* and in 1519 established his authority over the whole province. In 1536, he attacked *Hiraga Genshin* at *Uminokuchi*, but had to retreat ; his son *Harunobu* then came to his rescue and defeated *Genshin*. Some time after *Nobutora* resolved to disinherit *Harunobu* in favor of his second son *Nobushige*, whom he loved most particularly. *Harunobu* irritated, expelled his father from the province and delivered him to *Imagawa Yoshimoto, daimyō* of *Suruga*. *Nobutora* had to shave his head and was confined at *Sumpu* (1540). At the death of *Yoshitomo* (1560), he was allowed to retire to *Kyōto* and after the murder of the *Shōgun Yoshiteru* (1565) he returned into his old province, where *Harunobu* had him under surveillance at *Ina* (*Shinano*), till he died.

—— **Harunobu,** 晴信 (**Shingen**) (1521-1573). Eldest son of *Nobutora*. His father having planned to disinherit him in favor of a younger brother *Nobuyoshi*, *Harunobu* revolted and placed his father in custody with his father-in-law *Imagawa Yoshimoto* (1540), and assumed the government of the province of *Kai*. In 1547, he attacked and defeated *Murakami Yoshikiyo*, who then obtained help from *Uesugi Kenshin*. A war began between the two powerful *daimyō* which lasted for 20 years, and in which both distinguished themselves by skilful strategy. Their principal battlefield was the district of *Kawanakajima*, N. E. of *Shinano* where they fought many battles, the most important of which took place in 1553, 1554, 1555, 1556, and 1563, neither party however, gaining a decisive victory. Whilst

TAKEDA HARUNOBU.

engaged in this war, *Harunobu* occupied *Shinano, Hida* and a part of *Kōzuke*. In 1551, he shaved his head and took the name of *Shingen* (信玄), by which he is generally known. In 1568, he became master of *Suruga*. *Hōjō Ujimasa* attacked him but victory remained uncertain. The following year, he was in trouble with *Ieyasu* and made peace with the *Hōjō*. Then, joining the *Asai*, the *Asakura* and the bonzes of *Hiei-zan*, he answered the summons of the *Shōgun Yoshiaki* who tried to rid himself of *Nobunaga* (1571). Having gathered a large army, he offered battle to *Ieyasu* at *Mikata-ga-hara ;* then continuing his march to *Kyōto*, he passed into *Mikawa* and laid siege to the castle of *Noda :* during the siege, he was struck by a bullet, fell from his horse and died a few days after. His last request was to keep his death secret as long as possible. And indeed, he was buried only three years afterwards, in the temple of *Eirin-ji* at *Matsuzato* (*Kai*).

SEAL OF TAKEDA SHINGEN
(1578).

—— **Katsuyori,** 勝 賴 (1546-1582). 3rd son of *Harunobu*, was adopted by the *Ina* family and resided at the castle of *Takatō*. He succeeded his father, but soon made enemies of *Shingen's* companions in arms, by refusing to take their advice in important matters and by deciding all affairs according to his own pleasure. In 1574, he entered upon a campaign against *Ieyasu*, but was defeated at *Takatenjin* (*Tōtōmi*), and the following year, at *Nagashino* (*Mikawa*). From that time the glory of the *Takeda* began to decline rapidly. In 1578, he gave help to *Uesugi Kagekatsu* against his rival *Kagetora*, but the latter belonged to the *Hōjō* family, who all took up arms to defend their relative. Thus *Katsuyori* found himself at war with *Nobunaga*, *Ieyasu* and the *Hōjō* at the same time. The issue of such a war could not be doubtful. After having taken the castle of *Numata* (*Kōzuke*), he built forts at *Numazu*, and at *Sammaibashi* (*Suruga*), but was defeated at *Takatenjin* (1581). The following year, learning that *Kiso Yoshimasa* had made an alliance with *Nobunaga*, he marched against him, but *Nobutada* and *Ieyasu* joined forces, and after several battles, the army of *Katsuyori* was completely routed at the *Temmoku-zan* (*Kai*): *Katsuyori* and his son *Nobukatsu* killed themselves. —— Under the *Tokugawa*, two lateral branches of the *Takeda* family figure among the *Kōke*.

Takeda Izumo no Jō, 竹 田 出 雲 橡 (1646-1726). Born in *Awa* (*Shikoku*), he came to *Edo*, settled at *Asakusa*, where he gave theatrical shows with puppets, and had great success. At *Kyōto*, he was asked to give a performance at the Palace. In 1662, he settled at *Ōsaka* and opened a theatre, for which he composed pieces. Next to *Chikamatsu Monzaemon*, he was the greatest dramatist of his time. His most famous piece represents the vengeance of the 47 *rōnin* of *Akō*. The title of *Izumo no Jō* was given him in 1685. His descendants kept it for several generations and maintained the reputation of their theatre at *Ōsaka*.

Takeda Kōunsai, 武 田 耕 雲 齊 (1804-1865). *Samurai* of the *Mito* clan, enjoyed the confidence of his *daimyō Nariaki*. Two parties were then in power: the *Seitō*, which extolled the Imperial restoration and the expulsion of foreigners, and the *Kantō*, which desired to maintain the Shogunate and open the country to the world. *Kōunsai* was strongly inclined in favor of the first party and exercised great influence over his master in their behalf. After *Nariaki's* death (1860), he was called to *Kyōto* by *Keiki* and the Emperor honored him with the 5th rank at Court (*ju-go-i-ge*), but in 1864, the power of the *Shōgun* seemed to be in the ascendency and *Kōunsai* lost favor. He then joined the *Mito samurai* who had intrenched themselves on the *Tsukuba-san* where he was defeated with them. He fled to *Haibara* (*Echizen*) and asked pardon in vain: he was executed with a great number of his adherents.

Takehana, 竹 鼻. In *Mino*. Ancient castle belonging to *Oda Nobuo* and occupied by *Hideyoshi* in 1584.

Take-mikazuchi no kami, 健 御 雷 神. Shintoist god, sent to earth with *Futsunushi* to obtain the submission of *Ōkuninushi* and thus to prepare the way for the coming of *Ninigi no mikoto*. Also called

Takefutsu or *Toyofutsu*. A temple is dedicated to him at *Kashima* (*Hitachi*).

Take-minakata no kami, 健 御 名 方 神. Son of *Ōkuninushi*. When *Futsunushi* and *Take-mikazuchi* came to *Izumo* to have the sovereignty of *Ninigi no mikoto* recognized, he refused to obey and fought against the heavenly envoys. Defeated, he fled to *Suwa* (*Shinano*), where he is honored under the name of *Suwa-myōjin*.

Takemoto Gidayū, 竹 本 義 太 夫 (1651-1714). Famous dramatist was a follower of *Inoue Harima no Jō*, and later established his own school of *jōruri*. In 1685, he opened a theatre in which he made it a specialty to sing the pieces of the famous *Chikamatsu Monzaemon*. The name *gidayū* is given to the kind of performances he established.

Takenaka, 竹 中. *Daimyō* family, descended from the *Minamoto*. Resided at *Takata* (*Bungo*) in 1593; then in 1600 at *Funai* (*Bungo* — 20,000 k.).

—— **Shigetsuku,** 重 次 (+ 1634). In 1632, he was made *Naga-saki-bugyō*, but was accused of debauchery and extortions and condemned to kill himself. His domains returned to the *Shōgun*.

Takenokoshi, 竹 腰. Family descended from *Sasaki Nobutsuna* (+ 1242) (*Uda-Genji*) and vassal of the *Uesugi*.

—— **Masanobu,** 正 信. Served *Ieyasu*. When very young, he lost his father *Masatoki*; his mother, now a widow, bore *Ieyasu* a son who was the founder of the *Owari* branch. *Masanobu* followed the destinies of *Yoshinao* and in 1619, received a revenue of 30,000 k. at *Imao* (*Mino*), where his descendants remained to the Restoration. — Now Baron.

Takenoshita, 竹 下. In *Suruga* (*Ashigara-mura*). *Wakiya Yoshisuke* was defeated there by *Ashikaga Takauji* (1336).

Takenouchi, 竹 内. *Kuge* family descended from *Minamoto Yoshimitsu* (1056-1127) (*Seiwa-Genji*). — Now Viscount.

Takenouchi Shikibu, 竹 内 式 部 (1716-1771). Born in *Echigo*, he was a disciple of *Tamaki Isai*, a renovator of Shintoism; he went to *Kyōto* and opened a school where he expounded the doctrines of the Chinese philosopher *Shushi* (*Tchou-hi*: 1130-1200). His lectures attracted great crowds of students especially from among the *kuge*. Having been impeached for teaching his pupils military sciences, he was imprisoned by order of the *Shōgun*, and 17 *kuge* were disgraced at the same time (1758). Exiled from *Kyōto* the following year, he went to *Ise*. When *Yamagata Daini* and *Fujii Umon* were decapitated for favoring an Imperial restoration, (1767), *Shikibu* was arrested with them, imprisoned, and condemned to be exiled to *Hachijō-jima*. He died on the boat that was taking him thither.

Takenukawa-wake, 武 淳 川 別. Son of *Ōhiko* and grandson of the emperor *Kōgen*. In 88 B.C., he was named *Shōgun* of *Tōkaidō* and commissioned to repress the *Ebisu* of that region. His mission finished, he returned to his father, the *Shōgun* of *Hokurokudō*, and the name *Aizu* (meeting) was given to the place where they met.

Takeshiki, 竹 敷. Harbor of *Tsushima* island. It is within the bay called *Takeshiki no ura* or *Take no ura*. Naval station.

Takeshi-uchi no Sukune, 武內宿禰. Descendant of the emperor *Kōgen* in the 5th generation. He was born on the same day as the future emperor *Seimu* (85) and when the latter was declared heir to the throne, he received the title of *Omi* (minister). At the time of *Seimu's* accession, (131), he became *Ō-omi* (first minister). He accompanied *Chūai-tennō* in his campaign against the *Kumaso* of *Tsukushi* (199), and supported the opinion of the empress *Jingō* in reference to an expedition to Korea. When the emperor died, he followed the empress, helped her to subjugate the *San-kan*, and after her return to *Tsukushi, Jingō-kōgō* gave birth to *Ōjin* (201). The following year, two other sons of *Chūai, Kagosaka* and *Oshikuma*, attempted to succeed their father, and revolted. *Sukune* being sent against them, defeat~l and put them to death. In 278, he was commissioned to make a tour of inspection in *Tsukushi*. During his absence,

TAKESHI-UCHI NO SUKUNE.

his brother *Umashi-uchi* accused him of having levied troops under the pretence of sending them to Korea, but in reality to revolt. *Sukune* returned to Court, and justified himself by the ordeal of boiling water. His innocence having been admitted, he again became minister. He died, according to some in 367, at the age of 283, according to others, in 390, at the age 306.—It is presumed that under his name, the principal events of several generations of his family were collectively known.

Takeshiuchi no Sukune
{
Hata no Yashiro
Ki no Tsunu
Ishikawa-maro-Machi-Karako-Koma (*Soga*)
Kose no Ogara
Heguri no Tsuku-Matori-Shibi (*Heguri*)
Katsuragi no Sotsuhiko-Tamata-Tsubura (*Katsuragi*)
}

Takeshiuchi no Sukune is the ancestor of the *Soga, Heguri, Katsuragi* and other families.

Takeda no miya, 竹田宮. A family of royal blood, raised to be princes in 1906 in the person of *Tsunehisa*, the eldest son of prince *Kitashirakawa Yoshihisa* (1847-1895), when he was betrothed to *Masako, Tsune no miya*, 6th daughter of the Emperor.

Taketori-monogatari, 竹取物語 (Lit.: story of a bamboo gatherer). The oldest classical Japanese book. It is the story of a young girl banished from the moon and sent to the earth, where a woodman, whilst splitting a bamboo finds her, all sparkling with light. Some authors believe this book nothing but the translation of a Buddhist *sûtra*. The author and the date of its composition are unknown, but it is believed to date back as far as the 2nd half of the ninth century.

Taketsunumi no mikoto, 建津身命. A native of the province of *Kii*, who served as guide to *Jimmu-tennō* when he went to *Yamato* (663 B.C.). He, in reward, received the name of *Yata-garasu* (crow with 8 feet).

Takeya, 竹屋. *Kuge* family descended from *Fujiwara Manatsu* (771-830). — Now Viscount.

Takezono, 竹園. Family descended from *Fujiwara Sadakata* (868-932) and attached to the temple of *Kōfuku-ji* (*Nara*). — Now Baron.

Takibi no ma, 焚火間. Formerly a room in the *Shōgun's* palace, at *Kamakura*, which served as a meeting hall for the ministers and counsellors when they treated important matters. In order to obtain the greatest secrecy possible, not a word was uttered and each expressed his ideas by tracing characters in the ashes of the brazier (*irori*) which was burning in the room.

Takigawa Kazumasu, 瀧川一益. Vassal of *Oda Nobunaga*. Took part in all his campaigns as commander of the van-guard and distinguished himself by his bravery. In 1569, he received 5 districts of *Ise* as fief. He afterwards suppressed the army of the *Ikkō-shū* bonzes and built a castle at *Nagashima*. He besieged *Araki Murashige* in *Itami* (1579), then aided in the campaign against *Takeda Katsuyori*, at the end of which, he received the province of *Kōzuke* and 2 districts of *Shinano* (1582), but when *Nobunaga* was murdered, he returned to *Nagashima*, joined *Shibata Katsuie* and was defeated with him (1583). He then shaved his head and retired to *Echizen*, where he died.

Takiwaki, 瀧脇. *Daimyō* family, descended from *Minamoto Yoshishige* (+ 1202) (*Seiwa-Genji*). Resided at *Sakurai* (*Kazusa* — 10,000 k.), — Now Viscount.

Takiyama-jō, 瀧山城. In *Musashi* (*Kasumi-mura*). Ancient castle built in the 15th century by *Ōishi Sadahisa*, vassal of the *Uesugi*. In 1546, it passed into the possession of the *Hōjō* of *Odawara*, and in 1569 into that of the *Takeda*. Abandoned since 1590.

Tako, 多古. Small city (5000 inh.) of *Shimōsa*. From 1713 to 1868 was the residence of the *Hisamatsu daimyō* (12,000 k.).

Takuan, 澤庵 (1573-1645). Member of the *Miura* family, became bonze in the *Jōdo* sect. At the age of 14, he entered the temple of *Shōfuku-ji*, where he became known for his virtues. He travelled through the provinces, preaching and practising poverty and penance. Having offended the *Shōgun*, he was exiled to *Dewa*, but was pardoned 4 years after and returned to *Kyōto*. The ex-emperor *Go-Yōzei* and the *Shōgun Hidetada* gave him audience and favored him. In 1634, he founded the temple *Tōkai-ji* at *Shinagawa* (*Musashi*). *Takuan* found a manner of seasoning turnips (*daikon*), which is named *Takuanzuke*, after him.

Takuma-ryū, 宅麿流. School of painting, following the principles of *Kose Kanaoka*, and founded at the end of the 10th century by *Takuma Tameuji*, who was succeeded by *Tamenari* (towards 1030), *Tametō* (towards 1150), *Tamehisa* (1180) *Shōga* (t. 1200), *Chōga* (t. 1210), *Ryōga* (t. 1220), *Tameyuki* (t. 1230), *Eiga* (t. 1310), *Ryōson* (1265-1327), *Shikibu-tayū* (+ 1330), *Jōkō* (t. 1380), etc.

Takumi-ryō, 内匠寮. Bureau created in 728 and dependent upon the *Nakatsukasa-shō*. It was supervised by a *Kami* who attended to the preparation of festivals and to repairs in the Imperial Palace.

Tama-gawa, 多摩川, 玉川. River (139 Km.) that rises E. of *Kai*, passes through the province of *Musashi* and enters the bay of *Tōkyō* at *Haneda*, near *Kawasaki*. It is also called *Rokugō-gawa*. In

1653, an aqueduct was built which brought the water of this river to the city of *Edo*.

Tamamatsu, 玉松. *Kuge* family descendant from *Fujiwara (Saionji) Saneharu* (1600-1673). — Now Baron.

Tamaritsume-shū, 溜詰衆. Under the *Tokugawa*, a high official who assisted the *Rōjū*. He was so called because he exercised his office in the *Tamari no ma*, a room of the shogunal Palace. This title was created in 1675, and the first to receive it, was *Hoshina Masayasu*.

Tamaru, 田丸. In *Ise* (*Shirota-mura*). Ancient castle of a family of that name, vassal to the *Kitabatake*. *Oda Nabuo*, having inherited it from *Kitabatake Tomonori*, settled in that place in 1569. *Hideyoshi* gave it to *Ochi Michinao*. Under the *Tokugawa*, it belonged to *Inaba Michitō* (1600), then it became the property of the *Tokugawa* branch, *Kii*, and was ruled by a *jōdai* of the *Kunō* family.

Tamaru, 田丸. Ancient vassal family of the *Kitabatake*, governors of *Ise*. Since the 14th century, it resided at *Tamaru* (*Ise*). *Nobunaga* transferred it to *Miharu* (*Mutsu*) and *Hideyoshi* to *Iwamura* (*Mino* — 45,000 k). *Tomoyasu* the last of this family was dispossessed by *Ieyasu* and banished to *Aizu* (1600).

Tama-shizume no matsuri, 鎮魂祭. Shintoist ceremony dating from the time of *Jimmu-tennō*, during which prayers were said for the emperor's longevity and his peace of mind.

Tamatsukuri-gawa, 玉造川. River (98 Km.) rising on the boundary of *Uzen*, passes through *Rikuzen*, and flows into the *Kitakami-gawa* at *Wabuchi*. Also called *Eai-gawa*.

Tamayori-hime, 玉依姫. Daughter of *Watatsumi no kami* and sister of *Toyotama-hime*. Married *Ugaya-fuki-aezu no mikoto* and was the mother of *Jimmu-tennō*. Is honored under the name of *Mi-oya no kami*.

Tamba, 丹波. One of the 8 provinces of *San-in-dō*. Comprises 7 districts, 5 of which at present depend upon the *Kyōto-fu* and 2 on *Hyōgo-ken*. — Chinese name : *Tanshū* (with *Tango* and *Tajima*).

Tamenaga Shunsui, 爲永春水. Famous novel writer, author of the *Iroha-bunko* (story of the 47 *rōnin* of *Akō*), etc Imprisoned by order of the *Shōgun*, in 1842, he died shortly after.

Tamichi, 田道. Warrior of the 4th century, led an expedition to Korea in 365 to force *Shiragi* to pay tribute. He returned bringing inhabitants of 4 districts as prisoners. Two years later, he died during a campaign against the *Ebisu*. He is also called *Kamitsukenu Tamichi*.

Tami no tsukasa, 民部省. Ancient name of the *Mimbu-shō*.

Tamon, 多聞. — See *Anan*.

Tamon, 多門. — See *Bishamon*.

Tamon-jō, 多門城. In *Yamato*. Ancient castle built in 1567 by *Matsunaga Hisahide* on the *Tamon-zan* hill, near

TAMICHI.

Nara. In the construction of this castle, *Hisahide* departed from the customary rules and surrounded it with dependencies (*nagaya*). This inovation soon spread and is known under the name of *tamon*.

Tamu no mine, 多武峯. Or **Tan-zan, 談山**. Mountain in *Yamato* on which *Fujiwara Joe* in the 7th century constructed a temple to the memory of his father *Kamatari*. The temple became very prosperous. In the 14th century, the troops in the pay of the bonzes (*sōhei*) supported the S. dynasty and fought against *Kō Moronao*. — *Tamu no mine* is also called *Tabu no mine*, *Tō no mine*.

Tamura, 田村. Ancient *daimyō* family of *Mutsu* descendant from *Sakanoe no Tamura-maro*. *Date Masamune* dispossessed it in 1598, and some time after, chose his grandson *Muneyoshi* (whose mother was a descendant of the *Tamura*), to perpetuate the name. In 1695, *Take-aki*, son of *Muneyoshi* received the fief of *Ichinoseki* (*Mutsu* — 27,000 k.), which his descendants kept till the Restoration. — Now Viscount.

Tamura, 田村. Family of Confucianists at the service of the *Shōgun* of *Edo*. The best known are *Ransui* (+ 1776) and *Seiko* (+ 1793).

Tanabata, 棚機, 七夕. Popular feast celebrated on the 7th day of the 7th month. It owes its origin to a Chinese legend. The daughter of the master of heaven (*Tentei*) lived E. of the Milky Way (*Ama no kawa*) and passed her time in weaving cloth, whence the name of *Shokujo* (weaver), which was given to her. Her father chose a husband for her in the person of *Kengyū* (herdsman) who ruled on the other side of the Milky Way. But their honey moon lasted so long that the young wife neglected work altogether. *Tentei* condemned the couple to be separated. They were allowed to see each other only once a year, on the 7th night of the 7th month, and, when the time arrived, a raven extended its wings over the Milky Way to enable them to meet. This feast is especially kept by young girls who ask the *Shokujo* star to make them as skilful as she was in the art of sewing and perhaps also, one day to be united to a husband as faithful as *Kengyū*. According to popular belief, the petitions made on this day are sure to be fulfilled in less than a space of 3 years. This feast is also called *Kikōten*, and was celebrated for the first time in the Imperial Palace in the year 755, whence it gradually spread over the whole country. It is one of the *go-sekku*.

Tanabe, 田邊. In *Tango*. *Isshiki Mitsunori*, made governor of the province, settled there at the end of the 14th century. His descendants were dispossessed in 1584, by *Hosokawa Tadaoki*. Under the *Tokugawa*, it was the residence of the *Kyōgoku daimyō* (1604), and from 1668 to 1868, that of the *Makino* (35,000 k.). — At the time of the Restoration the name was changed to that of *Maizuru*. — (See that name).

Tanabe, 田邊. City (7,600 inh.) of *Kii*. Was from 1619 to 1868, the residence of the *Andō daimyō* (28,000 k.).

Tanaka, 田中. In *Suruga* (*Nishi-Mashizu-mura*). Ancient castle which successively belonged to the *daimyō Isshiki*, *Imagawa*, and *Takeda*. At the ruin of the latter (1582), it passed to *Ieyasu*. Under the *Tokugawa*, it was the residence of the *daimyō Sakai* (1601), *Tokugawa* (1625), *Sakurai* (1633), *Mizuno* (1635), *Matsudaira* (1642), *Hōjō* (1644)

Nishio (1649), *Sakai* (1679), *Tsuchiya* (1681), *Ōta* (1687), *Naito* (1705), *Toki* (1712), and from 1730 to 1868 that of *Honda* (40,000 k.).

Tanaka, 田中   Ancient *daimyō* family descendant from the *Tachibana* and installed at *Tanaka* (*Ōmi*).

—— **Yoshimasa,** 吉政 (+ 1609).   Served *Nobunaga*, then *Hideyoshi*, who in 1583 gave him a revenue of 30,000 k. at *Yawata* (*Ōmi*). In 1590, he was transferred to *Okazaki* (*Mikawa* — 100,000 k.). Named counsellor of *Hidetsugu*, he revealed to the *Taikō* the ambitious designs of his adopted son. After *Sekigahara* (1600), *Ieyasu* gave him the fief of *Kurume* (*Chikugo* — 320,000 k.).

—— **Tadamasa,** 忠政.   Son of *Yoshimasa*, died in 1620 without an heir, and his domains reverted to the *Shōgun*.

Tanaka, 田中.   *Samurai* family of the *Nagoya* clan (*Owari*), made noble in 1887. — Now Viscount.

Tanaka, 田中.   *Samurai* family of the *Kōchi* clan (*Tosa*) made noble in 1887. — Now Viscount.

Tanakura, 棚倉   In *Iwaki*. Was the residence of the *daimyō Tachibana* (1610), *Niwa* (1622), *Naitō* (1627), *Ōta* (1705), *Matsudaira* (1728), *Ogasawara* (1746) *Inoue* (1817), *Matsui* (1836), *Toda* (1865), and from 1866 to 1868 that of *Abe* (100,000 k.).

Tanasue no mitsugi, 手未調.   Or *Te-no-saki no mitsugi*. Formerly taxes in kind, paid with linen, thread, etc. — See *Soyōchō*.

Tandai, 探題.   Under the *Kamakura Shōgun*, title given to military governors of certain provinces. — See *Shikken, Rokuhara-tandai, Nagato-tandai, Kyūshū-tandai*, etc.

Tane-ga-shima, 種子嶋.   Island (148 Km. circ.) dependent upon the *Ōsumi* pro-

THE FIRST EUROPEANS AT TANE-GA-SHIMA (1542).

vince. During the Middle Ages, it belonged to the *Konoe* family, and later to the *Hōjō*, a branch of which took the name of *Tanegashima*. In 1362, *Yoritoki* sided with the *Ashikaga* and joined *Shimazu Ujihisa* against *Kikuchi Takemitsu*, but he was defeated and killed. — In 1542, the Portuguese *Fernand Mendez Pinto*, landed on that island and was the first European to set foot on the soil of Japan.

Tanegashima Tokitaka, 種嶋時堯. Was the governor of *Tanega-shima* island when the first Europeans landed in 1542. He learned from them the use and manufacture of firearms.

Tanehiko, 種彦 (1783-1842) Novelist. Author of the *Inaka-Genji*, a satire which caused him to lose the rank of *hatamoto*. His family name was *Yokose*, he is also called *Ryūtei*.

Tango, 丹後. One of the 8 provinces of *San-in-dō*. Comprises 5 districts which at present depend upon the *Kyōto-fu*. — Chinese name: *Tanshū* (with *Tamba* and *Tajima*). — In 713, it was separated from *Tamba* and called *Taniwa-no-michi no shiri*.

Tango, 端午. One of the 5 popular feasts (*go-sekku*), celebrated on the 5th day of the 5th month. It is the festival for boys. Each family raises a pole upon which flutter large carps made of paper or cloth, and intended to signify that as that fish ascends the strongest rapids, so also the child will surmount all obstacles in his path to fortune. This feast is also called *Ayame no sekku*.

Tani, 谷. *Daimyō* family descended from *Sasaki Nobutsuna* (+ 1242) (*Uda-Genji*). From 1600 to 1868, resided at *Yamaga* (*Tamba* — 13,000 k.). — Now Viscount.

Tani, 谷. *Samurai* family of the *Kōchi* clan (*Tosa*) made noble in 1884. — Now Viscount.

—— **Takeki,** 干城. Born in 1837. Became famous during the *Satsuma* war, by his brilliant defence of *Kumamoto* castle against the rebels (1877).

Tani Bunchō, 谷文晁 (1765-1842). Famous painter. Studied at first the principles of the *Kanō* school, and Chinese style, then established a school of his own. — His adopted son *Bun-ichi* (1787-1818) was also a celebrated artist. *Tani Bunchō's* disciples are: *Asano Baidō, Tahahisa Aigai, Watanabe Kwazan, Satake Eikai, Haruki Nanko*, etc.

Taniguchi Buson, 谷口蕪村. — See *Buson*.

Tani Jichū, 谷時中 (1598-1649). Born in *Tosa*, was at first a bonze, then studied the Chinese philosophy of *Shushi*. He established a school which contributed very much to the spreading of instruction among the *samurai* class of his district. He numbered among his pupils such men as: *Nonaka Kenzan, Yamazaki Ansai*, etc.

Tanikawa Shisei, 谷川士清 (1707-1776). Or *Kotokiyo* Man of letters and poet of *Ise*.

Taniwa, 丹波. Ancient name of the once united provinces of *Tamba, Tango* and *Tajima*, separated in 713.

Tankai, 探海. — See *Fujiwara Fuhito*.

Tannan, 丹南. In *Kawachi*. From 1623 to 1868 the residence of the *Takagi daimyō*. (10,000 k).

Tanomura Chikuden, 田 能 村 竹 田 (1777-1835). Confucianist and painter. Born at *Oka (Bungo)*, he resided in *Edo* and died at *Ōsaka*.

Tanshū, 淡 州 . Chinese name of *Awaji* province.

Tanshū, 丹 州 . Chinese name of the united provinces of *Tamba, Tango* and *Tajima*.

Tansui, 淡 水 . Port (6,000 inh.) N. of *Formosa*.

Tanuma, 田 沼 . *Daimyō* family descended from the *Fujiwara*.

—— **Okiyuki,** 意 行 . As *samurai* of *Kii* he accompanied his lord *Yoshimune* to *Edo*, when the latter was named *Shōgun* (1716),

—— **Okitsugu,** 意 次 (1719-1788). Son of *Motoyuki*, served the *Shogun Ieshige* and *Ieharu*. In 1772, he was named *Rōjū* and received the fief of *Sagara (Tōtōmi)*. His bad administration and ambitious views caused him to be dispossessed (1787).

—— **Okitomo,** 意 知 (+ 1784). Son of *Mototsugu*, was *Wakado-shiyori*. His arrogant behavior caused a quarrel with *Sano Masakoto*, who killed him in the palace of the *Shōgun*.

—— **Okikazu,** 意 壹 . At the death of *Mototsugu*, he received a revenue of 10,000 k. at *Shimomura (Mutsu)*. In 1823, the family was again transferred to *Sagara (Tōtōmi — 100,000 k.)*, where it remained till the Restoration. — Now Viscount.

Tappi-zaki, 龍 飛 崎 . Cape N. of *Mutsu*.

Tarumae-yama, 樽 前 山 . Volcano in *Iburi (Hokkaidō)*. Its last eruption in 1874.

Tashidaka, 足 高 . Under the *Tokugawa* an increase of pension given to officials who held a position superior to their rank.

Tataki, 敲 . Under the *Tokugawa*, a punishment, which consisted in giving 50 or 100 strokes on the back, with a rod called *hōkijiri*.

Tatara-hama, 多 々 良 濱 . Port of *Chikuzen*, a little N. of *Fuku-oka*. *Ashikaga Takauji* defeated *Kikuchi Taketoshi* (1336) there, and *Kobayakawa Takakage* gained a victory over the army of *Ōtomo Sōrin* (1569) at the same place.

Tatebayashi, 舘 林 . Town (9000 inh.) of *Kōzuke*. Ancient castle belonging to the *Uesugi*. In 1562, *Kenshin* entrusted it to *Nagao Akinaga*, and it then passed to the *Hōjō* of *Odawara* (1582). Under the *Tokugawa*, it was the residence of the *daimyō Sakakibara* (1590), *Matsudaira* (1645), *Tokugawa* (1661), *Matsudaira* (1706), *Ōta* (1728), *Matsudaira* (1746), *Inoue* (1836), and finally from 1845 to 1868, that of *Akimoto* (63,000 k.).

Tatebe, 建 部 . *Daimyō* family descended from *Sasaki Yoritsuna (Uda-Genji)*. From 1617 to 1868, it resided at *Hayashida (Harima — 10,000 k.)*. — Now Viscount.

Tate-eboshi-jō, 立 烏 帽 子 城 . In *Iyo (Sakuragi-mura)*. Ancient castle in which *Akabashi Shigetoki*, a relative of the *Hōjō*, was besieged in 1333.

Tate-ishi-zaki, 立 石 崎 . Cape S. W. of *Echizen*.

Tatemasa-jō, 建 昌 城 . In *Ōsumi (Mochida-mura)*. Ancient castle which towards the middle of the 15th century, was the residence of the *Shimazu daimyō*. Also called *Goma-jō*.

Tateshina-yama, 立科山. Mountain (2530 m.) E. of *Shinano*, also called *Iimori-yama*.

Tatewaki, 帶刀. Formerly, bodyguard of the Imperial Prince. The commanding officer had the title of *Tatewaki-senjō* (先生).

Tatewaki-senjō Yoshikata, 帶刀先生義賢. — See *Minamoto Yoshikata*.

Tateyama, 舘山. In *Awa* (*Tōkaidō*). Ancient castle built towards 1575 by *Satomi Yoshiyori*. Passed into the hands of the *Tokugawa* (1614), and from 1785 to 1868, was the residence of the *Inaba daimyō* (10,000 k.).

Tate-yama, 立山. Mountain (2800 m.) E. of *Etchū*. At its summit is a temple (*Oyama-jinja*), built in 701 and dedicated to *Oyama no kami*.

Tatsuno, 龍野. In *Harima*. Ancient castle built in 1334 by *Nitta Yoshisada*. It soon after fell into the possession of the *Akamatsu* who occupied it for 2 centuries. Under the *Tokugawa*, it was the residence of the *daimyō Ikeda* (1600), *Ogasawara* (1617), *Kyōgoku* (1637). Destroyed in 1658, it was rebuilt in 1672 by *Wakizaka Yasumasa*, and his descendants lived there till the Restoration (55,000 k.).

Tatsuta-gawa, 龍田川. River in *Yamato*, rises on Mount *Ikoma-yama* and flows into the *Yamato-gawa*. Also called *Ikoma-gawa, Heguri-gawa*. Formerly was often the theme of poets.

Tatsuta no seki, 龍田關. Barrier established between *Yamato* and *Kawachi*. Later on called *Tatsuno-seki*.

Tawara, 田原. In *Mikawa*. Was in the 16th century, the residence of the *Toda daimyō*. Under the *Tokugawa*, it belonged to the families *Ikeda* (1590), *Toda* (1600), and from 1664 to 1868, to *Miyake* (12,000 k.).

Tawara, 田原. *Daimyō* family which from the 13th to the 16th century resided at *Aki* (*Bungo*), but was dispossessed towards 1550 by *Ōtomo Sōrin*.

Tawara Tōda, 田原藤太. — See *Fujiwara Hidesato*.

Tayasu, 田安. Branch of the *Tokugawa* family descended from *Munetake* (+ 1769) son of the *Shōgun Yoshimune*. — See *Tokugawa, San-kyō.*

Tega-numa, 手賀沼. Lake (28 Km. circ.) in *Shimōsa*; it feeds the *Tone-gawa*.

Tei-ei, 貞永. *Nengō*: 1232.

Teiji-in, 亭子院. Ancient palace in *Kyōto*, residence of the emperor *Uda* after his abdication (897). Later, was changed into a temple. — *Uda* himself is often called *Teiji-in*.

Teika-ryū, 定家流. A writing used in some special kind of poetry. It was introduced in the 13th century by *Fujiwara Teika* (*Sadaie*).

Teikyō, 貞享. *Nengō*: 1684-1687.

Tei-ō, 貞應. *Nengō*: 1222-1223.

Tei-seikō, 鄭成功. — See *Kokusen-ya*.

Tei-shi, 禎子 (1013-1094). 4th daughter of the emperor *Sanjō*. Married *Go-Shujaku-tennō* and was the mother of *Go-Sanjō*. She shaved her head in 1069, and took the name of *Yōmei-mon-in*. It is under this title that she is generally known.

Teishin-shō, 遞信省. Department having charge of the Postal arrangements, telegraph, etc.; created in 1885.

Teishu-ha, 程朱派. School of Confucianism established in the beginning of the 17th century, by *Fujiwara Seikwa, Hayashi Razan,* etc. Their principal disciples were *Naba Kwassho* (1595-1648), *Matsunaga Sekigo* (1592-1657), *Miyake Kisai* (1580-1649), *Ishikawa Jōzan* (1583-1672), *Tani Jichū* (1598-1649), *Yamazaki Ansai* (1618-1682), *Nonaka Kenzan* (1616-1664), *Matsumoto Kunzan* (1692-1783), *Rai Shunsui* (1746-1816), *Koga Seiri* (1750-1817), etc.

Teiwa, 貞和. Nengō of the Northern dynasty: 1345-1349.

Tejō, 手鎖. Under the *Tokugawa*, a punishment which consisted in enclosing the hands of the condemned in two iron rings joined together. The duration of the punishment depended upon the gravity of the crime committed and ranged from 30 to 50 and even to 100 days.

Tekoshi-ga-hara, 手越河原. Plain in *Suruga*, on the western side of the river *Abe-kawa*. In 1335, *Nitta Yoshisada* defeated *Ashikaga Tadayoshi* there.

Tembun, 天文. Nengō: 1532-1554.

Temma, 傳馬. Formerly, horses at the service of the Imperial messengers; each district kept 5 relay horses in readiness for the bearers of a duly sealed commission (*dempu*).

Temmangū, 天滿宮.— See *Sugawara Michizane*.

Temman-zan, 天滿山. Hill in *Ōmi*, S. of the village of *Sekigahara*. At the time of the famous battle fought here (1600), *Hideyori's* army established itself on this hill: *Ukita Hideie* and *Shimazu Yoshihiro*, kept the centre; *Ishida Kazushige, Konishi Yukinaga*, the left; *Ōtani Yoshitaka*, the right. From these positions they attacked *Ieyasu* who however gained a complete victory.

Temmei, 天明. Nengō: 1781-1788.

Temmoku-zan, 天目山. Mountain in *Kai*, E. of the village of *Tokusa*. In 1582 *Takeda Katsuyori* being defeated in that place by *Oda Nobutada*, killed himself together with his whole family.

Temmon-kata, 天文方. Under the *Tokugawa*, officials who made astronomical observations, drew up the calendar, etc. They were divided into 4 branches each charged with a special subject: astronomy (*temmon*), calendar (*rekijutsu*), land-surveying (*sokuryō*) and topography (*chishi*). They also translated European, especially Dutch, books, which treated of these matters. The title, created in 1685, was for the first time bestowed on *Yasui Santetsu*, who later on took the name of *Shibukawa Shunkai*. The number of those who bore this title was reduced to 4 or 5 and were chosen from among the *Yoshida, Shibukawa, Yamaji*, etc. families.

Temmu-tennō, 天武天皇. 40th Emperor of Japan (673-686). *Ō-ama* or *Ama no nunahara-oki no mabito*, 3rd son of *Jomei-tennō*, was chosen heir to the throne in the 7th year (668) of the reign of his brother *Tenchi*. When the latter fell ill, he shaved his head and retired to the *Yoshino-zan*. But *Ōtomo no Ōji* (*Kōbun-tennō*), *Tenchi's* son, had scarcely ascended the throne when *Ō-ama* levied an army and revolted. This civil war (*Jinshin no ran*) did not last long: the Imperial troops were defeated everywhere and *Kōbun* killed himself. *Ō-ama* then ascended the throne, and during a reign of 14 years, proved himself a skilful administrator. He continued the reforms that had been begun during the *Teikwa* era (645-649), favored Buddhism, established rules for ceremonies at Court, prescribed the form of dress, family names, and fixed the limits of the provinces, etc. He died at the age of 65.

Tempai-zan, 天拜山. Hill in *Chikuzen*, near *Dazaifu*. It is from the top of this mountain that *Sugawara Michizane*, with his face turned towards *Kyōto*, venerated the Emperor who exiled him to *Kyūshū*. A temple (*Temman-gū*) has been erected in his honor on the summit of the mountain.

Tempō, 天保. *Nengō*: 1830-1843.

Tempuku, 天福. *Nengō*: 1223.

Tempyō, 天平. *Nengō*: 722-748.

Tempyō-hōji, 天平寶字. *Nengō*: 757-764.

Tempyō-shingo, 天平神護. *Nengō*: 765-766.

Tempyō-shōhō, 天平勝寶. *Nengō*: 749-756.

Temujin, 鐵木眞. Japanese name of *Genghis-khan* (*Tiemoutsin*: 1157-1226). They also call him *Tetsubokushin*.

Ten-an, 天安. *Nengō*: 857-858.

Tenazuchi, 手名椎. Wife of *Ashinazuchi* and mother of *Kushi-inada-hime*, who was saved by *Susano-o* and became his wife.

Tenchi-tennō, 天智天皇. 38th Emperor of Japan (662-671). *Ame-mikoto-hirakasu-wake*, also called *Katsuragi no Ōji* and *Naka no Ōe*, 2nd son of *Jomei-tennō* and of the empress *Kōgyoku*, succeeded his mother at the age of 36. In 645, he was actively engaged in the ruin of the *Soga*. Named crown-prince at the accession of *Kōtoku*, he took great interest in the *Taikwa* reform. When emperor, he proved to be a distinguished administrator and in 670 published a Code of laws in 22 volumes, known by the name of *Ōmi-ryō*. He gave his minister *Naka-tomi Kamatari* the name of *Fujiwara* (669). Under his reign the Japanese, defeated by the combined forces of China and *Shiragi*, definitely abandoned the Korean peninsula.

Tenchō, 天長. *Nengō*: 824-833.

Tendai-shū, 天臺宗. Buddhist sect, introduced from China in 806 by the bonze *Saichō* (*Dengyō-Daishi*). The aim of this sect is to encourage all men to attain perfection by the observance of the 3 precepts (*kai*): shun evil (*shōritsugi-kai*), do good works (*shōzenbō-kai*) and be kind to all existing beings (*shōshujō-kai*) — Having returned from China, *Saichō* settled at the *Hiei-zan* temple, which became the centre of the new sect. The *Tendai-shū* at present divided into 3 branches, numbers in Japan, 4,600 temples 2,800 chief-bonzes and 917,600 adherents.

Tendō, 天童. In *Uzen*. Ancient castle built in 1360 by *Shiba Yorinao*. In the 16th century, it fell into the possession of the *Satomi*. From 1767 to 1868, it was the residence of the *Oda daimyō* (20,000 k.).

Ten-ei, 天永. *Nengō*: 1110-1112.

Ten-en, 天延. *Nengō*: 973-975.

Tengen, 天元. *Nengō*: 978-982.

Tengi, 天喜. *Nengō*: 1053-1057.

Tengu, 天狗. Fabulous beings represented with wings and an extremely long nose. They are supposed to live in the woods and mountains, and are the subjects of many marvellous stories.

Tenji, 天治. *Nengō*: 1124-1125.

Tenji, 典侍. Formerly ladies in attendance at Court. Under the authority of the *Naishi-tsukasa*, their office was the same as that of the *Shōji*. They had no direct communication with the emperor, but were obliged to transmit his orders. The *Tenji* numbered 4 persons.

Tenjiku, 天竺. India.

Tenjiku Tokubei, 天竺徳兵衛 (1618-1686). Born at *Sendō* (*Harima*), he, at the age of 15, sailed to India in a boat manned by *Suminokura Mitsumasa*. He remained 3 years, then returned to *Nagasaki* (1636). The following year, he left for *Macao* and remained 2 years in that place. Having returned to Japan, he wrote an account of his travels, which however has been lost. Some time after, he shaved his head and took the name of *Sōshin*.

Tenjin, 天神. — See *Sugawara Michizane*.

Tenjin, 天神 (Lit.: heavenly spirits). Title given to the ancestors of the Imperial family before *Ama-terasu-ō-mikami*.

Tenjin shichi-dai, 天神七代. The 7 generations of heavenly spirits before *Ama-terasu-ō-mikami*. According the *Nihon-shoki*, they are: 1° *Kunitokotachi no mikoto*; 2° *Kunisatsuchi no mikoto*; 3° *Toyokunnu no mikoto*; 4° *Uijini no mikoto* and *Suijini no mikoto*; 5° *Ōtonoji no mikoto* and *Ōtomabe no mikoto*; 6° *Omotaru no mikoto* and *Kashikone no mikoto*; 7° *Izanagi no mikoto* and *Izanami no mikoto*.

Tenjin-yama, 天神山. In *Etchū* (*Nishi-fuse-mura*). In 1582, *Uesugi Kagekatsu* was defeated there by *Nobunaga's* generals: *Shibata Katsuie, Sasa Narimasa, Maeda Toshiie*, etc.

Tenjin-yama, 天神山. In *Harima* (*Shikata-mura*). Ancient castle built by *Akamatsu Ujinori*, who, having espoused the cause of the Southern dynasty, was besieged in it by *Yamana Ujikiyo*, fled to the *Shimizudera* and there killed himself, together with 137 companions in arms (1386).

Tenju, 天授. *Nengō*: 1124-1125.

Tenkai, 天海 († 1643). Born at *Takata* (*Rikuzen*) of the *Miura* family. At the age of 11 he entered the *Ben-yo-ji* temple and made a serious study of Buddhism. *Takeda Shingen* suggested to him the idea of gathering 3,000 bonzes of the *Tendai-shū* sect, to discuss Buddhist topics. *Tenkai* was president of the assembly and his learning excited the admiration of all. In 1599, *Ieyasu* named him chief of the *Nankō-in* temple, then *Sōjō*. About this time he settled at the *Bishamon-dō*. When *Hideyoshi* had erected the *Tō-ei-ji* temple at *Ueno* (*Edo*), *Tenkai* was named its superior (1625). Thus he at the same time directed the great temples of *Nikkō* and *Ueno*

TENKAI.

and enjoyed the full confidence of the first *Tokugawa Shōgun*. After his death, he received the posthumous title of *Jigen-Daishi*.

Tenkei, 天慶. *Nengō*: 936-948.

Tenkei no ran, 天慶亂. The civil war, brought about by the rebellion of *Taira Masakado* (See that name) during the *Tenkei* era.

Tenna, 天和. *Nengō*: 1681-1683. — Or *Tenwa*.

Tennin, 天仁. *Nengō*: 1108-1109.

Tennin, 天人. The angels of Buddhism. They are represented as young maidens, dressed in long robes of many colors hovering in the air and playing various musical instruments.

Tennō, 天皇. The Emperor.—The most common honorary titles given to the Emperor are: *Tennō* (lord of heaven) *Tenshi* (son of heaven), *Kōtei* (emperor), *Heika*, *Ichijin*, *Shison*, *Shujō*, *Ue*, *Ue Sama*, *Kinjō*, *Tōdai*, *Tōkon*, *Sume-mima no mikoto*, *Sumera-mikoto*, *Arahito-gami*, *Gosho*, *Dairi*, *Kinri*, *Ōyake*, *Ōkimi*, *Mikado*, *Hijiri no kimi*, *Banjō no Shu*, *Itten no Shu*, *Jūzen no Shu*, *Seichō*, *Seijō*, *Seishu*, *Seikō*, *Kokka*, *Chōtei*, *Waga-kimi*, *Kugo no Hijiri*, *Nammen no Ō*, etc.

IMPERIAL SEAL. (763.)

Tennō-ji, 天王寺. Or better **Shi-Tennō-ji,** 四天王寺. Large Buddhist temple built near the present city of *Ōsaka* (*Settsu*) by prince *Shōtoku-taishi* (593), of materials taken from the house of *Mononobe no Moriya*. From the 11th to the 16th century, it was governed by a prince of the Imperial household. Under the *Tokugawa*, it was a dependency of the *Rinnō-ji*. Burned in 1802, it was rebuilt 20 years after.—The Exposition of 1903 took place within its precincts.

Tennō-ki, 天皇記. Collection of the biographies of various emperors, published in 612 by *Shōtoku-taishi* and *Soga no Umako*. Was destroyed at the time of the *Soga's* ruin (645).

Ten-ō, 天應. *Nengō*: 781.

Tenri-kyō, 天理敎. Religious sect established by *Nakayama Miki*, usually called *O Miki* (1798-1887). Born near the village of *Mishima* (*Yamato*), of the *Maekawa* family, *O Miki* at the age of 14 married a certain *Nakayama*, and at the death of her husband, began to propagate his doctrines. The teaching, as much as cosmogonical ideas are concerned, is taken from Shintoism; the ethics, from popular Confucianism of the *Kyūō-dōwa* and of the *Shingaku-dōwa*, which mixture is intermingled with the recital of many pseudo-miracles and gross superstitions. — The *Tenri-kyō* is connected with the Shintoist branch called *Shintō-honkyoku*.

Tenroku, 天祿. *Nengō*: 970-972.

Tenryaku, 天曆. *Nengō*: 947-956.

Tenryō, 天領. Formerly name given to the domains of the *Shōgun*.

Tenryū-gawa, 天龍川. River (220 Km.), rises in lake *Suwa* (*Shinano*) passes through *Tōtōmi* and enters the Ocean a few miles E. of *Hamamatsu*. It is famous for its rapids.

Tenryū-ji, 天龍寺. Temple erected in the village of *Saga*, W. of *Kyōto*, by the bonze *Soseki* (*Musō-kokushi*) in 1342, At first a villa of the emperors *Saga*, *Go-Saga* and *Kameyama*, it was transformed into a Buddhist temple by *Ashikaga Takauji* and consecrated to the memory of *Go-Daigo*, whom he had dethroned. *Soseki* was its first superior. — Became the seat of the *Tenryū-ji*, a subdivision of the *Rinzai* branch of the *Zen-shū* sect.

Tenryūji-bune, 天龍寺船. When *Takauji* was erecting the temple *Tenryū-ji*, he sent the bonze *Soseki* to China to obtain the necessary articles for ornamenting the temple. The boats that carried these, were called *Tenryūji-bune*, and this name was later on applied to all boats that were authorized to do commerce with China.

Tenshō, 天承. *Nengō* : 1131.

Tenshō, 天正. *Nengō* : 1573-1591.

Tenshōkō-Daijin, 天照皇太神.—See *Amaterasu-ō-mikami*.

Tenshō no koku-naoshi, 天正石直.—See *Bunroku no kenchi*, *Kokudaka*, etc.

Tenshu, 天守. Square tower, several stories high, erected in the precincts of castles to serve as watch tower. *Matsunaga Hisahide* was the first to build such a structure in his castle of *Tamon* (1567). This word, was at first written with the two characters 天主 (master of heaven) the very same characters with which the Catholics designate God. Because of this, and to repudiate all connection with the proscribed religion the second character was changed into that of 守 (keeper). — Under the *Tokugawa*, the soldiers having the care of the *tenshu* were called *tenshu-ban*, and their chief, *tenshu-ban-gashira*. — *Tensu* is also used to designate it.

Tensō, 傳奏. Under the *Tokugawa*, officials at Court, serving as intermediaries between the Imperial Palace and the Shōgunate. When the *Shōgun* had to make a communication, a *Rōjū* transmitted it to the *Shoshidai* of *Kyōto*, the latter, to the *Tensō*, who with the *Kwampaku*, presented it to the Emperor. The answer was returned by the *Gisō*. — the *Tensō* were always two in number.

Tentoku, 天德. *Nengō*, 957-960.

Tenwa, 天和. *Nengō* : 1681-1683. — Or *Tenna*.

Ten-yaku-ryō, 典藥寮. Formerly a bureau subject to the *Kunaishō* and charged to look after the personnel of the Court physicians, their consultations, the medicines, and gardens containing medicinal herbs, etc. The chief had the title of *Ten-yaku*.

Ten-yō, 天養. *Nengō* : 1144.

Teppōdama-kusri-bugyō, 鐵砲玉藥奉行. Title created in 1632 and given to the official who directed the manufacture of powder.

Teppō-gata, 鐵砲方. Under the *Tokugawa*, officials who directed the manufacture of guns and canon, and who instructed others in the use of these weapons. This title was hereditary in the *Tatsuke* family for guns, and in the *Inoue* family for canon.

Teppō hyaku-nin-gumi, 砲鐵百人組. Under the *Tokugawa*, 25 squadrons of 100 men on horseback, armed with guns, and known as the *Kōga-gumi, Negoro-gumi, Iga-gumi*, etc. Their chief officers, 4 in number, each had a pension of 3000 k.

Teppō-tansu-bugyō, 鐵砲簞笥奉行. Title created in 1660 and given to 6 officers who had charge of the boxes where the guns to be used by the *Shōgun's* army, were kept.

Tera, 寺. Buddhist temple. — The words *ji* (in writing), *bukkaku, bonkyū, bonsetsu*, etc. are also used. — The word *tera* does not designate the temple only, but it includes in its signification all the dependences such as, dwellings of the bonzes, reception halls, etc.

Tera-bugyō, 寺奉行. Under the *Ashikaga Shōgun*, officials supervising the Buddhist bonzes and temples.

Tera-hōshi, 寺法師. Name formerly given to the bonzes of the *Mii-dera* temple (*Ōmi*). — See *Yama-hōshi*.

Terajima, 寺嶋. *Samurai* family of the *Kagoshima* clan (*Satsuma*), made noble after the Restoration. — Now Count

Terajima, 寺嶋. *Samurai* family, of the *Yamaguchi* clan (*Suwō*), made noble after the Restoration. — Now Baron.

Tera-koya, 寺子屋. Since the time of the *Kamakura Shōgun*, public instruction declined gradually. The bonzes then opened small schools in most of their temples, where boys from the ages of 10 to 15 were received and taught the most ordinary Chinese characters. The instruction consisted in reading and writing the copies placed in the hands of the children. These schools, called *tera-koya*, continued till the Restoration.

Terazawa, 寺澤. *Daimyō* family descended from *Ki no Haseo*.

—— **Hirotaka,** 廣高 (1563-1633). Called also *Masanari*, served *Hideyoshi*, who after the *Kyūshū* campaign (1587), gave him *Karatsu* (*Hizen* — 80,000 k.) in fief. He was governor of *Nagasaki* and took part in the Korean expedition. In 1600, he fought on the side of *Ieyasu* and received the *Amakusa* islands in reward, which brought him a revenue of 120,000 k. *Hirotaka* had been baptised in 1596, but when the edicts of persecution were published, he apostatized and became a persecutor.

—— **Katataka,** 堅高 (1609-1647). Son of *Hirotaka*, who through his exactions and tyranny, brought about the *Shimabara* insurrection, which being suppressed, he was dispossessed (1638). He became insane and committed suicide in the temple of *Asakusa* (*Edo*). — He was the last scion of the family.

Teruta-hime, 照手姫. — See *Oguri Hangwan*.

Teshi-ga-hara, 勅使河原. In *Musashi* (*Kami-mura*). In 1590, scene of battle between *Hōjō Ujinao* and *Takigawa Kazumasu*.

Teshima-ga-hara, 豐嶋河原. In *Settsu* (*Itami-machi*). In 1336, *Ashikaga Takauji* was defeated there by the Southern generals, *Nitta, Kitabatake*, etc.

Teshio, 天鹽. One of the 11 provinces of the *Hokkaidō*. Comprises 6 districts.

Teshio-gawa, 天鹽川. River (255 Km.) rises at the *Teshiotake*, passes through the province of the same name and enters the Japan sea at the village of *Teshio*. Also called *Nishi no Haha-gawa*.

Teshio-take, 天鹽嶽. The highest mountain (2,200 m.) of the *Teshio* province.

Tesshū, 鐡舟. Bonze of the 14th century, also called *Tokusai*. Disciple of *Soseki* (*Musō-kokushi*), he went to China and there received the title of *Entsū-Daishi*. Having returned to Japan, he founded the *Ryūkō-in* temple at *Saga* (*Yamashiro*). *Tesshū* was one of the most famous painters of his time.

Tetori-gawa, 手取川. River (79 Km.) which rises at the *Haku-san* mountain, passes through *Kaga* and enters the Japan sea at the *Mikawa* village.

Tetsubokushin, 鐡木眞. — See *Temujin*.

Tetsugen, 鐡眼 (1630-1682). Born in *Higo*, he became a bonze of the *Ikkō-shū* sect, which he left to join the *Ōbaku* when *Ingen* arrived in *Kyūshū* (1654). He distinguished himself at the time of a great famine. His principal work was the translation of the Buddhist Canon in 6,771 volumes, which undertaking he finished in 1681.

Tō, 東. *Daimyō* family — See *Endō*.

Toba, 鳥羽. Principal city (5200 inh.) of the *Shima* province. Ancient castle built towards 1570 by *Kuki Yoshitaka* Was the residence of the *daimyō Naitō* (1634), *Doi* (1681), *Matsudaira* (*Ōgyū*) (1691), *Itakura* (1710), *Toda* (1717), and from 1725 to 1868 that of *Inagaki* (30,000 k.).

Toba-e, 鳥羽繪. Popular drawings, caricatures, etc. introduced by the bonze *Toba-Sōjō*.

Toba-Sōjō, 鳥羽僧正 (1053-1114). Son of *Minamoto Takakuni*, became bonze of the *Tendai* sect under the name of *Kakuyū* and attained the dignity of *Sōjō*. As he lived in *Toba* (*Yamashiro*), he was given the name *Toba-Sōjō*. He cultivated painting and produced humorous pictures, since then called *toba-e*.

Toba-tennō, 鳥羽天皇. 74th Emperor of Japan (1108-1123). *Munehito*, eldest son of *Horikawa-tennō*, succeeded his father at the age of 5, his grandfather *Shirakawa* together with *Fujiwara Tada-zane* being regents. His reign was disturbed by the continuous wars between the bonzes of the great temples that surround *Kyōto*, *Enryaku-ji*, (*Hiei-zan*), *Onjō-ji* (*Mii-dera*), *Kōfuku-ji*, *Tō-daiji*, etc. At the age of 21, he abdicated in favor of his young son, *Sutoku*, and at the death of *Shirakawa* (1129), he again assumed power. In 1141, he shaved his head and took the name of *Kūkaku* and later, the title of *Hō-ō*. The same year he forced *Sutoku* to abdicate in favor of *Konoe*, a son of his favourite concubine *Toku-ko* (*Bifuku-mon-in*), but as *Konoe* died at the age of 17, (1155), *Toba* raised another of his sons, *Go-Shirakawa*, to the throne. He died the following year, at the age of 55 years. — During his administration, *Toba* multiplied the *shō-en* to excess in favor of his creatures, so much so that the provincial governors had jurisdiction only over one hundredth part of the territory they were supposed to administer. The great aim now was to become independent of Imperial protection, and for this purpose, the rich secured domains the names of which they assumed and enrolled themselves under the banner of the *Taira* or *Minamoto*. The

Imperial authority was steadily losing ground whilst the two rival clans, on the contrary, were daily gaining. War soon broke out between the two, a war which *Toba* had encouraged by his improvidence and his prodigality.

Tobi-no-su-yama, 鳶 巣 山. Hill in *Mikawa*, near *Nagashino*. *Takeda Nobuzane* was defeated there in 1573 by *Sakai Tadatsugu*.

Tochigi, 栃 木. City (22,400 inh.) of *Shimotsuke*, which gave its name to the department (*Tochigi-ken*) to which it belongs. In the 16th century, castle of the *Minagawa daimyō*.

Tochigi-ken, 栃 木 縣. Department formed by the *Shimotsuke* province. — Pop.: 859,000 inh. — Principal city: *Utsunomiya* (32,000 inh.); chief towns: *Tochigi* (22,400 inh.), *Ashikaga* (21,400 inh.), *Ashio* (19,000 inh.), *Kanuma* (12,500 inh.), *Tanuma* (11,650 inh.), etc.

Toda, 富 田. In *Izumo* (*Hirose-machi*). Ancient castle of the *Amako daimyō*. Passed in 1566 to the *Mōri* and was the residence of the *Kikkawa*. Abandoned in 1600.

Toda, 戸 田. *Daimyō* family from *Mikawa* and descended from *Fujiwara* (*Sanjō*) *Sanefusa* (1146-1224).

—— **Munemitsu,** 宗 光. The first lord of *Ueno* (*Mikawa*), he constructed the castle of *Tawara* (*Mikawa*), towards 1495, which his descendants kept for several generations.

Munemitsu
|
Norimitsu
|
| | |
Masamitsu | Ujikazu
Yasumitsu | Ujitern
| | |
Yoshimitsu | Mitsutada | Ujimitsu
Shigesada | Tadatsugu | Kazuaki
Yasunaga | Kiyomitsu | Ujikane
| | |
Yasunao | Takatsugu | Ujinobu   Ujitsune
Mitsushige | Tadayoshi | Ujiaki   Ujitoshi
| | |
Mitsunaga Tadamasa Tadatoshi Ujisada Ujishige
Mitsuhiro Tadazane Tadazono   Ujinaga Ujifusa
(a)   (b)   (c)   (d)   (e)

(*a*) — Senior branch. —— **Yasunaga,** 康 長 (1562-1632). Served *Ieyasu*, who allowed his family to assume the name of *Matsudaira*. After *Sekigahara* (1600), he received the fief of *Koga* (*Shimōsa* — 20,000 k.); then in 1609 he was transferred to *Minagawa* (*Shimotsuke*); in 1612, to *Kasama* (*Hitachi*) in 1616, to *Takasaki* (*Kōzuke*); in 1617, to *Matsumoto* (*Shinano* — 60,000 k). — In 1633 his descendants lived at *Akashi* (*Harima*); in 1639, at *Kanō* (*Mino*); in 1711, at *Yodo* (*Yamashiro*); in 1717, at *Toba* (*Shima*); finally from 1725 to 1868, at *Matsumoto* (*Shinano* — 60,000 k.). — Now Viscount.

(*b*) — Junior Branch. —— **Tadatsugu,** 忠 次 (1532-1598). Served *Ieyasu*, and in 1590 received a revenue of 5,000 k. at *Shimoda* (*Izu*).

—— **Takatsugu, 尊次** (1565-1615). In 1601 received the fief of *Tawara* (*Mikawa* — 10,000 k.).

—— **Tadamasa, 忠昌** (1632-1699). Was transferred in 1664, to *Tomioka* (*Higo*) ; in 1676, to *Shimodate* (*Hitachi*); in 1682, to *Iwatsuki* (*Musashi*) ; in 1686, to *Sakura* (*Shimōsa* — 72,000 k.). He was also *Jisha-bugyō*, *Shoshidai* of *Kyōto*, *Rōjū*, etc.

—— **Tadazane, 忠眞** (1651-1729). *Daimyō* of *Takata* (*Echigo*) (1701), then, in 1710, of *Utsunomiya* (*Shimotsuke*). — His descendants, transferred in 1749 to *Shimabara* (*Hizen*), returned to *Utsunomiya* in 1774 and resided in that place till the Restoration (77,000 k.). — Now Viscount. — A branch of this family was made noble in 1866 and received a revenue of 10,000 k. at *Takatoku* (*Shimotsuke*). — Now Viscount.

(*c*) — Branch which from 1682 to 1868, resided at *Ashikaga* (*Shimotsuke* — 10,000 k.). — Now Viscount.

(*d*) — Branch descended from *Ujikazu*, 2nd son of *Norimitsu*.

—— **Kazuaki, 一西** (1542-1604). Served *Ieyasu* and in 1601 received the fief of *Zeze* (*Ōmi* — 30,000 k.). — His descendants at first transferred to *Amagasaki* (*Settsu*) in 1617, resided at *Ōgaki* (*Mino* — 100,000 k.) from 1634 to 1868. — Now Count.

(*e*) — Branch descended from the above, which from 1698 to 1868, resided at *Nomura* (*Mino* — 13,000 k.). — Now Viscount.

Tō-dai-ji, 東大寺. Buddhist temple erected at *Nara* in 728 by the bonze *Ryōben*. It is the headquarters of the *Kegon-shū* sect. In 746, a large statue of Buddha (*Daibutsu*), was erected. This statue which represents him, as is customary, seated on a lotus flower, measures 15.9m. high. — Endowed with rich revenues by the emperors, the *Tōdaiji* became a great power and had a large body of men (*sōhei*) in its pay. As it sided against *Kiyomori*, he sent his son *Shigehira* who burnt it to the ground (1180). *Yoritomo* rebuilt it in 1195. The temple which shelters the *Daibutsu*, was burnt in 1567, during a battle between *Matsunaga Hisahide* and the *Miyoshi*, and was rebuilt only at the end of the 17th century by the *Shōgun Tsunayoshi*.

Toda Mosui, 戸田茂睡 (1629-1706). Famous poet of *Asakusa* (*Edo*).

Tōdō, 藤堂. *Daimyō* family descended from the *kuge Nakahara*, descendant of prince *Toneri-shinnō* (676-735), son of *Temmu-tennō*.

—— **Takatora, 高虎** (1556-1630). Served *Nobunaga*, then *Hideyoshi*, who placed him near his brother *Hidenaga*. At the death of the latter (1591), *Takatora* shaved his head and retired to the *Kōya-san* but *Hideyoshi* recalling him, made him counsellor of *Hidetoshi*, heir to *Hidenaga*. At the time of the Korean expedition, he commanded a part of the Japanese fleet. *Hidetoshi* died in 1594, and *Takatora* returned to *Kōya-san*. Recalled again by *Hideyoshi*, he received the fief of *Ōsu* (*Iyo* — 80,000 k.). After *Sekigahara* (1600), he was transferred to *Uwajima* (*Iyo* — 200,000 k.), then, in 1608, to *Tsu* (*Ise* — 323,900 k.), where his descendants remained till the Restoration. — Now Count. — A junior branch descended from *Taka-*

michi, grandson of *Takatora*, from 1632 to 1868 resided at *Hisai* (*Ise* — 53,000 k.). — Now Viscount.

Tō-ei-zan, 東 叡 山 . When the *Shōgun Iemitsu* erected the great temples of *Ueno* (*Edo*) (1625), he gave them, in distinction to the *Hiei-zan* of *Kyōto*, the name of *Tō-ei-zan* (*Hiei-zan* of the East). The principal temple was called *Kwan-ei-ji*, from the name of the era during which it was erected.

Tō-ei-zan mokudai, 東 叡 山 目 代 . Under the *Tokugawa*, official entrusted with the administration of the property belonging to the *Ueno* temples (*Edo*). This title was hereditary in the *Tamura* family. The *mokudai* was set over 6 *tedai* and 20 *dōshin*.

Tōfuku-ji, 東 福 寺 . Buddhist temple, S. E. of *Kyōto*. It took *Kujō Michiie* nearly 20 years (1236-1255) to build it, and its first superior was the bonze *Ben-en* (*Shōitsu-kokushi*). It became the headquarters of a subdivision of the *Rinzai* branch of the *Zenshū* sect.—The *Tōfuku-ji*, which was for a long time the most beautiful temple of the capital, possessed a *Daibutsu* 15 m. in height. It was burned with the temple in 1881.

Togashi, 富 樫 . Ancient *daimyō* family, descended from the *Chinjufu - Shōgun Fujiwara Toshihito* (10th century).

—— **Tadayori,** 忠 頼 . Great-grandson of *Toshihito*, who in the 11th century, received the governorship of the *Kaga* province with the title of *Kaga no suke*.

—— **Iekuni,** 家 國 . Son of *Tadayori*, built the castle of *Takao*, at *Togashi*. He was also known under the title of *Kaga no suke* or *Togashi no suke*, which he transmitted to his descendants.

—— **Ienao,** 家 直 . Great-grandson of *Iekuni*, served *Minamoto Yoritomo*.

—— **Takaie,** 高 家 . Lived in the 14th century, sided with *Ashikaga Takauji* and aided the Northern dynasty.

—— **Masachika,** 政 親 (+ 1488) Sided with *Hosokawa Katsumoto* at the time of the *Ōnin* war (1467). Later on, being besieged in his castle of *Togashi* by the troops of the bonzes of *Ikkō-shū*, he was defeated, fled to *Etchū* and killed himself. — He was the last scion of that family which had governed the *Kaga* province during 4 centuries.

Togawa, 戸 川 . Ancient *daimyō* family of *Bingo*.

—— **Hideyasu,** 秀 安 (+ 1598). Was vassal of the *Ukita* of *Okayama*, who granted him a revenue of 25,000 k.

—— **Satoyasu,** 達 安 (1569-1627). Son of *Hideyasu*, in 1600 received the fief of *Niwase* (*Bitchū* — 30,000 k). — The family became extinct in 1674.

Tōgō Heihachiro, 東 郷 平 八 郎 . Born in 1847 of a *samurai* family of *Satsuma*, he studied in England (1871-1878), and was Commander of the *Naniwa-kan* during the Chinese war (1894), Rear-Admiral in 1895, Vice-Admiral in 1900. He was in command of the fleet during the Russo-Japanese war and became Admiral in June 1904.

Tōgō no ike, 東 郷 池 . Lake (10 Km. circ.) in *Inaba*. Its outlet is the *Hashizu-gawa*.

Tōgū, 東 宮. Formerly a name given to the palace inhabited by the Crown Prince. His Court was formed on the model of the Imperial Court. Suppressed during the civil wars of the 14th century, it was lately re-established. — See *Kōtaishi*.

Tō-in, 洞 院. Branch of the *Saionji* family, which in the 14th century, became famous because of its attachment to the Southern emperors, at whose Court it held important offices. The best known of its members are ; *Kinkata* (1291-1360), *Saneyo* (1308-1358), *Kinsada* (1340-1399), etc.

Toi no zoku, 刀 伊 賊. Name given to pirates of the eastern provinces of China, who during the 11th century at various times devastated the coast of Japan. The country of *Toi* was formerly named *Shukushin Makkatsu* and later, was called *Nyoshin*. In 1019, more than 50 pirate boats attacked *Tsushima* and *Iki-shima*. The following year, they appeared off the coast of *Chikuzen*, but were repulsed by the chiefs of the *Dazaifu, Fujiwara Takaie, Ōkura Tanemoto*, etc. leaving 1280 prisoners and 380 horses or heads of cattle, in the hands of the victor.

Toi-saki, 都 井 崎. Cape, S. of *Hyūga*.

Toishi-jō, 戸 石 城. In *Shinano*. Ancient castle N. E. of the present city of *Ueda*. In the 16th century, it belonged to the *Murakami daimyō*. In 1545, *Takeda Shingen* stormed it and put the army of *Murakami Yoshikiyo* to flight

Toji, 刀 自. Formerly, female servants in the Imperial Palace, especially charged to look after the preparation of the meals.

Tō-ji, 東 寺. Buddhist temple of the *Shingon-shū* sect, S. of *Kyōto*, erected in 796 by *Kōbō-Daishi*. Its real name is *Kyō-ō-gokoku-ji*. It is the only remaining temple of that epoch.

Tōji-in, 東 寺 院. Temple of the *Zen-shū* sect, N. W. of *Kyōto*. Was established towards 1360 by *Ashikaga Takauji* wherefore his tomb is preserved in it. It was adorned with the statues of all the *Ashikaga Shōgun*, when, in 1863, some *samurai* of the Imperial party went to the temple, mutilated those of *Takauji, Yoshiakira* and *Yoshimitsu*, and carried their heads to the place where great criminals were exposed.

Tokachi, 十 勝. One of the 11 provinces of the *Hokkaidō*. Comprises 7 districts.

Tokachi-gawa, 十 勝 川. River (196 Km.) in *Tokachi*.

Tokachi-take, 十 勝 嶽. Mountain (2,100 m.) on the boarders of *Tokachi* and *Ishikari*.

Tōka-Ebisu, 十 日 惠 比 須. Feast celebrated on the 10th day of the 1st month, in honor of *Ebisu*, god of wealth.

Tōkaidō, 東 海 道. (Lit. : region of the Eastern Ocean). One of the large divisions of Japan. Comprises 15 provinces : *Iga, Ise, Shima, Owari, Mikawa, Tōtōmi, Suruga, Kai, Izu, Sagami, Musashi, Awa, Kazusa, Shimōsa*, and *Hitachi*. — The name *Tōkaidō* was also given to the road extending from *Kyōto* to *Tōkyō*, and passing through the provinces boardering the Pacific Ocean. — See *Go-kaidō*.

Tōka no sechie, 十 日 節 會. Formerly a feast which took place at the Palace at first in the *Hōgaku-den*, then in the *Shishin-den*, and during which the new year was celebrated by singing and dancing.

Young men celebrated it on the 15th of the 1st month and young girls on the following day. This feast which dates back as far as the 6th century, was called *Arare-hashiri*.

Tōkei, 東京. Ancient pronunciation of the word *Tōkyō*. — (See that name).

Toki, 土岐. *Daimyō* family descended from *Minamoto Yorimitsu* (944-1021) (*Seiwa-Genji*).

—— **Mitsunobu, 光信**. Descended from *Yorimitsu* in the 4th generation, settled at *Toki* (*Mino*) and took the name of that place. He served the ex-emperor *Toba* and was *Kebiishi* and *Dewa no kami*. He is the ancestor of the *Toki*, *Asano*, *Akechi*, etc. families.

—— **Yorisada, 頼貞**. Descended from *Mitsunobu* in the 6th generation and was on his mother's side grandson of *Hōjō Sadatoki*, *Shikken* of *Kamakura*. He was renowned for horsemanship, bow-shooting and poetry. He bore the title of *Hōki no kami*. He sided with the *Ashikaga* and fought with *Takauji* against the Southern dynasty.

—— **Yoritō, 頼遠**. Son of *Yorisada*, served *Ashikaga Tadayoshi*. He distinguished himself at the battle of *Tatara-hama* (1336) and besieged *Wakiya Yoshisuke* in the castle of *Somayama* (*Echizen*), which he occupied (1339). Some misunderstanding having arisen between him and *Tadayoshi*, he was beheaded by him at *Rokujō-ga-hara* (*Kyōto*) (1342).

—— **Yoriaki, 頼明** (+1348). Brother of *Yoritō*, whom he succeeded in the family domains of *Mino*. He was killed at the battle of *Shijō-nawate* whilst fighting *Kusunoki Masatsura*.

—— **Yorikane, 頼兼** (+1324). Brother to the preceding, sided with *Go-Daigo* when the latter resolved to destroy the *Hōjō*. But the inmates of the *Rokuhara* becoming aware of the plot, *Yorikane* was put to death together with his relative *Tajimi Kuninaga*.

—— **Yoriyasu, 頼康** (1318-1387). Son of *Yorikiyo*, became chief of all the *Toki* clan in 1348, under the title of *Mino no kami*. He served the *Shōgun Yoshiakira* and fought the Southern dynasty. At the death of *Takauji* (1358), he shaved his head and took the name of *Zenchū*.

—— **Yasuyuki, 康行**. Nephew and adopted son of the above, governed the provinces of *Mino, Ise* and *Owari*. When the *Shōgun* had tried to take *Owari* province from him and give it to his relative *Shimada Mitsusada, Yasuyuki* refused to submit and during two years (1389-1391) fought *Yorimasu*. After the restoration of peace, he fought against the *Yamana*.

—— **Yorimasu, 頼益**. Son of *Yoritada*, in 1399 he was ordered to march against his cousin *Yasuyuki*, whom he defeated. He then became chief of the *Mino* clan and governor of the province.

—— **Nariyori, 成頼** (+1497). Adopted son of *Yoritame*, succeeded *Mochimasu* (1474). During the *Ōnin* war, he sided with *Yamana Sōzen*. In 1487, he conquered the southern part of *Ōmi*. He shaved his head and took the name of *Sōan* (1396), and died the following year.

—— **Masafusa, 政房** (1467-1519). Son of *Nariyori*, had to repress some revolts in his province, *Mino*. He was successful owing to the help of *Asakura Takakage* of *Echizen* (1518).

—— **Yorizumi, 頼藝** (+1548). Eldest son of *Masafusa*, who, like his father, escaped into *Echizen* to ask the help of *Asakura Yoshikage* against his vassals, who had rebelled. With the same help he was able to defeat *Saitō Hidetatsu* (1546).

—— **Yoshiyori, 義頼** (1502-1583). Brother of *Yorizumi*, built the castle at *Ōkuwa* (*Mino*). In 1542, he was defeated by *Saitō Hidetatsu* and fled to *Echizen*, from whence he passed to *Kazusa*, where he lived in great misery.

—— **Sadamasa, 定政** (1551-1597). Descendant of *Akechi Kuniatsu*. When only two years old he lost his father *Sadaaki*, who was killed during the civil wars that desolated the *Mino* province (1552). Carried by his mother to *Mikawa*, he was adopted by *Suganuma Sadamitsu*. At the age of 14, he served in *Ieyasu's* army and took the name of *Saitō*. In 1590, he received a revenue of 10,000 k. in the *Sōma* district (*Shimōsa*) and revived the former glory of the *Toki*.

—— **Sadayoshi, 定義** (1579-1618). Son of *Sadamasa*, served *Hidetada* in his *Shinano* campaign (1600), then received charge of the *Mito* castle (*Hitachi*). In 1617, he received the fief of *Takatsuki* (*Settsu* — 30,000 k.). — His descendants successively resided : in 1619, at *Sōma* (*Shimōsa*) ; in 1627 at *Kami no yama* (*Dewa*) ; in 1712, at *Tanaka* (*Suruga*) ; and from 1742 to 1868, at *Numata* (*Kōzuke* — 35,000 k.). Now Viscount.

Tokibe, 解部. Formerly bureau of the *Gyōbu-shō* whose duty it was to establish and preserve the genealogies of families, etc.

Tokiwa Gozen, 常磐御前. At first a maid honour to the Empress, wife of *Konoe-tennō*, she became the concubine of *Minamoto Yoshitomo*, by whom she had 3 sons. When *Yoshitomo* perished in the *Heiji* war (1160), she fled with her 3 children. The youngest child then only a few months old, became the famous *Yoshitsune*. She lived a hidden life in the village of *Ryūmon* (*Yamato*). *Kiyomori* having made vain efforts to discover her, arrested her mother. Hearing of this, *Tokiwa* at once surrendered herself, whereupon her mother was set free, her children shaved their heads and she became the concubine of *Kiyomori*, to whom she bore a daughter. But this union did not last long and she soon after married *Fujiwara Naganari*, *Ōkura-kyō*.

Tokiwai, 常磐井. Family descended from prince *Tokiwai no Miya*, son of the emperor *Go-Kashiwabara*. He was named chief of the *Takada* branch of the *Zen-shū* sect when the headquarters of this sect were transferred (1465) from *Takada* (*Shimotsuke*) to *Isshinden* (*Ise*). Was by right of inheritance at the head of this temple (*Senshū-ji*). — Now Baron.

Tokiyo-shinnō, 齊世親王 (+927). Son of the emperor *Uda* and of *Tachibana Yoshi-ko*. Was *Hyōbukyō* and *Kazusa no taishu*. He lost the Imperial favor at the same time as his father-in-law *Sugawara Michizane*, and became a bonze in the *Enjō-ji* temple.

TOKIWA GOZEN.

Tokoro-gawa, 常呂川. River (118 Km.) in *Kitami* (*Hokkaido*).

Tokoyo no kuni, 常世國. Region repeatedly mentioned in history but difficult to identify. It is the place where *Sukuna-bikona* retired after having helped *Ōkuninushi* to pacify *Izumo*. There also, *Tajima Mori* found the orange tree (*tachibana*), etc. The most reliable authorities apply this name to the S. E. coasts of China (at present *Fokien*). These coasts were colonized by the same invaders who, coming from the South, also made their abode in Japan.

Tokudaiji, 德大寺. Branch of the *Fujiwara* family descended from *Kinzane* (1053-1107).

—— **Saneyoshi**, 實義 (1096-1157). Son of *Kinzane*, was the first to bear the name of *Tokudaiji*. His sister *Tama-ko*, married the emperor *Toba*, and was the mother of *Sutoku* and *Go-Shirakawa*; on account of this relationship, *Saneyoshi* enjoyed great favor. He was *Sadaijin* and helped *Toba* in his struggle against the *Taira*. — This family belonged to the *Kwazan-in*, the *Seikwa* and the *San-daijin-ke*. — Now Marquis.

Tokugawa, 德川. Hamlet in the *Serata* village, district of *Nitta* (*Kōzuke*). *Yoshisue*, 4th son of *Nitta Yoshishige*, lived there at the beginning of the 13th century and took the name of that place. He is the ancestor of the *Tokugawa, Matsudaira, Sakai*, etc. families. — In 1611, *Ieyasu* sent *Doi Toshikatsu* to *Nitta* his native district to make researches concerning his ancestry. He conceded special favors to the inhabitants of the village of *Serata*.

Tokugawa, 德川. Family descended from *Nitta Yoshishige* (+ 1202), grandson of *Minamoto Yoshiie (Seiwa-Genji)*.

—— **Yoshisue**, 義季. 4th son of *Yoshishige*. In the beginning of the 13th century he settled at *Tokugawa* (*Kōzuke*) and took the name of that place. He is often called *Tokugawa Shirō*.

—— **Chikauji**, 親氏. Son of *Arichika* and descended from *Yoshisue* in the 8th generation. He witnessed the ruin of the *Nitta* in their war against the *Ashikaga*. Threatened with death, he fled disguised as a bonze to the *Mikawa* province. Having arrived at the village of *Sakai*, he became a domestic in the household of *Gorōzaemon*, the chief of the village, who obliged him to marry his daughter. He had a son (1367), *Tadahiro*, who kept the name of *Sakai* and is the ancestor of the family of that name. The following year, having lost his wife, *Chikauji* went to the village of *Matsudaira*. There he married the daughter of *Nobushige*, chief of the village, and again had a son *Yasuchika*, born in 1369, who took the name of *Matsudaira*. *Chikauji* is believed to have died in 1407, but the documents of that epoch are not reliable and dates, as far back as the 16th century, can be taken only approximately.

—— **Yasuchika**, 泰親 (1369-1412). Was in charge of the castle of *Iwatsu*, then of *Okazaki* (*Mikawa*), and governor of the province.

—— **Nobumitsu**, 信光 (1390-1465). Son of *Yasuchika*. He strengthened the authority of his family in the province. He shaved his head and received the name of *Izumi-Nyūdō*.

—— **Chikatada**, 親忠 (1418-1480). Son of *Nobumitsu*, was *Shuri no suke*. Some of his vassals, the *Suzuki*, the *Miyake*, the *Nasu*, the *Abe*, and others, joined their forces and besieged him in his castle of *Iwatsu*, but *Chikatada* completely defeated them. Soon after, he shaved his head and took the name of *Saichū*.

—— **Nagachika**, 長親 (1442-1510). Son of *Chikatada*. He fought *Imagawa Ujichika*, governor of *Suruga*, who attempted to occupy *Mikawa*.

—— **Nobutada**, 信忠 (1489-1531). Son of *Nagachika*, resided at the castle of *Anjō* (*Mikawa*), and in the midst of the civil wars which were continuously waged about him, was able to retain all his hereditary possessions.

—— **Kiyoyasu**, 清康 (1511-1536). Son of *Nobutada*, was murdered at the age of 25, by one of his vassals, *Abe Masatoyo*.

—— **Hirotada**, 廣忠 (1526-1549). Son of *Kiyoyasu*, was under the tutorship of *Abe Sadayoshi*. Taking advantage of his youth, his uncle *Serata Nobusada*, sought to supplant him, but *Sadayoshi* took *Hirotada* to *Ise* and interested *Imagawa Yoshimoto* in his cause, who re-established him in his castle of *Okazaki*. In 1541, he married the daughter of

Mizuno Tadamasa, lord of *Kariya,* and the following year he had a son, who was *Ieyasu.* At the death of *Tadamasa* (1545), the latter's son, *Nobumoto,* made an alliance with the *Oda* of *Owari,* and *Hirotada,* repudiating his wife, sent her back to her brother. War ensued between *Hirotada* and *Oda Nobuhide.* He asked *Imagawa Yoshimoto* for help, and sent his son *Ieyasu* to him as hostage (1547), but *Nobuhide* succeeded in getting possession of the child and took him to *Nagoya. Hirotada* marched against *Nobuhide* and defeated him, but he died soon after in his castle of *Okazaki.*

———**Ieyasu,** 家康 (1542-1616). First *Tokugawa Shōgun,* ruled from 1603 to 1605. — Born at the castle of *Okazaki* (*Mikawa*), he received the name of *Takechiyo.* In 1547, his father having sought help from *Imagawa Yoshimoto* against *Oda Nobuhide,* sent, as was customary, *Takechiyo* with 50 other young *samurai,* as hostages to *Suruga.* During the journey, a certain *Norimitsu, Hirotada's* vassal, stopped the train and delivered *Takechiyo* into the hands of *Nobuhide,* who placed him in custody in the *Katō* family of *Atsuta* (*Owari*). *Nobuhide,* then offered peace to *Hirotada* but on such hard conditions that the latter preferred to continue the war, and *Takechiyo* was confined in the small temple *Tennō-bō,* where he had to undergo many hardships, notwithstanding the devotedness of *O Cha no Tsubone.* At the death of *Hirotada* (1549), the prince of *Mikawa* was in great perplexity. Peace had been concluded between the *Imagawa* and the *Oda,* but *Takechiyo* always remained a hostage. At the age of 12 (1554), he for the first time put on a coat of arms. Two years later, at the ceremony of the *gembuku,* he received the name of *Motonobu.* In 1558, he married the daughter of *Sekiguchi Chikanaga,* vassal of the *Imagawa,* and soon after received permission to return to his own province, where he changed his name to that of *Motoyasu.* He was scarcely at *Okazaki,* when he began to make preparations for war against *Nobunaga* who was threatening to attack *Mikawa.* Having regained possession of his two castles of *Terabe* and *Hirose,* as well as the western portion of *Mikawa* province, he entered *Suruga.* At that very time, (1560), *Imagawa Yoshimoto* was attacking *Nobunaga,* but was defeated and killed at *Okehazama* (*Owari*). *Motoyasu* having forced his uncle *Mizuno Nobumoto* to submit, after defeating him at *Ishi-ga-se* and at *Kariya,* returned to *Okazaki* to settle the terms of peace with *Nobunaga* (1561). He then applied himself to restore order in his province, established the *Bugyō,* then, in order to free himself from the *Imagawa* and to assert his independence, he put the name *Motoyasu* (a character of which had been given to him by *Yoshimoto*) aside and took that of *Ieyasu* (1565), by which he was to be henceforth known and under which he has become so renowned. In 1567, he received the title of *Mikawa no kami,* then obtained permission from the emperor to keep the name of *Tokugawa* for his own family, leaving that of *Matsudaira* to the lateral branch of the *Nitta* and the *Serata* families. At that time, he became acquainted with the famous *Takeda Shingen* and made an alliance with him against *Imagawa Ujizane.* The latter attacked by his two foes was routed and dispossessed of his domains, *Shingen* taking *Suruga*, *Ieyasu* receiving *Tōtōmi*. Leaving his son *Nobuyasu* at *Okazaki*, *Ieyasu* went to *Hikuma*, which name he changed to *Hamamatsu* and built a castle there (1570).

His fame spread by degrees and all the former vassals of the *Imagawa* offered him their services. At this time, he with 10,000 men aided *Nobunaga* to triumph over the *Ashikaga* and *Asai* at *Anegawa* (*Ōmi*). Meanwhile, *Takeda Shingen* was fighting the *Hōjō* of *Odawara*, who were trying to take the province of *Suruga* from him. He asked *Ieyasu* for help but was refused and war soon began. In

TOKUGAWA IEYASU.

1571, *Shingen* entered *Tōtōmi* and besieged the castles of *Takatenjin*, *Yoshida*, *Nire*, etc. *Uesugi Kenshin* attacked *Shinano*, and *Shingen* had to face this new enemy; but the following year, war recommenced between the two rivals, and *Ieyasu* found himself besieged in *Hamamatsu*. He sent to *Nobunaga* for help, and the latter sent him a great body of men under the command of *Sakuma Morinobu*. In the beginning of 1572, *Shingen* with 40,000 men was camping at *Mikata-ga-hara* and burned all the surroundings of the castle of *Hamamatsu*, but *Ieyasu* held his position. To induce him to accept battle, *Shingen* retired to *Iidani* and *Ieyasu* left his castle and camped at *Mikata-ga-hara*. He was at once attacked and defeated. *Morinobu* fled and *Ieyasu* was preparing for death, when one of his vassals, *Natsume Masayoshi*, whom he had left at *Hamamatsu*, arrived in haste, and obliged his lord to return to the castle. With a small body of faithful *samurai* he boldly met death, a sacrifice to his master's welfare. Having returned to *Hamamatsu*, *Ieyasu*, on the following night, made a sortie with 400 men, and attacked the enemy at daybreak. The vanquished of the preceding day came to his rescue, and defeat was soon changed into a decided victory. War was resumed the following year, but was interrupted for some time by *Shingen's* death (1573). *Katsuyori*, his son, renewed the struggle and invaded *Tōtōmi*. This time also, *Ieyasu* with *Oda Nobunaga's* help, defeated his enemy at *Nagashino* (1574). A truce followed which lasted for several years, during which time, both parties prepared for a final effort. In 1579, the eldest son of *Ieyasu*, *Nobuyasu*, was accused of having friendly relations with the *Takeda*, whereupon his father called him to *Hamamatsu*, and after an investigation, invited him to commit *harakiri*. War began in 1581, and *Ieyasu* took the castle of *Takatenjin* from *Katsuyori*. The following year, an expedition conducted by *Nobunaga* and *Ieyasu* was directed against *Katsuyori*. It ended with the ruin of the *Takeda* at *Temmoku-zan* (*Kai*), and *Ieyasu* received the *Suruga* province. He then paid a visit to *Nobunaga* in his castle of *Azuchi*, and *Akechi Mitsuhide* was chosen to receive so high a dignitary From here, he went to *Kyōto* and thence to *Ōsaka*, in which latter city he heard of the murder of *Nobunaga*. Not having enough troops with him to oppose *Mitsuhide*, he hastened to *Mikawi*, gathered a small army and marched towards *Kyōto*, but at *Atsuta*, he heard of the defeat and death of *Mitsuhide*. He returned to *Okazaki* and did not take part in the campaign of *Shizu-gatake* (1583). The following year, he accepted the advances made by *Oda Nobuo* and joined him to fight *Hideyoshi*. The army of the latter, was defeated at *Komaki-yama* (*Owari*), but soon after, *Ieyasu*, deserted his ally, and made peace with the future *Taikō* confirming it by his marriage with *Asahi no kata*, *Hideyoshi's* daughter. In the following years, he busied himself with the administration of his domains. In 1590, he resumed his military life in a campaign against the *Hōjō* of *Odawara*. In this expedition he gained the 8 provinces of *Kwantō*, but not those of *Shimotsuke* and *Awa*. He then had a revenue of 2,557,000 k., which enabled him freely to distribute domains among those who for 30 years had been fighting in his interests. As his residence, he chose the small port of *Edo*, in *Musashi*, and on the ruins of the fortress built there in the 15th century by *Ōta Dōkwan*, he erected an immense castle. He found a pretext for not taking part in the Korean expedition. *Hideyoshi*, who had chosen him as one of the *Go-Tairō*, called him near his person. When on the point of death, he ordered *Ieyasu* to lead the army from Korea back, and most particularly entrusted to him the guardianship of his son *Hideyori* (1598). After the *Taikō's* death, *Ieyasu* installed himself in the castle of *Fushimi* and began to rule as sole master. Troubles soon rose between him and the great *daimyō* who accused *Ieyasu* of usurping the power of his ward. The leaders of this faction were *Maeda Toshiie* and *Ishida Kazushige*. *Ieyasu* through much cunning was able to bring *Toshiie* to his side. But many *daimyō* returned to their domains, plainly showing their dissatisfaction. Among them were: *Ukita Hideie*, *Mōri Terumoto*, *Uesugi Kagekatsu*, etc. The last mentioned in particular, so openly refused to recognize the authority of *Ieyasu*, that the latter soon opened a campaign against him. He had scarcely left *Fushimi*, going north, when his enemies issued a proclamation accusing him of 13 serious charges and calling to arms all the vassals that remained faithful to the *Taikō*. *Ieyasu's* adherents however, were not idle and prepared for battle. Thus at very short notice, Japan was divided into two camps. The war began in August 1600. *Hosokawa Fujitaka*, *Ieyasu's* vassal, was attacked in the castle of *Tanabe* (*Tanjo*) and resisted heroically. *Torii Mototada* defended *Fushimi* well, but the assailants took the castle and *Mototada* died in battle. Meanwhile, *Fukushima Masanori* and *Ikeda Terumasa*, allied to the *Tokugawa* family, marched towards the East and occupied the castles of *Kiyosu* and *Gifu*. There *Nobunaga's* grandson, *Hidenobu*, whom *Ishida Kazushige* had won to his party, was taken prisoner and confined to the *Kôya-san*. *Ieyasu* however had come to *Oyama* (*Shimo-tsuke*), where he learned what had happened since his departure. He hastened to retrace his steps and gathering an army of 80,000 men, encountered *Kazushige's* army in *Mino*, 130,000 strong. A battle took place at *Sekigahara* where *Ieyasu* gained a complete victory over his enemies and 40,000 heads of the enemy were the trophy of the day (Oct. 21, 1600). This success gave *Ieyasu* undisputed authority, which he used most arbitrarily. Of his former adversaries, the principal, *Ishida Kazushige, Konishi Yukinaga, Ankokuji Ekei*, etc. were beheaded at *Kyôto*; *Ukita Hideie, Oda Hidenobu, Chôsokabe Morichika, Maeda Toshimasa, Masuda Nagamori, Tachibana Muneshige, Niwa Naga-shige*, and others were deprived of their domains; others again, such as *Môri Terumoto, Uesugi Kagekatsu, Satake Yoshinobu, Akita Sanesue*, etc. who submitted to the victor, found their revenues considerably reduced. His adherents, the *Kobayakawa, Date, Katô, Mogami, Asano, Fukushima, Gamô, Ikeda, Kuroda, Hosokawa, Tôdô, Tanaka, Yamanouchi, Oku-daira, Ii*, etc. received very large domains, and the distribution of fiefs was made in such a manner that the last to submit to the new power (*tozama-daimyô*) always found themselves near one or several of the ancient vassals (*fudai-daimyô*), who watched them so as to prevent even the possibility of a rebellion. — *Ieyasu* now securely established in power showered greater honors on the person of the Emperor than had thus far been accorded to him, but reserved the executive power to himself. Installed in *Fushi-mi*, he summoned the learned *Fujiwara Seikwa* and *Hayashi Dô-shun* to help him, with their sagacity, in the administration of affairs. He ordered the maps of the provinces and districts to be revised: brought the ancient books of the *Ashikaga-gakkô* and *Kanazawa-bunko*, to *Fu-shimi* or to *Edo* and had the most important and rarest rewritten. It was he too, who revived the edicts against Christianity and increased their severity. It was only in 1603, that he received from the Emperor *Go-Yôzei*, the title of *Sei-i-tai shôgun* and those connected with it, such as the titles of *Genji no chôja, Junwa-in* and *Shôgaku-in no Bettô*. Two years later, he abdicated in favor of his son *Hidetada*, then 26 years old, his principle motive being to secure the succession of his high dignity to his family. He retired to *Sumpu* (*Shizuoka*), and whilst taking an active part in the government, he devoted his leisure to literature and poetry. In 1611, he went to *Kyôto* and had an enterview with *Hideyori* to whom he betrothed his granddaughter *Sen-hime*, daughter of the *Shôgun Hidetada*. *Hideyori*, having become of age was, notwithstanding all the precautions taken by *Ieyasu* and the surveillance exercised over him, taught by his surroundings and in particular by his mother *Yodo-gimi*, to look upon *Ieyasu* as the usurper of his power. Thus the re-lations between him and the *Tokugawa* became steadily more strained and the latter only waited for an opportune moment to get rid of him. *Ieyasu* induced *Hideyori* to rebuild the *Hōkō-ji* temple at great expense. It had been previously built by *Hideyoshi* but was destroyed by an earthquake in 1596. *Ieyasu* well knew that the money used in this pious work, would not be employed in recruiting soldiers. When the temple was finished, *Hideyori* ordered a large bell to be cast and invited *Ieyasu* to the opening ceremony. Now, it happened that in the inscription placed on the bell, the two characters of the name of *Ieyasu* were employed, separated one from the other. (The inscription read as follows:

國家安康 *kokka-ankō*, peace and tranquillity of the country, the 2nd and the 4th of these characters form the name of *Ieyasu*). The *ex-Shōgun* affected to be insulted at this imprecation against him, bringing down the curse of heaven. He stopped the proceedings of the feast, asked an explanation and even wanted to force the emperor to suppress the ill-omened inscription. *Hideyori* refused to submit to such unreasonableness, and, some time after, *Ieyasu* and *Hidetaka*, at the head of 50,000 men were camping under the walls of *Ōsaka*. The castle was well fortified, and *Hideyori's* generals *Ōno Harunaga*, *Sanada Yukimura*, *Gotō Mototsugu*, etc. had assembled 60,000 *samurai*, mostly *rōnin* of ancient *daimyō*, dispossessed by *Ieyasu*. Every man was determined to sell his life dearly. After some doubtful encounters, *Ieyasu* sent *O Cha no Tsubone* to *Yodo-gimi*, and through her intermediary, peace was restored, *Hideyori* agreeing to dismiss his troops and to-

THE GREAT MEN OF 16TH CENTURY.

NOBUNAGA AND MITSUHIDE PILE THE RICE, HIDEYOSHI KNEADS THE DOUGH, IEYASU EATS THE CAKE (*mochi*).

fill the moats of the castle of *Ōsaka*. Thus ended what is known in history as the winter campaign of *Ōsaka (Ōsaka fuyu no eki)*, because it took place in the last months of the year 1614. *Ieyasu* had scarcely returned to *Sumpu*, when new difficulties arose. *Hideyori* consented to the demolition of the exterior defences and to the filling up of the moats, but he asked that his soldiers should be recognized as regular troops which request met with a flat refusal. He then proposed to exchange his provinces of *Settsu, Kawachi* and *Izumi* for those of *Awa, Sanuki* and *Iyo*, in *Shikoku*. *Ieyasu* offered him those of *Shimōsa, Kazusa* and *Awa (Tōkaidō)*, but to accept this proposition, would have been putting himself completely into the power of the former. *Hideyori* refused and the two parties again prepared for war. In May 1615, *Ieyasu* gathered his army and one month after, despite the bravery shown by the besieged garrison, *Ōsaka* fell. *Hideyori* and *Yodo-gimi* perished in the conflagration of the castle. This second siege is called the summer campaign of *Ōsaka (Ōsaka natsu no eki)*. The power of the *Tokugawa* was now supreme and secure for a long period. Before returning to *Suruga, Ieyasu* promulgated Regulations for the *samurai (Buke-hatto)* in 13 chapters, taken from the *Jōei-shikimoku* and the *Kembu-shikimoku* Codes. He likewise established the *Kuge* Code *(Kuge-hatto)* in 17 chapters, after having consulted the *Kwampaku Nijō Akizane* on the matter. Soon after his return to *Sumpu* in the beginning of 1616, *Ieyasu* fell ill. He received the title of *Dajō-daijin* from the Emperor, but in the month of May, departed this life, at the age of 74. Buried temporarily at the *Kunō-zan*, near *Shizuoka*, his body was carried with great solemnity, in the following year, to *Nikkō*, where a magnificent temple was erected in his honor He received the posthumous name of *Tōshōgū*.

	Kame-hime (married to *Okudaira Nobumasa*)					
	Nobuyasu					
	Hideyasu (*Matsudaira of Echizen*)					
		Sen-hime (married to *Toyotomi Hideyoshi*)				
		Daughter (married to *Maeda Toshinaga*)				
		" (" " *Matsudaira Tadanao*)				
		" (" " *Kyōgoku Tadataka*)				
Ieyasu (1)	**Hidetada** (2)	**Iemitsu** (3)	**Ietsuna** (4)			
			Tsunashige	**Ienobu** (6) - **Ietsugu** (7)		
				Kiyotake		
			Tsunayoshi (5)			
		Tadanaga				
		Daughter (married to the Emperor *Go-Mi-no-o*)				
		Masayuki (*Hoshina*)				
	Tadayoshi					
	Nobuyoshi					
	Daughter (married to *Hōjō Ujinao*)					
	" (" " *Gamō Hideyuki*, and then to *Asano Nagaakira*)					
	Tadateru					
	Yoshinao (*Owari*)					
	Yoshinobu - Mitsusada	**Yoshimune** (8) — See next Table				
		Tsunanori (*Kii*)				
	Yorifusa (*Mito*)					

Ieyasu was certainly a genius. He was a skilful warrior and a shrewd politician. He finished the work of pacifying the country, a work begun by *Nobunaga* and *Hideyoshi*, and endowed it with a powerful organisation, securing the power to his own family for two and a half centuries. As regards religion, he was under the influence of the bonzes *Tenkai* and *Den Chōrō*. Impartial history however, cannot hide his cruel persecution of the Christians, and the edict which he published in 1614 will always be a stain upon his memory.

—— **Nobuyasu,** 信 康 (1559-1579). Eldest son of *Ieyasu*, was left in the castle of *Okazaki*, when his father moved to *Hamamatsu* (1567). At the age of 16, under the command of *Ieyasu*, he undertook his first campaign against *Takeda Katsuyori*. He married a daughter of *Nobunaga*. Having been accused of treason against his father and father-in-law, for having entered into relations with their enemy *Katsuyori*, he was called to *Hamamatsu* and invited to commit *harakiri*. He was then 21 years old. His wife retired to *Kyōto* with her two daughters; the one *Fuku-hime*, married *Ogasawara Hidemasa*, and the other, *Kuni-hime*, married *Honda Tadamasa*.

—— **Hideyasu,** 秀 康 (1574-1607). 2nd son of *Ieyasu*. — See *Matsudaira (Echizen)*.

—— **Hidetada,** 秀 忠 (1579-1632). 2nd *Shōgun* of the *Tokugawa* family, from 1605 to 1622. — 3rd son of *Ieyasu*, was born at the castle of *Hamamatsu*, and at the age of 10, was sent to *Kyōto* to stay with *Hideyoshi*. In 1600, he accompanied his father in the projected campaign against *Uesugi Kagekatsu* and went as far as *Utsunomiya* but hearing that *Ishida Kazushige* had risen in arms, he marched South through *Tōsandō*, but allowed himself to be delayed at the siege of *Ueda* (*Shinano*) for 15 days and arrived in *Mino* after the battle of *Sekigahara*. *Ieyasu*, in his anger, refused to receive him, but at the intervention of *Honda Masazumi* consented to give him audience. In 1605, *Hidetada*, was named *Shōgun*. He aimed at maintaining and developing his father's policy. He took part with him in the two sieges of *Ōsaka* (1614-1615). In 1620, his daughter *Kazu-ko* married the emperor *Go-Mi-no-o*. He continued to persecute the Christians and under the most severe penalty forbade any Japanese to go out of the country. It is he who stopped commercial relations with all foreigners except the Dutch, Chinese and Koreans. In 1622, *Hidetada* abdicated the shōgunate in favor of his son *Iemitsu* and died 10 years later, at the age of 53 years. He was buried in the temple *Zōjō-ji*, at *Shiba* (*Edo*) and received the posthumous name of *Taitoku-in*.

—— **Tadayoshi,** 忠 吉 (1580-1607). 4th son of *Ieyasu*, was at first adopted by *Matsudaira Ietada* and was named *Tadayasu*. In 1592, he received the castle of *Ōshi* (*Musashi* — 100,000 k.) as fief. He took part in the battle of *Sekigahara* in which he opposed *Shimazu Yoshihiro*. After the campaign, he was transferred to *Kiyosu* (*Owari* — 240,000 k.), changed his name *Tadayasu* to that of *Tadayoshi*, and received the title of *Satsuma no kami*. He died at the age of 27, without an heir.

—— **Nobuyoshi,** 信 吉 (1583-1603). 5th son of *Ieyasu*, was chosen to represent the *Takeda* family which became extinct in 1582. He received the fief of *Sakura* (*Shimōsa* — 40,000 k.) (1594); after *Sekigahara* he was transferred to *Mito* (*Hitachi* — 240,000 k.), but being of a weak constitution, he died at the age of 20.

—— **Tadateru, 忠輝** (1593-1683). 6th son of *Ieyasu*, was chosen heir to *Matsudaira* (*Nagasawa*) *Yasutada* (+ 1600), and received the fief of *Sakura* (40,000 k.). In 1603, he was transferred to *Kawanaka-jima* (*Shinano* — 180,000 k.), and in 1610, to *Takata* (*Echigo* — 620,000 k.). When *Ōsaka* was besieged in 1615, he at first refused to lead his troops thither and came only towards the end of the campaign. The following year, being accused of wishing to overthrow his brother, the *Shōgun Hidetada*, and of badly administering his estates, he was dispossessed, shaved his head and retired to a temple at *Odawara*. Later on, he went to *Takayama* (*Hida*), then in 1626, to *Suwa* (*Shinano*), where he died at the age of 91 years.

—— **Yoshinao, 義直**. 7th son of *Ieyasu*. — See *Tokugawa* (*Owari*).

—— **Yorinobu, 頼宣**. 8th son of *Ieyasu*. — See *Tokugawa* (*Kii*).

—— **Yorifusa, 頼房**. 9th son of *Ieyasu*. — See *Tokugawa* (*Mito*).

—— **Sen-hime, 千姫** (1597-1666) Daughter of *Hidetada*, was promised in marriage to *Toyotomi Hideyori* in 1603. After the death of the latter (1615), she married *Honda Tadatoki*, *daimyō* of *Himeji* (*Harima*). Again a widow in 1626, she came to *Edo*, to live near her brother, the *Shōgun Iemitsu*, and as her residence was near the *Take-bashi* bridge, she was called *Takebashi-Goten*. She died at the age of 70, was buried in the temple *Denzū-in* and received the posthumous name of *Tenju-in*.

—— **Iemitsu, 家光** (1603-1651). 3rd *Tokugawa Shōgun*, from 1622 to 1651. — Eldest son of *Hidetada*, he was educated by *Naitō Tadashige*. He became *Shōgun* at the age of 19, when his father abdicated, and devoted all his time to the study and perfecting of the government methods introduced by *Ieyasu*. He closed the country entirely to all foreign commercial transactions; forbade the building of ships which would permit of long voyages (1636); by a cruel massacre suppressed the *Shimabara* insurrection (1638); put to death the *Macao* ambassadors who had come to ask for liberty of commerce (1640); confined the Dutch who were allowed to pursue commerce with the Japanese to *Deshima* (*Nagasaki*); bore a blind and ferocious hatred to Christianity and destroyed it by a fierce persecution; made the law (*Sankin-kōdai*) which obliged the *daimyō* to reside alternately at *Edo*, and in their domains, in which latter case they were obliged to leave their wife and children as hostages at *Edo*. He was a protector of Buddhism and Confucianism. For the former he built the *Kwan-ei-ji* (1626) at *Edo* and the *Eishō-ji* (1634) at *Kamakura*. He erected a temple in honor of Confucius and protected the learned *Hayashi Dōshun*, *Nakae Tōju*, etc. His sister *Kazu-ko*, had been married in 1620 to the emperor *Go-Mi-no-o*, and from this union was born a daughter (*Myōshō-tennō*) who was raised to the throne at the age of 7. Thus, *Iemitsu's* influence was great both at *Kyōto* and at *Edo*. To prevent any attempt of insubordination on the part of the Imperial Court, he required that a prince of royal blood should be always at the head of the *Ueno* (*Edo*) and *Nikkō* temples, whom he was ready to oppose to the legitimate sovereign should he prove troublesome. By all these manoeuvres, *Iemitsu* brought the government of the *Shōgun* to the highest degree of power. He died at the age of 47 and was buried at *Nikkō* where a magnificent temple was erected to his memory. His posthumous name is *Taiyū-in*. At his death, 10 of his most faithful subjects killed themselves; among these were: *Hotta Masamori, daimyō* of *Sakura, Abe Shigetsugu, daimyō* of *Iwatsuki, Uchida Masanobu, Saegusa Moriyoshi, Okuyama Yasu shige*, etc. At the same time, more than 3,700 maids of honour were dismissed from the Palace, and of this number, over 100 shaved their heads and embraced religious life (*ama*).

—— **Tadanaga,** 忠 長 (1605-1633). Son of *Hidetada* and brother of *Iemitsu*. In 1617, he received the fief *Komoro* (*Shinano*), and the following year was transferred to *Fuchū* (*Kai* — 240,000 k.). In 1624, the provinces of *Suruga* and of *Tōtōmi* were added to his domains and he took up his residence in the castle of *Sumpu* (*Suruga* — 550,000 k.). The same year, he received the title of *Dainagon*, hence the name of *Suruga-Dainagon* by which he is often known. He was accused of maladministration and of plotting against his brother, the *Shōgun Iemitsu*, wherefore he was banished in 1332, to the domain of *Andō Shigenaga, daimyō* of *Takazaki* (*Kōzuke*), and, the following year, invited to commit *harakiri*.

—— **Kazu-ko,** 和 子 (1607-1678). Daughter of *Hidetada*, who in 1620 married the Emperor *Go-Mi-no-o* and had 5 children; the eldest became the Empress *Myōshō-tennō*. She is known by the name of *Tōfuku-mon-in*.

—— **Masayuki,** 正 之 . — See *Hoshina Masayuki*.

—— **Ietsuna,** 家 綱 (1639-1680). 4th *Tokugawa Shōgun*, from 1651 to 1680. Eldest son of *Iemitsu*, and succeeded his father at the age of 12. In the year of his accession to the shōgunate, he repressed the rebellion of *Yui Shōsetsu* and *Marubashi Chūya*. *Ietsuna's* ministers were: *Sakai Tadakiyo, Matsudaira Nobutsuna, Ii Naozumi*, etc. They continued to govern according to the manner of *Iemitsu*. He forbade suicide (*junshi*) at the death of a master and prohibited any translation of European works and any writing concerning the government, *Edo* morals, etc. We need not wonder therefore at the great number of authors who were imprisoned or banished during his reign. *Ietsuna* died at the age of 41, and as he had no children, his brother *Tsunayoshi* succeeded him. He was buried in the *Kwan-ei-ji* (*Ueno*) and received the posthumous name of *Gen-yū-in*.

—— **Tsunashige,** 綱 重 (1644-1678). 3rd son of *Iemitsu*, received the fief of *Fuchū* (*Kai* — 250,000 k.) in 1661. He died at the age of 35. His son *Tsunatoyo* was *Shōgun* under the name of *Ienobu*.

—— **Tsunayoshi,** 綱 吉 (1646-1709). 5th *Tokugawa Shōgun*, from 1680 to 1709. 4th son of *Iemitsu*, he in 1661, received the fief of *Tatebayashi* (*Kōzuke* — 350,000 k.), and was called to succeed his brother *Ietsuna* who died without progeny. He was at that time 34 years old. He was a patron of letters and sciences, encouraged military studies, worked at the reform of the calendar, founded schools, protected artists, etc. The finances being in a bad condition, he sought to improve affairs by altering the value of money and by awarding land to the *hatamoto* instead of giving them a pension in rice. These measures wrought a notable increase in the prices of all necessaries of life and occasioned general dissatisfaction. *Tsunayoshi* had acted on the advice of *Yanagisawa Yoshiyasu*, and on representations made by the *Kanjō-bugyō Ogiwara Shigehide*. At that time, 30 million *koku* composed the revenues of the whole Empire; of which 23 million belonged to the *daimyō*, 3 million to the temples and *hatamoto*, and the remaining 4 million to the shōgunate. This last sum, from which 150,000 k. were deducted, being the allowance made to the Court of *Kyōto*, could certainly not suffice because of the prodigality of *Tsunayoshi*, who had to find divers expedients to increase his finances. Owing to the influence of the bonzes, he, under the strictest penalty, forbade the killing of any living being, and had places of refuge erected for disabled or infirm horses and dogs (See *Inu-Kubō*). Examples of the inhuman execution of this law are not wanting; thus, a vassal of the *daimyō Akita*, having killed a swallow was put to death and his children sent into exile (1686). — In 1704, *Tsunayoshi* having no children, adopted his nephew *Tsuna-toyo*, son of *Tsunashige*, who took the name of *Ienobu*. The fief of *Fuchū* (*Kai*), which he possessed up to that time, passed to *Yanagisawa Yoshiyasu*, who then was continually rising in favor. Abusing the influence he had acquired over the mind of the weak and aged *Shōgun*, *Yoshiyasu* asked that the province of *Suruga* be added to the fief which his son *Yoshisato* was to inherit. *Tsunayoshi* consented, but before placing his seal on the official document confirming the donation, his wife, *Mi-daidokoro*, daughter of the ex-*Kwampaku Takatsukasa Fu-sasuke*, exasperated that such an abnormal favor should be granted, stabbed the *Shōgun* and killed herself. *Tsunayoshi* was then 63 years old. He was buried at the *Kwan-ei-ji* (*Ueno*) and received the posthumous name of *Jōken-in*.

—— **Ienobu, 家宣** (1662-1712). 6th *Tokugawa Shōgun*, from 1709 to 1712. — Son of *Tsunashige*, he was *daimyō* of *Fuchū* (*Kai* — 350,000 k.) when his uncle *Tsunayoshi*, chose him as heir (1704). He then changed his name *Tsunatoyo* to that of *Ienobu*, and 5 years later, received the title of *Shōgun*, at the age of 47 years. The first act of his reign was to abrogate the severe laws enacted by his predecessors against those who killed animals or caused them to suffer. On the petition of *Arai Hakuseki* he suppressed the custom which obliged the greater number of the princes of the Imperial family to become bonzes and the princesses to become *ama*, and he allowed them to marry. He recoined the altered pieces of money that *Tsunayoshi* had introduced and gave them their former value. *Ienobu* took the famous and learned *Arai Hakuseki*, with him from *Kai*, for he loved to follow his advice. He died at the age of 50, was buried in the *Zōjō-ji* (*Shiba*) and received the posthumous name of *Bunshō-in*.

—— **Kiyotake, 清武** . — See *Matsudaira* (*Ochi*).

—— **Ietsugu, 家継** (1709-1716). 7th *Tokugawa Shōgun*, from 1713 to 1716. — Son of *Ienobu*, succeeded him at the age of 4. It was in his

name that a law was enacted, which obliged the *daimyō* of *Kyūshū* to
burn any European vessel that should land on their coasts and to kill the
crew. *Ietsugu* died when but 7 years old, was buried in the *Zōjō-ji*
(*Shiba*) and received the posthumous name of *Yūshō-in*.

—— **Yoshimune,** 吉宗 (1677-1751). 8th *Tokugawa Shōgun*, from
1716 to 1745. — 3rd son of *Tokugawa Mitsusada*, of the *Kii* branch, he
in 1797, received a revenue of 30,000 k. at *Nibu* (*Echizen*) and at the death
of his two elder brothers, he became *daimyō* of *Wakayama* and chief of
the *Kii* branch (1705). At the death of *Ietsugu*, he was chosen as his
successor, and though he refused the dignity of *Shōgun* three times, he
was obliged to submit to the decision of the family council. He was then
39 years old. When in power, his first endeavor was to extirpate abuses
and to bring about the happiness of his people. He entrusted the affairs of
justice to the upright *Ō-oka Tadasuke ;* made researches for the tombs of
the ancient emperors and had them repaired ; ordered boxes to be placed
in the cities of *Edo, Kyōto* and *Ōsaka*, to receive the petitions and complaints of the common people ; repressed luxury
and favored economy ; distributed a book on
popular medicine for the benefit of the poor ;
introduced the growing of sweet potatoes and the
making of sugar ; established a trade system for
the mutual benefit of the provinces ; etc. He was
also a protector of the learned, removed the prohibition to read or translate European books, and
personally supervised the printing of a great
number of books, etc. In short, he became so
popular by his wise administration, that the

TOKUGAWA YOSHIMUNE.

people called him *Kome-shōgun* (the *Shōgun* of the rice). *Yoshimune*
however did not revoke the laws closing the country to strangers, nay he
redoubled the watchfulness and did much for the protection of the
coasts. In 1729, a certain *Ten-ichi-bō*, a native of *Wakayama*, pretending to be the son of *Yoshimune* came to *Edo* to assert his rights but was
arrested, convicted of falsehood and put to death. At the age of 68, *Yoshimune* abdicated in favor of his son *Ieshige*. He died 6 years later, was
buried at the *Kwan-ei-ji* (*Ueno*) and received the posthumous name of
Yūtoku-in.

Yoshimune (8) { Ieshige (9) { Ieharu (10) - Iemoto / Shigeyoshi (*Shimizu*) ; Munetaka (*Tayasu*) } ; Munetada-Harunari { Ienari (11) { Ieyoshi (12) - Iesada (13) / Nariyuki { Yoshitomi (*Kii*) / Iemochi (14) } ; Nariatsu (*Hitotsubashi*) } ; Munenao (*Kii*) }

—— **Ieshige,** 家重 (1712-1761). 9th *Tokugawa Shōgun*, from 1745
to 1760.—Eldest son of *Yoshimune*, whom he succeeded at the age of 34.
He was of a weak constitution, and left the administration of public
affairs to his ministers. In 1758, the councilors of the *Shōgun*, began

to fear the doctrines taught by *Takenouchi Shikibu* at *Kyōto*, wherefore he was imprisoned and 17 *kuge*, were degraded or exiled. *Ieshige* abdicated at the age of 48, in favor of his son *Ieharu*, and died the following year. He was buried in the *Zōjō-ji* (*Shiba*), and received the posthumous name of *Junshin-in*.

—— **Ieharu, 家治** (1737-1786). 10th *Tokugawa Shōgun*, from 1760 to 1786. — Eldest son of *Ieshige*, whom he succeeded at the age of 23, he ordered Dutch books to be translated and encouraged letters and science. During his administration, *Yamagata Daini* and *Fujii Umon* were beheaded and *Takenouchi Shikibu* exiled, for having proclaimed the authority of the Emperor to the prejudice of that of the *Shōgun* (1767). — *Ieharu* died at the age of 50 and his son *Iemoto* having died before him, a successor was chosen in the *Hitotsubashi* branch. He was buried in the *Kwan-ei-ji* (*Ueno*) and received the posthumous name of *Shimmei-in*.

—— **Shigeyoshi, 重好**. — See *Tokugawa* (*Shimizu*).

—— **Iemoto, 家基** (1763-1779). Son of *Ieharu*. In 1766, was nominated heir to the *Shōgun* (*taishi*), but died at the age of 18. He was buried in the *Kwan-ei-ji* (*Ueno*) and received the posthumous name of *Kōkyō-in*.

—— **Ienari, 家齊** (1773-1841). 11th *Tokugawa Shōgun*, from 1786 to 1837. — Son of *Hitotsubashi Harunari*. In 1781 was chosen by the *Shōgun Ieharu* to be his heir, and was only 15 years old when he succeeded him. In 1789, troubles occurred in the island of *Ezo* but were repressed by *Matzumae Michihiro*. This is the last revolt of the *Ebisu* mentioned in history. During the rule of *Ienari*, the foreign powers again renewed their efforts to enter into communication with Japan: Russia, in 1792-1798-1804-1811-1814 ; England, in 1797-1801-1803-1808-1810-1813-1818-1824 ; America, in 1797-1806-1837 ; but all advances were met with a refusal. The *Shōgun* ordered the *daimyō* of the North, to keep a good watch on the coasts and to defend them. Forts were constructed in different parts of the country, communications with Annam and Luzon were interrupted, and the country was again secluded more than ever from the outside world. The famous *Matsudaira Sadanobu* reformed the regulations of the army and marine, obliged the *hatamoto* to pass examinations on military affairs, personally inspected the coasts, etc. In 1827, *Ienari* received the title of *Dajō-Daijin ;* he is the only one who bore that title whilst *Shōgun*. In 1837, *Ōshio Heihachirō* revolted and attempted to occupy the castle of *Ōsaka* but was defeated by the *Jōdai Doi Toshitsura*, and killed himself. Soon after, *Ienari* resigned the shōgunate to his son *Ieyoshi*. He had ruled during 50 years. He died 4 years later, at the age of 69. He had 51 children, 31 of whom died in their youth ; the others entering by adoption or by marriage into the noblest families. *Ienari* received the posthumous name of *Bunkyō-in* and was buried in the *Kwan-ei-ji* (*Ueno*).

—— **Ieyoshi, 家慶** (1792-1853). 12th *Tokugawa Shōgun*, from 1837 to 1858. — Succeeded his father *Ienari*, at the age of 45. As foreign vessels were more frequently sighted off Japan, orders were given to fire at those which came near the coasts (1842). In the mean time the *daimyō* of *Mito*, *Tokugawa Nariaki*, ordered canon to be cast guns and weapons to be made, drilled his troops, and all this in view of a war with the Europeans, but the *Edo* government began to fear that he had some other purpose in view, and confined *Nariaki* to his domains of *Komagome* (*Edo*) together with his counsellor *Fujita Tōko* (1844). The same year, King William II. of Holland wrote a letter to the *Shōgun*, requesting him to enter into commercial relations with the different powers of Europe The Catholic missionaries, in spite of long standing prohibitions, settled in the island of *Okinawa*, preparatory to their entrance into Japan. In 1846, an American vessel, the *Columbus*, entered the haven of *Suruga* (*Sagami*) and attempted in the name of her government to open commercial relations with Japan, similar to that carried on with China, but met with a polite refusal. However the French, English and Russian flags frequently appeared in Japanese waters. *Ii Naosuke* then minister, set *Nariaki* free, and entrusted him with the defence of the country (1852). *Nariaki* constructed the forts of *Shinagawa*, in order to protect *Edo*, presented the *Bakufu* with 72 canon that had been cast in his domains, ordered guns to be made, etc. Mean-

while the Emperor had prayers offered in the Shintoist and Buddhist temples. On July the 8th, 1853, an American fleet anchored in *Suruga* bay, and the commander, Commodore *Perry* asked to present a letter from President *Fillmore* to the *Shōgun*. At this news, all that district was greatly excited. The *Bugyō* of *Uraga* in all haste, informed the *Edo* government, which at once sent an order to all the *daimyō* to prepare for war. In the meantime, a temporary building had been erected on the sea

ARRIVAL OF COMMODORE PERRY'S FLEET. (1853)

coast near *Kurihama*, and the *Bugyō* of *Uraga* received the American envoy. On July 14, *Perry* landed with an escort of 300 armed sailors, handed over the President's letter and announced that he would return the following year to get an answer from the *Shōgun*, and after having made several soundings in *Kanagawa* bay, he sailed away.

On August the 20th, *Poutiatine*, a Russian, arrived at *Nagasaki* with a similar mission from his government, but *Ieyoshi* had just died 5 days before. He was buried in the *Zōjō-ji* (*Shiba*) and received the posthumous name of *Shintoku-in*.

—— **Iesada,** 家定 (1824-1858). 13th *Tokugawa Shōgun*, from 1853 to 1858. — Adopted by his brother, *Ieyoshi*, he succeeded him at the age of 30 years, at a time, when the arrival of foreigners and their petitions to enter into relation with Japan, was about to place the government of the *Shōgun* in a predicament. The Council of the *Shōgun* together with the principal *daimyō*, deliberated upon the answer to be given to the United States of America, but could not agree as to how the letter should be worded. In the mean time, the Russian envoy demanded the opening of diplomatic and commercial relations and the settlement of the disputed boundaries in the island of *Saghalien*. He was put off for another year. On February the 12th 1854, Commodore *Perry* with 7 vessels arrived in the harbor of *Uraga* Bay and asked for the answer to his communication of the preceding year. Opinion differed. *Nariaki* urged a refusal and *Hosokawa Narimori* of *Kumamoto* asked permission to fire upon the American vessels. But the *Shōgun*, after much vacillation, signed a temporary treaty which opened the two ports of *Shimoda* and *Hakodate* to the American vessels with permission to traffic there and get provisions (March 31, 1854). Soon after the port of *Nagasaki* was added to the two others. The *Bakufu* however continued its preparations for war. He sent *Yatabori Kō* and *Katsu Rintarō* to *Nagasaki* to obtain information from the Dutch about the construction and handling of European ships. The same year (1855), in the month of November, a most violent earthquake was felt at *Edo* and occasioned a big fire which destroyed several quarters of the city and killed 25,000 people. The following year, Mr. *Harris* arrived at *Shimoda* as Minister plenipotentiary of the United States, and the *Bakufu* sent *Hotta Masaatsu*, *Bitchū no kami* and *daimyō* of *Sakura* to settle all questions in reference to foreigners. Notwithstanding the opposition of his *daimyō*, the *Shōgun* gave audience to Mr. *Harris* and received a letter from him in which 10 ports were asked to be opened to American commerce. *Iesada* dared not take such responsibility upon himself and sent *Hotta Masaatsu* to the Emperor to confer with him. The counsellors of the *Kyōto* Court, through love for conservative traditions and also in opposition to the authority of the *Shōgun* were of opinion that every petition of the strangers should be refused and even those that had already been granted should be revoked. *Masaatsu* returned to *Edo* with this answer and the *Shōgun* read it to the assembled *daimyō* in order to have their opinion on the subject. At that time, *Ii Naosuke*, *Kamon no kami* and *daimyō* of *Hikone*, was named first Minister of the *Shōgun* (*tairō*) (1858), and his energy was destined to hasten the solution of the pending difficulties. *Masaatsu* at first tried to evade the formal answer which the American envoy seemed to be expecting: *Harris* then spoke of addressing himself directly to *Kyōto*. The *Bakufu*, in order to gain time, sent a tardy answer to the Washington government. *Harris* however gave them to understand that France and England, who, after the capture of *Canton*, had just concluded a treaty with China (Treaty of *Tientsin* — June, 27, 1858), would send their combined fleets to Japan, and, if need be, take extreme measures to effect the opening of the country. In view of this threat the *Bakufu* yielded, and on July 29th signed a treaty with the United States. At this juncture *Iesada* fell dangerously ill and having no children, the question of his succession brought about great difficulties. *Nariaki* of *Mito* proposed his son *Keiki*, but the *Tairō Ii Naosuke* was powerful enough to have this candidate set aside and secured the majority of votes for *Iemochi*, a boy of 12 years and a member of the *Kii* branch. This secured the continuation of his influence, and he at once profited by it to confine *Nariaki* to his domains and forbade *Keiki* to enter the Palace of the *Shōgun*. *Iesada* died, August the 15th, 1858, at the age.of 35. He was interred at *Ueno* and received the posthumous name of *Onkyō-in*.

—— **Iemochi,** 家茂 (1846-1866). 14th *Tokugawa Shōgun*, from 1858 to 1866. — Son of *Nariyuki*, of the *Kii* branch, he was chosen heir to *Iesada*, through the influence of the *Tairō Ii Naosuke*, despite the opposition of *Mito Nariaki*, who proposed his own son *Hitotsubashi Keiki*. *Iemochi* was then only 12 years old and the government remained in the hands of *Naosuke*. It was he who signed the treaties with Holland (*Donker Curtius*, Aug. 19, 1858) with Russia (*Poutiatine*, Aug. 20), with England (*Lord Elgin*, Aug. 27) and with France (Baron *Gros*, Oct. 9). This news caused great disturbance in *Kyōto*. The Emperor secretly wrote to *Nariaki*, and asked him to bring the *Bakufu* to change his line of conduct and to expel all foreigners. *Naosuke*, then sent the *Rōjū Manabe Norikatsu* to *Kyōto*, who imprisoned 57 *kuge* and *samurai* who were hostile to the shōgunate while 40 or 50 others received the same punishment at *Edo*. These measures calmed the people for some time. At the beginning of 1859, *Yokohama* was opened to foreigners, but the Japanese were strictly forbidden to dress in European style. The following year, the *Shōgun* sent an embassy to the United States. In the mean time, *Ii Naosuke* was assassinated by the *rōnin* of *Mito*, but his successor, *Andō Nobumasa*, *Tsushima no kami*, followed the same policy. Plenipotentiary ministers were sent to all the countries that had signed treaties with Japan (1861). Public opinion however did not abate in its resistance to the policy of opening the country, and foreigners were frequently murdered. The *Bakufu* then resolved to send an extraordinary embassy to the powers asking them to postpone the application of the treaties. The envoys to Europe left Japan, Jan. 22, 1862, and were received in audience by *Napoleon III*, April 13. But neither at Paris nor elsewhere did they find the government disposed to abandon the advantages promised in the treaties. The Emperor had meanwhile entrusted the keeping of *Kyōto* to the *daimyō* of *Tosa* and of *Satsuma*, who were hostile to the *Bakufu*, and sent the *kuge Ōhara Shigenori* with a large retinue commanded by *Shimazu Hisamitsu* to *Edo*. The Imperial envoy was to order the *Shōgun* to repair to *Kyōto* with the principal *daimyō* in order to treat about the interior and exterior affairs of the country ; to oblige him to name 5 *tairō* as in the days of *Hideyoshi*, and to receive *Hitotsubashi Keiki* and *Matsudaira Yoshinaga* (*Echizen*) as counsellors. Moreover, amnesty was given to all condemned in 1858 and the revenues of the *Ii* and the *Andō* families were diminished. It was on his return to *Kyōto*, that *Ōhara's* retinue met some Englishmen at *Namamugi*, near *Yokohama*. *Richardson*, one of the party was killed and two others wounded by the *Satsuma samurai*. At this time, the *Bakufu* abrogated the law (*Sankin-kōdai*) which obliged the *daimyō* to leave their wifes and children in *Edo*, and on all sides troops were raised. *Enomoto Kamajirō, Akamatsu Kosaburō* and *Uchida Tsunejirō* were sent to Holland to study the construction of war ships. The *Shōgun* meanwhile had sent *Keiki* and *Yoshinaga* to *Kyōto* whither he himself went in the beginning of 1863. The *samurai* at once asked him to be their leader and proceed to expel the barbarians, but finding *Iemochi* loathe to comply with their requests, they went to the *Tōji-in* temple, broke the statues of three *Ashikaga Shōgun* and exposed their heads at *Shijō-gahara*. Disorder soon reigned supreme in the capital. The Emperor *Kōmei* went to the temple *Hachiman* of *Otoko-yama*, where he intended to present *Iemochi* with a sword, the emblem of authority to expel all foreigners. The *Shōgun*, feigning sickness, requested *Keiki* to replace him at the ceremony, but *Keiki* likewise shunned this honor. This dissatisfied the *samurai* still more and they asked the Emperor to place himself at their head. Soon after, however, *Iemochi* went to the Imperial Palace and promised to enter upon the campaign before the lapse of another month. He also manifested the desire to return to *Edo*, but was detained at *Kyōto*, and replaced at his castle by *Mito Yoshiatsu*. At that time, England insisted on having the indemnity settled which she demanded for the murder of *Richardson*. *Keiki* was sent to settle the affair, and at the same time, *Ogasawara Nagayuki* went to *Yokohama* to ask the representatives of the powers to desist from entering into relation with Japan. His request did not even receive consideration, whereupon *Ikeda, Chikugo no kami*, was dispatched to Europe to treat directly with the governments, but he dared not attempt to accomplish his difficult mission, and on his return was degraded. Meanwhile, on the day appointed by the Emperor, the 10th of the 5th month, *Mōri Motonori*, the *Chōshū daimyō*, gave order to fire on the American vessel, the *Pembroke*, which was passing *Shimonoseki* strait, and in a few days, some French and Dutch ships experienced the same treatment. *Mōri* however received congratulations from *Kyōto* for this bold act. As England could obtain no redress for the *Namamugi* affair, admiral *Kuper* with 7 ships was sent to bombard *Kagoshima*. The *Bakufu* now offered the *Shimazu* a loan of 70,000 *ryō* (350,000 frs.) to pay the claimed indemnity. In September, 1863, the *Shōgun* despite the opposition of *Mōri*, succeeded in having the custody of the city of *Kyōto* taken from the *Chōshū* troops and given to those of *Satsuma* and *Aizu*. *Mōri Motozumi, Sanjō Sanetomi* and 6 other *kuge* fled to *Nagato* and were at once degraded. The *Bakufu* thus recovered a little influence, a semblance of calm set in, and the hostility against the foreigners quieted down somewhat. In the beginning of 1864, the *Shōgun*, after only a few months' stay in *Edo*, returned to *Kyōto*, and, to his great astonishment, was ordered by the Emperor to punish *Mōri* and to postpone the campaign against the foreigners. The *samurai* of *Chōshū*, unable to obtain the accomplishment of their wishes, openly rebelled and tried to overpower the guard of *Kyōto*. They were repulsed, but in the fight, some stray balls found their way into the Imperial Palace. *Mōri* apologized but was not heeded, and *Keiki* named *Tokugawa Yoshikatsu* (*Owari*) commander-in-chief of the army that was to march against the *Chōshū* troops. At the same time, prince *Arisugawa Taruhito*, *Ichijō Saneyoshi* and 70 other opponents of the *Bakufu* were imprisoned. In the month of November, the *Shōgun's* army arrived at *Hiroshima*; *Mōri*, finding it impossible to resist, concluded peace and the troops returned to *Kyōto*. Some time before, the powers made a call at *Shimonoseki* and their combined fleet bombarded and destroyed the forts (September 5-8). — The year 1865 was passed in preparing for an expedition against *Chōshū* which the *Shōgun* intended to lead in person. *Tokugawa Yoshikatsu* and *Katsu Yoshikuni* tried in vain to make him desist from his design. *Mōri* did not remain inactive, and, through the intervention of *Saigō Takamori*, he made peace with *Satsuma*. War began in July 1866, and the *Shōgun's* troops were defeated by those of *Chōshū*. On September 19, *Iemochi* died at *Ōsaka* at the age of 21. He received the posthumous name of *Shōtoku-in*, and his body, taken back to *Edo*, was buried in the *Zōjō-ji* (*Shiba*).

—— **Yoshinobu** or **Keiki**, 慶喜. 15th *Tokugawa Shōgun*, from 1866 to 1868. — Son of the prince of *Mito*, *Nariaki*. He was born in 1837 and was adopted by the *Hitotsubashi* family. At the death of the *Shōgun Iesada* (1858), his father presented him as a candidate to the shōgunate, but was opposed by *Ii Kamon no kami*. In 1862, he was made minister (*hosa*) to *Iemochi* and from that time was an important factor in politics. At *Iemochi's* death, he was chosen to succeed him. He took the name of *Yoshinobu* and received the title of *Se-i-tai-shōgun*. He was no sooner in office than he dispatched *Katsu Yoshikuni* to *Hiroshima*, to stop the war against *Chōshū*. Soon after, the emperor *Kōmei* died and his successor being only 15 years old, the influential *kuge* and *daimyō*, seeing they had nothing to fear from his personal initiative, openly expressed their intentions. Prince *Arisugawa* and the *kuge* who had been imprisoned were given freedom. In the middle of the year 1867, the *daimyō* of *Tosa*, *Yamanouchi Toyonobu*, addressed a memoir to the *Shōgun*, inviting him to resign his power into the hands of the Emperor. *Keiki* frightened at the difficulties of his position, accepted the advice and on October 14, he sent in his resignation. The Emperor reserved his answer till after the great assembly of *daimyō* and *kuge* which had been summoned for the 15th of December. In this assembly, *Mōri* and his *kuge* followers were reinstated in their dignities and offices; the guard of the city of *Kyōto* was taken from the troops of *Aizu* and *Kuwana* and again confided to the troops of *Satsuma*, *Chōshū*, *Aki*, *Echizen*, etc.; the titles of *Sesshō*, *Kwampaku*, *Sei-i-tai-shōgun*, *Gisō*,

Tensō, Shoshidai, were suppressed; the offices of *Sōsai, Gitei,* and *San-yo* were created, etc. These measures were promulgated Jan. 4th, 1868: it was the end of the shōgunate and the beginning of a new era for Japan. — *Keiki* was ready to accept the decision of the Emperor, and the princes of *Owari* and *Echizen* did all in their power to keep him in these dispositions, but a large number of great *daimyō,* protested against this forced resignation, and those of *Aizu* and *Kuwana* considered it an insult to have been relieved of the guard of *Kyōtō.* *Keiki* however resolved to submit and left the castle of *Ōsaka* to go to *Kyōtō* and to obey the will of the Emperor. He was entering the city, surrounded with a great retinue, when news arrived from *Edo,* that some *samurai* from *Satsuma* had fired on the barracks of his troops, and that the latter in turn attacked the residence of the *Shimazu* and dislodged its garrison. *Keiki* at once changed his mind for he had suspected that the suppression of the shōgunate had been decided upon on the suggestion of *Satsuma* and this incident confirmed him in his opinion. Thereupon he ordered all his adherents to prepare to march against the *Shimazu.* The *Aizu* and *Kuwana* troops were at hand ready to fight, but were defeated by the *Satsuma* and the *Chōshū* troops at *Fushimi* (Jan. 27), at *Toba* (Jan. 29), at *Ōsaka* (Feb. 5). *Keiki* then returned to *Edo* by sea. Guilty of having taken up arms against the Emperor, he was degraded from all his dignities and titles. The *daimyō* of *Aizu,* of *Kuwana* and 27 others shared his punishment, whilst those of *Tosa, Chōshū* and *Aki* were ordered to suppress the rebellion. On Feb. 9th, prince *Arisugawa Taruhito* was made commander-in-chief (*tai-sōtoku*) of the Imperial army, and on March the 5th, he entered *Sumpu (Shizuoka).* He was preparing to march against *Edo,* when the ex-Shōgun sent *Ōkubo Tadahiro, Katsu Yoshikuni,* etc. to treat of peace with *Saigō Takamori.* The conditions were submitted to the Emperor by *Takamori* himself, who had been sent to *Kyōtō* for that purpose, and on whose return, affairs were settled thus: the Imperial army was to take possession of *Edo, Keiki* was to retire to *Mito,* where a revenue of 700,000 k. was to be allotted to the *Tokugawa* family.—The *Shōgun's* adherents did not accept all these conditions, and a certain number intrenched themselves in the *Tōei-żan (Ueno)* where they were defeated (July 4). *Ōtori Keisuke* then retired to *Shimotsuke,* but was routed at *Utsunomiya* and at *Nikkō.* Meanwhile, *Enomoto Takeaki* took 8 ships of the *Shōgun's* fleet with him to *Ezo,* and intended to defend himself there. The Imperial army continued its march Northward and on Nov. 6, occupied the castle of *Wakamatsu.* This marked the end of the war in *Hondo.* *Matsudaira (Hoshina) Katamori, daimyō* of *Aizu,* was condemned to imprisonment, as were likewise the *daimyō* of *Sendai, Morioka* and *Tsurugaoka,* who submitted after the reduction of *Wakamatsu.* Finally, after a glorious defence, *Enomoto* capitulated at *Hakodate* (June 27, 1869) and the civil war was ended making the Imperial Restoration an accomplished fact. — *Keiki,* after having passed some time at *Mito,* retired to *Shizuoka,* and lived in retirement till 1897, when he came to *Tōkyō.* - - At the time of the capitulation of *Edo,* he had adopted *Iesato* 家達 (born in 1863), son of *Tayasu Yoshiyori* as heir. *Yoshiyori* has received the title of Duke. This title was also conceded to *Keiki* in 1902. — In 1887, a grandson of *Keiki* received the title of Baron.

Tokugawa (Owari). — Branch descended from *Yoshinao*, 7th son of *Ieyasu.* It was one of the 3 families (*san-ke*) in which the *Shōgun* could be chosen, but none was ever chosen from it.

Yoshinao - Mitsutomo {Tsunanobu - Tsugitomo - Muneharu ... (a)
Yoshiyuki - Yoshitaka - Yoshiatsu ... (b)

(*a*) — Senior branch —— **Yoshinao, 義直** (1600-1650). 7th son of *Ieyasu*, in 1603 received the fief of *Fuchū* (*Kai* — 250,000 k.), then in 1607, that of *Kiyosu* (*Owari* — 550,000 k.). *Ieyasu* was then building the castle of *Nagoya*, wherein *Yoshinao* was established in 1610, and which his descendants occupied till the Restoration (619,500 k.). — Now, Marquis. — After the Restoration, the 11th son of *Yoshikatsu*, last *daimyō* of *Nagoya*, was permitted to establish a separate branch with the title of Baron.

(*b*) — Junior branch. — See *Matsudaira* (*Owari*).

Tokugawa (Kii), — Branch descended from *Yorinobu*, 8th son of *Ieyasu.* It was one of the *San-ke*, and three *Shōgun* (1716-1786-1858) were chosen from among its members.

Yorinobu {Mitsusada - Tsunanori - Yorimoto - Yoshimune ... (a)
Yorizumi - Yoriyoshi - Yoriyasu - Yorimura ... (b)

(*a*) — Senior branch — **Yorinobu, 頼宣** (1602-1671). 8th son of *Ieyasu*, in 1603 received the fief of *Mito* (*Hitachi* — 250,000 k.), in 1606, that of *Fuchū* (*Suruga*) ; and in 1619. he was transferred to *Wakayama* (*Kii* — 555,000 k.), where his descendants remained till the Restoration. — Now Marquis.

(*b*) — Junior branch. — See *Matsudaira* (*Kii*).

Tokugawa (Mito). — Branch issued from *Yorifusa*, 9th son of *Ieyasu.* It was one of the *San-ke*, to which the last *Shōgun*, *Keiki*, belonged by right of birth.

Yorifusa {
Mitsukuni - Tsunaeda - Yoshizane - Munetaka ... (a)
Yorishige - Yoritsune- Yoritoyo - Yoritake ... (b)
Yorimoto - Yorisada - Yorihiro - Yoriaki ... (c)
Yoritaka - Yoriyuki - Yoriakira - Yorinaga ... (d)
Yorio - Yorimichi- Yorinori - Yorina ... (e)
}

(*a*) — Senior branch. — **Yorifusa, 頼房** (1603-1661). 9th son of *Ieyasu*, in 1606 received the fief of *Shimotsuma* (*Hitachi* — 100,000 k.) ; in 1609, he was transferred to *Mito* (*Hitachi* — 350,000 k.), where his descendants remained till the Restoration.

—— **Mitsukuni, 光圀** (1628-1700). 3rd son of *Yorifusa*, who, because of his intelligence, was chosen to succeed his father. He cultivated letters and history, and with predilection studied Japanese antiquity, gathering around him many learned men whom he made his co-laborers. In 1657, he was engaged in the great historical work, the *Dai-Nihon-shi.* At the death of his father, he prevented several *kerai* from committing suicide (*junshi*), and at his request the *Bakufu* again forbade this barbarous custom. When he learned of the arrival of the great Chinese *Shu-Shunsui* in Japan, he called him to his palace, modestly became one of his scholars (1665), and made him one of his principal co-laborers ·in the great work of the *Dai-Nihon-shi*. His researches into national antiquity, made him counteract the infatuation for things Chinese. He gave preference to Japanese literature over the Chinese classics, protected and propagated Shintoism rather than Buddhism which was of foreign origin, and was able to defend the Imperial dynasty against the encroachments of the shōgunate. He thus gave rise to ideas different from those of his forefathers, and prepared the work of the following century. He admitted the legitimacy of the Southern dynasty during the schism in the 14th century and recognized the rights of the Northern dynasty only when, on the day of *Go-Kameyama's* abdication, it was put into possession of the three Imperial emblems (1392). He sang the fidelity of the *Kusunoki, Masashige,* and *Masatsura,* and caused them to become the popular heroes we find them to be at the present day. In 1692, he ordered a monument to be erected in honor of *Masashige* on the very spot where he died (*Hyōgo*). He destroyed a thousand Buddhist temples that had been recently constructed in his domains, sparing only the most ancient, and in their place, constructed Shintoist temples for each village. It was only on the express order of his father and of the *Shōgun Iemitsu,* that he accepted the succession to the fief of *Mito,* to the prejudice of his elder brother *Yorishige,* but, in order to repair what he called an injustice, he chose *Tsunaeda* eldest son of *Yorishige* to be his heir, and in 1675, resigned the government of his domains in his favor in order to devote all his time to scientific and literary pursuits. Till then it had been the custom among learned Confucianists and others to shave their head and adopt a Buddhist name, but he abolished this custom, commanded all his literati to let their hair grow and elevated them to the rank of *samurai.* *Mitsukuni's* great work, the *Dai-Nihon-shi,* was completed only in 1715, but a great part of it was published in 1697. It consists of 243 volumes, comprises the history of Japan from the time of *Jimmu-tennō,* and to the present day has remained the best authority on historical matters. *Mitsukuni* is also known by the names of *Mito Kōmon, Gikō Seizan,* etc.

—— **Nariaki,** 齊昭 (1800-1860). Descendant of *Mitsukuni* and likewise, *daimyō* of *Mito.* He proved himself a staunch supporter of the Imperial restoration. He caused his *samurai* to study military art, and had war instruments made. The plausible cause of these preparations was the urgent necessity of repulsing the foreigners, whose ships were then frequently entering Japanese waters. The *Bakufu* fearing some disguised designs, became suspicious, and in 1844, *Nariaki* and his adviser *Fujita Tōko* were confined to *Komagome* (*Edo*). They were liberated only when Commodore *Perry's* arrival had brought the anxiety of the *Shōgun's* government to a climax, and *Nariaki* was entrusted with the preparations for the defence of the country (1853). He then ordered the forts of *Shinagawa* to be erected, established arsenals in *Edo* and

Ōsaka, etc., but found a fierce antagonist on questions relating to foreigners in the person of *Ii Naosuke, Kamon no kami*, minister of the *Shōgun*. This statesman believed that Japan would meet certain failure in trying to oppose the powers and therefore favored a policy of concilia-

CONFERENCE BETWEEN MITO NARIAKI (l) AND II NAOSUKE (.) IN THE GREAT HALL OF THE EDO PALACE

tion, which conviction he put in practice by signing treaties with the United States, Holland, etc. These two men thus became the leaders of two opposite parties : *Nariaki* working at the Imperial restoration and the expulsion of foreigners ; *Naosuke* attempting to save the government of the *Shōgun* and to open Japan to external commerce. To attain his ends, *Nariaki* proposed his son *Keiki* as successor to the *Shōgun Iesada* (1858), but at this time, *Naosuke* was the more influential and he obtained the election of *Iemochi* of the *Kii* branch, and *Nariaki* was again condemned to seclusion. The Emperor *Kōmei* however had secretly written to *Nariaki* asking him to bring about a change in the policy of the *Shōgun* and to expel the barbarians. This mark of confidence only increased the hatred of the *Mito* clan against *Naosuke*, who was assassinated whilst going to the Palace, March 1860. *Nariaki's* triumph was short : he died in September of the same year. He is often named *Rekkō*, 烈公. — The heir of the eldest branch of *Mito* has the title of Marquis. — After the Restoration, a branch received the title of Viscount.

(b) (c) (d) (e). — Junior branches. — See *Matsudaira* (*Mito*).

Tokugawa (**Tayasu**, 田安). Branch founded by *Munetake* 宗武 (+ 1769), son of the *Shōgun Yoshimune*. It was one of the *Sankyō*, that had no castle and resided at *Edo*. Its revenues were 130,000 k. — Now Count.

Tokugawa (**Hitotsubashi, 一橋**). Branch established in 1741 by the *Shōgun Yoshimune*, in favor of his son *Munetada* 宗尹 (1721-1764). It was one of the *San-kyō*. Its revenues were 130,000 k. — Now Count.

Tokugawa (**Shimizu, 清水**). Branch founded by *Shigeyoshi* 重好 (1745-1795), son of the *Shōgun Ieshige*. It was one of the *San-kyō*. Its revenues were 100,000 k. — Now Count.

Tokugawa-bakufu, 德川幕府. Government of the *Tokugawa Shōgun*, from 1603 to 1868.

Tokugawa-bakufu gakkō, 德川幕府學校. Schools establish-ed in the domains of the *Shōgun* under the *Tokugawa*. The principal of which were:

Shōhei-kō, 昌平校	Founded at *Edo*	in	1630.
Kiten-kwan, 徽典館	" *Kōfu*	towards	1795.
Meishin-kwan, 明新館	" *Sumpu*	"	1855.
Nikkō-gakkanjo, 日光學問所	" *Nikkō*	"	1862.
Shukyō-kwan, 修敎館	" *Sado*	"	1820.
Meirin-dō, 明倫堂	" *Nagasaki*	"	1645.

Instruction was given according to *Shōhei-kō* programs (See *Shōhei-kō*. To most of them a School of medicine was annexed. — See *Shohan-gakkō.*

Tokugawa-bakufu shokusei, 德川幕府職制. Officials direct-ly responsible for their administration to the *Shōgun*. At first they were, the *Tairō*, the 5 *Rōjū* and the 5 *Waka-doshiyori*, who formed the *Shōgun's* Council and assembled in the apartment of the Palace at *Edo*, called *Go-yō-beya*. Subject to them, were the *Jisha-bugyō*, the *Machi-bugyō* and the *Kanjō-bugyō*, high officials called the *San-bugyō*, who met at the *Hyōjō-sho*, once a month, to consider the important affairs of their department. Next in importance were the *Ōban-gashira, Ō-me-tsuke, Koshō-gumi-ban-gashira, Gosho-in-ban-gashira, Fushin-bugyō, Yari-buyyō, Hata-bugyō*, etc., all of whom lived in *Edo*. — The prin-cipal officials residing outside of *Edo*, were: the *Shoshidai* of *Kyōto ;* the *Jōdai, Jōban* and *Kaban* of the castles of *Nijō, Ōsaka* and *Sumpu ;* the *Machi-bugyō* of *Kyōto, Ōsaka, Nara, Fushimi* and *Sumpu ;* the *Bugyō* of *Nagasaki, Sado, Sakai, (Izumi), Yamada (Ise), Niigata (Echigo), Nikkō* and *Uraga (Sagami)* ; and finally, the *daikwan* who managed the domains of the *Shōgun*.

Tokugawa-jidai, 德川時代. Period of the *Tokugawa* govern-ment, between 1603 and 1868. It is also called *Edo-jidai*.

Tokugawa-jidai no keigaku-ha, 德川時代經學派. The principal schools of Chinese literature and philosophy under the *Toku-gawa :*

(*a*)—**Teishu 程朱 gaku-ha,** established by *Fujiwara Seikwa, Hayashi Razan*, etc. Explaining the most ancient Confucianist books, it claims that the road to wisdom lies in the development of human nature, intellect, heart and instinct.

(*b*)—**Yōmei 陽明 gaku-ha,** school of *Nakae Tōju, Kumazawa Ryōkai*, etc. It extolled the cooperation of science and action, accord-ing to the methods of *Mōshi* (Mencius, 372-289 B.C.).

(c)—**Fukko** 復 古 **gaku-ha,** established by *Itō Jinsai, Ogiu Sorai,* etc. It was the opponent of the *Teishu* school, and claimed that the doctrines (*riki no setsu*) of that school were due to a false interpretation of the words of *Confucius.* The road to wisdom, according to its tenets, lies in the imitation of the ancients. After 80 years of controversy between the two schools, *Inoue Kinga* (1733-1784) took from the theories of both what seemed best to him and founded another school.

(d)—**Setchū** 折 衷 **gaku-ha,** doctrine of the ancient Chinese sages, as interpreted by the philosophers of the *Kan* and *Tō* dynasties.

The curriculum of the *keigaku* embraced only a commentary of the Chinese classics, the *shi-sho* and the *go-kyo.* — The *shi-sho* were :

1.—*Daigaku,* 大 學 (Great study). Explanation of the teachings of *Confucius* by his disciple *Shōshi.*

2.—*Chūyō* 中 庸 (Central virtue). By *Shishi,* great-nephew of *Confucius.*

3.—*Mōshi* 孟 子 Philosopher (372-289 B.C.).

4.—*Rongo* 論 語 speeches of *Confucius* transmitted by his disciples. The *go-kyo* are :

1.—*Ekikyō* 易 經 (Book of mutations). Commentary on *Confucius* according to ancient historical books.

2.—*Shokyō* 書 經. Annals from the year 2350 to about 620 B. C.

3.—*Shikyō,* 詩 經. Moral instruction by examples.

4.—*Raiki,* 禮 記. Collection of customs and ceremonies.

5.—*Shunjū,* 春 秋. Annals of the time of *Shunjū* by *Confucius.*

Tokugawa-jikki, 德 川 實 記. History of the *Tokugawa* till the 10th *Shōgun,* by *Narushima Shichoku* (1778-1862).

Tokugawa-keihō, 德 川 刑 法. Punishments administered in the times of the *Tokugawa.* The principal ones were :

(a)—*Tataki* 敲. Scourging of two degrees of severity : 50 strokes (*keikō*) and 100 strokes (*jukō*).

(b)—*Tsuihō* 追 放. Banishment. — See *Tsuihō.*

(c)—*Entō* 遠 嶋. Exile to an island in *Izu, Satsuma, Hizen, Oki, Sado* or *Iki.*

(d)—*Shizai,* 死 罪. Capital punishment by decapitation (*kubi-kiri*), by fire (*hi-aburi*), by decapitation with exposure (*sarashi-kubi*), by crucifixion (*hari-tsuke*), and by sawing (*nokogiri-biki*).

For the *samurai,* the punishments inflicted were : *fukusoku* (surveillance), *heimon* (imprisonment for 50 or 100 days), *chikkyo* (seclusion), *kaieki* (degradation from the rank of *samurai*), *seppuku* (suicide by *hara-kiri*). For the bonzes : *sarashi* (exposition), *tsui-in,* (expulsion from the temple), *kamai* expulsion and prohibition to preach.

For women ; to have the head shaved and become servants.

Among the common classes ; censure (*shikari*), fine, seclusion, chaining of the hands.

Tokuji, 德 治. *Nengō* : 1306-1307.

Tokunaga, 德 永. Ancient *daimyō* family, coming from *Ōmi* and descended from the *Fujiwara.*

—— **Toshimasa,** 壽昌 (1549-1612). Served *Hideyoshi*, who in 1590, gave him the fief of *Matsunaga* (*Mino* — 20,000 k.). In 1600, *Ieyasu* transferred him to *Takasu* (*Mino* — 60,000 k.).

—— **Masashige,** 昌重 (1574-1642). Son of *Toshimasa*, was dispossessed in 1628, on account of his bad conduct, and exiled to *Shinjō* (*Dewa*) where he died.

Tokunō Michitoki, 得能通言 . — See *Doi Michiharu*.

Toku no shima, 德嶋 . Island (12 Km. circ.) belongs to the *Ōsumi* province, S. E. of *Ōshima*.

Tokusei, 德政 (Lit.: good doing government) This term was formerly applied to the reign of *Nintoku*, who, touched by the misery of the people set them free from taxes for several years. — Under the *Ashikaga*, the same name was given to a decree of the *Shōgun* remitting all debts contracted by his vassals. During the 15th century, most of the noblemen and officials, not being able to meet the expenses of their household because of the luxury prevailing at the time, borrowed money or bought on credit from the *Kyōto* merchants, and, when the latter became too exacting in the demand of their dues the former obtained, from the *Shōgun*, remission of all their obligations. In order to gain the favor of the great, *Yoshimasa* made use of this means as frequently as 13 times. This naturally estranged all the merchants from him. — Under the *Tokugawa*, this act was called *ki-en*.

Tokusen, 得選 . Office of maid-servants employed at the Imperial table. When chosen from among the *Uneme* they were called *Tokusen-ko*.

Tokushima, 德嶋 . Chief-town (63,000 inh.) of the department of the same name of the *Awa* province (*Shikoku*). Ancient castle belonging to the *Hosokawa*. *Chōsokabe Motochika* occupied it and placed his vassal *Yoshida Yasutoshi* therein. In 1585, *Hideyoshi* gave it and the whole province as fief, to *Hachisuka Iemasa*, whose descendants kept it till the Restoration (258,000 k.). — The city was formerly called *Iyama* or *Inotsu*, for it was only in 1678, that it received the name which it has to-day.

Tokushima-ken, 德嶋縣 . Department formed by the *Awa* province (*Shikoku*). — Pop.: 730,000 inh. — Chief town; *Tokushima* (63,000 inh.). — Principal cities: *Muya* (18,000 inh.) *Komatsujima* (12,500 inh.), etc.

Tokushitsu, 篤疾 . This name was formerly given to a certain class of persons exempted from taxes on account of infirmity such as the blind, paralytics, idiots, etc.

Tokushi-yoron, 讀史餘論 . Historical book in 12 volumes by *Arai Hakuseki*. Extends from the beginning of the world to the time of *Hideyoshi*.

Tokuyama, 德山 . Town (12,300 inh.) of the *Suwō* province. Was from 1634 to 1868, the residence of a branch of the *Mōri* family (30,000 k.).

Tōkwa-shō, 桐花章 . Order of the Paulownia (*kiri*). — See *Kunshō*.

Tōkyō, 東京 . Capital (1,819,000 inh.) of the Japanese Empire and chief-town of the *Tōkyō-fu*. Before the Imperial Restoration, it was called *Edo* (See that name) and was the residence of the *Tokugawa Shōgun*. The name of *Edo* was changed to that of *Tōkyō* (capital of the East) September 13th, 1868, and on March 26th, 1869, it became the residence of the Emperor and the seat of government. — *Tōkyō* is divided into 15 districts (*ku*): *Kōjimachi* 麹町 (73,210 inh.), *Kanda* 神田

THE NIHON-BASHI BRIDGE, AT EDO, AT THE TIME OF THE TOKUGAWA.

(138,590 inh.), *Nihonbashi* 日本橋 (138,070 inh.), *Kyōbashi* 京橋 (128,680 inh.), *Shiba* 芝 (127,740 inh.), *Azabu* 麻布 (53,080 inh.), *Akasaka* 赤坂 (43,365 inh.), *Yotsuya* 四谷 (40,160 inh.), *Ushigome* 牛込 (51,545 inh.), *Koishikawa* 小石川 (54,570 inh.), *Hongō* 本郷 (78,900 inh.), *Shitaya* 下谷 (107,410 inh.), *Asakusa* 淺草 (140,725 inh.), *Honjo* 本所 (130,090 inh.) and *Fukagawa* 深川 (100,470 inh.).

Tōkyō-fu, 東京府. Department formed by 8 districts of the *Musashi* province, the 7 islands of *Izu* and the *Ogasawara-jima* group. — Pop.: 2,219,000 inh. — Chief-town: *Tōkyō* (1,819,000 inh.). — Principal cities; *Hachiōji* (23,000 inh.), *Shinagawa* (18,300 inh.), *Minami-senju* (12,700 inh.), *Ōmori* (11,100 inh.), *Ōji* (10,670 inh.), etc.

Tōkyō-wan, 東京灣. *Tōkyō* bay. Its width from E., to W., varies between 15 and 30 Km., its length from N. to S., is about 80 Km. Its entrance is protected by capes *Kannon-saki* (*Sagami*) and *Futtsu-saki* (*Kazusa*), which are 9 Km. apart.

Tomiku, 富來. In *Bungo*. Ancient castle built by *Takeda Shima no kami*. Passed into the possession of the *Tomiku*, vassals of the *Ōtomo*. In 1587, *Hideyoshi* gave it to *Kakimi Iezumi*, who was dispossessed in 1600, and the castle was abandoned.

Tominokōji, 富小路. *Kuge* family descended from *Fujiwara Tadamichi* (1097-1164). — Now Viscount.

Tomioka, 富岡. In *Awa* (*Shikoku*). Ancient castle belonging to the *Hosokawa*. *Chōsokabe Motochika* stormed it in 1582 and entrusted its keeping to his brother *Chikayasu*. Three years later, the province was under the authority of *Hachisuka Iemasa,* who confided the custody of *Tomiku* castle to the *Kajima* family.

Tomita, 富田. Ancient *daimyō* family descended from the *Minamoto*.

—— **Nobuhiro,** 信廣. Served *Hideyoshi,* who in 1586, gave him the fief of *Anotsu* (*Ise* — 100,000 k).

—— **Tomonobu,** 知信. Son of *Nobuhiro,* bravely defended his castle of *Anotsu* against *Mōri Hidemoto, Kikkawa Hiroie,* etc. His wife, daughter of *Ukita Tadaie,* likewise distinguished herself and fought at his side. To reward him for his services, *Ieyasu* in 1608, transferred him to *Uwajima* (*Iyo* — 120,000 k). He was dispossessed in 1613 because he tried to save his father, *Sakazaki Samon,* guilty of murder, from the vengeance of justice. He died at *Iwakidaira* (*Mutsu*) the place of his exile.

Tomobayashi Mitsuhira, 伴林光平 (+ 1864). Native of *Settsu*. Was at first bonze, and studied national literature and poetry. His conferences which attracted many scholars were looked upon with suspicion by the government of the *Shōgun*. He was arrested by the *Bugyō* of *Nara* and beheaded.

Tomobe, 品部. Formerly a general term used to designate all officials of the Imperial palace. They were divided into several groups having a chief at their head, and distinguished by a characteristic *uji,* or a *kabane,* such as *Ōmi, Muraji, Tomo no miyatsuko,* etc. The whole body of officials was called *Yasotomo-no-o* or *Momo-yasobe* and later *Hyakkwan*. The *Ōmi* and the *Muraji* remained in the capital and attended to government affairs, whilst some of the *Tomo no miyatsuko* lived at Court, and others in their provinces.

Tomoe Gozen, 鞆繪御前. Daughter of *Nakahara Kanetō* and sister of *Imai Kanehira*. She married *Kiso Yoshinaka* and was remarkable for her beauty and courage. She followed her husband everywhere, and fought in all his battles, herself leading a troop of men. When *Yoshinaka* was defeated at *Uji* (1184), he had only 13 cavaliers around him, and *Tomoe* was with them. A certain *Uchida Ieyoshi,* of herculean strength, came to attack her, but *Tomoe* defeated him and cut off his head. After *Yoshinaka's* death, she retired to *Tomosugi* (*Echigo*). She was then 28 years old. — Another, rather doubtful tradition says she was overpowered by *Wada Yoshimori,* at the battle of *Awazu* where *Yoshinaka* met

TOMOE GOZEN.

his death. She became the mistress of her victor and bore him a son who was no other than the famous *Asahina Saburō*.

Tomohira-Shinnō, 具平王親 (963-1009). 9th son of the emperor *Murakami*. He was *Nakatsukasa-kyō*, and became famous as a poet and literary man. He is also called *Rokujō no Miya*. He is the ancestor of the *Murakami-Genji*.

Tomo no miyatsuko, 伴造. This word at first designated the chief of certain official sections, either at Court or in the provinces (See *Tomobe*). — Later on, it was applied to the body of officials, as a synonym of *Yaso-tomo-no-o*. The principal divisions were: *Nakatomi, Imibe* (ceremonies of the Shintoist religion); *Mononobe, Ōtomo, Saeki,* (guard of the Palace and war): *Fubitobe, Ekakibe,* (secretaries); *Yamabe, Tabe, Umibe* (rice-fields, waters and forests); *Kashiwabe, Umakaibe, Torikaibe, Takakaibe, Inukaibe, Yugebe, Yahagibe, Tatenuibe, Oribe, Hatori, Kinunuibe, Moku, Ishizukuri, Kajibe, Urushibe, Hanishibe,* etc.

Tomo-no-tsu, 鞆津. Port in *Bingo*. *Ashikaga Tadafuyu* settled there in 1349, when he was named *Tandai* of the *Saikoku*. The *Shōgun Yoshiaki* lived there in 1575. — To-day *Tomo*.

Ton-a, 頓阿 (1301-1384). By birth, *Nikaidō Sadamune*. He became a bonze and studied at the *Hiei-zan*, then at the *Kōya-san*. He was one of the most distinguished poets of his time and the emperor *Kōgon* requested him to finish the *Shūi-shū* collection which had been interrupted by the death of *Fujiwara Tameaki*. Together with *Kenkō, Jōben* and *Keiun*, he belonged, to the *Wa-ka shi-tennō*.

Tone-gawa, 利根川. River (280 Km.) which rises in the *Monju-san*, N. of *Kōzuke*, passes through *Numata, Maebashi*, then forms the boundary of the provinces *Musashi* and *Shimōsa*, receives the tributary *Watarasegawa* near *Kurihashi*, then divides into two branches called the *Gongendōgawa* and the *Akahori-gawa*, which join again at *Sekiya-do*, flow S. E. and enter the Pacific Ocean near *Chōshi*. It is also called *Bandō-Tarō*.

Toneri, 舎人. Formerly guards of the Imperial Palace and of the houses of princes and great lords. The Emperor *Yūryaku* created the *Ō-toneri*; *Ninken* divided them into *Sa-toneri* and *U-toneri*. The *Uchi-toneri* carried a sword and accompanied the Emperor's carriage.—See *Ō-toneri*, etc.

Toneri-Shinnō, 舎人親王 (676-735). 7th son of the emperor *Temmu* and of the princess *Niitabe*, daughter of *Tenchi*. He was entrusted with the composition of the *Nihon-shoki*, which was completed in 720. One of his sons ascended the throne in 759 under the name of *Junnin* and then bestowed upon his father the posthumous name of *Sudō-jinkyō-kōtei*.

TONERI-SHINNŌ.

Tone-zaka, 刀根坂. Hill near the village of *Arachi*, (*Echizen*). In 1572, *Nobunaga* there defeated *Asakura Yoshikage*.

Tonoi, 宿直. Formerly soldiers who guarded the Emperor's apartments during the night.

Tō no mine, 多武峯. — See *Tamu no mine*.

Tonomori, 主殿. Formerly a department of those domestics at the Imperial Palace who had charge of the heating, lighting, baths, etc.

These services were entrusted to women. Its chief officers (*Tonomori-zukasa*) were 1 *Shōden*, 2 *Tenden*, and 6 *Nyoju*.

Tonomo-ryō, 主殿寮. Bureau dependent upon the *Kunai-shō* and which succeeded the *Tonomori-zukasa*. It had the same functions and was directed by 1 *Kami*, 1 *Suke*, 1 *Jō* and 1 *Sakwan*.

Tori Busshi, 鳥佛師. — See *Kuratsukuribe no Tori*.

Torii, 鳥居. *Daimyō* family descended from *Fujiwara Moromasa* (+ 969) and coming from *Mikawa*.

—— **Mototada, 元忠** (1539-1600). Son of *Tadayoshi* ; in 1590 he received the domain of *Yahagi* (*Shimōsa* — 40,000 k.). When *Ieyasu* entered on a campaign against *Uesugi Kagekatsu*, he requested *Mototada* to defend the castle of *Fushimi*, where, being besieged by the troops of the *Shimazu* and the *Ukita*, he died at the moment when the place was reduced.

$$\text{Mototada} \begin{cases} \text{Tadamasa - Tadatsune - Tadaharu - Tadanori} & (a) \\ \text{Naritsugu} & (b) \end{cases}$$

(*a*) — Senior branch. —— **Tadamasa, 忠政** (1567-1628). In 1603 received the fief of *Iwakidaira* (*Mutsu* — 100,000 k.), then was transferred, in 1622, to *Yamagata* (*Dewa* — 260,000 k.).

—— **Tadatsune, 忠恒**. Died in 1636 without an heir, and his domains returned to the *Shōgun*.

—— **Tadaharu, 忠春** (1608-1651). Brother of *Tadatsune*, was chosen to perpetuate the name and in 1636, received the fief of *Takatō* (*Shinano* — 30,000 k.). — His descendants afterwards resided : in 1689, at *Shimomura* (*Noto*) ; in 1695, at *Minakuchi* (*Ōmi*) ; and from 1712 to 1868, at *Mibu* (*Shimotsnke* — 30,000 k.). — Now Viscount.

(*b*) — Junior branch. —— **Naritsugu, 成次**. In 1601 he received the fief of *Yamura* (*Kai* — 35,000 k.), and was dispossessed in 1632 for not having kept good watch over the *Suruga-Dainagon Tadanaga*, whose counsellor he was. He was at the same time banished to *Yamagata* where his nephew *Tadatsune* ruled.

Torii, 鳥井. Family of famous painters of the 18th century. The best known among them are : *Kiyonobu* (1664-1730), *Kiyomitsu* (1735-1785), *Kiyonobu* II, *Kiyomasu* (1706-1763), *Kiyonaga* (+ 1813) and *Kiyomine* (1787-1868), Their school, was a branch of that of *Hishikawa Moronobu*, and attained fame among the schools of realistic painting.

Torimi, 鳥海. In *Rikuchū*. *Minamoto Yoriyoshi* was defeated at that place by *Abe Sadatō* in 1056.

Tori-no-umi-yama, 鳥海山. — See *Chōkai-zan*.

Torio, 鳥尾. *Samurai* family of the *Yamaguchi* clan (*Suwō*) made noble after the Restoration. — Now Viscount.

Tosa, 土佐. One of the 6 provinces of the *Nankaidō*. Comprises 7 districts. — Chinese name : *Toshū*. — Is now the department of *Kōchi*.

Tosabō Shōshun, 土佐坊昌俊. At first bonze at *Nara*, he adhered to *Yoritomo*. When the latter became estranged from his brother *Yoshitsune*, he sent *Shōshun* to *Kyōto* to murder him. *Shōshun* despite treachery, failed in his attempt and fled to the temple of *Kurama-yama*, but the bonzes delivered him into the hands of *Yoshitsune*, who put him to death (1185).

Tosaka-jō, 鳥坂城. Ancient castle of the village of *Sekigawa* (*Echigo*). It was there that in 1201, *Jō Sukemori* rose in revolt against the *Kamakura* administration. The *Shōgun Yoriie* sent *Sasaki Moritsuna* against him. *Jō Sukemori* was defeated.

Tōsandō, 東山道 (Lit.: region of the Eastern mountains). One of the large divisions of Japan, including the whole North of *Hondo*. It comprises 13 provinces: *Ōmi, Mino, Hida, Shinano, Kōzuke, Shimotsuke, Iwaki, Iwashiro, Rikuzen, Rikuchū. Rikuoku* or *Mutsu, Uzen* and *Ugo*.

Tosa-nikki, 土佐日記. A classic, composed in 935, by *Ki no Tsurayuki* in which he with great ingenuity relates his return from *Tosa* where he had been governor.

Tosa no sampitsu, 土佐三筆. The 3 most famous painters of the *Tosa* school: *Kasuga Motomitsu, Tosa Mitsunobu* and *Tosa Mitsuoki*.

Tosa-ryū, 土佐派. School of painting established, during the 13th century, by *Fujiwara Tsunetaka*, and so called because *Tsunetaka* had the title of *Tosa Gon no kami*. It is the principal branch of the ancient Japanese school called *Yamato-ryū* or *Kasuga-ryū*.

```
                          Tsunetaka
                          Kunitaka

            Nagataka                        Mitsuhide    Takakane

      Yoshimitsu            Takasuke    Mitsumasa    Takamori
        Mitsuaki           Sukeyoshi    Nagayuki

Nagaharu  Yukimitsu  Jakusai  Takamitsu
Mitsukuni  Yukihiro           Tsunemitsu

   Mitsushige        Yukihide
   Mitsuhiro         Hirochika
   Mitsuchika        Mitsunobu (1434-1525)

                     Mitsushige

                     Mitsumoto (1530-1559)

                     Mitsuyoshi (1539-1613)

                     Mitsunori (1583-1638)

                     Mitsuoki (1617-1691)

                     Mitsunari (1646-1710)

                     Mitsusuke (1675-1710)

                     Mitsuyoshi (1700-1772)

  Mitsuatsu (1734-1764)  Mitsusada (1738-1806)
  Mitsutoki (1765-1819)  Mitsuzane (1782-1852)
  Mitsutomi       Mitsukiyo (+ 1862)
  Mitsubumi (1812-1879)
```

This school kept aloof from Chinese influence and retained primitive traditions. It made it a specialty to represent legendary scenes or such as were drawn from national history.

Toshigoi no matsuri, 祈 年 祭. Feast celebrated at the *Dajō-kwan*, on the 4th day of the 2nd month, and during which prayers were said for preservation from scourges, storms, floods, etc. and also to obtain a good harvest.

To-shima, 利嶋. Island (7 Km. circ.) dependent upon the *Izu* province.

To-shima, 戸嶋. Island (18 Km. circ.) S. W. of the *Iyo* province of which it is a dependency.

Tō-shi no shi-ke, 藤 氏 四 家. The 4 branches of the *Fujiwara* family descended from the 4 sons of *Fuhito* (*Tankai*): the *Nan-ke* of *Muchimaro ;* the *Hoku-ke* of *Fusasaki ;* the *Shiki-ke* of *Umakai ;* and the *Kyō-ke* of *Maro.*

Toshiyori, 年 寄 (Lit.: old man). — See *Rōjū* and *Waka doshiyori.*

Tōshō-dai-gongen, 東 照 大 權 現. Posthumous title given to *Tokugawa Ieyasu.*

Tōshō-gū, 東照宮. The temple erected over the tomb of *Ieyasu* and by extension applied to *Ieyasu* himself.

Toshū, 土 州. Chinese name of the province of *Tosa.*

Tōtōmi, 遠 江. One of the 15 provinces of the *Tōkaidō.* Comprises 6 distrcts, which belong to the *Shizuoka-ken.* — Chinese name: *Enshū.* — Formerly the lake *Hamana-ko* was called *Tōtsu-umi* (far off sea), in distinction to lake *Biwa* which is closer to the capital. *Tōtōmi,* the name of the whole province is derived from the above name.

Totoribe, 鳥 取 部. Formerly a corporation of men who made it a business to catch and breed birds. Their chief had the title of *Totoribe no Muraji.*

Totoribe no Yorozu, 捕 鳥 部 萬. Servant of *Mononobe no Moriya,* who after the death of his master (587), fled to the mountains. Pursued and surrounded by a large number of men, he killed 30 of his enemies then, an arrow striking his knee, he killed himself. Legend adds that *Yorozu* had a dog which, with its snout and paws, dug a hole for its master, covered him with earth and then, lying down on the tomb, starved itself to death.

Tōtsu-Asuka, 遠 飛 鳥. — See *Asuka.*

Tōtsuka no tsurugi, 十 握 劍 (Lit.: sword of 10 *tsuka*). The sword which *Susano-o* exchanged for the *Yasakani no magatama* of *Amaterasu.*

Tottori, 鳥 取. Chief-town (28,500 inh.) of the department of the same name of *Inaba* province. — Towards the middle of the 16th century, *Yamana Masamichi* built a castle there which he entrusted to the keeping of *Takeda Takanobu.* It passed into the possession of the *Mōri,* and later *Hideyoshi* bestowed it upon *Miyabe Tsugumasu.* In 1600, *Ieyasu* gave it to the *Ikeda daimyō* (320,000 k.), who kept it till the Restoration.

Tottori-ken, 鳥 取 縣. Department formed by the provinces of *Inaba* and *Hōki.* — Pop.: 439,000 inh. — Largest city: *Tottori* (28,500 inh.). — Principal town: *Yonago* (16,000 inh.)

Towada-numa, 十輪田沼 Lake (62 Km. circ.) N. of *Rikuchū*. It is drained by the *Rokunohe-gawa* and the *Yoneshiro-gawa*.

Toyama, 富山. Chief-town (56,000 inh.) of the department of the same name and of the *Etchū* province. In the 16th century, a certain *Jimbō* family had a castle there which in 1572 was occupied by *Uesugi Kenshin*. *Nobunaga* gave it to *Sasa Narimasa* (1578), who was dispossessed by *Hideyoshi* and replaced by *Maeda Toshiie* (1585). In 1639, *Toyama* became the domain of one of the branches of the *Maeda* (100,000 k.) which retained it till the Restoration.

Toyama, 外山. *Kuge* family descended from *Fujiwara Arinobu*. — Now Viscount.

Tōyama, 遠山. *Daimyō* family descended from *Fujiwara Taka-fusa*. Since 1600, resided at *Naeki* (*Mino*) (10,000 k.). — Now Viscount.

Toyama-ken, 富山縣. Department formed of the *Etchū* province. — Pop.: 815,000 inh. — Chief city: *Toyama* (56,000 inh.). — Pr. towns: *Takaoka* (31,500 inh.), *Shin-minato* (18,000 inh.), *Uozu* (13,500 inh.), *Himi* (12,500 inh.), *Namerikawa* (10,500 inh.), etc.

Toyama Masakazu, 外山正一 (1848-1900). *Samurai* of the *Shizuoka* clan, who studied in England and America, and was professor, then principal of the University and Minister of Public Instruction (1898).

Tōyama Kagetomo, 遠山景元. Official of the *Shōgun* government. Was successively *Metsuke, Kita-machi-bugyō* (1840) and *Saemon no Jō*. He greatly promoted the work of draining the city of *Edo* and of embellishing it, and was distinguished for his integrity. In 1852, he resigned his office and died in 1855.

Toyo-akitsu-shima, 豐秋津洲. ⎫ Names
Toyo-ashi-hara-mizuho no kuni, 豐葦原瑞穗國. ⎰ given to Japan in mythological times.

Toyoda, 豐田. In *Rikuchū* (*Fujisato-mura*). In the 11th century, it was the residence of the provincial governor, *Fujiwara Kiyohira*, who in 1060 went to *Hiraizumi*.

Toyohashi, 豐橋. Town (22,000 inh.) of *Mikawa*. Formerly called *Yoshida* (See *Yoshida*).

Toyoki-iri-hiko no mikoto, 豐城入彥命. Eldest son of the emperor *Sujin*; was ordered to pacify the Eastern provinces (50 B.C.). *Yatsunada* was his son.

Toyokuni no yashiro, 豐國神社. Shintoist temple of *Kyōto*, erected to the memory of *Hideyoshi* in 1599, who received the posthumous title of *Toyokuni-Daimyōjin*. Destroyed under the *Tokugawa*, it was rebuilt only in the year 1873. *Hideyoshi's* tomb is on the summit of a small neighboring hill, called *Amida-ga-mine*. — The *Toyokumi no yashiro* is also named *Hōkoku-jinja* (Chinese pronunciation of the same characters).

Toyo no kuni, 豐國. Ancient name of the *Buzen* and *Bungo* provinces.

Toyooka, 豊岡. Town (6,900 inh.) of *Tajima*. In the time of *Hideyoshi*, it belonged to *Miyabe Tsugumasu*, then to *Sugihara Nagafusa*. From 1668 to 1868, it was a fief of the *Kyōgoku daimyō* (15,000 k.).

Toyooka, 豊岡. *Kuge* family descended from *Fujiwara Tadamichi* (1097-1164). — Now Viscount.

Toyora, 豊浦. Western district of the *Nagato* province in which the Emperor *Chūai* resided from 193 to 199.

Toyora-dera, 豊浦寺. Name given to the first Buddhist temple erected in Japan by *Soga no Iname* in his domain of *Asuka* (*Yamato*) in 553. The real name of the temple was *Kōgen-ji* or *Katsuragi-dera*. It was destroyed at the time of the ruin of the *Soga* (645).

Toyo-shima, 豊嶋. Island (9 Km. circ.) of the Inland Sea, S.E. of the *Aki* province of which it is a dependency.

Toyotama-hime, 豊玉姫. Daughter of *Watatsumi no kami*; married *Hiko-hohodemi no mikoto* and was the grandmother of *Jimmu*.

Toyotomi, 豊臣. Family-name which *Hideyoshi* received in 1586, after he became *Kwampaku*, and by which he is known in history.

—— **Hideyoshi,** 秀吉 (1536-1598). He was the son of a certain *Nakamura Yanosuke*, and was born in the village of *Nakamura* in *Owari*. His father dying soon after, his mother married into the *Chikuami* family, by whom he was educated. In his childhoood, he was called *Hiyoshi*. His parents destined him to become a bonze, so they placed him in the *Kōmyō-ji*, a neighboring temple, but at the age of 15, he made his escape and went to *Tōtōmi*, where he entered the service of *Matsushita Yukitsuna*, castellan of *Kunō*. The latter, having learned one day that *Hideyoshi* was from *Owari*, gave him 6 *ryō* to purchase a coat of mail for his master, like the one *Nobunaga* wore. The young man took the money, used it to procure clothes and weapons, but instead of returning to his master, he changed his name to that of *Kinoshita Tōkichi*, and went to *Nobunaga*. The latter admitted him into his service and soon noticed his brilliant intellect; in 1559, he made him marry a daughter of *Sugihara Yoshifusa*, brought up by *Asano Nagakatsu*, and changed his name to that of *Hideyoshi* (1562). He distinguished himself in several campaigns, especially in those against the *Asai* and the *Asakura* and received the castle of *Nagahama* (*Ōmi*) in fief with a revenue of 220,000 k. and the title of *Chikuzen no kami* (1574). Borrowing a character from the name of his two companions in arms, *Niwa* and *Shibata* he formed the name of *Hashiba* and as he had no children, *Nobunaga* appointed *Hidekatsu* one of his own sons, to be his heir. At that time, *Mōri Terumoto* had gradually joined 10 provinces in the *San-yō-dō* and the *San-in-dō* to his domains and now refused to submit to *Nobunaga*. The latter prepared for war against him, and meanwhile sent *Hideyoshi* ahead, who, after having induced *Ukita Naoie*, *daimyō* of *Okayama* (*Bizen*) to join him, successively besieged all the castles of the *Mōri*, and, in 5 years, succeeded in taking the provinces of *Harima*, *Bizen*, *Mimasaka*, *Tajima*, and *Inaba*. In 1580, during an armistice, he came to *Azuchi* to give an account of his exploits to *Nobunaga* by whom he was received with great honor. Soon after, he exchanged his castle of *Nagahama* for that of *Himeji* (*Harima*), and resumed the war by laying siege to *Takamatsu* (*Bitchū*). *Mōri's* troops resisted with great energy and *Terumoto* himself came to their aid at the head of a great army. *Hideyoshi* asked *Nobunaga* for support and *Akechi Mitsuhide* received an order to reinforce him with 30,000 men. But *Akechi*, instead of leading his forces to the seat of war, brought them to *Kyōto*, besieged *Nobunaga* in the temple *Honnō-ji*, killed him, and prepared to succeed him (1582). *Hideyoshi*, on hearing this, hastened to conclude

peace with *Teru-moto*, condemning the defender of *Takamatsu*, *Shi-mizu Muneharu*, to kill himself and his soldiers to disperse. Going towards the capital, *Hideyoshi* met *Nobutaka*, *No-bunaga's* son, at *Amagasaki* (*Settsu*) with whom he de-cided at once to march against the traitor. The van-guard of his army, commanded by *Ta-kayama Ukon*, *Na-kagawa Kiyohide*, and *Ikeda Nobu-teru*, overtook *Mi-*

TOYOTOMI HIDEYOSHI.

tsuhide at *Yamazaki*, and defeated and killed him whilst he was trying to escape. *Hideyoshi* then went to the castle of *Kiyosu* (*Owari*), and after having conferred with the great vassals of *Oda*, he nominated *Sambōshi*, grandson of *Nobunaga*, heir and appointed *Nobuo* and *Nobutaka*, two uncles of *Sambōshi*, guardians till *Sambōshi* should attain majority. *Hideyoshi* expected to obtain *Nobunaga's* power in the government of the country, but in this he was opposed by the *Oda* who could not bear to see an upstart occupy a position their father had so much difficulty to obtain. *Nobutaka* was the first to revolt and calling *Shibata Katsuie* to his help he declared war against the usurper. *Hide-yoshi* sent *Nobuo* to besiege his brother in the castle of *Gifu* and *Nobu-taka* being defeated, killed himself. Meanwhile, *Hideyoshi* with a large army had gone to attack *Katsuie*, who, being defeated at *Shizu-ga-take* (*Ōmi*), re-entered his castle of *Kita-no-shō* (*Echizen*) and committed sui-cide (1583). *Nobuo* in his turn quarrelled with *Hideyoshi* and to be able to fight him, asked help from *Tokugawa Ieyasu*. The latter accepted, engaged *Hideyoshi's* vanguard at *Nagakute* (*Owari*), and routed it completely. The two armies camping at *Komaki-yama* for a long time, faced each other, neither daring to begin the battle, when finally *Hideyoshi* thought it prudent to negotiate. He first spoke to *Nobuo*, whom he easily brought to an agreement and who then served as intermediary between him and *Ieyasu*. To cement the peace, *Hideyoshi* gave his sister *Asahi no kata* in marriage to *Ieyasu* and the latter left his son *Hideyasu* as hostage (1584). *Hideyoshi* then began to build the castle of *Ōsaka*, which was to be his residence and which, in grandeur and richness, surpassed all that was ever seen in Japan. He then repressed the tumults occasioned by the bonzes of the temple *Negoro-dera* (*Kii*) and sent an expedition into *Shikoku* to reduce the *Chōsokabe* to submission, and to limit their domains to the sole province of *Tosa* (1585). After this triumph, *Hideyoshi's* power was no more contested, and he wished his honor to be proportionate to his importance. He at first thought of the shōgunate, but this dignity could be given only to the descendants of the *Minamoto*. The *Udaijin Kikutei Harusue* proposed the dignity of *Kwampaku*, and *Hideyoshi* having assented, *Nijō Akizane* was induced to resign that office. He soon after received the family name of *Toyotomi* (1586). His annual revenue at this time was 3,000,000 k. He created 5 *bugyō* to help him in the administration of the government : *Maeda Gen-i, Nagatsuka Masaie, Asano Nagamasa, Ishida Kazushige* and *Masuda Nagamori*. Then leading an army of 100,000 men towards the North, he had his authority recognized everywhere, almost without striking a blow : the *Sasa* in *Etchū*, the *Uesugi* in *Echigo*, the *Anenokōji* in *Hida*, the *Sanada* in *Shinano*, all made their submission and consented to be his vassals. At that time, *Shimazu Yoshihisa*, *daimyō* of *Satsuma*, waged war against his neighbors and threatened to subjugate all *Kyūshū*. The *Ōtomo*, the *Ryūzōji*, etc. called on *Hideyoshi*, who, by letter, ordered *Yoshihisa* to recall his troops and upon the latter refusing to obey, a large army was sent to the *Saikoku*, and in a few months the whole region was pacified. *Hideyoshi* then proceeded to divide the fiefs of *Kyūshū* anew, so as to weaken the power of the *Shimazu* (1587) After his return, he opened the palace (*Jurakutei*) which he had built at *Kyōto*, and in the midst of splendid festivities received the visit of the emperor *Go-Yōzei*, the ex-emperor *Ōgimachi*, and the whole Imperial Court. In 1589, he distributed 365,000 *ryō* to the civil and military officials. The following year, he invited all the *daimyō* to join in a campaign against the *Hōjō* of *Odawara* who after a siege of 4 months surrendered, and *Ieyasu* received all the provinces of the *Kwantō* in fief. Turning his attention to Korea, *Hideyoshi* sent *Sō Yoshitomo*, the *daimyō* of *Tsushima*, to invite the king of

SEAL OF HIDEYOSHI.

that country to become his vassal. The king refused and appealed to his sole lord, the Emperor of China. *Hideyoshi* then called upon all the *daimyō* and ordered them to prepare for an expedition into Korea, the following year. He resigned his title of *Kwam-*

paku in favor of his adopted son *Hidetsugu* and assumed that of *Taikō*. He now built a residence at *Nagoya* (*Hizen*), and upon arriving at that place, in April 1592, he found an army of 130,000 men assembled. The fleet was commanded by *Kuki Yoshitaka* and *Tōdō Takatora*. The vanguard left under the command of *Konishi Yukinaga* and *Katō Kiyomasa*. The main army soon followed, and in a short time, all Korea was in the possession of the Japanese. The king had fled to China demanding help from the emperor. On hearing of the intervention of the Chinese, *Hideyoshi* sent a reinforcement of 60,000 men in the month of July, but the Japanese being obliged to retreat, now engaged in preliminaries for peace. *Hideyoshi* presented 7 conditions, the principal being the marriage of a daughter of the Chinese Emperor to the Emperor of Japan, the continuation of former commercial relations between the two countries, the cession of the 4 southern provinces of Korea to Japan,

etc. *Naitō Joan* was sent to present these propositions to the Chinese Emperor. He had scarcely left on his mission, when *Hideyoshi* was informed that his wife *Yodogimi* had given birth to a son (May 1593), whereupon he placed *Maeda Toshiie* in charge of *Nagoya* and hastened to return to *Ōsaka*. He built a castle at *Fushimi*, whither he intended to retire in his old age. At this time he had a quarrel with his adopted son *Hidetsugu*, for the latter although invested with the office of *Kwampaku*, thought only of pleasure, and the fear of being disinherited in favor of the son just born to *Hideyoshi* probably caused him to use some offensive words

HIDEYOSHI AND THE CHINESE AMBASSADOR.

against his adopted father. Nevertheless, *Hideyoshi* accused him of having plotted against his life and he exiled him to mount *Kōya*, where he was invited to kill himself (1595). At the beginning of the following year, the answer of the Chinese Emperor arrived. Without mentioning any of the conditions conveyed through *Naitō*, three conditions were proposed : the immediate recall of the Japanese troops yet in *Fusan*, the resumption of commercial relations, and peace with Korea. If these conditions proved acceptable, the Chinese envoy, in the name of his master, was to confer the title of King of Japan upon *Hideyoshi* and to give him the golden seal and crown, emblems of his new dignity. At the reading of these propositions, *Hideyoshi* became furious, expelled the ambassador and decided to resume the war. In the following spring, 100,000 men, under the leadership of *Kobayakawa Hideaki*, the *Taikō's* nephew, crossed the straits and commenced hostilities, but, his army fatigued by continued fighting, decimated by sickness and privation, had no success and the expedition utterly failed. In May 1598, *Hideyoshi* fell sick and perceived that death was nigh. He ordered *Ieyasu* to call back the remnants of the army from Korea. Then, fearing for his son's future, he took great precautions to assure the succession to him. To that end, he created 5 *tairō*, who were to govern during the minority of his son. These were : *Tokugawa Ieyasu, Maeda Toshiie, Uesugi Kagekatsu, Mōri Terumoto,* and *Ukita Hideie*, the 5 greatest *daimyō* of *Hondo*. Subject to the *tairō*, 5 *bugyō*, created some 10 years before, had charge of the administration. Three *chūrō : Nakamura Kazuuji, Horio Yoshiharu* and *Ikoma Chikamasa*, were also chosen and ranked between the *tairō* and the *bugyō*. They were to settle any differences that might arise among the *daimyō*. Lastly, two most trustworthy men, *Katagiri Katsumoto* and *Koide Masahide*, were charged to educate *Hideyori*. *Hideyoshi* made all these dignitaries swear fealty to their young master, and having thus arranged all things, he died without concern for the future of his son, Sept. 15 1598, in his palace of *Fushimi*. He was then 62 years old. — *Hideyoshi* is certainly one of the greatest figures in Japanese history. Of low birth, he, by intelligence, rose to the first rank. A cunning politician rather than a skilful warrior, he was able to impose his authority upon the ambitious *daimyō* of these troubled times. He re-established order and prosperity in a country which had been ruined by civil wars during a century and a half. A dutiful servant of the Imperial dynasty, he rebuilt the *Kyōto* Palace and secured sufficient revenues for the Court to defray the necessary expenses, for which reason the Emperor *Go-Yōsei*, bestowed upon him the posthumous title of *Toyokuni-Daimyōjin*. To his discredit however history records the disastrous expedition to Korea, inspired either by pride or the desire to check the too warlike military caste of Japan. Nor is it to be forgotten that *Hideyoshi* inaugurated religious persecution in Japan, believing to save the country from great danger by crucifying the 26 first Martyrs at *Nagasaki* (Feb. 5, 1597).

—— **Hidetsugu, 秀次** (1568-1595). Was son of *Yoshifusa, Musashi no kami* and castellan of *Ōyama* (Owari), who successively bore the names of *Kinoshita, Nagao* and *Miyoshi*. His mother (*Zuiryū-in*) was a half-sister of *Hideyoshi*, who himself desired to educate his nephew. In 1583, he was ordered to fight *Takigawa Kazumasu* in *Ise*, and stormed the castle of *Mine*. The following year, he was defeated by *Ieyasu* at *Nagakute*. He took part in the campaign against the bonzes of *Negoro* and in the expedition of *Shikoku* against the *Chōsokabe* (1585). When *Hideyoshi* was named *Kwampaku*, *Hidetsugu* changed his name *Miyoshi* to that of *Hashiba*, which *Hideyoshi* bore till then. During the war against the *Hōjō* of *Odawara*, he besieged and took the *Yamanaka* castle (*Sagami*). After the campaign, he received 5 districts in *Owari* and *Ise* (1590). At the end of the same year, he with *Gamō Ujisato*, conducted an expedition against *Kunohe Masazane* who had caused trouble in *Mutsu* and had invaded the domains of *Kimura Hidetoshi*. In 1591, *Hideyoshi* adopted him, gave him the name of *Toyotomi* and made him *Naidaijin*. The following year, he created him *Kwampaku*, and desired him to lead the expedition against Korea, but *Hidetsugu* refused not daring to venture on such a distant and dangerous campaign. This irritated *Hideyoshi*, who soon found other reasons to complain of the conduct of his heir. The ex-emperor *Ōgimachi* died in the beginning of 1593, and before the official mourning was over, *Hidetsugu* organized a hunting expedition. He also had taken the liberty to enter the monasteries of the *Hiei-zan* with his wife and daughters, an act altogether prohibited to women. *Gamō Ujisato* and *Kuroda Josui* vainly tried to make him understand the impropriety of such acts, he listened to nothing. At this juncture, *Hideyori* was born and *Hideyoshi* thought of transmitting the succession, which he intended to withdraw from *Hidetsugu*, to his own son. From that moment, their relations gradually became strained. *Ishida Kazushige* and *Masuda Nagamori*, out of hatred to *Hidetsugu*, accused him of plotting against the *Tairō*. The latter, in a moment of fury, confined him to the temple of *Seigan-ji* on Mt. *Kōya* and *Hidetsugu* vainly tried to justify himself. In August, 1595, *Fukushima Masanori* and *Fukuhara Naotaka* with 10,000 men came to invest the place and communicated to *Hidetsugu* the order to kill himself. At the request of *Ishida Kazushige*, his head was exposed in *Kyōto*. The following month, his wife, daughters and ladies in waiting, 34 in all, were decapitated.

—— **Hideyori, 秀頼** (1593-1615). Son of *Hideyoshi* and *Yodogimi*, was born at the castle of *Fushimi*. At the age of 3, his father presented him for the first time at the Imperial Palace, where he received the title of *Sakon-e-chūjō*, and the following year, that of *Chūnagon*. At the death of the *Taikō* he with his mother went to the castle of *Ōsaka*, being then 5 years old. When his party was defeated at *Sekigahara* (1600), the *Ōsaka* castle was greatly alarmed, but *Ieyasu*, dared not lay hands on a child he had promised to protect and allowed him to retain his castle and the three provinces of *Settsu*, *Kawachi*, and *Izumi* with a revenue of 650,000 k. In 1603, *Hideyori* was named *Naidaijin*, and *Ieyasu* betrothed him to his granddaughter *Senhime*, then 6 years old. In 1611, *Ieyasu* came to *Kyōto* and desired to see *Hideyori*. The trusted servants of the *Toyotomi*, fearing lest *Ieyasu* entertained some evil design opposed the interview, but the widow of *Hideyoshi*, *Kōdai-in*, was of a contrary opinion, and *Katō Kiyomasa* and *Asano Nagamasa* vouched that nothing unpleasant would happen to the young man. Thus *Hideyori* went to *Kyōto*, saw his dreaded protector and returned without harm. The same year, he ordered the reconstruction of the temple *Hōkō-ji* (*Kyōto*), which his father had erected but which was destroyed during the great earthquake of 1596. He added a large bell to it (4m. 20 high—2m. 74 diameter, and 33 cm. thick) on which there was an in-scription, which served as a pretext to ruin the *Toyotomi*. For some time already, *Ōsaka* had become the refuge of all those *samurai* who had been reduced to misery by the rising power of the *Tokugawa*. *Ieyasu*, distrust-fully looked upon this centre of dissatisfaction and opposition, and longed for an occasion to destroy it. He thought he found it in the inscription on the bell. There happened to be two characters on the bell, which formed his name, but were separated by another character from each other. He affected to see an insult in this and a curse upon his head. Vainly did *Hideyori* send *Katagiri Katsumoto* to *Sumpu* to give explanations, he would listen to nothing and war was resolved upon. *Hideyori* called on all the friends and protégés of his father. None of the *daimyō* in power, answered his appeal, but some ancient *daimyō* and a great number of *samurai* came to increase his army which soon rose to 60,000 men. It was commanded by *Ōno Harunaga*, *Sanada Yukimura*, *Gotō Mototsugu*, *Chōsokabe Morichika*, *Mōri Katsunaga*, *Akashi Morishige*, etc. In November, 1614, *Ieyasu* with *Hidetada* and an army of 150,000 ap-peared before *Ōsaka*, but after some fighting, peace was concluded on con-dition that the walls of the castle should be destroyed and the moats filled in (Jan. 1615). When *Ieyasu* however sent *Honda Masazumi* to oversee the work to be done, *Hideyori* protested. War ensued and this time, it was to be decisive. After a month's siege, the castle of *Ōsaka* was reduced to ashes; *Hideyori*, *Yodo-gimi* and most of the surviving *samurai* perished in the flames. *Hideyori* was survived by *Kunimatsumaro*, a son of 7 years, and a daughter of 5, who, having been arrested in *Kyōto*, were beheaded (June 1615). Thus ended the short lineage of the *Toyotomi*. — Such at least is the version of the *Tokugawa*. But it seems more probable that, at the capture of *Ōsaka*, *Hideyori* and his family, with *Ieyasu's* consent, es-caped on vessels put at their disposal by *Hachisuka Iemasa* and retired to *Satsuma*, where under the name of *Tanimura*, they received rich presents from the great *daimyō*, ancient vassals of the *Taikō*, and their descendants have lived to be one of the richest families of the province. Moreover the annals tell us that in 1645, a certain *Tenshū*, 天 秀, daughter of *Hideyori*, died at *Kamakura*. She had been an *ama* of the *Tōkei-ji* temple.

Toyotomi go-bugyō, 豊 臣 五 奉 行. The 5 *bugyō* created by *Hideyoshi* in 1587: *Maeda Gen-i*, *Asano Nagamasa*, *Masuda Naga-mori*, *Ishida Kazushige*, and *Nagatsuka Masaie*.

Toyotomi go-tairō, 豊 臣 五 大 老. The 5 *tairō* designated by *Hideyoshi* to govern during the minority of his son *Hideyori*: *Tokugawa Ieyasu*, *Maeda Toshiie*, *Mōri Terumoto*, *Ukita Hideie* and *Uesugi Kagekatsu*.

Toyotomi san-chūrō, 豊臣三中老. The 3 *chūrō* created by *Hideyoshi* to settle disputes that might arise among the *daimyō*: *Horie Yoshiharu*, *Ikoma Chikamasa* and *Nakamura Kazuuji*.

Toyo-uke-bime no kami, 豊受姫神. Daughter of *Izanagi* and *Izanami*. Goddess of cereals (*Shintō*), also called *Uka no mitama*, *Ukemochi no kami*, *Ōketsu-hime*. Many identify her with *Wakamusubi no kami*. Is honored in the *Gekū* temple of *Ise*.

Toyoura, 豊浦.— See *Toyora*.

Tozama-daimyō, 外様大名. Formerly this term was applied to the *daimyō* who were not vassals of the *Shōgun*. *Ieyasu* gave that name to the 86 *daimyō* who submitted to him only after the battle of *Sekigahara*, (1600) whilst he called those who had sided with him from the beginning of the campaign, *fudai-daimyō*: these numbered 176.— The most powerful among the *tozama-daimyō* were: *Maeda* (*Kaga*), *Date* (*Sendai*), *Shimazu* (*Satsuma*) *Mōri* (*Chōshū*). They took rank immediately after the *go san-ke*; were the guests of the *Shōgun* when they came to *Edo* for their annual visit, and were received by a special envoy (*jōshi*) sent as far as *Shinagawa* or *Senju*.— It was natural that the *tozama-daimyō* were among the foremost to contribute to the ruin of the shōgunate and to the Imperial Restoration.

Tozama-shū, 外様衆. Under the *Ashikaga Shōgun*, the most powerful and richest families after the *kunimochi-shū*.

Tozawa, 戸沢. *Daimyō* family descended from *Taira Tadamasa*.

—— **Moriyasu,** 盛安 (1566-1590). Was, like his ancestors, vassal of the *Nambu* family and castellan of the *Kaku-no-tate* castle (*Dewa*).

—— **Masamori,** 政盛 (1585-1648). Son of the above, sided with *Ieyasu*, received 2 districts of *Hitachi* in fief and resided at *Matsuoka* (40,000 k.). In 1622, he was transferred to *Shinjō* (*Dewa* — 68,000 k.), where his descendants remained till the Restoration. — Now Viscount.

Tsu, 津. Chief-town (23,300 inh.) of the *Mie-ken* and the *Ise* province — This town was formerly called *Anotsu* and was the residence of a branch of the *Taira* family (*Ise-Heishi*). In 1575, *Nobunaga* gave it to his son *Nobuo*. *Hideyoshi* established *Tomita Tomonobu* (1589) there. Finally, from 1608 to 1868, it belonged to the *Tōdō daimyō* (320,000 k.).

Tsuboi, 坪井. *Samurai* family of the *Yamaguchi* clan (*Suwō*), made noble after the Restoration. — Now Baron.

Tsubokiri no tsurugi, 壺切劔. Sword which the Emperor presented to the prince chosen to be his heir (*kōtaishi*), on the day of his nomination. *Daigo-tennō* was the first to carry out this ceremony at the election of his son *Yasuakira-shinnō* (904), and from that time it became a custom. The sword has often been injured by fire, but the blade, it seems, is in good condition.

Tsuchi-gumo, 土蜘蛛. (Lit: ground spider). A tribe of Aborigines of *Yamato*, thus called, because they inhabited caves dug in the earth. They were subjugated by *Jimmu-tennō*.

Tsuchimikado, 土御門. *Kuge* family descended from *Abe no Kurahashimaro* — Now Viscount.

Tsuchimikado-tennō, 土御門天皇. 83rd Emperor of Japan (1199-1210). *Tamehito*, eldest son of *Go-Toba-tennō*, who succeeded his father at the age of 3 years, was put on the throne by *Yoritomo*. After a reign of 12 years, during which time the authority was in the hands of the *Hōjō*, *Tokimasa* and *Yoshitoki*, he abdicated, on the advice of his father, in favor of his brother *Juntoku*. He was then 15 years old. During the *Shokyū* war (1221), he sided with his father against the *Hōjō* and was banished to *Tosa* and then transferred to *Awa* (1223), where he died at the age of 36, in 1231.

Tsuchiura, 土浦. Town (11,700 inh.) of *Hitachi*. — Tradition refers to a castle which *Taira Masakado* is said to have built there in 939. *Hideyoshi* gave it to *Yūki Hideyasu*, son of *Ieyasu*. Under the *Tokugawa*, it successively was the residence of the *daimyō Matsudaira* (1601), *Nishio* (1617), *Kuchiki* (1649), *Tsuchiya* (1681), *Ōkōchi* (1681) ; and from 1688 to 1868, that of *Tsuchiya* (95,000 k.).

Tsuchiya, 土屋. *Daimyō* family descended from *Minamoto Yasuuji* (*Seiwa-Genji*). Made noble in the person of *Tadanao* (1585-1612) in 1602, it resided successively at *Kururi* (*Kazusa*) ; in 1669, at *Tsuchiura* (*Hitachi*) ; in 1681 at *Tanaka* (*Suruga*) : then from 1688 to 1686, again at *Tsuchiura* (95,000 k.). — Now Viscount.

Tsuda Kemmotsu, 津田監物. Born at *Ogura* (*Kii*), he went to *Tane-ga-shima*, where he studied mechanics and the use of fire arms, introduced sometime before by the Portuguese (1542). After 10 years, he returned and established a school (*Tsuda-ryū*) and a workshop at *Sakai* (*Izumi*) for the manufacture of guns. His son *Jiyūsai* succeeded him.

Tsuda Sanzō, 津田三藏 (1855-1891). *Samurai* of the *Tsu* clan (*Ise*), who as a policeman struck the Czarevitch (later on Nicolas II.) with his sword at *Ōtsu*, near lake *Biwa* (May 11th, 1891). Condemned to exportation to the *Hokkaidō*, he drowned himself, some say, whilst going thither.

Tsugaru, 津軽. District comprising the western part of the present province of *Mutsu* or *Rokuoku*. In 1878, it was divided into 5 parts: *Kita-Tsugaru*, *Higashi-Tsugaru*, *Naka-Tsugaru*, *Minami-Tsugaru* and *Nishi-Tsugaru*. — The name *Tsugaru* is also given to the present city of *Hirosaki*, which was the chief-city of the district and the residence of the *daimyō* of *Tsugaru*.

Tsugaru, 津軽. *Daimyō* family descended from *Fujiwara Tadamichi* (1097-1154). Was at first called *Kuji*, then *Ōura*, and governed the *Tsugaru* district.

—— **Tamenobu,** 爲信 (+ 1608). Son of *Ōura Morinobu*, was obliged to defend his domains against *Nambu Nobunao*, who attempted to give them to his brother *Masanobu*. He demanded help from *Akita Sanesue* (1589), and gained his cause. He then submitted to *Hideyoshi*, who confirmed him in the possession of his fief and gave him the name of *Tsugaru* (1590). The same year, he took part in the campaign against the *Hōjō* of *Odawara*, and at the time of the Korean expedition, he accompanied

Hideyoshi to *Nagoya* (*Hizen*). In 1600, he sided with *Ieyasu*, who increased his revenues to 47,000 k.

—— **Nobuhira,** 信 牧 (1586-1631). Son of *Tamenobu*, was baptized in 1596. He succeeded his father and in 1610, built the castle of *Hirosaki* where he lived. At the time of the persecution of 1614, he received many Christians who had been exiled, but later, he abandoned all religion.

—— **Yasuchika,** 寧 親. Descendant of the above, had his revenues raised to 117,000 k. in 1805.

—— **Nobuyuki,** 信 順. In 1808, his revenues were raised to 217,000 k. — The family continued to reside at *Hirosaki* till the Restoration. — Now Count. — A junior branch, descended from *Nobuhira*, in 1814 settled at *Kuroishi* (*Mutsu* — 10,000 k.). — Now Viscount.

Tsugaru-Fuji, 津 輕 富 士. — See *Iwaki-yama*.

Tsugaru-kaikyō, 津 輕 海 峽. Strait which separates the *Hokkaidō* from *Hondo*.

Tsuibushi, 追 捕 便. Title first conferred upon *Ono Yoshifuru* in 939, when he was sent to repress the revolt of *Fujiwara Sumitomo* in *Shikoku*. The title became synonymous to that of governor of the province. — See *Sōtsuibushi*.

Tsuihō, 追 放. Penalty of exile inflicted under the *Tokugawa*. — It comprised 6 degrees. The first (*tokoro-barai*) consisted in being forbidden to sojourn in one's native place. The second (*Edo-barai*), in being prohibited to sojourn in *Edo*. The third (*Edo ju-ri-shihō-barai*), in being prohibited to approach within 10 leagues of *Edo*. The fourth (*kei-tsuihō*), besides the above prohibiton, forbade the use of the roads to *Nikkō*, the *Tōkaidō* road, and entry into the cities of *Ōsaka* and *Kōfu*. The fifth (*chū-tsuihō*), added to the preceding list the road of *Kiso-kaidō* and residence in the cities of *Kyōto, Wakayama, Nagoya, Mito, Nara, Sakai, Fushimi* and *Nagasaki*. The sixth (*jū-tsuihō*) forbade residence in the 8 *Kwantō* provinces and those of *Yamashiro, Yamato, Settsu, Suruga, Kai, Owari, Kii*, the city of *Nagasaki* and the *Tōkaidō* and *Kiso-kaidō* roads.

Tsuina, 追 儺. Ceremony to chase away the devils; formerly it took place on the last night of the year. The Palace guards (*toneri*) shot arrows into the air and screamed furiously to put the devils to flight. At present this ceremony is replaced by the *setsubun* or *oni-yarai*, during which people spread peas throughout the house whilst saying : May good fortune enter, and all the devils depart (*fuku wa uchi, oni wa soto*).

Tsuison-tennō, 追 尊 天 皇. Name given to the princes who, though they did not ascend the throne during life, after death received a posthumous title from the Emperor. — Thus *Kusakabe-Ōji*, father of *Mommu* was named *Nagaoka-tennō* and *Oka-no-miya-tennō* ; *Toneri-shinnō*, father of *Junnin*, received the title of *Sudō-jinkyō-tennō* ; *Shiki-shinnō*, father of *Kōnin*, those of *Tawara-tennō*, and *Kasuga-no-miya-tennō* ; *Masahito*, father of *Go-Yōzei*, that of *Yōkō-in*, etc. It happened also that princes during their lifetime received the title of *In* : *Kō-Ichijō-in* (*Atsuakira-shinnō*), *Go-Takakura-in* (*Morisada-shinnō*), etc.

Tsuji, 辻. *Samurai* family of the *Hiroshima* clan (*Aki*), made noble after the Restoration. — Now Baron.

Tsuji-giri, 辻漸. Under the *Tokugawa* it sometimes happened that a *samurai*, to test the quality of his sword, went out at night and sought with one stroke to behead an unoffensive passer-by. This practice was called *tsuji-giri* (decapitation in the street) or *tameshi-giri* (trial decapitation).

Tsuka, 握, 束. Formerly a measure of about 4 fingers. The *Tōtsuka no tsurugi* was 10 times that length. Later on, the size of the arrows was limited to 13 *tsuka* 3 *buse* (*mitsubuse* is a width of 3 fingers)

Tsukai-ban, 使番. During the civil wars of the 16th century, officials inspecting the camps, transmitting the commander's orders, etc. They were sent as tutors to the great *daimyō* who were yet too young to govern their domains. They were changed every 11th day of the 1st month.

Tsukasa-meshi, 官召. — See *Jimoku.*

Tsuki Ikina, 調伊企難. Descendant of a Korean who established himself in Japan during the reign of *Ōjin-tennō.* He was born at *Naniwa.* In 562, being sent with *Ki no Omaro* to fight *Shiragi*, he was made prisoner. Brought before the king, he was asked to show contempt to the King of Japan by word and act. *Ikina*, not frightened in the least, turned sharply around and shouted the insulting words in a stentorian voice by applying them to the King of *Shiragi.* He had not finished the sentence when the soldiers killed him on the spot.

Tsukiyomi no kami, 月夜見神. Goddess of the moon. Came from the right eye of *Izanagi*; she was a sister to *Amaterasu* and *Susano-o.* She received the country of *Unabara* as her inheritance, which is believed to be Korea by some commentators, whilst others claim it to be the *Ryūkyū* islands.

Tsukuba-san, 筑波山. Mountain (960 m.) S. of *Hitachi.* It is the place where *Fujita Koshirō* stopped and intrenched himself in 1864, in order to fight the *Shōgun's* army. — Also called *Tsukuba-ne.*

Tsukushi, 筑紫. Ancient name of the *Chikuzen* and the *Chikugo* provinces. This name is also given to the whole *Kyūshū* island. — A district (*kōri*) of *Chikuzen* also bears that name. The country of *Tsukushi*, in olden times, formed a small kingdom whose chief, in close connection with China, was considered a vassal of the Middle Empire, which granted him a golden seal with the title of king of *Yamato.* In Japan, he was known only as governor of the district of *Itō.* Queen *Pimiho*, mentioned in the Chinese and Korean annals, and whom some historians wrongly identify with *Jingō-Kōgō*, governed the whole North of *Kyūshū.* This almost independent sovereignty ended in the defeat of *Iwai* (528), and to replace it, the *Dazaifu* was created.

Tsukushi, 筑紫. Ancient *daimyō* family descended from *Shōni Sukeyori*, who took his name from the village of *Chikuzen* where he resided.

—— **Korekado, 惟門.** Served the *Shōgun Yoshitane* and the *Ōuchi.* Joining *Akizuki Fumitane*, he sided with *Mōri Motonari*, but was defeated by *Ōtomo Sōrin* (1557) and had to seek refuge in *Yamaguchi*.

—— **Hirokado,** 廣 門 (1548-1615). Son of the above, was defeated by *Ōtomo Sōrin* (1567), then by *Shimazu Yoshihisa*. *Hideyoshi* allowed him to retain his domains, which formed the district of *Tsukushi*, and he settled in the castle of *Yamashita* (1587). He took part in the Korean expedition. In 1600, he sided against *Ieyasu*, was dispossessed and shaved his head. *Hirokado* had been baptized in 1593, as was also his son *Harukado*, and both persevered till the end.

Tsukushi-gata, 筑 紫 潟． Another name of the *Ariake no oki* (*Hizen*).

Tsukushi no Fuji, 筑 紫 富 士． Name given to Mt. *Uki-mine* (*Chikuzen*) and to *Yū no mine* (*Bungo*).

Tsukushi Saburō, 筑 紫 三 郎　Surname given to the *Chikugo-gawa*.

Tsumago, 妻 籠． In *Shinano*, *Azuma-mura*. During the 16th century, residence of the *Tsumago* family. Later on, *Kiso Yoshimasa* built a castle there which he entrusted to the care of *Yamamura Yoshikatsu*. At the time of the *Komaki-yama* war (1584), *Yoshimasa* sided with *Hideyoshi* and was besieged in his castle by *Suganuma Sadatoshi* acting under orders from *Ieyasu*, who however failed to take the place. After *Sekigahara*, it was abandoned — *Tsumago* was formerly one of the relay stations of the *Nakasendō*.

Tsumenami, 詰 並． Under the *Tokugawa*, name given to certain families of *fudai-daimyō*, — about 40 in numbers. During the ceremonies in the *Shōgun's* Palace, their places were in the Chrysanthemum hall (*kiku no ma*). They were dispensed from being guards.

Tsumeshū, 詰 衆　Under the *Tokugawa*, families of *fudai-daimyō*, which on days of ceremonies, took their places in the room called *Kari no ma*. They numbered about 25 and had a revenue inferior to the *Tsumenami*. Every day, 6 or 7 of them had to act as guards in the aforesaid hall.

Tsumori, 津 守　Family which was by right of inheritance at the head of the *Sumiyoshi* temple (*Settsu*). — Now Baron.

Tsunenaga-shinnō, 恒 良 親 王 (1324-1338)　8th son of the emperor *Go-Daigo*, he was named heir to the throne in 1334. He was the guest of *Nitta Yoshisada* in the castle of *Kana-ga-saki* (*Echizen*) (1336), but the following year, when the castle was stormed, he fled to *Kabukiura*, was made prisoner by *Shiba Takatsune*, taken to *Kyōto* and imprisoned in the *Kwazan-in*. He became ill, and *Ashikaga Tadayoshi* refused to give him the assistance of a physician and thus he died, when only 14 years of age.

Tsunesada-shinnō, 恒 貞 親 王 (823-884).　2nd son of the emperor *Junwa*, was named heir to the throne at the accession of *Nimmyō* (834). A plot was formed by *Tachibana Hayanari* to put him on the throne, for which reason he was deposed and became bonze under the name of *Kōseki*. He distinguished himself as a literary man and continued to direct the administration of public affairs. He had two sons who became bonzes at the same time with him.

Tsuneyo-shinnō, 恒世親王 (+ 826). Son of *Junwa-tennō.* Was *Nakatsukasa-kyō.*

Tsurezure-gusa, 徒然草. Classical work, composed in the 14th century by *Yoshida Kenkō* (1283-1350). It is a collection of essays and anecdotes on all kinds of subjects, and both for the matter it treats as for its style, it ranks high in Japanese literature. It contributed much to the spreading of Buddhist doctrines and the theories of *Confucius* and *Mencius.*

Tsurudono, 鶴殿. Family descended from the *Kujō* and established after the Restoration by *Iekatsu,* 5th son of *Naotada.* — Now Baron.

Tsuruga, 敦賀. Town (17,700 inh.) of *Echizen.* — A legend says that in the year 33 B.C. during the reign of *Sujin,* men with horns (*tsuno*) came there from *Mimana,* for which reason the place received the name of *Tsunoga.* The emperor *Chūai* resided there for some time (192). The castle of *Kana-ga-saki,* defended by *Nitta Yoshisada* (1337), was built on the site of the actual city. In the 16th century, the *Ashikaga* had a castle there which was taken and destroyed by *Nobunaga* (1573). From 1682 to 1868, it was the residence of a branch of the *Sakai* family (15,000 k.). It is at *Tsuruga,* that *Fujita Koshirō, Takeda Kōunsai,* etc. were imprisoned in 1864. It is the most frequented port on the W. coast of Japan.

Tsurugaoka, 鶴岡. Town (20,500 inh.) of *Uzen.* — Was formerly called *Shōnai.* Under the *Kamakura Shōgun, Musashi Sukeyori* built a castle there which was in the possession of the family for 6 generations. In the 16th century, it belonged to the *Mogami* family. From 1622 to 1868, it was the residence of the *Sakai daimyō* (145,000 k.).

Tsurugaoka Hachiman-gū, 鶴岡八幡宮. Famous temple at *Kamakura* dedicated to the god of war. — In 1073, *Minamoto Yoriyoshi* had erected a temple on *Yui-ga-hama,* in honor of *Hachiman,* the titulary god of his family. *Yoritomo* transported it (1193) to *Kamakura,* erected it on the *Tsuru-ga-oka* hill, where it can be seen to the present day. In 1219, the *Shōgun Sanetomo* in great pomp went there to render thanks for his nomination to the dignity of *Udaijin.* After the ceremony, on descending the steps leading from the temple, his nephew, *Kugyō,* assassinated him. In 1526, *Satomi Yoshihiro,* the governor of the province *Awa,* plundered the treasures of the temple, but *Hōjō Ujitsuna* obliged him to retreat. — The temple of *Tsurugaoka* is one of the last remnants of the grandeur of *Kamakura.* Interesting souvenirs of the Middle Ages are kept in it.

Tsurugi-saki, 剣崎. Cape S. E. of *Sagami,* at the entrance of *Tōkyō* bay.

Tsurugi-san, 劍山. Mountain (2240 m.) W. of *Awa* (*Shikoku*). — Also called *Ken-zan.*

Tsurumaki, 鶴巻. In *Kazusa.* From 1827 to 1868, the residence of a branch of the *Mizuno* family (15,000 k.).

Tsurumaru-jō, 鶴丸城. Ancient name of the castle built at the beginning of the 17th century at *Kagoshima* (*Satsuma*) by *Shimazu Iehisa.*

Tsurumi-saki, 鶴見崎. Cape E, of *Bungo*.

Tsurumi-yama, 鶴見山. Volcano (1600 m.) of *Bungo*.

Tsurunuma-gawa, 鶴沼川. River (118 Km.) which rises in *Iwashiro*, irrigates that province and by its union with the *Hibashi-gawa* and the *Tadami-gawa*, forms the *Agano-gawa*.

Tsushima, 對馬. Group of islands situated in the middle of the strait that separates Japan from Korea. It forms one of the 12 provinces of the *Saikai-dō*. — Chinese name : *Taishū*. — The group comprises one large island and 5 small ones. The large one (811 Km. circ.) is almost entirely divided into two parts *Kami-agata* and *Shimo-agata* by the *Asajiura* bay. The population of *Tsushima* is estimated at 35,000 inh.; the chief-town is *Izu-no-hara* (10,000 inh.). Since the 12th century, the island was the fief of the *Sō daimyō*, who frequently had to defend himself against Korean and Chinese pirates. It was completely devastated by the Mongols in 1274 and in 1281. In 1861 Russia tried to get a concession on it, but the intervention of England caused her to renounce her claim. — *Tsushima* at present belongs to *Nagasaki-ken*.

Tsutsui, 筒井. Village in *Yamato*, where the *Tsutsui daimyō* had a castle in the 16th century. *Junkei* was besieged there in 1569, by *Matsunaga Hisahide*.

Tsutsui, 筒井. Ancient *daimyō* family descended from the *Fujiwara*. Vassal of the big temple of *Kōkoku-ji*, it received the domains of *Tsutsui* (*Yamato*) and took its name.

—— **Junkei,** 順慶 (1549-1584). Was at first called *Fujimasa* or *Fujikatsu*. When he entered into possession of his father's estate, a large number of *samurai* were enlisting in the army of the then all powerful *daimyō Matsunaga Hisahide*. To oppose such an adversary, *Junkei* placed himself under the protection of *Nobunaga* and thus was not molested in his domains. When *Hisahide* revolted against *Nobunaga*, *Junkei* was ordered to besiege him in his castle of *Shigi-san*. He stormed the place and in reward received the *Yamato* province (1577). At the death of *Nobunaga*, he sided with his relative *Akechi Mitsuhide*, and brought his troops to *Yamazaki*, to take part in the battle, but remarking the great strength of *Hideyoshi's* army, he kept his army on the *Hora-ga-take*, to watch the issue of the fight and when victory favored *Hideyoshi*, he joined him, thus contributing to defeat his relative *Mitsuhide*. Hence the nickname he received, *Hiyorimi-Junkei* (*Junkei* who observes how omens appear in the heavens). *Hideyoshi* however was not much inclined to acknowledge such a tardy assistance and reduced his revenue to 70,000 k. (1582).

—— **Sadatsugu,** 定次 (+ 1615). Was adopted in 1571 by *Junkei*, his uncle. At the latter's death, he received the castle of *Ueno* (*Iga*), with a revenue of 120,000 k. in *Yamashiro* and *Ise*. In 1585, he joined *Hori Hidemasa* in their fight against the bonzes of the *Negoro-dera* (*Kii*), killed them all and burned their temple. In 1600, he sided with *Ieyasu*, accompanied him in the expedition against *Uesugi Kagekatsu*, and returned in time to assist at the battle of *Sekigahara*. Accused by his *kerai* of maladministration, he was dispossessed, banished to *Matsu-*

yama (*Iyo*, 1608), and invited to commit *harakiri* (1615). — *Sadatsugu* was a Christian and had received baptism in 1592. This fact may have been one of the causes of his disgrace.

Tsutsui Junkei san-rō, 筒井順慶三老. The 3 principal *kerai* of *Tsutsui Junkei: Shima Tomoyuki, Matsukura Katsushige,* and *Mōri Yoshiyuki.*

Tsutsuji-ga-saki, 躑躅崎. In *Kai, Aikawa-mura.* Ancient castle built in 1538 by *Takeda Nobutora* and destroyed by *Nobunaga* (1582).

Tsutsumi, 堤. *Kuge* family descended from *Fujiwara Tamefusa.* — Now Viscount.

Tsuwamono no tsukasa, 兵部省. Ancient name of the *Hyōbu-shō.*

Tsuwano, 津和野. Town (5300 inh.) of the *Iwami* province. Was also called *Sambommatsu.* Ancient castle which, in the 16th century, belonged successively to the *Yoshimi, Ōuchi,* and *Mōri* families. Under the *Tokugawa* it was the residence of the *Sakazaki daimyō* (1600), then from 1617 to 1868 that of the *Kamei* (43,000 k.).

Tsuyama, 津山. Town (12,350 inh.) of *Mimasaka* province. Ancient castle built in 1442 by *Yamana Norikiyo.* Towards the middle of the 16th century, it passed to the *Ukita.* Under the *Tokugawa,* it was the residence of the *daimyō Mori* (1604), then from 1697 to 1868, it belonged to *Matsudaira* (100,000 k.).

Tsuyama-gawa, 津山川. Name given to the *Higashi-ōkawa,* whilst it passes through *Mimasaka.* It is also called *Higashi-gawa, In-no-shō-gawa,* etc.

U

Ubusuna no kami, 産土神. — See *Uji-gami*.

Uchibito, 内人. In ancient times, officials who resided at the great temple of *Ise* and were entrusted with its management, offerings, etc.

Uchida, 内田. *Daimyō* family descended from *Fujiwara Muchimaro*. Made noble in 1639 in the person of *Masanobu* (+ 1651), it resided at first at *Shikanuma* (*Shimotsuke*), then from 1724 to 1868, at *Omigawa* (*Shimōsa* — 10,000 k.). — Now Viscount.

Uchide no hama, 打出濱. In *Settsu*. *Nitta Yoshisada* there defeated *Ashikaga Tadayoshi* (1336).

Uchi-ko Naishinnō, 有智子内親王 (807-847). Daughter of the Emperor *Saga*, she distinguished herself in literature and poetry. She was the first who received the title of *Sai-in* in the temple of *Kamo* (814).

Uchi-kura, 内藏. In olden times, a storehouse (*kura*) erected for storing away the presents that were regularly brought by the messengers of the *San-kan* (Korea). Later on, it became the title of those who had the keeping of them. This office belonged to the *Shin* and the *Kan* families. As the presents increased, the *Ōkura* was erected and its superintendence given to *Shin Shukō*. *Shin* then became a family name, and in 702 was changed into that of *Ōkura*.

Uchino, 内野. At *Kyōto*, the site of the ancient Imperial Palace destroyed by fire and left uncultivated. It was the scene of several battles, especially in 1391, when the *Shōgun Yoshimitsu* defeated *Yamana Ujikiyo* there.

Uchi no kanimori-zukasa, 内掃部司. Official of the *Kunaishō*, having charge of the mats, seats, etc. — See *Kanimori-zukasa*.

Uchi no kashiwade no tsukasa, 内膳司. — See *Naizen-shi*.

Uchi no kura no tsukasa, 内藏司. — See *Kura-ryō*.

Uchi no kusuri no tsukasa, 内藥司. — See *Naigaku-shi*.

Uchi no miyabito, 内宮人. Formerly name given to the employees of the *Naikū* temple of *Ise*. (The Japanese reading of *Naikū* is *Uchi no miya*).

Uchi no miyake, 内宮家. Or *Uchitsu-miyake*, or *Watari-tamuroke*. Formerly Japanese military stations in Korea. Each *kan* had a central establishment. The one of *Mimana* had the *Mimana kōgungensui* as its chief; the one of *Kudara*, the *Kudara-sai*; the one of *Shiragi*, the *Shiragi-sai*.

Uchi no ō-omi, 内大臣. — See *Naidaijin*.

Uchi no otodo, 内大臣. — See *Naidaijin*.

Uchi no shirusu-tsukasa, 内記. Or *Naiki*. Officials of the *Nakatsukasa-shō* entrusted with the making of the decrees (*mikotonori*, *semmyō*, etc.) that were to be promulgated in the name of the Emperor.

There were the *dai-naiki*, secretaries of the first class, and the *shō-naiki*, secretaries of the second class.

Uchi no somemono no tsukasa, 内 染 司 . Department under the *Kunai-shō* which attended to the dyeing of the stuffs and clothes used by the Emperor. Later on, was joined to the *Nui-no tsukasa*.

Uchi no takumi no tsukasa, 内 匠 司 . — See *Takumi-ryō*.

Uchi no toneri, 内 舎 人 . — See *Toneri*.

Uchūben, 右 中 辨 . Official of the *Dajōkwan*, created by the *Taihō* Code (702) to assist the *Udaiben*. — See *Benkwan*.

Uchūjō, 右 中 將 . Abbreviation of *Ukon-e-chūjō*.

Uda, 宇 陀, 雨 多 . District of *Yamato*, through which *Jimmu-tennō* passed when going from *Kumano* to *Yoshino*. The legendary crow *Yata-garasu* guided him on his journey and a temple has been erected there in honor of the crow.

Udagawa Genzui, 宇 田 川 玄 隨 (1753-1795). Confucianist from *Tsuyama* (*Mimasaka*) who knew the Dutch language perfectly. — His son *Shinsai* (1769-1834) was also a distinguished savant and continued to teach his father's doctrines.

Uda-Genji, 宇 多 源 氏 . Branch of the *Minamoto* descended from the Emperor *Uda*, whose grandson, *Masanobu* (920-993), son of *Atsuzane-shinnō*, received the name of *Minamoto* for himself and his descendants. The following table indicates the principal families descended from this stock.

Masanobu - Tokinaka	Narimasa - Sukemichi - Masanaga	Niwata
		Aya-no-kōji
	Sukeyoshi- Noriyori - Akitsune	Sasaki
		Rokkaku
		Kyōgoku
		Kuroda
		Enya
		Amako
		Tō
		Kamei
	Tokikata - Nakayori - Nakachika ...	Itsutsuji
	Yasutsuna- Tokinobu - Ujiyori	Mori
		Morikawa

Uda-tennō, 宇 多 天 皇 . 59th Emperor of Japan (889-897). — *Sadayoshi*, 3rd son of *Kōkō-tennō*, succeeded his father at the age of 21 years. He instituted the ceremonies of the *Shihō-hai* (1st day of the year) and of the *Nanakusa no kayu* (7th day of the 1st month). He protected *Sugawara Michizane*, raised him to the dignity of *Dainagon*, and on his advice, stopped sending ambassadors to China, which had been regularly done before (894). After a reign of 9 years, he abdicated in favor of his son *Daigo* and retired to the *Shujaku-in*, where he shaved his head and thus became the first *Hō-ō*. When he resigned the throne to his son, he left him written instructions which were called *Kwampyō-go-ikai* (Imperial precepts of the *Kwampyō* era). In 901, he did all in his power to prevent the disgrace of *Michizane*, but could not succeed. He then more and more retired into solitude, faithfully practiced the Bud-

dhist law, and died in 631 at the age of 65 years. He was cremated at
Ōuchi-yama.

UDA HŌ-Ō.

Udaiben, 右大辨. First secretary in the Ministries of war (*Hyōbu*),
Justice (*Gyōbu*), Finance (*Ōkura*) and Palace (*Kunai*). He was superior
to the *Uchūben* and the *Ushōben.* — See *Benkwan.*

Udaijin, 右大臣 (Lit.: minister of the right). From 645 to 1885,
the 3rd of the 3 principal ministers, inferior to the *Sadaijin.* — See
Dajō-kwan, Sadaijin, San-kō, etc.

Udo, 宇土. Town (5,500 inh.) of *Higo.* Ancient castle of the *Murakami daimyō,* who resided there from 1480 to 1587. In 1588, *Hideyoshi* gave it as fief to *Konishi Yukinaga* with half of the province.
After 1600, it belonged to the domains of the *Kumamoto daimyō.*

Ueda, 上田. Town (24,100 inh.) of *Shinano.* Ancient castle which
at first belonged to the *Murakami.* Under the *Tokugawa,* was the residence of the *daimyō Sanada* (1582), *Sengoku* (1622), then from 1706 to
1868, that of the *Matsudaira* (53,000 k.).

Ueda Akinari, 上田秋成 (1732-1809). Writer of *Kyōto.* Left
several works.

Uematsu, 植松. *Kuge* family descended from *Minamoto Masazane*
(*Murakami-Genji*). — Now Viscount.

Uemura, 植村. *Daimyō* family descended from *Minamoto Yoshikuni* (*Seiwa-Genji*). Made noble in 1640 in the person of *Iemasa* (1589-

1650), it resided from that time till the Restoration at *Takatori* (*Yamato* — 25,000 k.). — Now Viscount.

Ueno, 上野. Chief-town (14,600 inh.) of the *Iga* province. Towards 1570, *Takigawa Katsutoshi, Kitabatake's* vassal, built a castle there, which in 1593 passed to the *Tsutsui*. From 1608, it became part of the domains of the *Tōdō daimyō* of *Tsu* (*Ise*).

Ueno, 上野. An ancient castle in *Mikawa* which in the 16th century, belonged to the *Matsudaira* family, then to the *Sakai* and the *Naitō*. It was abandoned towards the end of the same century.

Ueno, 上野. Park N. E. of *Tōkyō* (*Shitaya-ku*) famous for its temples, which possess the tombs of several *Tokugawa Shōgun* (See

UENO TEMPLE ON A FEAST DAY.

Tōei-zan). Also famous for its museum, botanical garden, *Daibutsu*, etc. — On July 4, 1868, a battle was fought at *Ueno* and the *Shōgun's* army was defeated by the adherents of the Emperor. It brought about *Keiki's* submission. During the battle, the famous *Kwanei-ji* temple was burned.

Ueno, 上野. Ancient *daimyō* family descended from *Ashikaga Yasuuji*. Ceased to exist towards the end of the 14th century. It had faithfully served the *Ashikaga*.

Ueno, 上野. Noble family founded by *Masao*, 3rd son of prince *Kita-shirakawa Yoshihisa* (+ 1895). — Now Count.

Ue no mitsubone, 上御局. Or *Fujitsubo-no-ue no mitsubone*. Apartment reserved for Ladies of the Imperial Palace : *Kisaki, Nyōgo, Kōi*, etc.

Uesugi, 上杉. Famous *daimyō* family descended from *Fujiwara Yoshikado*.

—— **Shigefusa,** 重房. Decendant of *Yoshikado* in the 13th generation. Towards the 13th century he received the domain of *Uesugi* (*Tango*) and took its name. He had a daughter who married *Ashikaga Yoriuji* and was the mother of *Ietoki,* grandfather of *Takauji.* — His descendants formed the three branches of *Inukake, Yamanouchi* and *Ōgigayatsu.*

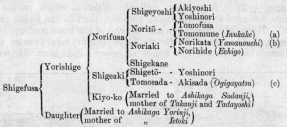

(*a*) — (**Inukake,** 犬懸). —— **Norifusa,** 憲房. Grandson of *Shigefusa,* served *Ashikaga Takauji,* whose complete confidence he enjoyed. He was killed at *Shijō-ga-hara,* when *Takauji* again took possession of *Kyōto* (1336). — His sister *Kiyo-ko* married *Ashikaga Sadauji* and was the mother of *Takauji* and of *Tadayoshi. Norifusa* was their uncle, hence the great influence he exercised over them.

—— **Shigeyoshi,** 重能 (+1349). Adopted son of *Norifusa,* was *Izu no kami.* He helped *Takauji* when the latter had been defeated by *Nitta Yoshisada,* but he was himself defeated in *Izumo* and had to escape to *Kyūshū.* He then fought against *Kō Moronao,* was defeated and banished to *Echizen,* where *Moronao* had him assassinated.

```
           ⎧Shigeyoshi ⎧Yoshinori - Noritaka
           ⎪           ⎨
           ⎪           ⎩Akiyoshi
Norifusa  ⎨                      ⎧Tomofusa        ⎧Noriaki
           ⎪Noritō -   ⎨                ⎧Ujinori -⎨Norikata
           ⎪           ⎩Tomomune ⎨                ⎪Noritomo
           ⎩                     ⎩Ujitomo - Mochifusa - Norihide
```

—— **Akiyoshi,** 顕能 (+1351). Son of *Shigeyoshi.* In order to revenge the death of his father, he killed *Kō Moronao* and *Moroyasu* when they were returning to *Kyōto. Takauji* irritated, condemned him to death, but *Tadayoshi,* who was entrusted with the execution of the Imperial order, was content with banishing him.

—— **Tomomune,** 朝宗 (1339-1414). Succeeded his father *Noritō,* who had been killed during the wars with *Takauji,* and was *Kazusa no suke.* In 1395, he was named *Shitsuji* (minister) of *Ashikaga Ujimitsu.* At the death of *Mitsukane* (1409), he shaved his head, took the name of *Jōsho* and retired to a temple.

—— **Ujinori,** 氏憲 (+1417). Was *Shitsuji* of the *Kwanryō* of *Kamakura, Ashikaga Mochiuji.* Having been dismissed, he shaved his head and took the name of *Zenshū*. Calling to him *Yoshitsugu*, brother of the *Shōgun Yoshimochi*, and *Mitsutaka*, brother of *Mitsukane*, he revolted against *Mochiuji*, expelled him from *Kamakura*, and again took the title of minister. But the *Shōgun* ordered all the *daimyō* of the country to support *Mochiuji*. At the beginning of the following year, the rebels found themselves nearly deserted, and being defeated, retired to the temple *Hōshō-in* at *Yuki-no-shita*, and more than 40, committed *harakiri*.

—— **Mochifusa,** 持房. Son of *Ujinori*. In 1438 he sided with his relative *Uesugi Norizane*, and by order of the *Shōgun Yoshinori*, marched against the *Kwanryō Mochiuji*, whom he defeated at *Hakone* (1439).

—— **Noritomo,** 教朝 (+1461) Brother of the above. In 1456, he was *Shitsuji* of the *Kwanryō Masatomo*. He died during an epidemic to which many fell victims all over Japan. — With him, the *Inukake* branch disappears from history.

(*b*) — (**Yamanouchi,** 山內).—— **Noriaki,** 憲顯 (1306-1368). Son of *Norifusa*, served *Takauji*. In 1337, when *Kitabatake Akiie* again became master of *Kamakura*, *Noriaki*, who had joined *Hosokawa Tomouji*, marched against and defeated him on the *Tone-gawa*. He likewise defeated *Nitta Yoshioki*. When *Ashikaga Motouji* became *Kwanryō* of *Kamakura* (1349), *Noriaki* was his *Shitsuji* together with *Kō Morofuyu*. At the same time he received the titles of *Echigo no kami* and *Izu no kami*. When his brother *Shigeyoshi* was murdered by *Kō Moronao* (1349), he was exasperated and with *Ashikaga Tadayoshi* passed to the ranks of the Southern party. Defeated in *Musashi*, he fled to *Shinano*, where he enlisted under the banner of prince *Munenaga-shinnō*, a protégé of *Nitta Yoshimune*, but was again defeated at the *Fuefuki-take*. *Motouji*, however lacking the good advice of *Noriaki*, forgave him his defection and again gave him the title of *Shitsuji*, which dignity he kept when *Ujimitsu* succeeded *Motouji* (1367).

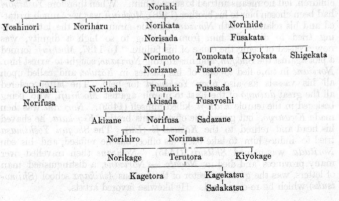

—— **Yoshinori, 能 憲** (+1378). Son of *Noriaki*, was adopted by his uncle *Shigeyoshi*, and when the latter had been murdered by *Kō Moronao* (1349), *Yoshinori* resolved to take revenge. He with *Ashikaga Tada-yoshi* passed to the Southern side, and with the help of *Suwa Katashige*, defeated and killed *Morofuyu*, brother of *Moronao*. At the death of *Noriaki* (1368), he succeeded him as *Shitsuji*.

—— **Noriharu, 憲 春** (+1379). Son of *Noriaki*, was *Shitsuji* of the *Kwanryō Ujimitsu*. This latter was ambitious to supplant the *Shōgun Yoshimitsu* and *Noriharu* vainly sought to dissuade him from his project. Seeing the futility of his remonstrances, he went home, wrote a last letter to the *Kwanryō*, and killed himself.

—— **Norikata, 憲 方** (1335-1394). Repressed a revolt of the *Toki* in *Mino* in 1378. At the death of his brother *Noriharu*, he replaced him in the office of *Shitsuji* to the *Kwanryō Ujimitsu*. He settled in the village of *Yamanouchi*, near *Kamakura*, hence the name given to the branch of the *Uesugi* of which he is the ancestor. In 1382, he defeated *Oyama Yoshimasa*, who had sided with the Southern dynasty. Sickness forced him to resign the office of *Shitsuji*.

—— **Norimoto, 憲 基** (1383-1418). Grandson of *Norikata*. He was named *Shitsuji* when *Ujinori* was deprived of this title (1415). The latter rose in revolt the following year, and *Norimoto* was defeated. Whilst the *Kwanryō Mochiuji* escaped to *Suruga*, he sought refuge in the temple *Kokusei-ji*, at *Nirayama* (*Izu*). Pursued even to that place by his enemies he went to *Echigo*. In the beginning of 1417, he levied troops, re-entered *Kamakura*, defeated *Ujinori's* army and again took up his functions.

—— **Norizane, 憲 實** (+1455). One of the most illustrious men of the *Uesugi* line, was *Norizane*, son of *Fusakata*. In 1419, he was named *Shitsuji* and *Awa no kami*, and secured the succession of *Norimoto*. *Mochi-uji, Kwanryō*, of *Kamakura*, seeing that the *Shōgun Yoshimochi* had no children, left no means untried to succeed him. When therefore *Yoshinori* had been chosen heir to his brother (1428), *Mochiuji* was very much irritated and his relations with *Norizane* became strained, for the latter, having tried to dissuade him from aspiring to so high a dignity, was now accused of being the cause of his failure. In 1437, *Mochiuji* formed a plot against the *Shōgun*, and mistrusting *Norizane*, sought to arrest him. *Norizane* in time fled to one of his castles in *Kōzuke*, and called upon all his vassals as also upon *Yoshinori* for help. The latter ordered all the great *daimyō* of the East to march against *Mochiuji*, who being besieged in the temple *Eian-ji*, killed himself (1439). *Norizane* was then made *Kwanryō*, but giving the office to his brother *Kiyokata*, he shaved his head and retired to the *Kokusei-ji* (*Izu*). The *Shōgun Yoshimasa* tried to induce him to take back his office, but he refused, and his son *Noritada* was named *Shitsuji* (1445). *Norizane* then travelled over many provinces and died in *Nagato*. — *Norizane*, a distinguished man of letters, was the great protector of the famous *Ashikaga* school (*Shimo-tsuke*) which he re-organized. He likewise favored artists.

—— **Kiyokata, 清方** (+1442). 5th son of *Fusakata*, governor of *Echigo* and was *Shitsuji* of the *Kwanryō* of *Kamakura* (1439). The following year, *Yūki Ujitomo* brought the two sons of *Mochiuji*, *Haru-ō* and *Yasu-ō*, to his castle of *Koga* (*Shimotsuke*) and was their protector against the *Uesugi*. *Kiyokata* besieged them and stormed the castle. *Ujitomo* was killed during the battle, and his wards, then 12 and 10 years old respectively, were put to death (1441). Some time after, *Kiyokata* went to *Kyōto* to give an account of the campaign to the *Shōgun*, and as he returned from the city, he was assassinated.

—— **Noritada, 憲忠** (1433-1454). Son of *Norizane*, was named *Shitsuji* when *Nagao Masakata* reinstalled *Ashikaga Shigeuji* in the office of *Kwanryō* (1445), but, as *Noritada* was only 12 years old, *Masakata* acted in his stead. *Shigeuji* had resolved to avenge the death of his father and brothers. He sought a favorable occasion, and one day, he sent *Yūki Shigetomo* and *Satomi Yoshizane* to invest the house of *Noritada*, who died whilst defending himself.

—— **Fusaaki, 房顕** (1432-1466). Son of *Norizane*, was named *Kwantō-kwanryō* by *Nagao Masakata* after the murder of his brother *Noritada* (1454). He forced *Shigeuji* to seek refuge in *Koga* and then took up his residence at *Kamakura*. He then asked the *Shōgun Yoshimasa* to appoint a successor to *Shigeuji*. *Yoshimasa* named his own brother *Masatomo*, who had settled at *Horikoshi* (*Izu*) (1461). *Shigeuji* however, supported by the *daimyō* of *Shimotsuke*, took the field, and before the war was over, *Fusaaki* fell sick and died in his camp at *Ikago* (*Musashi*).

—— **Akisada, 顕定** (1454-1510). Son of *Fusasada*. He was brought from *Echigo* by *Nagao Masakata* to acquire the inheritance of *Fusaaki* by marrying his only surviving child. *Masakata* declared himself the tutor of his protégé, and asked the *Shōgun* to give him the title of *Kwanryō* of *Kwantō* (1470). At the death of *Masakata*, *Akisada* disregarding *Kageharu* the son of the former, chose *Nagao Tadakage* as the successor. *Kageharu* now passed to the other branch of the *Uesugi*, the *Ōgigayatsu*, and, then began the rivalry between these two families which was to cause the ruin of both. In 1477 *Kageharu* levied troops, and attacked *Akisada* at *Ikago*. *Akisada* retired to *Kōzuke*, where he built the castle of *Shirai*, and from there governed the *Kwantō*. The first period of the war finished in 1486. *Akisada* victorious over his competitor *Sadamasa* (*Ōgigayatsu*), ordered *Ōta Dōkwan*, the principal *kerai* of *Sadamasa* to be put to death. The war was resumed in 1493 ; this time, *Sadamasa* met with death but his successor *Tomoyoshi* continued the war. During these continual dissensions, a new power had risen. *Hōjō Sōun* had occupied the castle of *Odawara* (1494), and gradually enlarged his estates at the expense of his neighbors. After having for a long time fought in the environs of *Kawagoe* (*Musashi*), the two *Uesugi* factions were reconciled, and met their common foe (1505). *Akisada* shaved his head and took the name of *Kajun*. The following year, *Nagao Tamekage* rebelled in *Echigo* and put his lord *Fusayoshi*, brother of *Akisada*, to death. The latter, marched against the rebel and defeated him. But many of the *samurai* of *Echigo*, breaking their alliance with the *Uesugi*, enlisted in the army of *Tamekage*. *Akisada* resumed the campaign, but was defeated and killed himself. He had ruled over the *Kwantō* for 40 years.

—— **Norifusa,** 憲 房 (1466-1524). Adopted son of *Akisada*. He strengthened his castle of *Hirai* (*Kōzuke*) and soon after had to oppose the *Nagao, Tamekage* and *Kageharu*, and *Hōjō Sōun*. *Nagao Kagenaga* came to his rescue and had him made *Kwanryō* of *Kamakura* (1512). In 1524, *Uesugi Tomooki* (*Ōgigayatsu*) was defeated at *Kawagoe* by *Hōjō Ujitsuna*, who occupied the castle of *Edo*. *Norifusa* was prepar-- ing an expedition against *Ujitsuna*, when he fell sick and died.

—— **Norimasa,** 憲 政 (1522-1579). Son of *Norifusa*. He continued the war against the *Hōjō* of *Odawara*. In 1537, he united his forces with those of *Ōgigayatsu Tomosada*, but *Hōjō Ujiyasu* was victorious in the battle and occupied the castle of *Kawagoe*: *Tomosada* was killed and *Norimasa* fled to *Hirai*. He formed a second army and re-entered the field but he was again defeated in 1540 and 1543. The whole *Kwantō* now acknowledged the authority of the *Hōjō*. *Norimasa* then possessed only the castle of *Hirai* and in 1551, *Ujiyasu* occupied it. *Norimasa* fled to *Echigo* and placed himself under the protection of his vassal *Nagao Kagetora*, whom he adopted as his son and who afterwards took the name of *Uesugi*. He was to be the famous *Kenshin*, and to support the glory of the family.

—— **Terutora,** 輝 虎 (**Kenshin,** 謙 信) (1530-1578). Was the 3rd son of *Nagao Tamekage*, vassal of the *Uesugi*. Born at *Tochio* (*Echigo*), he received the name of *Sarumatsu-maru*, then that of *Kagetora*. At the death of his father, his elder brother, *Harukage*, succeeded him, but being feeble and sickly, he showed little ability to govern. *Kagetora*, then 11 years old, suffered to such an extent from this state of affairs, that he asked permission to become a bonze and took the name of *Shūshimbō*. He travelled over several provinces and at the *Hiei-zan* he met *Usami Sadayuki*, who advised him to return to his native province. He followed this advice, and in 1543, he returned to *Echigo*, deposed his brother, and supported by *Sadayuki*, assumed the administration of the paternal domains. He began his career by forcing his brother-in-law, *Nagao Masakage*, to sue for peace and submit to him. At that time, *Murakami Yoshikiyo* was at war with *Takeda Shingen*. Defeated, he called on *Kagetora* for help, and thus began a struggle between these two fearless opponents which was to endure for more than 10 years. In 1551, *Uesugi Norimasa*, defeated by *Hōjō Ujiyasu*, sought protection and refuge at his powerful vassal's castle, but the latter made his conditions. *Norimasa* was to invest him with the office of *Kwanryō*, adopt him as his son, give him the name of *Uesugi* and the title of *Echigo no kami*. The following year, *Kagetora* shaved his head and took the name of *Kenshin*, by which he is better known. He then went to *Kyōto* and was ordered by the *Shōgun* to fight the *Hōjō*. He thus had to combat *Takeda Shingen* and the *daimyō* of *Odawara* at the same time. The war with *Shingen* was mostly fought in the *Kawanaka-jima* district, N. of *Shinano*. Here the two champions met every year and displayed their strategic skill, each campaign ending without decisive results. In 1558, *Kenshin* declared war against the *Hōjō*, and stormed the castles of *Numata* and of *Umayabashi* (*Kōzuke*). The *Shōgun Yoshiteru* then gave him the title of *Kwantō-kwanryō*, and allowed him to use one of the characters of his own name, and the name *Kagetora* became *Terutora*. Pursuing his exploits, he besieged *Odawara*, fought *Takeda Shingen* at *Kawanaka-jima*, where *Nobushige*, *Shingen's* brother, was killed; conquered *Etchū* and achieved the conquest of *Kōzuke* province (1564). At this stage of the war, the *Shōgun* offered to arbitrate, and forced him to make peace with the *Hōjō*, one of the clauses of the treaty being that *Kenshin*, who was a bonze since childhood and had no heir, should adopt *Ujiyasu's* son, *Saburō*, to whom he was to give the name of *Kagetora*. When peace was signed, *Kenshin* was able to give his undivided attention to *Shingen* who had just invaded *Etchū*, and whom he pursued as far as *Kaga* and *Noto*. Whilst thus waging war far from his own estates, he heard that *Nobunaga* was besieging several of his castles in *Kwantō*. He hastened to face this new foe and hesitated not to enter

UESUGI KENSHIN.

into contest with him who had become master of all Japan. He joined the coalition against *Nobunaga* formed by *Takeda Katsuyori*, son of *Shingen*. Before personally entering upon a campaign against this dreaded foe, *Nobunaga* sent *Shibata Katsuie*, *Maeda Toshiie*, etc. against him. After some months, *Kenshin* fell sick and died at the age of 48. He received the Buddhist posthumous name of *Shinkō*. The question of his succession brought about fresh troubles.

—— **Kagetora,** 景虎 (1552-1579). 7th son of *Hōjō Ujiyasu*, adopted by *Kenshin*. In 1564, he governed *Noto* and *Sado*. At the death of *Kenshin* he received a part of his inheritance, but *Kagekatsu*, *Kenshin's* nephew, claimed his rights. War followed and *Kagetora* was defeated. *Hōjō Nagakuni* was sent to help him, but *Takeda Katsuyori* supported *Kagekatsu*. War was renewed and after a short space *Nagakuni* was killed in battle, and *Kagetora* was again defeated and killed himself at *Kitagawa*.

—— **Kagekatsu,** 景勝 (1555-1623) Son of *Nagao Masakage*, who married a sister of *Kenshin*. He was first called *Kiheida* and was brought up by his uncle, whom he accompanied in all his campaigns, as soon as he could carry arms. When *Kenshin* had adopted *Kagetora*, he divided his immense domains in half to satisfy both his sons. But at the death of *Kenshin*, *Kagekatsu* claimed the whole inheritance, and the following year, *Kagetora* being defeated, killed himself. Being sole master, *Kagekatsu* restored order in his provinces, reconquered *Etchū* and *Kaga*, served *Nobunaga* and then *Hideyoshi*, who bestowed upon him the title of *Chūnagon* and chose him as one of the 5 *Tairō* who were entrusted with the government of affairs during the minority of

Hideyori. In the beginning of 1598, *Kagekatsu* exchanged his fief of *Echigo* for that of *Aizu* with a revenue of 1,200,000 k. Some months later *Hideyoshi* died and disunion quickly followed among the *Tairō*, all of whom returned to their domains. *Ieyasu* soon after hearing that *Kagekatsu* was preparing for war, and not wishing to give him time to finish his preparations, at once took the field against him. He had scarcely reached *Oyama* (*Shimotsuke*), when he learned of the coalition that had been formed against him by *Ishida Kazushige*, and he hastened to retrace his steps. *Naoe Kanetsugu*, who was leading the *Aizu* troops, intended to attack him at this juncture but *Kagekatsu* opposed this plan. After *Sekigahara* (1600), when the *daimyō* were vying with each other in their submission to the victor, *Kagekatsu* kept aloof. *Ieyasu* at last called him to *Kyōto* and there exchanged his fief of *Aizu* for that of *Yonezawa* (*Dewa* — 300,000 k.). In 1615, *Kagekatsu* took his place among the *daimyō* who were besieging *Ōsaka*, his submission being complete.

—— **Sadakatsu,** 定勝 (1603-1645). Son of *Kagekatsu*, succeeded him in the fief of *Yonezawa*, and proved himself a good administrator.

—— **Tsunakatsu,** 綱勝 (+ 1664). Son of *Sadakatsu*, had no children, and adopted *Tsunanori*, son of *Kira Yoshinaka*; but at his death, the revenues of the fief were reduced to 150,000 k.

—— **Harunori,** 治憲 (1751-1822). Son of *Akizuki Tanemitsu*, was adopted by *Uesugi Shigesada* and succeeded him in the fief of *Yonezawa*. In 1785, he entrusted the administration of his domains to his son and devoted his time to literature. He established a school at *Yonezawa*, called *Kōjō-kwan* (1797). — The descendants of the family resided at *Yonezawa* (*Dewa*), till the Restoration. — Now Count. — A side branch, descended from *Tsunanori* and having a revenue of 10,000 k., now bears the title of Viscount.

(c) —— (**Ōgigayatsu, 扇 谷**). — **Akisada,** 顯 定. Grandson of *Shigeaki*, settled at *Ōgigayatsu* (*Sagami*) and took the name of the place.

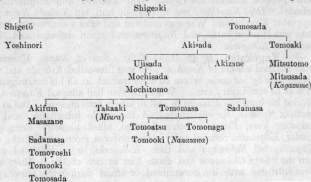

	Shigeaki		
Shigetō		Tomosada	
Yoshinori	Akisada		Tomoaki
	Ujisada Akizane		Mitsutomo
	Mochisada		Mitsusada (*Kagazume*)
	Mochitomo		
Akifusa	Takaaki (*Miura*) Tomomasa Sadamasa		
Masazane			
	Tomoatsu Tomonaga		
Sadamasa	Tomooki (*Nanazawa*)		
Tomoyoshi			
Tomooki			
Tomosada			

—— **Mochitomo,** 持朝 (1416-1467). Sided with his relative *Norizane* during the *Eikyō* civil war (1438), and, when *Shigeuji* had been made *Kwanryō* (1449), he shaved his head, took the name of *Dōchō*, resigned his domains in favor of his son *Akifusa* and retired to *Kawagoe* (*Musashi*). When *Ashikaga Shigeuji* murdered *Uesugi* (*Yamanouchi*) *Noritada* (1454), *Mochitomo* joined *Fusaaki*, marched against *Shigeuji* and obliged him to seek refuge in *Koga*. In 1457, he built the castle of *Kawagoe*, supported *Ashikaga Masatomo* against *Shigeuji*, and maintained the struggle for several years. At that epoch, the *Yamanouchi* branch of the *Uesugi* was in the height of its power and *Nagao Masakata*, its principal *herai*, served it with intelligence and energy, and maintained its authority in *Echigo, Kōzuke, Musashi, Izu*. In the mean time, *Ōta Dōkwan*, principal vassal of the *Ōgigayatsu*, was engaged in extending the influence of his own lord, and rivalry soon became so intense between the two families that war broke out. The immediate occasion was found in an order of the *Shōgun Yoshimasa* commanding his brother *Masatomo* and the *Uesugi* clan to begin another campaign against *Shigeuji* (1462). *Mochitomo*, contrary to expectations sided with *Shigeuji*. *Masatomo, Yamanouchi Fusasada* marched against him and he died during the war.

—— **Sadamasa,** 定正 (1442-1493). Son of *Mochitomo*, continued the war in which his father had been engaged, and was especially aided by *Ōta Dōkwan*. Two servants, jealous of the favor enjoyed by *Ōta*, and probably bribed by the *Yamanouchi*, calumniated him to his master and he was put to death. Disorder having broken out in the domains of the *Ōgigayatsu* and *Yamanouchi, Akisada* took up arms to restore peace. *Sadamasa* asked *Ashikaga Shigeuji* for help, who sent his son *Masauji* with some troops and the *Yamanouchi* were defeated. The *Shigeuji* and the *Ōgigayatsu* party gained the ascendency for some time, especially when *Hōjō Sōun* joined it. In a battle against *Akisada, Sadamasa* fell from his horse and was killed.

—— **Tomoyoshi,** 朝良 (+1518). Son of *Tomomasa*, was chosen heir by his uncle *Sadamasa*. When he heard that *Hōjō Sōun* had occupied *Odawara*, he levied troops and marched against him ; *Sōun*, fearing to begin war so soon, acknowledged, for the time being at least, the suzerainty of the *Uesugi* (1494). *Tomiyoshi* then turned against *Yamanouchi Akisada*, but despite the support of *Sōun* and *Imagawa Ujichika*, he was defeated after having fought several battles in *Musashi*. He retired to *Kawagoe*, where he was obliged to capitulate. He was transferred to the castle of *Edo* (1504).

—— **Tomooki,** 朝興 (1488-1537). Had attempted to relieve *Miura Yoshiatsu* then besieged by *Hōjō Sōun* in his castle of *Arai* (*Sagami*), but was defeated (1517). Aided by *Hōjō Ujitsuna*, he later reconquered *Kawagoe*. In 1530, in a war agrinst the *Hōjō*, he was defeated by *Ujiyasu*.

—— **Tomosada,** 朝定 (+1544). Son of *Tomooki*, erected the castle of *Kandaiji* to resist the *Hōjō* of *Odawara*. *Ujiyasu* then laid siege to *Kawagoe* (1537), stormed it and *Tomosada* took refuge in *Matsuyama*

(*Musashi*). In 1543, he joined *Yamanouchi Norimasa* and tried to recover *Kawagoe*. The siege lastened a long time, and *Tomosada* was killed. With him, the name of the *Ōgigayatsu* disappears from history.

Uesugi Echigo shi-rō, 上杉越後四老. The 4 principal vassal families of the *Uesugi* in *Echigo: Nagao, Ishikawa, Chisaka* and *Saitō*.

Uesugi Kwantō shi-rō, 上杉關東四老. The 4 principal vassal families of the *Uesugi* in *Kwantō: Nagao, Ōishi, Kobata* and *Shirokura*.

Uga-no-mitama no kami, 倉御魂神. — See *Toyo-uke-hime*.

Ugayafuki-aezu no mikoto, 鸕鶿草葺不合尊. — See *Hikonagi-satake-ugayafuki-aezu no mikoto*.

Ugo, 羽後. One of the 13 provinces of the *Tōsandō*. Comprises 9 districts — Chinese name: *Ushū* (with *Uzen*). — At present it belongs to the *Akita-ken*. — Formerly with *Uzen*, it formed the province of *Dewa* which in 1869, was divided in two.

Uji, 氏. Family name, partronymic name. *Nakatomi, Fujiwara, Taira, Minamoto*, are known as *uji*. In ancient books, the word *kabane* (*sei*) is often used for *uji* (*shi*), but not vice versâ. (See *Kabane*). Distinction was made between the *ō-uji* (reserved to the senior family) and the *ko-uji* (applied to the branches). The chief of the family had the title of *Uji no kami*. The vassals were called *Tomobe, Mimbu*, etc.

Uji, 宇治, 宇遅. District of the *Yamashiro* province, to which the city of *Kyōto* belongs. The tea of that place enjoys a great reputation, and was formerly reserved for the Emperors and the *Shōgun*. The bonze *Eisai* was the first to cultivate it at *Toga-no-o*, from where it was carried to *Uji* (15th century).

Uji, 宇治. Small city (3500 inh.) of the *Yamashiro* province, and the *Kuze* district, on the *Uji-kawa* river; also a village of the same province, *Uji* district, on the opposite side of the river, spanned by the famous bridge *Uji-bashi*. — *Ōjin-tennō* had his palace there and *Uji no Waki-iratsuko* was born in that place.

Uji-bashi, 宇治橋. Bridge joining the two sides of the *Uji-kawa* river near the city of *Uji* (*Yamashiro*). Was constructed in 647 by the bonze *Dōchō*. As it was on the road leading from *Kyōto* to *Yamato, Iga*, etc. it became the scene of many encounters. — See *Uji-kawa*.

Uji-bito, 氏人. Name formerly given to all the members of a family who honored the same *Uji-gami*. *Uji-ko* has the same meaning.

Uji-dera, 氏寺. Formerly, name given to the Buddhist temple erected by a family in honor of its *Uji-gami*. Thus the *Kōfuku-ji* at *Nara* was the *uji-dera* of the *Fujiwara*.

Ujie, 氏家. Ancient *daimyō* family native of *Shimotsuke* and descended from the *Fujiwara*.

—— **Kinyori,** 君頼. At the end of the 12th century, settled at *Ujie* (*Shimotsuke*) where he built a castle.

—— **Tadamoto,** 直 元 (+1571). Had the title of *Hitachi no suke*. He shaved his head and took the name of *Bakuzen*. In 1559, he was in command of the castle of *Ōgaki*. He was killed during the war against the troops of *Ikkō-shū* of *Nagashima*.

—— **Yukihiro,** 行 廣 (+1615). Son of the above, became *daimyō* of *Kuwana* (*Ise* — 25,000 k.), but in 1600, he sided against *Ieyasu* and was dispossessed. He enlisted in the army of *Hideyoshi*, and at the fall of *Ōsaka*, was ordered to commit *harakiri*.

—— **Yukitsugu,** 行 次. *Shima no kami*, brother of the above and *daimyō* of *Moriyama* (*Ōmi* — 15,000 k.), was likewise dispossessed in 1600.

Uji-gami, 氏 神. Titulary god of the hearth. In the Middle Ages, every family had its own god and erected a temple to him (*uji-dera*), where they gathered at stated times to venerate their ancestors and pray for the prosperity of their descendants. This god was either the first ancestor of the lineage or a god who was already honored by the family, from time immemorial. The *Uji-gami* must then be distinguished from the *Ubusuna no kami* : the first being a god protector of the family, the second, the titulary god of the place of birth. All the members of one clan, who venerated the same *Uji-gami*, were called *ujibito* or *ujiko*. It is commonly known that the *Uji-gami* of the *Minamoto* was *Hachiman*, god of war.

Uji-gawa, 宇 治 川. River, known as an outlet of lake *Biwa* (*Ōmi*) by the name of *Seta-gawa*, flows through *Yamashiro* and skirts the *Uji* district, whence its name, then passes *Fushimi*, and joining the *Katsura-gawa*, forms the *Yodo-gawa*. On its banks many battles were fought, the most famous being the one of 1180, in which *Minamoto Yorimasa*, after having performed prodigies of valor, being defeated by *Taira Tomomori*, committed *harakiri* in a neighboring temple, *Byōdō-in*. Another was fought in 1184, when *Kiso Yoshinaka* met his death on its banks.

Uji-monogatari, 宇 治 物 語. (Lit.: recitals of *Uji*). Classical book in 60 volumes, composed by *Minamoto Takakuni* (+1077), known by the name of *Uji-Dainagon*.

Uji no kami, 氏 上. Or *Uji no Chōja*, 氏 長 者. Title or Office created to remedy the disorder introduced by the assumption of such family names as *uji*, *kabane*, etc. From researches made in the 10th century, it appears that there existed more than 2,800 such titles. In the principal families an *Uji no kami* was established, who verified the right of those bearing such patronymic names. He was at the same time the chief of the clan. Practically the title existed only in the *Fujiwara*, *Tachibana*, *Taira* and *Minamoto* families. One of the *Tokugawa Shōgun's* titles was *Genji no chōja* or chief of the *Minamoto* clan.

Uji no Waki-iratsuko, 蒐 道 稚 郎 子 (+312). Son of the Emperor *Ōjin* and younger brother of *Nintoku*. His teacher was the famous Korean *Wani*. In 297 he received an order to punish the king of *Koma* (Korea), who had written an insulting letter to *Ōjin*. In 309, he was chosen heir to the throne, but at the death of his father, he refused to succeed him to the detriment of his elder brother *Nintoku*. The latter, however, in respect to the will of his father, refused to ascend the throne. This contest of disinterestedness lasted for 3 years, after which lapse of time, *Waki-iratsuko*, to force his brother to ascend the throne, fled to *Uji* and there committed *harakiri*.

Ukemochi no kami, 保倉神 . — See *Toyo-uke-hime*.

Ukita, 宇喜多 . Ancient *daimyō* family descended from *Kojima Takanori*, and therefore from *Minamoto* (*Seiwa-Genji*).

—— **Yoshiie,** 義家 . Was vassal of *Urakami Muramune, daimyō* of *Mimasaka*. *Munekage*, son of *Muramune*, had him put to death.

—— **Naoie,** 直家 (1530-1582). Son of *Yoshiie*, at first served *Munekage*, then to avenge the death of his father, revolted and obliged *Munekage* to flee to *Sanuki*. He then rid himself of *Nakayama Nobumasa* and of his brother-in-law *Tanigawa Hisataka*, and was sole master of the *Bitchū* province. But he had to fight against the *Mōri* and asked help from *Nobunaga*, who confirmed him in the possession of his fief.

—— **Hideie,** 秀家 (+ 1662). Being a child at the death of his father, he was brought up by *Hideyoshi*. When the latter made peace with the *Mōri*, he added the *Mimasaka* province (1582) to the fief of the *Ukita*. At the time of the Korean expedition, *Hideie* was made general in chief (*gensui*). After *Hideyoshi's* death, he opposed *Ieyasu* and stormed the castle of *Fushimi*. When the armies met in *Mino*, *Hideie* advised an night attack but *Ishida Kazushige* refused. After the defeat of his party at *Sekigahara*, *Hideie* fled to *Satsuma* and was deprived of his fief of *Okayama* (*Bizen* — 475,000 k.), which comprised 3 provinces. In the beginning of 1603, *Shimazu Iehisa* revealed the retreat of *Hideie* to *Ieyasu* and the *Shōgun* condemned him to death, but commuted this penalty to perpetual exile to the island of *Hachijō-jima* (*Izu*), whither he was transported with his son *Hidekatsu*. Upon arrival at the place of his exile, he shaved his head and took the name of *Raifu*. He died at an advanced age being more than 90 years old. — A brother of *Naoie*, *Tadaie*, took the family name of *Sakazaki*. His son *Narimasa*, served *Hideie*, then *Maeda Gen-i*, and later *Ieyasu*, who gave him the fief of *Tsuwano* (*Iwami* — 20,000 k.). He killed himself in 1616.

Ukiyo-e, 浮世繪 . Style of painting inaugurated in the 17th century by *Iwasa Matabei*. He endeavored to represent the scenes of every day life exactly, for which reason it is called the vulgar or re-alistic school. His works are more esteemed by foreigners than by Japanese. The best painters the school has produced besides *Matabei*, are : *Hishikawa Moronobu, Hanabusa Itchō, Kitagawa Utamaro, Hokusai, Miyagawa Chōshun*, etc.

Ukiyo Matabei, 浮世又兵衛 . — See *Iwasa Matabei*.

Ukon, 右近 . — See *Kon-e-efu*.

Uku-shima, 宇久嶋 . Island (34 Km. circ.) N. of the *Gotō* group (*Hizen*).

Ukwanshō, 右官掌 . — See *Sakwanshō*.

Uma-azukari, 馬預 . Under the *Tokugawa*, functionaries who trained horses for the *Shōgun*. This charge was hereditary in the

Suwabe and *Manaki* families; they received an allowance of 200 k. of rice.

Umashimate no mikoto, 可美眞手命. Son of *Nigihayahi no mikoto*, resided in *Yamato* when *Jimmu* came to conquer that land. His uncle *Nagasune-hiko* having refused to submit, he killed him, wherefore he was named chief of the interior guard of the Imperial Palace. He is the ancestor of the *Mononobe*.

Umayabashi, 厩橋. Ancient name of the present city of *Maebashi*, (*Kōzuke*).

Umayado no Ōji, 厩戸皇子.—See *Shōtoku-taishi*.

Umeda Umbin, 梅田雲濱 (1816-1859). Confucianist of *Kyōto* and distinguished poet. He promoted the cause of the Imperial Restoration by word and writing, and was on that account arrested by order of the *Shōgun*. He died in prison.

UMASHIMATE.

Umedani, 梅溪. *Kuge* family descended from the *Fujiwara*. — Now Viscount.

Umenokōji, 梅小路. *Kuge* family descended from the *Fujiwara*. — Now Viscount.

Umetsubo, 梅坪. In *Mikawa*. *Matsudaira Hirotada*, father of *Ieyasu*, defeated *Miyake Yasusada*, *Nobunaga's* general, (1548) at that place.

Umewaka, 梅若. Family descended from *Tachibana Moroe*, became famous for composing and performing the *nō* or *sarugaku*.

—— **Kagehisa,** 景久 (1466-1529). Left the *Kwanze* to establish a special school and in 1481, received the name of *Umewaka* from the Emperor *Go-Tsuchimikado*. The best known after him, are: *Iehisa*, *Hironaga*, *Ujimori*, *Ujiyoshi*, (1744-1818), *Rokurō* (1776-1854), etc.

Umezono, 梅園. *Kuge* family descended from the *Fujiwara*. — Now Viscount.

Ummei-den, 温明殿. Apartment in the Imperial Palace, reserved for the ladies of the Court. Also called *Naishi-dokoro*.

Unabara, 海原. Country which *Izanagi* left as an inheritance to *Tsukiyomi*, or according to others, to *Susano-o*. Some commentators believe it to be a part of Korea, others, the *Ryūkyū* islands; the first opinion is the most generally admitted.

Unagaya, 湯長谷 or **Yunagaya**. In *Iwashiro*. Was from 1670 to 1868, the residence of a branch of the *Naitō* family (15,000 k.).

Unebi-yama, 畝火山. Hill between the villages of *Shirakashi* and *Masuge*, in *Yamato*, near which *Jimmu-tennō* fixed his residence (*Kashiwabara no miya*) (660 B.C.) and was buried (*Unebi-yama no ushitora no sumi*). — In its vicinity are likewise found the tombs of the Emperors *Annei* (*Unebi-yama no hitsuji-saru no mi-hodoi no sumi*), *Itoku* (*Unebi-yama no minami-masago-dani-no-ue no sumi*). — Mount *Unebi* is also called *Jimyōji-zan*. In 1889, a temple (*Kashiwabara-jingū*) was erected on its summit in honor of the first Emperor of Japan.

Uneme, 釆女. Formerly female attendants of the Palace. The daughters of the district governors were usually chosen for that office (*kōri-zukasa*), giving preference to those who were remarkable for their beauty and poetical or musical talents. At their head was the *Uneme-zukasa*.

Unjō, 運上. Under the *Tokugawa*, taxes levied on merchants, artisans, etc. Corresponds to what is known to-day as the *eigyō-zei*. The taxes on public pawn shops, inns, etc. were called *myōga-kin*.

Unkei, 運慶. Famous sculptor of the 12th and the 13th centuries. Son of *Kōkei* and a descendant of *Jōchō*, he at first resided at *Kyōto*, then went to *Kamakura* and is the ancestor of many sculptors of Buddhist statues (*busshi*). He received the title of *Bitchū-hōin*.—His son *Tankei* and his grandson *Kōen* were also great sculptors.

UNKEI.

Unkoku-ryū, 雲谷流. School of painting of Chinese style, founded by *Sesshū* (1420-1507), bonze of the *Unkoku-ji* temple. Its principal masters are: *Shūgetsu, Shūtoku, Tōseki, Tōsatsu, Shūkō, Sesson, Tōgan*, etc. The so called *Settei-ryū* and *Hasegawa-ryū* are branches of this school.

Un-no-kuchi, 海野口. In *Shinano*, *Minami-maki-mura*. A castle had been built there which belonged to the *Murakami daimyō*. In the 16th century, it was entrusted to *Hiraga Genshin* who was besieged therein by *Takeda Nobutora*. Later on, it was taken by *Shingen*, son of *Nobutora*.

Unno Yukisuke, 海野幸典 (1789-1858). Literary man. Disciple of *Motoori Ōhira*, studied especially national antiquity.

Uno Shishin, 宇野士新 (1698-1745). Scholar of *Kyōto*, made a special study of Chinese literature.

Unsen-ga-take, 温泉嶽. Volcano (1250 m) in *Shimabara* (*Hizen*) peninsula, in eruption in 1792.

Unshū, 雲州. Chinese name for the *Izumo* province.

Unuma, 鵜沼. In *Mino*. Ancient castle which was defended by *Ōsawa Jirōemon* and stormed by *Nobunaga* (1564).

Uotsu, 魚津. In *Etchū*. Ancient castle which during the 14th century belonged to the *Shiina* family and was taken by *Nagoshi Tokikane*. At the end of the 16th century, *Itaya Masahiro* was besieged there and defeated by *Uesugi Kenshin*. The latter in turn was expelled by *Shibata Katsuie*.

Urabe, 卜部. Ancient family descended from *Ame-no-koyane no mikoto*. Several of its members are distinguished literati and poets: *Mushimaro, Kotatsu, Hirokata* (8th century), *Hiramaro* (9th century), etc.

Urabe Kenkō, 卜部兼好. — See *Yoshida Kenkō*.

Urabe Suetake, 卜部季武 (950-1022). Warrior, and one of the *shi-tennō* of *Minamoto Yorimitsu*.

Urado, 浦戸. In *Tosa*. When *Chōsokabe Motochika* had been defeated by *Hideyoshi* and his domains were reduced to the single province of *Tosa*, he left his castle of *Asakura*, and built another at *Urado*, where he resided (1585). His son *Morichika* having been dispossessed in 1600, the castle was abandoned.

Uraga, 浦賀. Town (14,000 inh.) of *Sagami*. Under the *Tokugawa*, a bureau for inspecting all ships entering or leaving the port. In 1818, an English ship, the *Gordon*, visited it. In 1837, an American man-of-war (*Morrison's* expedition) entered it and was fired upon. The *Mercator* (1845) and the *Columbus* (1846) visited it also. In July, Commodore *Perry* arrived and soon after Japan was opened to the outer world.

Uraga-bugyō, 浦賀奉行. Under the *Tokugawa*, the official who supervised the port of *Uraga*. He had also judiciary powers over *Sagami* province. He was at first stationed at *Shimoda* (*Izu*), but, in 1721, was transferred to *Uraga*.

Uraga-kaikyō, 浦賀海峽. Strait that separates *Sagami* from *Awa*, and gives access to *Tōkyō* bay.

Urakami, 浦上. Ancient *daimyō* family descended from *Ki no Kosami*.

—— **Norimune,** 則宗. Was vassal of the *Akamatsu*. During the *Ōnin* civil war (1468), he sided with *Yamana Sōzen* and was defeated by the *Hosokawa*. He then went to *Kyōto* where his lord *Akamatsu Masanori*, who was at the head of the *Samurai-dokoro*, made him *Shoshidai*. *Masanori* died in 1494 and was succeeded by his son *Masamura*, who was then only a child, and *Norimune* was administrator of his domains.

—— **Muramune,** 村宗 (+1524). Grandson of *Norimune*. At the time of the ruin of the *Akamatsu*, he received the provinces of *Harima* and *Mimasaka*. *Masamura* vainly tried to regain possession of his domains ; he was defeated (1505) and later on, put to death by *Muramune* (1522). Some former *kerai* of the *Akamatsu* attempted to revolt, but were subjugated by *Ukita Yoshiie* (1523). The same year, *Hosokawa Takakuni* asked help from *Muramune*, who then besieged *Hosokawa Harumoto* in the castle of *Takamatsu*. He took the castle and gave it to *Takakuni*. The following year, *Harumoto* returned with a large army and defeated *Takakuni* at *Imamiya* (*Settsu*), and *Muramune* was killed in the battle.

—— **Munekage,** 宗景. Son of *Muramune*, was dispossessed by his vassal *Ukita Naoie* towards 1550, and the family disappears from history.

Uramatsu, 裏松. *Kuge* family descended from *Fujiwara Toshimitsu*. — Now Viscount.

Urashima Tarō, 浦嶋太郎. Hero of a very popular legend. A fisherman living on the coasts of *Yura* (*Tango*), had gone out fishing (it being the year 478, according to the legend) when a sea tortoise transported him to the sub-marine palaces of the goddess *Oto-hime*, where he was detained for 200, according to others for 350 years. Longing to see his family again, he asked to return to his village. The goddess after having vainly tried to dissuade him from his request, presented him with a casket containing the years of his life that had glided away without his knowledge, but with the strict injunction, never to open it. The imprudent man however could not overcome his curiosity, and scarcely had he raised the lid when he noticed a light smoke issuing from the box. He at once died of old age.

Uratsuji, 裏辻. *Kuge* family descended from *Fujiwara Toshimitsu.* — Now Viscount.

Urawa, 浦和. Chief town (6,900 inh.) of the *Saitama-ken* (*Musashi*).

Urin, 羽林. In China, the name of the superior officers of the Imperial guard.

Urin-ke, 羽林家. Formerly, families which acquired the offices (*chūjō, shōshō*) of *Kon-e-fu* and those of *Nagon, Sangi.* They were thus named because in China the *Kon-e-fu* were called *Urin.* The foremost of these families were: *Ōgimachi, Nakayama, Washio, Sono, Aburanokōji, Matsuki, Anenokōji, Higashizono, Ōmiya, Nishiōji, Niwata, Asukai, Reizei, Rokujō,* etc.

Uriuno, 瓜生野. In *Settsu, Suminoe-mura. Kusunoki Masatsura* there defeated *Yamana Tokiuji* and *Hosokawa Akiuji* (1347).

Uruppu-jima, 得撫嶋. Island (95 Km. in length and 24 Km. in width) of the *Chishima* archipelago (*Kurile*).

Usa, 宇佐. District and city (3,800 inh.) of *Buzen.* Was formerly called *Usa no kuni.* At the time of *Jimmu,* the ruler of the land came to meet the conqueror, made his submission and acted as pilot to his fleet. In the city, may be seen the famous temple *Usa-Hachiman,* dedicated to *Ōjin-tennō* and erected, according to some, in the year 570, and according to others, in 712. It is the temple to which *Wake no Kiyomaro* was sent to consult the god whether *Shōtoku* should abdicate in favor of the bonze *Dōkyō* (768). During the 16th century, *Ōtomo Sōrin,* profiting by the civil wars, burned the temple and seized its domains. His son *Yoshimune* rebuilt it.

Usami Sadayuki, 宇佐美定行. Also called *Yoshikatsu.* Son of *Takatada* and likewise vassal of the *Uesugi,* he supported *Nagao Tamekage,* then *Terutora,* who, accepting his counsels, again brought glory to the *Uesugi* family and became the illustrious *Kenshin.* In 1564, *Nagao Yoshikage* was calumniated to *Kenshin,* who ordered him to be put to death. *Sadayuki* invited *Yoshikage* to go out boating with him and, suddenly threw him overboard. After *Kenshin's* death, *Kagekatsu,* his successor and son of *Yoshikage,* resolved to avenge the death of his father on *Katsuyuki,* the son of *Sadayuki.* The latter then left the *Uesugi* clan and took service in *Hideyoshi's* army.

Usami Sensui, 宇佐美灊水 (1710-1776). Confucianist. Born in *Kazusa,* was a disciple of *Ogiu Sorai,* and entered the service of the *Matsudaira daimyō* of *Matsue* (*Izumo*). Left several works.

Usa-yama, 宇佐山. Hill in *Ōmi,* near the *Shiga* village. A temple was erected on its summit in honor of *Hachiman,* hence the name given to it. In 1570, *Nobunaga* constructed a castle upon this hill, and entrusted it to *Mori Yoshinari*, who was besieged in it by *Asai Naga-masa* and *Asakura Yoshikage*. *Mori Yoshinari* died during the siege.

Ushiku, 牛久. In *Hitachi*. Ancient castle which during the 16th century, belonged to a family bearing that name. Under the *Toku-gawa*, it became the residence of the *daimyō Yura*, and from 1628 to 1868, that of the *Yamaguchi* (10,000 k.).

Ushikubo, 牛窪. Small city (3,600 inh.) of *Mikawa*. Ancient castle, defended by *Makino Narisada*, in the middle of the 16th century. He was a vassal of the *Imagawa*, who surrendered it to the *Tokugawa*. It was abandoned in 1590.

Ushiku-numa, 牛久沼. Lake (24 Km. circ.) in *Hitachi*.

Ushiromi-shoku, 後見職. Under the *Tokugawa*, applied to the tutor of a *Shōgun* during his minority. He was chosen, either by the *Shōgun* before his death, or by the Emperor, and was always selected from the *San-ke* or the *San-kyō*. Thus *Ietsugu's* tutor was *Yoshimune* of *Kii*, who became his successor (1716). *Iemochi*, elected at the age of 12 (1858) was directed by *Tayasu Yoshiyori*, then by *Hitotsubashi Keiki*.

Ushi-zaki, 牛裂. Formerly a penalty inflicted upon great crimi-nals : quartered by 4 oxen.

Ushō, 右相. Chinese name of the *Udaijin*. *Ufu* was also used.

Ushōben, 右少辨. Formerly an official of the *Dajōkwan*, who assisted the *Udaiben* and *Uchūben*. — See *Benkwan*.

Ushōshō, 右少將. Abbreviation of *Ukon-e-shōshō*.

Ushū, 羽州. Chinese name for the ancient province of *Dewa*, which forms the actual provinces of *Uzen* and *Ugo*.

Usui, 碓井. Western district of *Kōzuke*. The group of mountains that separate *Kōzuke* from *Shinano* are called *Usui-ryō*, and the road that joins the two provinces, *Usui-saka*. According to the *Nihon-ki*, it was from the summit of the *Usui* (*Torii-tōge*) that *Yamato-takeru*, at the thought of his wife *Tachibana-hime*, exclaimed " *Azuma wa ya !* " (The *Kojiki* relates the incident as having taken place in *Sagami*, on *Ashigara-yama*, *Usui-zaka*). As the mountains are on the borders of the *Kwantō* and the *Tōsan-dō*, a barrier (*seki*) guarded by soldiers was formerly placed there. During the 16th century, this vicinity was the scene of several battles between the *Takeda* and the *Uesugi*.

Usuki, 臼杵. Town (10,500 inh.) of *Bungo*. Ancient castle built in 1564 by *Ōtomo Sōrin :* it was called *Niūjima-jō*. In 1593, *Hideyoshi* gave it to *Fukuwara Naotaka*, who entrusted it to *Ōta Masayuki*. Under the *Tokugawa* it became the residence of the *Inaba daimyō* (56,000 k.) from 1600 to 1868.

Usuki Kanren, 臼杵鑑連. Vassal of the *Ōtomo* of *Bungo*. He constantly urged *Sōrin* to enlarge his domains. He was made governor of *Chikuzen* and settled in the castle of *Tachibana*, which name he took. After his death the *Ōtomo* declined. — His adopted son was *Tachibana Muneshige* (See that name).

Uta-dokoro, 歌所. — See *Waka-dokoro*.

Utae-tadasu tsukasa, 刑部省. Ancient name of the *Gyōbu-shō*.

Utagaki, 歌 垣 . Ancient dance performed whilst singing, and during which the young men chose the girl they wished to marry.

Utagawa-ryū, 歌 川 流 . Realistic school of painting (*ukiyo-e*), thus called from its founder *Utagawa Toyoharu*. The best known painters are :

Toyoharu (1735-1814)	Toyokuni I (1769-1825)	Kuninao (1793-1854)
		Kuninobu
		Kunifusa
		Kuniie
		Toyokuni II-Toyokuni III (1786-1864)-Toyokuni IV (1823-1880)
		Kuniyoshi (1797-1861)
		Kunishige (1777-1835)
		Kuninaga
		Kunimasa (1773-1810)
		Kunimaru
		Kunimitzu
		Kuniyasu (1802-1836)
	Toyohiro (1765-1829)	Toyonobu
		Toyoyoshi
		Hiromasa
		Hiroshige I - Hiroshige II - Hiroshige III (*Andō*)
		(1797-1858) (1842-1894)
	Toyohisa	
	Toyomaru	

Utoneri, 内 舍 人 . Originally, the body guard of the Emperor was called *toneri*. In 701, 90 *utoneri* were appointed ; this number reduced to 40, was later on raised to 60, then to 100. The most intelligent young men belonging to families of the 5th rank (*go-i*) and upwards were chosen to form this guard.

Utsumi, 内 海 . In *Owari*. *Minamoto Yoshitomo* was put to death in that place by *Osada Tadamune* (1160). There also, *Oda Nobutaka* committed suicide after his defeat — (1583).

Utsumine, 宇 津 峰 . Mountain in *Iwaki*, upon which *Kitabatake Akinobu* when made *Chinjufu-Shōgun*, built a castle (1340) which was called *Utsumine-jō* or *Hoshi-ga-shiro*. He was expelled from it in 1352 by the troops of the *Kira*, *Yūki*, etc. of the Northern dynasty.

Utsunomiya, 宇 都 宮 . Chief town (32,100 inh) of the *Tochigi-ken* and of the province of *Shimotsuke*. Ancient castle built in the Middle Ages, by the *Utsunomiya* family. *Hideyoshi* gave it to *Asano Nagayoshi* (1591), then to *Gamō Hideyuki* (1596). Under the *Tokugawa* it was successively the residence of the *daimyō Okudaira* (1601), *Honda* (1619) *Okudaira* (1622), *Honda* (1681), *Okudaira* (1685), *Abe* (1697), *Toda* (1710), *Matsudaira* (1749), and from 1774 to 1868, that of the *Toda* (70,000 k.).

Utsunomiya, 宇 都 宮 . Ancient *daimyō* family descended from the *Kwampaku Fujiwara Michikane* (955-995). A great-grandson of *Michikane* became bonze under the name of *Sōen* and was placed at the head of the temple of *Futara* (now, *Nikkō*). His son *Munetsuna* built the castle of *Utsunomiya* and took his name from that place.

—— **Kintsuna,** 公 綱 (1302-1356). Son of *Sadatsuna*, was governor of *Bizen*. Sent by *Hōjō Takatoki* to defend the *Rokuhara* (*Kyōto*) in 1332, he joined the Imperial cause after the capture of *Kamakura* and fought under *Nitta Yoshisada.* Seeing his party defeated everywhere, he returned to *Utsunomiya.* He re-entered the field in 1337 and defeated *Ashikaga Yoshiakira, Uesugi Noriaki,* etc. When his lord (*Kitabatake Akiie*) had suffered defeat, he returned to *Utsunomiya,* shaved his head and took the name of *Riren.*

—— **Ujitsuna,** 氏綱 (+1370). Son of *Kintsuna,* continued the war against the *Ashikaga* and defeated *Tadayoshi* and *Momonoi Naoyoshi.* He afterwards surrendered to the *Kwanryō Motouji.*

—— **Toshitsuna,** 等綱 (1437-1477). Son of *Mochitsuna,* sided with *Shigeuji* against the *Uesugi,* but was defeated, obliged to shave his head and was confined to *Shirakawa* (*Mutsu*).

—— **Tadatsuna,** 忠綱. His domains being invaded by *Satake Yoshiaki* and *Iwaki Shigekata, Yūki Masatomo* came to his aid (1499). Instead of being grateful for the favor received, *Tadatsuna* plotted against his benefactor. *Masatomo* therefore returned, deposed him and replaced him by his uncle *Okitsuna.*

—— **Hisatsuna,** 尚綱 (1519-1546). Son of *Okitsuna,* was killed at *Saotome* (*Shimotsuke*) in a war against his neighbor *Nasu.*

—— **Hirotsuna,** 廣綱 (1544-1590). Reinstated in his domains by *Satake Yoshiaki* (1557), he was again defeated by *Nasu Takasuke,* but later on was victorious. He sided with the *Uesugi,* then with the *Hōjō,* and brought troops to *Hideyoshi* at the siege of *Odawara.* Was confirmed in his fief, but died the same year and with him the family disappears from history.

Uwajima, 宇和嶋. Town (13,400 inh.) in *Iyo.* Ancient castle built by *Toda Katsutaka* (1600); passed into the possession of the *Tomita* (1608), then from 1614 to 1868, was the residence of the *Date daimyō* (100,000 k.).

Uzen, 羽前. One of the 13 provinces of the *Tōsan-dō.* Comprises 10 districts. — Chinese name: *Ushū* (with *Ugo*). — At present belongs to the *Yamagata-ken.* — Formerly *Uzen* and *Ugo* formed one province, *Dewa,* which was divided in 1869 into two parts.

Uzumasa, 太秦. Family descended from *Fujiwara Kanetoshi* and attached to the *Kōfuku-ji* temple (*Nara*). — Now Baron.

W

Wada, 和田. In *Izumi, Kuze-mura*. The *Wada* family, from which the *Kusunoki* descended, had its castle in that place during the 14th century.

Wada, 和田. In *Mikawa, Kasumi-mura*. Towards 1560, *Ōkubo Tadatoshi* acting under the command of *Ieyasu*, defeated the troops of *Ikkōshū* in that place. In 1570, *Matsudaira Tadanori* who resided at *Wada* entered into negotiations with *Nobunaga* intending to join him, wherefore he was put to death by *Ieyasu*.

Wada, 和田. In *Ōmi, Aburahi-mura*. The future *Shōgun Yoshiaki*, whilst in that place, heard of the murder of his brother *Yoshiteru* (1565) and asked *Wada Koremasa* to give him shelter. Sometime after, having conferred with *Hosokawa Fujitaka*, he sought refuge in the temple *Shōrin-ji*, in the village of *Tamatsu*.

Wada, 輪田. Or *Ōwada*. Ancient name of the city of *Hyōgo* (*Settsu*).

Wada, 和田. Family descended from *Miura Yoshiaki* and through him, from the *Taira*. It was very powerful in the beginning of the 13th century.

—— Yoshimori, 義盛 (1147-1213). Grandson of *Miura Yoshiaki* and son of *Sugimoto Yoshimune*, he took the name of *Wada* from the village where he lived. He joined *Yorimoto* as soon as the latter revolted against the *Taira*, and after the triumph of the *Minamoto*, received the title of *Bettō* of the *Samurai-dokoro*. With *Yoshitsune*, he undertook the campaign against *Kiso Yoshinaka*, assisted at the battles of *Ichi no tani* (1184), *Dan no ura* (1185), and in the expedition in *Mutsu* against *Fujiwara Yasuhira* (1189). When *Izumi Chikahira* revolted against the *Hōjō* (1213), 2 of the sons of *Yoshimori*, *Yoshinao* and *Yoshishige*, and his nephew *Tanenaga* joined him and were arrested. *Yoshimori*, then in *Shimōsa*, hastened to *Kamakura* and asked pardon for his two sons, which the *Shōgun Sanetomo* granted. Emboldened by this success he made a like request in favor of his nephew, but met with a refusal. Believing this to be due to the influence of *Hōjō Yoshitoki*, he conceived a violent hatred against the latter, and levying troops, prepared to attack him. *Yoshitoki*, forewarned, took refuge in the *Shōgun's* palace which *Yoshimori* ventured to invest, but was repulsed and perished with his two sons.

Wada, 和田. Ancient *daimyō* family of *Izumi*, related to the *Kusunoki*.

—— **Masauji,** 正氏 (+1336). Junior brother of *Kusunoki Masashige*, and with him fought for the Southern dynasty and died at *Minatogawa*.

—— **Sukehide** or **Kenshū,** 賢秀. Son of *Masauji*, companion in arms of *Kusunoki Masatsura*, his cousin.

—— **Masatomo,** 正朝 (1352). Brother of *Sukehide*, distinguished himself by his wars against the *Kō, Moronao* and *Morofuyu*.

—— **Masatake,** 正武. Supported the cause of *Go-Murakami* and fought against the *Shōgun Yoshiakira* (1360) and *Sasaki Hideaki*, whom he defeated and killed. When *Kusunoki Masanori* joined the Northern dynasty (1369), he fought against him, remaining faithful to the Southern dynasty.

—— **Masatada,** 正忠. He with *Kusunoki Masanori* and *Hosokawa Akiuji*, became master

WADA MASATOMO.

of *Kyōto* (1352), and reinstalled *Go-Murakami*, but soon after, *Ashikaga Yoshiakira*, returned with a large body of men whom he levied in *Ōmi*, and attacked him on the *Otoko-yama*. *Masatada* died during the battle. He was then only 17 years old.

Wada Koremasa, 和田惟政 (1536-1583). Vassal of the *Sasaki* of *Ōmi*, he fixed his residence at *Wada*, and there gave shelter to the future *Shōgun Yoshiaki*, after the murder of his brother *Yoshiteru* (1565). After the ruin of the *Sasaki*, he offered his services to *Nobunaga*, who entrusted the *Akutagawa* castle (*Settsu*) to him (1568). The following year he defeated *Miyoshi Yoshitsugu* and was made governor of *Kyōto*. When the *Shōgun* resolved to rid himself of the yoke of *Nobunaga*, *Koremasa* fortified his castle of *Akutagawa*. Attacked by *Nakagawa Kiyohide*, he was defeated and put to death.

Wada no misaki, 和田岬. Cape in *Settsu*, S. of *Kōbe*.

Wada-yama, 和田山. In *Ōmi, Kita-gokashō-mura*. Ancient castle of *Rokkaku Takayori*. Taken by *Nobunaga* in 1568.

Wadō, 和銅. *Nengō*: 708-714. — The first pieces of copper-money were struck during this era. (*Wadō-kaichin*).

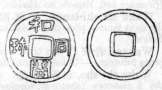

WADŌ-KAICHIN.

Wagaku-jo, 和學所. School of Japanese literature, established in 1793 by *Hanawa Hokiichi*. It was at first called *Wagaku-kōdan-sho,* and placed under the supervision of the *Hayashi*. In 1805, new buildings were erected, the name of the school was changed to that of *Wagaku-jo* and the direction given to the *Hanawa* family.

Wakabayashi, 若林. In *Kawachi, Ega-mura*. In 1547, scene of a battle between *Miyoshi Norinaga* and *Hatakeyama Takamasa*.

Waka-dokoro, 和歌所. Department created in 951 in the Imperial Palace and entrusted with all that pertained to poetry. *Fujiwara Koretada* was its first *Bettō*. By it the poetical works of *Kōsen-waka-shū, Shin-kokin-shū,* etc. were compiled and published.

Waka-doshiyori, 若年寄. Under the *Tokugawa,* members of the Council of the *Shōgun,* below the *Rōjū*. Their functions were to supervise officials and the *hatamoto*. In 1633, the *Shōgun Iemitsu* created the following 6 : *Matsudaira Nobutsuna, Miura Masatsugu, Abe Tadaoki, Ōta Sukemune, Hotta Masamori* and *Abe Shigetsugu*. This number was always retained.

Wakae, 若江. In *Kawachi*. Ancient castle built in the 15th century by the *Yuza* family, which, as vassal of the *Hatakeyama* governed the province in their stead. Towards 1550, *Miyoshi Yoshinaga, Shitsuji* of the *Shōgun Yoshiteru,* took up his residence at that place, but he was killed by *Matsunaga Hisahide* and replaced by *Miyoshi Yoshitsugu* (1561), who, in his turn was expelled by *Nobunaga*. The *Shōgun Yoshiaki* was confined there for some time after his deposition (1573). In 1615, during the siege of *Ōsaka,* a battle took place at *Wakae* between *Kimura Shigenari, Hideyori's* general, and *Ii Naotaka,* the first being defeated and killed.

Wakamatsu, 若松. Town (29,200 inh.) of the *Iwashiro* province, chief-town of the *Aizu* district. Ancient castle which was called *Kurokawa* (See that word). *Gamō Ujisato* who was *daimyō* of that place in 1590, changed its name to *Wakamatsu*. At the death of *Ujisato* (1596), it passed to the *Uesugi*. Under the *Tokugawa,* it belonged to the *daimyō Gamō* (1601), *Katō* (1627), then from 1644 to 1868, to *Matsudaira* (*Hoshina*) (280,000 k.). The *Wakamatsu* clan, at the time of the Restoration remained faithful to the *Shōgun,* and the capture of the castle (Nov. 6, 1868) closed the civil war in *Hondo*.

Wakamatsu-jima, 若松嶋. Island (75 Km. circ.) of the *Gotō* group (*Hizen*). Also called *Nishi-jima*.

Waka ni-sei, 和歌二聖. The two ancient poets, *Kakinomoto no Hitomaro* and *Yamabe no Akahito,* now considered as gods of poetry.

Waka no shi-tennō, 和歌四天王. 4 bonzes considered to be the most famous poets of the *Ashikaga* period : *Kinkō, Ton-a, Jōben* and *Keiun*.

Wakasa, 若狭. One of the 7 provinces of the *Hokuroku-dō*. Comprises 3 districts. — Chinese name : *Jakushū*. — Depends on the *Fukui-ken*.

Waka shi-sho, 和歌四書. 4 famous poetical works regarded as the 4 classics : *Yamato-monogatari, Sumiyoshi-monogatari, Taketori-monogatari* and *Utsubo-monogatari*.

Wakayama, 和歌山. Chief-town (68,000 inh.) of the department of the same name and of the *Kii* province. — In 1585, *Hideyoshi* after having checked the bonzes of the *Negoro-dera*, gave this province to his brother *Hidenaga*. The latter built a castle at *Wakayama* and entrusted it to *Kuwayama Shigeharu*. In 1600, *Ieyasu* placed *Asano Yukinaga* there. Then in 1619, *Wakayama* became the domain of *Yorinobu*, 8th son of *Ieyasu*. The descendants of *Yorinobu*, formed one of the 3 principal branches (*San-ke*) of the *Tokugawa* family (555,000 k.). — The present castle, one of the best preserved in Japan, dates only from 1850.

Wakayama-ken, 和歌山縣. Department formed by 9 districts in the *Kii* province. — Pop.: 722,000 inh. — Chief cities: *Wakayama* (68,000 inh.). — Pr. towns: *Shingū* (14,000 inh.), *Yuasa* (10,500 inh.).

Wakaza, 若櫻. In *Inaba*. Under the *Tokugawa*, residence of a branch (20,000 k.) of the *Ikeda* of *Tottori*.

Wake, 別. Formerly a title synonymous with that of governor or master. It was generally applied to princes of the Imperial family. The Emperor *Keikō* gave it to more than 70 princes. Thus we find the *Chinu-wake* (*Izumi*), *Kadono-wake* (*Yamashiro*), *Mikawaho-wake* (*Mikawa*), etc.

Wake, 和氣. Ancient family which played a prominent part during the 8th and the 9th centuries.

—— **Kiyomaro,** 清麿 (733-799). Born in *Bizen*, in 797 was made *Inaba no suke*. At that time, the bonze *Dōkyō*, who enjoyed the entire confidence of the empress *Shōtoku*, and who had already received the title of *Dajō-daijin-zenshi*, aspired even to the throne, and, supported by *Nakatomi Asomaro*, spread the rumor that the god *Hachiman* had chosen him for that exalted position. The empress, despite her predilection for her favorite, did not dare to consent to such a usurpation and deputed *Kiyomaro* to the famous *Usa* temple (*Buzen*) to consult *Hachiman*. Before leaving, *Kiyomaro* was called by *Dōkyō*, who promised to invest him with the dignity of *Dajō-daijin* if he returned with a favorable answer, and threatened him with the most horrible tortures, if he were to baffle his hopes. *Hachiman's* answer was that the Imperial dignity was never to leave the progeny of the gods. *Kiyomaro* faithfully transmitted the message, and *Dōkyō* in his fury, ridiculed him by changing his name to that of *Wakebe Kegaremaro*, and cutting the sinews of his legs exiled him to *Ōsumi* (769). But *Fujiwara Momokawa* moved by such great fidelity, offered him a part of his domains in *Bingo*. Soon after, the empress died and the first act of her successor *Kōnin*, was to recall *Kiyomaro* and to banish *Dōkyō* to *Shimotsuke*.

WAKE KIYOMARO.

Kiyomaro lived 30 years longer and was loaded with favors and honors. In 1854, the emperor *Kōmei*, raised him to the 1st rank (*Zō-shō-ichi-i*) and bestowed upon him the title of *Go-ō-dai-myōjin*, his rank and title being confirmed March 18, 1898. *Kiyomaro* is honored at the *Takao-zan*, near *Hachiōji* (*Musashi*).

—— **Hiromushi,** 廣蟲 (730-799). Eldest sister of *Kiyomaro*. Married to *Katsurai Konushi*, she, later on, became one of the ladies in waiting upon the Empress *Kōken*, who was greatly attached to her. When *Kōken* abdicated and shaved her head (758), *Hiromushi* did the same and took the name of *Hōkin*. At the time of the revolt of *Fujiwara Nakamaro* (764), several hundreds of *Fujiwara's* adherents were being massacred together with their leader. *Hōkin*, on hearing this, hastened to the battle field and by her intercession saved the life of all who remained. Some time after, wars, famine, and epidemics having made many orphans, *Hōkin* gathered some 83 whom she adopted. They were called *Katsuragi-obito*. When her brother *Kiyomaro* was exiled, *Hōkin* left her place of retreat, resumed her first name and was banished to *Bingo* (769). She returned to Court with her brother and shared the honors bestowed on him.

—— **Hiroyo,** 廣世. Son of *Kiyomaro*, studied medicine and is the ancestor of the *Wake* who distinguished themselves in this science. He was *Ten-yaku no kami* and *Daigaku-bettō*, endowed the University and transformed his own house into a school, called the *Kōbun-in*, in which he established a rich library.

Wakebe, 分部. *Daimyō* family, descended from *Fujiwara Tokinobu*.

—— **Mitsuyoshi,** 光嘉. In 1592 received from *Hideyoshi*, a revenue of 10,000 k. in *Ise*. — His descendants resided from 1619 to 1868 at *Ōmizo* (*Ōmi* — 20,000 k.). — Now Viscount.

Waki-iratsuko, 稚郎子. — See *Uji no Waki-iratsuko*.

Wakíya, 脇屋. Branch of the *Nitta* family, which, in the 14th century, distinguished itself by its fidelity to the Southern dynasty.

WAKIYA YOSHISUKE.

—— **Yoshisuke,** 義助 (+1340). Brother of *Nitta Yoshisada*, fought by his side. In 1336, he helped to drive *Takauji* from *Kyōto* and *Go-Daigo* returned and made him *Musha-dokoro* and governor of *Suruga*. The following year, defeated by *Takauji* at *Yamazaki*, he fled to the *Hiei-zan*, then returned to *Kyōto*. He afterwards accompanied *Yoshisada* to the castle of *Somayama*, and later to *Kana-ga-saki*. After the death of his brother he fled to *Mino*, then to *Owari* and finally went to the *Yoshino*, thus living near the emperor *Go-Murakami*. In 1340, he was sent to *Iyo*, which he nearly conquered, but he fell sick and died soon after.

—— **Yoshiharu,** 義治. Son of *Yoshisuke*.
He was taught the use of arms under his father's direction. At the age of 13, he assisted at the battle of *Takenoshita* (*Suruga*) where his father was defeated by *Takauji* (1337). He fought in *Echizen* against *Shiba Takatsune* and after the death of *Yoshisuke*, fixed his abode in *Shimotsuke*. In 1345, he joined *Kojima Takanori* to be able to take the field again, but he was defeated and fled to *Shinano*. With the help of his cousins *Yoshioki* and *Yoshimune*, he took *Kamakura*, but was soon after, expelled from that place by *Takauji* (1352). He then

WAKIYA YOSHIHARU.

retired to *Echigo*. Being again defeated in 1368, he retired to *Dewa*, and is from that time lost to history.

Wakizaka, 脇坂. *Daimyō* family, descended from the *Fujiwara*.

—— **Yasuharu,** 安治 (1554-1626). Served *Akechi Mitsuhide*, then *Hideyoshi*. In 1585, he received the island of *Awaji* in fief and established himself in the castle of *Sumoto* (30,000 k.). During the Korean expedition, he commanded a part of the Japanese fleet. In 1600, he placed himself under the command of *Kobayakawa Hideaki*, whom he followed when the latter in the midst of the batttle of *Sekigahara* passed to the side of *Ieyasu*. He contributed to the defeat of *Ishida Kazushige*, and then stormed the castle of *Sawayama*. In 1609, he was transferred to *Ōsu* (*Iyo* — 50,000 k.), and in 1617, to *Iida* (*Shinano*).

—— **Yasumoto,** 安元 (1581-1654). Son of *Yasuharu*. He took part in the siege of *Ōsaka* (1615), replacing his father, who refused to go under the plea that he had been a *kerai* of *Hideyoshi*. He inherited the fief of *Iida*. — In 1672, the family was transferred to *Tatsuno* (*Harima* — 55,000 k.), where it resided till the Restoration. — Now Viscount.

Wani, 王仁. Learned man from *Kudara* (Korea), who came to Japan in 285 and was the preceptor of prince *Uji no Waki-iratsuko*. He brought 10 volumes of the *Rongo* and the *Senji-mon* with him. — History relying upon Korean documents, places *Wani's* arrival in the year 405, which would indicate a difference of 120 years in the dates furnished by Japanese history for this period. It is difficult however to admit that *Wani* brought the *Senji-mon* to Japan in 285, or even in 405, it being composed only about the year 525. — To *Wani* is attributed the construction of the first storehouse (*uchi-kura*) used for preserving the presents sent from Korea and this during the reign of *Richū* (400-405), which would suppose him to have lived for at least 150 years.

Warabi, 蕨. In *Musashi*. *Shibukawa Yoshikane* having been made *Kwantō-tandai* by the *Shōgun Yoshinori*, built a castle there (1457) which was inhabited by his descendants during several generations. They were dispossessed towards 1525, by the *Hōjō* of *Odawara*. — Under the *Tokugawa*, *Warabi* was one of the relay stations (*eki*) of the *Nakasendō*.

Warai-botoke, 笑佛. — See *Fu-Daishi*.

Warifu, 割符. In former times, a small piece of wood on which a seal was impressed. It was then divided into two parts, one being kept by the officials and the other, used as a passport by the person entrusted with a mission. The *warifu* had to be shown at every barrier (*seki*) and to the provincial administration.

Waseda, 早稲田. District of *Tōkyō* (ward of *Ushigome*), in which Count *Ōkuma*, chief of the progressive party, built a school (*Waseda-Semmon-gakkō*), which became very flourishing and, in 1902, obtained the title of Free University (*Shiritsu Daigakkō*).

Washi no saki, 鷲岬. Cape in *Tango*.

Washio, 鷲尾. *Kuge* family, descended from *Fujiwara Ienari*. — Now Count. — A junior branch has received the title of Baron.

Washizu, 鷲津. In *Owari*, *Ōtaka-machi*. In 1558, *Nobunaga* erected a castle there. *Imagawa Yoshimoto* took it in 1560, and entrusted it to *Tokugawa Ieyasu*.

Washū, 和州. Chinese name of the *Yamato* province.

Watanabe, 渡邊. *Daimyō* family, descended from the *Saga-Genji*. Made noble in 1661, it resided at *Hakata* (*Izumi* — 13,000 k.), till the Restoration. — Now Viscount.

Watanabe, 渡邊. *Samurai* family of the *Ōmura* clan (*Hizen*), made noble after the Restoration. — Now Viscount. — A lateral branch has the title of Baron.

Watanabe, 渡邊. *Samurai* family of the *Suwa* clan (*Shinano*), made noble after the Restoration. — Now Viscount.

Watanabe Kwazan, 渡邊華山 (1793-1841). Also called *Noboru*. Born on the domains of the *Miyake daimyō* of *Tawara* (*Mikawa*), he studied sciences as taught in Europe and wrote several books in which whilst insisting on coast defence, he supported the policy of opening the country to foreign commerce. The *Bakufu* took offence at these opinions and in 1839, *Kwazan* was arrested together with his friend and fellow labourer *Takano Chōei*. Condemned to death, his penalty was commuted to imprisonment, which he suffered in his own province. From his prison he passed some letters to his friends, for which the *Bakufu* censured the *Miyake daimyō*. *Kwazan* hearing this, and wishing to avoid all annoyance to his lord, committed suicide.

Watarase-gawa, 渡瀬川. River (118 Km.) which rises at Mt. *Kōshin-zan* (*Shimotsuke*), passes through *Ashio*, enters *Kōzuke*, then reenters *Shimotsuke*, receives the *Kiriu-gawa*, and passes through *Koga* (*Shimōsa*) joining the *Tone-gawa*.

Watari-gawa, 渡川. River (80 Km.) rising in *Tosa*, irrigates that province and enters the Pacific Ocean.

Watari-shima, 渡嶋. Ancient name of the island of *Ezo* and also of *Sado*.

Watazumi, 渡海. Sea god (*Shintō*). *Hiko-hohodemi no mikoto*, son of *Ninigi no mikoto*, returned to his residence, — believed by some to be the *Ryūkyū* archipelago, — and married his daughter *Toyotama-hime*, who became the mother of *Ugaya-fuki-aezu no mikoto*, the father of *Jimmu-tennō*.

Y

Yabu, 藪. *Kuge* family, descended from *Fujiwara Kosemaro.* — Now Viscount.

Yabuhara, 藪原. In *Shinano, Kiso-mura.* *Takeda Shingen* built a castle there in 1555.

Yabusame, 流鏑馬. Sport during the time of the *Kamakura Shōgun.* The competitors on horse back, galloped at full speed, and in

YABUSAME.

the act of leaping shot arrows (*kabura-ya*) at 3 or 5 targets along the line.

Yaeyama-jima, 八重山嶋. Southern group of the *Ryūkyū* archipelago, comprising 9 islands, the principal of which are: *Ishigaki-jima,* (143 Km. circ.), *Iri-omote-jima* (114 Km.), *Yonakuni-jima* (32 Km.).

Yagimoto, 柳本. Or *Yanagimoto.* In *Yamato.* From 1615 to 1868, residence of a branch of the *Oda* family (10,000 k.).

Yagiu, 柳生. In *Yamato.* From 1636 to 1868, residence of the *Yagiu daimyō* (10,000 k.).

Yagiu, 柳生. *Daimyō* family, descended from *Sugawara Michizane.* Made noble by the *Shōgun Iemitsu* in 1636, it resided at *Yagiu* (*Yamato* — 10,000 k.) till the Restoration.

Yaguchi no watari, 矢口渡. Formerly a place, near the actual village of *Yaguchi* (*Musashi*), where the *Rokugō-gawa* could be forded. It is the spot, where *Ashikaga Motouji* drowned *Nitta Yoshioki* in 1358. A temple has been erected in honor of the latter (*Nitta-myōjin*).

Yahagi - gawa, 矢作川. River (92 Km.) which rises near the borders of *Mino* and *Shinano*, passes *Mikawa* and enters the *Owari* gulf. Also called *Washizuka-gawa*. — On its shores, in 1335, *Nitta Yoshisada* defeated *Ashikaga Tadayoshi*.

Yahiro-dono, 八尋殿. (Lit.: Palace of 8 fathoms). Name given to the palace built by *Izanagi* and *Izanami* at *Onokoro-jima*.

Ya-iro no kabane, 八色姓. The 8 *kabane* created by *Temmu-tennō* in 685. — See *Kabane, Hassei*.

Yaizu, 燒津. In *Suruga*. According to legend, *Yamatotakeru no mikoto* there escaped from the fire which surrounded him and which had been kindled by the *Ebisu*. He is said to have succeeded in this by mowing down the grass with his sword. — See *Ame-no-mura-kumo no tsurugi*.

Yakami, 八上. In *Tamba*. Towards 1525, *Hatano Tanemichi* built a castle there, and revolting against his lord *Hosokawa Takakuni*, made himself governor of the province. *Akechi Mitsuhide* took the castle of *Yakami* and the possessions of the *Hatano*. He fixed his residence at *Kameyama*. In 1582, *Hideyoshi* replaced him by *Maeda Gen-i*. From 1608 to 1615, was the residence of the *Matsudaira daimyō* (*Matsui*), and then was abandoned.

Yake-yama, 燒山. Mountain (2,400 m.) on the borders of *Shinano* and *Echigo*.

Yaku-daka, 役高. Under the *Tokugawa*, the revenues were proportionate to the offices held: this was called *yaku-daka* (1723).

Yakushiji, 藥師寺. Village in *Shimotsuke*, thus called because of an old temple dedicated to *Yakushi-Nyorai*. In 770, the intriguing bonze *Dōkyō*, banished from Court, was made *Bettō* of that temple.

Yakushi-Nyorai, 藥師如來. One of the 5 gods of wisdom (Buddh.). — See *Go-chi-Nyorai*.

Yakushin, 益信 (827-906). Famous bonze of the *Shingon* sect. Was chief of the temple *Ninna-ji*. Received the posthumous title of *Hongaku-Daishi*.

Yamabe no Akahito, 山邊赤人. Famous poet of the 8th century. He was protected by the emperor *Shōmu*. Many of his poems are cited by the *Man-yō-shū*. He is known as one of the gods of poetry.

Yamabushi, 山伏. Or *Shugenja*. Follower of the *Shugendō* sect.

Yamada, 山田. Town (28,000 inh.) of the *Ise* province, famous for its *Shintō* temples, *Naikū, Gekū*, etc., the most ancient and venerated temples of Japan. The real name of the city is *Uji-Yamada*. The *Tokugawa* placed a *Bugyō* in it to supervise pilgrims and shrines.

Yamada, 山田. *Samurai* family of the *Yamaguchi* clan (*Suwō*), made noble after the Restoration. — Now Count.

—— **Akiyoshi, 顯義** (1844-1892). Born at *Hagi* (*Nagato*), took an active part in the wars of the Restoration. Brigadier General in 1871, he studied the military organisation of foreign countries. He afterwards helped to repress the *Saga* rebellion (1874) and the *Satsuma* insurrection (1877). He was made General of a division, became *Sangi* and Minister of Public Works (1879), of the Interior (1880), of Justice (1883). In this latter position he had a leading part in compiling the Code of Justice now in force. In 1884, he was made Count.

Yamada Nagamasa, 山 田 長 政 (1578-1633). Famous adventurer of the 17th century. Born in *Suruga*, he pretended to be the grandson of *Nobunaga*. In 1615, he secretly sailed from *Ōsaka* in a vessel bound for Formosa. After having sojourned for some time in that island, he sailed for Siam, and took up his abode in the capital where his

SHIP OF YAMADA NAGAMASA.

business prospered in a short time. During a revolt, *Yamada* gave the king good advice, wherefore he was given command of the troops and succeeded in restoring order. The king then chose him as his minister and gave him his daughter in marriage. *Nagamasa* made good use of his position, encouraged commerce and thus caused many Japanese to settle in Siam. The king becoming old, confided the whole administration to him, but during a revolt brought about by the jealousy of a minister, *Nagamasa* was poisoned. His daughter, *A-in* sought to avenge the death of her father, but was defeated and killed.

Yamaga, 山家. In *Tamba*. From 1600 to 1868, residence of the *Tani daimyō* (10,000 k.).

Yamaga Sokō, 山鹿素行 (1622-1685). *Samurai* of the *Aizu* clan, also called *Takasuke, Enzan*. Was a disciple of *Hayashi Razan* and of *Hōjō Ujinaga*. In 1652, the *daimyō* of *Akō* (*Harima*), *Asano Naganao*, invited him to instruct the young *samurai* of his clan. In 1660, he returned to *Edo*, where his lectures on the art of warfare attracted many hearers. At the age of 40 he burned all the books he had written thus far and under the title "*Seikyō-yōroku*," published a résumé of his philosophy, in which he strongly attacked the doctrines of *Shushi* highly esteemed at that time. This displeased the *Bakufu* and *Sokō* was imprisoned at *Akō* (1666). Pardoned after 10 years of confinement, he returned to *Edo*. He is the founder of a military school which retained his name (*Yamaga-ryū*). He is also supposed to have codified the rules of the *Bushidō*, which he commented upon in his books. *Ōishi Yoshio*, the chief of the 47 *rōnin*, was his disciple at *Akō*.

Yamagata, 山形. Chief-town (35,500 inh.) of the department of that name and of *Uzen* province. Its name formerly was *Mogami*. In 1335, *Ashikaga Takauji* gave the *Dewa* province to one of his relatives *Shiba Kaneyori*, whose descendants took the name of *Mogami* and remained in that place till they were dispossessed in 1622. *Yamagata* was afterwards the residence of the *daimyō Torii* (1622), *Hoshina* (1636), *Matsudaira* (1644), *Okudaira* (1648), *Hotta* (1685), *Matsudaira* (1686), *Okudaira* (1692), *Hotta* (1700), *Ōgyū* (1745), *Akimoto* (1767), and from 1845 to 1868, that of *Mizuno* (50,000 k.).

Yamagata, 山縣. *Samurai* family of the *Yamaguchi* clan (*Suwō*), made noble after the Restoration.

—— **Aritomo,** 有朋. Born in 1838, he took a leading part in the Restoration. Was successively Minister of Justice, President of the Privy-Council, Commander of the 1st army during the Chinese war (1894), Minister of War (1895), etc. — Now Marquis.

Yamagata Daini, 山縣大貳 (1725-1767). *Samurai* of *Kai*. He zealously advocated the cause of the Imperial Restoration. He came to *Edo* in 1756, and joined *Fujii Umon, Takenouchi Shikibu*, etc., who were defending the same cause. The *Bakufu* took offence at the theories they were spreading broadcast by word and pen. They were arrested, *Daini* and *Umon* being condemned to death.

Yamagata-ken, 山形縣. Department formed by the *Uzen* province and a district of *Ugo*. — Pop.: 899,000. — Chief city: *Yamagata* (35,500 inh.). — Pr. towns: *Yonezawa* (30,600 inh.), *Tsurugaoka* (20,500 inh.), *Shinjō* (11,600 inh.), etc.

Yamagata Masakage, 山縣昌景 (+ 1575). Vassal of *Takeda Shingen* and castellan of *Ejiri* (*Suruga*). At the time of the *Nagakute* campaign, he remonstrated with his lord, but seeing the futility of his efforts, killed himself.

Yamaguchi, 山口. Chief-town (17,500 inh.) of the department of the same name and of *Suwō* province. Towards 1350, *Ōuchi Hiroyo*, made governor of the province, built a castle there, which for 2 centuries was inhabited by his descendants, and from where they governed as many as 7 provinces. In addition to their titles they added that of *Dazai-Shōni*. The city of *Yamaguchi* became very flourishing and a great number of *daimyō* to get rid of the incessant annoyances to which they were exposed in *Kyōto*, sought the hospitality of the *Ōuchi*, bringing with them a love of the pleasures to which they were accustomed at Court. These new diversions gradually replaced the sports in use among the warriors and hastened the ruin of the powerful *daimyō*. In 1551, Saint Francis Xavier remained in that city for two months, and established a Christian community which gave the brightest hopes. But soon after his departure for *Funai* (*Bungo*), *Sue Harukata* rebelled against his lord *Yoshitaka* and perished with his whole family. He was replaced by *Yoshinaga*, brother of *Ōtomo Sōrin*, who was dispossessed by *Mōri Motonari* in 1557. From that time the castle of *Yamaguchi* belonged to the *Mōri*, who however occupied it only during a short period, from 1863 to the Restoration.

Yamaguchi, 山口. *Daimyō* family, descended from *Mochimori*, 2nd son of *Ōuchi Yoshihiro*. From 1601 to 1868, resided at *Ushiku* (*Hitachi* — 10,000 k.). — Now Viscount.

Yamaguchi, 山口. *Samurai* family of the *Yamaguchi* clan (*Suwō*), made noble after the Restoration. — Now Baron.

Yamaguchi-ken, 山口縣. Department formed by the provinces of *Suwō* and *Nagato*. — Pop.: 1,033,000 inh. — Chief city: *Yamaguchi* (17,500 inh.) — Pr. towns: *Shimonoseki* (41,500 inh.), *Hagi* (16,000 inh.), *Tokuyama* (12,500 inh.), *Mitajiri* (11,700 inh.), *Kamuro-nishigata* (10,500 inh.) etc.

Yamaguchi no Atae Ōkuchi, 山口直大口. Famous sculptor of the 7th century.

Yama-hōshi, 山法師. In the Middle Ages, a name given to the bonzes of *Hiei-zan*, to distinguish them from those of the *Onjō-ji*, called *Tera-hōshi*.

Yamakami, 山上. In *Ōmi*. From 1685 to 1868, residence of the *Inagaki daimyō* (13,000 k.).

Yamamoto, 山本. In *Ōmi*. Ancient castle of the *Asai daimyō*, who resided in that place from 1516 to 1573. It then passed to the *Abe*, and was abandoned in 1582.

Yamamoto, 山本. *Kuge* family, descended from *Fujiwara* (*Sanjō*) *Kinnori* (1103-1160). — Now Viscount.

Yamamoto, 山本. Family of *Satsuma*, made noble in 1902 in the person of *Gombei*, then Vice-Admiral and Minister of the Navy. — Now Baron.

Yamamoto Hokuzan, 山本北山 (1752-1812). Famous Confucianist of *Edo*.

Yamamoto Yoshitsune, 山本義經. Descendant of *Minamoto Yoshimitsu*. He was exiled by the *Taira* to *Sado* (1176). Pardoned after 3 years, he fought under the banner of *Yoritomo*, intrenched himself in the temple *Onjō-ji* (*Ōmi*), but was defeated and fled to *Kamakura*.

He then joined *Yoshinaka* and entered *Kyōto* with him (1181). His teeth protruded very much (*soppa*), hence to distinguish him from *Minamoto Yoshitsune*, whose name had a similar pronunciation, he was called *Soppa no Yoshitsune*.

Yamana, 山名. Ancient *daimyō* family, descended from *Minamoto Yoshishige* (+ 1202) (*Seiwa-Genji*).

—— **Yoshinori**, 義範. Son of *Yoshishige*. He was the first to take the name of *Yamana*.

—— **Tokiuji**, 時氏 (+ 1372). Descendant of *Yoshinori* in the 8th generation. He sided with *Ashikaga Takauji*, assisted at the battle of *Takenoshita* (*Suruga*) and in the campaign in *Kyūshū* (1336). In 1340, he put *Enya Takasada* to death in *Izumo*, and was made *Bettō* of the *Samurai-dokoro* and governor of *Inaba* and *Hōki* at the same time. Sent by *Takauji* to rescue *Hosokawa Akiuji*, defeated by *Kusunoki Masatsura*, he was completely defeated at *Uriuno* (*Settsu*) and received 7 wounds in the battle (1347). Later he sided with the Southern dynasty (1352) and fought against the *Ashikaga*. In 1362, he conquered the provinces of *Mimasaka*, *Bizen*, *Bitchū*, *Inaba*, and *Tamba*. He renewed his allegiance to the Northern dynasty and the *Shōgun Yoshiakira* allowed him to retain these 5 provinces in fief. He then shaved his head and took the name of *Dōjō*. He left 11 sons.

Tokiuji			
Moroyoshi	Ujiyuki-	-Hiroyuki	-Noriyuki
	Mitsuyuki		
	Tokiyoshi	-Tokihiro	-Mochitoyo (*See next table*)
Yoshimasa -	Yoshikiyo	-Norikiyo	-Masakiyo
Ujifuyu			
Ujikiyo -	- Mitsuuji		
Tokiyoshi			
Yoshinori			
Yoshitsugu			
Ujishige-	- Ujiie	- -Hirotaka	
Takayoshi			
Yoshiharu			
Ujiyori			

—— **Moroyoshi**, 師義 (+ 1376). Eldest son of *Tokiuji*. At the age of 14 he took part in the campaigns of his father. The *Shōgun Takauji* promised him the *Wakasa* province, but he died before investing him officially. After the victory of *Otoko-yama* he renewed his petition to the *Shōgun Yoshiakira* but met with a refusal. Exasperated, he returned to *Hōki* and induced his father to join the Southern dynasty (1352). The following year, he defeated *Yoshiakira* at *Kyōto*, but was in turn defeated in 1355. After having conquered *Mimasaka*, *Bizen*, etc., he returned to the party of *Ashikaga* and became *Bettō* of the *Samurai-dokoro*. He then shaved his head and took the name of *Dōkō*.

—— **Yoshimasa**, 義理. Brother of *Moroyoshi*, he occupied *Izumi* and *Kii* in the name of the *Ashikaga*. Then having quarrelled with the *Shōgun Yoshimitsu*, he ventured to attack him, but was defeated in a battle where his brother *Ujikiyo* was slain. He submitted to the victors and was condemned to shave his head. He took the name of *Sōkō* and retired to *Kōkoku-ji*.

—— **Ujikiyo, 氏清** (1345-1392). 4th son of *Tokiuji*, was governor of *Tamba*, then of *Izumi*. He opposed the *Ashikaga*, but was defeated and killed by *Isshiki Akinori*.

—— **Ujiyuki, 氏幸**. Son of *Moroyoshi*, revolted in 1390 against the *Shōgun Yoshimitsu* but was defeated, made his submission and 2 years later, at the partition of the domains of his family, he received the *Hōki* province.

—— **Mitsuyuki, 満幸** (+ 1395). Brother of the above, he in 1384 was made governor of *Izumo* and *Tamba*. He, together with *Ujikiyo*, was ordered to repress the rebellion of his brother *Ujiyuki* and his nephew *Tokihiro* (1390). Some time after *Ujiyuki* resigned his possession to him and thus he governed the provinces of *Hōki* and *Oki* in addition to his own. At that time the *Yamana* family possessed 11 provinces, i.e. $\frac{1}{6}$ of the whole country, for which reason the people had called them *Roku bun no ichi dono* (the lords of one sixth). The *Shōgun Yoshimitsu* became jealous of such power, and resolved to crush it. *Mitsuyuki* furnished a pretext when he dared to appropriate some domains in *Izumo* that belonged to the ex-emperor. *Yoshimitsu* at once recalled his exiled Minister *Hosokawa Yoriyuki* and with him prepared an expedition against the *Yamana*. *Mitsuyuki* did not wait to be attacked and with his father-in-law, *Ujikiyo*, came to invest *Kyōto*. *Yoshimitsu*, aided by *Isshiki Akinori*, of *Hatakeyama Motokuni*, etc. defeated them. *Ujikiyo* was killed and *Mitsuyuki* escaped to *Kyūshū*. Their large estates were divided and the family was allowed to retain the two provinces of *Tajima* and *Hōki*, (1392). Three years later, *Mitsuyuki* was assassinated.

—— **Tokihiro, 時熈** (+ 1435). Son of *Tokiyoshi*, in 1392, received *Tajima*. The following year he rebelled, was despoiled of his domains and ordered to shave his head.

—— **Mochitoyo, 持豊 (Sōzen)** (1404-1473). Son of *Tokihiro*, inherited the domains of the family in 1435, which at that time consisted of the *Tajima*, *Inaba*, and *Hōki* provinces. In 1441, he assisted at the siege of *Shirahata* castle, which completed the ruin of the *Akamatsu*, and he in reward received the *Harima* province. He then shaved his head and took the name of *Sōzen*, by which name he is especially known. Having offended the *Shōgun Yoshimasa*, he retired to *Tajima* and sent his son *Noritoyo* to replace him at *Kyōto* (1454). The following year, *Akamatsu Norinao* entered the province of *Harima*, but *Sōzen* marched against him, defeated and put him to death. Continuing his march, he went to *Kyōto*. At the time of the division of the *Hosokawa* clan, *Sōzen* sided with *Yoshinari*. He likewise supported the rights of *Yoshihisa*, son of the *Shōgun*, against *Yoshimi*. His rival *Hosokawa Katsumoto* supported *Yoshimi*, and all the great *daimyō* were divided into two factions. A civil war, known as the *Ōnin* war (1467), broke out. It continued for 10 years, and before its end, *Sōzen* 宗全 died, two months before his rival

Katsumoto. The result of the war was then yet undecided, so much so that it was impossible to surmise the ultimate victor.

```
                              ┌ Toshitoyo
                    ┌Masatoyo ┤ Naritoyo-Toyosada-Toyokuni ┌Toyomasa
          ┌Noritoyo ┤         └ Akitoyo -Suketoyo          └Toyoyoshi
          │         └Toyoyasu
          │ Koretoyo - Yoritada
Mochitoyo ┤ Katsutoyo
          │ Tokitoyo
          │ Toyohisa
          │ Daughter (married to Hosokawa Katsumoto)
          └ Daughter (married to Shiba Yoshikado)
```

—— **Koretoyo,** 是豐. Son of *Sōzen,* defeated *Hosokawa Yoshi-nari* at *Kintaiji (Kawachi)* (1462). During the *Ōnin* war, he left his father and fought on the side of his brother-in-law, *Hosokawa Katsumoto.*

—— **Masatoyo,** 政豐. Son of *Noritoyo,* took part in the campaign of the *Shōgun Yoshihisa* in *Ōmi* against *Sasaki Takayori* (1487).

—— **Toyokuni,** 豐國 (1548-1626). Great-grandson of *Masatoyo,* was governor of *Inaba* and resided at the castle of *Tottori.* He refused to acknowledge the authority of *Hideyoshi* for a long time, but at last, had to yield (1580). The conqueror allotted to him two districts of the province as his domain, but *Toyokuni* divided them among his servants and preferred to wander about till his death. — During the shōgunate of the *Tokugawa* his descendants remained at *Muraoka (Inaba)* and after the Restoration received the title of Baron.

Yamanaka, 山中. In *Sagami.* — See *Ogino.*

Yamanaka-jō, 山中城. In *Izu, Nishikida-mura.* Ancient castle belonging to the *Hōjō* of *Odawara.* Besieged in 1580 by *Nakamura Kazuuji, Tanaka Yoshimasa,* etc. it was captured, and *Matsuda Yasunaga* who defended it killed himself.

Yamanaka-jō, 山中城. In *Mikawa.* Ancient castle built in 1526, by *Matsudaira Kiyoyasu,* who entrusted it to his vassal *Shigehiro.* The *Ikkō-shū* troops took this castle about the year 1560 and from it were able to resist *Ieyasu,* but *Ishikawa Ienari* defeated them and reoccupied the castle.

Yamanaka-ko, 山中湖. Lake (13 Km. circ.) in *Kai,* which is drained by the *Katsura-gawa* river. Also called *Gayyū-ko.* It is one of the 8 lakes that surround Mt. *Fuji.*

Yamanaka Tensui, 山中天水 (1758-1790). Man of letters and philosopher.

Yamanashi-ken, 山梨縣. Department formed by the *Kai* province. — Pop.: 538,000 inh. — Chief-town: *Kōfu* (37,600 inh.).

Yamane, 山根. *Samurai* family of the *Yamaguchi* clan (*Suwō*), made noble after the Restoration. — Now Baron.

Yamanoi, 山井. *Kuge* family, descended from *Fujiwara Ujinari.*— Now Viscount.

Yamanouchi, 山內. Hamlet of *Kosaka* village (*Sagami*). In 1349, when *Uesugi Noriaki* was named *Shitsuji* to the *Kwanryō* of

Kamakura, he fixed his residence in that place and his family received
the name of *Yamanouchi no Uesugi.*

Yamanouchi, 山內. *Daimyō* family, descended
from *Fujiwara Hidesato.*

—— **Toshimichi,** 俊通. Descended from *Hidesato*
in the 10th generation, was the first to take the name
of *Yamanouchi.*

—— **Moritoyo,** 盛豐. In the 16th century governed the castles of *Iwakura* and *Kuroda,* in *Owari.*

—— **Kazutoyo,** 一豐 (1546-1605). Son of *Moritoyo.* At the age
of 13 he entered the service of *Nobunaga. Hideyoshi* in 1582, gave him
the fief of *Takahama* (*Wakasa*), then in 1585, that of *Nagahama* (*Ōmi*)
and the title of *Tsushima no kami.* Transferred, in 1590, to *Kakegawa*
(*Tōtōmi* — 50,000 k.), he later on sided with *Ieyasu,* who in 1600,
bestowed upon him the whole province of *Tosa.* (242,000 k.) with a residence at *Kōchi.* — His descendants remained there till the Restoration.

—— **Yōdō,** 容堂 (1827-1872). His real name was *Toyonobu,* 豐
信. He took a leading part in the Imperial Restoration. He was the
first, who on the advice of *Gotō Shōjirō,* wrote to the *Shōgun* asking him
to remit the government of the country to the Emperor. Later he was
councillor, senator, etc. — Now Marquis. — Two junior branches of the
family have received the title of Viscount and one of Baron.

Yamanouchi-kwanryō, 山內管領. Under the *Ashikaga,* the
Shōgun resided at *Kyōto* and the *Kwantō-kwanryō* at *Kamakura* ; but
both had a first minister who represented them and who was called
Shitsuji. Later the *Shōgun* was called *Kubō,* and the *Shitsuji* became *Kwanryō* ; likewise at *Kamakura* the *Kwanryō* was called *Kubō,*
and the *Shitsuji, Kwanryō.* As the latter was generally chosen from the
Yamanouchi branch of the *Uesugi,* the *Shitsuji* was known by the name
of *Yamanouchi-kwanryō.*

Yamanoue Okura, 山上憶良 (660-733). Ambassador to China
(701), then governor of *Hōki* (725), and *Chikuzen* (725) ; is known as a
man of letters and a poet.

Yamao, 山尾. *Samurai* family of the *Yamaguchi* clan (*Suwō*), made
noble after the Restoration. — Now Viscount.

Yamaoka, 山岡. *Samurai* family of the *Shizuoka* clan (*Suruga*),
made noble after the Restoration. — Now Viscount.

Yamashina, 山階. Family of princes of the royal blood, descended
from the *Fushimi* branch. The present chief is prince *Kikumaro* (born
in 1873). He married (1902) the daughter of Duke *Shimazu Tadayoshi.*
The prince is an officer of the navy.

Yamashina, 山科. *Kuge* family, descended from *Fujiwara Ienari.*
— Now Count.

Yamashina no Miya, 山科宮. Name by which prince *Saneyasu-
shinnō* (+872), son of *Nimmyō-tennō* and brother of the emperors *Montoku* and *Kōkō,* is known. He is also called *Kitano-shinnō, Yamashina
no Miko.*

Yamashiro, 山城. One of the 5 provinces of *Kinai*. Chief-town: *Kyōto*. Comprises 8 districts which depend upon the *Kyōto-fu*. — Chinese name: *Jōshu*. Formerly the name *Yamashiro* was written 山背 (*yama-ushiro*, behind the mountains), on account of its stuation in reference to *Nara* the capital. When *Kwammu* came to establish his residence at that place, he changed the characters to 山城 (castle of the mountain).

Yamata no orochi, 八頭大蛇. Fabulous monster, having the form of a serpent wtih 8 heads and 8 tails, is said to have ravaged the *Izumo* district when *Susano-ō* went to that place. Having heard of its desire for *sake* (wine made from rice), the hero was able to intoxicate and kill it during its torpor. It was in its tail that he found the sword *Murakumo no tsurugi*. — Some commentators believe the monster to have been a swift river having 8 mouths; others a notorious chief of robbers.

Yamato, 大和. One of the 5 provinces of *Kinai*. Chief-town: *Nara*. Comprises 10 districts, which form the *Nara-ken*. — Chinese name: *Washū*. — Formerly the name of the province was written 大倭; in 737, the characters were changed to 大和. Till the end of the 8th century, the capital was generally in that province. When it was transferred to *Kyōto* (794), *Nara* became *Nanto* (capital of the South). During the schism of the 14th century, the mountains of *Yamato* served as a place of refuge for the legitimate dynasty, i.e. that of the South. Under the *Ashikaga*, *Yamato* became the fief of the *Hatakeyama* family. The *Tokugawa* divided it into 7 districts: *Kōriyama, Takatori, Koizumi, Shibamura, Yagimoto, Yagiu* and *Kushira*.

Yamato, 邪馬臺. — See *Yame*.

Yamato-gawa, 大和川. River (52 Km.) which rises in *Yamato*, and in its upper course bears the name *Hatsuse-gawa*. It separates the 2 provinces of *Kawachi* and *Izumi* and enters the Ocean near *Sakai*. — Formerly it was a tributary of the *Yodo-gawa* N. E. of *Ōsaka*; towards the end of the 17th century a direct way to the Ocean was opened to it.

Yamato-mai, 大和舞. Ancient dance performed for the first time before the emperor *Ōjin* by the villagers of *Kuzu* (*Yamato*). It was afterwards introduced into certain ceremonies: *Daijō-e, Chinkon-sai*, etc.

Yamato no mikotomochi, 日本府. Formerly head-quarters of the Japanese envoy in Korea, at the epoch of the *San-kan*. Its chief had the title of *Ikusa no kimi*.

Yamato-ryū, 倭流. School of painting established in the 11th century by *Fujiwara Motomitsu*, and much favored at Court. From it came the *Tosa* school.

Yamatotakeru no mikoto, 日本武尊 (81-113). 3rd son of the emperor *Keikō*. Also called *Ousu* and *Yamato-ogena*. At the age of 16, he was ordered to repress the rebellion of the *Kumaso* in *Kyūshū*. Disguised as a lady, he was introduced to the chief and killed him. This secured the submission of the rebels. Having returned to the capital after peace had been

YAMATOTAKERU.

restored to *Izumo*, he left it again to fight the *Ebisu* of the East. Following the *Tōkaidō*, he went as far as *Mutsu*, and after having subdued the barbarians, he returned by way of *Kōzuke*, *Shinano*, *Kai*, *Mino* and *Ōmi*. He was attacked on Mount *Ibuki* by a malignant fever and died at *Nobono* (*Ise*), being only 33 years old. *Yamatotakeru* is the most famous hero of legendary times.

Yamazaki, 山崎. Village S. of *Yamashiro*, where *Akechi Mitsushide*, the murderer of *Nobunaga*, was defeated by *Hideyoshi* (1582).

Yamazaki, 山崎. In *Harima*. Was the residence of the *daimyō Okabe* (1602), *Ikeda* (1615), then from 1639 to 1868, that of *Honda* (10,000 k.).

Yamazaki Ansai, 山崎闇齋 (1618-1682). Born at *Kyōto*, he was placed in the temple *Myōshin-ji* and destined to become a bonze. From there he went to the *Kyūkō-ji* (*Tosa*), where he received lessons from *Tani Jichū* and *Nonaka Kenzan*, and studied Japanese antiquities, at the same time devoting himself to Chinese sciences. He went to *Edo*, opened a school for young *samurai* and was protected by *Masayuki*, *daimyō* of *Aizu* and son of the *Shōgun Hidetada*. At the death of the latter (1672), he returned to *Kyōto* where he died. He established a new sect, the *Suiga-Shintō*, and left very many works in which he applies the doctrines of the Chinese philosophers of the *Sō* dynasty to Shintoism (960-1279).

Yamazawa, 山澤. *Samurai* family of the *Kagoshima* clan (*Satsuma*), made noble after the Restoration. — Now Baron.

Yame, 八女. Or *Yametsu-kuni*. — Formerly a country in the North of *Kyūshū*, which nearly became independent and accepted the suzerainty of China. Its governors, descendants of *Watatsumi*, resided at the port of *Na-no-tsu* (at present *Hakata*) and had regular commercial transactions with Korea and the continent. One of them received a golden seal with the title of king from the Emperor *Kōmu* 光武. The Chinese represent the name of *Yametsu* with the characters 邪馬臺 *Yamato* ; this *Yamato* refers only to *Yame* and not to all Japan. The same region was also called the district of *Ito*, 怡土. The Chinese wrote it 倭奴 (*Ito*), and gave the governor the title of king of the country of *Ito* (倭奴國王). The queen *Pimiho*, mentioned in the Chinese and Korean annals, was at the head of that district. *Kami-tsuma-gōri* and *Shimo-tsuma-gōri*, joined in 1896, under the name of *Yame-gōri*.

Yametsu-hime, 八女津媛. She is a descendant of *Watatsumi* and ruled the country of *Yame*, north of *Kyūshū*, from 190 to 247. The Chinese and Korean annals give her the name *Pimiho* 卑彌呼 which is a corruption of *Hime-ko* 媛子. She conquered the savage tribes of southern *Tsukushi* and received from the Chinese Emperor *Ming-ti* (明帝, *Mei-tei*) a golden seal with the title of king of the country of *Wo* 倭 (238). At her death, over 100 of her servants buried themselves alive around her tomb. Her successor was her daughter *Iyo-hime*, who succeeded her at the age of 13.

Yanagase, 柳瀬. In *Ōmi*, *Kataoka-mura*. *Nobunaga* there defeated *Asakura Yoshikage* (1572). In 1583, *Shibata Katsuie* was defeated by *Hideyoshi* at the same place and from there fled to his castle of *Kita no shō (Echizen)*. The *Tokugawa* erected a barrier *(seki)* there for inspecting travellers.

Yanagawa, 柳川. Town (7,500 inh.) of *Chikugo*. Ancient castle built by *Kamachi Shigenari* in 1560, and which passed into the hands of the *Ryūzōji* and the *Nabeshima*. *Hideyoshi* gave it to *Tachibana Muneshige* (1587). Under the *Tokugawa*, was the residence of the *daimyō Tanaka* (1600), then from 1620 to 1868, that of *Tachibana* (119,000 k.).

Yanagiwara, 柳原. *Kuge* family, descended from *Fujiwara Kanemitsu*. — Now Count.

Yanagizawa, 柳澤. *Daimyō* family, descended from *Takeda Nobuyoshi (Seiwa-Genji)*.

—— **Yoshiyasu,** 吉保 (1658-1714). Son of a simple *samurai* who had a revenue of 150 k., was the protégé of the *Shōgun Tsunayoshi* who gave him the titles of *Dewa no kami, Mino no kami, Rōjū*, then the fiefs of *Sanuki (Kazusa* — 22,000 k.) (1690), *Kawagoe (Musashi* — 82,000 k.) (1694). When *Tsunayoshi* adopted his nephew *Tsunatoyo*, the latter left his fief of *Kōfu*, which was given to *Yoshiyasu* (150,000 k) (1704).

Yoshiyasu {
Yoshisato - Nobutoki - Yasumitsu - Yasuhiro   (a)
Tsunetaka - Satozumi - Satoakira - Yasutaka   (b)
Tokichika - Yasutsune - Nobuaki - Satoyuki   (c)
}

(a) — Senior branch, descended from *Yoshisato (1687-1745)*, which in 1724, was transferred to *Kōriyama (Yamato* — 150,000 k.), where it resided till the Restoration, — Now Count.

(b) — Junior Branch which from 1723 to 1868, resided at *Kurokawa (Echigo* — 10,000 k.). — Now Viscount.

(c) — Junior Branch which from 1723 to 1868 resided at *Mikkaichi (Echigo* — 10,000 k.). — Now Viscount.

Yanagizawa Kien, 柳澤淇園 (1576-1758). An erudite man of the *Kōriyama* clan *(Yamato)*, who distinguished himself in all sciences of his time.

Yao, 八尾. Small city (7,000 inh.) of *Kawachi*. Ancient castle which in 1337 was besieged by the Southern army. In 1348, *Hosokawa Akiuji* came to attack *Kusunoki Masatsura*, who feigning to retreat to his castle, inflicted a bloody defeat on his adversary in the forest of *Handa*. The Southern army in its turn was defeated there by *Hatakeyama Dōyo* (1360). During the siege of *Ōsaka* (1615), *Chōsokabe Morichika* there defeated *Tōdō Takatora*.

Yari-bugyō, 鎗奉行. Under the *Tokugawa*, an official who furnished the *Shōgun's* army with spears. He was chief of a body of 1,000 men at *Hachiōji (Musashi)*. This office was a sinecure for 250 years.

Yari-ga-take, 鎗嶽. Mountain (3.000 m.) on the borders of *Hida, Shinano* and *Etchū*.

Yasaka-Hōkwanji, 八坂法観寺. Formerly one of the principal Buddhist temples of *Kyōto*, constructed, it is said, by *Shōtoku-Taishi*. At the present time there remains only a pagoda, 5 stories high.

Yasaka-jinja, 八坂神社. — See *Gion no yashiro.*

Yasakani no magatama, 八尺瓊曲玉. Sacred jewel made by *Tama-no-oya no mikoto,* when *Amaterasu* had hidden herself in the cave *Ama no iwato.* Given to *Ninigi no mikoto,* when he descended from heaven to rule Japan, it remained one of the 3 treasures or emblems which the emperors transmitted to their progeny.

Yashiki-aratame, 屋敷改. Title created in 1670 and given to 3 officials charged to survey the property of the *daimyō* at *Edo,* etc.

Yashima, 屋嶋. In *Sanuki, Katamoto-mura.* In 1184, *Taira Munemori* went there with the emperor *Antoku,* but besieged by *Minamoto Yoshitsune,* he escaped to *Nagato.*

Ya-shima, 屋嶋. Island (16 Km. circ.) S. of the *Suwo* province, to which it belongs.

Ya-shima, 屋嶋. Another name for *Noto-jima* island (*Noto*).

Yashiro, 社. Shintoist temple. — See *Miya.*

Yashiro, 屋代. *Daimyō* family, descended from *Murakami Tamekuni* (*Murakami-Genji*).

—— **Yorikuni,** 頼國. Settled at *Yashiro* (*Shinano*) whose name he took.

—— **Hidemasa,** 秀正 (+ 1623). In 1600 received the fief of *Hōjō* (*Awa* — 10,000 k.).

—— **Tadamasa,** 忠正 (1594-1662). Was dispossessed in 1632 and banished to *Takata* (*Echigo*) for not having kept stricter watch on the *Suruga-Dainagon Tadanaga,* whom he kept prisoner. Pardoned after 6 years, he regained his former domains.

—— **Tadanori,** 忠位. Was definitively dispossessed in 1712, because of bad administration.

Yashiro Hirokata, 屋代弘賢 (1758-1841). Also called *Rinchi.* Man of letters from *Edo* in attendance upon the *Bakufu.*

Yashū, 野州. Chinese name of *Shimotsuke* province.

Yashū ryō-tō, 野州兩黨. In the Middle Ages, the two principal clans of *Shimotsuke, Ki* and *Kiyowara.*

Yaso-tomo-no-o, 八十伴緒. In ancient times, generic name applied to an assemblage of officials. *Hyaku-kwan* is at present used. — See *Tomobe.*

Yasuba, 安塲. *Samurai* family of *Kumamoto* (*Higo*), made noble after the Restoration. — Now Baron.

Yasui Shunkai, 安井春海 (1639-1715). Astronomer who reformed the calendar (*Semmei-reki*) in use at that time, and in 1684, replaced it by the more exact *Teikyō-reki.* (See *Koyomi*). — *Shunkai* at first bore the family name of *Shibukawa,* by which he is sometimes known.

Yasui Shokken, 安井息軒 (1799-1876). Born at *Obi* (*Hyūga*), he studied at the *Shōhei-kō,* and became a distinguished professor. Left several books.

Yasunaga-shinnō, 懷良親王 (1326-1383). Son of the emperor *Go-Daigo.* He was taken to *Kyūshū* by *Kikuchi Takeshige,* a defender of the Southern dynasty (1338), who succeeded in governing nearly all *Kyūshū.* With the help of *Takemitsu,* son of *Takeshige,* he gained several victories over the troops of the North. He is also called *Chinzei no Miya, Higo no Miya*.

Yatabe, 谷田部. In *Hitachi*. From 1616 to 1868, residence of the *Hosokawa daimyō* (16,000 k.).

Yata no kagami, 八咫鏡. Sacred mirror that was made by *Ishikoridome no mikoto*, when *Amaterasu* was hidden in the cave *Ama no iwato*. It was given to *Ninigi no mikoto* when he left heaven to rule Japan, and it remained one of the 3 treasures or emblems of the Imperial dynasty. It was at first preserved in the Imperial Palace, but the emperor *Sujin*, fearing some profanation, entrusted it to his daughter *Toyo-suki-iri-hime*, who became the high-priestess of the temple erected for its preservation at *Kasanui* (*Yamato*) (92 B.C.). Under the reign of *Suinin*, *Yamato-hime* succeeded *Toyo-suki-iri*; the temple was taken to *Ise* (5 B.C.) and is the famous *Daijin-gū* temple. A reproduction of the mirror, made as exact as possible, was kept at the Palace in the *Kashi-ko-dokoro*, but during the reign of *Murakami-tennō* (947-967), it was often damaged, although not destroyed by fire. — Its diameter is about 25 cm., and the mirror is said to have the form of a flower with 8 petals.

Yata no karasu, 八咫烏. The raven sent by *Amaterasu* to guide *Jimmu-tennō* in his expedition to *Yamato*. — Some authors believe this to be a surname given to *Taketsunumi no mikoto* by *Jimmu* for having been his guide; others see in it a metaphor signifying the compass used by the conqueror (*yata* indicating the 8 directions marked on the instrument).

Yatsu-ga-take, 八ヶ嶽. Group of Mountains on the borders of *Kai* and *Shinano*. The principal peaks are: *Amigasa-dake* (2530 m.), *Gongen-dake* (2740 m.), *Nishi-dake* (2420 m.) and *Aka-dake* (2930 m.).

Yatsuhashi Kengyō, 八橋檢校. Artist of the 17th century, considered the creator of modern Japanese music. He greatly improved the *koto* (sort of harp with 13 cords), an instrument for which he composed many pieces. Died at the age of 71.

Yatsu-mimi no Ōji, 八耳王子 (Lit.: prince having eight ears). Surname given to *Shōtoku-taishi*, because, it is said, he could listen to 8 persons at one time and give each an appropriate answer.

Yatsuomo, 八面. In *Ōmi, Kumaku-mura*. In 1564, *Ieyasu* there defeated *Arakawa Yorimochi*, who had joined the *Ikkō-shū* troops.

Yatsushiro, 八代. Town (10,500 inh.) of *Higo*. Prince *Yasunaga-shinnō* resided there during the civil wars of the 14th century. Belonged to the *Sagara* family, then to the *Shimazu*. In 1588, was a part of the domains of *Konishi Yukinaga*. Under the *Tokugawa*, it belonged to the *Kumamoto* fief. The castle was defended by the *Nagaoka*, vassals of the *Hosokawa daimyō*.

Yatsushiro-kai, 八代海. Inland Sea, between the *Higo* province and the *Amakusa* islands.

Yawata, 八幡. In *Mino*. — See *Gujō*.

Yawata-yama, 八幡山. Other name for Mt. *Otoko-yama*, near *Kyōto*. Thus called on account of the *Hachiman* temple erected on its summit.

Yedo, 江戸. — See *Edo*.

Yezo, 蝦夷. — See *Ezo*.

Yodo, 淀, In *Yamashiro*. Ancient castle which, in the beginning of the 16th century, belonged to the *Hosokawa*, then passed to the *Miyoshi*. *Hosokawa Fujitaka* occupied it in 1573. Towards 1590, *Hideyoshi* had it enlarged and his wife, *Asai Nagamasa's* daughter, resided there, hence its name *Yodo-gimi* or *Yodo-dono*. Under the *Tokugawa*, the castle being reconstructed in 1623-1625, was successively the residence of the *daimyō Hisamatsu* (1625), *Nagai* (1634), *Ishikawa* (1669), *Toda* (1711), *Ōgyū* (1717), and from 1723 to 1868, that of *Inaba* (115,000 k.). — In 1868, the *Shōgun's* army sought refuge there after its defeat at *Fushimi*.

Yodo-gawa, 淀川. River (78 Km.) formed by the junction of the *Uji-gawa* and the *Katsura-gawa*. It passes *Ōsaka* and flows into the sea by many outlets.

Yodo-gawa-kwasho-bune, 淀川過書船. Under the *Tokugawa*, boats authorized to sail on the *Yodo-gawa* and carrying mail. Established in 1603, this service was entrusted to the *Suminokura* and *Kimura* families, who likewise inspected boats on the *Ōi-gawa* and the *Takase-gawa*, and levied a tax on every boat.

Yodo-gimi, 淀君 (1569-1615). Daughter of *Asai Nagamasa* and of *Odani no kata*, sister to *Nobunaga*. She was called *Chacha*. Being 4 years old at the death of her father, she as well as her two sisters were taken care of by *Shibata Katsuie*. At the overthrow of the latter, *Hideyoshi* became their protector, and married the eldest one; he gave the second in marriage to *Kyōgoku Takatsugu* and the 3rd to the future *Shōgun Hidetada*. *Chacha* being the wife of *Hideyoshi*, received the castle of *Yodo* (*Yamashiro*); hence her name *Yodo-gimi* or *Yodo-dono*. In the Month of May 1593, she gave birth to *Hideyori*, which fact secured her the *Taikō's* favor. When a widow (1598), she retired with her son to the castle of *Ōsaka*, and bore great hatred to *Ieyasu*, the usurper of *Hideyori's* rights. She prepared to revenge her wrongs, but as she had to deal with a man of great ability, her efforts did not meet with success. She perished at the age of 46, during the great fire of *Ōsaka* which consummated the ruin of the *Toyotomi*.

Yōgaku-jo, 洋學所. School founded at *Edo* in 1855, to teach European sciences. The following year, its name was changed to that of *Bansho-shirabe-dokoro* (See that word). — At first the Dutch language alone was taught, but in 1860, French, English, German and Russian were added to the curriculum.

Yoita, 與板. Small city (5700 inh.) of *Echigo*, formerly called *Ōtsu*. Ancient castle, which, at the end of the 16th century, belonged to the *Naoe Kanetsugu*, vassal of the *Uesugi*. In 1601, was a part of the domains of the *Makino daimyō*, and from 1705 to 1868, was the residence of a branch of the *Ii* family (20,000 k.).

Yōjō-sho, 養生所. Dispensary established at *Edo, Koishikawa*, in 1722, by order of the *Shōgun Yoshimune*, in consequence of a petition of *Ogawa Shōsen*. Was suppressed in 1868. The botanical garden (*Shokubutsu-en*) nas been established on its premises.

Yokohama, 横濱．Chief-town of the *Kanagawa-ken*.—Population 396,700, of whom are 10,000 foreigners. The latter include 8,000 Chinese. Port opened to foreigners in 1859.

YOKOHAMA IN 1851.

Yokoi Shōnan, 横井小楠 (+ 1869). *Samurai* of the *Kumamoto* clan (*Higo*). At the time of the Restoration, was eminent for his liberal views. He was murdered by the opponents of the new regime.

Yokoi Yayū, 横井也有 (+ 1783). *Samurai* of *Owari*. Founded a School for military science and became famous as a poet (*haikai*).

Yokosuka, 横須賀．Port (24,800 inh.) of *Sagami*; seat of a maritime prefecture (*chinjufu*). The Englishman, *Will Adams* lived there from 1600 to 1620. He was a pilot on a Dutch ship which was confiscated by *Ieyasu*. He became ship builder for the *Shōgun* and served as intermediary between the *Bakufu* and the foreign merchants. His tomb is in the village of *Hemi*. — An arsenal was established there in 1866 under the direction of French engineers, at whose head were MM. *Verny* (1866-1876), *Dupont* (1876-1877) and *Thibaudier* (1877-1878). At present it is directed by the Japanese Navy. A French engineer however, M. *Bertin* (1886-1890), made the plans of several Japanese men of war and supervised their construction at *Yokosuka*.

Yokosuka, 横須賀．In *Tōtōmi, Ōsuka-mura*. Ancient castle built in 1578 by *Ieyasu*, who entrusted it to *Ōsuka Yasutaka*. *Hideyoshi* gave it to *Arima Toyouji* (1593). Under the *Tokugawa*, was successively the residence of the *daimyō Ōsuka* (1601), *Matsudaira* (1619), *Inoue* (1623), *Honda* (1645), and from 1682 to 1868, that of *Nishio* (35,000 k.).

Yokota, 横田．In *Shimotsuke, Yokokawa-mura*. In the 13th century, castle of the *daimyō Utsunomiya*.

Yokota-ga-hara, 横田河原．In *Shinano, Sakae-mura*. Scene of several battles; between *Kiso Yoshinaka* and *Jō Nagamochi* (1181), between *Takeda Shingen* and *Uesugi Kenshin* (1553-1561).

Yokota-gawa, 横田川．River (60 Km.) in the *Ōmi* province.

Yokote, 横手．City (12,300 inh.) of *Ugo*. Before the 17th century castle of the *Onodera* family.

Yokote-yama, 横手山. Mountain (2,150 m.) between *Shinano* and *Kōzuke*.

Yokoyama-jō, 横山城. In *Ōmi*, *Kita-gōri-mura*. Ancient castle of the *Asai daimyō*. *Nobunaga* occupied it in 1570.

Yōmei-ha, 陽明派. Under the *Tokugawa*, one of the 4 large schools of Chinese classical literature, established by *Nakae Tōju* (1608-1648), *Kumazawa Ryōkai* (1619-1691), etc. Their principal disciples were: *Nakae Jōsei* (1666-1709), *Nakagawa Giemon* (1763-1830), etc. — See *Tokugawa-jidai no keigaku-ha.*

Yōmei-mon-in, 陽明門院. — See *Tei-shi.*

Yōmei-tennō, 用明天皇. 31st Emperor of Japan (586-587). *Tachibana no Toyohi*, 4th son of *Kimmei*, succeeded his brother *Bidatsu*. In the beginning of 587, he fell sick and on the advice of his son *Shōtoku-taishi*, then 15 years old, he resolved to embrace Buddhism. *Mononobe no Moriya* and *Nakatomi no Katsumi* vainly tried to impress upon him that such an act would be most displeasing to the gods of the country and provoke their anger, *Yōmei* persisted in his intentions. He was the first emperor converted to the doctrines of Buddha. He died soon after, according to some at the age of 41, according to others at 48. — A 3rd opinion is that he lived 69 years, but in that case his father, *Kimmei* of whom he was not the first child, would have been only 10 years old when *Yōmei* was born.

Yome-tori-bugyō, 嫁娶奉行. Title created in 1230 and given to the official charged to negotiate the marriage of the *Shōgun* of *Kamakura*.

Yomotsu-kami, 黄泉神. God of hell (*Shintō*).

Yōmyō, 幼名. Or *Osana-na*. Formerly name given to children till the ceremony of the *gembuku*, when they received the *eboshi-na* or *kammei*. Thus the *yōmyō* of *Minamoto Yoshiie* was *Genda;* his *eboshi-na* was *Hachiman-Tarō;* *Yoshiie* was his *jitsumyō* or *nanori*.

Yonago, 米子. Town (16,100 inh.) of *Hōki*. Ancient castle built by *Kikkawa Hiroie* towards 1580. In 1600, it passed to *Nakamura Kazuuji*, then in 1610 to *Katō Sadayasu*. Since 1617, was a part of the domains of *Ikeda* of *Tottori* (*Inaba*).

Yoneda, 米田. *Samurai* family of the *Kumamoto* clan (*Higo*) made noble after the Restoration. — Now Baron.

Yonekura, 米倉. *Daimyō* family, descended from *Minamoto Yoshimitsu* (*Seiwa-Genji*). Made noble in 1696, it resided at *Kanazawa* till the Restoration (*Musashi* — 12,000 k.). — Now Viscount.

Yoneyama, 米山. In *Echigo*. *Nagao Kagetora* (*Kenshin*) defeated *Nagao Masakage* (1547) there.

Yonezawa, 米澤. Town (30,750 inh.) of *Uzen*, formerly called *Maizuru*. Ancient castle built in 1238 by the *Nagai* family. Passed to the *Endō*, vassals of the *Date*. In 1590, was a part of the domains of *Gamō Ujisato*. Under the *Tokugawa*, from 1601, was a fief of the *Uesugi* (150,000 k.).

Yonezu, 米津. *Daimyō* family, descended from *Minamoto Yorimitsu* (*Seiwa-Genji*). Made noble in 1601, it resided at *Nagatoro* (*Dewa* — 11,000 k.) from 1698 to 1868. — Now Viscount.

Yoriai-gumi, 寄合組. Under the *Tokugawa*, *samurai* without office but having a revenue of 3,000 to 10,000 k. As they guarded the castle of *Edo* or the houses of their *daimyō* during their absence, they were called *Rusui-gumi*.

Yoriai-shū, 寄合衆. Under the *Kamakura Shōgun*, high officials who with the *Shikken* and the *Hyōjō-shū* belonged to the Council of the *Shōgun*.

Yoriki-dōshin, 與力同心. Under the *Tokugawa*, minor officials subject to a *Bugyō*. These offices were hereditary. The *yoriki* were divided into two classes: *Go-fudai-gumi* and *O-kakae-gumi*. The *dōshin* belonged to the *kakae-gumi*.

Yōrō, 養老. *Nengō*: 717-723.

Yōrō no taki, 養老瀧. Waterfall on Mount *Tado-zan*, in the district of *Yōrō* (*Mino*): height, 40 m; width, 2 m. 70. In 717, the empress *Genshō* saw it, gave it this name and changed the name of the era into that of *Yōrō*.

Yōrō-ryōritsu, 養老令律. — See *Taihō-ryō*.

Yoroi-gata, 鎧潟. Lake (8 Km. circ.) in *Echigo*. Also called *Hishi no ko*.

Yosami no ike, 依羅池. Lake dug in the reign of *Sujin* (36 B.C.) in *Settsu*. When a new bed was dug for the *Yamato-gawa* to lead the stream to *Sakai* (*Izumi*), the water of the lake flowed into the new river (1704).

Yoseba-bugyō, 寄場奉行. Title created in 1790 and given to the official having charge of the penitentiary erected on the isle of *Ishikawa-jima*, near the mouth of the *Sumida* river (*Edo*). Besides prisoners, exiles and vagabonds were confined there. They were all dressed in red. After 3 years they were liberated and a small sum of money was given them, to make a new attempt in life. Subject to the *Yoseba-bugyō* were: the *Motojime-yaku* (controller), *Tewaza-gakari* (superintendent of manual labor), *Kagi-ban-yaku* (turnkey), *Kakibai-seisho-gakari* (kiln-officer), *Hatake-gakari* (fieldwork-officer) *Abura-shime-gata* (officer supervising the oil presses), etc.

Yoshida, 吉田. In *Mikawa*, *Toyohashi-machi*. Ancient castle built at the end of the 15th century by *Makino Naritoki*. He fought *Toda Danjō*, who received help from *Imagawa Ujichika* and invested *Yoshida*. *Naritoki* was killed and the castle passed to the possession of the *Imagawa* (1506). *Nobunari*, son of *Naritoki*, retook it, but afterwards was defeated and killed by *Matsudaira Kiyoyasu* (1532) who settled in that place. Given back to the *Imagawa*, it was stormed by *Ieyasu* (1564) who placed *Sakai Tadatsugu* there. *Hideyoshi* gave it to *Ikeda Terumasa* (1590). Under the *Tokugawa*, was successively the residence of the *daimyō Matsudaira* (1601), *Mizuno* (1632), *Ogasawara* (1645), *Kuze* (1697), *Makino* (1705), *Ōkōchi* (1712), *Honjō* (1749) and from 1749 to 1868, that of *Ōkōchi* (*Matsudaira*) (73,000 k.) — At present called *Toyohashi*.

Yoshida, 吉田. In *Iyo*. From 1614 to 1868, residence of a branch of the *Date* family (30,000 k.).

Yoshida, 吉 田 . In *Aki*. *Mōri Tokichika* fixed his residence in that place towards 1335. Two centuries later his descendant *Motonari* became master of the province. Besieged in *Yoshida* by *Amako Haruhisa* (1540), he called on *Ōuchi Yoshitaka* for help, defeated *Haruhisa* and following up his conquests, he gradually gained possession of 10 provinces. His grandson *Terumoto* left *Yoshida* castle and came to *Hiroshima* in 1592.

Yoshida, 吉 田 . Branch of the *Urabe* family, which under the *Ashikaga* exercised great influence in things pertaining to Shintoism, and under the *Tokugawa* obtained the office of Vice-Minister of Cults (*Jingi-kwan*) with the right of inheritance. It gave new vigor to the old religion by establishing the *Yui-itsu-Shintō*. — Now Viscount.

—— **Kenkō,** 兼 好 (1283-1350). Or *Kaneyoshi*. Also called *Urabe Kenkō*. He cultivated literature. At the death of the emperor *Go-Uda*, his protector, he shaved his head and retired to the *Shūgaku-in* (1324). In 1340, accepting an invitation from *Tachibana Naritada*, he fixed his abode at the foot of the *Kunimi-yama* (*Iga*). *Kenkō* is the author of the *Tsurezure-gusa*.

Yoshida, 吉 田 . *Samurai* family of the *Kagoshima* clan (*Satsuma*), made noble after the Restoration. — Now Viscount.

Yoshida-Kōyu, 吉 田 光 由 (1598-1672). Famous mathematician.

Yoshida Shōin, 吉 田 松 陰 (1831-1860). Also called *Torajirō*. *Samurai* of the *Chōshū* clan and a zealous promoter of the Imperial cause and the expulsion of foreigners. In *Edo*, he with *Sakuma Shōzan* studied things foreign and wishing to see Europeans at home, they went to *Nagasaki*, secretly to embark on a Russian ship, but at their arrival found the ship had already left. The following year (1854), when Commodore *Perry's* fleet returned to *Shimoda*, they asked to be taken to America, but were refused. The *Bakufu* hearing of this put them in prison. Once released though confined in his house, *Shōin* continued to oppose the foreigners. When *Manabe Norikatsu* was sent to *Kyōto* to obtain the consent of the Court for the opening to the country to foreign commerce (1859), *Shōin* sought to take his life, but was arrested and put to death.

Yoshii, 吉 井 . In *Kōzuke*. Ancient castle, which in the 16th century belonged to the *Uesugi*, then passed to the *Hōjō* of *Odawara*. Under the *Tokugawa*, residence of the *daimyō Suganuma* (1590), *Hotta* (1682); then from 1709 to 1868, that of the *Yoshii* (*Matsudaira* 10,000 k.).

Yoshii, 吉 井 . *Daimyō* family, descended from *Fujiwara* (*Takatsu-kasa*) *Kanehira* (1228-1294).

—— **Nobuhira,** 信 平 (1564-1657). Son of the *Kwampaku Taka-tsukasa Nobufusa*. He received the name of *Matsudaira* from the *Shōgun Iemitsu* because he had married the daughter of *Tokugawa Yorinobu* (*Kii*), son of *Ieyasu*.

—— **Nobukiyo,** 信 清 . Grandson of *Nobuhira*, who in 1709, settled at *Yoshii* (*Kōzuke* — 10,000 k.), where his descendants remained till the Restoration, at which time, the family took the name of *Yoshii*. — Now Viscount.

Yoshii, 吉井 . *Samurai* family of the *Kagoshima* clan (*Satsuma*), made noble after the Restoration. — Now Count.

Yoshikawa, 吉 川 . *Samurai* family of *Tokushima* (*Awa*), made noble in 1896. — Now Viscount.

Yoshimine, 良 岑 . Ancient family, descended from the emperor *Kwammu.*

—— **Yasuyo,** 安世 (785-830). 14th son of *Kwammu-tennō.* In 802, he received the family name of *Yoshimine.* He loved literature and with others labored at several books edited in his time, such as : *Nihon-kōki* (819), *Dairi-shiki* (821), *Keikoku-shū* (827), etc. The erection of the first waterwheels, or *noria* for the irrigation of rice-fields are attributed to him.

—— **Munesada,** 宗 貞 (816-890). Son of *Yasuyo,* served the emperor *Nimmyō* at whose death (850) he became a bonze, took the name of *Henjō* and placed himself under the guidance of the famous *Ennin* (*Jikaku-Daishi*), whom he succeeded in the dignity of *Sōjō.* Hence the name of *Sōjō Henjō,* by which he is known. A renowned poet, he is ranked among the *Rokkasen.* — He left two sons who also became bonzes.

Yoshimizu Sōjō, 吉 水 僧 正 (1155-1225). Son of the *Kwampaku Fujiwara Tadamichi,* became bonze, took the name of *Jichin,* was *Sōjō* and chief (*zasu*) of the *Tendai* sect. He is known as a man of letters and as a poet.

Yoshinaka no shi-tennō, 義 仲 四 天 王 . The 4 faithful body guards of *Minamoto* (*Kiso*) *Yoshinaka*: *Imai Kanehira, Higuchi Kane-mitsu, Tate Chikatada* and *Nenoi Yukichika.*

Yoshino, 吉 野 , 芳 野 . Mountainous district forming the southern half of the *Yamato* province. *Jimmu-tennō* ascending the *Kumano-gawa,* here fought *Nagasune-hiko.* The emperor *Ōjin* had a villa in that part of the country. Prince *Ō-ama* (*Temmu-tennō*) also retired here when he prepared to attack *Kōbun-tennō* (672). At a very remote time, a Shintoist temple called *Kane-no-mine-jinja* was erected in that village which was affiliated to the *Ryōbu-shintō* and was named *Kongō-zō-ō-gongen* or *Kongōbu-ji.* The bonzes of this temple became very powerful, being protected by the emperors who, frequently came to that place, attracted by the beauty of the landscape. In 1185, *Yoshitsune* pursued by the hatred of his brother *Yoritomo,* sought shelter at *Yoshino.* Prince *Morinaga-shinnō* transformed the temple into a fortress and thus was able to oppose the attacks of *Nikaidō Dōun,* general of the *Hōjō* (1333). Three years later, the emperor *Go-Daigo,* expelled from *Kyōto,* sought refuge in the temple and established his Court at *Yoshino.* He died there and was buried in the N. E. corner of the temple (1338). His son *Go-Murakami* succeeded him, but being attacked by *Kō Moronao* in 1348, he escaped to *Kawachi,* and the temporary palace of the exiled sovereigns was burned. — The scenery around *Yoshino* has been the theme of many poems. — The principal mountain peaks are : *Misen, Saka-ga-take, Ō-mine, Inamura* and *Shichimen-zan.* Their average height is from 1500 to 1800 meters.

Yoshino-gawa, 吉野川. River (161 Km.) which rises in the *Kame-ga-mori-yama* (*Tosa*), passes through *Awa* and enters the Pacific Ocean at *Tokushima*. It is surnamed *Shikoku-Saburō* because it is considered the 3rd largest river of Japan.

Yoshi no hōhei, 由奉幣. Formerly official proclamation made in the principal Shintoist temples on the accession of an emperor At first it was made only in the *Daijingū* of *Ise*, but was extended to the temples of *Kamo* and *Iwashimizu :* it was then called *San-sha-hōhei*.

Yoshitsune no shi-tennō, 義經四天王. The 4 faithful companions in arms of *Minamoto Yoshitsune :* *Kamada Morimasa* and his brother *Mitsumasa*, *Satō Tsuginobu* and his brother *Tadanobu*.

Yoshizaki, 吉崎. In *Echizen*. *Rennyo-Shōnin* built a temple (*Yosizaki-dōjō*) there in 1471, which became the headquarters of the troops of *Ikkō-shū* in the *Hokuroku-dō*.

Yoshū, 豫州. Chinese name of the *Iyo* province.

Yōwa, 養和. *Nengō :* 1181.

Yōzei-tennō, 陽成天皇. 57th Emperor of Japan (877-884). *Sada-akira*, eldest son of *Seiwa-tennō*, succeeded his father at the age of 10. *Fujiwara Mototsune* was regent (*Sesshō*), and when the emperor attained his majority (882), he was the first to receive the title of *Kwampaku*. Soon after, believing that *Yōzei* by his dangerous sports and eccentric habits showed signs of mental weakness, he deposed him and replaced him by his grand uncle *Kōkō*. *Yōzei* was then only 18 years old and lived in retreat to the age of 82.

Yuasa Gentei, 湯淺元禎 (1735-1781). Famous Confucianist of *Okayama* (*Bizen*).

Yuba-dono, 弓塲殿. Formerly a pavilion in the Imperial Palace in which the Emperor assisted at the competition of the *kuge* in such sports as bow-shooting, etc. These exhibitions took place annually on the 5th day of the 10th month. — See *Nori-yumi*.

Yubu-dake, 由布嶽. Volcano (1700 m.) in *Bungo*. Also called *Bungo no Fuji, Tsukushi no Fuji*.

Yuchishi-den, 輸地子田. Formerly rice-fields that were subject to taxes in kind (*chishi*).

Yuge Dōkyō, 弓削道鏡. — See *Dōkyō* (*Yuge* is the ancient name of the *Kawachi* province from which *Dōkyō* came).

Yuge-jima, 弓削嶋. Island (20 Km. circ.) N. of the *Iyo* province.

Yuhazu no mitsugi, 弓弭調. (Lit.: taxes of the bow). In ancient times taxes consisted of meat, skins of deer, boars, and other game. This custom was introduced at the time of the emperor *Sujin* (86 B. C.).

Yui-ga-hama, 由比濱. Sea coast near *Kamakura* (*Sagami*). *Wada Yoshimori* was defeated there when he revolted against the *Hōjō* (1213). There also *Nitta Yoshisada* began his attack upon *Kamakura* (1333).

Yui Shōsetsu, 由井正雪 (+ 1651). Son of a dyer of the village of *Yui* (*Suruga*). He resolved to rise to the rank of a *samurai* and for that reason he came to *Edo*, studied military science, started a school which became very flourishing and which gave him a high reputation. Implicated with *Marubashi Chūya* in a plot against the *Shōgun*, he was arrested and committed suicide.

Yui-itsu-Shintō, 唯一神道. Reform of Shintoism introduced during the 17th century by the *Yoshida* family, vice-minister of the *Jingi-kwan*. Being a reaction against the *Ryōbu-shintō* and pretending to re-establish the pure Shintoism of ancient times, this doctrine is a medley of Buddhism, Confucianism and Chinese philosophy (*In-yō*). The tendency to add a philosophical system to Shintoism, is still more pronounced in the subsequent works of such men as : *Watarai Enka, Yamasaki Ansai, Motoori Norinaga, Hirata Atsutane,* etc.

Yuima-e, 維摩會. In 669, *Nakatomi no Kamatari* being dangerously ill, the Emperor sent for the *ama Hōmyō-ni* to recite the *Yuima-kyō* (buddhist book) over him. This custom was adopted, and the ceremony took place every year at the *Kōfuku-ji*, from the 10th to the 16th of the 10th month, the last date being the anniversary of the death of *Kamatari*. The same ceremony took place at the Imperial Palace.

Yūki, 結城. Town (10,600 inh.) of *Shimōsa* — In 940, *Fujiwara Hidesato* after the defeat of the rebel *Taira Masakado*, received the title of *Chinjufu-Shōgun*. He built a castle at *Oyama* where he fixed his residence, and another at *Yūki*, which he entrusted to one of his relatives. Under the *Kamakura Shōgun*, it belonged to the *Ōyama* family which later on changed its name to that of *Yūki*. — Demolished in 1611, the castle was rebuilt in 1703 by *Mizuno Katsunaga* whose descendants remained there till the Restoration (18,000 k.).

Yūki, 結城. *Daimyō* family, descended from *Fujiwara Hidesato*.

—— **Tomomitsu,** 朝光 (1168-1254). Son of *Oyama Masamitsu* and descendant of *Hidesato* in the 10th generation. He received the fief of *Yūki* (*Shimōsa*) and took the name of the place. His mother had been the nurse of *Yoritomo* and she advised her son to side with him against the *Taira*. He entered upon a campaign against *Fujiwara Yasuhira* in *Mutsu* (1189). When *Kajiwara Kagetoki* revolted, he marched against him and defeated him in *Suruga* (1200). He later on received the title of *Kazusa no suke*.

—— **Tomohiro,** 朝廣. Son of *Tomomitsu*. He had two sons : the elder one, *Hirotsugu*, kept the fief of *Yūki* and transmitted it to his descendants ; the other, *Sukehiro*, settled (1289) at *Shirakawa* (*Mutsu*), where his family resided for several centuries.

—— **Munehiro,** 宗廣. Son of *Sukehiro*, was *Kōzuke no suke*. He shaved his head and took the name of *Dōchū*. Castellan of *Shirakawa* (*Mutsu*), he at first served the *Hōjō* and joined them in the fight against *Go-Daigo* on Mt. *Kasagi* (1331). When the emperor escaped from *Oki* and fled to *Funanoe-sen* (*Hōki*), he called all his faithful servants round. *Munehiro* then abandoned the *Hōjō* party, joined *Nitta Yoshisada* and with him entered *Kamakura* (1333). With prince *Yoshinaga-shinnō* he went to *Mutsu* and fought against *Ashikaga Takauji*. Defeated with *Kitabatake Akiie* at *Nara*, he took refuge at *Yoshino* (1338). Having returned to *Mutsu* he levied another army which he took to *Anotsu* (*Ise*) by sea, but had scarcely landed, when he fell sick and died.

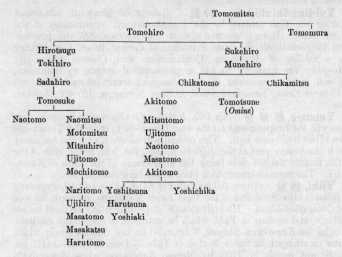

```
                                    Tomomitsu
                                        |
                    Tomohiro                           Tomomura
                        |
        Hirotsugu                          Sukehiro
        Tokihiro                           Munehiro
            |                                  |
        Sadahiro                  Chikatomo          Chikamitsu
            |                         |
        Tomosuke              Akitomo      Tomotsune
                                          (Omine)
    Naotomo   Naomitsu     Mitsutomo
              Motomitsu     Ujitomo
              Mitsuhiro     Naotomo
              Ujitomo      Masatomo
              Mochitomo     Akitomo
                  |            |
              Naritomo  Yoshitsuna     Yoshichika
              Ujihiro   Harutsuna
              Masatomo  Yoshiaki
              Masakatsu
              Harutomo
```

—— **Chikatomo,** 親朝 (+ 1382). Eldest son of *Munehiro*, sided with *Go-Daigo* against the *Hōjō* and then against the *Ashikaga*, but seeing his opponents successful everywhere, he finally submitted to the Northern dynasty (1340).

—— **Chikamitsu,** 親光 (+ 1336). Brother of *Chikatomo*. He sided with *Daibutsu Sadanao* against *Kusunoki Masashige* whom he besieged in his castle of *Akasaka* (*Kawachi*), then defended the *Roku-hara* (*Kyōto*) against the Imperial army (1333). Later he fought the *Ashikaga* and defeated *Takauji* at *Seta*. When *Go-Daigo* fled to the *Hiei-zan*, *Chikamitsu* remained in *Kyōto*, but being attacked by superior forces, he asked to surrender. *Takauji* mistrusting his intentions, sent *Ōtomo Sadanori* to negotiate with him. During the conference *Chikamitsu* attacked *Sadanori* and killed him with one stroke. He then fell under the spears of the soldiers of the *Ashikaga*.

—— **Akitomo,** 顕朝. Son of *Chikatomo*. He served the *Ashikaga* and together with *Hatakeyama Takakuni* fought *Kitabatake Chikafusa*, who was forced to escape to *Yoshino*. In 1350, when *Ashikaga Tadayoshi* joined the Southern dynasty, *Akitomo* intended to follow him, but *Takauji* prevented him by threatening to confiscate all his domains. He then joined him against *Kitabatake Akinobu*. In 1369, he transferred his domains to his son *Mitsutomo*. — His descendants for 2 centuries kept their fief of *Shirakawa*, the last, *Yoshiaki*, being dispossessed by *Hideyoshi* in 1590.

—— **Ujitomo,** 氏朝 (1398-1441). Descendant of the senior Branch, he inherited the fief of *Yūki*. In 1440, he sided with *Haru-ō* and *Yasu-ō*, the two sons of the ex-*kwanryō Ashikaga Mochiuji*. Besieged in his castle of *Koga* by *Uesugi Kiyokata*, he was defeated and killed and his two wards were put to death.

—— **Naritomo,** 成朝 (1439-1462). Was only 2 years old when *Ujitomo* died. Taken to *Hitachi* by a faithful servant, he was received as a guest by *Satake Yoshitoshi*. In 1454, *Ashikaga* gave his domains back to him. He was continually at war with the *Uesugi*.

—— **Masatomo,** 政朝 (1477-1545). Grandson of *Naritomo*. He was obliged to fight the *Utsunomiya* his neighbors, who sought to despoil him of his domains but were defeated. In 1525, he gave his domains to his son *Masakatsu* and shaved his head taking the name of *Kōshō*.

—— **Masakatsu,** 政勝 (1504-1559). Son of *Masatomo*, was continually obliged to wage war against his vassals *Oda, Tagaya*, and others, who attempted to become independent.

—— **Harutomo,** 晴朝 (1534-1614). Son of *Oyama Takatomo*, was adopted by his uncle *Masakatsu* and succeeded him. He continued the war against his neighbors. As he had no children, to retain the favor of *Hideyoshi*, he asked him to chose an heir. *Hideyoshi* selected *Hideyasu*, son of *Ieyasu*, who took the name of *Yūki*, and some time after, *Harutomo* transferred the administration of his domains to him (1590). When *Hideyasu* was transferred to *Echizen*, *Harutomo* accompanied him, retired to *Katakasu* and died there.

—— **Hideyasu,** 秀康．— See *Matsudaira (Echizen)*.— After his transfer to *Echizen*, he gave the name of *Yūki* to his 4th son *Naomoto*, but the family kept the name *Matsudaira*.

Yūki shi-ten, 結城四天． The 4 great vassals of the *Yūki* family : *Tagaya, Mizutani, Yamakawa* and *Iwakami*.

Yukihito-shinnō, 幸仁親王 (1656-1699). 3rd son of the emperor *Go-Sai-in*, was adopted by the princely family of *Takamatsu no Miya*, whose name was changed to that of *Arisugawa no Miya* (1672). He is known as a poet, a man of letters and a painter.

Yumi-ya san-ten, 弓矢三天． The 3 divinities that protected warriors : *Marishi-ten, Benzai-ten* and *Daikoku-ten*.

Yumi-ya-yari-bugyō, 弓矢鎗奉行． Title created in 1637 and given to 2 officials who had charge of the bows, arrows and spears of the *Shōgun's* army. In 1863, these offices were joined to those of the *Gusoku-bugyō* under the title of *Bugu-bugyō*.

Yura, 由良． Ancient family vassal of the *Nitta*. In the 16th century it was established at *Kanayama (Kōzuke)*. Transferred afterwards to *Hitachi* (10,000 k.) it died out in 1621.

Yura-gawa, 由良川． River (106 Km.) which rises in *Tamba*, where it bears the name of *Fukuchi-gawa*, passes through *Tango* and enters the sea of Japan at *Yura*. Also called *Ōkawa, Ōkumo-gawa*.

Yura-kaikyō, 由良海峽． Strait between the island of *Awaji* and the *Kii* peninsula. Also called *Izumi-kaikyō, Kitan-kaikyō*.

Yūrappu-gawa, 勇拉川. River (133 Km.) in *Iburi* (*Hokkaidō*).

Yūrappu-take, 勇拉嶽. Mountain (1230 m.) on the boundary of *Iburi*, and *Shiribeshi* (*Hokkaidō*).

Yuri, 由利. *Samurai* family of the *Fukui* clan (*Echizen*), made noble in 1887. — Now Viscount.

Yūryaku-tennō, 雄畧天皇. 21st Emperor of Japan (457-479). *Ō-hatsuse-wakatake no mikoto*, 5th son of *Inkyō*, succeeded his brother *Ankō*, when 29 years old. *Ankō* had been murdered by *Mayuwa-Ō*. *Yūryaku* before ascending the throne, avenged his death and at the same time put his cousin and rival prince *Ichinobe-oshiba* to death. During his reign, whilst continuing the Korean war, he applied himself to the development of agriculture and commerce, planted mulberry trees, and ordered potters, builders, weavers, etc. to come from Korea. He added a second story to the Imperial Palace : this being the first two story structure seen in Japan (468). *Yūryaku* died at the age of 62. (The *Koji-ki* believes him to have been 124 years old, so that he would have been born 20 years before his father).

Yuso-den, 輸租田. Formerly rice-fields taxed by the Imperial Court. They were of several kinds :

(*a*) — **Kubun-den, 口分田**. Rice-fields distributed in each village according to the number of members in the family, at 2 *tan* (20 ares) per man and 1⅓ *tan* (13 ares 33) per woman.

(*b*) — **I-den, 位田**. Rice-fields allotted to princes and nobles of the 5th rank and above.

(*c*) — **Shi-den, 賜田**. Domains given by special decree of the Emperor.

(*d*) — **Kō-den, 功田**. Rice-fields given as rewards for services rendered to the Empire.

(*e*) — **Kon-den, 墾田**. Concessions of uncultivated land to be tilled.

Yuzawa, 湯澤. Small city (8200 inh.) of the *Ugo* province. Ancient castle of the *Miharu* family, vassal to the *Onodera*. Passed to the *Satake*, and was abandoned in 1620.

Yuzuki-jō, 湯月城. — See *Dōgo*.

Yuzuki no Kimi, 弓月君. Descendant of the Chinese *Shin* dynasty (秦, *Tsin* — 249-206 B.C.) who had become a Korean prince and who in 283, emigrated to Japan with a great number of his countrymen. He is the ancestor of the *Hata* clan whose office it was for a long time, to spread the cultivation of the silkworm.

Yūzū-nembutsu-shū, 融通念佛宗. Buddhist sect established towards the year 1100 by the bonze *Ryōnin* (*Shōō-Daishi*). At present it possesses 350 temples and 200 bonzes, chiefs of *tera*.

Z

Zaimoku-ishi-bugyō, 材木石奉行. Title created in 1647 and given to an official who was entrusted with buying, transporting and using materials (wood, stones, etc.) required for constructions on the *Shōgun's* properties.

Zanshitsu, 殘疾. Formerly infirm persons exempted from taxation. They were the half-blind, persons having their thumb, two fingers or three toes cut off, etc.

Zasu, 座主. Formerly title of the chief bonze of the *Hiei-zan* temple and of all the temples of the *Tendai* sect.

Zatsumu-bugyō, 雜務奉行.—See *Kuni-bugyō*.

Zen-bugyō, 膳奉行. Under the *Tokugawa*, officials charged to provide the *Shōgun's* table with victuals. At first called *Oni-tori-yaku*, this office, at the end of the 17th century, had 8 titularies, which number was afterwards reduced to 4. In 1861, they were joined to the *Konando-shū*.

Zeniya Gohei, 錢屋五兵衞 (1798-1855). Born at *Miyakoshi-ura* (at present *Kanaiwa*) in *Kaga* and a descendant of a family of money-changers, whence his name, *Zeniya*. In his early childhood, he worked for a ship builder, named *Kitani Tōemon*. One day, borrowing 1,000 *ryō* from his master, he speculated but failed, and being insolvent, he was imprisoned. *Tōemon* himself asked for his pardon. During a famine he built many ships, sent them to all the ports of the Empire and by his commercial transactions, procured rice for his country-men and enriched the province. He formed the project of filling up lake *Kahoku-gata* and of transforming it into rice-fields. Having obtained permission from his lord, he set to work, but the expense was too great; moreover the fishermen about the lake, complained and *Gohei* was put in prison where he died.

Zenji, 禪師. At first a name given to the bonzes who distinguished themselves by their learning, became afterwards a title officially given to those who were considered as being the most virtuous.

Zenkō, 禪閣. Title given to a *Kwampaku* who transmitted his office to his son, shaved his head and became a bonze. When he remained in public life after his resignation, he took the title of *Taikō*.

Zenkō-ji, 善光寺. Famous Buddhist temple of the city of *Nagano* (*Shinano*). Established in 670, it at first belonged to the *Tendai* sect, then passed to the *Shingon*. Towards 1630, it returned to the *Tendai-shū* and became a dependency of the great temple *Tōei-zan* of *Ueno* (*Edo*). It is dedicated to *Amida*, *Kwannon* and *Daiseishi*, whose statues according to legend have been miraculously carried there from Korea in the 7th century.—The town of *Nagano* is often called *Zenkōji*, on account of this temple.

Zen-ku-nen no eki, 前 九 年 役. The war brought about by the rebellion of *Abe Yoritoki* and his sons (1056-1064). It lasted 9 years, whence the name by which it is often known. — See *Abe Yoritoki.*

Zenshin-ni, 善信尼. Daughter of the Chinese *Shibatatsu* or *Shiba Dattō,* who emigrated to Japan in 522. At first called *Shima,* she was confided to the bonze *Eben* and in 584 became the first *ama* or *bikuni* (female-bonze). Having collected some companions, she was placed in a house built by *Soga Umako.* Sent to Korea in 588, she returned after two year's absence, bringing statues, Buddhist books, etc. with her. She died at the temple *Sakurai-dera.*

Zen-shū, 禪宗. Buddhist sect, which when first introduced from China in the 7th century had no success in Japan (See *Busshin-shū*). Later on, the bonze *Eisai* after having made two voyages to the Continent, returned to Japan in 1192, built the *Shōfuku-ji* temple at *Hakata* (*Chikuzen*) and began to preach the doctrines of the sect. 10 years later, the *Shōgun Yoriie* having founded the *Kennin-ji* at *Kyōto* chose *Eisai* to be its first superior, and from that time, the sect spread rapidly.—This sect which may be called the "sect of contemplation" is based upon the principle that every one may arrive at the knowledge of the law and nature of Buddha by meditating upon one's self and this without being influenced by other dissenting doctrines on this matter. These various explanations seem to reach the great number of 84,000. The sect was introduced by *Daruma* (520) from China. Two of his disciples were *Enō* and *Jinshū,* the first preached in the North, and the second in the South, hence the two branches. The doctrines brought by *Eisai* conform to the Southern branch which is called *Rinzai-shū.* In 1227, *Dōsen* founded the *Sōdō-shū* and *Ingen,* in 1661, the *Ōbaku-shū :* these are the three branches of the *Zen-shū* sect.

Zeze, 膳所. In *Ōmi.* Castle built in 1601 and successively occupied by the *daimyō Toda* (1601), *Honda* (1617), *Suganuma* (1619), *Ishikawa* (1634) then from 1651 to 1868, by *Honda* (60,000 k.).

Zōchō, 増長. One of the Buddhist gods who keep watch over the 4 cardinal points : he protects the West.

Zōhei-shi, 造兵司. Formerly officials who supervised the manufacture of arms and kept a record of patents filed by gunsmiths. In 896, this office was joined to that of the *Hyōgo-ryō.*

Zōjō-ji, 増上寺. Great Buddhist temple at *Shiba* (*Tōkyō*). Established in 1393, it belonged to the *Jōdo-shū* sect and was chosen by *Ieyasu* to contain the funeral tablets of his family. In its precincts are found the tombs of the *Shōgun Hidetada* (+ 1632), *Ienobu* (+ 1713), *Ietsugu* (+ 1716), *Ieshige* (+ 1761), *Ieyoshi* (+ 1853) and *Iemochi* (+ 1866).

Zōkwan, 贈官. Honorary title conferred after death. This custom, borrowed from China, was introduced into Japan at the death of the *Dainagon Ōtomo Miyuki,* who then received the title of *Udaijin* (701). In 735, prince *Toneri-shinnō* was honored with the posthumous dignity of *Dajō-daijin,* and from that time forward the custom was established. It exists to the present day.

Zōkwa no san-jin, 造化三神. The 3 Shintoist divinities who preside over the motions of the stars, and produce all earthly beings. They are: *Ame no minakanushi, Takamimusubi* and *Kammimusubi.*

Zokumyō, 俗名. Name corresponding to the Christian name. Also called *tsūshō. Genjirō, Kōnosuke,* etc. are *zokumyō.*

Zōō-zan-jō, 藏王山城.—See *Nagaoka (Echigo).*

Zōshiki, 雜色 (Lit.: different colors). Formerly servants who had no court rank (*i*). The possessors (*ihō*) of a court rank wore dresses of a certain color as fixed by the ceremonial. The others dressed as they chose: hence the generic name given to them.

Zuihō-shō, 瑞寳章. Order of the sacred Treasury. — See *Kunshō.*

Zui-jin, 隨神. Name given to the two statues placed one on each side of the principal entrance of Shintoist temples. They are also called *Yadai-jin, Sadaijin, Kado no osa.* They are supposed to guard the higher divinities that are venerated in the temple.

Zuiryū-in-ni, 瑞龍院尼. By birth, *Chie-ko;* sister of *Hideyoshi.* Married *Miyoshi Yoshifusa* and was the mother of *Hidetsugu* and of *Hidekatsu.* Later she shaved her head and retired to the *Zuiryū-in* temple whence her name.

Zuishin, 隨身. Formerly bodyguard which accompanied high personages when going out. There were two kinds: the *hompu no zuishin,* attached to the Palace and guarding the Emperor, and the *shō-zuishin,* attendants upon high officers of the imperial guard. The *zuishin* carried a bow, arrows and a sword. Their number was limited according to the rank of the persons guarded thus the *Kwampaku* were allowed 10, the *Daijin* and *Taishō* 8, the *Nagon* and *Sangi* 6, the *Chūjō* 4, the *Shōshō* 2.

Zushoryō, 圖書寮. Formerly bureau dependent upon the *Naka-tsukasashō* and charged to preserve books and manuscripts, to write historical annals, etc.

Zushū, 豆州. Chinese name of the *Izu* province.

SUPPLEMENT.

PRINCIPAL FOREIGNERS

CONNECTED WITH JAPAN BEFORE THE RESTORATION.

(1542-1868).

Adami (John-Matthew). — Jesuit from Sicily. Arrived in Japan in 1604, was exiled to *Macao* in 1614, returned in 1624, and after laboring for 19 years in *Echigo, Sado, Ōshū*, at *Edo*, etc., was buried alive at *Nagasaki* (1633).

Adams (Will) (+ 1520). English pilot on the Dutch ship "*Erasmus*" which stranded on the shores of *Bungo* in April 1600. Taken to *Ōsaka*, he had an enterview with *Ieyasu* the following month, and was engaged to build several small schooners, one of which, the *San Bonaventura*, made a voyage as far as Mexico (1610). He was likewise employed in several commerical transactions with the Dutch and English concerning their factories at *Hirado*. He was not permitted to return to his country. He married a Japanese woman and died at *Hemi*, near the present port of *Yokosuka*. — The Japanese designate him by the name of *Anjin* (pilot) : his tomb is called *Anjin-zuka* and a street in *Edo* bears his name (*Anjin-chō*).

Adnet (Matthew) (1813-1848). Priest of the Foreign Missions of Paris. Born in *Lorraine*, he came to the *Ryūkyū* in 1846 and died at *Naha* after a two years' vain effort to enter Japan.

Aguire (Martin d') or of the Ascension (1567-1597). — Spanish Friar of the Fraanciscan order. Arrived in Japan in April 1596, and is one of the 26 Martyrs crucified at *Nagasaki* Feb. 5. 1597.

Alberto del Spirito Santo. — Belonged to the order of the Trinity, and was born at Messina. Captured by Turkish privateers on his way to Genoa, he was taken to Constantinople where a merchant bought him and took him to Japan. He was martyred at *Nagasaki* in 1634.

Albuquerque (Dom John d') — Bishop of the Indies. On Pentecost, 1548, he baptized the three first Japanese Christians at Goa : Paul John and Anthony, who the following year, accompanied St. Francis Xavier.

Albuquerque (Dom Mathias d'). — Viceroy of the Indies. Sent a letter with presents to the *Taikō Hideyoshi*, in 1596.

Alcock (Sir Rutherford). — Chargé d'affaires of England (1864), he assisted at the bombardment of *Shimonoseki*. It was he who was addressed by two young Japanese, *Itō Shunsuke* (later on, Marquis *Itō Hirobumi*) and *Inoue Bunda* (Count *Inoue Kaoru*) recently returned from Europe. These young men promised to obtain from their *daimyō Mōri Motonori* the concessions demanded by the powers. They were given 12 days to make their negotiations successful, but having failed, *Shimonoseki* was bombarded (Sept, 5-9, 1864). — Sir Alcock has published a book (The Capital of the Tycoon), a very interesting account of the events that occurred in *Edo* from 1859 to 1862.

Almeyda (Louis) (1525-1583). — Portuguese Jesuit. Came to Japan in 1556. He labored chiefly in *Kyūshū*. At *Nara* he received a visit from *Miyoshi Yoshitsugu* (1565). He baptized *Arima Harunobu* (1576), and died at *Amakusa* at the age of 58.

Amorin (Juan de). — Spanish Augustinian who perished on the ship " *Madre de Dios* " which was sunk in the harbor of *Nagasaki* by *Arima Harunobu* (1610).

Angelis (Jerome de). (1568-1623). — Jesuit from Sicily. Arrived in Japan in 1602. He was the superior of the *Fushimi* house and established a residence at *Sumpu*. In 1614, he remained hidden in *Nagasaki*. Later on, he evangelized the N. of *Hondo* and even *Yezo* island. He, with 50 Christains, was burned alive at *Edo*, Dec. 4, 1623.

Antonio de Saint-Bonaventure (1587-1628). — Spanish Franciscan. Born at Valladolid, he arrived in Japan in 1618, was arrested Jan. 21, 1627 and burned alive at *Nagasaki*, Sept. 8, 1628.

Arroyo (Alonzo de) (1592-?). — Spanish Jesuit. Born at Malaga, he came to Japan in 1643, was at once arrested with his companions and enclosed in the *Kirishitan-yashiki* at *Edo*. The date of his death is uncertain.

Baeza (Joan-Bapt. de) (1558-1626). — Spanish Jesuit. Born in Andalusia, he came to Japan in 1590, was Vicar-General of Mgr de Cerqueira. At the time of the expulsion of all the missionaries (1614) he remained hidden. — Writing one day (1615) to Rev. Zola, he finished his letter with these words : " Ab illo benedicaris in cujus honore cremaberis," and, in fact, Father Zola was burned alive the following year. — Father de Baeza died worn out by fatigue at *Nagasaki*. It is said that no missionary has ever converted so many infidels in Japan as did this zealous apostle.

Baldwin — English Major, who was assassinated at *Kamakura*, Nov. 24, 1864.

Beechey — Captain in the English navy, and commander of the " *Blossom*," which visited the *Ryūkyū* islands and the *Ogasawara* archipelago in 1827 and gave a name to the principal islands.

Beltran (Louis) (+1627) — Spanish Dominican Friar. Born at Barcelona, he came to Japan in 1622 and was burned alive at *Ōmura* after having been enclosed for a whole year in a small hut.

Benyowski (Maurice-August, Count of) (1741-1786). — Hungarian adventurer, who being banished to *Kamtchatka* for having plotted against the Czar, escaped, touched at the *Ryūkyū* islands, tried to settle in Formosa (1771), then left for Madagascar. Has published a book of " Voyages et Mémoires."

Bettelheim—Protestant missionary sent to the *Ryūkyū* islands in 1846, by the Britannic-Mission Society. He remained for several years at *Naha* and sent a Japanese translation of the New-Testament to London (1853.)

Biddle—American Commodore. Commander of the " *Columbus*," he came to *Uraga* in 1846 and asked to make a treaty with Japan similar to that made with China, but his petition was rejected.

Bird—Lieutenant in the English army, assassinated at *Kamakura*, November 24, 1864.

Black (J. R.)—One of the first residents of Japan after the country had been opened to foreigners. His book " Young Japan " is, so to say, the diary of events that interested the European colony of *Yokohama* between the years 1858 and 1879. He started the first newspaper (*Nisshin-shinji-shi*) printed in Japan.

Blanco (Francesco) (1566-1597). Spanish Franciscan. Born in Galicia, he came to Japan in 1596 and was one of the 26 Holy Martyrs of 1597.

Blumhoff (Sir Knight).—Director of the Factory at *Deshima* in 1817, had brought his young wife with him, but the Japanese obliged him at once to reembark her for home.

Borghes (Manoel) (1582-1633).—Portuguese Jesuit. Landed in Japan in 1612, was exiled in 1614, returned in 1621 and after 12 years of laborious ministry, was arrested and condemned to the torment of the pit. He died on the third day.

Broeckhorst—Director of the Dutch Factory at *Deshima*, he had an audience with the *Shōgun Iemitsu*, in 1645.

Broek (Abraham Van den).—Envoy of the Dutch East India Company who, in 1609, was received in audience by *Ieyasu*, and owing to a letter supposed to be from the Statholder Mauricius of Nassau, obtained authorization to trade with Japan and to open factories at *Hirado*.

Brouwer (Hendrick)—Director of the Dutch Factory at *Hirado* from 1613 to 1618.

Bulcher (Sir Ed.).—Officer of the English navy. He commanded the " *Samarang*," which, in 1845, landed at the *Ryūkyū* island and at *Nagasaki*.

Cabral (Francisco) (1529-1609).—Portuguese Jesuit. Came to Japan in 1570 with the title of Vice-Provincial. He soon after baptized *Ōmura Sumitada* and his whole family. At *Kyōto* he was received by the *Shōgun Yoshiaki* and at *Azuchi* by *Nobunaga* (1572). He baptized *Ōtomo Yoshimune* and his brother-in-law *Ichijō Kanesada* (1575), *Ōtomo Sōrin* (1578), etc. returned to Macao in 1581.

Camus—French officer. Lieutenant in the 3rd African battallion assassinated by the *rōnin* near *Yokohama*, Oct. 14, 1863.

Capece (Antonio) (1606-1643).—Jesuit from Naples. Came to Japan in 1642 was at once arrested and put to death at *Nagasaki* after enduring 7 months of torture.

Carnero (Melchior), S. J.—Titular Bishop of Nicea. Made Bishop of Japan, he died at Macao whilst on his way to his mission (1567).

Caron (Francis).—Born in Holland of French parents, he came to Japan whilst very young and by his intelligence, rose to the position of Director of the Dutch Factory (1629-1641). In 1636, he was sent with presents to the *Shōgun Iemitsu* and obtained Nuyts' freedom. In 1640, he was obliged to destroy all the storehouses newly erected at *Hirado* and all the houses whose front bore a date of the Christian era. Moreover, the Dutch were from that time forbidden to celebrate Sunday, to use the Christian calendar, to kill animals, to carry weapons, etc. The following year, Caron was replaced by Max. Lemaire. He hoped the Company would appoint him to a higher position, but was disappointed. He then sought employment in France and obtained an appointment from Colbert in the Cie des Indes, being commissioned to try to open communications with Japan. He set sail in 1665, but fell sick and died at Lisbon.

Carvalho (Diego de) (1577-1624).—Portuguese Jesuit. Born at Coimbre. He came to Japan in 1609. Exiled in 1614, he went to Cochin-China, then returned to Japan in 1616, worked much in the North, in *Ō-u* and *Yezo*. Arrested at *Sendai*, he was plunged into the icy waters of the river.

Carvalho (Gonzalo de Monteiro de) (1590-1640).—One of the 4 ambassadors from Macao put to death at *Nagasaki*, with all their attendants.

Carvalho (Miguel) (1578-1624).—Portuguese Jesuit. Born at Braga, he came to Japan in 1616 and was burned alive at *Nagasaki*, Aug. 25, 1624.

Carvalho (Valentine) (+ 1631).—Portuguese Jesuit. He was for 6 years Provincial of Japan and became Superior of the mission at the death of Mgr. de Cerqueira. Died at Goa.

Carvalho (Vincente) or de S. Antonio (+ 1632).—Augustinian brother. Born at Lisbon, came to Japan in 1622. Ten years later, he was burned alive at *Nagasaki* after 7 months' of torture.

Cassola (Francisco).—Italian Jesuit. He came to Japan in 1643, was at once arrested and imprisoned in the *Kirishitan-yashiki*. The Japanese assert that he married a Japanese woman and lived for several years in the house of the *Kirishitan-bugyō, Inoue Masashige, Chikugo no kami*. The date of his death is uncertain.

Castellet (Domingos) (1592-1628).—Spanish Dominican. Born in Catalonia, he came to Japan in 1621, and after 7 years' of laborious ministry, was burned alive at *Nagasaki*.

Castro (Gaspard de) (1561-1626).—Portuguese Jesuit. Born at Braga, he came to Japan in 1596 and died of exhaustion after 30 years of toil and fatigue.

Cécille (John-Bapt.).—French admiral. In 1847, he made a cruise to the *Ryūkyū* islands and to *Nagasaki* with the 3 ships, *Cléopâtre, Sabine* and *Victorieuse*.

Cerqueira (Luis de) (1552-1614).—Portuguese Jesuit. He was professor in the college of Evora, when he was appointed Coadjutor to Mgr,

P. Martinez (1591). Consecrated at Lisbon, he left for the Indies in 1594 and came to *Nagasaki* in 1596. He governed the Japanese missions for 18 years. In 1606, he was received in audience by *Ieyasu* at *Fushimi*. Died at *Nagasaki*.

Cespedes (Gregorio de) (1552-1611).—Portuguese Jesuit. Came to Japan in 1578, built a church at *Akashi* (*Harima*), had an audience with *Hideyoshi* (1585), accompanied *Konishi Yukinaga* to Korea, and died at *Kokura* (*Buzen*).

Chanoine — French officer. Captain of the Staff, and chief of the first military mission to *Edo*, from 1866 to 1868. Afterwards General of division, Minister of War, etc.

Chiara (Giuseppe). — See Dict. art. *Chiara*.

Cocks (Capt. Richard). — Chief of the English factory of *Hirado* in the year of its establishment (1613). The factory was besieged by the Dutch (1618), who were then at war with the English, but he was delivered by Japanese intervention. He retired in 1621, when the factory was suppressed.

Collado (Diego) (+ 1633). — Spanish Dominican. Born in Estremadure, he came to Japan in 1619. Recalled by his superiors for having written letters and memoirs against the Jesuits, he died when the ship carrying him to Europe was wrecked. He published a Japanese Grammar.

Correa (Duarte). — Captain of a Portuguese ship. Arrested in 1637, he was burned alive at *Ōmura* (*Hizen*) after two years of hard captivity. He wrote an account of the *Shimabara* revolt.

Costa (Joan da) (1576-1633). — Portuguese Jesuit. Born near Lisbon, he came to Japan in 1609, was exiled to Macao (1614) and returned via Manila. Arrested in *Suwō*, he was brought to *Nagasaki* and condemned to the torture of the pit. He died three days after.

Costanzo (Camilo) (1571-1622). — Jesuit from Naples. Came to Japan in 1605, was exiled to Macao in 1614, returned in 1615 and three years after, was burned alive at *Hirado*.

Couros (Matheus de) (1571-1633). — Portuguese Jesuit. Born at Lisbon, he came to Japan in 1603, was banished in 1614, returned soon after, became Provincial of the Company and died worn out by labours at *Fushimi*.

Courtet (William), in religion, Fr. Thomas de Santo-Domingo. — French Dominican. Born at Beziers, he landed in the *Ryūkyū* islands in 1636, was at once arrested, the following year brought to *Kagoshima*, then to *Nagasaki*, where he was subjected to what is known as the " water torture."

Critana (Antonio-Francisco) (1551-1614). — Spanish Jesuit. Born near Toledo, he came to Japan in 1583, was banished in 1614 and died when entering the harbor of Manila.

Cuello (Gaspard) (+ 1590). — Portuguese Jesuit. Vice-Provincial in 1580, he was received several times in audience by *Hideyoshi*. In 1587, he received notification of the banishment of all the missionaries.

Curtius (Donker). — Dutch commissary at *Deshima*, in the middle of the 19th century. He was the first who signed a treaty with Japan. He published a Japanese Grammar (1857).

Decker. — Dutch Captain assassinated at *Yokohama*, Feb. 1862.

Diego de Santa Catalina (+ 1636). — Franciscan Friar. Entrusted by the Spanish king Philip III. with an embassy to the *Shōgun*, he arrived in Japan with two companions at the end of 1615. *Ieyasu* already ill, refused to receive them, but *Hidetada* admitted them to his presence, received them coldly and refused to accept their presents. They returned by way of Mexico.

Doeff (Hendrik). — Came to Japan in 1798, was director of the *Deshima* factory from 1805 to 1817. He defeated the attempt of the English, then masters of Batavia, to take the *Deshima* factory in 1813. He lived 19 years in Japan and 3 times went as ambassador to *Edo* : the first time, he witnessed an immense fire (1806).

Duchesne de Bellecourt — Chargé d'affaires and General-Consul of France in Japan from 1859 to 1864.

Dury (Leo) (+ 1891). — At first officer in the navy on board the *Charles Martel*, he was Vice-Consul of France at *Nagasaki* from 1862 to 1870, then professor of French at *Nagasaki*, *Kyōto* and *Tōkyō*. Having returned to France, he remained Honorary Consul of Japan at Marseilles until his death.

Elgin (George-Charles-Constantine Bruce, Count of). — Plenipotentiary Minister of England, signed the first treaty with Japan in *Edo* (Aug. 26, 1858).

Eloriaga (Dom Miguel de). — Portuguese Captain. He commanded the ship which carried the Abbé *Sidotti* from Manila to Japan (1709).

Elserak (Johan Van). — Director of the *Deshima* factory from 1641 to 1646. He obtained the release of the officers of the ship *Breskens* arrested at *Nambu* and taken as prisoners to *Edo* (1643).

Erquicia (Domingo de) (+ 1633). — Spanish Dominican. Born at St. Sebastian, he came to Japan in 1623, was Superior of his Order, and, after 10 years of apostolic labors, endured the torture of the pit at *Nagasaki*.

Esquival (Jacinto de) (+ 1633). — Spanish Dominican. Born in Biscaye. He passed several years in Formosa, then embarked on a Chinese junk sailing for Japan but during the voyage, he was massacred by the crew.

Fernandez (Ambrosio) (1551-1620). — Portuguese Jesuit brother. Born at Xisto, he went to the Indies at the age of 20. He had been a merchant, then a soldier, and finally entered the Society, was sent to Japan and died in the prison of *Ōmura*.

Fernandez (Benedict) (1580-1633). — Portuguese Jesuit. Came to Japan in 1606, endured the torture of the pit at *Nagasaki*, after having labored for 27 years under most trying circumstances.

Fernandez (John) (+ 1566). — Portuguese Jesuit. Came to Japan with St. Francis Xavier (1549), labored especially in *Kyūshū* and died at *Hirado*.

Ferreira (Christopher). — Portuguese Jesuit. Came to Japan in 1610. Distinguished for virtue and apostolic zeal, he was chosen Provincial of his Order after the death of Father de Couros. Arrested at *Nagasaki*, he was condemned to the torture of the pit (1633), but after 5 hours of torments, his courage failed him and he apostatized. He was released and employed by the governors of *Nagasaki* as interpreter and in that capacity often assisted at the examination and martyrdom of his former companions. It is said that he originated the idea of obliging Christians to trample on the cross and the holy images. After 20 years of such a miserable existence, he retracted his apostacy which he expiated by martyrdom.

Figueiredo (Melchior). — Portuguese Jesuit. Came to Japan in 1564, worked at first at *Ōmura* and in the *Gotō* islands, then was sent to *Kyōto* where he converted the famous doctor *Manase Dōsan* (1584).

Flores (Luis). — Flemish Dominican. Born at Gand, he for a long time labored in Mexico, and left for Japan in 1620. In sight of Formosa, he was captured by the crew of the English ship *Elisabeth* and delivered into the hands of the Dutch, who, after having kept him at *Hirado* handed him over to the Japanese. He was condemned to be burned alive (1622).

Fonseca (Joan da) (1569-1620). — Portuguese Jesuit. Born at Lisbon, he was sent to Japan in 1604 and died worn out by fatigue after 16 years of ministry.

Forcade (Theodore-Augustin) (1818-1885). — Priest of the Society of the Foreign Missions of Paris. Born at Versailles, he was sent to the *Ryūkyū* Islands, where he lived two years (1844-1846). Named Bishop of Samos and Vicar-Apostolic of Japan, he made his abode, for the time being at Hongkong. Seeing the impossibility of entering Japan, he left the Society (1852), and having returned to France, successively became Bishop of Guadelupe (1853), of Nevers, then Archbishop of Aix.

Francisco de Gracia, (+ 1633). — Portuguese religious of the Order of St. Augustine. Came to Japan in 1632 and was arrested the following year. Condemned to the torture of the pit, he was bled at the forehead and temples to enable him to live longer : his sufferings lasted 30 h.

Francisco de Jesus or **de San Fulgencio** (+1631). — Spanish Augustinian. Came to Japan in 1623, passed two years and a half in the mountains of *Nagasaki* to study the language, then evangelized the *Ōshū* province. Named Provincial of his Order, he returned to *Kyūshū* (1628), was arrested the following year, and after a long and painful imprisonment, was plunged on 33 consecutive days into the sulphurous and boiling waters of Mount *Unsen* (*Hizen*).

Francisco de Santa Maria (+1627). — Spanish Franciscan Friar. Came to Japan in 1623 and was burned alive at *Nagasaki* 4 years later.

Francisco (Domingo). — Ambassador of the Viceroy of the Philippines, who asked that the Portuguese and the Spaniards sojourning in Japan without the authorization of the king of Spain, be delivered to him and taken to Manila : *Ieyasu* refused (1613).

Franco (Apollinarius) (+1622). — Spanish Franciscan Friar. Burned alive at *Ōmura* (*Hizen*) after 5 years of imprisonment.

Francis-Xavier (Saint) (1506-1552). — Religious of the Company of Jesus, Apostle of the Indies and of Japan. Came to *Kagoshima* (*Satsuma*) Aug. 15, 1549, went to *Hirado* Sept. 1550, then to *Hakata* and to *Yamaguchi*, and arrived at *Kyōto* Feb. 1551. He remained there only 15 days on account of the disturbances reigning in that city, and returned to *Yamaguchi*, whence, on Sept. 15th, he departed for *Funai* (*Bungo*). Recalled by his Superiors, he sailed back to the Indies Nov. 20, 1551. He had passed two years and 3 months in Japan. He died Dec. 2nd of the following year in the island of *Sancian.*

Freitas (Lucia de) (+1622). — Japanese woman, born at *Nagasaki* and married to Philip de Freitas, a Portuguese. Burned alive for the faith at the age of 80.

Frisius — Ambassador sent by the governor of the Dutch Indies to thank the *Shōgun* for his kindness towards the Dutch (1650). He was not received on account of *Ieyasu's* illness.

Froez (Louis) (+1597).— Portuguese Jesuit. Came to Japan in 1563 and was sent to *Kyōto* the following year. Together with Father Vilela he was received in audience by the *Shōgun Yoshiteru* and his mother (1565). Received by *Nobunaga* at *Kyōto* (1568), he obtained permission to settle in the capital, his residence being called *Eiroku-ji* and *Namban-ji*. In 1576, he went to *Bungo* and took up his abode at *Usuki*. In 1592, he left this latter place to return to Macao where he died 6 years later.

Gabriel de la Madeleine (+1632) — Spanish Franciscan brother. Arrested in 1630, he was imprisoned for a long time in *Ōmura*, plunged twice into the waters of Mt. *Unsen*, then burned alive at *Nagasaki*.

Gago (Balthazar). — Portuguese Jesuit. Was sent to Japan in 1552, by Saint Francis Xavier, who gave him presents for *Ōtomo Sōrin*. After several years of ministry in *Kyūshū*, he returned to Goa (1561).

Galves (Francisco) (1577-1623). — Spanish Franciscan. Came to Japan in 1603 was banished in 1614, returned in 1618, evangelized the northern provinces, then the city of *Edo*. Arrested at *Kamakura*, he was burned alive at *Edo*.

Garcia (Gonzalo) (+1597). — Portuguese Franciscan brother. Educated by the Jesuits, he came to Japan with them at the age of 15 and served them for 8 years. In 1588, he entered the Order of Saint-Francis at Manila. Chosen as interpreter to the Rev. Pierre Baptiste, he accompanied him to Japan and was crucified with him at *Nagasaki*. He is one of the 26 Martyrs canonized in 1862.

Gerritszoon (Dirck). — The first Dutchman who landed in Japan. He came thither from *Macao*, in 1585-1586, on board the Portuguese ship "*la Santa Cruz.*"

Giannone (Giacomo-Antonio) (+1633). — Jesuit from Naples. Came to Japan in 1609, and after 24 years of labor in *Kyūshū* was plunged into the waters of Mt. *Unsen*.

Giordano di S. Stephano (+1634). — Dominican of Sicily. Came to Japan in 1632, was arrested two years later and after most frightful torments suffered the torture of the pit for 8 days.

Girard (Prudence) (1820-1867). — Priest of the Society of the Foreign Missions of Paris. Born at *Bourges*, he left France in 1847 and after waiting for two years at *Hongkong*, labored at *Wampu* near *Canton*. In the beginning of 1855 he went to the *Ryūkyū*, then returned to *Hongkong*, Oct. 1858. Named Superior of the mission of Japan, he settled in *Edo* the following year, built the church at *Yokohama* (1861), went to France, returned in July 1863 and died at the age of 48, on Dec. 9th, 1867.

Gnecchi (Organtino) or **Soldi** (1530-1609). — Portuguese Jesuit. Came to Japan in 1570, was sent to *Kyōto* and evangelized the neighboring provinces. *Nobunaga* gave him some land at *Azuchi* to erect a school destined for young noblemen (1577). He was also treated well by *Hideyoshi*, hid himself at *Ōsaka* at the time of the edict of banishment (1587), then was authorized to stay in Japan. He died at *Nagasaki* at the age of 79. His infirmities obliged him during his last 3 years to seek rest from the fatigues of his laborious ministry.

Golownine (Captain). — Officer of the Russian navy. Commanded the ship "*Diana*," on a voyage of exploration to the seas N. of Japan. Having landed on the *Kunashiri* island he was arrested, led to *Matsumae* and imprisoned. He escaped with some of his companions, but was recaptured and released only 2 years afterwards, when Russia sent a formal disavowel of the conduct of Chwostoff and Dawidoff (See Resanoff). During his captivity, he gave lessons in astronomy and in the Russian language to *Takahashi Sakuzaemon*.

Gomez (Luis) (+1634). — Portuguese Franciscan. At the age of 80, suffered the torture of the pit, after having worked in Japan for 30 years.

Gomez (Pedro) (1535-1600). — Spanish Jesuit. Sent to Japan in 1582, he was Vice-Provincial in 1591. Many books on religion were printed by his orders at *Amakusa*.

Gonzalez (Antonio) (+1637). — Spanish Dominican. Was arrested upon landing at *Nagasaki*, and 3 days later, was subjected to the "water torture."

Gonzalvez (Alphonse) (1547-1601). — Portuguese Jesuit. Came to Japan in 1577, and labored especially in *Higo*. At the capture of *Udo* by *Katō Kiyomasa*, he was imprisoned and died of exhaustion.

Gros (Baron J. B. Louis). — French plenipotentiary. Signed the first treaty with Japan (Oct. 9th, 1858.) at *Edo*.

Guérin (Nicolas-François). — Officer in the French navy. Commanded the sloop of war "*Sabine*," which put in at the *Ryūkyū* Islands in 1846, and the following year followed Admiral Cecille to *Nagasaki*. When Vice-Admiral, he signed a treaty with the king of the *Ryūkyū* (1855) which was never ratified by the French government.

Gutierrez (Bartholomew) (1580-1632). — Augustinian. Born in Mexico of Spanish parents, he came to Japan in 1612. Banished in 1614, he returned in 1618. Arrested in November 1629, he was imprisoned at *Ōmura*, was twice plunged into the waters of Mt. *Unsen* (Dec. 1631), and was burned alive September 3, 1632.

Harris (Towsend). — Plenipotentiary Minister and Consul of the U. S. Came to *Shimoda* (Aug. 1856) and made a new treaty with Japan at *Kanagawa* (Jul. 28, 1858).

Hemmy (Gysbert) (1747-1798). — Director of the Dutch factory of *Deshima*. He died on a journey to *Edo* and was buried near *Kakegawa* (*Tōtōmi*), where his tomb can yet be seen.

Hernando de Ayala or **de S. Joseph** (1575-1617). — Spanish Augustinian. Came to Japan in 1605 and after 12 years of fruitful labor in *Kyūshū*, was arrested and beheaded.

Heusken (J.). — A Hollander. Secretary of the U. S. Legation, he was murdered at *Edo* Jan. 14, 1861.

Jaurès (Admiral). — Commander in the French navy, he arrived at *Yokohama* in the month of April 1863 ; on July 15, he destroyed the battery at *Shimonoseki* that had fired on his ships. The following year he assisted the combined action of the powers against this same city (Sept. 5-9, 1864).

Jerome de Jesus (+1602). — Franciscan Friar. Born at Lisbon, he came to Japan in 1594, was expelled in 1596, returned the following year and built the first Catholic chapel in *Edo*.

Jorge- (Domingos) (+1618). Portuguese who after having been soldier in India, came to Japan and was put to death for having sheltered some proscribed religious. His wife and three children, arrested at the same time, were also executed in 1621.

Joseph de S. Jacinthe (+1622). — Spanish Dominican. Came to Japan in 1607, and built a church at *Kyōto*. Arrested in 1621, he was imprisoned at *Ōmura* and after one year's captivity, was burned alive at *Nagasaki*.

Juan de Rueda or **de los Angelos** (+1626). — Spanish Dominican. Came to Japan in 1604, returned to Manila in 1619 where he had some books printed in the Japanese language. He tried to re-enter Japan by way of the *Ryūkyū* islands and succeeded, but was arrested and condemned to death. He was thrown into the sea.

Juan de S. Domingo (+1619). — Spanish Dominican. Arrested soon after his arrival in Japan, he was imprisoned at *Ōmura* and died of exhaustion after 4 months' captivity.

Juan de Santa-Marta (+1618). Spanish Franciscan. Came to Japan in 1605, was arrested at *Ōmura* in 1615, and was sent to *Kyōto*, where he was imprisoned for 3 years, then beheaded and his body torn to pieces.

Kaempfer (Engelbert) (1651-1716). — Doctor attached to the Dutch East India Company. He came to Japan in September 1690 and remained a little over two years. He published two very interesting books : " *Amoenitatum exoticarum.........fasciculi quinque* " and " *Histoire naturelle, civile and ecclésiastique de l'Empire du Japon.*"

Koeckebaecker, (Nicholas). — Director of the Dutch factory of *Deshima* from 1633 to 1639. Having received orders from the Japanese authorities to help in repressing the *Shimabara* insurrection, he went there on board the " *de Ryp,*" which ship, from Feb. 21, to March 12th, 1638, fired 425 guns against the *Hara* castle, in which the insurgents had fortified themselves. One Dutchman was killed on the top of the mast, and falling down, killed another. Koeckebaecker then left the fight, leaving 6 pieces of ordnance to the assailing forces, in addition to the battery they had already received at the beginning of the strife.

Kramer (Conrad). — Director of the Dutch factory of *Deshima*, he had an audience with the *Shōgun Iemitsu* and the ex-*Shōgun Hidetada* in 1626. On his return from *Edo*, he assisted at the feasts in *Kyōto* which celebrated the official visit of *Hidetada* to the emperor *Go-Mi-no-o*, his son-in-law. He has left a very interesting narrative of this journey.

Krusenstern. — Russian naval officer. He in 1804, commanded the ship which brought Resanoff to *Nagasaki*. The following year he explored the coasts of *Ezo*, Kurils, Saghalien, etc. His name was given to the strait that separates Japan from *Tsushima*.

Kuper (Admiral). — Commander of an English fleet which came to *Yokohama*, March 1863, bombarded *Kagoshima* the following August, and aided in the attack upon *Shimonoseki* (Sept. 1864).

Landecho (Dom Mathias). — Commander of the Spanish galleon " *San Felipe* " which stranded in the port of *Urado* (*Tosa*) 1596, and was confiscated by the *daimyō Chōsokabe Morichika*.

La Pérouse — French navigator. In 1787, he explored the coasts of *Ezo* and the Kurils. Has given his name to the strait that separates *Ezo* from *Saghalien*.

Laxman (Captain Adam). — Russian naval officer. In 1792, he brought back to *Matsumae* some Japanese who had suffered shipwreck on the coasts of Siberia. He profited by the occasion to propose to open commercial relations between the two countries : he was told to go to *Nagasaki*, but circumstances did not allow him to go there.

Layrle (Admiral). — Was chief of staff to Admiral Jaurès at the time of the bombardment of *Shimonoseki* (July 19, 1863). He returned to Japan as Commander-in-chief of the naval division in the Far East (1887-1888), and has since published an interesting volume on " *la Restoration Impériale au Japon.*"

Lemaire (Maximilian). — Director of the Dutch factory, he went to *Edo* soon after his arrival in Japan (1641), but the *Shōgun Iemitsu* refused to receive him and through his ministers, ordered him to transfer the factory then at *Hirado* to *Deshima* (*Nagasaki*). It meant to exchange the kind protection of the *Hirado daimyō* for the tyrannical supervision of the Governors of *Nagasaki*, but they were obliged to obey, so on May 22, 1641, *Hirado* was abandoned and *Deshima*, for two centuries, became the place of confinement of the only Europeans allowed to sojourn in Japan.

Liano (Lopez de). — Sent by the Governor of the Philippines, 1592, with a letter to *Hideyoshi* asking him to favor Spaniards in preference to Portuguese. He was received at *Nagoya* (*Hizen*), but his mission failed and on his return, he was lost in a storm at sea.

Linschooten (John-Hughes de). — Dutch navigator who explored the coasts of Japan in 1584. His report excited the greed of the Dutch, who from that time tried to supplant the Portuguese in their commercial relations with Japan.

Lopez (Antonio) (1547-1598). Portuguese Jesuit, rector of the *Nagasaki* house, where he died after having been in the mission for 22 years.

Lopez (Balthazar) (1535-1605). — Portuguese Jesuit who labored in Japan for 37 years.

Lucas del Espiritu Santo (1594-1633). — Spanish Dominican. Came to Japan in 1623, evangelized especially in the city of *Edo*. Arrested at *Ōsaka*, he was conducted to *Nagasaki* and endured the torture of the pit.

Machado (Joan-Bapt. de) (1581-1617). — Portuguese Jesuit. Born in the Azores, he came to Japan in 1609, evangelized *Kyōto* and *Fushimi*, hid himself at the time of the expulsion of 1614, but was arrested in the *Gotō* islands and was beheaded.

Mahay (James). — Dutch Admiral, who with 5 ships received orders to pass through Magellan strait to go to the Indies. Leaving Holland in June 1598, he died at the beginning of the voyage and the fleet was dispersed by a storm ; one of the vessels the "*Erasmus*" landed in April 1600 on the coasts of *Bungo*. Her pilot was the Scotch Will Adams.

Mansdale (Gaspard Van). — Was director of the *Deshima* factory in 1708 and served as interpreter during the first examination of Abbé Sidotti at *Nagasaki*.

Marinas (Dom Gomez Perez de). — Governor of the Philippines. In 1591, he received a letter from *Hideyoshi* inviting him to do him homage as vassal and to pay him tribute. He answered through Lopez de Liano, and in 1593, by the ambassador P. Pierre-Baptiste.

Marquez (Francisco) (1611-1643). — Born at *Nagasaki*, of a Portuguese father and a Japanese mother descendant from *Ōtomo Sōrin*. He studied at Macao, entered the Company of Jesus, returned to Japan in 1642, was arrested and taken to *Nagasaki*, where after 7 months of incredible tortures he suffered the torment of the pit.

Marquez (Pedro) (1575-1657). Portuguese Jesuit. Came to Japan in 1643, was at once arrested, taken to *Edo* and enclosed in the *Kirishi-tan-yashiki*, where he lived 13 years.

Martin de S. Nicolas (1592-1632). Spanish Augustinian. Born at Saragossa, he came to Japan in 1632, was arrested soon after and burned alive at *Nagasaki*.

Martinez (Bartholomew). — Spanish Dominican. Built the first Catholic Church in Formosa, near Kelung (1626).

Martinez (Pedro) (+ 1598). — Portuguese Jesuit. Born at Coimbre, he was named Bishop of Japan (1591), consecrated at Goa (1595) and came to *Nagasaki* in August 1596. He at once went to *Kyōto* to offer the presents to *Hideyoshi* which he brought from the Viceroy of the Indies, Dom Mathias d'Albuquerque. The *Taikō* received him with kindness. On his return to *Nagasaki*, he witnessed the death of the 26 martyrs (Feb. 5, 1597). Towards the end of the year, he left for Goa to arrange different affairs concerning his diocese, but he died of a fever during the voyage and was buried at Malacca.

Mastrilli (Marcello-Francisco) (1603-1637). — Jesuit from Naples. Cured in 1633, by the intercession of St. Francis Xavier, from a serious wound he had accidentally received, he resolved to devote himself to the missions, and was sent to Japan, where he arrived in 1637. Arrested a few days after his arrival in *Satsuma*, he was taken to *Nagasaki* and put to death amidst horrible tortures, which his executioners prolonged for the space of 12 days.

Mattos (Gabriel de). — Portuguese Jesuit. He was rector of the house of *Kyōto* when the edict of banishment was promulgated (1614). Having gone to *Nagasaki*, he was sent to Rome to give an account of the mission. He was in *Tonkin* during the year 1632, and died at Macao the following year.

Mecinski (Albert). — Polish Jesuit. Came to Japan in 1642 and was immediately arrested. He was put to death at *Nagasaki* after being daily tortured for 7 months.

Melchior de S. Augustin (1599-1632). Spanish Augustinian. He came to Japan in 1632, was arrested soon after, imprisoned at *Nagasaki* and burned alive.

Mena (Alonso de) (+ 1622). — Spanish Dominican. He was one of the 5 first religious of his Order sent to Japan (1602). Arrested in 1619, he endured a severe captivity of 3 years, and was burned alive at *Nagasaki*.

Menesez (Eduard de). — Viceroy of the Indies at Goa. Sent an embassy with rich presents to *Hideyoshi* in 1590 : the chief of the embassy was Rev. P. Valegnani, Provincial of the Jesuits.

Mesquita (Diego de) (1554-1614). — Portuguese Jesuit. He served as interpreter to Rev. P. Valegnani when on his embassy to *Hideyoshi* (1590). He was for a long time rector of the college at *Nagasaki* and died of exhaustion after 38 years of missionary life.

Meylan (G. F.). — Hollander. Was director of the *Deshima* factory from 1827 to 1830.

Moralez (Diego de) (1604-1643). — Spanish Jesuit. Came to Japan in 1642, was arrested at once and after several months of suffering, endured the torture of the pit.

Moralez (Francisco de) (+ 1622). — Spanish Dominican. Born at Madrid, he came to Japan in 1602, was arrested in 1619 and after 3 years' captivity at *Ōmura*, was burned alive at *Nagasaki*.

Moralez (Sebastian de). Portuguese Jesuit. Born at Funchal (Madeira Is.), he was Provincial of his Order, when Pope Sixtus V. named him Bishop of Japan in 1587. Consecrated at Lisbon, he sailed for his mission but died in Mozambique.

Navarrete (Alonso) (+ 1617). — Spanish Dominican. Came to Japan in 1611, and after 6 years of ministry was beheaded near *Nagasaki.*

Navarrete (Louis). — Ambassador of the governor of the Philippines to the *Taikō Hideyoshi* in 1597.

Navarro (Pietro-Paolo) (1560-1622). — Jesuit from Naples. Came to Japan in 1588, and after 33 years of apostolic work, was arrested, imprisoned at *Shimabara* for 10 months and burned alive.

Neale (Colonel). — The first Chargé d'affaires of England to Japan, from 1859 to 1863.

Norogna (Dom Alphonse de). — Viceroy of the Indies, who in 1554 received a letter and presents from *Ōtomo Sōrin.* He ordered Fernandez Mendez Pinto to carry the answer the following year.

Nuyts (Peter). — Hollander who being sent by the Dutch Company of Batavia, presented himself as ambassador of the king of Holland (1628). The imposture was discovered and the envoy dismissed without a reply. The following year, he was made governor of the Dutch establishments of Formosa and a chance offered itself to take revenge for the affront he had received at *Edo.* Two Japanese boats, belonging to the adventurer *Hamada Yahei,* touched at Formosa on their way to China. Nuyts had the sails, artillery, etc. brought to him, and under some pretext or other, kept the boats in the harbor, so that they missed the monsoon. After a year of vain expectation, the Japanese lost patience. *Yahei,* his brother *Kozaemon,* his son *Shinzō* and several other determined men made their way into the house of Nuyts, took him prisoner and released him only after having obtained the rigging of their vessel, the permission to sail away and a large indemnity for the losses they had sustained on his account. Having returned to their country, they lodged a complaint before the *Shōgun. Iemitsu* at once ordered the seizure of 9 Dutch ships that were in the *Hirado* harbor and demanded that the guilty party be delivered to him. The Dutch did not dare to refuse. In the month of July 1631, the unfortunate Nuyts was handed over to the *Shōgun* who had him at once put into the prison of *Ōmura.* He remained there 5 years and left it only on the earnest entreaties of Caron (1636).

Nyenrode (Cornelis Van). — Succeeded Specx at the head of the *Hirado* factory (1621).

Orfanel (Jacinthe) (+ 1622). — Spanish Dominican. Came to Japan in 1607, labored in *Kyūshū,* was arrested in 1621 and burned alive the following year.

Organtin — See *Gnecchi.*

Orsucci (Angel) (1572-1622). — Italian Dominican. Born at Lucques he came to Japan in 1618, was arrested soon after and burned alive after 3 years' captivity.

Ortiz (Estacio). — Augustinian. Born in Mexico, came to Japan in 1602, labored in *Bungo* and returned to Manila at the time of the decree of expulsion of 1614.

Outrey (Maxime). — Plenipotentiary Minister and Consul General of France to Japan from 1868 to 1871.

Ozaraza (Miguel de) (+ 1637).—Spanish Dominican. He landed in the *Ryūkyū* islands in 1636 but was arrested immediately; he was imprisoned for one year, then taken to *Kagoshima* and from there to *Nagasaki*, where after divers tortures he was subjected to the torment of the pit.

Pacheco (Francisco) (1566-1626). — Portuguese Jesuit Came to Japan in 1604 was the administrator of the diocese during the absence of Mgr. de Cerqueira (1612), then Provincial of the Order (1622). Arrested in 1625, he was imprisoned at *Shimabara* and the following year burned alive at *Nagasaki*.

Pacheco (Luis Paez) (1572-1640). — Chief of the embassy sent from Macao to the *Shōgun Iemitsu*. Was beheaded with all his companions: 3 co-ambassadors and 57 sailors or servants (12 Portuguese, 4 Spaniards, 17 Chinese, 6 Bengalese 18 Malayans). Thirteen sailors were spared and sent back to Macao with the information that "henceforth any one who would put his foot on Japanese soil, were he the king of Portugal, were he even the God of the Christians, would be put to death ! "

Paez (Francisco) or **Pasio.** — Portuguese Jesuit. He assisted the 26 Martyrs of 1597, at their death, giving them consolations and encouraging them. Made Vice-Provincial in 1600, he resumed the official visits that had been interrupted for some years and was received in audience by *Ieyasu* at *Sumpu*, by *Hidetada* at *Edo*, and by *Hideyori* at *Ōsaka* (1607). He returned to Macao in 1612.

Paiva (Francisco de) (1570-1609) — Portuguese Jesuit. Died at *Ōsaka* after an apostolate of 9 years in that city.

Paiva (Simon Vaz de) (1587-1640). — Born at Lisbon and transacting business at Macao, he commanded the commercial expedition of 1631. He was at *Nagasaki* at the time of the martyrdom of Rev. Barth. Gutierrez and his companions, and he pledged himself to answer for their perseverance. Was later on, one of the 4 ambassadors who were beheaded by order of the *Shōgun Iemitsu*.

Paredes (Rodrigo Sanchez de) (1585-1640). — Senator of Macao, one of the 4 ambassadors put to death at *Nagasaki*.

Parilla (Francesco de la) or **de S. Miguel** (1544-1597). — Lay-brother of the Order of St. Francis, and one of the 26 Holy Martyrs of Feb. 5, 1597.

Pedro de Avila (+ 1622). Spanish Franciscan. Came to Japan in 1619, was arrested the following year, suffered 2 years' imprisonment at *Ōmura*, then was burned alive at *Nagasaki*.

Pedro de la Asuncion (+ 1617). — Spanish Franciscan. Came to Japan in 1609 and after 8 years' work, was arrested and beheaded near *Nagasaki*.

Peixota (Antonio). — One of the 3 Portuguese who, whilst going to China, were driven by a storm upon the coasts of *Kyūshū* and landed at *Kagoshima* in 1542. They maintained that they discovered Japan before Mendez Pinto.

Pellew (Captain Fleetwood). — Officer of the English navy. Commander of the "*Phaeton*," he, in 1808, entered the bay of *Nagasaki*, seized the two Dutchmen of the *Deshima* factory, who came on board his ship to inspect as was their custom. After two days he released them and went away. The *bugyō* of *Nagasaki*, *Matsudaira Yasuhide*, and several of his subordinates committed *harakiri* for not having been able to prevent this violation of the laws of the Empire.

Pereira (William) (1537-1603). — Portuguese Jesuit. Was taken to Japan whilst a seminarist, and died after 40 years especially devoted to the education of youth.

Perry (Commodore Matthew C). — Officer of the American navy. On the 8th of July 1853, he reached *Uraga* bay (*Sagami*) with a fleet, and was bearer of a message from President Millard Fillmore to the *Shōgun Ieyoshi*. 6 days later, he handed the letter to *Toda Ujiaki*, *daimyō* of *Ōgaki* (*Mino*), sent from *Edo* to interview him and after having made some soundings, he departed declaring that he would return the following year for an answer to his letter. On Feb. 12th, 1854, he returned with 7 ships, and after more than a month's parley, the *Bakufu* signed a provisional treaty which opened the ports of *Shimoda* and *Hakodate* to Americans.

Pessoa (Andrew). — Was Commander of the port of Macao in 1608. A Japanese ship, chartered by *Arima Harunobu* passed the winter in the port, and a quarrel ensued between the crew and the natives. Pessoa showed himself severe in repressing the disturbance and obliged the Japanese to sign a paper stating that they were guilty. But they had scarcely returned to their country, when they sent a complaint to *Ieyasu* at *Sumpu*. The following year, Pessoa arrived at *Nagasaki* commanding the carack "*Madre de Dios*." He at once sent explanations that were accepted. But *Harunobu* and *Hasegawa Fujihiro*, *bugyō* of *Nagasaki*, persuaded *Ieyasu* to revoke his decision and to sign an order to seize the Portuguese vessel. They gathered 1200 men and a great number of boats, and for 3 days, endeavored to set the ship on fire. Finally Pessoa despairing of saving himself, set fire to the casks of powder and blew up his ship, causing the ruin of a great number of Japanese junks. (Jan. 7th, 1610).

Petitjean (Bernard) (1829-1884). — Priest of the Society of the Foreign Missions of Paris. Born at Blanzy (Saône et Loire), he left for Japan in 1860 and remained 2 years at *Naha* (*Ryūkyū*). In 1862, he was at *Yokohama*, and the following year at *Nagasaki*. On March the 17th 1865, he discovered the descendants of the ancient Christians. Made Bishop of Myriophyte and Vicar-Apostolic of Japan in 1866, he remained at the head of the Southern Vicariate, when the Northern Mission was formed (1876). He died at *Nagasaki* at the age of 55.

Philippe de las Casas or de Jesus (+ 1597). — Portuguese Franciscan-brother and one of the 26 Holy Martyrs of Feb. 5, 1597.

Piano (Giulio) (1537-1605). Portuguese Jesuit. He labored in Japan for 27 years.

Pierre-Baptiste (Saint) (1545-1597). — Spanish Franciscan. Born near Avila, he was Commissary of his Order in the Philippines, when the governor Dom Gomez Perez de las Marinas, chose him as ambassador to *Hideyoshi* (1593). After having fulfilled his mission, he remained at *Kyōto*, awaiting the ratification of the treaty with the Spanish king, and in the meantime established a flourishing Christian community in the capital. When the disposition of the *Taikō* changed, he was arrested, taken to *Nagasaki* and crucified with 25 others, 19 of whom were Japanese (Feb. 5, 1597). These 26 Martyrs were beatified in 1627 and canonized on June the 8th, 1862.

Pierre-Baptiste (+ 1630). — Spanish Franciscan. Was Commissary of his Order. Left Japan in 1624 to assist at the General Chapter of the Order, then was charged to procure the beatification of the Martyrs of 1597.

Pinto (Fernand Mendez). — Portuguese who is said to have been the first to land in Japan, in 1542. Having boarded the ship of a Chinese corsair at Macao together with two other Portuguese, Diego Zeimoto and Christopher Borrello, they could not land at the *Ryūkyū* Islands and were carried by a storm to *Tane-ga-shima* island, where they landed in the port of *Nishi-mura*. The governor of the island, *Tanegashima Tokitaka*, marvelling at the sight of the firearms brought by the strangers, sent one of his officers *Sasagawa Koshirō*, to study their construction and manipulation, whereupon he had some made. *Ōtomo Yoshinori, daimyō* of *Bungo*, invited the Portuguese to *Funai*. On his return to the Indies, Pinto loved to relate and probably to exaggerate the details of his voyage. In 1554, he succeeded in having himself made ambassador of the Viceroy, Dom Alphonsus de Norogna, to *Ōtomo Sōrin*, and then entered the Company of Jesus. When his embassy was finished he had himself released from his vows and returned to Portugal, where he published an account of his voyages.

Porro (John-Baptist). (1575-1639). — Jesuit from Milan. At first labored in *Kyūshū*, then went to *Chūgoku*. In 1609, he served as interpreter to the ancient governor of the Philippines, Dom Rodrigo de Vivero y Velazco, in the different audiences he obtained from *Hidetada* at *Edo*, and from *Ieyasu* at *Sumpu*. After 40 years of ministry in Japan, Father Porro was burned with all the inhabitants of a village he had converted.

Poutiatine. — Russian Admiral. He arrived at *Nagasaki* on Aug. 20, 1854 and handed to the governor the despatches of his government in reference to treaties to be signed between the two countries. He returned in the beginning of 1855 and signed a convention similar to that of the U. S., and a supplementary treaty in 1858.

Puik (James). — Companion of Abraham Van den Broek in his pseudo-embassy to the *Shōgun Ieyasu* (1609).

Quast (Matthew). — Dutch navigator who in 1639, explored the *Ogasawara* Isl. the coasts of *Mutsu*, Formosa, etc. The man who was first mate in this expedition, was Abel Jansz Tasman, who 3 years later discovered the island which bears his name, *Tasmania*.

Quesada (Gines de). — Spanish Franciscan who arrived in Japan in 1632, was arrested the same year and burned alive at *Nagasaki*.

Raimondo (Pedro) (1550-1611). — Spanish Jesuit who died at *Nagasaki* after 34 years of apostolic labor in Japan.

Resanoff (Count). — Russian diplomat sent to negotiate a treaty with Japan. On board the ship commanded by Captain Krusenstern, he arrived at *Nagasaki* Oct. 7, 1804, and communicated the object of his mission to the governors. These referred the matter to *Edo*, and the first interview with the envoy of the *Shōgun* took place only on April 4, of the following year. It was followed by others, and ended in a dismissal. Resanoff irritated on account of the protracted stay and the humiliating treatment he had undergone, swore to take revenge and in 1806, sent two of his officers, Chwostoff and Dawidoff, to pillage several villages of Saghalien. The *daimyō* of *Matsumae* was dispossessed for want of supervision, and *Yezo* became a province of the *Shōgun* with a governor named by the *Bakufu*. The Japanese retaliated by keeping Captain Golownine (See that name) and a part of his crew in prison for 2 years (1811-1813).

Ribadeneyra (Marcel de). — Spanish Franciscan. Came to Japan in 1594 with a letter and presents from the governor of the Philippines to the *Shōgun Hideyoshi*. He left for Spain 4 years later with documents relating to the Martyrs of 1597.

Richard de Sainte-Anne — Franciscan. Born in Flanders, he came to Japan in 1614, was exiled the same year, returned in 1619, was arrested 2 years later, imprisoned at *Ōmura* and burned alive at *Nagasaki* (1622).

Richardson — Englishman murdered at *Namamugi*, near *Yokohama*, by the *samurai* in the train of *Ōhara Shigenori*, envoy of the Emperor to the *Shōgun* (1862). This escort was under the command of *Shimazu Saburō Hisamitsu*. As the indemnity asked for this murder was not paid at the appointed time, the English fleet (Admiral Kuper) bombarded *Kagoshima* (1863).

Roches (Leo). — Plenipotentiary Minister and Consul General of France to Japan from 1864 to 1868.

Rodriguez (John) (1559-1633). — Portuguese Jesuit. Came to Japan in 1585, thoroughly studied the Japanese language and was chosen by *Hideyoshi* and *Ieyasu* as interpreter for all business to be transacted with the Portuguese. He was in special favor with the *Taikō*, so much so that he was excepted from the edict of banishment enacted against the religious in 1597. *Ieyasu* treated him with the same benevolence. He died at *Macao*. He published a Dictionary and a Grammar (1604) of the Japanese language.

Rubino (Antonio) (1578-1643). — Jesuit from Savoy. Born at Turin, he came to Japan in 1642, was at once apprehended and put to death after 7 months of horrible tortures.

Saris (John). — Salesman of the English factory of *Bantam*, he came to *Hirado* in June 1613 and was well received by the *daimyō*, *Matsuura Shigenobu*, to whom he remitted a letter from the king of England. Whilst at *Hirado*, he invited Will Adams then at *Edo*, to join him and in his company left for *Sumpu* where he had an audience with *Ieyasu* and presented him a letter from James I. He spent several days in *Edo*, was received by the *Shōgun Hidetada* and returned by way of *Sumpu* where he received the answer of *Ieyasu* to the king of England and a charter of privileges for his countrymen. The English thereby received full liberty of commerce in all the ports of Japan, exemption from custom taxes, authorization to establish factories, permission to explore *Yezo* and the adjacent islands, etc. On his return to *Hirado*, (Nov. 1613), he built a factory, supervised by Richards Cocks: W. Adams (at £ 100 per year) with 6 other Englishmen was associated with him. Saris returned from *Hirado* the following month, taking with him 15 Japanese, and in Sept. 1614, he reached Plymouth. The English factory of *Hirado* was abandoned in 1621.

Sarmiento de Carvalho (Lopo). — Captain of a Portuguese ship, he in 1617, paid a visit to the *Shōgun Hidetada* to apply for some land at *Nagasaki* to establish custom houses. Hendrick Brouwer, chief of the Dutch factory at *Hirado*, was strongly opposed to this plan and the request was not granted.

Schaep (Henry-Cornelius). — Dutch sailor. Commander of the " *Breskens.*" he left Batavia in Feb. 1643 to explore the coasts of *Yezo* and the *Kurils*. He passed *Tsugaru* strait, sailed along the coasts of *Yezo* and the Kurils, then returned to Japan. Having landed at *Nambu* with 9 of his crew, he was taken prisoner, sent to *Edo*, and obtained his freedom after having made the declaration that he had no missionaries on board, and that if some guns had been fired on his ship, it was because he did not know that such an act was forbidden.

Sequeyra (Gonzalo de). — Portuguese nobleman. Sent as ambassador to Japan by the new King John to announce to the *Shōgun* the accession of his master to the throne and the separation of the two kingdoms of Portugal and Spain, and also to ask for a renewal of former commercial relations. Having arrived at *Nagasaki* in the beginning of 1647, he gave notice of the object of his embassy to the governors; these referred the matter to *Edo*, but the answer was a decided refusal.

Sidotti — See Dict., art. *Sidotti.*

Siebold (Philipp-Franz von) (1796-1866). — Came to *Nagasaki* in August 1823, and as a companion of Colonel Van Sturler went to *Edo* (1826) and obtained permission to stay in order to give lessons in medecine and surgery. He was later on permitted to travel in the interior of the country, on condition that he would make no sketches, nor maps. He was however able to get the map of Japan drawn by *Inō Chūkei* from *Takahashi Sakuzaemon*, but was imprisoned for doing so. He was released only in 1830, and then was forbidden ever again to set foot on Japanese soil. Thirty years later he returned, sent by his government on a semi-official mission which produced no results. Siebold wrote a book "*Nippon*," which is a precious mine of useful information on the Japan of his time.

Sotelo (Luis) (1574-1624). Spanish Franciscan. Born at Sevilla, he came to Japan in 1606, built an oratory in the middle of a leprous settlement at *Asakusa* (*Edo*) (1613), was arrested the same year and released at the request of the *daimyō* of *Sendai, Date Masamune*, who asked him to join the embassy he was sending to Madrid and Rome under the leadership of *Hasekura Rokuemon Tsunenaga*. In Rome, the Pope named him 2nd Bishop of Japan, with jurisdiction in the Northern provinces (1615). On his return he was detained at Manila and arrived in Japan only in 1622. He was immediately arrested, imprisoned at *Ōmura* and burned alive after two years of confinement. — Father Sotelo endeavored to open commercial relations between Japan and Mexico and thus alienated the affections of his countrymen at Manila. The king of Spain himself opposed his consecration as bishop. Under his signature appeared a letter to the Holy Father full of calumnies against the bishops of Japan and the Jesuit missionaries ; but it has proved to be a forgery.

Sotomayor (Nuño de). — Ambassador of the Viceroy of Mexico, was received in audience by *Ieyasu* at *Sumpu*, by *Hidetada* at *Edo* and by *Hideyori* at *Ōsaka* (1611), but did not attain his object, especially in reference to the expulsion of the Dutch.

Souza (Antonio de) (1589-1633). — Portuguese Jesuit. Suffered the torment of the pit at *Nagasaki* after having labored for 17 years in Japan.

Souza (Pascal Correa de) (1605-1643). — Portuguese who at Manila, joined the 5 Jesuits on their way to Japan in 1643 ; he was martyred with them.

Spangberg (Martin). — Russian navigator who left *Kamschatka* in 1739 on an exploration tour to the Northern coasts of Japan.

Specx (James). — Dutch envoy who in 1609, went to the Court at *Sumpu* and obtained a commercial charter from *Ieyasu*, which enabled him to open a factory at *Hirado*. He was its first director. In 1620, he delivered 2 religious to the Japanese authorities, who had been captured at sea by an English vessel and transferred to a Dutch ship. These two religious were martyred after a long captivity. Specx returned to Java in 1621. Later on, he became Governor General of the Dutch Indies and gave a strong impulse to commerce with Japan.

Spinola (Carlo) (1564-1622). — Italian Jesuit. Came to Japan in 1602, fulfilled the duties of his ministry at *Kyōto* (1605), where he established a school of science, then went to *Nagasaki* (1612). At the time of the edict of banishment he remained hidden, was arrested in 1618 and burned alive after 4 years of hard imprisonment.

Stewart (William-Robert).　American navigator.　Commander of the "*Eliza*," he obtained entrance into the harbor of *Nagasaki* in 1797, by hoisting the Dutch flag.　He returned the following year, but was shipwrecked on leaving the port.　He came back on the "*Emperor of Japan*" in 1800 and in 1803.

Stirling (Admiral). — English plenipotentiary.　Signed the first treaty with Japan at *Nagasaki*, Oct. 14, 1854.　One of the clauses was that the ports of *Nagasaki* and *Hakodate* were to be open to English commerce.

Sturler (Colonel Van). — Director of the *Deshima* factory from 1824 to 1826.　In 1826, he travelled to *Edo* in company with Siebold.

Tello (Dom Francisco). — Governor of the Philippines who in 1597, sent an embassy to *Hideyoshi*, under the direction of Louis Navarrete to complain about the seizure of the gallion "*San-Felipe*" and the execution of the religious in the beginning of the same year.　The answer was that commercial relations could be opened on condition that no missionary be introduced into Japan by ships coming from the Philippines.

Thunberg (P.). — Director of the Dutch factory at *Deshima* in 1775.

Titsingh (Isaac) (1745-1812) — Director of the *Deshima* factory from 1779-1780, and from 1781 to 1784.　Travelled twice to *Edo*, in 1780 and 1782.　He left several works on Japan as well as a translation of the *Nihon-ō-dai ichiran* (Annals of the *Dairi*.).

Torrella (Juan). — Spanish Franciscan, who arrived in Japan in 1632, was arrested three months later and burned alive.

Torres (Baltasar de) (1563-1626).　Spanish Jesuit.　Born at Granada, was sent to Japan in 1600, for a long time labored in *Kyōto* and *Ōsaka*, then in *Kaga* and *Noto*.　Arrested in 1626, he was burned alive at *Nagasaki*.

Torrez (Côme de). (1497-1570). — Portuguese Jesuit.　He came to Japan with St. Francis Xavier, established a Christian community at *Hirado*, then had charge of the one in *Yamaguchi*.　Superior of the mission till his death.

Valegnani (Alexander) (1537-1606). — Visitor of the Company of Jesus, resided in Japan at 3 different times, in 1577-82, 1590-92, and 1598-1601.　He established numerous residences, colleges, churches, confraternities, hospitals, seminaries, printing offices, etc.　Nothing escaped his vigilant eye ; he is for this reason considered as one of the founders of the missions of Japan.　He suggested the idea of an embassy to Rome to the Christian *daimyō* of *Kyūshū*.　He sailed with the ambassadors (1582), left them at *Goa*, then returned to Japan (1590) with them, bearer of a message from the Viceroy of the Indies.　He died at Macao.

Valens (Diego). — Portuguese Jesuit.　Named Bishop of Japan at the death of Mgr. de Cerqueyra (1614), he came to the Indies (1618) and stopped at Macao, where he died.

Vasquez (Pedro) or de Sainte Catherine (+1624). — Spanish Dominican.　Came to Japan in 1621, was arrested two years after, imprisoned at *Ōmura* and was burnt alive.

Verny — French engineer. Founder and director of the arsenal of *Yokosuka*, from 1865 to 1875.

Vieyra (Andrew). — Brother of the Company of Jesus. Japanese by birth, he came from Manila in 1643, was enclosed in the *Kirishitan-yashiki*, took the name of *Nampō* there and died in 1678. He was buried at the *Muryō-in* temple.

Vieyra (Sebastian) (1571-1634). — Roman Jesuit. Visitor of his Order, he was sent to Rome on business concerning the mission (1623). Having returned to Japan in 1632, he was arrested the following year, taken to *Edo* and burned alive.

Vilela (Gaspard) (+1570). — Portuguese Jesuit. Came to Japan and labored especially in *Kyōto* and the surrounding districts. After 16 years of ministry, he returned to the Indies and died at Malacca.

Vincent de Saint-Joseph — Lay-brother of the Order of St. Francis. Born in Spain, he came to Japan in 1618, was arrested two years after, imprisoned at *Ōmura* and burned alive in 1622.

Vivero y Velasco (Dom Rodrigo de). — Governor of the Philippines in 1608-1609. When his term of office expired, he sailed for Mexico, but was wrecked and stranded on the coasts of *Kazusa*, at *Iwawada*. He was taken before the *daimyō* of *Ōtaki, Honda Tadatomo*, then to *Edo* where he was presented to the *Shōgun Hidetada*. He afterwards went to *Sumpu* where he obtained an audience from *Ieyasu*, whom he asked to protect the Catholic missionaries, to confirm his alliance with Spain and to expel the Dutch. The two first petitions only were granted. Vivero left on a boat constructed by Will Adams and placed at his disposal by *Ieyasu* (1610). On his return to Spain, he was given the title of Count of Valle and then of Orizaba.

Vos. — Dutch Captain assassinated at *Yokohama* in Feb., 1862.

Vries (Martin Heritzoom de). — Dutch navigator. Commander of the " *Castricoom*," he in 1643, explored the coasts of *Yezo* and the *Kurils* and *Saghalien*. He discovered the strait that separates the two islands *Etorū* (Itorup) and *Uruppu* and gave it his name, which was likewise given to *Ōshima* island (*Izu*) and its volcano, the *Mihara*.

Waardenaar (Willem). — Director of the *Deshima* factory from 1798 to 1805. He returned in 1813 as an envoy of England which country being at war with Holland (then annexed to France), had occupied Batavia and intended to seize *Deshima*, but was prevented by Doeff, the director of the factory.

Wagenaar (Zachary). — Director of the *Deshima* factory in 1656. The following year he went to *Edo*, where he distributed more than 14,000 florins as presents. He returned to that city in 1659.

Woddel (Lord). — English Admiral who in 1637, came to *Nagasaki* with 4 vessels and tried to open commercial relations with Japan, but met with a formal refusal.

Zeimoto (Diego). — One of the companions of Mendez Pinto when he landed at *Tane-ga-shima* (1542).

Zola (John-Baptist) (1575-1626). — Italian Jesuit. Born at Brescia, he came to Japan in 1606 and labored in *Kyūshū*. Arrested in 1625, he was burned alive the following year.

Zumarraga (Thomas de) or of the Holy Ghost (+1622). Spanish Dominican. Came to Japan in 1606, labored in *Kyūshū*, was arrested in 1617, detained for 5 years at *Ōmura* and finally burned alive.

Zuniga (Peter de) (+1622). — Spanish Augustinian. Son of a Viceroy of New Spain, he came to Japan in 1618, and returned to Manila, at the urgent entreaties of the governor of *Nagasaki*. He returned to Japan in 1620, with Father Flores, on a ship which was captured by an English vessel. The two missionaries were handed over to the Dutch at *Hirado* who delivered them to the Japanese. They were tormented with water and finally were burned alive at *Nagasaki*.

APPENDIXES.

I.—ALPHABETICAL INDEX

OF A NUMBER OF ENGLISH TERMS REFERRING TO ARTICLES IN THE
DICTIONARY WHERE THE MATTERS ARE FULLY TREATED.

Abdication. — See *Jō-i*, etc.

Abuse. — See *Jōkō-jūnin*, *shō-en*, etc.

Ainos. — See *Ebisu*.

Amusements, Diversions, Sports. — See *Inu-ou-mono*, *jun no o-mari-bugyō*, *kasagake*, *kyokusui no en*, *ne-no-hi no asobi*, *yabusame*, etc.

Army, Imperial Guard. — See *Efu*, *ejifu*, *emonfu*, *gebu-kwan*, *go-efu*, *gundan*, *hashiri-shū*, *hayato*, *hyōbu-shō*, *hyōgo-ryō*, *kon-efu*, *ko-saburai-dokoro*, *mononobe*, *ōtoneri*, *roku-efu*, *sei-i-shi*, *shichi-hon-yari*, *taishō*, *utoneri*, etc.

Barriers. — See *Fuwa no seki*, *Kikuta no seki*, *Nakoso no seki*, etc.

Bonzes. — See *Ama*, *bōzu*, *daishi*, *dai-sōjō*, *Dōchō*, *Hiei-zan*, *Kūkai*, *Nichiren*, *Rennyo-Shōnin*, *risshi*, *Ryōnin*, *Saigyō-Hōshi*, *Shinran-Shō-nin*, *sō-kwan*, etc.

Buddhism. — See *Bukkyō*, *daijō*, *gongen*, *honchi-suijaku*, *Ryōbu-Shintō*, *san-ji-kyō*, *Shaka*, *shōjō*, *sōhei*, etc.

Calendar. — See *Genka-reki*, *hi-oki*, *koyomi*, and Append. XVII.

Capital. — See *Edo*, *Heian-kyō*, *Heijō-kyō*, *Kamakura*, *Kyōto*, *Nanto*, *Nara*, *Taira no miyako*, *Tōkyō*, etc.

Castes, Classes. — See *Eta*, *hatamoto*, *heimin*, *hinin*, *kwazoku*, *samu-rai*, *shimbetsu*, *shizoku*, etc.

Castles, Forts. — See *Shiro*, *tenshu*, *Tamon-jō*, etc.

Ceremonies. — Civil. — See *Chōga*, *daijō-e*, *genshi-sai*, *haraka no sō*, *iki-shiki ko-chōhai*, *kokki*, *kōsaku*, *tsuina*, etc.

—— Religious. — See *Daigen no hō*, *daishi*, *go-sai-e*, *kajō*, *kwambutsu-e*, *kwanjō*, *ni-ō-e*, *saishi*, *tama-shizume*, etc.

Chastisements, Penalties. — See *Bōhan*, *chikura-okido*, *chokkwan*, *hei-mon*, *hiki-mawashi*, *hissoku*, *kaieki*, *kamae*, *kessho*, *roku-gi*, *shizai*, *tata-ki*, *tejō*, *Tokugawa-keihō*, *tsuihō*, *yoseba-bugyō*, etc.

Chivalry, Knighthood. — See *Bushidō*, *shi-ten*, etc.

Christianity. — See *Chiara*, *Kirishitan-shū*, *Namban-ji*, *shŭmon-ara-tame*, *Sidotti*, and Supplement *passim*.

Civil Condition. — See *Nimbetsu-chō*.

Clothing. — See *Ihō*, *kamishimo*, etc.

Commerce — See *Go-shŭin-bune*, etc.

Confucianism. — See *Judō*, *Kwansei-igaku no kin*, *Rongo*, *Shigaku-dōwa*, *Teishu-ha*, *Tokugawa-jidai*, *keigaku-ha*, *Yōmei-ha*, etc.

Court Ladies. — See *Fujin*, *gyōgesha*, *higyōsha*, *kokiden*, *Naishi no tsukasa*, *nyo-in nyokwan*, *tenji*, *tokusen*, *Ummei-den*, *Uneme*.

Customs, Usages. — See *Bunshin*, *dembu*, *futomani*, *gembuku*, *haimu*, *hassaku, kugatachi, meyasu-bako, nanakusa no kayu, shōbi-kōchin, so-kue, suikotō, sumō-shiki, taisha, tsuji-giri, warifu,* etc.

Dances. — See *Dengaku, go-sechie no mai, hayato-mai, kabuki, kagu-ra, kume-mai, mi-ko, samurai-odori, shirabyōshi, utagaki, Yamato-mai.*

Decorations. — See *Kunshō.*

Departments. —- See *Ken* and Append. III, IV.

Districts. — See *Agata, Aizu, gun, kōri,* and Append. V.

Divinities. — Buddhist. — See *Aizen-myō-ō, Amida, Anan, Ashuku, Binzuru, bosatsu, Dainichi, Daiseishi, Emma-Ō, Fu-Daishi, Fudō, Fugen, Go-chi-nyorai, Jizō, Kwannon, Marishi-ten, Ni-ō, Roshana,* etc.

—— Shintoist. — See *Amaterasu-ō-mikami, Ashinazuchi, Atago, Ben-ten, Bishamon, Daikoku, Ebisu, Fukurokuju, Hachiman, Hotei, Ikazuchi, Inari, Izanagi, Kasuga, Kōjin, Shichi-fukujin, Susa-no-o, Ujigami,* etc.

Domains. — See *Han, jikifu, kantokoro,* etc.

Embassies (to China). — See *Kentō-shi,* etc.

Emperor. — See *Dajō-tennō, go-kō, Hō-ō, Jōkō, Mikado, mi-yuki, senso, soku-i, Sumera, taisō, taka-mikura, Tennō,* etc.

Empress. — See *Gyōkei, kisaki, kōtaifujin, kōtaigō, nyo-in, nyo-tei, sangū, taikōtaigō,* etc.

Eras. — See *Ichibu-ichigen, kigen, nanchin, nengō.*

Escutcheon, Blazon. — See *Bukan, mon.*

Feasts. — Civil. — See *Chōyō, Ebisu-kō, go-sechi-e, go-sekku, jōmi, kigen-setsu, rekken, san-sechi-e, tanabata, tōka no sechi-e,* etc.

—— Religious. — See *Bon, chūshi, hana-shizume, kanname-matsuri, kōshin, niiname-matsuri, shōshi, shūki-kōrei-sai, shunki-kōrei-sai,* etc.

Feudal System. — See *Daimyō, fudai, han, shō-en,* etc.

Geographical Division, Regions.—See *Dō, Go-kinai, hachi-dō, Hok-kaidō, Hokurokudō, Hondo, Saikaidō, Sai-in-dō, San-yō-dō, Tōkaidō, Tōsandō,* etc.

Government. — See *Bakufu, buke-seiji, Chinjufu, Chinzei, Dazaifu, ekiba, gunken, insei, kaitakushi, Kamakura-bakufu-kwansei, Muro-machi, Sekkwan-seiji, Taikwa no kaishin, tokusei,* etc.

Granaries (Public). — See *Kokusō-in, miyake, uchi-kura.*

Headgear. — See *Kammuri,* etc.

Hierarchy, Ranks at Court. — See *Ikai, iroku,'kun-i, kwan-i, kwantō, shaku-i,* etc.

History. — See *Dai-Nihon-shi, Gempei-seisui-ki, Heiji-monogatari, Honchō-tsūgan, Junkōshōtō-ki, Koji-ki, Kuji-ki, Mizu-kagami, Nihon-gwaishi, Nihon-ki, Nihon-seiki, Riku-kokushi, San-kagami, Tennō-ki,* etc.

Hospitals. — See *Hiden-in, Yōjō-sho,* etc.

Japan. —- See *Dai-Nihon, Fusō-koku,* etc. and Appendixes.

Justice. — See *Danjōdai, Gyōbu-shō, hon-bugyō, Monchūjo,* etc.

Laws, Codes. — See *Buke-keihō, buke-shohatto, chakudasei, Engishi-ki, hatto-gaki, Jōei-shikimoku, Kemmu-shikimoku, kempō 17 jō, kinchū-jōmoku, kōkwa-senjo, kuge-shohatto, Kwampyō go-ikai, mikoto, Ōmi-ryō, ritsuryō-kyakushiki, Ryō no gige, Ryō no shūge, sankin-kōdai, senji, shōsho, Taihō-ryōritsu,* etc.

Library. — See *Go-sho-dokoro, Kanazawa-bunko,* etc.

Literature. — See *Azuma-kagami, Eigwa-monogatari, Genji-monogatari, Gunsho-ruijū, Heiji-monogatari, Heike-monogatari, Hōgen-monogatari, Hōjō-ki, Ise-monogatari, Makura no sōshi, Senjimon, Taketori-monogatari, Tosa-nikki, Tsurezure-gusa, Uji-monogatari,* etc.

Measures. — See *Chō, koku, Koma-shaku, ri, senji-masu, shiro, tsuka.*

Medicine. — See *Igaku-kwan, Yōjō-sho,* etc.

Ministries, Bureaus of Administration. — See *Daijin, Daizen-shiki, Dajō-kwan, E-dokoro, Gagaku-ryō, Gemba-ryō, Go-yō-beya, Gwaimushō, Gyōbu-shō, Hyōbu-shō, Hyōjō-sho, Jibu-sho, Jingi-kwan, Kaigun-shō, Kebiishi-chō, Kiroku-sho, Kumonjo, Kunai-shō, Kura-ryō, Kurōdo-dokoro, Mandokoro, Mimbu-shō, Naidaijin, Nakatsukasa-shō, Nōshōmu-shō, Ōi-ryō, Ōkura-shō, On-yō-ryō, Rikugun-shō, Saigū-ryō, Samurai-dokoro, Shikibu-shō, Shuri-shiki, Shuzei-ryō, Sūmitsu-in, Takumi-ryō, Teishin-shō, Ten-yaku-ryō, Tonomori, Zusho-ryō,* etc.

Money. — See *Dairyō, hansatsu, kaiki-shōhō, Wadō,* etc.

Morals. — See *Bushidō, otokodate,* etc.

Mourning. — See *Fukki, haichō,* etc.

Names. — See *Azana, bambetsu, eboshi-na, hassei, kabane, kaimyō, myōji, nanori, okurina, ō-uji, uji, uji no kami, yōmyō, zokumyō,* etc.

Nobility. — See *Daimyō, fudai-daimyō, gekkei-unkaku, go-sekke, kwazoku, san-ke, san-kyō, seikwa, tozama-daimyō, urin-ke,* etc.

Nomination. Promotion. — See *Jimoku, nin, rinji,* etc.

Painting, Drawing, Calligraphy. — See *Kanō, Kasuga-ryū, Kose-ryū, Nansō-gwa, Nishiki-e, Sesshū, Sesson, Shijō-ha, Shūbun, Takuma-ryū, Toba-e, Tosa-ryū, Ukiyo-e, Yamato-ryū,* etc.

Offices. — See *Agata no miyatsuko, azechi, azukarimōsu, benkwan, bettō, bugyō, Chinzei-bugyō, chūnagon, daikwan, dainagon, dai-ni, dajō-daijin, Dazai no gon-no-sotsu, denjō-bito, Fushimi-bugyō, gensui, gisō, gusoku-bugyō, han-chiji, hikitsukeshū, hyōjō-shū, jisha-bugyō, jitō, jōdai, junsatsu-shi, kami, kanimori-zukasa, kanjō-bugyō, kashiwade, kebiishi-chō, kōke, kokushi, kōmon, kubō, kurōdo, kwanryō, Kyōto-shoshidai, machi-bugyō, metsuke, moitori, nairan, nanushi, ōryōshi, ōsuke, rensho, rōjū, sadaijin, sangi, shikken, shitsuji, shōnagon, shō-ni, shugo, sōtsui-bushi, suke, taikō, tairō, tandai, tensō, tomobe, waka-doshiyori,* etc., etc.

Palace. — Imperial. — See *Dai-dairi, Daigoku-den, Daikyō, Dairi, Futama, Go-sho, Higashi-Sanjō-dairi, In no chō, Kan-in-dairi, Kinri, Miya, Miyasu-dokoro, Seiryō-den, Sentō, Shishin-den, Shūhōsha,* etc.

—— Shōgunal. — See *Fukuwara, Imadegawa no tei, Juraku-tei, Nijō-jō, Oku, Rokuhara, takibi no ma,* etc.

Pensions, Revenues. — See *Kirimai, kiroku, koku-daka, kuge-ryō, kwan-daka, tashi-daka,* etc.

Periods (Historical), Data. — See *Ashikaga-jidai, Bakufu-jidai, Buke-jidai, Chūko, Edo-jidai, Heian-chō-jidai, Jindai, Jōko, Kamakura-jidai, Kemmu-chūko, Kinko, Kinsei, Muromachi-jidai, Namboku-chō-jidai, Nara-jidai, Ōchō-jidai, Sengoku-jidai, Taiko, Tokugawa-jidai,* etc.

Poetry. — See *Chokusenka-shū, Hachi-daishū, Hyaku-nin-isshū, Iro-ha-uta, Kokin-shū, Kwaifūsō, Man-yō-shū, Nashitsubo no go-kasen, Nijū-ichi-daishū, Rokkasen, San-gyoku-shū, San-jū-rokkasen, Waka-dokoro.*

Porcelain. — See *Hanibe, hanishi, haniwa, Kutani, Kyōtōshi.*

Printing. — See *Keichō no Kwatsuji-hon.*

Princes. — See *Arisugawa, Fushimi, Hiko, Hime-miko, Hō-shinnō, Kan-in, Kōtaishi, Kōtaitei, Kuni, Kwachō, Miko, Miya, Miya-monzeki, Nyūdō-shinnō, Shinnō, Shi-shinnō-ke, Taishi, Tōgū, Tsuison-tennō.*

Provinces. — See *Kokushi, kuni, shūmei,* and Appendix III.

Regency. — See *Sesshō, Sekkwan-seiji,* etc.

Rice-Fields. — See *Fukanden-sō, fu-yuso-den, handen-shuju-hō, iden, kōden, kwangaku-den, mitoshiro, myōden, yuso-den,* etc.

Roads. — See *Go-kaidō, Hakone-ji, Nakasendō, Ōshū-kaidō, Reiheishi-kaidō, Tōkaidō,* etc.

Religious Sects. — See *Busshin-shū, Chinzei, Fuju-fuze, Fuke-shū, Fusō, hasshū, Hongwanji, Hossō-shū, Ikkō-shū, Ji-shū, Jōdo-shinshū, Jōdo-shū, Jōjitsu-shū, Kairitsu-shū, Ko-ha, Kusha-shū, Misshū, Nichi-ren-shū, Ōbaku-shū, Remmon-kyō, Rinzai-shū, Risshū, Sanron-shū, Seizan, Shingon-shū, Shugen-dō, Sōdō-shū, Tendai-shū, Tenri-kyō, Yūzū-nembutsu-shū, Zen-shū,* etc.

Schools (Education). — See *Ashikaga-gakkō, Bansho-shirabe-dokoro, Gakkwan-in, Gakumon-jo, Gakushū-in, Keiō-gijuku, Kōbun-in, Shōgaku-in, shohan-gakkō Shōhei-kō, tera-koya, Tokugawa-bafuku-gakkō, Wagaku-jo, Yōgaku-jo.*

Schools (Arts). — See *Busshi-ryū, Enshū-ryū, Fukko-ha, Tokugawa-jidai-keigaku-ha, Tosa-ryū, Yamato-ryū,* etc.

Shintoism. — See *Ryōbu-Shintō, Shintō, Yui-itsu-Shintō,* etc.

Shōgun. — See *Fuji-no maki-gari, Sei-i-shi, Sei-i-taishōgun,* etc.

Suicide. — See *Harakiri, junshi.*

Survey. — See *Bunroku no kenchi.*

Taxes. — See *Haishitsu, Jōmen-dori, Kemmei-tori, Ko-mononari, Kutō-ko, So-yō-chō, Tanasue no mitsugi, Yuhazu no mitsugi, Zanshitsu,* etc.

Temples. — Buddhist. — See *Bikuni-gosho, Enryaku-ji, garan, Go-zan, Hongwan-ji, Honji-fure-gashira, Ishiyama-dera, Jingū-ji, Kiyo-mizu-dera, Kōfuku-ji, Kokawa, Kokubun-ji, Kōya-san, Kurama-dera, Mangwan-ji, Minobu, Naidōjō, Negoro-dera, Nikkō, Ninna-ji, Onjō-ji, Shinshō-ji, tera, Zenkō-ji, Zōjō-ji,* etc.

—— Shintoist — See *Daijingū, Gion no yashiro, Hirano-jinja, Hiyoshi, Ikuta-jinja, Izumo no ō-yashiro, Kamo, Kashima, Kasuga, Katori, Kitano, Kotohira-jinja, Kumano-jinja, Matsuo, miya, Naikū, Shingū, Shōkon-sha,* etc.

Theatres. — See *Dengaku, kabuki, kyōgen, nō, sarugaku,* etc.

Tombs. — See *Misasagi, Nikkō, Sanryō-bugyō, Unebi-yama,* etc.

Tutor. — See *Kōken.*

University. — See *Daigaku-ryō, Kiden-dō, Myōkyō-dō, San-dō,* etc.

Vassals. — See *Baishin, fudai, jikisan,* etc.

Vengeance. — See *Ōishi Yoshio, Shi-jū-shichi gishi, Soga Tokimune.*

Wars. — See *Bun-ei no eki, Eikyō no ran, Genkō no ran, Go-sannen no eki, Heiji no ran, Hōgen no ran, Ikkō-to no ran, Jinshin no ran, Kakitsu no hen, Nichiro-sensō, Nishin-sensō, Ōnin no ran, Sankan-seibatsu, Shōkyū no ran, Tenkei no ran,* etc.

II. — ALPHABETICAL INDEX OF THE FORENAMES.

REFERRING TO THE FAMILY NAMES UNDER WHICH HEADING THE
BIOGRAPHICAL NOTICES ARE COLLECTED.

Hiromushi	See Wake	Iwazumi	See Sakaibe	Kawanari	See Kudara
Hironari	— Hineno			Kazu-ko	— Tokugawa
Hironari	-- Inube	**J**		Kazumasa	— Ikoma
Hirotada	— Tokugawa			Kazumasu	— Takigawa
Hirotaka	— Terazawa	Jikkyū	See Miyoshi	Kazunori	— Aoki
Hiroteru	— Minagawa	Jingorō	— Hidari	Kazushige	— Ishida
Hirotsugu	— Fujiwara	Jinsai	— Itō	Kazutoyo	— Yamanouchi
Hirotsuna	— Utsunomiya	Jōzan	— Ishikawa	Kazuuji	— Nakamura
Hirotsune	— Taira	Jōzen	— Hosokawa	Keifuku	— Kudara
Hiroyo	— Ōuchi	Jun-an	— Kinoshita	Keiki	— Tokugawa
Hiroyo	— Wake	Junkei	— Tsutsui	Keisai	— Asami
Hirozumi	— Ki	Junzō	— Ōhashi	Keisuke	— Ōtori
Hisahide	— Matsunaga	Jussai	— Hayashi	Kemmotsu	— Tsuda
Hisamasa	— Asai			Kengyō	— Yatsuhashi
Hisamitsu	— Shimazu	**K**		Kenkō	— Yoshida
Hisaoi	— Arakida			Ken-shi	— Fujiwara
Hitomaro	— Kakinomoto	Kachi-ko	See Tachibana	Kenshin	— Uesugi
Hōitsu	— Sakai	Kagechika	— Ōba	Kenzan	— Nonaki
Hokiichi	— Hanawa	Kageharu	— Nagao	Kenzan	— Ogata
Hōshū	— Amenomori	Kagekatsu	— Uesugi	Kigin	— Kitamura
		Kagekazu	— Katō	Kimi-ko	— Fujiwara
I		Kageki	— Kagawa	Kimimaro	— Kuninaka
		Kagekiyo	— Taira	Kimmochi	— Saionji
Ichi-ō	See Ōkubo	Kagemasa	— Kamakura	Kimmune	— ,,
Ieharu	— Tokugawa	Kagemori	— Adachi	Kinhira	— ,,
Iehira	— Kiyowara	Kagemoto	— Toyama	Kinjō	— Ōta
Iehisa	— Shimazu	Kagesuke	— Shōni	Kintaka	— Koremune
Iekane	— Ryūzōji	Kagetoki	— Kajiwara	Kinsue	— Fujiwara
Iemasa	— Hachisuka	Kagetora	— Uesugi	Kintō	— ,,
Iemitsu	— Tokugawa	Kageyoshi	— Ōba	Kintsugu	— ,,
Iemochi	— ,,	Kahei	— Takadaya	Kintsune	— Saionji
Iemoto	— ,,	Kamako	— Nakatomi	Kintsune	— Utsunomiya
Ienari	— ,,	Kamatari	— Fujiwara	Kinyori	— Sanjō
Ienobu	— ,,	Kanamura	— Ōtomo	Kinzane	— Fujiwara
Ienori	— Matsudaira	Kanaoka	— Koss	Kiyogimi	— Sugawara
Iesada	— Kinoshita	Kanehira	— Fujiwara	Kiyohide	— Nakagawa
Iesada	— Taira	Kanehira	— Imai	Kiyokata	— Uesugi
Iesada	— Tokugawa	Kaneie	— Fujiwara	Kiyokawa	— Fujiwara
Ieshige	— ,,	Kanemichi	— ,,	Kiyomaro	— Wake
Ietada	— Matsudaira	Kanemitsu	— Higuchi	Kiyomasa	— Katō
Ietaka	— Fujiwara	Kanemitsu	— Hino	Kiyomori	— Taira
Ietoki	— Ashikaga	Kanesada	— Ichijō	Kiyoshige	— Kasai
Ietsugu	— Sakai	Kanesue	— Fujiwara	Kiyosuke	— Fujiwara
Ietsugu	— Tokugawa	Kanesue	— Kikutei	Kiyotada	— Bōmon
Ietsuna	— ,,	Kanetane	— Chiba	Kiyotsugu	— Kwanze
Ieyasu	— ,,	Kanetsugu	— Naoe	Kiyotsura	— Miyoshi
Ieyoshi	— ,,	Kaneyasu	— Se-no-o	Kiyouji	— Hosokawa
Iezane	— Fujiwara	Kaneyoshi	— Ichijō	Kiyoyasu	— Tokugawa
Iezane	— Saigō	Kanezane	— Fujiwara	Kiyozumi	— Arima
Iezumi	— Kakimi	Kanren	— Usuki	Kōetsu	— Honnami
Ikina	— Tsuki	Katahide	— Gamō	Kōkan	— Shiba
Ikku	— Jippensha	Katana	— Kamitsukenu	Komachi	— Ono
Imakebito	— Saeki	Katataka	— Terazawa	Komaro	— Shimotsukenu
Imoko	— Ono	Katsuhisa	— Amako	Kon-yō	— Aoki
Iname	— Soga	Katsuie	— Shibata	Korechika	— Fujiwara
In-ei	— Hōzō-in	Katsumi	— Nakatomi	Korehisa	— Taira
Iruka	— Soga	Katsumoto	— Hosokawa	Korekado	— Tsukuhisa
I-shi	— Fujiwara	Katsunaga	— Mōri	Koremasa	— Wada
Issai	— Satō	Katsunobu	— ,,	Koremichi	— Fujiwara
Issei	— Maebara	Katsushige	— Itakura	Koremitsu	— Aso
Itchō	— Hanabusa	Katsushige	— Mizuno	Koremochi	— Taira
Iwao	— Ōyama	Katsushige	— Nabeshima	Koremori	— ,,
Izu-ko	— Fujiwara	Katsutoshi	— Kinoshita	Korenao	— Aso
Izumo no Jō	— Takeda	Katsuyori	— Takeda	Korenari	— Fujiwara

Koretada	See	Fujiwara	Masatomo	See	Ashikaga	Mitsuzumi	See	Iwamatsu
Koretada	—	„	Masatemo	—	Honda	Michifusa	—	Uesugi
Koretoyo	—	Aso	Masatomo	—	Wada	Mochikuni	—	Hatakeyama
Koretoyo	—	Yamana	Masatomo	—	Yūki	Mochimoto	—	Nijō
Koretsuna	—	Anenokōji	Masatora	—	Hotta	Mochimoto	—	Uesugi
Korezumi	—	Aso	Masatoshi	—	„	Mochitoyo	—	Yamana
Kōrin	—	Ogata	Masatoshi	—	Ikoma	Mochiuji	—	Ashikaga
Kosami	—	Ki	Masatoyo	—	Yamana	Mochiyo	—	Ōuchi
Koshirō	—	Fujita	Masatsugu	—	Abe	Mochiyuki	—	Hosokawa
Kōunsai	—	Takeda	Masatsugu	—	Heki	Momokawa	—	Fujiwara
Kumpei	—	Gamō	Masatsuna	—	Ōkōchi	Mondo	—	Hara
Kunichika	—	Chōsokabe	Masatsura	—	Kusunoki	Monzaemon	—	Chikamatsu
Kunihisa	—	Amako	Masauji	—	Ashikaga	Morichika	—	Chōsokabe
Kunikiyo	—	Hatakeyama	Masauji	—	Wada	Morikiyo	—	Ashina
Kunimitsu	—	Hino	Masayasu	—	Hotta	Morikuni	—	Tachibana
Kurajimaro	—	Fujiwara	Masayori	—	Fukushima	Morimasa	—	Ashina
Kuranosuke	—	Ōishi	Masayuki	—	Hoshina	Morimasa	—	Sakuma
Kuromaro	—	Takamuku	Masayuki	—	Sanada	Morinaga	—	Adachi
Kuronushi	—	Ōtomo	Masayuki	—	Takayama	Morishige	—	Akashi
Kusuri-ko	—	Fujiwara	Masazane	—	Minamoto	Morishige	—	Ashina
Kwazan	—	Watanabe	Masazumi	—	Honda	Morishige	—	Kondō
Kyōsai	—	Kawanabe	Masujirō	—	Ōmura	Moritaka	—	Ashina
Kyusō	—	Muro	Masu-ko	—	Fujiwara	Moritaka	—	Kuki
			Matabei]	—	Iwasa	Moritō	—	Endō
M			Matarokurō	—	Kōsai	Moritō	—	Nishina
			Matate	—	Fujiwara	Moritoki	—	Akabashi
Mabuchi	See	Kamo	Me	—	Mononobe	Moritoshi	—	Taira
Makoto	—	Minamoto	Michiari	—	Kōno	Moritsuna	—	Sasaki
Mamichi	—	Sugeno	Michichika	—	Minamoto	Moriuji	—	Ashina
Marise	—	Sakaibe	Michifusa	—	Kurushima	Moriya	—	Mononobe
Maro	—	Fujiwara	Michiharu	—	Doi	Moroe	—	Tachibana
Masachika	—	Togashi	Michihira	—	Nijō	Morofusa	—	Minamoto
Masahide	—	Koide	Michiie	—	Fujiwara	Morofuyu	—	Kō
Masahiro	—	Ōuchi	Michikane	—	„	Morokata	—	Kwazan-in
Masaie	—	Nagatsuka	Michikaze	—	Ono	Moromichi	—	Fujiwara
Masaie	—	Ryūzōji	Michimori	—	Kōno	Moromitsu	—	„
Masakado	—	Taira	Michinaga	—	Fujiwara	Moronaga	—	„
Masakage	—	Yamagata	Michinao	—	Kōno	Moronao	—	Kō
Masakatsu	—	Hachisuka	Michinobu	—	„	Moronobu	—	Hishigawa
Masakatsu	—	Honda	Michinori	—	Fujiwara	Morosuke	—	Fujiwara
Masakatsu	—	Saigō	Michitaka	—	„	Moroyasu	—	Kō
Masakatsu	—	Yūki	Michitaka	—	Kōno	Moroyoshi	—	Yamana
Masakazu	—	Kobori	Michitsura	—	Nozu	Morozane	—	Fujiwara
Masa-ko	—	Fujiwara	Michizane	—	Sugawara	Motochika	—	Chōsokabe
Masamitsu	—	Hoshina	Mifune	—	Ōmi	Motochika	—	Kōsai
Masamitsu	—	Oyama	Mikisaburō	—	Rai	Motofusa	—	Fujiwara
Masamori	—	Hotta	Mitsuharu	—	Akechi	Motoharu	—	Kikkawa
Masamoto	—	Hosokawa	Mitsuhide	—	„	Motokazu	—	Tanuma
Masamune	—	Date	Mitsuie	—	Hatakeyama	Motokiyo	—	Mōri
Masamune	—	Okazaki	Mitsukane	—	Ashikaga	Motokuni	—	Hatakeyama
Masamura	—	Hōjō	Mitskuni	—	Tokugawa	Motomichi	—	Fujiwara
Masamutsu	—	Hotta	Mitsumasa	—	Ikeda	Motonaga	—	Kikkawa
Masanaga	—	Hatakeyama	Mitsumasa	—	Kitabatake	Motonari	—	Mōri
Masanaka	—	Hosokawa	Mitsumoto	—	Hosokawa	Motonori	—	„
Masanari	—	Inaba	Mitsumura	—	Miura	Mototada	—	Torii
Masanobu	—	Honda	Mitsunaga	—	Matsudaira	Mototane	—	Takahashi
Masanobu	—	Hotta	Mitsunaka	—	Minamoto	Mototomo	—	Tanuma
Masanori	—	Fukushima	Mitsunari	—	Ishida	Mototoshi	—	Fujiwara
Masanori	—	Kusunoki	Mitsusada	—	Kira	Mototsugu	—	Tanuma
Masanori	—	Rokugō	Mitsusue	—	Iga	Mototsuna	—	Kuchiki
Masasato	—	Kitabatake	Mitsusuke	—	Akamatsu	Mototsune	—	Fujiwara
Masashige	—	Kusunoki	Mitsutaka	—	Rokkaku	Motouji	—	Ashikaga
Masatada	—	Wada	Mitsuyuki	—	Yamana	Motoyasu	—	Mōri
Masatake	—	„				Motozane	—	Fujiwara

Muchimaro	See *Fujiwara*	Naozumi	See *Arima*	Norikatsu	See *Manabe*
Munehiro	— *Yūki*	Naramaro	— *Tachibana*	Norikuni	— *Imagawa*
Munehisa	— *Maeda*	Nariaki	— *Tokugawa*	Norimasa	— *Imagawa*
Munekiyo	— *Taira*	Nariakira	— *Shimazu*	Norimasa	— *Uesugi*
Munemori	— "	Narichika	— *Fujiwara*	Norimichi	— *Fujiwara*
Munesada	— *Yoshimine*	Narihira	— *Ariwara*	Norimori	— *Taira*
Muneshige	— *Tachibana*	Narihiro	— *Mōri*	Norimoto	— *Uesugi*
Munesuke	— *Honjō*	Narimasa	— *Sasa*	Norimune	— *Urakami*
Munetō	— *Abe*	Naritomo	— *Yūki*	Norimura	— *Akamatsu*
Munetsugu	— *Tachiiri*	Naritsune	— *Fujiwara*	Norinaga	— *Motoori*
Muramune	— *Urakami*	Natsui	— *Ki*	Norisuke	— *Akamatsu*
Murashige	— *Araki*	Natsuno	— *Kiyowara*	Noritada	— *Imagawa*
		Nobuharu	— *Baba*	Noritada	— *Uesugi*
N		Nobuhide	— *Oda*	Noritomo	— *Kitabatake*
		Nobuhira	— *Tsugaru*	Noritsune	— *Taira*
Nagaakira	See *Asano*	Nobuhiro	— *Konoe*	Noriuji	— *Imagawa*
Nagachika	— *Tokugawa*	Nobuhiro	— *Matsumae*	Noriyori	— *Minamoto*
Nagafusa	— *Takayama*	Nobuhiro	— *Oda*	Norizane	— *Kujō*
Nagaharu	— *Bessho*	Nobukane	— "	Norizane	— *Uesugi*
Nagahide	— *Niwa*	Nobukata	— *Itagaki*		
Nagamasa	— *Asai*	Nobukatsu	— *Baba*	**O**	
Nagamasa	— *Asano*	Nobukazu	— *Matsudaira*		
Nagamasa	— *Kuroda*	Nobumasa	— *Andō*	Oguromaro	See *Fujiwara*
Nagamasa	— *Yamada*	Nobumasa	— *Asakura*	Oiwa	— *Ki*
Nagamasu	— *Oda*	Nobumasa	— *Okudaira*	Okimoto	— *Hosokawa*
Nagamochi	— *Jō*	Nobumasa	— *Takeda*	Okoshi	— *Mononobe*
Nagamori	— *Masuda*	Nobumitsu	— "	Okura	— *Yamanouchi*
Nagamori	— *Okabe*	Nobumitsu	— *Tokugawa*	Okyo	— *Maruyama*
Nagamoto	— *Miyoshi*	Nobumori	— *Nishina*	Omaro	— *Ki*
Naganori	— *Asano*	Nobumori	— *Sakuma*	On-shi	— *Fujiwara*
Nagashige	— *Niwa*	Nobumoto	— *Mizuno*	Otomaro	— *Otomo*
Nagate	— *Fujiwara*	Nobunaga	— *Oda*	Otondo	— *Ōe*
Nagateru	— *Miyoshi*	Nobunao	— *Nambu*	Otsugu	— *Fujiwara*
Nagatoki	— *Hōjō*	Nobunari	— *Naitō*	Oyori	— *Murakuni*
Nagatoki	— *Ogasawara*	Nobuo	— *Oda*	Oyumi	— *Ki*
Nagatomo	— *Akimoto*	Nobuoki	— *Kitabatake*		
Nagatoshi	— *Nawa*	Nobutada	— *Konoe*	**R**	
Nagatsune	— *Ikeda*	Nobutada	— *Oda*		
Nagauji	— *Hōjō*	Nobutada	— *Tokugawa*	Razan	See *Hayashi*
Nagayasu	— *Ōkubo*	Nobutaka	— *Oda*	Ren-shi	— *Fujiwara*
Nagayoshi	— *Ikeda*	Nobuteru	— *Ikeda*	Rikyū	— *Sen*
Nagayoshi	— *Mori*	Nobutomi	— *Matsudaira*	Rinzō	— *Mamiya*
Nagayuki	— *Ikeda*	Nobutora	— *Takeda*	Ritsuzan	— *Shibano*
Nakahira	— *Fujiwara*	Nobutoshi	— *Kinoshita*	Rokuemon	— *Hasekura*
Nakamaro	— *Abe*	Nobutsuna	— *Okōchi*	Ryōi	— *Suminokura*
Nakamaro	— *Fujiwara*	Nobutsuna	— *Sasaki*	Ryōkai	— *Kumazawa*
Nakanari	— "	Nobutsura	— *Hasabe*	Ryōshun	— *Imagawa*
Nambo	— *Ōta*	Nobuyasu	— *Tokugawa*		
Nankai	— *Gion*	Nobuyori	— *Fujiwara*	**S**	
Naoie	— *Ukita*	Nobuyoshi	— *Hosokawa*		
Naokatsu	— *Ii*	Nobuyoshi	— *Takeda*	Sadafuji	See *Nikaidō*
Naomasa	— "	Nobuyoshi	— *Tokugawa*	Sadafusa	— *Hisamatsu*
Naomasa	— *Nagai*	Nobuyuki	— *Oda*	Sadaie	— *Fujiwara*
Naomitsu	— "	Nobuyuki	— *Sanada*	Sadakata	— *Nitta*
Naonaga	— "	Nobuzumi	— *Oda*	Sadakatsu	— *Hisamatsu*
Naonobu	— *Hatakeyama*	Noriaki	— *Uesugi*	Sadakiyo	— *Ishikawa*
Naoshige	— *Nabeshima*	Norifusa	— *Ichijō*	Sada-ko	— *Fujiwara*
Noasuke	— *Ii*	Norifusa	— *Manabe*	Sadamasa	— *Toki*
Naotaka	— "	Norifusa	— *Uesugi*	Sadamasa	— *Uesugi*
Naotsugu	— *Andō*	Noriharu	— "	Sadamori	— *Sō*
Naotsugu	— *Hanawa*	Norihiro	— *Ouchi*	Sadamori	— *Taira*
Naotsune	— *Momonoi*	Norikage	— *Asakura*	Sadamune	— *Ogasawara*
Naoyori	— *Shinjō*	Norikata	— *Uesugi*	Sadamune	— *Otomo*
Naozane	— *Kumagaya*			Sadanao	— *Osaragi*
				Sadanobu	— *Matsudaira*

Sadanushi	See	Shigeno
Sadataka	—	Iwaki
Sadatane	—	Chiba
Sadatō	—	Abe
Sadatoki	—	Hōjō
Sadatsugu	—	Tsutsui
Sadatsuna	—	Matsudaira
Sadatsuna	—	Sasaki
Sadatsune	—	Shōni
Sadauji	—	Ashikaga
Sadayo	—	Imagawa
Sadayori	—	Fujiwara
Sadayori	—	Rokkaku
Sadayoshi	—	Taira
Sadayoshi	—	Toki
Sadayuki	—	Usami
Sadehiko	—	Ōtomo
Sake no kimi	—	Hata
Sake no kimi	—	Kudara
Sakihisa	—	Konoe
Sakuzaemon	—	Takahashi
Samba	—	Sekütei
Sanefusa	—	Sanjō
Sanehira	—	Doi
Sanekuni	—	Nikki
Sanemori	—	Saitō
Sanesue	—	Akita
Sanetane	—	Chiba
Sanetomi	—	Sanjō
Sanetomo	—	Minamoto
Saneyoshi	—	Tokudaiji
Saneyuki	—	Sanjō
San-yō	—	Rai
Sanzō	—	Tsuda
Saru	—	Kose
Sayo-hime	—	Matsuura
Seikwa	—	Fujiwara
Seikwaku	—	Ibara
Seimei	—	Abe
Seiri	—	Koga
Sen-hime	—	Tokugawa
Senju-maru	—	Minamoto
Sensai	—	Emura
Sen-shi	—	Fujiwara
Shigeharu	—	Matsukura
Shigehide	—	Ogiwara
Shigehira	—	Taira
Shigehiro	—	Itakura
Shigekata	—	Hosokawa
Shigekatsu	—	Furuta
Shigekatsu	—	Onoki
Shigekore	—	Kimura
Shigemasa	—	Itakura
Shigemasa	—	Matsukura
Shigemasa	—	Okamoto
Shigemitsu	—	Kudō
Shigemori	—	Taira
Shigemune	—	Itakura
Shigenao	—	Nabeshima
Shigenari	—	Furuta
Shigenari	—	Kimura
Shigenobu	—	Andō
Shigenobu	—	Matsuura
Shigenobu	—	Ōkuma

Shigenori	See	Itakura
Shigetada	—	Hatakeyama
Shigetane	—	Chiba
Shigetane	—	Itakura
Shigetane	—	Takahashi
Shigetoki	—	Hōjō
Shigetoshi	—	Morikawa
Shigetsune	—	Furuta
Shigeuji	—	Ashikaga
Shigeyoshi	—	Taguchi
Shigeyoshi	—	Uesugi
Shihei	—	Hayashi
Shikibu	—	Murasaki
Shikibu	—	Takenouchi
Shimpei	—	Etō
Shingen	—	Takeda
Shinsaku	—	Takasugi
Shinzaemon	—	Sorori
Shirōzaemon	—	Katō
Shitagau	—	Minamoto
Shōan	—	Minabuchi
Shōin	—	Yoshida
Shōnagon	—	Sei
Shōsetsu	—	Yui
Shōshun	—	Tosabō
Shōzau	—	Sakuma
Shōzui	—	Ise
Shunkai	—	Yasui
Shunkei	—	Katō
Shunsai	—	Hayashi
Shunsui	—	Shu
Shunsui	—	Tamenaga
Shuntai	—	Dazai
Sōdan	—	Kamiya
Sōgorō	—	Sakura
Sōi	—	Mori
Sokō	—	Yamaga
Sōkun	—	Imai
Sorai	—	Ogiu
Sōrin	—	Ōtomo
Sosen	—	Mori
Sōun	—	Hōjō
Sōzen	—	Yamana
Suefusa	—	Akamatsu
Suehiro	—	Matsumae
Sugane	—	Fujiwara
Sukeaki	—	Hino
Sukechika	—	Itō
Sukekiyo	—	„
Sukekiyo	—	Ōta
Sukemasa	—	Asai
Sukemasa	—	Fujiwara
Sukemori	—	Jō
Sukemoto	—	Shōni
Sukemune	—	Ōta
Sukena	—	Hino
Sukenaga	—	Jō
Sukenaga	—	Ōta
Sukenari	—	Soga
Sukeshige	—	Oguri
Suketaka	—	Itō
Suketaka	—	Ōta
Suketomo	—	Hino

Suketsune	See	Kudō
Sukeyori	—	Shōni
Sukeyoshi	—	Itō
Sukezane	—	Kujō
Sukune	—	Nomi
Sukune	—	Takeshiuchi
Sumimoto	—	Hosokawa
Sumitada	—	Ōmura
Sumitomo	—	Fujiwara
Sumiyori	—	Ōmura
Sumiyuki	—	Hosokawa
Surugamaro	—	Ōtomo

T

Tadaaki	See	Matsudaira
Tadabumi	—	Fujiwara
Tadachika	—	Nakayama
Tadachika	—	Ōkubo
Tadafusa	—	Ishikawa
Tadafusa	—	Ōe
Tadafuyu	—	Askikaga
Tadaharu	—	Horio
Tadahide	—	Homma
Tadahira	—	Fujiwara
Tadahiro	—	Katō
Tadahiro	—	Matsudaira
Tadahisa	—	Shimazu
Tadakatsu	—	Honda
Tadakatsu	—	Sakai
Tadakiyo	—	„
Tadamasa	—	Honda
Tadamasa	—	Ina
Tadamasa	—	Matsudaira
Tadamasa	—	Mizuno
Tadamasa	—	Mori
Tadamichi	—	Fujiwara
Tadamori	—	Taira
Tadamoto	—	Ōkubo
Tadanaga	—	Tokugawa
Tadanao	—	Matsudaira
Tadanobu	—	Fujiwara
Tadanori	—	Ōkubo
Tadanori	—	Taira
Tadao	—	Ikeda
Tadaoki	—	Hosokawa
Tadasato	—	Gamō
Tadashige	—	Mizuno
Tadasuke	—	Ōkubo
Tadasuke	—	Ō-oka
Tadataka	—	Honda
Tadataka	—	Kyōgoku
Tadateru	—	Tokugawa
Tadatomo	—	Gamō
Tadatomo	—	Honda
Tadatoshi	—	Hosokawa
Tadatoshi	—	Matsudaira
Tadatsugu	—	Honda
Tadatsugu	—	Ikeda
Tadatsugu	—	Ina
Tadatsugu	—	Sakai
Tadatsuna	—	Anenokōji
Tadatsuna	—	Utsunomiya

III. — TABLE OF PROVINCES.

AND THEIR DEPARTMENTS.

PROVINCES	CHINESE NAME	DEPARTMENTS	PROVINCES	CHINESE NAME	DEPARTMENTS
Go-Kinai			**Hokurokudō**		
1. Yamashiro	*Jōshū*	Kyōto	5. Etchū	*Esshū*	Toyama
2. Yamato	*Washū*	Nara	6. Echigo	„	Niigata
3. Kawachi	*Kashū*	Ōsaka	7. Sado	*Sashū*	„
4. Izumi	*Senshū*	„			
5. Settsu	*Sesshū*	„ , Hyōgo	**San-in-dō**		
Tōkaidō			1. Tamba	*Tanshū*	Kyōto, Hyōgo
			2. Tango	„	„
			3. Tajima	„	Hyōgo
1. Iga	*Ishū*	Mie	4. Inaba	*Inshū*	Tottori
2. Ise	*Seishū*	„	5. Hōki	*Hakushū*	„
3. Shima	*Shishū*	„	6. Izumo	*Unshū*	Shimane
4. Owari	*Bishū*	Aichi	7. Iwami	*Sekishū*	„
5. Mikawa	*Sanshū*	„	8. Oki	*Inshū*	„
6. Tōtōmi	*Eushū*	Shizuoka			
7. Suruga	*Sunshū*	„	**San-yō-dō**		
8. Kai	*Kōshū*	Yamanashi			
9. Izu	*Zushū*	Shizuoka	1. Harima	*Banshū*	Hyōgo
10. Sagami	*Sōshū*	Kanagawa	2. Mimasaka	*Sakushū*	Okayama
11. Musashi	*Bushū*	Tōkyō, Kana-gawa, Saitama	3. Bizen	*Bishū*	„
			4. Bitchū	„	Hiroshima
12. Awa	*Bōshū*	Chiba	5. Bingo	„	
13. Kazusa	*Sōshū*	„	6. Aki	*Geishū*	„
14. Shimōsa	„	„ , Ibaraki	7. Suwō	*Bōshū*	Yamaguchi
15. Hitachi	*Jōshū*	Ibaraki	8. Nagato	*Chōshū*	„
Tōsandō			**Nankaidō**		
1. Ōmi	*Gōshū*	Shiga	1. Kii	*Kishū*	Wakayama, Mie
2. Mino	*Nōshū*	Gifu			
3. Hida	*Hishū*	„	2. Awaji	*Tanshū*	Hyōgo
4. Shinano	*Shinshū*	Nagano	3. Awa	*Ashū*	Tokushima
5. Kōzuke	*Jōshū*	Gumma	4. Sanuki	*Sanshū*	Kagawa
6. Shimotsuke	*Yashū*	Tochigi	5. Iyo	*Yoshū*	Ehime
7. Iwaki	*Ōshū*	Fukushima, Miyagi	6. Tosa	*Toshū*	Kōchi
8. Iwashiro	„	„	**Saikaidō**		
9. Rikuzen	„	Miyagi, Iwate			
10. Rikuchū	„	Iwate, Akita	1. Chikuzen	*Chikushū*	Fukuoka
11. Mutsu	„	Aomori	2. Chikugo	„	„
12. Uzen	*Ushū*	Yamagata	3. Buzen	*Hōshū*	„ , Ōita
13. Ugo	„	Akita, Yamagata	4. Bungo	„	Ōita
			5. Hizen	*Hishū*	Nagasaki, Saga
			6. Higo	„	Kumamoto
Hokurokudō			7. Hyūga	*Nisshū*	Miyazaki, Kagoshima
1. Wakasa	*Jakushū*	Fukui	8. Ōsumi	*Gūshū*	Kagoshima
2. Kaga	*Kashū*	Ishikawa	9. Satsuma	*Sasshū*	„
3. Noto	*Nōshū*	„	10. Iki	*Ishū*	Nagasaki
4. Echizen	*Esshū*	Fukui	11. Tsushima	*Taishū*	„
			12. Ryūkyū		Okinawa

PROVINCES	CHINESE NAME	DEPARTMENTS	PROVINCES	CHINESE NAME	DEPARTMENTS
Hokkaidō			**Hokkaidō**		
1. Oshima		Hokkaidō-chō	7. Hidaka		Hokkaidō-chō
2. Shiribeshi		,,	8. Tokachi		,,
3. Ishikari		,,	9. Kushiro		,,
4. Teshio		,,	10. Nemuro		,,
5. Kitami		,,	11. Chishima		,,
6. Iburi		,,			

IV. — TABLE OF THE DEPARTMENTS. *(ken)*

WITH THEIR AREA, POPULATION, ETC.

(December 31, 1903)

RE-GION.	DEPARTMENTS	AREA IN KM².	POPULA-TION	POPULA-TION PER KM.²	CHIEF-TOWN	POPULA-TION
	Tōkyō (*fu*)	1,940.28	1,668,198	859	Tōkyō	1.518,655
	Kanagawa	2,400.97	866,264	361	Yokohama	326,035
	Saitama	4,102.50	1,248,596	304	Urawa	7,000
	Chiba	5,030.37	1,329,350	264	Chiba	28,768
	Ibaraki	5,940.82	1,205,207	203	Mito	36,928
	Tochigi	6,350.94	858,862	135	Utsunomiya	35,953
	Gumma	6 281.22	850,075	132	Maebashi	41,714
	Nagano	13,167.97	1,321,564	100	Nagano	37,202
	Yamanashi	4,470.50	537,934	120	Kōfu	44.188
	Shizuoka	7,770.67	1,294,904	162	Shizuoka	48,744
	Aichi	4,824.16	1,692,744	350	Nagoya	288,639
	Mie	5,684.33	1,051,052	185	Tsu	36,408
	Gifu	10,356.11	1,046,519	101	Gifu	40,168
	Shiga	3,986.05	739,608	185	Ōtsu	39,595
	Fukui	4,201.36	655,711	156	Fukui	50,155
	Ishikawa	4,175.45	806,745	193	Kanazawa	99,657
	Toyama	4,108.98	814,876	198	Toyama	56,275
Honshū	Niigata	12,718.06	1,882,559	148	Niigata	59,576
	Fukushima	13,049.36	1,145,582	87	Fukushima	27,233
	Miyagi	8,340.87	898,513	108	Sendai	100,231
	Yamagata	9,256.41	889,502	96	Yamagata	40,248
	Akita	11,629.32	834,779	72	Akita	34,350
	Iwate	13,868.66	761,281	55	Morioka	31,861
	Aomori	9,362.53	663,284	71	Aomori	34,857
	Kyōto (*fu*)	4,573.84	984,285	215	Kyōto	380,568
	Ōsaka (*fu*)	I,784.81	1,432,881	802	Ōsaka	995,945
	Nara	3,106.60	568,265	182	Nara	33,735
	Wakayama	4,790.85	721,402	150	Wakayama	68,527
	Hyōgo	8,585.95	1,776,202	206	Kōbe	285,002
	Okayama	6,492.99	1,181,200	181	Okayama	81,025
	Hiroshima	8,032.25	1,517,164	188	Hiroshima	121,196
	Yamaguchi	6,015.01	1,032,852	171	Yamaguchi	18,000
	Shimane	6,721.87	742,834	110	Matsue	35,081
	Tottori	3,457.33	439,199	127	Tottori	31,023

RE-GION	DEPARTMENTS	AREA IN KM².	POPULA-TION	POPULA-TION PER KM.²	CHIEF-TOWN	POPULA-TION
Shikoku	Tokushima	4,184.09	729,950	174	Tokushima	63,710
	Kagawa	1,750.57	730,944	417	Takamatsu	37,430
	Ehime	5,262.03	1,056,047	200	Matsuyama	37,842
	Kōchi	7,013.37	650,754	92	Kōchi	35,518
Kyūshū	Nagasaki	3,626.83	878,662	242	Nagasaki	153,293
	Saga	2.468.99	666,157	269	Saga	35,083
	Fukuoka	4,901.74	1,476,485	301	Fukuoka	71,047
	Kumamoto	7.179.18	1,212,182	168	Kumemoto	59,717
	Oita	6,211.51	873,650	140	Oita	14,000
	Miyazaki	7,516.49	490,269	65	Miyazaki	8,000
	Kagoshima	9,289.73	1,194,226	128	Kagoshima	59,001
	Okinawa	2,420.10	469,203	193	Naha	43,132

REGION	AREA IN KM².	POPULA-TION	POPULA-TION PER KM.²	KWA-ZOKU	SHIZOKU	HEIMIN
Honshū	226,579.39	35,460,507	157	4,473	1,115,172	34,340,862
Shikoku	18,210.06	3,167,696	174	52	131,981	3,035,663
Kyūshū	43,614.57	7,260,834	166	502	860,578	6,399,854
Hokkaidō	94,011.79	843,615	9	28	59,658	783,929
Taiwan	34,973.87	3,025,564	86	„	2,000	3,023,564
Japanese Empire	417,389.68	49,758,216	119	5,055	2,169,389	47,583,772

DENSITY OF POPULATION.

ACCORDING TO FORMER CENSUSES.

YEAR	POPULATION	POPULA-TION PER KM.²	YEAR	POPULATION	POPULA-TION PER KM.²
1871	33,110,825	86	1895	44,620,620	107
1875	34,338,404	89	1896	45,158,264	108
1880	36,358,944	95	1897	45,778,863	109
1885	38,151,217	99	1898	46,410,815	111
1890	40,453,461	105	1899	47,019,152	112
1891	40,718,677	106	1900	47,656,853	114
1892	41,089,940	107	1901	48,362,096	115
1893	41,388,313	108	1902	49,022,572	117
1894	41,813,215	109	1903	49,758,216	119

V. — TABLE OF THE DISTRICTS (*kōri = gun*)

BY PROVINCES

WITH THE DEPARTMENTS TO WHICH THEY BELONG.

DISTRICTS	DEPART-MENTS	DISTRICTS	DEPART-MENTS
Yamashiro		**Ise**	
1. Otokuni, 乙訓	*Kyōto*	1. Ano, 安濃	*Mie*
2. Kadono, 葛野	,,	2. Mie, 三重	,,
3. Kii, 紀伊	,,	3. Kuwana, 桑名	,,
4. Otagi, 愛宕	,,	4. Inabe, 員弁	,,
5. Uji, 宇治	,,	5. Suzuga, 鈴鹿	,,
6. Kuze, 久世	,,	6. Kawage, 河藝	,,
7. Tsuzuki, 綴喜	,,	7. Isshi, 一志	,,
8. Sōraku, 相樂	,,	8. Iinami, 飯南	,,
		9. Take, 多氣	,,
Yamato		10. Watarai, 度會	,,
1. Sō-no-Kami, 添上	*Nara*	**Shima**	
2. Ikoma, 生駒	,,		
3. Yamabe, 山邊	,,	1. Shima, 志摩	*Mie*
4. Kita-Katsuragi, 北葛城	,,		
5. Minami-Katsuragi, 南葛城	,,	**Owari**	
6. Uda, 宇陀	,,	1. Aichi, 愛知	*Aichi*
7. Uchi, 宇智	,,	2. Nishi-Kasugai, 西春日井	,,
8. Takaichi, 高市	,,	3. Chita, 知多	,,
9. Yoshino, 吉野	,,	4. Kaitō, 海東	,,
10. Shiki, 磯城	,,	5. Kaisai, 海西	,,
		6. Higashi-Kasugai, 東春日井	,,
Kawachi		7. Niwa, 丹羽	,,
1. Minami-Kawachi, 南河內	*Ōsaka*	8. Haguri, 葉栗	,,
2. Naka-Kawachi, 中河內	,,	9. Nakajima, 中島	,,
3. Kita-Kawachi, 北河內	,,	**Mikawa**	
Izumi		1. Atsumi, 渥美	*Aichi*
		2. Yana, 八名	,,
1. Sennan, 泉南	*Ōsaka*	3. Hoi, 寶飯	,,
2. Semboku, 泉北	,,	4. Nukada, 額田	,,
		5. Aomi, 碧海	,,
Settsu		6. Minami-Shidara, 南設樂	,,
1. Higashi-Nari, 東成	*Ōsaka*	7. Kita-Shidara, 地設樂	,,
2. Nishi-Nari, 西成	,,	8. Hazu, 幡豆	,,
3. Mishima, 三島	,,	9. Higashi-Kamo, 東加茂	,,
4. Toyono, 豐能	,,	10. Nishi-Kamo, 西加茂	,,
5. Muko, 武庫	*Hyōgo*	**Tōtōmi**	
6. Kawabe, 川邊	,,		
7. Arima, 有馬	,,	1. Inasa, 引佐	*Shizuoka*
		2. Hamana, 濱名	,,
Iga		3. Iwata, 磐田	,,
1. Ayama, 阿山	*Mie*	4. Ogasa, 小笠	,,
2. Naga, 名賀	,,		

Districts	Departments	Districts	Departments
Tōtōmi		**Musashi**	
5. Suchi, 榛知	*Shizuoka*	8. Kita-Saitama, 北埼玉	*Saitama*
6. Haibara, 捧原	,,	9. Kita-Katsushika,	,,
		北葛飾	
Suruga		10. Kita-Toshima, 北豐島	*Tōkyō*
		11. Ebara, 荏原	,,
1. Suntō, 駿東	*Shizuoka*	12. Toyotama, 豐多摩	,,
2. Ibara, 庵原	,,	13. Minami-Katsushika,	,,
3. Abe, 阿倍	,,	南葛飾	
4. Shida, 志太	,,	14. Nishi-Tama, 西多摩	,,
5. Fuji, 富士	,,	15. Minami-Tama, 南多摩	,,
		16. Kita-Tama, 北多摩	,,
Kai		17. Minami-Adachi,	,,
		南足立	
1. Minami-Tsuru, 南都留	*Yamanashi*	18. Kuraki, 久良岐	*Kanagawa*
2. Kita-Tsuru, 地都留	,,	19. Tachibana, 橘樹	,,
3. Higashi-Yatsushiro,	,,	20. Tsuzuki, 都築	,,
東八代			
4. Nishi-Yatsushiro,	,,	**Awa**	
西八代			
5. Higashi-Yamanashi,	,,	1. Awa, 安房	*Chiba*
東山梨			
6. Nishi-Yamanashi,		**Kazusa**	
西山梨	,,		
7. Minami-Koma, 南巨摩	,,	1. Sambu, 山武	*Chiba*
8. Naka-Koma, 中巨摩	,,	2. Ichihara, 市原	,,
9. Kita-Koma, 北巨摩	,,	3. Isumi, 夷隅	,,
		4. Chōsei, 長生	,,
Izu		5. Kimitsu, 君津	,,
1. Tagata, 田方	*Shizuoka*	**Shimōsa**	
2. Kamo, 賀茂	,,		
		1. Higashi-Katsushika	*Chiba*
Sagami		東葛飾	
		2. Katori, 香取	,,
1 Ashigara-Kami, 足柄上	*Kanagawa*	3. Sōsa, 匝嵯	,,
2. Ashigara-Shimo,	,,	4. Unagami, 海上	,,
足柄下		5. Chiba, 千葉	,,
3. Miura, 三浦	,,	6. Imba, 印藩	,,
4. Kamakura, 鎌倉	,,	7. Yūki, 結城	*Ibaraki*
5. Kōza, 高度	,,	8. Kita-Sōma, 北相馬	,,
6. Naka, 中	,,	9. Sashima, 猿島	,,
7. Aikō, 愛甲	,,		
8. Tsukui, 津久井	,,	**Hitachi**	
		1. Higashi-Ibaraki,	*Ibaraki*
Musashi		東茨木	
		2. Nishi-Ibaraki, 西茨木	,,
1. Chichibu, 秩父	*Saitama*	3. Tsukuba, 筑波	,,
2. Kita-Adachi, 北足立	,,	4. Niiharu, 新治	,,
3. Iruma, 入間	,,	5. Kuji, 久慈	,,
4. Hiki, 比企	,,	6. Inashiki, 稻敷	,,
5. Kodama, 兒玉	,,	7. Makabe, 眞壁	,,
6. Ōsato, 大里	,,	8. Naka, 那珂	,,
7. Minami-Saitama,	,,	9. Taga, 多賀	,,
南埼玉		10. Namekata, 行方	,,
		11. Kashima, 鹿島	,,

Districts	Depart-ments	Districts	Depart-ments
Ōmi		**Kōzuke**	
1. Shiga, 滋賀	*Shiga*	1. Seta, 勢多	*Gumma*
2. Kōga, 甲賀	,,	2. Gunma, 群馬	,,
3. Higashi-Asai, 東淺井	,,	3. Tano, 多野	,,
4. Takashima, 高嶋	,,	4. Kita-Kanra, 北甘樂	,,
5. Yasu, 野洲	,,	5. Ora, 邑樂	,,
6. Ika, 伊香	,,	6. Sawa, 佐波	,,
7. Kurita, 栗太	,,	7. Usui, 碓氷	,,
8. Gamō, 蒲生	,,	8. Azuma, 吾妻	,,
9. Kanzaki, 神崎	,,	9. Tone, 利根	,,
10. Eichi, 愛知	,,	10. Yamada, 山田	,,
11. Inukami, 犬上	,,	11. Nitta, 新田	,,
12. Sakata, 坂田	,,		
Mino		**Shimotsuke**	
1. Inaba, 稻葉	*Gifu*	1. Kawachi, 河內	*Tochigi*
2. Ena, 惠那	,,	2. Kami-Tsuga, 上都賀	,,
3. Toki, 土岐	,,	3. Shimo-Tsuga, 下都賀	,,
4. Kani, 可兒	,,	4. Aso, 安蘇	,,
5. Kamo, 加茂	,,	5. Ashikaga, 足利	,,
6. Hashima, 羽島	,,	6. Haga, 芳賀	,,
7. Mugi, 武儀	,,	7. Shioya, 鹽谷	,,
8. Yōrō, 養老	,,	8. Nasu, 那須	,,
9. Kaizu, 海津	,,	**Iwaki**	
10. Fuwa, 不破	,,		
11. Ibi, 揖斐	,,	1. Higashi-Shirakawa,	*Fukushima*
12. Ampachi, 安八	,,	東白河	
13. Gunjō, 郡上	,,	2. Nishi-Shirakawa	,,
14. Yamagata, 山縣	,,	西白河	
15. Motosu, 本巣	,,	3. Iwaki, 石城	,,
Hida		4. Futaba, 雙葉	,,
		5. Sōma, 相馬	,,
1. Masuda, 益田	*Gifu*	6. Ishikawa, 石川	,,
2. Ōno, 大野	,,	7. Tamura, 田村	,,
3. Yoshiki, 吉城	,,	8. Watari, 亘理	*Miyagi*
		9. Katta, 刈田	,,
Shinano		10. Igu, 伊具	,,
1. Minami-Saku, 南佐久	*Nagano*	**Iwashiro**	
2. Kita Saku, 北佐久	,,		
3. Chiisagata, 小縣	,,	1. Asaka, 安積	*Fukushima*
4. Suwa, 諏訪	,,	2. Iwase, 岩瀨	,,
5. Kami-Ina, 上伊那	,,	3. Adachi, 安達	,,
6. Shimo-Ina, 下伊那	,,	4. Date, 伊達	,,
7. Nishi-Tsukuma, 西筑摩	,,	5. Shinobu, 信夫	,,
8. Higashi-Tsukuma,	,,	6. Minami-Aizu, 南會津	,,
東筑摩		7. Kita-Aizu, 北會津	,,
9. Minami-Azumi, 南安曇	,,	8. Kawanuma, 河沼	,,
10. Kita-Azumi, 北安曇	,,	9. Yama, 耶麻	,,
11. Sarashina, 更科	,,	10. Onuma, 大沼	,,
12. Hanishina, 埴科	,,	**Rikuzen**	
13. Kami-Takai, 上高井	,,		
14. Shimo-Takai, 下高井	,,	1. Miyagi, 宮城	*Miyagi*
15. Kami-Minochi, 上水內	,,	2. Natori, 名取	,,
16. Shimo-Minochi, 下水內	,,	3. Shibata, 柴田	,,

Districts	Departments	Districts	Departments

Rikuzen

4. Kurokawa, 黑川	*Miyagi*	
5. Shida, 志田	,,	
6. Tamatsukuri, 玉造	,,	
7. Kami, 加美	,,	
8. Kurihara, 栗原	,,	
9. Oshika, 牡鹿	,,	
10. Motoyoshi, 本吉	,,	
11. Toyoma, 登米	,,	
12. Tōda, 遠田	,,	
13. Monō, 桃生	,,	
14. Kesen, 氣仙	*Iwate*	

Rikuchū

1. Iwate, 巖手	*Iwate*
2. Shibata, 紫波	,,
3. Shimo-Hei, 下閉伊	,,
4. Kami-Hei, 上閉伊	,,
5. Hienuki, 稗貫	,,
6. Ezashi, 江刺	,,
7. Kunohe, 九戸	,,
8. Waga, 和賀	,,
9. Higashi-Iwai, 東磐井	,,
10. Nishi-Iwai, 西磐井	,,
11. Izawa, 膽澤	,,
12. Kazuno, 鹿角	*Akita*

Mutsu

1. Higashi-Tsugaru, 東津輕	*Aomori*
2. Nishi-Tsugaru, 西津輕	,,
3. Naka-Tsugaru, 中津輕	,,
4. Minami-Tsugaru, 南津輕	,,
5. Kita-Tsugaru, 北津輕	,,
6. Kami-Kita, 上北	,,
7. Shimo-Kita, 下北	,,
8. Sannohe, 三戸	,,
9. Ninohe, 二戸	*Iwate*

Uzen

1. Higashi-Murayama, 東村山	*Yamagata*
2. Nishi-Murayama, 西村山	,,
3. Minami-Murayama, 南村山	,,
4. Kita-Murayama, 北村山	,,
5. Higashi-Tagawa, 東田川	,,
6. Nishi-Tagawa, 西田川	,,
7. Higashi-Oitama, 東置賜	,,
8. Nishi-Oitama, 西置賜	,,
9. Minami-Oitama, 南置賜	,,
10. Mogami, 最上	,,

Ugo

1. Akumi, 飽海	*Yamagata*
2. Kawabe, 川邊	*Akita*
3. Okachi, 雄勝	,,
4. Hiraga, 平鹿	,,
5. Sembobu, 泉北	,,
6. Minami-Akita, 南秋田	,,
7. Kita-Akita, 北秋田	,,
8. Yamamoto, 山本	,,
9. Yuri, 由利	,,

Wakasa

1. Onyū, 遠敷	*Fukui*
2. Oi, 大飯	,,
3. Mikata, 三方	,,

Echizen

1. Tsuruga, 敦賀,	*Fukui*
2. Nanjō, 南條,	,,
3. Niū, 丹生	,,
4. Imadachi, 今立	,,
5. Asuha, 足羽	,,
6. Ono, 大野	,,
7. Yoshida, 吉田	,,
8. Sakai, 坂井	,,

Kaga

1. Ishikawa, 石川	*Ishikawa*
2. Kahoku, 河北	,,
3. Nomi, 能美	,,
4. Enuma, 江沼	,,

Noto

1. Suzu, 珠洲	*Ishikawa*
2. Hakui, 羽咋	,,
3. Kashima, 鹿島	,,
4. Fugeshi, 鳳至	,,

Etchū

1. Kami-Niikawa, 上新川	*Toyama*
2. Naka-Niikawa, 中新川	,,
3. Nei, 婦負	,,
4. Shimo-Niikawa, 下新川	,,
5. Imizu, 射水	,,
6. Himi, 冰見	,,
7. Higashi-Tonami, 東礪波	,,
8. Nishi-Tonami, 西礪波	,,

Districts	Depart-ments	Districts	Depart-ments
Echigo		**Hōki**	
1. Iwafune, 岩船	*Niigata*		
2. Kita-Kambara, 北蒲原	,,	1. Tō-Haku, 東伯	*Tottori*
3. Naka-Kambara, 中蒲原	,,	2. Sai-Haku, 西伯	,,
4. Minami-Kambara, 南蒲原	,,	3. Hino, 日野	,,
5. Higashi-Kambara, 東蒲原	,,	**Izumo**	
6. Nishi-Kambara, 西蒲原	,,		
7. Koshi, 古志	,,	1. Yatsuka, 八束	*Shimane*
8. Mishima, 三島	,,	2. Nogi, 能義	,,
9. Kariha, 刈羽	,,	3. Nita, 仁多	,,
10. Minami-Uonuma, 南魚沼	,,	4. Iishi, 飯石	,,
11. Naka-Uonuma, 中魚沼	,,	5. Ōhara, 大原	,,
12. Kita-Uonuma, 北魚沼	,,	6. Hikawa, 簸川	,,
13. Higashi-Kubiki, 東頸城	,,	**Iwami**	
14. Naka-Kubiki, 中頸城	,,		
15. Nishi-Kubiki, 西頸城	,,	1. Ōchi, 邑智	*Shimane*
Sado		2. Nima, 邇摩	,,
		3. Ano, 安濃	,,
1. Sado, 佐渡	*Niigata*	4. Naka, 那賀	,,
Tamba		5. Mino, 美濃	,,
		6. Ka-no-ashi, 鹿足	,,
1. Minami-Kuwada, 南桑田	*Kyōto*	**Oki**	
2. Kita-Kuwada, 北桑田	,,		
3. Funai, 船井	,,	1. Chiburi, 知夫	*Shimane*
4. Amada, 天田	,,	2. Ama, 海士	,,
5. Ikaruga, 何鹿	,,	3. Sukitsu, 周吉	,,
6. Taki, 多紀	*Hyōgo*	4. Ochi, 穏地	,,
7. Hikami, 氷上	,,	**Harima**	
Tango			
		1 Akashi, 明石	*Hyōgo*
1. Kasa, 加佐	*Kyōto*	2. Kako, 加古	,,
2. Yosa, 與佐	,,	3. Innami, 印南	,,
3. Naka, 中	,,	4. Mino, 美囊	,,
4. Takeno, 竹野	,,	5. Taka, 多可	,,
5. Kumano, 熊野	,,	6. Shizawa, 宍粟	,,
Tajima		7. Kanzaki, 神崎	,,
		8. Kasai, 加西	,,
1. Ki-no-saki, 城崎	*Hyōgo*	9. Katō, 加東	,,
2. Izushi, 出石	,,	10. Sayo, 佐用	,,
3. Asako, 朝來	,,	11. Akō, 赤穂	,,
4. Mikata, 美方	,,	12. Ibo, 揖保	,,
5. Yabu, 養父	,,	13. Shikama, 飾磨	,,
Inaba		**Mimasaka**	
1. Iwami, 岩美	*Tottori*	1. Maniwa, 眞庭	*Okayama*
2. Ketaka, 氣高	,,	2. Tomada, 苫田	,,
3. Yazu, 八頭	,,	3. Kume, 久米	,,
		4. Katsuda, 勝田	,,
		5. Aita, 英田	,,

Districts	Departments
Bizen	
1. Wake, 和氣	Okayama
2. Oku, 邑久	,,
3. Jōdō, 上道	,,
4. Akaiwa, 赤磐	,,
5. Mitsu, 御津	,,
6. Kojima, 兒島	,,
Bitchū	
1. Tsukubo, 都窪	Okayama
2. Asakuchi, 淺口	,,
3. Kibi, 吉備	,,
4. Oda, 小田	,,
5. Shitsuki, 後月	,,
6. Jōbō, 上房	,,
7. Atetsu, 阿哲	,,
Bingo	
1. Ashina, 蘆品	Hiroshima
2. Jinseki, 神石	,,
3. Sera, 世羅	,,
4. Mitsugi, 御調	,,
5. Fukayasu, 深安	,,
6. Kōnu, 甲奴	,,
7. Futami, 雙三	,,
8. Numakuma, 沼隈	,,
9. Hiba, 比婆	,,
Aki	
1. Asa, 安佐	Hiroshima
2. Takata, 高田	,,
3. Yamagata, 山縣	,,
4. Kamo, 賀茂	,,
5. Aki, 安藝	,,
6. Saeki, 佐伯	,,
7. Toyoda, 豐田	,,
Suwō	
1. Ōshima, 大嶋	Yamaguchi
2. Yoshiki, 吉敷	,,
3. Saba, 佐波	,,
4. Tsuno, 都濃	,,
5. Kamage, 熊毛	,,
6. Kuka, 玖珂	,,
Nagato	
1. Toyora, 豐浦	Yamaguchi
2. Asa, 厚狹	,,
3. Ōtsu, 大津	,,
4. Abu, 阿武	,,
5. Mine, 美禰	,,

Districts	Departments
Kii	
1. Minami-Muro, 南牟婁	Mie
2. Kita-Muro, 北牟婁	,,
3. Higashi-Muro, 東牟婁	Wakayama
4. Nishi-Muro, 西牟婁	,,
5. Hitaka, 日高	,,
6. Arita, 有田	,,
7. Ito, 伊都	,,
8. Naka, 那賀	,,
9. Kaisō, 海草	,,
Awaji	
1. Tsuna, 津名	Hyōgo
2. Mihara, 三原	,,
Awa	
1. Myōdō, 名東	Tokushima
2. Katsuura, 勝浦	,,
3. Naka, 那賀	,,
4. Oe, 麻植	,,
5. Kaibu, 海部	,,
6. Myōsai, 名西	,,
7. Itano, 板野	,,
8. Awa, 阿波	,,
9. Mima, 美馬	,,
10. Miyoshi, 三好	,,
Sanuki	
1. Shōzu, 小豆	Kagawa
2. Ōkawa, 大川	,,
3. Kida, 木田	,,
4. Kagawa, 香川	,,
5. Ayauta, 綾歌	,,
6. Naka-Tado, 仲多度	,,
7. Mitoyo, 三豐	,,
Iyo	
1. Uma, 宇麿	Ehime
2. Nii, 新居	,,
3. Shūso, 周桑	,,
4. Ochi, 越智	,,
5. Onsen, 溫泉	,,
6. Kami-Ukena, 上浮穴	,,
7. Iyo, 伊像	,,
8. Kita, 喜多	,,
9. Higashi-Uwa, 東宇和	,,
10. Nishi-Uwa, 西宇和	,,
11. Minami-Uwa, 南宇和	,,
12. Kita-Uwa, 北宇和	,,

Districts	Depart-ments	Districts	Depart-ments
Tosa		**Hizen**	
1. Aki, 安藝	*Kōchi*	1. Higashi-Sonoki, 東彼杵	*Nagasaki*
2. Kami, 香美	,,	2. Nishi-Sonoki, 西彼杵	,,
3. Tosa, 土佐	,,	3. Min.-Takaku, 南高來	,,
4. Agawa, 吾川	,,	4. Kita-Takaku, 北高來	,,
5. Nagaoka, 長岡	,,	5. Minami-Matsuura, 南松浦	,,
6. Takaoka. 高岡	,,	6. Kita-Matsuura, 北松浦	,,
7. Hata, 幡多	,,	7. Saga, 佐賀	*Saga*
Chikuzen		8. Miyaki, 三養基	,,
		9. Kanzaki, 神埼	,,
1. Kasuya, 糟屋	*Fukuoka*	10. Ogi, 小城	,,
2. Tsukushi, 筑紫	,,	11. Kinoshima, 杵島	,,
3. Sawara, 早良	,,	12. Fujitsu, 藤津	,,
4. Asakura, 朝倉	,,	13. Higashi-Matsuura, 東松浦	,,
5. Onga, 遠賀	,,	14. Nishi-Matsuura, 西松浦	,,
6. Kurate, 鞍手	,,	**Higo**	
7. Munakata, 宗像	,,		
8. Kaho, 嘉穗	,,	1. Hōtaku, 飽託	*Kumamoto*
9. Itoshima, 糸島	,,	2. Tamana, 玉名	,,
Chikugo		3. Kamoto, 鹿本	,,
		4. Kikuchi, 菊池	,,
1. Mii, 三井	*Fukuoka*	5. Yatsushiro, 八代	,,
2. Yame, 八女	,,	6. Kuma, 球磨	,,
3. Miike, 三池	,,	7. Kami-Mashiki, 上益城	,,
4. Yamato, 山門	,,	8. Shimo-Mashiki, 下益城	,,
5. Mitsuma, 三潴	,,	9. Aso, 阿蘇	,,
6. Ukiha, 浮羽	,,	10. Udo, 宇土	,,
Buzen		11. Ashikita, 葦北	,,
		12. Amakusa, 天草	,,
1. Tagawa, 田川	*Fukuoka*	**Hyūga**	
2. Chikujō, 築上	,,		
3. Kiku, 企救	,,	1. Higashi-Usuki, 東臼杵	*Miyazaki*
4. Kyōto, 京都	,,	2. Nishi-Usuki, 西臼杵	,,
5. Shimoke, 下毛	*Ōita*	3. Koyu, 兒湯	,,
6. Usa, 宇佐	,,	4. Miyazaki, 宮崎	,,
Bungo		5. Minami-Naka, 南那賀	,,
		6. Kita-Naka, 北那賀	,,
1. Ōita, 大分	*Ōita*	7. Higashi-Morokata, 東諸縣	,,
2. Hayami, 速見	,,	8. Nishi-Morokata, 西諸縣	,,
3. Ono, 大野	,,	**Ōsumi**	
4. Minami-Amabe, 南天蓋	,,		
5. Kita-Amabe, 北天蓋	,,	1. Kimotsuki, 肝屬	*Kagoshima*
6. Naori, 直入	,,	2. Soo, 囎唹	,,
7. Kusu, 玖珠	,,	3. Aira, 姶良	,,
8. Hida, 日田	,,	4. Ōshima, 大島	,,
9. Higashi-Kunisaki, 東國東	,,	5. Kumage, 熊毛	,,
10. Nishi-Kunisaki, 西國東	,,		

Districts	Depart-ments	Districts	Depart-ments
Satsuma		**Kitami**	
1. Izumi, 出水	*Kagoshima*	1. Sōya, 崇谷	*Hokkaidō-chō*
2. Hioki, 日置	,,	2. Esashi, 枝幸	,,
3. Kawanabe, 川邊	,,	3. Riijiri, 利尻	,,
4. Kagoshima. 鹿兒島	,,	4. Rebunjiri, 禮文	,,
5. Satsuma, 薩摩	,,	5. Tokoro, 常呂	,,
6. Isa, 伊佐	,,	6. Shari, 斜里	,,
7. Ibusuki, 揖宿	,,	7. Mombetsu, 紋別	,,
		8. Abashiri, 網走	,,
Iki		**Iburi**	
1. Iki, 壹歧	*Nagasaki*	1. Yamakushi, 山越	*Hokkaidō-chō*
		2. Abuta, 虻田	,,
Tsushima		3. Usu, 有珠	,,
		4. Mororan, 室蘭	,,
1. Kami-Agata, 上縣	*Nagasaki*	5. Horobetsu, 幌別	,,
2. Shimo-Agata, 下縣	,,	6. Shiraoi, 白老	,,
		7. Yūbutsu, 勇拂	,,
Ryukyu		8. Chitose, 千歲	,,
1. Shimajiri, 島尻	*Okinawa*	**Hidaka**	
2. Nakagami, 中頭	,,		
3. Kunigami, 國頭	,,	1. Saru, 沙流	*Hokkaidō-chō*
4. Miyako, 宮古	,,	2. Shizunai, 靜內	,,
5. Yaeyama, 八重山	,,	3. Mitsuishi, 三石	,,
		4. Urakawa, 浦河	,,
Shiribeshi		5. Shamani, 樣似	,,
		6. Horoizumi, 幌泉	,,
1. Otaru, 小樽	*Hokkaidō-chō*	7. Niikappu, 新冠	,,
2. Takashima, 高島	,,		
3. Oshiyoro, 忍路	,,	**Tokachi**	
4. Yoichi, 余市	,,		
5. Furuhira, 古平	,,	1. Hiro-o, 廣尾	*Hokkaidō-chō*
6. Shakotan, 積丹	,,	2. Tōbuchi, 當緣	,,
7. Furu-u, 古宇	,,	3. Tokachi, 十勝	,,
8. Iwanai, 岩內	,,	4. Nakagawa, 中川	,,
9. Isoya, 磯谷	,,	5. Kamikawa, 上川	,,
10. Utasutsu, 歌棄	,,	6. Katō, 河東	,,
11. Sutsu, 壽都	,,	7. Kasai, 河西	,,
12. Shimakomaki, 島牧	,,		
13. Setanai, 瀬棚	,,	**Kushiro**	
14. Futoro, 太櫓	,,		
15. Kudō, 久遠	,,	1. Shiranuka, 白糠	*Hokkaidō-chō*
16. Okujiri, 奧尻	,,	2. Ashiyoro, 足寄	,,
17. Bikuni, 美國	,,	3. Kushiro, 釧路	,,
		4. Akan, 阿寒	,,
Teshiro		5. Kawakami, 川上	,,
		6. Akkeshi, 厚岸	,,
1. Mashige, 增毛	*Hokkaidō-chō*	**Nemuro**	
2. Rurumoppe, 留萌	,,		
3. Teshio, 天鹽	,,	1. Hanasaki, 花咲	*Hokkaidō-chō*
4. Tomamae, 苫前	,,	2. Nemuro, 根室	,,
5. Kamikawa, 上川	,,	3. Notsuke, 野付	,,
6. Nakagawa, 中川	,,	4. Shibetsu, 標津	,,
		5. Menashi, 目梨	,,

Districts	Depart-ments	Districts	Depart-ments
Oshima		**Chishima**	
1. Kameda, 龜田	*Hokkaidō-chō*	1. Kunajiri, 國後	*Hokkaidō-chō*
2. Kayabe, 茅部	,,	2. Etorū, 擇捉	,,
3. Kami-Iso, 上磯	,,	3. Shikitan, 色丹	,,
4. Matsumae, 松前	,,	4. Shimushu, 占守	,,
5. Hiyama, 檜山	,,	5. Shinshiru, 新知	,,
6. Nishi, 爾志	,,	6. Uruppu, 得撫	,,
		7. Fūrebetsu, 振別	,,
Kushiro		8. Shibetoro, 蘂取	,,
		9. Shana, 紗那	,,
1. Sapporo, 札幌	*Hokkaidō-chō*		
2. Kamikawa, 上川	,,		
3. Kabato, 樺戸	,,		
4. Uryū, 雨龍	,,		
5. Sorachi, 穴知	,,	Total = 638 Districts.	
6. Yūbari, 夕張	,,		
7. Ishikari, 石狩	,,		
8. Atsuta, 厚田	,,		
9. Hamamashike, 濱益	,,		

AFTER A BATTLE.

VI. — GENERATIONS OF MYTHOLOGICAL TIMES

(JINDAI or TAIKO).

A. — **The 7 generations of celestial Spirits** (*Tenjin shichi-dai*).

1. — Kuni-toko-tachi no Mikoto
2. — Kuni-satsuchi no Mikoto
3. — Toyo-kunnu no Mikoto
4. — { Uijini no Mikoto
      { Suijini no Mikoto
5. — { Ōtonochi no Mikoto
      { Ōtomabe no Mikoto
6. — { Omotaru no Mikoto
      { Kashikone no Mikoto
7. — { Izanagi no Mikoto
      { Izanami no Mikoto

B. — **The 5 generations of terrestrial Spirits** (*Chijin go-dai*).

Izanagi Izanami

1. Amaterasu-ō-mikami   Tsukiyomi no Mikoto   Susano-o no Mikoto

2. Masaya-akatsu-kachi- Ama-no-hoi Amatsu-hikone Ikutsu-hikone Kumano-kusuhi
   hayahi-ama-no-oshiho-
   mimi no Mikoto

3. Amatsu-hiko-hikoho-no-ninigi no Mikoto

Hosuseri no Mikoto   4. Hiko-hohodemi no Mikoto   Ho-no-akari no Mikoto

5. Hiko-nagisatake-ugaya-fuki-aezu no Mikoto

Hiko-itsuse   Inahi no   Mike-irino   Kamu-Yamato-Iwarehiko no Mikoto
no Mikoto   Mikoto   no Mikoto   (*Jimmu-tennō*)

VII. — CHRONOLOGICAL LIST OF EMPERORS.

Posthumous Name	Birth	Accession	Abdication	Death
	B.C.	B.C.	B.C.	B.C.
1. Jimıru	711	660		585
2. Suisei	632	581		549
3. Annei	567	548		511
4. Itoku	553?	510		477
5. Kōshō	506	475		393
6. Kōan	427	392		291
7. Kōrei	342	290		215
8. Kōgen	273	214		158
9. Kaikwa	208	157		98
10. Sujin	148	97		30
				A.D.
11. Suinin	70	31		70
		A.D.	*A.D.*	
12. Keikō	12	71		130
	A.D.			
13. Seimu	83	131		190
14. Chūai	149	192		200
Jingō (Reg.)	170	201		269
15. Ōjin	201	201		310
16. Nintoku	290	313		399
17. Richū	336	400		405
18. Hanshō	352	406		411
19. Inkyō	374	412		453
20. Ankō	401	454		456
21. Yūryaku	418	457		479
22. Seinei	444	480		484
23. Kensō	440	485		487
24. Ninken	448	488		498
25. Buretsu	489	499		506
26. Keitai	450	507	531	531
27. Ankan	466	534		535
28. Senkwa	467	536		539
29. Kimmei	510	540		571
30. Bitatsu	538	572		585
31. Yōmei	540	586		587
32. Sushun	523	588		592
33. Suiko (Empress)	554	593		628
34. Jomei	593	629		641
35. Kōgyoku (Empress)	594	642	645	
36. Kōtoku	596	646		654
37. Saimei (Empr.)		655		661
38. Tenchi	626	662		671
39. Kōbun	648	672		672
40. Temmu	622	673		686
41. Jitō (Empress)	646	687	696	703
42. Mommu	683	697		707
43. Gemmei (Empress)	662	708	· 714	722
	681	715	723	748
44. Genshō (Empr.)	699	724	748	756
45. Shōmu	718	749	758	
46. Kōken (Empr.)	733	759	764	765
47. Junnin				

Posthumous Name	Birth	Accession	Abdication	Death
	A.D.	A.D.	A.D.	A.D.
48. Shōtoku (Empress)		765		769
49. Kōnin	719	770		781
50. Kwammu	736	782		805
51. Heijō	774	806	809	824
52. Saga	785	810	823	842
53. Junwa	786	824	833	840
54. Nimmyō	810	834		850
55. Montoku	827	851		858
56. Seiwa	851	859	876	881
57. Yōzei	868	877	884	949
58. Kōkō	830	885		887
59. Uda	867	888	897	931
60. Daigo	885	898		930
61. Shujaku	923	931	946	952
62. Murakami	926	947		967
63. Reizei	950	968	969	1011
64. En-yū	959	970	984	991
65. Kwazan	968	985	986	1008
66. Ichijō	980	987		1011
67. Sanjō	976	1012	1016	1017
68. Go-Ichijō	1008	1017		1036
69. Go-Shujaku	1009	1037		1045
70. Go-Reizei	1025	1046		1068
71. Go-Sanjō	1034	1069	1072	1073
72. Shirakawa	1053	1073	1086	1129
73. Horikawa	1078	1087		1107
74. Toba	1103	1108	1123	1156
75. Sutoku	1119	1124	1141	1164
76. Konoe	1139	1142		1155
77. Go-Shirakawa	1127	1156	1158	1192
78. Nijō	1143	1159		1165
79. Rokujō	1164	1166	1168	1176
80. Takakura	1161	1169	1180	1181
81. Antoku	1178	1181	1183	1185
82. Go-Toba	1179	1184	1198	1239
83. Tsuchimikado	1195	1199	1210	1231
84. Juntoku	1197	1211	1221	1242
85. Chūkyō	1218	1221	1221	1234
86. Go-Horikawa	1212	1222	1232	1234
87. Shijō	1231	1233		1242
88. Go-Saga	1220	1243	1246	1272
89. Go-Fukakusa	1243	1247	1259	1304
90. Kameyama	1259	1260	1274	1305
91. Go-Uda	1267	1275	1287	1324
92. Fushimi	1265	1288	1298	1317
93. Go-Fushimi	1288	1299	1301	1336
94. Go-Nijō	1285	1302		1308
95. Hanazono	1297	1309	1318	1348
96. Go-Daigo	1287	1319		1338
97. Go-Murakami	1328	1339		1368
98. Chōkei	?	1369	1372	?
99. Go-Kameyama	1347	1373	1392	1424

Posthumous name	Birth	Accession	Abdication	Death
	A.D.	A.D.	A.D.	A.D.
100. Go-Komatsu		1392	1412	1433
101. Shōkō	1401	1413		1428
102. Go-Hanazono	1419	1429	1464	1471
103. Go-Tsuchimikado	1442	1465		1500
104. Go-Kashiwabara	1464	1501		1526
105. Go-Nara	1497	1527		1557
106. Ōgimachi	1517	1558	1586	1593
107. Go-Yōzei	1571	1587	1611	1617
108. Go-Mi-no-o	1596	1612	1629	1680
109. Myōshō (Empr.)	1623	1630	1643	1696
110. Go-Kōmyō	1633	1644		1654
111. Go-Saiin	1637	1655	1662	1685
112. Reigen	1654	1663	1686	1732
113. Higashi-yama	1675	1687	1709	1709
114. Nakamikado	1702	1710	1735	1737
115. Sakuramachi	1720	1736	1746	1750
116. Momozono	1741	1746		1762
117. Go-Sakuramachi (Empress)	1740	1763	1770	1813

POSTHUMOUS NAME	BIRTH	ACCESSION	ABDICATION	DEATH
	A.D.	A.D.	A.D.	A.D.
118. Go-Momozono	1758	1771		1779
119. Kōkaku	1771	1780	1816	1840
120. Ninkō	1800	1817		1846
121. Kōmei	1831	1847		1867
122. Mutsuhito	1852	1868		

Northern Dynasty.

(1) Kōgon	1313	1331	1333	1364
(2) Kōmyō	1322	1336	1348	1380
(3) Sūkō	1334	1349	1352	1398
(4) Go-Kōgon	1338	1353	1371	1374
(5) Go-En-yū	1359	1372	1381	1393
(6) Go-Komatsu	1377	1383	1302	

The 122nd Emperor *Mutsuhito* descends from *Jimmu-tennō* in the 68th generation

VIII.—GENEALOGICAL TABLE OF THE EMPERORS.

1. JIMMU

Takishi-mimi　　Kan-yai-mimi　　2. SUISEI　　Kishi-mimi　　Hiko-yai-mimi

3. ANNEI

Okishi-mimi　　　Tokotsu-hiko-irone　　4. ITOKU　　　Shikitsu-hiko

5. KŌSHŌ　　　　　　　　　　　Tagishi-hiko

Ama-tarashi-hiko-kuni-oshi-hiko　　　　6. KŌAN

7. KŌREI

8. KŌGEN　　Chiji-haya-hime　　Hiko-isosaseri-hiko　　Hiko-sashima
　　　　　　　　　　　　　　　　(O-kibitsu-hiko)

Ōhiko　　9. KAIKWA　　Hiko-futa-oshi-makoto　　Take-haniyasu-hiko

Hiko-yumu-sumi　　10. SUJIN　　Hiko-imasu　　Taketoyo-hatsura-wake

Toyoki-iri-hiko　　11. SUININ　　Yasaka-iri-hiko　　Iza-no-mawaka

Homutsu-wake　　12. KEIKŌ　　Yamato-hime

Ō-usu　　Yamato-takeru　　13. SEIMU　　Ihoki-iri-hiko　　Oshi-no-wake

Inayori-wake　　14. CHŪAI　　Waka-take　　Isome-hiko

Kagusaka　　Oshikuma　　Homuya-wake　　15. ŌJIN

Ōyamamori　　16. NINTOKU　　Uji no Waki-iratsuko　　Wakanuke-futamata

17. RICHŪ　　　18. HANSHŌ　　19. INKYŌ　　　Ōkusaka　Ōhodo

Ichinobe no Oshiwa　Kinashi-karu　20. ANKŌ　21. YŪRYAKU　Mayuwa　Uhi

24. NINKEN　23. KENSŌ　Oshinumi no Iitoyo-ao　22. SEINEI　　Hiko-ushi-bito
25. BURETSU　　　　　　　　　　　　　　　　　　　26. KEITAI

27. ANKAN　　28. SENKWA　　29. KIMMEI　　Ō-Iratsuko

30. BITATSU　　31. YŌMEI　　33. SUIKO　　Anahobe　32. SUSHUN
Osaka no hiko-bito-oi-ne　　Toyodo-mimi (*Shōtoku-taishi*)

34. JOMEI　　Nakatsu　　Kuwada　　　　Chinu

38. TENCHI　　　　　40. TEMMU　　⎰35. KŌGYOKU　36. KŌTOKU
　　　　　　　　　　　　　　　　　⎱37. SAIMEI

41. JITŌ　43. GEMMEI　39. KŌBUN　Shiki　　Kusakabe　　　　　Toneri

49. KŌNIN　42. MOMMU　44. GENSHŌ　47. JUNNIN

49. KŌNIN   42. MOMMU

50. KWAMMU   Sawara   Osabe   45. SHŌMU

51. HEIJŌ   52. SAGA   53. JUNWA   Katsurabara {46. KŌKEN
                     (*Taira*)   {48. SHŌTOKU

54. NIMMYŌ   Makoto   Hiromu   Sadamu   Tōru

55. MONTOKU   Muneyasu   58. KŌKŌ

Koretaka   56. SEIWA   Yoshiari   Koretada   59. UDA   Kiyozane

57. YŌZEI   Sadazumi (*Seiwa-Genji*)   60. DAIGO   Atsuyoshi   Atsuzane (*Uda-Genji*)

61. SHUJAKU   62. MURAKAMI   Kaneakira

Hirohira   63. REIZEI   Tamehira   64. EN-YŪ   Tomohira (*Murakami-Genji*)

65. KWAZAN   67. SANJŌ   66. ICHIJŌ

Atsuakira (*Ko-Ichijō*)   Atsuyasu   68. GO-ICHIJŌ   69. GO-SHUJAKU

70. GO-REIZEI   71. GO-SANJŌ

72. SHIRAKAWA   Sanehito   Sukehito

Atsubumi   73. HORIKAWA

74. TOBA

75. SUTOKU   77. GO-SHIRAKAWA   76. KONOE

Shigehito   78. NIJŌ   Mochihito   80. TAKAKURA

79. ROKUJŌ

81. ANTOKU   Morisada (*Go-Takakura*)   82. GO-TOBA

86. GO-HORIKAWA   83. TSUCHIMIKADO   84. JUNTOKU

87. SHIJŌ   88. GO-SAGA   85. CHUKYŌ

Munetaka (*Shōgun*)   89. GO-FUKAKUSA   90. KAMEYAMA

Koreyasu (*Shōgun*)   92. FUSHIMI   Hisaakira (*Shōgun*)   91. GO-UDA

93. GO-FUSHIMI   95. HANAZONO   Morikuni (*Shōgun*)   94. GO-NIJŌ   96. GO-DAIGO

(N. 1) *Kōgon*   (N. 2) *Kōmyō*   Takanaga   97 GO-MURAKAMI   Morinaga

(N. 3) *Sukō*   (N. 4) *Go-Kōgon*   98. CHŌKEI   99. GO-KAMEYAMA

Einin   (N. 5) *Go-En-yū*   Ogura

Sadafusa *Go-Sukō*   (N. 6) 100. GO-KOMATSU   Takayoshi

102. GO-HANAZONO   Sadatsune   101. SHŌKŌ   Takahide

103. GO-TSUCHIMIKADO   (*Fushimi*)

104. GO-KASHIWABARA

104. Go-KASHIWABARA
    105. Go-NARA
    106. OGIMACHI
      Masahito (*Yōkō-in*)

107. Go-YŌZEI   Tomohito (*Hachijō no Miya*)

108. Go-MI-NO-O   Yoshihito (*Takamatsu no Miya*)

109. MYŌSHŌ   110. Go-KŌMYŌ   111. Go-SAIIN   112. REIGEN
                             Yukihito ((*Arisugawa*)   113. HIGASHI-YAMA

114. NAKAMIKADO   Naohito (*Kan-in*)
    115. SAKURAMACHI   Sukehito

118. Go-SAKURAMACHI   116. MOMOZONO   Haruhito (*Kan-in*)   119. KŌKAKU
              117. Go-MOMOZONO   120. NINKŌ
                                             121 KŌMEI
                                             122 MUTSUHITO
                                     Yoshihito (*Haru no Miya*)

Hirohito (*Michi no Miya*)   Yasuhito (*Atsu no Miya*)   Nobuhito (*Teru no Miya*)

TRAIN OF

IX. — PRINCELY FAMILIES (*SHI-SHINNŌ-KE.*

Sukō ...14 gen...Sadayoshi	Kuniie	Sadanori-Sadanaru	Kunika Akinori	Fushimi
		Akihito (Komatsu)-Yorihito		Higashi-Fushimi
		Hirotsune-Hiroatsu - Hiroyasu		Kwachō
		Satonari-Yoshihis (Kitashirakawa)	Narihisa	Taketa
			Yoshi- yuki	Count *Futara*
			Masao	Count *Ueno*
		Ienori		Count *Kiyozumi*
		Akira-Kikumaro-Takehiko		Yamashina
		Moriosa Morimasa		Nashimoto
		Asahiko-Kunihiko		Kuni Asaka
Ogimachi-Masahito	Go-Yōzei	Go-Minoo-Reigen-Hig.-yama-Naohito...		Kan-in
		Yoshihito-Go-Saiin-Yukihito -Masahito..		Arisugawa
	Tomohito	Tomotada-Yasuhito-Osahito - Toshihito...		Katsura
		Tadayuki-Toyotada		Marquis *Hirohata*

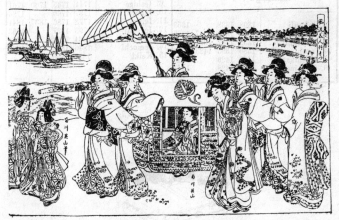

A PRINCESS.

X. — CHRONOLOGICAL LIST OF THE *SHŌGUN*.

NAME	Birth	Nomi-nation	Abdi-cation	Death	NAME	Birth	Nomi-nation	Abdi-cation	Death
Minamoto (*Kamakura*)					7. Yoshikatsu	1433	1441		1443
					8. Yoshimasa	1435	1449	1474	1490
					9. Yoshihisa	1465	1474		1489
1. Yoritomo	1147	1192		1199	10. Yoshitane (1)	1465	1490	1493	
2. Yoriie	1182	1202	1203	1204	11. Yoshizumi	1478	1493	1508	1511
3. Sanetomo	1192	1203		1219	Yoshitane (2)		1508	1521	1522
					12. Yoshiharu	1510	1521	1545	1550
					13. Yoshiteru	1535	1545		1565
Fujiwara (*Kamakura*)					14. Yoshihide	1564	1568		1568
					15. Yoshiaki	1537	1568	1573	1597
1. Yoritsune	1218	1226	1244	1256					
2. Yoritsugu	1239	1244	1252	1256	**Tokugawa** (*Edo*)				
Imperial Princes (*Kamakura*)									
1. Munetaka	1242	1252	1266	1274	1. Ieyasu	1542	1603	1605	1616
2. Koreyasu	1264	1266	1289	1326	2. Hidetada	1579	1605	1623	1632
3. Hisa-akira	1274	1289	1308	1328	3. Iemitsu	1604	1623		1651
4. Morikuni	1302	1308		1333	4. Ietsuna	1641	1651		1680
5. Morinaga	1308	1333	1334	1335	5. Tsunayoshi	1646	1680		1709
6. Naringa	1325	1334	1338	1338	6. Ienobu	1662	1709		1712
					7. Ietsugu	1709	1712		1716
Ashikaga (*Kyōto*)					8. Yoshimune	1684	1716	1745	1751
					9. Ieshige	1711	1745	1760	1761
					10. Ieharu	1737	1760		1786
1. Takauji	1308	1338		1358	11. Ienari	1773	1786	1837	1841
2. Yoshiakira	1330	1358	1367	1368	12. Ieyoshi	1793	1837		1853
3. Yoshimitsu	1358	1367	1395	1408	13. Iesada	1824	1853		1858
4. Yoshimochi	1386	1395	1423	1428	14. Iemochi	1846	1858		1866
5. Yoshikazu	1407	1423		1425	15. Keiki	1837	1866	1868	
6. Yoshinori	1394	1428		1441					

XI. — CHRONOLOGICAL LIST OF *NENGŌ*.

Taikwa	645-650	Manju	1024-1028	Shōgen	1207-1211
Hakuchi	650-655	Chōgen	1028-1037	Kenryaku	1211-1213
....	....	Chōryaku	1037-1040	Kempo	1213-1219
Sujaku	672	Chōkyū	1040-1044	Shōkyō	1219-1222
Hakuhō	673-686	Kwantoku	1044-1046	Tei-ō	1222-1224
Shuchō	686-701	Eishō	1046-1053	Gennin	1224-1225
Taihō	701-704	Tenki	1053-1058	Karoku	1225-1227
Keiun	704-708	Kōhei	1058-1065	Antei	1227-1229
Wadō	708-715	Chiryaku	1065-1069	Kwanki	1229-1232
Reiki	715-717	Enkyū	1066-1074	Tei-ei	1232-1233
Yōrō	717-724	Shōhō	1074-1077	Tempuku	1233-1234
Shinki	724-729	Shōryaku	1077-1081	Bunryakū	1234-1235
Tempyō	729-749	Eihō	1081-1084	Katei	1235-1238
Tempyō-shōhō	749-757	Otoku	1084-1087	Ryakunin	1238-1239
Tempyō-hōji	757-765	Kwanji	1087-1094	En-ō	1239-1240
Tempyō-jingo	765-767	Kahō	1094-1096	Ninji	1240-1243
Jingo-keiun	767-770	Eichō	1096-1097	Kwangen	1243-1247
Hōki	770-781	Shōtoku	1097-1099	Hōji	1247-1249
Ten-ō	781-782	Kōwa	1099-1104	Kenchō	1249-1256
Enryaku	782-806	Chōji	1104-1106	Kōgen	1256-1257
Daidō	806-810	Kashō	1106-1108	Shōka	1257-1259
Kōnin	810-824	Tennin	1108-1110	Shōgen	1259-1260
Tenchō	824-834	Ten-ei	1110-1113	Bun-ō	1260-1261
Shōwa	834-848	Eikyū	1113-1118	Kōchō	1261-1264
Kashō	848-851	Gwan-ei	1118-1120	Bun-ei	1264-1275
Ninju	851-854	Hōan	1120-1124	Kenji	1275-1278
Seikō	854-857	Tenji	1124-1126	Kōan	1278-1288
Ten-an	857-859	Taiji	1126-1131	Shōō	1288-1293
Jōkwan	859-877	Tenshō	1131-1132	Einin	1293-1299
Genkei	877-885	Chōshō	1132-1135	Shōan	1299-1302
Ninwa	885-889	Hōen	1135-1141	Kengen	1302-1303
Kwampyō	889-898	Eiji	1141-1142	Kagen	1303-1306
Shōtai	898-901	Kōji	1142-1144	Tokuji	1306-1309
Engi	901-923	Ten-yō	1144-1145	Enkei	1309-1311
Enchō	923-931	Kyūan	1145-1151	Ochō	1311-1312
Shōhyō	931-938	Nimpyō	1151-1154	Shōwa	1312-1317
Tenkei	938-947	Kyūju	1154-1156	Bumpō	1317-1319
Tenryaku	947-957	Hōgen	1156-1159	Gen-ō	1319-1321
Tentoku	957-961	Heiji	1159-1160	Genkyō	1321-1324
Owa	961-964	Eiryaku	1160-1161	Shōchū	1324-1326
Kōhō	964-968	Ōhō	1161-1163	Kareki	1326-1329
Anwa	968-970	Chōkwan	1163-1165	Gentoku	1329-1331
Tenroku	970-973	Eiman	1165-1166	Genkō	1331-1334
Ten-en	973-976	Nin-an	1166-1169	Kemmu	1334-1336
Teigen	976-978	Kaō	1169-1171	Engen	1336-1340
Tengen	978-983	Shōan	1171-1175	Kōkoku	1340-1346
Eikwan	983-985	Angen	1175-1177	Shōhei	1346-1370
Kwanwa	985-987	Jishō	1177-1181	Kentoku	1370-1372
Eien	987-989	Yōwa	1181-1182	Bunchō	1372-1375
Eiso	989-990	Juei	1182-1184	Tenju	1375-1381
Shōryaku	990-995	Gwanryaku	1184-1185	Kōwa	1381-1384
Chōtoku	995-999	Bunji	1185-1190	Genchū	1384-1393
Chōhō	999-1004	Kenkyū	1190-1199		
Kwankō	1004-1012	Shōji	1199-1201	**Northern dynasty.**	
Chōwa	1012-1017	Kennin	1201-1204		
Kwannin	1017-1021	Genkyū	1204-1206	Ryaku-ō	1338-1342
Chian	1021-1024	Ken-ei	1206-1207	Kōei	1342-1345

Teiwa	1345-1350	Bunshō	1466-1467	Teikyō	1684-1688
Kwan-ō	1350-1352	Ōnin	1467-1469	Genroku	1688-1704
Bunwa	1352-1356	Bummei	1469-1487	Hōei	1704-1711
Embun	1356-1361	Chōkyō	1487-1489	Shōtoku	1711-1716
Kōan	1361-1362	Entoku	1489-1492	Kōhō	1716-1736
Jōji	1362-1368	Meiō	1492-1501	Gembun	1736-1741
Ō-an	1368-1375	Bunki	1501-1504	Kwampō	1741-1744
Eiwa	1375-1379	Eishō	1504-1521	Eikyō	1744-1748
Kōryaku	1379-1381	Tai-ei	1521-1528	Kwan-en	1748-1751
Eitoku	1381-1384	Kyōroku	1528-1532	Hōreki	1751-1764
Shitoku	1384-1387	Tembun	1532-1555	Meiwa	1764-1772
Kakei	1387-1389	Kōji	1555-1558	An-ei	1772-1781
Kōō	1389-1390	Eiroku	1558-1570	Temmei	1781-1789
Meitoku	1390-1393	Genki	1570-1573	Kwansei	1789-1801
		Tenshō	1573-1592	Kyōwa	1801-1804
		Bunroku	1592-1596	Bunkwa	1804-1818
Meitoku	1393-1394	Keichō	1596-1615	Bunsei	1818-1830
Ō-ei	1394-1428	Genwa	1615-1624	Tempū	1830-1844
Shōchō	1428-1429	Kwan-ei	1624-1644	Kōkwa	1844-1848
Eikyō	1429-1441	Shōhō	1644-1648	Kaei	1848-1854
Kakitsu	1441-1444	Keian	1648-1652	Ansei	1854-1860
Bun-an	1444-1449	Shōō	1652-1655	Man-en	1860-1861
Hōtoku	1449-1452	Meireki	1655-1658	Bunkyū	1861-1864
Kyōtoku	1452-1455	Manji	1658-1661	Gwanji	1864-1865
Kōshō	1455-1457	Kwambun	1661-1673	Keiō	1865-1868
Chōroku	1457-1460	Empō	1673-1681	Meiji	1868
Kwanshō	1460-1466	Tenwa	1681-1684		

XII.—TABLE OF THE BUDDHIST SECTS.

Sects, Branches, etc.	Founder	Central Seat	Number of temples.
Sanron	Ekwan —625	......	...
Jōjitsu	Ekwan —625	......	...
Hossō {Nanji-den / Hokuji-den	Chitsū —657 / Chihō —703	Genkō-ji (Settsu) / Kōfuku-ji (Yamato)	45
Kusha	Chitsū —660	......	...
Kegon	Dōsen —735	Tō-daiji (Yamato)	21
Ritsu	Kanshin —754	Tōshō-daiji (Yamato)	...
Tendai {Sammon / Jimon / Shinjō	Saichō —805 / Enchin —858 / Shinjō —1486	Enryaku - ji (Ōmi) / Onjō-ji (Ōmi) / Saikyō-ji (Ōmi)	4,602
Shingon {Kogi / Shingi	Kūkai —806 / Kakuhan —t.1130	Tō-ji (Yamashiro) / Dempō-in (Musashi)	12,920
Yūzū-nembutsu	Ryōnin —1123	Sumiyoshi (Settsu)	350
Jōdo { Chinzei {Shirahata / Fujita / Nagoshi / Obata / Sanjō / Ichijō} Seizan {Nishidani / Fukakusa / Higashi-yama / Saga} Chōraku-ji / Kuhon-jgi / Ichinengi	Jaku-ei —13 cent. / Ji-a — „ / Sonkwan— „ / Ryōkū — „ / Dōkō — „ / Rei-a — „ / Jōon — „ / Enkū — „ / Kwanshō— „ / Dōkwan — „ / Ryūkwan— „ / Kakumyō— „ / Jōkaku — „	Kōmyō-ji (Yamashiro) / Muryō-ji „ / Zendō-ji (Kōzuke) / Sonshō-ji (Yamashiro) / Goshin-ji (Mikawa) / Kōmyō-in (Yamashiro) / Kōmyō-ji „ / Shinsō-in „ / Amida-in „ / Kongō-in „ / Chōraku-ji / Kuhon-ji	8,320
Zen { Rinzai {Kennin-ji / Tōfuku-ji / Kenchō-ji / Engaku-ji / Nanzen-ji / Eigen-ji / Daitoku-ji / Tenryū-ji / Myōshin-ji / Shōkoku-ji} Fuke {Kinsen / Kwassō / Kichiku / Kogiku / Kozasa / Umeji} Sōdō Obaku	Eisai —1202 / Ben-en —1255 / Dōryū —1249 / Sogen —1282 / Busshin —1293 / Genkō —1320 / Myōchō —1323 / Soseki —1339 / Egen —1337 / Myōha —1383 / Rōan —t.1475 / . . . . / . . . . / . . . . / . . . . / . . . . / . . . . / Dōgen —1228 / Ingen —1655	Kyōto (Yamashiro) / Fushimi „ / Kamakura (Sagami) / . . . . / Kyōto (Yamashiro) / Eigen-ji (Ōmi) / Ōmiya (Yamashiro) / Saga „ / Hanazono „ / Kyōto „ / Ichigetsu-ji (Shimōsa) / Reihō-ji (Musashi) / Myōan-ji (Yamashiro) / Shingetsu-ji (Hitachi) / Rikō-ji (Kōzuke) / Jijō-ji / Eihei-ji (Echizen) / Mampuku-ji (Yamash.)	6,120 / 18,706 / 556

Sects, Branches, etc.		Founder	Central Seat	Number of temples
Ji	Honzan	Ippen —t.1275	Shojōkō-ji (Sagami)	857
	Yūkō		Kinkō-ji (Yamashiro)	
	Ikkō		Renge-ji (Ōmi)	
	Okudani		Hōgwan-ji (Iyo)	
	Taima	Chishin —1261	Muryōkō-ji (Sagami)	
	Shijō		Kinrenji (Yamashiro)	
	Rokujō		Kwankikō-ji „	
	Kaii		Shinzenkō-ji (Hitachi)	
	Reizan		Shōhōji (Yamashiro)	
	Kokua		Sōrin-ji „	
	Ichiya		Kinkō-ji „	
	Tendō		Bukkō-ji (Dewa)	
	Mikagedō		Shinzenkō-ji (Yamash.)	
Jōdo-Shinshū or **Monto** or **Ikkō**	Hongwan-ji	Shinran —1224	Nishi-Hongwan-ji (Kyōto)	19,608
	Ōtani	Kōjū —1602	Hig.-Hongwan-ji „	
	Takada	Shimbutsu —1226	Senshū-ji (Ise)	
	Bukkō-ji	Ryōgen —14c.	Bukkō-ji (Yamashiro)	
	Kōshō-ji	Renkyō — „	Kōshō-ji „	
	Kibe	Shōshin —13c.	Kinshoku-ji (Ōmi)	
	Senshō-ji	Jodō — „	Senshō-ji (Echizen)	
	Chōsei-ji	Dōshō —14c.	Chōsei-ji „	
	Jōshō-ji	Jogaku — „	Jōshō-ji „	
	Gōshō-ji	Shōsen — „	Gōshō-ji „	
Hokke or **Nichiren**	Itchi	Nichirō —13c.	Ikegami (Musashi)	5,194
	Shōretsu	Nichigetsu—14c.	„ „	
	Honsei-ji (*Hokke*)	Nichi-in —1320	Honsei-ji (Echigo)	
	Myōman-ji (*Kempon-Hokke*)	Nisshū —1381	Myōman-ji(Yamashiro)	
	Hachihon (*Hommon-Hokke*)	Nichiryū —1420	Ikegami (Musashi)	
	Houryū-ji (*Hommyō-Hokke*)	Nisshin —1585	Hanazono (Higo)	
	Fuju-fuze	Nichiō —1595	Myōgaku-ji (Bizen)	
	Fuju-fuze-kōmon	Nikkō —16c.	„ „	
	Kōmon (*Hommon*)	Nikkō —1280	Ikegami (Musashi)	

XIII. — TABLE OF FIEFS (*HAN*) BY PROVINCES AT THE TIME OF THE RESTORATION (1867).

Residence	Daimyō	Revenues in *koku*	Residence	Daimyō	Revenues in *koku*
Yamashiro			**Mikawa**		
Yodo	Inaba	115,000	Okazaki	Honda	50,000
			Yoshida	Ōkōchi (*Matsud.*)	73,000
Yamato			Kariya	Doi	23,000
			Nishio	Ōgyū (*Matsud*).	60,000
Yagimoto	Oda	10,000	Tawara	Miyake	12,000
Koizumi	Katagiri	12,000	Okudono	Ōgyū (*Matsud*).	16,000
Shibamura	Oda	10,000	Koromo	Naitō	20,000
Shinjō	Nagai	10,000	Nishi-Ōhira	Ō-oka	10,000
Yagiu	Yagiu	10,000			
Kōriyama	Yanagisawa	150,000	**Tōtōmi**		
Kawachi			Hamamatsu	Inoue	60,000
			Kakegawa	Ōta	50,000
Sayama	Hōjō	10,000	Yokosuka	Nishio	35,000
Tannan	Takagi	10,000	Sagara	Tanuma	10,000
Izumi			**Suruga**		
			Shizuoka	Tokugawa	(Shōg. dom.)
Kishiwada	Okabe	60,000	Tanaka	Honda	40,000
Hakata	Watanabe	14,000	Numazu	Mizuno	50,000
			Kojima	Matsudaira	10,000
Settsu					
			Kai		
Amagasaki	Sakurai	40,000			
Takatsuki	Nagai	36,000	Kōfu	Tokugawa	(Shōg. dom.)
Sanda	Kuki	36,000			
Asada	Aoki	10,000	**Sagami**		
Ise			Odawara	Ōkubo	116,000
			Ogino	Ōkubo	16,000
Tsu	Tōdō	324,000	**Musashi**		
Kambe	Honda	15,000			
Kuwana	Hisamatsu	100,000			
Kameyama	Ishikawa	70,000	Edo	Tokugawa	5.000,000
Nagashima	Masuyama	33,000	„	Tayasu	130,000
Hisai	Tōdō	53,000	„	Hitotsubashi	130,000
Komono	Hijikata	11,000	„	Shimizu	100,000
			Ōshi	Okudaira	100,000
Shima			Kawagoe	Matsudaira	95,000
			Iwatsuki	Ō-oka	23,000
Toba	Inagaki	30,000	Okabe	Abe	20,000
			Kanazawa	Yonekura	13,000
Owari			**Awa**		
Nagoya	Tokugawa	619,500	Tateyama	Inaba	10,000
Inuyama	Naruse	35,000	Katsuyama	Sakai	12,000

Residence	Daimyō	Revenues in *koku*	Residence	Daimyō	Revenues in *koku*
	Kazusa			**Shinano**	
			Matsumoto	Toda	60,000
Ōtaki	Ōkōchi	20,000	Komoro	Makino	15,000
Kururi	Kuroda	30,000	Ueda	Matsudaira	53,000
Sanuki	Abe	16,000	Iiyama	Honda	20,000
Iino	Hoshina	20,000	Takatō	Naitō	33,000
Tsurumaki	Mizuno	15,000	Matsushiro	Sanada	100,000
Ichinomiya	Kanō	14,000	Takashima	Suwa	30,000
	(*Matsud.*)		Susaka	Hori (*Okuda*)	10,000
Kaibuchi	Hayashi	10,000	Iwámurata	Naitō	15,000
			Iida	Hori	15,000
	Shimōsa			**Kōzuke**	
Yūki	Mizuno	18,000	Takasaki	Ōkōchi	82,000
Sakura	Hotta	115,000		(*Matsud.*).	
Koga	Doi	80,000	Obata	Okudaira	20,000
Omigawa	Uchida	10,000	Maebashi	Matsudaira	170,000
Sekiyado	Kuze	48,000	Yoshii	Yoshii	12,000
Takaoka	Inoue	14,000	Tatebayashi	Akimoto	63,000
Oimi	Morikawa	10,000	Numata	Toki	35,000
Tako	Hisamatsu	12,000	Annaka	Itakura	30,000
			Isezaki	Sakai	20,000
	Hitachi		Nanukaichi	Maeda	10,000
Mito	Tokugawa	350,000		**Shimotsuke**	
Tsuchiura	Tsuchiya	95,000	Ashikaga	Toda	12,000
Kasama	Makino	80,000	Sano	Hotta	18,000
Ushiku	Yamaguchi	10,000	Karasuyama	Ōkubo	30,000
Yatabe	Hosokawa	16,000	Ōtawara	Ōtawara	12,000
Shimotsuma	Inoue	10,000	Kurobane	Ōseki	18,000
Shimodate	Ishikawa	22,000	Kitsuregawa	Ashikaga	10,000
Fuchū	Matsudaira	20,000	Utsunomiya	Toda	77,000
Asō	Shinjō	10,000	Mibu	Torii	30,000
			Fukiage	Arima	10,000
	Mino			**Mutsu**	
Hachiman	Aoyama	50,000	Iwakidaira	Andō	50,000
Iwanuma	Ishikawa	30,000	Wakamatsu	Hoshina	280,000
Ogaki	Toda	100,000		(*Matsud.*)	
Takasu	Matsudaira	30,000	Morioka	Nambu	200,000
Naeki	Tōyama	10,000	Hachinohe	Nambu	20,000
Kanō	Nagai	33,000	Hirosaki	Tsugaru	217,000
Takatomi	Honjō	10,000	Kuroishi	Tsugaru	10,000
			Tanakura	Matsudaira	95,000
	Ōmi		Shirakawa	Abe	100,000
			Nakamura	Sōma	60,000
			Miharu	Akita	50,000
Minakuchi	Katō	25,000	Nihommatsu	Niwa	100,000
Zeze	Honda	60,000	Fukushima	Itakura	30,000
Hikone	Ii	240,000	Sendai	Date	620,000
Ōmizo	Wakebe	20,000	Ichinoseki	Tamura (*Date*)	30,000
Nishi-Oji	Ichibashi	18,000	Unagaya	Naitō	15,000
Mikami	Endō	12,000	Moriyama	Matsudaira	20,000
Yamakami	Inagaki	13,000	Izumi	Honda	20,000
Miyagawa	Hotta	13,000	Shimotedo	Tachibana	10,000

Residence	Daimyō	Revenues in *koku*	Residence	Daimyō	Revenues in *koku*
Dewa			**Tango**		
Yamagata	Mizuno	50,000	Miyazu	Honjō	70,000
Akita	Satake	205,000		(*Matsud.*)	
Yonezawa	Uesugi	180,000	Tanabe	Makino	35,000
Kamiyama	Matsudaira	30,000	Mineyama	Kyōgoku	13,000
Kameda	Iwaki	20,000			
Shinjō	Tozawa	68,000	**Tajima**		
Tsurugaoka	Sakai	145,000			
Honjō	Rokugō	20,000	Izushi	Sengoku	30,000
Matsumine	Sakai	25,000	Toyooka	Kyōgoku	15,000
Nagatoro	Yonezu	11,000			
Tendō	Oda	20,000	**Inaba**		
Wakasa			Tottori	Ikeda	325,000
Obama	Sakai	103,000	**Izumo**		
Kaga			Matsue	Matsudaira	186,000
			Hirose	Matsudaira	30,000
Kanazawa	Maeda	1.027,000	Hori	Matsudaira	10,000
Daishōji	Maeda	100,000			
Echizen			**Iwami**		
			Tsuwano	Kamei	43,000
Fukui	Matsudaira	320,000	Hamada	Matsudaira	61,000
Tsuruga	Sakai	10,000			
Maruoka	Arima	50,000	**Harima**		
Ōno	Doi	40,000			
Sabae	Manabe	40,000	Himeji	Sakai	155,000
Katsuyama	Ogasawara	22,000	Yamazaki	Honda	10,000
			Akō	Mori	20,000
Etchū			Tatsuno	Wakizaka	55,000
			Ono	Hitotsuyanagi	10,000
Toyama	Maeda	100,000	Akashi	Matsudaira	100,000
			Hayashida	Tatebe	10,000
Echigo			Ashi	Ogasawara	10,000
			Mikazuki	Mori	15,000
Shibata	Mizoguchi	50,000	Mikusa	Niwa	10,000
Takata	Sakakibara	150,000			
Murakami	Naitō	70,000	**Mimasaka**		
Nagaoka	Makino	74,000			
Muramatsu	Hori (*Okuda*)	30,000	Tsuyama	Matsudaira	100,000
Shiiya	Hori (*Okuda*)	10,000	Katsuyama	Miura	23,000
Itoigawa	Matsudaira	10,000			
Yoita	Ii	20,000	**Bizen**		
Mikkaichi	Yanagisawa	10,000			
Kurokawa	Yanagisawa	10,000	Okayama	Ikeda	315,000
				(*Matsud.*)	
Tamba			**Bitchū**		
Kameyama	Matsudaira	50,000			
Fukuchiyama	Kuchiki	32,000	Matsuyama	Itakura	55,000
Sasayama	Aoyama	60,000	Niwase	Itakura	20,000
Yamaga	Tani	10,000	Ashimori	Kinoshita	25,000
Sonobe	Koide	30,000	Okada	Itō	10,000
Ayabe	Kuki	20,000	Niimi	Seki	18,000
Kashiwabara	Oda	20,000			

Residence	Daimyō	Revenues in *koku*
Bingo		
Fukuyama	Abe	110,000
Aki		
Hiroshima	Asano	426,000
Suwō		
Iwakuni	Kikkawa	60,000
Tokuyama	Mōri	40,000
Nagato		
Hagi	Mōri	369,000
Fuchū	Mōri	40,000
Kii		
Wakayama	Tokugawa	555,000
Tanabe	Andō	40,000
Shingū	Mizuno	35,000
Awa		
Tokushima	Hachisuka	258,000
Tosa		
Kōchi	Yamanouchi	242,000
Sanuki		
Takamatsu	Matsudaira	120,000
Marugame	Kyōgoku	50,000
Tadotsu	Kyōgoku	10,000
Iyo		
Matsuyama	Hisamatsu	150,000
Imabaru	Hisamatsu	35,000
Uwajima	Date	100,000
Osu	Katō	60,000
Saijō	Matsudaira	30,000
Komatsu	Hitotsuyanagi	10,000
Yoshida	Date	30,000
Niiya	Katō	10,000
Chikuzen		
Fukuoka	Kuroda	520,000
Akizuki	Kuroda	50,000
Chikugo		
Kurume	Arima	210,000
Yanagawa	Tachibana	119,000

Residence	Daimyō	Revenues in *koku*
Buzen		
Kokura	Ogasawara	150,000
Nakatsu	Okudaira	100,000
Bungo		
Ōita (*Funai*)	Matsudaira	21,000
Usuki	Inaba	56,000
Takeda	Nakagawa	70,000
Hiji	Kinoshita	25,000
Saeki	Mōri	20,000
Mori	Kurushima	12,000
Kizuki	Matsudaira	32,000
Hizen		
Saga	Nabeshima	357,000
Hirado	Matsuura	61,000
Karatsu	Ogasawara	60,000
Shimabara	Matsudaira	70,000
Hasuike	Nabeshima	52,000
Ogi	Nabeshima	73,000
Kashima	Nabeshima	20,000
Ōmura	Ōmura	28,000
Fukue (*Gotō*)	Gotō	12,000
Higo		
Kumamoto	Hosokawa	540,000
Udo	Hosokawa	30,000
Hitoyoshi	Sagara	22,000
Hyūga		
Nobeoka	Naitō	70,000
Sadowara	Shimazu	27,000
Obi	Itō	50,000
Takanabe	Akizuki	27,000
Satsuma		
Kagoshima	Shimazu	778,000
Iki		
Katsumoto	Matsuura	10,000
Tsushima		
Fuchū	Sō	100,000
Ezo		
Matsumae	Matsumae	80,000

Total—258 Daimyō
Sankei 3   Kamon 18
Fudai 139   Tozama 98

XIV.—MINISTRIES SINCE 1885.

	President of the Council	Foreign Affairs	Interior	Finances	War	Marine	Justice	Public Instruction	Agriculture Culture and Commerce	Communications
Dec. 1885	Itō	Inoue, Itō, Okuma	Yamagata	Matsukata	Oyama	Saigō	Yamada	Mori	Tani, Hijikata, Kuroda	Enomoto
April 88	Kuroda	Okuma	Yamagata	Matsukata	Oyama	Saigō	Yamada	Mori, Enomoto	Inoue	Gotō
Dec. 89	Yamagata	Aoki	Yamagata, Saigō	Matsukata	Oyama	Saigō, Kabayama	Yamada	Yoshikawa	Mutsu	Gotō
May 91	Matsukata	Enomoto	Shinagawa, Soejima, Kōno	Matsukata	Takashima	Kabayama	Oki	Oki	Mutsu, Kōno, Sano	Gotō
Aug. 92	Itō	Mutsu	Inoue, Nomura, Itagaki	Watanabe, Matsukata, Watanabe	Oyama, Yamagata, Oyama	Nire, Saigō	Yamagata, Yoshikawa	Kōno, Inoue, Saionji	Gotō, Enomoto	Kuroda, Watanabe, Shirane
Sept. 96	Matsukata	Okuma, Nishi	Itagaki	Matsukata	Takashima	Saigō	Kiyoura	Hachisuka, Hamano	Enomoto	Nomura
Jan. 98	Itō	Nishi	Yoshikawa	Inoue	Katsura	Saigō	Sone	Saionji, Toyama	Itō (Miyoji), Kaneko	Suematsu
June 98	Okuma	Okuma	Itagaki	Matsuda	Katsura	Saigō	Okiyoshi	Ozaki, Inukai	Oishi	Hayashi
Nov. 98	Yamagata	Aoki	Saigō	Matsuda	Katsura	Yamamoto	Kiyoura	Kabayama	Sone	Yoshikawa
Oct. 1900	Itō	Katō	Suematsu	Watanabe	Katsura, Kodama	Yamamoto	Kaneko	Matsuda	Hayashi	Hoshi, Hara
June 01	Katsura	Sone, Komura	Utsumi, Kodama, Katsura, Yoshikawa	Sone	Kodama, Kodama, Terauchi	Yamamoto	Kiyoura, Hatano	Kikuchi, Kodama, Kubota	Hirata, Kiyoura	Yoshikawa, Sone, Oura
Jan. 06	Saionji	Katō, Hayashi	Hara	Sakatani	Terauchi	Saitō	Matsuda	Makino	Matsuoka	Yamagata

XV. — KOREA.

Korea forms a peninsula of about 1250 Km., long, and 500 Km., of average width; it has an area of 218,000 Km². Its population is estimated at 15 million inhabitants, the density being 69 per Km².

The name Korea is a corruption of *Kôrie* (高 麗, Chin. *Kaoli*, Jap. *Kôrai*). Since the end of the 14th century, it was called *Tchao-sien* 朝 鮮 (Jap. *Chôsen*). Its official name in China, is *Han-kouo* 韓 國 (Jap. *Kan-koku* or *Kara no kuni*).

Korea is divided into 8 provinces (道, *tao*; Jap. *dô*), 5 of which, since the Sino-Japanese war (1894-1895) have been divided into 2 prefectures. In the table given below, the ancient capitals are in the first line, the new prefectures below it.

PROVINCES			PREFECTURES		
KOREAN NAME.	CHINESE.	JAPAN-ESE.	KOREAN NAME	CHINESE	JAPAN-ESE.
咸 鏡, Hamkyeng	Hienkin	Kankei	咸 興, Hamheung 吉 州, Kiltjyou	Hienhing Kitcheou	Kankō Kishū
平 安, Hpyen-an	Pingngan	Heian	平 壤, Hpyeng-yang 安 州, Antjyou	Ping-yang Ngantcheou	Heijō Anshū
黄 海, Hoang-hai	Hoang-hai	Kōkai	海 州, Hai-tjyou	Haitcheou	Kaishū
江 原, Kang-ouen	Kiang-yuen	Kōgen	原 州, Ouen-tjyou	Yuentcheou	Genshū
京 畿, Kyeng-keuei	King-ki	Kyōki	水 原, Syou-ouen (Seoul)	Choei-yuen	Suigen (Keijō)
忠 淸, Tchyoung-tchyeng	Tchoung-tsing	Chūsei	忠 州, Tchyoung-tjyou 公 州, Kong-tjyou	Tchongtcheou Kongtcheou	Chūshū Kōshū
慶 尙, Kieng-syang	King-chang	Keishō	太 公, Taikou 晋 州, Tjin-tjyou	Taikong Tsintcheou	Taikō Shinshū
全 羅, Tjyen-la	Tsiuen-la	Zenra	全 州, Tjyen-tjyou 維 州, La-tjyou	Tsiuentcheou Latcheou	Zenshū Rashū

The principal cities are: *Seoul*, or *Syou-ouen*, or *Hang-yang-tcheng* 漢 陽 城 (Jap.: *Kan-yo-jô*) (200,000 inh.), capital; — *Tchemulpo* or *Tjyei-moul-hpo* 濟 物 浦 or *Jen-tchoan* 仁 川 (Jap. *Jinsen*) (20,000 inh.), open port; — *Fusan* 釜 山 (Jap. *Fusan*) (48,000 inh.), open port; — *Yuenchan* 元 山 (Jap. *Gensan*) (18,000 inh.) open port; — *Kaisong* or *Song-do* 松 都 (Jap. *Shôto*) (60,000 inh.), was the capital from 910 to 1392; — *Hpyeng-yang* (Jap. *Heijô*) (30,000 inh.), etc.

The principal rivers are the *Yalu* 鴨綠, and the *Tumen* 圖門, which form the boundary nearly all along the Northern border ; the *Han-kiang*, 漢江 which passes through *Seoul*, and the *Tatong*, 大同, which flows through *Hpyeng-yang*.

Many islands are along the S. and the W. coast ; the principal ones are : *Tsitcheou-tao* 濟州島 (*Quelpaert* Isl.), *Kiuwen-tao* 巨文島 (*Port Hamilton*), *Kiutsi-tao* 巨齊島 opposite the Japanese island of *Tsushima*, etc.

XVI.—CHINA.

(A). — Political Divisions.

Provinces		Area in KM.²	Population (1902)	Pop. per KM.²	Capital		Popula- tion
直隸	Tcheli	300,000	20,930,000	70	京	Peking	700,000
山東	Changtong	145,000	38,247,900	264	濟南	Tsinan	100,000
山西	Chansi	212,000	12,200,000	57	太原	Taiyuen	230,000
河南	Honan	176,000	25,317,820	144	開封	Kaifong	200,000
江蘇	Kiangsou	100,000	23,980,230	239	南京	Nanking	350,000
安徽	Nganhoei	142,000	23,672,300	167	安慶	Nganking	40,000
江西	Kiangsi	180,000	26,532,000	148	南昌	Nantchang	300,000
浙江	Tchekiang	95,000	11,580,000	122	杭州	Hangtcheou	300,000
福建	Foukien	120,000	22,870,000	191	福州	Foutcheou	625,000
湖北	Houpe	185,000	35,280,000	191	武昌	Ouchang	500,000
湖南	Hounan	216,000	22,169,000	103	長沙	Tchangcha	500,000
甘肅	Kansou	325,000	10,386,000	32	蘭州	Lancheou	500,000
陝西	Chensi	195,000	8,450,000	43	西安	Singnan	1,000,000
四川	Setchoan	566,000	68,724,800	120	成都	Tchengtou	650,000
廣東	Koangtong	259,000	31,865,000	123	廣東	Canton	900,000
廣西	Koangsi	200,000	5,142,000	26	桂林	Koeilin	80,000
貴州	Koeitcheou	174,000	7,650,000	44	貴陽	Koeiyang	100,000
雲南	Yunnan	380,000	12,721,500	34	雲南	Yunnan	45,000
The 18 Provinces		3,970,000	407,518,750	103			
盛京	Chengking				奉天	Mukden	180,000
吉林	Kilin (Kirin)				吉林	Kirin	100,000
黑龍江	Helongkiang				齊々哈爾	Tsitsikar	30,000
滿洲	Manchuria	942,000	8,500,000	9			
蒙古	Mongolia	3,543,000	2,580,000	0,7	庫倫	Ourga	40,000
西藏	Thibet	1,200,000	6,430,000	5	拉薩	Lhassa	10,000
新疆	Turkestan	1,426,000	1 200,000	0,8	疏附	Kachgar	65,000
Chinese Empire		11,081,000	426,228,750	38,5			

(B). — The Chinese Dynasties.

After the 5 legendary sovereigns: *Fouhi* 伏羲, *Chennong* 神農, *Hoangti* 黃帝, *Chaohao* 少昊 and *Tchoan-hiu* 顓頊, and the 3 great Emperors: *Yao* 堯 (2357-2257 B.C.), *Choen* 舜 and *Yu* 禹, China was governed by 22 dynasties, 9 of which were called the great dynasties, and 13, the smaller ones.

1—Hia, 夏 (*Ka*)		2205 B.C.—	1766 B.C.	17	Emperors
2—	Chang, 商 (*Shō*)	1766	—1401	} 28	"
	In, 殷 (*In*)	1401	—1122		"
3—Tcheou, 周 (*Shū*)		1122	— 249	38	"
4—Tsin, 秦 (*Shin*)		249	— 206	4	"
5—	Han, 漢 (*Kan*)	206	— 25	} 25	"
	Tong-Han 東漢 (*Tō-Kan*)	25	— 221 A.D.		"
6—Chou, 蜀 (*Shoku*)		321 A.D.—	165	2	"
7—	Tsin, 晉 (*Shin*)	265	— 317	} 15	"
	Tong-Tsin, 東晉 (*Tō-Shin*)	317	— 420		"
8—Song, 宋 (*Sō*)		420	— 479	8	"
9—Nan-Tsi, 南齊 (*Nan-Sai*)		479	— 502	5	"
10—Nan-Liang, 南梁 (*Nan-Ryo*)		502	— 557	4	"
11—Nan-Tchen, 南陳 (*Nan-Chin*)		557	— 590	5	"
12—Soei, 隋 (*Zui*)		590	— 620	3	"
13—Tang, 唐 (*Tō*)		620	— 907	20	"
14—Heou-Liang, 後梁		907	— 923	2	"
15—Heou-Tang, 後唐		923	— 936	2	"
16—Heou-Tsin, 後晉		936	— 947	2	"
17—Heou-Han, 後漢		947	— 951	2	"
18—Heou-Tcheou 後周		951	— 960	3	"
19—	Song, 宋 (*Sō*)	960	—1127	} 18	"
	Nan-Song, 南宋 (*Nan-Sō*)	1127	—1280		"
20—Yuen 元 (*Gen*)		1280	—1368	10	"
21—Ming, 明 (*Min*)		1368	—1644	16	"
22—Tsing, 清 (*Shin*)		1644	—	11	"

(The data given in this table are taken from the "*Geographie de l'Empire de Chine*," by *L. Richard, S. J. — Chang-hai*).

XIII.—ANCIENT COMPUTATION OF YEARS, MONTHS, DAYS, HOURS, ETC.

In the beginning of the 7th century (604), Japan adopted the Chinese calendar, which, if we except some small modifications was in use till the year 1872.

It is a Luna-solar calendar, regulated according to the true movements of Sun and Moon.—The month was strictly lunar, and the first lunar month of the year was that in which the Sun enters the sign of the Fish; this placed the beginning of the year between Jan. the 20th and Feb. the 19th.

The year ordinarily contained 12 months, i.e. 354 or 355 days: this was the common year (*hei-nen*, 平 年); but when the delay in the solar year had become such as not to bring the 13th lunation to the sign of the Fish, a 13th month was added and called intercalar month (*urŭ-tsuki*, 閏 月), and the year then had 383 or 384 days; it was the full year (*urŭ-doshi, jun-nen*, 閏 年). The intercalar month was the one during which the Sun remained in the same sign. Thus in 1903, the Sun had entered Cancer on the 27th of the 5th month, remained in it during the whole following lunation (intercalar), and entered the Lion on the 1st of the 6th month. Thus, the same sign always corresponded to each lunation.

A.—YEARS.

Besides the *nengō* and the era of *Jimmu-tennō* (660 B.C.), of which, 1906 is the 2,566 year, the Japanese used the sexagesimal cycle of the Chinese, which is in its turn composed of the decimal cycle of the 10 trunks (*jikkan*, 十 干) and the duodecimal cycle of the 12 twigs (*ju-ni-shi*, 十 二 支). By combining these two series, we come to 60 terms which served in denominating the years.

The 10 trunks are formed of the 5 elements : wood, fire, earth, metal and water, each one counted twice, once as senior (*e*) and then as junior (*to*) brothers.

1.	甲	.	*Ki-no-e*	Elder brother of the wood		
2.	乙	.	*Ki-no-to*	Junior	,,	,,	,,
3.	丙	.	*Hi-no-e*	Elder	,,	,,	fire
4.	丁	.	*Hi-no-to*	Junior	,,	,,	,,
5.	戊	.	*Tsuchi-no-e*	Elder	,,	,,	earth
6.	己	.	*Tsuchi-no-to*	Junior	,,	,,	,,
7.	庚	.	*Ka-no-e*	Elder	,,	,,	metal
8.	辛	.	*Ka-no-to*	Junior	,,	,,	,,
9.	壬	.	*Mizu-no-e*	Elder	,,	,,	water
10.	癸	.	*Mizu-no-to*	Junior	,,	,,	,,

The 12 twigs are :

1.	子	*Ne*	Rat	5.	辰	*Tatsu*	Dragon	9. 申 *Saru* Monkey
2.	丑	*Ushi*	Ox	6.	巳	*Mi*	Serpent	10. 酉 *Tori* Cock
3.	寅	*Tora*	Tiger	7.	午	*Uma*	Horse	11. 戌 *Inu* Dog
4.	卯	*U*	Hare	8.	未	*Hitsuji*	Goat	12. 亥 *I* Boar

The combinations of the two series are indicated in the table below, with the corresponding years of the Christian era.

No.	干支	Name	Year	Animal	Year
1	甲子	Ki-no-e Ne	Year of the Rat		1864
2	乙丑	Ki-no-to Ushi	"	Ox	1865
3	丙寅	Hi-no-e Tora	"	Tiger	1866
4	丁卯	Hi-no-to U	"	Hare	1867
5	戊辰	Tsuchi-no-e Tatsu	"	Dragon	1868
6	己巳	Tsuchi-no-to Mi	"	Serpent	1869
7	庚午	Ka-no-e Uma	"	Horse	1870
8	辛未	Ka-no-to Hitsuji	"	Goat	1871
9	壬申	Mizu-no-e Saru	"	Monkey	1872
10	癸酉	Mizu-no-to Tori	"	Cock	1873
11	甲戌	Ki-no-e Inu	"	Dog	1874
12	乙亥	Ki-no-to I	"	Boar	1875
13	丙子	Hi-no-e Ne	"	Rat	1876
14	丁丑	Hi-no-to Ushi	"	Ox	1877
15	戊寅	Tsuchi-no-e Tora	"	Tiger	1878
16	己卯	Tsuchi-no-to U	"	Hare	1879
17	庚辰	Ka-no-e Tatsu	"	Dragon	1880
18	辛巳	Ka-no-to Mi	"	Serpent	1881
19	壬午	Mizu-no-e Uma	"	Horse	1882
20	癸未	Mizu-no-to Hitsuji	"	Goat	1883
21	甲申	Ki-no-e Saru	"	Monkey	1884
22	乙酉	Ki-no-to Tori	"	Cock	1885
23	丙戌	Hi-no-e Inu	"	Dog	1886
24	丁亥	Hi-no-to I	"	Boar	1887
25	戊子	Tsuchi-no-e Ne	"	Rat	1888
26	己丑	Tsuchi-no-to Ushi	"	Ox	1889
27	庚寅	Ka-no-e Tora	"	Tiger	1890
28	辛卯	Ka-no-to U	"	Hare	1891
29	壬辰	Mizu-no-e Tatsu	"	Dragon	1892
30	癸巳	Mizu-no-to Mi	"	Serpent	1893
31	甲午	Ki-no-e Uma	"	Horse	1894
32	乙未	Ki-no-to Hitsuji	"	Goat	1895
33	丙申	Hi-no-e Saru	"	Monkey	1896
34	丁酉	Hi-no-to Tori	"	Cock	1897
35	戊戌	Tsuchi-no-e Inu	"	Dog	1898
36	己亥	Tsuchi-no-to I	"	Boar	1899
37	庚子	Ka-no-e Ne	"	Rat	1900
38	辛丑	Ka-no-to Ushi	"	Ox	1901
39	壬寅	Mizu-no-e Tora	"	Tiger	1902
40	癸卯	Mizu-no-to U	"	Hare	1903
41	甲辰	Ki-no-e Tatsu	"	Dragon	1904
42	乙巳	Ki-no-to Mi	"	Serpent	1905
43	丙午	Hi-no-e Uma	"	Horse	1906
44	丁未	Hi-no-to Hitsuji	"	Goat	1907
45	戊申	Tsuchi-no-e Saru	"	Monkey	1908
46	己酉	Tsuchi-no-to Tori	"	Cock	1909
47	庚戌	Ka-no-e Inu	"	Dog	1910
48	辛亥	Ka-no-to I	"	Boar	1911
49	壬子	Mizu-no-e Ne	"	Rat	1912
50	癸丑	Mizu-no-to Ushi	"	Ox	1913
51	甲寅	Ki-no-e Tora	"	Tiger	1914
52	乙卯	Ki-no-to U	"	Hare	1915
53	丙辰	Hi-no-e Tatsu	"	Dragon	1916
54	丁巳	Hi-no-to Mi	"	Serpent	1917
55	戊午	Tsuchi-no-e Uma	"	Horse	1918
56	己未	Tsuchi-no-to Hitsuji	"	Goat	1919
57	庚申	Ka-no-e Saru	"	Monkey	1920
58	辛酉	Ka-no-to Tori	"	Cock	1921
59	壬戌	Mizu-no-e Inu	"	Dog	1922
60	癸亥	Mizu-no-to I	"	Boar	1923

B.—Months.

Each month was named by its number to which was added a special name derived from the temperature or some traditional custom, etc.

1st Month	Shō-gwatsu	Mutsuki	Month of good relations
2nd „	Ni- „	Kisaragi	„ when clothes are double-lined
3rd „	San- „	Yayoi	„ of nature's awakening
4th „	Shi- „	U-tsuki	„ of the flower U (Deutzia scabra)
5th „	Go- „	Sa-tsuki	„ of sowing
6th „	Roku- „	Mi-na-zuki	„ without water
7th „	Shichi- „	Fumi-zuki	„ of letters
8th „	Hachi- „ {	Ha-zuki	„ of leaves (that fall)
		Tsuki-mi-zuki	„ of viewing the moon
9th „	Ku- „ {	Naga-zuki	„ long?
		Kiku-zuki	„ of the Chrysanthemum
10th „	Jū- „	Kami-na-zuki	„ without gods
11th „	Jū-ichi- „	Shimo-tsuki	„ of the white frost
12th „	Jū-ni- „	Shiwasu	„ final

The months had 30 or 29 days: the former were called *dai no tsuki* (great), the latter, *shō no tsuki* (small). When a month was inserted, it took its name from the preceding one; for ex : *Urū-ni-gwatsu.*

C.—Seasons and Subdivisions of the Seasons.

The equinoxes and the solstices which mark the beginning of the European seasons, marked the middle of the Chinese seasons. Each season is divided into 6 nearly equal periods, according to the positions of the Sun moving from 15 to 15 degrees of longitude. These 24 subdivisions of the year are called *ki, setsu* or *sekki.* They are given in the table below with the corresponding dates of the European calendar.

Spring.....春	立春	Risshun	Beginning of spring	Feb.	5th
	雨水	U-sui	Rain water	„	19th
	驚蟄	Keichitsu	Awakening of the insects	March	5th
	春分	Shumbun	Equinox of spring	„	20th
	清明	Seimei	Pure lustre (clear weather)	April	5th
	穀雨	Koku-u	Rain for the cereals	„	20th
Summer...夏	立夏	Rikka	Beginning of summer	May	5th
	小満	Shōman	Small plenitude	„	21st
	芒種	Bōshū	Work of sowing	June	6th
	夏至	Geji	Solstice of summer	„	21st
	小暑	Shosho	Little heat	July	7th
	大暑	Daisho	Great heat	„	23rd
Autumn...秋	立秋	Risshū	Beginning of fall	Aug.	7th
	處暑	Shosho	End of heat	„	23rd
	白露	Hakuro	White dew	Sept.	8th
	秋分	Shūbun	Equinox of autumn	„	23rd
	寒露	Kanro	Cold dew	Oct.	8th
	霜降	Sōkō	Descent of the frost	„	23rd
Winter....冬	立冬	Rittō	Beginning of winter	Nov.	7th
	小雪	Shōsetsu	Little snow	„	22nd
	大雪	Daisetsu	Great snow	Dec.	7th
	冬至	Tōji	Solstice of winter	„	22nd
	小寒	Shōkan	Little cold	Jan.	6th
	大寒	Daikan	Great cold	„	21st

D.—Days.

The days of the month are known by their number. The first is also called *Tsuitachi* (*tsuki-tachi*, beginning of the moon). The last day of the month is called *misoka* (ancient form of the 30th day) and the last day of the year, *ō-misoka* (great 30th day). The 10th, 20th and 30th of each month, that were formerly days of rest, were also called *kami no tōka*, *naka no tōka* and *shimo no tōka*. The 10 first days of a month form the *jō-jun* (superior decade), the 10 following, the *chū-jun* (middle decade), and the last 10, the *ge-jun* (inferior decade).

The 60 signs of the sexagesimal cycle used for the years are also employed for the days and recur in the same order every 60 days. Thus the first, *ki-no-e ne* occurred in 1905, on the 25th of January, the 26th of March, the 25th of May, the 24th of July, the 23rd of September, the 22nd of November and so on.

E.—Hours.

The day was divided into 12 equal intervals (*toki*, 時), named according to the 12 twigs of the duodecimal cycle : *Ne no toki*, *Ushi no toki*, etc. These *toki* of two hours, were divided into two equal parts distinguished by the prefixes *sho* (初) and *sei* (正); each half comprised 8 *koku* (刻), each *koku* 15 *fun* (分), each *fun* 60 *byō* (秒).

Another manner of counting the hours was to give them a number according to order, which decreased from 9 to 4 and was repeated twice, once for the hours of night and once for those of the day.

The table on the next page shows the relation that exists between these two methods of reckoning.

AN OLD CLOCK.

Night	*Ne no toki*—Hour of the Rat	*Kokonotsu no toki*—9th hour	11	p.m.
	Ushi „ — „ Ox	*Yatsu* „ —8th „	1	a.m.
	Tora „ — „ Tiger	*Nanatsu* „ —7th „	3	„
Morning	*U* „ — „ Hare	*Mutsu* „ —6th „	5	„
	Tatsu „ — „ Dragon	*Itsutsu* „ —5th „	7	„
	Mi „ — „ Serpent	*Yotsu* „ —4th „	9	„
Day	*Uma* „ — „ Horse	*Kokonotsu* „ —9th „	11	„
	Hitsuji „ — „ Goat	*Yatsu* „ —8th „	1	p.m.
	Saru „ — „ Monkey	*Nanatsu* „ —7th „	3	„
Evening	*Tori* „ — „ Cock	*Mutsu* „ —6th „	5	„
	Inu „ — „ Dog	*Itsutsu* „ —5th „	7	„
	I „ — „ Boar	*Yotsu* „ —4th „	9	„

A third manner of reckoning the hours was to give them a different number of *koku* according as the days and nights were on the decrease or on the increase, in the different seasons of the year. For more details consult an old Chinese Calendar.

B.—Hours.

XVIII.—TABLE FOR COMPARING JAPANESE WITH FRENCH AND ENGLISH MEASURES.

MEASURES	JAPANESE		FRENCH		ENGLISH	
Length	里	*Ri* (league)	3,927 mèt.	2727	2 miles	4403
	海里	*Ri* (marine l.)	1,851 ,,	8181	1 mile	1507
	町	*Chō* (60 *ken*)	109 ,,	0910	5 chains	4230
	間	*Ken* (6 feet)	1 ,,	8181	1 yard	9884
	丈	*Jō* (10 feet)	3 ,,	0303	3 yards	3140
	尺	*Shaku* (foot)	0 ,,	3030	11 inches	9305
	寸	*Sun* (inch)	0 ,,	0303	1 inch	1930
	分	*Bu* (line)	0 ,,	0030	1 line	4317
Area	方里	*Ri* square	15 kil.²	4235	5 sq. miles	9552
	町	*Chō* (10 *tan*)	99 ares	1735	2 acres	4507
	反	*Tan* (300 *tsubo*)	9 ,,	9173	0 ,,	2450
	坪	*Tsubo* (1 *ken*².)	3 mèt.²	3058	3 sq. yards	9538
Capacity	石	*Koku* (10 *tō*)	180 litres	3906	39 gall. 703—4 bush.	963
	斗	*Tō* (½ bush.)	18 ,,	0391	3 ,, 970—1 peck	985
	升	*Shō* (pint)	1 ,,	8039	1 quart 588—0 ,,	199
	合	*Gō*	0 ,,	1804	1 gill 271—0 ,,	020
	勺	*Seki*	0 ,,	0180		
Weight	貫	*Kwan*	3,750 grammes		8 lb. 267 av. d. p.	
	斤	*Kin* (pound)	600 ,,		1 ,, 323 ,,	
	匁	*Momme*	3 ,, 750		33 oz. 86 ,,	
Money	圓	*Yen*	2 fr. 5832		2 s. 3 d.	

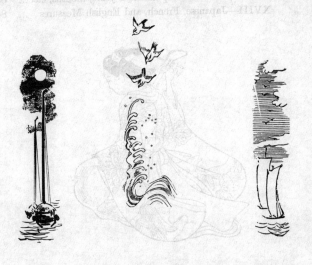

INDEX OF THE APPENDIXES.